A SHIPWRECKED ANTHOLOGY

A Collection of Timeless Tales of Shipwrecks & Survival At Sea

EDGAR ALLAN POE   JACK LONDON   DANIEL DEFOE
JONATHAN SWIFT   ROBERT LOUIS STEVENSON
JOSEPH CONRAD   STEPHEN CRANE
GERARD MANLEY HOPKINS

The Life & Adventures of Robinson Crusoe: The version of this work in this volume is derived from the 1919 printing of Defoe's work originally published in 1719, and therefore is in the public domain.

Gulliver's Travels: Originally published in 1727, this work is in the public domain.

Kidnapped: Originally published in 1886, this work is in the public domain.

Ms. Found In a Bottle: Originally published in 1833, this work is in the public domain.

Amy Foster: Originally published in *Typhoon & Other Stories* in 1903, this work in the public domain.

The Open Boat: Originally published in 1897, this work is in the public domain.

The "Francis Spaight": Originally published in *When God Laughs & Other Stories* in 1911, this work is in the public domain

The Wreck of the Deutschland: Originally published in 1918, this work is the public domain.

No copyright claim is made with respect to public domain works.

This edition reflects minor editorial revisions to the original texts.

CONTENTS

DANIEL DEFOE	The Life & Adventures of Robinson Crusoe	1
JONATHAN SWIFT	Gulliver's Travels	317
ROBERT LOUIS STEVENSON	Kidnapped	509
EDGAR ALLAN POE	Ms. Found In A Bottle	647
JOSEPH CONRAD	Amy Foster	657
STEPHEN CRANE	The Open Boat	677
JACK LONDON	The "Francis Spaight"	695
GERARD MANLEY HOPKINS	The Wreck of the Deutschland	703

THE LIFE & ADVENTURES OF ROBINSON CRUSOE

DANIEL DEFOE

VOLUME ONE

I

START IN LIFE

I was born in the year 1632, in the city of York, of a good family, though not of that country, my father being a foreigner of Bremen, who settled first at Hull. He got a good estate by merchandise, and leaving off his trade, lived afterwards at York, from whence he had married my mother, whose relations were named Robinson, a very good family in that country, and from whom I was called Robinson Kreutznaer; but, by the usual corruption of words in England, we are now called—nay we call ourselves and write our name—Crusoe; and so my companions always called me.

I had two elder brothers, one of whom was lieutenant-colonel to an English regiment of foot in Flanders, formerly commanded by the famous Colonel Lockhart, and was killed at the battle near Dunkirk against the Spaniards. What became of my second brother I never knew, any more than my father or mother knew what became of me.

Being the third son of the family and not bred to any trade, my head began to be filled very early with rambling thoughts. My father, who was very ancient, had given me a competent share of learning, as far as house-education and a country free school generally go, and designed me for the law; but I would be satisfied with nothing but going to sea; and my inclination to this led me so strongly against the will, nay, the commands of my father, and against all the entreaties and persuasions of my mother and other friends, that there seemed to be something fatal in that propensity of nature, tending directly to the life of misery which was to befall me.

My father, a wise and grave man, gave me serious and excellent counsel against what he foresaw was my design. He called me one morning into his chamber, where he was confined by the gout, and expostulated very warmly with me upon this subject. He asked me what reasons, more than a mere wandering inclination, I had for leaving father's house and my native country, where I might be well introduced, and had a prospect of raising my fortune by application and industry, with a life of ease and pleasure. He told me it was men of desperate fortunes on one hand, or of aspiring, superior fortunes on the other, who went abroad upon adventures, to rise by enterprise, and make themselves famous in undertakings of a nature out of the common road; that these things were all either too far above me or too far below me; that mine was the middle state, or what might be called the upper station of low life, which he had found, by long experience, was the best state in the world, the most suited to human happiness, not exposed to the miseries and hardships, the labour and sufferings of the mechanic part of mankind, and not embarrassed with the pride, luxury, ambition, and envy of the upper part of mankind. He told me I might judge of the happiness of this state by this one thing—viz. that this was the state of life which all other people envied; that kings have frequently lamented the miserable consequence of being born to great things, and wished they had been placed in the middle of the two extremes, between the mean and the great; that the wise man gave his testimony to this, as the standard of felicity, when he prayed to have neither poverty nor riches.

He bade me observe it, and I should always find that the calamities of life were shared among the upper and lower part of mankind, but that the middle station had the fewest disasters, and was not exposed to so many vicissitudes as the higher or lower part of mankind; nay, they were not subjected to so many distempers and uneasinesses, either of body or mind, as those were who, by vicious living, luxury, and extravagances on the one hand, or by hard labour, want of necessaries, and mean or insufficient diet on the other hand, bring distemper upon themselves by the natural consequences of their way of living; that the middle station of life was calculated for all kind of virtue and all kind of enjoyments; that peace and plenty were the handmaids of a middle fortune; that temperance, moderation, quietness, health, society, all agreeable diversions, and all desirable pleasures, were the blessings attending the middle station of life; that this way men went silently and smoothly through the world, and comfortably out of it, not embarrassed with the labours of the hands or of the head, not sold to a life of slavery for daily bread, nor harassed with perplexed circumstances, which rob the soul of peace and the body of rest, nor enraged with the passion of envy, or the secret burning lust of ambition for great things; but, in easy circumstances, sliding gently through the world, and sensibly tasting the sweets of living, without the bitter; feeling that they are happy, and learning by every day's experience to know it more sensibly.

After this he pressed me earnestly, and in the most affectionate manner, not to play the young man, nor to precipitate myself into miseries which nature, and the station of life I was born in, seemed to have provided against; that I was under no necessity of seeking my bread; that he would do well for me, and endeavour to enter me fairly into the station of life which he had just been recommending to me; and that if I was not very easy and happy in the world, it must be my mere fate or fault that must hinder it; and that he should have nothing to answer for, having thus discharged his duty in warning me against measures which he knew would be to my hurt; in a word, that as he would do very kind things for me if I would stay and settle at home as he directed, so he would not have so much hand in my misfortunes as to give me any encouragement to go away; and to close all, he told me I had my elder brother for an example, to whom he had used the same earnest persuasions to keep him from going into the Low Country wars, but could not prevail, his young desires prompting him to run into the army, where he was killed; and though he said he would not cease to pray for me, yet he would venture to say to me, that if I did take this foolish step, God would not bless me, and I should have leisure hereafter to reflect upon having neglected his counsel when there might be none to assist in my recovery.

I observed in this last part of his discourse, which was truly prophetic, though I suppose my father did not know it to be so himself—I say, I observed the tears run down his face very plentifully, especially when he spoke of my brother who was killed: and that when he spoke of my having leisure to repent, and none to assist me, he was so moved that he broke off the discourse, and told me his heart was so full he could say no more to me.

I was sincerely affected with this discourse, and, indeed, who could be otherwise? and I resolved not to think of going abroad any more, but to settle at home according to my father's desire. But alas! a few days wore it all off; and, in short, to prevent any of my father's further importunities, in a few weeks after I resolved to run quite away from him. However, I did not act quite so hastily as the first heat of my resolution prompted; but I took my mother at a time when I thought her a little more pleasant than ordinary, and told her that my thoughts were so entirely bent upon seeing the world that I should never settle to anything with resolution enough to go through with it, and my father had better give me his consent than force me to go without it; that I was now eighteen years old, which was too late to go apprentice to a trade or clerk to an attorney; that I was sure if I did I should never serve out my time, but I should certainly run away from my master before my time was out, and go to sea; and if she would speak to my father to let me go one voyage abroad, if I came home again, and did not like it, I would go no more; and I would promise, by a double diligence, to recover the time that I had lost.

This put my mother into a great passion; she told me she knew it would be to no purpose to speak to my father upon any such subject; that he knew too well what was my interest to give his consent to anything so much for my hurt; and that she wondered how I could think of any such thing after the discourse I had had with my father, and such kind and tender expressions as she knew my father had used to me; and that, in short, if I would ruin myself, there was no help for me; but I might depend I should never have their consent to it; that for her part she would not have so much hand in my destruction; and I should never have it to say that my mother was willing when my father was not.

Though my mother refused to move it to my father, yet I heard afterwards that she reported all the discourse to him, and that my father, after showing a great concern at it, said to her, with a sigh, "That boy might be happy if he would stay at home; but if he goes abroad, he will be the most miserable wretch that ever was born: I can give no consent to it."

It was not till almost a year after this that I broke loose, though, in the meantime, I continued obstinately deaf to all proposals of settling to business, and frequently expostulated with my father and mother about their being so positively determined against what they knew my inclinations prompted me to. But being one day at Hull, where I went casually, and without any purpose of making an elopement at that time; but, I say, being there, and one of my companions being about to sail to London in his father's ship, and prompting me to go with them with the common allurement of seafaring men, that it should cost me nothing for my passage, I consulted neither father nor mother any more, nor so much as sent them word of it; but leaving them to hear of it as they might, without asking God's blessing or my father's, without any consideration of circumstances or consequences, and in an ill hour, God knows, on the 1st of September 1651, I went on board a ship bound for London. Never any young adventurer's misfortunes, I believe, began sooner, or continued longer than mine. The ship was no sooner out of the Humber than the wind began to blow and the sea to rise in a most frightful manner; and, as I had never been at sea before, I was most inexpressibly sick in body and terrified in mind. I began now seriously to reflect upon what I had done, and how justly I was overtaken by the judgment of Heaven for my wicked leaving my father's house, and abandoning my duty. All the good counsels of my parents, my father's tears and my mother's entreaties, came now fresh into my mind; and my conscience, which was not yet come to the pitch of hardness to which it has since, reproached me with the contempt of advice, and the breach of my duty to God and my father.

All this while the storm increased, and the sea went very high, though nothing like what I have seen many times since; no, nor what I saw a few days after; but it was enough to affect me then, who was but a young sailor, and had never known anything of the matter. I expected every wave would have swallowed us up, and that every time the ship fell down, as I thought it did, in the trough or hollow of the sea, we should never rise more; in this agony of mind, I made many vows and resolutions that if it would please God to spare my life in this one voyage, if ever I got once my foot upon dry land again, I would go directly home to my father, and never set it into a ship again while I lived; that I would take his advice, and never run myself into such miseries as these any more. Now I saw plainly the goodness of his observations about the middle station of life, how easy, how comfortably he had lived all his days, and never had been exposed to tempests at sea or troubles on shore; and I resolved that I would, like a true repenting prodigal, go home to my father.

These wise and sober thoughts continued all the while the storm lasted, and indeed some time after; but the next day the wind was abated, and the sea calmer, and I began to be a little inured to it; however, I was very grave for all that day, being also a little sea-sick still; but towards night the weather cleared up, the wind was quite over, and a charming fine evening followed; the sun went down perfectly clear, and rose so the next morning; and having little or no wind, and a smooth sea, the sun shining upon it, the sight was, as I thought, the most delightful that ever I saw.

I had slept well in the night, and was now no more sea-sick, but very cheerful, looking with wonder upon the sea that was so rough and terrible the day before, and could be so calm and so pleasant in so little a time after. And now, lest my good resolutions should continue, my companion, who had enticed me away, comes to me; "Well, Bob," says he, clapping me upon the shoulder, "how do you do after it? I warrant you were frighted, wer'n't you, last night, when it blew but a capful of wind?" "A capful d'you call it?" said I; "'twas a terrible storm." "A storm, you fool you," replies he; "do you call that a storm? why, it was nothing at all; give us but a good ship and sea-room, and we think nothing of such a squall of wind as that; but you're but a fresh-water sailor, Bob. Come, let us make a bowl of punch, and we'll forget all that; d'ye see what charming weather 'tis now?" To make short this sad part of my story, we went the way of all sailors; the punch was made and I was made half drunk with it: and in that one night's wickedness I drowned all my repentance, all my reflections upon my past conduct, all my resolutions for the future. In a word, as the sea was returned to its smoothness of surface and settled calmness by the abatement of that storm, so the hurry of my thoughts being over, my fears and apprehensions of being swallowed up by the sea being forgotten, and the current of my former desires returned, I entirely forgot the vows and promises that I made in my distress. I found, indeed, some intervals of reflection; and the serious thoughts did, as it were, endeavour to return again sometimes; but I shook them off, and roused myself from them as it were from a distemper, and applying myself to drinking and company, soon mastered the return of those fits—for so I called them; and I had in five or six days got as complete a victory over conscience as any young fellow that resolved not to be troubled with it could desire. But I was to have another trial for it still; and Providence, as in such cases generally it does, resolved to leave me entirely without excuse; for if I would not take this for a deliverance, the next was to be such a one as the worst and most hardened wretch among us would confess both the danger and the mercy of.

The sixth day of our being at sea we came into Yarmouth Roads; the wind having been contrary and the weather calm, we had made but little way since the storm. Here we were obliged to come to an anchor, and here we lay, the wind continuing contrary—viz. at south-west—for seven or eight days, during which time a great many ships from Newcastle came into the same Roads, as the common harbour where the ships might wait for a wind for the river.

We had not, however, rid here so long but we should have tided it up the river, but that the wind blew too fresh, and after we had lain four or five days, blew very hard. However, the Roads being reckoned as good as a harbour, the anchorage good, and our ground-tackle very strong, our men were unconcerned, and not in the least apprehensive of danger, but spent the time in rest and mirth, after the manner of the sea; but the eighth day, in the morning, the wind increased, and we had all hands at work to strike our topmasts, and make everything snug and close, that the ship might ride as easy as possible. By noon the sea went very high indeed, and our ship rode forecastle in, shipped several seas, and we thought once or twice our anchor had come home; upon which our master ordered out the sheet-anchor, so that we rode with two anchors ahead, and the cables veered out to the bitter end.

By this time it blew a terrible storm indeed; and now I began to see terror and amazement in the faces even of the seamen themselves. The master, though vigilant in the business of preserving the ship, yet as he went in and out of his cabin by me, I could hear him softly to himself say, several times, "Lord be merciful to us! we shall be all lost! we shall be all undone!" and the like. During these first hurries I was stupid, lying still in my cabin, which was in the steerage, and cannot describe my temper: I could ill resume the first penitence which I had so apparently trampled upon and hardened myself against: I thought the bitterness of death had been past, and that this would be nothing like the first; but when the master himself came by me, as I said just now, and said we should be all lost, I was dreadfully frighted. I got up out of my cabin and looked out; but such a dismal sight I never saw: the sea ran mountains high, and broke upon us every three or four minutes; when I could look about, I could see nothing but distress round us; two ships that rode near us, we found, had cut their masts by the board, being deep laden; and our men cried out that a ship which rode about a mile ahead of us was foundered. Two more ships, being driven from their anchors, were run out of the Roads to sea, at all adventures, and that with not a mast standing. The light ships fared the best, as not so much labouring in the sea; but two or three of them drove, and came close by us, running away with only their spritsail out before the wind.

Towards evening the mate and boatswain begged the master of our ship to let them cut away the fore-mast, which he was very unwilling to do; but the boatswain protesting to him that if he did not the ship would founder, he consented; and when they had cut away the fore-mast, the main-mast stood so loose, and shook the ship so much, they were obliged to cut that away also, and make a clear deck.

Any one may judge what a condition I must be in at all this, who was but a young sailor, and who had been in such a fright before at but a little. But if I can express at this distance the thoughts I had about me at that time, I was in tenfold more horror of mind upon account of my former convictions, and the having returned from them to the resolutions I had wickedly taken at first, than I was at death itself; and these, added to the terror of the storm, put me into such a condition that I can by no words describe it. But the worst was not come yet; the storm continued with such fury that the seamen themselves acknowledged they had never seen a worse. We had a good ship, but she was deep laden, and wallowed in the sea, so that the seamen every now and then cried out she would founder. It was my advantage in one respect, that I did not know what they meant by *founder* till I inquired. However, the storm was so violent that I saw, what is not often seen, the master, the boatswain, and some others more sensible than the rest, at their prayers, and expecting every moment when the ship would go to the bottom. In the middle of the night, and under all the rest of our distresses, one of the men that had been down to see cried out we had sprung a leak; another said there was four feet water in the hold. Then all hands were called to the pump. At that word, my heart, as I thought, died within me: and I fell backwards upon the side of my bed where I sat, into the cabin. However, the men roused me, and told me that I, that was able to do nothing before, was as well able to pump as another; at which I stirred up and went to the pump, and worked very heartily. While this was doing the master, seeing some light colliers, who, not able to ride out the storm were obliged to slip and run away to sea, and would come near us, ordered to fire a gun as a signal of distress. I, who knew nothing what they meant, thought the ship had broken, or some dreadful thing happened. In a word, I was so surprised that I fell down in a swoon. As this was a time when everybody had his own life to think of, nobody minded me, or what was become of me; but another man stepped up to the pump, and thrusting me aside with his foot, let me lie, thinking I had been dead; and it was a great while before I came to myself.

We worked on; but the water increasing in the hold, it was apparent that the ship would founder; and though the storm began to abate a little, yet it was not possible she could swim till we might run into any port; so the master continued firing guns for help; and a light ship, who had rid it out just ahead of us, ventured a boat out to help us. It was with the utmost hazard the boat came near us; but it was impossible for us to get on board, or for the boat to lie near the ship's side, till at last the men rowing very heartily, and venturing their lives to save ours, our men cast them a rope over the stern with a buoy to it, and then veered it out a great length, which they, after much labour and hazard, took hold of, and we hauled them close under our stern, and got all into their boat. It was to no purpose for them or us, after we were in the boat, to think of reaching their own ship; so all agreed to let her drive, and only to pull her in towards shore as much as we could; and our master promised them, that if the boat was staved upon shore, he would make it good to their master: so partly rowing and partly driving, our boat went away to the northward, sloping towards the shore almost as far as Winterton Ness.

We were not much more than a quarter of an hour out of our ship till we saw her sink, and then I understood for the first time what was meant by a ship foundering in the sea. I must acknowledge I had hardly eyes to look up when the seamen told me she was sinking; for from the moment that they rather put me into the boat than that I might be said to go in, my heart was, as it were, dead within me, partly with fright, partly with horror of mind, and the thoughts of what was yet before me.

While we were in this condition—the men yet labouring at the oar to bring the boat near the shore—we could see (when, our boat mounting the waves, we were able to see the shore) a great many people running along the strand to assist us when we should come near; but we made but slow way towards the shore; nor were we able to reach the shore till, being past the lighthouse at Winterton, the shore falls off to the westward towards Cromer, and so the land broke off a little the violence of the wind. Here we got in, and though not without much difficulty, got all safe on shore, and walked afterwards on foot to Yarmouth, where, as unfortunate men, we were used with great humanity, as well by the magistrates of the town, who assigned us good quarters, as by particular merchants and owners of ships, and had money given us sufficient to carry us either to London or back to Hull as we thought fit.

Had I now had the sense to have gone back to Hull, and have gone home, I had been happy, and my father, as in our blessed Saviour's parable, had even killed the fatted calf for me; for hearing the ship I went away in was cast away in Yarmouth Roads, it was a great while before he had any assurances that I was not drowned.

But my ill fate pushed me on now with an obstinacy that nothing could resist; and though I had several times loud calls from my reason and my more composed judgment to go home, yet I had no power to do it. I know not what to call this, nor will I urge that it is a secret overruling decree, that hurries us on to be the instruments of our own destruction, even though it be before us, and that we rush upon it with our eyes open. Certainly, nothing but some such decreed unavoidable misery, which it was impossible for me to escape, could have pushed me forward against the calm reasonings and persuasions of my most retired thoughts, and against two such visible instructions as I had met with in my first attempt.

My comrade, who had helped to harden me before, and who was the master's son, was now less forward than I. The first time he spoke to me after we were at Yarmouth, which was not till two or three days, for we were separated in the town to several quarters; I say, the first time he saw me, it appeared his tone was altered; and, looking very melancholy, and shaking his head, he asked me how I did, and telling his father who I was, and how I had come this voyage only for a trial, in order to go further abroad, his father, turning to me with a very grave and concerned tone "Young man," says he, "you ought never to go to sea any more; you ought to take this for a plain and visible token that you are not to be a seafaring man." "Why, sir," said I, "will you go to sea no more?" "That is another case," said he; "it is my calling, and therefore my duty; but as you made this voyage on trial, you see what a taste Heaven has given you of what you are to expect if you persist. Perhaps this has all befallen us on your account, like Jonah in the ship of Tarshish. Pray," continues he, "what are you; and on what account did you go to sea?" Upon that I told him some of my story; at the end of which he burst out into a strange kind of passion: "What had I done," says he, "that such an unhappy wretch should come into my ship? I would not set my foot in the same ship with thee again for a thousand pounds." This indeed was, as I said, an excursion of his spirits, which were yet agitated by the sense of his loss, and was farther than he could have authority to go. However, he afterwards talked very gravely to me, exhorting me to go back to my father, and not tempt Providence to my ruin, telling me I might see a visible hand of Heaven against me. "And, young man," said he, "depend upon it, if you do not go back, wherever you go, you will meet with nothing but disasters and disappointments, till your father's words are fulfilled upon you."

We parted soon after; for I made him little answer, and I saw him no more; which way he went I knew not. As for me, having some money in my pocket, I travelled to London by land; and there, as well as on the road, had many struggles with myself what course of life I should take, and whether I should go home or to sea.

As to going home, shame opposed the best motions that offered to my thoughts, and it immediately occurred to me how I should be laughed at among the neighbours, and should be ashamed to see, not my father and mother only, but even everybody else; from whence I have since often observed, how incongruous and irrational the common temper of mankind is, especially of youth, to that reason which ought to guide them in such cases—viz. that they are not ashamed to sin, and yet are ashamed to repent; not ashamed of the action for which they ought justly to be esteemed fools, but are ashamed of the returning, which only can make them be esteemed wise men.

In this state of life, however, I remained some time, uncertain what measures to take, and what course of life to lead. An irresistible reluctance continued to going home; and as I stayed away a while, the remembrance of the distress I had been in wore off, and as that abated, the little motion I had in my desires to return wore off with it, till at last I quite laid aside the thoughts of it, and looked out for a voyage.

2

SLAVERY AND ESCAPE

That evil influence which carried me first away from my father's house—which hurried me into the wild and indigested notion of raising my fortune, and that impressed those conceits so forcibly upon me as to make me deaf to all good advice, and to the entreaties and even the commands of my father—I say, the same influence, whatever it was, presented the most unfortunate of all enterprises to my view; and I went on board a vessel bound to the coast of Africa; or, as our sailors vulgarly called it, a voyage to Guinea.

It was my great misfortune that in all these adventures I did not ship myself as a sailor; when, though I might indeed have worked a little harder than ordinary, yet at the same time I should have learnt the duty and office of a fore-mast man, and in time might have qualified myself for a mate or lieutenant, if not for a master. But as it was always my fate to choose for the worse, so I did here; for having money in my pocket and good clothes upon my back, I would always go on board in the habit of a gentleman; and so I neither had any business in the ship, nor learned to do any.

It was my lot first of all to fall into pretty good company in London, which does not always happen to such loose and misguided young fellows as I then was; the devil generally not omitting to lay some snare for them very early; but it was not so with me. I first got acquainted with the master of a ship who had been on the coast of Guinea; and who, having had very good success there, was resolved to go again. This captain taking a fancy to my conversation, which was not at all disagreeable at that time, hearing me say I had a mind to see the world, told me if I would go the voyage with him I should be at no expense; I should be his messmate and his companion; and if I could carry anything with me, I should have all the advantage of it that the trade would admit; and perhaps I might meet with some encouragement.

I embraced the offer; and entering into a strict friendship with this captain, who was an honest, plain-dealing man, I went the voyage with him, and carried a small adventure with me, which, by the disinterested honesty of my friend the captain, I increased very considerably; for I carried about £40 in such toys and trifles as the captain directed me to buy. These £40 I had mustered together by the assistance of some of my relations whom I corresponded with; and who, I believe, got my father, or at least my mother, to contribute so much as that to my first adventure.

This was the only voyage which I may say was successful in all my adventures, which I owe to the integrity and honesty of my friend the captain; under whom also I got a competent knowledge of the mathematics and the rules of navigation, learned how to keep an account of the ship's course, take an observation, and, in short, to understand some things that were needful to be understood by a sailor; for, as he took delight to instruct me, I took delight to learn; and, in a word, this voyage made me both a sailor and a merchant; for I brought home five pounds nine ounces of gold-dust for my adventure, which yielded me in London, at my return, almost £300; and this filled me with those aspiring thoughts which have since so completed my ruin.

Yet even in this voyage I had my misfortunes too; particularly, that I was continually sick, being thrown into a violent calenture by the excessive heat of the climate; our principal trading being upon the coast, from latitude of 15 degrees north even to the line itself.

I was now set up for a Guinea trader; and my friend, to my great misfortune, dying soon after his arrival, I resolved to go the same voyage again, and I embarked in the same vessel with one who was his mate in the former voyage, and had now got the command of the ship. This was the unhappiest voyage that ever man made; for though I did not carry quite £100 of my new-gained wealth, so that I had £200 left, which I had lodged with my friend's widow, who was very just to me, yet I fell into terrible misfortunes. The first was this: our ship making her course towards the Canary Islands, or rather between those islands and the African shore, was surprised in the grey of the morning by a Turkish rover of Sallee, who gave chase to us with all the sail she could make. We crowded also as much canvas as our yards would spread, or our masts carry, to get clear; but finding the pirate gained upon us, and would certainly come up with us in a few hours, we prepared to fight; our ship having twelve guns, and the rogue eighteen. About three in the afternoon he came up with us, and bringing to, by mistake, just athwart our quarter, instead of athwart our stern, as he intended, we brought eight of our guns to bear on that side, and poured in a broadside upon him, which made him sheer off again, after returning our fire, and pouring in also his small shot from near two hundred men which he had on board. However, we had not a man touched, all our men keeping close. He prepared to attack us again, and we to defend ourselves. But laying us on board the next time upon our other quarter, he entered sixty men upon our decks, who immediately fell to cutting and hacking the sails and rigging. We plied them with small shot, half-pikes, powder-chests, and such like, and cleared our deck of them twice. However, to cut short this melancholy part of our story, our ship being disabled, and three of our men killed, and eight wounded, we were obliged to yield, and were carried all prisoners into Sallee, a port belonging to the Moors.

The usage I had there was not so dreadful as at first I apprehended; nor was I carried up the country to the emperor's court, as the rest of our men were, but was kept by the captain of the rover as his proper prize, and made his slave, being young and nimble, and fit for his business. At this surprising change of my circumstances, from a merchant to a miserable slave, I was perfectly overwhelmed; and now I looked back upon my father's prophetic discourse to me, that I should be miserable and have none to relieve me, which I thought was now so effectually brought to pass that I could not be worse; for now the hand of Heaven had overtaken me, and I was undone without redemption; but, alas! this was but a taste of the misery I was to go through, as will appear in the sequel of this story.

As my new patron, or master, had taken me home to his house, so I was in hopes that he would take me with him when he went to sea again, believing that it would some time or other be his fate to be taken by a Spanish or Portugal man-of-war; and that then I should be set at liberty. But this hope of mine was soon taken away; for when he went to sea, he left me on shore to look after his little garden, and do the common drudgery of slaves about his house; and when he came home again from his cruise, he ordered me to lie in the cabin to look after the ship.

Here I meditated nothing but my escape, and what method I might take to effect it, but found no way that had the least probability in it; nothing presented to make the supposition of it rational; for I had nobody to communicate it to that would embark with me—no fellow-slave, no Englishman, Irishman, or Scotchman there but myself; so that for two years, though I often pleased myself with the imagination, yet I never had the least encouraging prospect of putting it in practice.

After about two years, an odd circumstance presented itself, which put the old thought of making some attempt for my liberty again in my head. My patron lying at home longer than usual without fitting out his ship, which, as I heard, was for want of money, he used constantly, once or twice a week, sometimes oftener if the weather was fair, to take the ship's pinnace and go out into the road a-fishing; and as he always took me and young Maresco with him to row the boat, we made him very merry, and I proved very dexterous in catching fish; insomuch that sometimes he would send me with a Moor, one of his kinsmen, and the youth—the Maresco, as they called him—to catch a dish of fish for him.

It happened one time, that going a-fishing in a calm morning, a fog rose so thick that, though we were not half a league from the shore, we lost sight of it; and rowing we knew not whither or which way, we laboured all day, and all the next night; and when the morning came we found we had pulled off to sea instead of pulling in for the shore; and that we were at least two leagues from the shore. However, we got well in again, though with a great deal of labour and some danger; for the wind began to blow pretty fresh in the morning; but we were all very hungry.

But our patron, warned by this disaster, resolved to take more care of himself for the future; and having lying by him the longboat of our English ship that he had taken, he resolved he would not go a-fishing any more without a compass and some provision; so he ordered the carpenter of his ship, who also was an English slave, to build a little state-room, or cabin, in the middle of the long-boat, like that of a barge, with a place to stand behind it to steer, and haul home the main-sheet; the room before for a hand or two to stand and work the sails. She sailed with what we call a shoulder-of-mutton sail; and the boom jibed over the top of the cabin, which lay very snug and low, and had in it room for him to lie, with a slave or two, and a table to eat on, with some small lockers to put in some bottles of such liquor as he thought fit to drink; and his bread, rice, and coffee.

We went frequently out with this boat a-fishing; and as I was most dexterous to catch fish for him, he never went without me. It happened that he had appointed to go out in this boat, either for pleasure or for fish, with two or three Moors of some distinction in that place, and for whom he had provided extraordinarily, and had, therefore, sent on board the boat overnight a larger store of provisions than ordinary; and had ordered me to get ready three fusees with powder and shot, which were on board his ship, for that they designed some sport of fowling as well as fishing.

I got all things ready as he had directed, and waited the next morning with the boat washed clean, her ancient and pendants out, and everything to accommodate his guests; when by-and-by my patron came on board alone, and told me his guests had put off going from some business that fell out, and ordered me, with the man and boy, as usual, to go out with the boat and catch them some fish, for that his friends were to sup at his house, and commanded that as soon as I got some fish I should bring it home to his house; all which I prepared to do.

This moment my former notions of deliverance darted into my thoughts, for now I found I was likely to have a little ship at my command; and my master being gone, I prepared to furnish myself, not for fishing business, but for a voyage; though I knew not, neither did I so much as consider, whither I should steer—anywhere to get out of that place was my desire.

My first contrivance was to make a pretence to speak to this Moor, to get something for our subsistence on board; for I told him we must not presume to eat of our patron's bread. He said that was true; so he brought a large basket of rusk or biscuit, and three jars of fresh water, into the boat. I knew where my patron's case of bottles stood, which it was evident, by the make, were taken out of some English prize, and I conveyed them into the boat while the Moor was on shore, as if they had been there before for our master. I conveyed also a great lump of beeswax into the boat, which weighed about half a hundred-weight, with a parcel of twine or thread, a hatchet, a saw, and a hammer, all of which were of great use to us afterwards, especially the wax, to make candles. Another trick I tried upon him, which he innocently came into also: his name was Ismael, which they call Muley, or Moely; so I called to him—"Moely," said I, "our patron's guns are on board the boat; can you not get a little powder and shot? It may be we may kill some alcamies (a fowl like our curlews) for ourselves, for I know he keeps the gunner's stores in the ship." "Yes," says he, "I'll bring some;" and accordingly he brought a great leather pouch, which held a pound and a half of powder, or rather more; and another with shot, that had five or six pounds, with some bullets, and put all into the boat. At the same time I had found some powder of my master's in the great cabin, with which I filled one of the large bottles in the case, which was almost empty, pouring what was in it into another; and thus furnished with everything needful, we sailed out of the port to fish. The castle, which is at the entrance of the port, knew who we were, and took no notice of us; and we were not above a mile out of the port before we hauled in our sail and set us down to fish. The wind blew from the N.N.E., which was contrary to my desire, for had it blown southerly I had been sure to have made the coast of Spain, and at least reached to the bay of Cadiz; but my resolutions were, blow which way it would, I would be gone from that horrid place where I was, and leave the rest to fate.

After we had fished some time and caught nothing—for when I had fish on my hook I would not pull them up, that he might not see them—I said to the Moor, "This will not do; our master will not be thus served; we must stand farther off." He, thinking no harm, agreed, and being in the head of the boat, set the sails; and, as I had the helm, I ran the boat out near a league farther, and then brought her to, as if I would fish; when, giving the boy the helm, I stepped forward to where the Moor was, and making as if I stooped for something behind him, I took him by surprise with my arm under his waist, and tossed him clear overboard into the sea. He rose immediately, for he swam like a cork, and called to me, begged to be taken in, told me he would go all over the world with me. He swam so strong after the boat that he would have reached me very quickly, there being but little wind; upon which I stepped into the cabin, and fetching one of the fowling-pieces, I presented it at him, and told him I had done him no hurt, and if he would be quiet I would do him none. "But," said I, "you swim well enough to reach to the shore, and the sea is calm; make the best of your way to shore, and I will do you no harm; but if you come near the boat I'll shoot you through the head, for I am resolved to have my liberty;" so he turned himself about, and swam for the shore, and I make no doubt but he reached it with ease, for he was an excellent swimmer.

I could have been content to have taken this Moor with me, and have drowned the boy, but there was no venturing to trust him. When he was gone, I turned to the boy, whom they called Xury, and said to him, "Xury, if you will be faithful to me, I'll make you a great man; but if you will not stroke your face to be true to me"—that is, swear by Mahomet and his father's beard—"I must throw you into the sea too." The boy smiled in my face, and spoke so innocently that I could not distrust him, and swore to be faithful to me, and go all over the world with me.

While I was in view of the Moor that was swimming, I stood out directly to sea with the boat, rather stretching to windward, that they might think me gone towards the Straits' mouth (as indeed any one that had been in their wits must have been supposed to do): for who would have supposed we were sailed on to the southward, to the truly Barbarian coast, where whole nations of negroes were sure to surround us with their canoes and destroy us; where we could not go on shore but we should be devoured by savage beasts, or more merciless savages of human kind.

But as soon as it grew dusk in the evening, I changed my course, and steered directly south and by east, bending my course a little towards the east, that I might keep in with the shore; and having a fair, fresh gale of wind, and a smooth, quiet sea, I made such sail that I believe by the next day, at three o'clock in the afternoon, when I first made the land, I could not be less than one hundred and fifty miles south of Sallee; quite beyond the Emperor of Morocco's dominions, or indeed of any other king thereabouts, for we saw no people.

Yet such was the fright I had taken of the Moors, and the dreadful apprehensions I had of falling into their hands, that I would not stop, or go on shore, or come to an anchor; the wind continuing fair till I had sailed in that manner five days; and then the wind shifting to the southward, I concluded also that if any of our vessels were in chase of me, they also would now give over; so I ventured to make to the coast, and came to an anchor in the mouth of a little river, I knew not what, nor where, neither what latitude, what country, what nation, or what river. I neither saw, nor desired to see any people; the principal thing I wanted was fresh water. We came into this creek in the evening, resolving to swim on shore as soon as it was dark, and discover the country; but as soon as it was quite dark, we heard such dreadful noises of the barking, roaring, and howling of wild creatures, of we knew not what kinds, that the poor boy was ready to die with fear, and begged of me not to go on shore till day. "Well, Xury," said I, "then I won't; but it may be that we may see men by day, who will be as bad to us as those lions." "Then we give them the shoot gun," says Xury, laughing, "make them run wey." Such English Xury spoke by conversing among us slaves. However, I was glad to see the boy so cheerful, and I gave him a dram (out of our patron's case of bottles) to cheer him up. After all, Xury's advice was good, and I took it; we dropped our little anchor, and lay still all night; I say still, for we slept none; for in two or three hours we saw vast great creatures (we knew not what to call them) of many sorts, come down to the sea-shore and run into the water, wallowing and washing themselves for the pleasure of cooling themselves; and they made such hideous howlings and yellings, that I never indeed heard the like.

Xury was dreadfully frighted, and indeed so was I too; but we were both more frighted when we heard one of these mighty creatures come swimming towards our boat; we could not see him, but we might hear him by his blowing to be a monstrous huge and furious beast. Xury said it was a lion, and it might be so for aught I know; but poor Xury cried to me to weigh the anchor and row away; "No," says I, "Xury; we can slip our cable, with the buoy to it, and go off to sea; they cannot follow us far." I had no sooner said so, but I perceived the creature (whatever it was) within two oars' length, which something surprised me; however,

I immediately stepped to the cabin door, and taking up my gun, fired at him; upon which he immediately turned about and swam towards the shore again.

But it is impossible to describe the horrid noises, and hideous cries and howlings that were raised, as well upon the edge of the shore as higher within the country, upon the noise or report of the gun, a thing I have some reason to believe those creatures had never heard before: this convinced me that there was no going on shore for us in the night on that coast, and how to venture on shore in the day was another question too; for to have fallen into the hands of any of the savages had been as bad as to have fallen into the hands of the lions and tigers; at least we were equally apprehensive of the danger of it.

Be that as it would, we were obliged to go on shore somewhere or other for water, for we had not a pint left in the boat; when and where to get to it was the point. Xury said, if I would let him go on shore with one of the jars, he would find if there was any water, and bring some to me. I asked him why he would go? why I should not go, and he stay in the boat? The boy answered with so much affection as made me love him ever after. Says he, "If wild mans come, they eat me, you go wey." "Well, Xury," said I, "we will both go and if the wild mans come, we will kill them, they shall eat neither of us." So I gave Xury a piece of rusk bread to eat, and a dram out of our patron's case of bottles which I mentioned before; and we hauled the boat in as near the shore as we thought was proper, and so waded on shore, carrying nothing but our arms and two jars for water.

I did not care to go out of sight of the boat, fearing the coming of canoes with savages down the river; but the boy seeing a low place about a mile up the country, rambled to it, and by-and-by I saw him come running towards me. I thought he was pursued by some savage, or frighted with some wild beast, and I ran forward towards him to help him; but when I came nearer to him I saw something hanging over his shoulders, which was a creature that he had shot, like a hare, but different in colour, and longer legs; however, we were very glad of it, and it was very good meat; but the great joy that poor Xury came with, was to tell me he had found good water and seen no wild mans.

But we found afterwards that we need not take such pains for water, for a little higher up the creek where we were we found the water fresh when the tide was out, which flowed but a little way up; so we filled our jars, and feasted on the hare he had killed, and prepared to go on our way, having seen no footsteps of any human creature in that part of the country.

As I had been one voyage to this coast before, I knew very well that the islands of the Canaries, and the Cape de Verde Islands also, lay not far off from the coast. But as I had no instruments to take an observation to know what latitude we were in, and not exactly knowing, or at least remembering, what latitude they were in, I knew not where to look for them, or when to stand off to sea towards them; otherwise I might now easily have found some of these islands. But my hope was, that if I stood along this coast till I came to that part where the English traded, I should find some of their vessels upon their usual design of trade, that would relieve and take us in.

By the best of my calculation, that place where I now was must be that country which, lying between the Emperor of Morocco's dominions and the negroes, lies waste and uninhabited, except by wild beasts; the negroes having abandoned it and gone farther south for fear of the Moors, and the Moors not thinking it worth inhabiting by reason of its barrenness; and indeed, both forsaking it because of the prodigious number of tigers, lions, leopards, and other furious creatures which harbour there; so that the Moors use it for their hunting only, where they go like an army, two or three thousand men at a time; and indeed for near a hundred miles together upon this coast we saw nothing but a waste, uninhabited country by day, and heard nothing but howlings and roaring of wild beasts by night.

Once or twice in the daytime I thought I saw the Pico of Teneriffe, being the high top of the Mountain Teneriffe in the Canaries, and had a great mind to venture out, in hopes of reaching thither; but having tried twice, I was forced in again by contrary winds, the sea also going too high for my little vessel; so, I resolved to pursue my first design, and keep along the shore.

Several times I was obliged to land for fresh water, after we had left this place; and once in particular, being early in morning, we came to an anchor under a little point of land, which was pretty high; and the tide beginning to flow, we lay still to go farther in. Xury, whose eyes were more about him than it seems mine were, calls softly to me, and tells me that we had best go farther off the shore; "For," says he, "look, yonder lies a dreadful monster on the side of that hillock, fast asleep." I looked where he pointed, and saw a dreadful monster indeed, for it was a terrible, great lion that lay on the side of the shore, under the shade of a piece of the hill that hung as it were a little over him. "Xury," says I, "you shall on shore and kill him." Xury, looked frighted, and said, "Me kill! he eat me at one mouth!"—one mouthful he meant. However, I said no more to the boy, but bade him lie still, and I took our biggest gun, which was almost musket-bore, and loaded it with a good charge of powder, and with two slugs, and laid it down; then I loaded another gun with two bullets; and the third (for we had three pieces) I loaded with five smaller bullets. I took the best aim I could with the first piece to have shot him in the head, but he lay so with his leg raised a little above his nose, that the slugs hit his leg about the knee and broke the bone. He started up, growling at first, but finding his leg broken, fell down again; and then got upon three legs, and gave the most hideous roar that ever I heard. I was a little surprised that I had not hit him on the head; however, I took up the second piece immediately, and though he began to move off, fired again, and shot him in the head, and had the pleasure to see him drop and make but little noise, but lie struggling for life. Then Xury took heart, and would have me let him go on shore. "Well, go," said I: so the boy jumped into the water and taking a little gun in one hand, swam to shore with the other hand, and coming close to the creature, put the muzzle of the piece to his ear, and shot him in the head again, which despatched him quite.

This was game indeed to us, but this was no food; and I was very sorry to lose three charges of powder and shot upon a creature that was good for nothing to us. However, Xury said he would have some of him; so he comes on board, and asked me to give him the hatchet. "For what, Xury?" said I. "Me cut off his head," said he. However, Xury could not cut off his head, but he cut off a foot, and brought it with him, and it was a monstrous great one.

I bethought myself, however, that, perhaps the skin of him might, one way or other, be of some value to us; and I resolved to take off his skin if I could. So Xury and I went to work with him; but Xury was much the better workman at it, for I knew very ill how to do it. Indeed, it took us both up the whole day, but at last we got off the hide of him, and spreading it on the top of our cabin, the sun effectually dried it in two days' time, and it afterwards served me to lie upon.

WRECKED ON A DESERT ISLAND

After this stop, we made on to the southward continually for ten or twelve days, living very sparingly on our provisions, which began to abate very much, and going no oftener to the shore than we were obliged to for fresh water. My design in this was to make the river Gambia or Senegal, that is to say anywhere about the Cape de Verde, where I was in hopes to meet with some European ship; and if I did not, I knew not what course I had to take, but to seek for the islands, or perish there among the negroes. I knew that all the ships from Europe, which sailed either to the coast of Guinea or to Brazil, or to the East Indies, made this cape, or those islands; and, in a word, I put the whole of my fortune upon this single point, either that I must meet with some ship or must perish.

When I had pursued this resolution about ten days longer, as I have said, I began to see that the land was inhabited; and in two or three places, as we sailed by, we saw people stand upon the shore to look at us; we could also perceive they were quite black and naked. I was once inclined to have gone on shore to them; but Xury was my better counsellor, and said to me, "No go, no go." However, I hauled in nearer the shore that I might talk to them, and I found they ran along the shore by me a good way. I observed they had no weapons in their hand, except one, who had a long slender stick, which Xury said was a lance, and that they could throw them a great way with good aim; so I kept at a distance, but talked with them by signs as well as I could; and particularly made signs for something to eat: they beckoned to me to stop my boat, and they would fetch me some meat. Upon this I lowered the top of my sail and lay by, and two of them ran up into the country, and in less than half-an-hour came back, and brought with them two pieces of dried flesh and some corn, such as is the produce of their country; but we neither knew what the one or the other was; however, we were willing to accept it, but how to come at it was our next dispute, for I would not venture on shore to them, and they were as much afraid of us; but they took a safe way for us all, for they brought it to the shore and laid it down, and went and stood a great way off till we fetched it on board, and then came close to us again.

We made signs of thanks to them, for we had nothing to make them amends; but an opportunity offered that very instant to oblige them wonderfully; for while we were lying by the shore came two mighty creatures, one pursuing the other (as we took it) with great fury from the mountains towards the sea; whether it was the male pursuing the female, or whether they were in sport or in rage, we could not tell, any more than we could tell whether it was usual or strange, but I believe it was the latter; because, in the first place, those ravenous creatures seldom appear but in the night; and, in the second place, we found the people terribly frighted, especially the women. The man that had the lance or dart did not fly from them, but the rest did; however, as the two creatures ran directly into the water, they did not offer to fall upon any of the negroes, but plunged themselves into the sea, and swam about, as if they had come for their diversion; at last one of them began to come nearer our boat than at first I expected; but I lay ready for him, for I had loaded my gun with all possible expedition, and bade Xury load both the others. As soon as he came fairly within my reach, I fired, and shot him directly in the head; immediately he sank down into the water, but rose instantly, and plunged up and down, as if he were struggling for life, and so indeed he was; he immediately made to the shore; but between the wound, which was his mortal hurt, and the strangling of the water, he died just before he reached the shore.

It is impossible to express the astonishment of these poor creatures at the noise and fire of my gun: some of them were even ready to die for fear, and fell down as dead with the very terror; but when they saw the creature dead, and sunk in the water, and that I made signs to them to come to the shore, they took heart and came, and began to search for the creature. I found him by his blood staining the water; and by the help of a rope, which I slung round him, and gave the negroes to haul, they dragged him on shore, and found that it was a most curious leopard, spotted, and fine to an admirable degree; and the negroes held up their hands with admiration, to think what it was I had killed him with.

The other creature, frighted with the flash of fire and the noise of the gun, swam on shore, and ran up directly to the mountains from whence they came; nor could I, at that distance, know what it was. I found quickly the negroes wished to eat the flesh of this creature, so I was willing to have them take it as a favour from me; which, when I made signs to them that they might take him, they were very thankful for. Immediately they fell to work with him; and though they had no knife, yet, with a sharpened piece of wood, they took off his skin as readily, and much more readily, than we could have done with a knife. They offered me some of the flesh, which I declined, pointing out that I would give it them; but made signs for the skin, which they gave me very freely, and brought me a great deal more of their provisions, which, though I did not understand, yet I accepted. I then made signs to them for some water, and held out one of my jars to them, turning it bottom upward, to show that it was empty, and that I wanted to have it filled. They called immediately to some of their friends, and there came two women, and brought a great vessel made of earth, and burnt, as I supposed, in the sun, this they set down to me, as before, and I sent Xury on shore with my jars, and filled them all three. The women were as naked as the men.

I was now furnished with roots and corn, such as it was, and water; and leaving my friendly negroes, I made forward for about eleven days more, without offering to go near the shore, till I saw the land run out a great length into the sea, at about the distance of four or five leagues before me; and the sea being very calm, I kept a large offing to make this point. At length, doubling the point, at about two leagues from the land, I saw plainly land on the other side, to seaward; then I concluded, as it was most certain indeed, that this was the Cape de Verde, and those the islands called, from thence, Cape de Verde Islands. However, they were at a great distance, and I could not well tell what I had best to do; for if I should be taken with a fresh of wind, I might neither reach one or other.

In this dilemma, as I was very pensive, I stepped into the cabin and sat down, Xury having the helm; when, on a sudden, the boy cried out, "Master, master, a ship with a sail!" and the foolish boy was frighted out of his wits, thinking it must needs be some of his master's ships sent to pursue us, but I knew we were far enough out of their reach. I jumped out of the cabin, and immediately saw, not only the ship, but that it was a Portuguese ship; and, as I thought, was bound to the coast of Guinea, for negroes. But, when I observed the course she steered, I was soon convinced they were bound some other way, and did not design to come any nearer to the shore; upon which I stretched out to sea as much as I could, resolving to speak with them if possible.

With all the sail I could make, I found I should not be able to come in their way, but that they would be gone by before I could make any signal to them: but after I had crowded to the utmost, and began to despair, they, it seems, saw by the help of their glasses that it was some European boat, which they supposed must belong to some ship that was lost; so they shortened sail to let me come up. I was encouraged with this, and as I had my patron's ancient on board, I made a waft of it to them, for a signal of distress, and fired a gun, both which they saw; for they told me they saw the smoke, though they did not hear the gun. Upon these signals they very kindly brought to, and lay by for me; and in about three hours; time I came up with them.

They asked me what I was, in Portuguese, and in Spanish, and in French, but I understood none of them; but at last a Scotch sailor, who was on board, called to me: and I answered him, and told him I was an Englishman, that I had made my escape out of slavery from the Moors, at Sallee; they then bade me come on board, and very kindly took me in, and all my goods.

It was an inexpressible joy to me, which any one will believe, that I was thus delivered, as I esteemed it, from such a miserable and almost hopeless condition as I was in; and I immediately offered all I had to the captain of the ship, as a return for my deliverance; but he generously told me he would take nothing from me, but that all I had should be delivered safe to me when I came to the Brazils. "For," says he, "I have saved your life on no other terms than I would be glad to be saved myself: and it may, one time or other, be my lot to be taken up in the same condition. Besides," said he, "when I carry you to the Brazils, so great a way from your own country, if I should take from you what you have, you will be starved there, and then I only take away that life I have given. No, no," says he: "Seignior Inglese" (Mr. Englishman), "I will carry you thither in charity, and those things will help to buy your subsistence there, and your passage home again."

As he was charitable in this proposal, so he was just in the performance to a tittle; for he ordered the seamen that none should touch anything that I had: then he took everything into his own possession, and gave me back an exact inventory of them, that I might have them, even to my three earthen jars.

As to my boat, it was a very good one; and that he saw, and told me he would buy it of me for his ship's use; and asked me what I would have for it? I told him he had been so generous to me in everything that I could not offer to make any price of the boat, but left it entirely to him: upon which he told me he would give me a note of hand to pay me eighty pieces of eight for it at Brazil; and when it came there, if any one offered to give more, he would make it up. He offered me also sixty pieces of eight more for my boy Xury, which I was loth to take; not that I was unwilling to let the captain have him, but I was very loth to sell the poor boy's liberty, who had assisted me so faithfully in procuring my own. However, when I let him know my reason, he owned it to be just, and offered me this medium, that he would give the boy an obligation to set him free in ten years, if he turned Christian: upon this, and Xury saying he was willing to go to him, I let the captain have him.

We had a very good voyage to the Brazils, and I arrived in the Bay de Todos los Santos, or All Saints' Bay, in about twenty-two days after. And now I was once more delivered from the most miserable of all conditions of life; and what to do next with myself I was to consider.

The generous treatment the captain gave me I can never enough remember: he would take nothing of me for my passage, gave me twenty ducats for the leopard's skin, and forty for the lion's skin, which I had in my boat, and caused everything I had in the ship to be punctually delivered to me; and what I was willing to sell he bought of me, such as the case of bottles, two of my guns, and a piece of the lump of beeswax—for I had made candles of the rest: in a word, I made about two hundred and twenty pieces of eight of all my cargo; and with this stock I went on shore in the Brazils.

I had not been long here before I was recommended to the house of a good honest man like himself, who had an *ingenio*, as they call it (that is, a plantation and a sugar-house). I lived with him some time, and acquainted myself by that means with the manner of planting and making of sugar; and seeing how well the planters lived, and how they got rich suddenly, I resolved, if I could get a licence to settle there, I would turn planter among them: resolving in the meantime to find out some way to get my money, which I had left in London, remitted to me. To this purpose, getting a kind of letter of naturalisation, I purchased as much land that was uncured as my money would reach, and formed a plan for my plantation and settlement; such a one as might be suitable to the stock which I proposed to myself to receive from England.

I had a neighbour, a Portuguese, of Lisbon, but born of English parents, whose name was Wells, and in much such circumstances as I was. I call him my neighbour, because his plantation lay next to mine, and we went on very sociably together. My stock was but low, as well as his; and we rather planted for food than anything else, for about two years. However, we began to increase, and our land began to come into order; so that the third year we planted some tobacco, and made each of us a large piece of ground ready for planting canes in the year to come. But we both wanted help; and now I found, more than before, I had done wrong in parting with my boy Xury.

But, alas! for me to do wrong that never did right, was no great wonder. I had no remedy but to go on: I had got into an employment quite remote to my genius, and directly contrary to the life I delighted in, and for which I forsook my father's house, and broke through all his good advice. Nay, I was coming into the very middle station, or upper degree of low life, which my father advised me to before, and which, if I resolved to go on with, I might as well have stayed at home, and never have fatigued myself in the world as I had done; and I used often to say to myself, I could have done this as well in England, among my friends, as have gone five thousand miles off to do it among strangers and savages, in a wilderness, and at such a distance as never to hear from any part of the world that had the least knowledge of me.

In this manner I used to look upon my condition with the utmost regret. I had nobody to converse with, but now and then this neighbour; no work to be done, but by the labour of my hands; and I used to say, I lived just like a man cast away upon some desolate island, that had nobody there but himself. But how just has it been—and how should all men reflect, that when they compare their present conditions with others that are worse, Heaven may oblige them to make the exchange, and be convinced of their former felicity by their experience—I say, how just has it been, that the truly solitary life I reflected on, in an island of mere desolation, should be my lot, who had so often unjustly compared it with the life which I then led, in which, had I continued, I had in all probability been exceeding prosperous and rich.

I was in some degree settled in my measures for carrying on the plantation before my kind friend, the captain of the ship that took me up at sea, went back—for the ship remained there, in providing his lading and preparing for his voyage, nearly three months—when telling him what little stock I had left behind me in London, he gave me this friendly and sincere advice:—"Seignior Inglese," says he (for so he always called me), "if you will give me letters, and a procuration in form to me, with orders to the person who has your money in London to send your effects to Lisbon, to such persons as I shall direct, and in such goods as are proper for this country, I will bring you the produce of them, God willing, at my return; but, since human affairs are all subject to changes and disasters, I would have you give orders but for one hundred pounds sterling, which, you say, is half your stock, and let the hazard be run for the first; so that, if it come safe, you may order the rest the same way, and, if it miscarry, you may have the other half to have recourse to for your supply."

This was so wholesome advice, and looked so friendly, that I could not but be convinced it was the best course I could take; so I accordingly prepared letters to the gentlewoman with whom I had left my money, and a procuration to the Portuguese captain, as he desired.

I wrote the English captain's widow a full account of all my adventures—my slavery, escape, and how I had met with the Portuguese captain at sea, the humanity of his behaviour, and what condition I was now in, with all other necessary directions for my supply; and when this honest captain came to Lisbon, he found means, by some of the English merchants there, to send over, not the order only, but a full account of my story to a merchant in London, who represented it effectually to her; whereupon she not only delivered the money, but out of her own pocket sent the Portugal captain a very handsome present for his humanity and charity to me.

The merchant in London, vesting this hundred pounds in English goods, such as the captain had written for, sent them directly to him at Lisbon, and he brought them all safe to me to the Brazils; among which, without my direction (for I was too young in my business to think of them), he had taken care to have all sorts of tools, ironwork, and utensils necessary for my plantation, and which were of great use to me.

When this cargo arrived I thought my fortune made, for I was surprised with the joy of it; and my stood steward, the captain, had laid out the five pounds, which my friend had sent him for a present for himself, to purchase and bring me over a servant, under bond for six years' service, and would not accept of any consideration, except a little tobacco, which I would have him accept, being of my own produce.

Neither was this all; for my goods being all English manufacture, such as cloths, stuffs, baize, and things particularly valuable and desirable in the country, I found means to sell them to a very great advantage; so that I might say I had more than four times the value of my first cargo, and was now infinitely beyond my poor neighbour—I mean in the advancement of my plantation; for the first thing I did, I bought me a negro slave, and an European servant also—I mean another besides that which the captain brought me from Lisbon.

But as abused prosperity is oftentimes made the very means of our greatest adversity, so it was with me. I went on the next year with great success in my plantation: I raised fifty great rolls of tobacco on my own ground, more than I had disposed of for necessaries among my neighbours; and these fifty rolls, being each of above a hundredweight, were well cured, and laid by against the return of the fleet from Lisbon: and now increasing in business and wealth, my head began to be full of projects and undertakings beyond my reach; such as are, indeed, often the ruin of the best heads in business. Had I continued in the station I was now in, I had room for all the happy things to have yet befallen me for which my father so earnestly recommended a quiet, retired life, and of which he had so sensibly described the middle station of life to be full of; but other things attended me, and I was still to be the wilful agent of all my own miseries; and particularly, to increase my fault, and double the reflections upon myself, which in my future sorrows I should have leisure to make, all these miscarriages were procured by my apparent obstinate adhering to my foolish inclination of wandering abroad, and pursuing that inclination, in contradiction to the clearest views of doing myself good in a fair and plain pursuit of those prospects, and those measures of life, which nature and Providence concurred to present me with, and to make my duty.

As I had once done thus in my breaking away from my parents, so I could not be content now, but I must go and leave the happy view I had of being a rich and thriving man in my new plantation, only to pursue a rash and immoderate desire of rising faster than the nature of the thing admitted; and thus I cast myself down again into the deepest gulf of human misery that ever man fell into, or perhaps could be consistent with life and a state of health in the world.

To come, then, by the just degrees to the particulars of this part of my story. You may suppose, that having now lived almost four years in the Brazils, and beginning to thrive and prosper very well upon my plantation, I had not only learned the language, but had contracted acquaintance and friendship among my fellow-planters, as well as among the merchants at St. Salvador, which was our port; and that, in my discourses among them, I had frequently given them an account of my two voyages to the coast of Guinea: the manner of trading with the negroes there, and how easy it was to purchase upon the coast for trifles—such as beads, toys, knives, scissors, hatchets, bits of glass, and the like—not only gold-dust, Guinea grains, elephants' teeth, &c., but negroes, for the service of the Brazils, in great numbers.

They listened always very attentively to my discourses on these heads, but especially to that part which related to the buying of negroes, which was a trade at that time, not only not far entered into, but, as far as it was, had been carried on by assientos, or permission of the kings of Spain and Portugal, and engrossed in the public stock: so that few negroes were bought, and these excessively dear.

It happened, being in company with some merchants and planters of my acquaintance, and talking of those things very earnestly, three of them came to me next morning, and told me they had been musing very much upon what I had discoursed with them of the last night, and they came to make a secret proposal to me; and, after enjoining me to secrecy, they told me that they had a mind to fit out a ship to go to Guinea; that they had all plantations as well as I, and were straitened for nothing so much as servants; that as it was a trade that could not be carried on, because they could not publicly sell the negroes when they came home, so they desired to make but one voyage, to bring the negroes on shore privately, and divide them among their own plantations; and, in a word, the question was whether I would go their supercargo in the ship, to manage the trading part upon the coast of Guinea; and they offered me that I should have my equal share of the negroes, without providing any part of the stock.

This was a fair proposal, it must be confessed, had it been made to any one that had not had a settlement and a plantation of his own to look after, which was in a fair way of coming to be very considerable, and with a good stock upon it; but for me, that was thus entered and established, and had nothing to do but to go on as I had begun, for three or four years more, and to have sent for the other hundred pounds from England; and who in that time, and with that little addition, could scarce have failed of being worth three or four thousand pounds sterling, and that increasing too—for me to think of such a voyage was the most preposterous thing that ever man in such circumstances could be guilty of.

But I, that was born to be my own destroyer, could no more resist the offer than I could restrain my first rambling designs when my father's good counsel was lost upon me. In a word, I told them I would go with all my heart, if they would undertake to look after my plantation in my absence, and would dispose of it to such as I should direct, if I miscarried. This they all engaged to do, and entered into writings or covenants to do so; and I made a formal will, disposing of my plantation and effects in case of my death, making the captain of the ship that had saved my life, as before, my universal heir, but obliging him to dispose of my effects as I had directed in my will; one half of the produce being to himself, and the other to be shipped to England.

In short, I took all possible caution to preserve my effects and to keep up my plantation. Had I used half as much prudence to have looked into my own interest, and have made a judgment of what I ought to have done and not to have done, I had certainly never gone away from so prosperous an undertaking, leaving all the probable views of a thriving circumstance, and gone upon a voyage to sea, attended with all its common hazards, to say nothing of the reasons I had to expect particular misfortunes to myself.

But I was hurried on, and obeyed blindly the dictates of my fancy rather than my reason; and, accordingly, the ship being fitted out, and the cargo furnished, and all things done, as by agreement, by my partners in the voyage, I went on board in an evil hour, the 1st September 1659, being the same day eight years that I went from my father and mother at Hull, in order to act the rebel to their authority, and the fool to my own interests.

Our ship was about one hundred and twenty tons burden, carried six guns and fourteen men, besides the master, his boy, and myself. We had on board no large cargo of goods, except of such toys as were fit for our trade with the negroes, such as beads, bits of glass, shells, and other trifles, especially little looking-glasses, knives, scissors, hatchets, and the like.

The same day I went on board we set sail, standing away to the northward upon our own coast, with design to stretch over for the African coast when we came about ten or twelve degrees of northern latitude, which, it seems, was the manner of course in those days. We had very good weather, only excessively hot, all the way upon our own coast, till we came to the height of Cape St. Augustino; from whence, keeping further off at sea, we lost sight of land, and steered as if we were bound for the isle Fernando de Noronha, holding our course N.E. by N., and leaving those isles on the east. In this course we passed the line in about twelve days' time, and were, by our last observation, in seven degrees twenty-two minutes northern latitude, when a violent tornado, or hurricane, took us quite out of our knowledge. It began from the south-east, came about to the north-west, and then settled in the north-east; from whence it blew in such a terrible manner, that for twelve days together we could do nothing but drive, and, scudding away before it, let it carry us whither fate and the fury of the winds directed; and, during these twelve days, I need not say that I expected every day to be swallowed up; nor, indeed, did any in the ship expect to save their lives.

In this distress we had, besides the terror of the storm, one of our men die of the calenture, and one man and the boy washed overboard. About the twelfth day, the weather abating a little, the master made an observation as well as he could, and found that he was in about eleven degrees north latitude, but that he was twenty-two degrees of longitude difference west from Cape St. Augustino; so that he found he was upon the coast of Guiana, or the north part of Brazil, beyond the river Amazon, toward that of the river Orinoco, commonly called the Great River; and began to consult with me what course he should take, for the ship was leaky, and very much disabled, and he was going directly back to the coast of Brazil.

I was positively against that; and looking over the charts of the sea-coast of America with him, we concluded there was no inhabited country for us to have recourse to till we came within the circle of the Caribbee Islands, and therefore resolved to stand away for Barbadoes; which, by keeping off at sea, to avoid the indraft of the Bay or Gulf of Mexico, we might easily perform, as we hoped, in about fifteen days' sail; whereas we could not possibly make our voyage to the coast of Africa without some assistance both to our ship and to ourselves.

With this design we changed our course, and steered away N.W. by W., in order to reach some of our English islands, where I hoped for relief. But our voyage was otherwise determined; for, being in the latitude of twelve degrees eighteen minutes, a second storm came upon us, which carried us away with the same impetuosity westward, and drove us so out of the way of all human commerce, that, had all our lives been saved as to the sea, we were rather in danger of being devoured by savages than ever returning to our own country.

In this distress, the wind still blowing very hard, one of our men early in the morning cried out, "Land!" and we had no sooner run out of the cabin to look out, in hopes of seeing whereabouts in the world we were, than the ship struck upon a sand, and in a moment her motion being so stopped, the sea broke over her in such a manner that we expected we should all have perished immediately; and we were immediately driven into our close quarters, to shelter us from the very foam and spray of the sea.

It is not easy for any one who has not been in the like condition to describe or conceive the consternation of men in such circumstances. We knew nothing where we were, or upon what land it was we were driven—whether an island or the main, whether inhabited or not inhabited. As the rage of the wind was still great, though rather less than at first, we could not so much as hope to have the ship hold many minutes without breaking into pieces, unless the winds, by a kind of miracle, should turn immediately about. In a word, we sat looking upon one another, and expecting death every moment, and every man, accordingly, preparing for another world; for there was little or nothing more for us to do in this. That which was our present comfort, and all the comfort we had, was that, contrary to our expectation, the ship did not break yet, and that the master said the wind began to abate.

Now, though we thought that the wind did a little abate, yet the ship having thus struck upon the sand, and sticking too fast for us to expect her getting off, we were in a dreadful condition indeed, and had nothing to do but to think of saving our lives as well as we could. We had a boat at our stern just before the storm, but she was first staved by dashing against the ship's rudder, and in the next place she broke away, and either sunk or was driven off to sea; so there was no hope from her. We had another boat on board, but how to get her off into the sea was a doubtful thing. However, there was no time to debate, for we fancied that the ship would break in pieces every minute, and some told us she was actually broken already.

In this distress the mate of our vessel laid hold of the boat, and with the help of the rest of the men got her slung over the ship's side; and getting all into her, let go, and committed ourselves, being eleven in number, to God's mercy and the wild sea; for though the storm was abated considerably, yet the sea ran dreadfully high upon the shore, and might be well called *den wild zee*, as the Dutch call the sea in a storm.

And now our case was very dismal indeed; for we all saw plainly that the sea went so high that the boat could not live, and that we should be inevitably drowned. As to making sail, we had none, nor if we had could we have done anything with it; so we worked at the oar towards the land, though with heavy hearts, like men going to execution; for we all knew that when the boat came near the shore she would be dashed in a thousand pieces by the breach of the sea. However, we committed our souls to God in the most earnest manner; and the wind driving us towards the shore, we hastened our destruction with our own hands, pulling as well as we could towards land.

What the shore was, whether rock or sand, whether steep or shoal, we knew not. The only hope that could rationally give us the least shadow of expectation was, if we might find some bay or gulf, or the mouth of some river, where by great chance we might have run our boat in, or got under the lee of the land, and perhaps made smooth water. But there was nothing like this appeared; but as we made nearer and nearer the shore, the land looked more frightful than the sea.

After we had rowed, or rather driven about a league and a half, as we reckoned it, a raging wave, mountain-like, came rolling astern of us, and plainly bade us expect the *coup de grâce*. It took us with such a fury, that it overset the boat at once; and separating us as well from the boat as from one another, gave us no time to say, "O God!" for we were all swallowed up in a moment.

Nothing can describe the confusion of thought which I felt when I sank into the water; for though I swam very well, yet I could not deliver myself from the waves so as to draw breath, till that wave having driven me, or rather carried me, a vast way on towards the shore, and having spent itself, went back, and left me upon the land almost dry, but half dead with the water I took in. I had so much presence of mind, as well as breath left, that seeing myself nearer the mainland than I expected, I got upon my feet, and endeavoured to make on towards the land as fast as I could before another wave should return and take me up again; but I soon found it was impossible to avoid it; for I saw the sea come after me as high as a great hill, and as furious as an enemy, which I had no means or strength to contend with: my business was to hold my breath, and raise myself upon the water if I could; and so, by swimming, to preserve my breathing, and pilot myself towards the shore, if possible, my greatest concern now being that the sea, as it would carry me a great way towards the shore when it came on, might not carry me back again with it when it gave back towards the sea.

The wave that came upon me again buried me at once twenty or thirty feet deep in its own body, and I could feel myself carried with a mighty force and swiftness towards the shore—a very great way; but I held my breath, and assisted myself to swim still forward with all my might. I was ready to burst with holding my breath, when, as I felt myself rising up, so, to my immediate relief, I found my head and hands shoot out above the surface of the water; and though it was not two seconds of time that I could keep myself so, yet it relieved me greatly, gave me breath, and new courage. I was covered again with water a good while, but not so long but I held it out; and finding the water had spent itself, and began to return, I struck forward against the return of the waves, and felt ground again with my feet. I stood still a few moments to recover breath, and till the waters went from me, and then took to my heels and ran with what strength I had further towards the shore. But neither would this deliver me from the fury of the sea, which came pouring in after me again; and twice more I was lifted up by the waves and carried forward as before, the shore being very flat.

The last time of these two had well-nigh been fatal to me, for the sea having hurried me along as before, landed me, or rather dashed me, against a piece of rock, and that with such force, that it left me senseless, and indeed helpless, as to my own deliverance; for the blow taking my side and breast, beat the breath as it were quite out of my body; and had it returned again immediately, I must have been strangled in the water; but I recovered a little before the return of the waves, and seeing I should be covered again with the water, I resolved to hold fast by a piece of the rock, and so to hold my breath, if possible, till the wave went back. Now, as the waves were not so high as at first, being nearer land, I held my hold till the wave abated, and then fetched another run, which brought me so near the shore that the next wave, though it went over me, yet did not so swallow me up as to carry me away; and the next run I took, I got to the mainland, where, to my great comfort, I clambered up the cliffs of the shore and sat me down upon the grass, free from danger and quite out of the reach of the water.

I was now landed and safe on shore, and began to look up and thank God that my life was saved, in a case wherein there was some minutes before scarce any room to hope. I believe it is impossible to express, to the life, what the ecstasies and transports of the soul are, when it is so saved, as I may say, out of the very grave: and I do not wonder now at the custom, when a malefactor, who has the halter about his neck, is tied up, and just going to be turned off, and has a reprieve brought to him—I say, I do not wonder that they bring a surgeon with it, to let him blood that very moment they tell him of it, that the surprise may not drive the animal spirits from the heart and overwhelm him.

"For sudden joys, like griefs, confound at first."

I walked about on the shore lifting up my hands, and my whole being, as I may say, wrapped up in a contemplation of my deliverance; making a thousand gestures and motions, which I cannot describe; reflecting upon all my comrades that were drowned, and that there should not be one soul saved but myself; for, as for them, I never saw them afterwards, or any sign of them, except three of their hats, one cap, and two shoes that were not fellows.

I cast my eye to the stranded vessel, when, the breach and froth of the sea being so big, I could hardly see it, it lay so far of; and considered, Lord! how was it possible I could get on shore?

After I had solaced my mind with the comfortable part of my condition, I began to look round me, to see what kind of place I was in, and what was next to be done; and I soon found my comforts abate, and that, in a word, I had a dreadful deliverance; for I was wet, had no clothes to shift me, nor anything either to eat or drink to comfort me; neither did I see any prospect before me but that of perishing with hunger or being devoured by wild beasts; and that which was particularly afflicting to me was, that I had no weapon, either to hunt and kill any creature for my sustenance, or to defend myself against any other creature that might desire to kill me for theirs. In a word, I had nothing about me but a knife, a tobacco-pipe, and a little tobacco in a box. This was all my provisions; and this threw me into such terrible agonies of mind, that for a while I ran about like a madman. Night coming upon me, I began with a heavy heart to consider what would be my lot if there were any ravenous beasts in that country, as at night they always come abroad for their prey.

All the remedy that offered to my thoughts at that time was to get up into a thick bushy tree like a fir, but thorny, which grew near me, and where I resolved to sit all night, and consider the next day what death I should die, for as yet I saw no prospect of life. I walked about a furlong from the shore, to see if I could find any fresh water to drink, which I did, to my great joy; and having drank, and put a little tobacco into my mouth to prevent hunger, I went to the tree, and getting up into it, endeavoured to place myself so that if I should sleep I might not fall. And having cut me a short stick, like a truncheon, for my defence, I took up my lodging; and having been excessively fatigued, I fell fast asleep, and slept as comfortably as, I believe, few could have done in my condition, and found myself more refreshed with it than, I think, I ever was on such an occasion.

4

FIRST WEEKS ON THE ISLAND

When I waked it was broad day, the weather clear, and the storm abated, so that the sea did not rage and swell as before. But that which surprised me most was, that the ship was lifted off in the night from the sand where she lay by the swelling of the tide, and was driven up almost as far as the rock which I at first mentioned, where I had been so bruised by the wave dashing me against it. This being within about a mile from the shore where I was, and the ship seeming to stand upright still, I wished myself on board, that at least I might save some necessary things for my use.

When I came down from my apartment in the tree, I looked about me again, and the first thing I found was the boat, which lay, as the wind and the sea had tossed her up, upon the land, about two miles on my right hand. I walked as far as I could upon the shore to have got to her; but found a neck or inlet of water between me and the boat which was about half a mile broad; so I came back for the present, being more intent upon getting at the ship, where I hoped to find something for my present subsistence.

A little after noon I found the sea very calm, and the tide ebbed so far out that I could come within a quarter of a mile of the ship. And here I found a fresh renewing of my grief; for I saw evidently that if we had kept on board we had been all safe—that is to say, we had all got safe on shore, and I had not been so miserable as to be left entirely destitute of all comfort and company as I now was. This forced tears to my eyes again; but as there was little relief in that, I resolved, if possible, to get to the ship; so I pulled off my clothes—for the weather was hot to extremity—and took the water. But when I came to the ship my difficulty was still greater to know how to get on board; for, as she lay aground, and high out of the water, there was nothing within my reach to lay hold of. I swam round her twice, and the second time I spied a small piece of rope, which I wondered I did not see at first, hung down by the fore-chains so low, as that with great difficulty I got hold of it, and by the help of that rope I got up into the forecastle of the ship. Here I found that the ship was bulged, and had a great deal of water in her hold, but that she lay so on the side of a bank of hard sand, or, rather earth, that her stern lay lifted up upon the bank, and her head low, almost to the water. By this means all her quarter was free, and all that was in that part was dry; for you may be sure my first work was to search, and to see what was spoiled and what was free. And, first, I found that all the ship's provisions were dry and untouched by the water, and being very well disposed to eat, I went to the bread room and filled my pockets with biscuit, and ate it as I went about other things, for I had no time to lose. I also found some rum in the great cabin, of which I took a large dram, and which I had, indeed, need enough of to spirit me for what was before me. Now I wanted nothing but a boat to furnish myself with many things which I foresaw would be very necessary to me.

It was in vain to sit still and wish for what was not to be had; and this extremity roused my application. We had several spare yards, and two or three large spars of wood, and a spare topmast or two in the ship; I resolved to fall to work with these, and I flung as many of them overboard as I could manage for their weight, tying every one with a rope, that they might not drive away. When this was done I went down the ship's side, and pulling them to me, I tied four of them together at both ends as well as I could, in the form of a raft, and laying two or three short pieces of plank upon them crossways, I found I could walk upon it very well, but that it was not able to bear any great weight, the pieces being too light. So I went to work, and with a carpenter's saw I cut a spare topmast into three lengths, and added them to my raft, with a great deal of labour and pains. But the hope of furnishing myself with necessaries encouraged me to go beyond what I should have been able to have done upon another occasion.

My raft was now strong enough to bear any reasonable weight. My next care was what to load it with, and how to preserve what I laid upon it from the surf of the sea; but I was not long considering this. I first laid all the planks or boards upon it that I could get, and having considered well what I most wanted, I got three of the seamen's chests, which I had broken open, and emptied, and lowered them down upon my raft; the first of these I filled with provisions—viz. bread, rice, three Dutch cheeses, five pieces of dried goat's flesh (which we lived much upon), and a little remainder of European corn, which had been laid by for some fowls which we brought to sea with us, but the fowls were killed. There had been some barley and wheat together; but, to my great disappointment, I found afterwards that the rats had eaten or spoiled it all. As for liquors, I found several, cases of bottles belonging to our skipper, in which were some cordial waters; and, in all, about five or six gallons of rack. These I stowed by themselves, there being no need to put them into the chest, nor any room for them. While I was doing this, I found the tide begin to flow, though very calm; and I had the mortification to see my coat, shirt, and waistcoat, which I had left on the shore, upon the sand, swim away. As for my breeches, which were only linen, and open-kneed, I swam on board in them and my stockings. However, this set me on rummaging for clothes, of which I found enough, but took no more than I wanted for present use, for I had others things which my eye was more upon—as, first, tools to work with on shore. And it was after long searching that I found out the carpenter's chest, which was, indeed, a very useful prize to me, and much more valuable than a shipload of gold would have been at that time. I got it down to my raft, whole as it was, without losing time to look into it, for I knew in general what it contained.

My next care was for some ammunition and arms. There were two very good fowling-pieces in the great cabin, and two pistols. These I secured first, with some powder-horns and a small bag of shot, and two old rusty swords. I knew there were three barrels of powder in the ship, but knew not where our gunner had stowed them; but with much search I found them, two of them dry and good, the third had taken water. Those two I got to my raft with the arms. And now I thought myself pretty well freighted, and began to think how I should get to shore with them, having neither sail, oar, nor rudder; and the least capful of wind would have overset all my navigation.

I had three encouragements—1st, a smooth, calm sea; 2ndly, the tide rising, and setting in to the shore; 3rdly, what little wind there was blew me towards the land. And thus, having found two or three broken oars belonging to the boat—and, besides the tools which were in the chest, I found two saws, an axe, and a hammer; with this cargo I put to sea. For a mile or thereabouts my raft went very well, only that I found it drive a little distant from the place where I had landed before; by which I perceived that there was some indraft of the water, and consequently I hoped to find some creek or river there, which I might make use of as a port to get to land with my cargo.

As I imagined, so it was. There appeared before me a little opening of the land, and I found a strong current of the tide set into it; so I guided my raft as well as I could, to keep in the middle of the stream.

But here I had like to have suffered a second shipwreck, which, if I had, I think verily would have broken my heart; for, knowing nothing of the coast, my raft ran aground at one end of it upon a shoal, and not being aground at the other end, it wanted but a little that all my cargo had slipped off towards the end that was afloat, and to fallen into the water. I did my utmost, by setting my back against the chests, to keep them in their places, but could not thrust off the raft with all my strength; neither durst I stir from the posture I was in; but holding up the chests with all my might, I stood in that manner near half-an-hour, in which time the rising of the water brought me a little more upon a level; and a little after, the water still-rising, my raft floated again, and I thrust her off with the oar I had into the channel, and then driving up higher, I at length found myself in the mouth of a little river, with land on both sides, and a strong current of tide running up. I looked on both sides for a proper place to get to shore, for I was not willing to be driven too high up the river: hoping in time to see some ships at sea, and therefore resolved to place myself as near the coast as I could.

At length I spied a little cove on the right shore of the creek, to which with great pain and difficulty I guided my raft, and at last got so near that, reaching ground with my oar, I could thrust her directly in. But here I had like to have dipped all my cargo into the sea again; for that shore lying pretty steep—that is to say sloping—there was no place to land, but where one end of my float, if it ran on shore, would lie so high, and the other sink lower, as before, that it would endanger my cargo again. All that I could do was to wait till the tide was at the highest, keeping the raft with my oar like an anchor, to hold the side of it fast to the shore, near a flat piece of ground, which I expected the water would flow over; and so it did. As soon as I found water enough—for my raft drew about a foot of water—I thrust her upon that flat piece of ground, and there fastened or moored her, by sticking my two broken oars into the ground, one on one side near one end, and one on the other side near the other end; and thus I lay till the water ebbed away, and left my raft and all my cargo safe on shore.

My next work was to view the country, and seek a proper place for my habitation, and where to stow my goods to secure them from whatever might happen. Where I was, I yet knew not; whether on the continent or on an island; whether inhabited or not inhabited; whether in danger of wild beasts or not. There was a hill not above a mile from me, which rose up very steep and high, and which seemed to overtop some other hills, which lay as in a ridge from it northward. I took out one of the fowling-pieces, and one of the pistols, and a horn of powder; and thus armed, I travelled for discovery up to the top of that hill, where, after I had with great labour and difficulty got to the top, I saw my fate, to my great affliction —viz. that I was in an island environed every way with the sea: no land to be seen except some rocks, which lay a great way off; and two small islands, less than this, which lay about three leagues to the west.

I found also that the island I was in was barren, and, as I saw good reason to believe, uninhabited except by wild beasts, of whom, however, I saw none. Yet I saw abundance of fowls, but knew not their kinds; neither when I killed them could I tell what was fit for food, and what not. At my coming back, I shot at a great bird which I saw sitting upon a tree on the side of a great wood. I believe it was the first gun that had been fired there since the creation of the world. I had no sooner fired, than from all parts of the wood there arose an innumerable number of fowls, of many sorts, making a confused screaming and crying, and every one according to his usual note, but not one of them of any kind that I knew. As for the creature I killed, I took it to be a kind of hawk, its colour and beak resembling it, but it had no talons or claws more than common. Its flesh was carrion, and fit for nothing.

Contented with this discovery, I came back to my raft, and fell to work to bring my cargo on shore, which took me up the rest of that day. What to do with myself at night I knew not, nor indeed where to rest, for I was afraid to lie down on the ground, not knowing but some wild beast might devour me, though, as I afterwards found, there was really no need for those fears.

However, as well as I could, I barricaded myself round with the chest and boards that I had brought on shore, and made a kind of hut for that night's lodging. As for food, I yet saw not which way to supply myself, except that I had seen two or three creatures like hares run out of the wood where I shot the fowl.

I now began to consider that I might yet get a great many things out of the ship which would be useful to me, and particularly some of the rigging and sails, and such other things as might come to land; and I resolved to make another voyage on board the vessel, if possible. And as I knew that the first storm that blew must necessarily break her all in pieces, I resolved to set all other things apart till I had got everything out of the ship that I could get. Then I called a council—that is to say in my thoughts—whether I should take back the raft; but this appeared impracticable: so I resolved to go as before, when the tide was down; and I did so, only that I stripped before I went from my hut, having nothing on but my chequered shirt, a pair of linen drawers, and a pair of pumps on my feet.

I got on board the ship as before, and prepared a second raft; and, having had experience of the first, I neither made this so unwieldy, nor loaded it so hard, but yet I brought away several things very useful to me; as first, in the carpenters stores I found two or three bags full of nails and spikes, a great screw-jack, a dozen or two of hatchets, and, above all, that most useful thing called a grindstone. All these I secured, together with several things belonging to the gunner, particularly two or three iron crows, and two barrels of musket bullets, seven muskets, another fowling-piece, with some small quantity of powder more; a large bagful of small shot, and a great roll of sheet-lead; but this last was so heavy, I could not hoist it up to get it over the ship's side.

Besides these things, I took all the men's clothes that I could find, and a spare fore-topsail, a hammock, and some bedding; and with this I loaded my second raft, and brought them all safe on shore, to my very great comfort.

I was under some apprehension, during my absence from the land, that at least my provisions might be devoured on shore: but when I came back I found no sign of any visitor; only there sat a creature like a wild cat upon one of the chests, which, when I came towards it, ran away a little distance, and then stood still. She sat very composed and unconcerned, and looked full in my face, as if she had a mind to be acquainted with me. I presented my gun at her, but, as she did not understand it, she was perfectly unconcerned at it, nor did she offer to stir away; upon which I tossed her a bit of biscuit, though by the way, I was not very free of it, for my store was not great: however, I spared her a bit, I say, and she went to it, smelled at it, and ate it, and looked (as if pleased) for more; but I thanked her, and could spare no more: so she marched off.

Having got my second cargo on shore—though I was fain to open the barrels of powder, and bring them by parcels, for they were too heavy, being large casks—I went to work to make me a little tent with the sail and some poles which I cut for that purpose: and into this tent I brought everything that I knew would spoil either with rain or sun; and I piled all the empty chests and casks up in a circle round the tent, to fortify it from any sudden attempt, either from man or beast.

When I had done this, I blocked up the door of the tent with some boards within, and an empty chest set up on end without; and spreading one of the beds upon the ground, laying my two pistols just at my head, and my gun at length by me, I went to bed for the first time, and slept very quietly all night, for I was very weary and heavy; for the night before I had slept little, and had laboured very hard all day to fetch all those things from the ship, and to get them on shore.

I had the biggest magazine of all kinds now that ever was laid up, I believe, for one man: but I was not satisfied still, for while the ship sat upright in that posture, I thought I ought to get everything out of her that I could; so every day at low water I went on board, and brought away something or other; but particularly the third time I went I brought away as much of the rigging as I could, as also all the small ropes and rope-twine I could get, with a piece of spare canvas, which was to mend the sails upon occasion, and the barrel of wet gunpowder. In a word, I brought away all the sails, first and last; only that I was fain to cut them in pieces, and bring as much at a time as I could, for they were no more useful to be sails, but as mere canvas only.

But that which comforted me more still, was, that last of all, after I had made five or six such voyages as these, and thought I had nothing more to expect from the ship that was worth my meddling with—I say, after all this, I found a great hogshead of bread, three large runlets of rum, or spirits, a box of sugar, and a barrel of fine flour; this was surprising to me, because I had given over expecting any more provisions, except what was spoiled by the water. I soon emptied the hogshead of the bread, and wrapped it up, parcel by parcel, in pieces of the sails, which I cut out; and, in a word, I got all this safe on shore also.

The next day I made another voyage, and now, having plundered the ship of what was portable and fit to hand out, I began with the cables. Cutting the great cable into pieces, such as I could move, I got two cables and a hawser on shore, with all the ironwork I could get; and having cut down the spritsail-yard, and the mizzen-yard, and everything I could, to make a large raft, I loaded it with all these heavy goods, and came away. But my good luck began now to leave me; for this raft was so unwieldy, and so overladen, that, after I had entered the little cove where I had landed the rest of my goods, not being able to guide it so handily as I did the other, it overset, and threw me and all my cargo into the water. As for myself, it was no great harm, for I was near the shore; but as to my cargo, it was a great part of it lost, especially the iron, which I expected would have been of great use to me; however, when the tide was out, I got most of the pieces of the cable ashore, and some of the iron, though with infinite labour; for I was fain to dip for it into the water, a work which fatigued me very much. After this, I went every day on board, and brought away what I could get.

I had been now thirteen days on shore, and had been eleven times on board the ship, in which time I had brought away all that one pair of hands could well be supposed capable to bring; though I believe verily, had the calm weather held, I should have brought away the whole ship, piece by piece. But preparing the twelfth time to go on board, I found the wind began to rise: however, at low water I went on board, and though I thought I had rummaged the cabin so effectually that nothing more could be found, yet I discovered a locker with drawers in it, in one of which I found two or three razors, and one pair of large scissors, with some ten or a dozen of good knives and forks: in another I found about thirty-six pounds value in money—some European coin, some Brazil, some pieces of eight, some gold, and some silver.

I smiled to myself at the sight of this money: "O drug!" said I, aloud, "what art thou good for? Thou art not worth to me—no, not the taking off the ground; one of those knives is worth all this heap; I have no manner of use for thee—e'en remain where thou art, and go to the bottom as a creature whose life is not worth saying." However, upon second thoughts I took it away; and wrapping all this in a piece of canvas, I began to think of making another raft; but while I was preparing this, I found the sky overcast, and the wind began to rise, and in a quarter of an hour it blew a fresh gale from the shore. It presently occurred to me that it was in vain to pretend to make a raft with the wind offshore; and that it was my business to be gone before the tide of flood began, otherwise I might not be able to reach the shore at all. Accordingly, I let myself down into the water, and swam across the channel, which lay between the ship and the sands, and even that with difficulty enough, partly with the weight of the things I had about me, and partly the roughness of the water; for the wind rose very hastily, and before it was quite high water it blew a storm.

But I had got home to my little tent, where I lay, with all my wealth about me, very secure. It blew very hard all night, and in the morning, when I looked out, behold, no more ship was to be seen! I was a little surprised, but recovered myself with the satisfactory reflection that I had lost no time, nor abated any diligence, to get everything out of her that could be useful to me; and that, indeed, there was little left in her that I was able to bring away, if I had had more time.

I now gave over any more thoughts of the ship, or of anything out of her, except what might drive on shore from her wreck; as, indeed, divers pieces of her afterwards did; but those things were of small use to me.

My thoughts were now wholly employed about securing myself against either savages, if any should appear, or wild beasts, if any were in the island; and I had many thoughts of the method how to do this, and what kind of dwelling to make—whether I should make me a cave in the earth, or a tent upon the earth; and, in short, I resolved upon both; the manner and description of which, it may not be improper to give an account of.

I soon found the place I was in was not fit for my settlement, because it was upon a low, moorish ground, near the sea, and I believed it would not be wholesome, and more particularly because there was no fresh water near it; so I resolved to find a more healthy and more convenient spot of ground.

I consulted several things in my situation, which I found would be proper for me: 1st, health and fresh water, I just now mentioned; 2ndly, shelter from the heat of the sun; 3rdly, security from ravenous creatures, whether man or beast; 4thly, a view to the sea, that if God sent any ship in sight, I might not lose any advantage for my deliverance, of which I was not willing to banish all my expectation yet.

In search of a place proper for this, I found a little plain on the side of a rising hill, whose front towards this little plain was steep as a house-side, so that nothing could come down upon me from the top. On the one side of the rock there was a hollow place, worn a little way in, like the entrance or door of a cave but there was not really any cave or way into the rock at all.

On the flat of the green, just before this hollow place, I resolved to pitch my tent. This plain was not above a hundred yards broad, and about twice as long, and lay like a green before my door; and, at the end of it, descended irregularly every way down into the low ground by the seaside. It was on the N.N.W. side of the hill; so that it was sheltered from the heat every day, till it came to a W. and by S. sun, or thereabouts, which, in those countries, is near the setting.

Before I set up my tent I drew a half-circle before the hollow place, which took in about ten yards in its semi-diameter from the rock, and twenty yards in its diameter from its beginning and ending.

In this half-circle I pitched two rows of strong stakes, driving them into the ground till they stood very firm like piles, the biggest end being out of the ground above five feet and a half, and sharpened on the top. The two rows did not stand above six inches from one another.

Then I took the pieces of cable which I had cut in the ship, and laid them in rows, one upon another, within the circle, between these two rows of stakes, up to the top, placing other stakes in the inside, leaning against them, about two feet and a half high, like a spur to a post; and this fence was so strong, that neither man nor beast could get into it or over it. This cost me a great deal of time and labour, especially to cut the piles in the woods, bring them to the place, and drive them into the earth.

The entrance into this place I made to be, not by a door, but by a short ladder to go over the top; which ladder, when I was in, I lifted over after me; and so I was completely fenced in and fortified, as I thought, from all the world, and consequently slept secure in the night, which otherwise I could not have done; though, as it appeared afterwards, there was no need of all this caution from the enemies that I apprehended danger from.

Into this fence or fortress, with infinite labour, I carried all my riches, all my provisions, ammunition, and stores, of which you have the account above; and I made a large tent, which to preserve me from the rains that in one part of the year are very violent there, I made double—one smaller tent within, and one larger tent above it; and covered the uppermost with a large tarpaulin, which I had saved among the sails.

And now I lay no more for a while in the bed which I had brought on shore, but in a hammock, which was indeed a very good one, and belonged to the mate of the ship.

Into this tent I brought all my provisions, and everything that would spoil by the wet; and having thus enclosed all my goods, I made up the entrance, which till now I had left open, and so passed and repassed, as I said, by a short ladder.

When I had done this, I began to work my way into the rock, and bringing all the earth and stones that I dug down out through my tent, I laid them up within my fence, in the nature of a terrace, so that it raised the ground within about a foot and a half; and thus I made me a cave, just behind my tent, which served me like a cellar to my house.

It cost me much labour and many days before all these things were brought to perfection; and therefore I must go back to some other things which took up some of my thoughts. At the same time it happened, after I had laid my scheme for the setting up my tent, and making the cave, that a storm of rain falling from a thick, dark cloud, a sudden flash of lightning happened, and after that a great clap of thunder, as is naturally the effect of it. I was not so much surprised with the lightning as I was with the thought which darted into my mind as swift as the lightning itself—Oh, my powder! My very heart sank within me when I thought that, at one blast, all my powder might be destroyed; on which, not my defence only, but the providing my food, as I thought, entirely depended. I was nothing near so anxious about my own danger, though, had the powder took fire, I should never have known who had hurt me.

Such impression did this make upon me, that after the storm was over I laid aside all my works, my building and fortifying, and applied myself to make bags and boxes, to separate the powder, and to keep it a little and a little in a parcel, in the hope that, whatever might come, it might not all take fire at once; and to keep it so apart that it should not be possible to make one part fire another. I finished this work in about a fortnight; and I think my powder, which in all was about two hundred and forty pounds weight, was divided in not less than a hundred parcels. As to the barrel that had been wet, I did not apprehend any danger from that; so I placed it in my new cave, which, in my fancy, I called my kitchen; and the rest I hid up and down in holes among the rocks, so that no wet might come to it, marking very carefully where I laid it.

In the interval of time while this was doing, I went out once at least every day with my gun, as well to divert myself as to see if I could kill anything fit for food; and, as near as I could, to acquaint myself with what the island produced. The first time I went out, I presently discovered that there were goats in the island, which was a great satisfaction to me; but then it was attended with this misfortune to me—viz. that they were so shy, so subtle, and so swift of foot, that it was the most difficult thing in the world to come at them; but I was not discouraged at this, not doubting but I might now and then shoot one, as it soon happened; for after I had found their haunts a little, I laid wait in this manner for them: I observed if they saw me in the valleys, though they were upon the rocks, they would run away, as in a terrible fright; but if they were feeding in the valleys, and I was upon the rocks, they took no notice of me; from whence I concluded that, by the position of their optics, their sight was so directed downward that they did not readily see objects that were above them; so afterwards I took this method—I always climbed the rocks first, to get above them, and then had frequently a fair mark.

The first shot I made among these creatures, I killed a she-goat, which had a little kid by her, which she gave suck to, which grieved me heartily; for when the old one fell, the kid stood stock still by her, till I came and took her up; and not only so, but when I carried the old one with me, upon my shoulders, the kid followed me quite to my enclosure; upon which I laid down the dam, and took the kid in my arms, and carried it over my pale, in hopes to have bred it up tame; but it would not eat; so I was forced to kill it and eat it myself. These two supplied me with flesh a great while, for I ate sparingly, and saved my provisions, my bread especially, as much as possibly I could.

Having now fixed my habitation, I found it absolutely necessary to provide a place to make a fire in, and fuel to burn: and what I did for that, and also how I enlarged my cave, and what conveniences I made, I shall give a full account of in its place; but I must now give some little account of myself, and of my thoughts about living, which, it may well be supposed, were not a few.

I had a dismal prospect of my condition; for as I was not cast away upon that island without being driven, as is said, by a violent storm, quite out of the course of our intended voyage, and a great way, viz. some hundreds of leagues, out of the ordinary course of the trade of mankind, I had great reason to consider it as a determination of Heaven, that in this desolate place, and in this desolate manner, I should end my life. The tears would run plentifully down my face when I made these reflections; and sometimes I would expostulate with myself why Providence should thus completely ruin His creatures, and render them so absolutely miserable; so without help, abandoned, so entirely depressed, that it could hardly be rational to be thankful for such a life.

But something always returned swift upon me to check these thoughts, and to reprove me; and particularly one day, walking with my gun in my hand by the seaside, I was very pensive upon the subject of my present condition, when reason, as it were, expostulated with me the other way, thus: "Well, you are in a desolate condition, it is true; but, pray remember, where are the rest of you? Did not you come, eleven of you in the boat? Where are the ten? Why were they not saved, and you lost? Why were you singled out? Is it better to be here or there?" And then I pointed to the sea. All evils are to be considered with the good that is in them, and with what worse attends them.

Then it occurred to me again, how well I was furnished for my subsistence, and what would have been my case if it had not happened (which was a hundred thousand to one) that the ship floated from the place where she first struck, and was driven so near to the shore that I had time to get all these things out of her; what would have been my case, if I had been forced to have lived in the condition in which I at first came on shore, without necessaries of life, or necessaries to supply and procure them? "Particularly," said I, aloud (though to myself), "what should I have done without a gun, without ammunition, without any tools to make anything, or to work with, without clothes, bedding, a tent, or any manner of covering?" and that now I had all these to sufficient quantity, and was in a fair way to provide myself in such a manner as to live without my gun, when my ammunition was spent: so that I had a tolerable view of subsisting, without any want, as long as I lived; for I considered from the beginning how I would provide for the accidents that might happen, and for the time that was to come, even not only after my ammunition should be spent, but even after my health and strength should decay.

I confess I had not entertained any notion of my ammunition being destroyed at one blast —I mean my powder being blown up by lightning; and this made the thoughts of it so surprising to me, when it lightened and thundered, as I observed just now.

And now being about to enter into a melancholy relation of a scene of silent life, such, perhaps, as was never heard of in the world before, I shall take it from its beginning, and continue it in its order. It was by my account the 30th of September, when, in the manner as above said, I first set foot upon this horrid island; when the sun, being to us in its autumnal equinox, was almost over my head; for I reckoned myself, by observation, to be in the latitude of nine degrees twenty-two minutes north of the line.

After I had been there about ten or twelve days, it came into my thoughts that I should lose my reckoning of time for want of books, and pen and ink, and should even forget the Sabbath days; but to prevent this, I cut with my knife upon a large post, in capital letters— and making it into a great cross, I set it up on the shore where I first landed—"I came on shore here on the 30th September 1659."

Upon the sides of this square post I cut every day a notch with my knife, and every seventh notch was as long again as the rest, and every first day of the month as long again as that long one; and thus I kept my calendar, or weekly, monthly, and yearly reckoning of time.

In the next place, we are to observe that among the many things which I brought out of the ship, in the several voyages which, as above mentioned, I made to it, I got several things of less value, but not at all less useful to me, which I omitted setting down before; as, in particular, pens, ink, and paper, several parcels in the captain's, mate's, gunner's and carpenter's keeping; three or four compasses, some mathematical instruments, dials, perspectives, charts, and books of navigation, all which I huddled together, whether I might want them or no; also, I found three very good Bibles, which came to me in my cargo from England, and which I had packed up among my things; some Portuguese books also; and among them two or three Popish prayer-books, and several other books, all which I carefully secured. And I must not forget that we had in the ship a dog and two cats, of whose eminent history I may have occasion to say something in its place; for I carried both the cats with me; and as for the dog, he jumped out of the ship of himself, and swam on shore to me the day after I went on shore with my first cargo, and was a trusty servant to me many years; I wanted nothing that he could fetch me, nor any company that he could make up to me; I only wanted to have him talk to me, but that would not do. As I observed before, I found pens, ink, and paper, and I husbanded them to the utmost; and I shall show that while my ink lasted, I kept things very exact, but after that was gone I could not, for I could not make any ink by any means that I could devise.

And this put me in mind that I wanted many things notwithstanding all that I had amassed together; and of these, ink was one; as also a spade, pickaxe, and shovel, to dig or remove the earth; needles, pins, and thread; as for linen, I soon learned to want that without much difficulty.

This want of tools made every work I did go on heavily; and it was near a whole year before I had entirely finished my little pale, or surrounded my habitation. The piles, or stakes, which were as heavy as I could well lift, were a long time in cutting and preparing in the woods, and more, by far, in bringing home; so that I spent sometimes two days in cutting and bringing home one of those posts, and a third day in driving it into the ground; for which purpose I got a heavy piece of wood at first, but at last bethought myself of one of the iron crows; which, however, though I found it, made driving those posts or piles very laborious and tedious work.

But what need I have been concerned at the tediousness of anything I had to do, seeing I had time enough to do it in? nor had I any other employment, if that had been over, at least that I could foresee, except the ranging the island to seek for food, which I did, more or less, every day.

I now began to consider seriously my condition, and the circumstances I was reduced to; and I drew up the state of my affairs in writing, not so much to leave them to any that were to come after me—for I was likely to have but few heirs—as to deliver my thoughts from daily poring over them, and afflicting my mind; and as my reason began now to master my despondency, I began to comfort myself as well as I could, and to set the good against the evil, that I might have something to distinguish my case from worse; and I stated very impartially, like debtor and creditor, the comforts I enjoyed against the miseries I suffered, thus:—

Evil.........Good

I am cast upon a horrible, desolate island, void of all hope of recovery..........But I am alive; and not drowned, as all my ship's company were.

I am singled out and separated, as it were, from all the world, to be miserable..........But I am singled out, too, from all the ship's crew, to be spared from death; and He that miraculously saved me from death can deliver me from this condition.

I am divided from mankind—a solitaire; one banished from human society..........But I am not starved, and perishing on a barren place, affording no sustenance.

I have no clothes to cover me..........But I am in a hot climate, where, if I had clothes, I could hardly wear them.

I am without any defence, or means to resist any violence of man or beast..........But I am cast on an island where I see no wild beasts to hurt me, as I saw on the coast of Africa; and what if I had been shipwrecked there?

I have no soul to speak to or relieve me..........But God wonderfully sent the ship in near enough to the shore, that I have got out as many necessary things as will either supply my wants or enable me to supply myself, even as long as I live.

Upon the whole, here was an undoubted testimony that there was scarce any condition in the world so miserable but there was something negative or something positive to be thankful for in it; and let this stand as a direction from the experience of the most miserable of all conditions in this world: that we may always find in it something to comfort ourselves from, and to set, in the description of good and evil, on the credit side of the account.

Having now brought my mind a little to relish my condition, and given over looking out to sea, to see if I could spy a ship—I say, giving over these things, I began to apply myself to arrange my way of living, and to make things as easy to me as I could.

I have already described my habitation, which was a tent under the side of a rock, surrounded with a strong pale of posts and cables: but I might now rather call it a wall, for I raised a kind of wall up against it of turfs, about two feet thick on the outside; and after some time (I think it was a year and a half) I raised rafters from it, leaning to the rock, and thatched or covered it with boughs of trees, and such things as I could get, to keep out the rain; which I found at some times of the year very violent.

I have already observed how I brought all my goods into this pale, and into the cave which I had made behind me. But I must observe, too, that at first this was a confused heap of goods, which, as they lay in no order, so they took up all my place; I had no room to turn myself: so I set myself to enlarge my cave, and work farther into the earth; for it was a loose sandy rock, which yielded easily to the labour I bestowed on it: and so when I found I was pretty safe as to beasts of prey, I worked sideways, to the right hand, into the rock; and then, turning to the right again, worked quite out, and made me a door to come out on the outside of my pale or fortification. This gave me not only egress and regress, as it was a back way to my tent and to my storehouse, but gave me room to store my goods.

And now I began to apply myself to make such necessary things as I found I most wanted, particularly a chair and a table; for without these I was not able to enjoy the few comforts I had in the world; I could not write or eat, or do several things, with so much pleasure without a table: so I went to work. And here I must needs observe, that as reason is the substance and origin of the mathematics, so by stating and squaring everything by reason, and by making the most rational judgment of things, every man may be, in time, master of every mechanic art. I had never handled a tool in my life; and yet, in time, by labour, application, and contrivance, I found at last that I wanted nothing but I could have made it, especially if I had had tools. However, I made abundance of things, even without tools; and some with no more tools than an adze and a hatchet, which perhaps were never made that way before, and that with infinite labour. For example, if I wanted a board, I had no other way but to cut down a tree, set it on an edge before me, and hew it flat on either side with my axe, till I brought it to be thin as a plank, and then dub it smooth with my adze. It is true, by this method I could make but one board out of a whole tree; but this I had no remedy for but patience, any more than I had for the prodigious deal of time and labour which it took me up to make a plank or board: but my time or labour was little worth, and so it was as well employed one way as another.

However, I made me a table and a chair, as I observed above, in the first place; and this I did out of the short pieces of boards that I brought on my raft from the ship. But when I had wrought out some boards as above, I made large shelves, of the breadth of a foot and a half, one over another all along one side of my cave, to lay all my tools, nails and ironwork on;

and, in a word, to separate everything at large into their places, that I might come easily at them. I knocked pieces into the wall of the rock to hang my guns and all things that would hang up; so that, had my cave been to be seen, it looked like a general magazine of all necessary things; and had everything so ready at my hand, that it was a great pleasure to me to see all my goods in such order, and especially to find my stock of all necessaries so great.

And now it was that I began to keep a journal of every day's employment; for, indeed, at first I was in too much hurry, and not only hurry as to labour, but in too much discomposure of mind; and my journal would have been full of many dull things; for example, I must have said thus: "30th.—After I had got to shore, and escaped drowning, instead of being thankful to God for my deliverance, having first vomited, with the great quantity of salt water which had got into my stomach, and recovering myself a little, I ran about the shore wringing my hands and beating my head and face, exclaiming at my misery, and crying out, 'I was undone, undone!' till, tired and faint, I was forced to lie down on the ground to repose, but durst not sleep for fear of being devoured."

Some days after this, and after I had been on board the ship, and got all that I could out of her, yet I could not forbear getting up to the top of a little mountain and looking out to sea, in hopes of seeing a ship; then fancy at a vast distance I spied a sail, please myself with the hopes of it, and then after looking steadily, till I was almost blind, lose it quite, and sit down and weep like a child, and thus increase my misery by my folly.

But having gotten over these things in some measure, and having settled my household staff and habitation, made me a table and a chair, and all as handsome about me as I could, I began to keep my journal; of which I shall here give you the copy (though in it will be told all these particulars over again) as long as it lasted; for having no more ink, I was forced to leave it off.

5

BUILDS A HOUSE—THE JOURNAL

September 30, 1659.—I, poor miserable Robinson Crusoe, being shipwrecked during a dreadful storm in the offing, came on shore on this dismal, unfortunate island, which I called "The Island of Despair"; all the rest of the ship's company being drowned, and myself almost dead.

All the rest of the day I spent in afflicting myself at the dismal circumstances I was brought to—viz. I had neither food, house, clothes, weapon, nor place to fly to; and in despair of any relief, saw nothing but death before me—either that I should be devoured by wild beasts, murdered by savages, or starved to death for want of food. At the approach of night I slept in a tree, for fear of wild creatures; but slept soundly, though it rained all night.

October 1.—In the morning I saw, to my great surprise, the ship had floated with the high tide, and was driven on shore again much nearer the island; which, as it was some comfort, on one hand—for, seeing her set upright, and not broken to pieces, I hoped, if the wind abated, I might get on board, and get some food and necessaries out of her for my relief—so, on the other hand, it renewed my grief at the loss of my comrades, who, I imagined, if we had all stayed on board, might have saved the ship, or, at least, that they would not have been all drowned as they were; and that, had the men been saved, we might perhaps have built us a boat out of the ruins of the ship to have carried us to some other part of the world. I spent great part of this day in perplexing myself on these things; but at length, seeing the ship almost dry, I went upon the sand as near as I could, and then swam on board. This day also it continued raining, though with no wind at all.

From the 1st of October to the 24th.—All these days entirely spent in many several voyages to get all I could out of the ship, which I brought on shore every tide of flood upon rafts. Much rain also in the days, though with some intervals of fair weather; but it seems this was the rainy season.

Oct. 20.—I overset my raft, and all the goods I had got upon it; but, being in shoal water, and the things being chiefly heavy, I recovered many of them when the tide was out.

Oct. 25.—It rained all night and all day, with some gusts of wind; during which time the ship broke in pieces, the wind blowing a little harder than before, and was no more to be seen, except the wreck of her, and that only at low water. I spent this day in covering and securing the goods which I had saved, that the rain might not spoil them.

Oct. 26.—I walked about the shore almost all day, to find out a place to fix my habitation, greatly concerned to secure myself from any attack in the night, either from wild beasts or men. Towards night, I fixed upon a proper place, under a rock, and marked out a semicircle for my encampment; which I resolved to strengthen with a work, wall, or fortification, made of double piles, lined within with cables, and without with turf.

From the 26th to the 30th I worked very hard in carrying all my goods to my new habitation, though some part of the time it rained exceedingly hard.

The 31st, in the morning, I went out into the island with my gun, to seek for some food, and discover the country; when I killed a she-goat, and her kid followed me home, which I afterwards killed also, because it would not feed.

November 1.—I set up my tent under a rock, and lay there for the first night; making it as large as I could, with stakes driven in to swing my hammock upon.

Nov. 2.—I set up all my chests and boards, and the pieces of timber which made my rafts, and with them formed a fence round me, a little within the place I had marked out for my fortification.

Nov. 3.—I went out with my gun, and killed two fowls like ducks, which were very good food. In the afternoon went to work to make me a table.

Nov. 4.—This morning I began to order my times of work, of going out with my gun, time of sleep, and time of diversion—viz. every morning I walked out with my gun for two or three hours, if it did not rain; then employed myself to work till about eleven o'clock; then eat what I had to live on; and from twelve to two I lay down to sleep, the weather being excessively hot; and then, in the evening, to work again. The working part of this day and of the next were wholly employed in making my table, for I was yet but a very sorry workman, though time and necessity made me a complete natural mechanic soon after, as I believe they would do any one else.

Nov. 5.—This day went abroad with my gun and my dog, and killed a wild cat; her skin pretty soft, but her flesh good for nothing; every creature that I killed I took of the skins and preserved them. Coming back by the sea-shore, I saw many sorts of sea-fowls, which I did not understand; but was surprised, and almost frightened, with two or three seals, which, while I was gazing at, not well knowing what they were, got into the sea, and escaped me for that time.

Nov. 6.—After my morning walk I went to work with my table again, and finished it, though not to my liking; nor was it long before I learned to mend it.

Nov. 7.—Now it began to be settled fair weather. The 7th, 8th, 9th, 10th, and part of the 12th (for the 11th was Sunday) I took wholly up to make me a chair, and with much ado brought it to a tolerable shape, but never to please me; and even in the making I pulled it in pieces several times.

Note.—I soon neglected my keeping Sundays; for, omitting my mark for them on my post, I forgot which was which.

Nov. 13.—This day it rained, which refreshed me exceedingly, and cooled the earth; but it was accompanied with terrible thunder and lightning, which frightened me dreadfully, for fear of my powder. As soon as it was over, I resolved to separate my stock of powder into as many little parcels as possible, that it might not be in danger.

Nov. 14, 15, 16.—These three days I spent in making little square chests, or boxes, which might hold about a pound, or two pounds at most, of powder; and so, putting the powder in, I stowed it in places as secure and remote from one another as possible. On one of these three days I killed a large bird that was good to eat, but I knew not what to call it.

Nov. 17.—This day I began to dig behind my tent into the rock, to make room for my further conveniency.

Note.—Three things I wanted exceedingly for this work—viz. a pickaxe, a shovel, and a wheelbarrow or basket; so I desisted from my work, and began to consider how to supply that want, and make me some tools. As for the pickaxe, I made use of the iron crows, which were proper enough, though heavy; but the next thing was a shovel or spade; this was so absolutely necessary, that, indeed, I could do nothing effectually without it; but what kind of one to make I knew not.

Nov. 18.—The next day, in searching the woods, I found a tree of that wood, or like it, which in the Brazils they call the iron-tree, for its exceeding hardness. Of this, with great labour, and almost spoiling my axe, I cut a piece, and brought it home, too, with difficulty enough, for it was exceeding heavy. The excessive hardness of the wood, and my having no other way, made me a long while upon this machine, for I worked it effectually by little and little into the form of a shovel or spade; the handle exactly shaped like ours in England, only that the board part having no iron shod upon it at bottom, it would not last me so long; however, it served well enough for the uses which I had occasion to put it to; but never was a shovel, I believe, made after that fashion, or so long in making.

I was still deficient, for I wanted a basket or a wheelbarrow. A basket I could not make by any means, having no such things as twigs that would bend to make wicker-ware—at least, none yet found out; and as to a wheelbarrow, I fancied I could make all but the wheel; but that I had no notion of; neither did I know how to go about it; besides, I had no possible way to make the iron gudgeons for the spindle or axis of the wheel to run in; so I gave it over, and so, for carrying away the earth which I dug out of the cave, I made me a thing like a hod which the labourers carry mortar in when they serve the bricklayers. This was not so difficult to me as the making the shovel: and yet this and the shovel, and the attempt which I made in vain to make a wheelbarrow, took me up no less than four days—I mean always excepting my morning walk with my gun, which I seldom failed, and very seldom failed also bringing home something fit to eat.

Nov. 23.—My other work having now stood still, because of my making these tools, when they were finished I went on, and working every day, as my strength and time allowed, I spent eighteen days entirely in widening and deepening my cave, that it might hold my goods commodiously.

Note.—During all this time I worked to make this room or cave spacious enough to accommodate me as a warehouse or magazine, a kitchen, a dining-room, and a cellar. As for my lodging, I kept to the tent; except that sometimes, in the wet season of the year, it rained so hard that I could not keep myself dry, which caused me afterwards to cover all my place within my pale with long poles, in the form of rafters, leaning against the rock, and load them with flags and large leaves of trees, like a thatch.

December 10.—I began now to think my cave or vault finished, when on a sudden (it seems I had made it too large) a great quantity of earth fell down from the top on one side; so much that, in short, it frighted me, and not without reason, too, for if I had been under it, I had never wanted a gravedigger. I had now a great deal of work to do over again, for I had the loose earth to carry out; and, which was of more importance, I had the ceiling to prop up, so that I might be sure no more would come down.

Dec. 11.—This day I went to work with it accordingly, and got two shores or posts pitched upright to the top, with two pieces of boards across over each post; this I finished the next day; and setting more posts up with boards, in about a week more I had the roof secured, and the posts, standing in rows, served me for partitions to part off the house.

Dec. 17.—From this day to the 20th I placed shelves, and knocked up nails on the posts, to hang everything up that could be hung up; and now I began to be in some order within doors.

Dec. 20.—Now I carried everything into the cave, and began to furnish my house, and set up some pieces of boards like a dresser, to order my victuals upon; but boards began to be very scarce with me; also, I made me another table.

Dec. 24.—Much rain all night and all day. No stirring out.

Dec. 25.—Rain all day.

Dec. 26.—No rain, and the earth much cooler than before, and pleasanter.

Dec. 27.—Killed a young goat, and lamed another, so that I caught it and led it home in a string; when I had it at home, I bound and splintered up its leg, which was broke.

N.B.—I took such care of it that it lived, and the leg grew well and as strong as ever; but, by my nursing it so long, it grew tame, and fed upon the little green at my door, and would not go away. This was the first time that I entertained a thought of breeding up some tame creatures, that I might have food when my powder and shot was all spent.

Dec. 28, 29, 30.—Great heats and no breeze, so that there was no stirring abroad except in the evening for food; this time I spent in putting all my things in order within doors.

January 1.—Very hot still: but I went abroad early and late with my gun, and lay still in the middle of the day. This evening, going farther into the valleys which lay towards the centre of the island, I found there were plenty of goats, though exceedingly shy, and hard to come at; however, I resolved to try if I could not bring my dog to hunt them down.

Jan. 2.—Accordingly, the next day I went out with my dog, and set him upon the goats, but I was mistaken, for they all faced about upon the dog, and he knew his danger too well, for he would not come near them.

Jan. 3.—I began my fence or wall; which, being still jealous of my being attacked by somebody, I resolved to make very thick and strong.

N.B.—This wall being described before, I purposely omit what was said in the journal; it is sufficient to observe, that I was no less time than from the 2nd of January to the 14th of April working, finishing, and perfecting this wall, though it was no more than about twenty-four yards in length, being a half-circle from one place in the rock to another place, about eight yards from it, the door of the cave being in the centre behind it.

All this time I worked very hard, the rains hindering me many days, nay, sometimes weeks together; but I thought I should never be perfectly secure till this wall was finished; and it is scarce credible what inexpressible labour everything was done with, especially the bringing piles out of the woods and driving them into the ground; for I made them much bigger than I needed to have done.

When this wall was finished, and the outside double fenced, with a turf wall raised up close to it, I perceived myself that if any people were to come on shore there, they would not perceive anything like a habitation; and it was very well I did so, as may be observed hereafter, upon a very remarkable occasion.

During this time I made my rounds in the woods for game every day when the rain permitted me, and made frequent discoveries in these walks of something or other to my advantage; particularly, I found a kind of wild pigeons, which build, not as wood-pigeons in a tree, but rather as house-pigeons, in the holes of the rocks; and taking some young ones, I endeavoured to breed them up tame, and did so; but when they grew older they flew away, which perhaps was at first for want of feeding them, for I had nothing to give them; however,

I frequently found their nests, and got their young ones, which were very good meat. And now, in the managing my household affairs, I found myself wanting in many things, which I thought at first it was impossible for me to make; as, indeed, with some of them it was: for instance, I could never make a cask to be hooped. I had a small runlet or two, as I observed before; but I could never arrive at the capacity of making one by them, though I spent many weeks about it; I could neither put in the heads, or join the staves so true to one another as to make them hold water; so I gave that also over. In the next place, I was at a great loss for candles; so that as soon as ever it was dark, which was generally by seven o'clock, I was obliged to go to bed. I remembered the lump of beeswax with which I made candles in my African adventure; but I had none of that now; the only remedy I had was, that when I had killed a goat I saved the tallow, and with a little dish made of clay, which I baked in the sun, to which I added a wick of some oakum, I made me a lamp; and this gave me light, though not a clear, steady light, like a candle. In the middle of all my labours it happened that, rummaging my things, I found a little bag which, as I hinted before, had been filled with corn for the feeding of poultry—not for this voyage, but before, as I suppose, when the ship came from Lisbon. The little remainder of corn that had been in the bag was all devoured by the rats, and I saw nothing in the bag but husks and dust; and being willing to have the bag for some other use (I think it was to put powder in, when I divided it for fear of the lightning, or some such use), I shook the husks of corn out of it on one side of my fortification, under the rock.

It was a little before the great rains just now mentioned that I threw this stuff away, taking no notice, and not so much as remembering that I had thrown anything there, when, about a month after, or thereabouts, I saw some few stalks of something green shooting out of the ground, which I fancied might be some plant I had not seen; but I was surprised, and perfectly astonished, when, after a little longer time, I saw about ten or twelve ears come out, which were perfect green barley, of the same kind as our European—nay, as our English barley.

It is impossible to express the astonishment and confusion of my thoughts on this occasion. I had hitherto acted upon no religious foundation at all; indeed, I had very few notions of religion in my head, nor had entertained any sense of anything that had befallen me otherwise than as chance, or, as we lightly say, what pleases God, without so much as inquiring into the end of Providence in these things, or His order in governing events for the world. But after I saw barley grow there, in a climate which I knew was not proper for corn, and especially that I knew not how it came there, it startled me strangely, and I began to suggest that God had miraculously caused His grain to grow without any help of seed sown, and that it was so directed purely for my sustenance on that wild, miserable place.

This touched my heart a little, and brought tears out of my eyes, and I began to bless myself that such a prodigy of nature should happen upon my account; and this was the more strange to me, because I saw near it still, all along by the side of the rock, some other straggling stalks, which proved to be stalks of rice, and which I knew, because I had seen it grow in Africa when I was ashore there.

I not only thought these the pure productions of Providence for my support, but not doubting that there was more in the place, I went all over that part of the island, where I had been before, peering in every corner, and under every rock, to see for more of it, but I could not find any. At last it occurred to my thoughts that I shook a bag of chickens' meat out in that place; and then the wonder began to cease; and I must confess my religious thankfulness to God's providence began to abate, too, upon the discovering that all this was nothing but what was common; though I ought to have been as thankful for so strange and unforeseen a providence as if it had been miraculous; for it was really the work of Providence to me, that should order or appoint that ten or twelve grains of corn should remain unspoiled, when the rats had destroyed all the rest, as if it had been dropped from heaven; as also, that I should throw it out in that particular place, where, it being in the shade of a high rock, it sprang up immediately; whereas, if I had thrown it anywhere else at that time, it had been burnt up and destroyed.

I carefully saved the ears of this corn, you may be sure, in their season, which was about the end of June; and, laying up every corn, I resolved to sow them all again, hoping in time to have some quantity sufficient to supply me with bread. But it was not till the fourth year that I could allow myself the least grain of this corn to eat, and even then but sparingly, as I shall say afterwards, in its order; for I lost all that I sowed the first season by not observing the proper time; for I sowed it just before the dry season, so that it never came up at all, at least not as it would have done; of which in its place.

Besides this barley, there were, as above, twenty or thirty stalks of rice, which I preserved with the same care and for the same use, or to the same purpose—to make me bread, or rather food; for I found ways to cook it without baking, though I did that also after some time.

But to return to my Journal.

I worked excessive hard these three or four months to get my wall done; and the 14th of April I closed it up, contriving to go into it, not by a door but over the wall, by a ladder, that there might be no sign on the outside of my habitation.

April 16.—I finished the ladder; so I went up the ladder to the top, and then pulled it up after me, and let it down in the inside. This was a complete enclosure to me; for within I had room enough, and nothing could come at me from without, unless it could first mount my wall.

The very next day after this wall was finished I had almost had all my labour overthrown at once, and myself killed. The case was thus: As I was busy in the inside, behind my tent, just at the entrance into my cave, I was terribly frighted with a most dreadful, surprising thing indeed; for all on a sudden I found the earth come crumbling down from the roof of my cave, and from the edge of the hill over my head, and two of the posts I had set up in the cave cracked in a frightful manner. I was heartily scared; but thought nothing of what was really the cause, only thinking that the top of my cave was fallen in, as some of it had done before: and for fear I should be buried in it I ran forward to my ladder, and not thinking myself safe there neither, I got over my wall for fear of the pieces of the hill, which I expected might roll down upon me. I had no sooner stepped down upon the firm ground, than I plainly saw it was a terrible earthquake, for the ground I stood on shook three times at about eight minutes' distance, with three such shocks as would have overturned the strongest building that could be supposed to have stood on the earth; and a great piece of the top of a rock which stood about half a mile from me next the sea fell down with such a terrible noise as I never heard in all my life. I perceived also the very sea was put into violent motion by it; and I believe the shocks were stronger under the water than on the island.

I was so much amazed with the thing itself, having never felt the like, nor discoursed with any one that had, that I was like one dead or stupefied; and the motion of the earth made my stomach sick, like one that was tossed at sea; but the noise of the falling of the rock awakened me, as it were, and rousing me from the stupefied condition I was in, filled me with horror; and I thought of nothing then but the hill falling upon my tent and all my household goods, and burying all at once; and this sunk my very soul within me a second time.

After the third shock was over, and I felt no more for some time, I began to take courage; and yet I had not heart enough to go over my wall again, for fear of being buried alive, but sat still upon the ground greatly cast down and disconsolate, not knowing what to do. All this while I had not the least serious religious thought; nothing but the common "Lord have mercy upon me!" and when it was over that went away too.

While I sat thus, I found the air overcast and grow cloudy, as if it would rain. Soon after that the wind arose by little and little, so that in less than half-an-hour it blew a most dreadful hurricane; the sea was all on a sudden covered over with foam and froth; the shore was covered with the breach of the water, the trees were torn up by the roots, and a terrible storm it was. This held about three hours, and then began to abate; and in two hours more it was quite calm, and began to rain very hard. All this while I sat upon the ground very much terrified and dejected; when on a sudden it came into my thoughts, that these winds and rain being the consequences of the earthquake, the earthquake itself was spent and over, and I might venture into my cave again. With this thought my spirits began to revive; and the rain also helping to persuade me, I went in and sat down in my tent. But the rain was so violent that my tent was ready to be beaten down with it; and I was forced to go into my cave, though very much afraid and uneasy, for fear it should fall on my head. This violent rain forced me to a new work—viz. to cut a hole through my new fortification, like a sink, to let the water go out, which would else have flooded my cave. After I had been in my cave for some time, and found still no more shocks of the earthquake follow, I began to be more composed. And now, to support my spirits, which indeed wanted it very much, I went to my little store, and took a small sup of rum; which, however, I did then and always very sparingly, knowing I could have no more when that was gone. It continued raining all that night and great part of the next day, so that I could not stir abroad; but my mind being more composed, I began to think of what I had best do; concluding that if the island was subject to these earthquakes, there would be no living for me in a cave, but I must consider of building a little hut in an open place which I might surround with a wall, as I had done here, and so make myself secure from wild beasts or men; for I concluded, if I stayed where I was, I should certainly one time or other be buried alive.

With these thoughts, I resolved to remove my tent from the place where it stood, which was just under the hanging precipice of the hill; and which, if it should be shaken again, would certainly fall upon my tent; and I spent the two next days, being the 19th and 20th of April, in contriving where and how to remove my habitation. The fear of being swallowed up alive made me that I never slept in quiet; and yet the apprehension of lying abroad without any fence was almost equal to it; but still, when I looked about, and saw how everything was put in order, how pleasantly concealed I was, and how safe from danger, it made me very loath to remove. In the meantime, it occurred to me that it would require a vast deal of time for me to do this, and that I must be contented to venture where I was, till I had formed a camp for myself, and had secured it so as to remove to it. So with this resolution I composed myself for a time, and resolved that I would go to work with all speed to build me a wall with piles and cables, &c., in a circle, as before, and set my tent up in it when it was finished; but that I would venture to stay where I was till it was finished, and fit to remove. This was the 21st.

April 22.—The next morning I begin to consider of means to put this resolve into execution; but I was at a great loss about my tools. I had three large axes, and abundance of hatchets (for we carried the hatchets for traffic with the Indians); but with much chopping and cutting knotty hard wood, they were all full of notches, and dull; and though I had a grindstone, I could not turn it and grind my tools too. This cost me as much thought as a statesman would have bestowed upon a grand point of politics, or a judge upon the life and death of a man. At length I contrived a wheel with a string, to turn it with my foot, that I might have both my hands at liberty. *Note.*—I had never seen any such thing in England, or at least, not to take notice how it was done, though since I have observed, it is very common there; besides that, my grindstone was very large and heavy. This machine cost me a full week's work to bring it to perfection.

April 28, 29.—These two whole days I took up in grinding my tools, my machine for turning my grindstone performing very well.

April 30.—Having perceived my bread had been low a great while, now I took a survey of it, and reduced myself to one biscuit cake a day, which made my heart very heavy.

May 1.—In the morning, looking towards the sea side, the tide being low, I saw something lie on the shore bigger than ordinary, and it looked like a cask; when I came to it, I found a small barrel, and two or three pieces of the wreck of the ship, which were driven on shore by the late hurricane; and looking towards the wreck itself, I thought it seemed to lie higher out of the water than it used to do. I examined the barrel which was driven on shore, and soon found it was a barrel of gunpowder; but it had taken water, and the powder was caked as hard as a stone; however, I rolled it farther on shore for the present, and went on upon the sands, as near as I could to the wreck of the ship, to look for more.

6

ILL AND CONSCIENCE-STRICKEN

When I came down to the ship I found it strangely removed. The forecastle, which lay before buried in sand, was heaved up at least six feet, and the stern, which was broke in pieces and parted from the rest by the force of the sea, soon after I had left rummaging her, was tossed as it were up, and cast on one side; and the sand was thrown so high on that side next her stern, that whereas there was a great place of water before, so that I could not come within a quarter of a mile of the wreck without swimming I could now walk quite up to her when the tide was out. I was surprised with this at first, but soon concluded it must be done by the earthquake; and as by this violence the ship was more broke open than formerly, so many things came daily on shore, which the sea had loosened, and which the winds and water rolled by degrees to the land.

This wholly diverted my thoughts from the design of removing my habitation, and I busied myself mightily, that day especially, in searching whether I could make any way into the ship; but I found nothing was to be expected of that kind, for all the inside of the ship was choked up with sand. However, as I had learned not to despair of anything, I resolved to pull everything to pieces that I could of the ship, concluding that everything I could get from her would be of some use or other to me.

May 3.—I began with my saw, and cut a piece of a beam through, which I thought held some of the upper part or quarter-deck together, and when I had cut it through, I cleared away the sand as well as I could from the side which lay highest; but the tide coming in, I was obliged to give over for that time.

May 4.—I went a-fishing, but caught not one fish that I durst eat of, till I was weary of my sport; when, just going to leave off, I caught a young dolphin. I had made me a long line of some rope-yarn, but I had no hooks; yet I frequently caught fish enough, as much as I cared to eat; all which I dried in the sun, and ate them dry.

May 5.—Worked on the wreck; cut another beam asunder, and brought three great fir planks off from the decks, which I tied together, and made to float on shore when the tide of flood came on.

May 6.—Worked on the wreck; got several iron bolts out of her and other pieces of ironwork. Worked very hard, and came home very much tired, and had thoughts of giving it over.

May 7.—Went to the wreck again, not with an intent to work, but found the weight of the wreck had broke itself down, the beams being cut; that several pieces of the ship seemed to lie loose, and the inside of the hold lay so open that I could see into it; but it was almost full of water and sand.

May 8.—Went to the wreck, and carried an iron crow to wrench up the deck, which lay now quite clear of the water or sand. I wrenched open two planks, and brought them on shore also with the tide. I left the iron crow in the wreck for next day.

May 9.—Went to the wreck, and with the crow made way into the body of the wreck, and felt several casks, and loosened them with the crow, but could not break them up. I felt also a roll of English lead, and could stir it, but it was too heavy to remove.

May 10-14.—Went every day to the wreck; and got a great many pieces of timber, and boards, or plank, and two or three hundredweight of iron.

May 15.—I carried two hatchets, to try if I could not cut a piece off the roll of lead by placing the edge of one hatchet and driving it with the other; but as it lay about a foot and a half in the water, I could not make any blow to drive the hatchet.

May 16.—It had blown hard in the night, and the wreck appeared more broken by the force of the water; but I stayed so long in the woods, to get pigeons for food, that the tide prevented my going to the wreck that day.

May 17.—I saw some pieces of the wreck blown on shore, at a great distance, near two miles off me, but resolved to see what they were, and found it was a piece of the head, but too heavy for me to bring away.

May 24.—Every day, to this day, I worked on the wreck; and with hard labour I loosened some things so much with the crow, that the first flowing tide several casks floated out, and two of the seamen's chests; but the wind blowing from the shore, nothing came to land that day but pieces of timber, and a hogshead, which had some Brazil pork in it; but the salt water and the sand had spoiled it. I continued this work every day to the 15th of June, except the time necessary to get food, which I always appointed, during this part of my employment, to be when the tide was up, that I might be ready when it was ebbed out; and by this time I had got timber and plank and ironwork enough to have built a good boat, if I had known how; and also I got, at several times and in several pieces, near one hundredweight of the sheet lead.

June 16.—Going down to the seaside, I found a large tortoise or turtle. This was the first I had seen, which, it seems, was only my misfortune, not any defect of the place, or scarcity; for had I happened to be on the other side of the island, I might have had hundreds of them every day, as I found afterwards; but perhaps had paid dear enough for them.

June 17.—I spent in cooking the turtle. I found in her three-score eggs; and her flesh was to me, at that time, the most savoury and pleasant that ever I tasted in my life, having had no flesh, but of goats and fowls, since I landed in this horrid place.

June 18.—Rained all day, and I stayed within. I thought at this time the rain felt cold, and I was something chilly; which I knew was not usual in that latitude.

June 19.—Very ill, and shivering, as if the weather had been cold.

June 20.—No rest all night; violent pains in my head, and feverish.

June 21.—Very ill; frighted almost to death with the apprehensions of my sad condition—to be sick, and no help. Prayed to God, for the first time since the storm off Hull, but scarce knew what I said, or why, my thoughts being all confused.

June 22.—A little better; but under dreadful apprehensions of sickness.

June 23.—Very bad again; cold and shivering, and then a violent headache.

June 24.—Much better.

June 25.—An ague very violent; the fit held me seven hours; cold fit and hot, with faint sweats after it.

June 26.—Better; and having no victuals to eat, took my gun, but found myself very weak. However, I killed a she-goat, and with much difficulty got it home, and broiled some of it, and ate. I would fain have stewed it, and made some broth, but had no pot.

June 27.—The ague again so violent that I lay a-bed all day, and neither ate nor drank. I was ready to perish for thirst; but so weak, I had not strength to stand up, or to get myself any water to drink. Prayed to God again, but was light-headed; and when I was not, I was so ignorant that I knew not what to say; only I lay and cried, "Lord, look upon me! Lord, pity me! Lord, have mercy upon me!" I suppose I did nothing else for two or three hours; till, the fit wearing off, I fell asleep, and did not wake till far in the night. When I awoke, I found myself much refreshed, but weak, and exceeding thirsty. However, as I had no water in my habitation, I was forced to lie till morning, and went to sleep again. In this second sleep I had this terrible dream: I thought that I was sitting on the ground, on the outside of my wall, where I sat when the storm blew after the earthquake, and that I saw a man descend from a great black cloud, in a bright flame of fire, and light upon the ground. He was all over as bright as a flame, so that I could but just bear to look towards him; his countenance was most inexpressibly dreadful, impossible for words to describe. When he stepped upon the ground with his feet, I thought the earth trembled, just as it had done before in the earthquake, and all the air looked, to my apprehension, as if it had been filled with flashes of fire. He was no sooner landed upon the earth, but he moved forward towards me, with a long spear or weapon in his hand, to kill me; and when he came to a rising ground, at some distance, he spoke to me—or I heard a voice so terrible that it is impossible to express the terror of it. All that I can say I understood was this: "Seeing all these things have not brought thee to repentance, now thou shalt die;" at which words, I thought he lifted up the spear that was in his hand to kill me.

No one that shall ever read this account will expect that I should be able to describe the horrors of my soul at this terrible vision. I mean, that even while it was a dream, I even dreamed of those horrors. Nor is it any more possible to describe the impression that remained upon my mind when I awaked, and found it was but a dream.

I had, alas! no divine knowledge. What I had received by the good instruction of my father was then worn out by an uninterrupted series, for eight years, of seafaring wickedness, and a constant conversation with none but such as were, like myself, wicked and profane to the last degree. I do not remember that I had, in all that time, one thought that so much as tended either to looking upwards towards God, or inwards towards a reflection upon my own ways; but a certain stupidity of soul, without desire of good, or conscience of evil, had entirely overwhelmed me; and I was all that the most hardened, unthinking, wicked creature among our common sailors can be supposed to be; not having the least sense, either of the fear of God in danger, or of thankfulness to God in deliverance.

In the relating what is already past of my story, this will be the more easily believed when I shall add, that through all the variety of miseries that had to this day befallen me, I never had so much as one thought of it being the hand of God, or that it was a just punishment for my sin—my rebellious behaviour against my father—or my present sins, which were great— or so much as a punishment for the general course of my wicked life. When I was on the desperate expedition on the desert shores of Africa, I never had so much as one thought of what would become of me, or one wish to God to direct me whither I should go, or to keep me from the danger which apparently surrounded me, as well from voracious creatures as cruel savages. But I was merely thoughtless of a God or a Providence, acted like a mere brute, from the principles of nature, and by the dictates of common sense only, and, indeed, hardly that. When I was delivered and taken up at sea by the Portugal captain, well used, and dealt justly and honourably with, as well as charitably, I had not the least thankfulness in my thoughts. When, again, I was shipwrecked, ruined, and in danger of drowning on this island, I was as far from remorse, or looking on it as a judgment. I only said to myself often, that I was an unfortunate dog, and born to be always miserable.

It is true, when I got on shore first here, and found all my ship's crew drowned and myself spared, I was surprised with a kind of ecstasy, and some transports of soul, which, had the grace of God assisted, might have come up to true thankfulness; but it ended where it began, in a mere common flight of joy, or, as I may say, being glad I was alive, without the least reflection upon the distinguished goodness of the hand which had preserved me, and had singled me out to be preserved when all the rest were destroyed, or an inquiry why Providence had been thus merciful unto me. Even just the same common sort of joy which seamen generally have, after they are got safe ashore from a shipwreck, which they drown all in the next bowl of punch, and forget almost as soon as it is over; and all the rest of my life was like it. Even when I was afterwards, on due consideration, made sensible of my condition, how I was cast on this dreadful place, out of the reach of human kind, out of all hope of relief, or prospect of redemption, as soon as I saw but a prospect of living and that I should not starve and perish for hunger, all the sense of my affliction wore off; and I began to be very easy, applied myself to the works proper for my preservation and supply, and was far enough from being afflicted at my condition, as a judgment from heaven, or as the hand of God against me: these were thoughts which very seldom entered my head.

The growing up of the corn, as is hinted in my Journal, had at first some little influence upon me, and began to affect me with seriousness, as long as I thought it had something miraculous in it; but as soon as ever that part of the thought was removed, all the impression that was raised from it wore off also, as I have noted already. Even the earthquake, though nothing could be more terrible in its nature, or more immediately directing to the invisible Power which alone directs such things, yet no sooner was the first fright over, but the impression it had made went off also. I had no more sense of God or His judgments—much less of the present affliction of my circumstances being from His hand—than if I had been in the most prosperous condition of life. But now, when I began to be sick, and a leisurely view of the miseries of death came to place itself before me; when my spirits began to sink under the burden of a strong distemper, and nature was exhausted with the violence of the fever; conscience, that had slept so long, began to awake, and I began to reproach myself with my past life, in which I had so evidently, by uncommon wickedness, provoked the justice of God to lay me under uncommon strokes, and to deal with me in so vindictive a manner. These reflections oppressed me for the second or third day of my distemper; and in the violence, as well of the fever as of the dreadful reproaches of my conscience, extorted some words from me like praying to God, though I cannot say they were either a prayer attended with desires or with hopes: it was rather the voice of mere fright and distress. My thoughts were confused, the convictions great upon my mind, and the horror of dying in such a miserable condition raised vapours into my head with the mere apprehensions; and in these hurries of my soul I knew not what my tongue might express. But it was rather exclamation, such as, "Lord, what a miserable creature am I! If I should be sick, I shall certainly die for want of help; and what will become of me!" Then the tears burst out of my eyes, and I could say no more for a good while. In this interval the good advice of my father came to my mind, and presently his prediction, which I mentioned at the beginning of this story—viz. that if I did take this foolish step, God would not bless me, and I would have leisure hereafter to reflect upon having neglected his counsel when there might be none to assist in my recovery. "Now," said I, aloud, "my dear father's words are come to pass; God's justice has overtaken me, and I have none to help or hear me. I rejected the voice of Providence, which had mercifully put me in a posture or station of life wherein I might have been happy and easy; but I would neither see it myself nor learn to know the blessing of it from my parents. I left them to mourn over my folly, and now I am left to mourn under the consequences of it. I abused their help and assistance, who would have lifted me in the world, and would have made everything easy to me; and now I have difficulties to struggle with, too great for even nature itself to support, and no assistance, no help, no comfort, no advice." Then I cried out, "Lord, be my help, for I am in great distress." This was the first prayer, if I may call it so, that I had made for many years.

But to return to my Journal.

June 28.—Having been somewhat refreshed with the sleep I had had, and the fit being entirely off, I got up; and though the fright and terror of my dream was very great, yet I considered that the fit of the ague would return again the next day, and now was my time to get something to refresh and support myself when I should be ill; and the first thing I did, I filled a large square case-bottle with water, and set it upon my table, in reach of my bed; and to take off the chill or aguish disposition of the water, I put about a quarter of a pint of rum into it, and mixed them together. Then I got me a piece of the goat's flesh and broiled it on the coals, but could eat very little. I walked about, but was very weak, and withal very sad and heavy-hearted under a sense of my miserable condition, dreading, the return of my distemper the next day. At night I made my supper of three of the turtle's eggs, which I roasted in the ashes, and ate, as we call it, in the shell, and this was the first bit of meat I had ever asked God's blessing to, that I could remember, in my whole life. After I had eaten I tried to walk, but found myself so weak that I could hardly carry a gun, for I never went out without that; so I went but a little way, and sat down upon the ground, looking out upon the sea, which was just before me, and very calm and smooth. As I sat here some such thoughts as these occurred to me: What is this earth and sea, of which I have seen so much? Whence is it produced? And what am I, and all the other creatures wild and tame, human and brutal? Whence are we? Sure we are all made by some secret Power, who formed the earth and sea, the air and sky. And who is that? Then it followed most naturally, it is God that has made all. Well, but then it came on strangely, if God has made all these things, He guides and governs them all, and all things that concern them; for the Power that could make all things must certainly have power to guide and direct them. If so, nothing can happen in the great circuit of His works, either without His knowledge or appointment.

And if nothing happens without His knowledge, He knows that I am here, and am in this dreadful condition; and if nothing happens without His appointment, He has appointed all this to befall me. Nothing occurred to my thought to contradict any of these conclusions, and therefore it rested upon me with the greater force, that it must needs be that God had appointed all this to befall me; that I was brought into this miserable circumstance by His direction, He having the sole power, not of me only, but of everything that happened in the world. Immediately it followed: Why has God done this to me? What have I done to be thus used? My conscience presently checked me in that inquiry, as if I had blasphemed, and methought it spoke to me like a voice: "Wretch! dost *thou* ask what thou hast done? Look back upon a dreadful misspent life, and ask thyself what thou hast *not* done? Ask, why is it that thou wert not long ago destroyed? Why wert thou not drowned in Yarmouth Roads;

killed in the fight when the ship was taken by the Sallee man-of-war; devoured by the wild beasts on the coast of Africa; or drowned *here*, when all the crew perished but thyself? Dost *thou* ask, what have I done?" I was struck dumb with these reflections, as one astonished, and had not a word to say—no, not to answer to myself, but rose up pensive and sad, walked back to my retreat, and went up over my wall, as if I had been going to bed; but my thoughts were sadly disturbed, and I had no inclination to sleep; so I sat down in my chair, and lighted my lamp, for it began to be dark. Now, as the apprehension of the return of my distemper terrified me very much, it occurred to my thought that the Brazilians take no physic but their tobacco for almost all distempers, and I had a piece of a roll of tobacco in one of the chests, which was quite cured, and some also that was green, and not quite cured.

I went, directed by Heaven no doubt; for in this chest I found a cure both for soul and body. I opened the chest, and found what I looked for, the tobacco; and as the few books I had saved lay there too, I took out one of the Bibles which I mentioned before, and which to this time I had not found leisure or inclination to look into. I say, I took it out, and brought both that and the tobacco with me to the table. What use to make of the tobacco I knew not, in my distemper, or whether it was good for it or no: but I tried several experiments with it, as if I was resolved it should hit one way or other. I first took a piece of leaf, and chewed it in my mouth, which, indeed, at first almost stupefied my brain, the tobacco being green and strong, and that I had not been much used to. Then I took some and steeped it an hour or two in some rum, and resolved to take a dose of it when I lay down; and lastly, I burnt some upon a pan of coals, and held my nose close over the smoke of it as long as I could bear it, as well for the heat as almost for suffocation. In the interval of this operation I took up the Bible and began to read; but my head was too much disturbed with the tobacco to bear reading, at least at that time; only, having opened the book casually, the first words that occurred to me were these, "Call on Me in the day of trouble, and I will deliver thee, and thou shalt glorify Me." These words were very apt to my case, and made some impression upon my thoughts at the time of reading them, though not so much as they did afterwards; for, as for being *delivered*, the word had no sound, as I may say, to me; the thing was so remote, so impossible in my apprehension of things, that I began to say, as the children of Israel did when they were promised flesh to eat, "Can God spread a table in the wilderness?" so I began to say, "Can God Himself deliver me from this place?" And as it was not for many years that any hopes appeared, this prevailed very often upon my thoughts; but, however, the words made a great impression upon me, and I mused upon them very often. It grew now late, and the tobacco had, as I said, dozed my head so much that I inclined to sleep; so I left my lamp burning in the cave, lest I should want anything in the night, and went to bed. But before I lay down, I did what I never had done in all my life—I kneeled down, and prayed to God to fulfil the promise to me, that if I called upon Him in the day of trouble, He would deliver me. After my broken and imperfect prayer was over, I drank the rum in which I had steeped the tobacco, which was so strong and rank of the tobacco that I could scarcely get it down; immediately upon this I went to bed. I found presently it flew up into my head violently; but I fell into a sound sleep, and waked no more till, by the sun, it must necessarily be near three o'clock in the afternoon the next day—nay, to this hour I am partly of opinion that I slept all the next day and night, and till almost three the day after; for otherwise I know not how I should lose a day out of my reckoning in the days of the week, as it appeared some years after I had done; for if I had lost it by crossing and recrossing the line, I should have lost more than one day; but certainly I lost a day in my account, and never knew which way. Be that, however, one way or the other, when I awaked I found myself exceedingly refreshed, and my spirits lively and cheerful; when I got up I was stronger than I was the day before, and my stomach better, for I was hungry; and, in short, I had no fit the next day, but continued much altered for the better. This was the 29th.

The 30th was my well day, of course, and I went abroad with my gun, but did not care to travel too far. I killed a sea-fowl or two, something like a brandgoose, and brought them home, but was not very forward to eat them; so I ate some more of the turtle's eggs, which were very good. This evening I renewed the medicine, which I had supposed did me good the day before—the tobacco steeped in rum; only I did not take so much as before, nor did I chew any of the leaf, or hold my head over the smoke; however, I was not so well the next day, which was the first of July, as I hoped I should have been; for I had a little spice of the cold fit, but it was not much.

July 2.—I renewed the medicine all the three ways; and dosed myself with it as at first, and doubled the quantity which I drank.

July 3.—I missed the fit for good and all, though I did not recover my full strength for some weeks after. While I was thus gathering strength, my thoughts ran exceedingly upon this Scripture, "I will deliver thee"; and the impossibility of my deliverance lay much upon my mind, in bar of my ever expecting it; but as I was discouraging myself with such thoughts, it occurred to my mind that I pored so much upon my deliverance from the main affliction, that I disregarded the deliverance I had received, and I was as it were made to ask myself such questions as these—viz. Have I not been delivered, and wonderfully too, from sickness—from the most distressed condition that could be, and that was so frightful to me? and what notice had I taken of it? Had I done my part? God had delivered me, but I had not glorified Him—that is to say, I had not owned and been thankful for that as a deliverance; and how could I expect greater deliverance? This touched my heart very much; and immediately I knelt down and gave God thanks aloud for my recovery from my sickness.

July 4.—In the morning I took the Bible; and beginning at the New Testament, I began seriously to read it, and imposed upon myself to read a while every morning and every night; not tying myself to the number of chapters, but long as my thoughts should engage me. It was not long after I set seriously to this work till I found my heart more deeply and sincerely affected with the wickedness of my past life. The impression of my dream revived; and the words, "All these things have not brought thee to repentance," ran seriously through my thoughts. I was earnestly begging of God to give me repentance, when it happened providentially, the very day, that, reading the Scripture, I came to these words: "He is exalted a Prince and a Saviour, to give repentance and to give remission." I threw down the book; and with my heart as well as my hands lifted up to heaven, in a kind of ecstasy of joy, I cried out aloud, "Jesus, thou son of David! Jesus, thou exalted Prince and Saviour! give me repentance!" This was the first time I could say, in the true sense of the words, that I prayed in all my life; for now I prayed with a sense of my condition, and a true Scripture view of hope, founded on the encouragement of the Word of God; and from this time, I may say, I began to hope that God would hear me.

Now I began to construe the words mentioned above, "Call on Me, and I will deliver thee," in a different sense from what I had ever done before; for then I had no notion of anything being called *deliverance*, but my being delivered from the captivity I was in; for though I was indeed at large in the place, yet the island was certainly a prison to me, and that in the worse sense in the world. But now I learned to take it in another sense: now I looked back upon my past life with such horror, and my sins appeared so dreadful, that my soul sought nothing of God but deliverance from the load of guilt that bore down all my comfort. As for my solitary life, it was nothing. I did not so much as pray to be delivered from it or think of it; it was all of no consideration in comparison to this. And I add this part here, to hint to whoever shall read it, that whenever they come to a true sense of things, they will find deliverance from sin a much greater blessing than deliverance from affliction.

But, leaving this part, I return to my Journal.

My condition began now to be, though not less miserable as to my way of living, yet much easier to my mind: and my thoughts being directed, by a constant reading the Scripture and praying to God, to things of a higher nature, I had a great deal of comfort within, which till now I knew nothing of; also, my health and strength returned, I bestirred myself to furnish myself with everything that I wanted, and make my way of living as regular as I could.

From the 4th of July to the 14th I was chiefly employed in walking about with my gun in my hand, a little and a little at a time, as a man that was gathering up his strength after a fit of sickness; for it is hardly to be imagined how low I was, and to what weakness I was reduced. The application which I made use of was perfectly new, and perhaps which had never cured an ague before; neither can I recommend it to any to practise, by this experiment: and though it did carry off the fit, yet it rather contributed to weakening me; for I had frequent convulsions in my nerves and limbs for some time. I learned from it also this, in particular, that being abroad in the rainy season was the most pernicious thing to my health that could be, especially in those rains which came attended with storms and hurricanes of wind; for as the rain which came in the dry season was almost always accompanied with such storms, so I found that rain was much more dangerous than the rain which fell in September and October.

7

AGRICULTURAL EXPERIENCE

I had now been in this unhappy island above ten months. All possibility of deliverance from this condition seemed to be entirely taken from me; and I firmly believe that no human shape had ever set foot upon that place. Having now secured my habitation, as I thought, fully to my mind, I had a great desire to make a more perfect discovery of the island, and to see what other productions I might find, which I yet knew nothing of.

It was on the 15th of July that I began to take a more particular survey of the island itself. I went up the creek first, where, as I hinted, I brought my rafts on shore. I found after I came about two miles up, that the tide did not flow any higher, and that it was no more than a little brook of running water, very fresh and good; but this being the dry season, there was hardly any water in some parts of it—at least not enough to run in any stream, so as it could be perceived. On the banks of this brook I found many pleasant savannahs or meadows, plain, smooth, and covered with grass; and on the rising parts of them, next to the higher grounds, where the water, as might be supposed, never overflowed, I found a great deal of tobacco, green, and growing to a great and very strong stalk. There were divers other plants, which I had no notion of or understanding about, that might, perhaps, have virtues of their own, which I could not find out. I searched for the cassava root, which the Indians, in all that climate, make their bread of, but I could find none. I saw large plants of aloes, but did not understand them. I saw several sugar-canes, but wild, and, for want of cultivation, imperfect. I contented myself with these discoveries for this time, and came back, musing with myself what course I might take to know the virtue and goodness of any of the fruits or plants which I should discover, but could bring it to no conclusion; for, in short, I had made so little observation while I was in the Brazils, that I knew little of the plants in the field; at least, very little that might serve to any purpose now in my distress.

The next day, the sixteenth, I went up the same way again; and after going something further than I had gone the day before, I found the brook and the savannahs cease, and the country become more woody than before. In this part I found different fruits, and particularly I found melons upon the ground, in great abundance, and grapes upon the trees. The vines had spread, indeed, over the trees, and the clusters of grapes were just now in their prime, very ripe and rich. This was a surprising discovery, and I was exceeding glad of them; but I was warned by my experience to eat sparingly of them; remembering that when I was ashore in Barbary, the eating of grapes killed several of our Englishmen, who were slaves there, by throwing them into fluxes and fevers. But I found an excellent use for these grapes; and that was, to cure or dry them in the sun, and keep them as dried grapes or raisins are kept, which I thought would be, as indeed they were, wholesome and agreeable to eat when no grapes could be had.

I spent all that evening there, and went not back to my habitation; which, by the way, was the first night, as I might say, I had lain from home. In the night, I took my first contrivance, and got up in a tree, where I slept well; and the next morning proceeded upon my discovery; travelling nearly four miles, as I might judge by the length of the valley, keeping still due north, with a ridge of hills on the south and north side of me. At the end of this march I came to an opening where the country seemed to descend to the west; and a little spring of fresh water, which issued out of the side of the hill by me, ran the other way, that is, due east; and the country appeared so fresh, so green, so flourishing, everything being in a constant verdure or flourish of spring that it looked like a planted garden. I descended a little on the side of that delicious vale, surveying it with a secret kind of pleasure, though mixed with my other afflicting thoughts, to think that this was all my own; that I was king and lord of all this country indefensibly, and had a right of possession; and if I could convey it, I might have it in inheritance as completely as any lord of a manor in England. I saw here abundance of cocoa trees, orange, and lemon, and citron trees; but all wild, and very few bearing any fruit, at least not then. However, the green limes that I gathered were not only pleasant to eat, but very wholesome; and I mixed their juice afterwards with water, which made it very wholesome, and very cool and refreshing. I found now I had business enough to gather and carry home; and I resolved to lay up a store as well of grapes as limes and lemons, to furnish myself for the wet season, which I knew was approaching. In order to do this, I gathered a great heap of grapes in one place, a lesser heap in another place, and a great parcel of limes and lemons in another place; and taking a few of each with me, I travelled homewards; resolving to come again, and bring a bag or sack, or what I could make, to carry the rest home. Accordingly, having spent three days in this journey, I came home (so I must now call my tent and my cave); but before I got thither the grapes were spoiled; the richness of the fruit and the weight of the juice having broken them and bruised them, they were good for little or nothing; as to the limes, they were good, but I could bring but a few.

The next day, being the nineteenth, I went back, having made me two small bags to bring home my harvest; but I was surprised, when coming to my heap of grapes, which were so rich and fine when I gathered them, to find them all spread about, trod to pieces, and dragged about, some here, some there, and abundance eaten and devoured. By this I concluded there were some wild creatures thereabouts, which had done this; but what they were I knew not. However, as I found there was no laying them up on heaps, and no carrying them away in a sack, but that one way they would be destroyed, and the other way they would be crushed with their own weight, I took another course; for I gathered a large quantity of the grapes, and hung upon the out-branches of the trees, that they might cure and dry in the sun; and as for the limes and lemons, I carried as many back as I could well stand under.

When I came home from this journey, I contemplated with great pleasure the fruitfulness of that valley, and the pleasantness of the situation; the security from storms on that side of the water, and the wood: and concluded that I had pitched upon a place to fix my abode which was by far the worst part of the country. Upon the whole, I began to consider of removing my habitation, and looking out for a place equally safe as where now I was situate, if possible, in that pleasant, fruitful part of the island.

This thought ran long in my head, and I was exceeding fond of it for some time, the pleasantness of the place tempting me; but when I came to a nearer view of it, I considered that I was now by the seaside, where it was at least possible that something might happen to my advantage, and, by the same ill fate that brought me hither might bring some other unhappy wretches to the same place; and though it was scarce probable that any such thing should ever happen, yet to enclose myself among the hills and woods in the centre of the island was to anticipate my bondage, and to render such an affair not only improbable, but impossible; and that therefore I ought not by any means to remove. However, I was so enamoured of this place, that I spent much of my time there for the whole of the remaining part of the month of July; and though upon second thoughts, I resolved not to remove, yet I built me a little kind of a bower, and surrounded it at a distance with a strong fence, being a double hedge, as high as I could reach, well staked and filled between with brushwood; and here I lay very secure, sometimes two or three nights together; always going over it with a ladder; so that I fancied now I had my country house and my sea-coast house; and this work took me up to the beginning of August.

I had but newly finished my fence, and began to enjoy my labour, when the rains came on, and made me stick close to my first habitation; for though I had made me a tent like the other, with a piece of a sail, and spread it very well, yet I had not the shelter of a hill to keep me from storms, nor a cave behind me to retreat into when the rains were extraordinary.

About the beginning of August, as I said, I had finished my bower, and began to enjoy myself. The 3rd of August, I found the grapes I had hung up perfectly dried, and, indeed, were excellent good raisins of the sun; so I began to take them down from the trees, and it was very happy that I did so, for the rains which followed would have spoiled them, and I had lost the best part of my winter food; for I had above two hundred large bunches of them. No sooner had I taken them all down, and carried the most of them home to my cave, than it began to rain; and from hence, which was the 14th of August, it rained, more or less, every day till the middle of October; and sometimes so violently, that I could not stir out of my cave for several days.

In this season I was much surprised with the increase of my family; I had been concerned for the loss of one of my cats, who ran away from me, or, as I thought, had been dead, and I heard no more tidings of her till, to my astonishment, she came home about the end of August with three kittens. This was the more strange to me because, though I had killed a wild cat, as I called it, with my gun, yet I thought it was quite a different kind from our European cats; but the young cats were the same kind of house-breed as the old one; and both my cats being females, I thought it very strange. But from these three cats I afterwards came to be so pestered with cats that I was forced to kill them like vermin or wild beasts, and to drive them from my house as much as possible.

From the 14th of August to the 26th, incessant rain, so that I could not stir, and was now very careful not to be much wet. In this confinement, I began to be straitened for food: but venturing out twice, I one day killed a goat; and the last day, which was the 26th, found a very large tortoise, which was a treat to me, and my food was regulated thus: I ate a bunch of raisins for my breakfast; a piece of the goat's flesh, or of the turtle, for my dinner, broiled—for, to my great misfortune, I had no vessel to boil or stew anything; and two or three of the turtle's eggs for my supper.

During this confinement in my cover by the rain, I worked daily two or three hours at enlarging my cave, and by degrees worked it on towards one side, till I came to the outside of the hill, and made a door or way out, which came beyond my fence or wall; and so I came in and out this way. But I was not perfectly easy at lying so open; for, as I had managed myself before, I was in a perfect enclosure; whereas now I thought I lay exposed, and open for anything to come in upon me; and yet I could not perceive that there was any living thing to fear, the biggest creature that I had yet seen upon the island being a goat.

Sept. 30.—I was now come to the unhappy anniversary of my landing. I cast up the notches on my post, and found I had been on shore three hundred and sixty-five days. I kept this day as a solemn fast, setting it apart for religious exercise, prostrating myself on the ground with the most serious humiliation, confessing my sins to God, acknowledging His righteous judgments upon me, and praying to Him to have mercy on me through Jesus Christ; and not having tasted the least refreshment for twelve hours, even till the going down of the sun, I then ate a biscuit-cake and a bunch of grapes, and went to bed, finishing the day as I began it. I had all this time observed no Sabbath day; for as at first I had no sense of religion upon my mind, I had, after some time, omitted to distinguish the weeks, by making a longer notch than ordinary for the Sabbath day, and so did not really know what any of the days were; but now, having cast up the days as above, I found I had been there a year; so I divided it into weeks, and set apart every seventh day for a Sabbath; though I found at the end of my account I had lost a day or two in my reckoning. A little after this, my ink began to fail me, and so I contented myself to use it more sparingly, and to write down only the most remarkable events of my life, without continuing a daily memorandum of other things.

The rainy season and the dry season began now to appear regular to me, and I learned to divide them so as to provide for them accordingly; but I bought all my experience before I had it, and this I am going to relate was one of the most discouraging experiments that I made.

I have mentioned that I had saved the few ears of barley and rice, which I had so surprisingly found spring up, as I thought, of themselves, and I believe there were about thirty stalks of rice, and about twenty of barley; and now I thought it a proper time to sow it, after the rains, the sun being in its southern position, going from me. Accordingly, I dug up a piece of ground as well as I could with my wooden spade, and dividing it into two parts, I sowed my grain; but as I was sowing, it casually occurred to my thoughts that I would not sow it all at first, because I did not know when was the proper time for it, so I sowed about two-thirds of the seed, leaving about a handful of each. It was a great comfort to me afterwards that I did so, for not one grain of what I sowed this time came to anything: for the dry months following, the earth having had no rain after the seed was sown, it had no moisture to assist its growth, and never came up at all till the wet season had come again, and then it grew as if it had been but newly sown. Finding my first seed did not grow, which I easily imagined was by the drought, I sought for a moister piece of ground to make another trial in, and I dug up a piece of ground near my new bower, and sowed the rest of my seed in February, a little before the vernal equinox; and this having the rainy months of March and April to water it, sprung up very pleasantly, and yielded a very good crop; but having part of the seed left only, and not daring to sow all that I had, I had but a small quantity at last, my whole crop not amounting to above half a peck of each kind. But by this experiment I was made master of my business, and knew exactly when the proper season was to sow, and that I might expect two seed-times and two harvests every year.

While this corn was growing I made a little discovery, which was of use to me afterwards. As soon as the rains were over, and the weather began to settle, which was about the month of November, I made a visit up the country to my bower, where, though I had not been some months, yet I found all things just as I left them. The circle or double hedge that I had made was not only firm and entire, but the stakes which I had cut out of some trees that grew thereabouts were all shot out and grown with long branches, as much as a willow-tree usually shoots the first year after lopping its head. I could not tell what tree to call it that these stakes were cut from. I was surprised, and yet very well pleased, to see the young trees grow; and I pruned them, and led them up to grow as much alike as I could; and it is scarce credible how beautiful a figure they grew into in three years; so that though the hedge made a circle of about twenty-five yards in diameter, yet the trees, for such I might now call them, soon covered it, and it was a complete shade, sufficient to lodge under all the dry season. This made me resolve to cut some more stakes, and make me a hedge like this, in a semi-circle round my wall (I mean that of my first dwelling), which I did; and placing the trees or stakes in a double row, at about eight yards distance from my first fence, they grew presently, and were at first a fine cover to my habitation, and afterwards served for a defence also, as I shall observe in its order.

I found now that the seasons of the year might generally be divided, not into summer and winter, as in Europe, but into the rainy seasons and the dry seasons, which were generally thus:—The half of February, the whole of March, and the half of April—rainy, the sun being then on or near the equinox.

The half of April, the whole of May, June, and July, and the half of August—dry, the sun being then to the north of the line.

The half of August, the whole of September, and the half of October—rainy, the sun being then come back.

The half of October, the whole of November, December, and January, and the half of February—dry, the sun being then to the south of the line.

The rainy seasons sometimes held longer or shorter as the winds happened to blow, but this was the general observation I made. After I had found by experience the ill consequences of being abroad in the rain, I took care to furnish myself with provisions beforehand, that I might not be obliged to go out, and I sat within doors as much as possible during the wet months. This time I found much employment, and very suitable also to the time, for I found great occasion for many things which I had no way to furnish myself with but by hard labour and constant application; particularly I tried many ways to make myself a basket, but all the twigs I could get for the purpose proved so brittle that they would do nothing. It proved of excellent advantage to me now, that when I was a boy, I used to take great delight in standing at a basket-maker's, in the town where my father lived, to see them make their wicker-ware; and being, as boys usually are, very officious to help, and a great observer of the manner in which they worked those things, and sometimes lending a hand, I had by these means full knowledge of the methods of it, and I wanted nothing but the materials, when it came into my mind that the twigs of that tree from whence I cut my stakes that grew might possibly be as tough as the sallows, willows, and osiers in England, and I resolved to try. Accordingly, the next day I went to my country house, as I called it, and cutting some of the smaller twigs, I found them to my purpose as much as I could desire; whereupon I came the next time prepared with a hatchet to cut down a quantity, which I soon found, for there was great plenty of them. These I set up to dry within my circle or hedge, and when they were fit for use I carried them to my cave; and here, during the next season, I employed myself in making, as well as I could, a great many baskets, both to carry earth or to carry or lay up anything, as I had occasion; and though I did not finish them very handsomely, yet I made them sufficiently serviceable for my purpose; thus, afterwards, I took care never to be without them; and as my wicker-ware decayed, I made more, especially strong, deep baskets to place my corn in, instead of sacks, when I should come to have any quantity of it.

Having mastered this difficulty, and employed a world of time about it, I bestirred myself to see, if possible, how to supply two wants. I had no vessels to hold anything that was liquid, except two runlets, which were almost full of rum, and some glass bottles—some of the common size, and others which were case bottles, square, for the holding of water, spirits, &c. I had not so much as a pot to boil anything, except a great kettle, which I saved out of the ship, and which was too big for such as I desired it—viz. to make broth, and stew a bit of meat by itself. The second thing I fain would have had was a tobacco-pipe, but it was impossible to me to make one; however, I found a contrivance for that, too, at last. I employed myself in planting my second rows of stakes or piles, and in this wicker-working all the summer or dry season, when another business took me up more time than it could be imagined I could spare.

8

SURVEYS HIS POSITION

I mentioned before that I had a great mind to see the whole island, and that I had travelled up the brook, and so on to where I built my bower, and where I had an opening quite to the sea, on the other side of the island. I now resolved to travel quite across to the sea-shore on that side; so, taking my gun, a hatchet, and my dog, and a larger quantity of powder and shot than usual, with two biscuit-cakes and a great bunch of raisins in my pouch for my store, I began my journey. When I had passed the vale where my bower stood, as above, I came within view of the sea to the west, and it being a very clear day, I fairly descried land—whether an island or a continent I could not tell; but it lay very high, extending from the W. to the W.S.W. at a very great distance; by my guess it could not be less than fifteen or twenty leagues off.

I could not tell what part of the world this might be, otherwise than that I knew it must be part of America, and, as I concluded by all my observations, must be near the Spanish dominions, and perhaps was all inhabited by savages, where, if I had landed, I had been in a worse condition than I was now; and therefore I acquiesced in the dispositions of Providence, which I began now to own and to believe ordered everything for the best; I say I quieted my mind with this, and left off afflicting myself with fruitless wishes of being there.

Besides, after some thought upon this affair, I considered that if this land was the Spanish coast, I should certainly, one time or other, see some vessel pass or repass one way or other; but if not, then it was the savage coast between the Spanish country and Brazils, where are found the worst of savages; for they are cannibals or men-eaters, and fail not to murder and devour all the human bodies that fall into their hands.

With these considerations, I walked very leisurely forward. I found that side of the island where I now was much pleasanter than mine—the open or savannah fields sweet, adorned with flowers and grass, and full of very fine woods. I saw abundance of parrots, and fain I would have caught one, if possible, to have kept it to be tame, and taught it to speak to me. I did, after some painstaking, catch a young parrot, for I knocked it down with a stick, and having recovered it, I brought it home; but it was some years before I could make him speak;

however, at last I taught him to call me by name very familiarly. But the accident that followed, though it be a trifle, will be very diverting in its place.

I was exceedingly diverted with this journey. I found in the low grounds hares (as I thought them to be) and foxes; but they differed greatly from all the other kinds I had met with, nor could I satisfy myself to eat them, though I killed several. But I had no need to be venturous, for I had no want of food, and of that which was very good too, especially these three sorts, viz. goats, pigeons, and turtle, or tortoise, which added to my grapes, Leadenhall market could not have furnished a table better than I, in proportion to the company; and though my case was deplorable enough, yet I had great cause for thankfulness that I was not driven to any extremities for food, but had rather plenty, even to dainties.

I never travelled in this journey above two miles outright in a day, or thereabouts; but I took so many turns and re-turns to see what discoveries I could make, that I came weary enough to the place where I resolved to sit down all night; and then I either reposed myself in a tree, or surrounded myself with a row of stakes set upright in the ground, either from one tree to another, or so as no wild creature could come at me without waking me.

As soon as I came to the sea-shore, I was surprised to see that I had taken up my lot on the worst side of the island, for here, indeed, the shore was covered with innumerable turtles, whereas on the other side I had found but three in a year and a half. Here was also an infinite number of fowls of many kinds, some which I had seen, and some which I had not seen before, and many of them very good meat, but such as I knew not the names of, except those called penguins.

I could have shot as many as I pleased, but was very sparing of my powder and shot, and therefore had more mind to kill a she-goat if I could, which I could better feed on; and though there were many goats here, more than on my side the island, yet it was with much more difficulty that I could come near them, the country being flat and even, and they saw me much sooner than when I was on the hills.

I confess this side of the country was much pleasanter than mine; but yet I had not the least inclination to remove, for as I was fixed in my habitation it became natural to me, and I seemed all the while I was here to be as it were upon a journey, and from home. However, I travelled along the shore of the sea towards the east, I suppose about twelve miles, and then setting up a great pole upon the shore for a mark, I concluded I would go home again, and that the next journey I took should be on the other side of the island east from my dwelling, and so round till I came to my post again.

I took another way to come back than that I went, thinking I could easily keep all the island so much in my view that I could not miss finding my first dwelling by viewing the country; but I found myself mistaken, for being come about two or three miles, I found myself descended into a very large valley, but so surrounded with hills, and those hills covered with wood, that I could not see which was my way by any direction but that of the sun, nor even then, unless I knew very well the position of the sun at that time of the day. It happened, to my further misfortune, that the weather proved hazy for three or four days while I was in the valley, and not being able to see the sun, I wandered about very uncomfortably, and at last was obliged to find the seaside, look for my post, and come back the same way I went: and then, by easy journeys, I turned homeward, the weather being exceeding hot, and my gun, ammunition, hatchet, and other things very heavy.

In this journey my dog surprised a young kid, and seized upon it; and I, running in to take hold of it, caught it, and saved it alive from the dog. I had a great mind to bring it home if I could, for I had often been musing whether it might not be possible to get a kid or two, and so raise a breed of tame goats, which might supply me when my powder and shot should be all spent. I made a collar for this little creature, and with a string, which I made of some rope-yarn, which I always carried about me, I led him along, though with some difficulty, till I came to my bower, and there I enclosed him and left him, for I was very impatient to be at home, from whence I had been absent above a month.

I cannot express what a satisfaction it was to me to come into my old hutch, and lie down in my hammock-bed. This little wandering journey, without settled place of abode, had been so unpleasant to me, that my own house, as I called it to myself, was a perfect settlement to me compared to that; and it rendered everything about me so comfortable, that I resolved I would never go a great way from it again while it should be my lot to stay on the island.

I reposed myself here a week, to rest and regale myself after my long journey; during which most of the time was taken up in the weighty affair of making a cage for my Poll, who began now to be a mere domestic, and to be well acquainted with me. Then I began to think of the poor kid which I had penned in within my little circle, and resolved to go and fetch it home, or give it some food; accordingly I went, and found it where I left it, for indeed it could not get out, but was almost starved for want of food. I went and cut boughs of trees, and branches of such shrubs as I could find, and threw it over, and having fed it, I tied it as I did before, to lead it away; but it was so tame with being hungry, that I had no need to have tied it, for it followed me like a dog: and as I continually fed it, the creature became so loving, so gentle, and so fond, that it became from that time one of my domestics also, and would never leave me afterwards.

The rainy season of the autumnal equinox was now come, and I kept the 30th of September in the same solemn manner as before, being the anniversary of my landing on the island, having now been there two years, and no more prospect of being delivered than the first day I came there, I spent the whole day in humble and thankful acknowledgments of the many wonderful mercies which my solitary condition was attended with, and without which it might have been infinitely more miserable. I gave humble and hearty thanks that God had been pleased to discover to me that it was possible I might be more happy in this solitary condition than I should have been in the liberty of society, and in all the pleasures of the world; that He could fully make up to me the deficiencies of my solitary state, and the want of human society, by His presence and the communications of His grace to my soul; supporting, comforting, and encouraging me to depend upon His providence here, and hope for His eternal presence hereafter.

It was now that I began sensibly to feel how much more happy this life I now led was, with all its miserable circumstances, than the wicked, cursed, abominable life I led all the past part of my days; and now I changed both my sorrows and my joys; my very desires altered, my affections changed their gusts, and my delights were perfectly new from what they were at my first coming, or, indeed, for the two years past.

Before, as I walked about, either on my hunting or for viewing the country, the anguish of my soul at my condition would break out upon me on a sudden, and my very heart would die within me, to think of the woods, the mountains, the deserts I was in, and how I was a prisoner, locked up with the eternal bars and bolts of the ocean, in an uninhabited wilderness, without redemption. In the midst of the greatest composure of my mind, this would break out upon me like a storm, and make me wring my hands and weep like a child. Sometimes it would take me in the middle of my work, and I would immediately sit down and sigh, and look upon the ground for an hour or two together; and this was still worse to me, for if I could burst out into tears, or vent myself by words, it would go off, and the grief, having exhausted itself, would abate.

But now I began to exercise myself with new thoughts: I daily read the word of God, and applied all the comforts of it to my present state. One morning, being very sad, I opened the Bible upon these words, "I will never, never leave thee, nor forsake thee." Immediately it occurred that these words were to me; why else should they be directed in such a manner, just at the moment when I was mourning over my condition, as one forsaken of God and man? "Well, then," said I, "if God does not forsake me, of what ill consequence can it be, or what matters it, though the world should all forsake me, seeing on the other hand, if I had all the world, and should lose the favour and blessing of God, there would be no comparison in the loss?"

From this moment I began to conclude in my mind that it was possible for me to be more happy in this forsaken, solitary condition than it was probable I should ever have been in any other particular state in the world; and with this thought I was going to give thanks to God for bringing me to this place. I know not what it was, but something shocked my mind at that thought, and I durst not speak the words. "How canst thou become such a hypocrite," said I, even audibly, "to pretend to be thankful for a condition which, however thou mayest endeavour to be contented with, thou wouldst rather pray heartily to be delivered from?" So I stopped there; but though I could not say I thanked God for being there, yet I sincerely gave thanks to God for opening my eyes, by whatever afflicting providences, to see the former condition of my life, and to mourn for my wickedness, and repent. I never opened the Bible, or shut it, but my very soul within me blessed God for directing my friend in England, without any order of mine, to pack it up among my goods, and for assisting me afterwards to save it out of the wreck of the ship.

Thus, and in this disposition of mind, I began my third year; and though I have not given the reader the trouble of so particular an account of my works this year as the first, yet in general it may be observed that I was very seldom idle, but having regularly divided my time according to the several daily employments that were before me, such as: first, my duty to God, and the reading the Scriptures, which I constantly set apart some time for thrice every day; secondly, the going abroad with my gun for food, which generally took me up three hours in every morning, when it did not rain; thirdly, the ordering, cutting, preserving, and cooking what I had killed or caught for my supply; these took up great part of the day. Also, it is to be considered, that in the middle of the day, when the sun was in the zenith, the violence of the heat was too great to stir out; so that about four hours in the evening was all the time I could be supposed to work in, with this exception, that sometimes I changed my hours of hunting and working, and went to work in the morning, and abroad with my gun in the afternoon.

To this short time allowed for labour I desire may be added the exceeding laboriousness of my work; the many hours which, for want of tools, want of help, and want of skill, everything I did took up out of my time. For example, I was full two and forty days in making a board for a long shelf, which I wanted in my cave; whereas, two sawyers, with their tools and a saw-pit, would have cut six of them out of the same tree in half a day.

My case was this: it was to be a large tree which was to be cut down, because my board was to be a broad one. This tree I was three days in cutting down, and two more cutting off the boughs, and reducing it to a log or piece of timber. With inexpressible hacking and hewing I reduced both the sides of it into chips till it began to be light enough to move; then I turned it, and made one side of it smooth and flat as a board from end to end; then, turning that side downward, cut the other side til I brought the plank to be about three inches thick, and smooth on both sides. Any one may judge the labour of my hands in such a piece of work; but labour and patience carried me through that, and many other things. I only observe this in particular, to show the reason why so much of my time went away with so little work—viz. that what might be a little to be done with help and tools, was a vast labour and required a prodigious time to do alone, and by hand. But notwithstanding this, with patience and labour I got through everything that my circumstances made necessary to me to do, as will appear by what follows.

I was now, in the months of November and December, expecting my crop of barley and rice. The ground I had manured and dug up for them was not great; for, as I observed, my seed of each was not above the quantity of half a peck, for I had lost one whole crop by sowing in the dry season. But now my crop promised very well, when on a sudden I found I was in danger of losing it all again by enemies of several sorts, which it was scarcely possible to keep from it; as, first, the goats, and wild creatures which I called hares, who, tasting the sweetness of the blade, lay in it night and day, as soon as it came up, and eat it so close, that it could get no time to shoot up into stalk.

This I saw no remedy for but by making an enclosure about it with a hedge; which I did with a great deal of toil, and the more, because it required speed. However, as my arable land was but small, suited to my crop, I got it totally well fenced in about three weeks' time; and shooting some of the creatures in the daytime, I set my dog to guard it in the night, tying him up to a stake at the gate, where he would stand and bark all night long; so in a little time the enemies forsook the place, and the corn grew very strong and well, and began to ripen apace.

But as the beasts ruined me before, while my corn was in the blade, so the birds were as likely to ruin me now, when it was in the ear; for, going along by the place to see how it throve, I saw my little crop surrounded with fowls, of I know not how many sorts, who stood, as it were, watching till I should be gone. I immediately let fly among them, for I always had my gun with me. I had no sooner shot, but there rose up a little cloud of fowls, which I had not seen at all, from among the corn itself.

This touched me sensibly, for I foresaw that in a few days they would devour all my hopes; that I should be starved, and never be able to raise a crop at all; and what to do I could not tell; however, I resolved not to lose my corn, if possible, though I should watch it night and day. In the first place, I went among it to see what damage was already done, and found they had spoiled a good deal of it; but that as it was yet too green for them, the loss was not so great but that the remainder was likely to be a good crop if it could be saved.

I stayed by it to load my gun, and then coming away, I could easily see the thieves sitting upon all the trees about me, as if they only waited till I was gone away, and the event proved it to be so; for as I walked off, as if I was gone, I was no sooner out of their sight than they dropped down one by one into the corn again. I was so provoked, that I could not have patience to stay till more came on, knowing that every grain that they ate now was, as it might be said, a peck-loaf to me in the consequence; but coming up to the hedge, I fired again, and killed three of them. This was what I wished for; so I took them up, and served them as we serve notorious thieves in England—hanged them in chains, for a terror to others. It is impossible to imagine that this should have such an effect as it had, for the fowls would not only not come at the corn, but, in short, they forsook all that part of the island, and I could never see a bird near the place as long as my scarecrows hung there. This I was very glad of, you may be sure, and about the latter end of December, which was our second harvest of the year, I reaped my corn.

I was sadly put to it for a scythe or sickle to cut it down, and all I could do was to make one, as well as I could, out of one of the broadswords, or cutlasses, which I saved among the arms out of the ship. However, as my first crop was but small, I had no great difficulty to cut it down; in short, I reaped it in my way, for I cut nothing off but the ears, and carried it away in a great basket which I had made, and so rubbed it out with my hands; and at the end of all my harvesting, I found that out of my half-peck of seed I had near two bushels of rice, and about two bushels and a half of barley; that is to say, by my guess, for I had no measure at that time.

However, this was a great encouragement to me, and I foresaw that, in time, it would please God to supply me with bread. And yet here I was perplexed again, for I neither knew how to grind or make meal of my corn, or indeed how to clean it and part it; nor, if made into meal, how to make bread of it; and if how to make it, yet I knew not how to bake it. These things being added to my desire of having a good quantity for store, and to secure a constant supply, I resolved not to taste any of this crop but to preserve it all for seed against the next season; and in the meantime to employ all my study and hours of working to accomplish this great work of providing myself with corn and bread.

It might be truly said, that now I worked for my bread. I believe few people have thought much upon the strange multitude of little things necessary in the providing, producing, curing, dressing, making, and finishing this one article of bread.

I, that was reduced to a mere state of nature, found this to my daily discouragement; and was made more sensible of it every hour, even after I had got the first handful of seed-corn, which, as I have said, came up unexpectedly, and indeed to a surprise.

First, I had no plough to turn up the earth—no spade or shovel to dig it. Well, this I conquered by making me a wooden spade, as I observed before; but this did my work but in a wooden manner; and though it cost me a great many days to make it, yet, for want of iron, it not only wore out soon, but made my work the harder, and made it be performed much worse. However, this I bore with, and was content to work it out with patience, and bear with the badness of the performance. When the corn was sown, I had no harrow, but was forced to go over it myself, and drag a great heavy bough of a tree over it, to scratch it, as it may be called, rather than rake or harrow it. When it was growing, and grown, I have observed already how many things I wanted to fence it, secure it, mow or reap it, cure and carry it home, thrash, part it from the chaff, and save it. Then I wanted a mill to grind it, sieves to dress it, yeast and salt to make it into bread, and an oven to bake it; but all these things I did without, as shall be observed; and yet the corn was an inestimable comfort and advantage to me too. All this, as I said, made everything laborious and tedious to me; but that there was no help for. Neither was my time so much loss to me, because, as I had divided it, a certain part of it was every day appointed to these works; and as I had resolved to use none of the corn for bread till I had a greater quantity by me, I had the next six months to apply myself wholly, by labour and invention, to furnish myself with utensils proper for the performing all the operations necessary for making the corn, when I had it, fit for my use.

9

A BOAT

But first I was to prepare more land, for I had now seed enough to sow above an acre of ground. Before I did this, I had a week's work at least to make me a spade, which, when it was done, was but a sorry one indeed, and very heavy, and required double labour to work with it. However, I got through that, and sowed my seed in two large flat pieces of ground, as near my house as I could find them to my mind, and fenced them in with a good hedge, the stakes of which were all cut off that wood which I had set before, and knew it would grow; so that, in a year's time, I knew I should have a quick or living hedge, that would want but little repair. This work did not take me up less than three months, because a great part of that time was the wet season, when I could not go abroad. Within-doors, that is when it rained and I could not go out, I found employment in the following occupations—always observing, that all the while I was at work I diverted myself with talking to my parrot, and teaching him to speak; and I quickly taught him to know his own name, and at last to speak it out pretty loud, "Poll," which was the first word I ever heard spoken in the island by any mouth but my own. This, therefore, was not my work, but an assistance to my work; for now, as I said, I had a great employment upon my hands, as follows: I had long studied to make, by some means or other, some earthen vessels, which, indeed, I wanted sorely, but knew not where to come at them. However, considering the heat of the climate, I did not doubt but if I could find out any clay, I might make some pots that might, being dried in the sun, be hard enough and strong enough to bear handling, and to hold anything that was dry, and required to be kept so; and as this was necessary in the preparing corn, meal, &c., which was the thing I was doing, I resolved to make some as large as I could, and fit only to stand like jars, to hold what should be put into them.

It would make the reader pity me, or rather laugh at me, to tell how many awkward ways I took to raise this paste; what odd, misshapen, ugly things I made; how many of them fell in and how many fell out, the clay not being stiff enough to bear its own weight; how many cracked by the over-violent heat of the sun, being set out too hastily; and how many fell in pieces with only removing, as well before as after they were dried; and, in a word, how, after having laboured hard to find the clay—to dig it, to temper it, to bring it home, and work it—I could not make above two large earthen ugly things (I cannot call them jars) in about two months' labour.

However, as the sun baked these two very dry and hard, I lifted them very gently up, and set them down again in two great wicker baskets, which I had made on purpose for them, that they might not break; and as between the pot and the basket there was a little room to spare, I stuffed it full of the rice and barley straw; and these two pots being to stand always dry I thought would hold my dry corn, and perhaps the meal, when the corn was bruised.

Though I miscarried so much in my design for large pots, yet I made several smaller things with better success; such as little round pots, flat dishes, pitchers, and pipkins, and any things my hand turned to; and the heat of the sun baked them quite hard.

But all this would not answer my end, which was to get an earthen pot to hold what was liquid, and bear the fire, which none of these could do. It happened after some time, making a pretty large fire for cooking my meat, when I went to put it out after I had done with it, I found a broken piece of one of my earthenware vessels in the fire, burnt as hard as a stone, and red as a tile. I was agreeably surprised to see it, and said to myself, that certainly they might be made to burn whole, if they would burn broken.

This set me to study how to order my fire, so as to make it burn some pots. I had no notion of a kiln, such as the potters burn in, or of glazing them with lead, though I had some lead to do it with; but I placed three large pipkins and two or three pots in a pile, one upon another, and placed my firewood all round it, with a great heap of embers under them. I plied the fire with fresh fuel round the outside and upon the top, till I saw the pots in the inside red-hot quite through, and observed that they did not crack at all. When I saw them clear red, I let them stand in that heat about five or six hours, till I found one of them, though it did not crack, did melt or run; for the sand which was mixed with the clay melted by the violence of the heat, and would have run into glass if I had gone on; so I slacked my fire gradually till the pots began to abate of the red colour; and watching them all night, that I might not let the fire abate too fast, in the morning I had three very good (I will not say handsome) pipkins, and two other earthen pots, as hard burnt as could be desired, and one of them perfectly glazed with the running of the sand.

After this experiment, I need not say that I wanted no sort of earthenware for my use; but I must needs say as to the shapes of them, they were very indifferent, as any one may suppose, when I had no way of making them but as the children make dirt pies, or as a woman would make pies that never learned to raise paste.

No joy at a thing of so mean a nature was ever equal to mine, when I found I had made an earthen pot that would bear the fire; and I had hardly patience to stay till they were cold before I set one on the fire again with some water in it to boil me some meat, which it did admirably well; and with a piece of a kid I made some very good broth, though I wanted oatmeal, and several other ingredients requisite to make it as good as I would have had it been.

My next concern was to get me a stone mortar to stamp or beat some corn in; for as to the mill, there was no thought of arriving at that perfection of art with one pair of hands. To supply this want, I was at a great loss; for, of all the trades in the world, I was as perfectly unqualified for a stone-cutter as for any whatever; neither had I any tools to go about it with. I spent many a day to find out a great stone big enough to cut hollow, and make fit for a mortar, and could find none at all, except what was in the solid rock, and which I had no way to dig or cut out; nor indeed were the rocks in the island of hardness sufficient, but were all of a sandy, crumbling stone, which neither would bear the weight of a heavy pestle, nor would break the corn without filling it with sand. So, after a great deal of time lost in searching for a stone, I gave it over, and resolved to look out for a great block of hard wood, which I found, indeed, much easier; and getting one as big as I had strength to stir, I rounded it, and formed it on the outside with my axe and hatchet, and then with the help of fire and infinite labour, made a hollow place in it, as the Indians in Brazil make their canoes. After this, I made a great heavy pestle or beater of the wood called the iron-wood; and this I prepared and laid by against I had my next crop of corn, which I proposed to myself to grind, or rather pound into meal to make bread.

My next difficulty was to make a sieve or searce, to dress my meal, and to part it from the bran and the husk; without which I did not see it possible I could have any bread. This was a most difficult thing even to think on, for to be sure I had nothing like the necessary thing to make it—I mean fine thin canvas or stuff to searce the meal through. And here I was at a full stop for many months; nor did I really know what to do. Linen I had none left but what was mere rags; I had goat's hair, but neither knew how to weave it or spin it; and had I known how, here were no tools to work it with. All the remedy that I found for this was, that at last I did remember I had, among the seamen's clothes which were saved out of the ship, some neckcloths of calico or muslin; and with some pieces of these I made three small sieves proper enough for the work; and thus I made shift for some years: how I did afterwards, I shall show in its place.

The baking part was the next thing to be considered, and how I should make bread when I came to have corn; for first, I had no yeast. As to that part, there was no supplying the want, so I did not concern myself much about it. But for an oven I was indeed in great pain. At length I found out an experiment for that also, which was this: I made some earthen-vessels very broad but not deep, that is to say, about two feet diameter, and not above nine inches deep. These I burned in the fire, as I had done the other, and laid them by; and when I wanted to bake, I made a great fire upon my hearth, which I had paved with some square tiles of my own baking and burning also; but I should not call them square.

When the firewood was burned pretty much into embers or live coals, I drew them forward upon this hearth, so as to cover it all over, and there I let them lie till the hearth was very hot. Then sweeping away all the embers, I set down my loaf or loaves, and whelming down the earthen pot upon them, drew the embers all round the outside of the pot, to keep in and add to the heat; and thus as well as in the best oven in the world, I baked my barley-loaves, and became in little time a good pastrycook into the bargain; for I made myself several cakes and puddings of the rice; but I made no pies, neither had I anything to put into them supposing I had, except the flesh either of fowls or goats.

It need not be wondered at if all these things took me up most part of the third year of my abode here; for it is to be observed that in the intervals of these things I had my new harvest and husbandry to manage; for I reaped my corn in its season, and carried it home as well as I could, and laid it up in the ear, in my large baskets, till I had time to rub it out, for I had no floor to thrash it on, or instrument to thrash it with.

And now, indeed, my stock of corn increasing, I really wanted to build my barns bigger; I wanted a place to lay it up in, for the increase of the corn now yielded me so much, that I had of the barley about twenty bushels, and of the rice as much or more; insomuch that now I resolved to begin to use it freely; for my bread had been quite gone a great while; also I resolved to see what quantity would be sufficient for me a whole year, and to sow but once a year.

Upon the whole, I found that the forty bushels of barley and rice were much more than I could consume in a year; so I resolved to sow just the same quantity every year that I sowed the last, in hopes that such a quantity would fully provide me with bread, &c.

All the while these things were doing, you may be sure my thoughts ran many times upon the prospect of land which I had seen from the other side of the island; and I was not without secret wishes that I were on shore there, fancying that, seeing the mainland, and an inhabited country, I might find some way or other to convey myself further, and perhaps at last find some means of escape.

But all this while I made no allowance for the dangers of such an undertaking, and how I might fall into the hands of savages, and perhaps such as I might have reason to think far worse than the lions and tigers of Africa: that if I once came in their power, I should run a hazard of more than a thousand to one of being killed, and perhaps of being eaten; for I had heard that the people of the Caribbean coast were cannibals or man-eaters, and I knew by the latitude that I could not be far from that shore. Then, supposing they were not cannibals, yet they might kill me, as many Europeans who had fallen into their hands had been served, even when they had been ten or twenty together—much more I, that was but one, and could make little or no defence; all these things, I say, which I ought to have considered well; and did come into my thoughts afterwards, yet gave me no apprehensions at first, and my head ran mightily upon the thought of getting over to the shore.

Now I wished for my boy Xury, and the long-boat with shoulder-of-mutton sail, with which I sailed above a thousand miles on the coast of Africa; but this was in vain: then I thought I would go and look at our ship's boat, which, as I have said, was blown up upon the shore a great way, in the storm, when we were first cast away. She lay almost where she did at first, but not quite; and was turned, by the force of the waves and the winds, almost bottom upward, against a high ridge of beachy, rough sand, but no water about her. If I had had hands to have refitted her, and to have launched her into the water, the boat would have done well enough, and I might have gone back into the Brazils with her easily enough; but I might have foreseen that I could no more turn her and set her upright upon her bottom than I could remove the island; however, I went to the woods, and cut levers and rollers, and brought them to the boat resolving to try what I could do; suggesting to myself that if I could but turn her down, I might repair the damage she had received, and she would be a very good boat, and I might go to sea in her very easily.

I spared no pains, indeed, in this piece of fruitless toil, and spent, I think, three or four weeks about it; at last finding it impossible to heave it up with my little strength, I fell to digging away the sand, to undermine it, and so to make it fall down, setting pieces of wood to thrust and guide it right in the fall.

But when I had done this, I was unable to stir it up again, or to get under it, much less to move it forward towards the water; so I was forced to give it over; and yet, though I gave over the hopes of the boat, my desire to venture over for the main increased, rather than decreased, as the means for it seemed impossible.

This at length put me upon thinking whether it was not possible to make myself a canoe, or periagua, such as the natives of those climates make, even without tools, or, as I might say, without hands, of the trunk of a great tree. This I not only thought possible, but easy, and pleased myself extremely with the thoughts of making it, and with my having much more convenience for it than any of the negroes or Indians; but not at all considering the particular inconveniences which I lay under more than the Indians did—viz. want of hands to move it, when it was made, into the water—a difficulty much harder for me to surmount than all the consequences of want of tools could be to them; for what was it to me, if when I had chosen a vast tree in the woods, and with much trouble cut it down, if I had been able with my tools to hew and dub the outside into the proper shape of a boat, and burn or cut out the inside to make it hollow, so as to make a boat of it—if, after all this, I must leave it just there where I found it, and not be able to launch it into the water?

One would have thought I could not have had the least reflection upon my mind of my circumstances while I was making this boat, but I should have immediately thought how I should get it into the sea; but my thoughts were so intent upon my voyage over the sea in it, that I never once considered how I should get it off the land: and it was really, in its own nature, more easy for me to guide it over forty-five miles of sea than about forty-five fathoms of land, where it lay, to set it afloat in the water.

I went to work upon this boat the most like a fool that ever man did who had any of his senses awake. I pleased myself with the design, without determining whether I was ever able to undertake it; not but that the difficulty of launching my boat came often into my head; but I put a stop to my inquiries into it by this foolish answer which I gave myself—"Let me first make it; I warrant I will find some way or other to get it along when it is done."

This was a most preposterous method; but the eagerness of my fancy prevailed, and to work I went. I felled a cedar-tree, and I question much whether Solomon ever had such a one for the building of the Temple of Jerusalem; it was five feet ten inches diameter at the lower part next the stump, and four feet eleven inches diameter at the end of twenty-two feet; after which it lessened for a while, and then parted into branches. It was not without infinite labour that I felled this tree; I was twenty days hacking and hewing at it at the bottom; I was fourteen more getting the branches and limbs and the vast spreading head cut off, which I hacked and hewed through with axe and hatchet, and inexpressible labour; after this, it cost me a month to shape it and dub it to a proportion, and to something like the bottom of a boat, that it might swim upright as it ought to do. It cost me near three months more to clear the inside, and work it out so as to make an exact boat of it; this I did, indeed, without fire, by mere mallet and chisel, and by the dint of hard labour, till I had brought it to be a very handsome periagua, and big enough to have carried six-and-twenty men, and consequently big enough to have carried me and all my cargo.

When I had gone through this work I was extremely delighted with it. The boat was really much bigger than ever I saw a canoe or periagua, that was made of one tree, in my life. Many a weary stroke it had cost, you may be sure; and had I gotten it into the water, I make no question, but I should have begun the maddest voyage, and the most unlikely to be performed, that ever was undertaken.

But all my devices to get it into the water failed me; though they cost me infinite labour too. It lay about one hundred yards from the water, and not more; but the first inconvenience was, it was up hill towards the creek. Well, to take away this discouragement, I resolved to dig into the surface of the earth, and so make a declivity: this I began, and it cost me a prodigious deal of pains (but who grudge pains who have their deliverance in view?); but when this was worked through, and this difficulty managed, it was still much the same, for I could no more stir the canoe than I could the other boat. Then I measured the distance of ground, and resolved to cut a dock or canal, to bring the water up to the canoe, seeing I could not bring the canoe down to the water. Well, I began this work; and when I began to enter upon it, and calculate how deep it was to be dug, how broad, how the stuff was to be thrown out, I found that, by the number of hands I had, being none but my own, it must have been ten or twelve years before I could have gone through with it; for the shore lay so high, that at the upper end it must have been at least twenty feet deep; so at length, though with great reluctancy, I gave this attempt over also.

This grieved me heartily; and now I saw, though too late, the folly of beginning a work before we count the cost, and before we judge rightly of our own strength to go through with it.

In the middle of this work I finished my fourth year in this place, and kept my anniversary with the same devotion, and with as much comfort as ever before; for, by a constant study and serious application to the Word of God, and by the assistance of His grace, I gained a different knowledge from what I had before. I entertained different notions of things. I looked now upon the world as a thing remote, which I had nothing to do with, no expectations from, and, indeed, no desires about: in a word, I had nothing indeed to do with it, nor was ever likely to have, so I thought it looked, as we may perhaps look upon it hereafter—viz. as a place I had lived in, but was come out of it; and well might I say, as Father Abraham to Dives, "Between me and thee is a great gulf fixed."

In the first place, I was removed from all the wickedness of the world here; I had neither the lusts of the flesh, the lusts of the eye, nor the pride of life. I had nothing to covet, for I had all that I was now capable of enjoying; I was lord of the whole manor; or, if I pleased, might call myself king or emperor over the whole country which I had possession of: there were no rivals; I had no competitor, none to dispute sovereignty or command with me: I might have raised ship-loadings of corn, but I had no use for it; so I let as little grow as I thought enough for my occasion. I had tortoise or turtle enough, but now and then one was as much as I could put to any use: I had timber enough to have built a fleet of ships; and I had grapes enough to have made wine, or to have cured into raisins, to have loaded that fleet when it had been built.

But all I could make use of was all that was valuable: I had enough to eat and supply my wants, and what was all the rest to me? If I killed more flesh than I could eat, the dog must eat it, or vermin; if I sowed more corn than I could eat, it must be spoiled; the trees that I cut down were lying to rot on the ground; I could make no more use of them but for fuel, and that I had no occasion for but to dress my food.

In a word, the nature and experience of things dictated to me, upon just reflection, that all the good things of this world are no farther good to us than they are for our use; and that, whatever we may heap up to give others, we enjoy just as much as we can use, and no more. The most covetous, griping miser in the world would have been cured of the vice of covetousness if he had been in my case; for I possessed infinitely more than I knew what to do with. I had no room for desire, except it was of things which I had not, and they were but trifles, though, indeed, of great use to me. I had, as I hinted before, a parcel of money, as well gold as silver, about thirty-six pounds sterling. Alas! there the sorry, useless stuff lay; I had no more manner of business for it; and often thought with myself that I would have given a handful of it for a gross of tobacco-pipes; or for a hand-mill to grind my corn; nay, I would have given it all for a sixpenny-worth of turnip and carrot seed out of England, or for a handful of peas and beans, and a bottle of ink. As it was, I had not the least advantage by it or benefit from it; but there it lay in a drawer, and grew mouldy with the damp of the cave in the wet seasons; and if I had had the drawer full of diamonds, it had been the same case—they had been of no manner of value to me, because of no use.

I had now brought my state of life to be much easier in itself than it was at first, and much easier to my mind, as well as to my body. I frequently sat down to meat with thankfulness, and admired the hand of God's providence, which had thus spread my table in the wilderness. I learned to look more upon the bright side of my condition, and less upon the dark side, and to consider what I enjoyed rather than what I wanted; and this gave me sometimes such secret comforts, that I cannot express them; and which I take notice of here, to put those discontented people in mind of it, who cannot enjoy comfortably what God has given them, because they see and covet something that He has not given them. All our discontents about what we want appeared to me to spring from the want of thankfulness for what we have.

Another reflection was of great use to me, and doubtless would be so to any one that should fall into such distress as mine was; and this was, to compare my present condition with what I at first expected it would be; nay, with what it would certainly have been, if the good providence of God had not wonderfully ordered the ship to be cast up nearer to the shore, where I not only could come at her, but could bring what I got out of her to the shore, for my relief and comfort; without which, I had wanted for tools to work, weapons for defence, and gunpowder and shot for getting my food.

I spent whole hours, I may say whole days, in representing to myself, in the most lively colours, how I must have acted if I had got nothing out of the ship. How I could not have so much as got any food, except fish and turtles; and that, as it was long before I found any of them, I must have perished first; that I should have lived, if I had not perished, like a mere savage; that if I had killed a goat or a fowl, by any contrivance, I had no way to flay or open it, or part the flesh from the skin and the bowels, or to cut it up; but must gnaw it with my teeth, and pull it with my claws, like a beast.

These reflections made me very sensible of the goodness of Providence to me, and very thankful for my present condition, with all its hardships and misfortunes; and this part also I cannot but recommend to the reflection of those who are apt, in their misery, to say, "Is any affliction like mine?" Let them consider how much worse the cases of some people are, and their case might have been, if Providence had thought fit.

I had another reflection, which assisted me also to comfort my mind with hopes; and this was comparing my present situation with what I had deserved, and had therefore reason to expect from the hand of Providence. I had lived a dreadful life, perfectly destitute of the knowledge and fear of God. I had been well instructed by father and mother; neither had they been wanting to me in their early endeavours to infuse a religious awe of God into my mind, a sense of my duty, and what the nature and end of my being required of me. But, alas! falling early into the seafaring life, which of all lives is the most destitute of the fear of God, though His terrors are always before them; I say, falling early into the seafaring life, and into seafaring company, all that little sense of religion which I had entertained was laughed out of me by my messmates; by a hardened despising of dangers, and the views of death, which grew habitual to me by my long absence from all manner of opportunities to converse with anything but what was like myself, or to hear anything that was good or tended towards it.

So void was I of everything that was good, or the least sense of what I was, or was to be, that, in the greatest deliverances I enjoyed—such as my escape from Sallee; my being taken up by the Portuguese master of the ship; my being planted so well in the Brazils; my receiving the cargo from England, and the like—I never had once the words "Thank God!" so much as on my mind, or in my mouth; nor in the greatest distress had I so much as a thought to pray to Him, or so much as to say, "Lord, have mercy upon me!" no, nor to mention the name of God, unless it was to swear by, and blaspheme it.

I had terrible reflections upon my mind for many months, as I have already observed, on account of my wicked and hardened life past; and when I looked about me, and considered what particular providences had attended me since my coming into this place, and how God had dealt bountifully with me—had not only punished me less than my iniquity had deserved, but had so plentifully provided for me—this gave me great hopes that my repentance was accepted, and that God had yet mercy in store for me.

With these reflections I worked my mind up, not only to a resignation to the will of God in the present disposition of my circumstances, but even to a sincere thankfulness for my condition; and that I, who was yet a living man, ought not to complain, seeing I had not the due punishment of my sins; that I enjoyed so many mercies which I had no reason to have expected in that place; that I ought never more to repine at my condition, but to rejoice, and to give daily thanks for that daily bread, which nothing but a crowd of wonders could have brought; that I ought to consider I had been fed even by a miracle, even as great as that of feeding Elijah by ravens, nay, by a long series of miracles; and that I could hardly have named a place in the uninhabitable part of the world where I could have been cast more to my advantage; a place where, as I had no society, which was my affliction on one hand, so I found no ravenous beasts, no furious wolves or tigers, to threaten my life; no venomous creatures, or poisons, which I might feed on to my hurt; no savages to murder and devour me. In a word, as my life was a life of sorrow one way, so it was a life of mercy another; and I wanted nothing to make it a life of comfort but to be able to make my sense of God's goodness to me, and care over me in this condition, be my daily consolation; and after I did make a just improvement on these things, I went away, and was no more sad. I had now been here so long that many things which I had brought on shore for my help were either quite gone, or very much wasted and near spent.

My ink, as I observed, had been gone some time, all but a very little, which I eked out with water, a little and a little, till it was so pale, it scarce left any appearance of black upon the paper. As long as it lasted I made use of it to minute down the days of the month on which any remarkable thing happened to me; and first, by casting up times past, I remembered that there was a strange concurrence of days in the various providences which befell me, and which, if I had been superstitiously inclined to observe days as fatal or fortunate, I might have had reason to have looked upon with a great deal of curiosity.

First, I had observed that the same day that I broke away from my father and friends and ran away to Hull, in order to go to sea, the same day afterwards I was taken by the Sallee man-of-war, and made a slave; the same day of the year that I escaped out of the wreck of that ship in Yarmouth Roads, that same day-year afterwards I made my escape from Sallee in a boat; the same day of the year I was born on—viz. the 30th of September, that same day I had my life so miraculously saved twenty-six years after, when I was cast on shore in this island; so that my wicked life and my solitary life began both on a day.

The next thing to my ink being wasted was that of my bread—I mean the biscuit which I brought out of the ship; this I had husbanded to the last degree, allowing myself but one cake of bread a-day for above a year; and yet I was quite without bread for near a year before I got any corn of my own, and great reason I had to be thankful that I had any at all, the getting it being, as has been already observed, next to miraculous.

My clothes, too, began to decay; as to linen, I had had none a good while, except some chequered shirts which I found in the chests of the other seamen, and which I carefully preserved; because many times I could bear no other clothes on but a shirt; and it was a very great help to me that I had, among all the men's clothes of the ship, almost three dozen of shirts. There were also, indeed, several thick watch-coats of the seamen's which were left, but they were too hot to wear; and though it is true that the weather was so violently hot that there was no need of clothes, yet I could not go quite naked—no, though I had been inclined to it, which I was not—nor could I abide the thought of it, though I was alone. The reason why I could not go naked was, I could not bear the heat of the sun so well when quite naked as with some clothes on; nay, the very heat frequently blistered my skin: whereas, with a shirt on, the air itself made some motion, and whistling under the shirt, was twofold cooler than without it. No more could I ever bring myself to go out in the heat of the sun without a cap or a hat; the heat of the sun, beating with such violence as it does in that place, would give me the headache presently, by darting so directly on my head, without a cap or hat on, so that I could not bear it; whereas, if I put on my hat it would presently go away.

Upon these views I began to consider about putting the few rags I had, which I called clothes, into some order; I had worn out all the waistcoats I had, and my business was now to try if I could not make jackets out of the great watch-coats which I had by me, and with such other materials as I had; so I set to work, tailoring, or rather, indeed, botching, for I made most piteous work of it. However, I made shift to make two or three new waistcoats, which I hoped would serve me a great while: as for breeches or drawers, I made but a very sorry shift indeed till afterwards.

I have mentioned that I saved the skins of all the creatures that I killed, I mean four-footed ones, and I had them hung up, stretched out with sticks in the sun, by which means some of them were so dry and hard that they were fit for little, but others were very useful. The first thing I made of these was a great cap for my head, with the hair on the outside, to shoot off the rain; and this I performed so well, that after I made me a suit of clothes wholly of these skins—that is to say, a waistcoat, and breeches open at the knees, and both loose, for they were rather wanting to keep me cool than to keep me warm. I must not omit to acknowledge that they were wretchedly made; for if I was a bad carpenter, I was a worse tailor. However, they were such as I made very good shift with, and when I was out, if it happened to rain, the hair of my waistcoat and cap being outermost, I was kept very dry.

After this, I spent a great deal of time and pains to make an umbrella; I was, indeed, in great want of one, and had a great mind to make one; I had seen them made in the Brazils, where they are very useful in the great heats there, and I felt the heats every jot as great here, and greater too, being nearer the equinox; besides, as I was obliged to be much abroad, it was a most useful thing to me, as well for the rains as the heats. I took a world of pains with it, and was a great while before I could make anything likely to hold: nay, after I had thought I had hit the way, I spoiled two or three before I made one to my mind: but at last I made one that answered indifferently well: the main difficulty I found was to make it let down. I could make it spread, but if it did not let down too, and draw in, it was not portable for me any way but just over my head, which would not do. However, at last, as I said, I made one to answer, and covered it with skins, the hair upwards, so that it cast off the rain like a pent-house, and kept off the sun so effectually, that I could walk out in the hottest of the weather with greater advantage than I could before in the coolest, and when I had no need of it could close it, and carry it under my arm.

Thus I lived mighty comfortably, my mind being entirely composed by resigning myself to the will of God, and throwing myself wholly upon the disposal of His providence. This made my life better than sociable, for when I began to regret the want of conversation I would ask myself, whether thus conversing mutually with my own thoughts, and (as I hope I may say) with even God Himself, by ejaculations, was not better than the utmost enjoyment of human society in the world?

10

TAMES GOATS

I cannot say that after this, for five years, any extraordinary thing happened to me, but I lived on in the same course, in the same posture and place, as before; the chief things I was employed in, besides my yearly labour of planting my barley and rice, and curing my raisins, of both which I always kept up just enough to have sufficient stock of one year's provisions beforehand; I say, besides this yearly labour, and my daily pursuit of going out with my gun, I had one labour, to make a canoe, which at last I finished: so that, by digging a canal to it of six feet wide and four feet deep, I brought it into the creek, almost half a mile. As for the first, which was so vastly big, for I made it without considering beforehand, as I ought to have done, how I should be able to launch it, so, never being able to bring it into the water, or bring the water to it, I was obliged to let it lie where it was as a memorandum to teach me to be wiser the next time: indeed, the next time, though I could not get a tree proper for it, and was in a place where I could not get the water to it at any less distance than, as I have said, near half a mile, yet, as I saw it was practicable at last, I never gave it over; and though I was near two years about it, yet I never grudged my labour, in hopes of having a boat to go off to sea at last.

However, though my little periagua was finished, yet the size of it was not at all answerable to the design which I had in view when I made the first; I mean of venturing over to the *terra firma*, where it was above forty miles broad; accordingly, the smallness of my boat assisted to put an end to that design, and now I thought no more of it. As I had a boat, my next design was to make a cruise round the island; for as I had been on the other side in one place, crossing, as I have already described it, over the land, so the discoveries I made in that little journey made me very eager to see other parts of the coast; and now I had a boat, I thought of nothing but sailing round the island.

For this purpose, that I might do everything with discretion and consideration, I fitted up a little mast in my boat, and made a sail too out of some of the pieces of the ship's sails which lay in store, and of which I had a great stock by me. Having fitted my mast and sail, and tried the boat, I found she would sail very well; then I made little lockers or boxes at each end of my boat, to put provisions, necessaries, ammunition, &c., into, to be kept dry, either from rain or the spray of the sea; and a little, long, hollow place I cut in the inside of the boat, where I could lay my gun, making a flap to hang down over it to keep it dry.

I fixed my umbrella also in the step at the stern, like a mast, to stand over my head, and keep the heat of the sun off me, like an awning; and thus I every now and then took a little voyage upon the sea, but never went far out, nor far from the little creek. At last, being eager to view the circumference of my little kingdom, I resolved upon my cruise; and accordingly I victualled my ship for the voyage, putting in two dozen of loaves (cakes I should call them) of barley-bread, an earthen pot full of parched rice (a food I ate a good deal of), a little bottle of rum, half a goat, and powder and shot for killing more, and two large watch-coats, of those which, as I mentioned before, I had saved out of the seamen's chests; these I took, one to lie upon, and the other to cover me in the night.

It was the 6th of November, in the sixth year of my reign—or my captivity, which you please—that I set out on this voyage, and I found it much longer than I expected; for though the island itself was not very large, yet when I came to the east side of it, I found a great ledge of rocks lie out about two leagues into the sea, some above water, some under it; and beyond that a shoal of sand, lying dry half a league more, so that I was obliged to go a great way out to sea to double the point.

When I first discovered them, I was going to give over my enterprise, and come back again, not knowing how far it might oblige me to go out to sea; and above all, doubting how I should get back again: so I came to an anchor; for I had made a kind of an anchor with a piece of a broken grappling which I got out of the ship.

Having secured my boat, I took my gun and went on shore, climbing up a hill, which seemed to overlook that point where I saw the full extent of it, and resolved to venture.

In my viewing the sea from that hill where I stood, I perceived a strong, and indeed a most furious current, which ran to the east, and even came close to the point; and I took the more notice of it because I saw there might be some danger that when I came into it I might be carried out to sea by the strength of it, and not be able to make the island again; and indeed, had I not got first upon this hill, I believe it would have been so; for there was the same current on the other side the island, only that it set off at a further distance, and I saw there was a strong eddy under the shore; so I had nothing to do but to get out of the first current, and I should presently be in an eddy.

I lay here, however, two days, because the wind blowing pretty fresh at ESE., and that being just contrary to the current, made a great breach of the sea upon the point: so that it was not safe for me to keep too close to the shore for the breach, nor to go too far off, because of the stream.

The third day, in the morning, the wind having abated overnight, the sea was calm, and I ventured: but I am a warning to all rash and ignorant pilots; for no sooner was I come to the point, when I was not even my boat's length from the shore, but I found myself in a great depth of water, and a current like the sluice of a mill; it carried my boat along with it with such violence that all I could do could not keep her so much as on the edge of it; but I found it hurried me farther and farther out from the eddy, which was on my left hand. There was no wind stirring to help me, and all I could do with my paddles signified nothing: and now I began to give myself over for lost; for as the current was on both sides of the island, I knew in a few leagues distance they must join again, and then I was irrecoverably gone; nor did I see any possibility of avoiding it; so that I had no prospect before me but of perishing, not by the sea, for that was calm enough, but of starving from hunger. I had, indeed, found a tortoise on the shore, as big almost as I could lift, and had tossed it into the boat; and I had a great jar of fresh water, that is to say, one of my earthen pots; but what was all this to being driven into the vast ocean, where, to be sure, there was no shore, no mainland or island, for a thousand leagues at least?

And now I saw how easy it was for the providence of God to make even the most miserable condition of mankind worse. Now I looked back upon my desolate, solitary island as the most pleasant place in the world and all the happiness my heart could wish for was to be but there again. I stretched out my hands to it, with eager wishes—"O happy desert!" said I, "I shall never see thee more. O miserable creature! whither am going?" Then I reproached myself with my unthankful temper, and that I had repined at my solitary condition; and now what would I give to be on shore there again! Thus, we never see the true state of our condition till it is illustrated to us by its contraries, nor know how to value what we enjoy, but by the want of it. It is scarcely possible to imagine the consternation I was now in, being driven from my beloved island (for so it appeared to me now to be) into the wide ocean, almost two leagues, and in the utmost despair of ever recovering it again. However, I worked hard till, indeed, my strength was almost exhausted, and kept my boat as much to the northward, that is, towards the side of the current which the eddy lay on, as possibly I could; when about noon, as the sun passed the meridian, I thought I felt a little breeze of wind in my face, springing up from SSE. This cheered my heart a little, and especially when, in about half-an-hour more, it blew a pretty gentle gale. By this time I had got at a frightful distance from the island, and had the least cloudy or hazy weather intervened, I had been undone another way, too; for I had no compass on board, and should never have known how to have steered towards the island, if I had but once lost sight of it; but the weather continuing clear, I applied myself to get up my mast again, and spread my sail, standing away to the north as much as possible, to get out of the current.

Just as I had set my mast and sail, and the boat began to stretch away, I saw even by the clearness of the water some alteration of the current was near; for where the current was so strong the water was foul; but perceiving the water clear, I found the current abate; and presently I found to the east, at about half a mile, a breach of the sea upon some rocks: these rocks I found caused the current to part again, and as the main stress of it ran away more southerly, leaving the rocks to the north-east, so the other returned by the repulse of the rocks, and made a strong eddy, which ran back again to the north-west, with a very sharp stream.

They who know what it is to have a reprieve brought to them upon the ladder, or to be rescued from thieves just going to murder them, or who have been in such extremities, may guess what my present surprise of joy was, and how gladly I put my boat into the stream of this eddy; and the wind also freshening, how gladly I spread my sail to it, running cheerfully before the wind, and with a strong tide or eddy underfoot.

This eddy carried me about a league on my way back again, directly towards the island, but about two leagues more to the northward than the current which carried me away at first; so that when I came near the island, I found myself open to the northern shore of it, that is to say, the other end of the island, opposite to that which I went out from.

When I had made something more than a league of way by the help of this current or eddy, I found it was spent, and served me no further. However, I found that being between two great currents—viz. that on the south side, which had hurried me away, and that on the north, which lay about a league on the other side; I say, between these two, in the wake of the island, I found the water at least still, and running no way; and having still a breeze of wind fair for me, I kept on steering directly for the island, though not making such fresh way as I did before.

About four o'clock in the evening, being then within a league of the island, I found the point of the rocks which occasioned this disaster stretching out, as is described before, to the southward, and casting off the current more southerly, had, of course, made another eddy to the north; and this I found very strong, but not directly setting the way my course lay, which was due west, but almost full north. However, having a fresh gale, I stretched across this eddy, slanting north-west; and in about an hour came within about a mile of the shore, where, it being smooth water, I soon got to land.

When I was on shore, God I fell on my knees and gave God thanks for my deliverance, resolving to lay aside all thoughts of my deliverance by my boat; and refreshing myself with such things as I had, I brought my boat close to the shore, in a little cove that I had spied under some trees, and laid me down to sleep, being quite spent with the labour and fatigue of the voyage.

I was now at a great loss which way to get home with my boat! I had run so much hazard, and knew too much of the case, to think of attempting it by the way I went out; and what might be at the other side (I mean the west side) I knew not, nor had I any mind to run any more ventures; so I resolved on the next morning to make my way westward along the shore, and to see if there was no creek where I might lay up my frigate in safety, so as to have her again if I wanted her. In about three miles or thereabouts, coasting the shore, I came to a very good inlet or bay, about a mile over, which narrowed till it came to a very little rivulet or brook, where I found a very convenient harbour for my boat, and where she lay as if she had been in a little dock made on purpose for her. Here I put in, and having stowed my boat very safe, I went on shore to look about me, and see where I was.

I soon found I had but a little passed by the place where I had been before, when I travelled on foot to that shore; so taking nothing out of my boat but my gun and umbrella, for it was exceedingly hot, I began my march. The way was comfortable enough after such a voyage as I had been upon, and I reached my old bower in the evening, where I found everything standing as I left it; for I always kept it in good order, being, as I said before, my country house.

I got over the fence, and laid me down in the shade to rest my limbs, for I was very weary, and fell asleep; but judge you, if you can, that read my story, what a surprise I must be in when I was awaked out of my sleep by a voice calling me by my name several times, "Robin, Robin, Robin Crusoe: poor Robin Crusoe! Where are you, Robin Crusoe? Where are you? Where have you been?"

I was so dead asleep at first, being fatigued with rowing, or part of the day, and with walking the latter part, that I did not wake thoroughly; but dozing thought I dreamed that somebody spoke to me; but as the voice continued to repeat, "Robin Crusoe, Robin Crusoe," at last I began to wake more perfectly, and was at first dreadfully frightened, and started up in the utmost consternation; but no sooner were my eyes open, but I saw my Poll sitting on the top of the hedge; and immediately knew that it was he that spoke to me; for just in such bemoaning language I had used to talk to him and teach him; and he had learned it so perfectly that he would sit upon my finger, and lay his bill close to my face and cry, "Poor Robin Crusoe! Where are you? Where have you been? How came you here?" and such things as I had taught him.

However, even though I knew it was the parrot, and that indeed it could be nobody else, it was a good while before I could compose myself. First, I was amazed how the creature got thither; and then, how he should just keep about the place, and nowhere else; but as I was well satisfied it could be nobody but honest Poll, I got over it; and holding out my hand, and calling him by his name, "Poll," the sociable creature came to me, and sat upon my thumb, as he used to do, and continued talking to me, "Poor Robin Crusoe! and how did I come here?

and where had I been?" just as if he had been overjoyed to see me again; and so I carried him home along with me.

I had now had enough of rambling to sea for some time, and had enough to do for many days to sit still and reflect upon the danger I had been in. I would have been very glad to have had my boat again on my side of the island; but I knew not how it was practicable to get it about. As to the east side of the island, which I had gone round, I knew well enough there was no venturing that way; my very heart would shrink, and my very blood run chill, but to think of it; and as to the other side of the island, I did not know how it might be there; but supposing the current ran with the same force against the shore at the east as it passed by it on the other, I might run the same risk of being driven down the stream, and carried by the island, as I had been before of being carried away from it: so with these thoughts, I contented myself to be without any boat, though it had been the product of so many months' labour to make it, and of so many more to get it into the sea.

In this government of my temper I remained near a year; and lived a very sedate, retired life, as you may well suppose; and my thoughts being very much composed as to my condition, and fully comforted in resigning myself to the dispositions of Providence, I thought I lived really very happily in all things except that of society.

I improved myself in this time in all the mechanic exercises which my necessities put me upon applying myself to; and I believe I should, upon occasion, have made a very good carpenter, especially considering how few tools I had.

Besides this, I arrived at an unexpected perfection in my earthenware, and contrived well enough to make them with a wheel, which I found infinitely easier and better; because I made things round and shaped, which before were filthy things indeed to look on. But I think I was never more vain of my own performance, or more joyful for anything I found out, than for my being able to make a tobacco-pipe; and though it was a very ugly, clumsy thing when it was done, and only burned red, like other earthenware, yet as it was hard and firm, and would draw the smoke, I was exceedingly comforted with it, for I had been always used to smoke; and there were pipes in the ship, but I forgot them at first, not thinking there was tobacco in the island; and afterwards, when I searched the ship again, I could not come at any pipes.

In my wicker-ware also I improved much, and made abundance of necessary baskets, as well as my invention showed me; though not very handsome, yet they were such as were very handy and convenient for laying things up in, or fetching things home. For example, if I killed a goat abroad, I could hang it up in a tree, flay it, dress it, and cut it in pieces, and bring it home in a basket; and the like by a turtle; I could cut it up, take out the eggs and a piece or two of the flesh, which was enough for me, and bring them home in a basket, and leave the rest behind me. Also, large deep baskets were the receivers of my corn, which I always rubbed out as soon as it was dry and cured, and kept it in great baskets.

I began now to perceive my powder abated considerably; this was a want which it was impossible for me to supply, and I began seriously to consider what I must do when I should have no more powder; that is to say, how I should kill any goats. I had, as is observed in the third year of my being here, kept a young kid, and bred her up tame, and I was in hopes of getting a he-goat; but I could not by any means bring it to pass, till my kid grew an old goat; and as I could never find in my heart to kill her, she died at last of mere age.

But being now in the eleventh year of my residence, and, as I have said, my ammunition growing low, I set myself to study some art to trap and snare the goats, to see whether I could not catch some of them alive; and particularly I wanted a she-goat great with young. For this purpose I made snares to hamper them; and I do believe they were more than once taken in them; but my tackle was not good, for I had no wire, and I always found them broken and my bait devoured. At length I resolved to try a pitfall; so I dug several large pits in the earth, in places where I had observed the goats used to feed, and over those pits I placed hurdles of my own making too, with a great weight upon them; and several times I put ears of barley and dry rice without setting the trap; and I could easily perceive that the goats had gone in and eaten up the corn, for I could see the marks of their feet. At length I set three traps in one night, and going the next morning I found them, all standing, and yet the bait eaten and gone; this was very discouraging. However, I altered my traps; and not to trouble you with particulars, going one morning to see my traps, I found in one of them a large old he-goat; and in one of the others three kids, a male and two females.

As to the old one, I knew not what to do with him; he was so fierce I durst not go into the pit to him; that is to say, to bring him away alive, which was what I wanted. I could have killed him, but that was not my business, nor would it answer my end; so I even let him out, and he ran away as if he had been frightened out of his wits. But I did not then know what I afterwards learned, that hunger will tame a lion. If I had let him stay three or four days without food, and then have carried him some water to drink and then a little corn, he would have been as tame as one of the kids; for they are mighty sagacious, tractable creatures, where they are well used.

However, for the present I let him go, knowing no better at that time: then I went to the three kids, and taking them one by one, I tied them with strings together, and with some difficulty brought them all home.

It was a good while before they would feed; but throwing them some sweet corn, it tempted them, and they began to be tame. And now I found that if I expected to supply myself with goats' flesh, when I had no powder or shot left, breeding some up tame was my only way, when, perhaps, I might have them about my house like a flock of sheep. But then it occurred to me that I must keep the tame from the wild, or else they would always run wild when they grew up; and the only way for this was to have some enclosed piece of ground, well fenced either with hedge or pale, to keep them in so effectually, that those within might not break out, or those without break in.

This was a great undertaking for one pair of hands yet, as I saw there was an absolute necessity for doing it, my first work was to find out a proper piece of ground, where there was likely to be herbage for them to eat, water for them to drink, and cover to keep them from the sun.

Those who understand such enclosures will think I had very little contrivance when I pitched upon a place very proper for all these (being a plain, open piece of meadow land, or savannah, as our people call it in the western colonies), which had two or three little drills of fresh water in it, and at one end was very woody—I say, they will smile at my forecast, when I shall tell them I began by enclosing this piece of ground in such a manner that, my hedge or pale must have been at least two miles about. Nor was the madness of it so great as to the compass, for if it was ten miles about, I was like to have time enough to do it in; but I did not consider that my goats would be as wild in so much compass as if they had had the whole island, and I should have so much room to chase them in that I should never catch them.

My hedge was begun and carried on, I believe, about fifty yards when this thought occurred to me; so I presently stopped short, and, for the beginning, I resolved to enclose a piece of about one hundred and fifty yards in length, and one hundred yards in breadth, which, as it would maintain as many as I should have in any reasonable time, so, as my stock increased, I could add more ground to my enclosure.

This was acting with some prudence, and I went to work with courage. I was about three months hedging in the first piece; and, till I had done it, I tethered the three kids in the best part of it, and used them to feed as near me as possible, to make them familiar; and very often I would go and carry them some ears of barley, or a handful of rice, and feed them out of my hand; so that after my enclosure was finished and I let them loose, they would follow me up and down, bleating after me for a handful of corn.

This answered my end, and in about a year and a half I had a flock of about twelve goats, kids and all; and in two years more I had three-and-forty, besides several that I took and killed for my food. After that, I enclosed five several pieces of ground to feed them in, with little pens to drive them to take them as I wanted, and gates out of one piece of ground into another.

But this was not all; for now I not only had goat's flesh to feed on when I pleased, but milk too—a thing which, indeed, in the beginning, I did not so much as think of, and which, when it came into my thoughts, was really an agreeable surprise, for now I set up my dairy, and had sometimes a gallon or two of milk in a day. And as Nature, who gives supplies of food to every creature, dictates even naturally how to make use of it, so I, that had never milked a cow, much less a goat, or seen butter or cheese made only when I was a boy, after a great many essays and miscarriages, made both butter and cheese at last, also salt (though I found it partly made to my hand by the heat of the sun upon some of the rocks of the sea), and never wanted it afterwards. How mercifully can our Creator treat His creatures, even in those conditions in which they seemed to be overwhelmed in destruction! How can He sweeten the bitterest providences, and give us cause to praise Him for dungeons and prisons! What a table was here spread for me in the wilderness, where I saw nothing at first but to perish for hunger!

11

FINDS PRINT OF MAN'S FOOT ON THE SAND

It would have made a Stoic smile to have seen me and my little family sit down to dinner. There was my majesty the prince and lord of the whole island; I had the lives of all my subjects at my absolute command; I could hang, draw, give liberty, and take it away, and no rebels among all my subjects. Then, to see how like a king I dined, too, all alone, attended by my servants! Poll, as if he had been my favourite, was the only person permitted to talk to me. My dog, who was now grown old and crazy, and had found no species to multiply his kind upon, sat always at my right hand; and two cats, one on one side of the table and one on the other, expecting now and then a bit from my hand, as a mark of especial favour.

But these were not the two cats which I brought on shore at first, for they were both of them dead, and had been interred near my habitation by my own hand; but one of them having multiplied by I know not what kind of creature, these were two which I had preserved tame; whereas the rest ran wild in the woods, and became indeed troublesome to me at last, for they would often come into my house, and plunder me too, till at last I was obliged to shoot them, and did kill a great many; at length they left me. With this attendance and in this plentiful manner I lived; neither could I be said to want anything but society; and of that, some time after this, I was likely to have too much.

I was something impatient, as I have observed, to have the use of my boat, though very loath to run any more hazards; and therefore sometimes I sat contriving ways to get her about the island, and at other times I sat myself down contented enough without her. But I had a strange uneasiness in my mind to go down to the point of the island where, as I have said in my last ramble, I went up the hill to see how the shore lay, and how the current set, that I might see what I had to do: this inclination increased upon me every day, and at length I resolved to travel thither by land, following the edge of the shore. I did so; but had any one in England met such a man as I was, it must either have frightened him, or raised a great deal of laughter; and as I frequently stood still to look at myself, I could not but smile at the notion of my travelling through Yorkshire with such an equipage, and in such a dress. Be pleased to take a sketch of my figure, as follows.

I had a great high shapeless cap, made of a goat's skin, with a flap hanging down behind, as well to keep the sun from me as to shoot the rain off from running into my neck, nothing being so hurtful in these climates as the rain upon the flesh under the clothes.

I had a short jacket of goat's skin, the skirts coming down to about the middle of the thighs, and a pair of open-kneed breeches of the same; the breeches were made of the skin of an old he-goat, whose hair hung down such a length on either side that, like pantaloons, it reached to the middle of my legs; stockings and shoes I had none, but had made me a pair of somethings, I scarce knew what to call them, like buskins, to flap over my legs, and lace on either side like spatterdashes, but of a most barbarous shape, as indeed were all the rest of my clothes.

I had on a broad belt of goat's skin dried, which I drew together with two thongs of the same instead of buckles, and in a kind of a frog on either side of this, instead of a sword and dagger, hung a little saw and a hatchet, one on one side and one on the other. I had another belt not so broad, and fastened in the same manner, which hung over my shoulder, and at the end of it, under my left arm, hung two pouches, both made of goat's skin too, in one of which hung my powder, in the other my shot. At my back I carried my basket, and on my shoulder my gun, and over my head a great clumsy, ugly, goat's-skin umbrella, but which, after all, was the most necessary thing I had about me next to my gun. As for my face, the colour of it was really not so mulatto-like as one might expect from a man not at all careful of it, and living within nine or ten degrees of the equinox. My beard I had once suffered to grow till it was about a quarter of a yard long; but as I had both scissors and razors sufficient, I had cut it pretty short, except what grew on my upper lip, which I had trimmed into a large pair of Mahometan whiskers, such as I had seen worn by some Turks at Sallee, for the Moors did not wear such, though the Turks did; of these moustachios, or whiskers, I will not say they were long enough to hang my hat upon them, but they were of a length and shape monstrous enough, and such as in England would have passed for frightful.

But all this is by-the-bye; for as to my figure, I had so few to observe me that it was of no manner of consequence, so I say no more of that. In this kind of dress I went my new journey, and was out five or six days. I travelled first along the sea-shore, directly to the place where I first brought my boat to an anchor to get upon the rocks; and having no boat now to take care of, I went over the land a nearer way to the same height that I was upon before, when, looking forward to the points of the rocks which lay out, and which I was obliged to double with my boat, as is said above, I was surprised to see the sea all smooth and quiet—no rippling, no motion, no current, any more there than in other places. I was at a strange loss to understand this, and resolved to spend some time in the observing it, to see if nothing from the sets of the tide had occasioned it; but I was presently convinced how it was—viz. that the tide of ebb setting from the west, and joining with the current of waters from some great river on the shore, must be the occasion of this current, and that, according as the wind blew more forcibly from the west or from the north, this current came nearer or went farther from the shore; for, waiting thereabouts till evening, I went up to the rock again, and then the tide of ebb being made, I plainly saw the current again as before, only that it ran farther off, being near half a league from the shore, whereas in my case it set close upon the shore, and hurried me and my canoe along with it, which at another time it would not have done.

This observation convinced me that I had nothing to do but to observe the ebbing and the flowing of the tide, and I might very easily bring my boat about the island again; but when I began to think of putting it in practice, I had such terror upon my spirits at the remembrance of the danger I had been in, that I could not think of it again with any patience, but, on the contrary, I took up another resolution, which was more safe, though more laborious—and this was, that I would build, or rather make, me another periagua or canoe, and so have one for one side of the island, and one for the other.

You are to understand that now I had, as I may call it, two plantations in the island—one my little fortification or tent, with the wall about it, under the rock, with the cave behind me, which by this time I had enlarged into several apartments or caves, one within another. One of these, which was the driest and largest, and had a door out beyond my wall or fortification —that is to say, beyond where my wall joined to the rock—was all filled up with the large earthen pots of which I have given an account, and with fourteen or fifteen great baskets, which would hold five or six bushels each, where I laid up my stores of provisions, especially my corn, some in the ear, cut off short from the straw, and the other rubbed out with my hand.

As for my wall, made, as before, with long stakes or piles, those piles grew all like trees, and were by this time grown so big, and spread so very much, that there was not the least appearance, to any one's view, of any habitation behind them.

Near this dwelling of mine, but a little farther within the land, and upon lower ground, lay my two pieces of corn land, which I kept duly cultivated and sowed, and which duly yielded me their harvest in its season; and whenever I had occasion for more corn, I had more land adjoining as fit as that.

Besides this, I had my country seat, and I had now a tolerable plantation there also; for, first, I had my little bower, as I called it, which I kept in repair—that is to say, I kept the hedge which encircled it in constantly fitted up to its usual height, the ladder standing always in the inside. I kept the trees, which at first were no more than stakes, but were now grown very firm and tall, always cut, so that they might spread and grow thick and wild, and make the more agreeable shade, which they did effectually to my mind. In the middle of this I had my tent always standing, being a piece of a sail spread over poles, set up for that purpose, and which never wanted any repair or renewing; and under this I had made me a squab or couch with the skins of the creatures I had killed, and with other soft things, and a blanket laid on them, such as belonged to our sea-bedding, which I had saved; and a great watch-coat to cover me. And here, whenever I had occasion to be absent from my chief seat, I took up my country habitation.

Adjoining to this I had my enclosures for my cattle, that is to say my goats, and I had taken an inconceivable deal of pains to fence and enclose this ground. I was so anxious to see it kept entire, lest the goats should break through, that I never left off till, with infinite labour, I had stuck the outside of the hedge so full of small stakes, and so near to one another, that it was rather a pale than a hedge, and there was scarce room to put a hand through between them; which afterwards, when those stakes grew, as they all did in the next rainy season, made the enclosure strong like a wall, indeed stronger than any wall.

This will testify for me that I was not idle, and that I spared no pains to bring to pass whatever appeared necessary for my comfortable support, for I considered the keeping up a breed of tame creatures thus at my hand would be a living magazine of flesh, milk, butter, and cheese for me as long as I lived in the place, if it were to be forty years; and that keeping them in my reach depended entirely upon my perfecting my enclosures to such a degree that I might be sure of keeping them together; which by this method, indeed, I so effectually secured, that when these little stakes began to grow, I had planted them so very thick that I was forced to pull some of them up again.

In this place also I had my grapes growing, which I principally depended on for my winter store of raisins, and which I never failed to preserve very carefully, as the best and most agreeable dainty of my whole diet; and indeed they were not only agreeable, but medicinal, wholesome, nourishing, and refreshing to the last degree.

As this was also about half-way between my other habitation and the place where I had laid up my boat, I generally stayed and lay here in my way thither, for I used frequently to visit my boat; and I kept all things about or belonging to her in very good order. Sometimes I went out in her to divert myself, but no more hazardous voyages would I go, scarcely ever above a stone's cast or two from the shore, I was so apprehensive of being hurried out of my knowledge again by the currents or winds, or any other accident. But now I come to a new scene of my life.

It happened one day, about noon, going towards my boat, I was exceedingly surprised with the print of a man's naked foot on the shore, which was very plain to be seen on the sand. I stood like one thunderstruck, or as if I had seen an apparition. I listened, I looked round me, but I could hear nothing, nor see anything; I went up to a rising ground to look farther; I went up the shore and down the shore, but it was all one; I could see no other impression but that one. I went to it again to see if there were any more, and to observe if it might not be my fancy; but there was no room for that, for there was exactly the print of a foot—toes, heel, and every part of a foot. How it came thither I knew not, nor could I in the least imagine; but after innumerable fluttering thoughts, like a man perfectly confused and out of myself, I came home to my fortification, not feeling, as we say, the ground I went on, but terrified to the last degree, looking behind me at every two or three steps, mistaking every bush and tree, and fancying every stump at a distance to be a man. Nor is it possible to describe how many various shapes my affrighted imagination represented things to me in, how many wild ideas were found every moment in my fancy, and what strange, unaccountable whimsies came into my thoughts by the way.

When I came to my castle (for so I think I called it ever after this), I fled into it like one pursued. Whether I went over by the ladder, as first contrived, or went in at the hole in the rock, which I had called a door, I cannot remember; no, nor could I remember the next morning, for never frightened hare fled to cover, or fox to earth, with more terror of mind than I to this retreat.

I slept none that night; the farther I was from the occasion of my fright, the greater my apprehensions were, which is something contrary to the nature of such things, and especially to the usual practice of all creatures in fear; but I was so embarrassed with my own frightful ideas of the thing, that I formed nothing but dismal imaginations to myself, even though I was now a great way off. Sometimes I fancied it must be the devil, and reason joined in with me in this supposition, for how should any other thing in human shape come into the place? Where was the vessel that brought them? What marks were there of any other footstep? And how was it possible a man should come there? But then, to think that Satan should take human shape upon him in such a place, where there could be no manner of occasion for it, but to leave the print of his foot behind him, and that even for no purpose too, for he could not be sure I should see it—this was an amusement the other way. I considered that the devil might have found out abundance of other ways to have terrified me than this of the single print of a foot; that as I lived quite on the other side of the island, he would never have been so simple as to leave a mark in a place where it was ten thousand to one whether I should ever see it or not, and in the sand too, which the first surge of the sea, upon a high wind, would have defaced entirely. All this seemed inconsistent with the thing itself and with all the notions we usually entertain of the subtlety of the devil.

Abundance of such things as these assisted to argue me out of all apprehensions of its being the devil; and I presently concluded then that it must be some more dangerous creature—viz. that it must be some of the savages of the mainland opposite who had wandered out to sea in their canoes, and either driven by the currents or by contrary winds, had made the island, and had been on shore, but were gone away again to sea; being as loath, perhaps, to have stayed in this desolate island as I would have been to have had them.

While these reflections were rolling in my mind, I was very thankful in my thoughts that I was so happy as not to be thereabouts at that time, or that they did not see my boat, by which they would have concluded that some inhabitants had been in the place, and perhaps have searched farther for me. Then terrible thoughts racked my imagination about their having found out my boat, and that there were people here; and that, if so, I should certainly have them come again in greater numbers and devour me; that if it should happen that they should not find me, yet they would find my enclosure, destroy all my corn, and carry away all my flock of tame goats, and I should perish at last for mere want.

Thus my fear banished all my religious hope, all that former confidence in God, which was founded upon such wonderful experience as I had had of His goodness; as if He that had fed me by miracle hitherto could not preserve, by His power, the provision which He had made for me by His goodness. I reproached myself with my laziness, that would not sow any more corn one year than would just serve me till the next season, as if no accident could intervene to prevent my enjoying the crop that was upon the ground; and this I thought so just a reproof, that I resolved for the future to have two or three years' corn beforehand; so that, whatever might come, I might not perish for want of bread.

How strange a chequer-work of Providence is the life of man! and by what secret different springs are the affections hurried about, as different circumstances present! To-day we love what to-morrow we hate; to-day we seek what to-morrow we shun; to-day we desire what to-morrow we fear, nay, even tremble at the apprehensions of. This was exemplified in me, at this time, in the most lively manner imaginable; for I, whose only affliction was that I seemed banished from human society, that I was alone, circumscribed by the boundless ocean, cut off from mankind, and condemned to what I call silent life; that I was as one whom Heaven thought not worthy to be numbered among the living, or to appear among the rest of His creatures; that to have seen one of my own species would have seemed to me a raising me from death to life, and the greatest blessing that Heaven itself, next to the supreme blessing of salvation, could bestow; I say, that I should now tremble at the very apprehensions of seeing a man, and was ready to sink into the ground at but the shadow or silent appearance of a man having set his foot in the island.

Such is the uneven state of human life; and it afforded me a great many curious speculations afterwards, when I had a little recovered my first surprise. I considered that this was the station of life the infinitely wise and good providence of God had determined for me; that as I could not foresee what the ends of Divine wisdom might be in all this, so I was not to dispute His sovereignty; who, as I was His creature, had an undoubted right, by creation, to govern and dispose of me absolutely as He thought fit; and who, as I was a creature that had offended Him, had likewise a judicial right to condemn me to what punishment He thought fit; and that it was my part to submit to bear His indignation, because I had sinned against Him. I then reflected, that as God, who was not only righteous but omnipotent, had thought fit thus to punish and afflict me, so He was able to deliver me: that if He did not think fit to do so, it was my unquestioned duty to resign myself absolutely and entirely to His will; and, on the other hand, it was my duty also to hope in Him, pray to Him, and quietly to attend to the dictates and directions of His daily providence.

These thoughts took me up many hours, days, nay, I may say weeks and months: and one particular effect of my cogitations on this occasion I cannot omit. One morning early, lying in my bed, and filled with thoughts about my danger from the appearances of savages, I found it discomposed me very much; upon which these words of the Scripture came into my thoughts, "Call upon Me in the day of trouble, and I will deliver thee, and thou shalt glorify Me." Upon this, rising cheerfully out of my bed, my heart was not only comforted, but I was guided and encouraged to pray earnestly to God for deliverance: when I had done praying I took up my Bible, and opening it to read, the first words that presented to me were, "Wait on the Lord, and be of good cheer, and He shall strengthen thy heart; wait, I say, on the Lord." It is impossible to express the comfort this gave me. In answer, I thankfully laid down the book, and was no more sad, at least on that occasion.

In the middle of these cogitations, apprehensions, and reflections, it came into my thoughts one day that all this might be a mere chimera of my own, and that this foot might be the print of my own foot, when I came on shore from my boat: this cheered me up a little, too, and I began to persuade myself it was all a delusion; that it was nothing else but my own foot; and why might I not come that way from the boat, as well as I was going that way to the boat? Again, I considered also that I could by no means tell for certain where I had trod, and where I had not; and that if, at last, this was only the print of my own foot, I had played the part of those fools who try to make stories of spectres and apparitions, and then are frightened at them more than anybody.

Now I began to take courage, and to peep abroad again, for I had not stirred out of my castle for three days and nights, so that I began to starve for provisions; for I had little or nothing within doors but some barley-cakes and water; then I knew that my goats wanted to be milked too, which usually was my evening diversion: and the poor creatures were in great pain and inconvenience for want of it; and, indeed, it almost spoiled some of them, and almost dried up their milk. Encouraging myself, therefore, with the belief that this was nothing but the print of one of my own feet, and that I might be truly said to start at my own shadow, I began to go abroad again, and went to my country house to milk my flock: but to see with what fear I went forward, how often I looked behind me, how I was ready every now and then to lay down my basket and run for my life, it would have made any one have thought I was haunted with an evil conscience, or that I had been lately most terribly frightened; and so, indeed, I had. However, I went down thus two or three days, and having seen nothing, I began to be a little bolder, and to think there was really nothing in it but my own imagination; but I could not persuade myself fully of this till I should go down to the shore again, and see this print of a foot, and measure it by my own, and see if there was any similitude or fitness, that I might be assured it was my own foot: but when I came to the place, first, it appeared evidently to me, that when I laid up my boat I could not possibly be on shore anywhere thereabouts; secondly, when I came to measure the mark with my own foot, I found my foot not so large by a great deal. Both these things filled my head with new imaginations, and gave me the vapours again to the highest degree, so that I shook with cold like one in an ague; and I went home again, filled with the belief that some man or men had been on shore there; or, in short, that the island was inhabited, and I might be surprised before I was aware; and what course to take for my security I knew not.

Oh, what ridiculous resolutions men take when possessed with fear! It deprives them of the use of those means which reason offers for their relief. The first thing I proposed to myself was, to throw down my enclosures, and turn all my tame cattle wild into the woods, lest the enemy should find them, and then frequent the island in prospect of the same or the like booty: then the simple thing of digging up my two corn-fields, lest they should find such a grain there, and still be prompted to frequent the island: then to demolish my bower and tent, that they might not see any vestiges of habitation, and be prompted to look farther, in order to find out the persons inhabiting.

These were the subject of the first night's cogitations after I was come home again, while the apprehensions which had so overrun my mind were fresh upon me, and my head was full of vapours. Thus, fear of danger is ten thousand times more terrifying than danger itself, when apparent to the eyes; and we find the burden of anxiety greater, by much, than the evil which we are anxious about: and what was worse than all this, I had not that relief in this trouble that from the resignation I used to practise I hoped to have. I looked, I thought, like Saul, who complained not only that the Philistines were upon him, but that God had forsaken him; for I did not now take due ways to compose my mind, by crying to God in my distress, and resting upon His providence, as I had done before, for my defence and deliverance; which, if I had done, I had at least been more cheerfully supported under this new surprise, and perhaps carried through it with more resolution.

This confusion of my thoughts kept me awake all night; but in the morning I fell asleep; and having, by the amusement of my mind, been as it were tired, and my spirits exhausted, I slept very soundly, and waked much better composed than I had ever been before. And now I began to think sedately; and, upon debate with myself, I concluded that this island (which was so exceedingly pleasant, fruitful, and no farther from the mainland than as I had seen) was not so entirely abandoned as I might imagine; that although there were no stated inhabitants who lived on the spot, yet that there might sometimes come boats off from the shore, who, either with design, or perhaps never but when they were driven by cross winds, might come to this place; that I had lived there fifteen years now and had not met with the least shadow or figure of any people yet; and that, if at any time they should be driven here, it was probable they went away again as soon as ever they could, seeing they had never thought fit to fix here upon any occasion; that the most I could suggest any danger from was from any casual accidental landing of straggling people from the main, who, as it was likely, if they were driven hither, were here against their wills, so they made no stay here, but went off again with all possible speed; seldom staying one night on shore, lest they should not have the help of the tides and daylight back again; and that, therefore, I had nothing to do but to consider of some safe retreat, in case I should see any savages land upon the spot.

Now, I began sorely to repent that I had dug my cave so large as to bring a door through again, which door, as I said, came out beyond where my fortification joined to the rock: upon maturely considering this, therefore, I resolved to draw me a second fortification, in the manner of a semicircle, at a distance from my wall, just where I had planted a double row of trees about twelve years before, of which I made mention: these trees having been planted so thick before, they wanted but few piles to be driven between them, that they might be thicker and stronger, and my wall would be soon finished. So that I had now a double wall; and my outer wall was thickened with pieces of timber, old cables, and everything I could think of, to make it strong; having in it seven little holes, about as big as I might put my arm out at. In the inside of this I thickened my wall to about ten feet thick with continually bringing earth out of my cave, and laying it at the foot of the wall, and walking upon it; and through the seven holes I contrived to plant the muskets, of which I took notice that I had got seven on shore out of the ship; these I planted like my cannon, and fitted them into frames, that held them like a carriage, so that I could fire all the seven guns in two minutes' time; this wall I was many a weary month in finishing, and yet never thought myself safe till it was done.

When this was done I stuck all the ground without my wall, for a great length every way, as full with stakes or sticks of the osier-like wood, which I found so apt to grow, as they could well stand; insomuch that I believe I might set in near twenty thousand of them, leaving a pretty large space between them and my wall, that I might have room to see an enemy, and they might have no shelter from the young trees, if they attempted to approach my outer wall.

Thus in two years' time I had a thick grove; and in five or six years' time I had a wood before my dwelling, growing so monstrously thick and strong that it was indeed perfectly impassable: and no men, of what kind so ever, could ever imagine that there was anything beyond it, much less a habitation. As for the way which I proposed to myself to go in and out (for I left no avenue), it was by setting two ladders, one to a part of the rock which was low, and then broke in, and left room to place another ladder upon that; so when the two ladders were taken down no man living could come down to me without doing himself mischief; and if they had come down, they were still on the outside of my outer wall.

Thus I took all the measures human prudence could suggest for my own preservation; and it will be seen at length that they were not altogether without just reason; though I foresaw nothing at that time more than my mere fear suggested to me.

12

A CAVE RETREAT

While this was doing, I was not altogether careless of my other affairs; for I had a great concern upon me for my little herd of goats: they were not only a ready supply to me on every occasion, and began to be sufficient for me, without the expense of powder and shot, but also without the fatigue of hunting after the wild ones; and I was loath to lose the advantage of them, and to have them all to nurse up over again.

For this purpose, after long consideration, I could think of but two ways to preserve them: one was, to find another convenient place to dig a cave underground, and to drive them into it every night; and the other was to enclose two or three little bits of land, remote from one another, and as much concealed as I could, where I might keep about half-a-dozen young goats in each place; so that if any disaster happened to the flock in general, I might be able to raise them again with little trouble and time: and this though it would require a good deal of time and labour, I thought was the most rational design.

Accordingly, I spent some time to find out the most retired parts of the island; and I pitched upon one, which was as private, indeed, as my heart could wish: it was a little damp piece of ground in the middle of the hollow and thick woods, where, as is observed, I almost lost myself once before, endeavouring to come back that way from the eastern part of the island. Here I found a clear piece of land, near three acres, so surrounded with woods that it was almost an enclosure by nature; at least, it did not want near so much labour to make it so as the other piece of ground I had worked so hard at.

I immediately went to work with this piece of ground; and in less than a month's time I had so fenced it round that my flock, or herd, call it which you please, which were not so wild now as at first they might be supposed to be, were well enough secured in it: so, without any further delay, I removed ten young she-goats and two he-goats to this piece, and when they were there I continued to perfect the fence till I had made it as secure as the other; which, however, I did at more leisure, and it took me up more time by a great deal. All this labour I was at the expense of, purely from my apprehensions on account of the print of a man's foot; for as yet I had never seen any human creature come near the island; and I had now lived two years under this uneasiness, which, indeed, made my life much less comfortable than it was before, as may be well imagined by any who know what it is to live in the constant snare of the fear of man. And this I must observe, with grief, too, that the discomposure of my mind had great impression also upon the religious part of my thoughts; for the dread and terror of falling into the hands of savages and cannibals lay so upon my spirits, that I seldom found myself in a due temper for application to my Maker; at least, not with the sedate calmness and resignation of soul which I was wont to do: I rather prayed to God as under great affliction and pressure of mind, surrounded with danger, and in expectation every night of being murdered and devoured before morning; and I must testify, from my experience, that a temper of peace, thankfulness, love, and affection, is much the more proper frame for prayer than that of terror and discomposure: and that under the dread of mischief impending, a man is no more fit for a comforting performance of the duty of praying to God than he is for a repentance on a sick-bed; for these discomposures affect the mind, as the others do the body; and the discomposure of the mind must necessarily be as great a disability as that of the body, and much greater; praying to God being properly an act of the mind, not of the body.

But to go on. After I had thus secured one part of my little living stock, I went about the whole island, searching for another private place to make such another deposit; when, wandering more to the west point of the island than I had ever done yet, and looking out to sea, I thought I saw a boat upon the sea, at a great distance. I had found a perspective glass or two in one of the seamen's chests, which I saved out of our ship, but I had it not about me; and this was so remote that I could not tell what to make of it, though I looked at it till my eyes were not able to hold to look any longer; whether it was a boat or not I do not know, but as I descended from the hill I could see no more of it, so I gave it over; only I resolved to go no more out without a perspective glass in my pocket. When I was come down the hill to the end of the island, where, indeed, I had never been before, I was presently convinced that the seeing the print of a man's foot was not such a strange thing in the island as I imagined: and but that it was a special providence that I was cast upon the side of the island where the savages never came, I should easily have known that nothing was more frequent than for the canoes from the main, when they happened to be a little too far out at sea, to shoot over to that side of the island for harbour: likewise, as they often met and fought in their canoes, the victors, having taken any prisoners, would bring them over to this shore, where, according to their dreadful customs, being all cannibals, they would kill and eat them; of which hereafter.

When I was come down the hill to the shore, as I said above, being the SW. point of the island, I was perfectly confounded and amazed; nor is it possible for me to express the horror of my mind at seeing the shore spread with skulls, hands, feet, and other bones of human bodies; and particularly I observed a place where there had been a fire made, and a circle dug in the earth, like a cockpit, where I supposed the savage wretches had sat down to their human feastings upon the bodies of their fellow-creatures.

I was so astonished with the sight of these things, that I entertained no notions of any danger to myself from it for a long while: all my apprehensions were buried in the thoughts of such a pitch of inhuman, hellish brutality, and the horror of the degeneracy of human nature, which, though I had heard of it often, yet I never had so near a view of before; in short, I turned away my face from the horrid spectacle; my stomach grew sick, and I was just at the point of fainting, when nature discharged the disorder from my stomach; and having vomited with uncommon violence, I was a little relieved, but could not bear to stay in the place a moment; so I got up the hill again with all the speed I could, and walked on towards my own habitation.

When I came a little out of that part of the island I stood still awhile, as amazed, and then, recovering myself, I looked up with the utmost affection of my soul, and, with a flood of tears in my eyes, gave God thanks, that had cast my first lot in a part of the world where I was distinguished from such dreadful creatures as these; and that, though I had esteemed my present condition very miserable, had yet given me so many comforts in it that I had still more to give thanks for than to complain of: and this, above all, that I had, even in this miserable condition, been comforted with the knowledge of Himself, and the hope of His blessing: which was a felicity more than sufficiently equivalent to all the misery which I had suffered, or could suffer.

In this frame of thankfulness I went home to my castle, and began to be much easier now, as to the safety of my circumstances, than ever I was before: for I observed that these wretches never came to this island in search of what they could get; perhaps not seeking, not wanting, or not expecting anything here; and having often, no doubt, been up the covered, woody part of it without finding anything to their purpose. I knew I had been here now almost eighteen years, and never saw the least footsteps of human creature there before; and I might be eighteen years more as entirely concealed as I was now, if I did not discover myself to them, which I had no manner of occasion to do; it being my only business to keep myself entirely concealed where I was, unless I found a better sort of creatures than cannibals to make myself known to. Yet I entertained such an abhorrence of the savage wretches that I have been speaking of, and of the wretched, inhuman custom of their devouring and eating one another up, that I continued pensive and sad, and kept close within my own circle for almost two years after this: when I say my own circle, I mean by it my three plantations—viz. my castle, my country seat (which I called my bower), and my enclosure in the woods: nor did I look after this for any other use than an enclosure for my goats; for the aversion which nature gave me to these hellish wretches was such, that I was as fearful of seeing them as of seeing the devil himself. I did not so much as go to look after my boat all this time, but began rather to think of making another; for I could not think of ever making any more attempts to bring the other boat round the island to me, lest I should meet with some of these creatures at sea; in which case, if I had happened to have fallen into their hands, I knew what would have been my lot.

Time, however, and the satisfaction I had that I was in no danger of being discovered by these people, began to wear off my uneasiness about them; and I began to live just in the same composed manner as before, only with this difference, that I used more caution, and kept my eyes more about me than I did before, lest I should happen to be seen by any of them; and particularly, I was more cautious of firing my gun, lest any of them, being on the island, should happen to hear it. It was, therefore, a very good providence to me that I had furnished myself with a tame breed of goats, and that I had no need to hunt any more about the woods, or shoot at them; and if I did catch any of them after this, it was by traps and snares, as I had done before; so that for two years after this I believe I never fired my gun once off, though I never went out without it; and what was more, as I had saved three pistols out of the ship, I always carried them out with me, or at least two of them, sticking them in my goat-skin belt. I also furbished up one of the great cutlasses that I had out of the ship, and made me a belt to hang it on also; so that I was now a most formidable fellow to look at when I went abroad, if you add to the former description of myself the particular of two pistols, and a broadsword hanging at my side in a belt, but without a scabbard.

Things going on thus, as I have said, for some time, I seemed, excepting these cautions, to be reduced to my former calm, sedate way of living. All these things tended to show me more and more how far my condition was from being miserable, compared to some others;

nay, to many other particulars of life which it might have pleased God to have made my lot. It put me upon reflecting how little repining there would be among mankind at any condition of life if people would rather compare their condition with those that were worse, in order to be thankful, than be always comparing them with those which are better, to assist their murmurings and complainings.

As in my present condition there were not really many things which I wanted, so indeed I thought that the frights I had been in about these savage wretches, and the concern I had been in for my own preservation, had taken off the edge of my invention, for my own conveniences; and I had dropped a good design, which I had once bent my thoughts upon, and that was to try if I could not make some of my barley into malt, and then try to brew myself some beer. This was really a whimsical thought, and I reproved myself often for the simplicity of it: for I presently saw there would be the want of several things necessary to the making my beer that it would be impossible for me to supply; as, first, casks to preserve it in, which was a thing that, as I have observed already, I could never compass: no, though I spent not only many days, but weeks, nay months, in attempting it, but to no purpose. In the next place, I had no hops to make it keep, no yeast to make it work, no copper or kettle to make it boil; and yet with all these things wanting, I verily believe, had not the frights and terrors I was in about the savages intervened, I had undertaken it, and perhaps brought it to pass too; for I seldom gave anything over without accomplishing it, when once I had it in my head to began it. But my invention now ran quite another way; for night and day I could think of nothing but how I might destroy some of the monsters in their cruel, bloody entertainment, and if possible save the victim they should bring hither to destroy. It would take up a larger volume than this whole work is intended to be to set down all the contrivances I hatched, or rather brooded upon, in my thoughts, for the destroying these creatures, or at least frightening them so as to prevent their coming hither any more: but all this was abortive; nothing could be possible to take effect, unless I was to be there to do it myself: and what could one man do among them, when perhaps there might be twenty or thirty of them together with their darts, or their bows and arrows, with which they could shoot as true to a mark as I could with my gun?

Sometimes I thought if digging a hole under the place where they made their fire, and putting in five or six pounds of gunpowder, which, when they kindled their fire, would consequently take fire, and blow up all that was near it: but as, in the first place, I should be unwilling to waste so much powder upon them, my store being now within the quantity of one barrel, so neither could I be sure of its going off at any certain time, when it might surprise them; and, at best, that it would do little more than just blow the fire about their ears and fright them, but not sufficient to make them forsake the place: so I laid it aside; and then proposed that I would place myself in ambush in some convenient place, with my three guns all double-loaded, and in the middle of their bloody ceremony let fly at them, when I should be sure to kill or wound perhaps two or three at every shot; and then falling in upon them with my three pistols and my sword, I made no doubt but that, if there were twenty, I should kill them all. This fancy pleased my thoughts for some weeks, and I was so full of it that I often dreamed of it, and, sometimes, that I was just going to let fly at them in my sleep. I went so far with it in my imagination that I employed myself several days to find out proper places to put myself in ambuscade, as I said, to watch for them, and I went frequently to the place itself, which was now grown more familiar to me; but while my mind was thus filled with thoughts of revenge and a bloody putting twenty or thirty of them to the sword, as I may call it, the horror I had at the place, and at the signals of the barbarous wretches devouring one another, abetted my malice. Well, at length I found a place in the side of the hill where I was satisfied I might securely wait till I saw any of their boats coming; and might then, even before they would be ready to come on shore, convey myself unseen into some thickets of trees, in one of which there was a hollow large enough to conceal me entirely; and there I might sit and observe all their bloody doings, and take my full aim at their heads, when they were so close together as that it would be next to impossible that I should miss my shot, or that I could fail wounding three or four of them at the first shot. In this place, then, I resolved to fulfil my design; and accordingly I prepared two muskets and my ordinary fowling-piece. The two muskets I loaded with a brace of slugs each, and four or five smaller bullets, about the size of pistol bullets; and the fowling-piece I loaded with near a handful of swan-shot of the largest size; I also loaded my pistols with about four bullets each; and, in this posture, well provided with ammunition for a second and third charge, I prepared myself for my expedition.

After I had thus laid the scheme of my design, and in my imagination put it in practice, I continually made my tour every morning to the top of the hill, which was from my castle, as I called it, about three miles or more, to see if I could observe any boats upon the sea, coming near the island, or standing over towards it; but I began to tire of this hard duty, after I had for two or three months constantly kept my watch, but came always back without any discovery; there having not, in all that time, been the least appearance, not only on or near the shore, but on the whole ocean, so far as my eye or glass could reach every way.

As long as I kept my daily tour to the hill, to look out, so long also I kept up the vigour of my design, and my spirits seemed to be all the while in a suitable frame for so outrageous an execution as the killing twenty or thirty naked savages, for an offence which I had not at all entered into any discussion of in my thoughts, any farther than my passions were at first fired by the horror I conceived at the unnatural custom of the people of that country, who, it seems, had been suffered by Providence, in His wise disposition of the world, to have no other guide than that of their own abominable and vitiated passions; and consequently were left, and perhaps had been so for some ages, to act such horrid things, and receive such dreadful customs, as nothing but nature, entirely abandoned by Heaven, and actuated by some hellish degeneracy, could have run them into. But now, when, as I have said, I began to be weary of the fruitless excursion which I had made so long and so far every morning in vain, so my opinion of the action itself began to alter; and I began, with cooler and calmer thoughts, to consider what I was going to engage in; what authority or call I had to pretend to be judge and executioner upon these men as criminals, whom Heaven had thought fit for so many ages to suffer unpunished to go on, and to be as it were the executioners of His judgments one upon another; how far these people were offenders against me, and what right I had to engage in the quarrel of that blood which they shed promiscuously upon one another. I debated this very often with myself thus: "How do I know what God Himself judges in this particular case? It is certain these people do not commit this as a crime; it is not against their own consciences reproving, or their light reproaching them; they do not know it to be an offence, and then commit it in defiance of divine justice, as we do in almost all the sins we commit. They think it no more a crime to kill a captive taken in war than we do to kill an ox; or to eat human flesh than we do to eat mutton."

When I considered this a little, it followed necessarily that I was certainly in the wrong; that these people were not murderers, in the sense that I had before condemned them in my thoughts, any more than those Christians were murderers who often put to death the prisoners taken in battle; or more frequently, upon many occasions, put whole troops of men to the sword, without giving quarter, though they threw down their arms and submitted. In the next place, it occurred to me that although the usage they gave one another was thus brutish and inhuman, yet it was really nothing to me: these people had done me no injury: that if they attempted, or I saw it necessary, for my immediate preservation, to fall upon them, something might be said for it: but that I was yet out of their power, and they really had no knowledge of me, and consequently no design upon me; and therefore it could not be just for me to fall upon them; that this would justify the conduct of the Spaniards in all their barbarities practised in America, where they destroyed millions of these people; who, however they were idolators and barbarians, and had several bloody and barbarous rites in their customs, such as sacrificing human bodies to their idols, were yet, as to the Spaniards, very innocent people; and that the rooting them out of the country is spoken of with the utmost abhorrence and detestation by even the Spaniards themselves at this time, and by all other Christian nations of Europe, as a mere butchery, a bloody and unnatural piece of cruelty, unjustifiable either to God or man; and for which the very name of a Spaniard is reckoned to be frightful and terrible, to all people of humanity or of Christian compassion; as if the kingdom of Spain were particularly eminent for the produce of a race of men who were without principles of tenderness, or the common bowels of pity to the miserable, which is reckoned to be a mark of generous temper in the mind.

These considerations really put me to a pause, and to a kind of a full stop; and I began by little and little to be off my design, and to conclude I had taken wrong measures in my resolution to attack the savages; and that it was not my business to meddle with them, unless they first attacked me; and this it was my business, if possible, to prevent: but that, if I were discovered and attacked by them, I knew my duty. On the other hand, I argued with myself that this really was the way not to deliver myself, but entirely to ruin and destroy myself; for unless I was sure to kill every one that not only should be on shore at that time, but that should ever come on shore afterwards, if but one of them escaped to tell their country-people what had happened, they would come over again by thousands to revenge the death of their fellows, and I should only bring upon myself a certain destruction, which, at present, I had no manner of occasion for. Upon the whole, I concluded that I ought, neither in principle nor in policy, one way or other, to concern myself in this affair: that my business was, by all possible means to conceal myself from them, and not to leave the least sign for them to guess by that there were any living creatures upon the island—I mean of human shape. Religion joined in with this prudential resolution; and I was convinced now, many ways, that I was perfectly out of my duty when I was laying all my bloody schemes for the destruction of innocent creatures—I mean innocent as to me. As to the crimes they were guilty of towards one another, I had nothing to do with them; they were national, and I ought to leave them to the justice of God, who is the Governor of nations, and knows how, by national punishments, to make a just retribution for national offences, and to bring public judgments upon those who offend in a public manner, by such ways as best please Him. This appeared so clear to me now, that nothing was a greater satisfaction to me than that I had not been suffered to do a thing which I now saw so much reason to believe would have been no less a sin than that of wilful murder if I had committed it; and I gave most humble thanks on my knees to God, that He had thus delivered me from blood-guiltiness; beseeching Him to grant me the protection of His providence, that I might not fall into the hands of the barbarians, or that I might not lay my hands upon them, unless I had a more clear call from Heaven to do it, in defence of my own life.

In this disposition I continued for near a year after this; and so far was I from desiring an occasion for falling upon these wretches, that in all that time I never once went up the hill to see whether there were any of them in sight, or to know whether any of them had been on shore there or not, that I might not be tempted to renew any of my contrivances against them, or be provoked by any advantage that might present itself to fall upon them; only this I did: I went and removed my boat, which I had on the other side of the island, and carried it down to the east end of the whole island, where I ran it into a little cove, which I found under some high rocks, and where I knew, by reason of the currents, the savages durst not, at least would not, come with their boats upon any account whatever. With my boat I carried away everything that I had left there belonging to her, though not necessary for the bare going thither—viz. a mast and sail which I had made for her, and a thing like an anchor, but which, indeed, could not be called either anchor or grapnel; however, it was the best I could make of its kind: all these I removed, that there might not be the least shadow for discovery, or appearance of any boat, or of any human habitation upon the island. Besides this, I kept myself, as I said, more retired than ever, and seldom went from my cell except upon my constant employment, to milk my she-goats, and manage my little flock in the wood, which, as it was quite on the other part of the island, was out of danger; for certain, it is that these savage people, who sometimes haunted this island, never came with any thoughts of finding anything here, and consequently never wandered off from the coast, and I doubt not but they might have been several times on shore after my apprehensions of them had made me cautious, as well as before. Indeed, I looked back with some horror upon the thoughts of what my condition would have been if I had chopped upon them and been discovered before that; when, naked and unarmed, except with one gun, and that loaded often only with small shot, I walked everywhere, peeping and peering about the island, to see what I could get; what a surprise should I have been in if, when I discovered the print of a man's foot, I had, instead of that, seen fifteen or twenty savages, and found them pursuing me, and by the swiftness of their running no possibility of my escaping them! The thoughts of this sometimes sank my very soul within me, and distressed my mind so much that I could not soon recover it, to think what I should have done, and how I should not only have been unable to resist them, but even should not have had presence of mind enough to do what I might have done; much less what now, after so much consideration and preparation, I might be able to do. Indeed, after serious thinking of these things, I would be melancholy, and sometimes it would last a great while; but I resolved it all at last into thankfulness to that Providence which had delivered me from so many unseen dangers, and had kept me from those mischiefs which I could have no way been the agent in delivering myself from, because I had not the least notion of any such thing depending, or the least supposition of its being possible. This renewed a contemplation which often had come into my thoughts in former times, when first I began to see the merciful dispositions of Heaven, in the dangers we run through in this life; how wonderfully we are delivered when we know nothing of it; how, when we are in a quandary as we call it, a doubt or hesitation whether to go this way or that way, a secret hint shall direct us this way, when we intended to go that way: nay, when sense, our own inclination, and perhaps business has called us to go the other way, yet a strange impression upon the mind, from we know not what springs, and by we know not what power, shall overrule us to go this way; and it shall afterwards appear that had we gone that way, which we should have gone, and even to our imagination ought to have gone, we should have been ruined and lost. Upon these and many like reflections I afterwards made it a certain rule with me, that whenever I found those secret hints or pressings of mind to doing or not doing anything that presented, or going this way or that way, I never failed to obey the secret dictate; though I knew no other reason for it than such a pressure or such a hint hung upon my mind. I could give many examples of the success of this conduct in the course of my life, but more especially in the latter part of my inhabiting this unhappy island; besides many occasions which it is very likely I might have taken notice of, if I had seen with the same eyes then that I see with now. But it is never too late to be wise; and I cannot but advise all considering men, whose lives are attended with such extraordinary incidents as mine, or even though not so extraordinary, not to slight such secret intimations of Providence, let them come from what invisible intelligence they will. That I shall not discuss, and perhaps cannot account for; but certainly they are a proof of the converse of spirits, and a secret communication between those embodied and those unembodied, and such a proof as can never be withstood; of which I shall have occasion to give some remarkable instances in the remainder of my solitary residence in this dismal place.

I believe the reader of this will not think it strange if I confess that these anxieties, these constant dangers I lived in, and the concern that was now upon me, put an end to all invention, and to all the contrivances that I had laid for my future accommodations and conveniences. I had the care of my safety more now upon my hands than that of my food. I cared not to drive a nail, or chop a stick of wood now, for fear the noise I might make should be heard: much less would I fire a gun for the same reason: and above all I was intolerably uneasy at making any fire, lest the smoke, which is visible at a great distance in the day, should betray me. For this reason, I removed that part of my business which required fire, such as burning of pots and pipes, &c., into my new apartment in the woods; where, after I had been some time, I found, to my unspeakable consolation, a mere natural cave in the earth, which went in a vast way, and where, I daresay, no savage, had he been at the mouth of it, would be so hardy as to venture in; nor, indeed, would any man else, but one who, like me, wanted nothing so much as a safe retreat.

The mouth of this hollow was at the bottom of a great rock, where, by mere accident (I would say, if I did not see abundant reason to ascribe all such things now to Providence), I was cutting down some thick branches of trees to make charcoal; and before I go on I must observe the reason of my making this charcoal, which was this—I was afraid of making a smoke about my habitation, as I said before; and yet I could not live there without baking my bread, cooking my meat, &c.; so I contrived to burn some wood here, as I had seen done in England, under turf, till it became chark or dry coal: and then putting the fire out, I preserved the coal to carry home, and perform the other services for which fire was wanting, without danger of smoke. But this is by-the-bye. While I was cutting down some wood here, I perceived that, behind a very thick branch of low brushwood or underwood, there was a kind of hollow place: I was curious to look in it; and getting with difficulty into the mouth of it, I found it was pretty large, that is to say, sufficient for me to stand upright in it, and perhaps another with me: but I must confess to you that I made more haste out than I did in, when looking farther into the place, and which was perfectly dark, I saw two broad shining eyes of some creature, whether devil or man I knew not, which twinkled like two stars; the dim light from the cave's mouth shining directly in, and making the reflection. However, after some pause I recovered myself, and began to call myself a thousand fools, and to think that he that was afraid to see the devil was not fit to live twenty years in an island all alone; and that I might well think there was nothing in this cave that was more frightful than myself. Upon this, plucking up my courage, I took up a firebrand, and in I rushed again, with the stick flaming in my hand: I had not gone three steps in before I was almost as frightened as before; for I heard a very loud sigh, like that of a man in some pain, and it was followed by a broken noise, as of words half expressed, and then a deep sigh again. I stepped back, and was indeed struck with such a surprise that it put me into a cold sweat, and if I had had a hat on my head, I will not answer for it that my hair might not have lifted it off. But still plucking up my spirits as well as I could, and encouraging myself a little with considering that the power and presence of God was everywhere, and was able to protect me, I stepped forward again, and by the light of the firebrand, holding it up a little over my head, I saw lying on the ground a monstrous, frightful old he-goat, just making his will, as we say, and gasping for life, and, dying, indeed, of mere old age. I stirred him a little to see if I could get him out, and he essayed to get up, but was not able to raise himself; and I thought with myself he might even lie there—for if he had frightened me, so he would certainly fright any of the savages, if any of them should be so hardy as to come in there while he had any life in him.

I was now recovered from my surprise, and began to look round me, when I found the cave was but very small—that is to say, it might be about twelve feet over, but in no manner of shape, neither round nor square, no hands having ever been employed in making it but those of mere Nature. I observed also that there was a place at the farther side of it that went in further, but was so low that it required me to creep upon my hands and knees to go into it, and whither it went I knew not; so, having no candle, I gave it over for that time, but resolved to go again the next day provided with candles and a tinder-box, which I had made of the lock of one of the muskets, with some wildfire in the pan.

Accordingly, the next day I came provided with six large candles of my own making (for I made very good candles now of goat's tallow, but was hard set for candle-wick, using sometimes rags or rope-yarn, and sometimes the dried rind of a weed like nettles); and going into this low place I was obliged to creep upon all-fours as I have said, almost ten yards—which, by the way, I thought was a venture bold enough, considering that I knew not how far it might go, nor what was beyond it. When I had got through the strait, I found the roof rose higher up, I believe near twenty feet; but never was such a glorious sight seen in the island, I daresay, as it was to look round the sides and roof of this vault or cave—the wall reflected a hundred thousand lights to me from my two candles. What it was in the rock—whether diamonds or any other precious stones, or gold which I rather supposed it to be—I knew not. The place I was in was a most delightful cavity, or grotto, though perfectly dark; the floor was dry and level, and had a sort of a small loose gravel upon it, so that there was no nauseous or venomous creature to be seen, neither was there any damp or wet on the sides or roof. The only difficulty in it was the entrance—which, however, as it was a place of security, and such a retreat as I wanted; I thought was a convenience; so that I was really rejoiced at the discovery, and resolved, without any delay, to bring some of those things which I was most anxious about to this place: particularly, I resolved to bring hither my magazine of powder, and all my spare arms—viz. two fowling-pieces—for I had three in all—and three muskets—for of them I had eight in all; so I kept in my castle only five, which stood ready mounted like pieces of cannon on my outmost fence, and were ready also to take out upon any expedition. Upon this occasion of removing my ammunition I happened to open the barrel of powder which I took up out of the sea, and which had been wet, and I found that the water had penetrated about three or four inches into the powder on every side, which caking and growing hard, had preserved the inside like a kernel in the shell, so that I had near sixty pounds of very good powder in the centre of the cask. This was a very agreeable discovery to me at that time; so I carried all away thither, never keeping above two or three pounds of powder with me in my castle, for fear of a surprise of any kind; I also carried thither all the lead I had left for bullets.

I fancied myself now like one of the ancient giants who were said to live in caves and holes in the rocks, where none could come at them; for I persuaded myself, while I was here, that if five hundred savages were to hunt me, they could never find me out—or if they did, they would not venture to attack me here. The old goat whom I found expiring died in the mouth of the cave the next day after I made this discovery; and I found it much easier to dig a great hole there, and throw him in and cover him with earth, than to drag him out; so I interred him there, to prevent offence to my nose.

13

WRECK OF A SPANISH SHIP

I was now in the twenty-third year of my residence in this island, and was so naturalised to the place and the manner of living, that, could I but have enjoyed the certainty that no savages would come to the place to disturb me, I could have been content to have capitulated for spending the rest of my time there, even to the last moment, till I had laid me down and died, like the old goat in the cave. I had also arrived to some little diversions and amusements, which made the time pass a great deal more pleasantly with me than it did before—first, I had taught my Poll, as I noted before, to speak; and he did it so familiarly, and talked so articulately and plain, that it was very pleasant to me; and he lived with me no less than six-and-twenty years. How long he might have lived afterwards I know not, though I know they have a notion in the Brazils that they live a hundred years. My dog was a pleasant and loving companion to me for no less than sixteen years of my time, and then died of mere old age. As for my cats, they multiplied, as I have observed, to that degree that I was obliged to shoot several of them at first, to keep them from devouring me and all I had; but at length, when the two old ones I brought with me were gone, and after some time continually driving them from me, and letting them have no provision with me, they all ran wild into the woods, except two or three favourites, which I kept tame, and whose young, when they had any, I always drowned; and these were part of my family. Besides these I always kept two or three household kids about me, whom I taught to feed out of my hand; and I had two more parrots, which talked pretty well, and would all call "Robin Crusoe," but none like my first; nor, indeed, did I take the pains with any of them that I had done with him. I had also several tame sea-fowls, whose name I knew not, that I caught upon the shore, and cut their wings; and the little stakes which I had planted before my castle-wall being now grown up to a good thick grove, these fowls all lived among these low trees, and bred there, which was very agreeable to me; so that, as I said above, I began to be very well contented with the life I led, if I could have been secured from the dread of the savages. But it was otherwise directed; and it may not be amiss for all people who shall meet with my story to make this just observation from it: How frequently, in the course of our lives, the evil which in itself we seek most to shun, and which, when we are fallen into, is the most dreadful to us, is oftentimes the very means or door of our deliverance, by which alone we can be raised again from the affliction we are fallen into. I could give many examples of this in the course of my unaccountable life; but in nothing was it more particularly remarkable than in the circumstances of my last years of solitary residence in this island.

It was now the month of December, as I said above, in my twenty-third year; and this, being the southern solstice (for winter I cannot call it), was the particular time of my harvest, and required me to be pretty much abroad in the fields, when, going out early in the morning, even before it was thorough daylight, I was surprised with seeing a light of some fire upon the shore, at a distance from me of about two miles, toward that part of the island where I had observed some savages had been, as before, and not on the other side; but, to my great affliction, it was on my side of the island.

I was indeed terribly surprised at the sight, and stopped short within my grove, not daring to go out, lest I might be surprised; and yet I had no more peace within, from the apprehensions I had that if these savages, in rambling over the island, should find my corn standing or cut, or any of my works or improvements, they would immediately conclude that there were people in the place, and would then never rest till they had found me out. In this extremity I went back directly to my castle, pulled up the ladder after me, and made all things without look as wild and natural as I could.

Then I prepared myself within, putting myself in a posture of defence. I loaded all my cannon, as I called them—that is to say, my muskets, which were mounted upon my new fortification—and all my pistols, and resolved to defend myself to the last gasp—not forgetting seriously to commend myself to the Divine protection, and earnestly to pray to God to deliver me out of the hands of the barbarians. I continued in this posture about two hours, and began to be impatient for intelligence abroad, for I had no spies to send out. After sitting a while longer, and musing what I should do in this case, I was not able to bear sitting in ignorance longer; so setting up my ladder to the side of the hill, where there was a flat place, as I observed before, and then pulling the ladder after me, I set it up again and mounted the top of the hill, and pulling out my perspective glass, which I had taken on purpose, I laid me down flat on my belly on the ground, and began to look for the place. I presently found there were no less than nine naked savages sitting round a small fire they had made, not to warm them, for they had no need of that, the weather being extremely hot, but, as I supposed, to dress some of their barbarous diet of human flesh which they had brought with them, whether alive or dead I could not tell.

They had two canoes with them, which they had hauled up upon the shore; and as it was then ebb of tide, they seemed to me to wait for the return of the flood to go away again. It is not easy to imagine what confusion this sight put me into, especially seeing them come on my side of the island, and so near to me; but when I considered their coming must be always with the current of the ebb, I began afterwards to be more sedate in my mind, being satisfied that I might go abroad with safety all the time of the flood of tide, if they were not on shore before; and having made this observation, I went abroad about my harvest work with the more composure.

As I expected, so it proved; for as soon as the tide made to the westward I saw them all take boat and row (or paddle as we call it) away. I should have observed, that for an hour or more before they went off they were dancing, and I could easily discern their postures and gestures by my glass. I could not perceive, by my nicest observation, but that they were stark naked, and had not the least covering upon them; but whether they were men or women I could not distinguish.

As soon as I saw them shipped and gone, I took two guns upon my shoulders, and two pistols in my girdle, and my great sword by my side without a scabbard, and with all the speed I was able to make went away to the hill where I had discovered the first appearance of all; and as soon as I got thither, which was not in less than two hours (for I could not go quickly, being so loaded with arms as I was), I perceived there had been three canoes more of the savages at that place; and looking out farther, I saw they were all at sea together, making over for the main. This was a dreadful sight to me, especially as, going down to the shore, I could see the marks of horror which the dismal work they had been about had left behind it —viz. the blood, the bones, and part of the flesh of human bodies eaten and devoured by those wretches with merriment and sport. I was so filled with indignation at the sight, that I now began to premeditate the destruction of the next that I saw there, let them be whom or how many so ever. It seemed evident to me that the visits which they made thus to this island were not very frequent, for it was above fifteen months before any more of them came on shore there again—that is to say, I neither saw them nor any footsteps or signals of them in all that time; for as to the rainy seasons, then they are sure not to come abroad, at least not so far. Yet all this while I lived uncomfortably, by reason of the constant apprehensions of their coming upon me by surprise: from whence I observe, that the expectation of evil is more bitter than the suffering, especially if there is no room to shake off that expectation or those apprehensions.

During all this time I was in a murdering humour, and spent most of my hours, which should have been better employed, in contriving how to circumvent and fall upon them the very next time I should see them—especially if they should be divided, as they were the last time, into two parties; nor did I consider at all that if I killed one party—suppose ten or a dozen—I was still the next day, or week, or month, to kill another, and so another, even *ad infinitum*, till I should be, at length, no less a murderer than they were in being man-eaters— and perhaps much more so. I spent my days now in great perplexity and anxiety of mind, expecting that I should one day or other fall into the hands of these merciless creatures; and if I did at any time venture abroad, it was not without looking around me with the greatest care and caution imaginable. And now I found, to my great comfort, how happy it was that I had provided a tame flock or herd of goats, for I durst not upon any account fire my gun, especially near that side of the island where they usually came, lest I should alarm the savages; and if they had fled from me now, I was sure to have them come again with perhaps two or three hundred canoes with them in a few days, and then I knew what to expect. However, I wore out a year and three months more before I ever saw any more of the savages, and then I found them again, as I shall soon observe. It is true they might have been there once or twice; but either they made no stay, or at least I did not see them; but in the month of May, as near as I could calculate, and in my four-and-twentieth year, I had a very strange encounter with them; of which in its place.

The perturbation of my mind during this fifteen or sixteen months' interval was very great; I slept unquietly, dreamed always frightful dreams, and often started out of my sleep in the night. In the day great troubles overwhelmed my mind; and in the night I dreamed often of killing the savages and of the reasons why I might justify doing it.

But to waive all this for a while. It was in the middle of May, on the sixteenth day, I think, as well as my poor wooden calendar would reckon, for I marked all upon the post still; I say, it was on the sixteenth of May that it blew a very great storm of wind all day, with a great deal of lightning and thunder, and; a very foul night it was after it. I knew not what was the particular occasion of it, but as I was reading in the Bible, and taken up with very serious thoughts about my present condition, I was surprised with the noise of a gun, as I thought, fired at sea. This was, to be sure, a surprise quite of a different nature from any I had met with before; for the notions this put into my thoughts were quite of another kind. I started up in the greatest haste imaginable; and, in a trice, clapped my ladder to the middle place of the rock, and pulled it after me; and mounting it the second time, got to the top of the hill the very moment that a flash of fire bid me listen for a second gun, which, accordingly, in about half a minute I heard; and by the sound, knew that it was from that part of the sea where I was driven down the current in my boat. I immediately considered that this must be some ship in distress, and that they had some comrade, or some other ship in company, and fired these for signals of distress, and to obtain help. I had the presence of mind at that minute to think, that though I could not help them, it might be that they might help me; so I brought together all the dry wood I could get at hand, and making a good handsome pile, I set it on fire upon the hill. The wood was dry, and blazed freely; and, though the wind blew very hard, yet it burned fairly out; so that I was certain, if there was any such thing as a ship, they must needs see it. And no doubt they did; for as soon as ever my fire blazed up, I heard another gun, and after that several others, all from the same quarter. I plied my fire all night long, till daybreak: and when it was broad day, and the air cleared up, I saw something at a great distance at sea, full east of the island, whether a sail or a hull I could not distinguish— no, not with my glass: the distance was so great, and the weather still something hazy also; at least, it was so out at sea.

 I looked frequently at it all that day, and soon perceived that it did not move; so I presently concluded that it was a ship at anchor; and being eager, you may be sure, to be satisfied, I took my gun in my hand, and ran towards the south side of the island to the rocks where I had formerly been carried away by the current; and getting up there, the weather by this time being perfectly clear, I could plainly see, to my great sorrow, the wreck of a ship, cast away in the night upon those concealed rocks which I found when I was out in my boat; and which rocks, as they checked the violence of the stream, and made a kind of counter-stream, or eddy, were the occasion of my recovering from the most desperate, hopeless condition that ever I had been in in all my life. Thus, what is one man's safety is another man's destruction; for it seems these men, whoever they were, being out of their knowledge, and the rocks being wholly under water, had been driven upon them in the night, the wind blowing hard at ENE. Had they seen the island, as I must necessarily suppose they did not, they must, as I thought, have endeavoured to have saved themselves on shore by the help of their boat; but their firing off guns for help, especially when they saw, as I imagined, my fire, filled me with many thoughts. First, I imagined that upon seeing my light they might have put themselves into their boat, and endeavoured to make the shore: but that the sea running very high, they might have been cast away. Other times I imagined that they might have lost their boat before, as might be the case many ways; particularly by the breaking of the sea upon their ship, which many times obliged men to stave, or take in pieces, their boat, and sometimes to throw it overboard with their own hands. Other times I imagined they had some other ship or ships in company, who, upon the signals of distress they made, had taken them up, and carried them off. Other times I fancied they were all gone off to sea in their boat, and being hurried away by the current that I had been formerly in, were carried out into the great ocean, where there was nothing but misery and perishing: and that, perhaps, they might by this time think of starving, and of being in a condition to eat one another.

 As all these were but conjectures at best, so, in the condition I was in, I could do no more than look on upon the misery of the poor men, and pity them; which had still this good effect upon my side, that it gave me more and more cause to give thanks to God, who had so happily and comfortably provided for me in my desolate condition; and that of two ships' companies, who were now cast away upon this part of the world, not one life should be spared but mine. I learned here again to observe, that it is very rare that the providence of God casts us into any condition so low, or any misery so great, but we may see something or other to be thankful for, and may see others in worse circumstances than our own. Such certainly was the case of these men, of whom I could not so much as see room to suppose any were saved; nothing could make it rational so much as to wish or expect that they did not all perish there, except the possibility only of their being taken up by another ship in company; and this was but mere possibility indeed, for I saw not the least sign or appearance of any such thing. I cannot explain, by any possible energy of words, what a strange longing I felt in my soul upon this sight, breaking out sometimes thus: "Oh that there had been but one or two, nay, or but one soul saved out of this ship, to have escaped to me, that I might but have had one companion, one fellow-creature, to have spoken to me and to have conversed with!" In all the time of my solitary life I never felt so earnest, so strong a desire after the society of my fellow-creatures, or so deep a regret at the want of it.

There are some secret springs in the affections which, when they are set a-going by some object in view, or, though not in view, yet rendered present to the mind by the power of imagination, that motion carries out the soul, by its impetuosity, to such violent, eager embracings of the object, that the absence of it is insupportable. Such were these earnest wishings that but one man had been saved. I believe I repeated the words, "Oh that it had been but one!" a thousand times; and my desires were so moved by it, that when I spoke the words my hands would clinch together, and my fingers would press the palms of my hands, so that if I had had any soft thing in my hand I should have crushed it involuntarily; and the teeth in my head would strike together, and set against one another so strong, that for some time I could not part them again. Let the naturalists explain these things, and the reason and manner of them. All I can do is to describe the fact, which was even surprising to me when I found it, though I knew not from whence it proceeded; it was doubtless the effect of ardent wishes, and of strong ideas formed in my mind, realising the comfort which the conversation of one of my fellow-Christians would have been to me. But it was not to be; either their fate or mine, or both, forbade it; for, till the last year of my being on this island, I never knew whether any were saved out of that ship or no; and had only the affliction, some days after, to see the corpse of a drowned boy come on shore at the end of the island which was next the shipwreck. He had no clothes on but a seaman's waistcoat, a pair of open-kneed linen drawers, and a blue linen shirt; but nothing to direct me so much as to guess what nation he was of. He had nothing in his pockets but two pieces of eight and a tobacco pipe—the last was to me of ten times more value than the first.

It was now calm, and I had a great mind to venture out in my boat to this wreck, not doubting but I might find something on board that might be useful to me. But that did not altogether press me so much as the possibility that there might be yet some living creature on board, whose life I might not only save, but might, by saving that life, comfort my own to the last degree; and this thought clung so to my heart that I could not be quiet night or day, but I must venture out in my boat on board this wreck; and committing the rest to God's providence, I thought the impression was so strong upon my mind that it could not be resisted—that it must come from some invisible direction, and that I should be wanting to myself if I did not go.

Under the power of this impression, I hastened back to my castle, prepared everything for my voyage, took a quantity of bread, a great pot of fresh water, a compass to steer by, a bottle of rum (for I had still a great deal of that left), and a basket of raisins; and thus, loading myself with everything necessary. I went down to my boat, got the water out of her, got her afloat, loaded all my cargo in her, and then went home again for more. My second cargo was a great bag of rice, the umbrella to set up over my head for a shade, another large pot of water, and about two dozen of small loaves, or barley cakes, more than before, with a bottle of goat's milk and a cheese; all which with great labour and sweat I carried to my boat; and praying to God to direct my voyage, I put out, and rowing or paddling the canoe along the shore, came at last to the utmost point of the island on the north-east side. And now I was to launch out into the ocean, and either to venture or not to venture. I looked on the rapid currents which ran constantly on both sides of the island at a distance, and which were very terrible to me from the remembrance of the hazard I had been in before, and my heart began to fail me; for I foresaw that if I was driven into either of those currents, I should be carried a great way out to sea, and perhaps out of my reach or sight of the island again; and that then, as my boat was but small, if any little gale of wind should rise, I should be inevitably lost.

These thoughts so oppressed my mind that I began to give over my enterprise; and having hauled my boat into a little creek on the shore, I stepped out, and sat down upon a rising bit of ground, very pensive and anxious, between fear and desire, about my voyage; when, as I was musing, I could perceive that the tide was turned, and the flood come on; upon which my going was impracticable for so many hours. Upon this, presently it occurred to me that I should go up to the highest piece of ground I could find, and observe, if I could, how the sets of the tide or currents lay when the flood came in, that I might judge whether, if I was driven one way out, I might not expect to be driven another way home, with the same rapidity of the currents. This thought was no sooner in my head than I cast my eye upon a little hill which sufficiently overlooked the sea both ways, and from whence I had a clear view of the currents or sets of the tide, and which way I was to guide myself in my return. Here I found, that as the current of ebb set out close by the south point of the island, so the current of the flood set in close by the shore of the north side; and that I had nothing to do but to keep to the north side of the island in my return, and I should do well enough.

Encouraged by this observation, I resolved the next morning to set out with the first of the tide; and reposing myself for the night in my canoe, under the watch-coat I mentioned, I launched out. I first made a little out to sea, full north, till I began to feel the benefit of the current, which set eastward, and which carried me at a great rate; and yet did not so hurry me as the current on the south side had done before, so as to take from me all government of the boat; but having a strong steerage with my paddle, I went at a great rate directly for the wreck, and in less than two hours I came up to it. It was a dismal sight to look at; the ship, which by its building was Spanish, stuck fast, jammed in between two rocks. All the stern and quarter of her were beaten to pieces by the sea; and as her forecastle, which stuck in the rocks, had run on with great violence, her mainmast and foremast were brought by the board —that is to say, broken short off; but her bowsprit was sound, and the head and bow appeared firm. When I came close to her, a dog appeared upon her, who, seeing me coming, yelped and cried; and as soon as I called him, jumped into the sea to come to me. I took him into the boat, but found him almost dead with hunger and thirst. I gave him a cake of my bread, and he devoured it like a ravenous wolf that had been starving a fortnight in the snow; I then gave the poor creature some fresh water, with which, if I would have let him, he would have burst himself. After this I went on board; but the first sight I met with was two men drowned in the cook-room, or forecastle of the ship, with their arms fast about one another. I concluded, as is indeed probable, that when the ship struck, it being in a storm, the sea broke so high and so continually over her, that the men were not able to bear it, and were strangled with the constant rushing in of the water, as much as if they had been under water. Besides the dog, there was nothing left in the ship that had life; nor any goods, that I could see, but what were spoiled by the water. There were some casks of liquor, whether wine or brandy I knew not, which lay lower in the hold, and which, the water being ebbed out, I could see; but they were too big to meddle with. I saw several chests, which I believe belonged to some of the seamen; and I got two of them into the boat, without examining what was in them. Had the stern of the ship been fixed, and the forepart broken off, I am persuaded I might have made a good voyage; for by what I found in those two chests I had room to suppose the ship had a great deal of wealth on board; and, if I may guess from the course she steered, she must have been bound from Buenos Ayres, or the Rio de la Plata, in the south part of America, beyond the Brazils to the Havannah, in the Gulf of Mexico, and so perhaps to Spain. She had, no doubt, a great treasure in her, but of no use, at that time, to anybody; and what became of the crew I then knew not.

I found, besides these chests, a little cask full of liquor, of about twenty gallons, which I got into my boat with much difficulty. There were several muskets in the cabin, and a great powder-horn, with about four pounds of powder in it; as for the muskets, I had no occasion for them, so I left them, but took the powder-horn. I took a fire-shovel and tongs, which I wanted extremely, as also two little brass kettles, a copper pot to make chocolate, and a gridiron; and with this cargo, and the dog, I came away, the tide beginning to make home again—and the same evening, about an hour within night, I reached the island again, weary and fatigued to the last degree. I reposed that night in the boat and in the morning I resolved to harbour what I had got in my new cave, and not carry it home to my castle. After refreshing myself, I got all my cargo on shore, and began to examine the particulars. The cask of liquor I found to be a kind of rum, but not such as we had at the Brazils; and, in a word, not at all good; but when I came to open the chests, I found several things of great use to me—for example, I found in one a fine case of bottles, of an extraordinary kind, and filled with cordial waters, fine and very good; the bottles held about three pints each, and were tipped with silver. I found two pots of very good succades, or sweetmeats, so fastened also on the top that the salt-water had not hurt them; and two more of the same, which the water had spoiled. I found some very good shirts, which were very welcome to me; and about a dozen and a half of white linen handkerchiefs and coloured neckcloths; the former were also very welcome, being exceedingly refreshing to wipe my face in a hot day. Besides this, when I came to the till in the chest, I found there three great bags of pieces of eight, which held about eleven hundred pieces in all; and in one of them, wrapped up in a paper, six doubloons of gold, and some small bars or wedges of gold; I suppose they might all weigh near a pound. In the other chest were some clothes, but of little value; but, by the circumstances, it must have belonged to the gunner's mate; though there was no powder in it, except two pounds of fine glazed powder, in three flasks, kept, I suppose, for charging their fowling-pieces on occasion. Upon the whole, I got very little by this voyage that was of any use to me; for, as to the money, I had no manner of occasion for it; it was to me as the dirt under my feet, and I would have given it all for three or four pair of English shoes and stockings, which were things I greatly wanted, but had had none on my feet for many years. I had, indeed, got two pair of shoes now, which I took off the feet of two drowned men whom I saw in the wreck, and I found two pair more in one of the chests, which were very welcome to me; but they were not like our English shoes, either for ease or service, being rather what we call pumps than shoes. I found in this seaman's chest about fifty pieces of eight, in rials, but no gold: I supposed this belonged to a poorer man than the other, which seemed to belong to some officer. Well, however, I lugged this money home to my cave, and laid it up, as I had done that before which I had brought from our own ship; but it was a great pity, as I said, that the other part of this ship had not come to my share: for I am satisfied I might have loaded my canoe several times over with money; and, thought I, if I ever escape to England, it might lie here safe enough till I come again and fetch it.

14

A DREAM REALISED

Having now brought all my things on shore and secured them, I went back to my boat, and rowed or paddled her along the shore to her old harbour, where I laid her up, and made the best of my way to my old habitation, where I found everything safe and quiet. I began now to repose myself, live after my old fashion, and take care of my family affairs; and for a while I lived easy enough, only that I was more vigilant than I used to be, looked out oftener, and did not go abroad so much; and if at any time I did stir with any freedom, it was always to the east part of the island, where I was pretty well satisfied the savages never came, and where I could go without so many precautions, and such a load of arms and ammunition as I always carried with me if I went the other way.

I lived in this condition near two years more; but my unlucky head, that was always to let me know it was born to make my body miserable, was all these two years filled with projects and designs how, if it were possible, I might get away from this island: for sometimes I was for making another voyage to the wreck, though my reason told me that there was nothing left there worth the hazard of my voyage; sometimes for a ramble one way, sometimes another—and I believe verily, if I had had the boat that I went from Sallee in, I should have ventured to sea, bound anywhere, I knew not whither.

I have been, in all my circumstances, a memento to those who are touched with the general plague of mankind, whence, for aught I know, one half of their miseries flow: I mean that of not being satisfied with the station wherein God and Nature hath placed them—for, not to look back upon my primitive condition, and the excellent advice of my father, the opposition to which was, as I may call it, my *original sin*, my subsequent mistakes of the same kind had been the means of my coming into this miserable condition; for had that Providence which so happily seated me at the Brazils as a planter blessed me with confined desires, and I could have been contented to have gone on gradually, I might have been by this time—I mean in the time of my being in this island—one of the most considerable planters in the Brazils—nay, I am persuaded, that by the improvements I had made in that little time I lived there, and the increase I should probably have made if I had remained, I might have been worth a hundred thousand moidores—and what business had I to leave a settled fortune, a well-stocked plantation, improving and increasing, to turn supercargo to Guinea to fetch negroes, when patience and time would have so increased our stock at home, that we could have bought them at our own door from those whose business it was to fetch them? and though it had cost us something more, yet the difference of that price was by no means worth saving at so great a hazard.

But as this is usually the fate of young heads, so reflection upon the folly of it is as commonly the exercise of more years, or of the dear-bought experience of time—so it was with me now; and yet so deep had the mistake taken root in my temper, that I could not satisfy myself in my station, but was continually poring upon the means and possibility of my escape from this place; and that I may, with greater pleasure to the reader, bring on the remaining part of my story, it may not be improper to give some account of my first conceptions on the subject of this foolish scheme for my escape, and how, and upon what foundation, I acted.

I am now to be supposed retired into my castle, after my late voyage to the wreck, my frigate laid up and secured under water, as usual, and my condition restored to what it was before: I had more wealth, indeed, than I had before, but was not at all the richer; for I had no more use for it than the Indians of Peru had before the Spaniards came there.

It was one of the nights in the rainy season in March, the four-and-twentieth year of my first setting foot in this island of solitude, I was lying in my bed or hammock, awake, very well in health, had no pain, no distemper, no uneasiness of body, nor any uneasiness of mind more than ordinary, but could by no means close my eyes, that is, so as to sleep; no, not a wink all night long, otherwise than as follows:

It is impossible to set down the innumerable crowd of thoughts that whirled through that great thoroughfare of the brain, the memory, in this night's time. I ran over the whole history of my life in miniature, or by abridgment, as I may call it, to my coming to this island, and also of that part of my life since I came to this island. In my reflections upon the state of my case since I came on shore on this island, I was comparing the happy posture of my affairs in the first years of my habitation here, with the life of anxiety, fear, and care which I had lived in ever since I had seen the print of a foot in the sand. Not that I did not believe the savages had frequented the island even all the while, and might have been several hundreds of them at times on shore there; but I had never known it, and was incapable of any apprehensions about it; my satisfaction was perfect, though my danger was the same, and I was as happy in not knowing my danger as if I had never really been exposed to it. This furnished my thoughts with many very profitable reflections, and particularly this one: How infinitely good that Providence is, which has provided, in its government of mankind, such narrow bounds to his sight and knowledge of things; and though he walks in the midst of so many thousand dangers, the sight of which, if discovered to him, would distract his mind and sink his spirits, he is kept serene and calm, by having the events of things hid from his eyes, and knowing nothing of the dangers which surround him.

After these thoughts had for some time entertained me, I came to reflect seriously upon the real danger I had been in for so many years in this very island, and how I had walked about in the greatest security, and with all possible tranquillity, even when perhaps nothing but the brow of a hill, a great tree, or the casual approach of night, had been between me and the worst kind of destruction—viz. that of falling into the hands of cannibals and savages, who would have seized on me with the same view as I would on a goat or turtle; and have thought it no more crime to kill and devour me than I did of a pigeon or a curlew. I would unjustly slander myself if I should say I was not sincerely thankful to my great Preserver, to whose singular protection I acknowledged, with great humanity, all these unknown deliverances were due, and without which I must inevitably have fallen into their merciless hands.

When these thoughts were over, my head was for some time taken up in considering the nature of these wretched creatures, I mean the savages, and how it came to pass in the world that the wise Governor of all things should give up any of His creatures to such inhumanity—nay, to something so much below even brutality itself—as to devour its own kind: but as this ended in some (at that time) fruitless speculations, it occurred to me to inquire what part of the world these wretches lived in? how far off the coast was from whence they came? what they ventured over so far from home for? what kind of boats they had? and why I might not order myself and my business so that I might be able to go over thither, as they were to come to me?

I never so much as troubled myself to consider what I should do with myself when I went thither; what would become of me if I fell into the hands of these savages; or how I should escape them if they attacked me; no, nor so much as how it was possible for me to reach the coast, and not to be attacked by some or other of them, without any possibility of delivering myself; and if I should not fall into their hands, what I should do for provision, or whither I should bend my course; none of these thoughts, I say, so much as came in my way; but my mind was wholly bent upon the notion of my passing over in my boat to the mainland. I looked upon my present condition as the most miserable that could possibly be; that I was not able to throw myself into anything but death, that could be called worse; and if I reached the shore of the main I might perhaps meet with relief, or I might coast along, as I did on the African shore, till I came to some inhabited country, and where I might find some relief; and after all, perhaps I might fall in with some Christian ship that might take me in: and if the worst came to the worst, I could but die, which would put an end to all these miseries at once. Pray note, all this was the fruit of a disturbed mind, an impatient temper, made desperate, as it were, by the long continuance of my troubles, and the disappointments I had met in the wreck I had been on board of, and where I had been so near obtaining what I so earnestly longed for—somebody to speak to, and to learn some knowledge from them of the place where I was, and of the probable means of my deliverance. I was agitated wholly by these thoughts; all my calm of mind, in my resignation to Providence, and waiting the issue of the dispositions of Heaven, seemed to be suspended; and I had as it were no power to turn my thoughts to anything but to the project of a voyage to the main, which came upon me with such force, and such an impetuosity of desire, that it was not to be resisted.

When this had agitated my thoughts for two hours or more, with such violence that it set my very blood into a ferment, and my pulse beat as if I had been in a fever, merely with the extraordinary fervour of my mind about it, Nature—as if I had been fatigued and exhausted with the very thoughts of it—threw me into a sound sleep. One would have thought I should have dreamed of it, but I did not, nor of anything relating to it, but I dreamed that as I was going out in the morning as usual from my castle, I saw upon the shore two canoes and eleven savages coming to land, and that they brought with them another savage whom they were going to kill in order to eat him; when, on a sudden, the savage that they were going to kill jumped away, and ran for his life; and I thought in my sleep that he came running into my little thick grove before my fortification, to hide himself; and that I seeing him alone, and not perceiving that the others sought him that way, showed myself to him, and smiling upon him, encouraged him: that he kneeled down to me, seeming to pray me to assist him; upon which I showed him my ladder, made him go up, and carried him into my cave, and he became my servant; and that as soon as I had got this man, I said to myself, "Now I may certainly venture to the mainland, for this fellow will serve me as a pilot, and will tell me what to do, and whither to go for provisions, and whither not to go for fear of being devoured; what places to venture into, and what to shun." I waked with this thought; and was under such inexpressible impressions of joy at the prospect of my escape in my dream, that the disappointments which I felt upon coming to myself, and finding that it was no more than a dream, were equally extravagant the other way, and threw me into a very great dejection of spirits.

Upon this, however, I made this conclusion: that my only way to go about to attempt an escape was, to endeavour to get a savage into my possession: and, if possible, it should be one of their prisoners, whom they had condemned to be eaten, and should bring hither to kill. But these thoughts still were attended with this difficulty: that it was impossible to effect this without attacking a whole caravan of them, and killing them all; and this was not only a very desperate attempt, and might miscarry, but, on the other hand, I had greatly scrupled the lawfulness of it to myself; and my heart trembled at the thoughts of shedding so much blood, though it was for my deliverance. I need not repeat the arguments which occurred to me against this, they being the same mentioned before; but though I had other reasons to offer now—viz. that those men were enemies to my life, and would devour me if they could; that it was self-preservation, in the highest degree, to deliver myself from this death of a life, and was acting in my own defence as much as if they were actually assaulting me, and the like; I say though these things argued for it, yet the thoughts of shedding human blood for my deliverance were very terrible to me, and such as I could by no means reconcile myself to for a great while. However, at last, after many secret disputes with myself, and after great perplexities about it (for all these arguments, one way and another, struggled in my head a long time), the eager prevailing desire of deliverance at length mastered all the rest; and I resolved, if possible, to get one of these savages into my hands, cost what it would. My next thing was to contrive how to do it, and this, indeed, was very difficult to resolve on; but as I could pitch upon no probable means for it, so I resolved to put myself upon the watch, to see them when they came on shore, and leave the rest to the event; taking such measures as the opportunity should present, let what would be.

With these resolutions in my thoughts, I set myself upon the scout as often as possible, and indeed so often that I was heartily tired of it; for it was above a year and a half that I waited; and for great part of that time went out to the west end, and to the south-west corner of the island almost every day, to look for canoes, but none appeared. This was very discouraging, and began to trouble me much, though I cannot say that it did in this case (as it had done some time before) wear off the edge of my desire to the thing; but the longer it seemed to be delayed, the more eager I was for it: in a word, I was not at first so careful to shun the sight of these savages, and avoid being seen by them, as I was now eager to be upon them. Besides, I fancied myself able to manage one, nay, two or three savages, if I had them, so as to make them entirely slaves to me, to do whatever I should direct them, and to prevent their being able at any time to do me any hurt. It was a great while that I pleased myself with this affair; but nothing still presented itself; all my fancies and schemes came to nothing, for no savages came near me for a great while.

About a year and a half after I entertained these notions (and by long musing had, as it were, resolved them all into nothing, for want of an occasion to put them into execution), I was surprised one morning by seeing no less than five canoes all on shore together on my side the island, and the people who belonged to them all landed and out of my sight. The number of them broke all my measures; for seeing so many, and knowing that they always came four or six, or sometimes more in a boat, I could not tell what to think of it, or how to take my measures to attack twenty or thirty men single-handed; so lay still in my castle, perplexed and discomforted. However, I put myself into the same position for an attack that I had formerly provided, and was just ready for action, if anything had presented. Having waited a good while, listening to hear if they made any noise, at length, being very impatient, I set my guns at the foot of my ladder, and clambered up to the top of the hill, by my two stages, as usual; standing so, however, that my head did not appear above the hill, so that they could not perceive me by any means. Here I observed, by the help of my perspective glass, that they were no less than thirty in number; that they had a fire kindled, and that they had meat dressed. How they had cooked it I knew not, or what it was; but they were all dancing, in I know not how many barbarous gestures and figures, their own way, round the fire.

While I was thus looking on them, I perceived, by my perspective, two miserable wretches dragged from the boats, where, it seems, they were laid by, and were now brought out for the slaughter. I perceived one of them immediately fall; being knocked down, I suppose, with a club or wooden sword, for that was their way; and two or three others were at work immediately, cutting him open for their cookery, while the other victim was left standing by himself, till they should be ready for him. In that very moment this poor wretch, seeing himself a little at liberty and unbound, Nature inspired him with hopes of life, and he started away from them, and ran with incredible swiftness along the sands, directly towards me; I mean towards that part of the coast where my habitation was. I was dreadfully frightened, I must acknowledge, when I perceived him run my way; and especially when, as I thought, I saw him pursued by the whole body: and now I expected that part of my dream was coming to pass, and that he would certainly take shelter in my grove; but I could not depend, by any means, upon my dream, that the other savages would not pursue him thither and find him there. However, I kept my station, and my spirits began to recover when I found that there was not above three men that followed him; and still more was I encouraged, when I found that he outstripped them exceedingly in running, and gained ground on them; so that, if he could but hold out for half-an-hour, I saw easily he would fairly get away from them all.

There was between them and my castle the creek, which I mentioned often in the first part of my story, where I landed my cargoes out of the ship; and this I saw plainly he must necessarily swim over, or the poor wretch would be taken there; but when the savage escaping came thither, he made nothing of it, though the tide was then up; but plunging in, swam through in about thirty strokes, or thereabouts, landed, and ran with exceeding strength and swiftness. When the three persons came to the creek, I found that two of them could swim, but the third could not, and that, standing on the other side, he looked at the others, but went no farther, and soon after went softly back again; which, as it happened, was very well for him in the end. I observed that the two who swam were yet more than twice as strong swimming over the creek as the fellow was that fled from them. It came very warmly upon my thoughts, and indeed irresistibly, that now was the time to get me a servant, and, perhaps, a companion or assistant; and that I was plainly called by Providence to save this poor creature's life. I immediately ran down the ladders with all possible expedition, fetched my two guns, for they were both at the foot of the ladders, as I observed before, and getting up again with the same haste to the top of the hill, I crossed towards the sea; and having a very short cut, and all down hill, placed myself in the way between the pursuers and the pursued, hallowing aloud to him that fled, who, looking back, was at first perhaps as much frightened at me as at them; but I beckoned with my hand to him to come back; and, in the meantime, I slowly advanced towards the two that followed; then rushing at once upon the foremost, I knocked him down with the stock of my piece. I was loath to fire, because I would not have the rest hear; though, at that distance, it would not have been easily heard, and being out of sight of the smoke, too, they would not have known what to make of it. Having knocked this fellow down, the other who pursued him stopped, as if he had been frightened, and I advanced towards him: but as I came nearer, I perceived presently he had a bow and arrow, and was fitting it to shoot at me: so I was then obliged to shoot at him first, which I did, and killed him at the first shot. The poor savage who fled, but had stopped, though he saw both his enemies fallen and killed, as he thought, yet was so frightened with the fire and noise of my piece that he stood stock still, and neither came forward nor went backward, though he seemed rather inclined still to fly than to come on. I hallooed again to him, and made signs to come forward, which he easily understood, and came a little way; then stopped again, and then a little farther, and stopped again; and I could then perceive that he stood trembling, as if he had been taken prisoner, and had just been to be killed, as his two enemies were. I beckoned to him again to come to me, and gave him all the signs of encouragement that I could think of; and he came nearer and nearer, kneeling down every ten or twelve steps, in token of acknowledgment for saving his life. I smiled at him, and looked pleasantly, and beckoned to him to come still nearer; at length he came close to me; and then he kneeled down again, kissed the ground, and laid his head upon the ground, and taking me by the foot, set my foot upon his head; this, it seems, was in token of swearing to be my slave for ever. I took him up and made much of him, and encouraged him all I could. But there was more work to do yet; for I perceived the savage whom I had knocked down was not killed, but stunned with the blow, and began to come to himself: so I pointed to him, and showed him the savage, that he was not dead; upon this he spoke some words to me, and though I could not understand them, yet I thought they were pleasant to hear; for they were the first sound of a man's voice that I had heard, my own excepted, for above twenty-five years. But there was no time for such reflections now; the savage who was knocked down recovered himself so far as to sit up upon the ground, and I perceived that my savage began to be afraid; but when I saw that, I presented my other piece at the man, as if I would shoot him: upon this my savage, for so I call him now, made a motion to me to lend him my sword, which hung naked in a belt by my side, which I did. He no sooner had it, but he runs to his enemy, and at one blow cut off his head so cleverly, no executioner in Germany could have done it sooner or better; which I thought very strange for one who, I had reason to believe, never saw a sword in his life before, except their own wooden swords: however, it seems, as I learned afterwards, they make their wooden swords so sharp, so heavy, and the wood is so hard, that they will even cut off heads with them, ay, and arms, and that at one blow, too. When he had done this, he comes laughing to me in sign of triumph, and brought me the sword again, and with abundance of gestures which I did not understand, laid it down, with the head of the savage that he had killed, just before me. But that which astonished him most was to know how I killed the other Indian so far off; so, pointing to him, he made signs to me to let him go to him; and I bade him go, as well as I could. When he came to him, he stood like one amazed, looking at him, turning him first on one side, then on the other; looked at the wound the bullet had made, which it seems was just in his breast, where it had made a hole, and no great quantity of blood had followed; but he had bled inwardly, for he was quite dead. He took up his bow and arrows, and came back; so I turned to go away, and beckoned him to follow me, making signs to him that more might come after them. Upon this he made signs to me that he should bury them with sand, that they might not be seen by the rest, if they followed; and so I made signs to him again to do so. He fell to work; and in an instant he had scraped a hole in the sand with his hands big enough to bury the first in, and then dragged him into it, and covered him; and did so by the other also; I believe he had him buried them both in a quarter of an hour. Then, calling away, I carried him, not to my castle, but quite away to my cave, on the farther part of the island: so I did not let my dream come to pass in that part, that he came into my grove for shelter. Here I gave him bread and a bunch of raisins to eat, and a draught of water, which I found he was indeed in great distress for, from his running: and having refreshed him, I made signs for him to go and lie down to sleep, showing him a place where I had laid some rice-straw, and a blanket upon it, which I used to sleep upon myself sometimes; so the poor creature lay down, and went to sleep.

He was a comely, handsome fellow, perfectly well made, with straight, strong limbs, not too large; tall, and well-shaped; and, as I reckon, about twenty-six years of age. He had a very good countenance, not a fierce and surly aspect, but seemed to have something very manly in his face; and yet he had all the sweetness and softness of a European in his countenance, too, especially when he smiled. His hair was long and black, not curled like wool; his forehead very high and large; and a great vivacity and sparkling sharpness in his eyes. The colour of his skin was not quite black, but very tawny; and yet not an ugly, yellow, nauseous tawny, as the Brazilians and Virginians, and other natives of America are, but of a bright kind of a dun olive-colour, that had in it something very agreeable, though not very easy to describe. His face was round and plump; his nose small, not flat, like the negroes; a very good mouth, thin lips, and his fine teeth well set, and as white as ivory.

After he had slumbered, rather than slept, about half-an-hour, he awoke again, and came out of the cave to me, for I had been milking my goats which I had in the enclosure just by: when he espied me he came running to me, laying himself down again upon the ground, with all the possible signs of an humble, thankful disposition, making a great many antic gestures to show it. At last he lays his head flat upon the ground, close to my foot, and sets my other foot upon his head, as he had done before; and after this made all the signs to me of subjection, servitude, and submission imaginable, to let me know how he would serve me so long as he lived. I understood him in many things, and let him know I was very well pleased with him. In a little time I began to speak to him; and teach him to speak to me; and first, I let him know his name should be Friday, which was the day I saved his life; I called him so for the memory of the time. I likewise taught him to say Master; and then let him know that was to be my name; I likewise taught him to say Yes and No and to know the meaning of them. I gave him some milk in an earthen pot, and let him see me drink it before him, and sop my bread in it; and gave him a cake of bread to do the like, which he quickly complied with, and made signs that it was very good for him. I kept there with him all that night; but as soon as it was day I beckoned to him to come with me, and let him know I would give him some clothes; at which he seemed very glad, for he was stark naked. As we went by the place where he had buried the two men, he pointed exactly to the place, and showed me the marks that he had made to find them again, making signs to me that we should dig them up again and eat them. At this I appeared very angry, expressed my abhorrence of it, made as if I would vomit at the thoughts of it, and beckoned with my hand to him to come away, which he did immediately, with great submission. I then led him up to the top of the hill, to see if his enemies were gone; and pulling out my glass I looked, and saw plainly the place where they had been, but no appearance of them or their canoes; so that it was plain they were gone, and had left their two comrades behind them, without any search after them.

But I was not content with this discovery; but having now more courage, and consequently more curiosity, I took my man Friday with me, giving him the sword in his hand, with the bow and arrows at his back, which I found he could use very dexterously, making him carry one gun for me, and I two for myself; and away we marched to the place where these creatures had been; for I had a mind now to get some further intelligence of them. When I came to the place my very blood ran chill in my veins, and my heart sunk within me, at the horror of the spectacle; indeed, it was a dreadful sight, at least it was so to me, though Friday made nothing of it. The place was covered with human bones, the ground dyed with their blood, and great pieces of flesh left here and there, half-eaten, mangled, and scorched; and, in short, all the tokens of the triumphant feast they had been making there, after a victory over their enemies. I saw three skulls, five hands, and the bones of three or four legs and feet, and abundance of other parts of the bodies; and Friday, by his signs, made me understand that they brought over four prisoners to feast upon; that three of them were eaten up, and that he, pointing to himself, was the fourth; that there had been a great battle between them and their next king, of whose subjects, it seems, he had been one, and that they had taken a great number of prisoners; all which were carried to several places by those who had taken them in the fight, in order to feast upon them, as was done here by these wretches upon those they brought hither.

I caused Friday to gather all the skulls, bones, flesh, and whatever remained, and lay them together in a heap, and make a great fire upon it, and burn them all to ashes. I found Friday had still a hankering stomach after some of the flesh, and was still a cannibal in his nature; but I showed so much abhorrence at the very thoughts of it, and at the least appearance of it, that he durst not discover it: for I had, by some means, let him know that I would kill him if he offered it.

When he had done this, we came back to our castle; and there I fell to work for my man Friday; and first of all, I gave him a pair of linen drawers, which I had out of the poor gunner's chest I mentioned, which I found in the wreck, and which, with a little alteration, fitted him very well; and then I made him a jerkin of goat's skin, as well as my skill would allow (for I was now grown a tolerably good tailor); and I gave him a cap which I made of hare's skin, very convenient, and fashionable enough; and thus he was clothed, for the present, tolerably well, and was mighty well pleased to see himself almost as well clothed as his master. It is true he went awkwardly in these clothes at first: wearing the drawers was very awkward to him, and the sleeves of the waistcoat galled his shoulders and the inside of his arms; but a little easing them where he complained they hurt him, and using himself to them, he took to them at length very well.

The next day, after I came home to my hutch with him, I began to consider where I should lodge him: and that I might do well for him and yet be perfectly easy myself, I made a little tent for him in the vacant place between my two fortifications, in the inside of the last, and in the outside of the first. As there was a door or entrance there into my cave, I made a formal framed door-case, and a door to it, of boards, and set it up in the passage, a little within the entrance; and, causing the door to open in the inside, I barred it up in the night, taking in my ladders, too; so that Friday could no way come at me in the inside of my innermost wall, without making so much noise in getting over that it must needs awaken me; for my first wall had now a complete roof over it of long poles, covering all my tent, and leaning up to the side of the hill; which was again laid across with smaller sticks, instead of laths, and then thatched over a great thickness with the rice-straw, which was strong, like reeds; and at the hole or place which was left to go in or out by the ladder I had placed a kind of trap-door, which, if it had been attempted on the outside, would not have opened at all, but would have fallen down and made a great noise—as to weapons, I took them all into my side every night. But I needed none of all this precaution; for never man had a more faithful, loving, sincere servant than Friday was to me: without passions, sullenness, or designs, perfectly obliged and engaged; his very affections were tied to me, like those of a child to a father; and

I daresay he would have sacrificed his life to save mine upon any occasion whatsoever—the many testimonies he gave me of this put it out of doubt, and soon convinced me that I needed to use no precautions for my safety on his account.

This frequently gave me occasion to observe, and that with wonder, that however it had pleased God in His providence, and in the government of the works of His hands, to take from so great a part of the world of His creatures the best uses to which their faculties and the powers of their souls are adapted, yet that He has bestowed upon them the same powers, the same reason, the same affections, the same sentiments of kindness and obligation, the same passions and resentments of wrongs, the same sense of gratitude, sincerity, fidelity, and all the capacities of doing good and receiving good that He has given to us; and that when He pleases to offer them occasions of exerting these, they are as ready, nay, more ready, to apply them to the right uses for which they were bestowed than we are. This made me very melancholy sometimes, in reflecting, as the several occasions presented, how mean a use we make of all these, even though we have these powers enlightened by the great lamp of instruction, the Spirit of God, and by the knowledge of His word added to our understanding; and why it has pleased God to hide the like saving knowledge from so many millions of souls, who, if I might judge by this poor savage, would make a much better use of it than we did. From hence I sometimes was led too far, to invade the sovereignty of Providence, and, as it were, arraign the justice of so arbitrary a disposition of things, that should hide that sight from some, and reveal it to others, and yet expect a like duty from both; but I shut it up, and checked my thoughts with this conclusion: first, that we did not know by what light and law these should be condemned; but that as God was necessarily, and by the nature of His being, infinitely holy and just, so it could not be, but if these creatures were all sentenced to absence from Himself, it was on account of sinning against that light which, as the Scripture says, was a law to themselves, and by such rules as their consciences would acknowledge to be just, though the foundation was not discovered to us; and secondly, that still as we all are the clay in the hand of the potter, no vessel could say to him, "Why hast thou formed me thus?"

But to return to my new companion. I was greatly delighted with him, and made it my business to teach him everything that was proper to make him useful, handy, and helpful; but especially to make him speak, and understand me when I spoke; and he was the aptest scholar that ever was; and particularly was so merry, so constantly diligent, and so pleased when he could but understand me, or make me understand him, that it was very pleasant for me to talk to him. Now my life began to be so easy that I began to say to myself that could I but have been safe from more savages, I cared not if I was never to remove from the place where I lived.

15

FRIDAY'S EDUCATION

After I had been two or three days returned to my castle, I thought that, in order to bring Friday off from his horrid way of feeding, and from the relish of a cannibal's stomach, I ought to let him taste other flesh; so I took him out with me one morning to the woods. I went, indeed, intending to kill a kid out of my own flock; and bring it home and dress it; but as I was going I saw a she-goat lying down in the shade, and two young kids sitting by her. I catched hold of Friday. "Hold," said I, "stand still;" and made signs to him not to stir: immediately I presented my piece, shot, and killed one of the kids. The poor creature, who had at a distance, indeed, seen me kill the savage, his enemy, but did not know, nor could imagine how it was done, was sensibly surprised, trembled, and shook, and looked so amazed that I thought he would have sunk down. He did not see the kid I shot at, or perceive I had killed it, but ripped up his waistcoat to feel whether he was not wounded; and, as I found presently, thought I was resolved to kill him: for he came and kneeled down to me, and embracing my knees, said a great many things I did not understand; but I could easily see the meaning was to pray me not to kill him.

I soon found a way to convince him that I would do him no harm; and taking him up by the hand, laughed at him, and pointing to the kid which I had killed, beckoned to him to run and fetch it, which he did: and while he was wondering, and looking to see how the creature was killed, I loaded my gun again. By-and-by I saw a great fowl, like a hawk, sitting upon a tree within shot; so, to let Friday understand a little what I would do, I called him to me again, pointed at the fowl, which was indeed a parrot, though I thought it had been a hawk; I say, pointing to the parrot, and to my gun, and to the ground under the parrot, to let him see I would make it fall, I made him understand that I would shoot and kill that bird; accordingly, I fired, and bade him look, and immediately he saw the parrot fall. He stood like one frightened again, notwithstanding all I had said to him; and I found he was the more amazed, because he did not see me put anything into the gun, but thought that there must be some wonderful fund of death and destruction in that thing, able to kill man, beast, bird, or anything near or far off; and the astonishment this created in him was such as could not wear off for a long time; and I believe, if I would have let him, he would have worshipped me and my gun. As for the gun itself, he would not so much as touch it for several days after; but he would speak to it and talk to it, as if it had answered him, when he was by himself; which, as I afterwards learned of him, was to desire it not to kill him. Well, after his astonishment was a little over at this, I pointed to him to run and fetch the bird I had shot, which he did, but stayed some time; for the parrot, not being quite dead, had fluttered away a good distance from the place where she fell: however, he found her, took her up, and brought her to me; and as I had perceived his ignorance about the gun before, I took this advantage to charge the gun again, and not to let him see me do it, that I might be ready for any other mark that might present; but nothing more offered at that time: so I brought home the kid, and the same evening I took the skin off, and cut it out as well as I could; and having a pot fit for that purpose, I boiled or stewed some of the flesh, and made some very good broth. After I had begun to eat some I gave some to my man, who seemed very glad of it, and liked it very well; but that which was strangest to him was to see me eat salt with it. He made a sign to me that the salt was not good to eat; and putting a little into his own mouth, he seemed to nauseate it, and would spit and sputter at it, washing his mouth with fresh water after it: on the other hand, I took some meat into my mouth without salt, and I pretended to spit and sputter for want of salt, as much as he had done at the salt; but it would not do; he would never care for salt with meat or in his broth; at least, not for a great while, and then but a very little.

Having thus fed him with boiled meat and broth, I was resolved to feast him the next day by roasting a piece of the kid: this I did by hanging it before the fire on a string, as I had seen many people do in England, setting two poles up, one on each side of the fire, and one across the top, and tying the string to the cross stick, letting the meat turn continually. This Friday admired very much; but when he came to taste the flesh, he took so many ways to tell me how well he liked it, that I could not but understand him: and at last he told me, as well as he could, he would never eat man's flesh any more, which I was very glad to hear.

The next day I set him to work beating some corn out, and sifting it in the manner I used to do, as I observed before; and he soon understood how to do it as well as I, especially after he had seen what the meaning of it was, and that it was to make bread of; for after that I let him see me make my bread, and bake it too; and in a little time Friday was able to do all the work for me as well as I could do it myself.

I began now to consider, that having two mouths to feed instead of one, I must provide more ground for my harvest, and plant a larger quantity of corn than I used to do; so I marked out a larger piece of land, and began the fence in the same manner as before, in which Friday worked not only very willingly and very hard, but did it very cheerfully: and I told him what it was for; that it was for corn to make more bread, because he was now with me, and that I might have enough for him and myself too. He appeared very sensible of that part, and let me know that he thought I had much more labour upon me on his account than I had for myself; and that he would work the harder for me if I would tell him what to do.

This was the pleasantest year of all the life I led in this place. Friday began to talk pretty well, and understand the names of almost everything I had occasion to call for, and of every place I had to send him to, and talked a great deal to me; so that, in short, I began now to have some use for my tongue again, which, indeed, I had very little occasion for before. Besides the pleasure of talking to him, I had a singular satisfaction in the fellow himself: his simple, unfeigned honesty appeared to me more and more every day, and I began really to love the creature; and on his side I believe he loved me more than it was possible for him ever to love anything before.

I had a mind once to try if he had any inclination for his own country again; and having taught him English so well that he could answer me almost any question, I asked him whether the nation that he belonged to never conquered in battle? At which he smiled, and said—"Yes, yes, we always fight the better;" that is, he meant always get the better in fight; and so we began the following discourse:—

Master.—You always fight the better; how came you to be taken prisoner, then, Friday?

Friday.—My nation beat much for all that.

Master.—How beat? If your nation beat them, how came you to be taken?

Friday.—They more many than my nation, in the place where me was; they take one, two, three, and me: my nation over-beat them in the yonder place, where me no was; there my nation take one, two, great thousand.

Master.—But why did not your side recover you from the hands of your enemies, then?

Friday.—They run, one, two, three, and me, and make go in the canoe; my nation have no canoe that time.

Master.—Well, Friday, and what does your nation do with the men they take? Do they carry them away and eat them, as these did?

Friday.—Yes, my nation eat mans too; eat all up.

Master.—Where do they carry them?

Friday.—Go to other place, where they think.

Master.—Do they come hither?

Friday.—Yes, yes, they come hither; come other else place.

Master.—Have you been here with them?

Friday.—Yes, I have been here (points to the NW. side of the island, which, it seems, was their side).

By this I understood that my man Friday had formerly been among the savages who used to come on shore on the farther part of the island, on the same man-eating occasions he was now brought for; and some time after, when I took the courage to carry him to that side, being the same I formerly mentioned, he presently knew the place, and told me he was there once, when they ate up twenty men, two women, and one child; he could not tell twenty in English, but he numbered them by laying so many stones in a row, and pointing to me to tell them over.

I have told this passage, because it introduces what follows: that after this discourse I had with him, I asked him how far it was from our island to the shore, and whether the canoes were not often lost. He told me there was no danger, no canoes ever lost: but that after a little way out to sea, there was a current and wind, always one way in the morning, the other in the afternoon. This I understood to be no more than the sets of the tide, as going out or coming in; but I afterwards understood it was occasioned by the great draft and reflux of the mighty river Orinoco, in the mouth or gulf of which river, as I found afterwards, our island lay; and that this land, which I perceived to be W. and NW., was the great island Trinidad, on the north point of the mouth of the river. I asked Friday a thousand questions about the country, the inhabitants, the sea, the coast, and what nations were near; he told me all he knew with the greatest openness imaginable. I asked him the names of the several nations of his sort of people, but could get no other name than Caribs; from whence I easily understood that these were the Caribbees, which our maps place on the part of America which reaches from the mouth of the river Orinoco to Guiana, and onwards to St. Martha. He told me that up a great way beyond the moon, that was beyond the setting of the moon, which must be west from their country, there dwelt white bearded men, like me, and pointed to my great whiskers, which I mentioned before; and that they had killed much mans, that was his word: by all which I understood he meant the Spaniards, whose cruelties in America had been spread over the whole country, and were remembered by all the nations from father to son.

I inquired if he could tell me how I might go from this island, and get among those white men. He told me, "Yes, yes, you may go in two canoe." I could not understand what he meant, or make him describe to me what he meant by two canoe, till at last, with great difficulty, I found he meant it must be in a large boat, as big as two canoes. This part of Friday's discourse I began to relish very well; and from this time I entertained some hopes that, one time or other, I might find an opportunity to make my escape from this place, and that this poor savage might be a means to help me.

During the long time that Friday had now been with me, and that he began to speak to me, and understand me, I was not wanting to lay a foundation of religious knowledge in his mind; particularly I asked him one time, who made him. The creature did not understand me at all, but thought I had asked who was his father—but I took it up by another handle, and asked him who made the sea, the ground we walked on, and the hills and woods. He told me, "It was one Benamuckee, that lived beyond all;" he could describe nothing of this great person, but that he was very old, "much older," he said, "than the sea or land, than the moon or the stars." I asked him then, if this old person had made all things, why did not all things worship him? He looked very grave, and, with a perfect look of innocence, said, "All things say O to him." I asked him if the people who die in his country went away anywhere? He said, "Yes; they all went to Benamuckee." Then I asked him whether those they eat up went thither too. He said, "Yes."

From these things, I began to instruct him in the knowledge of the true God; I told him that the great Maker of all things lived up there, pointing up towards heaven; that He governed the world by the same power and providence by which He made it; that He was omnipotent, and could do everything for us, give everything to us, take everything from us; and thus, by degrees, I opened his eyes. He listened with great attention, and received with pleasure the notion of Jesus Christ being sent to redeem us; and of the manner of making our prayers to God, and His being able to hear us, even in heaven. He told me one day, that if our God could hear us, up beyond the sun, he must needs be a greater God than their Benamuckee, who lived but a little way off, and yet could not hear till they went up to the great mountains where he dwelt to speak to them. I asked him if ever he went thither to speak to him. He said, "No; they never went that were young men; none went thither but the old men," whom he called their Oowokakee; that is, as I made him explain to me, their religious, or clergy; and that they went to say O (so he called saying prayers), and then came back and told them what Benamuckee said. By this I observed, that there is priestcraft even among the most blinded, ignorant pagans in the world; and the policy of making a secret of religion, in order to preserve the veneration of the people to the clergy, not only to be found in the Roman, but, perhaps, among all religions in the world, even among the most brutish and barbarous savages.

I endeavoured to clear up this fraud to my man Friday; and told him that the pretence of their old men going up to the mountains to say O to their god Benamuckee was a cheat; and their bringing word from thence what he said was much more so; that if they met with any answer, or spake with any one there, it must be with an evil spirit; and then I entered into a long discourse with him about the devil, the origin of him, his rebellion against God, his enmity to man, the reason of it, his setting himself up in the dark parts of the world to be worshipped instead of God, and as God, and the many stratagems he made use of to delude mankind to their ruin; how he had a secret access to our passions and to our affections, and to adapt his snares to our inclinations, so as to cause us even to be our own tempters, and run upon our destruction by our own choice.

I found it was not so easy to imprint right notions in his mind about the devil as it was about the being of a God. Nature assisted all my arguments to evidence to him even the necessity of a great First Cause, an overruling, governing Power, a secret directing Providence, and of the equity and justice of paying homage to Him that made us, and the like; but there appeared nothing of this kind in the notion of an evil spirit, of his origin, his being, his nature, and above all, of his inclination to do evil, and to draw us in to do so too; and the poor creature puzzled me once in such a manner, by a question merely natural and innocent, that I scarce knew what to say to him. I had been talking a great deal to him of the power of God, His omnipotence, His aversion to sin, His being a consuming fire to the workers of iniquity; how, as He had made us all, He could destroy us and all the world in a moment; and he listened with great seriousness to me all the while. After this I had been telling him how the devil was God's enemy in the hearts of men, and used all his malice and skill to defeat the good designs of Providence, and to ruin the kingdom of Christ in the world, and the like. "Well," says Friday, "but you say God is so strong, so great; is He not much strong, much might as the devil?" "Yes, yes," says I, "Friday; God is stronger than the devil—God is above the devil, and therefore we pray to God to tread him down under our feet, and enable us to resist his temptations and quench his fiery darts." "But," says he again, "if God much stronger, much might as the wicked devil, why God no kill the devil, so make him no more do wicked?" I was strangely surprised at this question; and, after all, though I was now an old man, yet I was but a young doctor, and ill qualified for a casuist or a solver of difficulties; and at first I could not tell what to say; so I pretended not to hear him, and asked him what he said; but he was too earnest for an answer to forget his question, so that he repeated it in the very same broken words as above. By this time I had recovered myself a little, and I said, "God will at last punish him severely; he is reserved for the judgment, and is to be cast into the bottomless pit, to dwell with everlasting fire." This did not satisfy Friday; but he returns upon me, repeating my words, "'*Reserve at last!*' me no understand—but why not kill the devil now; not kill great ago?" "You may as well ask me," said I, "why God does not kill you or me, when we do wicked things here that offend Him—we are preserved to repent and be pardoned." He mused some time on this. "Well, well," says he, mighty affectionately, "that well—so you, I, devil, all wicked, all preserve, repent, God pardon all." Here I was run down again by him to the last degree; and it was a testimony to me, how the mere notions of nature, though they will guide reasonable creatures to the knowledge of a God, and of a worship or homage due to the supreme being of God, as the consequence of our nature, yet nothing but divine revelation can form the knowledge of Jesus Christ, and of redemption purchased for us; of a Mediator of the new covenant, and of an Intercessor at the footstool of God's throne; I say, nothing but a revelation from Heaven can form these in the soul; and that, therefore, the gospel of our Lord and Saviour Jesus Christ, I mean the Word of God, and the Spirit of God, promised for the guide and sanctifier of His people, are the absolutely necessary instructors of the souls of men in the saving knowledge of God and the means of salvation.

I therefore diverted the present discourse between me and my man, rising up hastily, as upon some sudden occasion of going out; then sending him for something a good way off, I seriously prayed to God that He would enable me to instruct savingly this poor savage; assisting, by His Spirit, the heart of the poor ignorant creature to receive the light of the knowledge of God in Christ, reconciling him to Himself, and would guide me so to speak to him from the Word of God that his conscience might be convinced, his eyes opened, and his soul saved. When he came again to me, I entered into a long discourse with him upon the subject of the redemption of man by the Saviour of the world, and of the doctrine of the gospel preached from Heaven, viz. of repentance towards God, and faith in our blessed Lord Jesus. I then explained to him as well as I could why our blessed Redeemer took not on Him the nature of angels but the seed of Abraham; and how, for that reason, the fallen angels had no share in the redemption; that He came only to the lost sheep of the house of Israel, and the like.

I had, God knows, more sincerity than knowledge in all the methods I took for this poor creature's instruction, and must acknowledge, what I believe all that act upon the same principle will find, that in laying things open to him, I really informed and instructed myself in many things that either I did not know or had not fully considered before, but which occurred naturally to my mind upon searching into them, for the information of this poor savage; and I had more affection in my inquiry after things upon this occasion than ever I felt before: so that, whether this poor wild wretch was better for me or no, I had great reason to be thankful that ever he came to me; my grief sat lighter, upon me; my habitation grew comfortable to me beyond measure: and when I reflected that in this solitary life which I have been confined to, I had not only been moved to look up to heaven myself, and to seek the Hand that had brought me here, but was now to be made an instrument, under Providence, to save the life, and, for aught I knew, the soul of a poor savage, and bring him to the true knowledge of religion and of the Christian doctrine, that he might know Christ Jesus, in whom is life eternal; I say, when I reflected upon all these things, a secret joy ran through every part of My soul, and I frequently rejoiced that ever I was brought to this place, which I had so often thought the most dreadful of all afflictions that could possibly have befallen me.

I continued in this thankful frame all the remainder of my time; and the conversation which employed the hours between Friday and me was such as made the three years which we lived there together perfectly and completely happy, if any such thing as complete happiness can be formed in a sublunary state. This savage was now a good Christian, a much better than I; though I have reason to hope, and bless God for it, that we were equally penitent, and comforted, restored penitents. We had here the Word of God to read, and no farther off from His Spirit to instruct than if we had been in England. I always applied myself, in reading the Scripture, to let him know, as well as I could, the meaning of what I read; and he again, by his serious inquiries and questionings, made me, as I said before, a much better scholar in the Scripture knowledge than I should ever have been by my own mere private reading. Another thing I cannot refrain from observing here also, from experience in this retired part of my life, viz. how infinite and inexpressible a blessing it is that the knowledge of God, and of the doctrine of salvation by Christ Jesus, is so plainly laid down in the Word of God, so easy to be received and understood, that, as the bare reading the Scripture made me capable of understanding enough of my duty to carry me directly on to the great work of sincere repentance for my sins, and laying hold of a Saviour for life and salvation, to a stated reformation in practice, and obedience to all God's commands, and this without any teacher or instructor, I mean human; so the same plain instruction sufficiently served to the enlightening this savage creature, and bringing him to be such a Christian as I have known few equal to him in my life.

As to all the disputes, wrangling, strife, and contention which have happened in the world about religion, whether niceties in doctrines or schemes of church government, they were all perfectly useless to us, and, for aught I can yet see, they have been so to the rest of the world. We had the sure guide to heaven, viz. the Word of God; and we had, blessed be God, comfortable views of the Spirit of God teaching and instructing by His word, leading us into all truth, and making us both willing and obedient to the instruction of His word. And I cannot see the least use that the greatest knowledge of the disputed points of religion, which have made such confusion in the world, would have been to us, if we could have obtained it. But I must go on with the historical part of things, and take every part in its order.

After Friday and I became more intimately acquainted, and that he could understand almost all I said to him, and speak pretty fluently, though in broken English, to me, I acquainted him with my own history, or at least so much of it as related to my coming to this place: how I had lived there, and how long; I let him into the mystery, for such it was to him, of gunpowder and bullet, and taught him how to shoot. I gave him a knife, which he was wonderfully delighted with; and I made him a belt, with a frog hanging to it, such as in England we wear hangers in; and in the frog, instead of a hanger, I gave him a hatchet, which was not only as good a weapon in some cases, but much more useful upon other occasions.

I described to him the country of Europe, particularly England, which I came from; how we lived, how we worshipped God, how we behaved to one another, and how we traded in ships to all parts of the world. I gave him an account of the wreck which I had been on board of, and showed him, as near as I could, the place where she lay; but she was all beaten in pieces before, and gone. I showed him the ruins of our boat, which we lost when we escaped, and which I could not stir with my whole strength then; but was now fallen almost all to pieces. Upon seeing this boat, Friday stood, musing a great while, and said nothing. I asked him what it was he studied upon. At last says he, "Me see such boat like come to place at my nation." I did not understand him a good while; but at last, when I had examined further into it, I understood by him that a boat, such as that had been, came on shore upon the country where he lived: that is, as he explained it, was driven thither by stress of weather. I presently imagined that some European ship must have been cast away upon their coast, and the boat might get loose and drive ashore; but was so dull that I never once thought of men making their escape from a wreck thither, much less whence they might come: so I only inquired after a description of the boat.

Friday described the boat to me well enough; but brought me better to understand him when he added with some warmth, "We save the white mans from drown." Then I presently asked if there were any white mans, as he called them, in the boat. "Yes," he said; "the boat full of white mans." I asked him how many. He told upon his fingers seventeen. I asked him then what became of them. He told me, "They live, they dwell at my nation."

This put new thoughts into my head; for I presently imagined that these might be the men belonging to the ship that was cast away in the sight of my island, as I now called it; and who, after the ship was struck on the rock, and they saw her inevitably lost, had saved themselves in their boat, and were landed upon that wild shore among the savages. Upon this I inquired of him more critically what was become of them. He assured me they lived still there; that they had been there about four years; that the savages left them alone, and gave them victuals to live on. I asked him how it came to pass they did not kill them and eat them. He said, "No, they make brother with them;" that is, as I understood him, a truce; and then he added, "They no eat mans but when make the war fight;" that is to say, they never eat any men but such as come to fight with them and are taken in battle.

It was after this some considerable time, that being upon the top of the hill at the east side of the island, from whence, as I have said, I had, in a clear day, discovered the main or continent of America, Friday, the weather being very serene, looks very earnestly towards the mainland, and, in a kind of surprise, falls a jumping and dancing, and calls out to me, for I was at some distance from him. I asked him what was the matter. "Oh, joy!" says he; "Oh, glad! there see my country, there my nation!" I observed an extraordinary sense of pleasure appeared in his face, and his eyes sparkled, and his countenance discovered a strange eagerness, as if he had a mind to be in his own country again. This observation of mine put a great many thoughts into me, which made me at first not so easy about my new man Friday as I was before; and I made no doubt but that, if Friday could get back to his own nation again, he would not only forget all his religion but all his obligation to me, and would be forward enough to give his countrymen an account of me, and come back, perhaps with a hundred or two of them, and make a feast upon me, at which he might be as merry as he used to be with those of his enemies when they were taken in war. But I wronged the poor honest creature very much, for which I was very sorry afterwards. However, as my jealousy increased, and held some weeks, I was a little more circumspect, and not so familiar and kind to him as before: in which I was certainly wrong too; the honest, grateful creature having no thought about it but what consisted with the best principles, both as a religious Christian and as a grateful friend, as appeared afterwards to my full satisfaction.

While my jealousy of him lasted, you may be sure I was every day pumping him to see if he would discover any of the new thoughts which I suspected were in him; but I found everything he said was so honest and so innocent, that I could find nothing to nourish my suspicion; and in spite of all my uneasiness, he made me at last entirely his own again; nor did he in the least perceive that I was uneasy, and therefore I could not suspect him of deceit.

One day, walking up the same hill, but the weather being hazy at sea, so that we could not see the continent, I called to him, and said, "Friday, do not you wish yourself in your own country, your own nation?" "Yes," he said, "I be much O glad to be at my own nation." "What would you do there?" said I. "Would you turn wild again, eat men's flesh again, and be a savage as you were before?" He looked full of concern, and shaking his head, said, "No, no, Friday tell them to live good; tell them to pray God; tell them to eat corn-bread, cattle flesh, milk; no eat man again." "Why, then," said I to him, "they will kill you." He looked grave at that, and then said, "No, no, they no kill me, they willing love learn." He meant by this, they would be willing to learn. He added, they learned much of the bearded mans that came in the boat. Then I asked him if he would go back to them. He smiled at that, and told me that he could not swim so far. I told him I would make a canoe for him. He told me he would go if I would go with him. "I go!" says I; "why, they will eat me if I come there." "No, no," says he, "me make they no eat you; me make they much love you." He meant, he would tell them how I had killed his enemies, and saved his life, and so he would make them love me. Then he told me, as well as he could, how kind they were to seventeen white men, or bearded men, as he called them who came on shore there in distress.

From this time, I confess, I had a mind to venture over, and see if I could possibly join with those bearded men, who I made no doubt were Spaniards and Portuguese; not doubting but, if I could, we might find some method to escape from thence, being upon the continent, and a good company together, better than I could from an island forty miles off the shore, alone and without help. So, after some days, I took Friday to work again by way of discourse, and told him I would give him a boat to go back to his own nation; and, accordingly, I carried him to my frigate, which lay on the other side of the island, and having cleared it of water (for I always kept it sunk in water), I brought it out, showed it him, and we both went into it. I found he was a most dexterous fellow at managing it, and would make it go almost as swift again as I could. So when he was in, I said to him, "Well, now, Friday, shall we go to your nation?" He looked very dull at my saying so; which it seems was because he thought the boat was too small to go so far. I then told him I had a bigger; so the next day I went to the place where the first boat lay which I had made, but which I could not get into the water. He said that was big enough; but then, as I had taken no care of it, and it had lain two or three and twenty years there, the sun had so split and dried it, that it was rotten. Friday told me such a boat would do very well, and would carry "much enough vittle, drink, bread;" this was his way of talking.

16

RESCUE OF PRISONERS FROM CANNIBALS

Upon the whole, I was by this time so fixed upon my design of going over with him to the continent that I told him we would go and make one as big as that, and he should go home in it. He answered not one word, but looked very grave and sad. I asked him what was the matter with him. He asked me again, "Why you angry mad with Friday?—what me done?" I asked him what he meant. I told him I was not angry with him at all. "No angry!" says he, repeating the words several times; "why send Friday home away to my nation?" "Why," says I, "Friday, did not you say you wished you were there?" "Yes, yes," says he, "wish we both there; no wish Friday there, no master there." In a word, he would not think of going there without me. "I go there, Friday?" says I; "what shall I do there?" He turned very quick upon me at this. "You do great deal much good," says he; "you teach wild mans be good, sober, tame mans; you tell them know God, pray God, and live new life." "Alas, Friday!" says I, "thou knowest not what thou sayest; I am but an ignorant man myself." "Yes, yes," says he, "you teachee me good, you teachee them good." "No, no, Friday," says I, "you shall go without me; leave me here to live by myself, as I did before." He looked confused again at that word; and running to one of the hatchets which he used to wear, he takes it up hastily, and gives it to me. "What must I do with this?" says I to him. "You take kill Friday," says he. "What must kill you for?" said I again. He returns very quick—"What you send Friday away for? Take kill Friday, no send Friday away." This he spoke so earnestly that I saw tears stand in his eyes. In a word, I so plainly discovered the utmost affection in him to me, and a firm resolution in him, that I told him then and often after, that I would never send him away from me if he was willing to stay with me.

Upon the whole, as I found by all his discourse a settled affection to me, and that nothing could part him from me, so I found all the foundation of his desire to go to his own country was laid in his ardent affection to the people, and his hopes of my doing them good; a thing which, as I had no notion of myself, so I had not the least thought or intention, or desire of undertaking it. But still I found a strong inclination to attempting my escape, founded on the supposition gathered from the discourse, that there were seventeen bearded men there; and therefore, without any more delay, I went to work with Friday to find out a great tree proper to fell, and make a large periagua, or canoe, to undertake the voyage. There were trees enough in the island to have built a little fleet, not of periaguas or canoes, but even of good, large vessels; but the main thing I looked at was, to get one so near the water that we might launch it when it was made, to avoid the mistake I committed at first. At last Friday pitched upon a tree; for I found he knew much better than I what kind of wood was fittest for it; nor can I tell to this day what wood to call the tree we cut down, except that it was very like the tree we call fustic, or between that and the Nicaragua wood, for it was much of the same colour and smell. Friday wished to burn the hollow or cavity of this tree out, to make it for a boat, but I showed him how to cut it with tools; which, after I had showed him how to use, he did very handily; and in about a month's hard labour we finished it and made it very handsome; especially when, with our axes, which I showed him how to handle, we cut and hewed the outside into the true shape of a boat. After this, however, it cost us near a fortnight's time to get her along, as it were inch by inch, upon great rollers into the water; but when she was in, she would have carried twenty men with great ease.

When she was in the water, though she was so big, it amazed me to see with what dexterity and how swift my man Friday could manage her, turn her, and paddle her along. So I asked him if he would, and if we might venture over in her. "Yes," he said, "we venture over in her very well, though great blow wind." However I had a further design that he knew nothing of, and that was, to make a mast and a sail, and to fit her with an anchor and cable. As to a mast, that was easy enough to get; so I pitched upon a straight young cedar-tree, which I found near the place, and which there were great plenty of in the island, and I set Friday to work to cut it down, and gave him directions how to shape and order it. But as to the sail, that was my particular care. I knew I had old sails, or rather pieces of old sails, enough; but as I had had them now six-and-twenty years by me, and had not been very careful to preserve them, not imagining that I should ever have this kind of use for them, I did not doubt but they were all rotten; and, indeed, most of them were so. However, I found two pieces which appeared pretty good, and with these I went to work; and with a great deal of pains, and awkward stitching, you may be sure, for want of needles, I at length made a three-cornered ugly thing, like what we call in England a shoulder-of-mutton sail, to go with a boom at bottom, and a little short sprit at the top, such as usually our ships' long-boats sail with, and such as I best knew how to manage, as it was such a one as I had to the boat in which I made my escape from Barbary, as related in the first part of my story.

I was near two months performing this last work, viz. rigging and fitting my masts and sails; for I finished them very complete, making a small stay, and a sail, or foresail, to it, to assist if we should turn to windward; and, what was more than all, I fixed a rudder to the stern of her to steer with. I was but a bungling shipwright, yet as I knew the usefulness and even necessity of such a thing, I applied myself with so much pains to do it, that at last I brought it to pass; though, considering the many dull contrivances I had for it that failed, I think it cost me almost as much labour as making the boat.

After all this was done, I had my man Friday to teach as to what belonged to the navigation of my boat; though he knew very well how to paddle a canoe, he knew nothing of what belonged to a sail and a rudder; and was the most amazed when he saw me work the boat to and again in the sea by the rudder, and how the sail jibed, and filled this way or that way as the course we sailed changed; I say when he saw this he stood like one astonished and amazed. However, with a little use, I made all these things familiar to him, and he became an expert sailor, except that of the compass I could make him understand very little. On the other hand, as there was very little cloudy weather, and seldom or never any fogs in those parts, there was the less occasion for a compass, seeing the stars were always to be seen by night, and the shore by day, except in the rainy seasons, and then nobody cared to stir abroad either by land or sea.

I was now entered on the seven-and-twentieth year of my captivity in this place; though the three last years that I had this creature with me ought rather to be left out of the account, my habitation being quite of another kind than in all the rest of the time. I kept the anniversary of my landing here with the same thankfulness to God for His mercies as at first: and if I had such cause of acknowledgment at first, I had much more so now, having such additional testimonies of the care of Providence over me, and the great hopes I had of being effectually and speedily delivered; for I had an invincible impression upon my thoughts that my deliverance was at hand, and that I should not be another year in this place. I went on, however, with my husbandry; digging, planting, and fencing as usual. I gathered and cured my grapes, and did every necessary thing as before.

The rainy season was in the meantime upon me, when I kept more within doors than at other times. We had stowed our new vessel as secure as we could, bringing her up into the creek, where, as I said in the beginning, I landed my rafts from the ship; and hauling her up to the shore at high-water mark, I made my man Friday dig a little dock, just big enough to hold her, and just deep enough to give her water enough to float in; and then, when the tide was out, we made a strong dam across the end of it, to keep the water out; and so she lay, dry as to the tide from the sea: and to keep the rain off we laid a great many boughs of trees, so thick that she was as well thatched as a house; and thus we waited for the months of November and December, in which I designed to make my adventure.

When the settled season began to come in, as the thought of my design returned with the fair weather, I was preparing daily for the voyage. And the first thing I did was to lay by a certain quantity of provisions, being the stores for our voyage; and intended in a week or a fortnight's time to open the dock, and launch out our boat. I was busy one morning upon something of this kind, when I called to Friday, and bid him to go to the sea-shore and see if he could find a turtle or a tortoise, a thing which we generally got once a week, for the sake of the eggs as well as the flesh. Friday had not been long gone when he came running back, and flew over my outer wall or fence, like one that felt not the ground or the steps he set his foot on; and before I had time to speak to him he cries out to me, "O master! O master! O sorrow! O bad!"—"What's the matter, Friday?" says I. "O yonder there," says he, "one, two, three canoes; one, two, three!" By this way of speaking I concluded there were six; but on inquiry I found there were but three. "Well, Friday," says I, "do not be frightened." So I heartened him up as well as I could. However, I saw the poor fellow was most terribly scared, for nothing ran in his head but that they were come to look for him, and would cut him in pieces and eat him; and the poor fellow trembled so that I scarcely knew what to do with him. I comforted him as well as I could, and told him I was in as much danger as he, and that they would eat me as well as him. "But," says I, "Friday, we must resolve to fight them. Can you fight, Friday?" "Me shoot," says he, "but there come many great number." "No matter for that," said I again; "our guns will fright them that we do not kill." So I asked him whether, if I resolved to defend him, he would defend me, and stand by me, and do just as I bid him. He said, "Me die when you bid die, master." So I went and fetched a good dram of rum and gave him; for I had been so good a husband of my rum that I had a great deal left. When we had drunk it, I made him take the two fowling-pieces, which we always carried, and loaded them with large swan-shot, as big as small pistol-bullets. Then I took four muskets, and loaded them with two slugs and five small bullets each; and my two pistols I loaded with a brace of bullets each. I hung my great sword, as usual, naked by my side, and gave Friday his hatchet. When I had thus prepared myself, I took my perspective glass, and went up to the side of the hill, to see what I could discover; and I found quickly by my glass that there were one-and-twenty savages, three prisoners, and three canoes; and that their whole business seemed to be the triumphant banquet upon these three human bodies: a barbarous feast, indeed! but nothing more than, as I had observed, was usual with them. I observed also that they had landed, not where they had done when Friday made his escape, but nearer to my creek, where the shore was low, and where a thick wood came almost close down to the sea. This, with the abhorrence of the inhuman errand these wretches came about, filled me with such indignation that I came down again to Friday, and told him I was resolved to go down to them and kill them all; and asked him if he would stand by me. He had now got over his fright, and his spirits being a little raised with the dram I had given him, he was very cheerful, and told me, as before, he would die when I bid die.

In this fit of fury I divided the arms which I had charged, as before, between us; I gave Friday one pistol to stick in his girdle, and three guns upon his shoulder, and I took one pistol and the other three guns myself; and in this posture we marched out. I took a small bottle of rum in my pocket, and gave Friday a large bag with more powder and bullets; and as to orders, I charged him to keep close behind me, and not to stir, or shoot, or do anything till I bid him, and in the meantime not to speak a word. In this posture I fetched a compass to my right hand of near a mile, as well to get over the creek as to get into the wood, so that I could come within shot of them before I should be discovered, which I had seen by my glass it was easy to do.

While I was making this march, my former thoughts returning, I began to abate my resolution: I do not mean that I entertained any fear of their number, for as they were naked, unarmed wretches, it is certain I was superior to them—nay, though I had been alone. But it occurred to my thoughts, what call, what occasion, much less what necessity I was in to go and dip my hands in blood, to attack people who had neither done or intended me any wrong? who, as to me, were innocent, and whose barbarous customs were their own disaster, being in them a token, indeed, of God's having left them, with the other nations of that part of the world, to such stupidity, and to such inhuman courses, but did not call me to take upon me to be a judge of their actions, much less an executioner of His justice—that whenever He thought fit He would take the cause into His own hands, and by national vengeance punish them as a people for national crimes, but that, in the meantime, it was none of my business—that it was true Friday might justify it, because he was a declared enemy and in a state of war with those very particular people, and it was lawful for him to attack them—but I could not say the same with regard to myself. These things were so warmly pressed upon my thoughts all the way as I went, that I resolved I would only go and place myself near them that I might observe their barbarous feast, and that I would act then as God should direct; but that unless something offered that was more a call to me than yet I knew of, I would not meddle with them.

With this resolution I entered the wood, and, with all possible wariness and silence, Friday following close at my heels, I marched till I came to the skirts of the wood on the side which was next to them, only that one corner of the wood lay between me and them. Here I called softly to Friday, and showing him a great tree which was just at the corner of the wood, I bade him go to the tree, and bring me word if he could see there plainly what they were doing. He did so, and came immediately back to me, and told me they might be plainly viewed there—that they were all about their fire, eating the flesh of one of their prisoners, and that another lay bound upon the sand a little from them, whom he said they would kill next; and this fired the very soul within me. He told me it was not one of their nation, but one of the bearded men he had told me of, that came to their country in the boat. I was filled with horror at the very naming of the white bearded man; and going to the tree, I saw plainly by my glass a white man, who lay upon the beach of the sea with his hands and his feet tied with flags, or things like rushes, and that he was an European, and had clothes on.

There was another tree and a little thicket beyond it, about fifty yards nearer to them than the place where I was, which, by going a little way about, I saw I might come at undiscovered, and that then I should be within half a shot of them; so I withheld my passion, though I was indeed enraged to the highest degree; and going back about twenty paces, I got behind some bushes, which held all the way till I came to the other tree, and then came to a little rising ground, which gave me a full view of them at the distance of about eighty yards.

I had now not a moment to lose, for nineteen of the dreadful wretches sat upon the ground, all close huddled together, and had just sent the other two to butcher the poor Christian, and bring him perhaps limb by limb to their fire, and they were stooping down to untie the bands at his feet. I turned to Friday. "Now, Friday," said I, "do as I bid thee." Friday said he would. "Then, Friday," says I, "do exactly as you see me do; fail in nothing." So I set down one of the muskets and the fowling-piece upon the ground, and Friday did the like by his, and with the other musket I took my aim at the savages, bidding him to do the like; then asking him if he was ready, he said, "Yes." "Then fire at them," said I; and at the same moment I fired also.

Friday took his aim so much better than I, that on the side that he shot he killed two of them, and wounded three more; and on my side I killed one, and wounded two. They were, you may be sure, in a dreadful consternation: and all of them that were not hurt jumped upon their feet, but did not immediately know which way to run, or which way to look, for they knew not from whence their destruction came. Friday kept his eyes close upon me, that, as I had bid him, he might observe what I did; so, as soon as the first shot was made, I threw down the piece, and took up the fowling-piece, and Friday did the like; he saw me cock and present; he did the same again. "Are you ready, Friday?" said I. "Yes," says he. "Let fly, then," says I, "in the name of God!" and with that I fired again among the amazed wretches, and so did Friday; and as our pieces were now loaded with what I call swan-shot, or small pistol-bullets, we found only two drop; but so many were wounded that they ran about yelling and screaming like mad creatures, all bloody, and most of them miserably wounded; whereof three more fell quickly after, though not quite dead.

"Now, Friday," says I, laying down the discharged pieces, and taking up the musket which was yet loaded, "follow me," which he did with a great deal of courage; upon which I rushed out of the wood and showed myself, and Friday close at my foot. As soon as I perceived they saw me, I shouted as loud as I could, and bade Friday do so too, and running as fast as I could, which, by the way, was not very fast, being loaded with arms as I was, I made directly towards the poor victim, who was, as I said, lying upon the beach or shore, between the place where they sat and the sea. The two butchers who were just going to work with him had left him at the surprise of our first fire, and fled in a terrible fright to the seaside, and had jumped into a canoe, and three more of the rest made the same way. I turned to Friday, and bade him step forwards and fire at them; he understood me immediately, and running about forty yards, to be nearer them, he shot at them; and I thought he had killed them all, for I saw them all fall of a heap into the boat, though I saw two of them up again quickly; however, he killed two of them, and wounded the third, so that he lay down in the bottom of the boat as if he had been dead.

While my man Friday fired at them, I pulled out my knife and cut the flags that bound the poor victim; and loosing his hands and feet, I lifted him up, and asked him in the Portuguese tongue what he was. He answered in Latin, *Christianus*; but was so weak and faint that he could scarce stand or speak. I took my bottle out of my pocket and gave it him, making signs that he should drink, which he did; and I gave him a piece of bread, which he ate. Then I asked him what countryman he was: and he said, Espagniole; and being a little recovered, let me know, by all the signs he could possibly make, how much he was in my debt for his deliverance. "Seignior," said I, with as much Spanish as I could make up, "we will talk afterwards, but we must fight now: if you have any strength left, take this pistol and sword, and lay about you." He took them very thankfully; and no sooner had he the arms in his hands, but, as if they had put new vigour into him, he flew upon his murderers like a fury, and had cut two of them in pieces in an instant; for the truth is, as the whole was a surprise to them, so the poor creatures were so much frightened with the noise of our pieces that they fell down for mere amazement and fear, and had no more power to attempt their own escape than their flesh had to resist our shot; and that was the case of those five that Friday shot at in the boat; for as three of them fell with the hurt they received, so the other two fell with the fright.

I kept my piece in my hand still without firing, being willing to keep my charge ready, because I had given the Spaniard my pistol and sword: so I called to Friday, and bade him run up to the tree from whence we first fired, and fetch the arms which lay there that had been discharged, which he did with great swiftness; and then giving him my musket, I sat down myself to load all the rest again, and bade them come to me when they wanted. While I was loading these pieces, there happened a fierce engagement between the Spaniard and one of the savages, who made at him with one of their great wooden swords, the weapon that was to have killed him before, if I had not prevented it. The Spaniard, who was as bold and brave as could be imagined, though weak, had fought the Indian a good while, and had cut two great wounds on his head; but the savage being a stout, lusty fellow, closing in with him, had thrown him down, being faint, and was wringing my sword out of his hand; when the Spaniard, though undermost, wisely quitting the sword, drew the pistol from his girdle, shot the savage through the body, and killed him upon the spot, before I, who was running to help him, could come near him.

Friday, being now left to his liberty, pursued the flying wretches, with no weapon in his hand but his hatchet: and with that he despatched those three who as I said before, were wounded at first, and fallen, and all the rest he could come up with: and the Spaniard coming to me for a gun, I gave him one of the fowling-pieces, with which he pursued two of the savages, and wounded them both; but as he was not able to run, they both got from him into the wood, where Friday pursued them, and killed one of them, but the other was too nimble for him; and though he was wounded, yet had plunged himself into the sea, and swam with all his might off to those two who were left in the canoe; which three in the canoe, with one wounded, that we knew not whether he died or no, were all that escaped our hands of one-and-twenty. The account of the whole is as follows: Three killed at our first shot from the tree; two killed at the next shot; two killed by Friday in the boat; two killed by Friday of those at first wounded; one killed by Friday in the wood; three killed by the Spaniard; four killed, being found dropped here and there, of the wounds, or killed by Friday in his chase of them; four escaped in the boat, whereof one wounded, if not dead—twenty-one in all.

Those that were in the canoe worked hard to get out of gun-shot, and though Friday made two or three shots at them, I did not find that he hit any of them. Friday would fain have had me take one of their canoes, and pursue them; and indeed I was very anxious about their escape, lest, carrying the news home to their people, they should come back perhaps with two or three hundred of the canoes and devour us by mere multitude; so I consented to pursue them by sea, and running to one of their canoes, I jumped in and bade Friday follow me: but when I was in the canoe I was surprised to find another poor creature lie there, bound hand and foot, as the Spaniard was, for the slaughter, and almost dead with fear, not knowing what was the matter; for he had not been able to look up over the side of the boat, he was tied so hard neck and heels, and had been tied so long that he had really but little life in him.

I immediately cut the twisted flags or rushes which they had bound him with, and would have helped him up; but he could not stand or speak, but groaned most piteously, believing, it seems, still, that he was only unbound in order to be killed. When Friday came to him I bade him speak to him, and tell him of his deliverance; and pulling out my bottle, made him give the poor wretch a dram, which, with the news of his being delivered, revived him, and he sat up in the boat. But when Friday came to hear him speak, and look in his face, it would have moved any one to tears to have seen how Friday kissed him, embraced him, hugged him, cried, laughed, hallooed, jumped about, danced, sang; then cried again, wrung his hands, beat his own face and head; and then sang and jumped about again like a distracted creature. It was a good while before I could make him speak to me or tell me what was the matter; but when he came a little to himself he told me that it was his father.

It is not easy for me to express how it moved me to see what ecstasy and filial affection had worked in this poor savage at the sight of his father, and of his being delivered from death; nor indeed can I describe half the extravagances of his affection after this: for he went into the boat and out of the boat a great many times: when he went in to him he would sit down by him, open his breast, and hold his father's head close to his bosom for many minutes together, to nourish it; then he took his arms and ankles, which were numbed and stiff with the binding, and chafed and rubbed them with his hands; and I, perceiving what the case was, gave him some rum out of my bottle to rub them with, which did them a great deal of good.

This affair put an end to our pursuit of the canoe with the other savages, who were now almost out of sight; and it was happy for us that we did not, for it blew so hard within two hours after, and before they could be got a quarter of their way, and continued blowing so hard all night, and that from the north-west, which was against them, that I could not suppose their boat could live, or that they ever reached their own coast.

But to return to Friday; he was so busy about his father that I could not find in my heart to take him off for some time; but after I thought he could leave him a little, I called him to me, and he came jumping and laughing, and pleased to the highest extreme: then I asked him if he had given his father any bread. He shook his head, and said, "None; ugly dog eat all up self." I then gave him a cake of bread out of a little pouch I carried on purpose; I also gave him a dram for himself; but he would not taste it, but carried it to his father. I had in my pocket two or three bunches of raisins, so I gave him a handful of them for his father. He had no sooner given his father these raisins but I saw him come out of the boat, and run away as if he had been bewitched, for he was the swiftest fellow on his feet that ever I saw: I say, he ran at such a rate that he was out of sight, as it were, in an instant; and though I called, and hallooed out too after him, it was all one—away he went; and in a quarter of an hour I saw him come back again, though not so fast as he went; and as he came nearer I found his pace slacker, because he had something in his hand. When he came up to me I found he had been quite home for an earthen jug or pot, to bring his father some fresh water, and that he had got two more cakes or loaves of bread: the bread he gave me, but the water he carried to his father; however, as I was very thirsty too, I took a little of it. The water revived his father more than all the rum or spirits I had given him, for he was fainting with thirst.

When his father had drunk, I called to him to know if there was any water left. He said, "Yes"; and I bade him give it to the poor Spaniard, who was in as much want of it as his father; and I sent one of the cakes that Friday brought to the Spaniard too, who was indeed very weak, and was reposing himself upon a green place under the shade of a tree; and whose limbs were also very stiff, and very much swelled with the rude bandage he had been tied with. When I saw that upon Friday's coming to him with the water he sat up and drank, and took the bread and began to eat, I went to him and gave him a handful of raisins. He looked up in my face with all the tokens of gratitude and thankfulness that could appear in any countenance; but was so weak, notwithstanding he had so exerted himself in the fight, that he could not stand up upon his feet—he tried to do it two or three times, but was really not able, his ankles were so swelled and so painful to him; so I bade him sit still, and caused Friday to rub his ankles, and bathe them with rum, as he had done his father's.

I observed the poor affectionate creature, every two minutes, or perhaps less, all the while he was here, turn his head about to see if his father was in the same place and posture as he left him sitting; and at last he found he was not to be seen; at which he started up, and, without speaking a word, flew with that swiftness to him that one could scarce perceive his feet to touch the ground as he went; but when he came, he only found he had laid himself down to ease his limbs, so Friday came back to me presently; and then I spoke to the Spaniard to let Friday help him up if he could, and lead him to the boat, and then he should carry him to our dwelling, where I would take care of him. But Friday, a lusty, strong fellow, took the Spaniard upon his back, and carried him away to the boat, and set him down softly upon the side or gunnel of the canoe, with his feet in the inside of it; and then lifting him quite in, he set him close to his father; and presently stepping out again, launched the boat off, and paddled it along the shore faster than I could walk, though the wind blew pretty hard too; so he brought them both safe into our creek, and leaving them in the boat, ran away to fetch the other canoe. As he passed me I spoke to him, and asked him whither he went. He told me, "Go fetch more boat;" so away he went like the wind, for sure never man or horse ran like him; and he had the other canoe in the creek almost as soon as I got to it by land; so he wafted me over, and then went to help our new guests out of the boat, which he did; but they were neither of them able to walk; so that poor Friday knew not what to do.

To remedy this, I went to work in my thought, and calling to Friday to bid them sit down on the bank while he came to me, I soon made a kind of hand-barrow to lay them on, and Friday and I carried them both up together upon it between us.

But when we got them to the outside of our wall, or fortification, we were at a worse loss than before, for it was impossible to get them over, and I was resolved not to break it down; so I set to work again, and Friday and I, in about two hours' time, made a very handsome tent, covered with old sails, and above that with boughs of trees, being in the space without our outward fence and between that and the grove of young wood which I had planted; and here we made them two beds of such things as I had—viz. of good rice-straw, with blankets laid upon it to lie on, and another to cover them, on each bed.

My island was now peopled, and I thought myself very rich in subjects; and it was a merry reflection, which I frequently made, how like a king I looked. First of all, the whole country was my own property, so that I had an undoubted right of dominion. Secondly, my people were perfectly subjected—I was absolutely lord and lawgiver—they all owed their lives to me, and were ready to lay down their lives, if there had been occasion for it, for me. It was remarkable, too, I had but three subjects, and they were of three different religions—my man Friday was a Protestant, his father was a Pagan and a cannibal, and the Spaniard was a Papist. However, I allowed liberty of conscience throughout my dominions. But this is by the way.

As soon as I had secured my two weak, rescued prisoners, and given them shelter, and a place to rest them upon, I began to think of making some provision for them; and the first thing I did, I ordered Friday to take a yearling goat, betwixt a kid and a goat, out of my particular flock, to be killed; when I cut off the hinder-quarter, and chopping it into small pieces, I set Friday to work to boiling and stewing, and made them a very good dish, I assure you, of flesh and broth; and as I cooked it without doors, for I made no fire within my inner wall, so I carried it all into the new tent, and having set a table there for them, I sat down, and ate my own dinner also with them, and, as well as I could, cheered them and encouraged them. Friday was my interpreter, especially to his father, and, indeed, to the Spaniard too; for the Spaniard spoke the language of the savages pretty well.

After we had dined, or rather supped, I ordered Friday to take one of the canoes, and go and fetch our muskets and other firearms, which, for want of time, we had left upon the place of battle; and the next day I ordered him to go and bury the dead bodies of the savages, which lay open to the sun, and would presently be offensive. I also ordered him to bury the horrid remains of their barbarous feast, which I could not think of doing myself; nay, I could not bear to see them if I went that way; all which he punctually performed, and effaced the very appearance of the savages being there; so that when I went again, I could scarce know where it was, otherwise than by the corner of the wood pointing to the place.

I then began to enter into a little conversation with my two new subjects; and, first, I set Friday to inquire of his father what he thought of the escape of the savages in that canoe, and whether we might expect a return of them, with a power too great for us to resist. His first opinion was, that the savages in the boat never could live out the storm which blew that night they went off, but must of necessity be drowned, or driven south to those other shores, where they were as sure to be devoured as they were to be drowned if they were cast away; but, as to what they would do if they came safe on shore, he said he knew not; but it was his opinion that they were so dreadfully frightened with the manner of their being attacked, the noise, and the fire, that he believed they would tell the people they were all killed by thunder and lightning, not by the hand of man; and that the two which appeared—viz. Friday and I—were two heavenly spirits, or furies, come down to destroy them, and not men with weapons. This, he said, he knew; because he heard them all cry out so, in their language, one to another; for it was impossible for them to conceive that a man could dart fire, and speak thunder, and kill at a distance, without lifting up the hand, as was done now: and this old savage was in the right; for, as I understood since, by other hands, the savages never attempted to go over to the island afterwards, they were so terrified with the accounts given by those four men (for it seems they did escape the sea), that they believed whoever went to that enchanted island would be destroyed with fire from the gods. This, however, I knew not; and therefore was under continual apprehensions for a good while, and kept always upon my guard, with all my army: for, as there were now four of us, I would have ventured upon a hundred of them, fairly in the open field, at any time.

17

VISIT OF MUTINEERS

In a little time, however, no more canoes appearing, the fear of their coming wore off; and I began to take my former thoughts of a voyage to the main into consideration; being likewise assured by Friday's father that I might depend upon good usage from their nation, on his account, if I would go. But my thoughts were a little suspended when I had a serious discourse with the Spaniard, and when I understood that there were sixteen more of his countrymen and Portuguese, who having been cast away and made their escape to that side, lived there at peace, indeed, with the savages, but were very sore put to it for necessaries, and, indeed, for life. I asked him all the particulars of their voyage, and found they were a Spanish ship, bound from the Rio de la Plata to the Havanna, being directed to leave their loading there, which was chiefly hides and silver, and to bring back what European goods they could meet with there; that they had five Portuguese seamen on board, whom they took out of another wreck; that five of their own men were drowned when first the ship was lost, and that these escaped through infinite dangers and hazards, and arrived, almost starved, on the cannibal coast, where they expected to have been devoured every moment. He told me they had some arms with them, but they were perfectly useless, for that they had neither powder nor ball, the washing of the sea having spoiled all their powder but a little, which they used at their first landing to provide themselves with some food.

I asked him what he thought would become of them there, and if they had formed any design of making their escape. He said they had many consultations about it; but that having neither vessel nor tools to build one, nor provisions of any kind, their councils always ended in tears and despair. I asked him how he thought they would receive a proposal from me, which might tend towards an escape; and whether, if they were all here, it might not be done. I told him with freedom, I feared mostly their treachery and ill-usage of me, if I put my life in their hands; for that gratitude was no inherent virtue in the nature of man, nor did men always square their dealings by the obligations they had received so much as they did by the advantages they expected. I told him it would be very hard that I should be made the instrument of their deliverance, and that they should afterwards make me their prisoner in New Spain, where an Englishman was certain to be made a sacrifice, what necessity or what accident so ever brought him thither; and that I had rather be delivered up to the savages, and be devoured alive, than fall into the merciless claws of the priests, and be carried into the Inquisition. I added that, otherwise, I was persuaded, if they were all here, we might, with so many hands, build a barque large enough to carry us all away, either to the Brazils southward, or to the islands or Spanish coast northward; but that if, in requital, they should, when I had put weapons into their hands, carry me by force among their own people, I might be ill-used for my kindness to them, and make my case worse than it was before.

He answered, with a great deal of candour and ingenuousness, that their condition was so miserable, and that they were so sensible of it, that he believed they would abhor the thought of using any man unkindly that should contribute to their deliverance; and that, if I pleased, he would go to them with the old man, and discourse with them about it, and return again and bring me their answer; that he would make conditions with them upon their solemn oath, that they should be absolutely under my direction as their commander and captain; and they should swear upon the holy sacraments and gospel to be true to me, and go to such Christian country as I should agree to, and no other; and to be directed wholly and absolutely by my orders till they were landed safely in such country as I intended, and that he would bring a contract from them, under their hands, for that purpose. Then he told me he would first swear to me himself that he would never stir from me as long as he lived till I gave him orders; and that he would take my side to the last drop of his blood, if there should happen the least breach of faith among his countrymen. He told me they were all of them very civil, honest men, and they were under the greatest distress imaginable, having neither weapons nor clothes, nor any food, but at the mercy and discretion of the savages; out of all hopes of ever returning to their own country; and that he was sure, if I would undertake their relief, they would live and die by me.

Upon these assurances, I resolved to venture to relieve them, if possible, and to send the old savage and this Spaniard over to them to treat. But when we had got all things in readiness to go, the Spaniard himself started an objection, which had so much prudence in it on one hand, and so much sincerity on the other hand, that I could not but be very well satisfied in it; and, by his advice, put off the deliverance of his comrades for at least half a year. The case was thus: he had been with us now about a month, during which time I had let him see in what manner I had provided, with the assistance of Providence, for my support; and he saw evidently what stock of corn and rice I had laid up; which, though it was more than sufficient for myself, yet it was not sufficient, without good husbandry, for my family, now it was increased to four; but much less would it be sufficient if his countrymen, who were, as he said, sixteen, still alive, should come over; and least of all would it be sufficient to victual our vessel, if we should build one, for a voyage to any of the Christian colonies of America; so he told me he thought it would be more advisable to let him and the other two dig and cultivate some more land, as much as I could spare seed to sow, and that we should wait another harvest, that we might have a supply of corn for his countrymen, when they should come; for want might be a temptation to them to disagree, or not to think themselves delivered, otherwise than out of one difficulty into another. "You know," says he, "the children of Israel, though they rejoiced at first for their being delivered out of Egypt, yet rebelled even against God Himself, that delivered them, when they came to want bread in the wilderness."

His caution was so seasonable, and his advice so good, that I could not but be very well pleased with his proposal, as well as I was satisfied with his fidelity; so we fell to digging, all four of us, as well as the wooden tools we were furnished with permitted; and in about a month's time, by the end of which it was seed-time, we had got as much land cured and trimmed up as we sowed two-and-twenty bushels of barley on, and sixteen jars of rice, which was, in short, all the seed we had to spare: indeed, we left ourselves barely sufficient, for our own food for the six months that we had to expect our crop; that is to say reckoning from the time we set our seed aside for sowing; for it is not to be supposed it is six months in the ground in that country.

Having now society enough, and our numbers being sufficient to put us out of fear of the savages, if they had come, unless their number had been very great, we went freely all over the island, whenever we found occasion; and as we had our escape or deliverance upon our thoughts, it was impossible, at least for me, to have the means of it out of mine. For this purpose I marked out several trees, which I thought fit for our work, and I set Friday and his father to cut them down; and then I caused the Spaniard, to whom I imparted my thoughts on that affair, to oversee and direct their work. I showed them with what indefatigable pains I had hewed a large tree into single planks, and I caused them to do the like, till they made about a dozen large planks, of good oak, near two feet broad, thirty-five feet long, and from two inches to four inches thick: what prodigious labour it took up any one may imagine.

At the same time I contrived to increase my little flock of tame goats as much as I could; and for this purpose I made Friday and the Spaniard go out one day, and myself with Friday the next day (for we took our turns), and by this means we got about twenty young kids to breed up with the rest; for whenever we shot the dam, we saved the kids, and added them to our flock. But above all, the season for curing the grapes coming on, I caused such a prodigious quantity to be hung up in the sun, that, I believe, had we been at Alicant, where the raisins of the sun are cured, we could have filled sixty or eighty barrels; and these, with our bread, formed a great part of our food—very good living too, I assure you, for they are exceedingly nourishing.

It was now harvest, and our crop in good order: it was not the most plentiful increase I had seen in the island, but, however, it was enough to answer our end; for from twenty-two bushels of barley we brought in and thrashed out above two hundred and twenty bushels; and the like in proportion of the rice; which was store enough for our food to the next harvest, though all the sixteen Spaniards had been on shore with me; or, if we had been ready for a voyage, it would very plentifully have victualled our ship to have carried us to any part of the world; that is to say, any part of America. When we had thus housed and secured our magazine of corn, we fell to work to make more wicker-ware, viz. great baskets, in which we kept it; and the Spaniard was very handy and dexterous at this part, and often blamed me that I did not make some things for defence of this kind of work; but I saw no need of it.

And now, having a full supply of food for all the guests I expected, I gave the Spaniard leave to go over to the main, to see what he could do with those he had left behind him there. I gave him a strict charge not to bring any man who would not first swear in the presence of himself and the old savage that he would in no way injure, fight with, or attack the person he should find in the island, who was so kind as to send for them in order to their deliverance; but that they would stand by him and defend him against all such attempts, and wherever they went would be entirely under and subjected to his command; and that this should be put in writing, and signed in their hands. How they were to have done this, when I knew they had neither pen nor ink, was a question which we never asked. Under these instructions, the Spaniard and the old savage, the father of Friday, went away in one of the canoes which they might be said to have come in, or rather were brought in, when they came as prisoners to be devoured by the savages. I gave each of them a musket, with a firelock on it, and about eight charges of powder and ball, charging them to be very good husbands of both, and not to use either of them but upon urgent occasions.

This was a cheerful work, being the first measures used by me in view of my deliverance for now twenty-seven years and some days. I gave them provisions of bread and of dried grapes, sufficient for themselves for many days, and sufficient for all the Spaniards—for about eight days' time; and wishing them a good voyage, I saw them go, agreeing with them about a signal they should hang out at their return, by which I should know them again when they came back, at a distance, before they came on shore. They went away with a fair gale on the day that the moon was at full, by my account in the month of October; but as for an exact reckoning of days, after I had once lost it I could never recover it again; nor had I kept even the number of years so punctually as to be sure I was right; though, as it proved when I afterwards examined my account, I found I had kept a true reckoning of years.

It was no less than eight days I had waited for them, when a strange and unforeseen accident intervened, of which the like has not, perhaps, been heard of in history. I was fast asleep in my hutch one morning, when my man Friday came running in to me, and called aloud, "Master, master, they are come, they are come!" I jumped up, and regardless of danger I went, as soon as I could get my clothes on, through my little grove, which, by the way, was by this time grown to be a very thick wood; I say, regardless of danger I went without my arms, which was not my custom to do; but I was surprised when, turning my eyes to the sea, I presently saw a boat at about a league and a half distance, standing in for the shore, with a shoulder-of-mutton sail, as they call it, and the wind blowing pretty fair to bring them in: also I observed, presently, that they did not come from that side which the shore lay on, but from the southernmost end of the island. Upon this I called Friday in, and bade him lie close, for these were not the people we looked for, and that we might not know yet whether they were friends or enemies. In the next place I went in to fetch my perspective glass to see what I could make of them; and having taken the ladder out, I climbed up to the top of the hill, as I used to do when I was apprehensive of anything, and to take my view the plainer without being discovered. I had scarce set my foot upon the hill when my eye plainly discovered a ship lying at anchor, at about two leagues and a half distance from me, SSE., but not above a league and a half from the shore. By my observation it appeared plainly to be an English ship, and the boat appeared to be an English long-boat.

I cannot express the confusion I was in, though the joy of seeing a ship, and one that I had reason to believe was manned by my own countrymen, and consequently friends, was such as I cannot describe; but yet I had some secret doubts hung about me—I cannot tell from whence they came—bidding me keep upon my guard. In the first place, it occurred to me to consider what business an English ship could have in that part of the world, since it was not the way to or from any part of the world where the English had any traffic; and I knew there had been no storms to drive them in there in distress; and that if they were really English it was most probable that they were here upon no good design; and that I had better continue as I was than fall into the hands of thieves and murderers.

Let no man despise the secret hints and notices of danger which sometimes are given him when he may think there is no possibility of its being real. That such hints and notices are given us I believe few that have made any observation of things can deny; that they are certain discoveries of an invisible world, and a converse of spirits, we cannot doubt; and if the tendency of them seems to be to warn us of danger, why should we not suppose they are from some friendly agent (whether supreme, or inferior and subordinate, is not the question), and that they are given for our good?

The present question abundantly confirms me in the justice of this reasoning; for had I not been made cautious by this secret admonition, come it from whence it will, I had been done inevitably, and in a far worse condition than before, as you will see presently. I had not kept myself long in this posture till I saw the boat draw near the shore, as if they looked for a creek to thrust in at, for the convenience of landing; however, as they did not come quite far enough, they did not see the little inlet where I formerly landed my rafts, but ran their boat on shore upon the beach, at about half a mile from me, which was very happy for me; for otherwise they would have landed just at my door, as I may say, and would soon have beaten me out of my castle, and perhaps have plundered me of all I had. When they were on shore I was fully satisfied they were Englishmen, at least most of them; one or two I thought were Dutch, but it did not prove so; there were in all eleven men, whereof three of them I found were unarmed and, as I thought, bound; and when the first four or five of them were jumped on shore, they took those three out of the boat as prisoners: one of the three I could perceive using the most passionate gestures of entreaty, affliction, and despair, even to a kind of extravagance; the other two, I could perceive, lifted up their hands sometimes, and appeared concerned indeed, but not to such a degree as the first. I was perfectly confounded at the sight, and knew not what the meaning of it should be. Friday called out to me in English, as well as he could, "O master! you see English mans eat prisoner as well as savage mans." "Why, Friday," says I, "do you think they are going to eat them, then?" "Yes," says Friday, "they will eat them." "No no," says I, "Friday; I am afraid they will murder them, indeed; but you may be sure they will not eat them."

All this while I had no thought of what the matter really was, but stood trembling with the horror of the sight, expecting every moment when the three prisoners should be killed; nay, once I saw one of the villains lift up his arm with a great cutlass, as the seamen call it, or sword, to strike one of the poor men; and I expected to see him fall every moment; at which all the blood in my body seemed to run chill in my veins. I wished heartily now for the Spaniard, and the savage that had gone with him, or that I had any way to have come undiscovered within shot of them, that I might have secured the three men, for I saw no firearms they had among them; but it fell out to my mind another way. After I had observed the outrageous usage of the three men by the insolent seamen, I observed the fellows run scattering about the island, as if they wanted to see the country. I observed that the three other men had liberty to go also where they pleased; but they sat down all three upon the ground, very pensive, and looked like men in despair. This put me in mind of the first time when I came on shore, and began to look about me; how I gave myself over for lost; how wildly I looked round me; what dreadful apprehensions I had; and how I lodged in the tree all night for fear of being devoured by wild beasts. As I knew nothing that night of the supply I was to receive by the providential driving of the ship nearer the land by the storms and tide, by which I have since been so long nourished and supported; so these three poor desolate men knew nothing how certain of deliverance and supply they were, how near it was to them, and how effectually and really they were in a condition of safety, at the same time that they thought themselves lost and their case desperate. So little do we see before us in the world, and so much reason have we to depend cheerfully upon the great Maker of the world, that He does not leave His creatures so absolutely destitute, but that in the worst circumstances they have always something to be thankful for, and sometimes are nearer deliverance than they imagine; nay, are even brought to their deliverance by the means by which they seem to be brought to their destruction.

It was just at high-water when these people came on shore; and while they rambled about to see what kind of a place they were in, they had carelessly stayed till the tide was spent, and the water was ebbed considerably away, leaving their boat aground. They had left two men in the boat, who, as I found afterwards, having drunk a little too much brandy, fell asleep; however, one of them waking a little sooner than the other and finding the boat too fast aground for him to stir it, hallooed out for the rest, who were straggling about: upon which they all soon came to the boat: but it was past all their strength to launch her, the boat being very heavy, and the shore on that side being a soft oozy sand, almost like a quicksand. In this condition, like true seamen, who are, perhaps, the least of all mankind given to forethought, they gave it over, and away they strolled about the country again; and I heard one of them say aloud to another, calling them off from the boat, "Why, let her alone, Jack, can't you? she'll float next tide;" by which I was fully confirmed in the main inquiry of what countrymen they were. All this while I kept myself very close, not once daring to stir out of my castle any farther than to my place of observation near the top of the hill: and very glad I was to think how well it was fortified. I knew it was no less than ten hours before the boat could float again, and by that time it would be dark, and I might be at more liberty to see their motions, and to hear their discourse, if they had any. In the meantime I fitted myself up for a battle as before, though with more caution, knowing I had to do with another kind of enemy than I had at first. I ordered Friday also, whom I had made an excellent marksman with his gun, to load himself with arms. I took myself two fowling-pieces, and I gave him three muskets. My figure, indeed, was very fierce; I had my formidable goat-skin coat on, with the great cap I have mentioned, a naked sword by my side, two pistols in my belt, and a gun upon each shoulder.

It was my design, as I said above, not to have made any attempt till it was dark; but about two o'clock, being the heat of the day, I found that they were all gone straggling into the woods, and, as I thought, laid down to sleep. The three poor distressed men, too anxious for their condition to get any sleep, had, however, sat down under the shelter of a great tree, at about a quarter of a mile from me, and, as I thought, out of sight of any of the rest. Upon this I resolved to discover myself to them, and learn something of their condition; immediately I marched as above, my man Friday at a good distance behind me, as formidable for his arms as I, but not making quite so staring a spectre-like figure as I did. I came as near them undiscovered as I could, and then, before any of them saw me, I called aloud to them in Spanish, "What are ye, gentlemen?" They started up at the noise, but were ten times more confounded when they saw me, and the uncouth figure that I made. They made no answer at all, but I thought I perceived them just going to fly from me, when I spoke to them in English. "Gentlemen," said I, "do not be surprised at me; perhaps you may have a friend near when you did not expect it." "He must be sent directly from heaven then," said one of them very gravely to me, and pulling off his hat at the same time to me; "for our condition is past the help of man." "All help is from heaven, sir," said I, "but can you put a stranger in the way to help you? for you seem to be in some great distress. I saw you when you landed; and when you seemed to make application to the brutes that came with you, I saw one of them lift up his sword to kill you."

The poor man, with tears running down his face, and trembling, looking like one astonished, returned, "Am I talking to God or man? Is it a real man or an angel?" "Be in no fear about that, sir," said I; "if God had sent an angel to relieve you, he would have come better clothed, and armed after another manner than you see me; pray lay aside your fears; I am a man, an Englishman, and disposed to assist you; you see I have one servant only; we have arms and ammunition; tell us freely, can we serve you? What is your case?" "Our case, sir," said he, "is too long to tell you while our murderers are so near us; but, in short, sir, I was commander of that ship—my men have mutinied against me; they have been hardly prevailed on not to murder me, and, at last, have set me on shore in this desolate place, with these two men with me—one my mate, the other a passenger—where we expected to perish, believing the place to be uninhabited, and know not yet what to think of it." "Where are these brutes, your enemies?" said I; "do you know where they are gone? There they lie, sir," said he, pointing to a thicket of trees; "my heart trembles for fear they have seen us and heard you speak; if they have, they will certainly murder us all." "Have they any firearms?" said I. He answered, "They had only two pieces, one of which they left in the boat." "Well, then," said I, "leave the rest to me; I see they are all asleep; it is an easy thing to kill them all; but shall we rather take them prisoners?" He told me there were two desperate villains among them that it was scarce safe to show any mercy to; but if they were secured, he believed all the rest would return to their duty. I asked him which they were. He told me he could not at that distance distinguish them, but he would obey my orders in anything I would direct. "Well," says I, "let us retreat out of their view or hearing, lest they awake, and we will resolve further." So they willingly went back with me, till the woods covered us from them.

"Look you, sir," said I, "if I venture upon your deliverance, are you willing to make two conditions with me?" He anticipated my proposals by telling me that both he and the ship, if recovered, should be wholly directed and commanded by me in everything; and if the ship was not recovered, he would live and die with me in what part of the world so ever I would send him; and the two other men said the same. "Well," says I, "my conditions are but two; first, that while you stay in this island with me, you will not pretend to any authority here; and if I put arms in your hands, you will, upon all occasions, give them up to me, and do no prejudice to me or mine upon this island, and in the meantime be governed by my orders; secondly, that if the ship is or may be recovered, you will carry me and my man to England passage free."

He gave me all the assurances that the invention or faith of man could devise that he would comply with these most reasonable demands, and besides would owe his life to me, and acknowledge it upon all occasions as long as he lived. "Well, then," said I, "here are three muskets for you, with powder and ball; tell me next what you think is proper to be done." He showed all the testimonies of his gratitude that he was able, but offered to be wholly guided by me. I told him I thought it was very hard venturing anything; but the best method I could think of was to fire on them at once as they lay, and if any were not killed at the first volley, and offered to submit, we might save them, and so put it wholly upon God's providence to direct the shot. He said, very modestly, that he was loath to kill them if he could help it; but that those two were incorrigible villains, and had been the authors of all the mutiny in the ship, and if they escaped, we should be undone still, for they would go on board and bring the whole ship's company, and destroy us all. "Well, then," says I, "necessity legitimates my advice, for it is the only way to save our lives." However, seeing him still cautious of shedding blood, I told him they should go themselves, and manage as they found convenient.

In the middle of this discourse we heard some of them awake, and soon after we saw two of them on their feet. I asked him if either of them were the heads of the mutiny? He said, "No." "Well, then," said I, "you may let them escape; and Providence seems to have awakened them on purpose to save themselves. Now," says I, "if the rest escape you, it is your fault." Animated with this, he took the musket I had given him in his hand, and a pistol in his belt, and his two comrades with him, with each a piece in his hand; the two men who were with him going first made some noise, at which one of the seamen who was awake turned about, and seeing them coming, cried out to the rest; but was too late then, for the moment he cried out they fired—I mean the two men, the captain wisely reserving his own piece. They had so well aimed their shot at the men they knew, that one of them was killed on the spot, and the other very much wounded; but not being dead, he started up on his feet, and called eagerly for help to the other; but the captain stepping to him, told him it was too late to cry for help, he should call upon God to forgive his villainy, and with that word knocked him down with the stock of his musket, so that he never spoke more; there were three more in the company, and one of them was slightly wounded. By this time I was come; and when they saw their danger, and that it was in vain to resist, they begged for mercy. The captain told them he would spare their lives if they would give him an assurance of their abhorrence of the treachery they had been guilty of, and would swear to be faithful to him in recovering the ship, and afterwards in carrying her back to Jamaica, from whence they came. They gave him all the protestations of their sincerity that could be desired; and he was willing to believe them, and spare their lives, which I was not against, only that I obliged him to keep them bound hand and foot while they were on the island.

While this was doing, I sent Friday with the captain's mate to the boat with orders to secure her, and bring away the oars and sails, which they did; and by-and-by three straggling men, that were (happily for them) parted from the rest, came back upon hearing the guns fired; and seeing the captain, who was before their prisoner, now their conqueror, they submitted to be bound also; and so our victory was complete.

It now remained that the captain and I should inquire into one another's circumstances. I began first, and told him my whole history, which he heard with an attention even to amazement—and particularly at the wonderful manner of my being furnished with provisions and ammunition; and, indeed, as my story is a whole collection of wonders, it affected him deeply. But when he reflected from thence upon himself, and how I seemed to have been preserved there on purpose to save his life, the tears ran down his face, and he could not speak a word more. After this communication was at an end, I carried him and his two men into my apartment, leading them in just where I came out, viz. at the top of the house, where I refreshed them with such provisions as I had, and showed them all the contrivances I had made during my long, long inhabiting that place.

All I showed them, all I said to them, was perfectly amazing; but above all, the captain admired my fortification, and how perfectly I had concealed my retreat with a grove of trees, which having been now planted nearly twenty years, and the trees growing much faster than in England, was become a little wood, so thick that it was impassable in any part of it but at that one side where I had reserved my little winding passage into it. I told him this was my castle and my residence, but that I had a seat in the country, as most princes have, whither I could retreat upon occasion, and I would show him that too another time; but at present our business was to consider how to recover the ship. He agreed with me as to that, but told me he was perfectly at a loss what measures to take, for that there were still six-and-twenty hands on board, who, having entered into a cursed conspiracy, by which they had all forfeited their lives to the law, would be hardened in it now by desperation, and would carry it on, knowing that if they were subdued they would be brought to the gallows as soon as they came to England, or to any of the English colonies, and that, therefore, there would be no attacking them with so small a number as we were.

I mused for some time on what he had said, and found it was a very rational conclusion, and that therefore something was to be resolved on speedily, as well to draw the men on board into some snare for their surprise as to prevent their landing upon us, and destroying us. Upon this, it presently occurred to me that in a little while the ship's crew, wondering what was become of their comrades and of the boat, would certainly come on shore in their other boat to look for them, and that then, perhaps, they might come armed, and be too strong for us: this he allowed to be rational. Upon this, I told him the first thing we had to do was to stave the boat which lay upon the beach, so that they might not carry her of, and taking everything out of her, leave her so far useless as not to be fit to swim. Accordingly, we went on board, took the arms which were left on board out of her, and whatever else we found there—which was a bottle of brandy, and another of rum, a few biscuit-cakes, a horn of powder, and a great lump of sugar in a piece of canvas (the sugar was five or six pounds): all which was very welcome to me, especially the brandy and sugar, of which I had had none left for many years.

When we had carried all these things on shore (the oars, mast, sail, and rudder of the boat were carried away before), we knocked a great hole in her bottom, that if they had come strong enough to master us, yet they could not carry off the boat. Indeed, it was not much in my thoughts that we could be able to recover the ship; but my view was, that if they went away without the boat, I did not much question to make her again fit to carry as to the Leeward Islands, and call upon our friends the Spaniards in my way, for I had them still in my thoughts.

18

THE SHIP RECOVERED

While we were thus preparing our designs, and had first, by main strength, heaved the boat upon the beach, so high that the tide would not float her off at high-water mark, and besides, had broke a hole in her bottom too big to be quickly stopped, and were set down musing what we should do, we heard the ship fire a gun, and make a waft with her ensign as a signal for the boat to come on board—but no boat stirred; and they fired several times, making other signals for the boat. At last, when all their signals and firing proved fruitless, and they found the boat did not stir, we saw them, by the help of my glasses, hoist another boat out and row towards the shore; and we found, as they approached, that there were no less than ten men in her, and that they had firearms with them.

As the ship lay almost two leagues from the shore, we had a full view of them as they came, and a plain sight even of their faces; because the tide having set them a little to the east of the other boat, they rowed up under shore, to come to the same place where the other had landed, and where the boat lay; by this means, I say, we had a full view of them, and the captain knew the persons and characters of all the men in the boat, of whom, he said, there were three very honest fellows, who, he was sure, were led into this conspiracy by the rest, being over-powered and frightened; but that as for the boatswain, who it seems was the chief officer among them, and all the rest, they were as outrageous as any of the ship's crew, and were no doubt made desperate in their new enterprise; and terribly apprehensive he was that they would be too powerful for us. I smiled at him, and told him that men in our circumstances were past the operation of fear; that seeing almost every condition that could be was better than that which we were supposed to be in, we ought to expect that the consequence, whether death or life, would be sure to be a deliverance. I asked him what he thought of the circumstances of my life, and whether a deliverance were not worth venturing for? "And where, sir," said I, "is your belief of my being preserved here on purpose to save your life, which elevated you a little while ago? For my part," said I, "there seems to be but one thing amiss in all the prospect of it." "What is that?" say he. "Why," said I, "it is, that as you say there are three or four honest fellows among them which should be spared, had they been all of the wicked part of the crew I should have thought God's providence had singled them out to deliver them into your hands; for depend upon it, every man that comes ashore is our own, and shall die or live as they behave to us." As I spoke this with a raised voice and cheerful countenance, I found it greatly encouraged him; so we set vigorously to our business.

We had, upon the first appearance of the boat's coming from the ship, considered of separating our prisoners; and we had, indeed, secured them effectually. Two of them, of whom the captain was less assured than ordinary, I sent with Friday, and one of the three delivered men, to my cave, where they were remote enough, and out of danger of being heard or discovered, or of finding their way out of the woods if they could have delivered themselves. Here they left them bound, but gave them provisions; and promised them, if they continued there quietly, to give them their liberty in a day or two; but that if they attempted their escape they should be put to death without mercy. They promised faithfully to bear their confinement with patience, and were very thankful that they had such good usage as to have provisions and light left them; for Friday gave them candles (such as we made ourselves) for their comfort; and they did not know but that he stood sentinel over them at the entrance.

The other prisoners had better usage; two of them were kept pinioned, indeed, because the captain was not able to trust them; but the other two were taken into my service, upon the captain's recommendation, and upon their solemnly engaging to live and die with us; so with them and the three honest men we were seven men, well armed; and I made no doubt we should be able to deal well enough with the ten that were coming, considering that the captain had said there were three or four honest men among them also. As soon as they got to the place where their other boat lay, they ran their boat into the beach and came all on shore, hauling the boat up after them, which I was glad to see, for I was afraid they would rather have left the boat at an anchor some distance from the shore, with some hands in her to guard her, and so we should not be able to seize the boat. Being on shore, the first thing they did, they ran all to their other boat; and it was easy to see they were under a great surprise to find her stripped, as above, of all that was in her, and a great hole in her bottom. After they had mused a while upon this, they set up two or three great shouts, hallooing with all their might, to try if they could make their companions hear; but all was to no purpose. Then they came all close in a ring, and fired a volley of their small arms, which indeed we heard, and the echoes made the woods ring. But it was all one; those in the cave, we were sure, could not hear; and those in our keeping, though they heard it well enough, yet durst give no answer to them. They were so astonished at the surprise of this, that, as they told us afterwards, they resolved to go all on board again to their ship, and let them know that the men were all murdered, and the long-boat staved; accordingly, they immediately launched their boat again, and got all of them on board.

The captain was terribly amazed, and even confounded, at this, believing they would go on board the ship again and set sail, giving their comrades over for lost, and so he should still lose the ship, which he was in hopes we should have recovered; but he was quickly as much frightened the other way.

They had not been long put off with the boat, when we perceived them all coming on shore again; but with this new measure in their conduct, which it seems they consulted together upon, viz. to leave three men in the boat, and the rest to go on shore, and go up into the country to look for their fellows. This was a great disappointment to us, for now we were at a loss what to do, as our seizing those seven men on shore would be no advantage to us if we let the boat escape; because they would row away to the ship, and then the rest of them would be sure to weigh and set sail, and so our recovering the ship would be lost. However we had no remedy but to wait and see what the issue of things might present. The seven men came on shore, and the three who remained in the boat put her off to a good distance from the shore, and came to an anchor to wait for them; so that it was impossible for us to come at them in the boat. Those that came on shore kept close together, marching towards the top of the little hill under which my habitation lay; and we could see them plainly, though they could not perceive us. We should have been very glad if they would have come nearer us, so that we might have fired at them, or that they would have gone farther off, that we might come abroad. But when they were come to the brow of the hill where they could see a great way into the valleys and woods, which lay towards the north-east part, and where the island lay lowest, they shouted and hallooed till they were weary; and not caring, it seems, to venture far from the shore, nor far from one another, they sat down together under a tree to consider it. Had they thought fit to have gone to sleep there, as the other part of them had done, they had done the job for us; but they were too full of apprehensions of danger to venture to go to sleep, though they could not tell what the danger was they had to fear.

The captain made a very just proposal to me upon this consultation of theirs, viz. that perhaps they would all fire a volley again, to endeavour to make their fellows hear, and that we should all sally upon them just at the juncture when their pieces were all discharged, and they would certainly yield, and we should have them without bloodshed. I liked this proposal, provided it was done while we were near enough to come up to them before they could load their pieces again. But this event did not happen; and we lay still a long time, very irresolute what course to take. At length I told them there would be nothing done, in my opinion, till night; and then, if they did not return to the boat, perhaps we might find a way to get between them and the shore, and so might use some stratagem with them in the boat to get them on shore. We waited a great while, though very impatient for their removing; and were very uneasy when, after long consultation, we saw them all start up and march down towards the sea; it seems they had such dreadful apprehensions of the danger of the place that they resolved to go on board the ship again, give their companions over for lost, and so go on with their intended voyage with the ship.

As soon as I perceived them go towards the shore, I imagined it to be as it really was that they had given over their search, and were going back again; and the captain, as soon as I told him my thoughts, was ready to sink at the apprehensions of it; but I presently thought of a stratagem to fetch them back again, and which answered my end to a tittle. I ordered Friday and the captain's mate to go over the little creek westward, towards the place where the savages came on shore, when Friday was rescued, and so soon as they came to a little rising round, at about half a mile distant, I bid them halloo out, as loud as they could, and wait till they found the seamen heard them; that as soon as ever they heard the seamen answer them, they should return it again; and then, keeping out of sight, take a round, always answering when the others hallooed, to draw them as far into the island and among the woods as possible, and then wheel about again to me by such ways as I directed them.

They were just going into the boat when Friday and the mate hallooed; and they presently heard them, and answering, ran along the shore westward, towards the voice they heard, when they were stopped by the creek, where the water being up, they could not get over, and called for the boat to come up and set them over; as, indeed, I expected. When they had set themselves over, I observed that the boat being gone a good way into the creek, and, as it were, in a harbour within the land, they took one of the three men out of her, to go along with them, and left only two in the boat, having fastened her to the stump of a little tree on the shore. This was what I wished for; and immediately leaving Friday and the captain's mate to their business, I took the rest with me; and, crossing the creek out of their sight, we surprised the two men before they were aware—one of them lying on the shore, and the other being in the boat. The fellow on shore was between sleeping and waking, and going to start up; the captain, who was foremost, ran in upon him, and knocked him down; and then called out to him in the boat to yield, or he was a dead man. They needed very few arguments to persuade a single man to yield, when he saw five men upon him and his comrade knocked down: besides, this was, it seems, one of the three who were not so hearty in the mutiny as the rest of the crew, and therefore was easily persuaded not only to yield, but afterwards to join very sincerely with us. In the meantime, Friday and the captain's mate so well managed their business with the rest that they drew them, by hallooing and answering, from one hill to another, and from one wood to another, till they not only heartily tired them, but left them where they were, very sure they could not reach back to the boat before it was dark; and, indeed, they were heartily tired themselves also, by the time they came back to us.

We had nothing now to do but to watch for them in the dark, and to fall upon them, so as to make sure work with them. It was several hours after Friday came back to me before they came back to their boat; and we could hear the foremost of them, long before they came quite up, calling to those behind to come along; and could also hear them answer, and complain how lame and tired they were, and not able to come any faster: which was very welcome news to us. At length they came up to the boat: but it is impossible to express their confusion when they found the boat fast aground in the creek, the tide ebbed out, and their two men gone. We could hear them call one to another in a most lamentable manner, telling one another they were got into an enchanted island; that either there were inhabitants in it, and they should all be murdered, or else there were devils and spirits in it, and they should be all carried away and devoured. They hallooed again, and called their two comrades by their names a great many times; but no answer. After some time we could see them, by the little light there was, run about, wringing their hands like men in despair, and sometimes they would go and sit down in the boat to rest themselves: then come ashore again, and walk about again, and so the same thing over again. My men would fain have had me give them leave to fall upon them at once in the dark; but I was willing to take them at some advantage, so as to spare them, and kill as few of them as I could; and especially I was unwilling to hazard the killing of any of our men, knowing the others were very well armed. I resolved to wait, to see if they did not separate; and therefore, to make sure of them, I drew my ambuscade nearer, and ordered Friday and the captain to creep upon their hands and feet, as close to the ground as they could, that they might not be discovered, and get as near them as they could possibly before they offered to fire.

They had not been long in that posture when the boatswain, who was the principal ringleader of the mutiny, and had now shown himself the most dejected and dispirited of all the rest, came walking towards them, with two more of the crew; the captain was so eager at having this principal rogue so much in his power, that he could hardly have patience to let him come so near as to be sure of him, for they only heard his tongue before: but when they came nearer, the captain and Friday, starting up on their feet, let fly at them. The boatswain was killed upon the spot: the next man was shot in the body, and fell just by him, though he did not die till an hour or two after; and the third ran for it. At the noise of the fire I immediately advanced with my whole army, which was now eight men, viz. myself, generalissimo; Friday, my lieutenant-general; the captain and his two men, and the three prisoners of war whom we had trusted with arms. We came upon them, indeed, in the dark, so that they could not see our number; and I made the man they had left in the boat, who was now one of us, to call them by name, to try if I could bring them to a parley, and so perhaps might reduce them to terms; which fell out just as we desired: for indeed it was easy to think, as their condition then was, they would be very willing to capitulate. So he calls out as loud as he could to one of them, "Tom Smith! Tom Smith!" Tom Smith answered immediately, "Is that Robinson?" for it seems he knew the voice. The other answered, "Ay, ay; for God's sake, Tom Smith, throw down your arms and yield, or you are all dead men this moment." "Who must we yield to? Where are they?" says Smith again. "Here they are," says he; "here's our captain and fifty men with him, have been hunting you these two hours; the boatswain is killed; Will Fry is wounded, and I am a prisoner; and if you do not yield you are all lost." "Will they give us quarter, then?" says Tom Smith, "and we will yield." "I'll go and ask, if you promise to yield," said Robinson: so he asked the captain, and the captain himself then calls out, "You, Smith, you know my voice; if you lay down your arms immediately and submit, you shall have your lives, all but Will Atkins."

Upon this Will Atkins cried out, "For God's sake, captain, give me quarter; what have I done? They have all been as bad as I:" which, by the way, was not true; for it seems this Will Atkins was the first man that laid hold of the captain when they first mutinied, and used him barbarously in tying his hands and giving him injurious language. However, the captain told him he must lay down his arms at discretion, and trust to the governor's mercy: by which he meant me, for they all called me governor. In a word, they all laid down their arms and begged their lives; and I sent the man that had parleyed with them, and two more, who bound them all; and then my great army of fifty men, which, with those three, were in all but eight, came up and seized upon them, and upon their boat; only that I kept myself and one more out of sight for reasons of state.

Our next work was to repair the boat, and think of seizing the ship: and as for the captain, now he had leisure to parley with them, he expostulated with them upon the villainy of their practices with him, and upon the further wickedness of their design, and how certainly it must bring them to misery and distress in the end, and perhaps to the gallows. They all appeared very penitent, and begged hard for their lives. As for that, he told them they were not his prisoners, but the commander's of the island; that they thought they had set him on shore in a barren, uninhabited island; but it had pleased God so to direct them that it was inhabited, and that the governor was an Englishman; that he might hang them all there, if he pleased; but as he had given them all quarter, he supposed he would send them to England, to be dealt with there as justice required, except Atkins, whom he was commanded by the governor to advise to prepare for death, for that he would be hanged in the morning.

Though this was all but a fiction of his own, yet it had its desired effect; Atkins fell upon his knees to beg the captain to intercede with the governor for his life; and all the rest begged of him, for God's sake, that they might not be sent to England.

It now occurred to me that the time of our deliverance was come, and that it would be a most easy thing to bring these fellows in to be hearty in getting possession of the ship; so I retired in the dark from them, that they might not see what kind of a governor they had, and called the captain to me; when I called, at a good distance, one of the men was ordered to speak again, and say to the captain, "Captain, the commander calls for you;" and presently the captain replied, "Tell his excellency I am just coming." This more perfectly amazed them, and they all believed that the commander was just by, with his fifty men. Upon the captain coming to me, I told him my project for seizing the ship, which he liked wonderfully well, and resolved to put it in execution the next morning. But, in order to execute it with more art, and to be secure of success, I told him we must divide the prisoners, and that he should go and take Atkins, and two more of the worst of them, and send them pinioned to the cave where the others lay. This was committed to Friday and the two men who came on shore with the captain. They conveyed them to the cave as to a prison: and it was, indeed, a dismal place, especially to men in their condition. The others I ordered to my bower, as I called it, of which I have given a full description: and as it was fenced in, and they pinioned, the place was secure enough, considering they were upon their behaviour.

To these in the morning I sent the captain, who was to enter into a parley with them; in a word, to try them, and tell me whether he thought they might be trusted or not to go on board and surprise the ship. He talked to them of the injury done him, of the condition they were brought to, and that though the governor had given them quarter for their lives as to the present action, yet that if they were sent to England they would all be hanged in chains; but that if they would join in so just an attempt as to recover the ship, he would have the governor's engagement for their pardon.

Any one may guess how readily such a proposal would be accepted by men in their condition; they fell down on their knees to the captain, and promised, with the deepest imprecations, that they would be faithful to him to the last drop, and that they should owe their lives to him, and would go with him all over the world; that they would own him as a father to them as long as they lived. "Well," says the captain, "I must go and tell the governor what you say, and see what I can do to bring him to consent to it." So he brought me an account of the temper he found them in, and that he verily believed they would be faithful. However, that we might be very secure, I told him he should go back again and choose out those five, and tell them, that they might see he did not want men, that he would take out those five to be his assistants, and that the governor would keep the other two, and the three that were sent prisoners to the castle (my cave), as hostages for the fidelity of those five; and that if they proved unfaithful in the execution, the five hostages should be hanged in chains alive on the shore. This looked severe, and convinced them that the governor was in earnest; however, they had no way left them but to accept it; and it was now the business of the prisoners, as much as of the captain, to persuade the other five to do their duty.

Our strength was now thus ordered for the expedition: first, the captain, his mate, and passenger; second, the two prisoners of the first gang, to whom, having their character from the captain, I had given their liberty, and trusted them with arms; third, the other two that I had kept till now in my bower, pinioned, but on the captain's motion had now released; fourth, these five released at last; so that there were twelve in all, besides five we kept prisoners in the cave for hostages.

I asked the captain if he was willing to venture with these hands on board the ship; but as for me and my man Friday, I did not think it was proper for us to stir, having seven men left behind; and it was employment enough for us to keep them asunder, and supply them with victuals. As to the five in the cave, I resolved to keep them fast, but Friday went in twice a day to them, to supply them with necessaries; and I made the other two carry provisions to a certain distance, where Friday was to take them.

When I showed myself to the two hostages, it was with the captain, who told them I was the person the governor had ordered to look after them; and that it was the governor's pleasure they should not stir anywhere but by my direction; that if they did, they would be fetched into the castle, and be laid in irons: so that as we never suffered them to see me as governor, I now appeared as another person, and spoke of the governor, the garrison, the castle, and the like, upon all occasions.

The captain now had no difficulty before him, but to furnish his two boats, stop the breach of one, and man them. He made his passenger captain of one, with four of the men; and himself, his mate, and five more, went in the other; and they contrived their business very well, for they came up to the ship about midnight. As soon as they came within call of the ship, he made Robinson hail them, and tell them they had brought off the men and the boat, but that it was a long time before they had found them, and the like, holding them in a chat till they came to the ship's side; when the captain and the mate entering first with their arms, immediately knocked down the second mate and carpenter with the butt-end of their muskets, being very faithfully seconded by their men; they secured all the rest that were upon the main and quarter decks, and began to fasten the hatches, to keep them down that were below; when the other boat and their men, entering at the forechains, secured the forecastle of the ship, and the scuttle which went down into the cook-room, making three men they found there prisoners. When this was done, and all safe upon deck, the captain ordered the mate, with three men, to break into the round-house, where the new rebel captain lay, who, having taken the alarm, had got up, and with two men and a boy had got firearms in their hands; and when the mate, with a crow, split open the door, the new captain and his men fired boldly among them, and wounded the mate with a musket ball, which broke his arm, and wounded two more of the men, but killed nobody. The mate, calling for help, rushed, however, into the round-house, wounded as he was, and, with his pistol, shot the new captain through the head, the bullet entering at his mouth, and came out again behind one of his ears, so that he never spoke a word more: upon which the rest yielded, and the ship was taken effectually, without any more lives lost.

As soon as the ship was thus secured, the captain ordered seven guns to be fired, which was the signal agreed upon with me to give me notice of his success, which, you may be sure, I was very glad to hear, having sat watching upon the shore for it till near two o'clock in the morning. Having thus heard the signal plainly, I laid me down; and it having been a day of great fatigue to me, I slept very sound, till I was surprised with the noise of a gun; and presently starting up, I heard a man call me by the name of "Governor! Governor!" and presently I knew the captain's voice; when, climbing up to the top of the hill, there he stood, and, pointing to the ship, he embraced me in his arms, "My dear friend and deliverer," says he, "there's your ship; for she is all yours, and so are we, and all that belong to her." I cast my eyes to the ship, and there she rode, within little more than half a mile of the shore; for they had weighed her anchor as soon as they were masters of her, and, the weather being fair, had brought her to an anchor just against the mouth of the little creek; and the tide being up, the captain had brought the pinnace in near the place where I had first landed my rafts, and so landed just at my door. I was at first ready to sink down with the surprise; for I saw my deliverance, indeed, visibly put into my hands, all things easy, and a large ship just ready to carry me away whither I pleased to go. At first, for some time, I was not able to answer him one word; but as he had taken me in his arms I held fast by him, or I should have fallen to the ground. He perceived the surprise, and immediately pulled a bottle out of his pocket and gave me a dram of cordial, which he had brought on purpose for me. After I had drunk it, I sat down upon the ground; and though it brought me to myself, yet it was a good while before I could speak a word to him. All this time the poor man was in as great an ecstasy as I, only not under any surprise as I was; and he said a thousand kind and tender things to me, to compose and bring me to myself; but such was the flood of joy in my breast, that it put all my spirits into confusion: at last it broke out into tears, and in a little while after I recovered my speech; I then took my turn, and embraced him as my deliverer, and we rejoiced together. I told him I looked upon him as a man sent by Heaven to deliver me, and that the whole transaction seemed to be a chain of wonders; that such things as these were the testimonies we had of a secret hand of Providence governing the world, and an evidence that the eye of an infinite Power could search into the remotest corner of the world, and send help to the miserable whenever He pleased. I forgot not to lift up my heart in thankfulness to Heaven; and what heart could forbear to bless Him, who had not only in a miraculous manner provided for me in such a wilderness, and in such a desolate condition, but from whom every deliverance must always be acknowledged to proceed.

When we had talked a while, the captain told me he had brought me some little refreshment, such as the ship afforded, and such as the wretches that had been so long his masters had not plundered him of. Upon this, he called aloud to the boat, and bade his men bring the things ashore that were for the governor; and, indeed, it was a present as if I had been one that was not to be carried away with them, but as if I had been to dwell upon the island still. First, he had brought me a case of bottles full of excellent cordial waters, six large bottles of Madeira wine (the bottles held two quarts each), two pounds of excellent good tobacco, twelve good pieces of the ship's beef, and six pieces of pork, with a bag of peas, and about a hundred-weight of biscuit; he also brought me a box of sugar, a box of flour, a bag full of lemons, and two bottles of lime-juice, and abundance of other things. But besides these, and what was a thousand times more useful to me, he brought me six new clean shirts, six very good neckcloths, two pair of gloves, one pair of shoes, a hat, and one pair of stockings, with a very good suit of clothes of his own, which had been worn but very little: in a word, he clothed me from head to foot. It was a very kind and agreeable present, as any one may imagine, to one in my circumstances, but never was anything in the world of that kind so unpleasant, awkward, and uneasy as it was to me to wear such clothes at first.

After these ceremonies were past, and after all his good things were brought into my little apartment, we began to consult what was to be done with the prisoners we had; for it was worth considering whether we might venture to take them with us or no, especially two of them, whom he knew to be incorrigible and refractory to the last degree; and the captain said he knew they were such rogues that there was no obliging them, and if he did carry them away, it must be in irons, as malefactors, to be delivered over to justice at the first English colony he could come to; and I found that the captain himself was very anxious about it. Upon this, I told him that, if he desired it, I would undertake to bring the two men he spoke of to make it their own request that he should leave them upon the island. "I should be very glad of that," says the captain, "with all my heart." "Well," says I, "I will send for them up and talk with them for you." So I caused Friday and the two hostages, for they were now discharged, their comrades having performed their promise; I say, I caused them to go to the cave, and bring up the five men, pinioned as they were, to the bower, and keep them there till I came. After some time, I came thither dressed in my new habit; and now I was called governor again. Being all met, and the captain with me, I caused the men to be brought before me, and I told them I had got a full account of their villainous behaviour to the captain, and how they had run away with the ship, and were preparing to commit further robberies, but that Providence had ensnared them in their own ways, and that they were fallen into the pit which they had dug for others. I let them know that by my direction the ship had been seized; that she lay now in the road; and they might see by-and-by that their new captain had received the reward of his villainy, and that they would see him hanging at the yard-arm; that, as to them, I wanted to know what they had to say why I should not execute them as pirates taken in the fact, as by my commission they could not doubt but I had authority so to do.

One of them answered in the name of the rest, that they had nothing to say but this, that when they were taken the captain promised them their lives, and they humbly implored my mercy. But I told them I knew not what mercy to show them; for as for myself, I had resolved to quit the island with all my men, and had taken passage with the captain to go to England;

and as for the captain, he could not carry them to England other than as prisoners in irons, to be tried for mutiny and running away with the ship; the consequence of which, they must needs know, would be the gallows; so that I could not tell what was best for them, unless they had a mind to take their fate in the island. If they desired that, as I had liberty to leave the island, I had some inclination to give them their lives, if they thought they could shift on shore. They seemed very thankful for it, and said they would much rather venture to stay there than be carried to England to be hanged. So I left it on that issue.

However, the captain seemed to make some difficulty of it, as if he durst not leave them there. Upon this I seemed a little angry with the captain, and told him that they were my prisoners, not his; and that seeing I had offered them so much favour, I would be as good as my word; and that if he did not think fit to consent to it I would set them at liberty, as I found them: and if he did not like it he might take them again if he could catch them. Upon this they appeared very thankful, and I accordingly set them at liberty, and bade them retire into the woods, to the place whence they came, and I would leave them some firearms, some ammunition, and some directions how they should live very well if they thought fit. Upon this I prepared to go on board the ship; but told the captain I would stay that night to prepare my things, and desired him to go on board in the meantime, and keep all right in the ship, and send the boat on shore next day for me; ordering him, at all events, to cause the new captain, who was killed, to be hanged at the yard-arm, that these men might see him.

When the captain was gone I sent for the men up to me to my apartment, and entered seriously into discourse with them on their circumstances. I told them I thought they had made a right choice; that if the captain had carried them away they would certainly be hanged. I showed them the new captain hanging at the yard-arm of the ship, and told them they had nothing less to expect.

When they had all declared their willingness to stay, I then told them I would let them into the story of my living there, and put them into the way of making it easy to them. Accordingly, I gave them the whole history of the place, and of my coming to it; showed them my fortifications, the way I made my bread, planted my corn, cured my grapes; and, in a word, all that was necessary to make them easy. I told them the story also of the seventeen Spaniards that were to be expected, for whom I left a letter, and made them promise to treat them in common with themselves. Here it may be noted that the captain, who had ink on board, was greatly surprised that I never hit upon a way of making ink of charcoal and water, or of something else, as I had done things much more difficult.

I left them my firearms—viz. five muskets, three fowling-pieces, and three swords. I had above a barrel and a half of powder left; for after the first year or two I used but little, and wasted none. I gave them a description of the way I managed the goats, and directions to milk and fatten them, and to make both butter and cheese. In a word, I gave them every part of my own story; and told them I should prevail with the captain to leave them two barrels of gunpowder more, and some garden-seeds, which I told them I would have been very glad of. Also, I gave them the bag of peas which the captain had brought me to eat, and bade them be sure to sow and increase them.

19

RETURN TO ENGLAND

Having done all this I left them the next day, and went on board the ship. We prepared immediately to sail, but did not weigh that night. The next morning early, two of the five men came swimming to the ship's side, and making the most lamentable complaint of the other three, begged to be taken into the ship for God's sake, for they should be murdered, and begged the captain to take them on board, though he hanged them immediately. Upon this the captain pretended to have no power without me; but after some difficulty, and after their solemn promises of amendment, they were taken on board, and were, some time after, soundly whipped and pickled; after which they proved very honest and quiet fellows.

Some time after this, the boat was ordered on shore, the tide being up, with the things promised to the men; to which the captain, at my intercession, caused their chests and clothes to be added, which they took, and were very thankful for. I also encouraged them, by telling them that if it lay in my power to send any vessel to take them in, I would not forget them.

When I took leave of this island, I carried on board, for relics, the great goat-skin cap I had made, my umbrella, and one of my parrots; also, I forgot not to take the money I formerly mentioned, which had lain by me so long useless that it was grown rusty or tarnished, and could hardly pass for silver till it had been a little rubbed and handled, as also the money I found in the wreck of the Spanish ship. And thus I left the island, the 19th of December, as I found by the ship's account, in the year 1686, after I had been upon it eight-and-twenty years, two months, and nineteen days; being delivered from this second captivity the same day of the month that I first made my escape in the long-boat from among the Moors of Sallee. In this vessel, after a long voyage, I arrived in England the 11th of June, in the year 1687, having been thirty-five years absent.

When I came to England I was as perfect a stranger to all the world as if I had never been known there. My benefactor and faithful steward, whom I had left my money in trust with, was alive, but had had great misfortunes in the world; was become a widow the second time, and very low in the world. I made her very easy as to what she owed me, assuring her I would give her no trouble; but, on the contrary, in gratitude for her former care and faithfulness to me, I relieved her as my little stock would afford; which at that time would, indeed, allow me to do but little for her; but I assured her I would never forget her former kindness to me; nor did I forget her when I had sufficient to help her, as shall be observed in its proper place. I went down afterwards into Yorkshire; but my father was dead, and my mother and all the family extinct, except that I found two sisters, and two of the children of one of my brothers; and as I had been long ago given over for dead, there had been no provision made for me; so that, in a word, I found nothing to relieve or assist me; and that the little money I had would not do much for me as to settling in the world.

I met with one piece of gratitude indeed, which I did not expect; and this was, that the master of the ship, whom I had so happily delivered, and by the same means saved the ship and cargo, having given a very handsome account to the owners of the manner how I had saved the lives of the men and the ship, they invited me to meet them and some other merchants concerned, and all together made me a very handsome compliment upon the subject, and a present of almost £200 sterling.

But after making several reflections upon the circumstances of my life, and how little way this would go towards settling me in the world, I resolved to go to Lisbon, and see if I might not come at some information of the state of my plantation in the Brazils, and of what was become of my partner, who, I had reason to suppose, had some years past given me over for dead. With this view I took shipping for Lisbon, where I arrived in April following, my man Friday accompanying me very honestly in all these ramblings, and proving a most faithful servant upon all occasions. When I came to Lisbon, I found out, by inquiry, and to my particular satisfaction, my old friend, the captain of the ship who first took me up at sea off the shore of Africa. He was now grown old, and had left off going to sea, having put his son, who was far from a young man, into his ship, and who still used the Brazil trade. The old man did not know me, and indeed I hardly knew him. But I soon brought him to my remembrance, and as soon brought myself to his remembrance, when I told him who I was.

After some passionate expressions of the old acquaintance between us, I inquired, you may be sure, after my plantation and my partner. The old man told me he had not been in the Brazils for about nine years; but that he could assure me that when he came away my partner was living, but the trustees whom I had joined with him to take cognisance of my part were both dead: that, however, he believed I would have a very good account of the improvement of the plantation; for that, upon the general belief of my being cast away and drowned, my trustees had given in the account of the produce of my part of the plantation to the procurator-fiscal, who had appropriated it, in case I never came to claim it, one-third to the king, and two-thirds to the monastery of St. Augustine, to be expended for the benefit of the poor, and for the conversion of the Indians to the Catholic faith: but that, if I appeared, or any one for me, to claim the inheritance, it would be restored; only that the improvement, or annual production, being distributed to charitable uses, could not be restored: but he assured me that the steward of the king's revenue from lands, and the providore, or steward of the monastery, had taken great care all along that the incumbent, that is to say my partner, gave every year a faithful account of the produce, of which they had duly received my moiety. I asked him if he knew to what height of improvement he had brought the plantation, and whether he thought it might be worth looking after; or whether, on my going thither, I should meet with any obstruction to my possessing my just right in the moiety. He told me he could not tell exactly to what degree the plantation was improved; but this he knew, that my partner was grown exceeding rich upon the enjoying his part of it; and that, to the best of his remembrance, he had heard that the king's third of my part, which was, it seems, granted away to some other monastery or religious house, amounted to above two hundred moidores a year: that as to my being restored to a quiet possession of it, there was no question to be made of that, my partner being alive to witness my title, and my name being also enrolled in the register of the country; also he told me that the survivors of my two trustees were very fair, honest people, and very wealthy; and he believed I would not only have their assistance for putting me in possession, but would find a very considerable sum of money in their hands for my account, being the produce of the farm while their fathers held the trust, and before it was given up, as above; which, as he remembered, was for about twelve years.

I showed myself a little concerned and uneasy at this account, and inquired of the old captain how it came to pass that the trustees should thus dispose of my effects, when he knew that I had made my will, and had made him, the Portuguese captain, my universal heir, &c.

He told me that was true; but that as there was no proof of my being dead, he could not act as executor until some certain account should come of my death; and, besides, he was not willing to intermeddle with a thing so remote: that it was true he had registered my will, and put in his claim; and could he have given any account of my being dead or alive, he would have acted by procuration, and taken possession of the ingenio (so they call the sugar-house), and have given his son, who was now at the Brazils, orders to do it. "But," says the old man, "I have one piece of news to tell you, which perhaps may not be so acceptable to you as the rest; and that is, believing you were lost, and all the world believing so also, your partner and trustees did offer to account with me, in your name, for the first six or eight years' profits, which I received. There being at that time great disbursements for increasing the works, building an ingenio, and buying slaves, it did not amount to near so much as afterwards it produced; however," says the old man, "I shall give you a true account of what I have received in all, and how I have disposed of it."

After a few days' further conference with this ancient friend, he brought me an account of the first six years' income of my plantation, signed by my partner and the merchant-trustees, being always delivered in goods, viz. tobacco in roll, and sugar in chests, besides rum, molasses, &c., which is the consequence of a sugar-work; and I found by this account, that every year the income considerably increased; but, as above, the disbursements being large, the sum at first was small: however, the old man let me see that he was debtor to me four hundred and seventy moidores of gold, besides sixty chests of sugar and fifteen double rolls of tobacco, which were lost in his ship; he having been shipwrecked coming home to Lisbon, about eleven years after my having the place. The good man then began to complain of his misfortunes, and how he had been obliged to make use of my money to recover his losses, and buy him a share in a new ship. "However, my old friend," says he, "you shall not want a supply in your necessity; and as soon as my son returns you shall be fully satisfied." Upon this he pulls out an old pouch, and gives me one hundred and sixty Portugal moidores in gold; and giving the writings of his title to the ship, which his son was gone to the Brazils in, of which he was quarter-part owner, and his son another, he puts them both into my hands for security of the rest.

I was too much moved with the honesty and kindness of the poor man to be able to bear this; and remembering what he had done for me, how he had taken me up at sea, and how generously he had used me on all occasions, and particularly how sincere a friend he was now to me, I could hardly refrain weeping at what he had said to me; therefore I asked him if his circumstances admitted him to spare so much money at that time, and if it would not straiten him? He told me he could not say but it might straiten him a little; but, however, it was my money, and I might want it more than he.

Everything the good man said was full of affection, and I could hardly refrain from tears while he spoke; in short, I took one hundred of the moidores, and called for a pen and ink to give him a receipt for them: then I returned him the rest, and told him if ever I had possession of the plantation I would return the other to him also (as, indeed, I afterwards did); and that as to the bill of sale of his part in his son's ship, I would not take it by any means; but that if I wanted the money, I found he was honest enough to pay me; and if I did not, but came to receive what he gave me reason to expect, I would never have a penny more from him.

When this was past, the old man asked me if he should put me into a method to make my claim to my plantation. I told him I thought to go over to it myself. He said I might do so if I pleased, but that if I did not, there were ways enough to secure my right, and immediately to appropriate the profits to my use: and as there were ships in the river of Lisbon just ready to go away to Brazil, he made me enter my name in a public register, with his affidavit, affirming, upon oath, that I was alive, and that I was the same person who took up the land for the planting the said plantation at first. This being regularly attested by a notary, and a procuration affixed, he directed me to send it, with a letter of his writing, to a merchant of his acquaintance at the place; and then proposed my staying with him till an account came of the return.

Never was anything more honourable than the proceedings upon this procuration; for in less than seven months I received a large packet from the survivors of my trustees, the merchants, for whose account I went to sea, in which were the following, particular letters and papers enclosed:—

First, there was the account-current of the produce of my farm or plantation, from the year when their fathers had balanced with my old Portugal captain, being for six years; the balance appeared to be one thousand one hundred and seventy-four moidores in my favour.

Secondly, there was the account of four years more, while they kept the effects in their hands, before the government claimed the administration, as being the effects of a person not to be found, which they called civil death; and the balance of this, the value of the plantation increasing, amounted to nineteen thousand four hundred and forty-six crusadoes, being about three thousand two hundred and forty moidores.

Thirdly, there was the Prior of St. Augustine's account, who had received the profits for above fourteen years; but not being able to account for what was disposed of by the hospital, very honestly declared he had eight hundred and seventy-two moidores not distributed, which he acknowledged to my account: as to the king's part, that refunded nothing.

There was a letter of my partner's, congratulating me very affectionately upon my being alive, giving me an account how the estate was improved, and what it produced a year; with the particulars of the number of squares, or acres that it contained, how planted, how many slaves there were upon it: and making two-and-twenty crosses for blessings, told me he had said so many *Ave Marias* to thank the Blessed Virgin that I was alive; inviting me very passionately to come over and take possession of my own, and in the meantime to give him orders to whom he should deliver my effects if I did not come myself; concluding with a hearty tender of his friendship, and that of his family; and sent me as a present seven fine leopards' skins, which he had, it seems, received from Africa, by some other ship that he had sent thither, and which, it seems, had made a better voyage than I. He sent me also five chests of excellent sweetmeats, and a hundred pieces of gold uncoined, not quite so large as moidores. By the same fleet my two merchant-trustees shipped me one thousand two hundred chests of sugar, eight hundred rolls of tobacco, and the rest of the whole account in gold.

I might well say now, indeed, that the latter end of Job was better than the beginning. It is impossible to express the flutterings of my very heart when I found all my wealth about me; for as the Brazil ships come all in fleets, the same ships which brought my letters brought my goods: and the effects were safe in the river before the letters came to my hand. In a word, I turned pale, and grew sick; and, had not the old man run and fetched me a cordial, I believe the sudden surprise of joy had overset nature, and I had died upon the spot: nay, after that I continued very ill, and was so some hours, till a physician being sent for, and something of the real cause of my illness being known, he ordered me to be let blood; after which I had relief, and grew well: but I verily believe, if I had not been eased by a vent given in that manner to the spirits, I should have died.

I was now master, all on a sudden, of above five thousand pounds sterling in money, and had an estate, as I might well call it, in the Brazils, of above a thousand pounds a year, as sure as an estate of lands in England: and, in a word, I was in a condition which I scarce knew how to understand, or how to compose myself for the enjoyment of it. The first thing I did was to recompense my original benefactor, my good old captain, who had been first charitable to me in my distress, kind to me in my beginning, and honest to me at the end. I showed him all that was sent to me; I told him that, next to the providence of Heaven, which disposed all things, it was owing to him; and that it now lay on me to reward him, which I would do a hundred-fold: so I first returned to him the hundred moidores I had received of him; then I sent for a notary, and caused him to draw up a general release or discharge from the four hundred and seventy moidores, which he had acknowledged he owed me, in the fullest and firmest manner possible. After which I caused a procuration to be drawn, empowering him to be the receiver of the annual profits of my plantation: and appointing my partner to account with him, and make the returns, by the usual fleets, to him in my name; and by a clause in the end, made a grant of one hundred moidores a year to him during his life, out of the effects, and fifty moidores a year to his son after him, for his life: and thus I requited my old man.

I had now to consider which way to steer my course next, and what to do with the estate that Providence had thus put into my hands; and, indeed, I had more care upon my head now than I had in my state of life in the island where I wanted nothing but what I had, and had nothing but what I wanted; whereas I had now a great charge upon me, and my business was how to secure it. I had not a cave now to hide my money in, or a place where it might lie without lock or key, till it grew mouldy and tarnished before anybody would meddle with it; on the contrary, I knew not where to put it, or whom to trust with it. My old patron, the captain, indeed, was honest, and that was the only refuge I had. In the next place, my interest in the Brazils seemed to summon me thither; but now I could not tell how to think of going thither till I had settled my affairs, and left my effects in some safe hands behind me. At first I thought of my old friend the widow, who I knew was honest, and would be just to me; but then she was in years, and but poor, and, for aught I knew, might be in debt: so that, in a word, I had no way but to go back to England myself and take my effects with me.

It was some months, however, before I resolved upon this; and, therefore, as I had rewarded the old captain fully, and to his satisfaction, who had been my former benefactor, so I began to think of the poor widow, whose husband had been my first benefactor, and she, while it was in her power, my faithful steward and instructor. So, the first thing I did, I got a merchant in Lisbon to write to his correspondent in London, not only to pay a bill, but to go find her out, and carry her, in money, a hundred pounds from me, and to talk with her, and comfort her in her poverty, by telling her she should, if I lived, have a further supply: at the same time I sent my two sisters in the country a hundred pounds each, they being, though not in want, yet not in very good circumstances; one having been married and left a widow;

and the other having a husband not so kind to her as he should be. But among all my relations or acquaintances I could not yet pitch upon one to whom I durst commit the gross of my stock, that I might go away to the Brazils, and leave things safe behind me; and this greatly perplexed me.

I had once a mind to have gone to the Brazils and have settled myself there, for I was, as it were, naturalised to the place; but I had some little scruple in my mind about religion, which insensibly drew me back. However, it was not religion that kept me from going there for the present; and as I had made no scruple of being openly of the religion of the country all the while I was among them, so neither did I yet; only that, now and then, having of late thought more of it than formerly, when I began to think of living and dying among them, I began to regret having professed myself a Papist, and thought it might not be the best religion to die with.

But, as I have said, this was not the main thing that kept me from going to the Brazils, but that really I did not know with whom to leave my effects behind me; so I resolved at last to go to England, where, if I arrived, I concluded that I should make some acquaintance, or find some relations, that would be faithful to me; and, accordingly, I prepared to go to England with all my wealth.

In order to prepare things for my going home, I first (the Brazil fleet being just going away) resolved to give answers suitable to the just and faithful account of things I had from thence; and, first, to the Prior of St. Augustine I wrote a letter full of thanks for his just dealings, and the offer of the eight hundred and seventy-two moidores which were undisposed of, which I desired might be given, five hundred to the monastery, and three hundred and seventy-two to the poor, as the prior should direct; desiring the good padre's prayers for me, and the like. I wrote next a letter of thanks to my two trustees, with all the acknowledgment that so much justice and honesty called for: as for sending them any present, they were far above having any occasion of it. Lastly, I wrote to my partner, acknowledging his industry in the improving the plantation, and his integrity in increasing the stock of the works; giving him instructions for his future government of my part, according to the powers I had left with my old patron, to whom I desired him to send whatever became due to me, till he should hear from me more particularly; assuring him that it was my intention not only to come to him, but to settle myself there for the remainder of my life. To this I added a very handsome present of some Italian silks for his wife and two daughters, for such the captain's son informed me he had; with two pieces of fine English broadcloth, the best I could get in Lisbon, five pieces of black baize, and some Flanders lace of a good value.

Having thus settled my affairs, sold my cargo, and turned all my effects into good bills of exchange, my next difficulty was which way to go to England: I had been accustomed enough to the sea, and yet I had a strange aversion to go to England by the sea at that time, and yet I could give no reason for it, yet the difficulty increased upon me so much, that though I had once shipped my baggage in order to go, yet I altered my mind, and that not once but two or three times.

It is true I had been very unfortunate by sea, and this might be one of the reasons; but let no man slight the strong impulses of his own thoughts in cases of such moment: two of the ships which I had singled out to go in, I mean more particularly singled out than any other, having put my things on board one of them, and in the other having agreed with the captain; I say two of these ships miscarried. One was taken by the Algerines, and the other was lost on the Start, near Torbay, and all the people drowned except three; so that in either of those vessels I had been made miserable.

THE LIFE & ADVENTURES OF ROBINSON CRUSOE

Having been thus harassed in my thoughts, my old pilot, to whom I communicated everything, pressed me earnestly not to go by sea, but either to go by land to the Groyne, and cross over the Bay of Biscay to Rochelle, from whence it was but an easy and safe journey by land to Paris, and so to Calais and Dover; or to go up to Madrid, and so all the way by land through France. In a word, I was so prepossessed against my going by sea at all, except from Calais to Dover, that I resolved to travel all the way by land; which, as I was not in haste, and did not value the charge, was by much the pleasanter way: and to make it more so, my old captain brought an English gentleman, the son of a merchant in Lisbon, who was willing to travel with me; after which we picked up two more English merchants also, and two young Portuguese gentlemen, the last going to Paris only; so that in all there were six of us and five servants; the two merchants and the two Portuguese, contenting themselves with one servant between two, to save the charge; and as for me, I got an English sailor to travel with me as a servant, besides my man Friday, who was too much a stranger to be capable of supplying the place of a servant on the road.

In this manner I set out from Lisbon; and our company being very well mounted and armed, we made a little troop, whereof they did me the honour to call me captain, as well because I was the oldest man, as because I had two servants, and, indeed, was the origin of the whole journey.

As I have troubled you with none of my sea journals, so I shall trouble you now with none of my land journals; but some adventures that happened to us in this tedious and difficult journey I must not omit.

When we came to Madrid, we, being all of us strangers to Spain, were willing to stay some time to see the court of Spain, and what was worth observing; but it being the latter part of the summer, we hastened away, and set out from Madrid about the middle of October; but when we came to the edge of Navarre, we were alarmed, at several towns on the way, with an account that so much snow was falling on the French side of the mountains, that several travellers were obliged to come back to Pampeluna, after having attempted at an extreme hazard to pass on.

When we came to Pampeluna itself, we found it so indeed; and to me, that had been always used to a hot climate, and to countries where I could scarce bear any clothes on, the cold was insufferable; nor, indeed, was it more painful than surprising to come but ten days before out of Old Castile, where the weather was not only warm but very hot, and immediately to feel a wind from the Pyrenean Mountains so very keen, so severely cold, as to be intolerable and to endanger benumbing and perishing of our fingers and toes.

Poor Friday was really frightened when he saw the mountains all covered with snow, and felt cold weather, which he had never seen or felt before in his life. To mend the matter, when we came to Pampeluna it continued snowing with so much violence and so long, that the people said winter was come before its time; and the roads, which were difficult before, were now quite impassable; for, in a word, the snow lay in some places too thick for us to travel, and being not hard frozen, as is the case in the northern countries, there was no going without being in danger of being buried alive every step. We stayed no less than twenty days at Pampeluna; when (seeing the winter coming on, and no likelihood of its being better, for it was the severest winter all over Europe that had been known in the memory of man) I proposed that we should go away to Fontarabia, and there take shipping for Bordeaux, which was a very little voyage. But, while I was considering this, there came in four French gentlemen, who, having been stopped on the French side of the passes, as we were on the Spanish, had found out a guide, who, traversing the country near the head of Languedoc, had brought them over the mountains by such ways that they were not much incommoded with the snow; for where they met with snow in any quantity, they said it was frozen hard enough to bear them and their horses. We sent for this guide, who told us he would undertake to carry us the same way, with no hazard from the snow, provided we were armed sufficiently to protect ourselves from wild beasts; for, he said, in these great snows it was frequent for some wolves to show themselves at the foot of the mountains, being made ravenous for want of food, the ground being covered with snow. We told him we were well enough prepared for such creatures as they were, if he would insure us from a kind of two-legged wolves, which we were told we were in most danger from, especially on the French side of the mountains. He satisfied us that there was no danger of that kind in the way that we were to go; so we readily agreed to follow him, as did also twelve other gentlemen with their servants, some French, some Spanish, who, as I said, had attempted to go, and were obliged to come back again.

Accordingly, we set out from Pampeluna with our guide on the 15th of November; and indeed I was surprised when, instead of going forward, he came directly back with us on the same road that we came from Madrid, about twenty miles; when, having passed two rivers, and come into the plain country, we found ourselves in a warm climate again, where the country was pleasant, and no snow to be seen; but, on a sudden, turning to his left, he approached the mountains another way; and though it is true the hills and precipices looked dreadful, yet he made so many tours, such meanders, and led us by such winding ways, that we insensibly passed the height of the mountains without being much encumbered with the snow; and all on a sudden he showed us the pleasant and fruitful provinces of Languedoc and Gascony, all green and flourishing, though at a great distance, and we had some rough way to pass still.

We were a little uneasy, however, when we found it snowed one whole day and a night so fast that we could not travel; but he bid us be easy; we should soon be past it all: we found, indeed, that we began to descend every day, and to come more north than before; and so, depending upon our guide, we went on.

It was about two hours before night when, our guide being something before us, and not just in sight, out rushed three monstrous wolves, and after them a bear, from a hollow way adjoining to a thick wood; two of the wolves made at the guide, and had he been far before us, he would have been devoured before we could have helped him; one of them fastened upon his horse, and the other attacked the man with such violence, that he had not time, or presence of mind enough, to draw his pistol, but hallooed and cried out to us most lustily. My man Friday being next me, I bade him ride up and see what was the matter. As soon as Friday came in sight of the man, he hallooed out as loud as the other, "O master! O master!" but like a bold fellow, rode directly up to the poor man, and with his pistol shot the wolf in the head that attacked him.

It was happy for the poor man that it was my man Friday; for, having been used to such creatures in his country, he had no fear upon him, but went close up to him and shot him; whereas, any other of us would have fired at a farther distance, and have perhaps either missed the wolf or endangered shooting the man.

But it was enough to have terrified a bolder man than I; and, indeed, it alarmed all our company, when, with the noise of Friday's pistol, we heard on both sides the most dismal howling of wolves; and the noise, redoubled by the echo of the mountains, appeared to us as if there had been a prodigious number of them; and perhaps there was not such a few as that we had no cause of apprehension: however, as Friday had killed this wolf, the other that had fastened upon the horse left him immediately, and fled, without doing him any damage, having happily fastened upon his head, where the bosses of the bridle had stuck in his teeth.

But the man was most hurt; for the raging creature had bit him twice, once in the arm, and the other time a little above his knee; and though he had made some defence, he was just tumbling down by the disorder of his horse, when Friday came up and shot the wolf.

It is easy to suppose that at the noise of Friday's pistol we all mended our pace, and rode up as fast as the way, which was very difficult, would give us leave, to see what was the matter. As soon as we came clear of the trees, which blinded us before, we saw clearly what had been the case, and how Friday had disengaged the poor guide, though we did not presently discern what kind of creature it was he had killed.

20

FIGHT BETWEEN FRIDAY AND A BEAR

But never was a fight managed so hardily, and in such a surprising manner as that which followed between Friday and the bear, which gave us all, though at first we were surprised and afraid for him, the greatest diversion imaginable. As the bear is a heavy, clumsy creature, and does not gallop as the wolf does, who is swift and light, so he has two particular qualities, which generally are the rule of his actions; first, as to men, who are not his proper prey (he does not usually attempt them, except they first attack him, unless he be excessively hungry, which it is probable might now be the case, the ground being covered with snow), if you do not meddle with him, he will not meddle with you; but then you must take care to be very civil to him, and give him the road, for he is a very nice gentleman; he will not go a step out of his way for a prince; nay, if you are really afraid, your best way is to look another way and keep going on; for sometimes if you stop, and stand still, and look steadfastly at him, he takes it for an affront; but if you throw or toss anything at him, though it were but a bit of stick as big as your finger, he thinks himself abused, and sets all other business aside to pursue his revenge, and will have satisfaction in point of honour—that is his first quality: the next is, if he be once affronted, he will never leave you, night or day, till he has his revenge, but follows at a good round rate till he overtakes you.

My man Friday had delivered our guide, and when we came up to him he was helping him off his horse, for the man was both hurt and frightened, when on a sudden we espied the bear come out of the wood; and a monstrous one it was, the biggest by far that ever I saw. We were all a little surprised when we saw him; but when Friday saw him, it was easy to see joy and courage in the fellow's countenance. "O! O! O!" says Friday, three times, pointing to him; "O master, you give me te leave, me shakee te hand with him; me makee you good laugh."

I was surprised to see the fellow so well pleased. "You fool," says I, "he will eat you up."—"Eatee me up! eatee me up!" says Friday, twice over again; "me eatee him up; me makee you good laugh; you all stay here, me show you good laugh." So down he sits, and gets off his boots in a moment, and puts on a pair of pumps (as we call the flat shoes they wear, and which he had in his pocket), gives my other servant his horse, and with his gun away he flew, swift like the wind.

    The bear was walking softly on, and offered to meddle with nobody, till Friday coming pretty near, calls to him, as if the bear could understand him. "Hark ye, hark ye," says Friday, "me speakee with you." We followed at a distance, for now being down on the Gascony side of the mountains, we were entered a vast forest, where the country was plain and pretty open, though it had many trees in it scattered here and there. Friday, who had, as we say, the heels of the bear, came up with him quickly, and took up a great stone, and threw it at him, and hit him just on the head, but did him no more harm than if he had thrown it against a wall; but it answered Friday's end, for the rogue was so void of fear that he did it purely to make the bear follow him, and show us some laugh as he called it. As soon as the bear felt the blow, and saw him, he turns about and comes after him, taking very long strides, and shuffling on at a strange rate, so as would have put a horse to a middling gallop; away reins Friday, and takes his course as if he ran towards us for help; so we all resolved to fire at once upon the bear, and deliver my man; though I was angry at him for bringing the bear back upon us, when he was going about his own business another way; and especially I was angry that he had turned the bear upon us, and then ran away; and I called out, "You dog! is this your making us laugh? Come away, and take your horse, that we may shoot the creature." He heard me, and cried out, "No shoot, no shoot; stand still, and you get much laugh:" and as the nimble creature ran two feet for the bear's one, he turned on a sudden on one side of us, and seeing a great oak-tree fit for his purpose, he beckoned to us to follow; and doubling his pace, he got nimbly up the tree, laying his gun down upon the ground, at about five or six yards from the bottom of the tree. The bear soon came to the tree, and we followed at a distance: the first thing he did he stopped at the gun, smelt at it, but let it lie, and up he scrambles into the tree, climbing like a cat, though so monstrous heavy. I was amazed at the folly, as I thought it, of my man, and could not for my life see anything to laugh at, till seeing the bear get up the tree, we all rode near to him.

    When we came to the tree, there was Friday got out to the small end of a large branch, and the bear got about half-way to him. As soon as the bear got out to that part where the limb of the tree was weaker, "Ha!" says he to us, "now you see me teachee the bear dance:" so he began jumping and shaking the bough, at which the bear began to totter, but stood still, and began to look behind him, to see how he should get back; then, indeed, we did laugh heartily. But Friday had not done with him by a great deal; when seeing him stand still, he called out to him again, as if he had supposed the bear could speak English, "What, you come no farther? pray you come farther;" so he left jumping and shaking the tree; and the bear, just as if he understood what he said, did come a little farther; then he began jumping again, and the bear stopped again. We thought now was a good time to knock him in the head, and called to Friday to stand still and we should shoot the bear: but he cried out earnestly, "Oh, pray! Oh, pray! no shoot, me shoot by and then:" he would have said by-and-by. However, to shorten the story, Friday danced so much, and the bear stood so ticklish, that we had laughing enough, but still could not imagine what the fellow would do: for first we thought he depended upon shaking the bear off; and we found the bear was too cunning for that too; for he would not go out far enough to be thrown down, but clung fast with his great broad claws and feet, so that we could not imagine what would be the end of it, and what the jest would be at last. But Friday put us out of doubt quickly: for seeing the bear cling fast to the bough, and that he would not be persuaded to come any farther, "Well, well," says Friday, "you no come farther, me go; you no come to me, me come to you;" and upon this he went out to the smaller end, where it would bend with his weight, and gently let himself down by it, sliding down the bough till he came near enough to jump down on his feet, and away he ran to his gun, took it up, and stood still. "Well," said I to him, "Friday, what will you do now? Why don't you shoot him?" "No shoot," says Friday, "no yet; me shoot now, me no kill; me stay, give you one more laugh:" and, indeed, so he did; for when the bear saw his enemy gone, he came back from the bough, where he stood, but did it very cautiously, looking behind him every step, and coming backward till he got into the body of the tree, then, with the same hinder end foremost, he came down the tree, grasping it with his claws, and moving one foot at a time, very leisurely. At this juncture, and just before he could set his hind foot on the ground, Friday stepped up close to him, clapped the muzzle of his piece into his ear, and shot him dead. Then the rogue turned about to see if we did not laugh; and when he saw we were pleased by our looks, he began to laugh very loud. "So we kill bear in my country," says Friday. "So you kill them?" says I; "why, you have no guns."—"No," says he, "no gun, but shoot great much long arrow." This was a good diversion to us; but we were still in a wild place, and our guide very much hurt, and what to do we hardly knew; the howling of wolves ran much in my head; and, indeed, except the noise I once heard on the shore of Africa, of which I have said something already, I never heard anything that filled me with so much horror.

These things, and the approach of night, called us off, or else, as Friday would have had us, we should certainly have taken the skin of this monstrous creature off, which was worth saving; but we had near three leagues to go, and our guide hastened us; so we left him, and went forward on our journey.

The ground was still covered with snow, though not so deep and dangerous as on the mountains; and the ravenous creatures, as we heard afterwards, were come down into the forest and plain country, pressed by hunger, to seek for food, and had done a great deal of mischief in the villages, where they surprised the country people, killed a great many of their sheep and horses, and some people too.

We had one dangerous place to pass, and our guide told us if there were more wolves in the country we should find them there; and this was a small plain, surrounded with woods on every side, and a long, narrow defile, or lane, which we were to pass to get through the wood, and then we should come to the village where we were to lodge.

It was within half-an-hour of sunset when we entered the wood, and a little after sunset when we came into the plain: we met with nothing in the first wood, except that in a little plain within the wood, which was not above two furlongs over, we saw five great wolves cross the road, full speed, one after another, as if they had been in chase of some prey, and had it in view; they took no notice of us, and were gone out of sight in a few moments. Upon this, our guide, who, by the way, was but a fainthearted fellow, bid us keep in a ready posture, for he believed there were more wolves a-coming. We kept our arms ready, and our eyes about us; but we saw no more wolves till we came through that wood, which was near half a league, and entered the plain. As soon as we came into the plain, we had occasion enough to look about us. The first object we met with was a dead horse; that is to say, a poor horse which the wolves had killed, and at least a dozen of them at work, we could not say eating him, but picking his bones rather; for they had eaten up all the flesh before. We did not think fit to disturb them at their feast, neither did they take much notice of us. Friday would have let fly at them, but I would not suffer him by any means; for I found we were like to have more business upon our hands than we were aware of. We had not gone half over the plain when we began to hear the wolves howl in the wood on our left in a frightful manner, and presently after we saw about a hundred coming on directly towards us, all in a body, and most of them in a line, as regularly as an army drawn up by experienced officers. I scarce knew in what manner to receive them, but found to draw ourselves in a close line was the only way; so we formed in a moment; but that we might not have too much interval, I ordered that only every other man should fire, and that the others, who had not fired, should stand ready to give them a second volley immediately, if they continued to advance upon us; and then that those that had fired at first should not pretend to load their fusees again, but stand ready, every one with a pistol, for we were all armed with a fusee and a pair of pistols each man; so we were, by this method, able to fire six volleys, half of us at a time; however, at present we had no necessity; for upon firing the first volley, the enemy made a full stop, being terrified as well with the noise as with the fire. Four of them being shot in the head, dropped; several others were wounded, and went bleeding off, as we could see by the snow. I found they stopped, but did not immediately retreat; whereupon, remembering that I had been told that the fiercest creatures were terrified at the voice of a man, I caused all the company to halloo as loud as they could; and I found the notion not altogether mistaken; for upon our shout they began to retire and turn about. I then ordered a second volley to be fired in their rear, which put them to the gallop, and away they went to the woods. This gave us leisure to charge our pieces again; and that we might lose no time, we kept going; but we had but little more than loaded our fusees, and put ourselves in readiness, when we heard a terrible noise in the same wood on our left, only that it was farther onward, the same way we were to go.

The night was coming on, and the light began to be dusky, which made it worse on our side; but the noise increasing, we could easily perceive that it was the howling and yelling of those hellish creatures; and on a sudden we perceived three troops of wolves, one on our left, one behind us, and one in our front, so that we seemed to be surrounded with them: however, as they did not fall upon us, we kept our way forward, as fast as we could make our horses go, which, the way being very rough, was only a good hard trot. In this manner, we came in view of the entrance of a wood, through which we were to pass, at the farther side of the plain; but we were greatly surprised, when coming nearer the lane or pass, we saw a confused number of wolves standing just at the entrance. On a sudden, at another opening of the wood, we heard the noise of a gun, and looking that way, out rushed a horse, with a saddle and a bridle on him, flying like the wind, and sixteen or seventeen wolves after him, full speed: the horse had the advantage of them; but as we supposed that he could not hold it at that rate, we doubted not but they would get up with him at last: no question but they did.

But here we had a most horrible sight; for riding up to the entrance where the horse came out, we found the carcasses of another horse and of two men, devoured by the ravenous creatures; and one of the men was no doubt the same whom we heard fire the gun, for there lay a gun just by him fired off; but as to the man, his head and the upper part of his body was eaten up. This filled us with horror, and we knew not what course to take; but the creatures resolved us soon, for they gathered about us presently, in hopes of prey; and I verily believe there were three hundred of them. It happened, very much to our advantage, that at the entrance into the wood, but a little way from it, there lay some large timber-trees, which had been cut down the summer before, and I suppose lay there for carriage. I drew my little troop in among those trees, and placing ourselves in a line behind one long tree, I advised them all to alight, and keeping that tree before us for a breastwork, to stand in a triangle, or three fronts, enclosing our horses in the centre. We did so, and it was well we did; for never was a more furious charge than the creatures made upon us in this place. They came on with a growling kind of noise, and mounted the piece of timber, which, as I said, was our breastwork, as if they were only rushing upon their prey; and this fury of theirs, it seems, was principally occasioned by their seeing our horses behind us. I ordered our men to fire as before, every other man; and they took their aim so sure that they killed several of the wolves at the first volley; but there was a necessity to keep a continual firing, for they came on like devils, those behind pushing on those before.

When we had fired a second volley of our fusees, we thought they stopped a little, and I hoped they would have gone off, but it was but a moment, for others came forward again; so we fired two volleys of our pistols; and I believe in these four firings we had killed seventeen or eighteen of them, and lamed twice as many, yet they came on again. I was loth to spend our shot too hastily; so I called my servant, not my man Friday, for he was better employed, for, with the greatest dexterity imaginable, he had charged my fusee and his own while we were engaged—but, as I said, I called my other man, and giving him a horn of powder, I had him lay a train all along the piece of timber, and let it be a large train. He did so, and had but just time to get away, when the wolves came up to it, and some got upon it, when I, snapping an unchanged pistol close to the powder, set it on fire; those that were upon the timber were scorched with it, and six or seven of them fell; or rather jumped in among us with the force and fright of the fire; we despatched these in an instant, and the rest were so frightened with the light, which the night—for it was now very near dark—made more terrible that they drew back a little; upon which I ordered our last pistols to be fired off in one volley, and after that we gave a shout; upon this the wolves turned tail, and we sallied immediately upon near twenty lame ones that we found struggling on the ground, and fell to cutting them with our swords, which answered our expectation, for the crying and howling they made was better understood by their fellows; so that they all fled and left us.

We had, first and last, killed about threescore of them, and had it been daylight we had killed many more. The field of battle being thus cleared, we made forward again, for we had still near a league to go. We heard the ravenous creatures howl and yell in the woods as we went several times, and sometimes we fancied we saw some of them; but the snow dazzling our eyes, we were not certain. In about an hour more we came to the town where we were to lodge, which we found in a terrible fright and all in arms; for, it seems, the night before the wolves and some bears had broken into the village, and put them in such terror that they were obliged to keep guard night and day, but especially in the night, to preserve their cattle, and indeed their people.

The next morning our guide was so ill, and his limbs swelled so much with the rankling of his two wounds, that he could go no farther; so we were obliged to take a new guide here, and go to Toulouse, where we found a warm climate, a fruitful, pleasant country, and no snow, no wolves, nor anything like them; but when we told our story at Toulouse, they told us it was nothing but what was ordinary in the great forest at the foot of the mountains, especially when the snow lay on the ground; but they inquired much what kind of guide we had got who would venture to bring us that way in such a severe season, and told us it was surprising we were not all devoured. When we told them how we placed ourselves and the horses in the middle, they blamed us exceedingly, and told us it was fifty to one but we had been all destroyed, for it was the sight of the horses which made the wolves so furious, seeing their prey, and that at other times they are really afraid of a gun; but being excessively hungry, and raging on that account, the eagerness to come at the horses had made them senseless of danger, and that if we had not by the continual fire, and at last by the stratagem of the train of powder, mastered them, it had been great odds but that we had been torn to pieces; whereas, had we been content to have sat still on horseback, and fired as horsemen, they would not have taken the horses so much for their own, when men were on their backs, as otherwise; and withal, they told us that at last, if we had stood altogether, and left our horses, they would have been so eager to have devoured them, that we might have come off safe, especially having our firearms in our hands, being so many in number. For my part, I was never so sensible of danger in my life; for, seeing above three hundred devils come roaring and open-mouthed to devour us, and having nothing to shelter us or retreat to, I gave myself over for lost; and, as it was, I believe I shall never care to cross those mountains again: I think I would much rather go a thousand leagues by sea, though I was sure to meet with a storm once a-week.

I have nothing uncommon to take notice of in my passage through France—nothing but what other travellers have given an account of with much more advantage than I can. I travelled from Toulouse to Paris, and without any considerable stay came to Calais, and landed safe at Dover the 14th of January, after having had a severe cold season to travel in.

I was now come to the centre of my travels, and had in a little time all my new-discovered estate safe about me, the bills of exchange which I brought with me having been currently paid.

My principal guide and privy-counsellor was my good ancient widow, who, in gratitude for the money I had sent her, thought no pains too much nor care too great to employ for me; and I trusted her so entirely that I was perfectly easy as to the security of my effects; and, indeed, I was very happy from the beginning, and now to the end, in the unspotted integrity of this good gentlewoman.

And now, having resolved to dispose of my plantation in the Brazils, I wrote to my old friend at Lisbon, who, having offered it to the two merchants, the survivors of my trustees, who lived in the Brazils, they accepted the offer, and remitted thirty-three thousand pieces of eight to a correspondent of theirs at Lisbon to pay for it.

In return, I signed the instrument of sale in the form which they sent from Lisbon, and sent it to my old man, who sent me the bills of exchange for thirty-two thousand eight hundred pieces of eight for the estate, reserving the payment of one hundred moidores a year to him (the old man) during his life, and fifty moidores afterwards to his son for his life, which I had promised them, and which the plantation was to make good as a rent-charge. And thus I have given the first part of a life of fortune and adventure—a life of Providence's chequer-work, and of a variety which the world will seldom be able to show the like of; beginning foolishly, but closing much more happily than any part of it ever gave me leave so much as to hope for.

Any one would think that in this state of complicated good fortune I was past running any more hazards—and so, indeed, I had been, if other circumstances had concurred; but I was inured to a wandering life, had no family, nor many relations; nor, however rich, had I contracted fresh acquaintance; and though I had sold my estate in the Brazils, yet I could not keep that country out of my head, and had a great mind to be upon the wing again; especially I could not resist the strong inclination I had to see my island, and to know if the poor Spaniards were in being there. My true friend, the widow, earnestly dissuaded me from it, and so far prevailed with me, that for almost seven years she prevented my running abroad, during which time I took my two nephews, the children of one of my brothers, into my care; the eldest, having something of his own, I bred up as a gentleman, and gave him a settlement of some addition to his estate after my decease. The other I placed with the captain of a ship; and after five years, finding him a sensible, bold, enterprising young fellow, I put him into a good ship, and sent him to sea; and this young fellow afterwards drew me in, as old as I was, to further adventures myself.

In the meantime, I in part settled myself here; for, first of all, I married, and that not either to my disadvantage or dissatisfaction, and had three children, two sons and one daughter;

but my wife dying, and my nephew coming home with good success from a voyage to Spain, my inclination to go abroad, and his importunity, prevailed, and engaged me to go in his ship as a private trader to the East Indies; this was in the year 1694.

In this voyage I visited my new colony in the island, saw my successors the Spaniards, had the old story of their lives and of the villains I left there; how at first they insulted the poor Spaniards, how they afterwards agreed, disagreed, united, separated, and how at last the Spaniards were obliged to use violence with them; how they were subjected to the Spaniards, how honestly the Spaniards used them—a history, if it were entered into, as full of variety and wonderful accidents as my own part—particularly, also, as to their battles with the Caribbeans, who landed several times upon the island, and as to the improvement they made upon the island itself, and how five of them made an attempt upon the mainland, and brought away eleven men and five women prisoners, by which, at my coming, I found about twenty young children on the island.

Here I stayed about twenty days, left them supplies of all necessary things, and particularly of arms, powder, shot, clothes, tools, and two workmen, which I had brought from England with me, viz. a carpenter and a smith.

Besides this, I shared the lands into parts with them, reserved to myself the property of the whole, but gave them such parts respectively as they agreed on; and having settled all things with them, and engaged them not to leave the place, I left them there.

From thence I touched at the Brazils, from whence I sent a bark, which I bought there, with more people to the island; and in it, besides other supplies, I sent seven women, being such as I found proper for service, or for wives to such as would take them. As to the Englishmen, I promised to send them some women from England, with a good cargo of necessaries, if they would apply themselves to planting—which I afterwards could not perform. The fellows proved very honest and diligent after they were mastered and had their properties set apart for them. I sent them, also, from the Brazils, five cows, three of them being big with calf, some sheep, and some hogs, which when I came again were considerably increased.

But all these things, with an account how three hundred Caribbees came and invaded them, and ruined their plantations, and how they fought with that whole number twice, and were at first defeated, and one of them killed; but at last, a storm destroying their enemies' canoes, they famished or destroyed almost all the rest, and renewed and recovered the possession of their plantation, and still lived upon the island.

All these things, with some very surprising incidents in some new adventures of my own, for ten years more, I shall give a farther account of in the Second Part of my Story.

VOLUME TWO

❦ I ❦

REVISITS ISLAND

That homely proverb, used on so many occasions in England, viz. "That what is bred in the bone will not go out of the flesh," was never more verified than in the story of my Life. Any one would think that after thirty-five years' affliction, and a variety of unhappy circumstances, which few men, if any, ever went through before, and after near seven years of peace and enjoyment in the fulness of all things; grown old, and when, if ever, it might be allowed me to have had experience of every state of middle life, and to know which was most adapted to make a man completely happy; I say, after all this, any one would have thought that the native propensity to rambling which I gave an account of in my first setting out in the world to have been so predominant in my thoughts, should be worn out, and I might, at sixty one years of age, have been a little inclined to stay at home, and have done venturing life and fortune any more.

Nay, farther, the common motive of foreign adventures was taken away in me, for I had no fortune to make; I had nothing to seek: if I had gained ten thousand pounds I had been no richer; for I had already sufficient for me, and for those I had to leave it to; and what I had was visibly increasing; for, having no great family, I could not spend the income of what I had unless I would set up for an expensive way of living, such as a great family, servants, equipage, gaiety, and the like, which were things I had no notion of, or inclination to; so that I had nothing, indeed, to do but to sit still, and fully enjoy what I had got, and see it increase daily upon my hands. Yet all these things had no effect upon me, or at least not enough to resist the strong inclination I had to go abroad again, which hung about me like a chronic distemper. In particular, the desire of seeing my new plantation in the island, and the colony I left there, ran in my head continually. I dreamed of it all night, and my imagination ran upon it all day: it was uppermost in all my thoughts, and my fancy worked so steadily and strongly upon it that I talked of it in my sleep; in short, nothing could remove it out of my mind: it even broke so violently into all my discourses that it made my conversation tiresome, for I could talk of nothing else; all my discourse ran into it, even to impertinence; and I saw it myself.

I have often heard persons of good judgment say that all the stir that people make in the world about ghosts and apparitions is owing to the strength of imagination, and the powerful operation of fancy in their minds; that there is no such thing as a spirit appearing, or a ghost walking; that people's poring affectionately upon the past conversation of their deceased friends so realises it to them that they are capable of fancying, upon some extraordinary circumstances, that they see them, talk to them, and are answered by them, when, in truth, there is nothing but shadow and vapour in the thing, and they really know nothing of the matter.

For my part, I know not to this hour whether there are any such things as real apparitions, spectres, or walking of people after they are dead; or whether there is anything in the stories they tell us of that kind more than the product of vapours, sick minds, and wandering fancies: but this I know, that my imagination worked up to such a height, and brought me into such excess of vapours, or what else I may call it, that I actually supposed myself often upon the spot, at my old castle, behind the trees; saw my old Spaniard, Friday's father, and the reprobate sailors I left upon the island; nay, I fancied I talked with them, and looked at them steadily, though I was broad awake, as at persons just before me; and this I did till I often frightened myself with the images my fancy represented to me. One time, in my sleep, I had the villainy of the three pirate sailors so lively related to me by the first Spaniard, and Friday's father, that it was surprising: they told me how they barbarously attempted to murder all the Spaniards, and that they set fire to the provisions they had laid up, on purpose to distress and starve them; things that I had never heard of, and that, indeed, were never all of them true in fact: but it was so warm in my imagination, and so realised to me, that, to the hour I saw them, I could not be persuaded but that it was or would be true; also how I resented it, when the Spaniard complained to me; and how I brought them to justice, tried them, and ordered them all three to be hanged. What there was really in this shall be seen in its place; for however I came to form such things in my dream, and what secret converse of spirits injected it, yet there was, I say, much of it true. I own that this dream had nothing in it literally and specifically true; but the general part was so true— the base, villainous behaviour of these three hardened rogues was such, and had been so much worse than all I can describe, that the dream had too much similitude of the fact; and as I would afterwards have punished them severely, so, if I had hanged them all, I had been much in the right, and even should have been justified both by the laws of God and man.

But to return to my story. In this kind of temper I lived some years; I had no enjoyment of my life, no pleasant hours, no agreeable diversion but what had something or other of this in it; so that my wife, who saw my mind wholly bent upon it, told me very seriously one night that she believed there was some secret, powerful impulse of Providence upon me, which had determined me to go thither again; and that she found nothing hindered me going but my being engaged to a wife and children. She told me that it was true she could not think of parting with me: but as she was assured that if she was dead it would be the first thing I would do, so, as it seemed to her that the thing was determined above, she would not be the only obstruction; for, if I thought fit and resolved to go—[Here she found me very intent upon her words, and that I looked very earnestly at her, so that it a little disordered her, and she stopped. I asked her why she did not go on, and say out what she was going to say? But I perceived that her heart was too full, and some tears stood in her eyes.] "Speak out, my dear," said I; "are you willing I should go?"—"No," says she, very affectionately, "I am far from willing; but if you are resolved to go," says she, "rather than I would be the only hindrance, I will go with you: for though I think it a most preposterous thing for one of your years, and in your condition, yet, if it must be," said she, again weeping, "I would not leave you; for if it be of Heaven you must do it, there is no resisting it; and if Heaven make it your duty to go, He will also make it mine to go with you, or otherwise dispose of me, that I may not obstruct it."

This affectionate behaviour of my wife's brought me a little out of the vapours, and I began to consider what I was doing; I corrected my wandering fancy, and began to argue with myself sedately what business I had after threescore years, and after such a life of tedious sufferings and disasters, and closed in so happy and easy a manner; I, say, what business had I to rush into new hazards, and put myself upon adventures fit only for youth and poverty to run into?

With those thoughts I considered my new engagement; that I had a wife, one child born, and my wife then great with child of another; that I had all the world could give me, and had no need to seek hazard for gain; that I was declining in years, and ought to think rather of leaving what I had gained than of seeking to increase it; that as to what my wife had said of its being an impulse from Heaven, and that it should be my duty to go, I had no notion of that; so, after many of these cogitations, I struggled with the power of my imagination, reasoned myself out of it, as I believe people may always do in like cases if they will: in a word, I conquered it, composed myself with such arguments as occurred to my thoughts, and which my present condition furnished me plentifully with; and particularly, as the most effectual method, I resolved to divert myself with other things, and to engage in some business that might effectually tie me up from any more excursions of this kind; for I found that thing return upon me chiefly when I was idle, and had nothing to do, nor anything of moment immediately before me. To this purpose, I bought a little farm in the county of Bedford, and resolved to remove myself thither. I had a little convenient house upon it, and the land about it, I found, was capable of great improvement; and it was many ways suited to my inclination, which delighted in cultivating, managing, planting, and improving of land; and particularly, being an inland country, I was removed from conversing among sailors and things relating to the remote parts of the world. I went down to my farm, settled my family, bought ploughs, harrows, a cart, waggon-horses, cows, and sheep, and, setting seriously to work, became in one half-year a mere country gentleman. My thoughts were entirely taken up in managing my servants, cultivating the ground, enclosing, planting, &c.; and I lived, as I thought, the most agreeable life that nature was capable of directing, or that a man always bred to misfortunes was capable of retreating to.

I farmed upon my own land; I had no rent to pay, was limited by no articles; I could pull up or cut down as I pleased; what I planted was for myself, and what I improved was for my family; and having thus left off the thoughts of wandering, I had not the least discomfort in any part of life as to this world. Now I thought, indeed, that I enjoyed the middle state of life which my father so earnestly recommended to me, and lived a kind of heavenly life, something like what is described by the poet, upon the subject of a country life:—

"Free from vices, free from care,
Age has no pain, and youth no snare."

But in the middle of all this felicity, one blow from unseen Providence unhinged me at once; and not only made a breach upon me inevitable and incurable, but drove me, by its consequences, into a deep relapse of the wandering disposition, which, as I may say, being born in my very blood, soon recovered its hold of me; and, like the returns of a violent distemper, came on with an irresistible force upon me. This blow was the loss of my wife. It is not my business here to write an elegy upon my wife, give a character of her particular virtues, and make my court to the sex by the flattery of a funeral sermon. She was, in a few words, the stay of all my affairs; the centre of all my enterprises; the engine that, by her prudence, reduced me to that happy compass I was in, from the most extravagant and ruinous project that filled my head, and did more to guide my rambling genius than a mother's tears, a father's instructions, a friend's counsel, or all my own reasoning powers could do. I was happy in listening to her, and in being moved by her entreaties; and to the last degree desolate and dislocated in the world by the loss of her.

When she was gone, the world looked awkwardly round me. I was as much a stranger in it, in my thoughts, as I was in the Brazils, when I first went on shore there; and as much alone, except for the assistance of servants, as I was in my island. I knew neither what to think nor what to do. I saw the world busy around me: one part labouring for bread, another part squandering in vile excesses or empty pleasures, but equally miserable because the end they proposed still fled from them; for the men of pleasure every day surfeited of their vice, and heaped up work for sorrow and repentance; and the men of labour spent their strength in daily struggling for bread to maintain the vital strength they laboured with: so living in a daily circulation of sorrow, living but to work, and working but to live, as if daily bread were the only end of wearisome life, and a wearisome life the only occasion of daily bread.

This put me in mind of the life I lived in my kingdom, the island; where I suffered no more corn to grow, because I did not want it; and bred no more goats, because I had no more use for them; where the money lay in the drawer till it grew mouldy, and had scarce the favour to be looked upon in twenty years. All these things, had I improved them as I ought to have done, and as reason and religion had dictated to me, would have taught me to search farther than human enjoyments for a full felicity; and that there was something which certainly was the reason and end of life superior to all these things, and which was either to be possessed, or at least hoped for, on this side of the grave.

But my sage counsellor was gone; I was like a ship without a pilot, that could only run afore the wind. My thoughts ran all away again into the old affair; my head was quite turned with the whimsies of foreign adventures; and all the pleasant, innocent amusements of my farm, my garden, my cattle, and my family, which before entirely possessed me, were nothing to me, had no relish, and were like music to one that has no ear, or food to one that has no taste. In a word, I resolved to leave off housekeeping, let my farm, and return to London; and in a few months after I did so.

When I came to London, I was still as uneasy as I was before; I had no relish for the place, no employment in it, nothing to do but to saunter about like an idle person, of whom it may be said he is perfectly useless in God's creation, and it is not one farthing's matter to the rest of his kind whether he be dead or alive. This also was the thing which, of all circumstances of life, was the most my aversion, who had been all my days used to an active life; and I would often say to myself, "A state of idleness is the very dregs of life;" and, indeed, I thought I was much more suitably employed when I was twenty-six days making a deal board.

It was now the beginning of the year 1693, when my nephew, whom, as I have observed before, I had brought up to the sea, and had made him commander of a ship, was come home from a short voyage to Bilbao, being the first he had made. He came to me, and told me that some merchants of his acquaintance had been proposing to him to go a voyage for them to the East Indies, and to China, as private traders. "And now, uncle," says he, "if you will go to sea with me, I will engage to land you upon your old habitation in the island; for we are to touch at the Brazils."

Nothing can be a greater demonstration of a future state, and of the existence of an invisible world, than the concurrence of second causes with the idea of things which we form in our minds, perfectly reserved, and not communicated to any in the world.

My nephew knew nothing how far my distemper of wandering was returned upon me, and I knew nothing of what he had in his thought to say, when that very morning, before he came to me, I had, in a great deal of confusion of thought, and revolving every part of my circumstances in my mind, come to this resolution, that I would go to Lisbon, and consult with my old sea-captain; and if it was rational and practicable, I would go and see the island again, and what was become of my people there. I had pleased myself with the thoughts of peopling the place, and carrying inhabitants from hence, getting a patent for the possession and I know not what; when, in the middle of all this, in comes my nephew, as I have said, with his project of carrying me thither in his way to the East Indies.

I paused a while at his words, and looking steadily at him, "What devil," said I, "sent you on this unlucky errand?" My nephew stared as if he had been frightened at first; but perceiving that I was not much displeased at the proposal, he recovered himself. "I hope it may not be an unlucky proposal, sir," says he. "I daresay you would be pleased to see your new colony there, where you once reigned with more felicity than most of your brother monarchs in the world." In a word, the scheme hit so exactly with my temper, that is to say, the prepossession I was under, and of which I have said so much, that I told him, in a few words, if he agreed with the merchants, I would go with him; but I told him I would not promise to go any further than my own island. "Why, sir," says he, "you don't want to be left there again, I hope?" "But," said I, "can you not take me up again on your return?" He told me it would not be possible to do so; that the merchants would never allow him to come that way with a laden ship of such value, it being a month's sail out of his way, and might be three or four. "Besides, sir, if I should miscarry," said he, "and not return at all, then you would be just reduced to the condition you were in before."

This was very rational; but we both found out a remedy for it, which was to carry a framed sloop on board the ship, which, being taken in pieces, might, by the help of some carpenters, whom we agreed to carry with us, be set up again in the island, and finished fit to go to sea in a few days. I was not long resolving, for indeed the importunities of my nephew joined so effectually with my inclination that nothing could oppose me; on the other hand, my wife being dead, none concerned themselves so much for me as to persuade me one way or the other, except my ancient good friend the widow, who earnestly struggled with me to consider my years, my easy circumstances, and the needless hazards of a long voyage; and above all, my young children. But it was all to no purpose, I had an irresistible desire for the voyage; and I told her I thought there was something so uncommon in the impressions I had upon my mind, that it would be a kind of resisting Providence if I should attempt to stay at home; after which she ceased her expostulations, and joined with me, not only in making provision for my voyage, but also in settling my family affairs for my absence, and providing for the education of my children. In order to do this, I made my will, and settled the estate I had in such a manner for my children, and placed in such hands, that I was perfectly easy and satisfied they would have justice done them, whatever might befall me; and for their education, I left it wholly to the widow, with a sufficient maintenance to herself for her care: all which she richly deserved; for no mother could have taken more care in their education, or understood it better; and as she lived till I came home, I also lived to thank her for it.

My nephew was ready to sail about the beginning of January 1694-5; and I, with my man Friday, went on board, in the Downs, the 8th; having, besides that sloop which I mentioned above, a very considerable cargo of all kinds of necessary things for my colony, which, if I did not find in good condition, I resolved to leave so.

First, I carried with me some servants whom I purposed to place there as inhabitants, or at least to set on work there upon my account while I stayed, and either to leave them there or carry them forward, as they should appear willing; particularly, I carried two carpenters, a smith, and a very handy, ingenious fellow, who was a cooper by trade, and was also a general mechanic; for he was dexterous at making wheels and hand-mills to grind corn, was a good turner and a good pot-maker; he also made anything that was proper to make of earth or of wood: in a word, we called him our Jack-of-all-trades. With these I carried a tailor, who had offered himself to go a passenger to the East Indies with my nephew, but afterwards consented to stay on our new plantation, and who proved a most necessary handy fellow as could be desired in many other businesses besides that of his trade; for, as I observed formerly, necessity arms us for all employments.

My cargo, as near as I can recollect, for I have not kept account of the particulars, consisted of a sufficient quantity of linen, and some English thin stuffs, for clothing the Spaniards that I expected to find there; and enough of them, as by my calculation might comfortably supply them for seven years; if I remember right, the materials I carried for clothing them, with gloves, hats, shoes, stockings, and all such things as they could want for wearing, amounted to about two hundred pounds, including some beds, bedding, and household stuff, particularly kitchen utensils, with pots, kettles, pewter, brass, &c.; and near a hundred pounds more in ironwork, nails, tools of every kind, staples, hooks, hinges, and every necessary thing I could think of.

I carried also a hundred spare arms, muskets, and fusees; besides some pistols, a considerable quantity of shot of all sizes, three or four tons of lead, and two pieces of brass cannon; and, because I knew not what time and what extremities I was providing for, I carried a hundred barrels of powder, besides swords, cutlasses, and the iron part of some pikes and halberds. In short, we had a large magazine of all sorts of store; and I made my nephew carry two small quarter-deck guns more than he wanted for his ship, to leave behind if there was occasion; so that when we came there we might build a fort and man it against all sorts of enemies. Indeed, I at first thought there would be need enough for all, and much more, if we hoped to maintain our possession of the island, as shall be seen in the course of that story.

I had not such bad luck in this voyage as I had been used to meet with, and therefore shall have the less occasion to interrupt the reader, who perhaps may be impatient to hear how matters went with my colony; yet some odd accidents, cross winds and bad weather happened on this first setting out, which made the voyage longer than I expected it at first; and I, who had never made but one voyage, my first voyage to Guinea, in which I might be said to come back again, as the voyage was at first designed, began to think the same ill fate attended me, and that I was born to be never contented with being on shore, and yet to be always unfortunate at sea. Contrary winds first put us to the northward, and we were obliged to put in at Galway, in Ireland, where we lay wind-bound two-and-twenty days; but we had this satisfaction with the disaster, that provisions were here exceeding cheap, and in the utmost plenty; so that while we lay here we never touched the ship's stores, but rather added to them. Here, also, I took in several live hogs, and two cows with their calves, which I resolved, if I had a good passage, to put on shore in my island; but we found occasion to dispose otherwise of them.

We set out on the 5th of February from Ireland, and had a very fair gale of wind for some days. As I remember, it might be about the 20th of February in the evening late, when the mate, having the watch, came into the round-house and told us he saw a flash of fire, and heard a gun fired; and while he was telling us of it, a boy came in and told us the boatswain heard another. This made us all run out upon the quarter-deck, where for a while we heard nothing; but in a few minutes we saw a very great light, and found that there was some very terrible fire at a distance; immediately we had recourse to our reckonings, in which we all agreed that there could be no land that way in which the fire showed itself, no, not for five hundred leagues, for it appeared at WNW. Upon this, we concluded it must be some ship on fire at sea; and as, by our hearing the noise of guns just before, we concluded that it could not be far off, we stood directly towards it, and were presently satisfied we should discover it, because the further we sailed, the greater the light appeared; though, the weather being hazy, we could not perceive anything but the light for a while. In about half-an-hour's sailing, the wind being fair for us, though not much of it, and the weather clearing up a little, we could plainly discern that it was a great ship on fire in the middle of the sea.

I was most sensibly touched with this disaster, though not at all acquainted with the persons engaged in it; I presently recollected my former circumstances, and what condition I was in when taken up by the Portuguese captain; and how much more deplorable the circumstances of the poor creatures belonging to that ship must be, if they had no other ship in company with them. Upon this I immediately ordered that five guns should be fired, one soon after another, that, if possible, we might give notice to them that there was help for them at hand and that they might endeavour to save themselves in their boat; for though we could see the flames of the ship, yet they, it being night, could see nothing of us.

We lay by some time upon this, only driving as the burning ship drove, waiting for daylight; when, on a sudden, to our great terror, though we had reason to expect it, the ship blew up in the air; and in a few minutes all the fire was out, that is to say, the rest of the ship sunk. This was a terrible, and indeed an afflicting sight, for the sake of the poor men, who, I concluded, must be either all destroyed in the ship, or be in the utmost distress in their boat, in the middle of the ocean; which, at present, as it was dark, I could not see. However, to direct them as well as I could, I caused lights to be hung out in all parts of the ship where we could, and which we had lanterns for, and kept firing guns all the night long, letting them know by this that there was a ship not far off.

About eight o'clock in the morning we discovered the ship's boats by the help of our perspective glasses, and found there were two of them, both thronged with people, and deep in the water. We perceived they rowed, the wind being against them; that they saw our ship, and did their utmost to make us see them. We immediately spread our ancient, to let them know we saw them, and hung a waft out, as a signal for them to come on board, and then made more sail, standing directly to them. In little more than half-an-hour we came up with them; and took them all in, being no less than sixty-four men, women, and children; for there were a great many passengers.

Upon inquiry we found it was a French merchant ship of three-hundred tons, homebound from Quebec. The master gave us a long account of the distress of his ship; how the fire began in the steerage by the negligence of the steersman, which, on his crying out for help, was, as everybody thought, entirely put out; but they soon found that some sparks of the first fire had got into some part of the ship so difficult to come at that they could not effectually quench it; and afterwards getting in between the timbers, and within the ceiling of the ship, it proceeded into the hold, and mastered all the skill and all the application they were able to exert.

They had no more to do then but to get into their boats, which, to their great comfort, were pretty large; being their long-boat, and a great shallop, besides a small skiff, which was of no great service to them, other than to get some fresh water and provisions into her, after they had secured their lives from the fire. They had, indeed, small hopes of their lives by getting into these boats at that distance from any land; only, as they said, that they thus escaped from the fire, and there was a possibility that some ship might happen to be at sea, and might take them in. They had sails, oars, and a compass; and had as much provision and water as, with sparing it so as to be next door to starving, might support them about twelve days, in which, if they had no bad weather and no contrary winds, the captain said he hoped he might get to the banks of Newfoundland, and might perhaps take some fish, to sustain them till they might go on shore. But there were so many chances against them in all these cases, such as storms, to overset and founder them; rains and cold, to benumb and perish their limbs; contrary winds, to keep them out and starve them; that it must have been next to miraculous if they had escaped.

In the midst of their consternation, every one being hopeless and ready to despair, the captain, with tears in his eyes, told me they were on a sudden surprised with the joy of hearing a gun fire, and after that four more: these were the five guns which I caused to be fired at first seeing the light. This revived their hearts, and gave them the notice, which, as above, I desired it should, that there was a ship at hand for their help. It was upon the hearing of these guns that they took down their masts and sails: the sound coming from the windward, they resolved to lie by till morning. Some time after this, hearing no more guns, they fired three muskets, one a considerable while after another; but these, the wind being contrary, we never heard. Some time after that again they were still more agreeably surprised with seeing our lights, and hearing the guns, which, as I have said, I caused to be fired all the rest of the night. This set them to work with their oars, to keep their boats ahead, at least that we might the sooner come up with them; and at last, to their inexpressible joy, they found we saw them.

It is impossible for me to express the several gestures, the strange ecstasies, the variety of postures which these poor delivered people ran into, to express the joy of their souls at so unexpected a deliverance. Grief and fear are easily described: sighs, tears, groans, and a very few motions of the head and hands, make up the sum of its variety; but an excess of joy, a surprise of joy, has a thousand extravagances in it. There were some in tears; some raging and tearing themselves, as if they had been in the greatest agonies of sorrow; some stark raving and downright lunatic; some ran about the ship stamping with their feet, others wringing their hands; some were dancing, some singing, some laughing, more crying, many quite dumb, not able to speak a word; others sick and vomiting; several swooning and ready to faint; and a few were crossing themselves and giving God thanks.

I would not wrong them either; there might be many that were thankful afterwards; but the passion was too strong for them at first, and they were not able to master it: then were thrown into ecstasies, and a kind of frenzy, and it was but a very few that were composed and serious in their joy. Perhaps also, the case may have some addition to it from the particular circumstance of that nation they belonged to: I mean the French, whose temper is allowed to be more volatile, more passionate, and more sprightly, and their spirits more fluid than in other nations. I am not philosopher enough to determine the cause; but nothing I had ever seen before came up to it. The ecstasies poor Friday, my trusty savage, was in when he found his father in the boat came the nearest to it; and the surprise of the master and his two companions, whom I delivered from the villains that set them on shore in the island, came a little way towards it; but nothing was to compare to this, either that I saw in Friday, or anywhere else in my life.

It is further observable, that these extravagances did not show themselves in that different manner I have mentioned, in different persons only; but all the variety would appear, in a short succession of moments, in one and the same person. A man that we saw this minute dumb, and, as it were, stupid and confounded, would the next minute be dancing and hallooing like an antic; and the next moment be tearing his hair, or pulling his clothes to pieces, and stamping them under his feet like a madman; in a few moments after that we would have him all in tears, then sick, swooning, and, had not immediate help been had, he would in a few moments have been dead. Thus it was, not with one or two, or ten or twenty, but with the greatest part of them; and, if I remember right, our surgeon was obliged to let blood of about thirty persons.

There were two priests among them: one an old man, and the other a young man; and that which was strangest was, the oldest man was the worst. As soon as he set his foot on board our ship, and saw himself safe, he dropped down stone dead to all appearance. Not the least sign of life could be perceived in him; our surgeon immediately applied proper remedies to recover him, and was the only man in the ship that believed he was not dead. At length he opened a vein in his arm, having first chafed and rubbed the part, so as to warm it as much as possible. Upon this the blood, which only dropped at first, flowing freely, in three minutes after the man opened his eyes; a quarter of an hour after that he spoke, grew better, and after the blood was stopped, he walked about, told us he was perfectly well, and took a dram of cordial which the surgeon gave him. About a quarter of an hour after this they came running into the cabin to the surgeon, who was bleeding a Frenchwoman that had fainted, and told him the priest was gone stark mad. It seems he had begun to revolve the change of his circumstances in his mind, and again this put him into an ecstasy of joy. His spirits whirled about faster than the vessels could convey them, the blood grew hot and feverish, and the man was as fit for Bedlam as any creature that ever was in it. The surgeon would not bleed him again in that condition, but gave him something to doze and put him to sleep; which, after some time, operated upon him, and he awoke next morning perfectly composed and well. The younger priest behaved with great command of his passions, and was really an example of a serious, well-governed mind. At his first coming on board the ship he threw himself flat on his face, prostrating himself in thankfulness for his deliverance, in which I unhappily and unseasonably disturbed him, really thinking he had been in a swoon; but he spoke calmly, thanked me, told me he was giving God thanks for his deliverance, begged me to leave him a few moments, and that, next to his Maker, he would give me thanks also. I was heartily sorry that I disturbed him, and not only left him, but kept others from interrupting him also. He continued in that posture about three minutes, or little more, after I left him, then came to me, as he had said he would, and with a great deal of seriousness and affection, but with tears in his eyes, thanked me, that had, under God, given him and so many miserable creatures their lives. I told him I had no need to tell him to thank God for it, rather than me, for I had seen that he had done that already; but I added that it was nothing but what reason and humanity dictated to all men, and that we had as much reason as he to give thanks to God, who had blessed us so far as to make us the instruments of His mercy to so many of His creatures. After this the young priest applied himself to his countrymen, and laboured to compose them: he persuaded, entreated, argued, reasoned with them, and did his utmost to keep them within the exercise of their reason; and with some he had success, though others were for a time out of all government of themselves.

I cannot help committing this to writing, as perhaps it may be useful to those into whose hands it may fall, for guiding themselves in the extravagances of their passions; for if an excess of joy can carry men out to such a length beyond the reach of their reason, what will not the extravagances of anger, rage, and a provoked mind carry us to? And, indeed, here I saw reason for keeping an exceeding watch over our passions of every kind, as well those of joy and satisfaction as those of sorrow and anger.

We were somewhat disordered by these extravagances among our new guests for the first day; but after they had retired to lodgings provided for them as well as our ship would allow, and had slept heartily—as most of them did, being fatigued and frightened—they were quite another sort of people the next day. Nothing of good manners, or civil acknowledgments for the kindness shown them, was wanting; the French, it is known, are naturally apt enough to exceed that way. The captain and one of the priests came to me the next day, and desired to speak with me and my nephew; the commander began to consult with us what should be done with them; and first, they told us we had saved their lives, so all they had was little enough for a return to us for that kindness received. The captain said they had saved some money and some things of value in their boats, caught hastily out of the flames, and if we would accept it they were ordered to make an offer of it all to us; they only desired to be set on shore somewhere in our way, where, if possible, they might get a passage to France. My nephew wished to accept their money at first word, and to consider what to do with them afterwards; but I overruled him in that part, for I knew what it was to be set on shore in a strange country; and if the Portuguese captain that took me up at sea had served me so, and taken all I had for my deliverance, I must have been starved, or have been as much a slave at the Brazils as I had been at Barbary, the mere being sold to a Mahometan excepted; and perhaps a Portuguese is not a much better master than a Turk, if not in some cases much worse.

I therefore told the French captain that we had taken them up in their distress, it was true, but that it was our duty to do so, as we were fellow-creatures; and we would desire to be so delivered if we were in the like or any other extremity; that we had done nothing for them but what we believed they would have done for us if we had been in their case and they in ours; but that we took them up to save them, not to plunder them; and it would be a most barbarous thing to take that little from them which they had saved out of the fire, and then set them on shore and leave them; that this would be first to save them from death, and then kill them ourselves: save them from drowning, and abandon them to starving; and therefore I would not let the least thing be taken from them. As to setting them on shore, I told them indeed that was an exceeding difficulty to us, for that the ship was bound to the East Indies; and though we were driven out of our course to the westward a very great way, and perhaps were directed by Heaven on purpose for their deliverance, yet it was impossible for us wilfully to change our voyage on their particular account; nor could my nephew, the captain, answer it to the freighters, with whom he was under charter to pursue his voyage by way of Brazil; and all I knew we could do for them was to put ourselves in the way of meeting with other ships homeward bound from the West Indies, and get them a passage, if possible, to England or France.

The first part of the proposal was so generous and kind they could not but be very thankful for it; but they were in very great consternation, especially the passengers, at the notion of being carried away to the East Indies; they then entreated me that as I was driven so far to the westward before I met with them, I would at least keep on the same course to the banks of Newfoundland, where it was probable I might meet with some ship or sloop that they might hire to carry them back to Canada.

I thought this was but a reasonable request on their part, and therefore I inclined to agree to it; for indeed I considered that to carry this whole company to the East Indies would not only be an intolerable severity upon the poor people, but would be ruining our whole voyage by devouring all our provisions; so I thought it no breach of charter-party, but what an unforeseen accident made absolutely necessary to us, and in which no one could say we were to blame; for the laws of God and nature would have forbid that we should refuse to take up two boats full of people in such a distressed condition; and the nature of the thing, as well respecting ourselves as the poor people, obliged us to set them on shore somewhere or other for their deliverance. So I consented that we would carry them to Newfoundland, if wind and weather would permit: and if not, I would carry them to Martinico, in the West Indies.

The wind continued fresh easterly, but the weather pretty good; and as the winds had continued in the points between NE. and SE. a long time, we missed several opportunities of sending them to France; for we met several ships bound to Europe, whereof two were French, from St. Christopher's, but they had been so long beating up against the wind that they durst take in no passengers, for fear of wanting provisions for the voyage, as well for themselves as for those they should take in; so we were obliged to go on. It was about a week after this that we made the banks of Newfoundland; where, to shorten my story, we put all our French people on board a bark, which they hired at sea there, to put them on shore, and afterwards to carry them to France, if they could get provisions to victual themselves with. When I say all the French went on shore, I should remember that the young priest I spoke of, hearing we were bound to the East Indies, desired to go the voyage with us, and to be set on shore on the coast of Coromandel; which I readily agreed to, for I wonderfully liked the man, and had very good reason, as will appear afterwards; also four of the seamen entered themselves on our ship, and proved very useful fellows.

From hence we directed our course for the West Indies, steering away S. and S. by E. for about twenty days together, sometimes little or no wind at all; when we met with another subject for our humanity to work upon, almost as deplorable as that before.

2

INTERVENING HISTORY OF COLONY

It was in the latitude of 27 degrees 5 minutes N., on the 19th day of March 1694-95, when we spied a sail, our course SE. and by S. We soon perceived it was a large vessel, and that she bore up to us, but could not at first know what to make of her, till, after coming a little nearer, we found she had lost her main-topmast, fore-mast, and bowsprit; and presently she fired a gun as a signal of distress. The weather was pretty good, wind at NNW. a fresh gale, and we soon came to speak with her. We found her a ship of Bristol, bound home from Barbadoes, but had been blown out of the road at Barbadoes a few days before she was ready to sail, by a terrible hurricane, while the captain and chief mate were both gone on shore; so that, besides the terror of the storm, they were in an indifferent case for good mariners to bring the ship home. They had been already nine weeks at sea, and had met with another terrible storm, after the hurricane was over, which had blown them quite out of their knowledge to the westward, and in which they lost their masts. They told us they expected to have seen the Bahama Islands, but were then driven away again to the south-east, by a strong gale of wind at NNW., the same that blew now: and having no sails to work the ship with but a main course, and a kind of square sail upon a jury fore-mast, which they had set up, they could not lie near the wind, but were endeavouring to stand away for the Canaries.

But that which was worst of all was, that they were almost starved for want of provisions, besides the fatigues they had undergone; their bread and flesh were quite gone—they had not one ounce left in the ship, and had had none for eleven days. The only relief they had was, their water was not all spent, and they had about half a barrel of flour left; they had sugar enough; some succades, or sweetmeats, they had at first, but these were all devoured; and they had seven casks of rum. There was a youth and his mother and a maid-servant on board, who were passengers, and thinking the ship was ready to sail, unhappily came on board the evening before the hurricane began; and having no provisions of their own left, they were in a more deplorable condition than the rest: for the seamen being reduced to such an extreme necessity themselves, had no compassion, we may be sure, for the poor passengers; and they were, indeed, in such a condition that their misery is very hard to describe.

I had perhaps not known this part, if my curiosity had not led me, the weather being fair and the wind abated, to go on board the ship. The second mate, who upon this occasion commanded the ship, had been on board our ship, and he told me they had three passengers in the great cabin that were in a deplorable condition. "Nay," says he, "I believe they are dead, for I have heard nothing of them for above two days; and I was afraid to inquire after them," said he, "for I had nothing to relieve them with." We immediately applied ourselves to give them what relief we could spare; and indeed I had so far overruled things with my nephew, that I would have victualled them though we had gone away to Virginia, or any other part of the coast of America, to have supplied ourselves; but there was no necessity for that.

But now they were in a new danger; for they were afraid of eating too much, even of that little we gave them. The mate, or commander, brought six men with him in his boat; but these poor wretches looked like skeletons, and were so weak that they could hardly sit to their oars. The mate himself was very ill, and half starved; for he declared he had reserved nothing from the men, and went share and share alike with them in every bit they ate. I cautioned him to eat sparingly, and set meat before him immediately, but he had not eaten three mouthfuls before he began to be sick and out of order; so he stopped a while, and our surgeon mixed him up something with some broth, which he said would be to him both food and physic; and after he had taken it he grew better. In the meantime I forgot not the men. I ordered victuals to be given them, and the poor creatures rather devoured than ate it: they were so exceedingly hungry that they were in a manner ravenous, and had no command of themselves; and two of them ate with so much greediness that they were in danger of their lives the next morning. The sight of these people's distress was very moving to me, and brought to mind what I had a terrible prospect of at my first coming on shore in my island, where I had not the least mouthful of food, or any prospect of procuring any; besides the hourly apprehensions I had of being made the food of other creatures. But all the while the mate was thus relating to me the miserable condition of the ship's company, I could not put out of my thought the story he had told me of the three poor creatures in the great cabin, viz. the mother, her son, and the maid-servant, whom he had heard nothing of for two or three days, and whom, he seemed to confess, they had wholly neglected, their own extremities being so great; by which I understood that they had really given them no food at all, and that therefore they must be perished, and be all lying dead, perhaps, on the floor or deck of the cabin.

As I therefore kept the mate, whom we then called captain, on board with his men, to refresh them, so I also forgot not the starving crew that were left on board, but ordered my own boat to go on board the ship, and, with my mate and twelve men, to carry them a sack of bread, and four or five pieces of beef to boil. Our surgeon charged the men to cause the meat to be boiled while they stayed, and to keep guard in the cook-room, to prevent the men taking it to eat raw, or taking it out of the pot before it was well boiled, and then to give every man but a very little at a time: and by this caution he preserved the men, who would otherwise have killed themselves with that very food that was given them on purpose to save their lives.

At the same time I ordered the mate to go into the great cabin, and see what condition the poor passengers were in; and if they were alive, to comfort them, and give them what refreshment was proper: and the surgeon gave him a large pitcher, with some of the prepared broth which he had given the mate that was on board, and which he did not question would restore them gradually. I was not satisfied with this; but, as I said above, having a great mind to see the scene of misery which I knew the ship itself would present me with, in a more lively manner than I could have it by report, I took the captain of the ship, as we now called him, with me, and went myself, a little after, in their boat.

I found the poor men on board almost in a tumult to get the victuals out of the boiler before it was ready; but my mate observed his orders, and kept a good guard at the cook-room door, and the man he placed there, after using all possible persuasion to have patience, kept them off by force; however, he caused some biscuit-cakes to be dipped in the pot, and softened with the liquor of the meat, which they called brewis, and gave them every one some to stay their stomachs, and told them it was for their own safety that he was obliged to give them but little at a time. But it was all in vain; and had I not come on board, and their own commander and officers with me, and with good words, and some threats also of giving them no more, I believe they would have broken into the cook-room by force, and torn the meat out of the furnace—for words are indeed of very small force to a hungry belly; however, we pacified them, and fed them gradually and cautiously at first, and the next time gave them more, and at last filled their bellies, and the men did well enough.

But the misery of the poor passengers in the cabin was of another nature, and far beyond the rest; for as, first, the ship's company had so little for themselves, it was but too true that they had at first kept them very low, and at last totally neglected them: so that for six or seven days it might be said they had really no food at all, and for several days before very little. The poor mother, who, as the men reported, was a woman of sense and good breeding, had spared all she could so affectionately for her son, that at last she entirely sank under it; and when the mate of our ship went in, she sat upon the floor on deck, with her back up against the sides, between two chairs, which were lashed fast, and her head sunk between her shoulders like a corpse, though not quite dead. My mate said all he could to revive and encourage her, and with a spoon put some broth into her mouth. She opened her lips, and lifted up one hand, but could not speak: yet she understood what he said, and made signs to him, intimating, that it was too late for her, but pointed to her child, as if she would have said they should take care of him. However, the mate, who was exceedingly moved at the sight, endeavoured to get some of the broth into her mouth, and, as he said, got two or three spoonfuls down—though I question whether he could be sure of it or not; but it was too late, and she died the same night.

The youth, who was preserved at the price of his most affectionate mother's life, was not so far gone; yet he lay in a cabin bed, as one stretched out, with hardly any life left in him. He had a piece of an old glove in his mouth, having eaten up the rest of it; however, being young, and having more strength than his mother, the mate got something down his throat, and he began sensibly to revive; though by giving him, some time after, but two or three spoonfuls extraordinary, he was very sick, and brought it up again.

But the next care was the poor maid: she lay all along upon the deck, hard by her mistress, and just like one that had fallen down in a fit of apoplexy, and struggled for life. Her limbs were distorted; one of her hands was clasped round the frame of the chair, and she gripped it so hard that we could not easily make her let it go; her other arm lay over her head, and her feet lay both together, set fast against the frame of the cabin table: in short, she lay just like one in the agonies of death, and yet she was alive too. The poor creature was not only starved with hunger, and terrified with the thoughts of death, but, as the men told us afterwards, was broken-hearted for her mistress, whom she saw dying for two or three days before, and whom she loved most tenderly. We knew not what to do with this poor girl; for when our surgeon, who was a man of very great knowledge and experience, had, with great application, recovered her as to life, he had her upon his hands still; for she was little less than distracted for a considerable time after.

Whoever shall read these memorandums must be desired to consider that visits at sea are not like a journey into the country, where sometimes people stay a week or a fortnight at a place. Our business was to relieve this distressed ship's crew, but not lie by for them; and though they were willing to steer the same course with us for some days, yet we could carry no sail to keep pace with a ship that had no masts. However, as their captain begged of us to help him to set up a main-topmast, and a kind of a topmast to his jury fore-mast, we did, as it were, lie by him for three or four days; and then, having given him five barrels of beef, a barrel of pork, two hogsheads of biscuit, and a proportion of peas, flour, and what other things we could spare; and taking three casks of sugar, some rum, and some pieces of eight from them for satisfaction, we left them, taking on board with us, at their own earnest request, the youth and the maid, and all their goods.

The young lad was about seventeen years of age, a pretty, well-bred, modest, and sensible youth, greatly dejected with the loss of his mother, and also at having lost his father but a few months before, at Barbadoes. He begged of the surgeon to speak to me to take him out of the ship; for he said the cruel fellows had murdered his mother: and indeed so they had, that is to say, passively; for they might have spared a small sustenance to the poor helpless widow, though it had been but just enough to keep her alive; but hunger knows no friend, no relation, no justice, no right, and therefore is remorseless, and capable of no compassion.

The surgeon told him how far we were going, and that it would carry him away from all his friends, and put him, perhaps, in as bad circumstances almost as those we found him in, that is to say, starving in the world. He said it mattered not whither he went, if he was but delivered from the terrible crew that he was among; that the captain (by which he meant me, for he could know nothing of my nephew) had saved his life, and he was sure would not hurt him; and as for the maid, he was sure, if she came to herself, she would be very thankful for it, let us carry them where we would. The surgeon represented the case so affectionately to me that I yielded, and we took them both on board, with all their goods, except eleven hogsheads of sugar, which could not be removed or come at; and as the youth had a bill of lading for them, I made his commander sign a writing, obliging himself to go, as soon as he came to Bristol, to one Mr. Rogers, a merchant there, to whom the youth said he was related, and to deliver a letter which I wrote to him, and all the goods he had belonging to the deceased widow; which, I suppose, was not done, for I could never learn that the ship came to Bristol, but was, as is most probable, lost at sea, being in so disabled a condition, and so far from any land, that I am of opinion the first storm she met with afterwards she might founder, for she was leaky, and had damage in her hold when we met with her.

I was now in the latitude of 19 degrees 32 minutes, and had hitherto a tolerable voyage as to weather, though at first the winds had been contrary. I shall trouble nobody with the little incidents of wind, weather, currents, &c., on the rest of our voyage; but to shorten my story, shall observe that I came to my old habitation, the island, on the 10th of April 1695. It was with no small difficulty that I found the place; for as I came to it and went to it before on the south and east side of the island, coming from the Brazils, so now, coming in between the main and the island, and having no chart for the coast, nor any landmark, I did not know it when I saw it, or, know whether I saw it or not. We beat about a great while, and went on shore on several islands in the mouth of the great river Orinoco, but none for my purpose; only this I learned by my coasting the shore, that I was under one great mistake before, viz. that the continent which I thought I saw from the island I lived in was really no continent, but a long island, or rather a ridge of islands, reaching from one to the other side of the extended mouth of that great river; and that the savages who came to my island were not properly those which we call Caribbees, but islanders, and other barbarians of the same kind, who inhabited nearer to our side than the rest.

In short, I visited several of these islands to no purpose; some I found were inhabited, and some were not; on one of them I found some Spaniards, and thought they had lived there; but speaking with them, found they had a sloop lying in a small creek hard by, and came thither to make salt, and to catch some pearl-mussels if they could; but that they belonged to the Isle de Trinidad, which lay farther north, in the latitude of 10 and 11 degrees.

Thus coasting from one island to another, sometimes with the ship, sometimes with the Frenchman's shallop, which we had found a convenient boat, and therefore kept her with their very good will, at length I came fair on the south side of my island, and presently knew the very countenance of the place: so I brought the ship safe to an anchor, broadside with the little creek where my old habitation was. As soon as I saw the place I called for Friday, and asked him if he knew where he was? He looked about a little, and presently clapping his hands, cried, "Oh yes, Oh there, Oh yes, Oh there!" pointing to our old habitation, and fell dancing and capering like a mad fellow; and I had much ado to keep him from jumping into the sea to swim ashore to the place.

"Well, Friday," says I, "do you think we shall find anybody here or no? and do you think we shall see your father?" The fellow stood mute as a stock a good while; but when I named his father, the poor affectionate creature looked dejected, and I could see the tears run down his face very plentifully. "What is the matter, Friday? are you troubled because you may see your father?" "No, no," says he, shaking his head, "no see him more: no, never more see him again." "Why so, Friday? how do you know that?" "Oh no, Oh no," says Friday, "he long ago die, long ago; he much old man." "Well, well, Friday, you don't know; but shall we see any one else, then?" The fellow, it seems, had better eyes than I, and he points to the hill just above my old house; and though we lay half a league off, he cries out, "We see! we see! yes, we see much man there, and there, and there." I looked, but I saw nobody, no, not with a perspective glass, which was, I suppose, because I could not hit the place: for the fellow was right, as I found upon inquiry the next day; and there were five or six men all together, who stood to look at the ship, not knowing what to think of us.

As soon as Friday told me he saw people, I caused the English ancient to be spread, and fired three guns, to give them notice we were friends; and in about a quarter of an hour after we perceived a smoke arise from the side of the creek; so I immediately ordered the boat out, taking Friday with me, and hanging out a white flag, I went directly on shore, taking with me the young friar I mentioned, to whom I had told the story of my living there, and the manner of it, and every particular both of myself and those I left there, and who was on that account extremely desirous to go with me. We had, besides, about sixteen men well armed, if we had found any new guests there which we did not know of; but we had no need of weapons.

As we went on shore upon the tide of flood, near high water, we rowed directly into the creek; and the first man I fixed my eye upon was the Spaniard whose life I had saved, and whom I knew by his face perfectly well: as to his habit, I shall describe it afterwards. I ordered nobody to go on shore at first but myself; but there was no keeping Friday in the boat, for the affectionate creature had spied his father at a distance, a good way off the Spaniards, where, indeed, I saw nothing of him; and if they had not let him go ashore, he would have jumped into the sea. He was no sooner on shore, but he flew away to his father like an arrow out of a bow. It would have made any man shed tears, in spite of the firmest resolution, to have seen the first transports of this poor fellow's joy when he came to his father: how he embraced him, kissed him, stroked his face, took him up in his arms, set him down upon a tree, and lay down by him; then stood and looked at him, as any one would look at a strange picture, for a quarter of an hour together; then lay down on the ground, and stroked his legs, and kissed them, and then got up again and stared at him; one would have thought the fellow bewitched. But it would have made a dog laugh the next day to see how his passion ran out another way: in the morning he walked along the shore with his father several hours, always leading him by the hand, as if he had been a lady; and every now and then he would come to the boat to fetch something or other for him, either a lump of sugar, a dram, a biscuit, or something or other that was good. In the afternoon his frolics ran another way; for then he would set the old man down upon the ground, and dance about him, and make a thousand antic gestures; and all the while he did this he would be talking to him, and telling him one story or another of his travels, and of what had happened to him abroad to divert him. In short, if the same filial affection was to be found in Christians to their parents in our part of the world, one would be tempted to say there would hardly have been any need of the fifth commandment.

But this is a digression: I return to my landing. It would be needless to take notice of all the ceremonies and civilities that the Spaniards received me with. The first Spaniard, whom, as I said, I knew very well, was he whose life I had saved. He came towards the boat, attended by one more, carrying a flag of truce also; and he not only did not know me at first, but he had no thoughts, no notion of its being me that was come, till I spoke to him. "Seignior," said I, in Portuguese, "do you not know me?" At which he spoke not a word, but giving his musket to the man that was with him, threw his arms abroad, saying something in Spanish that I did not perfectly hear, came forward and embraced me, telling me he was inexcusable not to know that face again that he had once seen, as of an angel from heaven sent to save his life; he said abundance of very handsome things, as a well-bred Spaniard always knows how, and then, beckoning to the person that attended him, bade him go and call out his comrades. He then asked me if I would walk to my old habitation, where he would give me possession of my own house again, and where I should see they had made but mean improvements. I walked along with him, but, alas! I could no more find the place than if I had never been there; for they had planted so many trees, and placed them in such a position, so thick and close to one another, and in ten years' time they were grown so big, that the place was inaccessible, except by such windings and blind ways as they themselves only, who made them, could find.

I asked them what put them upon all these fortifications; he told me I would say there was need enough of it when they had given me an account how they had passed their time since their arriving in the island, especially after they had the misfortune to find that I was gone. He told me he could not but have some pleasure in my good fortune, when he heard that I was gone in a good ship, and to my satisfaction; and that he had oftentimes a strong persuasion that one time or other he should see me again, but nothing that ever befell him in his life, he said, was so surprising and afflicting to him at first as the disappointment he was under when he came back to the island and found I was not there.

As to the three barbarians (so he called them) that were left behind, and of whom, he said, he had a long story to tell me, the Spaniards all thought themselves much better among the savages, only that their number was so small: "And," says he, "had they been strong enough, we had been all long ago in purgatory;" and with that he crossed himself on the breast. "But, sir," says he, "I hope you will not be displeased when I shall tell you how, forced by necessity, we were obliged for our own preservation to disarm them, and make them our subjects, as they would not be content with being moderately our masters, but would be our murderers." I answered I was afraid of it when I left them there, and nothing troubled me at my parting from the island but that they were not come back, that I might have put them in possession of everything first, and left the others in a state of subjection, as they deserved; but if they had reduced them to it I was very glad, and should be very far from finding any fault with it; for I knew they were a parcel of refractory, ungoverned villains, and were fit for any manner of mischief.

While I was saying this, the man came whom he had sent back, and with him eleven more. In the dress they were in it was impossible to guess what nation they were of; but he made all clear, both to them and to me. First, he turned to me, and pointing to them, said, "These, sir, are some of the gentlemen who owe their lives to you;" and then turning to them, and pointing to me, he let them know who I was; upon which they all came up, one by one, not as if they had been sailors, and ordinary fellows, and the like, but really as if they had been ambassadors or noblemen, and I a monarch or great conqueror: their behaviour was, to the last degree, obliging and courteous, and yet mixed with a manly, majestic gravity, which very well became them; and, in short, they had so much more manners than I, that I scarce knew how to receive their civilities, much less how to return them in kind.

The history of their coming to, and conduct in, the island after my going away is so very remarkable, and has so many incidents which the former part of my relation will help to understand, and which will in most of the particulars, refer to the account I have already given, that I cannot but commit them, with great delight, to the reading of those that come after me.

In order to do this as intelligibly as I can, I must go back to the circumstances in which I left the island, and the persons on it, of whom I am to speak. And first, it is necessary to repeat that I had sent away Friday's father and the Spaniard (the two whose lives I had rescued from the savages) in a large canoe to the main, as I then thought it, to fetch over the Spaniard's companions that he left behind him, in order to save them from the like calamity that he had been in, and in order to succour them for the present; and that, if possible, we might together find some way for our deliverance afterwards. When I sent them away I had no visible appearance of, or the least room to hope for, my own deliverance, any more than I had twenty years before—much less had I any foreknowledge of what afterwards happened, I mean, of an English ship coming on shore there to fetch me off; and it could not be but a very great surprise to them, when they came back, not only to find that I was gone, but to find three strangers left on the spot, possessed of all that I had left behind me, which would otherwise have been their own.

The first thing, however, which I inquired into, that I might begin where I left off, was of their own part; and I desired the Spaniard would give me a particular account of his voyage back to his countrymen with the boat, when I sent him to fetch them over. He told me there was little variety in that part, for nothing remarkable happened to them on the way, having had very calm weather and a smooth sea. As for his countrymen, it could not be doubted, he said, but that they were overjoyed to see him (it seems he was the principal man among them, the captain of the vessel they had been shipwrecked in having been dead some time): they were, he said, the more surprised to see him, because they knew that he was fallen into the hands of the savages, who, they were satisfied, would devour him as they did all the rest of their prisoners; that when he told them the story of his deliverance, and in what manner he was furnished for carrying them away, it was like a dream to them, and their astonishment, he said, was somewhat like that of Joseph's brethren when he told them who he was, and the story of his exaltation in Pharaoh's court; but when he showed them the arms, the powder, the ball, the provisions that he brought them for their journey or voyage, they were restored to themselves, took a just share of the joy of their deliverance, and immediately prepared to come away with him.

Their first business was to get canoes; and in this they were obliged not to stick so much upon the honesty of it, but to trespass upon their friendly savages, and to borrow two large canoes, or periaguas, on pretence of going out a-fishing, or for pleasure. In these they came away the next morning. It seems they wanted no time to get themselves ready; for they had neither clothes nor provisions, nor anything in the world but what they had on them, and a few roots to eat, of which they used to make their bread. They were in all three weeks absent; and in that time, unluckily for them, I had the occasion offered for my escape, as I mentioned in the other part, and to get off from the island, leaving three of the most impudent, hardened, ungoverned, disagreeable villains behind me that any man could desire to meet with—to the poor Spaniards' great grief and disappointment.

The only just thing the rogues did was, that when the Spaniards came ashore, they gave my letter to them, and gave them provisions, and other relief, as I had ordered them to do; also they gave them the long paper of directions which I had left with them, containing the particular methods which I took for managing every part of my life there; the way I baked my bread, bred up tame goats, and planted my corn; how I cured my grapes, made my pots, and, in a word, everything I did. All this being written down, they gave to the Spaniards (two of them understood English well enough): nor did they refuse to accommodate the Spaniards with anything else, for they agreed very well for some time. They gave them an equal admission into the house or cave, and they began to live very sociably; and the head Spaniard, who had seen pretty much of my methods, together with Friday's father, managed all their affairs; but as for the Englishmen, they did nothing but ramble about the island, shoot parrots, and catch tortoises; and when they came home at night, the Spaniards provided their suppers for them.

The Spaniards would have been satisfied with this had the others but let them alone, which, however, they could not find in their hearts to do long: but, like the dog in the manger, they would not eat themselves, neither would they let the others eat. The differences, nevertheless, were at first but trivial, and such as are not worth relating, but at last it broke out into open war: and it began with all the rudeness and insolence that can be imagined—without reason, without provocation, contrary to nature, and indeed to common sense; and though, it is true, the first relation of it came from the Spaniards themselves, whom I may call the accusers, yet when I came to examine the fellows they could not deny a word of it.

But before I come to the particulars of this part, I must supply a defect in my former relation; and this was, I forgot to set down among the rest, that just as we were weighing the anchor to set sail, there happened a little quarrel on board of our ship, which I was once afraid would have turned to a second mutiny; nor was it appeased till the captain, rousing up his courage, and taking us all to his assistance, parted them by force, and making two of the most refractory fellows prisoners, he laid them in irons: and as they had been active in the former disorders, and let fall some ugly, dangerous words the second time, he threatened to carry them in irons to England, and have them hanged there for mutiny and running away with the ship. This, it seems, though the captain did not intend to do it, frightened some other men in the ship; and some of them had put it into the head of the rest that the captain only gave them good words for the present, till they should come to same English port, and that then they should be all put into gaol, and tried for their lives. The mate got intelligence of this, and acquainted us with it, upon which it was desired that I, who still passed for a great man among them, should go down with the mate and satisfy the men, and tell them that they might be assured, if they behaved well the rest of the voyage, all they had done for the time past should be pardoned. So I went, and after passing my honour's word to them they appeared easy, and the more so when I caused the two men that were in irons to be released and forgiven.

But this mutiny had brought us to an anchor for that night; the wind also falling calm next morning, we found that our two men who had been laid in irons had stolen each of them a musket and some other weapons (what powder or shot they had we knew not), and had taken the ship's pinnace, which was not yet hauled up, and run away with her to their companions in roguery on shore. As soon as we found this, I ordered the long-boat on shore, with twelve men and the mate, and away they went to seek the rogues; but they could neither find them nor any of the rest, for they all fled into the woods when they saw the boat coming on shore. The mate was once resolved, in justice to their roguery, to have destroyed their plantations, burned all their household stuff and furniture, and left them to shift without it; but having no orders, he let it all alone, left everything as he found it, and bringing the pinnace way, came on board without them. These two men made their number five; but the other three villains were so much more wicked than they, that after they had been two or three days together they turned the two newcomers out of doors to shift for themselves, and would have nothing to do with them; nor could they for a good while be persuaded to give them any food: as for the Spaniards, they were not yet come.

When the Spaniards came first on shore, the business began to go forward: the Spaniards would have persuaded the three English brutes to have taken in their countrymen again, that, as they said, they might be all one family; but they would not hear of it, so the two poor fellows lived by themselves; and finding nothing but industry and application would make them live comfortably, they pitched their tents on the north shore of the island, but a little more to the west, to be out of danger of the savages, who always landed on the east parts of the island. Here they built them two huts, one to lodge in, and the other to lay up their magazines and stores in; and the Spaniards having given them some corn for seed, and some of the peas which I had left them, they dug, planted, and enclosed, after the pattern I had set for them all, and began to live pretty well. Their first crop of corn was on the ground; and though it was but a little bit of land which they had dug up at first, having had but a little time, yet it was enough to relieve them, and find them with bread and other eatables; and one of the fellows being the cook's mate of the ship, was very ready at making soup, puddings, and such other preparations as the rice and the milk, and such little flesh as they got, furnished him to do.

They were going on in this little thriving position when the three unnatural rogues, their own countrymen too, in mere humour, and to insult them, came and bullied them, and told them the island was theirs: that the governor, meaning me, had given them the possession of it, and nobody else had any right to it; and that they should build no houses upon their ground unless they would pay rent for them. The two men, thinking they were jesting at first, asked them to come in and sit down, and see what fine houses they were that they had built, and to tell them what rent they demanded; and one of them merrily said if they were the ground-landlords, he hoped if they built tenements upon their land, and made improvements, they would, according to the custom of landlords, grant a long lease: and desired they would get a scrivener to draw the writings. One of the three, cursing and raging, told them they should see they were not in jest; and going to a little place at a distance, where the honest men had made a fire to dress their victuals, he takes a firebrand, and claps it to the outside of their hut, and set it on fire: indeed, it would have been all burned down in a few minutes if one of the two had not run to the fellow, thrust him away, and trod the fire out with his feet, and that not without some difficulty too.

The fellow was in such a rage at the honest man's thrusting him away, that he returned upon him, with a pole he had in his hand, and had not the man avoided the blow very nimbly, and run into the hut, he had ended his days at once. His comrade, seeing the danger they were both in, ran after him, and immediately they came both out with their muskets, and the man that was first struck at with the pole knocked the fellow down that began the quarrel with the stock of his musket, and that before the other two could come to help him; and then, seeing the rest come at them, they stood together, and presenting the other ends of their pieces to them, bade them stand off.

The others had firearms with them too; but one of the two honest men, bolder than his comrade, and made desperate by his danger, told them if they offered to move hand or foot they were dead men, and boldly commanded them to lay down their arms. They did not, indeed, lay down their arms, but seeing him so resolute, it brought them to a parley, and they consented to take their wounded man with them and be gone: and, indeed, it seems the fellow was wounded sufficiently with the blow. However, they were much in the wrong, since they had the advantage, that they did not disarm them effectually, as they might have done, and have gone immediately to the Spaniards, and given them an account how the rogues had treated them; for the three villains studied nothing but revenge, and every day gave them some intimation that they did so.

3

FIGHT WITH CANNIBALS

But not to crowd this part with an account of the lesser part of the rogueries with which they plagued them continually, night and day, it forced the two men to such a desperation that they resolved to fight them all three, the first time they had a fair opportunity. In order to do this they resolved to go to the castle (as they called my old dwelling), where the three rogues and the Spaniards all lived together at that time, intending to have a fair battle, and the Spaniards should stand by to see fair play: so they got up in the morning before day, and came to the place, and called the Englishmen by their names telling a Spaniard that answered that they wanted to speak with them.

It happened that the day before two of the Spaniards, having been in the woods, had seen one of the two Englishmen, whom, for distinction, I called the honest men, and he had made a sad complaint to the Spaniards of the barbarous usage they had met with from their three countrymen, and how they had ruined their plantation, and destroyed their corn, that they had laboured so hard to bring forward, and killed the milch-goat and their three kids, which was all they had provided for their sustenance, and that if he and his friends, meaning the Spaniards, did not assist them again, they should be starved. When the Spaniards came home at night, and they were all at supper, one of them took the freedom to reprove the three Englishmen, though in very gentle and mannerly terms, and asked them how they could be so cruel, they being harmless, inoffensive fellows: that they were putting themselves in a way to subsist by their labour, and that it had cost them a great deal of pains to bring things to such perfection as they were then in.

One of the Englishmen returned very briskly, "What had they to do there? that they came on shore without leave; and that they should not plant or build upon the island; it was none of their ground." "Why," says the Spaniard, very calmly, "Seignior Inglese, they must not starve." The Englishman replied, like a rough tarpaulin, "They might starve; they should not plant nor build in that place." "But what must they do then, seignior?" said the Spaniard. Another of the brutes returned, "Do? they should be servants, and work for them." "But how can you expect that of them?" says the Spaniard; "they are not bought with your money; you have no right to make them servants." The Englishman answered, "The island was theirs; the governor had given it to them, and no man had anything to do there but themselves;" and with that he swore that he would go and burn all their new huts; they should build none upon their land. "Why, seignior," says the Spaniard, "by the same rule, we must be your servants, too." "Ay," returned the bold dog, "and so you shall, too, before we have done with you;" mixing two or three oaths in the proper intervals of his speech. The Spaniard only smiled at that, and made him no answer. However, this little discourse had heated them; and starting up, one says to the other. (I think it was he they called Will Atkins), "Come, Jack, let's go and have t'other brush with them; we'll demolish their castle, I'll warrant you; they shall plant no colony in our dominions."

Upon this they were all trooping away, with every man a gun, a pistol, and a sword, and muttered some insolent things among themselves of what they would do to the Spaniards, too, when opportunity offered; but the Spaniards, it seems, did not so perfectly understand them as to know all the particulars, only that in general they threatened them hard for taking the two Englishmen's part. Whither they went, or how they bestowed their time that evening, the Spaniards said they did not know; but it seems they wandered about the country part of the night, and them lying down in the place which I used to call my bower, they were weary and overslept themselves. The case was this: they had resolved to stay till midnight, and so take the two poor men when they were asleep, and as they acknowledged afterwards, intended to set fire to their huts while they were in them, and either burn them there or murder them as they came out. As malice seldom sleeps very sound, it was very strange they should not have been kept awake. However, as the two men had also a design upon them, as I have said, though a much fairer one than that of burning and murdering, it happened, and very luckily for them all, that they were up and gone abroad before the bloody-minded rogues came to their huts.

When they came there, and found the men gone, Atkins, who it seems was the forwardest man, called out to his comrade, "Ha, Jack, here's the nest, but the birds are flown." They mused a while, to think what should be the occasion of their being gone abroad so soon, and suggested presently that the Spaniards had given them notice of it; and with that they shook hands, and swore to one another that they would be revenged of the Spaniards. As soon as they had made this bloody bargain they fell to work with the poor men's habitation; they did not set fire, indeed, to anything, but they pulled down both their houses, and left not the least stick standing, or scarce any sign on the ground where they stood; they tore all their household stuff in pieces, and threw everything about in such a manner, that the poor men afterwards found some of their things a mile off. When they had done this, they pulled up all the young trees which the poor men had planted; broke down an enclosure they had made to secure their cattle and their corn; and, in a word, sacked and plundered everything as completely as a horde of Tartars would have done.

The two men were at this juncture gone to find them out, and had resolved to fight them wherever they had been, though they were but two to three; so that, had they met, there certainly would have been blood shed among them, for they were all very stout, resolute fellows, to give them their due.

But Providence took more care to keep them asunder than they themselves could do to meet; for, as if they had dogged one another, when the three were gone thither, the two were here; and afterwards, when the two went back to find them, the three were come to the old habitation again: we shall see their different conduct presently. When the three came back like furious creatures, flushed with the rage which the work they had been about had put them into, they came up to the Spaniards, and told them what they had done, by way of scoff and bravado; and one of them stepping up to one of the Spaniards, as if they had been a couple of boys at play, takes hold of his hat as it was upon his head, and giving it a twirl about, fleering in his face, says to him, "And you, Seignior Jack Spaniard, shall have the same sauce if you do not mend your manners." The Spaniard, who, though a quiet civil man, was as brave a man as could be, and withal a strong, well-made man, looked at him for a good while, and then, having no weapon in his hand, stepped gravely up to him, and, with one blow of his fist, knocked him down, as an ox is felled with a pole-axe; at which one of the rogues, as insolent as the first, fired his pistol at the Spaniard immediately; he missed his body, indeed, for the bullets went through his hair, but one of them touched the tip of his ear, and he bled pretty much. The blood made the Spaniard believe he was more hurt than he really was, and that put him into some heat, for before he acted all in a perfect calm; but now resolving to go through with his work, he stooped, and taking the fellow's musket whom he had knocked down, was just going to shoot the man who had fired at him, when the rest of the Spaniards, being in the cave, came out, and calling to him not to shoot, they stepped in, secured the other two, and took their arms from them.

When they were thus disarmed, and found they had made all the Spaniards their enemies, as well as their own countrymen, they began to cool, and giving the Spaniards better words, would have their arms again; but the Spaniards, considering the feud that was between them and the other two Englishmen, and that it would be the best method they could take to keep them from killing one another, told them they would do them no harm, and if they would live peaceably, they would be very willing to assist and associate with them as they did before; but that they could not think of giving them their arms again, while they appeared so resolved to do mischief with them to their own countrymen, and had even threatened them all to make them their servants.

The rogues were now quite deaf to all reason, and being refused their arms, they raved away like madmen, threatening what they would do, though they had no firearms. But the Spaniards, despising their threatening, told them they should take care how they offered any injury to their plantation or cattle; for if they did they would shoot them as they would ravenous beasts, wherever they found them; and if they fell into their hands alive, they should certainly be hanged. However, this was far from cooling them, but away they went, raging and swearing like furies. As soon as they were gone, the two men came back, in passion and rage enough also, though of another kind; for having been at their plantation, and finding it all demolished and destroyed, as above mentioned, it will easily be supposed they had provocation enough. They could scarce have room to tell their tale, the Spaniards were so eager to tell them theirs: and it was strange enough to find that three men should thus bully nineteen, and receive no punishment at all.

The Spaniards, indeed, despised them, and especially, having thus disarmed them, made light of their threatenings; but the two Englishmen resolved to have their remedy against them, what pains soever it cost to find them out. But the Spaniards interposed here too, and told them that as they had disarmed them, they could not consent that they (the two) should pursue them with firearms, and perhaps kill them. "But," said the grave Spaniard, who was their governor, "we will endeavour to make them do you justice, if you will leave it to us: for there is no doubt but they will come to us again, when their passion is over, being not able to subsist without our assistance. We promise you to make no peace with them without having full satisfaction for you; and upon this condition we hope you will promise to use no violence with them, other than in your own defence." The two Englishmen yielded to this very awkwardly, and with great reluctance; but the Spaniards protested that they did it only to keep them from bloodshed, and to make them all easy at last. "For," said they, "we are not so many of us; here is room enough for us all, and it is a great pity that we should not be all good friends." At length they did consent, and waited for the issue of the thing, living for some days with the Spaniards; for their own habitation was destroyed.

In about five days' time the vagrants, tired with wandering, and almost starved with hunger, having chiefly lived on turtles' eggs all that while, came back to the grove; and finding my Spaniard, who, as I have said, was the governor, and two more with him, walking by the side of the creek, they came up in a very submissive, humble manner, and begged to be received again into the society. The Spaniards used them civilly, but told them they had acted so unnaturally to their countrymen, and so very grossly to themselves, that they could not come to any conclusion without consulting the two Englishmen and the rest; but, however, they would go to them and discourse about it, and they should know in half-an-hour. It may be guessed that they were very hard put to it; for, as they were to wait this half-hour for an answer, they begged they would send them out some bread in the meantime, which they did, sending at the same time a large piece of goat's flesh and a boiled parrot, which they ate very eagerly.

After half-an-hour's consultation they were called in, and a long debate ensued, their two countrymen charging them with the ruin of all their labour, and a design to murder them; all which they owned before, and therefore could not deny now. Upon the whole, the Spaniards acted the moderators between them; and as they had obliged the two Englishmen not to hurt the three while they were naked and unarmed, so they now obliged the three to go and rebuild their fellows' two huts, one to be of the same and the other of larger dimensions than they were before; to fence their ground again, plant trees in the room of those pulled up, dig up the land again for planting corn, and, in a word, to restore everything to the same state as they found it, that is, as near as they could.

Well, they submitted to all this; and as they had plenty of provisions given them all the while, they grew very orderly, and the whole society began to live pleasantly and agreeably together again; only that these three fellows could never be persuaded to work—I mean for themselves—except now and then a little, just as they pleased. However, the Spaniards told them plainly that if they would but live sociably and friendly together, and study the good of the whole plantation, they would be content to work for them, and let them walk about and be as idle as they pleased; and thus, having lived pretty well together for a month or two, the Spaniards let them have arms again, and gave them liberty to go abroad with them as before.

It was not above a week after they had these arms, and went abroad, before the ungrateful creatures began to be as insolent and troublesome as ever. However, an accident happened presently upon this, which endangered the safety of them all, and they were obliged to lay by all private resentments, and look to the preservation of their lives.

It happened one night that the governor, the Spaniard whose life I had saved, who was now the governor of the rest, found himself very uneasy in the night, and could by no means get any sleep: he was perfectly well in body, only found his thoughts tumultuous; his mind ran upon men fighting and killing one another; but he was broad awake, and could not by any means get any sleep; in short, he lay a great while, but growing more and more uneasy, he resolved to rise. As they lay, being so many of them, on goat-skins laid thick upon such couches and pads as they made for themselves, so they had little to do, when they were willing to rise, but to get upon their feet, and perhaps put on a coat, such as it was, and their pumps, and they were ready for going any way that their thoughts guided them. Being thus got up, he looked out; but being dark, he could see little or nothing, and besides, the trees which I had planted, and which were now grown tall, intercepted his sight, so that he could only look up, and see that it was a starlight night, and hearing no noise, he returned and lay down again; but to no purpose; he could not compose himself to anything like rest; but his thoughts were to the last degree uneasy, and he knew not for what. Having made some noise with rising and walking about, going out and coming in, another of them waked, and asked who it was that was up. The governor told him how it had been with him. "Say you so?" says the other Spaniard; "such things are not to be slighted, I assure you; there is certainly some mischief working near us;" and presently he asked him, "Where are the Englishmen?" "They are all in their huts," says he, "safe enough." It seems the Spaniards had kept possession of the main apartment, and had made a place for the three Englishmen, who, since their last mutiny, were always quartered by themselves, and could not come at the rest. "Well," says the Spaniard, "there is something in it, I am persuaded, from my own experience. I am satisfied that our spirits embodied have a converse with and receive intelligence from the spirits unembodied, and inhabiting the invisible world; and this friendly notice is given for our advantage, if we knew how to make use of it. Come, let us go and look abroad; and if we find nothing at all in it to justify the trouble, I'll tell you a story to the purpose, that shall convince you of the justice of my proposing it."

They went out presently to go up to the top of the hill, where I used to go; but they being strong, and a good company, nor alone, as I was, used none of my cautions to go up by the ladder, and pulling it up after them, to go up a second stage to the top, but were going round through the grove unwarily, when they were surprised with seeing a light as of fire, a very little way from them, and hearing the voices of men, not of one or two, but of a great number.

Among the precautions I used to take on the savages landing on the island, it was my constant care to prevent them making the least discovery of there being any inhabitant upon the place: and when by any occasion they came to know it, they felt it so effectually that they that got away were scarce able to give any account of it; for we disappeared as soon as possible, nor did ever any that had seen me escape to tell any one else, except it was the three savages in our last encounter who jumped into the boat; of whom, I mentioned, I was afraid they should go home and bring more help. Whether it was the consequence of the escape of those men that so great a number came now together, or whether they came ignorantly, and by accident, on their usual bloody errand, the Spaniards could not understand; but whatever it was, it was their business either to have concealed themselves or not to have seen them at all, much less to have let the savages have seen there were any inhabitants in the place; or to have fallen upon them so effectually as not a man of them should have escaped, which could only have been by getting in between them and their boats; but this presence of mind was wanting to them, which was the ruin of their tranquillity for a great while.

We need not doubt but that the governor and the man with him, surprised with this sight, ran back immediately and raised their fellows, giving them an account of the imminent danger they were all in, and they again as readily took the alarm; but it was impossible to persuade them to stay close within where they were, but they must all run out to see how things stood. While it was dark, indeed, they were safe, and they had opportunity enough for some hours to view the savages by the light of three fires they had made at a distance from one another; what they were doing they knew not, neither did they know what to do themselves. For, first, the enemy were too many; and secondly, they did not keep together, but were divided into several parties, and were on shore in several places.

The Spaniards were in no small consternation at this sight; and, as they found that the fellows went straggling all over the shore, they made no doubt but, first or last, some of them would chop in upon their habitation, or upon some other place where they would see the token of inhabitants; and they were in great perplexity also for fear of their flock of goats, which, if they should be destroyed, would have been little less than starving them. So the first thing they resolved upon was to despatch three men away before it was light, two

Spaniards and one Englishman, to drive away all the goats to the great valley where the cave was, and, if need were, to drive them into the very cave itself. Could they have seen the savages all together in one body, and at a distance from their canoes, they were resolved, if there had been a hundred of them, to attack them; but that could not be done, for they were some of them two miles off from the other, and, as it appeared afterwards, were of two different nations.

After having mused a great while on the course they should take, they resolved at last, while it was still dark, to send the old savage, Friday's father, out as a spy, to learn, if possible, something concerning them, as what they came for, what they intended to do, and the like. The old man readily undertook it; and stripping himself quite naked, as most of the savages were, away he went. After he had been gone an hour or two, he brings word that he had been among them undiscovered, that he found they were two parties, and of two several nations, who had war with one another, and had a great battle in their own country; and that both sides having had several prisoners taken in the fight, they were, by mere chance, landed all on the same island, for the devouring their prisoners and making merry; but their coming so by chance to the same place had spoiled all their mirth—that they were in a great rage at one another, and were so near that he believed they would fight again as soon as daylight began to appear; but he did not perceive that they had any notion of anybody being on the island but themselves. He had hardly made an end of telling his story, when they could perceive, by the unusual noise they made, that the two little armies were engaged in a bloody fight. Friday's father used all the arguments he could to persuade our people to lie close, and not be seen; he told them their safety consisted in it, and that they had nothing to do but lie still, and the savages would kill one another to their hands, and then the rest would go away; and it was so to a tittle. But it was impossible to prevail, especially upon the Englishmen; their curiosity was so importunate that they must run out and see the battle. However, they used some caution too: they did not go openly, just by their own dwelling, but went farther into the woods, and placed themselves to advantage, where they might securely see them manage the fight, and, as they thought, not be seen by them; but the savages did see them, as we shall find hereafter.

The battle was very fierce, and, if I might believe the Englishmen, one of them said he could perceive that some of them were men of great bravery, of invincible spirit, and of great policy in guiding the fight. The battle, they said, held two hours before they could guess which party would be beaten; but then that party which was nearest our people's habitation began to appear weakest, and after some time more some of them began to fly; and this put our men again into a great consternation, lest any one of those that fled should run into the grove before their dwelling for shelter, and thereby involuntarily discover the place; and that, by consequence, the pursuers would also do the like in search of them. Upon this, they resolved that they would stand armed within the wall, and whoever came into the grove, they resolved to sally out over the wall and kill them, so that, if possible, not one should return to give an account of it; they ordered also that it should be done with their swords, or by knocking them down with the stocks of their muskets, but not by shooting them, for fear of raising an alarm by the noise.

As they expected it fell out; three of the routed army fled for life, and crossing the creek, ran directly into the place, not in the least knowing whither they went, but running as into a thick wood for shelter. The scout they kept to look abroad gave notice of this within, with this comforting addition, that the conquerors had not pursued them, or seen which way they were gone; upon this the Spanish governor, a man of humanity, would not suffer them to kill the three fugitives, but sending three men out by the top of the hill, ordered them to go round, come in behind them, and surprise and take them prisoners, which was done. The residue of the conquered people fled to their canoes, and got off to sea; the victors retired, made no pursuit, or very little, but drawing themselves into a body together, gave two great screaming shouts, most likely by way of triumph, and so the fight ended; the same day, about three o'clock in the afternoon, they also marched to their canoes. And thus the Spaniards had the island again free to themselves, their fright was over, and they saw no savages for several years after.

After they were all gone, the Spaniards came out of their den, and viewing the field of battle, they found about two-and-thirty men dead on the spot; some were killed with long arrows, which were found sticking in their bodies; but most of them were killed with great wooden swords, sixteen or seventeen of which they found in the field of battle, and as many bows, with a great many arrows. These swords were strange, unwieldy things, and they must be very strong men that used them; most of those that were killed with them had their heads smashed to pieces, as we may say, or, as we call it in English, their brains knocked out, and several their arms and legs broken; so that it is evident they fight with inexpressible rage and fury. We found not one man that was not stone dead; for either they stay by their enemy till they have killed him, or they carry all the wounded men that are not quite dead away with them.

This deliverance tamed our ill-disposed Englishmen for a great while; the sight had filled them with horror, and the consequences appeared terrible to the last degree, especially upon supposing that some time or other they should fall into the hands of those creatures, who would not only kill them as enemies, but for food, as we kill our cattle; and they professed to me that the thoughts of being eaten up like beef and mutton, though it was supposed it was not to be till they were dead, had something in it so horrible that it nauseated their very stomachs, made them sick when they thought of it, and filled their minds with such unusual terror, that they were not themselves for some weeks after. This, as I said, tamed even the three English brutes I have been speaking of; and for a great while after they were tractable, and went about the common business of the whole society well enough—planted, sowed, reaped, and began to be all naturalised to the country. But some time after this they fell into such simple measures again as brought them into a great deal of trouble.

They had taken three prisoners, as I observed; and these three being stout young fellows, they made them servants, and taught them to work for them, and as slaves they did well enough; but they did not take their measures as I did by my man Friday, viz. to begin with them upon the principle of having saved their lives, and then instruct them in the rational principles of life; much less did they think of teaching them religion, or attempt civilising and reducing them by kind usage and affectionate arguments. As they gave them their food every day, so they gave them their work too, and kept them fully employed in drudgery enough; but they failed in this by it, that they never had them to assist them and fight for them as I had my man Friday, who was as true to me as the very flesh upon my bones.

But to come to the family part. Being all now good friends—for common danger, as I said above, had effectually reconciled them—they began to consider their general circumstances; and the first thing that came under consideration was whether, seeing the savages particularly haunted that side of the island, and that there were more remote and retired parts of it equally adapted to their way of living, and manifestly to their advantage, they should not rather move their habitation, and plant in some more proper place for their safety, and especially for the security of their cattle and corn.

Upon this, after long debate, it was concluded that they would not remove their habitation; because that, some time or other, they thought they might hear from their governor again, meaning me; and if I should send any one to seek them, I should be sure to direct them to that side, where, if they should find the place demolished, they would conclude the savages had killed us all, and we were gone, and so our supply would go too. But as to their corn and cattle, they agreed to remove them into the valley where my cave was, where the land was as proper for both, and where indeed there was land enough. However, upon second thoughts they altered one part of their resolution too, and resolved only to remove part of their cattle thither, and part of their corn there; so that if one part was destroyed the other might be saved. And one part of prudence they luckily used: they never trusted those three savages which they had taken prisoners with knowing anything of the plantation they had made in that valley, or of any cattle they had there, much less of the cave at that place, which they kept, in case of necessity, as a safe retreat; and thither they carried also the two barrels of powder which I had sent them at my coming away. They resolved, however, not to change their habitation; yet, as I had carefully covered it first with a wall or fortification, and then with a grove of trees, and as they were now fully convinced their safety consisted entirely in their being concealed, they set to work to cover and conceal the place yet more effectually than before. For this purpose, as I planted trees, or rather thrust in stakes, which in time all grew up to be trees, for some good distance before the entrance into my apartments, they went on in the same manner, and filled up the rest of that whole space of ground from the trees I had set quite down to the side of the creek, where I landed my floats, and even into the very ooze where the tide flowed, not so much as leaving any place to land, or any sign that there had been any landing thereabouts: these stakes also being of a wood very forward to grow, they took care to have them generally much larger and taller than those which I had planted. As they grew apace, they planted them so very thick and close together, that when they had been three or four years grown there was no piercing with the eye any considerable way into the plantation. As for that part which I had planted, the trees were grown as thick as a man's thigh, and among them they had placed so many other short ones, and so thick, that it stood like a palisado a quarter of a mile thick, and it was next to impossible to penetrate it, for a little dog could hardly get between the trees, they stood so close.

But this was not all; for they did the same by all the ground to the right hand and to the left, and round even to the side of the hill, leaving no way, not so much as for themselves, to come out but by the ladder placed up to the side of the hill, and then lifted up, and placed again from the first stage up to the top: so that when the ladder was taken down, nothing but what had wings or witchcraft to assist it could come at them. This was excellently well contrived: nor was it less than what they afterwards found occasion for, which served to convince me, that as human prudence has the authority of Providence to justify it, so it has doubtless the direction of Providence to set it to work; and if we listened carefully to the voice of it, I am persuaded we might prevent many of the disasters which our lives are now, by our own negligence, subjected to.

They lived two years after this in perfect retirement, and had no more visits from the savages. They had, indeed, an alarm given them one morning, which put them into a great consternation; for some of the Spaniards being out early one morning on the west side or end of the island (which was that end where I never went, for fear of being discovered), they were surprised with seeing about twenty canoes of Indians just coming on shore. They made the best of their way home in hurry enough; and giving the alarm to their comrades, they kept close all that day and the next, going out only at night to make their observation: but they had the good luck to be undiscovered, for wherever the savages went, they did not land that time on the island, but pursued some other design.

4

RENEWED INVASION OF SAVAGES

And now they had another broil with the three Englishmen; one of whom, a most turbulent fellow, being in a rage at one of the three captive slaves, because the fellow had not done something right which he bade him do, and seemed a little untractable in his showing him, drew a hatchet out of a frog-belt which he wore by his side, and fell upon the poor savage, not to correct him, but to kill him. One of the Spaniards who was by, seeing him give the fellow a barbarous cut with the hatchet, which he aimed at his head, but stuck into his shoulder, so that he thought he had cut the poor creature's arm off, ran to him, and entreating him not to murder the poor man, placed himself between him and the savage, to prevent the mischief. The fellow, being enraged the more at this, struck at the Spaniard with his hatchet, and swore he would serve him as he intended to serve the savage; which the Spaniard perceiving, avoided the blow, and with a shovel, which he had in his hand (for they were all working in the field about their corn land), knocked the brute down. Another of the Englishmen, running up at the same time to help his comrade, knocked the Spaniard down; and then two Spaniards more came in to help their man, and a third Englishman fell in upon them. They had none of them any firearms or any other weapons but hatchets and other tools, except this third Englishman; he had one of my rusty cutlasses, with which he made at the two last Spaniards, and wounded them both. This fray set the whole family in an uproar, and more help coming in they took the three Englishmen prisoners. The next question was, what should be done with them? They had been so often mutinous, and were so very furious, so desperate, and so idle withal, they knew not what course to take with them, for they were mischievous to the highest degree, and cared not what hurt they did to any man; so that, in short, it was not safe to live with them.

The Spaniard who was governor told them, in so many words, that if they had been of his own country he would have hanged them; for all laws and all governors were to preserve society, and those who were dangerous to the society ought to be expelled out of it; but as they were Englishmen, and that it was to the generous kindness of an Englishman that they all owed their preservation and deliverance, he would use them with all possible lenity, and would leave them to the judgment of the other two Englishmen, who were their countrymen. One of the two honest Englishmen stood up, and said they desired it might not be left to them. "For," says he, "I am sure we ought to sentence them to the gallows;" and with that he gives an account how Will Atkins, one of the three, had proposed to have all the five Englishmen join together and murder all the Spaniards when they were in their sleep.

When the Spanish governor heard this, he calls to Will Atkins, "How, Seignior Atkins, would you murder us all? What have you to say to that?" The hardened villain was so far from denying it, that he said it was true, and swore they would do it still before they had done with them. "Well, but Seignior Atkins," says the Spaniard, "what have we done to you that you will kill us? What would you get by killing us? And what must we do to prevent you killing us? Must we kill you, or you kill us? Why will you put us to the necessity of this, Seignior Atkins?" says the Spaniard very calmly, and smiling. Seignior Atkins was in such a rage at the Spaniard's making a jest of it, that, had he not been held by three men, and withal had no weapon near him, it was thought he would have attempted to kill the Spaniard in the middle of all the company. This hare-brained carriage obliged them to consider seriously what was to be done. The two Englishmen and the Spaniard who saved the poor savage were of the opinion that they should hang one of the three for an example to the rest, and that particularly it should be he that had twice attempted to commit murder with his hatchet; indeed, there was some reason to believe he had done it, for the poor savage was in such a miserable condition with the wound he had received that it was thought he could not live. But the governor Spaniard still said No; it was an Englishman that had saved all their lives, and he would never consent to put an Englishman to death, though he had murdered half of them; nay, he said if he had been killed himself by an Englishman, and had time left to speak, it should be that they should pardon him.

This was so positively insisted on by the governor Spaniard, that there was no gainsaying it; and as merciful counsels are most apt to prevail where they are so earnestly pressed, so they all came into it. But then it was to be considered what should be done to keep them from doing the mischief they designed; for all agreed, governor and all, that means were to be used for preserving the society from danger. After a long debate, it was agreed that they should be disarmed, and not permitted to have either gun, powder, shot, sword, or any weapon; that they should be turned out of the society, and left to live where they would and how they would, by themselves; but that none of the rest, either Spaniards or English, should hold any kind of converse with them, or have anything to do with them; that they should be forbid to come within a certain distance of the place where the rest dwelt; and if they offered to commit any disorder, so as to spoil, burn, kill, or destroy any of the corn, plantings, buildings, fences, or cattle belonging to the society, they should die without mercy, and they would shoot them wherever they could find them.

The humane governor, musing upon the sentence, considered a little upon it; and turning to the two honest Englishmen, said, "Hold; you must reflect that it will be long ere they can raise corn and cattle of their own, and they must not starve; we must therefore allow them provisions." So he caused to be added, that they should have a proportion of corn given them to last them eight months, and for seed to sow, by which time they might be supposed to raise some of their own; that they should have six milch-goats, four he-goats, and six kids given them, as well for present subsistence as for a store; and that they should have tools given them for their work in the fields, but they should have none of these tools or provisions unless they would swear solemnly that they would not hurt or injure any of the Spaniards with them, or of their fellow-Englishmen.

Thus they dismissed them the society, and turned them out to shift for themselves. They went away sullen and refractory, as neither content to go away nor to stay: but, as there was no remedy, they went, pretending to go and choose a place where they would settle themselves; and some provisions were given them, but no weapons. About four or five days after, they came again for some victuals, and gave the governor an account where they had pitched their tents, and marked themselves out a habitation and plantation; and it was a very convenient place indeed, on the remotest part of the island, NE., much about the place where I providentially landed in my first voyage, when I was driven out to sea in my foolish attempt to sail round the island.

Here they built themselves two handsome huts, and contrived them in a manner like my first habitation, being close under the side of a hill, having some trees already growing on three sides of it, so that by planting others it would be very easily covered from the sight, unless narrowly searched for. They desired some dried goat-skins for beds and covering, which were given them; and upon giving their words that they would not disturb the rest, or injure any of their plantations, they gave them hatchets, and what other tools they could spare; some peas, barley, and rice, for sowing; and, in a word, anything they wanted, except arms and ammunition.

They lived in this separate condition about six months, and had got in their first harvest, though the quantity was but small, the parcel of land they had planted being but little. Indeed, having all their plantation to form, they had a great deal of work upon their hands; and when they came to make boards and pots, and such things, they were quite out of their element, and could make nothing of it; therefore when the rainy season came on, for want of a cave in the earth, they could not keep their grain dry, and it was in great danger of spoiling. This humbled them much: so they came and begged the Spaniards to help them, which they very readily did; and in four days worked a great hole in the side of the hill for them, big enough to secure their corn and other things from the rain: but it was a poor place at best compared to mine, and especially as mine was then, for the Spaniards had greatly enlarged it, and made several new apartments in it.

About three quarters of a year after this separation, a new frolic took these rogues, which, together with the former villainy they had committed, brought mischief enough upon them, and had very near been the ruin of the whole colony. The three new associates began, it seems, to be weary of the laborious life they led, and that without hope of bettering their circumstances: and a whim took them that they would make a voyage to the continent, from whence the savages came, and would try if they could seize upon some prisoners among the natives there, and bring them home, so as to make them do the laborious part of the work for them.

The project was not so preposterous, if they had gone no further. But they did nothing, and proposed nothing, but had either mischief in the design, or mischief in the event. And if I may give my opinion, they seemed to be under a blast from Heaven: for if we will not allow a visible curse to pursue visible crimes, how shall we reconcile the events of things with the divine justice? It was certainly an apparent vengeance on their crime of mutiny and piracy that brought them to the state they were in; and they showed not the least remorse for the crime, but added new villanies to it, such as the piece of monstrous cruelty of wounding a poor slave because he did not, or perhaps could not, understand to do what he was directed, and to wound him in such a manner as made him a cripple all his life, and in a place where no surgeon or medicine could be had for his cure; and, what was still worse, the intentional murder, for such to be sure it was, as was afterwards the formed design they all laid to murder the Spaniards in cold blood, and in their sleep.

The three fellows came down to the Spaniards one morning, and in very humble terms desired to be admitted to speak with them. The Spaniards very readily heard what they had to say, which was this: that they were tired of living in the manner they did, and that they were not handy enough to make the necessaries they wanted, and that having no help, they found they should be starved; but if the Spaniards would give them leave to take one of the canoes which they came over in, and give them arms and ammunition proportioned to their defence, they would go over to the main, and seek their fortunes, and so deliver them from the trouble of supplying them with any other provisions.

The Spaniards were glad enough to get rid of them, but very honestly represented to them the certain destruction they were running into; told them they had suffered such hardships upon that very spot, that they could, without any spirit of prophecy, tell them they would be starved or murdered, and bade them consider of it. The men replied audaciously, they should be starved if they stayed here, for they could not work, and would not work, and they could but be starved abroad; and if they were murdered, there was an end of them; they had no wives or children to cry after them; and, in short, insisted importunately upon their demand, declaring they would go, whether they gave them any arms or not.

The Spaniards told them, with great kindness, that if they were resolved to go they should not go like naked men, and be in no condition to defend themselves; and that though they could ill spare firearms, not having enough for themselves, yet they would let them have two muskets, a pistol, and a cutlass, and each man a hatchet, which they thought was sufficient for them. In a word, they accepted the offer; and having baked bread enough to serve them a month given them, and as much goats' flesh as they could eat while it was sweet, with a great basket of dried grapes, a pot of fresh water, and a young kid alive, they boldly set out in the canoe for a voyage over the sea, where it was at least forty miles broad. The boat, indeed, was a large one, and would very well have carried fifteen or twenty men, and therefore was rather too big for them to manage; but as they had a fair breeze and flood-tide with them, they did well enough. They had made a mast of a long pole, and a sail of four large goat-skins dried, which they had sewed or laced together; and away they went merrily together. The Spaniards called after them "*Bon voyajo;*" and no man ever thought of seeing them any more.

The Spaniards were often saying to one another, and to the two honest Englishmen who remained behind, how quietly and comfortably they lived, now these three turbulent fellows were gone. As for their coming again, that was the remotest thing from their thoughts that could be imagined; when, behold, after two-and-twenty days' absence, one of the Englishmen being abroad upon his planting work, sees three strange men coming towards him at a distance, with guns upon their shoulders.

Away runs the Englishman, frightened and amazed, as if he was bewitched, to the governor Spaniard, and tells him they were all undone, for there were strangers upon the island, but he could not tell who they were. The Spaniard, pausing a while, says to him, "How do you mean—you cannot tell who? They are the savages, to be sure." "No, no," says the Englishman, "they are men in clothes, with arms." "Nay, then," says the Spaniard, "why are you so concerned! If they are not savages they must be friends; for there is no Christian nation upon earth but will do us good rather than harm." While they were debating thus, came up the three Englishmen, and standing without the wood, which was new planted, hallooed to them. They presently knew their voices, and so all the wonder ceased. But now the admiration was turned upon another question—What could be the matter, and what made them come back again?

It was not long before they brought the men in, and inquiring where they had been, and what they had been doing, they gave them a full account of their voyage in a few words: that they reached the land in less than two days, but finding the people alarmed at their coming, and preparing with bows and arrows to fight them, they durst not go on shore, but sailed on to the northward six or seven hours, till they came to a great opening, by which they perceived that the land they saw from our island was not the main, but an island: that upon entering that opening of the sea they saw another island on the right hand north, and several more west; and being resolved to land somewhere, they put over to one of the islands which lay west, and went boldly on shore; that they found the people very courteous and friendly to them; and they gave them several roots and some dried fish, and appeared very sociable; and that the women, as well as the men, were very forward to supply them with anything they could get for them to eat, and brought it to them a great way, on their heads. They continued here for four days, and inquired as well as they could of them by signs, what nations were this way, and that way, and were told of several fierce and terrible people that lived almost every way, who, as they made known by signs to them, used to eat men; but, as for themselves, they said they never ate men or women, except only such as they took in the wars; and then they owned they made a great feast, and ate their prisoners.

The Englishmen inquired when they had had a feast of that kind; and they told them about two moons ago, pointing to the moon and to two fingers; and that their great king had two hundred prisoners now, which he had taken in his war, and they were feeding them to make them fat for the next feast. The Englishmen seemed mighty desirous of seeing those prisoners; but the others mistaking them, thought they were desirous to have some of them to carry away for their own eating. So they beckoned to them, pointing to the setting of the sun, and then to the rising; which was to signify that the next morning at sunrising they would bring some for them; and accordingly the next morning they brought down five women and eleven men, and gave them to the Englishmen to carry with them on their voyage, just as we would bring so many cows and oxen down to a seaport town to victual a ship.

As brutish and barbarous as these fellows were at home, their stomachs turned at this sight, and they did not know what to do. To refuse the prisoners would have been the highest affront to the savage gentry that could be offered them, and what to do with them they knew not. However, after some debate, they resolved to accept of them: and, in return, they gave the savages that brought them one of their hatchets, an old key, a knife, and six or seven of their bullets; which, though they did not understand their use, they seemed particularly pleased with; and then tying the poor creatures' hands behind them, they dragged the prisoners into the boat for our men.

The Englishmen were obliged to come away as soon as they had them, or else they that gave them this noble present would certainly have expected that they should have gone to work with them, have killed two or three of them the next morning, and perhaps have invited the donors to dinner. But having taken their leave, with all the respect and thanks that could well pass between people, where on either side they understood not one word they could say, they put off with their boat, and came back towards the first island; where, when they arrived, they set eight of their prisoners at liberty, there being too many of them for their occasion. In their voyage they endeavoured to have some communication with their prisoners; but it was impossible to make them understand anything. Nothing they could say to them, or give them, or do for them, but was looked upon as going to murder them. They first of all unbound them; but the poor creatures screamed at that, especially the women, as if they had just felt the knife at their throats; for they immediately concluded they were unbound on purpose to be killed. If they gave them thing to eat, it was the same thing; they then concluded it was for fear they should sink in flesh, and so not be fat enough to kill. If they looked at one of them more particularly, the party presently concluded it was to see whether he or she was fattest, and fittest to kill first; nay, after they had brought them quite over, and began to use them kindly, and treat them well, still they expected every day to make a dinner or supper for their new masters.

When the three wanderers had give this unaccountable history or journal of their voyage, the Spaniard asked them where their new family was; and being told that they had brought them on shore, and put them into one of their huts, and were come up to beg some victuals for them, they (the Spaniards) and the other two Englishmen, that is to say, the whole colony, resolved to go all down to the place and see them; and did so, and Friday's father with them. When they came into the hut, there they sat, all bound; for when they had brought them on shore they bound their hands that they might not take the boat and make their escape; there, I say, they sat, all of them stark naked. First, there were three comely fellows, well shaped, with straight limbs, about thirty to thirty-five years of age; and five women, whereof two might be from thirty to forty, two more about four or five and twenty; and the fifth, a tall, comely maiden, about seventeen. The women were well-favoured, agreeable persons, both in shape and features, only tawny; and two of them, had they been perfect white, would have passed for very handsome women, even in London, having pleasant countenances, and of a very modest behaviour; especially when they came afterwards to be clothed and dressed, though that dress was very indifferent, it must be confessed.

The sight, you may be sure, was something uncouth to our Spaniards, who were, to give them a just character, men of the most calm, sedate tempers, and perfect good humour, that ever I met with: and, in particular, of the utmost modesty: I say, the sight was very uncouth, to see three naked men and five naked women, all together bound, and in the most miserable circumstances that human nature could be supposed to be, viz. to be expecting every moment to be dragged out and have their brains knocked out, and then to be eaten up like a calf that is killed for a dainty.

The first thing they did was to cause the old Indian, Friday's father, to go in, and see first if he knew any of them, and then if he understood any of their speech. As soon as the old man came in, he looked seriously at them, but knew none of them; neither could any of them understand a word he said, or a sign he could make, except one of the women. However, this was enough to answer the end, which was to satisfy them that the men into whose hands they were fallen were Christians; that they abhorred eating men or women; and that they might be sure they would not be killed. As soon as they were assured of this, they discovered such a joy, and by such awkward gestures, several ways, as is hard to describe; for it seems they were of several nations. The woman who was their interpreter was bid, in the next place, to ask them if they were willing to be servants, and to work for the men who had brought them away, to save their lives; at which they all fell a-dancing; and presently one fell to taking up this, and another that, anything that lay next, to carry on their shoulders, to intimate they were willing to work.

The governor, who found that the having women among them would presently be attended with some inconvenience, and might occasion some strife, and perhaps blood, asked the three men what they intended to do with these women, and how they intended to use them, whether as servants or as wives? One of the Englishmen answered, very boldly and readily, that they would use them as both; to which the governor said: "I am not going to restrain you from it—you are your own masters as to that; but this I think is but just, for avoiding disorders and quarrels among you, and I desire it of you for that reason only, viz. that you will all engage, that if any of you take any of these women as a wife, he shall take but one; and that having taken one, none else shall touch her; for though we cannot marry any one of you, yet it is but reasonable that, while you stay here, the woman any of you takes shall be maintained by the man that takes her, and should be his wife—I mean," says he, "while he continues here, and that none else shall have anything to do with her." All this appeared so just, that every one agreed to it without any difficulty.

Then the Englishmen asked the Spaniards if they designed to take any of them? But every one of them answered "No." Some of them said they had wives in Spain, and the others did not like women that were not Christians; and all together declared that they would not touch one of them, which was an instance of such virtue as I have not met with in all my travels. On the other hand, the five Englishmen took them every one a wife, that is to say, a temporary wife; and so they set up a new form of living; for the Spaniards and Friday's father lived in my old habitation, which they had enlarged exceedingly within. The three servants which were taken in the last battle of the savages lived with them; and these carried on the main part of the colony, supplied all the rest with food, and assisted them in anything as they could, or as they found necessity required.

But the wonder of the story was, how five such refractory, ill-matched fellows should agree about these women, and that some two of them should not choose the same woman, especially seeing two or three of them were, without comparison, more agreeable than the others; but they took a good way enough to prevent quarrelling among themselves, for they set the five women by themselves in one of their huts, and they went all into the other hut, and drew lots among them who should choose first.

Him that drew to choose first went away by himself to the hut where the poor naked creatures were, and fetched out her he chose; and it was worth observing, that he that chose first took her that was reckoned the homeliest and oldest of the five, which made mirth enough amongst the rest; and even the Spaniards laughed at it; but the fellow considered better than any of them, that it was application and business they were to expect assistance in, as much as in anything else; and she proved the best wife of all the parcel.

When the poor women saw themselves set in a row thus, and fetched out one by one, the terrors of their condition returned upon them again, and they firmly believed they were now going to be devoured. Accordingly, when the English sailor came in and fetched out one of them, the rest set up a most lamentable cry, and hung about her, and took their leave of her with such agonies and affection as would have grieved the hardest heart in the world: nor was it possible for the Englishmen to satisfy them that they were not to be immediately murdered, till they fetched the old man, Friday's father, who immediately let them know that the five men, who were to fetch them out one by one, had chosen them for their wives. When they had done, and the fright the women were in was a little over, the men went to work, and the Spaniards came and helped them: and in a few hours they had built them every one a new hut or tent for their lodging apart; for those they had already were crowded with their tools, household stuff, and provisions. The three wicked ones had pitched farthest off, and the two honest ones nearer, but both on the north shore of the island, so that they continued separated as before; and thus my island was peopled in three places, and, as I might say, three towns were begun to be built.

And here it is very well worth observing that, as it often happens in the world (what the wise ends in God's providence are, in such a disposition of things, I cannot say), the two honest fellows had the two worst wives; and the three reprobates, that were scarce worth hanging, that were fit for nothing, and neither seemed born to do themselves good nor any one else, had three clever, careful, and ingenious wives; not that the first two were bad wives as to their temper or humour, for all the five were most willing, quiet, passive, and subjected creatures, rather like slaves than wives; but my meaning is, they were not alike capable, ingenious, or industrious, or alike cleanly and neat. Another observation I must make, to the honour of a diligent application on one hand, and to the disgrace of a slothful, negligent, idle temper on the other, that when I came to the place, and viewed the several improvements, plantings, and management of the several little colonies, the two men had so far out-gone the three, that there was no comparison. They had, indeed, both of them as much ground laid out for corn as they wanted, and the reason was, because, according to my rule, nature dictated that it was to no purpose to sow more corn than they wanted; but the difference of the cultivation, of the planting, of the fences, and indeed, of everything else, was easy to be seen at first view.

The two men had innumerable young trees planted about their huts, so that, when you came to the place, nothing was to be seen but a wood; and though they had twice had their plantation demolished, once by their own countrymen, and once by the enemy, as shall be shown in its place, yet they had restored all again, and everything was thriving and flourishing about them; they had grapes planted in order, and managed like a vineyard, though they had themselves never seen anything of that kind; and by their good ordering their vines, their grapes were as good again as any of the others. They had also found themselves out a retreat in the thickest part of the woods, where, though there was not a natural cave, as I had found, yet they made one with incessant labour of their hands, and where, when the mischief which followed happened, they secured their wives and children so as they could never be found; they having, by sticking innumerable stakes and poles of the wood which, as I said, grew so readily, made the grove impassable, except in some places, when they climbed up to get over the outside part, and then went on by ways of their own leaving.

As to the three reprobates, as I justly call them, though they were much civilised by their settlement compared to what they were before, and were not so quarrelsome, having not the same opportunity; yet one of the certain companions of a profligate mind never left them, and that was their idleness. It is true, they planted corn and made fences; but Solomon's words were never better verified than in them, "I went by the vineyard of the slothful, and it was all overgrown with thorns": for when the Spaniards came to view their crop they could not see it in some places for weeds, the hedge had several gaps in it, where the wild goats had got in and eaten up the corn; perhaps here and there a dead bush was crammed in, to stop them out for the present, but it was only shutting the stable-door after the steed was stolen. Whereas, when they looked on the colony of the other two, there was the very face of industry and success upon all they did; there was not a weed to be seen in all their corn, or a gap in any of their hedges; and they, on the other hand, verified Solomon's words in another place, "that the diligent hand maketh rich"; for everything grew and thrived, and they had plenty within and without; they had more tame cattle than the others, more utensils and necessaries within doors, and yet more pleasure and diversion too.

It is true, the wives of the three were very handy and cleanly within doors; and having learned the English ways of dressing, and cooking from one of the other Englishmen, who, as I said, was a cook's mate on board the ship, they dressed their husbands' victuals very nicely and well; whereas the others could not be brought to understand it; but then the husband, who, as I say, had been cook's mate, did it himself. But as for the husbands of the three wives, they loitered about, fetched turtles' eggs, and caught fish and birds: in a word, anything but labour; and they fared accordingly. The diligent lived well and comfortably, and the slothful hard and beggarly; and so, I believe, generally speaking, it is all over the world.

But I now come to a scene different from all that had happened before, either to them or to me; and the origin of the story was this: Early one morning there came on shore five or six canoes of Indians or savages, call them which you please, and there is no room to doubt they came upon the old errand of feeding upon their slaves; but that part was now so familiar to the Spaniards, and to our men too, that they did not concern themselves about it, as I did: but having been made sensible, by their experience, that their only business was to lie concealed, and that if they were not seen by any of the savages they would go off again quietly, when their business was done, having as yet not the least notion of there being any inhabitants in the island; I say, having been made sensible of this, they had nothing to do but to give notice to all the three plantations to keep within doors, and not show themselves, only placing a scout in a proper place, to give notice when the boats went to sea again.

This was, without doubt, very right; but a disaster spoiled all these measures, and made it known among the savages that there were inhabitants there; which was, in the end, the desolation of almost the whole colony. After the canoes with the savages were gone off, the Spaniards peeped abroad again; and some of them had the curiosity to go to the place where they had been, to see what they had been doing. Here, to their great surprise, they found three savages left behind, and lying fast asleep upon the ground. It was supposed they had either been so gorged with their inhuman feast, that, like beasts, they were fallen asleep, and would not stir when the others went, or they had wandered into the woods, and did not come back in time to be taken in.

The Spaniards were greatly surprised at this sight and perfectly at a loss what to do. The Spaniard governor, as it happened, was with them, and his advice was asked, but he professed he knew not what to do. As for slaves, they had enough already; and as to killing them, there were none of them inclined to do that: the Spaniard governor told me they could not think of shedding innocent blood; for as to them, the poor creatures had done them no wrong, invaded none of their property, and they thought they had no just quarrel against them, to take away their lives. And here I must, in justice to these Spaniards, observe that, let the accounts of Spanish cruelty in Mexico and Peru be what they will, I never met with seventeen men of any nation whatsoever, in any foreign country, who were so universally modest, temperate, virtuous, so very good-humoured, and so courteous, as these Spaniards: and as to cruelty, they had nothing of it in their very nature; no inhumanity, no barbarity, no outrageous passions; and yet all of them men of great courage and spirit. Their temper and calmness had appeared in their bearing the insufferable usage of the three Englishmen; and their justice and humanity appeared now in the case of the savages above. After some consultation they resolved upon this; that they would lie still a while longer, till, if possible, these three men might be gone. But then the governor recollected that the three savages had no boat; and if they were left to rove about the island, they would certainly discover that there were inhabitants in it; and so they should be undone that way. Upon this, they went back again, and there lay the fellows fast asleep still, and so they resolved to awaken them, and take them prisoners; and they did so. The poor fellows were strangely frightened when they were seized upon and bound; and afraid, like the women, that they should be murdered and eaten: for it seems those people think all the world does as they do, in eating men's flesh; but they were soon made easy as to that, and away they carried them.

It was very happy for them that they did not carry them home to the castle, I mean to my palace under the hill; but they carried them first to the bower, where was the chief of their country work, such as the keeping the goats, the planting the corn, &c.; and afterward they carried them to the habitation of the two Englishmen. Here they were set to work, though it was not much they had for them to do; and whether it was by negligence in guarding them, or that they thought the fellows could not mend themselves, I know not, but one of them ran away, and, taking to the woods, they could never hear of him any more. They had good reason to believe he got home again soon after in some other boats or canoes of savages who came on shore three or four weeks afterwards, and who, carrying on their revels as usual, went off in two days' time. This thought terrified them exceedingly; for they concluded, and that not without good cause indeed, that if this fellow came home safe among his comrades, he would certainly give them an account that there were people in the island, and also how few and weak they were; for this savage, as observed before, had never been told, and it was very happy he had not, how many there were or where they lived; nor had he ever seen or heard the fire of any of their guns, much less had they shown him any of their other retired places; such as the cave in the valley, or the new retreat which the two Englishmen had made, and the like.

The first testimony they had that this fellow had given intelligence of them was, that about two months after this six canoes of savages, with about seven, eight, or ten men in a canoe, came rowing along the north side of the island, where they never used to come before, and landed, about an hour after sunrise, at a convenient place, about a mile from the habitation of the two Englishmen, where this escaped man had been kept. As the chief Spaniard said, had they been all there the damage would not have been so much, for not a man of them would have escaped; but the case differed now very much, for two men to fifty was too much odds. The two men had the happiness to discover them about a league off, so that it was above an hour before they landed; and as they landed a mile from their huts, it was some time before they could come at them. Now, having great reason to believe that they were betrayed, the first thing they did was to bind the two slaves which were left, and cause two of the three men whom they brought with the women (who, it seems, proved very faithful to them) to lead them, with their two wives, and whatever they could carry away with them, to their retired places in the woods, which I have spoken of above, and there to bind the two fellows hand and foot, till they heard farther. In the next place, seeing the savages were all come on shore, and that they had bent their course directly that way, they opened the fences where the milch cows were kept, and drove them all out; leaving their goats to straggle in the woods, whither they pleased, that the savages might think they were all bred wild; but the rogue who came with them was too cunning for that, and gave them an account of it all, for they went directly to the place.

When the two poor frightened men had secured their wives and goods, they sent the other slave they had of the three who came with the women, and who was at their place by accident, away to the Spaniards with all speed, to give them the alarm, and desire speedy help, and, in the meantime, they took their arms and what ammunition they had, and retreated towards the place in the wood where their wives were sent; keeping at a distance, yet so that they might see, if possible, which way the savages took. They had not gone far but that from a rising ground they could see the little army of their enemies come on directly to their habitation, and, in a moment more, could see all their huts and household stuff flaming up together, to their great grief and mortification; for this was a great loss to them, irretrievable, indeed, for some time. They kept their station for a while, till they found the savages, like wild beasts, spread themselves all over the place, rummaging every way, and every place they could think of, in search of prey; and in particular for the people, of whom now it plainly appeared they had intelligence.

The two Englishmen seeing this, thinking themselves not secure where they stood, because it was likely some of the wild people might come that way, and they might come too many together, thought it proper to make another retreat about half a mile farther; believing, as it afterwards happened, that the further they strolled, the fewer would be together. Their next halt was at the entrance into a very thick-grown part of the woods, and where an old trunk of a tree stood, which was hollow and very large; and in this tree they both took their standing, resolving to see there what might offer. They had not stood there long before two of the savages appeared running directly that way, as if they had already had notice where they stood, and were coming up to attack them; and a little way farther they espied three more coming after them, and five more beyond them, all coming the same way; besides which, they saw seven or eight more at a distance, running another way; for in a word, they ran every way, like sportsmen beating for their game.

The poor men were now in great perplexity whether they should stand and keep their posture or fly; but after a very short debate with themselves, they considered that if the savages ranged the country thus before help came, they might perhaps find their retreat in the woods, and then all would be lost; so they resolved to stand them there, and if they were too many to deal with, then they would get up to the top of the tree, from whence they doubted not to defend themselves, fire excepted, as long as their ammunition lasted, though all the savages that were landed, which was near fifty, were to attack them.

Having resolved upon this, they next considered whether they should fire at the first two, or wait for the three, and so take the middle party, by which the two and the five that followed would be separated; at length they resolved to let the first two pass by, unless they should spy them the tree, and come to attack them. The first two savages confirmed them also in this resolution, by turning a little from them towards another part of the wood; but the three, and the five after them, came forward directly to the tree, as if they had known the Englishmen were there. Seeing them come so straight towards them, they resolved to take them in a line as they came: and as they resolved to fire but one at a time, perhaps the first shot might hit them all three; for which purpose the man who was to fire put three or four small bullets into his piece; and having a fair loophole, as it were, from a broken hole in the tree, he took a sure aim, without being seen, waiting till they were within about thirty yards of the tree, so that he could not miss.

While they were thus waiting, and the savages came on, they plainly saw that one of the three was the runaway savage that had escaped from them; and they both knew him distinctly, and resolved that, if possible, he should not escape, though they should both fire; so the other stood ready with his piece, that if he did not drop at the first shot, he should be sure to have a second. But the first was too good a marksman to miss his aim; for as the savages kept near one another, a little behind in a line, he fired, and hit two of them directly; the foremost was killed outright, being shot in the head; the second, which was the runaway Indian, was shot through the body, and fell, but was not quite dead; and the third had a little scratch in the shoulder, perhaps by the same ball that went through the body of the second; and being dreadfully frightened, though not so much hurt, sat down upon the ground, screaming and yelling in a hideous manner.

The five that were behind, more frightened with the noise than sensible of the danger, stood still at first; for the woods made the sound a thousand times bigger than it really was, the echoes rattling from one side to another, and the fowls rising from all parts, screaming, and every sort making a different noise, according to their kind; just as it was when I fired the first gun that perhaps was ever shot off in the island.

However, all being silent again, and they not knowing what the matter was, came on unconcerned, till they came to the place where their companions lay in a condition miserable enough. Here the poor ignorant creatures, not sensible that they were within reach of the same mischief, stood all together over the wounded man, talking, and, as may be supposed, inquiring of him how he came to be hurt; and who, it is very rational to believe, told them that a flash of fire first, and immediately after that thunder from their gods, had killed those two and wounded him. This, I say, is rational; for nothing is more certain than that, as they saw no man near them, so they had never heard a gun in all their lives, nor so much as heard of a gun; neither knew they anything of killing and wounding at a distance with fire and bullets: if they had, one might reasonably believe they would not have stood so unconcerned to view the fate of their fellows, without some apprehensions of their own.

Our two men, as they confessed to me, were grieved to be obliged to kill so many poor creatures, who had no notion of their danger; yet, having them all thus in their power, and the first having loaded his piece again, resolved to let fly both together among them; and singling out, by agreement, which to aim at, they shot together, and killed, or very much wounded, four of them; the fifth, frightened even to death, though not hurt, fell with the rest; so that our men, seeing them all fall together, thought they had killed them all.

The belief that the savages were all killed made our two men come boldly out from the tree before they had charged their guns, which was a wrong step; and they were under some surprise when they came to the place, and found no less than four of them alive, and of them two very little hurt, and one not at all. This obliged them to fall upon them with the stocks of their muskets; and first they made sure of the runaway savage, that had been the cause of all the mischief, and of another that was hurt in the knee, and put them out of their pain; then the man that was not hurt at all came and kneeled down to them, with his two hands held up, and made piteous moans to them, by gestures and signs, for his life, but could not say one word to them that they could understand. However, they made signs to him to sit down at the foot of a tree hard by; and one of the Englishmen, with a piece of rope-yarn, which he had by great chance in his pocket, tied his two hands behind him, and there they left him; and with what speed they could made after the other two, which were gone before, fearing they, or any more of them, should find way to their covered place in the woods, where their wives, and the few goods they had left, lay. They came once in sight of the two men, but it was at a great distance; however, they had the satisfaction to see them cross over a valley towards the sea, quite the contrary way from that which led to their retreat, which they were afraid of; and being satisfied with that, they went back to the tree where they left their prisoner, who, as they supposed, was delivered by his comrades, for he was gone, and the two pieces of rope-yarn with which they had bound him lay just at the foot of the tree.

They were now in as great concern as before, not knowing what course to take, or how near the enemy might be, or in what number; so they resolved to go away to the place where their wives were, to see if all was well there, and to make them easy. These were in fright enough, to be sure; for though the savages were their own countrymen, yet they were most terribly afraid of them, and perhaps the more for the knowledge they had of them. When they came there, they found the savages had been in the wood, and very near that place, but had not found it; for it was indeed inaccessible, from the trees standing so thick, unless the persons seeking it had been directed by those that knew it, which these did not: they found, therefore, everything very safe, only the women in a terrible fright. While they were here they had the comfort to have seven of the Spaniards come to their assistance; the other ten, with their servants, and Friday's father, were gone in a body to defend their bower, and the corn and cattle that were kept there, in case the savages should have roved over to that side of the country, but they did not spread so far. With the seven Spaniards came one of the three savages, who, as I said, were their prisoners formerly; and with them also came the savage whom the Englishmen had left bound hand and foot at the tree; for it seems they came that way, saw the slaughter of the seven men, and unbound the eighth, and brought him along with them; where, however, they were obliged to bind again, as they had the two others who were left when the third ran away.

The prisoners now began to be a burden to them; and they were so afraid of their escaping, that they were once resolving to kill them all, believing they were under an absolute necessity to do so for their own preservation. However, the chief of the Spaniards would not consent to it, but ordered, for the present, that they should be sent out of the way to my old cave in the valley, and be kept there, with two Spaniards to guard them, and have food for their subsistence, which was done; and they were bound there hand and foot for that night.

When the Spaniards came, the two Englishmen were so encouraged, that they could not satisfy themselves to stay any longer there; but taking five of the Spaniards, and themselves, with four muskets and a pistol among them, and two stout quarter-staves, away they went in quest of the savages. And first they came to the tree where the men lay that had been killed; but it was easy to see that some more of the savages had been there, for they had attempted to carry their dead men away, and had dragged two of them a good way, but had given it over. From thence they advanced to the first rising ground, where they had stood and seen their camp destroyed, and where they had the mortification still to see some of the smoke; but neither could they here see any of the savages. They then resolved, though with all possible caution, to go forward towards their ruined plantation; but, a little before they came thither, coming in sight of the sea-shore, they saw plainly the savages all embarked again in their canoes, in order to be gone. They seemed sorry at first that there was no way to come at them, to give them a parting blow; but, upon the whole, they were very well satisfied to be rid of them.

The poor Englishmen being now twice ruined, and all their improvements destroyed, the rest all agreed to come and help them to rebuild, and assist them with needful supplies. Their three countrymen, who were not yet noted for having the least inclination to do any good, yet as soon as they heard of it (for they, living remote eastward, knew nothing of the matter till all was over), came and offered their help and assistance, and did, very friendly, work for several days to restore their habitation and make necessaries for them. And thus in a little time they were set upon their legs again.

About two days after this they had the farther satisfaction of seeing three of the savages' canoes come driving on shore, and, at some distance from them, two drowned men, by which they had reason to believe that they had met with a storm at sea, which had overset some of them; for it had blown very hard the night after they went off. However, as some might miscarry, so, on the other hand, enough of them escaped to inform the rest, as well of what they had done as of what had happened to them; and to whet them on to another enterprise of the same nature, which they, it seems, resolved to attempt, with sufficient force to carry all before them; for except what the first man had told them of inhabitants, they could say little of it of their own knowledge, for they never saw one man; and the fellow being killed that had affirmed it, they had no other witness to confirm it to, them.

✼ 5 ✼

A GREAT VICTORY

It was five or six months after this before they heard any more of the savages, in which time our men were in hopes they had either forgot their former bad luck, or given over hopes of better; when, on a sudden, they were invaded with a most formidable fleet of no less than eight-and-twenty canoes, full of savages, armed with bows and arrows, great clubs, wooden swords, and such like engines of war; and they brought such numbers with them, that, in short, it put all our people into the utmost consternation.

As they came on shore in the evening, and at the easternmost side of the island, our men had that night to consult and consider what to do. In the first place, knowing that their being entirely concealed was their only safety before and would be much more so now, while the number of their enemies would be so great, they resolved, first of all, to take down the huts which were built for the two Englishmen, and drive away their goats to the old cave; because they supposed the savages would go directly thither, as soon as it was day, to play the old game over again, though they did not now land within two leagues of it. In the next place, they drove away all the flocks of goats they had at the old bower, as I called it, which belonged to the Spaniards; and, in short, left as little appearance of inhabitants anywhere as was possible; and the next morning early they posted themselves, with all their force, at the plantation of the two men, to wait for their coming. As they guessed, so it happened: these new invaders, leaving their canoes at the east end of the island, came ranging along the shore, directly towards the place, to the number of two hundred and fifty, as near as our men could judge. Our army was but small indeed; but, that which was worse, they had not arms for all their number. The whole account, it seems, stood thus: first, as to men, seventeen Spaniards, five Englishmen, old Friday, the three slaves taken with the women, who proved very faithful, and three other slaves, who lived with the Spaniards. To arm these, they had eleven muskets, five pistols, three fowling-pieces, five muskets or fowling-pieces which were taken by me from the mutinous seamen whom I reduced, two swords, and three old halberds.

To their slaves they did not give either musket or fusee; but they had each a halberd, or a long staff, like a quarter-staff, with a great spike of iron fastened into each end of it, and by his side a hatchet; also every one of our men had a hatchet. Two of the women could not be prevailed upon but they would come into the fight, and they had bows and arrows, which the Spaniards had taken from the savages when the first action happened, which I have spoken of, where the Indians fought with one another; and the women had hatchets too.

The chief Spaniard, whom I described so often, commanded the whole; and Will Atkins, who, though a dreadful fellow for wickedness, was a most daring, bold fellow, commanded under him. The savages came forward like lions; and our men, which was the worst of their fate, had no advantage in their situation; only that Will Atkins, who now proved a most useful fellow, with six men, was planted just behind a small thicket of bushes as an advanced guard, with orders to let the first of them pass by and then fire into the middle of them, and as soon as he had fired, to make his retreat as nimbly as he could round a part of the wood, and so come in behind the Spaniards, where they stood, having a thicket of trees before them.

When the savages came on, they ran straggling about every way in heaps, out of all manner of order, and Will Atkins let about fifty of them pass by him; then seeing the rest come in a very thick throng, he orders three of his men to fire, having loaded their muskets with six or seven bullets apiece, about as big as large pistol-bullets. How many they killed or wounded they knew not, but the consternation and surprise was inexpressible among the savages; they were frightened to the last degree to hear such a dreadful noise, and see their men killed, and others hurt, but see nobody that did it; when, in the middle of their fright, Will Atkins and his other three let fly again among the thickest of them; and in less than a minute the first three, being loaded again, gave them a third volley.

Had Will Atkins and his men retired immediately, as soon as they had fired, as they were ordered to do, or had the rest of the body been at hand to have poured in their shot continually, the savages had been effectually routed; for the terror that was among them came principally from this, that they were killed by the gods with thunder and lightning, and could see nobody that hurt them. But Will Atkins, staying to load again, discovered the cheat: some of the savages who were at a distance spying them, came upon them behind; and though Atkins and his men fired at them also, two or three times, and killed above twenty, retiring as fast as they could, yet they wounded Atkins himself, and killed one of his fellow-Englishmen with their arrows, as they did afterwards one Spaniard, and one of the Indian slaves who came with the women. This slave was a most gallant fellow, and fought most desperately, killing five of them with his own hand, having no weapon but one of the armed staves and a hatchet.

Our men being thus hard laid at, Atkins wounded, and two other men killed, retreated to a rising ground in the wood; and the Spaniards, after firing three volleys upon them, retreated also; for their number was so great, and they were so desperate, that though above fifty of them were killed, and more than as many wounded, yet they came on in the teeth of our men, fearless of danger, and shot their arrows like a cloud; and it was observed that their wounded men, who were not quite disabled, were made outrageous by their wounds, and fought like madmen.

When our men retreated, they left the Spaniard and the Englishman that were killed behind them: and the savages, when they came up to them, killed them over again in a wretched manner, breaking their arms, legs, and heads, with their clubs and wooden swords, like true savages; but finding our men were gone, they did not seem inclined to pursue them, but drew themselves up in a ring, which is, it seems, their custom, and shouted twice, in token of their victory; after which, they had the mortification to see several of their wounded men fall, dying with the mere loss of blood.

The Spaniard governor having drawn his little body up together upon a rising ground,

Atkins, though he was wounded, would have had them march and charge again all together at once: but the Spaniard replied, "Seignior Atkins, you see how their wounded men fight; let them alone till morning; all the wounded men will be stiff and sore with their wounds, and faint with the loss of blood; and so we shall have the fewer to engage." This advice was good: but Will Atkins replied merrily, "That is true, seignior, and so shall I too; and that is the reason I would go on while I am warm." "Well, Seignior Atkins," says the Spaniard, "you have behaved gallantly, and done your part; we will fight for you if you cannot come on; but I think it best to stay till morning:" so they waited.

But as it was a clear moonlight night, and they found the savages in great disorder about their dead and wounded men, and a great noise and hurry among them where they lay, they afterwards resolved to fall upon them in the night, especially if they could come to give them but one volley before they were discovered, which they had a fair opportunity to do; for one of the Englishmen in whose quarter it was where the fight began, led them round between the woods and the seaside westward, and then turning short south, they came so near where the thickest of them lay, that before they were seen or heard eight of them fired in among them, and did dreadful execution upon them; in half a minute more eight others fired after them, pouring in their small shot in such a quantity that abundance were killed and wounded; and all this while they were not able to see who hurt them, or which way to fly.

The Spaniards charged again with the utmost expedition, and then divided themselves into three bodies, and resolved to fall in among them all together. They had in each body eight persons, that is to say, twenty-two men and the two women, who, by the way, fought desperately. They divided the firearms equally in each party, as well as the halberds and staves. They would have had the women kept back, but they said they were resolved to die with their husbands. Having thus formed their little army, they marched out from among the trees, and came up to the teeth of the enemy, shouting and hallooing as loud as they could; the savages stood all together, but were in the utmost confusion, hearing the noise of our men shouting from three quarters together. They would have fought if they had seen us; for as soon as we came near enough to be seen, some arrows were shot, and poor old Friday was wounded, though not dangerously. But our men gave them no time, but running up to them, fired among them three ways, and then fell in with the butt-ends of their muskets, their swords, armed staves, and hatchets, and laid about them so well that, in a word, they set up a dismal screaming and howling, flying to save their lives which way soever they could.

Our men were tired with the execution, and killed or mortally wounded in the two fights about one hundred and eighty of them; the rest, being frightened out of their wits, scoured through the woods and over the hills, with all the speed that fear and nimble feet could help them to; and as we did not trouble ourselves much to pursue them, they got all together to the seaside, where they landed, and where their canoes lay. But their disaster was not at an end yet; for it blew a terrible storm of wind that evening from the sea, so that it was impossible for them to go off; nay, the storm continuing all night, when the tide came up their canoes were most of them driven by the surge of the sea so high upon the shore that it required infinite toil to get them off; and some of them were even dashed to pieces against the beach. Our men, though glad of their victory, yet got little rest that night; but having refreshed themselves as well as they could, they resolved to march to that part of the island where the savages were fled, and see what posture they were in. This necessarily led them over the place where the fight had been, and where they found several of the poor creatures not quite dead, and yet past recovering life; a sight disagreeable enough to generous minds, for a truly great man though obliged by the law of battle to destroy his enemy, takes no delight in his misery. However, there was no need to give any orders in this case; for their own savages, who were their servants, despatched these poor creatures with their hatchets.

At length they came in view of the place where the more miserable remains of the savages' army lay, where there appeared about a hundred still; their posture was generally sitting upon the ground, with their knees up towards their mouth, and the head put between the two hands, leaning down upon the knees. When our men came within two musket-shots of them, the Spaniard governor ordered two muskets to be fired without ball, to alarm them; this he did, that by their countenance he might know what to expect, whether they were still in heart to fight, or were so heartily beaten as to be discouraged, and so he might manage accordingly. This stratagem took: for as soon as the savages heard the first gun, and saw the flash of the second, they started up upon their feet in the greatest consternation imaginable; and as our men advanced swiftly towards them, they all ran screaming and yelling away, with a kind of howling noise, which our men did not understand, and had never heard before; and thus they ran up the hills into the country.

At first our men had much rather the weather had been calm, and they had all gone away to sea: but they did not then consider that this might probably have been the occasion of their coming again in such multitudes as not to be resisted, or, at least, to come so many and so often as would quite desolate the island, and starve them. Will Atkins, therefore, who notwithstanding his wound kept always with them, proved the best counsellor in this case: his advice was, to take the advantage that offered, and step in between them and their boats, and so deprive them of the capacity of ever returning any more to plague the island. They consulted long about this; and some were against it for fear of making the wretches fly to the woods and live there desperate, and so they should have them to hunt like wild beasts, be afraid to stir out about their business, and have their plantations continually rifled, all their tame goats destroyed, and, in short, be reduced to a life of continual distress.

Will Atkins told them they had better have to do with a hundred men than with a hundred nations; that, as they must destroy their boats, so they must destroy the men, or be all of them destroyed themselves. In a word, he showed them the necessity of it so plainly that they all came into it; so they went to work immediately with the boats, and getting some dry wood together from a dead tree, they tried to set some of them on fire, but they were so wet that they would not burn; however, the fire so burned the upper part that it soon made them unfit for use at sea.

When the Indians saw what they were about, some of them came running out of the woods, and coming as near as they could to our men, kneeled down and cried, "Oa, Oa, Waramokoa," and some other words of their language, which none of the others understood anything of; but as they made pitiful gestures and strange noises, it was easy to understand they begged to have their boats spared, and that they would be gone, and never come there again. But our men were now satisfied that they had no way to preserve themselves, or to save their colony, but effectually to prevent any of these people from ever going home again; depending upon this, that if even so much as one of them got back into their country to tell the story, the colony was undone; so that, letting them know that they should not have any mercy, they fell to work with their canoes, and destroyed every one that the storm had not destroyed before; at the sight of which, the savages raised a hideous cry in the woods, which our people heard plain enough, after which they ran about the island like distracted men, so that, in a word, our men did not really know what at first to do with them. Nor did the Spaniards, with all their prudence, consider that while they made those people thus desperate, they ought to have kept a good guard at the same time upon their plantations; for though it is true they had driven away their cattle, and the Indians did not find out their main retreat, I mean my old castle at the hill, nor the cave in the valley, yet they found out my plantation at the bower, and pulled it all to pieces, and all the fences and planting about it; trod all the corn under foot, tore up the vines and grapes, being just then almost ripe, and did our men inestimable damage, though to themselves not one farthing's worth of service.

Though our men were able to fight them upon all occasions, yet they were in no condition to pursue them, or hunt them up and down; for as they were too nimble of foot for our people when they found them single, so our men durst not go abroad single, for fear of being surrounded with their numbers. The best was they had no weapons; for though they had bows, they had no arrows left, nor any materials to make any; nor had they any edge-tool among them. The extremity and distress they were reduced to was great, and indeed deplorable; but, at the same time, our men were also brought to very bad circumstances by them, for though their retreats were preserved, yet their provision was destroyed, and their harvest spoiled, and what to do, or which way to turn themselves, they knew not. The only refuge they had now was the stock of cattle they had in the valley by the cave, and some little corn which grew there, and the plantation of the three Englishmen. Will Atkins and his comrades were now reduced to two; one of them being killed by an arrow, which struck him on the side of his head, just under the temple, so that he never spoke more; and it was very remarkable that this was the same barbarous fellow that cut the poor savage slave with his hatchet, and who afterwards intended to have murdered the Spaniards.

I looked upon their case to have been worse at this time than mine was at any time, after I first discovered the grains of barley and rice, and got into the manner of planting and raising my corn, and my tame cattle; for now they had, as I may say, a hundred wolves upon the island, which would devour everything they could come at, yet could be hardly come at themselves.

When they saw what their circumstances were, the first thing they concluded was, that they would, if possible, drive the savages up to the farther part of the island, south-west, that if any more came on shore they might not find one another; then, that they would daily hunt and harass them, and kill as many of them as they could come at, till they had reduced their number; and if they could at last tame them, and bring them to anything, they would give them corn, and teach them how to plant, and live upon their daily labour. In order to do this, they so followed them, and so terrified them with their guns, that in a few days, if any of them fired a gun at an Indian, if he did not hit him, yet he would fall down for fear. So dreadfully frightened were they that they kept out of sight farther and farther; till at last our men followed them, and almost every day killing or wounding some of them, they kept up in the woods or hollow places so much, that it reduced them to the utmost misery for want of food; and many were afterwards found dead in the woods, without any hurt, absolutely starved to death.

When our men found this, it made their hearts relent, and pity moved them, especially the generous-minded Spaniard governor; and he proposed, if possible, to take one of them alive and bring him to understand what they meant, so far as to be able to act as interpreter, and go among them and see if they might be brought to some conditions that might be depended upon, to save their lives and do us no harm.

It was some while before any of them could be taken; but being weak and half-starved, one of them was at last surprised and made a prisoner. He was sullen at first, and would neither eat nor drink; but finding himself kindly used, and victuals given to him, and no violence offered him, he at last grew tractable, and came to himself. They often brought old Friday to talk to him, who always told him how kind the others would be to them all; that they would not only save their lives, but give them part of the island to live in, provided they would give satisfaction that they would keep in their own bounds, and not come beyond it to injure or prejudice others; and that they should have corn given them to plant and make it grow for their bread, and some bread given them for their present subsistence; and old Friday bade the fellow go and talk with the rest of his countrymen, and see what they said to it; assuring them that, if they did not agree immediately, they should be all destroyed.

The poor wretches, thoroughly humbled, and reduced in number to about thirty-seven, closed with the proposal at the first offer, and begged to have some food given them; upon which twelve Spaniards and two Englishmen, well armed, with three Indian slaves and old Friday, marched to the place where they were. The three Indian slaves carried them a large quantity of bread, some rice boiled up to cakes and dried in the sun, and three live goats; and they were ordered to go to the side of a hill, where they sat down, ate their provisions very thankfully, and were the most faithful fellows to their words that could be thought of; for, except when they came to beg victuals and directions, they never came out of their bounds; and there they lived when I came to the island and I went to see them. They had taught them both to plant corn, make bread, breed tame goats, and milk them: they wanted nothing but wives in order for them soon to become a nation. They were confined to a neck of land, surrounded with high rocks behind them, and lying plain towards the sea before them, on the south-east corner of the island. They had land enough, and it was very good and fruitful; about a mile and a half broad, and three or four miles in length. Our men taught them to make wooden spades, such as I made for myself, and gave among them twelve hatchets and three or four knives; and there they lived, the most subjected, innocent creatures that ever were heard of.

After this the colony enjoyed a perfect tranquillity with respect to the savages, till I came to revisit them, which was about two years after; not but that, now and then, some canoes of savages came on shore for their triumphal, unnatural feasts; but as they were of several nations, and perhaps had never heard of those that came before, or the reason of it, they did not make any search or inquiry after their countrymen; and if they had, it would have been very hard to have found them out.

Thus, I think, I have given a full account of all that happened to them till my return, at least that was worth notice. The Indians were wonderfully civilised by them, and they frequently went among them; but they forbid, on pain of death, any one of the Indians coming to them, because they would not have their settlement betrayed again. One thing was very remarkable, viz. that they taught the savages to make wicker-work, or baskets, but they soon outdid their masters: for they made abundance of ingenious things in wicker-work, particularly baskets, sieves, bird-cages, cupboards, &c.; as also chairs, stools, beds, couches, being very ingenious at such work when they were once put in the way of it.

My coming was a particular relief to these people, because we furnished them with knives, scissors, spades, shovels, pick-axes, and all things of that kind which they could want. With the help of those tools they were so very handy that they came at last to build up their huts or houses very handsomely, raddling or working it up like basket-work all the way round. This piece of ingenuity, although it looked very odd, was an exceeding good fence, as well against heat as against all sorts of vermin; and our men were so taken with it that they got the Indians to come and do the like for them; so that when I came to see the two Englishmen's colonies, they looked at a distance as if they all lived like bees in a hive.

As for Will Atkins, who was now become a very industrious, useful, and sober fellow, he had made himself such a tent of basket-work as I believe was never seen; it was one hundred and twenty paces round on the outside, as I measured by my steps; the walls were as close worked as a basket, in panels or squares of thirty-two in number, and very strong, standing about seven feet high; in the middle was another not above twenty-two paces round, but built stronger, being octagon in its form, and in the eight corners stood eight very strong posts; round the top of which he laid strong pieces, knit together with wooden pins, from which he raised a pyramid for a handsome roof of eight rafters, joined together very well, though he had no nails, and only a few iron spikes, which he made himself, too, out of the old iron that I had left there. Indeed, this fellow showed abundance of ingenuity in several things which he had no knowledge of: he made him a forge, with a pair of wooden bellows to blow the fire; he made himself charcoal for his work; and he formed out of the iron crows a middling good anvil to hammer upon: in this manner he made many things, but especially hooks, staples, and spikes, bolts and hinges. But to return to the house: after he had pitched the roof of his innermost tent, he worked it up between the rafters with basket-work, so firm, and thatched that over again so ingeniously with rice-straw, and over that a large leaf of a tree, which covered the top, that his house was as dry as if it had been tiled or slated. He owned, indeed, that the savages had made the basket-work for him. The outer circuit was covered as a lean-to all round this inner apartment, and long rafters lay from the thirty-two angles to the top posts of the inner house, being about twenty feet distant, so that there was a space like a walk within the outer wicker-wall, and without the inner, near twenty feet wide.

The inner place he partitioned off with the same wickerwork, but much fairer, and divided into six apartments, so that he had six rooms on a floor, and out of every one of these there was a door: first into the entry, or coming into the main tent, another door into the main tent, and another door into the space or walk that was round it; so that walk was also divided into six equal parts, which served not only for a retreat, but to store up any necessaries which the family had occasion for. These six spaces not taking up the whole circumference, what other apartments the outer circle had were thus ordered: As soon as you were in at the door of the outer circle you had a short passage straight before you to the door of the inner house; but on either side was a wicker partition and a door in it, by which you went first into a large room or storehouse, twenty feet wide and about thirty feet long, and through that into another not quite so long; so that in the outer circle were ten handsome rooms, six of which were only to be come at through the apartments of the inner tent, and served as closets or retiring rooms to the respective chambers of the inner circle; and four large warehouses, or barns, or what you please to call them, which went through one another, two on either hand of the passage, that led through the outer door to the inner tent. Such a piece of basket-work, I believe, was never seen in the world, nor a house or tent so neatly contrived, much less so built. In this great bee-hive lived the three families, that is to say, Will Atkins and his companion; the third was killed, but his wife remained with three children, and the other two were not at all backward to give the widow her full share of everything, I mean as to their corn, milk, grapes, &c., and when they killed a kid, or found a turtle on the shore; so that they all lived well enough; though it was true they were not so industrious as the other two, as has been observed already.

One thing, however, cannot be omitted, viz. that as for religion, I do not know that there was anything of that kind among them; they often, indeed, put one another in mind that there was a God, by the very common method of seamen, swearing by His name: nor were their poor ignorant savage wives much better for having been married to Christians, as we must call them; for as they knew very little of God themselves, so they were utterly incapable of entering into any discourse with their wives about a God, or to talk anything to them concerning religion.

The utmost of all the improvement which I can say the wives had made from them was, that they had taught them to speak English pretty well; and most of their children, who were near twenty in all, were taught to speak English too, from their first learning to speak, though they at first spoke it in a very broken manner, like their mothers. None of these children were above six years old when I came thither, for it was not much above seven years since they had fetched these five savage ladies over; they had all children, more or less: the mothers were all a good sort of well-governed, quiet, laborious women, modest and decent, helpful to one another, mighty observant, and subject to their masters (I cannot call them husbands), and lacked nothing but to be well instructed in the Christian religion, and to be legally married; both of which were happily brought about afterwards by my means, or at least in consequence of my coming among them.

6

THE FRENCH CLERGYMAN'S COUNSEL

Having thus given an account of the colony in general, and pretty much of my runagate Englishmen, I must say something of the Spaniards, who were the main body of the family, and in whose story there are some incidents also remarkable enough.

I had a great many discourses with them about their circumstances when they were among the savages. They told me readily that they had no instances to give of their application or ingenuity in that country; that they were a poor, miserable, dejected handful of people; that even if means had been put into their hands, yet they had so abandoned themselves to despair, and were so sunk under the weight of their misfortune, that they thought of nothing but starving. One of them, a grave and sensible man, told me he was convinced they were in the wrong; that it was not the part of wise men to give themselves up to their misery, but always to take hold of the helps which reason offered, as well for present support as for future deliverance: he told me that grief was the most senseless, insignificant passion in the world, for that it regarded only things past, which were generally impossible to be recalled or to be remedied, but had no views of things to come, and had no share in anything that looked like deliverance, but rather added to the affliction than proposed a remedy; and upon this he repeated a Spanish proverb, which, though I cannot repeat in the same words that he spoke it in, yet I remember I made it into an English proverb of my own, thus:—

"In trouble to be troubled,
Is to have your trouble doubled."

He then ran on in remarks upon all the little improvements I had made in my solitude: my unwearied application, as he called it; and how I had made a condition, which in its circumstances was at first much worse than theirs, a thousand times more happy than theirs was, even now when they were all together. He told me it was remarkable that Englishmen had a greater presence of mind in their distress than any people that ever he met with; that their unhappy nation and the Portuguese were the worst men in the world to struggle with misfortunes; for that their first step in dangers, after the common efforts were over, was to despair, lie down under it, and die, without rousing their thoughts up to proper remedies for escape.

I told him their case and mine differed exceedingly; that they were cast upon the shore without necessaries, without supply of food, or present sustenance till they could provide for it; that, it was true, I had this further disadvantage and discomfort, that I was alone; but then the supplies I had providentially thrown into my hands, by the unexpected driving of the ship on the shore, was such a help as would have encouraged any creature in the world to have applied himself as I had done. "Seignior," says the Spaniard, "had we poor Spaniards been in your case, we should never have got half those things out of the ship, as you did: nay," says he, "we should never have found means to have got a raft to carry them, or to have got the raft on shore without boat or sail: and how much less should we have done if any of us had been alone!" Well, I desired him to abate his compliments, and go on with the history of their coming on shore, where they landed. He told me they unhappily landed at a place where there were people without provisions; whereas, had they had the common sense to put off to sea again, and gone to another island a little further, they had found provisions, though without people: there being an island that way, as they had been told, where there were provisions, though no people—that is to say, that the Spaniards of Trinidad had frequently been there, and had filled the island with goats and hogs at several times, where they had bred in such multitudes, and where turtle and sea-fowls were in such plenty, that they could have been in no want of flesh, though they had found no bread; whereas, here they were only sustained with a few roots and herbs, which they understood not, and which had no substance in them, and which the inhabitants gave them sparingly enough; and they could treat them no better, unless they would turn cannibals and eat men's flesh.

They gave me an account how many ways they strove to civilise the savages they were with, and to teach them rational customs in the ordinary way of living, but in vain; and how they retorted upon them as unjust that they who came there for assistance and support should attempt to set up for instructors to those that gave them food; intimating, it seems, that none should set up for the instructors of others but those who could live without them. They gave me dismal accounts of the extremities they were driven to; how sometimes they were many days without any food at all, the island they were upon being inhabited by a sort of savages that lived more indolent, and for that reason were less supplied with the necessaries of life, than they had reason to believe others were in the same part of the world; and yet they found that these savages were less ravenous and voracious than those who had better supplies of food. Also, they added, they could not but see with what demonstrations of wisdom and goodness the governing providence of God directs the events of things in this world, which, they said, appeared in their circumstances: for if, pressed by the hardships they were under, and the barrenness of the country where they were, they had searched after a better to live in, they had then been out of the way of the relief that happened to them by my means.

They then gave me an account how the savages whom they lived amongst expected them to go out with them into their wars; and, it was true, that as they had firearms with them, had they not had the disaster to lose their ammunition, they could have been serviceable not only to their friends, but have made themselves terrible both to friends and enemies; but being without powder and shot, and yet in a condition that they could not in reason decline to go out with their landlords to their wars; so when they came into the field of battle they were in a worse condition than the savages themselves, for they had neither bows nor arrows, nor could they use those the savages gave them. So they could do nothing but stand still and be wounded with arrows, till they came up to the teeth of the enemy; and then, indeed, the three halberds they had were of use to them; and they would often drive a whole little army before them with those halberds, and sharpened sticks put into the muzzles of their muskets. But for all this they were sometimes surrounded with multitudes, and in great danger from their arrows, till at last they found the way to make themselves large targets of wood, which they covered with skins of wild beasts, whose names they knew not, and these covered them from the arrows of the savages: that, notwithstanding these, they were sometimes in great danger; and five of them were once knocked down together with the clubs of the savages, which was the time when one of them was taken prisoner—that is to say, the Spaniard whom I relieved. At first they thought he had been killed; but when they afterwards heard he was taken prisoner, they were under the greatest grief imaginable, and would willingly have all ventured their lives to have rescued him.

They told me that when they were so knocked down, the rest of their company rescued them, and stood over them fighting till they were come to themselves, all but him whom they thought had been dead; and then they made their way with their halberds and pieces, standing close together in a line, through a body of above a thousand savages, beating down all that came in their way, got the victory over their enemies, but to their great sorrow, because it was with the loss of their friend, whom the other party finding alive, carried off with some others, as I gave an account before. They described, most affectionately, how they were surprised with joy at the return of their friend and companion in misery, who they thought had been devoured by wild beasts of the worst kind—wild men; and yet, how more and more they were surprised with the account he gave them of his errand, and that there was a Christian in any place near, much more one that was able, and had humanity enough, to contribute to their deliverance.

They described how they were astonished at the sight of the relief I sent them, and at the appearance of loaves of bread—things they had not seen since their coming to that miserable place; how often they crossed it and blessed it as bread sent from heaven; and what a reviving cordial it was to their spirits to taste it, as also the other things I had sent for their supply; and, after all, they would have told me something of the joy they were in at the sight of a boat and pilots, to carry them away to the person and place from whence all these new comforts came. But it was impossible to express it by words, for their excessive joy naturally driving them to unbecoming extravagances, they had no way to describe them but by telling me they bordered upon lunacy, having no way to give vent to their passions suitable to the sense that was upon them; that in some it worked one way and in some another; and that some of them, through a surprise of joy, would burst into tears, others be stark mad, and others immediately faint. This discourse extremely affected me, and called to my mind Friday's ecstasy when he met his father, and the poor people's ecstasy when I took them up at sea after their ship was on fire; the joy of the mate of the ship when he found himself delivered in the place where he expected to perish; and my own joy, when, after twenty-eight years' captivity, I found a good ship ready to carry me to my own country. All these things made me more sensible of the relation of these poor men, and more affected with it.

Having thus given a view of the state of things as I found them, I must relate the heads of what I did for these people, and the condition in which I left them. It was their opinion, and mine too, that they would be troubled no more with the savages, or if they were, they would be able to cut them off, if they were twice as many as before; so they had no concern about that. Then I entered into a serious discourse with the Spaniard, whom I call governor, about their stay in the island; for as I was not come to carry any of them off, so it would not be just to carry off some and leave others, who, perhaps, would be unwilling to stay if their strength was diminished. On the other hand, I told them I came to establish them there, not to remove them; and then I let them know that I had brought with me relief of sundry kinds for them; that I had been at a great charge to supply them with all things necessary, as well for their convenience as their defence; and that I had such and such particular persons with me, as well to increase and recruit their number, as by the particular necessary employments which they were bred to, being artificers, to assist them in those things in which at present they were in want.

They were all together when I talked thus to them; and before I delivered to them the stores I had brought, I asked them, one by one, if they had entirely forgot and buried the first animosities that had been among them, and would shake hands with one another, and engage in a strict friendship and union of interest, that so there might be no more misunderstandings and jealousies.

Will Atkins, with abundance of frankness and good humour, said they had met with affliction enough to make them all sober, and enemies enough to make them all friends; that, for his part, he would live and die with them, and was so far from designing anything against the Spaniards, that he owned they had done nothing to him but what his own mad humour made necessary, and what he would have done, and perhaps worse, in their case; and that he would ask them pardon, if I desired it, for the foolish and brutish things he had done to them, and was very willing and desirous of living in terms of entire friendship and union with them, and would do anything that lay in his power to convince them of it; and as for going to England, he cared not if he did not go thither these twenty years.

The Spaniards said they had, indeed, at first disarmed and excluded Will Atkins and his two countrymen for their ill conduct, as they had let me know, and they appealed to me for the necessity they were under to do so; but that Will Atkins had behaved himself so bravely in the great fight they had with the savages, and on several occasions since, and had showed himself so faithful to, and concerned for, the general interest of them all, that they had forgotten all that was past, and thought he merited as much to be trusted with arms and supplied with necessaries as any of them; that they had testified their satisfaction in him by committing the command to him next to the governor himself; and as they had entire confidence in him and all his countrymen, so they acknowledged they had merited that confidence by all the methods that honest men could merit to be valued and trusted; and they most heartily embraced the occasion of giving me this assurance, that they would never have any interest separate from one another.

Upon these frank and open declarations of friendship, we appointed the next day to dine all together; and, indeed, we made a splendid feast. I caused the ship's cook and his mate to come on shore and dress our dinner, and the old cook's mate we had on shore assisted. We brought on shore six pieces of good beef and four pieces of pork, out of the ship's provisions, with our punch-bowl and materials to fill it; and in particular I gave them ten bottles of French claret, and ten bottles of English beer; things that neither the Spaniards nor the English had tasted for many years, and which it may be supposed they were very glad of. The Spaniards added to our feast five whole kids, which the cooks roasted; and three of them were sent, covered up close, on board the ship to the seamen, that they might feast on fresh meat from on shore, as we did with their salt meat from on board.

After this feast, at which we were very innocently merry, I brought my cargo of goods; wherein, that there might be no dispute about dividing, I showed them that there was a sufficiency for them all, desiring that they might all take an equal quantity, when made up, of the goods that were for wearing. As, first, I distributed linen sufficient to make every one of them four shirts, and, at the Spaniard's request, afterwards made them up six; these were exceeding comfortable to them, having been what they had long since forgot the use of, or what it was to wear them. I allotted the thin English stuffs, which I mentioned before, to make every one a light coat, like a frock, which I judged fittest for the heat of the season, cool and loose; and ordered that whenever they decayed, they should make more, as they thought fit; the like for pumps, shoes, stockings, hats, &c. I cannot express what pleasure sat upon the countenances of all these poor men when they saw the care I had taken of them, and how well I had furnished them. They told me I was a father to them; and that having such a correspondent as I was in so remote a part of the world, it would make them forget that they were left in a desolate place; and they all voluntarily engaged to me not to leave the place without my consent.

Then I presented to them the people I had brought with me, particularly the tailor, the smith, and the two carpenters, all of them most necessary people; but, above all, my general artificer, than whom they could not name anything that was more useful to them; and the tailor, to show his concern for them, went to work immediately, and, with my leave, made them every one a shirt, the first thing he did; and, what was still more, he taught the women not only how to sew and stitch, and use the needle, but made them assist to make the shirts for their husbands, and for all the rest. As to the carpenters, I scarce need mention how useful they were; for they took to pieces all my clumsy, unhandy things, and made clever convenient tables, stools, bedsteads, cupboards, lockers, shelves, and everything they wanted of that kind. But to let them see how nature made artificers at first, I carried the carpenters to see Will Atkins' basket-house, as I called it; and they both owned they never saw an instance of such natural ingenuity before, nor anything so regular and so handily built, at least of its kind; and one of them, when he saw it, after musing a good while, turning about to me, "I am sure," says he, "that man has no need of us; you need do nothing but give him tools."

Then I brought them out all my store of tools, and gave every man a digging-spade, a shovel, and a rake, for we had no barrows or ploughs; and to every separate place a pickaxe, a crow, a broad axe, and a saw; always appointing, that as often as any were broken or worn out, they should be supplied without grudging out of the general stores that I left behind. Nails, staples, hinges, hammers, chisels, knives, scissors, and all sorts of ironwork, they had without reserve, as they required; for no man would take more than he wanted, and he must be a fool that would waste or spoil them on any account whatever; and for the use of the smith I left two tons of unwrought iron for a supply.

My magazine of powder and arms which I brought them was such, even to profusion, that they could not but rejoice at them; for now they could march as I used to do, with a musket upon each shoulder, if there was occasion; and were able to fight a thousand savages, if they had but some little advantages of situation, which also they could not miss, if they had occasion.

I carried on shore with me the young man whose mother was starved to death, and the maid also; she was a sober, well-educated, religious young woman, and behaved so inoffensively that every one gave her a good word; she had, indeed, an unhappy life with us, there being no woman in the ship but herself, but she bore it with patience. After a while, seeing things so well ordered, and in so fine a way of thriving upon my island, and considering that they had neither business nor acquaintance in the East Indies, or reason for taking so long a voyage, both of them came to me and desired I would give them leave to remain on the island, and be entered among my family, as they called it. I agreed to this readily; and they had a little plot of ground allotted to them, where they had three tents or houses set up, surrounded with a basket-work, palisadoed like Atkins's, adjoining to his plantation. Their tents were contrived so that they had each of them a room apart to lodge in, and a middle tent like a great storehouse to lay their goods in, and to eat and to drink in.

And now the other two Englishmen removed their habitation to the same place; and so the island was divided into three colonies, and no more—viz. the Spaniards, with old Friday and the first servants, at my habitation under the hill, which was, in a word, the capital city, and where they had so enlarged and extended their works, as well under as on the outside of the hill, that they lived, though perfectly concealed, yet full at large. Never was there such a little city in a wood, and so hid, in any part of the world; for I verify believe that a thousand men might have ranged the island a month, and, if they had not known there was such a thing, and looked on purpose for it, they would not have found it. Indeed the trees stood so thick and so close, and grew so fast woven one into another, that nothing but cutting them down first could discover the place, except the only two narrow entrances where they went in and out could be found, which was not very easy; one of them was close down at the water's edge, on the side of the creek, and it was afterwards above two hundred yards to the place; and the other was up a ladder at twice, as I have already described it; and they had also a large wood, thickly planted, on the top of the hill, containing above an acre, which grew apace, and concealed the place from all discovery there, with only one narrow place between two trees, not easily to be discovered, to enter on that side.

The other colony was that of Will Atkins, where there were four families of Englishmen, I mean those I had left there, with their wives and children; three savages that were slaves, the widow and children of the Englishman that was killed, the young man and the maid, and, by the way, we made a wife of her before we went away. There were besides the two carpenters and the tailor, whom I brought with me for them: also the smith, who was a very necessary man to them, especially as a gunsmith, to take care of their arms; and my other man, whom I called Jack-of-all-trades, who was in himself as good almost as twenty men; for he was not only a very ingenious fellow, but a very merry fellow, and before I went away we married him to the honest maid that came with the youth in the ship I mentioned before.

And now I speak of marrying, it brings me naturally to say something of the French ecclesiastic that I had brought with me out of the ship's crew whom I took up at sea. It is true this man was a Roman, and perhaps it may give offence to some hereafter if I leave anything extraordinary upon record of a man whom, before I begin, I must (to set him out in just colours) represent in terms very much to his disadvantage, in the account of Protestants; as, first, that he was a Papist; secondly, a Popish priest; and thirdly, a French Popish priest. But justice demands of me to give him a due character; and I must say, he was a grave, sober, pious, and most religious person; exact in his life, extensive in his charity, and exemplary in almost everything he did. What then can any one say against being very sensible of the value of such a man, notwithstanding his profession? though it may be my opinion perhaps, as well as the opinion of others who shall read this, that he was mistaken.

The first hour that I began to converse with him after he had agreed to go with me to the East Indies, I found reason to delight exceedingly in his conversation; and he first began with me about religion in the most obliging manner imaginable. "Sir," says he, "you have not only under God" (and at that he crossed his breast) "saved my life, but you have admitted me to go this voyage in your ship, and by your obliging civility have taken me into your family, giving me an opportunity of free conversation. Now, sir, you see by my habit what my profession is, and I guess by your nation what yours is; I may think it is my duty, and doubtless it is so, to use my utmost endeavours, on all occasions, to bring all the souls I can to the knowledge of the truth, and to embrace the Catholic doctrine; but as I am here under your permission, and in your family, I am bound, in justice to your kindness as well as in decency and good manners, to be under your government; and therefore I shall not, without your leave, enter into any debate on the points of religion in which we may not agree, further than you shall give me leave."

I told him his carriage was so modest that I could not but acknowledge it; that it was true we were such people as they call heretics, but that he was not the first Catholic I had conversed with without falling into inconveniences, or carrying the questions to any height in debate; that he should not find himself the worse used for being of a different opinion from us, and if we did not converse without any dislike on either side, it should be his fault, not ours.

He replied that he thought all our conversation might be easily separated from disputes; that it was not his business to cap principles with every man he conversed with; and that he rather desired me to converse with him as a gentleman than as a religionist; and that, if I would give him leave at any time to discourse upon religious subjects, he would readily comply with it, and that he did not doubt but I would allow him also to defend his own opinions as well as he could; but that without my leave he would not break in upon me with any such thing. He told me further, that he would not cease to do all that became him, in his office as a priest, as well as a private Christian, to procure the good of the ship, and the safety of all that was in her; and though, perhaps, we would not join with him, and he could not pray with us, he hoped he might pray for us, which he would do upon all occasions. In this manner we conversed; and as he was of the most obliging, gentlemanlike behaviour, so he was, if I may be allowed to say so, a man of good sense, and, as I believe, of great learning.

He gave me a most diverting account of his life, and of the many extraordinary events of it; of many adventures which had befallen him in the few years that he had been abroad in the world; and particularly, it was very remarkable, that in the voyage he was now engaged in he had had the misfortune to be five times shipped and unshipped, and never to go to the place whither any of the ships he was in were at first designed. That his first intent was to have gone to Martinico, and that he went on board a ship bound thither at St. Malo; but being forced into Lisbon by bad weather, the ship received some damage by running aground in the mouth of the river Tagus, and was obliged to unload her cargo there; but finding a Portuguese ship there bound for the Madeiras, and ready to sail, and supposing he should meet with a ship there bound to Martinico, he went on board, in order to sail to the Madeiras; but the master of the Portuguese ship being but an indifferent mariner, had been out of his reckoning, and they drove to Fayal; where, however, he happened to find a very good market for his cargo, which was corn, and therefore resolved not to go to the Madeiras, but to load salt at the Isle of May, and to go away to Newfoundland. He had no remedy in this exigence but to go with the ship, and had a pretty good voyage as far as the Banks (so they call the place where they catch the fish), where, meeting with a French ship bound from France to Quebec, and from thence to Martinico, to carry provisions, he thought he should have an opportunity to complete his first design, but when he came to Quebec, the master of the ship died, and the vessel proceeded no further; so the next voyage he shipped himself for France, in the ship that was burned when we took them up at sea, and then shipped with us for the East Indies, as I have already said. Thus he had been disappointed in five voyages; all, as I may call it, in one voyage, besides what I shall have occasion to mention further of him.

But I shall not make digression into other men's stories which have no relation to my own; so I return to what concerns our affair in the island. He came to me one morning (for he lodged among us all the while we were upon the island), and it happened to be just when I was going to visit the Englishmen's colony, at the furthest part of the island; I say, he came to me, and told me, with a very grave countenance, that he had for two or three days desired an opportunity of some discourse with me, which he hoped would not be displeasing to me, because he thought it might in some measure correspond with my general design, which was the prosperity of my new colony, and perhaps might put it, at least more than he yet thought it was, in the way of God's blessing.

I looked a little surprised at the last of his discourse, and turning a little short, "How, sir," said I, "can it be said that we are not in the way of God's blessing, after such visible assistances and deliverances as we have seen here, and of which I have given you a large account?" "If you had pleased, sir," said he, with a world of modesty, and yet great readiness, "to have heard me, you would have found no room to have been displeased, much less to think so hard of me, that I should suggest that you have not had wonderful assistances and deliverances; and I hope, on your behalf, that you are in the way of God's blessing, and your design is exceeding good, and will prosper. But, sir, though it were more so than is even possible to you, yet there may be some among you that are not equally right in their actions: and you know that in the story of the children of Israel, one Achan in the camp removed God's blessing from them, and turned His hand so against them, that six-and-thirty of them, though not concerned in the crime, were the objects of divine vengeance, and bore the weight of that punishment."

I was sensibly touched with this discourse, and told him his inference was so just, and the whole design seemed so sincere, and was really so religious in its own nature, that I was very sorry I had interrupted him, and begged him to go on; and, in the meantime, because it seemed that what we had both to say might take up some time, I told him I was going to the Englishmen's plantations, and asked him to go with me, and we might discourse of it by the way. He told me he would the more willingly wait on me thither, because there partly the thing was acted which he desired to speak to me about; so we walked on, and I pressed him to be free and plain with me in what he had to say.

"Why, then, sir," said he, "be pleased to give me leave to lay down a few propositions, as the foundation of what I have to say, that we may not differ in the general principles, though we may be of some differing opinions in the practice of particulars. First, sir, though we differ in some of the doctrinal articles of religion (and it is very unhappy it is so, especially in the case before us, as I shall show afterwards), yet there are some general principles in which we both agree—that there is a God; and that this God having given us some stated general rules for our service and obedience, we ought not willingly and knowingly to offend Him, either by neglecting to do what He has commanded, or by doing what He has expressly forbidden. And let our different religions be what they will, this general principle is readily owned by us all, that the blessing of God does not ordinarily follow presumptuous sinning against His command; and every good Christian will be affectionately concerned to prevent any that are under his care living in a total neglect of God and His commands. It is not your men being Protestants, whatever my opinion may be of such, that discharges me from being concerned for their souls, and from endeavouring, if it lies before me, that they should live in as little distance from enmity with their Maker as possible, especially if you give me leave to meddle so far in your circuit."

I could not yet imagine what he aimed at, and told him I granted all he had said, and thanked him that he would so far concern himself for us: and begged he would explain the particulars of what he had observed, that like Joshua, to take his own parable, I might put away the accursed thing from us.

"Why, then, sir," says he, "I will take the liberty you give me; and there are three things, which, if I am right, must stand in the way of God's blessing upon your endeavours here, and which I should rejoice, for your sake and their own, to see removed. And, sir, I promise myself that you will fully agree with me in them all, as soon as I name them; especially because I shall convince you, that every one of them may, with great ease, and very much to your satisfaction, be remedied. First, sir," says he, "you have here four Englishmen, who have fetched women from among the savages, and have taken them as their wives, and have had many children by them all, and yet are not married to them after any stated legal manner, as the laws of God and man require. To this, sir, I know, you will object that there was no clergyman or priest of any kind to perform the ceremony; nor any pen and ink, or paper, to write down a contract of marriage, and have it signed between them. And I know also, sir, what the Spaniard governor has told you, I mean of the agreement that he obliged them to make when they took those women, viz. that they should choose them out by consent, and keep separately to them; which, by the way, is nothing of a marriage, no agreement with the women as wives, but only an agreement among themselves, to keep them from quarrelling. But, sir, the essence of the sacrament of matrimony" (so he called it, being a Roman) "consists not only in the mutual consent of the parties to take one another as man and wife, but in the formal and legal obligation that there is in the contract to compel the man and woman, at all times, to own and acknowledge each other; obliging the man to abstain from all other women, to engage in no other contract while these subsist; and, on all occasions, as ability allows, to provide honestly for them and their children; and to oblige the women to the same or like conditions, on their side. Now, sir," says he, "these men may, when they please, or when occasion presents, abandon these women, disown their children, leave them to perish, and take other women, and marry them while these are living;" and here he added, with some warmth, "How, sir, is God honoured in this unlawful liberty? And how shall a blessing succeed your endeavours in this place, however good in themselves, and however sincere in your design, while these men, who at present are your subjects, under your absolute government and dominion, are allowed by you to live in open adultery?"

I confess I was struck with the thing itself, but much more with the convincing arguments he supported it with; but I thought to have got off my young priest by telling him that all that part was done when I was not there: and that they had lived so many years with them now, that if it was adultery, it was past remedy; nothing could be done in it now.

"Sir," says he, "asking your pardon for such freedom, you are right in this, that, it being done in your absence, you could not be charged with that part of the crime; but, I beseech you, flatter not yourself that you are not, therefore, under an obligation to do your utmost now to put an end to it. You should legally and effectually marry them; and as, sir, my way of marrying may not be easy to reconcile them to, though it will be effectual, even by your own laws, so your way may be as well before God, and as valid among men. I mean by a written contract signed by both man and woman, and by all the witnesses present, which all the laws of Europe would decree to be valid."

I was amazed to see so much true piety, and so much sincerity of zeal, besides the unusual impartiality in his discourse as to his own party or church, and such true warmth for preserving people that he had no knowledge of or relation to from transgressing the laws of God. But recollecting what he had said of marrying them by a written contract, which I knew he would stand to, I returned it back upon him, and told him I granted all that he had said to be just, and on his part very kind; that I would discourse with the men upon the point now, when I came to them; and I knew no reason why they should scruple to let him marry them all, which I knew well enough would be granted to be as authentic and valid in England as if they were married by one of our own clergymen.

I then pressed him to tell me what was the second complaint which he had to make, acknowledging that I was very much his debtor for the first, and thanking him heartily for it. He told me he would use the same freedom and plainness in the second, and hoped I would take it as well; and this was, that notwithstanding these English subjects of mine, as he called them, had lived with these women almost seven years, had taught them to speak English, and even to read it, and that they were, as he perceived, women of tolerable understanding, and capable of instruction, yet they had not, to this hour, taught them anything of the Christian religion—no, not so much as to know there was a God, or a worship, or in what manner God was to be served, or that their own idolatry, and worshipping they knew not whom, was false and absurd. This he said was an unaccountable neglect, and what God would certainly call them to account for, and perhaps at last take the work out of their hands. He spoke this very affectionately and warmly.

"I am persuaded," says he, "had those men lived in the savage country whence their wives came, the savages would have taken more pains to have brought them to be idolaters, and to worship the devil, than any of these men, so far as I can see, have taken with them to teach the knowledge of the true God. Now, sir," said he, "though I do not acknowledge your religion, or you mine, yet we would be glad to see the devil's servants and the subjects of his kingdom taught to know religion; and that they might, at least, hear of God and a Redeemer, and the resurrection, and of a future state—things which we all believe; that they might, at least, be so much nearer coming into the bosom of the true Church than they are now in the public profession of idolatry and devil-worship."

I could hold no longer: I took him in my arms and embraced him eagerly. "How far," said I to him, "have I been from understanding the most essential part of a Christian, viz. to love the interest of the Christian Church, and the good of other men's souls! I scarce have known what belongs to the being a Christian."—"Oh, sir! do not say so," replied he; "this thing is not your fault."—"No," said I; "but why did I never lay it to heart as well as you?"—"It is not too late yet," said he; "be not too forward to condemn yourself."—"But what can be done now?" said I: "you see I am going away."—"Will you give me leave to talk with these poor men about it?"—"Yes, with all my heart," said I: "and oblige them to give heed to what you say too."—"As to that," said he, "we must leave them to the mercy of Christ; but it is your business to assist them, encourage them, and instruct them; and if you give me leave, and God His blessing, I do not doubt but the poor ignorant souls shall be brought home to the great circle of Christianity, if not into the particular faith we all embrace, and that even while you stay here." Upon this I said, "I shall not only give you leave, but give you a thousand thanks for it."

I now pressed him for the third article in which we were to blame. "Why, really," says he, "it is of the same nature. It is about your poor savages, who are, as I may say, your conquered subjects. It is a maxim, sir, that is or ought to be received among all Christians, of what church or pretended church soever, that the Christian knowledge ought to be propagated by all possible means and on all possible occasions. It is on this principle that our Church sends missionaries into Persia, India, and China; and that our clergy, even of the superior sort, willingly engage in the most hazardous voyages, and the most dangerous residence amongst murderers and barbarians, to teach them the knowledge of the true God, and to bring them over to embrace the Christian faith. Now, sir, you have such an opportunity here to have six or seven and thirty poor savages brought over from a state of idolatry to the knowledge of God, their Maker and Redeemer, that I wonder how you can pass such an occasion of doing good, which is really worth the expense of a man's whole life."

I was now struck dumb indeed, and had not one word to say. I had here the spirit of true

THE LIFE & ADVENTURES OF ROBINSON CRUSOE

Christian zeal for God and religion before me. As for me, I had not so much as entertained a thought of this in my heart before, and I believe I should not have thought of it; for I looked upon these savages as slaves, and people whom, had we not had any work for them to do, we would have used as such, or would have been glad to have transported them to any part of the world; for our business was to get rid of them, and we would all have been satisfied if they had been sent to any country, so they had never seen their own. I was confounded at his discourse, and knew not what answer to make him.

He looked earnestly at me, seeing my confusion. "Sir," says he, "I shall be very sorry if what I have said gives you any offence."—"No, no," said I, "I am offended with nobody but myself; but I am perfectly confounded, not only to think that I should never take any notice of this before, but with reflecting what notice I am able to take of it now. You know, sir," said I, "what circumstances I am in; I am bound to the East Indies in a ship freighted by merchants, and to whom it would be an insufferable piece of injustice to detain their ship here, the men lying all this while at victuals and wages on the owners' account. It is true, I agreed to be allowed twelve days here, and if I stay more, I must pay three pounds sterling *per diem* demurrage; nor can I stay upon demurrage above eight days more, and I have been here thirteen already; so that I am perfectly unable to engage in this work unless I would suffer myself to be left behind here again; in which case, if this single ship should miscarry in any part of her voyage, I should be just in the same condition that I was left in here at first, and from which I have been so wonderfully delivered." He owned the case was very hard upon me as to my voyage; but laid it home upon my conscience whether the blessing of saving thirty-seven souls was not worth venturing all I had in the world for. I was not so sensible of that as he was. I replied to him thus: "Why, sir, it is a valuable thing, indeed, to be an instrument in God's hand to convert thirty-seven heathens to the knowledge of Christ: but as you are an ecclesiastic, and are given over to the work, so it seems so naturally to fall in the way of your profession; how is it, then, that you do not rather offer yourself to undertake it than to press me to do it?"

Upon this he faced about just before me, as he walked along, and putting me to a full stop, made me a very low bow. "I most heartily thank God and you, sir," said he, "for giving me so evident a call to so blessed a work; and if you think yourself discharged from it, and desire me to undertake it, I will most readily do it, and think it a happy reward for all the hazards and difficulties of such a broken, disappointed voyage as I have met with, that I am dropped at last into so glorious a work."

I discovered a kind of rapture in his face while he spoke this to me; his eyes sparkled like fire; his face glowed, and his colour came and went; in a word, he was fired with the joy of being embarked in such a work. I paused a considerable while before I could tell what to say to him; for I was really surprised to find a man of such sincerity, and who seemed possessed of a zeal beyond the ordinary rate of men. But after I had considered it a while, I asked him seriously if he was in earnest, and that he would venture, on the single consideration of an attempt to convert those poor people, to be locked up in an unplanted island for perhaps his life, and at last might not know whether he should be able to do them good or not? He turned short upon me, and asked me what I called a venture? "Pray, sir," said he, "what do you think I consented to go in your ship to the East Indies for?"—"ay," said I, "that I know not, unless it was to preach to the Indians."—"Doubtless it was," said he; "and do you think, if I can convert these thirty-seven men to the faith of Jesus Christ, it is not worth my time, though I should never be fetched off the island again?—nay, is it not infinitely of more worth to save so many souls than my life is, or the life of twenty more of the same profession? Yes, sir," says he, "I would give God thanks all my days if I could be made the happy instrument of saving the souls of those poor men, though I were never to get my foot off this island or see my native country any more. But since you will honour me with putting me into this work, for which I will pray for you all the days of my life, I have one humble petition to you besides."—"What is that?" said I.—"Why," says he, "it is, that you will leave your man Friday with me, to be my interpreter to them, and to assist me; for without some help I cannot speak to them, or they to me."

I was sensibly touched at his requesting Friday, because I could not think of parting with him, and that for many reasons: he had been the companion of my travels; he was not only faithful to me, but sincerely affectionate to the last degree; and I had resolved to do something considerable for him if he out-lived me, as it was probable he would. Then I knew that, as I had bred Friday up to be a Protestant, it would quite confound him to bring him to embrace another religion; and he would never, while his eyes were open, believe that his old master was a heretic, and would be damned; and this might in the end ruin the poor fellow's principles, and so turn him back again to his first idolatry. However, a sudden thought relieved me in this strait, and it was this: I told him I could not say that I was willing to part with Friday on any account whatever, though a work that to him was of more value than his life ought to be of much more value than the keeping or parting with a servant. On the other hand, I was persuaded that Friday would by no means agree to part with me; and I could not force him to it without his consent, without manifest injustice; because I had promised I would never send him away, and he had promised and engaged that he would never leave me, unless I sent him away.

He seemed very much concerned at it, for he had no rational access to these poor people, seeing he did not understand one word of their language, nor they one of his. To remove this difficulty, I told him Friday's father had learned Spanish, which I found he also understood, and he should serve him as an interpreter. So he was much better satisfied, and nothing could persuade him but he would stay and endeavour to convert them; but Providence gave another very happy turn to all this.

I come back now to the first part of his objections. When we came to the Englishmen, I sent for them all together, and after some account given them of what I had done for them, viz. what necessary things I had provided for them, and how they were distributed, which they were very sensible of, and very thankful for, I began to talk to them of the scandalous life they led, and gave them a full account of the notice the clergyman had taken of it; and arguing how unchristian and irreligious a life it was, I first asked them if they were married men or bachelors? They soon explained their condition to me, and showed that two of them were widowers, and the other three were single men, or bachelors. I asked them with what conscience they could take these women, and call them their wives, and have so many children by them, and not be lawfully married to them? They all gave me the answer I expected, viz. that there was nobody to marry them; that they agreed before the governor to keep them as their wives, and to maintain them and own them as their wives; and they thought, as things stood with them, they were as legally married as if they had been married by a parson and with all the formalities in the world.

I told them that no doubt they were married in the sight of God, and were bound in conscience to keep them as their wives; but that the laws of men being otherwise, they might desert the poor women and children hereafter; and that their wives, being poor desolate women, friendless and moneyless, would have no way to help themselves. I therefore told them that unless I was assured of their honest intent, I could do nothing for them, but would take care that what I did should be for the women and children without them; and that, unless they would give me some assurances that they would marry the women, I could not think it was convenient they should continue together as man and wife; for that it was both scandalous to men and offensive to God, who they could not think would bless them if they went on thus.

All this went on as I expected; and they told me, especially Will Atkins, who now seemed to speak for the rest, that they loved their wives as well as if they had been born in their own native country, and would not leave them on any account whatever; and they did verily believe that their wives were as virtuous and as modest, and did, to the utmost of their skill, as much for them and for their children, as any woman could possibly do: and they would not part with them on any account. Will Atkins, for his own particular, added that if any man would take him away, and offer to carry him home to England, and make him captain of the best man-of-war in the navy, he would not go with him if he might not carry his wife and children with him; and if there was a clergyman in the ship, he would be married to her now with all his heart.

This was just as I would have it. The priest was not with me at that moment, but he was not far off; so to try him further, I told him I had a clergyman with me, and, if he was sincere, I would have him married next morning, and bade him consider of it, and talk with the rest. He said, as for himself, he need not consider of it at all, for he was very ready to do it, and was glad I had a minister with me, and he believed they would be all willing also. I then told him that my friend, the minister, was a Frenchman, and could not speak English, but I would act the clerk between them. He never so much as asked me whether he was a Papist or Protestant, which was, indeed, what I was afraid of. We then parted, and I went back to my clergyman, and Will Atkins went in to talk with his companions. I desired the French gentleman not to say anything to them till the business was thoroughly ripe; and I told him what answer the men had given me.

Before I went from their quarter they all came to me and told me they had been considering what I had said; that they were glad to hear I had a clergyman in my company, and they were very willing to give me the satisfaction I desired, and to be formally married as soon as I pleased; for they were far from desiring to part with their wives, and that they meant nothing but what was very honest when they chose them. So I appointed them to meet me the next morning; and, in the meantime, they should let their wives know the meaning of the marriage law; and that it was not only to prevent any scandal, but also to oblige them that they should not forsake them, whatever might happen.

The women were easily made sensible of the meaning of the thing, and were very well satisfied with it, as, indeed, they had reason to be: so they failed not to attend all together at my apartment next morning, where I brought out my clergyman; and though he had not on a minister's gown, after the manner of England, or the habit of a priest, after the manner of France, yet having a black vest something like a cassock, with a sash round it, he did not look very unlike a minister; and as for his language, I was his interpreter. But the seriousness of his behaviour to them, and the scruples he made of marrying the women, because they were not baptized and professed Christians, gave them an exceeding reverence for his person; and there was no need, after that, to inquire whether he was a clergyman or not. Indeed, I was afraid his scruples would have been carried so far as that he would not have married them at all; nay, notwithstanding all I was able to say to him, he resisted me, though modestly, yet very steadily, and at last refused absolutely to marry them, unless he had first talked with the men and the women too; and though at first I was a little backward to it, yet at last I agreed to it with a good will, perceiving the sincerity of his design.

When he came to them he let them know that I had acquainted him with their circumstances, and with the present design; that he was very willing to perform that part of his function, and marry them, as I had desired; but that before he could do it, he must take the liberty to talk with them. He told them that in the sight of all indifferent men, and in the sense of the laws of society, they had lived all this while in a state of sin; and that it was true that nothing but the consenting to marry, or effectually separating them from one another, could now put an end to it; but there was a difficulty in it, too, with respect to the laws of Christian matrimony, which he was not fully satisfied about, that of marrying one that is a professed Christian to a savage, an idolater, and a heathen—one that is not baptized; and yet that he did not see that there was time left to endeavour to persuade the women to be baptized, or to profess the name of Christ, whom they had, he doubted, heard nothing of, and without which they could not be baptized. He told them he doubted they were but indifferent Christians themselves; that they had but little knowledge of God or of His ways, and, therefore, he could not expect that they had said much to their wives on that head yet; but that unless they would promise him to use their endeavours with their wives to persuade them to become Christians, and would, as well as they could, instruct them in the knowledge and belief of God that made them, and to worship Jesus Christ that redeemed them, he could not marry them; for he would have no hand in joining Christians with savages, nor was it consistent with the principles of the Christian religion, and was, indeed, expressly forbidden in God's law.

They heard all this very attentively, and I delivered it very faithfully to them from his mouth, as near his own words as I could; only sometimes adding something of my own, to convince them how just it was, and that I was of his mind; and I always very carefully distinguished between what I said from myself and what were the clergyman's words. They told me it was very true what the gentleman said, that they were very indifferent Christians themselves, and that they had never talked to their wives about religion. "Lord, sir," says Will Atkins, "how should we teach them religion? Why, we know nothing ourselves; and besides, sir," said he, "should we talk to them of God and Jesus Christ, and heaven and hell, it would make them laugh at us, and ask us what we believe ourselves. And if we should tell them that we believe all the things we speak of to them, such as of good people going to heaven, and wicked people to the devil, they would ask us where we intend to go ourselves, that believe all this, and are such wicked fellows as we indeed are? Why, sir; 'tis enough to give them a surfeit of religion at first hearing; folks must have some religion themselves before they begin to teach other people."—"Will Atkins," said I to him, "though I am afraid that what you say has too much truth in it, yet can you not tell your wife she is in the wrong; that there is a God and a religion better than her own; that her gods are idols; that they can neither hear nor speak; that there is a great Being that made all things, and that can destroy all that He has made; that He rewards the good and punishes the bad; and that we are to be judged by Him at last for all we do here? You are not so ignorant but even nature itself will teach you that all this is true; and I am satisfied you know it all to be true, and believe it yourself."—"That is true, sir," said Atkins; "but with what face can I say anything to my wife of all this, when she will tell me immediately it cannot be true?"—"Not true!" said I; "what do you mean by that?"—"Why, sir," said he, "she will tell me it cannot be true that this God I shall tell her of can be just, or can punish or reward, since I am not punished and sent to the devil, that have been such a wicked creature as she knows I have been, even to her, and to everybody else; and that I should be suffered to live, that have been always acting so contrary to what I must tell her is good, and to what I ought to have done."—"Why, truly, Atkins," said I, "I am afraid thou speakest too much truth;" and with that I informed the clergyman of what Atkins had said, for he was impatient to know. "Oh," said the priest, "tell him there is one thing will make him the best minister in the world to his wife, and that is repentance; for none teach repentance like true penitents. He wants nothing but to repent, and then he will be so much the better qualified to instruct his wife; he will then be able to tell her that there is not only a God, and that He is the just rewarder of good and evil, but that He is a merciful Being, and with infinite goodness and long-suffering forbears to punish those that offend; waiting to be gracious, and willing not the death of a sinner, but rather that he should return and live; and even reserves damnation to the general day of retribution; that it is a clear evidence of God and of a future state that righteous men receive not their reward, or wicked men their punishment, till they come into another world; and this will lead him to teach his wife the doctrine of the resurrection and of the last judgment. Let him but repent himself, he will be an excellent preacher of repentance to his wife."

I repeated all this to Atkins, who looked very serious all the while, and, as we could easily perceive, was more than ordinarily affected with it; when being eager, and hardly suffering me to make an end, "I know all this, master," says he, "and a great deal more; but I have not the impudence to talk thus to my wife, when God and my conscience know, and my wife will be an undeniable evidence against me, that I have lived as if I had never heard of a God or future state, or anything about it; and to talk of my repenting, alas!" (and with that he fetched a deep sigh, and I could see that the tears stood in his eyes) "'tis past all that with me."—"Past it, Atkins?" said I: "what dost thou mean by that?"—"I know well enough what I mean," says he; "I mean 'tis too late, and that is too true."

I told the clergyman, word for word, what he said, and this affectionate man could not refrain from tears; but, recovering himself, said to me, "Ask him but one question. Is he easy that it is too late; or is he troubled, and wishes it were not so?" I put the question fairly to Atkins; and he answered with a great deal of passion, "How could any man be easy in a condition that must certainly end in eternal destruction? that he was far from being easy; but that, on the contrary, he believed it would one time or other ruin him."—"What do you mean by that?" said I.—"Why," he said, "he believed he should one time or other cut his throat, to put an end to the terror of it."

The clergyman shook his head, with great concern in his face, when I told him all this; but turning quick to me upon it, says, "If that be his case, we may assure him it is not too late; Christ will give him repentance. But pray," says he, "explain this to him: that as no man is saved but by Christ, and the merit of His passion procuring divine mercy for him, how can it be too late for any man to receive mercy? Does he think he is able to sin beyond the power or reach of divine mercy? Pray tell him there may be a time when provoked mercy will no longer strive, and when God may refuse to hear, but that it is never too late for men to ask mercy; and we, that are Christ's servants, are commanded to preach mercy at all times, in the name of Jesus Christ, to all those that sincerely repent: so that it is never too late to repent."

I told Atkins all this, and he heard me with great earnestness; but it seemed as if he turned off the discourse to the rest, for he said to me he would go and have some talk with his wife; so he went out a while, and we talked to the rest. I perceived they were all stupidly ignorant as to matters of religion, as much as I was when I went rambling away from my father; yet there were none of them backward to hear what had been said; and all of them seriously promised that they would talk with their wives about it, and do their endeavours to persuade them to turn Christians.

The clergyman smiled upon me when I reported what answer they gave, but said nothing a good while; but at last, shaking his head, "We that are Christ's servants," says he, "can go no further than to exhort and instruct: and when men comply, submit to the reproof, and promise what we ask, 'tis all we can do; we are bound to accept their good words; but believe me, sir," said he, "whatever you may have known of the life of that man you call Will

Atkin's, I believe he is the only sincere convert among them: I will not despair of the rest; but that man is apparently struck with the sense of his past life, and I doubt not, when he comes to talk of religion to his wife, he will talk himself effectually into it: for attempting to teach others is sometimes the best way of teaching ourselves. If that poor Atkins begins but once to talk seriously of Jesus Christ to his wife, he will assuredly talk himself into a thorough convert, make himself a penitent, and who knows what may follow."

Upon this discourse, however, and their promising, as above, to endeavour to persuade their wives to embrace Christianity, he married the two other couple; but Will Atkins and his wife were not yet come in. After this, my clergyman, waiting a while, was curious to know where Atkins was gone, and turning to me, said, "I entreat you, sir, let us walk out of your labyrinth here and look; I daresay we shall find this poor man somewhere or other talking seriously to his wife, and teaching her already something of religion." I began to be of the same mind; so we went out together, and I carried him a way which none knew but myself, and where the trees were so very thick that it was not easy to see through the thicket of leaves, and far harder to see in than to see out: when, coming to the edge of the wood, I saw Atkins and his tawny wife sitting under the shade of a bush, very eager in discourse: I stopped short till my clergyman came up to me, and then having showed him where they were, we stood and looked very steadily at them a good while. We observed him very earnest with her, pointing up to the sun, and to every quarter of the heavens, and then down to the earth, then out to the sea, then to himself, then to her, to the woods, to the trees. "Now," says the clergyman, "you see my words are made good, the man preaches to her; mark him now, he is telling her that our God has made him, her, and the heavens, the earth, the sea, the woods, the trees, &c."—"I believe he is," said I. Immediately we perceived Will Atkins start upon his feet, fall down on his knees, and lift up both his hands. We supposed he said something, but we could not hear him; it was too far for that. He did not continue kneeling half a minute, but comes and sits down again by his wife, and talks to her again; we perceived then the woman very attentive, but whether she said anything to him we could not tell. While the poor fellow was upon his knees I could see the tears run plentifully down my clergyman's cheeks, and I could hardly forbear myself; but it was a great affliction to us both that we were not near enough to hear anything that passed between them. Well, however, we could come no nearer for fear of disturbing them: so we resolved to see an end of this piece of still conversation, and it spoke loud enough to us without the help of voice. He sat down again, as I have said, close by her, and talked again earnestly to her, and two or three times we could see him embrace her most passionately; another time we saw him take out his handkerchief and wipe her eyes, and then kiss her again with a kind of transport very unusual; and after several of these things, we saw him on a sudden jump up again, and lend her his hand to help her up, when immediately leading her by the hand a step or two, they both kneeled down together, and continued so about two minutes.

My friend could bear it no longer, but cries out aloud, "St. Paul! St. Paul! behold he prayeth." I was afraid Atkins would hear him, therefore I entreated him to withhold himself a while, that we might see an end of the scene, which to me, I must confess, was the most affecting that ever I saw in my life. Well, he strove with himself for a while, but was in such raptures to think that the poor heathen woman was become a Christian, that he was not able to contain himself; he wept several times, then throwing up his hands and crossing his breast, said over several things ejaculatory, and by the way of giving God thanks for so miraculous a testimony of the success of our endeavours. Some he spoke softly, and I could not well hear others; some things he said in Latin, some in French; then two or three times the tears would interrupt him, that he could not speak at all; but I begged that he would contain himself, and let us more narrowly and fully observe what was before us, which he did for a time, the scene not being near ended yet; for after the poor man and his wife were risen again from their knees, we observed he stood talking still eagerly to her, and we observed her motion, that she was greatly affected with what he said, by her frequently lifting up her hands, laying her hand to her breast, and such other postures as express the greatest seriousness and attention; this continued about half a quarter of an hour, and then they walked away, so we could see no more of them in that situation.

I took this interval to say to the clergyman, first, that I was glad to see the particulars we had both been witnesses to; that, though I was hard enough of belief in such cases, yet that I began to think it was all very sincere here, both in the man and his wife, however ignorant they might both be, and I hoped such a beginning would yet have a more happy end. "But, my friend," added I, "will you give me leave to start one difficulty here? I cannot tell how to object the least thing against that affectionate concern which you show for the turning of the poor people from their paganism to the Christian religion; but how does this comfort you, while these people are, in your account, out of the pale of the Catholic Church, without which you believe there is no salvation? so that you esteem these but heretics, as effectually lost as the pagans themselves."

To this he answered, with abundance of candour, thus: "Sir, I am a Catholic of the Roman Church, and a priest of the order of St. Benedict, and I embrace all the principles of the Roman faith; but yet, if you will believe me, and that I do not speak in compliment to you, or in respect to my circumstances and your civilities; I say nevertheless, I do not look upon you, who call yourselves reformed, without some charity. I dare not say (though I know it is our opinion in general) that you cannot be saved; I will by no means limit the mercy of Christ so far as think that He cannot receive you into the bosom of His Church, in a manner to us unperceivable; and I hope you have the same charity for us: I pray daily for you being all restored to Christ's Church, by whatsoever method He, who is all-wise, is pleased to direct. In the meantime, surely you will allow it consists with me as a Roman to distinguish far between a Protestant and a pagan; between one that calls on Jesus Christ, though in a way which I do not think is according to the true faith, and a savage or a barbarian, that knows no God, no Christ, no Redeemer; and if you are not within the pale of the Catholic Church, we hope you are nearer being restored to it than those who know nothing of God or of His Church: and I rejoice, therefore, when I see this poor man, who you say has been a profligate, and almost a murderer kneel down and pray to Jesus Christ, as we suppose he did, though not fully enlightened; believing that God, from whom every such work proceeds, will sensibly touch his heart, and bring him to the further knowledge of that truth in His own time; and if God shall influence this poor man to convert and instruct the ignorant savage, his wife, I can never believe that he shall be cast away himself. And have I not reason, then, to rejoice, the nearer any are brought to the knowledge of Christ, though they may not be brought quite home into the bosom of the Catholic Church just at the time when I desire it, leaving it to the goodness of Christ to perfect His work in His own time, and in his own way? Certainly, I would rejoice if all the savages in America were brought, like this poor woman, to pray to God, though they were all to be Protestants at first, rather than they should continue pagans or heathens; firmly believing, that He that had bestowed the first light on them would farther illuminate them with a beam of His heavenly grace, and bring them into the pale of His Church when He should see good."

7

CONVERSATION BETWIXT WILL ATKINS AND HIS WIFE

I was astonished at the sincerity and temper of this pious Papist, as much as I was oppressed by the power of his reasoning; and it presently occurred to my thoughts, that if such a temper was universal, we might be all Catholic Christians, whatever Church or particular profession we joined in; that a spirit of charity would soon work us all up into right principles; and as he thought that the like charity would make us all Catholics, so I told him I believed, had all the members of his Church the like moderation, they would soon all be Protestants. And there we left that part; for we never disputed at all. However, I talked to him another way, and taking him by the hand, "My friend," says I, "I wish all the clergy of the Romish Church were blessed with such moderation, and had an equal share of your charity. I am entirely of your opinion; but I must tell you that if you should preach such doctrine in Spain or Italy, they would put you into the Inquisition."—"It may be so," said he; "I know not what they would do in Spain or Italy; but I will not say they would be the better Christians for that severity; for I am sure there is no heresy in abounding with charity."

Well, as Will Atkins and his wife were gone, our business there was over, so we went back our own way; and when we came back, we found them waiting to be called in. Observing this, I asked my clergyman if we should discover to him that we had seen him under the bush or not; and it was his opinion we should not, but that we should talk to him first, and hear what he would say to us; so we called him in alone, nobody being in the place but ourselves, and I began by asking him some particulars about his parentage and education. He told me frankly enough that his father was a clergyman who would have taught him well, but that he, Will Atkins, despised all instruction and correction; and by his brutish conduct cut the thread of all his father's comforts and shortened his days, for that he broke his heart by the most ungrateful, unnatural return for the most affectionate treatment a father ever gave.

In what he said there seemed so much sincerity of repentance, that it painfully affected me. I could not but reflect that I, too, had shortened the life of a good, tender father by my bad conduct and obstinate self-will. I was, indeed, so surprised with what he had told me, that I thought, instead of my going about to teach and instruct him, the man was made a teacher and instructor to me in a most unexpected manner.

I laid all this before the young clergyman, who was greatly affected with it, and said to me, "Did I not say, sir, that when this man was converted he would preach to us all? I tell you, sir, if this one man be made a true penitent, there will be no need of me; he will make Christians of all in the island."—But having a little composed myself, I renewed my discourse with Will Atkins. "But, Will," said I, "how comes the sense of this matter to touch you just now?"

W.A.—Sir, you have set me about a work that has struck a dart though my very soul; I have been talking about God and religion to my wife, in order, as you directed me, to make a Christian of her, and she has preached such a sermon to me as I shall never forget while I live.

R.C.—No, no, it is not your wife has preached to you; but when you were moving religious arguments to her, conscience has flung them back upon you.

W.A.—Ay, sir, with such force as is not to be resisted.

R.C.—Pray, Will, let us know what passed between you and your wife; for I know something of it already.

W.A.—Sir, it is impossible to give you a full account of it; I am too full to hold it, and yet have no tongue to express it; but let her have said what she will, though I cannot give you an account of it, this I can tell you, that I have resolved to amend and reform my life.

R.C.—But tell us some of it: how did you begin, Will? For this has been an extraordinary case, that is certain. She has preached a sermon, indeed, if she has wrought this upon you.

W.A.—Why, I first told her the nature of our laws about marriage, and what the reasons were that men and women were obliged to enter into such compacts as it was neither in the power of one nor other to break; that otherwise, order and justice could not be maintained, and men would run from their wives, and abandon their children, mix confusedly with one another, and neither families be kept entire, nor inheritances be settled by legal descent.

R.C.—You talk like a civilian, Will. Could you make her understand what you meant by inheritance and families? They know no such things among the savages, but marry anyhow, without regard to relation, consanguinity, or family; brother and sister, nay, as I have been told, even the father and the daughter, and the son and the mother.

W.A.—I believe, sir, you are misinformed, and my wife assures me of the contrary, and that they abhor it; perhaps, for any further relations, they may not be so exact as we are; but she tells me never in the near relationship you speak of.

R.C.—Well, what did she say to what you told her?

W.A.—She said she liked it very well, as it was much better than in her country.

R.C.—But did you tell her what marriage was?

W.A.—Ay, ay, there began our dialogue. I asked her if she would be married to me our way. She asked me what way that was; I told her marriage was appointed by God; and here we had a strange talk together, indeed, as ever man and wife had, I believe.

N.B.—This dialogue between Will Atkins and his wife, which I took down in writing just after he told it me, was as follows:—

Wife.—Appointed by your God!—Why, have you a God in your country?

W.A.—Yes, my dear, God is in every country.

Wife.—No your God in my country; my country have the great old Benamuckee God.

W.A.—Child, I am very unfit to show you who God is; God is in heaven and made the heaven and the earth, the sea, and all that in them is.

Wife.—No makee de earth; no you God makee all earth; no makee my country.

[Will Atkins laughed a little at her expression of God not making her country.]

Wife.—No laugh; why laugh me? This no ting to laugh.

[He was justly reproved by his wife, for she was more serious than he at first.]

W.A.—That's true, indeed; I will not laugh any more, my dear.

Wife.—Why you say you God makee all?

W.A.—Yes, child, our God made the whole world, and you, and me, and all things; for He is the only true God, and there is no God but Him. He lives for ever in heaven.

Wife.—Why you no tell me long ago?

W.A.—That's true, indeed; but I have been a wicked wretch, and have not only forgotten to acquaint thee with anything before, but have lived without God in the world myself.

Wife.—What, have you a great God in your country, you no know Him? No say O to Him? No do good ting for Him? That no possible.

W.A.—It is true; though, for all that, we live as if there was no God in heaven, or that He had no power on earth.

Wife.—But why God let you do so? Why He no makee you good live?

W.A.—It is all our own fault.

Wife.—But you say me He is great, much great, have much great power; can makee kill when He will: why He no makee kill when you no serve Him? no say O to Him? no be good mans?

W.A.—That is true, He might strike me dead; and I ought to expect it, for I have been a wicked wretch, that is true; but God is merciful, and does not deal with us as we deserve.

Wife.—But then do you not tell God thankee for that too?

W. A.—No, indeed, I have not thanked God for His mercy, any more than I have feared God from His power.

Wife.—Then you God no God; me no think, believe He be such one, great much power, strong: no makee kill you, though you make Him much angry.

W.A.—What, will my wicked life hinder you from believing in God? What a dreadful creature am I! and what a sad truth is it, that the horrid lives of Christians hinder the conversion of heathens!

Wife.—How me tink you have great much God up there [she points up to heaven], and yet no do well, no do good ting? Can He tell? Sure He no tell what you do?

W.A.—Yes, yes, He knows and sees all things; He hears us speak, sees what we do, knows what we think though we do not speak.

Wife.—What! He no hear you curse, swear, speak de great damn?

W.A.—Yes, yes, He hears it all.

Wife.—Where be then the much great power strong?

W.A.—He is merciful, that is all we can say for it; and this proves Him to be the true God; He is God, and not man, and therefore we are not consumed.

[Here Will Atkins told us he was struck with horror to think how he could tell his wife so clearly that God sees, and hears, and knows the secret thoughts of the heart, and all that we do, and yet that he had dared to do all the vile things he had done.]

Wife.—Merciful! What you call dat?

W.A.—He is our Father and Maker, and He pities and spares us.

Wife.—So then He never makee kill, never angry when you do wicked; then He no good Himself, or no great able.

W.A.—Yes, yes, my dear, He is infinitely good and infinitely great, and able to punish too; and sometimes, to show His justice and vengeance, He lets fly His anger to destroy sinners and make examples; many are cut off in their sins.

Wife.—But no makee kill you yet; then He tell you, maybe, that He no makee you kill: so you makee the bargain with Him, you do bad thing, He no be angry at you when He be angry at other mans.

W.A.—No, indeed, my sins are all presumptions upon His goodness; and He would be infinitely just if He destroyed me, as He has done other men.

Wife.—Well, and yet no kill, no makee you dead: what you say to Him for that? You no tell Him thankee for all that too?

W.A.—I am an unthankful, ungrateful dog, that is true.

Wife.—Why He no makee you much good better? you say He makee you.

W.A.—He made me as He made all the world: it is I have deformed myself and abused His goodness, and made myself an abominable wretch.

Wife.—I wish you makee God know me. I no makee Him angry—I no do bad wicked thing.

[Here Will Atkins said his heart sunk within him to hear a poor untaught creature desire to be taught to know God, and he such a wicked wretch, that he could not say one word to her about God, but what the reproach of his own carriage would make most irrational to her to believe; nay, that already she had told him that she could not believe in God, because he, that was so wicked, was not destroyed.]

W.A.—My dear, you mean, you wish I could teach you to know God, not God to know you; for He knows you already, and every thought in your heart.

Wife.—Why, then, He know what I say to you now: He know me wish to know Him. How shall me know who makee me?

W.A.—Poor creature, He must teach thee: I cannot teach thee. I will pray to Him to teach thee to know Him, and forgive me, that am unworthy to teach thee.

[The poor fellow was in such an agony at her desiring him to make her know God, and her wishing to know Him, that he said he fell down on his knees before her, and prayed to God to enlighten her mind with the saving knowledge of Jesus Christ, and to pardon his sins, and accept of his being the unworthy instrument of instructing her in the principles of religion: after which he sat down by her again, and their dialogue went on. This was the time when we saw him kneel down and hold up his hands.]

Wife.—What you put down the knee for? What you hold up the hand for? What you say? Who you speak to? What is all that?

W.A.—My dear, I bow my knees in token of my submission to Him that made me: I said O to Him, as you call it, and as your old men do to their idol Benamuckee; that is, I prayed to Him.

Wife.—What say you O to Him for?

W.A.—I prayed to Him to open your eyes and your understanding, that you may know Him, and be accepted by Him.

Wife.—Can He do that too?

W.A.—Yes, He can: He can do all things.

Wife.—But now He hear what you say?

W.A.—Yes, He has bid us pray to Him, and promised to hear us.

Wife.—Bid you pray? When He bid you? How He bid you? What you hear Him speak?

W.A.—No, we do not hear Him speak; but He has revealed Himself many ways to us.

[Here he was at a great loss to make her understand that God has revealed Himself to us by His word, and what His word was; but at last he told it to her thus.]

W.A.—God has spoken to some good men in former days, even from heaven, by plain words; and God has inspired good men by His Spirit; and they have written all His laws down in a book.

Wife.—Me no understand that; where is book?

W.A.—Alas! my poor creature, I have not this book; but I hope I shall one time or other get it for you, and help you to read it.

[Here he embraced her with great affection, but with inexpressible grief that he had not a Bible.]

Wife.—But how you makee me know that God teachee them to write that book?

W.A.—By the same rule that we know Him to be God.

Wife.—What rule? What way you know Him?

W.A.—Because He teaches and commands nothing but what is good, righteous, and holy, and tends to make us perfectly good, as well as perfectly happy; and because He forbids and commands us to avoid all that is wicked, that is evil in itself, or evil in its consequence.

Wife.—That me would understand, that me fain see; if He teachee all good thing, He makee all good thing, He give all thing, He hear me when I say O to Him, as you do just now; He makee me good if I wish to be good; He spare me, no makee kill me, when I no be good: all this you say He do, yet He be great God; me take, think, believe Him to be great God; me say O to Him with you, my dear.

Here the poor man could forbear no longer, but raised her up, made her kneel by him, and he prayed to God aloud to instruct her in the knowledge of Himself, by His Spirit; and that by some good providence, if possible, she might, some time or other, come to have a Bible, that she might read the word of God, and be taught by it to know Him. This was the time that we saw him lift her up by the hand, and saw him kneel down by her, as above.

They had several other discourses, it seems, after this; and particularly she made him promise that, since he confessed his own life had been a wicked, abominable course of provocations against God, that he would reform it, and not make God angry any more, lest He should make him dead, as she called it, and then she would be left alone, and never be taught to know this God better; and lest he should be miserable, as he had told her wicked men would be after death.

This was a strange account, and very affecting to us both, but particularly to the young clergyman; he was, indeed, wonderfully surprised with it, but under the greatest affliction imaginable that he could not talk to her, that he could not speak English to make her understand him; and as she spoke but very broken English, he could not understand her; however, he turned himself to me, and told me that he believed that there must be more to do with this woman than to marry her. I did not understand him at first; but at length he explained himself, viz. that she ought to be baptized. I agreed with him in that part readily, and wished it to be done presently. "No, no; hold, sir," says he; "though I would have her be baptized, by all means, for I must observe that Will Atkins, her husband, has indeed brought her, in a wonderful manner, to be willing to embrace a religious life, and has given her just ideas of the being of a God; of His power, justice, and mercy: yet I desire to know of him if he has said anything to her of Jesus Christ, and of the salvation of sinners; of the nature of faith in Him, and redemption by Him; of the Holy Spirit, the resurrection, the last judgment, and the future state."

I called Will Atkins again, and asked him; but the poor fellow fell immediately into tears, and told us he had said something to her of all those things, but that he was himself so wicked a creature, and his own conscience so reproached him with his horrid, ungodly life, that he trembled at the apprehensions that her knowledge of him should lessen the attention she should give to those things, and make her rather contemn religion than receive it; but he was assured, he said, that her mind was so disposed to receive due impressions of all those things, and that if I would but discourse with her, she would make it appear to my satisfaction that my labour would not be lost upon her.

Accordingly I called her in, and placing myself as interpreter between my religious priest and the woman, I entreated him to begin with her; but sure such a sermon was never preached by a Popish priest in these latter ages of the world; and as I told him, I thought he had all the zeal, all the knowledge, all the sincerity of a Christian, without the error of a Roman Catholic; and that I took him to be such a clergyman as the Roman bishops were before the Church of Rome assumed spiritual sovereignty over the consciences of men. In a word, he brought the poor woman to embrace the knowledge of Christ, and of redemption by Him, not with wonder and astonishment only, as she did the first notions of a God, but with joy and faith; with an affection, and a surprising degree of understanding, scarce to be imagined, much less to be expressed; and, at her own request, she was baptized.

When he was preparing to baptize her, I entreated him that he would perform that office with some caution, that the man might not perceive he was of the Roman Church, if possible, because of other ill consequences which might attend a difference among us in that very religion which we were instructing the other in. He told me that as he had no consecrated chapel, nor proper things for the office, I should see he would do it in a manner that I should not know by it that he was a Roman Catholic myself, if I had not known it before; and so he did; for saying only some words over to himself in Latin, which I could not understand, he poured a whole dishful of water upon the woman's head, pronouncing in French, very loud, "Mary" (which was the name her husband desired me to give her, for I was her godfather), "I baptize thee in the name of the Father, and of the Son, and of the Holy Ghost;" so that none could know anything by it what religion he was of. He gave the benediction afterwards in Latin, but either Will Atkins did not know but it was French, or else did not take notice of it at that time.

As soon as this was over we married them; and after the marriage was over, he turned to Will Atkins, and in a very affectionate manner exhorted him, not only to persevere in that good disposition he was in, but to support the convictions that were upon him by a resolution to reform his life: told him it was in vain to say he repented if he did not forsake his crimes; represented to him how God had honoured him with being the instrument of bringing his wife to the knowledge of the Christian religion, and that he should be careful he did not dishonour the grace of God; and that if he did, he would see the heathen a better Christian than himself; the savage converted, and the instrument cast away. He said a great many good things to them both; and then, recommending them to God's goodness, gave them the benediction again, I repeating everything to them in English; and thus ended the ceremony. I think it was the most pleasant and agreeable day to me that ever I passed in my whole life. But my clergyman had not done yet: his thoughts hung continually upon the conversion of the thirty-seven savages, and fain he would have stayed upon the island to have undertaken it; but I convinced him, first, that his undertaking was impracticable in itself; and, secondly, that perhaps I would put it into a way of being done in his absence to his satisfaction.

Having thus brought the affairs of the island to a narrow compass, I was preparing to go on board the ship, when the young man I had taken out of the famished ship's company came to me, and told me he understood I had a clergyman with me, and that I had caused the Englishmen to be married to the savages; that he had a match too, which he desired might be finished before I went, between two Christians, which he hoped would not be disagreeable to me.

I knew this must be the young woman who was his mother's servant, for there was no other Christian woman on the island: so I began to persuade him not to do anything of that kind rashly, or because he found himself in this solitary circumstance. I represented to him that he had some considerable substance in the world, and good friends, as I understood by himself, and the maid also; that the maid was not only poor, and a servant, but was unequal to him, she being six or seven and twenty years old, and he not above seventeen or eighteen; that he might very probably, with my assistance, make a remove from this wilderness, and come into his own country again; and that then it would be a thousand to one but he would repent his choice, and the dislike of that circumstance might be disadvantageous to both. I was going to say more, but he interrupted me, smiling, and told me, with a great deal of modesty, that I mistook in my guesses—that he had nothing of that kind in his thoughts; and he was very glad to hear that I had an intent of putting them in a way to see their own country again; and nothing should have made him think of staying there, but that the voyage I was going was so exceeding long and hazardous, and would carry him quite out of the reach of all his friends; that he had nothing to desire of me but that I would settle him in some little property in the island where he was, give him a servant or two, and some few necessaries, and he would live here like a planter, waiting the good time when, if ever I returned to England, I would redeem him. He hoped I would not be unmindful of him when I came to England: that he would give me some letters to his friends in London, to let them know how good I had been to him, and in what part of the world and what circumstances I had left him in: and he promised me that whenever I redeemed him, the plantation, and all the improvements he had made upon it, let the value be what it would, should be wholly mine.

His discourse was very prettily delivered, considering his youth, and was the more agreeable to me, because he told me positively the match was not for himself. I gave him all possible assurances that if I lived to come safe to England, I would deliver his letters, and do his business effectually; and that he might depend I should never forget the circumstances I had left him in. But still I was impatient to know who was the person to be married; upon which he told me it was my Jack-of-all-trades and his maid Susan. I was most agreeably surprised when he named the match; for, indeed, I thought it very suitable. The character of that man I have given already; and as for the maid, she was a very honest, modest, sober, and religious young woman: had a very good share of sense, was agreeable enough in her person, spoke very handsomely and to the purpose, always with decency and good manners, and was neither too backward to speak when requisite, nor impertinently forward when it was not her business; very handy and housewifely, and an excellent manager; fit, indeed, to have been governess to the whole island; and she knew very well how to behave in every respect.

The match being proposed in this manner, we married them the same day; and as I was father at the altar, and gave her away, so I gave her a portion; for I appointed her and her husband a handsome large space of ground for their plantation; and indeed this match, and the proposal the young gentleman made to give him a small property in the island, put me upon parcelling it out amongst them, that they might not quarrel afterwards about their situation.

This sharing out the land to them I left to Will Atkins, who was now grown a sober, grave, managing fellow, perfectly reformed, exceedingly pious and religious; and, as far as I may be allowed to speak positively in such a case, I verily believe he was a true penitent. He divided things so justly, and so much to every one's satisfaction, that they only desired one general writing under my hand for the whole, which I caused to be drawn up, and signed and sealed, setting out the bounds and situation of every man's plantation, and testifying that I gave them thereby severally a right to the whole possession and inheritance of the respective plantations or farms, with their improvements, to them and their heirs, reserving all the rest of the island as my own property, and a certain rent for every particular plantation after eleven years, if I, or any one from me, or in my name, came to demand it, producing an attested copy of the same writing. As to the government and laws among them, I told them I was not capable of giving them better rules than they were able to give themselves; only I made them promise me to live in love and good neighbourhood with one another; and so I prepared to leave them.

One thing I must not omit, and that is, that being now settled in a kind of commonwealth among themselves, and having much business in hand, it was odd to have seven-and-thirty Indians live in a nook of the island, independent, and, indeed, unemployed; for except the providing themselves food, which they had difficulty enough to do sometimes, they had no manner of business or property to manage. I proposed, therefore, to the governor Spaniard that he should go to them, with Friday's father, and propose to them to remove, and either plant for themselves, or be taken into their several families as servants to be maintained for their labour, but without being absolute slaves; for I would not permit them to make them slaves by force, by any means; because they had their liberty given them by capitulation, as it were articles of surrender, which they ought not to break.

They most willingly embraced the proposal, and came all very cheerfully along with him: so we allotted them land and plantations, which three or four accepted of, but all the rest chose to be employed as servants in the several families we had settled. Thus my colony was in a manner settled as follows: The Spaniards possessed my original habitation, which was the capital city, and extended their plantations all along the side of the brook, which made the creek that I have so often described, as far as my bower; and as they increased their culture, it went always eastward. The English lived in the north-east part, where Will Atkins and his comrades began, and came on southward and south-west, towards the back part of the Spaniards; and every plantation had a great addition of land to take in, if they found occasion, so that they need not jostle one another for want of room. All the east end of the island was left uninhabited, that if any of the savages should come on shore there only for their customary barbarities, they might come and go; if they disturbed nobody, nobody would disturb them: and no doubt but they were often ashore, and went away again; for I never heard that the planters were ever attacked or disturbed any more.

8

SAILS FROM THE ISLAND FOR THE BRAZILS

It now came into my thoughts that I had hinted to my friend the clergyman that the work of converting the savages might perhaps be set on foot in his absence to his satisfaction, and I told him that now I thought that it was put in a fair way; for the savages, being thus divided among the Christians, if they would but every one of them do their part with those which came under their hands, I hoped it might have a very good effect.

He agreed presently in that, if they did their part. "But how," says he, "shall we obtain that of them?" I told him we would call them all together, and leave it in charge with them, or go to them, one by one, which he thought best; so we divided it—he to speak to the Spaniards, who were all Papists, and I to speak to the English, who were all Protestants; and we recommended it earnestly to them, and made them promise that they would never make any distinction of Papist or Protestant in their exhorting the savages to turn Christians, but teach them the general knowledge of the true God, and of their Saviour Jesus Christ; and they likewise promised us that they would never have any differences or disputes one with another about religion.

When I came to Will Atkins's house, I found that the young woman I have mentioned above, and Will Atkins's wife, were become intimates; and this prudent, religious young woman had perfected the work Will Atkins had begun; and though it was not above four days after what I have related, yet the new-baptized savage woman was made such a Christian as I have seldom heard of in all my observation or conversation in the world. It came next into my mind, in the morning before I went to them, that amongst all the needful things I had to leave with them I had not left them a Bible, in which I showed myself less considering for them than my good friend the widow was for me when she sent me the cargo of a hundred pounds from Lisbon, where she packed up three Bibles and a Prayer-book. However, the good woman's charity had a greater extent than ever she imagined, for they were reserved for the comfort and instruction of those that made much better use of them than I had done.

I took one of the Bibles in my pocket, and when I came to Will Atkins's tent, or house, and found the young woman and Atkins's baptized wife had been discoursing of religion together—for Will Atkins told it me with a great deal of joy—I asked if they were together now, and he said, "Yes"; so I went into the house, and he with me, and we found them together very earnest in discourse. "Oh, sir," says Will Atkins, "when God has sinners to reconcile to Himself, and aliens to bring home, He never wants a messenger; my wife has got a new instructor: I knew I was unworthy, as I was incapable of that work; that young woman has been sent hither from heaven—she is enough to convert a whole island of savages." The young woman blushed, and rose up to go away, but I desired her to sit-still; I told her she had a good work upon her hands, and I hoped God would bless her in it.

We talked a little, and I did not perceive that they had any book among them, though I did not ask; but I put my hand into my pocket, and pulled out my Bible. "Here," said I to Atkins, "I have brought you an assistant that perhaps you had not before." The man was so confounded that he was not able to speak for some time; but, recovering himself, he takes it with both his hands, and turning to his wife, "Here, my dear," says he, "did not I tell you our God, though He lives above, could hear what we have said? Here's the book I prayed for when you and I kneeled down under the bush; now God has heard us and sent it." When he had said so, the man fell into such passionate transports, that between the joy of having it, and giving God thanks for it, the tears ran down his face like a child that was crying.

The woman was surprised, and was like to have run into a mistake that none of us were aware of; for she firmly believed God had sent the book upon her husband's petition. It is true that providentially it was so, and might be taken so in a consequent sense; but I believe it would have been no difficult matter at that time to have persuaded the poor woman to have believed that an express messenger came from heaven on purpose to bring that individual book. But it was too serious a matter to suffer any delusion to take place, so I turned to the young woman, and told her we did not desire to impose upon the new convert in her first and more ignorant understanding of things, and begged her to explain to her that God may be very properly said to answer our petitions, when, in the course of His providence, such things are in a particular manner brought to pass as we petitioned for; but we did not expect returns from heaven in a miraculous and particular manner, and it is a mercy that it is not so.

This the young woman did afterwards effectually, so that there was no priestcraft used here; and I should have thought it one of the most unjustifiable frauds in the world to have had it so. But the effect upon Will Atkins is really not to be expressed; and there, we may be sure, was no delusion. Sure no man was ever more thankful in the world for anything of its kind than he was for the Bible, nor, I believe, never any man was glad of a Bible from a better principle; and though he had been a most profligate creature, headstrong, furious, and desperately wicked, yet this man is a standing rule to us all for the well instructing children, viz. that parents should never give over to teach and instruct, nor ever despair of the success of their endeavours, let the children be ever so refractory, or to appearance insensible to instruction; for if ever God in His providence touches the conscience of such, the force of their education turns upon them, and the early instruction of parents is not lost, though it may have been many years laid asleep, but some time or other they may find the benefit of it. Thus it was with this poor man: however ignorant he was of religion and Christian knowledge, he found he had some to do with now more ignorant than himself, and that the least part of the instruction of his good father that now came to his mind was of use to him.

Among the rest, it occurred to him, he said, how his father used to insist so much on the inexpressible value of the Bible, and the privilege and blessing of it to nations, families, and persons; but he never entertained the least notion of the worth of it till now, when, being to talk to heathens, savages, and barbarians, he wanted the help of the written oracle for his assistance. The young woman was glad of it also for the present occasion, though she had one, and so had the youth, on board our ship among their goods, which were not yet brought on shore. And now, having said so many things of this young woman, I cannot omit telling one story more of her and myself, which has something in it very instructive and remarkable.

I have related to what extremity the poor young woman was reduced; how her mistress was starved to death, and died on board that unhappy ship we met at sea, and how the whole ship's company was reduced to the last extremity. The gentlewoman, and her son, and this maid, were first hardly used as to provisions, and at last totally neglected and starved—that is to say, brought to the last extremity of hunger. One day, being discoursing with her on the extremities they suffered, I asked her if she could describe, by what she had felt, what it was to starve, and how it appeared? She said she believed she could, and told her tale very distinctly thus:—

"First, we had for some days fared exceedingly hard, and suffered very great hunger; but at last we were wholly without food of any kind except sugar, and a little wine and water. The first day after I had received no food at all, I found myself towards evening, empty and sick at the stomach, and nearer night much inclined to yawning and sleep. I lay down on the couch in the great cabin to sleep, and slept about three hours, and awaked a little refreshed, having taken a glass of wine when I lay down; after being about three hours awake, it being about five o'clock in the morning, I found myself empty, and my stomach sickish, and lay down again, but could not sleep at all, being very faint and ill; and thus I continued all the second day with a strange variety—first hungry, then sick again, with retchings to vomit. The second night, being obliged to go to bed again without any food more than a draught of fresh water, and being asleep, I dreamed I was at Barbadoes, and that the market was mightily stocked with provisions; that I bought some for my mistress, and went and dined very heartily. I thought my stomach was full after this, as it would have been after a good dinner; but when I awaked I was exceedingly sunk in my spirits to find myself in the extremity of family. The last glass of wine we had I drank, and put sugar in it, because of its having some spirit to supply nourishment; but there being no substance in the stomach for the digesting office to work upon, I found the only effect of the wine was to raise disagreeable fumes from the stomach into the head; and I lay, as they told me, stupid and senseless, as one drunk, for some time. The third day, in the morning, after a night of strange, confused, and inconsistent dreams, and rather dozing than sleeping, I awaked ravenous and furious with hunger; and I question, had not my understanding returned and conquered it, whether if I had been a mother, and had had a little child with me, its life would have been safe or not. This lasted about three hours, during which time I was twice raging mad as any creature in Bedlam, as my young master told me, and as he can now inform you.

"In one of these fits of lunacy or distraction I fell down and struck my face against the corner of a pallet-bed, in which my mistress lay, and with the blow the blood gushed out of my nose; and the cabin-boy bringing me a little basin, I sat down and bled into it a great deal; and as the blood came from me I came to myself, and the violence of the flame or fever I was in abated, and so did the ravenous part of the hunger. Then I grew sick, and retched to vomit, but could not, for I had nothing in my stomach to bring up. After I had bled some time I swooned, and they all believed I was dead; but I came to myself soon after, and then had a most dreadful pain in my stomach not to be described—not like the colic, but a gnawing, eager pain for food; and towards night it went off with a kind of earnest wishing or longing for food. I took another draught of water with sugar in it; but my stomach loathed the sugar and brought it all up again; then I took a draught of water without sugar, and that stayed with me; and I laid me down upon the bed, praying most heartily that it would please God to take me away; and composing my mind in hopes of it, I slumbered a while, and then waking, thought myself dying, being light with vapours from an empty stomach. I recommended my soul then to God, and then earnestly wished that somebody would throw me into the into the sea.

"All this while my mistress lay by me, just, as I thought, expiring, but she bore it with much more patience than I, and gave the last bit of bread she had left to her child, my young master, who would not have taken it, but she obliged him to eat it; and I believe it saved his life. Towards the morning I slept again, and when I awoke I fell into a violent passion of crying, and after that had a second fit of violent hunger. I got up ravenous, and in a most dreadful condition; and once or twice I was going to bite my own arm. At last I saw the basin in which was the blood I had bled at my nose the day before: I ran to it, and swallowed it with such haste, and such a greedy appetite, as if I wondered nobody had taken it before, and afraid it should be taken from me now. After it was down, though the thoughts of it filled me with horror, yet it checked the fit of hunger, and I took another draught of water, and was composed and refreshed for some hours after. This was the fourth day; and this I kept up till towards night, when, within the compass of three hours, I had all the several circumstances over again, one after another, viz. sick, sleepy, eagerly hungry, pain in the stomach, then ravenous again, then sick, then lunatic, then crying, then ravenous again, and so every quarter of an hour, and my strength wasted exceedingly; at night I lay me down, having no comfort but in the hope that I should die before morning.

"All this night I had no sleep; but the hunger was now turned into a disease; and I had a terrible colic and griping, by wind instead of food having found its way into the bowels; and in this condition I lay till morning, when I was surprised by the cries and lamentations of my young master, who called out to me that his mother was dead. I lifted myself up a little, for I had not strength to rise, but found she was not dead, though she was able to give very little signs of life. I had then such convulsions in my stomach, for want of some sustenance, as I cannot describe; with such frequent throes and pangs of appetite as nothing but the tortures of death can imitate; and in this condition I was when I heard the seamen above cry out, 'A sail! a sail!' and halloo and jump about as if they were distracted. I was not able to get off from the bed, and my mistress much less; and my young master was so sick that I thought he had been expiring; so we could not open the cabin door, or get any account what it was that occasioned such confusion; nor had we had any conversation with the ship's company for twelve days, they having told us that they had not a mouthful of anything to eat in the ship; and this they told us afterwards—they thought we had been dead. It was this dreadful condition we were in when you were sent to save our lives; and how you found us, sir, you know as well as I, and better too."

This was her own relation, and is such a distinct account of starving to death, as, I confess, I never met with, and was exceeding instructive to me. I am the rather apt to believe it to be a true account, because the youth gave me an account of a good part of it; though I must own, not so distinct and so feeling as the maid; and the rather, because it seems his mother fed him at the price of her own life: but the poor maid, whose constitution was stronger than that of her mistress, who was in years, and a weakly woman too, might struggle harder with it; nevertheless she might be supposed to feel the extremity something sooner than her mistress, who might be allowed to keep the last bit something longer than she parted with any to relieve her maid. No question, as the case is here related, if our ship or some other had not so providentially met them, but a few days more would have ended all their lives. I now return to my disposition of things among the people. And, first, it is to be observed here, that for many reasons I did not think fit to let them know anything of the sloop I had framed, and which I thought of setting up among them; for I found, at least at my first coming, such seeds of division among them, that I saw plainly, had I set up the sloop, and left it among them, they would, upon every light disgust, have separated, and gone away from one another; or perhaps have turned pirates, and so made the island a den of thieves, instead of a plantation of sober and religious people, as I intended it; nor did I leave the two pieces of brass cannon that I had on board, or the extra two quarter-deck guns that my nephew had provided, for the same reason. I thought it was enough to qualify them for a defensive war against any that should invade them, but not to set them up for an offensive war, or to go abroad to attack others; which, in the end, would only bring ruin and destruction upon them. I reserved the sloop, therefore, and the guns, for their service another way, as I shall observe in its place.

Having now done with the island, I left them all in good circumstances and in a flourishing condition, and went on board my ship again on the 6th of May, having been about twenty-five days among them: and as they were all resolved to stay upon the island till I came to remove them, I promised to send them further relief from the Brazils, if I could possibly find an opportunity. I particularly promised to send them some cattle, such as sheep, hogs, and cows: as to the two cows and calves which I brought from England, we had been obliged, by the length of our voyage, to kill them at sea, for want of hay to feed them.

The next day, giving them a salute of five guns at parting, we set sail, and arrived at the bay of All Saints in the Brazils in about twenty-two days, meeting nothing remarkable in our passage but this: that about three days after we had sailed, being becalmed, and the current setting strong to the ENE., running, as it were, into a bay or gulf on the land side, we were driven something out of our course, and once or twice our men cried out, "Land to the eastward!" but whether it was the continent or islands we could not tell by any means. But the third day, towards evening, the sea smooth, and the weather calm, we saw the sea as it were covered towards the land with something very black; not being able to discover what it was till after some time, our chief mate, going up the main shrouds a little way, and looking at them with a perspective, cried out it was an army. I could not imagine what he meant by an army, and thwarted him a little hastily. "Nay, sir," says he, "don't be angry, for 'tis an army, and a fleet too: for I believe there are a thousand canoes, and you may see them paddle along, for they are coming towards us apace."

I was a little surprised then, indeed, and so was my nephew the captain; for he had heard such terrible stories of them in the island, and having never been in those seas before, that he could not tell what to think of it, but said, two or three times, we should all be devoured. I must confess, considering we were becalmed, and the current set strong towards the shore, I liked it the worse; however, I bade them not be afraid, but bring the ship to an anchor as soon as we came so near as to know that we must engage them. The weather continued calm, and they came on apace towards us, so I gave orders to come to an anchor, and furl all our sails; as for the savages, I told them they had nothing to fear but fire, and therefore they should get their boats out, and fasten them, one close by the head and the other by the stern, and man them both well, and wait the issue in that posture: this I did, that the men in the boats might he ready with sheets and buckets to put out any fire these savages might endeavour to fix to the outside of the ship.

In this posture we lay by for them, and in a little while they came up with us; but never was such a horrid sight seen by Christians; though my mate was much mistaken in his calculation of their number, yet when they came up we reckoned about a hundred and twenty-six canoes; some of them had sixteen or seventeen men in them, and some more, and the least six or seven. When they came nearer to us, they seemed to be struck with wonder and astonishment, as at a sight which doubtless they had never seen before; nor could they at first, as we afterwards understood, know what to make of us; they came boldly up, however, very near to us, and seemed to go about to row round us; but we called to our men in the boats not to let them come too near them. This very order brought us to an engagement with them, without our designing it; for five or six of the large canoes came so near our long-boat, that our men beckoned with their hands to keep them back, which they understood very well, and went back: but at their retreat about fifty arrows came on board us from those boats, and one of our men in the long-boat was very much wounded. However, I called to them not to fire by any means; but we handed down some deal boards into the boat, and the carpenter presently set up a kind of fence, like waste boards, to cover them from the arrows of the savages, if they should shoot again.

About half-an-hour afterwards they all came up in a body astern of us, and so near that we could easily discern what they were, though we could not tell their design; and I easily found they were some of my old friends, the same sort of savages that I had been used to engage with. In a short time more they rowed a little farther out to sea, till they came directly broadside with us, and then rowed down straight upon us, till they came so near that they could hear us speak; upon this, I ordered all my men to keep close, lest they should shoot any more arrows, and made all our guns ready; but being so near as to be within hearing, I made Friday go out upon the deck, and call out aloud to them in his language, to know what they meant. Whether they understood him or not, that I knew not; but as soon as he had called to them, six of them, who were in the foremost or nighest boat to us, turned their canoes from us, and stooping down, showed us their naked backs; whether this was a defiance or challenge we knew not, or whether it was done in mere contempt, or as a signal to the rest; but immediately Friday cried out they were going to shoot, and, unhappily for him, poor fellow, they let fly about three hundred of their arrows, and to my inexpressible grief, killed poor Friday, no other man being in their sight. The poor fellow was shot with no less than three arrows, and about three more fell very near him; such unlucky marksmen they were!

I was so annoyed at the loss of my old trusty servant and companion, that I immediately ordered five guns to be loaded with small shot, and four with great, and gave them such a broadside as they had never heard in their lives before. They were not above half a cable's length off when we fired; and our gunners took their aim so well, that three or four of their canoes were overset, as we had reason to believe, by one shot only. The ill manners of turning up their bare backs to us gave us no great offence; neither did I know for certain whether that which would pass for the greatest contempt among us might be understood so by them or not; therefore, in return, I had only resolved to have fired four or five guns at them with powder only, which I knew would frighten them sufficiently: but when they shot at us directly with all the fury they were capable of, and especially as they had killed my poor Friday, whom I so entirely loved and valued, and who, indeed, so well deserved it, I thought myself not only justifiable before God and man, but would have been very glad if I could have overset every canoe there, and drowned every one of them.

I can neither tell how many we killed nor how many we wounded at this broadside, but sure such a fright and hurry never were seen among such a multitude; there were thirteen or fourteen of their canoes split and overset in all, and the men all set a-swimming: the rest, frightened out of their wits, scoured away as fast as they could, taking but little care to save those whose boats were split or spoiled with our shot; so I suppose that many of them were lost; and our men took up one poor fellow swimming for his life, above an hour after they were all gone. The small shot from our cannon must needs kill and wound a great many;

but, in short, we never knew how it went with them, for they fled so fast, that in three hours or thereabouts we could not see above three or four straggling canoes, nor did we ever see the rest any more; for a breeze of wind springing up the same evening, we weighed and set sail for the Brazils.

We had a prisoner, indeed, but the creature was so sullen that he would neither eat nor speak, and we all fancied he would starve himself to death. But I took a way to cure him: for I had made them take him and turn him into the long-boat, and make him believe they would toss him into the sea again, and so leave him where they found him, if he would not speak; nor would that do, but they really did throw him into the sea, and came away from him. Then he followed them, for he swam like a cork, and called to them in his tongue, though they knew not one word of what he said; however at last they took him in again, and then he began to be more tractable: nor did I ever design they should drown him.

We were now under sail again, but I was the most disconsolate creature alive for want of my man Friday, and would have been very glad to have gone back to the island, to have taken one of the rest from thence for my occasion, but it could not be: so we went on. We had one prisoner, as I have said, and it was a long time before we could make him understand anything; but in time our men taught him some English, and he began to be a little tractable. Afterwards, we inquired what country he came from; but could make nothing of what he said; for his speech was so odd, all gutturals, and he spoke in the throat in such a hollow, odd manner, that we could never form a word after him; and we were all of opinion that they might speak that language as well if they were gagged as otherwise; nor could we perceive that they had any occasion either for teeth, tongue, lips, or palate, but formed their words just as a hunting-horn forms a tune with an open throat. He told us, however, some time after, when we had taught him to speak a little English, that they were going with their kings to fight a great battle. When he said kings, we asked him how many kings? He said they were five nation (we could not make him understand the plural 's), and that they all joined to go against two nation. We asked him what made them come up to us? He said, "To makee te great wonder look." Here it is to be observed that all those natives, as also those of Africa when they learn English, always add two e's at the end of the words where we use one; and they place the accent upon them, as makée, takée, and the like; nay, I could hardly make Friday leave it off, though at last he did.

And now I name the poor fellow once more, I must take my last leave of him. Poor honest Friday! We buried him with all the decency and solemnity possible, by putting him into a coffin, and throwing him into the sea; and I caused them to fire eleven guns for him. So ended the life of the most grateful, faithful, honest, and most affectionate servant that ever man had.

We went now away with a fair wind for Brazil; and in about twelve days' time we made land, in the latitude of five degrees south of the line, being the north-easternmost land of all that part of America. We kept on S. by E., in sight of the shore four days, when we made Cape St. Augustine, and in three days came to an anchor off the bay of All Saints, the old place of my deliverance, from whence came both my good and evil fate. Never ship came to this port that had less business than I had, and yet it was with great difficulty that we were admitted to hold the least correspondence on shore: not my partner himself, who was alive, and made a great figure among them, not my two merchant-trustees, not the fame of my wonderful preservation in the island, could obtain me that favour. My partner, however, remembering that I had given five hundred moidores to the prior of the monastery of the Augustines, and two hundred and seventy-two to the poor, went to the monastery, and obliged the prior that then was to go to the governor, and get leave for me personally, with the captain and one more, besides eight seamen, to come on shore, and no more; and this upon condition, absolutely capitulated for, that we should not offer to land any goods out of the ship, or to carry any person away without licence. They were so strict with us as to landing any goods, that it was with extreme difficulty that I got on shore three bales of English goods, such as fine broadcloths, stuffs, and some linen, which I had brought for a present to my partner.

He was a very generous, open-hearted man, although he began, like me, with little at first. Though he knew not that I had the least design of giving him anything, he sent me on board a present of fresh provisions, wine, and sweetmeats, worth about thirty moidores, including some tobacco, and three or four fine medals of gold: but I was even with him in my present, which, as I have said, consisted of fine broadcloth, English stuffs, lace, and fine holland; also, I delivered him about the value of one hundred pounds sterling in the same goods, for other uses; and I obliged him to set up the sloop, which I had brought with me from England, as I have said, for the use of my colony, in order to send the refreshments I intended to my plantation.

Accordingly, he got hands, and finished the sloop in a very few days, for she was already framed; and I gave the master of her such instructions that he could not miss the place; nor did he, as I had an account from my partner afterwards. I got him soon loaded with the small cargo I sent them; and one of our seamen, that had been on shore with me there, offered to go with the sloop and settle there, upon my letter to the governor Spaniard to allot him a sufficient quantity of land for a plantation, and on my giving him some clothes and tools for his planting work, which he said he understood, having been an old planter at Maryland, and a buccaneer into the bargain. I encouraged the fellow by granting all he desired; and, as an addition, I gave him the savage whom we had taken prisoner of war to be his slave, and ordered the governor Spaniard to give him his share of everything he wanted with the rest.

When we came to fit this man out, my old partner told me there was a certain very honest fellow, a Brazil planter of his acquaintance, who had fallen into the displeasure of the Church. "I know not what the matter is with him," says he, "but, on my conscience, I think he is a heretic in his heart, and he has been obliged to conceal himself for fear of the Inquisition." He then told me that he would be very glad of such an opportunity to make his escape, with his wife and two daughters; and if I would let them go to my island, and allot them a plantation, he would give them a small stock to begin with—for the officers of the Inquisition had seized all his effects and estate, and he had nothing left but a little household stuff and two slaves; "and," adds he, "though I hate his principles, yet I would not have him fall into their hands, for he will be assuredly burned alive if he does." I granted this presently, and joined my Englishman with them; and we concealed the man, and his wife and daughters, on board our ship, till the sloop put out to go to sea; and then having put all their goods on board some time before, we put them on board the sloop after she was got out of the bay. Our seaman was mightily pleased with this new partner; and their stocks, indeed, were much alike, rich in tools, in preparations, and a farm—but nothing to begin with, except as above: however, they carried over with them what was worth all the rest, some materials for planting sugar-canes, with some plants of canes, which he, I mean the Brazil planter, understood very well.

Among the rest of the supplies sent to my tenants in the island, I sent them by the sloop three milch cows and five calves; about twenty-two hogs, among them three sows; two mares, and a stone-horse. For my Spaniards, according to my promise, I engaged three Brazil women to go, and recommended it to them to marry them, and use them kindly. I could have procured more women, but I remembered that the poor persecuted man had two daughters, and that there were but five of the Spaniards that wanted partners; the rest had wives of their own, though in another country. All this cargo arrived safe, and, as you may easily suppose, was very welcome to my old inhabitants, who were now, with this addition, between sixty and seventy people, besides little children, of which there were a great many. I found letters at London from them all, by way of Lisbon, when I came back to England.

I have now done with the island, and all manner of discourse about it: and whoever reads the rest of my memorandums would do well to turn his thoughts entirely from it, and expect to read of the follies of an old man, not warned by his own harms, much less by those of other men, to beware; not cooled by almost forty years' miseries and disappointments—not satisfied with prosperity beyond expectation, nor made cautious by afflictions and distress beyond example.

9

DREADFUL OCCURRENCES IN MADAGASCAR

I had no more business to go to the East Indies than a man at full liberty has to go to the turnkey at Newgate, and desire him to lock him up among the prisoners there, and starve him. Had I taken a small vessel from England and gone directly to the island; had I loaded her, as I did the other vessel, with all the necessaries for the plantation and for my people; taken a patent from the government here to have secured my property, in subjection only to that of England; had I carried over cannon and ammunition, servants and people to plant, and taken possession of the place, fortified and strengthened it in the name of England, and increased it with people, as I might easily have done; had I then settled myself there, and sent the ship back laden with good rice, as I might also have done in six months' time, and ordered my friends to have fitted her out again for our supply—had I done this, and stayed there myself, I had at least acted like a man of common sense. But I was possessed of a wandering spirit, and scorned all advantages: I pleased myself with being the patron of the people I placed there, and doing for them in a kind of haughty, majestic way, like an old patriarchal monarch, providing for them as if I had been father of the whole family, as well as of the plantation. But I never so much as pretended to plant in the name of any government or nation, or to acknowledge any prince, or to call my people subjects to any one nation more than another; nay, I never so much as gave the place a name, but left it as I found it, belonging to nobody, and the people under no discipline or government but my own, who, though I had influence over them as a father and benefactor, had no authority or power to act or command one way or other, further than voluntary consent moved them to comply. Yet even this, had I stayed there, would have done well enough; but as I rambled from them, and came there no more, the last letters I had from any of them were by my partner's means, who afterwards sent another sloop to the place, and who sent me word, though I had not the letter till I got to London, several years after it was written, that they went on but poorly; were discontented with their long stay there; that Will Atkins was dead; that five of the Spaniards were come away; and though they had not been much molested by the savages, yet they had had some skirmishes with them; and that they begged of him to write to me to think of the promise I had made to fetch them away, that they might see their country again before they died.

But I was gone a wildgoose chase indeed, and they that will have any more of me must be content to follow me into a new variety of follies, hardships, and wild adventures, wherein the justice of Providence may be duly observed; and we may see how easily Heaven can gorge us with our own desires, make the strongest of our wishes be our affliction, and punish us most severely with those very things which we think it would be our utmost happiness to be allowed to possess. Whether I had business or no business, away I went: it is no time now to enlarge upon the reason or absurdity of my own conduct, but to come to the history—I was embarked for the voyage, and the voyage I went.

I shall only add a word or two concerning my honest Popish clergyman, for let their opinion of us, and all other heretics in general, as they call us, be as uncharitable as it may, I verily believe this man was very sincere, and wished the good of all men: yet I believe he used reserve in many of his expressions, to prevent giving me offence; for I scarce heard him once call on the Blessed Virgin, or mention St. Jago, or his guardian angel, though so common with the rest of them. However, I say I had not the least doubt of his sincerity and pious intentions; and I am firmly of opinion, if the rest of the Popish missionaries were like him, they would strive to visit even the poor Tartars and Laplanders, where they have nothing to give them, as well as covet to flock to India, Persia, China, &c., the most wealthy of the heathen countries; for if they expected to bring no gains to their Church by it, it may well be admired how they came to admit the Chinese Confucius into the calendar of the Christian saints.

A ship being ready to sail for Lisbon, my pious priest asked me leave to go thither; being still, as he observed, bound never to finish any voyage he began. How happy it had been for me if I had gone with him. But it was too late now; all things Heaven appoints for the best: had I gone with him I had never had so many things to be thankful for, and the reader had never heard of the second part of the travels and adventures of Robinson Crusoe: so I must here leave exclaiming at myself, and go on with my voyage. From the Brazils we made directly over the Atlantic Sea to the Cape of Good Hope, and had a tolerably good voyage, our course generally south-east, now and then a storm, and some contrary winds; but my disasters at sea were at an end—my future rubs and cross events were to befall me on shore, that it might appear the land was as well prepared to be our scourge as the sea.

Our ship was on a trading voyage, and had a supercargo on board, who was to direct all her motions after she arrived at the Cape, only being limited to a certain number of days for stay, by charter-party, at the several ports she was to go to. This was none of my business, neither did I meddle with it; my nephew, the captain, and the supercargo adjusting all those things between them as they thought fit. We stayed at the Cape no longer than was needful to take in-fresh water, but made the best of our way for the coast of Coromandel. We were, indeed, informed that a French man-of-war, of fifty guns, and two large merchant ships, were gone for the Indies; and as I knew we were at war with France, I had some apprehensions of them; but they went their own way, and we heard no more of them.

I shall not pester the reader with a tedious description of places, journals of our voyage, variations of the compass, latitudes, trade-winds, &c.; it is enough to name the ports and places which we touched at, and what occurred to us upon our passages from one to another. We touched first at the island of Madagascar, where, though the people are fierce and treacherous, and very well armed with lances and bows, which they use with inconceivable dexterity, yet we fared very well with them a while. They treated us very civilly; and for some trifles which we gave them, such as knives, scissors, &c., they brought us eleven good fat bullocks, of a middling size, which we took in, partly for fresh provisions for our present spending, and the rest to salt for the ship's use.

We were obliged to stay here some time after we had furnished ourselves with provisions; and I, who was always too curious to look into every nook of the world wherever I came, went on shore as often as I could. It was on the east side of the island that we went on shore one evening: and the people, who, by the way, are very numerous, came thronging about us, and stood gazing at us at a distance. As we had traded freely with them, and had been kindly used, we thought ourselves in no danger; but when we saw the people, we cut three boughs out of a tree, and stuck them up at a distance from us; which, it seems, is a mark in that country not only of a truce and friendship, but when it is accepted the other side set up three poles or boughs, which is a signal that they accept the truce too; but then this is a known condition of the truce, that you are not to pass beyond their three poles towards them, nor they to come past your three poles or boughs towards you; so that you are perfectly secure within the three poles, and all the space between your poles and theirs is allowed like a market for free converse, traffic, and commerce. When you go there you must not carry your weapons with you; and if they come into that space they stick up their javelins and lances all at the first poles, and come on unarmed; but if any violence is offered them, and the truce thereby broken, away they run to the poles, and lay hold of their weapons, and the truce is at an end.

It happened one evening, when we went on shore, that a greater number of their people came down than usual, but all very friendly and civil; and they brought several kinds of provisions, for which we satisfied them with such toys as we had; the women also brought us milk and roots, and several things very acceptable to us, and all was quiet; and we made us a little tent or hut of some boughs or trees, and lay on shore all night. I know not what was the occasion, but I was not so well satisfied to lie on shore as the rest; and the boat riding at an anchor at about a stone's cast from the land, with two men in her to take care of her, I made one of them come on shore; and getting some boughs of trees to cover us also in the boat, I spread the sail on the bottom of the boat, and lay under the cover of the branches of the trees all night in the boat.

About two o'clock in the morning we heard one of our men making a terrible noise on the shore, calling out, for God's sake, to bring the boat in and come and help them, for they were all like to be murdered; and at the same time I heard the fire of five muskets, which was the number of guns they had, and that three times over; for it seems the natives here were not so easily frightened with guns as the savages were in America, where I had to do with them. All this while, I knew not what was the matter, but rousing immediately from sleep with the noise, I caused the boat to be thrust in, and resolved with three fusees we had on board to land and assist our men. We got the boat soon to the shore, but our men were in too much haste; for being come to the shore, they plunged into the water, to get to the boat with all the expedition they could, being pursued by between three and four hundred men. Our men were but nine in all, and only five of them had fusees with them; the rest had pistols and swords, indeed, but they were of small use to them.

We took up seven of our men, and with difficulty enough too, three of them being very ill wounded; and that which was still worse was, that while we stood in the boat to take our men in, we were in as much danger as they were in on shore; for they poured their arrows in upon us so thick that we were glad to barricade the side of the boat up with the benches, and two or three loose boards which, to our great satisfaction, we had by mere accident in the boat. And yet, had it been daylight, they are, it seems, such exact marksmen, that if they could have seen but the least part of any of us, they would have been sure of us. We had, by the light of the moon, a little sight of them, as they stood pelting us from the shore with darts and arrows; and having got ready our firearms, we gave them a volley that we could hear, by the cries of some of them, had wounded several; however, they stood thus in battle array on the shore till break of day, which we supposed was that they might see the better to take their aim at us.

In this condition we lay, and could not tell how to weigh our anchor, or set up our sail, because we must needs stand up in the boat, and they were as sure to hit us as we were to hit a bird in a tree with small shot. We made signals of distress to the ship, and though she rode a league off, yet my nephew, the captain, hearing our firing, and by glasses perceiving the posture we lay in, and that we fired towards the shore, pretty well understood us; and weighing anchor with all speed, he stood as near the shore as he durst with the ship, and then sent another boat with ten hands in her, to assist us. We called to them not to come too near, telling them what condition we were in; however, they stood in near to us, and one of the men taking the end of a tow-line in his hand, and keeping our boat between him and the enemy, so that they could not perfectly see him, swam on board us, and made fast the line to the boat: upon which we slipped out a little cable, and leaving our anchor behind, they towed us out of reach of the arrows; we all the while lying close behind the barricade we had made. As soon as we were got from between the ship and the shore, that we could lay her side to the shore, she ran along just by them, and poured in a broadside among them, loaded with pieces of iron and lead, small bullets, and such stuff, besides the great shot, which made a terrible havoc among them.

When we were got on board and out of danger, we had time to examine into the occasion of this fray; and indeed our supercargo, who had been often in those parts, put me upon it; for he said he was sure the inhabitants would not have touched us after we had made a truce, if we had not done something to provoke them to it. At length it came out that an old woman, who had come to sell us some milk, had brought it within our poles, and a young woman with her, who also brought us some roots or herbs; and while the old woman (whether she was mother to the young woman or no they could not tell) was selling us the milk, one of our men offered some rudeness to the girl that was with her, at which the old woman made a great noise: however, the seaman would not quit his prize, but carried her out of the old woman's sight among the trees, it being almost dark; the old woman went away without her, and, as we may suppose, made an outcry among the people she came from; who, upon notice, raised that great army upon us in three or four hours, and it was great odds but we had all been destroyed.

One of our men was killed with a lance thrown at him just at the beginning of the attack, as he sallied out of the tent they had made; the rest came off free, all but the fellow who was the occasion of all the mischief, who paid dear enough for his brutality, for we could not hear what became of him for a great while. We lay upon the shore two days after, though the wind presented, and made signals for him, and made our boat sail up shore and down shore several leagues, but in vain; so we were obliged to give him over; and if he alone had suffered for it, the loss had been less. I could not satisfy myself, however, without venturing on shore once more, to try if I could learn anything of him or them; it was the third night after the action that I had a great mind to learn, if I could by any means, what mischief we had done, and how the game stood on the Indians' side. I was careful to do it in the dark, lest we should be attacked again: but I ought indeed to have been sure that the men I went with had been under my command, before I engaged in a thing so hazardous and mischievous as I was brought into by it, without design.

We took twenty as stout fellows with us as any in the ship, besides the supercargo and myself, and we landed two hours before midnight, at the same place where the Indians stood drawn up in the evening before. I landed here, because my design, as I have said, was chiefly to see if they had quitted the field, and if they had left any marks behind them of the mischief we had done them, and I thought if we could surprise one or two of them, perhaps we might get our man again, by way of exchange.

We landed without any noise, and divided our men into two bodies, whereof the boatswain commanded one and I the other. We neither saw nor heard anybody stir when we landed: and we marched up, one body at a distance from another, to the place. At first we could see nothing, it being very dark; till by-and-by our boatswain, who led the first party, stumbled and fell over a dead body. This made them halt a while; for knowing by the circumstances that they were at the place where the Indians had stood, they waited for my coming up there. We concluded to halt till the moon began to rise, which we knew would be in less than an hour, when we could easily discern the havoc we had made among them. We told thirty-two bodies upon the ground, whereof two were not quite dead; some had an arm and some a leg shot off, and one his head; those that were wounded, we supposed, they had carried away. When we had made, as I thought, a full discovery of all we could come to the knowledge of, I resolved on going on board; but the boatswain and his party sent me word that they were resolved to make a visit to the Indian town, where these dogs, as they called them, dwelt, and asked me to go along with them; and if they could find them, as they still fancied they should, they did not doubt of getting a good booty; and it might be they might find Tom Jeffry there: that was the man's name we had lost.

Had they sent to ask my leave to go, I knew well enough what answer to have given them; for I should have commanded them instantly on board, knowing it was not a hazard fit for us to run, who had a ship and ship-loading in our charge, and a voyage to make which depended very much upon the lives of the men; but as they sent me word they were resolved to go, and only asked me and my company to go along with them, I positively refused it, and rose up, for I was sitting on the ground, in order to go to the boat. One or two of the men began to importune me to go; and when I refused, began to grumble, and say they were not under my command, and they would go. "Come, Jack," says one of the men, "will you go with me? I'll go for one." Jack said he would—and then another—and, in a word, they all left me but one, whom I persuaded to stay, and a boy left in the boat. So the supercargo and I, with the third man, went back to the boat, where we told them we would stay for them, and take care to take in as many of them as should be left; for I told them it was a mad thing they were going about, and supposed most of them would have the fate of Tom Jeffry.

They told me, like seamen, they would warrant it they would come off again, and they would take care, &c.; so away they went. I entreated them to consider the ship and the voyage, that their lives were not their own, and that they were entrusted with the voyage, in some measure; that if they miscarried, the ship might be lost for want of their help, and that they could not answer for it to God or man. But I might as well have talked to the mainmast of the ship: they were mad upon their journey; only they gave me good words, and begged I would not be angry; that they did not doubt but they would be back again in about an hour at furthest; for the Indian town, they said, was not above half-a mile off, though they found it above two miles before they got to it.

Well, they all went away, and though the attempt was desperate, and such as none but madmen would have gone about, yet, to give them their due, they went about it as warily as boldly; they were gallantly armed, for they had every man a fusee or musket, a bayonet, and a pistol; some of them had broad cutlasses, some of them had hangers, and the boatswain and two more had poleaxes; besides all which they had among them thirteen hand grenadoes. Bolder fellows, and better provided, never went about any wicked work in the world. When they went out their chief design was plunder, and they were in mighty hopes of finding gold there; but a circumstance which none of them were aware of set them on fire with revenge, and made devils of them all.

When they came to the few Indian houses which they thought had been the town, which was not above half a mile off, they were under great disappointment, for there were not above twelve or thirteen houses, and where the town was, or how big, they knew not. They consulted, therefore, what to do, and were some time before they could resolve; for if they fell upon these, they must cut all their throats; and it was ten to one but some of them might escape, it being in the night, though the moon was up; and if one escaped, he would run and raise all the town, so they should have a whole army upon them; on the other hand, if they went away and left those untouched, for the people were all asleep, they could not tell which way to look for the town; however, the last was the best advice, so they resolved to leave them, and look for the town as well as they could. They went on a little way, and found a cow tied to a tree; this, they presently concluded, would be a good guide to them; for, they said, the cow certainly belonged to the town before them, or the town behind them, and if they untied her, they should see which way she went: if she went back, they had nothing to say to her; but if she went forward, they would follow her. So they cut the cord, which was made of twisted flags, and the cow went on before them, directly to the town; which, as they reported, consisted of above two hundred houses or huts, and in some of these they found several families living together.

Here they found all in silence, as profoundly secure as sleep could make them: and first, they called another council, to consider what they had to do; and presently resolved to divide themselves into three bodies, and so set three houses on fire in three parts of the town; and as the men came out, to seize them and bind them (if any resisted, they need not be asked what to do then), and so to search the rest of the houses for plunder: but they resolved to march silently first through the town, and see what dimensions it was of, and if they might venture upon it or no.

They did so, and desperately resolved that they would venture upon them: but while they were animating one another to the work, three of them, who were a little before the rest, called out aloud to them, and told them that they had found—Tom Jeffry: they all ran up to the place, where they found the poor fellow hanging up naked by one arm, and his throat cut. There was an Indian house just by the tree, where they found sixteen or seventeen of the principal Indians, who had been concerned in the fray with us before, and two or three of them wounded with our shot; and our men found they were awake, and talking one to another in that house, but knew not their number.

The sight of their poor mangled comrade so enraged them, as before, that they swore to one another that they would be revenged, and that not an Indian that came into their hands should have any quarter; and to work they went immediately, and yet not so madly as might be expected from the rage and fury they were in. Their first care was to get something that would soon take fire, but, after a little search, they found that would be to no purpose; for most of the houses were low, and thatched with flags and rushes, of which the country is full; so they presently made some wildfire, as we call it, by wetting a little powder in the palm of their hands, and in a quarter of an hour they set the town on fire in four or five places, and particularly that house where the Indians were not gone to bed.

As soon as the fire begun to blaze, the poor frightened creatures began to rush out to save their lives, but met with their fate in the attempt; and especially at the door, where they drove them back, the boatswain himself killing one or two with his poleaxe. The house being large, and many in it, he did not care to go in, but called for a hand grenado, and threw it among them, which at first frightened them, but, when it burst, made such havoc among them that they cried out in a hideous manner. In short, most of the Indians who were in the open part of the house were killed or hurt with the grenado, except two or three more who pressed to the door, which the boatswain and two more kept, with their bayonets on the muzzles of their pieces, and despatched all that came in their way; but there was another apartment in the house, where the prince or king, or whatever he was, and several others were; and these were kept in till the house, which was by this time all in a light flame, fell in upon them, and they were smothered together.

All this while they fired not a gun, because they would not waken the people faster than they could master them; but the fire began to waken them fast enough, and our fellows were glad to keep a little together in bodies; for the fire grew so raging, all the houses being made of light combustible stuff, that they could hardly bear the street between them. Their business was to follow the fire, for the surer execution: as fast as the fire either forced the people out of those houses which were burning, or frightened them out of others, our people were ready at their doors to knock them on the head, still calling and hallooing one to another to remember Tom Jeffry.

While this was doing, I must confess I was very uneasy, and especially when I saw the flames of the town, which, it being night, seemed to be close by me. My nephew, the captain, who was roused by his men seeing such a fire, was very uneasy, not knowing what the matter was, or what danger I was in, especially hearing the guns too, for by this time they began to use their firearms; a thousand thoughts oppressed his mind concerning me and the supercargo, what would become of us; and at last, though he could ill spare any more men, yet not knowing what exigence we might be in, he took another boat, and with thirteen men and himself came ashore to me.

He was surprised to see me and the supercargo in the boat with no more than two men; and though he was glad that we were well, yet he was in the same impatience with us to know what was doing; for the noise continued, and the flame increased; in short, it was next to an impossibility for any men in the world to restrain their curiosity to know what had happened, or their concern for the safety of the men: in a word, the captain told me he would go and help his men, let what would come. I argued with him, as I did before with the men, the safety of the ship, the danger of the voyage, the interests of the owners and merchants, &c., and told him I and the two men would go, and only see if we could at a distance learn what was likely to be the event, and come back and tell him. It was in vain to talk to my nephew, as it was to talk to the rest before; he would go, he said; and he only wished he had left but ten men in the ship, for he could not think of having his men lost for want of help: he had rather lose the ship, the voyage, and his life, and all; and away he went.

I was no more able to stay behind now than I was to persuade them not to go; so the captain ordered two men to row back the pinnace, and fetch twelve men more, leaving the long-boat at an anchor; and that, when they came back, six men should keep the two boats, and six more come after us; so that he left only sixteen men in the ship: for the whole ship's company consisted of sixty-five men, whereof two were lost in the late quarrel which brought this mischief on.

Being now on the march, we felt little of the ground we trod on; and being guided by the fire, we kept no path, but went directly to the place of the flame. If the noise of the guns was surprising to us before, the cries of the poor people were now quite of another nature, and filled us with horror. I must confess I was never at the sacking a city, or at the taking a town by storm. I had heard of Oliver Cromwell taking Drogheda, in Ireland, and killing man, woman, and child; and I had read of Count Tilly sacking the city of Magdeburg and cutting the throats of twenty-two thousand of all sexes; but I never had an idea of the thing itself before, nor is it possible to describe it, or the horror that was upon our minds at hearing it. However, we went on, and at length came to the town, though there was no entering the streets of it for the fire. The first object we met with was the ruins of a hut or house, or rather the ashes of it, for the house was consumed; and just before it, plainly now to be seen by the light of the fire, lay four men and three women, killed, and, as we thought, one or two more lay in the heap among the fire; in short, there were such instances of rage, altogether barbarous, and of a fury something beyond what was human, that we thought it impossible our men could be guilty of it; or, if they were the authors of it, we thought they ought to be every one of them put to the worst of deaths. But this was not all: we saw the fire increase forward, and the cry went on just as the fire went on; so that we were in the utmost confusion. We advanced a little way farther, and behold, to our astonishment, three naked women, and crying in a most dreadful manner, came flying as if they had wings, and after them sixteen or seventeen men, natives, in the same terror and consternation, with three of our English butchers in the rear, who, when they could not overtake them, fired in among them, and one that was killed by their shot fell down in our sight. When the rest saw us, believing us to be their enemies, and that we would murder them as well as those that pursued them, they set up a most dreadful shriek, especially the women; and two of them fell down, as if already dead, with the fright.

My very soul shrunk within me, and my blood ran chill in my veins, when I saw this; and, I believe, had the three English sailors that pursued them come on, I had made our men kill them all; however, we took some means to let the poor flying creatures know that we would not hurt them; and immediately they came up to us, and kneeling down, with their hands lifted up, made piteous lamentation to us to save them, which we let them know we would: whereupon they crept all together in a huddle close behind us, as for protection. I left my men drawn up together, and, charging them to hurt nobody, but, if possible, to get at some of our people, and see what devil it was possessed them, and what they intended to do, and to command them off; assuring them that if they stayed till daylight they would have a hundred thousand men about their ears: I say I left them, and went among those flying people, taking only two of our men with me; and there was, indeed, a piteous spectacle among them. Some of them had their feet terribly burned with trampling and running through the fire; others their hands burned; one of the women had fallen down in the fire, and was very much burned before she could get out again; and two or three of the men had cuts in their backs and thighs, from our men pursuing; and another was shot through the body and died while I was there.

I would fain have learned what the occasion of all this was; but I could not understand one word they said; though, by signs, I perceived some of them knew not what was the occasion themselves. I was so terrified in my thoughts at this outrageous attempt that I could not stay there, but went back to my own men, and resolved to go into the middle of the town, through the fire, or whatever might be in the way, and put an end to it, cost what it would; accordingly, as I came back to my men, I told them my resolution, and commanded them to follow me, when, at the very moment, came four of our men, with the boatswain at their head, roving over heaps of bodies they had killed, all covered with blood and dust, as if they wanted more people to massacre, when our men hallooed to them as loud as they could halloo; and with much ado one of them made them hear, so that they knew who we were, and came up to us.

As soon as the boatswain saw us, he set up a halloo like a shout of triumph, for having, as he thought, more help come; and without waiting to hear me, "Captain," says he, "noble captain! I am glad you are come; we have not half done yet. Villainous hell-hound dogs! I'll kill as many of them as poor Tom has hairs upon his head: we have sworn to spare none of them; we'll root out the very nation of them from the earth;" and thus he ran on, out of breath, too, with action, and would not give us leave to speak a word. At last, raising my voice that I might silence him a little, "Barbarous dog!" said I, "what are you doing! I won't have one creature touched more, upon pain of death; I charge you, upon your life, to stop your hands, and stand still here, or you are a dead man this minute."—"Why, sir," says he, "do you know what you do, or what they have done? If you want a reason for what we have done, come hither;" and with that he showed me the poor fellow hanging, with his throat cut.

I confess I was urged then myself, and at another time would have been forward enough; but I thought they had carried their rage too far, and remembered Jacob's words to his sons Simeon and Levi: "Cursed be their anger, for it was fierce; and their wrath, for it was cruel." But I had now a new task upon my hands; for when the men I had carried with me saw the sight, as I had done, I had as much to do to restrain them as I should have had with the others; nay, my nephew himself fell in with them, and told me, in their hearing, that he was only concerned for fear of the men being overpowered; and as to the people, he thought not one of them ought to live; for they had all glutted themselves with the murder of the poor man, and that they ought to be used like murderers. Upon these words, away ran eight of my men, with the boatswain and his crew, to complete their bloody work; and I, seeing it quite out of my power to restrain them, came away pensive and sad; for I could not bear the sight, much less the horrible noise and cries of the poor wretches that fell into their hands.

I got nobody to come back with me but the supercargo and two men, and with these walked back to the boat. It was a very great piece of folly in me, I confess, to venture back, as it were, alone; for as it began now to be almost day, and the alarm had run over the country, there stood about forty men armed with lances and boughs at the little place where the twelve or thirteen houses stood, mentioned before: but by accident I missed the place, and came directly to the seaside, and by the time I got to the seaside it was broad day: immediately I took the pinnace and went on board, and sent her back to assist the men in what might happen. I observed, about the time that I came to the boat-side, that the fire was pretty well out, and the noise abated; but in about half-an-hour after I got on board, I heard a volley of our men's firearms, and saw a great smoke. This, as I understood afterwards, was our men falling upon the men, who, as I said, stood at the few houses on the way, of whom they killed sixteen or seventeen, and set all the houses on fire, but did not meddle with the women or children.

By the time the men got to the shore again with the pinnace our men began to appear; they came dropping in, not in two bodies as they went, but straggling here and there in such a manner, that a small force of resolute men might have cut them all off. But the dread of them was upon the whole country; and the men were surprised, and so frightened, that I believe a hundred of them would have fled at the sight of but five of our men. Nor in all this terrible action was there a man that made any considerable defence: they were so surprised between the terror of the fire and the sudden attack of our men in the dark, that they knew not which way to turn themselves; for if they fled one way they were met by one party, if back again by another, so that they were everywhere knocked down; nor did any of our men receive the least hurt, except one that sprained his foot, and another that had one of his hands burned.

10

HE IS LEFT ON SHORE

I was very angry with my nephew, the captain, and indeed with all the men, but with him in particular, as well for his acting so out of his duty as a commander of the ship, and having the charge of the voyage upon him, as in his prompting, rather than cooling, the rage of his blind men in so bloody and cruel an enterprise. My nephew answered me very respectfully, but told me that when he saw the body of the poor seaman whom they had murdered in so cruel and barbarous a manner, he was not master of himself, neither could he govern his passion; he owned he should not have done so, as he was commander of the ship; but as he was a man, and nature moved him, he could not bear it. As for the rest of the men, they were not subject to me at all, and they knew it well enough; so they took no notice of my dislike. The next day we set sail, so we never heard any more of it. Our men differed in the account of the number they had killed; but according to the best of their accounts, put all together, they killed or destroyed about one hundred and fifty people, men, women, and children, and left not a house standing in the town. As for the poor fellow Tom Jeffry, as he was quite dead (for his throat was so cut that his head was half off), it would do him no service to bring him away; so they only took him down from the tree, where he was hanging by one hand.

However just our men thought this action, I was against them in it, and I always, after that time, told them God would blast the voyage; for I looked upon all the blood they shed that night to be murder in them. For though it is true that they had killed Tom Jeffry, yet Jeffry was the aggressor, had broken the truce, and had ill-used a young woman of theirs, who came down to them innocently, and on the faith of the public capitulation.

The boatswain defended this quarrel when we were afterwards on board. He said it was true that we seemed to break the truce, but really had not; and that the war was begun the night before by the natives themselves, who had shot at us, and killed one of our men without any just provocation; so that as we were in a capacity to fight them now, we might also be in a capacity to do ourselves justice upon them in an extraordinary manner; that though the poor man had taken a little liberty with the girl, he ought not to have been murdered, and that in such a villainous manner: and that they did nothing but what was just and what the laws of God allowed to be done to murderers. One would think this should have been enough to have warned us against going on shore amongst the heathens and barbarians; but it is impossible to make mankind wise but at their own expense, and their experience seems to be always of most use to them when it is dearest bought.

We were now bound to the Gulf of Persia, and from thence to the coast of Coromandel, only to touch at Surat; but the chief of the supercargo's design lay at the Bay of Bengal, where, if he missed his business outward-bound, he was to go out to China, and return to the coast as he came home. The first disaster that befell us was in the Gulf of Persia, where five of our men, venturing on shore on the Arabian side of the gulf, were surrounded by the Arabians, and either all killed or carried away into slavery; the rest of the boat's crew were not able to rescue them, and had but just time to get off their boat. I began to upbraid them with the just retribution of Heaven in this case; but the boatswain very warmly told me, he thought I went further in my censures than I could show any warrant for in Scripture; and referred to Luke xiii. 4, where our Saviour intimates that those men on whom the Tower of Siloam fell were not sinners above all the Galileans; but that which put me to silence in the case was, that not one of these five men who were now lost were of those who went on shore to the massacre of Madagascar, so I always called it, though our men could not bear to hear the word *massacre* with any patience.

But my frequent preaching to them on this subject had worse consequences than I expected; and the boatswain, who had been the head of the attempt, came up boldly to me one time, and told me he found that I brought that affair continually upon the stage; that I made unjust reflections upon it, and had used the men very ill on that account, and himself in particular; that as I was but a passenger, and had no command in the ship, or concern in the voyage, they were not obliged to bear it; that they did not know but I might have some ill-design in my head, and perhaps to call them to an account for it when they came to England; and that, therefore, unless I would resolve to have done with it, and also not to concern myself any further with him, or any of his affairs, he would leave the ship; for he did not think it safe to sail with me among them.

I heard him patiently enough till he had done, and then told him that I confessed I had all along opposed the massacre of Madagascar, and that I had, on all occasions, spoken my mind freely about it, though not more upon him than any of the rest; that as to having no command in the ship, that was true; nor did I exercise any authority, only took the liberty of speaking my mind in things which publicly concerned us all; and what concern I had in the voyage was none of his business; that I was a considerable owner in the ship. In that claim I conceived I had a right to speak even further than I had done, and would not be accountable to him or any one else, and began to be a little warm with him. He made but little reply to me at that time, and I thought the affair had been over. We were at this time in the road at Bengal; and being willing to see the place, I went on shore with the supercargo in the ship's boat to divert myself; and towards evening was preparing to go on board, when one of the men came to me, and told me he would not have me trouble myself to come down to the boat, for they had orders not to carry me on board any more. Any one may guess what a surprise I was in at so insolent a message; and I asked the man who bade him deliver that message to me? He told me the coxswain.

I immediately found out the supercargo, and told him the story, adding that I foresaw there would be a mutiny in the ship; and entreated him to go immediately on board and acquaint the captain of it. But I might have spared this intelligence, for before I had spoken to him on shore the matter was effected on board. The boatswain, the gunner, the carpenter, and all the inferior officers, as soon as I was gone off in the boat, came up, and desired to speak with the captain; and then the boatswain, making a long harangue, and repeating all he had said to me, told the captain that as I was now gone peaceably on shore, they were loath to use any violence with me, which, if I had not gone on shore, they would otherwise have done, to oblige me to have gone. They therefore thought fit to tell him that as they shipped themselves to serve in the ship under his command, they would perform it well and faithfully; but if I would not quit the ship, or the captain oblige me to quit it, they would all leave the ship, and sail no further with him; and at that word *all* he turned his face towards the main-mast, which was, it seems, a signal agreed on, when the seamen, being got together there, cried out, "One and all! one and all!"

My nephew, the captain, was a man of spirit, and of great presence of mind; and though he was surprised, yet he told them calmly that he would consider of the matter, but that he could do nothing in it till he had spoken to me about it. He used some arguments with them, to show them the unreasonableness and injustice of the thing, but it was all in vain; they swore, and shook hands round before his face, that they would all go on shore unless he would engage to them not to suffer me to come any more on board the ship.

This was a hard article upon him, who knew his obligation to me, and did not know how I might take it. So he began to talk smartly to them; told them that I was a very considerable owner of the ship, and that if ever they came to England again it would cost them very dear; that the ship was mine, and that he could not put me out of it; and that he would rather lose the ship, and the voyage too, than disoblige me so much: so they might do as they pleased. However, he would go on shore and talk with me, and invited the boatswain to go with him, and perhaps they might accommodate the matter with me. But they all rejected the proposal, and said they would have nothing to do with me any more; and if I came on board they would all go on shore. "Well," said the captain, "if you are all of this mind, let me go on shore and talk with him." So away he came to me with this account, a little after the message had been brought to me from the coxswain.

I was very glad to see my nephew, I must confess; for I was not without apprehensions that they would confine him by violence, set sail, and run away with the ship; and then I had been stripped naked in a remote country, having nothing to help myself; in short, I had been in a worse case than when I was alone in the island. But they had not come to that length, it seems, to my satisfaction; and when my nephew told me what they had said to him, and how they had sworn and shook hands that they would, one and all, leave the ship if I was suffered to come on board, I told him he should not be concerned at it at all, for I would stay on shore. I only desired he would take care and send me all my necessary things on shore, and leave me a sufficient sum of money, and I would find my way to England as well as I could. This was a heavy piece of news to my nephew, but there was no way to help it but to comply; so, in short, he went on board the ship again, and satisfied the men that his uncle had yielded to their importunity, and had sent for his goods from on board the ship; so that the matter was over in a few hours, the men returned to their duty, and I began to consider what course I should steer.

I was now alone in a most remote part of the world, for I was near three thousand leagues by sea farther off from England than I was at my island; only, it is true, I might travel here by land over the Great Mogul's country to Surat, might go from thence to Bassora by sea, up the Gulf of Persia, and take the way of the caravans, over the desert of Arabia, to Aleppo and Scanderoon; from thence by sea again to Italy, and so overland into France. I had another way before me, which was to wait for some English ships, which were coming to Bengal from Achin, on the island of Sumatra, and get passage on board them from England. But as I came hither without any concern with the East Indian Company, so it would be difficult to go from hence without their licence, unless with great favour of the captains of the ships, or the company's factors: and to both I was an utter stranger.

Here I had the mortification to see the ship set sail without me; however, my nephew left me two servants, or rather one companion and one servant; the first was clerk to the purser, whom he engaged to go with me, and the other was his own servant. I then took a good lodging in the house of an Englishwoman, where several merchants lodged, some French, two Italians, or rather Jews, and one Englishman. Here I stayed above nine months, considering what course to take. I had some English goods with me of value, and a considerable sum of money; my nephew furnishing me with a thousand pieces of eight, and a letter of credit for more if I had occasion, that I might not be straitened, whatever might happen. I quickly disposed of my goods to advantage; and, as I originally intended, I bought here some very good diamonds, which, of all other things, were the most proper for me in my present circumstances, because I could always carry my whole estate about me.

During my stay here many proposals were made for my return to England, but none falling out to my mind, the English merchant who lodged with me, and whom I had contracted an intimate acquaintance with, came to me one morning, saying: "Countryman, I have a project to communicate, which, as it suits with my thoughts, may, for aught I know, suit with yours also, when you shall have thoroughly considered it. Here we are posted, you by accident and I by my own choice, in a part of the world very remote from our own country; but it is in a country where, by us who understand trade and business, a great deal of money is to be got. If you will put one thousand pounds to my one thousand pounds, we will hire a ship here, the first we can get to our minds. You shall be captain, I'll be merchant, and we'll go a trading voyage to China; for what should we stand still for? The whole world is in motion; why should we be idle?"

I liked this proposal very well; and the more so because it seemed to be expressed with so much goodwill. In my loose, unhinged circumstances, I was the fitter to embrace a proposal for trade, or indeed anything else. I might perhaps say with some truth, that if trade was not my element, rambling was; and no proposal for seeing any part of the world which I had never seen before could possibly come amiss to me. It was, however, some time before we could get a ship to our minds, and when we had got a vessel, it was not easy to get English sailors—that is to say, so many as were necessary to govern the voyage and manage the sailors which we should pick up there. After some time we got a mate, a boatswain, and a gunner, English; a Dutch carpenter, and three foremast men. With these we found we could do well enough, having Indian seamen, such as they were, to make up.

When all was ready we set sail for Achin, in the island of Sumatra, and from thence to Siam, where we exchanged some of our wares for opium and some arrack; the first a commodity which bears a great price among the Chinese, and which at that time was much wanted there. Then we went up to Saskan, were eight months out, and on our return to Bengal I was very well satisfied with my adventure. Our people in England often admire how officers, which the company send into India, and the merchants which generally stay there, get such very great estates as they do, and sometimes come home worth sixty or seventy thousand pounds at a time; but it is little matter for wonder, when we consider the innumerable ports and places where they have a free commerce; indeed, at the ports where the English ships come there is such great and constant demands for the growth of all other countries, that there is a certain vent for the returns, as well as a market abroad for the goods carried out.

I got so much money by my first adventure, and such an insight into the method of getting more, that had I been twenty years younger, I should have been tempted to have stayed here, and sought no farther for making my fortune; but what was all this to a man upwards of threescore, that was rich enough, and came abroad more in obedience to a restless desire of seeing the world than a covetous desire of gaining by it? A restless desire it really was, for when I was at home I was restless to go abroad; and when I was abroad I was restless to be at home. I say, what was this gain to me? I was rich enough already, nor had I any uneasy desires about getting more money; therefore the profit of the voyage to me was of no great force for the prompting me forward to further undertakings. Hence, I thought that by this voyage I had made no progress at all, because I was come back, as I might call it, to the place from whence I came, as to a home: whereas, my eye, like that which Solomon speaks of, was never satisfied with seeing. I was come into a part of the world which I was never in before, and that part, in particular, which I heard much of, and was resolved to see as much of it as I could: and then I thought I might say I had seen all the world that was worth seeing.

But my fellow-traveller and I had different notions: I acknowledge his were the more suited to the end of a merchant's life: who, when he is abroad upon adventures, is wise to stick to that, as the best thing for him, which he is likely to get the most money by. On the other hand, mine was the notion of a mad, rambling boy, that never cares to see a thing twice over. But this was not all: I had a kind of impatience upon me to be nearer home, and yet an unsettled resolution which way to go. In the interval of these consultations, my friend, who was always upon the search for business, proposed another voyage among the Spice Islands, to bring home a loading of cloves from the Manillas, or thereabouts.

We were not long in preparing for this voyage; the chief difficulty was in bringing me to come into it. However, at last, nothing else offering, and as sitting still, to me especially, was the unhappiest part of life, I resolved on this voyage too, which we made very successfully, touching at Borneo and several other islands, and came home in about five months, when we sold our spices, with very great profit, to the Persian merchants, who carried them away to the Gulf. My friend, when we made up this account, smiled at me: "Well, now," said he, with a sort of friendly rebuke on my indolent temper, "is not this better than walking about here, like a man with nothing to do, and spending our time in staring at the nonsense and ignorance of the Pagans?"—"Why, truly," said I, "my friend, I think it is, and I begin to be a convert to the principles of merchandising; but I must tell you, by the way, you do not know what I am doing; for if I once conquer my backwardness, and embark heartily, old as I am, I shall harass you up and down the world till I tire you; for I shall pursue it so eagerly, I shall never let you lie still."

11

WARNED OF DANGER BY A COUNTRYMAN

A little while after this there came in a Dutch ship from Batavia; she was a coaster, not an European trader, of about two hundred tons burden; the men, as they pretended, having been so sickly that the captain had not hands enough to go to sea with, so he lay by at Bengal; and having, it seems, got money enough, or being willing, for other reasons, to go for Europe, he gave public notice he would sell his ship. This came to my ears before my new partner heard of it, and I had a great mind to buy it; so I went to him and told him of it. He considered a while, for he was no rash man neither; and at last replied, "She is a little too big—however, we will have her." Accordingly, we bought the ship, and agreeing with the master, we paid for her, and took possession. When we had done so we resolved to engage the men, if we could, to join with those we had, for the pursuing our business; but, on a sudden, they having received not their wages, but their share of the money, as we afterwards learned, not one of them was to be found; we inquired much about them, and at length were told that they were all gone together by land to Agra, the great city of the Mogul's residence, to proceed from thence to Surat, and then go by sea to the Gulf of Persia.

Nothing had so much troubled me a good while as that I should miss the opportunity of going with them; for such a ramble, I thought, and in such company as would both have guarded and diverted me, would have suited mightily with my great design; and I should have both seen the world and gone homeward too. But I was much better satisfied a few days after, when I came to know what sort of fellows they were; for, in short, their history was, that this man they called captain was the gunner only, not the commander; that they had been a trading voyage, in which they had been attacked on shore by some of the Malays, who had killed the captain and three of his men; and that after the captain was killed, these men, eleven in number, having resolved to run away with the ship, brought her to Bengal, leaving the mate and five men more on shore.

Well, let them get the ship how they would, we came honestly by her, as we thought, though we did not, I confess, examine into things so exactly as we ought; for we never inquired anything of the seamen, who would certainly have faltered in their account, and contradicted one another. Somehow or other we should have had reason to have suspected, them; but the man showed us a bill of sale for the ship, to one Emanuel Clostershoven, or some such name, for I suppose it was all a forgery, and called himself by that name, and we could not contradict him: and withal, having no suspicion of the thing, we went through with our bargain. We picked up some more English sailors here after this, and some Dutch, and now we resolved on a second voyage to the south-east for cloves, &c.—that is to say, among the Philippine and Malacca isles. In short, not to fill up this part of my story with trifles when what is to come is so remarkable, I spent, from first to last, six years in this country, trading from port to port, backward and forward, and with very good success, and was now the last year with my new partner, going in the ship above mentioned, on a voyage to China, but designing first to go to Siam to buy rice.

In this voyage, being by contrary winds obliged to beat up and down a great while in the Straits of Malacca and among the islands, we were no sooner got clear of those difficult seas than we found our ship had sprung a leak, but could not discover where it was. This forced us to make some port; and my partner, who knew the country better than I did, directed the captain to put into the river of Cambodia; for I had made the English mate, one Mr. Thompson, captain, not being willing to take the charge of the ship upon myself. This river lies on the north side of the great bay or gulf which goes up to Siam. While we were here, and going often on shore for refreshment, there comes to me one day an Englishman, a gunner's mate on board an English East India ship, then riding in the same river. "Sir," says he, addressing me, "you are a stranger to me, and I to you; but I have something to tell you that very nearly concerns you. I am moved by the imminent danger you are in, and, for aught I see, you have no knowledge of it."—"I know no danger I am in," said I, "but that my ship is leaky, and I cannot find it out; but I intend to lay her aground to-morrow, to see if I can find it."—"But, sir," says he, "leaky or not leaky, you will be wiser than to lay your ship on shore to-morrow when you hear what I have to say to you. Do you know, sir," said he, "the town of Cambodia lies about fifteen leagues up the river; and there are two large English ships about five leagues on this side, and three Dutch?"—"Well," said I, "and what is that to me?"—"Why, sir," said be, "is it for a man that is upon such adventures as you are to come into a port, and not examine first what ships there are there, and whether he is able to deal with them? I suppose you do not think you are a match for them?" I could not conceive what he meant; and I turned short upon him, and said: "I wish you would explain yourself; I cannot imagine what reason I have to be afraid of any of the company's ships, or Dutch ships. I am no interloper. What can they have to say to me?"—"Well, sir," says he, with a smile, "if you think yourself secure you must take your chance; but take my advice, if you do not put to sea immediately, you will the very next tide be attacked by five longboats full of men, and perhaps if you are taken you will be hanged for a pirate, and the particulars be examined afterwards. I thought, sir," added he, "I should have met with a better reception than this for doing you a piece of service of such importance."—"I can never be ungrateful," said I, "for any service, or to any man that offers me any kindness; but it is past my comprehension what they should have such a design upon me for: however, since you say there is no time to be lost, and that there is some villainous design on hand against me, I will go on board this minute, and put to sea immediately, if my men can stop the leak; but, sir," said I, "shall I go away ignorant of the cause of all this? Can you give me no further light into it?"

"I can tell you but part of the story, sir," says he; "but I have a Dutch seaman here with me, and I believe I could persuade him to tell you the rest; but there is scarce time for it. But the short of the story is this—the first part of which I suppose you know well enough—that you were with this ship at Sumatra; that there your captain was murdered by the Malays, with three of his men; and that you, or some of those that were on board with you, ran away with the ship, and are since turned pirates. This is the sum of the story, and you will all be seized as pirates, I can assure you, and executed with very little ceremony; for you know merchant ships show but little law to pirates if they get them into their power."—"Now you speak plain English," said I, "and I thank you; and though I know nothing that we have done like what you talk of, for I am sure we came honestly and fairly by the ship; yet seeing such a work is doing, as you say, and that you seem to mean honestly, I will be upon my guard."—"Nay, sir," says he, "do not talk of being upon your guard; the best defence is to be out of danger. If you have any regard for your life and the lives of all your men, put to sea without fail at high-water; and as you have a whole tide before you, you will be gone too far out before they can come down; for they will come away at high-water, and as they have twenty miles to come, you will get near two hours of them by the difference of the tide, not reckoning the length of the way: besides, as they are only boats, and not ships, they will not venture to follow you far out to sea, especially if it blows."—"Well," said I, "you have been very kind in this: what shall I do to make you amends?"—"Sir," says he, "you may not be willing to make me any amends, because you may not be convinced of the truth of it. I will make an offer to you: I have nineteen months' pay due to me on board the ship ---, which I came out of England in; and the Dutchman that is with me has seven months' pay due to him. If you will make good our pay to us we will go along with you; if you find nothing more in it we will desire no more; but if we do convince you that we have saved your lives, and the ship, and the lives of all the men in her, we will leave the rest to you."

I consented to this readily, and went immediately on board, and the two men with me. As soon as I came to the ship's side, my partner, who was on board, came out on the quarter-deck, and called to me, with a great deal of joy, "We have stopped the leak—we have stopped the leak!"—"Say you so?" said I; "thank God; but weigh anchor, then, immediately."—"Weigh!" says he; "what do you mean by that? What is the matter?"—"Ask no questions," said I; "but set all hands to work, and weigh without losing a minute." He was surprised; however, he called the captain, and he immediately ordered the anchor to be got up; and though the tide was not quite down, yet a little land-breeze blowing, we stood out to sea. Then I called him into the cabin, and told him the story; and we called in the men, and they told us the rest of it; but as it took up a great deal of time, before we had done a seaman comes to the cabin door, and called out to us that the captain bade him tell us we were chased by five sloops, or boats, full of men. "Very well," said I, "then it is apparent there is something in it." I then ordered all our men to be called up, and told them there was a design to seize the ship, and take us for pirates, and asked them if they would stand by us, and by one another; the men answered cheerfully, one and all, that they would live and die with us. Then I asked the captain what way he thought best for us to manage a fight with them; for resist them I was resolved we would, and that to the last drop. He said readily, that the way was to keep them off with our great shot as long as we could, and then to use our small arms, to keep them from boarding us; but when neither of these would do any longer, we would retire to our close quarters, for perhaps they had not materials to break open our bulkheads, or get in upon us.

The gunner had in the meantime orders to bring two guns, to bear fore and aft, out of the steerage, to clear the deck, and load them with musket-bullets, and small pieces of old iron, and what came next to hand. Thus we made ready for fight; but all this while we kept out to sea, with wind enough, and could see the boats at a distance, being five large longboats, following us with all the sail they could make.

Two of those boats (which by our glasses we could see were English) outsailed the rest, were near two leagues ahead of them, and gained upon us considerably, so that we found they would come up with us; upon which we fired a gun without ball, to intimate that they should bring to: and we put out a flag of truce, as a signal for parley: but they came crowding after us till within shot, when we took in our white flag, they having made no answer to it, and hung out a red flag, and fired at them with a shot. Notwithstanding this, they came on till they were near enough to call to them with a speaking-trumpet, bidding them keep off at their peril.

It was all one; they crowded after us, and endeavoured to come under our stern, so as to board us on our quarter; upon which, seeing they were resolute for mischief, and depended upon the strength that followed them, I ordered to bring the ship to, so that they lay upon our broadside; when immediately we fired five guns at them, one of which had been levelled so true as to carry away the stern of the hindermost boat, and we then forced them to take down their sail, and to run all to the head of the boat, to keep her from sinking; so she lay by, and had enough of it; but seeing the foremost boat crowd on after us, we made ready to fire at her in particular. While this was doing one of the three boats that followed made up to the boat which we had disabled, to relieve her, and we could see her take out the men. We then called again to the foremost boat, and offered a truce, to parley again, and to know what her business was with us; but had no answer, only she crowded close under our stern. Upon this, our gunner who was a very dexterous fellow ran out his two case-guns, and fired again at her, but the shot missing, the men in the boat shouted, waved their caps, and came on. The gunner, getting quickly ready again, fired among them a second time, one shot of which, though it missed the boat itself, yet fell in among the men, and we could easily see did a great deal of mischief among them. We now wore the ship again, and brought our quarter to bear upon them, and firing three guns more, we found the boat was almost split to pieces; in particular, her rudder and a piece of her stern were shot quite away; so they handed her sail immediately, and were in great disorder. To complete their misfortune, our gunner let fly two guns at them again; where he hit them we could not tell, but we found the boat was sinking, and some of the men already in the water: upon this, I immediately manned out our pinnace, with orders to pick up some of the men if they could, and save them from drowning, and immediately come on board ship with them, because we saw the rest of the boats began to come up. Our men in the pinnace followed their orders, and took up three men, one of whom was just drowning, and it was a good while before we could recover him. As soon as they were on board we crowded all the sail we could make, and stood farther out to the sea; and we found that when the other boats came up to the first, they gave over their chase.

Being thus delivered from a danger which, though I knew not the reason of it, yet seemed to be much greater than I apprehended, I resolved that we should change our course, and not let any one know whither we were going; so we stood out to sea eastward, quite out of the course of all European ships, whether they were bound to China or anywhere else, within the commerce of the European nations. When we were at sea we began to consult with the two seamen, and inquire what the meaning of all this should be; and the Dutchman confirmed the gunner's story about the false sale of the ship and of the murder of the captain, and also how that he, this Dutchman, and four more got into the woods, where they wandered about a great while, till at length he made his escape, and swam off to a Dutch ship, which was sailing near the shore in its way from China.

He then told us that he went to Batavia, where two of the seamen belonging to the ship arrived, having deserted the rest in their travels, and gave an account that the fellow who had run away with the ship, sold her at Bengal to a set of pirates, who were gone a-cruising in her, and that they had already taken an English ship and two Dutch ships very richly laden. This latter part we found to concern us directly, though we knew it to be false; yet, as my partner said, very justly, if we had fallen into their hands, and they had had such a prepossession against us beforehand, it had been in vain for us to have defended ourselves, or to hope for any good quarter at their hands; especially considering that our accusers had been our judges, and that we could have expected nothing from them but what rage would have dictated, and an ungoverned passion have executed. Therefore it was his opinion we should go directly back to Bengal, from whence we came, without putting in at any port whatever—because where we could give a good account of ourselves, could prove where we were when the ship put in, of whom we bought her, and the like; and what was more than all the rest, if we were put upon the necessity of bringing it before the proper judges, we should be sure to have some justice, and not to be hanged first and judged afterwards.

I was some time of my partner's opinion; but after a little more serious thinking, I told him I thought it was a very great hazard for us to attempt returning to Bengal, for that we were on the wrong side of the Straits of Malacca, and that if the alarm was given, we should be sure to be waylaid on every side—that if we should be taken, as it were, running away, we should even condemn ourselves, and there would want no more evidence to destroy us. I also asked the English sailor's opinion, who said he was of my mind, and that we certainly should be taken. This danger a little startled my partner and all the ship's company, and we immediately resolved to go away to the coast of Tonquin, and so on to the coast of China—and pursuing the first design as to trade, find some way or other to dispose of the ship, and come back in some of the vessels of the country such as we could get. This was approved of as the best method for our security, and accordingly we steered away NNE., keeping above fifty leagues off from the usual course to the eastward. This, however, put us to some inconvenience: for, first, the winds, when we came that distance from the shore, seemed to be more steadily against us, blowing almost trade, as we call it, from the E. and ENE., so that we were a long while upon our voyage, and we were but ill provided with victuals for so long a run; and what was still worse, there was some danger that those English and Dutch ships whose boats pursued us, whereof some were bound that way, might have got in before us, and if not, some other ship bound to China might have information of us from them, and pursue us with the same vigour.

I must confess I was now very uneasy, and thought myself, including the late escape from the longboats, to have been in the most dangerous condition that ever I was in through my past life; for whatever ill circumstances I had been in, I was never pursued for a thief before; nor had I ever done anything that merited the name of dishonest or fraudulent, much less thievish. I had chiefly been my own enemy, or, as I may rightly say, I had been nobody's enemy but my own; but now I was woefully embarrassed: for though I was perfectly innocent, I was in no condition to make that innocence appear; and if I had been taken, it had been under a supposed guilt of the worst kind. This made me very anxious to make an escape, though which way to do it I knew not, or what port or place we could go to. My partner endeavoured to encourage me by describing the several ports of that coast, and told me he would put in on the coast of Cochin China, or the bay of Tonquin, intending afterwards to go to Macao, where a great many European families resided, and particularly the missionary priests, who usually went thither in order to their going forward to China.

Hither then we resolved to go; and, accordingly, though after a tedious course, and very much straitened for provisions, we came within sight of the coast very early in the morning; and upon reflection on the past circumstances of danger we were in, we resolved to put into a small river, which, however, had depth enough of water for us, and to see if we could, either overland or by the ship's pinnace, come to know what ships were in any port thereabouts. This happy step was, indeed, our deliverance: for though we did not immediately see any European ships in the bay of Tonquin, yet the next morning there came into the bay two Dutch ships; and a third without any colours spread out, but which we believed to be a Dutchman, passed by at about two leagues' distance, steering for the coast of China; and in the afternoon went by two English ships steering the same course; and thus we thought we saw ourselves beset with enemies both one way and the other. The place we were in was wild and barbarous, the people thieves by occupation; and though it is true we had not much to seek of them, and, except getting a few provisions, cared not how little we had to do with them, yet it was with much difficulty that we kept ourselves from being insulted by them several ways. We were in a small river of this country, within a few leagues of its utmost limits northward; and by our boat we coasted north-east to the point of land which opens the great bay of Tonquin; and it was in this beating up along the shore that we discovered we were surrounded with enemies. The people we were among were the most barbarous of all the inhabitants of the coast; and among other customs they have this one: that if any vessel has the misfortune to be shipwrecked upon their coast, they make the men all prisoners or slaves; and it was not long before we found a spice of their kindness this way, on the occasion following.

I have observed above that our ship sprung a leak at sea, and that we could not find it out; and it happened that, as I have said, it was stopped unexpectedly, on the eve of our being pursued by the Dutch and English ships in the bay of Siam; yet, as we did not find the ship so perfectly tight and sound as we desired, we resolved while we were at this place to lay her on shore, and clean her bottom, and, if possible, to find out where the leaks were. Accordingly, having lightened the ship, and brought all our guns and other movables to one side, we tried to bring her down, that we might come at her bottom; but, on second thoughts, we did not care to lay her on dry ground, neither could we find out a proper place for it.

12

THE CARPENTER'S WHIMSICAL CONTRIVANCE

The inhabitants came wondering down the shore to look at us; and seeing the ship lie down on one side in such a manner, and heeling in towards the shore, and not seeing our men, who were at work on her bottom with stages, and with their boats on the off-side, they presently concluded that the ship was cast away, and lay fast on the ground. On this supposition they came about us in two or three hours' time with ten or twelve large boats, having some of them eight, some ten men in a boat, intending, no doubt, to have come on board and plundered the ship, and if they found us there, to have carried us away for slaves.

When they came up to the ship, and began to row round her, they discovered us all hard at work on the outside of the ship's bottom and side, washing, and graving, and stopping, as every seafaring man knows how. They stood for a while gazing at us, and we, who were a little surprised, could not imagine what their design was; but being willing to be sure, we took this opportunity to get some of us into the ship, and others to hand down arms and ammunition to those that were at work, to defend themselves with if there should be occasion. And it was no more than need: for in less than a quarter of an hour's consultation, they agreed, it seems, that the ship was really a wreck, and that we were all at work endeavouring to save her, or to save our lives by the help of our boats; and when we handed our arms into the boat, they concluded, by that act, that we were endeavouring to save some of our goods. Upon this, they took it for granted we all belonged to them, and away they came directly upon our men, as if it had been in a line-of-battle.

Our men, seeing so many of them, began to be frightened, for we lay but in an ill posture to fight, and cried out to us to know what they should do. I immediately called to the men that worked upon the stages to slip them down, and get up the side into the ship, and bade those in the boat to row round and come on board. The few who were on board worked with all the strength and hands we had to bring the ship to rights; however, neither the men upon the stages nor those in the boats could do as they were ordered before the Cochin Chinese were upon them, when two of their boats boarded our longboat, and began to lay hold of the men as their prisoners.

The first man they laid hold of was an English seaman, a stout, strong fellow, who having a musket in his hand, never offered to fire it, but laid it down in the boat, like a fool, as I thought; but he understood his business better than I could teach him, for he grappled the Pagan, and dragged him by main force out of their boat into ours, where, taking him by the ears, he beat his head so against the boat's gunnel that the fellow died in his hands. In the meantime, a Dutchman, who stood next, took up the musket, and with the butt-end of it so laid about him, that he knocked down five of them who attempted to enter the boat. But this was doing little towards resisting thirty or forty men, who, fearless because ignorant of their danger, began to throw themselves into the longboat, where we had but five men in all to defend it; but the following accident, which deserved our laughter, gave our men a complete victory.

Our carpenter being prepared to grave the outside of the ship, as well as to pay the seams where he had caulked her to stop the leaks, had got two kettles just let down into the boat, one filled with boiling pitch, and the other with rosin, tallow, and oil, and such stuff as the shipwrights use for that work; and the man that attended the carpenter had a great iron ladle in his hand, with which he supplied the men that were at work with the hot stuff. Two of the enemy's men entered the boat just where this fellow stood in the foresheets; he immediately saluted them with a ladle full of the stuff, boiling hot which so burned and scalded them, being half-naked that they roared out like bulls, and, enraged with the fire, leaped both into the sea. The carpenter saw it, and cried out, "Well done, Jack! give them some more of it!" and stepping forward himself, takes one of the mops, and dipping it in the pitch-pot, he and his man threw it among them so plentifully that, in short, of all the men in the three boats, there was not one that escaped being scalded in a most frightful manner, and made such a howling and crying that I never heard a worse noise.

I was never better pleased with a victory in my life; not only as it was a perfect surprise to me, and that our danger was imminent before, but as we got this victory without any bloodshed, except of that man the seaman killed with his naked hands, and which I was very much concerned at. Although it maybe a just thing, because necessary (for there is no necessary wickedness in nature), yet I thought it was a sad sort of life, when we must be always obliged to be killing our fellow-creatures to preserve ourselves; and, indeed, I think so still; and I would even now suffer a great deal rather than I would take away the life even of the worst person injuring me; and I believe all considering people, who know the value of life, would be of my opinion, if they entered seriously into the consideration of it.

All the while this was doing, my partner and I, who managed the rest of the men on board, had with great dexterity brought the ship almost to rights, and having got the guns into their places again, the gunner called to me to bid our boat get out of the way, for he would let fly among them. I called back again to him, and bid him not offer to fire, for the carpenter would do the work without him; but bid him heat another pitch-kettle, which our cook, who was on broad, took care of. However, the enemy was so terrified with what they had met with in their first attack, that they would not come on again; and some of them who were farthest off, seeing the ship swim, as it were, upright, began, as we suppose, to see their mistake, and gave over the enterprise, finding it was not as they expected. Thus we got clear of this merry fight; and having got some rice and some roots and bread, with about sixteen hogs, on board two days before, we resolved to stay here no longer, but go forward, whatever came of it; for we made no doubt but we should be surrounded the next day with rogues enough, perhaps more than our pitch-kettle would dispose of for us. We therefore got all our things on board the same evening, and the next morning were ready to sail: in the meantime, lying at anchor at some distance from the shore, we were not so much concerned, being now in a fighting posture, as well as in a sailing posture, if any enemy had presented.

The next day, having finished our work within board, and finding our ship was perfectly healed of all her leaks, we set sail. We would have gone into the bay of Tonquin, for we wanted to inform ourselves of what was to be known concerning the Dutch ships that had been there; but we durst not stand in there, because we had seen several ships go in, as we supposed, but a little before; so we kept on NE. towards the island of Formosa, as much afraid of being seen by a Dutch or English merchant ship as a Dutch or English merchant ship in the Mediterranean is of an Algerine man-of-war.

When we were thus got to sea, we kept on NE., as if we would go to the Manillas or the Philippine Islands; and this we did that we might not fall into the way of any of the European ships; and then we steered north, till we came to the latitude of 22 degrees 30 seconds, by which means we made the island of Formosa directly, where we came to an anchor, in order to get water and fresh provisions, which the people there, who are very courteous in their manners, supplied us with willingly, and dealt very fairly and punctually with us in all their agreements and bargains. This is what we did not find among other people, and may be owing to the remains of Christianity which was once planted here by a Dutch missionary of Protestants, and it is a testimony of what I have often observed, viz. that the Christian religion always civilises the people, and reforms their manners, where it is received, whether it works saving effects upon them or no.

From thence we sailed still north, keeping the coast of China at an equal distance, till we knew we were beyond all the ports of China where our European ships usually come; being resolved, if possible, not to fall into any of their hands, especially in this country, where, as our circumstances were, we could not fail of being entirely ruined. Being now come to the latitude of 30 degrees, we resolved to put into the first trading port we should come at; and standing in for the shore, a boat came of two leagues to us with an old Portuguese pilot on board, who, knowing us to be an European ship, came to offer his service, which, indeed, we were glad of and took him on board; upon which, without asking us whither we would go, he dismissed the boat he came in, and sent it back. I thought it was now so much in our choice to make the old man carry us whither we would, that I began to talk to him about carrying us to the Gulf of Nankin, which is the most northern part of the coast of China. The old man said he knew the Gulf of Nankin very well; but smiling, asked us what we would do there? I told him we would sell our cargo and purchase China wares, calicoes, raw silks, tea, wrought silks, &c.; and so we would return by the same course we came. He told us our best port would have been to put in at Macao, where we could not have failed of a market for our opium to our satisfaction, and might for our money have purchased all sorts of China goods as cheap as we could at Nankin.

Not being able to put the old man out of his talk, of which he was very opinionated or conceited, I told him we were gentlemen as well as merchants, and that we had a mind to go and see the great city of Pekin, and the famous court of the monarch of China. "Why, then," says the old man, "you should go to Ningpo, where, by the river which runs into the sea there, you may go up within five leagues of the great canal. This canal is a navigable stream, which goes through the heart of that vast empire of China, crosses all the rivers, passes some considerable hills by the help of sluices and gates, and goes up to the city of Pekin, being in length near two hundred and seventy leagues."—"Well," said I, "Seignior Portuguese, but that is not our business now; the great question is, if you can carry us up to the city of Nankin, from whence we can travel to Pekin afterwards?" He said he could do so very well, and that there was a great Dutch ship gone up that way just before. This gave me a little shock, for a Dutch ship was now our terror, and we had much rather have met the devil, at least if he had not come in too frightful a figure; and we depended upon it that a Dutch ship would be our destruction, for we were in no condition to fight them; all the ships they trade with into those parts being of great burden, and of much greater force than we were.

The old man found me a little confused, and under some concern when he named a Dutch ship, and said to me, "Sir, you need be under no apprehensions of the Dutch; I suppose they are not now at war with your nation?"—"No," said I, "that's true; but I know not what liberties men may take when they are out of the reach of the laws of their own country."—"Why," says he, "you are no pirates; what need you fear? They will not meddle with peaceable merchants, sure." These words put me into the greatest disorder and confusion imaginable; nor was it possible for me to conceal it so, but the old man easily perceived it.

"Sir," says he, "I find you are in some disorder in your thoughts at my talk: pray be pleased to go which way you think fit, and depend upon it, I'll do you all the service I can." Upon this we fell into further discourse, in which, to my alarm and amazement, he spoke of the villainous doings of a certain pirate ship that had long been the talk of mariners in those seas; no other, in a word, than the very ship he was now on board of, and which we had so unluckily purchased. I presently saw there was no help for it but to tell him the plain truth, and explain all the danger and trouble we had suffered through this misadventure, and, in particular, our earnest wish to be speedily quit of the ship altogether; for which reason we had resolved to carry her up to Nankin.

The old man was amazed at this relation, and told us we were in the right to go away to the north; and that, if he might advise us, it should be to sell the ship in China, which we might well do, and buy, or build another in the country; adding that I should meet with customers enough for the ship at Nankin, that a Chinese junk would serve me very well to go back again, and that he would procure me people both to buy one and sell the other. "Well, but, seignior," said I, "as you say they know the ship so well, I may, perhaps, if I follow your measures, be instrumental to bring some honest, innocent men into a terrible broil; for wherever they find the ship they will prove the guilt upon the men, by proving this was the ship."—"Why," says the old man, "I'll find out a way to prevent that; for as I know all those commanders you speak of very well, and shall see them all as they pass by, I will be sure to set them to rights in the thing, and let them know that they had been so much in the wrong; that though the people who were on board at first might run away with the ship, yet it was not true that they had turned pirates; and that, in particular, these were not the men that first went off with the ship, but innocently bought her for their trade; and I am persuaded they will so far believe me as at least to act more cautiously for the time to come."

In about thirteen days' sail we came to an anchor, at the south-west point of the great Gulf of Nankin; where I learned by accident that two Dutch ships were gone the length before me, and that I should certainly fall into their hands. I consulted my partner again in this exigency, and he was as much at a loss as I was. I then asked the old pilot if there was no creek or harbour which I might put into and pursue my business with the Chinese privately, and be in no danger of the enemy. He told me if I would sail to the southward about forty-two leagues, there was a little port called Quinchang, where the fathers of the mission usually landed from Macao, on their progress to teach the Christian religion to the Chinese, and where no European ships ever put in; and if I thought to put in there, I might consider what further course to take when I was on shore. He confessed, he said, it was not a place for merchants, except that at some certain times they had a kind of a fair there, when the merchants from Japan came over thither to buy Chinese merchandises. The name of the port I may perhaps spell wrong, having lost this, together with the names of many other places set down in a little pocket-book, which was spoiled by the water by an accident; but this I remember, that the Chinese merchants we corresponded with called it by a different name from that which our Portuguese pilot gave it, who pronounced it Quinchang. As we were unanimous in our resolution to go to this place, we weighed the next day, having only gone twice on shore where we were, to get fresh water; on both which occasions the people of the country were very civil, and brought abundance of provisions to sell to us; but nothing without money.

We did not come to the other port (the wind being contrary) for five days; but it was very much to our satisfaction, and I was thankful when I set my foot on shore, resolving, and my partner too, that if it was possible to dispose of ourselves and effects any other way, though not profitably, we would never more set foot on board that unhappy vessel. Indeed, I must acknowledge, that of all the circumstances of life that ever I had any experience of, nothing makes mankind so completely miserable as that of being in constant fear. Well does the Scripture say, "The fear of man brings a snare"; it is a life of death, and the mind is so entirely oppressed by it, that it is capable of no relief.

Nor did it fail of its usual operations upon the fancy, by heightening every danger; representing the English and Dutch captains to be men incapable of hearing reason, or of distinguishing between honest men and rogues; or between a story calculated for our own turn, made out of nothing, on purpose to deceive, and a true, genuine account of our whole voyage, progress, and design; for we might many ways have convinced any reasonable creatures that we were not pirates; the goods we had on board, the course we steered, our frankly showing ourselves, and entering into such and such ports; and even our very manner, the force we had, the number of men, the few arms, the little ammunition, short provisions; all these would have served to convince any men that we were no pirates. The opium and other goods we had on board would make it appear the ship had been at Bengal. The Dutchmen, who, it was said, had the names of all the men that were in the ship, might easily see that we were a mixture of English, Portuguese, and Indians, and but two Dutchmen on board. These, and many other particular circumstances, might have made it evident to the understanding of any commander, whose hands we might fall into, that we were no pirates.

But fear, that blind, useless passion, worked another way, and threw us into the vapours; it bewildered our understandings, and set the imagination at work to form a thousand terrible things that perhaps might never happen. We first supposed, as indeed everybody had related to us, that the seamen on board the English and Dutch ships, but especially the Dutch, were so enraged at the name of a pirate, and especially at our beating off their boats and escaping, that they would not give themselves leave to inquire whether we were pirates or no, but would execute us off-hand, without giving us any room for a defence. We reflected that there really was so much apparent evidence before them, that they would scarce inquire after any more; as, first, that the ship was certainly the same, and that some of the seamen among them knew her, and had been on board her; and, secondly, that when we had intelligence at the river of Cambodia that they were coming down to examine us, we fought their boats and fled. Therefore we made no doubt but they were as fully satisfied of our being pirates as we were satisfied of the contrary; and, as I often said, I know not but I should have been apt to have taken those circumstances for evidence, if the tables were turned, and my case was theirs; and have made no scruple of cutting all the crew to pieces, without believing, or perhaps considering, what they might have to offer in their defence.

But let that be how it will, these were our apprehensions; and both my partner and I scarce slept a night without dreaming of halters and yard-arms; of fighting, and being taken; of killing, and being killed: and one night I was in such a fury in my dream, fancying the

Dutchmen had boarded us, and I was knocking one of their seamen down, that I struck my doubled fist against the side of the cabin I lay in with such a force as wounded my hand grievously, broke my knuckles, and cut and bruised the flesh, so that it awaked me out of my sleep. Another apprehension I had was, the cruel usage we might meet with from them if we fell into their hands; then the story of Amboyna came into my head, and how the Dutch might perhaps torture us, as they did our countrymen there, and make some of our men, by extremity of torture, confess to crimes they never were guilty of, or own themselves and all of us to be pirates, and so they would put us to death with a formal appearance of justice; and that they might be tempted to do this for the gain of our ship and cargo, worth altogether four or five thousand pounds. We did not consider that the captains of ships have no authority to act thus; and if we had surrendered prisoners to them, they could not answer the destroying us, or torturing us, but would be accountable for it when they came to their country. However, if they were to act thus with us, what advantage would it be to us that they should be called to an account for it?—or if we were first to be murdered, what satisfaction would it be to us to have them punished when they came home?

I cannot refrain taking notice here what reflections I now had upon the vast variety of my particular circumstances; how hard I thought it that I, who had spent forty years in a life of continual difficulties, and was at last come, as it were, to the port or haven which all men drive at, viz. to have rest and plenty, should be a volunteer in new sorrows by my own unhappy choice, and that I, who had escaped so many dangers in my youth, should now come to be hanged in my old age, and in so remote a place, for a crime which I was not in the least inclined to, much less guilty of. After these thoughts something of religion would come in; and I would be considering that this seemed to me to be a disposition of immediate Providence, and I ought to look upon it and submit to it as such. For, although I was innocent as to men, I was far from being innocent as to my Maker; and I ought to look in and examine what other crimes in my life were most obvious to me, and for which Providence might justly inflict this punishment as a retribution; and thus I ought to submit to this, just as I would to a shipwreck, if it had pleased God to have brought such a disaster upon me.

In its turn natural courage would sometimes take its place, and then I would be talking myself up to vigorous resolutions; that I would not be taken to be barbarously used by a parcel of merciless wretches in cold blood; that it were much better to have fallen into the hands of the savages, though I were sure they would feast upon me when they had taken me, than those who would perhaps glut their rage upon me by inhuman tortures and barbarities; that in the case of the savages, I always resolved to die fighting to the last gasp, and why should I not do so now? Whenever these thoughts prevailed, I was sure to put myself into a kind of fever with the agitation of a supposed fight; my blood would boil, and my eyes sparkle, as if I was engaged, and I always resolved to take no quarter at their hands; but even at last, if I could resist no longer, I would blow up the ship and all that was in her, and leave them but little booty to boast of.

13

ARRIVAL IN CHINA

The greater weight the anxieties and perplexities of these things were to our thoughts while we were at sea, the greater was our satisfaction when we saw ourselves on shore; and my partner told me he dreamed that he had a very heavy load upon his back, which he was to carry up a hill, and found that he was not able to stand longer under it; but that the Portuguese pilot came and took it off his back, and the hill disappeared, the ground before him appearing all smooth and plain: and truly it was so; they were all like men who had a load taken off their backs. For my part I had a weight taken off from my heart that it was not able any longer to bear; and as I said above we resolved to go no more to sea in that ship. When we came on shore, the old pilot, who was now our friend, got us a lodging, together with a warehouse for our goods; it was a little hut, with a larger house adjoining to it, built and also palisadoed round with canes, to keep out pilferers, of which there were not a few in that country: however, the magistrates allowed us a little guard, and we had a soldier with a kind of half-pike, who stood sentinel at our door, to whom we allowed a pint of rice and a piece of money about the value of three-pence per day, so that our goods were kept very safe.

The fair or mart usually kept at this place had been over some time; however, we found that there were three or four junks in the river, and two ships from Japan, with goods which they had bought in China, and were not gone away, having some Japanese merchants on shore.

The first thing our old Portuguese pilot did for us was to get us acquainted with three missionary Romish priests who were in the town, and who had been there some time converting the people to Christianity; but we thought they made but poor work of it, and made them but sorry Christians when they had done. One of these was a Frenchman, whom they called Father Simon; another was a Portuguese; and a third a Genoese. Father Simon was courteous, and very agreeable company; but the other two were more reserved, seemed rigid and austere, and applied seriously to the work they came about, viz. to talk with and insinuate themselves among the inhabitants wherever they had opportunity. We often ate and drank with those men; and though I must confess the conversion, as they call it, of the Chinese to Christianity is so far from the true conversion required to bring heathen people to the faith of Christ, that it seems to amount to little more than letting them know the name of Christ, and say some prayers to the Virgin Mary and her Son, in a tongue which they understood not, and to cross themselves, and the like; yet it must be confessed that the religionists, whom we call missionaries, have a firm belief that these people will be saved, and that they are the instruments of it; and on this account they undergo not only the fatigue of the voyage, and the hazards of living in such places, but oftentimes death itself, and the most violent tortures, for the sake of this work.

Father Simon was appointed, it seems, by order of the chief of the mission, to go up to Pekin, and waited only for another priest, who was ordered to come to him from Macao, to go along with him. We scarce ever met together but he was inviting me to go that journey; telling me how he would show me all the glorious things of that mighty empire, and, among the rest, Pekin, the greatest city in the world: "A city," said he, "that your London and our Paris put together cannot be equal to." But as I looked on those things with different eyes from other men, so I shall give my opinion of them in a few words, when I come in the course of my travels to speak more particularly of them.

Dining with Father Simon one day, and being very merry together, I showed some little inclination to go with him; and he pressed me and my partner very hard to consent. "Why, father," says my partner, "should you desire our company so much? you know we are heretics, and you do not love us, nor cannot keep us company with any pleasure."—"Oh," says he, "you may perhaps be good Catholics in time; my business here is to convert heathens, and who knows but I may convert you too?"—"Very well, father," said I, "so you will preach to us all the way?"—"I will not be troublesome to you," says he; "our religion does not divest us of good manners; besides, we are here like countrymen; and so we are, compared to the place we are in; and if you are Huguenots, and I a Catholic, we may all be Christians at last; at least, we are all gentlemen, and we may converse so, without being uneasy to one another." I liked this part of his discourse very well, and it began to put me in mind of my priest that I had left in the Brazils; but Father Simon did not come up to his character by a great deal; for though this friar had no appearance of a criminal levity in him, yet he had not that fund of Christian zeal, strict piety, and sincere affection to religion that my other good ecclesiastic had.

But to leave him a little, though he never left us, nor solicited us to go with him; we had something else before us at first, for we had all this while our ship and our merchandise to dispose of, and we began to be very doubtful what we should do, for we were now in a place of very little business. Once I was about to venture to sail for the river of Kilam, and the city of Nankin; but Providence seemed now more visibly, as I thought, than ever to concern itself in our affairs; and I was encouraged, from this very time, to think I should, one way or other, get out of this entangled circumstance, and be brought home to my own country again, though I had not the least view of the manner. Providence, I say, began here to clear up our way a little; and the first thing that offered was, that our old Portuguese pilot brought a Japan merchant to us, who inquired what goods we had: and, in the first place, he bought all our opium, and gave us a very good price for it, paying us in gold by weight, some in small pieces of their own coin, and some in small wedges, of about ten or twelves ounces each. While we were dealing with him for our opium, it came into my head that he might perhaps deal for the ship too, and I ordered the interpreter to propose it to him. He shrunk up his shoulders at it when it was first proposed to him; but in a few days after he came to me, with one of the missionary priests for his interpreter, and told me he had a proposal to make to me, which was this: he had bought a great quantity of our goods, when he had no thoughts of proposals made to him of buying the ship; and that, therefore, he had not money to pay for the ship: but if I would let the same men who were in the ship navigate her, he would hire the ship to go to Japan; and would send them from thence to the Philippine Islands with another loading, which he would pay the freight of before they went from Japan: and that at their return he would buy the ship. I began to listen to his proposal, and so eager did my head still run upon rambling, that I could not but begin to entertain a notion of going myself with him, and so to set sail from the Philippine Islands away to the South Seas; accordingly, I asked the Japanese merchant if he would not hire us to the Philippine Islands and discharge us there. He said No, he could not do that, for then he could not have the return of his cargo; but he would discharge us in Japan, at the ship's return. Well, still I was for taking him at that proposal, and going myself; but my partner, wiser than myself, persuaded me from it, representing the dangers, as well of the seas as of the Japanese, who are a false, cruel, and treacherous people; likewise those of the Spaniards at the Philippines, more false, cruel, and treacherous than they.

But to bring this long turn of our affairs to a conclusion; the first thing we had to do was to consult with the captain of the ship, and with his men, and know if they were willing to go to Japan. While I was doing this, the young man whom my nephew had left with me as my companion came up, and told me that he thought that voyage promised very fair, and that there was a great prospect of advantage, and he would be very glad if I undertook it; but that if I would not, and would give him leave, he would go as a merchant, or as I pleased to order him; that if ever he came to England, and I was there and alive, he would render me a faithful account of his success, which should be as much mine as I pleased. I was loath to part with him; but considering the prospect of advantage, which really was considerable, and that he was a young fellow likely to do well in it, I inclined to let him go; but I told him I would consult my partner, and give him an answer the next day. I discoursed about it with my partner, who thereupon made a most generous offer: "You know it has been an unlucky ship," said he, "and we both resolve not to go to sea in it again; if your steward" (so he called my man) "will venture the voyage, I will leave my share of the vessel to him, and let him make the best of it; and if we live to meet in England, and he meets with success abroad, he shall account for one half of the profits of the ship's freight to us; the other shall be his own."

If my partner, who was no way concerned with my young man, made him such an offer, I could not do less than offer him the same; and all the ship's company being willing to go with him, we made over half the ship to him in property, and took a writing from him, obliging him to account for the other, and away he went to Japan. The Japan merchant proved a very punctual, honest man to him: protected him at Japan, and got him a licence to come on shore, which the Europeans in general have not lately obtained. He paid him his freight very punctually; sent him to the Philippines loaded with Japan and China wares, and a supercargo of their own, who, trafficking with the Spaniards, brought back European goods again, and a great quantity of spices; and there he was not only paid his freight very well, and at a very good price, but not being willing to sell the ship, then the merchant furnished him goods on his own account; and with some money, and some spices of his own which he brought with him, he went back to the Manillas, where he sold his cargo very well. Here, having made a good acquaintance at Manilla, he got his ship made a free ship, and the governor of Manilla hired him to go to Acapulco, on the coast of America, and gave him a licence to land there, and to travel to Mexico, and to pass in any Spanish ship to Europe with all his men. He made the voyage to Acapulco very happily, and there he sold his ship: and having there also obtained allowance to travel by land to Porto Bello, he found means to get to Jamaica, with all his treasure, and about eight years after came to England exceeding rich.

But to return to our particular affairs, being now to part with the ship and ship's company, it came before us, of course, to consider what recompense we should give to the two men that gave us such timely notice of the design against us in the river Cambodia. The truth was, they had done us a very considerable service, and deserved well at our hands; though, by the way, they were a couple of rogues, too; for, as they believed the story of our being pirates, and that we had really run away with the ship, they came down to us, not only to betray the design that was formed against us, but to go to sea with us as pirates. One of them confessed afterwards that nothing else but the hopes of going a-roguing brought him to do it: however, the service they did us was not the less, and therefore, as I had promised to be grateful to them, I first ordered the money to be paid them which they said was due to them on board their respective ships: over and above that, I gave each of them a small sum of money in gold, which contented them very well. I then made the Englishman gunner in the ship, the gunner being now made second mate and purser; the Dutchman I made boatswain; so they were both very well pleased, and proved very serviceable, being both able seamen, and very stout fellows.

We were now on shore in China; if I thought myself banished, and remote from my own country at Bengal, where I had many ways to get home for my money, what could I think of myself now, when I was about a thousand leagues farther off from home, and destitute of all manner of prospect of return? All we had for it was this: that in about four months' time there was to be another fair at the place where we were, and then we might be able to purchase various manufactures of the country, and withal might possibly find some Chinese junks from Tonquin for sail, that would carry us and our goods whither we pleased. This I liked very well, and resolved to wait; besides, as our particular persons were not obnoxious, so if any English or Dutch ships came thither, perhaps we might have an opportunity to load our goods, and get passage to some other place in India nearer home. Upon these hopes we resolved to continue here; but, to divert ourselves, we took two or three journeys into the country.

First, we went ten days' journey to Nankin, a city well worth seeing; they say it has a million of people in it: it is regularly built, and the streets are all straight, and cross one another in direct lines. But when I come to compare the miserable people of these countries with ours, their fabrics, their manner of living, their government, their religion, their wealth, and their glory, as some call it, I must confess that I scarcely think it worth my while to mention them here. We wonder at the grandeur, the riches, the pomp, the ceremonies, the government, the manufactures, the commerce, and conduct of these people; not that there is really any matter for wonder, but because, having a true notion of the barbarity of those countries, the rudeness and the ignorance that prevail there, we do not expect to find any such thing so far off. Otherwise, what are their buildings to the palaces and royal buildings of Europe? What their trade to the universal commerce of England, Holland, France, and Spain? What are their cities to ours, for wealth, strength, gaiety of apparel, rich furniture, and infinite variety? What are their ports, supplied with a few junks and barks, to our navigation, our merchant fleets, our large and powerful navies? Our city of London has more trade than half their mighty empire: one English, Dutch, or French man-of-war of eighty guns would be able to fight almost all the shipping belonging to China: but the greatness of their wealth, their trade, the power of their government, and the strength of their armies, may be a little surprising to us, because, as I have said, considering them as a barbarous nation of pagans, little better than savages, we did not expect such things among them. But all the forces of their empire, though they were to bring two millions of men into the field together, would be able to do nothing but ruin the country and starve themselves; a million of their foot could not stand before one embattled body of our infantry, posted so as not to be surrounded, though they were not to be one to twenty in number; nay, I do not boast if I say that thirty thousand German or English foot, and ten thousand horse, well managed, could defeat all the forces of China. Nor is there a fortified town in China that could hold out one month against the batteries and attacks of an European army. They have firearms, it is true, but they are awkward and uncertain in their going off; and their powder has but little strength. Their armies are badly disciplined, and want skill to attack, or temper to retreat; and therefore, I must confess, it seemed strange to me, when I came home, and heard our people say such fine things of the power, glory, magnificence, and trade of the Chinese; because, as far as I saw, they appeared to be a contemptible herd or crowd of ignorant, sordid slaves, subjected to a government qualified only to rule such a people; and were not its distance inconceivably, great from Muscovy, and that empire in a manner as rude, impotent, and ill governed as they, the Czar of Muscovy might with ease drive them all out of their country, and conquer them in one campaign; and had the Czar (who is now a growing prince) fallen this way, instead of attacking the warlike Swedes, and equally improved himself in the art of war, as they say he has done; and if none of the powers of Europe had envied or interrupted him, he might by this time have been Emperor of China, instead of being beaten by the King of Sweden at Narva, when the latter was not one to six in number.

As their strength and their grandeur, so their navigation, commerce, and husbandry are very imperfect, compared to the same things in Europe; also, in their knowledge, their learning, and in their skill in the sciences, they are either very awkward or defective, though they have globes or spheres, and a smattering of the mathematics, and think they know more than all the world besides. But they know little of the motions of the heavenly bodies; and so grossly and absurdly ignorant are their common people, that when the sun is eclipsed, they think a great dragon has assaulted it, and is going to run away with it; and they fall a clattering with all the drums and kettles in the country, to fright the monster away, just as we do to hive a swarm of bees!

As this is the only excursion of the kind which I have made in all the accounts I have given of my travels, so I shall make no more such. It is none of my business, nor any part of my design; but to give an account of my own adventures through a life of inimitable wanderings, and a long variety of changes, which, perhaps, few that come after me will have heard the like of: I shall, therefore, say very little of all the mighty places, desert countries, and numerous people I have yet to pass through, more than relates to my own story, and which my concern among them will make necessary.

I was now, as near as I can compute, in the heart of China, about thirty degrees north of the line, for we were returned from Nankin. I had indeed a mind to see the city of Pekin, which I had heard so much of, and Father Simon importuned me daily to do it. At length his time of going away being set, and the other missionary who was to go with him being arrived from Macao, it was necessary that we should resolve either to go or not; so I referred it to my partner, and left it wholly to his choice, who at length resolved it in the affirmative, and we prepared for our journey. We set out with very good advantage as to finding the way; for we got leave to travel in the retinue of one of their mandarins, a kind of viceroy or principal magistrate in the province where they reside, and who take great state upon them, travelling with great attendance, and great homage from the people, who are sometimes greatly impoverished by them, being obliged to furnish provisions for them and all their attendants in their journeys. I particularly observed in our travelling with his baggage, that though we received sufficient provisions both for ourselves and our horses from the country, as belonging to the mandarin, yet we were obliged to pay for everything we had, after the market price of the country, and the mandarin's steward collected it duly from us. Thus our travelling in the retinue of the mandarin, though it was a great act of kindness, was not such a mighty favour to us, but was a great advantage to him, considering there were above thirty other people travelled in the same manner besides us, under the protection of his retinue; for the country furnished all the provisions for nothing to him, and yet he took our money for them.

We were twenty-five days travelling to Pekin, through a country exceeding populous, but I think badly cultivated; the husbandry, the economy, and the way of living miserable, though they boast so much of the industry of the people: I say miserable, if compared with our own, but not so to these poor wretches, who know no other. The pride of the poor people is infinitely great, and exceeded by nothing but their poverty, in some parts, which adds to that which I call their misery; and I must needs think the savages of America live much more happy than the poorer sort of these, because as they have nothing, so they desire nothing; whereas these are proud and insolent and in the main are in many parts mere beggars and drudges. Their ostentation is inexpressible; and, if they can, they love to keep multitudes of servants or slaves, which is to the last degree ridiculous, as well as their contempt of all the world but themselves.

I must confess I travelled more pleasantly afterwards in the deserts and vast wildernesses of Grand Tartary than here, and yet the roads here are well paved and well kept, and very convenient for travellers; but nothing was more awkward to me than to see such a haughty, imperious, insolent people, in the midst of the grossest simplicity and ignorance; and my friend Father Simon and I used to be very merry upon these occasions, to see their beggarly pride. For example, coming by the house of a country gentleman, as Father Simon called him, about ten leagues off the city of Nankin, we had first of all the honour to ride with the master of the house about two miles; the state he rode in was a perfect Don Quixotism, being a mixture of pomp and poverty. His habit was very proper for a merry-andrew, being a dirty calico, with hanging sleeves, tassels, and cuts and slashes almost on every side: it covered a taffety vest, so greasy as to testify that his honour must be a most exquisite sloven. His horse was a poor, starved, hobbling creature, and two slaves followed him on foot to drive the poor creature along; he had a whip in his hand, and he belaboured the beast as fast about the head as his slaves did about the tail; and thus he rode by us, with about ten or twelve servants, going from the city to his country seat, about half a league before us. We travelled on gently, but this figure of a gentleman rode away before us; and as we stopped at a village about an hour to refresh us, when we came by the country seat of this great man, we saw him in a little place before his door, eating a repast. It was a kind of garden, but he was easy to be seen; and we were given to understand that the more we looked at him the better he would be pleased. He sat under a tree, something like the palmetto, which effectually shaded him over the head, and on the south side; but under the tree was placed a large umbrella, which made that part look well enough. He sat lolling back in a great elbow-chair, being a heavy corpulent man, and had his meat brought him by two women slaves. He had two more, one of whom fed the squire with a spoon, and the other held the dish with one hand, and scraped off what he let fall upon his worship's beard and taffety vest.

Leaving the poor wretch to please himself with our looking at him, as if we admired his idle pomp, we pursued our journey. Father Simon had the curiosity to stay to inform himself what dainties the country justice had to feed on in all his state, which he had the honour to taste of, and which was, I think, a mess of boiled rice, with a great piece of garlic in it, and a little bag filled with green pepper, and another plant which they have there, something like our ginger, but smelling like musk, and tasting like mustard; all this was put together, and a small piece of lean mutton boiled in it, and this was his worship's repast. Four or five servants more attended at a distance, who we supposed were to eat of the same after their master. As for our mandarin with whom we travelled, he was respected as a king, surrounded always with his gentlemen, and attended in all his appearances with such pomp, that I saw little of him but at a distance. I observed that there was not a horse in his retinue but that our carrier's packhorses in England seemed to me to look much better; though it was hard to judge rightly, for they were so covered with equipage, mantles, trappings, &c., that we could scarce see anything but their feet and their heads as they went along.

I was now light-hearted, and all my late trouble and perplexity being over, I had no anxious thoughts about me, which made this journey the pleasanter to me; in which no ill accident attended me, only in passing or fording a small river, my horse fell and made me free of the country, as they call it—that is to say, threw me in. The place was not deep, but it wetted me all over. I mention it because it spoiled my pocket-book, wherein I had set down the names of several people and places which I had occasion to remember, and which not taking due care of, the leaves rotted, and the words were never after to be read.

At length we arrived at Pekin. I had nobody with me but the youth whom my nephew had given me to attend me as a servant and who proved very trusty and diligent; and my partner had nobody with him but one servant, who was a kinsman. As for the Portuguese pilot, he being desirous to see the court, we bore his charges for his company, and for our use of him as an interpreter, for he understood the language of the country, and spoke good French and a little English. Indeed, this old man was most useful to us everywhere; for we had not been above a week at Pekin, when he came laughing. "Ah, Seignior Inglese," says he, "I have something to tell will make your heart glad."—"My heart glad," says I; "what can that be? I don't know anything in this country can either give me joy or grief to any great degree."—"Yes, yes," said the old man, in broken English, "make you glad, me sorry."—"Why," said I, "will it make you sorry?"—"Because," said he, "you have brought me here twenty-five days' journey, and will leave me to go back alone; and which way shall I get to my port afterwards, without a ship, without a horse, without *pecune*?" so he called money, being his broken Latin, of which he had abundance to make us merry with. In short, he told us there was a great caravan of Muscovite and Polish merchants in the city, preparing to set out on their journey by land to Muscovy, within four or five weeks; and he was sure we would take the opportunity to go with them, and leave him behind, to go back alone.

I confess I was greatly surprised with this good news, and had scarce power to speak to him for some time; but at last I said to him, "How do you know this? are you sure it is true?"—"Yes," says he; "I met this morning in the street an old acquaintance of mine, an Armenian, who is among them. He came last from Astrakhan, and was designed to go to Tonquin, where I formerly knew him, but has altered his mind, and is now resolved to go with the caravan to Moscow, and so down the river Volga to Astrakhan."—"Well, Seignior," says I, "do not be uneasy about being left to go back alone; if this be a method for my return to England, it shall be your fault if you go back to Macao at all." We then went to consult together what was to be done; and I asked my partner what he thought of the pilot's news, and whether it would suit with his affairs? He told me he would do just as I would; for he had settled all his affairs so well at Bengal, and left his effects in such good hands, that as we had made a good voyage, if he could invest it in China silks, wrought and raw, he would be content to go to England, and then make a voyage back to Bengal by the Company's ships.

Having resolved upon this, we agreed that if our Portuguese pilot would go with us, we would bear his charges to Moscow, or to England, if he pleased; nor, indeed, were we to be esteemed over-generous in that either, if we had not rewarded him further, the service he had done us being really worth more than that; for he had not only been a pilot to us at sea, but he had been like a broker for us on shore; and his procuring for us a Japan merchant was some hundreds of pounds in our pockets. So, being willing to gratify him, which was but doing him justice, and very willing also to have him with us besides, for he was a most necessary man on all occasions, we agreed to give him a quantity of coined gold, which, as I computed it, was worth one hundred and seventy-five pounds sterling, between us, and to bear all his charges, both for himself and horse, except only a horse to carry his goods. Having settled this between ourselves, we called him to let him know what we had resolved. I told him he had complained of our being willing to let him go back alone, and I was now about to tell him we designed he should not go back at all. That as we had resolved to go to Europe with the caravan, we were very willing he should go with us; and that we called him to know his mind. He shook his head and said it was a long journey, and that he had no *pecune* to carry him thither, or to subsist himself when he came there. We told him we believed it was so, and therefore we had resolved to do something for him that should let him see how sensible we were of the service he had done us, and also how agreeable he was to us: and then I told him what we had resolved to give him here, which he might lay out as we would do our own; and that as for his charges, if he would go with us we would set him safe on shore (life and casualties excepted), either in Muscovy or England, as he would choose, at our own charge, except only the carriage of his goods. He received the proposal like a man transported, and told us he would go with us over all the whole world; and so we all prepared for our journey. However, as it was with us, so it was with the other merchants: they had many things to do, and instead of being ready in five weeks, it was four months and some days before all things were got together.

14

ATTACKED BY TARTARS

It was the beginning of February, new style, when we set out from Pekin. My partner and the old pilot had gone express back to the port where we had first put in, to dispose of some goods which we had left there; and I, with a Chinese merchant whom I had some knowledge of at Nankin, and who came to Pekin on his own affairs, went to Nankin, where I bought ninety pieces of fine damasks, with about two hundred pieces of other very fine silk of several sorts, some mixed with gold, and had all these brought to Pekin against my partner's return. Besides this, we bought a large quantity of raw silk, and some other goods, our cargo amounting, in these goods only, to about three thousand five hundred pounds sterling; which, together with tea and some fine calicoes, and three camels' loads of nutmegs and cloves, loaded in all eighteen camels for our share, besides those we rode upon; these, with two or three spare horses, and two horses loaded with provisions, made together twenty-six camels and horses in our retinue.

The company was very great, and, as near as I can remember, made between three and four hundred horses, and upwards of one hundred and twenty men, very well armed and provided for all events; for as the Eastern caravans are subject to be attacked by the Arabs, so are these by the Tartars. The company consisted of people of several nations, but there were above sixty of them merchants or inhabitants of Moscow, though of them some were Livonians; and to our particular satisfaction, five of them were Scots, who appeared also to be men of great experience in business, and of very good substance.

When we had travelled one day's journey, the guides, who were five in number, called all the passengers, except the servants, to a great council, as they called it. At this council every one deposited a certain quantity of money to a common stock, for the necessary expense of buying forage on the way, where it was not otherwise to be had, and for satisfying the guides, getting horses, and the like. Here, too, they constituted the journey, as they call it, viz. they named captains and officers to draw us all up, and give the word of command, in case of an attack, and give every one their turn of command; nor was this forming us into order any more than what we afterwards found needful on the way.

The road all on this side of the country is very populous, and is full of potters and earth-makers—that is to say, people, that temper the earth for the China ware. As I was coming along, our Portuguese pilot, who had always something or other to say to make us merry, told me he would show me the greatest rarity in all the country, and that I should have this to say of China, after all the ill-humoured things that I had said of it, that I had seen one thing which was not to be seen in all the world beside. I was very importunate to know what it was; at last he told me it was a gentleman's house built with China ware. "Well," says I, "are not the materials of their buildings the products of their own country, and so it is all China ware, is it not?"—"No, no," says he, "I mean it is a house all made of China ware, such as you call it in England, or as it is called in our country, porcelain."—"Well," says I, "such a thing may be; how big is it? Can we carry it in a box upon a camel? If we can we will buy it."—"Upon a camel!" says the old pilot, holding up both his hands; "why, there is a family of thirty people lives in it."

I was then curious, indeed, to see it; and when I came to it, it was nothing but this: it was a timber house, or a house built, as we call it in England, with lath and plaster, but all this plastering was really China ware—that is to say, it was plastered with the earth that makes China ware. The outside, which the sun shone hot upon, was glazed, and looked very well, perfectly white, and painted with blue figures, as the large China ware in England is painted, and hard as if it had been burnt. As to the inside, all the walls, instead of wainscot, were lined with hardened and painted tiles, like the little square tiles we call galley-tiles in England, all made of the finest china, and the figures exceeding fine indeed, with extraordinary variety of colours, mixed with gold, many tiles making but one figure, but joined so artificially, the mortar being made of the same earth, that it was very hard to see where the tiles met. The floors of the rooms were of the same composition, and as hard as the earthen floors we have in use in several parts of England; as hard as stone, and smooth, but not burnt and painted, except some smaller rooms, like closets, which were all, as it were, paved with the same tile; the ceiling and all the plastering work in the whole house were of the same earth; and, after all, the roof was covered with tiles of the same, but of a deep shining black. This was a China warehouse indeed, truly and literally to be called so, and had I not been upon the journey, I could have stayed some days to see and examine the particulars of it. They told me there were fountains and fishponds in the garden, all paved on the bottom and sides with the same; and fine statues set up in rows on the walks, entirely formed of the porcelain earth, burnt whole.

As this is one of the singularities of China, so they may be allowed to excel in it; but I am very sure they excel in their accounts of it; for they told me such incredible things of their performance in crockery-ware, for such it is, that I care not to relate, as knowing it could not be true. They told me, in particular, of one workman that made a ship with all its tackle and masts and sails in earthenware, big enough to carry fifty men. If they had told me he launched it, and made a voyage to Japan in it, I might have said something to it indeed; but as it was, I knew the whole of the story, which was, in short, that the fellow lied: so I smiled, and said nothing to it. This odd sight kept me two hours behind the caravan, for which the leader of it for the day fined me about the value of three shillings; and told me if it had been three days' journey without the wall, as it was three days' within, he must have fined me four times as much, and made me ask pardon the next council-day. I promised to be more orderly; and, indeed, I found afterwards the orders made for keeping all together were absolutely necessary for our common safety.

In two days more we passed the great China wall, made for a fortification against the Tartars: and a very great work it is, going over hills and mountains in an endless track, where the rocks are impassable, and the precipices such as no enemy could possibly enter, or indeed climb up, or where, if they did, no wall could hinder them. They tell us its length is near a thousand English miles, but that the country is five hundred in a straight measured line, which the wall bounds without measuring the windings and turnings it takes; it is about four fathoms high, and as many thick in some places.

I stood still an hour or thereabouts without trespassing on our orders (for so long the caravan was in passing the gate), to look at it on every side, near and far off; I mean what was within my view: and the guide, who had been extolling it for the wonder of the world, was mighty eager to hear my opinion of it. I told him it was a most excellent thing to keep out the Tartars; which he happened not to understand as I meant it and so took it for a compliment; but the old pilot laughed! "Oh, Seignior Inglese," says he, "you speak in colours."—"In colours!" said I; "what do you mean by that?"—"Why, you speak what looks white this way and black that way—gay one way and dull another. You tell him it is a good wall to keep out Tartars; you tell me by that it is good for nothing but to keep out Tartars. I understand you, Seignior Inglese, I understand you; but Seignior Chinese understood you his own way."—"Well," says I, "do you think it would stand out an army of our country people, with a good train of artillery; or our engineers, with two companies of miners? Would not they batter it down in ten days, that an army might enter in battalia; or blow it up in the air, foundation and all, that there should be no sign of it left?"—"Ay, ay," says he, "I know that." The Chinese wanted mightily to know what I said to the pilot, and I gave him leave to tell him a few days after, for we were then almost out of their country, and he was to leave us a little time after this; but when he knew what I said, he was dumb all the rest of the way, and we heard no more of his fine story of the Chinese power and greatness while he stayed.

After we passed this mighty nothing, called a wall, something like the Picts' walls so famous in Northumberland, built by the Romans, we began to find the country thinly inhabited, and the people rather confined to live in fortified towns, as being subject to the inroads and depredations of the Tartars, who rob in great armies, and therefore are not to be resisted by the naked inhabitants of an open country. And here I began to find the necessity of keeping together in a caravan as we travelled, for we saw several troops of Tartars roving about; but when I came to see them distinctly, I wondered more that the Chinese empire could be conquered by such contemptible fellows; for they are a mere horde of wild fellows, keeping no order and understanding no discipline or manner of it. Their horses are poor lean creatures, taught nothing, and fit for nothing; and this we found the first day we saw them, which was after we entered the wilder part of the country. Our leader for the day gave leave for about sixteen of us to go a hunting as they call it; and what was this but a hunting of sheep!—however, it may be called hunting too, for these creatures are the wildest and swiftest of foot that ever I saw of their kind! only they will not run a great way, and you are sure of sport when you begin the chase, for they appear generally thirty or forty in a flock, and, like true sheep, always keep together when they fly.

In pursuit of this odd sort of game it was our hap to meet with about forty Tartars: whether they were hunting mutton, as we were, or whether they looked for another kind of prey, we know not; but as soon as they saw us, one of them blew a hideous blast on a kind of horn. This was to call their friends about them, and in less than ten minutes a troop of forty or fifty more appeared, at about a mile distance; but our work was over first, as it happened.

One of the Scots merchants of Moscow happened to be amongst us; and as soon as he heard the horn, he told us that we had nothing to do but to charge them without loss of time; and drawing us up in a line, he asked if we were resolved. We told him we were ready to follow him; so he rode directly towards them. They stood gazing at us like a mere crowd, drawn up in no sort of order at all; but as soon as they saw us advance, they let fly their arrows, which missed us, very happily. Not that they mistook their aim, but their distance; for their arrows all fell a little short of us, but with so true an aim, that had we been about twenty yards nearer we must have had several men wounded, if not killed.

Immediately we halted, and though it was at a great distance, we fired, and sent them leaden bullets for wooden arrows, following our shot full gallop, to fall in among them sword in hand—for so our bold Scot that led us directed. He was, indeed, but a merchant, but he behaved with such vigour and bravery on this occasion, and yet with such cool courage too, that I never saw any man in action fitter for command. As soon as we came up to them we fired our pistols in their faces and then drew; but they fled in the greatest confusion imaginable. The only stand any of them made was on our right, where three of them stood, and, by signs, called the rest to come back to them, having a kind of scimitar in their hands, and their bows hanging to their backs. Our brave commander, without asking anybody to follow him, gallops up close to them, and with his fusee knocks one of them off his horse, killed the second with his pistol, and the third ran away. Thus ended our fight; but we had this misfortune attending it, that all our mutton we had in chase got away. We had not a man killed or hurt; as for the Tartars, there were about five of them killed—how many were wounded we knew not; but this we knew, that the other party were so frightened with the noise of our guns that they fled, and never made any attempt upon us.

We were all this while in the Chinese dominions, and therefore the Tartars were not so bold as afterwards; but in about five days we entered a vast wild desert, which held us three days' and nights' march; and we were obliged to carry our water with us in great leathern bottles, and to encamp all night, just as I have heard they do in the desert of Arabia. I asked our guides whose dominion this was in, and they told me this was a kind of border that might be called no man's land, being a part of Great Karakathy, or Grand Tartary: that, however, it was all reckoned as belonging to China, but that there was no care taken here to preserve it from the inroads of thieves, and therefore it was reckoned the worst desert in the whole march, though we were to go over some much larger.

In passing this frightful wilderness we saw, two or three times, little parties of the Tartars, but they seemed to be upon their own affairs, and to have no design upon us; and so, like the man who met the devil, if they had nothing to say to us, we had nothing to say to them: we let them go. Once, however, a party of them came so near as to stand and gaze at us. Whether it was to consider if they should attack us or not, we knew not; but when we had passed at some distance by them, we made a rear-guard of forty men, and stood ready for them, letting the caravan pass half a mile or thereabouts before us. After a while they marched off, but they saluted us with five arrows at their parting, which wounded a horse so that it disabled him, and we left him the next day, poor creature, in great need of a good farrier. We saw no more arrows or Tartars that time.

We travelled near a month after this, the ways not being so good as at first, though still in the dominions of the Emperor of China, but lay for the most part in the villages, some of which were fortified, because of the incursions of the Tartars. When we were come to one of these towns (about two days and a half's journey before we came to the city of Naum), I wanted to buy a camel, of which there are plenty to be sold all the way upon that road, and horses also, such as they are, because, so many caravans coming that way, they are often wanted. The person that I spoke to to get me a camel would have gone and fetched one for me; but I, like a fool, must be officious, and go myself along with him; the place was about two miles out of the village, where it seems they kept the camels and horses feeding under a guard.

I walked it on foot, with my old pilot and a Chinese, being very desirous of a little variety. When we came to the place it was a low, marshy ground, walled round with stones, piled up dry, without mortar or earth among them, like a park, with a little guard of Chinese soldiers at the door. Having bought a camel, and agreed for the price, I came away, and the Chinese that went with me led the camel, when on a sudden came up five Tartars on horseback. Two of them seized the fellow and took the camel from him, while the other three stepped up to me and my old pilot, seeing us, as it were, unarmed, for I had no weapon about me but my sword, which could but ill defend me against three horsemen. The first that came up stopped short upon my drawing my sword, for they are arrant cowards; but a second, coming upon my left, gave me a blow on the head, which I never felt till afterwards, and wondered, when I came to myself, what was the matter, and where I was, for he laid me flat on the ground; but my never-failing old pilot, the Portuguese, had a pistol in his pocket, which I knew nothing of, nor the Tartars either: if they had, I suppose they would not have attacked us, for cowards are always boldest when there is no danger. The old man seeing me down, with a bold heart stepped up to the fellow that had struck me, and laying hold of his arm with one hand, and pulling him down by main force a little towards him, with the other shot him into the head, and laid him dead upon the spot. He then immediately stepped up to him who had stopped us, as I said, and before he could come forward again, made a blow at him with a scimitar, which he always wore, but missing the man, struck his horse in the side of his head, cut one of the ears off by the root, and a great slice down by the side of his face. The poor beast, enraged with the wound, was no more to be governed by his rider, though the fellow sat well enough too, but away he flew, and carried him quite out of the pilot's reach; and at some distance, rising upon his hind legs, threw down the Tartar, and fell upon him.

In this interval the poor Chinese came in who had lost the camel, but he had no weapon; however, seeing the Tartar down, and his horse fallen upon him, away he runs to him, and seizing upon an ugly weapon he had by his side, something like a pole-axe, he wrenched it from him, and made shift to knock his Tartarian brains out with it. But my old man had the third Tartar to deal with still; and seeing he did not fly, as he expected, nor come on to fight him, as he apprehended, but stood stock still, the old man stood still too, and fell to work with his tackle to charge his pistol again: but as soon as the Tartar saw the pistol away he scoured, and left my pilot, my champion I called him afterwards, a complete victory.

By this time I was a little recovered. I thought, when I first began to wake, that I had been in a sweet sleep; but, as I said above, I wondered where I was, how I came upon the ground, and what was the matter. A few moments after, as sense returned, I felt pain, though I did not know where; so I clapped my hand to my head, and took it away bloody; then I felt my head ache: and in a moment memory returned, and everything was present to me again. I jumped upon my feet instantly, and got hold of my sword, but no enemies were in view: I found a Tartar lying dead, and his horse standing very quietly by him; and, looking further, I saw my deliverer, who had been to see what the Chinese had done, coming back with his hanger in his hand. The old man, seeing me on my feet, came running to me, and joyfully embraced me, being afraid before that I had been killed. Seeing me bloody, he would see how I was hurt; but it was not much, only what we call a broken head; neither did I afterwards find any great inconvenience from the blow, for it was well again in two or three days.

We made no great gain, however, by this victory, for we lost a camel and gained a horse. I paid for the lost camel, and sent for another; but I did not go to fetch it myself: I had had enough of that.

The city of Naum, which we were approaching, is a frontier of the Chinese empire, and is fortified in their fashion. We wanted, as I have said, above two days' journey of this city when messengers were sent express to every part of the road to tell all travellers and caravans to halt till they had a guard sent for them; for that an unusual body of Tartars, making ten thousand in all, had appeared in the way, about thirty miles beyond the city.

This was very bad news to travellers: however, it was carefully done of the governor, and we were very glad to hear we should have a guard. Accordingly, two days after, we had two hundred soldiers sent us from a garrison of the Chinese on our left, and three hundred more from the city of Naum, and with these we advanced boldly. The three hundred soldiers from Naum marched in our front, the two hundred in our rear, and our men on each side of our camels, with our baggage and the whole caravan in the centre; in this order, and well prepared for battle, we thought ourselves a match for the whole ten thousand Mogul Tartars, if they had appeared; but the next day, when they did appear, it was quite another thing.

15

DESCRIPTION OF AN IDOL, WHICH THEY DESTROY

Early in the morning, when marching from a little town called Changu, we had a river to pass, which we were obliged to ferry; and, had the Tartars had any intelligence, then had been the time to have attacked us, when the caravan being over, the rear-guard was behind; but they did not appear there. About three hours after, when we were entered upon a desert of about fifteen or sixteen miles over, we knew by a cloud of dust they raised, that the enemy was at hand, and presently they came on upon the spur.

Our Chinese guards in the front, who had talked so big the day before, began to stagger; and the soldiers frequently looked behind them, a certain sign in a soldier that he is just ready to run away. My old pilot was of my mind; and being near me, called out, "Seignior Inglese, these fellows must be encouraged, or they will ruin us all; for if the Tartars come on they will never stand it."—"If am of your mind," said I; "but what must be done?"—"Done?" says he, "let fifty of our men advance, and flank them on each wing, and encourage them. They will fight like brave fellows in brave company; but without this they will every man turn his back." Immediately I rode up to our leader and told him, who was exactly of our mind; accordingly, fifty of us marched to the right wing, and fifty to the left, and the rest made a line of rescue; and so we marched, leaving the last two hundred men to make a body of themselves, and to guard the camels; only that, if need were, they should send a hundred men to assist the last fifty.

At last the Tartars came on, and an innumerable company they were; how many we could not tell, but ten thousand, we thought, at the least. A party of them came on first, and viewed our posture, traversing the ground in the front of our line; and, as we found them within gunshot, our leader ordered the two wings to advance swiftly, and give them a salvo on each wing with their shot, which was done. They then went off, I suppose to give an account of the reception they were like to meet with; indeed, that salute cloyed their stomachs, for they immediately halted, stood a while to consider of it, and wheeling off to the left, they gave over their design for that time, which was very agreeable to our circumstances.

Two days after we came to the city of Naun, or Naum; we thanked the governor for his care of us, and collected to the value of a hundred crowns, or thereabouts, which we gave to the soldiers sent to guard us; and here we rested one day. This is a garrison indeed, and there were nine hundred soldiers kept here; but the reason of it was, that formerly the Muscovite frontiers lay nearer to them than they now do, the Muscovites having abandoned that part of the country, which lies from this city west for about two hundred miles, as desolate and unfit for use; and more especially being so very remote, and so difficult to send troops thither for its defence; for we were yet above two thousand miles from Muscovy properly so called. After this we passed several great rivers, and two dreadful deserts; one of which we were sixteen days passing over; and on the 13th of April we came to the frontiers of the Muscovite dominions. I think the first town or fortress, whichever it may he called, that belonged to the Czar, was called Arguna, being on the west side of the river Arguna.

I could not but feel great satisfaction that I was arrived in a country governed by Christians; for though the Muscovites do, in my opinion, but just deserve the name of Christians, yet such they pretend to be, and are very devout in their way. It would certainly occur to any reflecting man who travels the world as I have done, what a blessing it is to be brought into the world where the name of God and a Redeemer is known, adored, and worshipped; and not where the people, given up to strong delusions, worship the devil, and prostrate themselves to monsters, elements, horrid-shaped animals, and monstrous images. Not a town or city we passed through but had their pagodas, their idols, and their temples, and ignorant people worshipping even the works of their own hands. Now we came where, at least, a face of the Christian worship appeared; where the knee was bowed to Jesus: and whether ignorantly or not, yet the Christian religion was owned, and the name of the true God was called upon and adored; and it made my soul rejoice to see it. I saluted the brave Scots merchant with my first acknowledgment of this; and taking him by the hand, I said to him, "Blessed be God, we are once again amongst Christians." He smiled, and answered, "Do not rejoice too soon, countryman; these Muscovites are but an odd sort of Christians; and but for the name of it you may see very little of the substance for some months further of our journey."—"Well," says I, "but still it is better than paganism, and worshipping of devils."—"Why, I will tell you," says he; "except the Russian soldiers in the garrisons, and a few of the inhabitants of the cities upon the road, all the rest of this country, for above a thousand miles farther, is inhabited by the worst and most ignorant of pagans." And so, indeed, we found it.

We now launched into the greatest piece of solid earth that is to be found in any part of the world; we had, at least, twelve thousand miles to the sea eastward; two thousand to the bottom of the Baltic Sea westward; and above three thousand, if we left that sea, and went on west, to the British and French channels: we had full five thousand miles to the Indian or Persian Sea south; and about eight hundred to the Frozen Sea north.

We advanced from the river Arguna by easy and moderate journeys, and were very visibly obliged to the care the Czar has taken to have cities and towns built in as many places as it is possible to place them, where his soldiers keep garrison, something like the stationary soldiers placed by the Romans in the remotest countries of their empire; some of which I had read of were placed in Britain, for the security of commerce, and for the lodging of travellers. Thus it was here; for wherever we came, though at these towns and stations the garrisons and governors were Russians, and professed Christians, yet the inhabitants were mere pagans, sacrificing to idols, and worshipping the sun, moon, and stars, or all the host of heaven; and not only so, but were, of all the heathens and pagans that ever I met with, the most barbarous, except only that they did not eat men's flesh.

Some instances of this we met with in the country between Arguna, where we enter the Muscovite dominions, and a city of Tartars and Russians together, called Nortziousky, in which is a continued desert or forest, which cost us twenty days to travel over. In a village near the last of these places I had the curiosity to go and see their way of living, which is most brutish and unsufferable. They had, I suppose, a great sacrifice that day; for there stood out, upon an old stump of a tree, a diabolical kind of idol made of wood; it was dressed up, too, in the most filthy manner; its upper garment was of sheepskins, with the wool outward; a great Tartar bonnet on the head, with two horns growing through it; it was about eight feet high, yet had no feet or legs, nor any other proportion of parts.

This scarecrow was set up at the outer side of the village; and when I came near to it there were sixteen or seventeen creatures all lying flat upon the ground round this hideous block of wood; I saw no motion among them, any more than if they had been all logs, like the idol, and at first I really thought they had been so; but, when I came a little nearer, they started up upon their feet, and raised a howl, as if it had been so many deep-mouthed hounds, and walked away, as if they were displeased at our disturbing them. A little way off from the idol, and at the door of a hut, made of sheep and cow skins dried, stood three men with long knives in their hands; and in the middle of the tent appeared three sheep killed, and one young bullock. These, it seems, were sacrifices to that senseless log of an idol; the three men were priests belonging to it, and the seventeen prostrated wretches were the people who brought the offering, and were offering their prayers to that stock.

I confess I was more moved at their stupidity and brutish worship of a hobgoblin than ever I was at anything in my life, and, overcome with rage, I rode up to the hideous idol, and with my sword made a stroke at the bonnet that was on its head, and cut it in two; and one of our men that was with me, taking hold of the sheepskin that covered it, pulled at it, when, behold, a most hideous outcry ran through the village, and two or three hundred people came about my ears, so that I was glad to scour for it, for some had bows and arrows; but I resolved from that moment to visit them again. Our caravan rested three nights at the town, which was about four miles off, in order to provide some horses which they wanted, several of the horses having been lamed and jaded with the long march over the last desert; so we had some leisure here to put my design in execution. I communicated it to the Scots merchant, of whose courage I had sufficient testimony; I told him what I had seen, and with what indignation I had since thought that human nature could be so degenerate; I told him if I could get but four or five men well armed to go with me, I was resolved to go and destroy that vile, abominable idol, and let them see that it had no power to help itself, and consequently could not be an object of worship, or to be prayed to, much less help them that offered sacrifices to it.

He at first objected to my plan as useless, seeing that, owing to the gross ignorance of the people, they could not be brought to profit by the lesson I meant to teach them; and added that, from his knowledge of the country and its customs, he feared we should fall into great peril by giving offence to these brutal idol worshippers. This somewhat stayed my purpose, but I was still uneasy all that day to put my project in execution; and that evening, meeting the Scots merchant in our walk about the town, I again called upon him to aid me in it. When he found me resolute he said that, on further thoughts, he could not but applaud the design, and told me I should not go alone, but he would go with me; but he would go first and bring a stout fellow, one of his countrymen, to go also with us; "and one," said he, "as famous for his zeal as you can desire any one to be against such devilish things as these." So we agreed to go, only we three and my man-servant, and resolved to put it in execution the following night about midnight, with all possible secrecy.

We thought it better to delay it till the next night, because the caravan being to set forward in the morning, we suppose the governor could not pretend to give them any satisfaction upon us when we were out of his power. The Scots merchant, as steady in his resolution for the enterprise as bold in executing, brought me a Tartar's robe or gown of sheepskins, and a bonnet, with a bow and arrows, and had provided the same for himself and his countryman, that the people, if they saw us, should not determine who we were. All the first night we spent in mixing up some combustible matter, with aqua vitae, gunpowder, and such other materials as we could get; and having a good quantity of tar in a little pot, about an hour after night we set out upon our expedition.

We came to the place about eleven o'clock at night, and found that the people had not the least suspicion of danger attending their idol. The night was cloudy: yet the moon gave us light enough to see that the idol stood just in the same posture and place that it did before. The people seemed to be all at their rest; only that in the great hut, where we saw the three priests, we saw a light, and going up close to the door, we heard people talking as if there were five or six of them; we concluded, therefore, that if we set wildfire to the idol, those men would come out immediately, and run up to the place to rescue it from destruction; and what to do with them we knew not. Once we thought of carrying it away, and setting fire to it at a distance; but when we came to handle it, we found it too bulky for our carriage, so we were at a loss again. The second Scotsman was for setting fire to the hut, and knocking the creatures that were there on the head when they came out; but I could not join with that; I was against killing them, if it were possible to avoid it. "Well, then," said the Scots merchant, "I will tell you what we will do: we will try to make them prisoners, tie their hands, and make them stand and see their idol destroyed."

As it happened, we had twine or packthread enough about us, which we used to tie our firelocks together with; so we resolved to attack these people first, and with as little noise as we could. The first thing we did, we knocked at the door, when one of the priests coming to it, we immediately seized upon him, stopped his mouth, and tied his hands behind him, and led him to the idol, where we gagged him that he might not make a noise, tied his feet also together, and left him on the ground.

Two of us then waited at the door, expecting that another would come out to see what the matter was; but we waited so long till the third man came back to us; and then nobody coming out, we knocked again gently, and immediately out came two more, and we served them just in the same manner, but were obliged to go all with them, and lay them down by the idol some distance from one another; when, going back, we found two more were come out of the door, and a third stood behind them within the door. We seized the two, and immediately tied them, when the third, stepping back and crying out, my Scots merchant went in after them, and taking out a composition we had made that would only smoke and stink, he set fire to it, and threw it in among them. By that time the other Scotsman and my man, taking charge of the two men already bound, and tied together also by the arm, led them away to the idol, and left them there, to see if their idol would relieve them, making haste back to us.

When the fuze we had thrown in had filled the hut with so much smoke that they were almost suffocated, we threw in a small leather bag of another kind, which flamed like a candle, and, following it in, we found there were but four people, who, as we supposed, had been about some of their diabolical sacrifices. They appeared, in short, frightened to death, at least so as to sit trembling and stupid, and not able to speak either, for the smoke.

We quickly took them from the hut, where the smoke soon drove us out, bound them as we had done the other, and all without any noise. Then we carried them all together to the idol; when we came there, we fell to work with him. First, we daubed him all over, and his robes also, with tar, and tallow mixed with brimstone; then we stopped his eyes and ears and mouth full of gunpowder, and wrapped up a great piece of wildfire in his bonnet; then sticking all the combustibles we had brought with us upon him, we looked about to see if we could find anything else to help to burn him; when my Scotsman remembered that by the hut, where the men were, there lay a heap of dry forage; away he and the other Scotsman ran and fetched their arms full of that. When we had done this, we took all our prisoners, and brought them, having untied their feet and ungagged their mouths, and made them stand up, and set them before their monstrous idol, and then set fire to the whole.

We stayed by it a quarter of an hour or thereabouts, till the powder in the eyes and mouth and ears of the idol blew up, and, as we could perceive, had split altogether; and in a word, till we saw it burned so that it would soon be quite consumed. We then began to think of going away; but the Scotsman said, "No, we must not go, for these poor deluded wretches will all throw themselves into the fire, and burn themselves with the idol." So we resolved to stay till the forage has burned down too, and then came away and left them. After the feat was performed, we appeared in the morning among our fellow-travellers, exceedingly busy in getting ready for our journey; nor could any man suppose that we had been anywhere but in our beds.

But the affair did not end so; the next day came a great number of the country people to the town gates, and in a most outrageous manner demanded satisfaction of the Russian governor for the insulting their priests and burning their great Cham Chi-Thaungu. The people of Nertsinkay were at first in a great consternation, for they said the Tartars were already no less than thirty thousand strong. The Russian governor sent out messengers to appease them, assuring them that he knew nothing of it, and that there had not a soul in his garrison been abroad, so that it could not be from anybody there: but if they could let him know who did it, they should be exemplarily punished. They returned haughtily, that all the country reverenced the great Cham Chi-Thaungu, who dwelt in the sun, and no mortal would have dared to offer violence to his image but some Christian miscreant; and they therefore resolved to denounce war against him and all the Russians, who, they said, were miscreants and Christians.

The governor, unwilling to make a breach, or to have any cause of war alleged to be given by him, the Czar having strictly charged him to treat the conquered country with gentleness, gave them all the good words he could. At last he told them there was a caravan gone towards Russia that morning, and perhaps it was some of them who had done them this injury; and that if they would be satisfied with that, he would send after them to inquire into it. This seemed to appease them a little; and accordingly the governor sent after us, and gave us a particular account how the thing was; intimating withal, that if any in our caravan had done it they should make their escape; but that whether we had done it or no, we should make all the haste forward that was possible: and that, in the meantime, he would keep them in play as long as he could.

This was very friendly in the governor; however, when it came to the caravan, there was nobody knew anything of the matter; and as for us that were guilty, we were least of all suspected. However, the captain of the caravan for the time took the hint that the governor gave us, and we travelled two days and two nights without any considerable stop, and then we lay at a village called Plothus: nor did we make any long stop here, but hastened on towards Jarawena, another Muscovite colony, and where we expected we should be safe. But upon the second day's march from Plothus, by the clouds of dust behind us at a great distance, it was plain we were pursued. We had entered a vast desert, and had passed by a great lake called Schanks Oser, when we perceived a large body of horse appear on the other side of the lake, to the north, we travelling west. We observed they went away west, as we did, but had supposed we would have taken that side of the lake, whereas we very happily took the south side; and in two days more they disappeared again: for they, believing we were still before them, pushed on till they came to the Udda, a very great river when it passes farther north, but when we came to it we found it narrow and fordable.

The third day they had either found their mistake, or had intelligence of us, and came pouring in upon us towards dusk. We had, to our great satisfaction, just pitched upon a convenient place for our camp; for as we had just entered upon a desert above five hundred miles over, where we had no towns to lodge at, and, indeed, expected none but the city Jarawena, which we had yet two days' march to; the desert, however, had some few woods in it on this side, and little rivers, which ran all into the great river Udda; it was in a narrow strait, between little but very thick woods, that we pitched our camp that night, expecting to be attacked before morning. As it was usual for the Mogul Tartars to go about in troops in that desert, so the caravans always fortify themselves every night against them, as against armies of robbers; and it was, therefore, no new thing to be pursued. But we had this night a most advantageous camp: for as we lay between two woods, with a little rivulet running just before our front, we could not be surrounded, or attacked any way but in our front or rear. We took care also to make our front as strong as we could, by placing our packs, with the camels and horses, all in a line, on the inside of the river, and felling some trees in our rear.

In this posture we encamped for the night; but the enemy was upon us before we had finished. They did not come on like thieves, as we expected, but sent three messengers to us, to demand the men to be delivered to them that had abused their priests and burned their idol, that they might burn them with fire; and upon this, they said, they would go away, and do us no further harm, otherwise they would destroy us all. Our men looked very blank at this message, and began to stare at one another to see who looked with the most guilt in their faces; but nobody was the word—nobody did it. The leader of the caravan sent word he was well assured that it was not done by any of our camp; that we were peaceful merchants, travelling on our business; that we had done no harm to them or to any one else; and that, therefore, they must look further for the enemies who had injured them, for we were not the people; so they desired them not to disturb us, for if they did we should defend ourselves.

They were far from being satisfied with this for an answer: and a great crowd of them came running down in the morning, by break of day, to our camp; but seeing us so well posted, they durst come no farther than the brook in our front, where they stood in such number as to terrify us very much; indeed, some spoke of ten thousand. Here they stood and looked at us a while, and then, setting up a great howl, let fly a crowd of arrows among us; but we were well enough sheltered under our baggage, and I do not remember that one of us was hurt.

Some time after this we saw them move a little to our right, and expected them on the rear: when a cunning fellow, a Cossack of Jarawena, calling to the leader of the caravan, said to him, "I will send all these people away to Sibeilka." This was a city four or five days' journey at least to the right, and rather behind us. So he takes his bow and arrows, and getting on horseback, he rides away from our rear directly, as it were back to Nertsinskay; after this he takes a great circuit about, and comes directly on the army of the Tartars as if he had been sent express to tell them a long story that the people who had burned the Cham Chi-Thaungu were gone to Sibeilka, with a caravan of miscreants, as he called them—that is to say, Christians; and that they had resolved to burn the god Scal-Isar, belonging to the Tonguses. As this fellow was himself a Tartar, and perfectly spoke their language, he counterfeited so well that they all believed him, and away they drove in a violent hurry to Sibeilka. In less than three hours they were entirely out of our sight, and we never heard any more of them, nor whether they went to Sibeilka or no. So we passed away safely on to Jarawena, where there was a Russian garrison, and there we rested five days.

From this city we had a frightful desert, which held us twenty-three days' march. We furnished ourselves with some tents here, for the better accommodating ourselves in the night; and the leader of the caravan procured sixteen waggons of the country, for carrying our water or provisions, and these carriages were our defence every night round our little camp; so that had the Tartars appeared, unless they had been very numerous indeed, they would not have been able to hurt us. We may well be supposed to have wanted rest again after this long journey; for in this desert we neither saw house nor tree, and scarce a bush; though we saw abundance of the sable-hunters, who are all Tartars of Mogul Tartary; of which this country is a part; and they frequently attack small caravans, but we saw no numbers of them together.

After we had passed this desert we came into a country pretty well inhabited—that is to say, we found towns and castles, settled by the Czar with garrisons of stationary soldiers, to protect the caravans and defend the country against the Tartars, who would otherwise make it very dangerous travelling; and his czarish majesty has given such strict orders for the well guarding the caravans, that, if there are any Tartars heard of in the country, detachments of the garrison are always sent to see the travellers safe from station to station. Thus the governor of Adinskoy, whom I had an opportunity to make a visit to, by means of the Scots merchant, who was acquainted with him, offered us a guard of fifty men, if we thought there was any danger, to the next station.

I thought, long before this, that as we came nearer to Europe we should find the country better inhabited, and the people more civilised; but I found myself mistaken in both: for we had yet the nation of the Tonguses to pass through, where we saw the same tokens of paganism and barbarity as before; only, as they were conquered by the Muscovites, they were not so dangerous, but for rudeness of manners and idolatry no people in the world ever went beyond them. They are all clothed in skins of beasts, and their houses are built of the same; you know not a man from a woman, neither by the ruggedness of their countenances nor their clothes; and in the winter, when the ground is covered with snow, they live underground in vaults, which have cavities going from one to another. If the Tartars had their Cham Chi-Thaungu for a whole village or country, these had idols in every hut and every cave. This country, I reckon, was, from the desert I spoke of last, at least four hundred miles, half of it being another desert, which took us up twelve days' severe travelling, without house or tree; and we were obliged again to carry our own provisions, as well water as bread. After we were out of this desert and had travelled two days, we came to Janezay, a Muscovite city or station, on the great river Janezay, which, they told us there, parted Europe from Asia.

All the country between the river Oby and the river Janezay is as entirely pagan, and the people as barbarous, as the remotest of the Tartars. I also found, which I observed to the Muscovite governors whom I had an opportunity to converse with, that the poor pagans are not much wiser, or nearer Christianity, for being under the Muscovite government, which they acknowledged was true enough—but that, as they said, was none of their business; that if the Czar expected to convert his Siberian, Tonguse, or Tartar subjects, it should be done by sending clergymen among them, not soldiers; and they added, with more sincerity than I expected, that it was not so much the concern of their monarch to make the people Christians as to make them subjects.

From this river to the Oby we crossed a wild uncultivated country, barren of people and good management, otherwise it is in itself a pleasant, fruitful, and agreeable country. What inhabitants we found in it are all pagans, except such as are sent among them from Russia; for this is the country—I mean on both sides the river Oby—whither the Muscovite criminals that are not put to death are banished, and from whence it is next to impossible they should ever get away. I have nothing material to say of my particular affairs till I came to Tobolski, the capital city of Siberia, where I continued some time on the following account.

We had now been almost seven months on our journey, and winter began to come on apace; whereupon my partner and I called a council about our particular affairs, in which we found it proper, as we were bound for England, to consider how to dispose of ourselves. They told us of sledges and reindeer to carry us over the snow in the winter time, by which means, indeed, the Russians travel more in winter than they can in summer, as in these sledges they are able to run night and day: the snow, being frozen, is one universal covering to nature, by which the hills, vales, rivers, and lakes are all smooth and hard is a stone, and they run upon the surface, without any regard to what is underneath.

But I had no occasion to urge a winter journey of this kind. I was bound to England, not to Moscow, and my route lay two ways: either I must go on as the caravan went, till I came to Jarislaw, and then go off west for Narva and the Gulf of Finland, and so on to Dantzic, where I might possibly sell my China cargo to good advantage; or I must leave the caravan at a little town on the Dwina, from whence I had but six days by water to Archangel, and from thence might be sure of shipping either to England, Holland, or Hamburg.

Now, to go any one of these journeys in the winter would have been preposterous; for as to Dantzic, the Baltic would have been frozen up and I could not get passage; and to go by land in those countries was far less safe than among the Mogul Tartars; likewise, as to Archangel in October, all the ships would be gone from thence, and even the merchants who dwell there in summer retire south to Moscow in the winter, when the ships are gone; so that I could have nothing but extremity of cold to encounter, with a scarcity of provisions, and must lie in an empty town all the winter. Therefore, upon the whole, I thought it much my better way to let the caravan go, and make provision to winter where I was, at Tobolski, in Siberia, in the latitude of about sixty degrees, where I was sure of three things to wear out a cold winter with, viz. plenty of provisions, such as the country afforded, a warm house, with fuel enough, and excellent company.

I was now in quite a different climate from my beloved island, where I never felt cold, except when I had my ague; on the contrary, I had much to do to bear any clothes on my back, and never made any fire but without doors, which was necessary for dressing my food, &c. Now I had three good vests, with large robes or gowns over them, to hang down to the feet, and button close to the wrists; and all these lined with furs, to make them sufficiently warm. As to a warm house, I must confess I greatly dislike our way in England of making fires in every room of the house in open chimneys, which, when the fire is out, always keeps the air in the room cold as the climate. So I took an apartment in a good house in the town, and ordered a chimney to be built like a furnace, in the centre of six several rooms, like a stove; the funnel to carry the smoke went up one way, the door to come at the fire went in another, and all the rooms were kept equally warm, but no fire seen, just as they heat baths in England. By this means we had always the same climate in all the rooms, and an equal heat was preserved, and yet we saw no fire, nor were ever incommoded with smoke.

The most wonderful thing of all was, that it should be possible to meet with good company here, in a country so barbarous as this—one of the most northerly parts of Europe. But this being the country where the state criminals of Muscovy, as I observed before, are all banished, the city was full of Russian noblemen, gentlemen, soldiers, and courtiers. Here was the famous Prince Galitzin, the old German Robostiski, and several other persons of note, and some ladies. By means of my Scotch merchant, whom, nevertheless, I parted with here, I made an acquaintance with several of these gentlemen; and from these, in the long winter nights in which I stayed here, I received several very agreeable visits.

16

SAFE ARRIVAL IN ENGLAND

It was talking one night with a certain prince, one of the banished ministers of state belonging to the Czar, that the discourse of my particular case began. He had been telling me abundance of fine things of the greatness, the magnificence, the dominions, and the absolute power of the Emperor of the Russians: I interrupted him, and told him I was a greater and more powerful prince than ever the Czar was, though my dominion were not so large, or my people so many. The Russian grandee looked a little surprised, and, fixing his eyes steadily upon me, began to wonder what I meant. I said his wonder would cease when I had explained myself, and told him the story at large of my living in the island; and then how I managed both myself and the people that were under me, just as I have since minuted it down. They were exceedingly taken with the story, and especially the prince, who told me, with a sigh, that the true greatness of life was to be masters of ourselves; that he would not have exchanged such a state of life as mine to be Czar of Muscovy; and that he found more felicity in the retirement he seemed to be banished to there, than ever he found in the highest authority he enjoyed in the court of his master the Czar; that the height of human wisdom was to bring our tempers down to our circumstances, and to make a calm within, under the weight of the greatest storms without. When he came first hither, he said, he used to tear the hair from his head, and the clothes from his back, as others had done before him; but a little time and consideration had made him look into himself, as well as round him to things without; that he found the mind of man, if it was but once brought to reflect upon the state of universal life, and how little this world was concerned in its true felicity, was perfectly capable of making a felicity for itself, fully satisfying to itself, and suitable to its own best ends and desires, with but very little assistance from the world. That being now deprived of all the fancied felicity which he enjoyed in the full exercise of worldly pleasures, he said he was at leisure to look upon the dark side of them, where he found all manner of deformity; and was now convinced that virtue only makes a man truly wise, rich, and great, and preserves him in the way to a superior happiness in a future state; and in this, he said, they were more happy in their banishment than all their enemies were, who had the full possession of all the wealth and power they had left behind them. "Nor, sir," says he, "do I bring my mind to this politically, from the necessity of my circumstances, which some call miserable; but, if I know anything of myself, I would not now go back, though the Czar my master should call me, and reinstate me in all my former grandeur."

He spoke this with so much warmth in his temper, so much earnestness and motion of his spirits, that it was evident it was the true sense of his soul; there was no room to doubt his sincerity. I told him I once thought myself a kind of monarch in my old station, of which I had given him an account; but that I thought he was not only a monarch, but a great conqueror; for he that had got a victory over his own exorbitant desires, and the absolute dominion over himself, he whose reason entirely governs his will, is certainly greater than he that conquers a city.

I had been here eight months, and a dark, dreadful winter I thought it; the cold so intense that I could not so much as look abroad without being wrapped in furs, and a kind of mask of fur before my face, with only a hole for breath, and two for sight: the little daylight we had was for three months not above five hours a day, and six at most; only that the snow lying on the ground continually, and the weather being clear, it was never quite dark. Our horses were kept, or rather starved, underground; and as for our servants, whom we hired here to look after ourselves and horses, we had, every now and then, their fingers and toes to thaw and take care of, lest they should mortify and fall off.

It is true, within doors we were warm, the houses being close, the walls thick, the windows small, and the glass all double. Our food was chiefly the flesh of deer, dried and cured in the season; bread good enough, but baked as biscuits; dried fish of several sorts, and some flesh of mutton, and of buffaloes, which is pretty good meat. All the stores of provisions for the winter are laid up in the summer, and well cured: our drink was water, mixed with aqua vitae instead of brandy; and for a treat, mead instead of wine, which, however, they have very good. The hunters, who venture abroad all weathers, frequently brought us in fine venison, and sometimes bear's flesh, but we did not much care for the last. We had a good stock of tea, with which we treated our friends, and we lived cheerfully and well, all things considered.

It was now March, the days grown considerably longer, and the weather at least tolerable; so the other travellers began to prepare sledges to carry them over the snow, and to get things ready to be going; but my measures being fixed, as I have said, for Archangel, and not for Muscovy or the Baltic, I made no motion; knowing very well that the ships from the south do not set out for that part of the world till May or June, and that if I was there by the beginning of August, it would be as soon as any ships would be ready to sail. Therefore I made no haste to be gone, as others did: in a word, I saw a great many people, nay, all the travellers, go away before me. It seems every year they go from thence to Muscovy, for trade, to carry furs, and buy necessaries, which they bring back with them to furnish their shops: also others went on the same errand to Archangel.

In the month of May I began to make all ready to pack up; and, as I was doing this, it occurred to me that, seeing all these people were banished by the Czar to Siberia, and yet, when they came there, were left at liberty to go whither they would, why they did not then go away to any part of the world, wherever they thought fit: and I began to examine what should hinder them from making such an attempt. But my wonder was over when I entered upon that subject with the person I have mentioned, who answered me thus: "Consider, first, sir," said he, "the place where we are; and, secondly, the condition we are in; especially the generality of the people who are banished thither. We are surrounded with stronger things than bars or bolts; on the north side, an unnavigable ocean, where ship never sailed, and boat never swam; every other way we have above a thousand miles to pass through the Czar's own dominion, and by ways utterly impassable, except by the roads made by the government, and through the towns garrisoned by his troops; in short, we could neither pass undiscovered by the road, nor subsist any other way, so that it is in vain to attempt it."

I was silenced at once, and found that they were in a prison every jot as secure as if they had been locked up in the castle at Moscow: however, it came into my thoughts that I might certainly be made an instrument to procure the escape of this excellent person; and that, whatever hazard I ran, I would certainly try if I could carry him off. Upon this, I took an occasion one evening to tell him my thoughts. I represented to him that it was very easy for me to carry him away, there being no guard over him in the country; and as I was not going to Moscow, but to Archangel, and that I went in the retinue of a caravan, by which I was not obliged to lie in the stationary towns in the desert, but could encamp every night where I would, we might easily pass uninterrupted to Archangel, where I would immediately secure him on board an English ship, and carry him safe along with me; and as to his subsistence and other particulars, it should be my care till he could better supply himself.

He heard me very attentively, and looked earnestly on me all the while I spoke; nay, I could see in his very face that what I said put his spirits into an exceeding ferment; his colour frequently changed, his eyes looked red, and his heart fluttered, till it might be even perceived in his countenance; nor could he immediately answer me when I had done, and, as it were, hesitated what he would say to it; but after he had paused a little, he embraced me, and said, "How unhappy are we, unguarded creatures as we are, that even our greatest acts of friendship are made snares unto us, and we are made tempters of one another!" He then heartily thanked me for my offers of service, but withstood resolutely the arguments I used to urge him to set himself free. He declared, in earnest terms, that he was fully bent on remaining where he was rather than seek to return to his former miserable greatness, as he called it: where the seeds of pride, ambition, avarice, and luxury might revive, take root, and again overwhelm him. "Let me remain, dear sir," he said, in conclusion—"let me remain in this blessed confinement, banished from the crimes of life, rather than purchase a show of freedom at the expense of the liberty of my reason, and at the future happiness which I now have in my view, but should then, I fear, quickly lose sight of; for I am but flesh; a man, a mere man; and have passions and affections as likely to possess and overthrow me as any man: Oh, be not my friend and tempter both together!"

If I was surprised before, I was quite dumb now, and stood silent, looking at him, and, indeed, admiring what I saw. The struggle in his soul was so great that, though the weather was extremely cold, it put him into a most violent heat; so I said a word or two, that I would leave him to consider of it, and wait on him again, and then I withdrew to my own apartment.

About two hours after I heard somebody at or near the door of my room, and I was going to open the door, but he had opened it and come in. "My dear friend," says he, "you had almost overset me, but I am recovered. Do not take it ill that I do not close with your offer. I assure you it is not for want of sense of the kindness of it in you; and I came to make the most sincere acknowledgment of it to you; but I hope I have got the victory over myself."—"My lord," said I, "I hope you are fully satisfied that you do not resist the call of Heaven."—"Sir," said he, "if it had been from Heaven, the same power would have influenced me to have accepted it; but I hope, and am fully satisfied, that it is from Heaven that I decline it, and I have infinite satisfaction in the parting, that you shall leave me an honest man still, though not a free man."

I had nothing to do but to acquiesce, and make professions to him of my having no end in it but a sincere desire to serve him. He embraced me very passionately, and assured me he was sensible of that, and should always acknowledge it; and with that he offered me a very fine present of sables—too much, indeed, for me to accept from a man in his circumstances, and I would have avoided them, but he would not be refused. The next morning I sent my servant to his lordship with a small present of tea, and two pieces of China damask, and four little wedges of Japan gold, which did not all weigh above six ounces or thereabouts, but were far short of the value of his sables, which, when I came to England, I found worth near two hundred pounds. He accepted the tea, and one piece of the damask, and one of the pieces of gold, which had a fine stamp upon it, of the Japan coinage, which I found he took for the rarity of it, but would not take any more: and he sent word by my servant that he desired to speak with me.

When I came to him he told me I knew what had passed between us, and hoped I would not move him any more in that affair; but that, since I had made such a generous offer to him, he asked me if I had kindness enough to offer the same to another person that he would name to me, in whom he had a great share of concern. In a word, he told me it was his only son; who, though I had not seen him, was in the same condition with himself, and above two hundred miles from him, on the other side of the Oby; but that, if I consented, he would send for him.

I made no hesitation, but told him I would do it. I made some ceremony in letting him understand that it was wholly on his account; and that, seeing I could not prevail on him, I would show my respect to him by my concern for his son. He sent the next day for his son; and in about twenty days he came back with the messenger, bringing six or seven horses, loaded with very rich furs, which, in the whole, amounted to a very great value. His servants brought the horses into the town, but left the young lord at a distance till night, when he came incognito into our apartment, and his father presented him to me; and, in short, we concerted the manner of our travelling, and everything proper for the journey.

I had bought a considerable quantity of sables, black fox-skins, fine ermines, and such other furs as are very rich in that city, in exchange for some of the goods I had brought from China; in particular for the cloves and nutmegs, of which I sold the greatest part here, and the rest afterwards at Archangel, for a much better price than I could have got at London; and my partner, who was sensible of the profit, and whose business, more particularly than mine, was merchandise, was mightily pleased with our stay, on account of the traffic we made here.

It was the beginning of June when I left this remote place. We were now reduced to a very small caravan, having only thirty-two horses and camels in all, which passed for mine, though my new guest was proprietor of eleven of them. It was natural also that I should take more servants with me than I had before; and the young lord passed for my steward; what great man I passed for myself I know not, neither did it concern me to inquire. We had here the worst and the largest desert to pass over that we met with in our whole journey; I call it the worst, because the way was very deep in some places, and very uneven in others; the best we had to say for it was, that we thought we had no troops of Tartars or robbers to fear, as they never came on this side of the river Oby, or at least very seldom; but we found it otherwise.

My young lord had a faithful Siberian servant, who was perfectly acquainted with the country, and led us by private roads, so that we avoided coming into the principal towns and cities upon the great road, such as Tumen, Soloy Kamaskoy, and several others; because the Muscovite garrisons which are kept there are very curious and strict in their observation upon travellers, and searching lest any of the banished persons of note should make their escape that way into Muscovy; but, by this means, as we were kept out of the cities, so our whole journey was a desert, and we were obliged to encamp and lie in our tents, when we might have had very good accommodation in the cities on the way; this the young lord was so sensible of, that he would not allow us to lie abroad when we came to several cities on the way, but lay abroad himself, with his servant, in the woods, and met us always at the appointed places.

We had just entered Europe, having passed the river Kama, which in these parts is the boundary between Europe and Asia, and the first city on the European side was called Soloy Kamaskoy, that is, the great city on the river Kama. And here we thought to see some evident alteration in the people; but we were mistaken, for as we had a vast desert to pass, which is near seven hundred miles long in some places, but not above two hundred miles over where we passed it, so, till we came past that horrible place, we found very little difference between that country and Mogul Tartary. The people are mostly pagans; their houses and towns full of idols; and their way of living wholly barbarous, except in the cities and villages near them, where they are Christians, as they call themselves, of the Greek Church: but have their religion mingled with so many relics of superstition, that it is scarce to be known in some places from mere sorcery and witchcraft.

In passing this forest (after all our dangers were, to our imagination, escaped), I thought, indeed, we must have been plundered and robbed, and perhaps murdered, by a troop of thieves: of what country they were I am yet at a loss to know; but they were all on horseback, carried bows and arrows, and were at first about forty-five in number. They came so near to us as to be within two musket-shot, and, asking no questions, surrounded us with their horses, and looked very earnestly upon us twice; at length, they placed themselves just in our way; upon which we drew up in a little line, before our camels, being not above sixteen men in all. Thus drawn up, we halted, and sent out the Siberian servant, who attended his lord, to see who they were; his master was the more willing to let him go, because he was not a little apprehensive that they were a Siberian troop sent out after him. The man came up near them with a flag of truce, and called to them; but though he spoke several of their languages, or dialects of languages rather, he could not understand a word they said; however, after some signs to him not to come near them at his peril, the fellow came back no wiser than he went; only that by their dress, he said, he believed them to be some Tartars of Kalmuck, or of the Circassian hordes, and that there must be more of them upon the great desert, though he never heard that any of them were seen so far north before.

This was small comfort to us; however, we had no remedy: there was on our left hand, at about a quarter of a mile distance, a little grove, and very near the road. I immediately resolved we should advance to those trees, and fortify ourselves as well as we could there; for, first, I considered that the trees would in a great measure cover us from their arrows; and, in the next place, they could not come to charge us in a body: it was, indeed, my old Portuguese pilot who proposed it, and who had this excellency attending him, that he was always readiest and most apt to direct and encourage us in cases of the most danger. We advanced immediately, with what speed we could, and gained that little wood; the Tartars, or thieves, for we knew not what to call them, keeping their stand, and not attempting to hinder us. When we came thither, we found, to our great satisfaction, that it was a swampy piece of ground, and on the one side a very great spring of water, which, running out in a little brook, was a little farther joined by another of the like size; and was, in short, the source of a considerable river, called afterwards the Wirtska; the trees which grew about this spring were not above two hundred, but very large, and stood pretty thick, so that as soon as we got in, we saw ourselves perfectly safe from the enemy unless they attacked us on foot.

While we stayed here waiting the motion of the enemy some hours, without perceiving that they made any movement, our Portuguese, with some help, cut several arms of trees half off, and laid them hanging across from one tree to another, and in a manner fenced us in. About two hours before night they came down directly upon us; and though we had not perceived it, we found they had been joined by some more, so that they were near fourscore horse; whereof, however, we fancied some were women. They came on till they were within half-shot of our little wood, when we fired one musket without ball, and called to them in the Russian tongue to know what they wanted, and bade them keep off; but they came on with a double fury up to the wood-side, not imagining we were so barricaded that they could not easily break in. Our old pilot was our captain as well as our engineer, and desired us not to fire upon them till they came within pistol-shot, that we might be sure to kill, and that when we did fire we should be sure to take good aim; we bade him give the word of command, which he delayed so long that they were some of them within two pikes' length of us when we let fly. We aimed so true that we killed fourteen of them, and wounded several others, as also several of their horses; for we had all of us loaded our pieces with two or three bullets apiece at least.

They were terribly surprised with our fire, and retreated immediately about one hundred rods from us; in which time we loaded our pieces again, and seeing them keep that distance, we sallied out, and caught four or five of their horses, whose riders we supposed were killed; and coming up to the dead, we judged they were Tartars, but knew not how they came to make an excursion such an unusual length.

About an hour after they again made a motion to attack us, and rode round our little wood to see where they might break in; but finding us always ready to face them, they went off again; and we resolved not to stir for that night.

We slept little, but spent the most part of the night in strengthening our situation, and barricading the entrances into the wood, and keeping a strict watch. We waited for daylight, and when it came, it gave us a very unwelcome discovery indeed; for the enemy, who we thought were discouraged with the reception they met with, were now greatly increased, and had set up eleven or twelve huts or tents, as if they were resolved to besiege us; and this little camp they had pitched upon the open plain, about three-quarters of a mile from us. I confess I now gave myself over for lost, and all that I had; the loss of my effects did not lie so near me, though very considerable, as the thoughts of falling into the hands of such barbarians at the latter end of my journey, after so many difficulties and hazards as I had gone through, and even in sight of our port, where we expected safety and deliverance. As to my partner, he was raging, and declared that to lose his goods would be his ruin, and that he would rather die than be starved, and he was for fighting to the last drop.

The young lord, a most gallant youth, was for fighting to the last also; and my old pilot was of opinion that we were able to resist them all in the situation we were then in. Thus we spent the day in debates of what we should do; but towards evening we found that the number of our enemies still increased, and we did not know but by the morning they might still be a greater number: so I began to inquire of those people we had brought from Tobolski if there were no private ways by which we might avoid them in the night, and perhaps retreat to some town, or get help to guard us over the desert. The young lord's Siberian servant told us, if we designed to avoid them, and not fight, he would engage to carry us off in the night, to a way that went north, towards the river Petruz, by which he made no question but we might get away, and the Tartars never discover it; but, he said, his lord had told him he would not retreat, but would rather choose to fight. I told him he mistook his lord: for that he was too wise a man to love fighting for the sake of it; that I knew he was brave enough by what he had showed already; but that he knew better than to desire seventeen or eighteen men to fight five hundred, unless an unavoidable necessity forced them to it; and that if he thought it possible for us to escape in the night, we had nothing else to do but to attempt it. He answered, if his lordship gave him such orders, he would lose his life if he did not perform it; we soon brought his lord to give that order, though privately, and we immediately prepared for putting it in practice.

And first, as soon as it began to be dark, we kindled a fire in our little camp, which we kept burning, and prepared so as to make it burn all night, that the Tartars might conclude we were still there; but as soon as it was dark, and we could see the stars (for our guide would not stir before), having all our horses and camels ready loaded, we followed our new guide, who I soon found steered himself by the north star, the country being level for a long way.

After we had travelled two hours very hard, it began to be lighter still; not that it was dark all night, but the moon began to rise, so that, in short, it was rather lighter than we wished it to be; but by six o'clock the next morning we had got above thirty miles, having almost spoiled our horses. Here we found a Russian village, named Kermazinskoy, where we rested, and heard nothing of the Kalmuck Tartars that day. About two hours before night we set out again, and travelled till eight the next morning, though not quite so hard as before; and about seven o'clock we passed a little river, called Kirtza, and came to a good large town inhabited by Russians, called Ozomys; there we heard that several troops of Kalmucks had been abroad upon the desert, but that we were now completely out of danger of them, which was to our great satisfaction. Here we were obliged to get some fresh horses, and having need enough of rest, we stayed five days; and my partner and I agreed to give the honest Siberian who conducted us thither the value of ten pistoles.

In five days more we came to Veussima, upon the river Witzogda, and running into the Dwina: we were there, very happily, near the end of our travels by land, that river being navigable, in seven days' passage, to Archangel. From hence we came to Lawremskoy, the 3rd of July; and providing ourselves with two luggage boats, and a barge for our own convenience, we embarked the 7th, and arrived all safe at Archangel the 18th; having been a year, five months, and three days on the journey, including our stay of about eight months at Tobolski.

We were obliged to stay at this place six weeks for the arrival of the ships, and must have tarried longer, had not a Hamburgher come in above a month sooner than any of the English ships; when, after some consideration that the city of Hamburgh might happen to be as good a market for our goods as London, we all took freight with him; and, having put our goods on board, it was most natural for me to put my steward on board to take care of them; by which means my young lord had a sufficient opportunity to conceal himself, never coming on shore again all the time we stayed there; and this he did that he might not be seen in the city, where some of the Moscow merchants would certainly have seen and discovered him.

We then set sail from Archangel the 20th of August, the same year; and, after no extraordinary bad voyage, arrived safe in the Elbe the 18th of September. Here my partner and I found a very good sale for our goods, as well those of China as the sables, &c., of Siberia: and, dividing the produce, my share amounted to £3475, 17s 3d., including about six hundred pounds' worth of diamonds, which I purchased at Bengal.

Here the young lord took his leave of us, and went up the Elbe, in order to go to the court of Vienna, where he resolved to seek protection and could correspond with those of his father's friends who were left alive. He did not part without testimonials of gratitude for the service I had done him, and for my kindness to the prince, his father.

To conclude: having stayed near four months in Hamburgh, I came from thence by land to the Hague, where I embarked in the packet, and arrived in London the 10th of January 1705, having been absent from England ten years and nine months. And here, resolving to harass myself no more, I am preparing for a longer journey than all these, having lived seventy-two years a life of infinite variety, and learned sufficiently to know the value of retirement, and the blessing of ending our days in peace.

GULLIVER'S TRAVELS

JONATHAN SWIFT

THE PUBLISHER TO THE READER

[AS GIVEN IN THE ORIGINAL EDITION.]

The author of these Travels, Mr. Lemuel Gulliver, is my ancient and intimate friend; there is likewise some relation between us on the mother's side. About three years ago, Mr. Gulliver growing weary of the concourse of curious people coming to him at his house in Redriff, made a small purchase of land, with a convenient house, near Newark, in Nottinghamshire, his native country; where he now lives retired, yet in good esteem among his neighbours.

Although Mr. Gulliver was born in Nottinghamshire, where his father dwelt, yet I have heard him say his family came from Oxfordshire; to confirm which, I have observed in the churchyard at Banbury in that county, several tombs and monuments of the Gullivers.

Before he quitted Redriff, he left the custody of the following papers in my hands, with the liberty to dispose of them as I should think fit. I have carefully perused them three times. The style is very plain and simple; and the only fault I find is, that the author, after the manner of travellers, is a little too circumstantial. There is an air of truth apparent through the whole; and indeed the author was so distinguished for his veracity, that it became a sort of proverb among his neighbours at Redriff, when any one affirmed a thing, to say, it was as true as if Mr. Gulliver had spoken it.

By the advice of several worthy persons, to whom, with the author's permission, I communicated these papers, I now venture to send them into the world, hoping they may be, at least for some time, a better entertainment to our young noblemen, than the common scribbles of politics and party.

This volume would have been at least twice as large, if I had not made bold to strike out innumerable passages relating to the winds and tides, as well as to the variations and bearings in the several voyages, together with the minute descriptions of the management of the ship in storms, in the style of sailors; likewise the account of longitudes and latitudes; wherein I have reason to apprehend, that Mr. Gulliver may be a little dissatisfied. But I was resolved to fit the work as much as possible to the general capacity of readers. However, if my own ignorance in sea affairs shall have led me to commit some mistakes, I alone am answerable for them. And if any traveller hath a curiosity to see the whole work at large, as it came from the hands of the author, I will be ready to gratify him.

THE PUBLISHER TO THE READER

As for any further particulars relating to the author, the reader will receive satisfaction from the first pages of the book.

RICHARD SYMPSON.

A LETTER FROM CAPTAIN GULLIVER TO HIS COUSIN SYMPSON

WRITTEN IN THE YEAR 1727

I hope you will be ready to own publicly, whenever you shall be called to it, that by your great and frequent urgency you prevailed on me to publish a very loose and uncorrect account of my travels, with directions to hire some young gentleman of either university to put them in order, and correct the style, as my cousin Dampier did, by my advice, in his book called "A Voyage round the world." But I do not remember I gave you power to consent that any thing should be omitted, and much less that any thing should be inserted; therefore, as to the latter, I do here renounce every thing of that kind; particularly a paragraph about her majesty Queen Anne, of most pious and glorious memory; although I did reverence and esteem her more than any of human species. But you, or your interpolator, ought to have considered, that it was not my inclination, so was it not decent to praise any animal of our composition before my master *Houyhnhnm*: And besides, the fact was altogether false; for to my knowledge, being in England during some part of her majesty's reign, she did govern by a chief minister; nay even by two successively, the first whereof was the lord of Godolphin, and the second the lord of Oxford; so that you have made me say the thing that was not. Likewise in the account of the academy of projectors, and several passages of my discourse to my master *Houyhnhnm*, you have either omitted some material circumstances, or minced or changed them in such a manner, that I do hardly know my own work. When I formerly hinted to you something of this in a letter, you were pleased to answer that you were afraid of giving offence; that people in power were very watchful over the press, and apt not only to interpret, but to punish every thing which looked like an *innuendo* (as I think you call it). But, pray how could that which I spoke so many years ago, and at about five thousand leagues distance, in another reign, be applied to any of the *Yahoos*, who now are said to govern the herd; especially at a time when I little thought, or feared, the unhappiness of living under them? Have not I the most reason to complain, when I see these very *Yahoos* carried by *Houyhnhnms* in a vehicle, as if they were brutes, and those the rational creatures? And indeed to avoid so monstrous and detestable a sight was one principal motive of my retirement hither.

A LETTER FROM CAPTAIN GULLIVER TO HIS COUSIN SYMPSON

Thus much I thought proper to tell you in relation to yourself, and to the trust I reposed in you.

I do, in the next place, complain of my own great want of judgment, in being prevailed upon by the entreaties and false reasoning of you and some others, very much against my own opinion, to suffer my travels to be published. Pray bring to your mind how often I desired you to consider, when you insisted on the motive of public good, that the *Yahoos* were a species of animals utterly incapable of amendment by precept or example: and so it has proved; for, instead of seeing a full stop put to all abuses and corruptions, at least in this little island, as I had reason to expect; behold, after above six months warning, I cannot learn that my book has produced one single effect according to my intentions. I desired you would let me know, by a letter, when party and faction were extinguished; judges learned and upright; pleaders honest and modest, with some tincture of common sense, and Smithfield blazing with pyramids of law books; the young nobility's education entirely changed; the physicians banished; the female *Yahoos* abounding in virtue, honour, truth, and good sense; courts and levees of great ministers thoroughly weeded and swept; wit, merit, and learning rewarded; all disgracers of the press in prose and verse condemned to eat nothing but their own cotton, and quench their thirst with their own ink. These, and a thousand other reformations, I firmly counted upon by your encouragement; as indeed they were plainly deducible from the precepts delivered in my book. And it must be owned, that seven months were a sufficient time to correct every vice and folly to which *Yahoos* are subject, if their natures had been capable of the least disposition to virtue or wisdom. Yet, so far have you been from answering my expectation in any of your letters; that on the contrary you are loading our carrier every week with libels, and keys, and reflections, and memoirs, and second parts; wherein I see myself accused of reflecting upon great state folk; of degrading human nature (for so they have still the confidence to style it), and of abusing the female sex. I find likewise that the writers of those bundles are not agreed among themselves; for some of them will not allow me to be the author of my own travels; and others make me author of books to which I am wholly a stranger.

I find likewise that your printer has been so careless as to confound the times, and mistake the dates, of my several voyages and returns; neither assigning the true year, nor the true month, nor day of the month: and I hear the original manuscript is all destroyed since the publication of my book; neither have I any copy left: however, I have sent you some corrections, which you may insert, if ever there should be a second edition: and yet I cannot stand to them; but shall leave that matter to my judicious and candid readers to adjust it as they please.

I hear some of our sea *Yahoos* find fault with my sea-language, as not proper in many parts, nor now in use. I cannot help it. In my first voyages, while I was young, I was instructed by the oldest mariners, and learned to speak as they did. But I have since found that the sea *Yahoos* are apt, like the land ones, to become new-fangled in their words, which the latter change every year; insomuch, as I remember upon each return to my own country their old dialect was so altered, that I could hardly understand the new. And I observe, when any *Yahoo* comes from London out of curiosity to visit me at my house, we neither of us are able to deliver our conceptions in a manner intelligible to the other.

If the censure of the *Yahoos* could any way affect me, I should have great reason to complain, that some of them are so bold as to think my book of travels a mere fiction out of mine own brain, and have gone so far as to drop hints, that the *Houyhnhnms* and *Yahoos* have no more existence than the inhabitants of Utopia.

Indeed I must confess, that as to the people of *Lilliput, Brobdingrag* (for so the word should have been spelt, and not erroneously *Brobdingnag*), and *Laputa*, I have never yet heard of any *Yahoo* so presumptuous as to dispute their being, or the facts I have related concerning them; because the truth immediately strikes every reader with conviction. And is there less probability in my account of the *Houyhnhnms* or *Yahoos*, when it is manifest as to the latter, there are so many thousands even in this country, who only differ from their brother brutes in *Houyhnhnmland*, because they use a sort of jabber, and do not go naked? I wrote for their amendment, and not their approbation. The united praise of the whole race would be of less consequence to me, than the neighing of those two degenerate *Houyhnhnms* I keep in my stable; because from these, degenerate as they are, I still improve in some virtues without any mixture of vice.

Do these miserable animals presume to think, that I am so degenerated as to defend my veracity? *Yahoo* as I am, it is well known through all *Houyhnhnmland*, that, by the instructions and example of my illustrious master, I was able in the compass of two years (although I confess with the utmost difficulty) to remove that infernal habit of lying, shuffling, deceiving, and equivocating, so deeply rooted in the very souls of all my species; especially the Europeans.

I have other complaints to make upon this vexatious occasion; but I forbear troubling myself or you any further. I must freely confess, that since my last return, some corruptions of my *Yahoo* nature have revived in me by conversing with a few of your species, and particularly those of my own family, by an unavoidable necessity; else I should never have attempted so absurd a project as that of reforming the *Yahoo* race in this kingdom: But I have now done with all such visionary schemes for ever.

April 2, 1727

I
A VOYAGE TO LILLIPUT

I

THE AUTHOR GIVES SOME ACCOUNT OF HIMSELF AND FAMILY. HIS FIRST INDUCEMENTS TO TRAVEL. HE IS SHIPWRECKED, AND SWIMS FOR HIS LIFE. GETS SAFE ON SHORE IN THE COUNTRY OF LILLIPUT; IS MADE A PRISONER, AND CARRIED UP THE COUNTRY.

My father had a small estate in Nottinghamshire: I was the third of five sons. He sent me to Emanuel College in Cambridge at fourteen years old, where I resided three years, and applied myself close to my studies; but the charge of maintaining me, although I had a very scanty allowance, being too great for a narrow fortune, I was bound apprentice to Mr. James Bates, an eminent surgeon in London, with whom I continued four years. My father now and then sending me small sums of money, I laid them out in learning navigation, and other parts of the mathematics, useful to those who intend to travel, as I always believed it would be, some time or other, my fortune to do. When I left Mr. Bates, I went down to my father: where, by the assistance of him and my uncle John, and some other relations, I got forty pounds, and a promise of thirty pounds a year to maintain me at Leyden: there I studied physic two years and seven months, knowing it would be useful in long voyages.

Soon after my return from Leyden, I was recommended by my good master, Mr. Bates, to be surgeon to the Swallow, Captain Abraham Pannel, commander; with whom I continued three years and a half, making a voyage or two into the Levant, and some other parts. When I came back I resolved to settle in London; to which Mr. Bates, my master, encouraged me, and by him I was recommended to several patients. I took part of a small house in the Old Jewry; and being advised to alter my condition, I married Mrs. Mary Burton, second daughter to Mr. Edmund Burton, hosier, in Newgate-street, with whom I received four hundred pounds for a portion.

But my good master Bates dying in two years after, and I having few friends, my business began to fail; for my conscience would not suffer me to imitate the bad practice of too many among my brethren. Having therefore consulted with my wife, and some of my acquaintance, I determined to go again to sea. I was surgeon successively in two ships, and made several voyages, for six years, to the East and West Indies, by which I got some addition to my fortune. My hours of leisure I spent in reading the best authors, ancient and modern, being always provided with a good number of books; and when I was ashore, in observing the manners and dispositions of the people, as well as learning their language; wherein I had a great facility, by the strength of my memory.

JONATHAN SWIFT

The last of these voyages not proving very fortunate, I grew weary of the sea, and intended to stay at home with my wife and family. I removed from the Old Jewry to Fetter Lane, and from thence to Wapping, hoping to get business among the sailors; but it would not turn to account. After three years expectation that things would mend, I accepted an advantageous offer from Captain William Prichard, master of the Antelope, who was making a voyage to the South Sea. We set sail from Bristol, May 4, 1699, and our voyage was at first very prosperous.

It would not be proper, for some reasons, to trouble the reader with the particulars of our adventures in those seas; let it suffice to inform him, that in our passage from thence to the East Indies, we were driven by a violent storm to the north-west of Van Diemen's Land. By an observation, we found ourselves in the latitude of 30 degrees 2 minutes south. Twelve of our crew were dead by immoderate labour and ill food; the rest were in a very weak condition. On the 5th of November, which was the beginning of summer in those parts, the weather being very hazy, the seamen spied a rock within half a cable's length of the ship; but the wind was so strong, that we were driven directly upon it, and immediately split. Six of the crew, of whom I was one, having let down the boat into the sea, made a shift to get clear of the ship and the rock. We rowed, by my computation, about three leagues, till we were able to work no longer, being already spent with labour while we were in the ship. We therefore trusted ourselves to the mercy of the waves, and in about half an hour the boat was overset by a sudden flurry from the north. What became of my companions in the boat, as well as of those who escaped on the rock, or were left in the vessel, I cannot tell; but conclude they were all lost. For my own part, I swam as fortune directed me, and was pushed forward by wind and tide. I often let my legs drop, and could feel no bottom; but when I was almost gone, and able to struggle no longer, I found myself within my depth; and by this time the storm was much abated. The declivity was so small, that I walked near a mile before I got to the shore, which I conjectured was about eight o'clock in the evening. I then advanced forward near half a mile, but could not discover any sign of houses or inhabitants; at least I was in so weak a condition, that I did not observe them. I was extremely tired, and with that, and the heat of the weather, and about half a pint of brandy that I drank as I left the ship, I found myself much inclined to sleep. I lay down on the grass, which was very short and soft, where I slept sounder than ever I remembered to have done in my life, and, as I reckoned, about nine hours; for when I awaked, it was just day-light. I attempted to rise, but was not able to stir: for, as I happened to lie on my back, I found my arms and legs were strongly fastened on each side to the ground; and my hair, which was long and thick, tied down in the same manner. I likewise felt several slender ligatures across my body, from my arm-pits to my thighs. I could only look upwards; the sun began to grow hot, and the light offended my eyes. I heard a confused noise about me; but in the posture I lay, could see nothing except the sky. In a little time I felt something alive moving on my left leg, which advancing gently forward over my breast, came almost up to my chin; when, bending my eyes downwards as much as I could, I perceived it to be a human creature not six inches high, with a bow and arrow in his hands, and a quiver at his back. In the mean time, I felt at least forty more of the same kind (as I conjectured) following the first. I was in the utmost astonishment, and roared so loud, that they all ran back in a fright; and some of them, as I was afterwards told, were hurt with the falls they got by leaping from my sides upon the ground. However, they soon returned, and one of them, who ventured so far as to get a full sight of my face, lifting up his hands and eyes by way of admiration, cried out in a shrill but distinct voice, *Hekinah degul*: the others repeated the same words several times, but then I knew not what they meant. I lay all this while, as the reader may believe, in great uneasiness. At length, struggling to get loose, I had the fortune to break the strings, and wrench out the pegs that fastened my left arm to the ground; for, by lifting it up to my face, I discovered the methods they had taken to bind me, and at the same time with a violent pull, which gave me excessive pain, I a little loosened the strings that tied down my hair on the left side, so that I was just able to turn my head about two inches. But the creatures ran off a second time, before I could seize them; whereupon there was a great shout in a very shrill accent, and after it ceased I heard one of them cry aloud *Tolgo phonac*; when in an instant I felt above a hundred arrows discharged on my left hand, which, pricked me like so many needles; and besides, they shot another flight into the air, as we do bombs in Europe, whereof many, I suppose, fell on my body, (though I felt them not), and some on my face, which I immediately covered with my left hand. When this shower of arrows was over, I fell a groaning with grief and pain; and then striving again to get loose, they discharged another volley larger than the first, and some of them attempted with spears to stick me in the sides; but by good luck I had on a buff jerkin, which they could not pierce. I thought it the most prudent method to lie still, and my design was to continue so till night, when, my left hand being already loose, I could easily free myself: and as for the inhabitants, I had reason to believe I might be a match for the greatest army they could bring against me, if they were all of the same size with him that I saw. But fortune disposed otherwise of me. When the people observed I was quiet, they discharged no more arrows; but, by the noise I heard, I knew their numbers increased; and about four yards from me, over against my right ear, I heard a knocking for above an hour, like that of people at work; when turning my head that way, as well as the pegs and strings would permit me, I saw a stage erected about a foot and a half from the ground, capable of holding four of the inhabitants, with two or three ladders to mount it: from whence one of them, who seemed to be a person of quality, made me a long speech, whereof I understood not one syllable. But I should have mentioned, that before the principal person began his oration, he cried out three times, *Langro dehul san* (these words and the former were afterwards repeated and explained to me); whereupon, immediately, about fifty of the inhabitants came and cut the strings that fastened the left side of my head, which gave me the liberty of turning it to the right, and of observing the person and gesture of him that was to speak. He appeared to be of a middle age, and taller than any of the other three who attended him, whereof one was a page that held up his train, and seemed to be somewhat longer than my middle finger; the other two stood one on each side to support him. He acted every part of an orator, and I could observe many periods of threatenings, and others of promises, pity, and kindness. I answered in a few words, but in the most submissive manner, lifting up my left hand, and both my eyes to the sun, as calling him for a witness; and being almost famished with hunger, having not eaten a morsel for some hours before I left the ship, I found the demands of nature so strong upon me, that I could not forbear showing my impatience (perhaps against the strict rules of decency) by putting my finger frequently to my mouth, to signify that I wanted food. The *hurgo* (for so they call a great lord, as I afterwards learnt) understood me very well. He descended from the stage, and commanded that several ladders should be applied to my sides, on which above a hundred of the inhabitants mounted and walked towards my mouth, laden with baskets full of meat, which had been provided and sent thither by the king's orders, upon the first intelligence he received of me. I observed there was the flesh of several animals, but could not distinguish them by the taste. There were shoulders, legs, and loins, shaped like those of mutton, and very well dressed, but smaller than the wings of a lark. I ate them by two or three at a mouthful, and took three loaves at a time, about the bigness of musket bullets. They supplied me as fast as they could, showing a thousand marks of wonder and astonishment at my bulk and appetite. I then made another sign, that I wanted drink. They found by my eating that a small quantity would not suffice me; and being a most ingenious people, they slung up, with great dexterity, one of their largest hogsheads, then rolled it towards my hand, and beat out the top; I drank it off at a draught, which I might well do, for it did not hold half a pint, and tasted like a small wine of Burgundy, but much more delicious. They brought me a second hogshead, which I drank in the same manner, and made signs for more; but they had none to give me. When I had performed these wonders, they shouted for joy, and danced upon my breast, repeating several times as they did at first, *Hekinah degul*. They made me a sign that I should throw down the two hogsheads, but first warning the people below to stand out of the way, crying aloud, *Borach mevolah*; and when they saw the vessels in the air, there was a universal shout of *Hekinah degul*. I confess I was often tempted, while they were passing backwards and forwards on my body, to seize forty or fifty of the first that came in my reach, and dash them against the ground. But the remembrance of what I had felt, which probably might not be the worst they could do, and the promise of honour I made them—for so I interpreted my submissive behaviour—soon drove out these imaginations. Besides, I now considered myself as bound by the laws of hospitality, to a people who had treated me with so much expense and magnificence. However, in my thoughts I could not sufficiently wonder at the intrepidity of these diminutive mortals, who durst venture to mount and walk upon my body, while one of my hands was at liberty, without trembling at the very sight of so prodigious a creature as I must appear to them. After some time, when they observed that I made no more demands for meat, there appeared before me a person of high rank from his imperial majesty. His excellency, having mounted on the small of my right leg, advanced forwards up to my face, with about a dozen of his retinue; and producing his credentials under the signet royal, which he applied close to my eyes, spoke about ten minutes without any signs of anger, but with a kind of determinate resolution, often pointing forwards, which, as I afterwards found, was towards the capital city, about half a mile distant; whither it was agreed by his majesty in council that I must be conveyed. I answered in few words, but to no purpose, and made a sign with my hand that was loose, putting it to the other (but over his excellency's head for fear of hurting him or his train) and then to my own head and body, to signify that I desired my liberty. It appeared that he understood me well enough, for he shook his head by way of disapprobation, and held his hand in a posture to show that I must be carried as a prisoner. However, he made other signs to let me understand that I should have meat and drink enough, and very good treatment. Whereupon I once more thought of attempting to break my bonds; but again, when I felt the smart of their arrows upon my face and hands, which were all in blisters, and many of the darts still sticking in them, and observing likewise that the number of my enemies increased, I gave tokens to let them know that they might do with me what they pleased. Upon this, the *hurgo* and his train withdrew, with much civility and cheerful countenances. Soon after I heard a general shout, with frequent repetitions of the words *Peplom selan*; and I felt great numbers of people on my left side relaxing the cords to such a degree, that I was able to turn upon my right, and to ease myself with making water; which I very plentifully did, to the great astonishment of the people; who, conjecturing by my motion what I was going to do, immediately opened to the right and left on that side, to avoid the torrent, which fell with such noise and violence from me. But before this, they had daubed my face and both my hands with a sort of ointment, very pleasant to the smell, which, in a few minutes, removed all the smart of their arrows. These circumstances, added to the refreshment I had received by their victuals and drink, which were very nourishing, disposed me to sleep. I slept about eight hours, as I was afterwards assured; and it was no wonder, for the physicians, by the emperor's order, had mingled a sleepy potion in the hogsheads of wine.

It seems, that upon the first moment I was discovered sleeping on the ground, after my landing, the emperor had early notice of it by an express; and determined in council, that I should be tied in the manner I have related, (which was done in the night while I slept;) that plenty of meat and drink should be sent to me, and a machine prepared to carry me to the capital city.

This resolution perhaps may appear very bold and dangerous, and I am confident would not be imitated by any prince in Europe on the like occasion. However, in my opinion, it was extremely prudent, as well as generous: for, supposing these people had endeavoured to kill me with their spears and arrows, while I was asleep, I should certainly have awaked with the first sense of smart, which might so far have roused my rage and strength, as to have enabled me to break the strings wherewith I was tied; after which, as they were not able to make resistance, so they could expect no mercy.

These people are most excellent mathematicians, and arrived to a great perfection in mechanics, by the countenance and encouragement of the emperor, who is a renowned patron of learning. This prince has several machines fixed on wheels, for the carriage of trees and other great weights. He often builds his largest men of war, whereof some are nine feet long, in the woods where the timber grows, and has them carried on these engines three or four hundred yards to the sea. Five hundred carpenters and engineers were immediately set at work to prepare the greatest engine they had. It was a frame of wood raised three inches from the ground, about seven feet long, and four wide, moving upon twenty-two wheels. The shout I heard was upon the arrival of this engine, which, it seems, set out in four hours after my landing. It was brought parallel to me, as I lay. But the principal difficulty was to raise and place me in this vehicle. Eighty poles, each of one foot high, were erected for this purpose, and very strong cords, of the bigness of packthread, were fastened by hooks to many bandages, which the workmen had girt round my neck, my hands, my body, and my legs. Nine hundred of the strongest men were employed to draw up these cords, by many pulleys fastened on the poles; and thus, in less than three hours, I was raised and slung into the engine, and there tied fast. All this I was told; for, while the operation was performing, I lay in a profound sleep, by the force of that soporiferous medicine infused into my liquor. Fifteen hundred of the emperor's largest horses, each about four inches and a half high, were employed to draw me towards the metropolis, which, as I said, was half a mile distant.

About four hours after we began our journey, I awaked by a very ridiculous accident; for the carriage being stopped a while, to adjust something that was out of order, two or three of the young natives had the curiosity to see how I looked when I was asleep; they climbed up into the engine, and advancing very softly to my face, one of them, an officer in the guards, put the sharp end of his half-pike a good way up into my left nostril, which tickled my nose like a straw, and made me sneeze violently; whereupon they stole off unperceived, and it was three weeks before I knew the cause of my waking so suddenly. We made a long march the remaining part of the day, and, rested at night with five hundred guards on each side of me, half with torches, and half with bows and arrows, ready to shoot me if I should offer to stir. The next morning at sun-rise we continued our march, and arrived within two hundred yards of the city gates about noon. The emperor, and all his court, came out to meet us; but his great officers would by no means suffer his majesty to endanger his person by mounting on my body.

At the place where the carriage stopped there stood an ancient temple, esteemed to be the largest in the whole kingdom; which, having been polluted some years before by an unnatural murder, was, according to the zeal of those people, looked upon as profane, and therefore had been applied to common use, and all the ornaments and furniture carried away. In this edifice it was determined I should lodge. The great gate fronting to the north was about four feet high, and almost two feet wide, through which I could easily creep. On each side of the gate was a small window, not above six inches from the ground: into that on the left side, the king's smith conveyed fourscore and eleven chains, like those that hang to a lady's watch in Europe, and almost as large, which were locked to my left leg with six-and-thirty padlocks. Over against this temple, on the other side of the great highway, at twenty feet distance, there was a turret at least five feet high. Here the emperor ascended, with many principal lords of his court, to have an opportunity of viewing me, as I was told, for I could not see them. It was reckoned that above a hundred thousand inhabitants came out of the town upon the same errand; and, in spite of my guards, I believe there could not be fewer than ten thousand at several times, who mounted my body by the help of ladders. But a proclamation was soon issued, to forbid it upon pain of death. When the workmen found it was impossible for me to break loose, they cut all the strings that bound me; whereupon I rose up, with as melancholy a disposition as ever I had in my life. But the noise and astonishment of the people, at seeing me rise and walk, are not to be expressed. The chains that held my left leg were about two yards long, and gave me not only the liberty of walking backwards and forwards in a semicircle, but, being fixed within four inches of the gate, allowed me to creep in, and lie at my full length in the temple.

2

THE EMPEROR OF LILLIPUT, ATTENDED BY SEVERAL OF THE NOBILITY, COMES TO SEE THE AUTHOR IN HIS CONFINEMENT. THE EMPEROR'S PERSON AND HABIT DESCRIBED. LEARNED MEN APPOINTED TO TEACH THE AUTHOR THEIR LANGUAGE. HE GAINS FAVOUR BY HIS MILD DISPOSITION. HIS POCKETS ARE SEARCHED, AND HIS SWORD AND PISTOLS TAKEN FROM HIM.

When I found myself on my feet, I looked about me, and must confess I never beheld a more entertaining prospect. The country around appeared like a continued garden, and the enclosed fields, which were generally forty feet square, resembled so many beds of flowers. These fields were intermingled with woods of half a stang,[1] and the tallest trees, as I could judge, appeared to be seven feet high. I viewed the town on my left hand, which looked like the painted scene of a city in a theatre.

    I had been for some hours extremely pressed by the necessities of nature; which was no wonder, it being almost two days since I had last disburdened myself. I was under great difficulties between urgency and shame. The best expedient I could think of, was to creep into my house, which I accordingly did; and shutting the gate after me, I went as far as the length of my chain would suffer, and discharged my body of that uneasy load. But this was the only time I was ever guilty of so uncleanly an action; for which I cannot but hope the candid reader will give some allowance, after he has maturely and impartially considered my case, and the distress I was in. From this time my constant practice was, as soon as I rose, to perform that business in open air, at the full extent of my chain; and due care was taken every morning before company came, that the offensive matter should be carried off in wheel-barrows, by two servants appointed for that purpose. I would not have dwelt so long upon a circumstance that, perhaps, at first sight, may appear not very momentous, if I had not thought it necessary to justify my character, in point of cleanliness, to the world; which, I am told, some of my maligners have been pleased, upon this and other occasions, to call in question.

    When this adventure was at an end, I came back out of my house, having occasion for fresh air. The emperor was already descended from the tower, and advancing on horseback towards me, which had like to have cost him dear; for the beast, though very well trained, yet wholly unused to such a sight, which appeared as if a mountain moved before him, reared up on its hinder feet: but that prince, who is an excellent horseman, kept his seat, till his attendants ran in, and held the bridle, while his majesty had time to dismount. When he alighted, he surveyed me round with great admiration; but kept beyond the length of my chain. He ordered his cooks and butlers, who were already prepared, to give me victuals and drink, which they pushed forward in a sort of vehicles upon wheels, till I could reach them. I took these vehicles and soon emptied them all; twenty of them were filled with meat, and ten with liquor; each of the former afforded me two or three good mouthfuls; and I emptied the liquor of ten vessels, which was contained in earthen vials, into one vehicle, drinking it off at a draught; and so I did with the rest. The empress, and young princes of the blood of both sexes, attended by many ladies, sat at some distance in their chairs; but upon the accident that happened to the emperor's horse, they alighted, and came near his person, which I am now going to describe. He is taller by almost the breadth of my nail, than any of his court; which alone is enough to strike an awe into the beholders. His features are strong and masculine, with an Austrian lip and arched nose, his complexion olive, his countenance erect, his body and limbs well proportioned, all his motions graceful, and his deportment majestic. He was then past his prime, being twenty-eight years and three quarters old, of which he had reigned about seven in great felicity, and generally victorious. For the better convenience of beholding him, I lay on my side, so that my face was parallel to his, and he stood but three yards off: however, I have had him since many times in my hand, and therefore cannot be deceived in the description. His dress was very plain and simple, and the fashion of it between the Asiatic and the European; but he had on his head a light helmet of gold, adorned with jewels, and a plume on the crest. He held his sword drawn in his hand to defend himself, if I should happen to break loose; it was almost three inches long; the hilt and scabbard were gold enriched with diamonds. His voice was shrill, but very clear and articulate; and I could distinctly hear it when I stood up. The ladies and courtiers were all most magnificently clad; so that the spot they stood upon seemed to resemble a petticoat spread upon the ground, embroidered with figures of gold and silver. His imperial majesty spoke often to me, and I returned answers: but neither of us could understand a syllable. There were several of his priests and lawyers present (as I conjectured by their habits), who were commanded to address themselves to me; and I spoke to them in as many languages as I had the least smattering of, which were High and Low Dutch, Latin, French, Spanish, Italian, and Lingua Franca, but all to no purpose. After about two hours the court retired, and I was left with a strong guard, to prevent the impertinence, and probably the malice of the rabble, who were very impatient to crowd about me as near as they durst; and some of them had the impudence to shoot their arrows at me, as I sat on the ground by the door of my house, whereof one very narrowly missed my left eye. But the colonel ordered six of the ringleaders to be seized, and thought no punishment so proper as to deliver them bound into my hands; which some of his soldiers accordingly did, pushing them forward with the butt-ends of their pikes into my reach. I took them all in my right hand, put five of them into my coat-pocket; and as to the sixth, I made a countenance as if I would eat him alive. The poor man squalled terribly, and the colonel and his officers were in much pain, especially when they saw me take out my penknife: but I soon put them out of fear; for, looking mildly, and immediately cutting the strings he was bound with, I set him gently on the ground, and away he ran. I treated the rest in the same manner, taking them one by one out of my pocket; and I observed both the soldiers and people were highly delighted at this mark of my clemency, which was represented very much to my advantage at court.

Towards night I got with some difficulty into my house, where I lay on the ground, and continued to do so about a fortnight; during which time, the emperor gave orders to have a bed prepared for me. Six hundred beds of the common measure were brought in carriages, and worked up in my house; a hundred and fifty of their beds, sewn together, made up the breadth and length; and these were four double: which, however, kept me but very indifferently from the hardness of the floor, that was of smooth stone. By the same computation, they provided me with sheets, blankets, and coverlets, tolerable enough for one who had been so long inured to hardships.

As the news of my arrival spread through the kingdom, it brought prodigious numbers of rich, idle, and curious people to see me; so that the villages were almost emptied; and great neglect of tillage and household affairs must have ensued, if his imperial majesty had not provided, by several proclamations and orders of state, against this inconveniency. He directed that those who had already beheld me should return home, and not presume to come within fifty yards of my house, without license from the court; whereby the secretaries of state got considerable fees.

In the mean time the emperor held frequent councils, to debate what course should be taken with me; and I was afterwards assured by a particular friend, a person of great quality, who was as much in the secret as any, that the court was under many difficulties concerning me. They apprehended my breaking loose; that my diet would be very expensive, and might cause a famine. Sometimes they determined to starve me; or at least to shoot me in the face and hands with poisoned arrows, which would soon despatch me; but again they considered, that the stench of so large a carcass might produce a plague in the metropolis, and probably spread through the whole kingdom. In the midst of these consultations, several officers of the army went to the door of the great council-chamber, and two of them being admitted, gave an account of my behaviour to the six criminals above-mentioned; which made so favourable an impression in the breast of his majesty and the whole board, in my behalf, that an imperial commission was issued out, obliging all the villages, nine hundred yards round the city, to deliver in every morning six beeves, forty sheep, and other victuals for my sustenance; together with a proportionable quantity of bread, and wine, and other liquors; for the due payment of which, his majesty gave assignments upon his treasury: —for this prince lives chiefly upon his own demesnes; seldom, except upon great occasions, raising any subsidies upon his subjects, who are bound to attend him in his wars at their own expense. An establishment was also made of six hundred persons to be my domestics, who had board-wages allowed for their maintenance, and tents built for them very conveniently on each side of my door. It was likewise ordered, that three hundred tailors should make me a suit of clothes, after the fashion of the country; that six of his majesty's greatest scholars should be employed to instruct me in their language; and lastly, that the emperor's horses, and those of the nobility and troops of guards, should be frequently exercised in my sight, to accustom themselves to me. All these orders were duly put in execution; and in about three weeks I made a great progress in learning their language; during which time the emperor frequently honoured me with his visits, and was pleased to assist my masters in teaching me. We began already to converse together in some sort; and the first words I learnt, were to express my desire "that he would please give me my liberty;" which I every day repeated on my knees. His answer, as I could comprehend it, was, "that this must be a work of time, not to be thought on without the advice of his council, and that first I must *lumos kelmin pesso desmar lon emposo;*" that is, swear a peace with him and his kingdom. However, that I should be used with all kindness. And he advised me to "acquire, by my patience and discreet behaviour, the good opinion of himself and his subjects." He desired "I would not take it ill, if he gave orders to certain proper officers to search me; for probably I might carry about me several weapons, which must needs be dangerous things, if they answered the bulk of so prodigious a person." I said, "His majesty should be satisfied; for I was ready to strip myself, and turn up my pockets before him." This I delivered part in words, and part in signs. He replied, "that, by the laws of the kingdom, I must be searched by two of his officers; that he knew this could not be done without my consent and assistance; and he had so good an opinion of my generosity and justice, as to trust their persons in my hands; that whatever they took from me, should be returned when I left the country, or paid for at the rate which I would set upon them." I took up the two officers in my hands, put them first into my coat-pockets, and then into every other pocket about me, except my two fobs, and another secret pocket, which I had no mind should be searched, wherein I had some little necessaries that were of no consequence to any but myself. In one of my fobs there was a silver watch, and in the other a small quantity of gold in a purse. These gentlemen, having pen, ink, and paper, about them, made an exact inventory of every thing they saw; and when they had done, desired I would set them down, that they might deliver it to the emperor. This inventory I afterwards translated into English, and is, word for word, as follows:

"*Imprimis*: In the right coat-pocket of the great man-mountain" (for so I interpret the words *quinbus flestrin*,) "after the strictest search, we found only one great piece of coarse-cloth, large enough to be a foot-cloth for your majesty's chief room of state. In the left pocket we saw a huge silver chest, with a cover of the same metal, which we, the searchers, were not able to lift. We desired it should be opened, and one of us stepping into it, found himself up to the mid leg in a sort of dust, some part whereof flying up to our faces set us both a sneezing for several times together. In his right waistcoat-pocket we found a prodigious bundle of white thin substances, folded one over another, about the bigness of three men, tied with a strong cable, and marked with black figures; which we humbly conceive to be writings, every letter almost half as large as the palm of our hands. In the left there was a sort of engine, from the back of which were extended twenty long poles, resembling the pallisados before your majesty's court: wherewith we conjecture the man-mountain combs his head; for we did not always trouble him with questions, because we found it a great difficulty to make him understand us. In the large pocket, on the right side of his middle cover" (so I translate the word *ranfulo*, by which they meant my breeches,) "we saw a hollow pillar of iron, about the length of a man, fastened to a strong piece of timber larger than the pillar; and upon one side of the pillar, were huge pieces of iron sticking out, cut into strange figures, which we know not what to make of. In the left pocket, another engine of the same kind. In the smaller pocket on the right side, were several round flat pieces of white and red metal, of different bulk; some of the white, which seemed to be silver, were so large and heavy, that my comrade and I could hardly lift them. In the left pocket were two black pillars irregularly shaped: we could not, without difficulty, reach the top of them, as we stood at the bottom of his pocket. One of them was covered, and seemed all of a piece: but at the upper end of the other there appeared a white round substance, about twice the bigness of our heads. Within each of these was enclosed a prodigious plate of steel; which, by our orders, we obliged him to show us, because we apprehended they might be dangerous engines. He took them out of their cases, and told us, that in his own country his practice was to shave his beard with one of these, and cut his meat with the other. There were two pockets which we could not enter: these he called his fobs; they were two large slits cut into the top of his middle cover, but squeezed close by the pressure of his belly. Out of the right fob hung a great silver chain, with a wonderful kind of engine at the bottom. We directed him to draw out whatever was at the end of that chain; which appeared to be a globe, half silver, and half of some transparent metal; for, on the transparent side, we saw certain strange figures circularly drawn, and thought we could touch them, till we found our fingers stopped by the lucid substance. He put this engine into our ears, which made an incessant noise, like that of a water-mill: and we conjecture it is either some unknown animal, or the god that he worships; but we are more inclined to the latter opinion, because he assured us, (if we understood him right, for he expressed himself very imperfectly) that he seldom did any thing without consulting it. He called it his oracle, and said, it pointed out the time for every action of his life. From the left fob he took out a net almost large enough for a fisherman, but contrived to open and shut like a purse, and served him for the same use: we found therein several massy pieces of yellow metal, which, if they be real gold, must be of immense value.

"Having thus, in obedience to your majesty's commands, diligently searched all his pockets, we observed a girdle about his waist made of the hide of some prodigious animal, from which, on the left side, hung a sword of the length of five men; and on the right, a bag or pouch divided into two cells, each cell capable of holding three of your majesty's subjects. In one of these cells were several globes, or balls, of a most ponderous metal, about the bigness of our heads, and requiring a strong hand to lift them: the other cell contained a heap of certain black grains, but of no great bulk or weight, for we could hold above fifty of them in the palms of our hands.

"This is an exact inventory of what we found about the body of the man-mountain, who used us with great civility, and due respect to your majesty's commission. Signed and sealed on the fourth day of the eighty-ninth moon of your majesty's auspicious reign.

CLEFRIN FRELOCK, MARSI FRELOCK."

When this inventory was read over to the emperor, he directed me, although in very gentle terms, to deliver up the several particulars. He first called for my scimitar, which I took out, scabbard and all. In the mean time he ordered three thousand of his choicest troops (who then attended him) to surround me at a distance, with their bows and arrows just ready to discharge; but I did not observe it, for mine eyes were wholly fixed upon his majesty. He then desired me to draw my scimitar, which, although it had got some rust by the sea water, was, in most parts, exceeding bright. I did so, and immediately all the troops gave a shout between terror and surprise; for the sun shone clear, and the reflection dazzled their eyes, as I waved the scimitar to and fro in my hand. His majesty, who is a most magnanimous prince, was less daunted than I could expect: he ordered me to return it into the scabbard, and cast it on the ground as gently as I could, about six feet from the end of my chain. The next thing he demanded was one of the hollow iron pillars; by which he meant my pocket pistols. I drew it out, and at his desire, as well as I could, expressed to him the use of it; and charging it only with powder, which, by the closeness of my pouch, happened to escape wetting in the sea (an inconvenience against which all prudent mariners take special care to provide,) I first cautioned the emperor not to be afraid, and then I let it off in the air. The astonishment here was much greater than at the sight of my scimitar. Hundreds fell down as if they had been struck dead; and even the emperor, although he stood his ground, could not recover himself for some time. I delivered up both my pistols in the same manner as I had done my scimitar, and then my pouch of powder and bullets; begging him that the former might be kept from fire, for it would kindle with the smallest spark, and blow up his imperial palace into the air. I likewise delivered up my watch, which the emperor was very curious to see, and commanded two of his tallest yeomen of the guards to bear it on a pole upon their shoulders, as draymen in England do a barrel of ale. He was amazed at the continual noise it made, and the motion of the minute-hand, which he could easily discern; for their sight is much more acute than ours: he asked the opinions of his learned men about it, which were various and remote, as the reader may well imagine without my repeating; although indeed I could not very perfectly understand them. I then gave up my silver and copper money, my purse, with nine large pieces of gold, and some smaller ones; my knife and razor, my comb and silver snuff-box, my handkerchief and journal-book. My scimitar, pistols, and pouch, were conveyed in carriages to his majesty's stores; but the rest of my goods were returned me.

I had as I before observed, one private pocket, which escaped their search, wherein there was a pair of spectacles (which I sometimes use for the weakness of mine eyes,) a pocket perspective, and some other little conveniences; which, being of no consequence to the emperor, I did not think myself bound in honour to discover, and I apprehended they might be lost or spoiled if I ventured them out of my possession.

---

1. A stang is a pole or perch; sixteen feet and a half.

3

THE AUTHOR DIVERTS THE EMPEROR, AND HIS
NOBILITY OF BOTH SEXES, IN A VERY UNCOMMON
MANNER. THE DIVERSIONS OF THE COURT OF
LILLIPUT DESCRIBED. THE AUTHOR HAS HIS
LIBERTY GRANTED HIM UPON CERTAIN
CONDITIONS.

My gentleness and good behaviour had gained so far on the emperor and his court, and indeed upon the army and people in general, that I began to conceive hopes of getting my liberty in a short time. I took all possible methods to cultivate this favourable disposition. The natives came, by degrees, to be less apprehensive of any danger from me. I would sometimes lie down, and let five or six of them dance on my hand; and at last the boys and girls would venture to come and play at hide-and-seek in my hair. I had now made a good progress in understanding and speaking the language. The emperor had a mind one day to entertain me with several of the country shows, wherein they exceed all nations I have known, both for dexterity and magnificence. I was diverted with none so much as that of the rope-dancers, performed upon a slender white thread, extended about two feet, and twelve inches from the ground. Upon which I shall desire liberty, with the reader's patience, to enlarge a little.

This diversion is only practised by those persons who are candidates for great employments, and high favour at court. They are trained in this art from their youth, and are not always of noble birth, or liberal education. When a great office is vacant, either by death or disgrace (which often happens,) five or six of those candidates petition the emperor to entertain his majesty and the court with a dance on the rope; and whoever jumps the highest, without falling, succeeds in the office. Very often the chief ministers themselves are commanded to show their skill, and to convince the emperor that they have not lost their faculty. Flimnap, the treasurer, is allowed to cut a caper on the straight rope, at least an inch higher than any other lord in the whole empire. I have seen him do the summerset several times together, upon a trencher fixed on a rope which is no thicker than a common packthread in England. My friend Reldresal, principal secretary for private affairs, is, in my opinion, if I am not partial, the second after the treasurer; the rest of the great officers are much upon a par.

These diversions are often attended with fatal accidents, whereof great numbers are on record. I myself have seen two or three candidates break a limb. But the danger is much greater, when the ministers themselves are commanded to show their dexterity; for, by contending to excel themselves and their fellows, they strain so far that there is hardly one of them who has not received a fall, and some of them two or three. I was assured that, a year or two before my arrival, Flimnap would infallibly have broke his neck, if one of the king's cushions, that accidentally lay on the ground, had not weakened the force of his fall.

There is likewise another diversion, which is only shown before the emperor and empress, and first minister, upon particular occasions. The emperor lays on the table three fine silken threads of six inches long; one is blue, the other red, and the third green. These threads are proposed as prizes for those persons whom the emperor has a mind to distinguish by a peculiar mark of his favour. The ceremony is performed in his majesty's great chamber of state, where the candidates are to undergo a trial of dexterity very different from the former, and such as I have not observed the least resemblance of in any other country of the new or old world. The emperor holds a stick in his hands, both ends parallel to the horizon, while the candidates advancing, one by one, sometimes leap over the stick, sometimes creep under it, backward and forward, several times, according as the stick is advanced or depressed. Sometimes the emperor holds one end of the stick, and his first minister the other; sometimes the minister has it entirely to himself. Whoever performs his part with most agility, and holds out the longest in leaping and creeping, is rewarded with the blue-coloured silk; the red is given to the next, and the green to the third, which they all wear girt twice round about the middle; and you see few great persons about this court who are not adorned with one of these girdles.

The horses of the army, and those of the royal stables, having been daily led before me, were no longer shy, but would come up to my very feet without starting. The riders would leap them over my hand, as I held it on the ground; and one of the emperor's huntsmen, upon a large courser, took my foot, shoe and all; which was indeed a prodigious leap. I had the good fortune to divert the emperor one day after a very extraordinary manner. I desired he would order several sticks of two feet high, and the thickness of an ordinary cane, to be brought me; whereupon his majesty commanded the master of his woods to give directions accordingly; and the next morning six woodmen arrived with as many carriages, drawn by eight horses to each. I took nine of these sticks, and fixing them firmly in the ground in a quadrangular figure, two feet and a half square, I took four other sticks, and tied them parallel at each corner, about two feet from the ground; then I fastened my handkerchief to the nine sticks that stood erect; and extended it on all sides, till it was tight as the top of a drum; and the four parallel sticks, rising about five inches higher than the handkerchief, served as ledges on each side. When I had finished my work, I desired the emperor to let a troop of his best horses twenty-four in number, come and exercise upon this plain. His majesty approved of the proposal, and I took them up, one by one, in my hands, ready mounted and armed, with the proper officers to exercise them. As soon as they got into order they divided into two parties, performed mock skirmishes, discharged blunt arrows, drew their swords, fled and pursued, attacked and retired, and in short discovered the best military discipline I ever beheld. The parallel sticks secured them and their horses from falling over the stage; and the emperor was so much delighted, that he ordered this entertainment to be repeated several days, and once was pleased to be lifted up and give the word of command; and with great difficulty persuaded even the empress herself to let me hold her in her close chair within two yards of the stage, when she was able to take a full view of the whole performance. It was my good fortune, that no ill accident happened in these entertainments; only once a fiery horse, that belonged to one of the captains, pawing with his hoof, struck a hole in my handkerchief, and his foot slipping, he overthrew his rider and himself; but I immediately relieved them both, and covering the hole with one hand, I set down the troop with the other, in the same manner as I took them up. The horse that fell was strained in the left shoulder, but the rider got no hurt; and I repaired my handkerchief as well as I could: however, I would not trust to the strength of it any more, in such dangerous enterprises.

About two or three days before I was set at liberty, as I was entertaining the court with this kind of feat, there arrived an express to inform his majesty, that some of his subjects, riding near the place where I was first taken up, had seen a great black substance lying on the around, very oddly shaped, extending its edges round, as wide as his majesty's bedchamber, and rising up in the middle as high as a man; that it was no living creature, as they at first apprehended, for it lay on the grass without motion; and some of them had walked round it several times; that, by mounting upon each other's shoulders, they had got to the top, which was flat and even, and, stamping upon it, they found that it was hollow within; that they humbly conceived it might be something belonging to the man-mountain; and if his majesty pleased, they would undertake to bring it with only five horses. I presently knew what they meant, and was glad at heart to receive this intelligence. It seems, upon my first reaching the shore after our shipwreck, I was in such confusion, that before I came to the place where I went to sleep, my hat, which I had fastened with a string to my head while I was rowing, and had stuck on all the time I was swimming, fell off after I came to land; the string, as I conjecture, breaking by some accident, which I never observed, but thought my hat had been lost at sea. I entreated his imperial majesty to give orders it might be brought to me as soon as possible, describing to him the use and the nature of it: and the next day the waggoners arrived with it, but not in a very good condition; they had bored two holes in the brim, within an inch and half of the edge, and fastened two hooks in the holes; these hooks were tied by a long cord to the harness, and thus my hat was dragged along for above half an English mile; but, the ground in that country being extremely smooth and level, it received less damage than I expected.

Two days after this adventure, the emperor, having ordered that part of his army which quarters in and about his metropolis, to be in readiness, took a fancy of diverting himself in a very singular manner. He desired I would stand like a Colossus, with my legs as far asunder as I conveniently could. He then commanded his general (who was an old experienced leader, and a great patron of mine) to draw up the troops in close order, and march them under me; the foot by twenty-four abreast, and the horse by sixteen, with drums beating, colours flying, and pikes advanced. This body consisted of three thousand foot, and a thousand horse. His majesty gave orders, upon pain of death, that every soldier in his march should observe the strictest decency with regard to my person; which however could not prevent some of the younger officers from turning up their eyes as they passed under me: and, to confess the truth, my breeches were at that time in so ill a condition, that they afforded some opportunities for laughter and admiration.

I had sent so many memorials and petitions for my liberty, that his majesty at length mentioned the matter, first in the cabinet, and then in a full council; where it was opposed by none, except Skyresh Bolgolam, who was pleased, without any provocation, to be my mortal enemy. But it was carried against him by the whole board, and confirmed by the emperor. That minister was *galbet*, or admiral of the realm, very much in his master's confidence, and a person well versed in affairs, but of a morose and sour complexion. However, he was at length persuaded to comply; but prevailed that the articles and conditions upon which I should be set free, and to which I must swear, should be drawn up by himself. These articles were brought to me by Skyresh Bolgolam in person attended by two under-secretaries, and several persons of distinction. After they were read, I was demanded to swear to the performance of them; first in the manner of my own country, and afterwards in the method prescribed by their laws; which was, to hold my right foot in my left hand, and to place the middle finger of my right hand on the crown of my head, and my thumb on the tip of my right ear. But because the reader may be curious to have some idea of the style and manner of expression peculiar to that people, as well as to know the article upon which I recovered my liberty, I have made a translation of the whole instrument, word for word, as near as I was able, which I here offer to the public.

"Golbasto Momarem Evlame Gurdilo Shefin Mully Ully Gue, most mighty Emperor of Lilliput, delight and terror of the universe, whose dominions extend five thousand *blustrugs* (about twelve miles in circumference) to the extremities of the globe; monarch of all monarchs, taller than the sons of men; whose feet press down to the centre, and whose head strikes against the sun; at whose nod the princes of the earth shake their knees; pleasant as the spring, comfortable as the summer, fruitful as autumn, dreadful as winter: his most sublime majesty proposes to the man-mountain, lately arrived at our celestial dominions, the following articles, which, by a solemn oath, he shall be obliged to perform:—

"1st, The man-mountain shall not depart from our dominions, without our license under our great seal.

"2d, He shall not presume to come into our metropolis, without our express order; at which time, the inhabitants shall have two hours warning to keep within doors.

"3d, The said man-mountain shall confine his walks to our principal high roads, and not offer to walk, or lie down, in a meadow or field of corn.

"4th, As he walks the said roads, he shall take the utmost care not to trample upon the bodies of any of our loving subjects, their horses, or carriages, nor take any of our subjects into his hands without their own consent.

"5th, If an express requires extraordinary despatch, the man-mountain shall be obliged to carry, in his pocket, the messenger and horse a six days journey, once in every moon, and return the said messenger back (if so required) safe to our imperial presence.

"6th, He shall be our ally against our enemies in the island of Blefuscu, and do his utmost to destroy their fleet, which is now preparing to invade us.

"7th, That the said man-mountain shall, at his times of leisure, be aiding and assisting to our workmen, in helping to raise certain great stones, towards covering the wall of the principal park, and other our royal buildings.

"8th, That the said man-mountain shall, in two moons' time, deliver in an exact survey of the circumference of our dominions, by a computation of his own paces round the coast.

"Lastly, That, upon his solemn oath to observe all the above articles, the said man-mountain shall have a daily allowance of meat and drink sufficient for the support of 1724 of our subjects, with free access to our royal person, and other marks of our favour. Given at our palace at Belfaborac, the twelfth day of the ninety-first moon of our reign."

I swore and subscribed to these articles with great cheerfulness and content, although some of them were not so honourable as I could have wished; which proceeded wholly from the malice of Skyresh Bolgolam, the high-admiral: whereupon my chains were immediately unlocked, and I was at full liberty. The emperor himself, in person, did me the honour to be by at the whole ceremony. I made my acknowledgements by prostrating myself at his majesty's feet: but he commanded me to rise; and after many gracious expressions, which, to avoid the censure of vanity, I shall not repeat, he added, "that he hoped I should prove a useful servant, and well deserve all the favours he had already conferred upon me, or might do for the future."

The reader may please to observe, that, in the last article of the recovery of my liberty, the emperor stipulates to allow me a quantity of meat and drink sufficient for the support of 1724 Lilliputians. Some time after, asking a friend at court how they came to fix on that determinate number, he told me that his majesty's mathematicians, having taken the height of my body by the help of a quadrant, and finding it to exceed theirs in the proportion of twelve to one, they concluded from the similarity of their bodies, that mine must contain at least 1724 of theirs, and consequently would require as much food as was necessary to support that number of Lilliputians. By which the reader may conceive an idea of the ingenuity of that people, as well as the prudent and exact economy of so great a prince.

4

MILDENDO, THE METROPOLIS OF LILLIPUT, DESCRIBED, TOGETHER WITH THE EMPEROR'S PALACE. A CONVERSATION BETWEEN THE AUTHOR AND A PRINCIPAL SECRETARY, CONCERNING THE AFFAIRS OF THAT EMPIRE. THE AUTHOR'S OFFERS TO SERVE THE EMPEROR IN HIS WARS.

The first request I made, after I had obtained my liberty, was, that I might have license to see Mildendo, the metropolis; which the emperor easily granted me, but with a special charge to do no hurt either to the inhabitants or their houses. The people had notice, by proclamation, of my design to visit the town. The wall which encompassed it is two feet and a half high, and at least eleven inches broad, so that a coach and horses may be driven very safely round it; and it is flanked with strong towers at ten feet distance. I stepped over the great western gate, and passed very gently, and sidling, through the two principal streets, only in my short waistcoat, for fear of damaging the roofs and eaves of the houses with the skirts of my coat. I walked with the utmost circumspection, to avoid treading on any stragglers who might remain in the streets, although the orders were very strict, that all people should keep in their houses, at their own peril. The garret windows and tops of houses were so crowded with spectators, that I thought in all my travels I had not seen a more populous place. The city is an exact square, each side of the wall being five hundred feet long. The two great streets, which run across and divide it into four quarters, are five feet wide. The lanes and alleys, which I could not enter, but only view them as I passed, are from twelve to eighteen inches. The town is capable of holding five hundred thousand souls: the houses are from three to five stories: the shops and markets well provided.

The emperor's palace is in the centre of the city where the two great streets meet. It is enclosed by a wall of two feet high, and twenty feet distance from the buildings. I had his majesty's permission to step over this wall; and, the space being so wide between that and the palace, I could easily view it on every side. The outward court is a square of forty feet, and includes two other courts: in the inmost are the royal apartments, which I was very desirous to see, but found it extremely difficult; for the great gates, from one square into another, were but eighteen inches high, and seven inches wide. Now the buildings of the outer court were at least five feet high, and it was impossible for me to stride over them without infinite damage to the pile, though the walls were strongly built of hewn stone, and four inches thick. At the same time the emperor had a great desire that I should see the magnificence of his palace; but this I was not able to do till three days after, which I spent in cutting down with my knife some of the largest trees in the royal park, about a hundred yards distant from the city. Of these trees I made two stools, each about three feet high, and strong enough to bear my weight. The people having received notice a second time, I went again through the city to the palace with my two stools in my hands. When I came to the side of the outer court, I stood upon one stool, and took the other in my hand; this I lifted over the roof, and gently set it down on the space between the first and second court, which was eight feet wide. I then stept over the building very conveniently from one stool to the other, and drew up the first after me with a hooked stick. By this contrivance I got into the inmost court; and, lying down upon my side, I applied my face to the windows of the middle stories, which were left open on purpose, and discovered the most splendid apartments that can be imagined. There I saw the empress and the young princes, in their several lodgings, with their chief attendants about them. Her imperial majesty was pleased to smile very graciously upon me, and gave me out of the window her hand to kiss.

But I shall not anticipate the reader with further descriptions of this kind, because I reserve them for a greater work, which is now almost ready for the press; containing a general description of this empire, from its first erection, through along series of princes; with a particular account of their wars and politics, laws, learning, and religion; their plants and animals; their peculiar manners and customs, with other matters very curious and useful; my chief design at present being only to relate such events and transactions as happened to the public or to myself during a residence of about nine months in that empire.

One morning, about a fortnight after I had obtained my liberty, Reldresal, principal secretary (as they style him) for private affairs, came to my house attended only by one servant. He ordered his coach to wait at a distance, and desired I would give him an hours audience; which I readily consented to, on account of his quality and personal merits, as well as of the many good offices he had done me during my solicitations at court. I offered to lie down that he might the more conveniently reach my ear, but he chose rather to let me hold him in my hand during our conversation. He began with compliments on my liberty; said "he might pretend to some merit in it;" but, however, added, "that if it had not been for the present situation of things at court, perhaps I might not have obtained it so soon. For," said he, "as flourishing a condition as we may appear to be in to foreigners, we labour under two mighty evils: a violent faction at home, and the danger of an invasion, by a most potent enemy, from abroad. As to the first, you are to understand, that for about seventy moons past there have been two struggling parties in this empire, under the names of *Tramecksan* and *Slamecksan*, from the high and low heels of their shoes, by which they distinguish themselves. It is alleged, indeed, that the high heels are most agreeable to our ancient constitution; but, however this be, his majesty has determined to make use only of low heels in the administration of the government, and all offices in the gift of the crown, as you cannot but observe; and particularly that his majesty's imperial heels are lower at least by a *drurr* than any of his court (*drurr* is a measure about the fourteenth part of an inch). The animosities between these two parties run so high, that they will neither eat, nor drink, nor talk with each other. We compute the *Tramecksan*, or high heels, to exceed us in number; but the power is wholly on our side. We apprehend his imperial highness, the heir to the crown, to have some tendency towards the high heels; at least we can plainly discover that one of his heels is higher than the other, which gives him a hobble in his gait. Now, in the midst of these intestine disquiets, we are threatened with an invasion from the island of Blefuscu, which is the other great empire of the universe, almost as large and powerful as this of his majesty. For as to what we have heard you affirm, that there are other kingdoms and states in the world inhabited by human creatures as large as yourself, our philosophers are in much doubt, and would rather conjecture that you dropped from the moon, or one of the stars; because it is certain, that a hundred mortals of your bulk would in a short time destroy all the fruits and cattle of his majesty's dominions: besides, our histories of six thousand moons make no mention of any other regions than the two great empires of Lilliput and Blefuscu. Which two mighty powers have, as I was going to tell you, been engaged in a most obstinate war for six-and-thirty moons past. It began upon the following occasion. It is allowed on all hands, that the primitive way of breaking eggs, before we eat them, was upon the larger end; but his present majesty's grandfather, while he was a boy, going to eat an egg, and breaking it according to the ancient practice, happened to cut one of his fingers. Whereupon the emperor his father published an edict, commanding all his subjects, upon great penalties, to break the smaller end of their eggs. The people so highly resented this law, that our histories tell us, there have been six rebellions raised on that account; wherein one emperor lost his life, and another his crown. These civil commotions were constantly fomented by the monarchs of Blefuscu; and when they were quelled, the exiles always fled for refuge to that empire. It is computed that eleven thousand persons have at several times suffered death, rather than submit to break their eggs at the smaller end. Many hundred large volumes have been published upon this controversy: but the books of the Big-endians have been long forbidden, and the whole party rendered incapable by law of holding employments. During the course of these troubles, the emperors of Blefusca did frequently expostulate by their ambassadors, accusing us of making a schism in religion, by offending against a fundamental doctrine of our great prophet Lustrog, in the fifty-fourth chapter of the Blundecral (which is their Alcoran). This, however, is thought to be a mere strain upon the text; for the words are these: 'that all true believers break their eggs at the convenient end.' And which is the convenient end, seems, in my humble opinion to be left to every man's conscience, or at least in the power of the chief magistrate to determine. Now, the Big-endian exiles have found so much credit in the emperor of Blefuscu's court, and so much private assistance and encouragement from their party here at home, that a bloody war has been carried on between the two empires for six-and-thirty moons, with various success; during which time we have lost forty capital ships, and a much a greater number of smaller vessels, together with thirty thousand of our best seamen and soldiers; and the damage received by the enemy is reckoned to be somewhat greater than ours. However, they have now equipped a numerous fleet, and are just preparing to make a descent upon us; and his imperial majesty, placing great confidence in your valour and strength, has commanded me to lay this account of his affairs before you."

I desired the secretary to present my humble duty to the emperor; and to let him know, "that I thought it would not become me, who was a foreigner, to interfere with parties; but I was ready, with the hazard of my life, to defend his person and state against all invaders."

5

THE AUTHOR, BY AN EXTRAORDINARY STRATAGEM, PREVENTS AN INVASION. A HIGH TITLE OF HONOUR IS CONFERRED UPON HIM. AMBASSADORS ARRIVE FROM THE EMPEROR OF BLEFUSCU, AND SUE FOR PEACE. THE EMPRESS'S APARTMENT ON FIRE BY AN ACCIDENT; THE AUTHOR INSTRUMENTAL IN SAVING THE REST OF THE PALACE.

The empire of Blefuscu is an island situated to the north-east of Lilliput, from which it is parted only by a channel of eight hundred yards wide. I had not yet seen it, and upon this notice of an intended invasion, I avoided appearing on that side of the coast, for fear of being discovered, by some of the enemy's ships, who had received no intelligence of me; all intercourse between the two empires having been strictly forbidden during the war, upon pain of death, and an embargo laid by our emperor upon all vessels whatsoever. I communicated to his majesty a project I had formed of seizing the enemy's whole fleet; which, as our scouts assured us, lay at anchor in the harbour, ready to sail with the first fair wind. I consulted the most experienced seamen upon the depth of the channel, which they had often plumbed; who told me, that in the middle, at high-water, it was seventy *glumgluffs* deep, which is about six feet of European measure; and the rest of it fifty *glumgluffs* at most. I walked towards the north-east coast, over against Blefuscu, where, lying down behind a hillock, I took out my small perspective glass, and viewed the enemy's fleet at anchor, consisting of about fifty men of war, and a great number of transports: I then came back to my house, and gave orders (for which I had a warrant) for a great quantity of the strongest cable and bars of iron. The cable was about as thick as packthread and the bars of the length and size of a knitting-needle. I trebled the cable to make it stronger, and for the same reason I twisted three of the iron bars together, bending the extremities into a hook. Having thus fixed fifty hooks to as many cables, I went back to the north-east coast, and putting off my coat, shoes, and stockings, walked into the sea, in my leathern jerkin, about half an hour before high water. I waded with what haste I could, and swam in the middle about thirty yards, till I felt ground. I arrived at the fleet in less than half an hour. The enemy was so frightened when they saw me, that they leaped out of their ships, and swam to shore, where there could not be fewer than thirty thousand souls. I then took my tackling, and, fastening a hook to the hole at the prow of each, I tied all the cords together at the end. While I was thus employed, the enemy discharged several thousand arrows, many of which stuck in my hands and face, and, beside the excessive smart, gave me much disturbance in my work. My greatest apprehension was for mine eyes, which I should have infallibly lost, if I had not suddenly thought of an expedient. I kept, among other little necessaries, a pair of spectacles in a private pocket, which, as I observed before, had escaped the emperor's searchers. These I took out and fastened as strongly as I could upon my nose, and thus armed, went on boldly with my work, in spite of the enemy's arrows, many of which struck against the glasses of my spectacles, but without any other effect, further than a little to discompose them. I had now fastened all the hooks, and, taking the knot in my hand, began to pull; but not a ship would stir, for they were all too fast held by their anchors, so that the boldest part of my enterprise remained. I therefore let go the cord, and leaving the hooks fixed to the ships, I resolutely cut with my knife the cables that fastened the anchors, receiving about two hundred shots in my face and hands; then I took up the knotted end of the cables, to which my hooks were tied, and with great ease drew fifty of the enemy's largest men of war after me.

The Blefuscudians, who had not the least imagination of what I intended, were at first confounded with astonishment. They had seen me cut the cables, and thought my design was only to let the ships run adrift or fall foul on each other: but when they perceived the whole fleet moving in order, and saw me pulling at the end, they set up such a scream of grief and despair as it is almost impossible to describe or conceive. When I had got out of danger, I stopped awhile to pick out the arrows that stuck in my hands and face; and rubbed on some of the same ointment that was given me at my first arrival, as I have formerly mentioned. I then took off my spectacles, and waiting about an hour, till the tide was a little fallen, I waded through the middle with my cargo, and arrived safe at the royal port of Lilliput.

The emperor and his whole court stood on the shore, expecting the issue of this great adventure. They saw the ships move forward in a large half-moon, but could not discern me, who was up to my breast in water. When I advanced to the middle of the channel, they were yet more in pain, because I was under water to my neck. The emperor concluded me to be drowned, and that the enemy's fleet was approaching in a hostile manner: but he was soon eased of his fears; for the channel growing shallower every step I made, I came in a short time within hearing, and holding up the end of the cable, by which the fleet was fastened, I cried in a loud voice, "Long live the most puissant king of Lilliput!" This great prince received me at my landing with all possible encomiums, and created me a *nardac* upon the spot, which is the highest title of honour among them.

His majesty desired I would take some other opportunity of bringing all the rest of his enemy's ships into his ports. And so unmeasureable is the ambition of princes, that he seemed to think of nothing less than reducing the whole empire of Blefuscu into a province, and governing it, by a viceroy; of destroying the Big-endian exiles, and compelling that people to break the smaller end of their eggs, by which he would remain the sole monarch of the whole world. But I endeavoured to divert him from this design, by many arguments drawn from the topics of policy as well as justice; and I plainly protested, "that I would never be an instrument of bringing a free and brave people into slavery." And, when the matter was debated in council, the wisest part of the ministry were of my opinion.

This open bold declaration of mine was so opposite to the schemes and politics of his imperial majesty, that he could never forgive me. He mentioned it in a very artful manner at council, where I was told that some of the wisest appeared, at least by their silence, to be of my opinion; but others, who were my secret enemies, could not forbear some expressions which, by a side-wind, reflected on me. And from this time began an intrigue between his majesty and a junto of ministers, maliciously bent against me, which broke out in less than two months, and had like to have ended in my utter destruction. Of so little weight are the greatest services to princes, when put into the balance with a refusal to gratify their passions.

About three weeks after this exploit, there arrived a solemn embassy from Blefuscu, with humble offers of a peace, which was soon concluded, upon conditions very advantageous to our emperor, wherewith I shall not trouble the reader. There were six ambassadors, with a train of about five hundred persons, and their entry was very magnificent, suitable to the grandeur of their master, and the importance of their business. When their treaty was finished, wherein I did them several good offices by the credit I now had, or at least appeared to have, at court, their excellencies, who were privately told how much I had been their friend, made me a visit in form. They began with many compliments upon my valour and generosity, invited me to that kingdom in the emperor their master's name, and desired me to show them some proofs of my prodigious strength, of which they had heard so many wonders; wherein I readily obliged them, but shall not trouble the reader with the particulars.

When I had for some time entertained their excellencies, to their infinite satisfaction and surprise, I desired they would do me the honour to present my most humble respects to the emperor their master, the renown of whose virtues had so justly filled the whole world with admiration, and whose royal person I resolved to attend, before I returned to my own country. Accordingly, the next time I had the honour to see our emperor, I desired his general license to wait on the Blefuscudian monarch, which he was pleased to grant me, as I could perceive, in a very cold manner; but could not guess the reason, till I had a whisper from a certain person, "that Flimnap and Bolgolam had represented my intercourse with those ambassadors as a mark of disaffection;" from which I am sure my heart was wholly free. And this was the first time I began to conceive some imperfect idea of courts and ministers.

It is to be observed, that these ambassadors spoke to me, by an interpreter, the languages of both empires differing as much from each other as any two in Europe, and each nation priding itself upon the antiquity, beauty, and energy of their own tongue, with an avowed contempt for that of their neighbour; yet our emperor, standing upon the advantage he had got by the seizure of their fleet, obliged them to deliver their credentials, and make their speech, in the Lilliputian tongue. And it must be confessed, that from the great intercourse of trade and commerce between both realms, from the continual reception of exiles which is mutual among them, and from the custom, in each empire, to send their young nobility and richer gentry to the other, in order to polish themselves by seeing the world, and understanding men and manners; there are few persons of distinction, or merchants, or seamen, who dwell in the maritime parts, but what can hold conversation in both tongues; as I found some weeks after, when I went to pay my respects to the emperor of Blefuscu, which, in the midst of great misfortunes, through the malice of my enemies, proved a very happy adventure to me, as I shall relate in its proper place.

The reader may remember, that when I signed those articles upon which I recovered my liberty, there were some which I disliked, upon account of their being too servile; neither could anything but an extreme necessity have forced me to submit. But being now a *nardac* of the highest rank in that empire, such offices were looked upon as below my dignity, and the emperor (to do him justice), never once mentioned them to me. However, it was not long before I had an opportunity of doing his majesty, at least as I then thought, a most signal service. I was alarmed at midnight with the cries of many hundred people at my door; by which, being suddenly awaked, I was in some kind of terror. I heard the word *Burglum* repeated incessantly: several of the emperor's court, making their way through the crowd, entreated me to come immediately to the palace, where her imperial majesty's apartment was on fire, by the carelessness of a maid of honour, who fell asleep while she was reading a romance. I got up in an instant; and orders being given to clear the way before me, and it being likewise a moonshine night, I made a shift to get to the palace without trampling on any of the people. I found they had already applied ladders to the walls of the apartment, and were well provided with buckets, but the water was at some distance. These buckets were about the size of large thimbles, and the poor people supplied me with them as fast as they could: but the flame was so violent that they did little good. I might easily have stifled it with my coat, which I unfortunately left behind me for haste, and came away only in my leathern jerkin. The case seemed wholly desperate and deplorable; and this magnificent palace would have infallibly been burnt down to the ground, if, by a presence of mind unusual to me, I had not suddenly thought of an expedient. I had, the evening before, drunk plentifully of a most delicious wine called *glimigrim*, (the Blefuscudians call it *flunec*, but ours is esteemed the better sort,) which is very diuretic. By the luckiest chance in the world, I had not discharged myself of any part of it. The heat I had contracted by coming very near the flames, and by labouring to quench them, made the wine begin to operate by urine; which I voided in such a quantity, and applied so well to the proper places, that in three minutes the fire was wholly extinguished, and the rest of that noble pile, which had cost so many ages in erecting, preserved from destruction.

It was now day-light, and I returned to my house without waiting to congratulate with the emperor: because, although I had done a very eminent piece of service, yet I could not tell how his majesty might resent the manner by which I had performed it: for, by the fundamental laws of the realm, it is capital in any person, of what quality soever, to make water within the precincts of the palace. But I was a little comforted by a message from his majesty, "that he would give orders to the grand justiciary for passing my pardon in form:" which, however, I could not obtain; and I was privately assured, "that the empress, conceiving the greatest abhorrence of what I had done, removed to the most distant side of the court, firmly resolved that those buildings should never be repaired for her use: and, in the presence of her chief confidents could not forbear vowing revenge."

6

OF THE INHABITANTS OF LILLIPUT; THEIR
LEARNING, LAWS, AND CUSTOMS; THE MANNER OF
EDUCATING THEIR CHILDREN. THE AUTHOR'S WAY
OF LIVING IN THAT COUNTRY. HIS VINDICATION
OF A GREAT LADY.

Although I intend to leave the description of this empire to a particular treatise, yet, in the mean time, I am content to gratify the curious reader with some general ideas. As the common size of the natives is somewhat under six inches high, so there is an exact proportion in all other animals, as well as plants and trees: for instance, the tallest horses and oxen are between four and five inches in height, the sheep an inch and half, more or less: their geese about the bigness of a sparrow, and so the several gradations downwards till you come to the smallest, which to my sight, were almost invisible; but nature has adapted the eyes of the Lilliputians to all objects proper for their view: they see with great exactness, but at no great distance. And, to show the sharpness of their sight towards objects that are near, I have been much pleased with observing a cook pulling a lark, which was not so large as a common fly; and a young girl threading an invisible needle with invisible silk. Their tallest trees are about seven feet high: I mean some of those in the great royal park, the tops whereof I could but just reach with my fist clenched. The other vegetables are in the same proportion; but this I leave to the reader's imagination.

I shall say but little at present of their learning, which, for many ages, has flourished in all its branches among them: but their manner of writing is very peculiar, being neither from the left to the right, like the Europeans, nor from the right to the left, like the Arabians, nor from up to down, like the Chinese, but aslant, from one corner of the paper to the other, like ladies in England.

They bury their dead with their heads directly downward, because they hold an opinion, that in eleven thousand moons they are all to rise again; in which period the earth (which they conceive to be flat) will turn upside down, and by this means they shall, at their resurrection, be found ready standing on their feet. The learned among them confess the absurdity of this doctrine; but the practice still continues, in compliance to the vulgar.

There are some laws and customs in this empire very peculiar; and if they were not so directly contrary to those of my own dear country, I should be tempted to say a little in their justification. It is only to be wished they were as well executed. The first I shall mention, relates to informers. All crimes against the state, are punished here with the utmost severity;

but, if the person accused makes his innocence plainly to appear upon his trial, the accuser is immediately put to an ignominious death; and out of his goods or lands the innocent person is quadruply recompensed for the loss of his time, for the danger he underwent, for the hardship of his imprisonment, and for all the charges he has been at in making his defence; or, if that fund be deficient, it is largely supplied by the crown. The emperor also confers on him some public mark of his favour, and proclamation is made of his innocence through the whole city.

They look upon fraud as a greater crime than theft, and therefore seldom fail to punish it with death; for they allege, that care and vigilance, with a very common understanding, may preserve a man's goods from thieves, but honesty has no defence against superior cunning; and, since it is necessary that there should be a perpetual intercourse of buying and selling, and dealing upon credit, where fraud is permitted and connived at, or has no law to punish it, the honest dealer is always undone, and the knave gets the advantage. I remember, when I was once interceding with the emperor for a criminal who had wronged his master of a great sum of money, which he had received by order and ran away with; and happening to tell his majesty, by way of extenuation, that it was only a breach of trust, the emperor thought it monstrous in me to offer as a defence the greatest aggravation of the crime; and truly I had little to say in return, farther than the common answer, that different nations had different customs; for, I confess, I was heartily ashamed.[1]

Although we usually call reward and punishment the two hinges upon which all government turns, yet I could never observe this maxim to be put in practice by any nation except that of Lilliput. Whoever can there bring sufficient proof, that he has strictly observed the laws of his country for seventy-three moons, has a claim to certain privileges, according to his quality or condition of life, with a proportionable sum of money out of a fund appropriated for that use: he likewise acquires the title of *snilpall*, or legal, which is added to his name, but does not descend to his posterity. And these people thought it a prodigious defect of policy among us, when I told them that our laws were enforced only by penalties, without any mention of reward. It is upon this account that the image of Justice, in their courts of judicature, is formed with six eyes, two before, as many behind, and on each side one, to signify circumspection; with a bag of gold open in her right hand, and a sword sheathed in her left, to show she is more disposed to reward than to punish.

In choosing persons for all employments, they have more regard to good morals than to great abilities; for, since government is necessary to mankind, they believe, that the common size of human understanding is fitted to some station or other; and that Providence never intended to make the management of public affairs a mystery to be comprehended only by a few persons of sublime genius, of which there seldom are three born in an age: but they suppose truth, justice, temperance, and the like, to be in every man's power; the practice of which virtues, assisted by experience and a good intention, would qualify any man for the service of his country, except where a course of study is required. But they thought the want of moral virtues was so far from being supplied by superior endowments of the mind, that employments could never be put into such dangerous hands as those of persons so qualified; and, at least, that the mistakes committed by ignorance, in a virtuous disposition, would never be of such fatal consequence to the public weal, as the practices of a man, whose inclinations led him to be corrupt, and who had great abilities to manage, to multiply, and defend his corruptions.

In like manner, the disbelief of a Divine Providence renders a man incapable of holding any public station; for, since kings avow themselves to be the deputies of Providence, the

Lilliputians think nothing can be more absurd than for a prince to employ such men as disown the authority under which he acts.

In relating these and the following laws, I would only be understood to mean the original institutions, and not the most scandalous corruptions, into which these people are fallen by the degenerate nature of man. For, as to that infamous practice of acquiring great employments by dancing on the ropes, or badges of favour and distinction by leaping over sticks and creeping under them, the reader is to observe, that they were first introduced by the grandfather of the emperor now reigning, and grew to the present height by the gradual increase of party and faction.

Ingratitude is among them a capital crime, as we read it to have been in some other countries: for they reason thus; that whoever makes ill returns to his benefactor, must needs be a common enemy to the rest of mankind, from whom he has received no obligation, and therefore such a man is not fit to live.

Their notions relating to the duties of parents and children differ extremely from ours. For, since the conjunction of male and female is founded upon the great law of nature, in order to propagate and continue the species, the Lilliputians will needs have it, that men and women are joined together, like other animals, by the motives of concupiscence; and that their tenderness towards their young proceeds from the like natural principle: for which reason they will never allow that a child is under any obligation to his father for begetting him, or to his mother for bringing him into the world; which, considering the miseries of human life, was neither a benefit in itself, nor intended so by his parents, whose thoughts, in their love encounters, were otherwise employed. Upon these, and the like reasonings, their opinion is, that parents are the last of all others to be trusted with the education of their own children; and therefore they have in every town public nurseries, where all parents, except cottagers and labourers, are obliged to send their infants of both sexes to be reared and educated, when they come to the age of twenty moons, at which time they are supposed to have some rudiments of docility. These schools are of several kinds, suited to different qualities, and both sexes. They have certain professors well skilled in preparing children for such a condition of life as befits the rank of their parents, and their own capacities, as well as inclinations. I shall first say something of the male nurseries, and then of the female.

The nurseries for males of noble or eminent birth, are provided with grave and learned professors, and their several deputies. The clothes and food of the children are plain and simple. They are bred up in the principles of honour, justice, courage, modesty, clemency, religion, and love of their country; they are always employed in some business, except in the times of eating and sleeping, which are very short, and two hours for diversions consisting of bodily exercises. They are dressed by men till four years of age, and then are obliged to dress themselves, although their quality be ever so great; and the women attendant, who are aged proportionably to ours at fifty, perform only the most menial offices. They are never suffered to converse with servants, but go together in smaller or greater numbers to take their diversions, and always in the presence of a professor, or one of his deputies; whereby they avoid those early bad impressions of folly and vice, to which our children are subject. Their parents are suffered to see them only twice a year; the visit is to last but an hour; they are allowed to kiss the child at meeting and parting; but a professor, who always stands by on those occasions, will not suffer them to whisper, or use any fondling expressions, or bring any presents of toys, sweetmeats, and the like.

The pension from each family for the education and entertainment of a child, upon failure of due payment, is levied by the emperor's officers.

The nurseries for children of ordinary gentlemen, merchants, traders, and handicrafts, are managed proportionably after the same manner; only those designed for trades are put out apprentices at eleven years old, whereas those of persons of quality continue in their exercises till fifteen, which answers to twenty-one with us: but the confinement is gradually lessened for the last three years.

In the female nurseries, the young girls of quality are educated much like the males, only they are dressed by orderly servants of their own sex; but always in the presence of a professor or deputy, till they come to dress themselves, which is at five years old. And if it be found that these nurses ever presume to entertain the girls with frightful or foolish stories, or the common follies practised by chambermaids among us, they are publicly whipped thrice about the city, imprisoned for a year, and banished for life to the most desolate part of the country. Thus the young ladies are as much ashamed of being cowards and fools as the men, and despise all personal ornaments, beyond decency and cleanliness: neither did I perceive any difference in their education made by their difference of sex, only that the exercises of the females were not altogether so robust; and that some rules were given them relating to domestic life, and a smaller compass of learning was enjoined them: for their maxim is, that among peoples of quality, a wife should be always a reasonable and agreeable companion, because she cannot always be young. When the girls are twelve years old, which among them is the marriageable age, their parents or guardians take them home, with great expressions of gratitude to the professors, and seldom without tears of the young lady and her companions.

In the nurseries of females of the meaner sort, the children are instructed in all kinds of works proper for their sex, and their several degrees: those intended for apprentices are dismissed at seven years old, the rest are kept to eleven.

The meaner families who have children at these nurseries, are obliged, besides their annual pension, which is as low as possible, to return to the steward of the nursery a small monthly share of their gettings, to be a portion for the child; and therefore all parents are limited in their expenses by the law. For the Lilliputians think nothing can be more unjust, than for people, in subservience to their own appetites, to bring children into the world, and leave the burthen of supporting them on the public. As to persons of quality, they give security to appropriate a certain sum for each child, suitable to their condition; and these funds are always managed with good husbandry and the most exact justice.

The cottagers and labourers keep their children at home, their business being only to till and cultivate the earth, and therefore their education is of little consequence to the public: but the old and diseased among them, are supported by hospitals; for begging is a trade unknown in this empire.

And here it may, perhaps, divert the curious reader, to give some account of my domestics, and my manner of living in this country, during a residence of nine months, and thirteen days. Having a head mechanically turned, and being likewise forced by necessity, I had made for myself a table and chair convenient enough, out of the largest trees in the royal park. Two hundred sempstresses were employed to make me shirts, and linen for my bed and table, all of the strongest and coarsest kind they could get; which, however, they were forced to quilt together in several folds, for the thickest was some degrees finer than lawn. Their linen is usually three inches wide, and three feet make a piece. The sempstresses took my measure as I lay on the ground, one standing at my neck, and another at my mid-leg, with a strong cord extended, that each held by the end, while a third measured the length of the cord with a rule of an inch long. Then they measured my right thumb, and desired no more; for by a mathematical computation, that twice round the thumb is once round the wrist, and so on to the neck and the waist, and by the help of my old shirt, which I displayed on the ground before them for a pattern, they fitted me exactly. Three hundred tailors were employed in the same manner to make me clothes; but they had another contrivance for taking my measure. I kneeled down, and they raised a ladder from the ground to my neck; upon this ladder one of them mounted, and let fall a plumb-line from my collar to the floor, which just answered the length of my coat: but my waist and arms I measured myself. When my clothes were finished, which was done in my house (for the largest of theirs would not have been able to hold them), they looked like the patch-work made by the ladies in England, only that mine were all of a colour.

I had three hundred cooks to dress my victuals, in little convenient huts built about my house, where they and their families lived, and prepared me two dishes a-piece. I took up twenty waiters in my hand, and placed them on the table: a hundred more attended below on the ground, some with dishes of meat, and some with barrels of wine and other liquors slung on their shoulders; all which the waiters above drew up, as I wanted, in a very ingenious manner, by certain cords, as we draw the bucket up a well in Europe. A dish of their meat was a good mouthful, and a barrel of their liquor a reasonable draught. Their mutton yields to ours, but their beef is excellent. I have had a sirloin so large, that I have been forced to make three bites of it; but this is rare. My servants were astonished to see me eat it, bones and all, as in our country we do the leg of a lark. Their geese and turkeys I usually ate at a mouthful, and I confess they far exceed ours. Of their smaller fowl I could take up twenty or thirty at the end of my knife.

One day his imperial majesty, being informed of my way of living, desired "that himself and his royal consort, with the young princes of the blood of both sexes, might have the happiness," as he was pleased to call it, "of dining with me." They came accordingly, and I placed them in chairs of state, upon my table, just over against me, with their guards about them. Flimnap, the lord high treasurer, attended there likewise with his white staff; and I observed he often looked on me with a sour countenance, which I would not seem to regard, but ate more than usual, in honour to my dear country, as well as to fill the court with admiration. I have some private reasons to believe, that this visit from his majesty gave Flimnap an opportunity of doing me ill offices to his master. That minister had always been my secret enemy, though he outwardly caressed me more than was usual to the moroseness of his nature. He represented to the emperor "the low condition of his treasury; that he was forced to take up money at a great discount; that exchequer bills would not circulate under nine per cent. below par; that I had cost his majesty above a million and a half of *sprugs*" (their greatest gold coin, about the bigness of a spangle) "and, upon the whole, that it would be advisable in the emperor to take the first fair occasion of dismissing me."

I am here obliged to vindicate the reputation of an excellent lady, who was an innocent sufferer upon my account. The treasurer took a fancy to be jealous of his wife, from the malice of some evil tongues, who informed him that her grace had taken a violent affection for my person; and the court scandal ran for some time, that she once came privately to my lodging. This I solemnly declare to be a most infamous falsehood, without any grounds, further than that her grace was pleased to treat me with all innocent marks of freedom and friendship. I own she came often to my house, but always publicly, nor ever without three more in the coach, who were usually her sister and young daughter, and some particular acquaintance; but this was common to many other ladies of the court. And I still appeal to my servants round, whether they at any time saw a coach at my door, without knowing what persons were in it. On those occasions, when a servant had given me notice, my custom was to go immediately to the door, and, after paying my respects, to take up the coach and two horses very carefully in my hands (for, if there were six horses, the postillion always unharnessed four,) and place them on a table, where I had fixed a movable rim quite round, of five inches high, to prevent accidents. And I have often had four coaches and horses at once on my table, full of company, while I sat in my chair, leaning my face towards them; and when I was engaged with one set, the coachmen would gently drive the others round my table. I have passed many an afternoon very agreeably in these conversations. But I defy the treasurer, or his two informers (I will name them, and let them make the best of it) Clustril and Drunlo, to prove that any person ever came to me *incognito*, except the secretary Reldresal, who was sent by express command of his imperial majesty, as I have before related. I should not have dwelt so long upon this particular, if it had not been a point wherein the reputation of a great lady is so nearly concerned, to say nothing of my own; though I then had the honour to be a *nardac*, which the treasurer himself is not; for all the world knows, that he is only a *glumglum*, a title inferior by one degree, as that of a marquis is to a duke in England; yet I allow he preceded me in right of his post. These false informations, which I afterwards came to the knowledge of by an accident not proper to mention, made the treasurer show his lady for some time an ill countenance, and me a worse; and although he was at last undeceived and reconciled to her, yet I lost all credit with him, and found my interest decline very fast with the emperor himself, who was, indeed, too much governed by that favourite.

---

1. An act of parliament has been since passed by which some breaches of trust have been made capital.

7

THE AUTHOR, BEING INFORMED OF A DESIGN TO ACCUSE HIM OF HIGH-TREASON, MAKES HIS ESCAPE TO BLEFUSCU. HIS RECEPTION THERE.

Before I proceed to give an account of my leaving this kingdom, it may be proper to inform the reader of a private intrigue which had been for two months forming against me.

I had been hitherto, all my life, a stranger to courts, for which I was unqualified by the meanness of my condition. I had indeed heard and read enough of the dispositions of great princes and ministers, but never expected to have found such terrible effects of them, in so remote a country, governed, as I thought, by very different maxims from those in Europe.

When I was just preparing to pay my attendance on the emperor of Blefuscu, a considerable person at court (to whom I had been very serviceable, at a time when he lay under the highest displeasure of his imperial majesty) came to my house very privately at night, in a close chair, and, without sending his name, desired admittance. The chairmen were dismissed; I put the chair, with his lordship in it, into my coat-pocket: and, giving orders to a trusty servant, to say I was indisposed and gone to sleep, I fastened the door of my house, placed the chair on the table, according to my usual custom, and sat down by it. After the common salutations were over, observing his lordship's countenance full of concern, and inquiring into the reason, he desired "I would hear him with patience, in a matter that highly concerned my honour and my life." His speech was to the following effect, for I took notes of it as soon as he left me:—

"You are to know," said he, "that several committees of council have been lately called, in the most private manner, on your account; and it is but two days since his majesty came to a full resolution.

"You are very sensible that Skyresh Bolgolam" (*galbet*, or high-admiral) "has been your mortal enemy, almost ever since your arrival. His original reasons I know not; but his hatred is increased since your great success against Blefuscu, by which his glory as admiral is much obscured. This lord, in conjunction with Flimnap the high-treasurer, whose enmity against you is notorious on account of his lady, Limtoc the general, Lalcon the chamberlain, and Balmuff the grand justiciary, have prepared articles of impeachment against you, for treason and other capital crimes."

This preface made me so impatient, being conscious of my own merits and innocence, that I was going to interrupt him; when he entreated me to be silent, and thus proceeded:—

"Out of gratitude for the favours you have done me, I procured information of the whole proceedings, and a copy of the articles; wherein I venture my head for your service.

"'Articles of Impeachment against QUINBUS FLESTRIN, (the Man-Mountain.)
ARTICLE I.

"'Whereas, by a statute made in the reign of his imperial majesty Calin Deffar Plune, it is enacted, that, whoever shall make water within the precincts of the royal palace, shall be liable to the pains and penalties of high-treason; notwithstanding, the said Quinbus Flestrin, in open breach of the said law, under colour of extinguishing the fire kindled in the apartment of his majesty's most dear imperial consort, did maliciously, traitorously, and devilishly, by discharge of his urine, put out the said fire kindled in the said apartment, lying and being within the precincts of the said royal palace, against the statute in that case provided, etc. against the duty, etc.
ARTICLE II.

"'That the said Quinbus Flestrin, having brought the imperial fleet of Blefuscu into the royal port, and being afterwards commanded by his imperial majesty to seize all the other ships of the said empire of Blefuscu, and reduce that empire to a province, to be governed by a viceroy from hence, and to destroy and put to death, not only all the Big-endian exiles, but likewise all the people of that empire who would not immediately forsake the Big-endian heresy, he, the said Flestrin, like a false traitor against his most auspicious, serene, imperial majesty, did petition to be excused from the said service, upon pretence of unwillingness to force the consciences, or destroy the liberties and lives of an innocent people.
ARTICLE III.

"'That, whereas certain ambassadors arrived from the Court of Blefuscu, to sue for peace in his majesty's court, he, the said Flestrin, did, like a false traitor, aid, abet, comfort, and divert, the said ambassadors, although he knew them to be servants to a prince who was lately an open enemy to his imperial majesty, and in an open war against his said majesty.
ARTICLE IV.

"'That the said Quinbus Flestrin, contrary to the duty of a faithful subject, is now preparing to make a voyage to the court and empire of Blefuscu, for which he has received only verbal license from his imperial majesty; and, under colour of the said license, does falsely and traitorously intend to take the said voyage, and thereby to aid, comfort, and abet the emperor of Blefuscu, so lately an enemy, and in open war with his imperial majesty aforesaid.'

"There are some other articles; but these are the most important, of which I have read you an abstract.

"In the several debates upon this impeachment, it must be confessed that his majesty gave many marks of his great lenity; often urging the services you had done him, and endeavouring to extenuate your crimes. The treasurer and admiral insisted that you should be put to the most painful and ignominious death, by setting fire to your house at night, and the general was to attend with twenty thousand men, armed with poisoned arrows, to shoot you on the face and hands. Some of your servants were to have private orders to strew a poisonous juice on your shirts and sheets, which would soon make you tear your own flesh, and die in the utmost torture. The general came into the same opinion; so that for a long time there was a majority against you; but his majesty resolving, if possible, to spare your life, at last brought off the chamberlain.

"Upon this incident, Reldresal, principal secretary for private affairs, who always approved himself your true friend, was commanded by the emperor to deliver his opinion, which he accordingly did; and therein justified the good thoughts you have of him. He allowed your crimes to be great, but that still there was room for mercy, the most commendable virtue in a prince, and for which his majesty was so justly celebrated. He said, the friendship between you and him was so well known to the world, that perhaps the most honourable board might think him partial; however, in obedience to the command he had received, he would freely offer his sentiments. That if his majesty, in consideration of your services, and pursuant to his own merciful disposition, would please to spare your life, and only give orders to put out both your eyes, he humbly conceived, that by this expedient justice might in some measure be satisfied, and all the world would applaud the lenity of the emperor, as well as the fair and generous proceedings of those who have the honour to be his counsellors. That the loss of your eyes would be no impediment to your bodily strength, by which you might still be useful to his majesty; that blindness is an addition to courage, by concealing dangers from us; that the fear you had for your eyes, was the greatest difficulty in bringing over the enemy's fleet, and it would be sufficient for you to see by the eyes of the ministers, since the greatest princes do no more.

"This proposal was received with the utmost disapprobation by the whole board. Bolgolam, the admiral, could not preserve his temper, but, rising up in fury, said, he wondered how the secretary durst presume to give his opinion for preserving the life of a traitor; that the services you had performed were, by all true reasons of state, the great aggravation of your crimes; that you, who were able to extinguish the fire by discharge of urine in her majesty's apartment (which he mentioned with horror), might, at another time, raise an inundation by the same means, to drown the whole palace; and the same strength which enabled you to bring over the enemy's fleet, might serve, upon the first discontent, to carry it back; that he had good reasons to think you were a Big-endian in your heart; and, as treason begins in the heart, before it appears in overt-acts, so he accused you as a traitor on that account, and therefore insisted you should be put to death.

"The treasurer was of the same opinion: he showed to what straits his majesty's revenue was reduced, by the charge of maintaining you, which would soon grow insupportable; that the secretary's expedient of putting out your eyes, was so far from being a remedy against this evil, that it would probably increase it, as is manifest from the common practice of blinding some kind of fowls, after which they fed the faster, and grew sooner fat; that his sacred majesty and the council, who are your judges, were, in their own consciences, fully convinced of your guilt, which was a sufficient argument to condemn you to death, without the formal proofs required by the strict letter of the law.

"But his imperial majesty, fully determined against capital punishment, was graciously pleased to say, that since the council thought the loss of your eyes too easy a censure, some other way may be inflicted hereafter. And your friend the secretary, humbly desiring to be heard again, in answer to what the treasurer had objected, concerning the great charge his majesty was at in maintaining you, said, that his excellency, who had the sole disposal of the emperor's revenue, might easily provide against that evil, by gradually lessening your establishment; by which, for want of sufficient for you would grow weak and faint, and lose your appetite, and consequently, decay, and consume in a few months; neither would the stench of your carcass be then so dangerous, when it should become more than half diminished; and immediately upon your death five or six thousand of his majesty's subjects might, in two or three days, cut your flesh from your bones, take it away by cart-loads, and bury it in distant parts, to prevent infection, leaving the skeleton as a monument of admiration to posterity.

"Thus, by the great friendship of the secretary, the whole affair was compromised. It was strictly enjoined, that the project of starving you by degrees should be kept a secret; but the sentence of putting out your eyes was entered on the books; none dissenting, except Bolgolam the admiral, who, being a creature of the empress, was perpetually instigated by her majesty to insist upon your death, she having borne perpetual malice against you, on account of that infamous and illegal method you took to extinguish the fire in her apartment.

"In three days your friend the secretary will be directed to come to your house, and read before you the articles of impeachment; and then to signify the great lenity and favour of his majesty and council, whereby you are only condemned to the loss of your eyes, which his majesty does not question you will gratefully and humbly submit to; and twenty of his majesty's surgeons will attend, in order to see the operation well performed, by discharging very sharp-pointed arrows into the balls of your eyes, as you lie on the ground.

"I leave to your prudence what measures you will take; and to avoid suspicion, I must immediately return in as private a manner as I came."

His lordship did so; and I remained alone, under many doubts and perplexities of mind.

It was a custom introduced by this prince and his ministry (very different, as I have been assured, from the practice of former times,) that after the court had decreed any cruel execution, either to gratify the monarch's resentment, or the malice of a favourite, the emperor always made a speech to his whole council, expressing his great lenity and tenderness, as qualities known and confessed by all the world. This speech was immediately published throughout the kingdom; nor did any thing terrify the people so much as those encomiums on his majesty's mercy; because it was observed, that the more these praises were enlarged and insisted on, the more inhuman was the punishment, and the sufferer more innocent. Yet, as to myself, I must confess, having never been designed for a courtier, either by my birth or education, I was so ill a judge of things, that I could not discover the lenity and favour of this sentence, but conceived it (perhaps erroneously) rather to be rigorous than gentle. I sometimes thought of standing my trial, for, although I could not deny the facts alleged in the several articles, yet I hoped they would admit of some extenuation. But having in my life perused many state-trials, which I ever observed to terminate as the judges thought fit to direct, I durst not rely on so dangerous a decision, in so critical a juncture, and against such powerful enemies. Once I was strongly bent upon resistance, for, while I had liberty the whole strength of that empire could hardly subdue me, and I might easily with stones pelt the metropolis to pieces; but I soon rejected that project with horror, by remembering the oath I had made to the emperor, the favours I received from him, and the high title of *nardac* he conferred upon me. Neither had I so soon learned the gratitude of courtiers, to persuade myself, that his majesty's present seventies acquitted me of all past obligations.

At last, I fixed upon a resolution, for which it is probable I may incur some censure, and not unjustly; for I confess I owe the preserving of mine eyes, and consequently my liberty, to my own great rashness and want of experience; because, if I had then known the nature of princes and ministers, which I have since observed in many other courts, and their methods of treating criminals less obnoxious than myself, I should, with great alacrity and readiness, have submitted to so easy a punishment. But hurried on by the precipitancy of youth, and having his imperial majesty's license to pay my attendance upon the emperor of Blefuscu, I took this opportunity, before the three days were elapsed, to send a letter to my friend the secretary, signifying my resolution of setting out that morning for Blefuscu, pursuant to the leave I had got; and, without waiting for an answer, I went to that side of the island where our fleet lay. I seized a large man of war, tied a cable to the prow, and, lifting up the anchors,

I stripped myself, put my clothes (together with my coverlet, which I carried under my arm) into the vessel, and, drawing it after me, between wading and swimming arrived at the royal port of Blefuscu, where the people had long expected me: they lent me two guides to direct me to the capital city, which is of the same name. I held them in my hands, till I came within two hundred yards of the gate, and desired them "to signify my arrival to one of the secretaries, and let him know, I there waited his majesty's command." I had an answer in about an hour, "that his majesty, attended by the royal family, and great officers of the court, was coming out to receive me." I advanced a hundred yards. The emperor and his train alighted from their horses, the empress and ladies from their coaches, and I did not perceive they were in any fright or concern. I lay on the ground to kiss his majesty's and the empress's hands. I told his majesty, "that I was come according to my promise, and with the license of the emperor my master, to have the honour of seeing so mighty a monarch, and to offer him any service in my power, consistent with my duty to my own prince;" not mentioning a word of my disgrace, because I had hitherto no regular information of it, and might suppose myself wholly ignorant of any such design; neither could I reasonably conceive that the emperor would discover the secret, while I was out of his power; wherein, however, it soon appeared I was deceived.

I shall not trouble the reader with the particular account of my reception at this court, which was suitable to the generosity of so great a prince; nor of the difficulties I was in for want of a house and bed, being forced to lie on the ground, wrapped up in my coverlet.

8

THE AUTHOR, BY A LUCKY ACCIDENT, FINDS MEANS TO LEAVE BLEFUSCU; AND, AFTER SOME DIFFICULTIES, RETURNS SAFE TO HIS NATIVE COUNTRY.

Three days after my arrival, walking out of curiosity to the north-east coast of the island, I observed, about half a league off in the sea, somewhat that looked like a boat overturned. I pulled off my shoes and stockings, and, wailing two or three hundred yards, I found the object to approach nearer by force of the tide; and then plainly saw it to be a real boat, which I supposed might by some tempest have been driven from a ship. Whereupon, I returned immediately towards the city, and desired his imperial majesty to lend me twenty of the tallest vessels he had left, after the loss of his fleet, and three thousand seamen, under the command of his vice-admiral. This fleet sailed round, while I went back the shortest way to the coast, where I first discovered the boat. I found the tide had driven it still nearer. The seamen were all provided with cordage, which I had beforehand twisted to a sufficient strength. When the ships came up, I stripped myself, and waded till I came within a hundred yards off the boat, after which I was forced to swim till I got up to it. The seamen threw me the end of the cord, which I fastened to a hole in the fore-part of the boat, and the other end to a man of war; but I found all my labour to little purpose; for, being out of my depth, I was not able to work. In this necessity I was forced to swim behind, and push the boat forward, as often as I could, with one of my hands; and the tide favouring me, I advanced so far that I could just hold up my chin and feel the ground. I rested two or three minutes, and then gave the boat another shove, and so on, till the sea was no higher than my arm-pits; and now, the most laborious part being over, I took out my other cables, which were stowed in one of the ships, and fastened them first to the boat, and then to nine of the vessels which attended me; the wind being favourable, the seamen towed, and I shoved, until we arrived within forty yards of the shore; and, waiting till the tide was out, I got dry to the boat, and by the assistance of two thousand men, with ropes and engines, I made a shift to turn it on its bottom, and found it was but little damaged.

I shall not trouble the reader with the difficulties I was under, by the help of certain paddles, which cost me ten days making, to get my boat to the royal port of Blefuscu, where a mighty concourse of people appeared upon my arrival, full of wonder at the sight of so prodigious a vessel. I told the emperor "that my good fortune had thrown this boat in my way, to carry me to some place whence I might return into my native country; and begged his majesty's orders for getting materials to fit it up, together with his license to depart;" which, after some kind expostulations, he was pleased to grant.

I did very much wonder, in all this time, not to have heard of any express relating to me from our emperor to the court of Blefuscu. But I was afterward given privately to understand, that his imperial majesty, never imagining I had the least notice of his designs, believed I was only gone to Blefuscu in performance of my promise, according to the license he had given me, which was well known at our court, and would return in a few days, when the ceremony was ended. But he was at last in pain at my long absence; and after consulting with the treasurer and the rest of that cabal, a person of quality was dispatched with the copy of the articles against me. This envoy had instructions to represent to the monarch of Blefuscu, "the great lenity of his master, who was content to punish me no farther than with the loss of mine eyes; that I had fled from justice; and if I did not return in two hours, I should be deprived of my title of *nardac*, and declared a traitor." The envoy further added, "that in order to maintain the peace and amity between both empires, his master expected that his brother of Blefuscu would give orders to have me sent back to Lilliput, bound hand and foot, to be punished as a traitor."

The emperor of Blefuscu, having taken three days to consult, returned an answer consisting of many civilities and excuses. He said, "that as for sending me bound, his brother knew it was impossible; that, although I had deprived him of his fleet, yet he owed great obligations to me for many good offices I had done him in making the peace. That, however, both their majesties would soon be made easy; for I had found a prodigious vessel on the shore, able to carry me on the sea, which he had given orders to fit up, with my own assistance and direction; and he hoped, in a few weeks, both empires would be freed from so insupportable an encumbrance."

With this answer the envoy returned to Lilliput; and the monarch of Blefuscu related to me all that had passed; offering me at the same time (but under the strictest confidence) his gracious protection, if I would continue in his service; wherein, although I believed him sincere, yet I resolved never more to put any confidence in princes or ministers, where I could possibly avoid it; and therefore, with all due acknowledgments for his favourable intentions, I humbly begged to be excused. I told him, "that since fortune, whether good or evil, had thrown a vessel in my way, I was resolved to venture myself on the ocean, rather than be an occasion of difference between two such mighty monarchs." Neither did I find the emperor at all displeased; and I discovered, by a certain accident, that he was very glad of my resolution, and so were most of his ministers.

These considerations moved me to hasten my departure somewhat sooner than I intended; to which the court, impatient to have me gone, very readily contributed. Five hundred workmen were employed to make two sails to my boat, according to my directions, by quilting thirteen folds of their strongest linen together. I was at the pains of making ropes and cables, by twisting ten, twenty, or thirty of the thickest and strongest of theirs. A great stone that I happened to find, after a long search, by the sea-shore, served me for an anchor. I had the tallow of three hundred cows, for greasing my boat, and other uses. I was at incredible pains in cutting down some of the largest timber-trees, for oars and masts, wherein I was, however, much assisted by his majesty's ship-carpenters, who helped me in smoothing them, after I had done the rough work.

In about a month, when all was prepared, I sent to receive his majesty's commands, and to take my leave. The emperor and royal family came out of the palace; I lay down on my face to kiss his hand, which he very graciously gave me: so did the empress and young princes of the blood. His majesty presented me with fifty purses of two hundred *sprugs* a-piece, together with his picture at full length, which I put immediately into one of my gloves, to keep it from being hurt. The ceremonies at my departure were too many to trouble the reader with at this time.

I stored the boat with the carcases of a hundred oxen, and three hundred sheep, with bread and drink proportionable, and as much meat ready dressed as four hundred cooks could provide. I took with me six cows and two bulls alive, with as many ewes and rams, intending to carry them into my own country, and propagate the breed. And to feed them on board, I had a good bundle of hay, and a bag of corn. I would gladly have taken a dozen of the natives, but this was a thing the emperor would by no means permit; and, besides a diligent search into my pockets, his majesty engaged my honour "not to carry away any of his subjects, although with their own consent and desire."

Having thus prepared all things as well as I was able, I set sail on the twenty-fourth day of September 1701, at six in the morning; and when I had gone about four-leagues to the northward, the wind being at south-east, at six in the evening I descried a small island, about half a league to the north-west. I advanced forward, and cast anchor on the lee-side of the island, which seemed to be uninhabited. I then took some refreshment, and went to my rest. I slept well, and as I conjectured at least six hours, for I found the day broke in two hours after I awaked. It was a clear night. I ate my breakfast before the sun was up; and heaving anchor, the wind being favourable, I steered the same course that I had done the day before, wherein I was directed by my pocket compass. My intention was to reach, if possible, one of those islands which I had reason to believe lay to the north-east of Van Diemen's Land. I discovered nothing all that day; but upon the next, about three in the afternoon, when I had by my computation made twenty-four leagues from Blefuscu, I descried a sail steering to the south-east; my course was due east. I hailed her, but could get no answer; yet I found I gained upon her, for the wind slackened. I made all the sail I could, and in half an hour she spied me, then hung out her ancient, and discharged a gun. It is not easy to express the joy I was in, upon the unexpected hope of once more seeing my beloved country, and the dear pledges I left in it. The ship slackened her sails, and I came up with her between five and six in the evening, September 26th; but my heart leaped within me to see her English colours. I put my cows and sheep into my coat-pockets, and got on board with all my little cargo of provisions. The vessel was an English merchantman, returning from Japan by the North and South seas; the captain, Mr. John Biddel, of Deptford, a very civil man, and an excellent sailor.

We were now in the latitude of 30 degrees south; there were about fifty men in the ship; and here I met an old comrade of mine, one Peter Williams, who gave me a good character to the captain. This gentleman treated me with kindness, and desired I would let him know what place I came from last, and whither I was bound; which I did in a few words, but he thought I was raving, and that the dangers I underwent had disturbed my head; whereupon I took my black cattle and sheep out of my pocket, which, after great astonishment, clearly convinced him of my veracity. I then showed him the gold given me by the emperor of Blefuscu, together with his majesty's picture at full length, and some other rarities of that country. I gave him two purses of two hundreds *sprugs* each, and promised, when we arrived in England, to make him a present of a cow and a sheep big with young.

I shall not trouble the reader with a particular account of this voyage, which was very prosperous for the most part. We arrived in the Downs on the 13th of April, 1702. I had only one misfortune, that the rats on board carried away one of my sheep; I found her bones in a hole, picked clean from the flesh. The rest of my cattle I got safe ashore, and set them a-grazing in a bowling-green at Greenwich, where the fineness of the grass made them feed very heartily, though I had always feared the contrary: neither could I possibly have preserved them in so long a voyage, if the captain had not allowed me some of his best biscuit, which, rubbed to powder, and mingled with water, was their constant food. The short time I continued in England, I made a considerable profit by showing my cattle to many persons of quality and others: and before I began my second voyage, I sold them for six hundred pounds. Since my last return I find the breed is considerably increased, especially the sheep, which I hope will prove much to the advantage of the woollen manufacture, by the fineness of the fleeces.

I stayed but two months with my wife and family, for my insatiable desire of seeing foreign countries, would suffer me to continue no longer. I left fifteen hundred pounds with my wife, and fixed her in a good house at Redriff. My remaining stock I carried with me, part in money and part in goods, in hopes to improve my fortunes. My eldest uncle John had left me an estate in land, near Epping, of about thirty pounds a-year; and I had a long lease of the Black Bull in Fetter-Lane, which yielded me as much more; so that I was not in any danger of leaving my family upon the parish. My son Johnny, named so after his uncle, was at the grammar-school, and a towardly child. My daughter Betty (who is now well married, and has children) was then at her needle-work. I took leave of my wife, and boy and girl, with tears on both sides, and went on board the Adventure, a merchant ship of three hundred tons, bound for Surat, captain John Nicholas, of Liverpool, commander. But my account of this voyage must be referred to the Second Part of my Travels.

II
A VOYAGE TO BROBDINGNAG

I

A GREAT STORM DESCRIBED; THE LONG BOAT SENT TO FETCH WATER; THE AUTHOR GOES WITH IT TO DISCOVER THE COUNTRY. HE IS LEFT ON SHORE, IS SEIZED BY ONE OF THE NATIVES, AND CARRIED TO A FARMER'S HOUSE. HIS RECEPTION, WITH SEVERAL ACCIDENTS THAT HAPPENED THERE. A DESCRIPTION OF THE INHABITANTS.

Having been condemned, by nature and fortune, to active and restless life, in two months after my return, I again left my native country, and took shipping in the Downs, on the 20th day of June, 1702, in the Adventure, Captain John Nicholas, a Cornish man, commander, bound for Surat. We had a very prosperous gale, till we arrived at the Cape of Good Hope, where we landed for fresh water; but discovering a leak, we unshipped our goods and wintered there; for the captain falling sick of an ague, we could not leave the Cape till the end of March. We then set sail, and had a good voyage till we passed the Straits of Madagascar; but having got northward of that island, and to about five degrees south latitude, the winds, which in those seas are observed to blow a constant equal gale between the north and west, from the beginning of December to the beginning of May, on the 19th of April began to blow with much greater violence, and more westerly than usual, continuing so for twenty days together: during which time, we were driven a little to the east of the Molucca Islands, and about three degrees northward of the line, as our captain found by an observation he took the 2nd of May, at which time the wind ceased, and it was a perfect calm, whereat I was not a little rejoiced. But he, being a man well experienced in the navigation of those seas, bid us all prepare against a storm, which accordingly happened the day following: for the southern wind, called the southern monsoon, began to set in.

Finding it was likely to overblow, we took in our sprit-sail, and stood by to hand the fore-sail; but making foul weather, we looked the guns were all fast, and handed the mizen. The ship lay very broad off, so we thought it better spooning before the sea, than trying or hulling. We reefed the fore-sail and set him, and hauled aft the fore-sheet; the helm was hard a-weather. The ship wore bravely. We belayed the fore down-haul; but the sail was split, and we hauled down the yard, and got the sail into the ship, and unbound all the things clear of it. It was a very fierce storm; the sea broke strange and dangerous. We hauled off upon the laniard of the whip-staff, and helped the man at the helm. We would not get down our top-mast, but let all stand, because she scudded before the sea very well, and we knew that the top-mast being aloft, the ship was the wholesomer, and made better way through the sea, seeing we had sea-room. When the storm was over, we set fore-sail and main-sail, and brought the ship to. Then we set the mizen, main-top-sail, and the fore-top-sail. Our course was east-north-east, the wind was at south-west. We got the starboard tacks aboard, we cast off our weather-braces and lifts; we set in the lee-braces, and hauled forward by the weather-bowlings, and hauled them tight, and belayed them, and hauled over the mizen tack to windward, and kept her full and by as near as she would lie.

During this storm, which was followed by a strong wind west-south-west, we were carried, by my computation, about five hundred leagues to the east, so that the oldest sailor on board could not tell in what part of the world we were. Our provisions held out well, our ship was staunch, and our crew all in good health; but we lay in the utmost distress for water. We thought it best to hold on the same course, rather than turn more northerly, which might have brought us to the north-west part of Great Tartary, and into the Frozen Sea.

On the 16th day of June, 1703, a boy on the top-mast discovered land. On the 17th, we came in full view of a great island, or continent (for we knew not whether;) on the south side whereof was a small neck of land jutting out into the sea, and a creek too shallow to hold a ship of above one hundred tons. We cast anchor within a league of this creek, and our captain sent a dozen of his men well armed in the long-boat, with vessels for water, if any could be found. I desired his leave to go with them, that I might see the country, and make what discoveries I could. When we came to land we saw no river or spring, nor any sign of inhabitants. Our men therefore wandered on the shore to find out some fresh water near the sea, and I walked alone about a mile on the other side, where I observed the country all barren and rocky. I now began to be weary, and seeing nothing to entertain my curiosity, I returned gently down towards the creek; and the sea being full in my view, I saw our men already got into the boat, and rowing for life to the ship. I was going to holla after them, although it had been to little purpose, when I observed a huge creature walking after them in the sea, as fast as he could: he waded not much deeper than his knees, and took prodigious strides: but our men had the start of him half a league, and, the sea thereabouts being full of sharp-pointed rocks, the monster was not able to overtake the boat. This I was afterwards told, for I durst not stay to see the issue of the adventure; but ran as fast as I could the way I first went, and then climbed up a steep hill, which gave me some prospect of the country. I found it fully cultivated; but that which first surprised me was the length of the grass, which, in those grounds that seemed to be kept for hay, was about twenty feet high.

I fell into a high road, for so I took it to be, though it served to the inhabitants only as a foot-path through a field of barley. Here I walked on for some time, but could see little on either side, it being now near harvest, and the corn rising at least forty feet. I was an hour walking to the end of this field, which was fenced in with a hedge of at least one hundred and twenty feet high, and the trees so lofty that I could make no computation of their altitude. There was a stile to pass from this field into the next. It had four steps, and a stone to cross over when you came to the uppermost. It was impossible for me to climb this stile, because every step was six-feet high, and the upper stone about twenty. I was endeavouring to find some gap in the hedge, when I discovered one of the inhabitants in the next field, advancing towards the stile, of the same size with him whom I saw in the sea pursuing our boat. He appeared as tall as an ordinary spire steeple, and took about ten yards at every stride, as near as I could guess. I was struck with the utmost fear and astonishment, and ran to hide myself in the corn, whence I saw him at the top of the stile looking back into the next field on the right hand, and heard him call in a voice many degrees louder than a speaking-trumpet: but the noise was so high in the air, that at first I certainly thought it was thunder. Whereupon seven monsters, like himself, came towards him with reaping-hooks in their hands, each hook about the largeness of six scythes. These people were not so well clad as the first, whose servants or labourers they seemed to be; for, upon some words he spoke, they went to reap the corn in the field where I lay. I kept from them at as great a distance as I could, but was forced to move with extreme difficulty, for the stalks of the corn were sometimes not above a foot distant, so that I could hardly squeeze my body betwixt them. However, I made a shift to go forward, till I came to a part of the field where the corn had been laid by the rain and wind. Here it was impossible for me to advance a step; for the stalks were so interwoven, that I could not creep through, and the beards of the fallen ears so strong and pointed, that they pierced through my clothes into my flesh. At the same time I heard the reapers not a hundred yards behind me. Being quite dispirited with toil, and wholly overcome by grief and despair, I lay down between two ridges, and heartily wished I might there end my days. I bemoaned my desolate widow and fatherless children. I lamented my own folly and willfulness, in attempting a second voyage, against the advice of all my friends and relations. In this terrible agitation of mind, I could not forbear thinking of Lilliput, whose inhabitants looked upon me as the greatest prodigy that ever appeared in the world; where I was able to draw an imperial fleet in my hand, and perform those other actions, which will be recorded for ever in the chronicles of that empire, while posterity shall hardly believe them, although attested by millions. I reflected what a mortification it must prove to me, to appear as inconsiderable in this nation, as one single Lilliputian would be among us. But this I conceived was to be the least of my misfortunes; for, as human creatures are observed to be more savage and cruel in proportion to their bulk, what could I expect but to be a morsel in the mouth of the first among these enormous barbarians that should happen to seize me? Undoubtedly philosophers are in the right, when they tell us that nothing is great or little otherwise than by comparison. It might have pleased fortune, to have let the Lilliputians find some nation, where the people were as diminutive with respect to them, as they were to me. And who knows but that even this prodigious race of mortals might be equally overmatched in some distant part of the world, whereof we have yet no discovery.

Scared and confounded as I was, I could not forbear going on with these reflections, when one of the reapers, approaching within ten yards of the ridge where I lay, made me apprehend that with the next step I should be squashed to death under his foot, or cut in two with his reaping-hook. And therefore, when he was again about to move, I screamed as loud as fear could make me: whereupon the huge creature trod short, and, looking round about under him for some time, at last espied me as I lay on the ground. He considered awhile, with the caution of one who endeavours to lay hold on a small dangerous animal in such a manner that it shall not be able either to scratch or bite him, as I myself have sometimes done with a weasel in England. At length he ventured to take me behind, by the middle, between his fore-finger and thumb, and brought me within three yards of his eyes, that he might behold my shape more perfectly. I guessed his meaning, and my good fortune gave me so much presence of mind, that I resolved not to struggle in the least as he held me in the air above sixty feet from the ground, although he grievously pinched my sides, for fear I should slip through his fingers. All I ventured was to raise mine eyes towards the sun, and place my hands together in a supplicating posture, and to speak some words in a humble melancholy tone, suitable to the condition I then was in: for I apprehended every moment that he would dash me against the ground, as we usually do any little hateful animal, which we have a mind to destroy. But my good star would have it, that he appeared pleased with my voice and gestures, and began to look upon me as a curiosity, much wondering to hear me pronounce articulate words, although he could not understand them. In the mean time I was not able to forbear groaning and shedding tears, and turning my head towards my sides; letting him know, as well as I could, how cruelly I was hurt by the pressure of his thumb and finger. He seemed to apprehend my meaning; for, lifting up the lappet of his coat, he put me gently into it, and immediately ran along with me to his master, who was a substantial farmer, and the same person I had first seen in the field.

The farmer having (as I suppose by their talk) received such an account of me as his servant could give him, took a piece of a small straw, about the size of a walking-staff, and therewith lifted up the lappets of my coat; which it seems he thought to be some kind of covering that nature had given me. He blew my hairs aside to take a better view of my face. He called his hinds about him, and asked them, as I afterwards learned, whether they had ever seen in the fields any little creature that resembled me. He then placed me softly on the ground upon all fours, but I got immediately up, and walked slowly backward and forward, to let those people see I had no intent to run away. They all sat down in a circle about me, the better to observe my motions. I pulled off my hat, and made a low bow towards the farmer. I fell on my knees, and lifted up my hands and eyes, and spoke several words as loud as I could: I took a purse of gold out of my pocket, and humbly presented it to him. He received it on the palm of his hand, then applied it close to his eye to see what it was, and afterwards turned it several times with the point of a pin (which he took out of his sleeve,) but could make nothing of it. Whereupon I made a sign that he should place his hand on the ground. I then took the purse, and, opening it, poured all the gold into his palm. There were six Spanish pieces of four pistoles each, beside twenty or thirty smaller coins. I saw him wet the tip of his little finger upon his tongue, and take up one of my largest pieces, and then another; but he seemed to be wholly ignorant what they were. He made me a sign to put them again into my purse, and the purse again into my pocket, which, after offering it to him several times, I thought it best to do.

The farmer, by this time, was convinced I must be a rational creature. He spoke often to me; but the sound of his voice pierced my ears like that of a water-mill, yet his words were articulate enough. I answered as loud as I could in several languages, and he often laid his ear within two yards of me: but all in vain, for we were wholly unintelligible to each other. He then sent his servants to their work, and taking his handkerchief out of his pocket, he doubled and spread it on his left hand, which he placed flat on the ground with the palm upward, making me a sign to step into it, as I could easily do, for it was not above a foot in thickness. I thought it my part to obey, and, for fear of falling, laid myself at full length upon the handkerchief, with the remainder of which he lapped me up to the head for further security, and in this manner carried me home to his house. There he called his wife, and showed me to her; but she screamed and ran back, as women in England do at the sight of a toad or a spider. However, when she had a while seen my behaviour, and how well I observed the signs her husband made, she was soon reconciled, and by degrees grew extremely tender of me.

It was about twelve at noon, and a servant brought in dinner. It was only one substantial dish of meat (fit for the plain condition of a husbandman,) in a dish of about four-and-twenty feet diameter. The company were, the farmer and his wife, three children, and an old grandmother. When they were sat down, the farmer placed me at some distance from him on the table, which was thirty feet high from the floor. I was in a terrible fright, and kept as far as I could from the edge, for fear of falling. The wife minced a bit of meat, then crumbled some bread on a trencher, and placed it before me. I made her a low bow, took out my knife and fork, and fell to eat, which gave them exceeding delight. The mistress sent her maid for a small dram cup, which held about two gallons, and filled it with drink; I took up the vessel with much difficulty in both hands, and in a most respectful manner drank to her ladyship's health, expressing the words as loud as I could in English, which made the company laugh so heartily, that I was almost deafened with the noise. This liquor tasted like a small cider, and was not unpleasant. Then the master made me a sign to come to his trencher side; but as I walked on the table, being in great surprise all the time, as the indulgent reader will easily conceive and excuse, I happened to stumble against a crust, and fell flat on my face, but received no hurt. I got up immediately, and observing the good people to be in much concern, I took my hat (which I held under my arm out of good manners,) and waving it over my head, made three huzzas, to show I had got no mischief by my fall. But advancing forward towards my master (as I shall henceforth call him,) his youngest son, who sat next to him, an arch boy of about ten years old, took me up by the legs, and held me so high in the air, that I trembled every limb: but his father snatched me from him, and at the same time gave him such a box on the left ear, as would have felled an European troop of horse to the earth, ordering him to be taken from the table. But being afraid the boy might owe me a spite, and well remembering how mischievous all children among us naturally are to sparrows, rabbits, young kittens, and puppy dogs, I fell on my knees, and pointing to the boy, made my master to understand, as well as I could, that I desired his son might be pardoned. The father complied, and the lad took his seat again, whereupon I went to him, and kissed his hand, which my master took, and made him stroke me gently with it.

In the midst of dinner, my mistress's favourite cat leaped into her lap. I heard a noise behind me like that of a dozen stocking-weavers at work; and turning my head, I found it proceeded from the purring of that animal, who seemed to be three times larger than an ox, as I computed by the view of her head, and one of her paws, while her mistress was feeding and stroking her. The fierceness of this creature's countenance altogether discomposed me; though I stood at the farther end of the table, above fifty feet off; and although my mistress held her fast, for fear she might give a spring, and seize me in her talons. But it happened there was no danger, for the cat took not the least notice of me when my master placed me within three yards of her. And as I have been always told, and found true by experience in my travels, that flying or discovering fear before a fierce animal, is a certain way to make it pursue or attack you, so I resolved, in this dangerous juncture, to show no manner of concern. I walked with intrepidity five or six times before the very head of the cat, and came within half a yard of her; whereupon she drew herself back, as if she were more afraid of me: I had less apprehension concerning the dogs, whereof three or four came into the room, as it is usual in farmers' houses; one of which was a mastiff, equal in bulk to four elephants, and another a greyhound, somewhat taller than the mastiff, but not so large.

When dinner was almost done, the nurse came in with a child of a year old in her arms, who immediately spied me, and began a squall that you might have heard from London-Bridge to Chelsea, after the usual oratory of infants, to get me for a plaything. The mother, out of pure indulgence, took me up, and put me towards the child, who presently seized me by the middle, and got my head into his mouth, where I roared so loud that the urchin was frighted, and let me drop, and I should infallibly have broke my neck, if the mother had not held her apron under me. The nurse, to quiet her babe, made use of a rattle which was a kind of hollow vessel filled with great stones, and fastened by a cable to the child's waist: but all in vain; so that she was forced to apply the last remedy by giving it suck. I must confess no object ever disgusted me so much as the sight of her monstrous breast, which I cannot tell what to compare with, so as to give the curious reader an idea of its bulk, shape, and colour. It stood prominent six feet, and could not be less than sixteen in circumference. The nipple was about half the bigness of my head, and the hue both of that and the dug, so varied with spots, pimples, and freckles, that nothing could appear more nauseous: for I had a near sight of her, she sitting down, the more conveniently to give suck, and I standing on the table. This made me reflect upon the fair skins of our English ladies, who appear so beautiful to us, only because they are of our own size, and their defects not to be seen but through a magnifying glass; where we find by experiment that the smoothest and whitest skins look rough, and coarse, and ill-coloured.

I remember when I was at Lilliput, the complexion of those diminutive people appeared to me the fairest in the world; and talking upon this subject with a person of learning there, who was an intimate friend of mine, he said that my face appeared much fairer and smoother when he looked on me from the ground, than it did upon a nearer view, when I took him up in my hand, and brought him close, which he confessed was at first a very shocking sight. He said, "he could discover great holes in my skin; that the stumps of my beard were ten times stronger than the bristles of a boar, and my complexion made up of several colours altogether disagreeable:" although I must beg leave to say for myself, that I am as fair as most of my sex and country, and very little sunburnt by all my travels. On the other side, discoursing of the ladies in that emperor's court, he used to tell me, "one had freckles; another too wide a mouth; a third too large a nose;" nothing of which I was able to distinguish. I confess this reflection was obvious enough; which, however, I could not forbear, lest the reader might think those vast creatures were actually deformed: for I must do them the justice to say, they are a comely race of people, and particularly the features of my master's countenance, although he was but a farmer, when I beheld him from the height of sixty feet, appeared very well proportioned.

When dinner was done, my master went out to his labourers, and, as I could discover by his voice and gesture, gave his wife strict charge to take care of me. I was very much tired, and disposed to sleep, which my mistress perceiving, she put me on her own bed, and covered me with a clean white handkerchief, but larger and coarser than the main-sail of a man-of-war.

I slept about two hours, and dreamt I was at home with my wife and children, which aggravated my sorrows when I awaked, and found myself alone in a vast room, between two and three hundred feet wide, and above two hundred high, lying in a bed twenty yards wide. My mistress was gone about her household affairs, and had locked me in. The bed was eight yards from the floor. Some natural necessities required me to get down; I durst not presume to call; and if I had, it would have been in vain, with such a voice as mine, at so great a distance from the room where I lay to the kitchen where the family kept. While I was under these circumstances, two rats crept up the curtains, and ran smelling backwards and forwards on the bed. One of them came up almost to my face, whereupon I rose in a fright, and drew out my hanger to defend myself. These horrible animals had the boldness to attack me on both sides, and one of them held his fore-feet at my collar; but I had the good fortune to rip up his belly before he could do me any mischief. He fell down at my feet; and the other, seeing the fate of his comrade, made his escape, but not without one good wound on the back, which I gave him as he fled, and made the blood run trickling from him. After this exploit, I walked gently to and fro on the bed, to recover my breath and loss of spirits. These creatures were of the size of a large mastiff, but infinitely more nimble and fierce; so that if I had taken off my belt before I went to sleep, I must have infallibly been torn to pieces and devoured. I measured the tail of the dead rat, and found it to be two yards long, wanting an inch; but it went against my stomach to drag the carcass off the bed, where it lay still bleeding; I observed it had yet some life, but with a strong slash across the neck, I thoroughly despatched it.

Soon after my mistress came into the room, who seeing me all bloody, ran and took me up in her hand. I pointed to the dead rat, smiling, and making other signs to show I was not hurt; whereat she was extremely rejoiced, calling the maid to take up the dead rat with a pair of tongs, and throw it out of the window. Then she set me on a table, where I showed her my hanger all bloody, and wiping it on the lappet of my coat, returned it to the scabbard. I was pressed to do more than one thing which another could not do for me, and therefore endeavoured to make my mistress understand, that I desired to be set down on the floor; which after she had done, my bashfulness would not suffer me to express myself farther, than by pointing to the door, and bowing several times. The good woman, with much difficulty, at last perceived what I would be at, and taking me up again in her hand, walked into the garden, where she set me down. I went on one side about two hundred yards, and beckoning to her not to look or to follow me, I hid myself between two leaves of sorrel, and there discharged the necessities of nature.

I hope the gentle reader will excuse me for dwelling on these and the like particulars, which, however insignificant they may appear to groveling vulgar minds, yet will certainly help a philosopher to enlarge his thoughts and imagination, and apply them to the benefit of public as well as private life, which was my sole design in presenting this and other accounts of my travels to the world; wherein I have been chiefly studious of truth, without affecting any ornaments of learning or of style. But the whole scene of this voyage made so strong an impression on my mind, and is so deeply fixed in my memory, that, in committing it to paper I did not omit one material circumstance: however, upon a strict review, I blotted out several passages of less moment which were in my first copy, for fear of being censured as tedious and trifling, whereof travellers are often, perhaps not without justice, accused.

2

A DESCRIPTION OF THE FARMER'S DAUGHTER. THE AUTHOR CARRIED TO A MARKET-TOWN, AND THEN TO THE METROPOLIS. THE PARTICULARS OF HIS JOURNEY.

My mistress had a daughter of nine years old, a child of towardly parts for her age, very dexterous at her needle, and skilful in dressing her baby. Her mother and she contrived to fit up the baby's cradle for me against night: the cradle was put into a small drawer of a cabinet, and the drawer placed upon a hanging shelf for fear of the rats. This was my bed all the time I staid with those people, though made more convenient by degrees, as I began to learn their language and make my wants known. This young girl was so handy, that after I had once or twice pulled off my clothes before her, she was able to dress and undress me, though I never gave her that trouble when she would let me do either myself. She made me seven shirts, and some other linen, of as fine cloth as could be got, which indeed was coarser than sackcloth; and these she constantly washed for me with her own hands. She was likewise my school-mistress, to teach me the language: when I pointed to any thing, she told me the name of it in her own tongue, so that in a few days I was able to call for whatever I had a mind to. She was very good-natured, and not above forty feet high, being little for her age. She gave me the name of *Grildrig*, which the family took up, and afterwards the whole kingdom. The word imports what the Latins call *nanunculus*, the Italians *homunceletino*, and the English *mannikin*. To her I chiefly owe my preservation in that country: we never parted while I was there; I called her my *Glumdalclitch*, or little nurse; and should be guilty of great ingratitude, if I omitted this honourable mention of her care and affection towards me, which I heartily wish it lay in my power to requite as she deserves, instead of being the innocent, but unhappy instrument of her disgrace, as I have too much reason to fear.

It now began to be known and talked of in the neighbourhood, that my master had found a strange animal in the field, about the bigness of a *splacnuck*, but exactly shaped in every part like a human creature; which it likewise imitated in all its actions; seemed to speak in a little language of its own, had already learned several words of theirs, went erect upon two legs, was tame and gentle, would come when it was called, do whatever it was bid, had the finest limbs in the world, and a complexion fairer than a nobleman's daughter of three years old. Another farmer, who lived hard by, and was a particular friend of my master, came on a visit on purpose to inquire into the truth of this story. I was immediately produced, and placed upon a table, where I walked as I was commanded, drew my hanger, put it up again, made my reverence to my master's guest, asked him in his own language how he did, and told him *he was welcome*, just as my little nurse had instructed me. This man, who was old and dim-sighted, put on his spectacles to behold me better; at which I could not forbear laughing very heartily, for his eyes appeared like the full moon shining into a chamber at two windows. Our people, who discovered the cause of my mirth, bore me company in laughing, at which the old fellow was fool enough to be angry and out of countenance. He had the character of a great miser; and, to my misfortune, he well deserved it, by the cursed advice he gave my master, to show me as a sight upon a market-day in the next town, which was half an hour's riding, about two-and-twenty miles from our house. I guessed there was some mischief when I observed my master and his friend whispering together, sometimes pointing at me; and my fears made me fancy that I overheard and understood some of their words. But the next morning Glumdalclitch, my little nurse, told me the whole matter, which she had cunningly picked out from her mother. The poor girl laid me on her bosom, and fell a weeping with shame and grief. She apprehended some mischief would happen to me from rude vulgar folks, who might squeeze me to death, or break one of my limbs by taking me in their hands. She had also observed how modest I was in my nature, how nicely I regarded my honour, and what an indignity I should conceive it, to be exposed for money as a public spectacle, to the meanest of the people. She said, her papa and mamma had promised that Grildrig should be hers; but now she found they meant to serve her as they did last year, when they pretended to give her a lamb, and yet, as soon as it was fat, sold it to a butcher. For my own part, I may truly affirm, that I was less concerned than my nurse. I had a strong hope, which never left me, that I should one day recover my liberty: and as to the ignominy of being carried about for a monster, I considered myself to be a perfect stranger in the country, and that such a misfortune could never be charged upon me as a reproach, if ever I should return to England, since the king of Great Britain himself, in my condition, must have undergone the same distress.

My master, pursuant to the advice of his friend, carried me in a box the next market-day to the neighbouring town, and took along with him his little daughter, my nurse, upon a pillion behind him. The box was close on every side, with a little door for me to go in and out, and a few gimlet holes to let in air. The girl had been so careful as to put the quilt of her baby's bed into it, for me to lie down on. However, I was terribly shaken and discomposed in this journey, though it was but of half an hour: for the horse went about forty feet at every step and trotted so high, that the agitation was equal to the rising and falling of a ship in a great storm, but much more frequent. Our journey was somewhat farther than from London to St. Alban's. My master alighted at an inn which he used to frequent; and after consulting awhile with the inn-keeper, and making some necessary preparations, he hired the *grultrud*, or crier, to give notice through the town of a strange creature to be seen at the sign of the Green Eagle, not so big as a *splacnuck* (an animal in that country very finely shaped, about six feet long,) and in every part of the body resembling a human creature, could speak several words, and perform a hundred diverting tricks.

I was placed upon a table in the largest room of the inn, which might be near three hundred feet square. My little nurse stood on a low stool close to the table, to take care of me, and direct what I should do. My master, to avoid a crowd, would suffer only thirty people at a time to see me. I walked about on the table as the girl commanded; she asked me questions, as far as she knew my understanding of the language reached, and I answered them as loud as I could. I turned about several times to the company, paid my humble respects, said *they were welcome*, and used some other speeches I had been taught. I took up a thimble filled with liquor, which Glumdalclitch had given me for a cup, and drank their health, I drew out my hanger, and flourished with it after the manner of fencers in England. My nurse gave me a part of a straw, which I exercised as a pike, having learnt the art in my youth. I was that day shown to twelve sets of company, and as often forced to act over again the same fopperies, till I was half dead with weariness and vexation; for those who had seen me made such wonderful reports, that the people were ready to break down the doors to come in. My master, for his own interest, would not suffer any one to touch me except my nurse; and to prevent danger, benches were set round the table at such a distance as to put me out of every body's reach. However, an unlucky school-boy aimed a hazel nut directly at my head, which very narrowly missed me; otherwise it came with so much violence, that it would have infallibly knocked out my brains, for it was almost as large as a small pumpkin, but I had the satisfaction to see the young rogue well beaten, and turned out of the room.

My master gave public notice that he would show me again the next market-day; and in the meantime he prepared a convenient vehicle for me, which he had reason enough to do; for I was so tired with my first journey, and with entertaining company for eight hours together, that I could hardly stand upon my legs, or speak a word. It was at least three days before I recovered my strength; and that I might have no rest at home, all the neighbouring gentlemen from a hundred miles round, hearing of my fame, came to see me at my master's own house. There could not be fewer than thirty persons with their wives and children (for the country is very populous;) and my master demanded the rate of a full room whenever he showed me at home, although it were only to a single family; so that for some time I had but little ease every day of the week (except Wednesday, which is their Sabbath,) although I were not carried to the town.

My master, finding how profitable I was likely to be, resolved to carry me to the most considerable cities of the kingdom. Having therefore provided himself with all things necessary for a long journey, and settled his affairs at home, he took leave of his wife, and upon the 17th of August, 1703, about two months after my arrival, we set out for the metropolis, situate near the middle of that empire, and about three thousand miles distance from our house. My master made his daughter Glumdalclitch ride behind him. She carried me on her lap, in a box tied about her waist. The girl had lined it on all sides with the softest cloth she could get, well quilted underneath, furnished it with her baby's bed, provided me with linen and other necessaries, and made everything as convenient as she could. We had no other company but a boy of the house, who rode after us with the luggage.

My master's design was to show me in all the towns by the way, and to step out of the road for fifty or a hundred miles, to any village, or person of quality's house, where he might expect custom. We made easy journeys, of not above seven or eight score miles a-day; for Glumdalclitch, on purpose to spare me, complained she was tired with the trotting of the horse. She often took me out of my box, at my own desire, to give me air, and show me the country, but always held me fast by a leading-string. We passed over five or six rivers, many degrees broader and deeper than the Nile or the Ganges: and there was hardly a rivulet so small as the Thames at London-bridge. We were ten weeks in our journey, and I was shown in eighteen large towns, besides many villages, and private families.

On the 26th day of October we arrived at the metropolis, called in their language *Lorbrulgrud*, or Pride of the Universe. My master took a lodging in the principal street of the city, not far from the royal palace, and put out bills in the usual form, containing an exact description of my person and parts. He hired a large room between three and four hundred feet wide. He provided a table sixty feet in diameter, upon which I was to act my part, and pallisadoed it round three feet from the edge, and as many high, to prevent my falling over. I was shown ten times a-day, to the wonder and satisfaction of all people. I could now speak the language tolerably well, and perfectly understood every word, that was spoken to me. Besides, I had learnt their alphabet, and could make a shift to explain a sentence here and there; for Glumdalclitch had been my instructor while we were at home, and at leisure hours during our journey. She carried a little book in her pocket, not much larger than a Sanson's Atlas; it was a common treatise for the use of young girls, giving a short account of their religion: out of this she taught me my letters, and interpreted the words.

3

THE AUTHOR SENT FOR TO COURT. THE QUEEN BUYS HIM OF HIS MASTER THE FARMER, AND PRESENTS HIM TO THE KING. HE DISPUTES WITH HIS MAJESTY'S GREAT SCHOLARS. AN APARTMENT AT COURT PROVIDED FOR THE AUTHOR. HE IS IN HIGH FAVOUR WITH THE QUEEN. HE STANDS UP FOR THE HONOUR OF HIS OWN COUNTRY. HIS QUARRELS WITH THE QUEEN'S DWARF.

The frequent labours I underwent every day, made, in a few weeks, a very considerable change in my health: the more my master got by me, the more insatiable he grew. I had quite lost my stomach, and was almost reduced to a skeleton. The farmer observed it, and concluding I must soon die, resolved to make as good a hand of me as he could. While he was thus reasoning and resolving with himself, a *sardral*, or gentleman-usher, came from court, commanding my master to carry me immediately thither for the diversion of the queen and her ladies. Some of the latter had already been to see me, and reported strange things of my beauty, behaviour, and good sense. Her majesty, and those who attended her, were beyond measure delighted with my demeanour. I fell on my knees, and begged the honour of kissing her imperial foot; but this gracious princess held out her little finger towards me, after I was set on the table, which I embraced in both my arms, and put the tip of it with the utmost respect to my lip. She made me some general questions about my country and my travels, which I answered as distinctly, and in as few words as I could. She asked, "whether I could be content to live at court?" I bowed down to the board of the table, and humbly answered "that I was my master's slave: but, if I were at my own disposal, I should be proud to devote my life to her majesty's service." She then asked my master, "whether he was willing to sell me at a good price?" He, who apprehended I could not live a month, was ready enough to part with me, and demanded a thousand pieces of gold, which were ordered him on the spot, each piece being about the bigness of eight hundred moidores; but allowing for the proportion of all things between that country and Europe, and the high price of gold among them, was hardly so great a sum as a thousand guineas would be in England. I then said to the queen, "since I was now her majesty's most humble creature and vassal, I must beg the favour, that Glumdalclitch, who had always tended me with so much care and kindness, and understood to do it so well, might be admitted into her service, and continue to be my nurse and instructor."

Her majesty agreed to my petition, and easily got the farmer's consent, who was glad enough to have his daughter preferred at court, and the poor girl herself was not able to hide her joy. My late master withdrew, bidding me farewell, and saying he had left me in a good service; to which I replied not a word, only making him a slight bow.

The queen observed my coldness; and, when the farmer was gone out of the apartment, asked me the reason. I made bold to tell her majesty, "that I owed no other obligation to my late master, than his not dashing out the brains of a poor harmless creature, found by chance in his fields: which obligation was amply recompensed, by the gain he had made in showing me through half the kingdom, and the price he had now sold me for. That the life I had since led was laborious enough to kill an animal of ten times my strength. That my health was much impaired, by the continual drudgery of entertaining the rabble every hour of the day; and that, if my master had not thought my life in danger, her majesty would not have got so cheap a bargain. But as I was out of all fear of being ill-treated under the protection of so great and good an empress, the ornament of nature, the darling of the world, the delight of her subjects, the phoenix of the creation, so I hoped my late master's apprehensions would appear to be groundless; for I already found my spirits revive, by the influence of her most august presence."

This was the sum of my speech, delivered with great improprieties and hesitation. The latter part was altogether framed in the style peculiar to that people, whereof I learned some phrases from Glumdalclitch, while she was carrying me to court.

The queen, giving great allowance for my defectiveness in speaking, was, however, surprised at so much wit and good sense in so diminutive an animal. She took me in her own hand, and carried me to the king, who was then retired to his cabinet. His majesty, a prince of much gravity and austere countenance, not well observing my shape at first view, asked the queen after a cold manner "how long it was since she grew fond of a *splacnuck*?" for such it seems he took me to be, as I lay upon my breast in her majesty's right hand. But this princess, who has an infinite deal of wit and humour, set me gently on my feet upon the scrutoire, and commanded me to give his majesty an account of myself, which I did in a very few words: and Glumdalclitch who attended at the cabinet door, and could not endure I should be out of her sight, being admitted, confirmed all that had passed from my arrival at her father's house.

The king, although he be as learned a person as any in his dominions, had been educated in the study of philosophy, and particularly mathematics; yet when he observed my shape exactly, and saw me walk erect, before I began to speak, conceived I might be a piece of clock-work (which is in that country arrived to a very great perfection) contrived by some ingenious artist. But when he heard my voice, and found what I delivered to be regular and rational, he could not conceal his astonishment. He was by no means satisfied with the relation I gave him of the manner I came into his kingdom, but thought it a story concerted between Glumdalclitch and her father, who had taught me a set of words to make me sell at a better price. Upon this imagination, he put several other questions to me, and still received rational answers: no otherwise defective than by a foreign accent, and an imperfect knowledge in the language, with some rustic phrases which I had learned at the farmer's house, and did not suit the polite style of a court.

His majesty sent for three great scholars, who were then in their weekly waiting, according to the custom in that country. These gentlemen, after they had a while examined my shape with much nicety, were of different opinions concerning me. They all agreed that I could not be produced according to the regular laws of nature, because I was not framed with a capacity of preserving my life, either by swiftness, or climbing of trees, or digging holes in the earth. They observed by my teeth, which they viewed with great exactness, that I was a carnivorous animal; yet most quadrupeds being an overmatch for me, and field mice, with some others, too nimble, they could not imagine how I should be able to support myself, unless I fed upon snails and other insects, which they offered, by many learned arguments, to evince that I could not possibly do. One of these virtuosi seemed to think that I might be an embryo, or abortive birth. But this opinion was rejected by the other two, who observed my limbs to be perfect and finished; and that I had lived several years, as it was manifest from my beard, the stumps whereof they plainly discovered through a magnifying glass. They would not allow me to be a dwarf, because my littleness was beyond all degrees of comparison; for the queen's favourite dwarf, the smallest ever known in that kingdom, was near thirty feet high. After much debate, they concluded unanimously, that I was only *relplum scalcath*, which is interpreted literally *lusus naturæ*; a determination exactly agreeable to the modern philosophy of Europe, whose professors, disdaining the old evasion of occult causes, whereby the followers of Aristotle endeavoured in vain to disguise their ignorance, have invented this wonderful solution of all difficulties, to the unspeakable advancement of human knowledge.

After this decisive conclusion, I entreated to be heard a word or two. I applied myself to the king, and assured his majesty, "that I came from a country which abounded with several millions of both sexes, and of my own stature; where the animals, trees, and houses, were all in proportion, and where, by consequence, I might be as able to defend myself, and to find sustenance, as any of his majesty's subjects could do here; which I took for a full answer to those gentlemen's arguments." To this they only replied with a smile of contempt, saying, "that the farmer had instructed me very well in my lesson." The king, who had a much better understanding, dismissing his learned men, sent for the farmer, who by good fortune was not yet gone out of town. Having therefore first examined him privately, and then confronted him with me and the young girl, his majesty began to think that what we told him might possibly be true. He desired the queen to order that a particular care should be taken of me; and was of opinion that Glumdalclitch should still continue in her office of tending me, because he observed we had a great affection for each other. A convenient apartment was provided for her at court: she had a sort of governess appointed to take care of her education, a maid to dress her, and two other servants for menial offices; but the care of me was wholly appropriated to herself. The queen commanded her own cabinet-maker to contrive a box, that might serve me for a bedchamber, after the model that Glumdalclitch and I should agree upon. This man was a most ingenious artist, and according to my direction, in three weeks finished for me a wooden chamber of sixteen feet square, and twelve high, with sash-windows, a door, and two closets, like a London bed-chamber. The board, that made the ceiling, was to be lifted up and down by two hinges, to put in a bed ready furnished by her majesty's upholsterer, which Glumdalclitch took out every day to air, made it with her own hands, and letting it down at night, locked up the roof over me. A nice workman, who was famous for little curiosities, undertook to make me two chairs, with backs and frames, of a substance not unlike ivory, and two tables, with a cabinet to put my things in. The room was quilted on all sides, as well as the floor and the ceiling, to prevent any accident from the carelessness of those who carried me, and to break the force of a jolt, when I went in a coach. I desired a lock for my door, to prevent rats and mice from coming in. The smith, after several attempts, made the smallest that ever was seen among them, for I have known a larger at the gate of a gentleman's house in England. I made a shift to keep the key in a pocket of my own, fearing Glumdalclitch might lose it. The queen likewise ordered the thinnest silks that could be gotten, to make me clothes, not much thicker than an English blanket, very cumbersome till I was accustomed to them. They were after the fashion of the kingdom, partly resembling the Persian, and partly the Chinese, and are a very grave and decent habit.

The queen became so fond of my company, that she could not dine without me. I had a table placed upon the same at which her majesty ate, just at her left elbow, and a chair to sit on. Glumdalclitch stood on a stool on the floor near my table, to assist and take care of me. I had an entire set of silver dishes and plates, and other necessaries, which, in proportion to those of the queen, were not much bigger than what I have seen in a London toy-shop for the furniture of a baby-house: these my little nurse kept in her pocket in a silver box, and gave me at meals as I wanted them, always cleaning them herself. No person dined with the queen but the two princesses royal, the eldest sixteen years old, and the younger at that time thirteen and a month. Her majesty used to put a bit of meat upon one of my dishes, out of which I carved for myself, and her diversion was to see me eat in miniature: for the queen (who had indeed but a weak stomach) took up, at one mouthful, as much as a dozen English farmers could eat at a meal, which to me was for some time a very nauseous sight. She would craunch the wing of a lark, bones and all, between her teeth, although it were nine times as large as that of a full-grown turkey; and put a bit of bread into her mouth as big as two twelve-penny loaves. She drank out of a golden cup, above a hogshead at a draught. Her knives were twice as long as a scythe, set straight upon the handle. The spoons, forks, and other instruments, were all in the same proportion. I remember when Glumdalclitch carried me, out of curiosity, to see some of the tables at court, where ten or a dozen of those enormous knives and forks were lifted up together, I thought I had never till then beheld so terrible a sight.

It is the custom, that every Wednesday (which, as I have observed, is their Sabbath) the king and queen, with the royal issue of both sexes, dine together in the apartment of his majesty, to whom I was now become a great favourite; and at these times, my little chair and table were placed at his left hand, before one of the salt-cellars. This prince took a pleasure in conversing with me, inquiring into the manners, religion, laws, government, and learning of Europe; wherein I gave him the best account I was able. His apprehension was so clear, and his judgment so exact, that he made very wise reflections and observations upon all I said. But I confess, that, after I had been a little too copious in talking of my own beloved country, of our trade and wars by sea and land, of our schisms in religion, and parties in the state; the prejudices of his education prevailed so far, that he could not forbear taking me up in his right hand, and stroking me gently with the other, after a hearty fit of laughing, asked me, "whether I was a whig or tory?" Then turning to his first minister, who waited behind him with a white staff, near as tall as the mainmast of the Royal Sovereign, he observed "how contemptible a thing was human grandeur, which could be mimicked by such diminutive insects as I: and yet," says he, "I dare engage these creatures have their titles and distinctions of honour; they contrive little nests and burrows, that they call houses and cities; they make a figure in dress and equipage; they love, they fight, they dispute, they cheat, they betray!" And thus he continued on, while my colour came and went several times, with indignation, to hear our noble country, the mistress of arts and arms, the scourge of France, the arbitress of Europe, the seat of virtue, piety, honour, and truth, the pride and envy of the world, so contemptuously treated.

But as I was not in a condition to resent injuries, so upon mature thoughts I began to doubt whether I was injured or no. For, after having been accustomed several months to the sight and converse of this people, and observed every object upon which I cast mine eyes to be of proportionable magnitude, the horror I had at first conceived from their bulk and aspect was so far worn off, that if I had then beheld a company of English lords and ladies in their finery and birth-day clothes, acting their several parts in the most courtly manner of strutting, and bowing, and prating, to say the truth, I should have been strongly tempted to laugh as much at them as the king and his grandees did at me. Neither, indeed, could I forbear smiling at myself, when the queen used to place me upon her hand towards a looking-glass, by which both our persons appeared before me in full view together; and there could be nothing more ridiculous than the comparison; so that I really began to imagine myself dwindled many degrees below my usual size.

Nothing angered and mortified me so much as the queen's dwarf; who being of the lowest stature that was ever in that country (for I verily think he was not full thirty feet high), became so insolent at seeing a creature so much beneath him, that he would always affect to swagger and look big as he passed by me in the queen's antechamber, while I was standing on some table talking with the lords or ladies of the court, and he seldom failed of a smart word or two upon my littleness; against which I could only revenge myself by calling him brother, challenging him to wrestle, and such repartees as are usually in the mouths of court pages. One day, at dinner, this malicious little cub was so nettled with something I had said to him, that, raising himself upon the frame of her majesty's chair, he took me up by the middle, as I was sitting down, not thinking any harm, and let me drop into a large silver bowl of cream, and then ran away as fast as he could. I fell over head and ears, and, if I had not been a good swimmer, it might have gone very hard with me; for Glumdalclitch in that instant happened to be at the other end of the room, and the queen was in such a fright, that she wanted presence of mind to assist me. But my little nurse ran to my relief, and took me out, after I had swallowed above a quart of cream. I was put to bed: however, I received no other damage than the loss of a suit of clothes, which was utterly spoiled. The dwarf was soundly whipt, and as a farther punishment, forced to drink up the bowl of cream into which he had thrown me: neither was he ever restored to favour; for soon after the queen bestowed him on a lady of high quality, so that I saw him no more, to my very great satisfaction; for I could not tell to what extremities such a malicious urchin might have carried his resentment.

He had before served me a scurvy trick, which set the queen a-laughing, although at the same time she was heartily vexed, and would have immediately cashiered him, if I had not been so generous as to intercede. Her majesty had taken a marrow-bone upon her plate, and, after knocking out the marrow, placed the bone again in the dish erect, as it stood before; the dwarf, watching his opportunity, while Glumdalclitch was gone to the side-board, mounted the stool that she stood on to take care of me at meals, took me up in both hands, and squeezing my legs together, wedged them into the marrow bone above my waist, where I stuck for some time, and made a very ridiculous figure. I believe it was near a minute before any one knew what was become of me; for I thought it below me to cry out. But, as princes seldom get their meat hot, my legs were not scalded, only my stockings and breeches in a sad condition. The dwarf, at my entreaty, had no other punishment than a sound whipping.

I was frequently rallied by the queen upon account of my fearfulness; and she used to ask me whether the people of my country were as great cowards as myself? The occasion was this: the kingdom is much pestered with flies in summer; and these odious insects, each of them as big as a Dunstable lark, hardly gave me any rest while I sat at dinner, with their continual humming and buzzing about mine ears. They would sometimes alight upon my victuals, and leave their loathsome excrement, or spawn behind, which to me was very visible, though not to the natives of that country, whose large optics were not so acute as mine, in viewing smaller objects. Sometimes they would fix upon my nose, or forehead, where they stung me to the quick, smelling very offensively; and I could easily trace that viscous matter, which, our naturalists tell us, enables those creatures to walk with their feet upwards upon a ceiling. I had much ado to defend myself against these detestable animals, and could not forbear starting when they came on my face. It was the common practice of the dwarf, to catch a number of these insects in his hand, as schoolboys do among us, and let them out suddenly under my nose, on purpose to frighten me, and divert the queen. My remedy was to cut them in pieces with my knife, as they flew in the air, wherein my dexterity was much admired.

    I remember, one morning, when Glumdalclitch had set me in a box upon a window, as she usually did in fair days to give me air (for I durst not venture to let the box be hung on a nail out of the window, as we do with cages in England), after I had lifted up one of my sashes, and sat down at my table to eat a piece of sweet cake for my breakfast, above twenty wasps, allured by the smell, came flying into the room, humming louder than the drones of as many bagpipes. Some of them seized my cake, and carried it piecemeal away; others flew about my head and face, confounding me with the noise, and putting me in the utmost terror of their stings. However, I had the courage to rise and draw my hanger, and attack them in the air. I dispatched four of them, but the rest got away, and I presently shut my window. These insects were as large as partridges: I took out their stings, found them an inch and a half long, and as sharp as needles. I carefully preserved them all; and having since shown them, with some other curiosities, in several parts of Europe, upon my return to England I gave three of them to Gresham College, and kept the fourth for myself.

4

THE COUNTRY DESCRIBED. A PROPOSAL FOR CORRECTING MODERN MAPS. THE KING'S PALACE; AND SOME ACCOUNT OF THE METROPOLIS. THE AUTHOR'S WAY OF TRAVELLING. THE CHIEF TEMPLE DESCRIBED.

I now intend to give the reader a short description of this country, as far as I travelled in it, which was not above two thousand miles round Lorbrulgrud, the metropolis. For the queen, whom I always attended, never went farther when she accompanied the king in his progresses, and there staid till his majesty returned from viewing his frontiers. The whole extent of this prince's dominions reaches about six thousand miles in length, and from three to five in breadth: whence I cannot but conclude, that our geographers of Europe are in a great error, by supposing nothing but sea between Japan and California; for it was ever my opinion, that there must be a balance of earth to counterpoise the great continent of Tartary; and therefore they ought to correct their maps and charts, by joining this vast tract of land to the north-west parts of America, wherein I shall be ready to lend them my assistance.

    The kingdom is a peninsula, terminated to the north-east by a ridge of mountains thirty miles high, which are altogether impassable, by reason of the volcanoes upon the tops: neither do the most learned know what sort of mortals inhabit beyond those mountains, or whether they be inhabited at all. On the three other sides, it is bounded by the ocean. There is not one seaport in the whole kingdom: and those parts of the coasts into which the rivers issue, are so full of pointed rocks, and the sea generally so rough, that there is no venturing with the smallest of their boats; so that these people are wholly excluded from any commerce with the rest of the world. But the large rivers are full of vessels, and abound with excellent fish; for they seldom get any from the sea, because the sea fish are of the same size with those in Europe, and consequently not worth catching; whereby it is manifest, that nature, in the production of plants and animals of so extraordinary a bulk, is wholly confined to this continent, of which I leave the reasons to be determined by philosophers. However, now and then they take a whale that happens to be dashed against the rocks, which the common people feed on heartily. These whales I have known so large, that a man could hardly carry one upon his shoulders; and sometimes, for curiosity, they are brought in hampers to Lorbrulgrud; I saw one of them in a dish at the king's table, which passed for a rarity, but I did not observe he was fond of it; for I think, indeed, the bigness disgusted him, although I have seen one somewhat larger in Greenland.

The country is well inhabited, for it contains fifty-one cities, near a hundred walled towns, and a great number of villages. To satisfy my curious reader, it may be sufficient to describe Lorbrulgrud. This city stands upon almost two equal parts, on each side the river that passes through. It contains above eighty thousand houses, and about six hundred thousand inhabitants. It is in length three *glomglungs* (which make about fifty-four English miles,) and two and a half in breadth; as I measured it myself in the royal map made by the king's order, which was laid on the ground on purpose for me, and extended a hundred feet: I paced the diameter and circumference several times barefoot, and, computing by the scale, measured it pretty exactly.

The king's palace is no regular edifice, but a heap of buildings, about seven miles round: the chief rooms are generally two hundred and forty feet high, and broad and long in proportion. A coach was allowed to Glumdalclitch and me, wherein her governess frequently took her out to see the town, or go among the shops; and I was always of the party, carried in my box; although the girl, at my own desire, would often take me out, and hold me in her hand, that I might more conveniently view the houses and the people, as we passed along the streets. I reckoned our coach to be about a square of Westminster-hall, but not altogether so high: however, I cannot be very exact. One day the governess ordered our coachman to stop at several shops, where the beggars, watching their opportunity, crowded to the sides of the coach, and gave me the most horrible spectacle that ever a European eye beheld. There was a woman with a cancer in her breast, swelled to a monstrous size, full of holes, in two or three of which I could have easily crept, and covered my whole body. There was a fellow with a wen in his neck, larger than five wool-packs; and another, with a couple of wooden legs, each about twenty feet high. But the most hateful sight of all, was the lice crawling on their clothes. I could see distinctly the limbs of these vermin with my naked eye, much better than those of a European louse through a microscope, and their snouts with which they rooted like swine. They were the first I had ever beheld, and I should have been curious enough to dissect one of them, if I had had proper instruments, which I unluckily left behind me in the ship, although, indeed, the sight was so nauseous, that it perfectly turned my stomach.

Besides the large box in which I was usually carried, the queen ordered a smaller one to be made for me, of about twelve feet square, and ten high, for the convenience of travelling; because the other was somewhat too large for Glumdalclitch's lap, and cumbersome in the coach; it was made by the same artist, whom I directed in the whole contrivance. This travelling-closet was an exact square, with a window in the middle of three of the squares, and each window was latticed with iron wire on the outside, to prevent accidents in long journeys. On the fourth side, which had no window, two strong staples were fixed, through which the person that carried me, when I had a mind to be on horseback, put a leathern belt, and buckled it about his waist. This was always the office of some grave trusty servant, in whom I could confide, whether I attended the king and queen in their progresses, or were disposed to see the gardens, or pay a visit to some great lady or minister of state in the court, when Glumdalclitch happened to be out of order; for I soon began to be known and esteemed among the greatest officers, I suppose more upon account of their majesties' favour, than any merit of my own. In journeys, when I was weary of the coach, a servant on horseback would buckle on my box, and place it upon a cushion before him; and there I had a full prospect of the country on three sides, from my three windows. I had, in this closet, a field-bed and a hammock, hung from the ceiling, two chairs and a table, neatly screwed to the floor, to prevent being tossed about by the agitation of the horse or the coach. And having been long used to sea-voyages, those motions, although sometimes very violent, did not much discompose me.

Whenever I had a mind to see the town, it was always in my travelling-closet; which Glumdalclitch held in her lap in a kind of open sedan, after the fashion of the country, borne by four men, and attended by two others in the queen's livery. The people, who had often heard of me, were very curious to crowd about the sedan, and the girl was complaisant enough to make the bearers stop, and to take me in her hand, that I might be more conveniently seen.

I was very desirous to see the chief temple, and particularly the tower belonging to it, which is reckoned the highest in the kingdom. Accordingly one day my nurse carried me thither, but I may truly say I came back disappointed; for the height is not above three thousand feet, reckoning from the ground to the highest pinnacle top; which, allowing for the difference between the size of those people and us in Europe, is no great matter for admiration, nor at all equal in proportion (if I rightly remember) to Salisbury steeple. But, not to detract from a nation, to which, during my life, I shall acknowledge myself extremely obliged, it must be allowed, that whatever this famous tower wants in height, is amply made up in beauty and strength: for the walls are near a hundred feet thick, built of hewn stone, whereof each is about forty feet square, and adorned on all sides with statues of gods and emperors, cut in marble, larger than the life, placed in their several niches. I measured a little finger which had fallen down from one of these statues, and lay unperceived among some rubbish, and found it exactly four feet and an inch in length. Glumdalclitch wrapped it up in her handkerchief, and carried it home in her pocket, to keep among other trinkets, of which the girl was very fond, as children at her age usually are.

The king's kitchen is indeed a noble building, vaulted at top, and about six hundred feet high. The great oven is not so wide, by ten paces, as the cupola at St. Paul's: for I measured the latter on purpose, after my return. But if I should describe the kitchen grate, the prodigious pots and kettles, the joints of meat turning on the spits, with many other particulars, perhaps I should be hardly believed; at least a severe critic would be apt to think I enlarged a little, as travellers are often suspected to do. To avoid which censure I fear I have run too much into the other extreme; and that if this treatise should happen to be translated into the language of Brobdingnag (which is the general name of that kingdom,) and transmitted thither, the king and his people would have reason to complain that I had done them an injury, by a false and diminutive representation.

His majesty seldom keeps above six hundred horses in his stables: they are generally from fifty-four to sixty feet high. But, when he goes abroad on solemn days, he is attended, for state, by a military guard of five hundred horse, which, indeed, I thought was the most splendid sight that could be ever beheld, till I saw part of his army in battalia, whereof I shall find another occasion to speak.

5

SEVERAL ADVENTURERS THAT HAPPENED TO THE AUTHOR. THE EXECUTION OF A CRIMINAL. THE AUTHOR SHOWS HIS SKILL IN NAVIGATION.

I should have lived happy enough in that country, if my littleness had not exposed me to several ridiculous and troublesome accidents; some of which I shall venture to relate. Glumdalclitch often carried me into the gardens of the court in my smaller box, and would sometimes take me out of it, and hold me in her hand, or set me down to walk. I remember, before the dwarf left the queen, he followed us one day into those gardens, and my nurse having set me down, he and I being close together, near some dwarf apple trees, I must needs show my wit, by a silly allusion between him and the trees, which happens to hold in their language as it does in ours. Whereupon, the malicious rogue, watching his opportunity, when I was walking under one of them, shook it directly over my head, by which a dozen apples, each of them near as large as a Bristol barrel, came tumbling about my ears; one of them hit me on the back as I chanced to stoop, and knocked me down flat on my face; but I received no other hurt, and the dwarf was pardoned at my desire, because I had given the provocation.

Another day, Glumdalclitch left me on a smooth grass-plot to divert myself, while she walked at some distance with her governess. In the meantime, there suddenly fell such a violent shower of hail, that I was immediately by the force of it, struck to the ground: and when I was down, the hailstones gave me such cruel bangs all over the body, as if I had been pelted with tennis-balls; however, I made a shift to creep on all fours, and shelter myself, by lying flat on my face, on the lee-side of a border of lemon-thyme, but so bruised from head to foot, that I could not go abroad in ten days. Neither is this at all to be wondered at, because nature, in that country, observing the same proportion through all her operations, a hailstone is near eighteen hundred times as large as one in Europe; which I can assert upon experience, having been so curious as to weigh and measure them.

But a more dangerous accident happened to me in the same garden, when my little nurse, believing she had put me in a secure place (which I often entreated her to do, that I might enjoy my own thoughts,) and having left my box at home, to avoid the trouble of carrying it, went to another part of the garden with her governess and some ladies of her acquaintance. While she was absent, and out of hearing, a small white spaniel that belonged to one of the chief gardeners, having got by accident into the garden, happened to range near the place where I lay: the dog, following the scent, came directly up, and taking me in his mouth, ran straight to his master wagging his tail, and set me gently on the ground. By good fortune he had been so well taught, that I was carried between his teeth without the least hurt, or even tearing my clothes. But the poor gardener, who knew me well, and had a great kindness for me, was in a terrible fright: he gently took me up in both his hands, and asked me how I did? but I was so amazed and out of breath, that I could not speak a word. In a few minutes I came to myself, and he carried me safe to my little nurse, who, by this time, had returned to the place where she left me, and was in cruel agonies when I did not appear, nor answer when she called. She severely reprimanded the gardener on account of his dog. But the thing was hushed up, and never known at court, for the girl was afraid of the queen's anger; and truly, as to myself, I thought it would not be for my reputation, that such a story should go about.

This accident absolutely determined Glumdalclitch never to trust me abroad for the future out of her sight. I had been long afraid of this resolution, and therefore concealed from her some little unlucky adventures, that happened in those times when I was left by myself. Once a kite, hovering over the garden, made a stoop at me, and if I had not resolutely drawn my hanger, and run under a thick espalier, he would have certainly carried me away in his talons. Another time, walking to the top of a fresh mole-hill, I fell to my neck in the hole, through which that animal had cast up the earth, and coined some lie, not worth remembering, to excuse myself for spoiling my clothes. I likewise broke my right shin against the shell of a snail, which I happened to stumble over, as I was walking alone and thinking on poor England.

I cannot tell whether I were more pleased or mortified to observe, in those solitary walks, that the smaller birds did not appear to be at all afraid of me, but would hop about within a yard's distance, looking for worms and other food, with as much indifference and security as if no creature at all were near them. I remember, a thrush had the confidence to snatch out of my hand, with his bill, a of cake that Glumdalclitch had just given me for my breakfast. When I attempted to catch any of these birds, they would boldly turn against me, endeavouring to peck my fingers, which I durst not venture within their reach; and then they would hop back unconcerned, to hunt for worms or snails, as they did before. But one day, I took a thick cudgel, and threw it with all my strength so luckily, at a linnet, that I knocked him down, and seizing him by the neck with both my hands, ran with him in triumph to my nurse. However, the bird, who had only been stunned, recovering himself gave me so many boxes with his wings, on both sides of my head and body, though I held him at arm's-length, and was out of the reach of his claws, that I was twenty times thinking to let him go. But I was soon relieved by one of our servants, who wrung off the bird's neck, and I had him next day for dinner, by the queen's command. This linnet, as near as I can remember, seemed to be somewhat larger than an English swan.

The maids of honour often invited Glumdalclitch to their apartments, and desired she would bring me along with her, on purpose to have the pleasure of seeing and touching me. They would often strip me naked from top to toe, and lay me at full length in their bosoms; wherewith I was much disgusted because, to say the truth, a very offensive smell came from their skins; which I do not mention, or intend, to the disadvantage of those excellent ladies, for whom I have all manner of respect; but I conceive that my sense was more acute in proportion to my littleness, and that those illustrious persons were no more disagreeable to their lovers, or to each other, than people of the same quality are with us in England. And, after all, I found their natural smell was much more supportable, than when they used perfumes, under which I immediately swooned away. I cannot forget, that an intimate friend of mine in Lilliput, took the freedom in a warm day, when I had used a good deal of exercise, to complain of a strong smell about me, although I am as little faulty that way, as most of my sex: but I suppose his faculty of smelling was as nice with regard to me, as mine was to that of this people. Upon this point, I cannot forbear doing justice to the queen my mistress, and Glumdalclitch my nurse, whose persons were as sweet as those of any lady in England.

That which gave me most uneasiness among these maids of honour (when my nurse carried me to visit then) was, to see them use me without any manner of ceremony, like a creature who had no sort of consequence: for they would strip themselves to the skin, and put on their smocks in my presence, while I was placed on their toilet, directly before their naked bodies, which I am sure to me was very far from being a tempting sight, or from giving me any other emotions than those of horror and disgust: their skins appeared so coarse and uneven, so variously coloured, when I saw them near, with a mole here and there as broad as a trencher, and hairs hanging from it thicker than packthreads, to say nothing farther concerning the rest of their persons. Neither did they at all scruple, while I was by, to discharge what they had drank, to the quantity of at least two hogsheads, in a vessel that held above three tuns. The handsomest among these maids of honour, a pleasant, frolicsome girl of sixteen, would sometimes set me astride upon one of her nipples, with many other tricks, wherein the reader will excuse me for not being over particular. But I was so much displeased, that I entreated Glumdalclitch to contrive some excuse for not seeing that young lady any more.

One day, a young gentleman, who was nephew to my nurse's governess, came and pressed them both to see an execution. It was of a man, who had murdered one of that gentleman's intimate acquaintance. Glumdalclitch was prevailed on to be of the company, very much against her inclination, for she was naturally tender-hearted: and, as for myself, although I abhorred such kind of spectacles, yet my curiosity tempted me to see something that I thought must be extraordinary. The malefactor was fixed in a chair upon a scaffold erected for that purpose, and his head cut off at one blow, with a sword of about forty feet long. The veins and arteries spouted up such a prodigious quantity of blood, and so high in the air, that the great *jet d'eau* at Versailles was not equal to it for the time it lasted: and the head, when it fell on the scaffold floor, gave such a bounce as made me start, although I was at least half an English mile distant.

The queen, who often used to hear me talk of my sea-voyages, and took all occasions to divert me when I was melancholy, asked me whether I understood how to handle a sail or an oar, and whether a little exercise of rowing might not be convenient for my health? I answered, that I understood both very well: for although my proper employment had been to be surgeon or doctor to the ship, yet often, upon a pinch, I was forced to work like a common mariner. But I could not see how this could be done in their country, where the smallest wherry was equal to a first-rate man of war among us; and such a boat as I could manage would never live in any of their rivers. Her majesty said, if I would contrive a boat, her own joiner should make it, and she would provide a place for me to sail in. The fellow was an ingenious workman, and by my instructions, in ten days, finished a pleasure-boat with all its tackling, able conveniently to hold eight Europeans. When it was finished, the queen was so delighted, that she ran with it in her lap to the king, who ordered it to be put into a cistern full of water, with me in it, by way of trial, where I could not manage my two sculls, or little oars, for want of room. But the queen had before contrived another project. She ordered the joiner to make a wooden trough of three hundred feet long, fifty broad, and eight deep; which, being well pitched, to prevent leaking, was placed on the floor, along the wall, in an outer room of the palace. It had a cock near the bottom to let out the water, when it began to grow stale; and two servants could easily fill it in half an hour. Here I often used to row for my own diversion, as well as that of the queen and her ladies, who thought themselves well entertained with my skill and agility. Sometimes I would put up my sail, and then my business was only to steer, while the ladies gave me a gale with their fans; and, when they were weary, some of their pages would blow my sail forward with their breath, while I showed my art by steering starboard or larboard as I pleased. When I had done, Glumdalclitch always carried back my boat into her closet, and hung it on a nail to dry.

In this exercise I once met an accident, which had like to have cost me my life; for, one of the pages having put my boat into the trough, the governess who attended Glumdalclitch very officiously lifted me up, to place me in the boat: but I happened to slip through her fingers, and should infallibly have fallen down forty feet upon the floor, if, by the luckiest chance in the world, I had not been stopped by a corking-pin that stuck in the good gentlewoman's stomacher; the head of the pin passing between my shirt and the waistband of my breeches, and thus I was held by the middle in the air, till Glumdalclitch ran to my relief.

Another time, one of the servants, whose office it was to fill my trough every third day with fresh water, was so careless as to let a huge frog (not perceiving it) slip out of his pail. The frog lay concealed till I was put into my boat, but then, seeing a resting-place, climbed up, and made it lean so much on one side, that I was forced to balance it with all my weight on the other, to prevent overturning. When the frog was got in, it hopped at once half the length of the boat, and then over my head, backward and forward, daubing my face and clothes with its odious slime. The largeness of its features made it appear the most deformed animal that can be conceived. However, I desired Glumdalclitch to let me deal with it alone. I banged it a good while with one of my sculls, and at last forced it to leap out of the boat.

But the greatest danger I ever underwent in that kingdom, was from a monkey, who belonged to one of the clerks of the kitchen. Glumdalclitch had locked me up in her closet, while she went somewhere upon business, or a visit. The weather being very warm, the closet-window was left open, as well as the windows and the door of my bigger box, in which I usually lived, because of its largeness and conveniency. As I sat quietly meditating at my table, I heard something bounce in at the closet-window, and skip about from one side to the other: whereat, although I was much alarmed, yet I ventured to look out, but not stirring from my seat; and then I saw this frolicsome animal frisking and leaping up and down, till at last he came to my box, which he seemed to view with great pleasure and curiosity, peeping in at the door and every window. I retreated to the farther corner of my room; or box; but the monkey looking in at every side, put me in such a fright, that I wanted presence of mind to conceal myself under the bed, as I might easily have done. After some time spent in peeping, grinning, and chattering, he at last espied me; and reaching one of his paws in at the door, as a cat does when she plays with a mouse, although I often shifted place to avoid him, he at length seized the lappet of my coat (which being made of that country silk, was very thick and strong), and dragged me out. He took me up in his right fore-foot and held me as a nurse does a child she is going to suckle, just as I have seen the same sort of creature do with a kitten in Europe; and when I offered to struggle he squeezed me so hard, that I thought it more prudent to submit. I have good reason to believe, that he took me for a young one of his own species, by his often stroking my face very gently with his other paw. In these diversions he was interrupted by a noise at the closet door, as if somebody were opening it: whereupon he suddenly leaped up to the window at which he had come in, and thence upon the leads and gutters, walking upon three legs, and holding me in the fourth, till he clambered up to a roof that was next to ours. I heard Glumdalclitch give a shriek at the moment he was carrying me out. The poor girl was almost distracted: that quarter of the palace was all in an uproar; the servants ran for ladders; the monkey was seen by hundreds in the court, sitting upon the ridge of a building, holding me like a baby in one of his forepaws, and feeding me with the other, by cramming into my mouth some victuals he had squeezed out of the bag on one side of his chaps, and patting me when I would not eat; whereat many of the rabble below could not forbear laughing; neither do I think they justly ought to be blamed, for, without question, the sight was ridiculous enough to every body but myself. Some of the people threw up stones, hoping to drive the monkey down; but this was strictly forbidden, or else, very probably, my brains had been dashed out.

The ladders were now applied, and mounted by several men; which the monkey observing, and finding himself almost encompassed, not being able to make speed enough with his three legs, let me drop on a ridge tile, and made his escape. Here I sat for some time, five hundred yards from the ground, expecting every moment to be blown down by the wind, or to fall by my own giddiness, and come tumbling over and over from the ridge to the eaves; but an honest lad, one of my nurse's footmen, climbed up, and putting me into his breeches pocket, brought me down safe.

I was almost choked with the filthy stuff the monkey had crammed down my throat: but my dear little nurse picked it out of my mouth with a small needle, and then I fell a-vomiting, which gave me great relief. Yet I was so weak and bruised in the sides with the squeezes given me by this odious animal, that I was forced to keep my bed a fortnight. The king, queen, and all the court, sent every day to inquire after my health; and her majesty made me several visits during my sickness. The monkey was killed, and an order made, that no such animal should be kept about the palace.

When I attended the king after my recovery, to return him thanks for his favours, he was pleased to rally me a good deal upon this adventure. He asked me, "what my thoughts and speculations were, while I lay in the monkey's paw; how I liked the victuals he gave me; his manner of feeding; and whether the fresh air on the roof had sharpened my stomach." He desired to know, "what I would have done upon such an occasion in my own country." I told his majesty, "that in Europe we had no monkeys, except such as were brought for curiosity from other places, and so small, that I could deal with a dozen of them together, if they presumed to attack me. And as for that monstrous animal with whom I was so lately engaged (it was indeed as large as an elephant), if my fears had suffered me to think so far as to make use of my hanger," (looking fiercely, and clapping my hand on the hilt, as I spoke) "when he poked his paw into my chamber, perhaps I should have given him such a wound, as would have made him glad to withdraw it with more haste than he put it in." This I delivered in a firm tone, like a person who was jealous lest his courage should be called in question. However, my speech produced nothing else beside a loud laughter, which all the respect due to his majesty from those about him could not make them contain. This made me reflect, how vain an attempt it is for a man to endeavour to do himself honour among those who are out of all degree of equality or comparison with him. And yet I have seen the moral of my own behaviour very frequent in England since my return; where a little contemptible varlet, without the least title to birth, person, wit, or common sense, shall presume to look with importance, and put himself upon a foot with the greatest persons of the kingdom.

I was every day furnishing the court with some ridiculous story: and Glumdalclitch, although she loved me to excess, yet was arch enough to inform the queen, whenever I committed any folly that she thought would be diverting to her majesty. The girl, who had been out of order, was carried by her governess to take the air about an hour's distance, or thirty miles from town. They alighted out of the coach near a small foot-path in a field, and Glumdalclitch setting down my travelling box, I went out of it to walk. There was a cow-dung in the path, and I must need try my activity by attempting to leap over it. I took a run, but unfortunately jumped short, and found myself just in the middle up to my knees. I waded through with some difficulty, and one of the footmen wiped me as clean as he could with his handkerchief, for I was filthily bemired; and my nurse confined me to my box, till we returned home; where the queen was soon informed of what had passed, and the footmen spread it about the court: so that all the mirth for some days was at my expense.

6

SEVERAL CONTRIVANCES OF THE AUTHOR TO PLEASE THE KING AND QUEEN. HE SHOWS HIS SKILL IN MUSIC. THE KING INQUIRES INTO THE STATE OF ENGLAND, WHICH THE AUTHOR RELATES TO HIM. THE KING'S OBSERVATIONS THEREON.

I used to attend the king's levee once or twice a week, and had often seen him under the barber's hand, which indeed was at first very terrible to behold; for the razor was almost twice as long as an ordinary scythe. His majesty, according to the custom of the country, was only shaved twice a-week. I once prevailed on the barber to give me some of the suds or lather, out of which I picked forty or fifty of the strongest stumps of hair. I then took a piece of fine wood, and cut it like the back of a comb, making several holes in it at equal distances with as small a needle as I could get from Glumdalclitch. I fixed in the stumps so artificially, scraping and sloping them with my knife toward the points, that I made a very tolerable comb; which was a seasonable supply, my own being so much broken in the teeth, that it was almost useless: neither did I know any artist in that country so nice and exact, as would undertake to make me another.

And this puts me in mind of an amusement, wherein I spent many of my leisure hours. I desired the queen's woman to save for me the combings of her majesty's hair, whereof in time I got a good quantity; and consulting with my friend the cabinet-maker, who had received general orders to do little jobs for me, I directed him to make two chair-frames, no larger than those I had in my box, and to bore little holes with a fine awl, round those parts where I designed the backs and seats; through these holes I wove the strongest hairs I could pick out, just after the manner of cane chairs in England. When they were finished, I made a present of them to her majesty; who kept them in her cabinet, and used to show them for curiosities, as indeed they were the wonder of every one that beheld them. The queen would have me sit upon one of these chairs, but I absolutely refused to obey her, protesting I would rather die than place a dishonourable part of my body on those precious hairs, that once adorned her majesty's head. Of these hairs (as I had always a mechanical genius) I likewise made a neat little purse, about five feet long, with her majesty's name deciphered in gold letters, which I gave to Glumdalclitch, by the queen's consent. To say the truth, it was more for show than use, being not of strength to bear the weight of the larger coins, and therefore she kept nothing in it but some little toys that girls are fond of.

The king, who delighted in music, had frequent concerts at court, to which I was sometimes carried, and set in my box on a table to hear them: but the noise was so great that I could hardly distinguish the tunes. I am confident that all the drums and trumpets of a royal army, beating and sounding together just at your ears, could not equal it. My practice was to have my box removed from the place where the performers sat, as far as I could, then to shut the doors and windows of it, and draw the window curtains; after which I found their music not disagreeable.

I had learned in my youth to play a little upon the spinet. Glumdalclitch kept one in her chamber, and a master attended twice a-week to teach her: I called it a spinet, because it somewhat resembled that instrument, and was played upon in the same manner. A fancy came into my head, that I would entertain the king and queen with an English tune upon this instrument. But this appeared extremely difficult: for the spinet was near sixty feet long, each key being almost a foot wide, so that with my arms extended I could not reach to above five keys, and to press them down required a good smart stroke with my fist, which would be too great a labour, and to no purpose. The method I contrived was this: I prepared two round sticks, about the bigness of common cudgels; they were thicker at one end than the other, and I covered the thicker ends with pieces of a mouse's skin, that by rapping on them I might neither damage the tops of the keys nor interrupt the sound. Before the spinet a bench was placed, about four feet below the keys, and I was put upon the bench. I ran sideling upon it, that way and this, as fast as I could, banging the proper keys with my two sticks, and made a shift to play a jig, to the great satisfaction of both their majesties; but it was the most violent exercise I ever underwent; and yet I could not strike above sixteen keys, nor consequently play the bass and treble together, as other artists do; which was a great disadvantage to my performance.

The king, who, as I before observed, was a prince of excellent understanding, would frequently order that I should be brought in my box, and set upon the table in his closet: he would then command me to bring one of my chairs out of the box, and sit down within three yards distance upon the top of the cabinet, which brought me almost to a level with his face. In this manner I had several conversations with him. I one day took the freedom to tell his majesty, "that the contempt he discovered towards Europe, and the rest of the world, did not seem answerable to those excellent qualities of mind that he was master of; that reason did not extend itself with the bulk of the body; on the contrary, we observed in our country, that the tallest persons were usually the least provided with it; that among other animals, bees and ants had the reputation of more industry, art, and sagacity, than many of the larger kinds; and that, as inconsiderable as he took me to be, I hoped I might live to do his majesty some signal service." The king heard me with attention, and began to conceive a much better opinion of me than he had ever before. He desired "I would give him as exact an account of the government of England as I possibly could; because, as fond as princes commonly are of their own customs (for so he conjectured of other monarchs, by my former discourses), he should be glad to hear of any thing that might deserve imitation."

Imagine with thyself, courteous reader, how often I then wished for the tongue of Demosthenes or Cicero, that might have enabled me to celebrate the praise of my own dear native country in a style equal to its merits and felicity.

I began my discourse by informing his majesty, that our dominions consisted of two islands, which composed three mighty kingdoms, under one sovereign, beside our plantations in America. I dwelt long upon the fertility of our soil, and the temperature of our climate. I then spoke at large upon the constitution of an English parliament; partly made up of an illustrious body called the House of Peers; persons of the noblest blood, and of the most ancient and ample patrimonies. I described that extraordinary care always taken of their education in arts and arms, to qualify them for being counsellors both to the king and kingdom; to have a share in the legislature; to be members of the highest court of judicature, whence there can be no appeal; and to be champions always ready for the defence of their prince and country, by their valour, conduct, and fidelity. That these were the ornament and bulwark of the kingdom, worthy followers of their most renowned ancestors, whose honour had been the reward of their virtue, from which their posterity were never once known to degenerate. To these were joined several holy persons, as part of that assembly, under the title of bishops, whose peculiar business is to take care of religion, and of those who instruct the people therein. These were searched and sought out through the whole nation, by the prince and his wisest counsellors, among such of the priesthood as were most deservedly distinguished by the sanctity of their lives, and the depth of their erudition; who were indeed the spiritual fathers of the clergy and the people.

That the other part of the parliament consisted of an assembly called the House of Commons, who were all principal gentlemen, freely picked and culled out by the people themselves, for their great abilities and love of their country, to represent the wisdom of the whole nation. And that these two bodies made up the most august assembly in Europe; to whom, in conjunction with the prince, the whole legislature is committed.

I then descended to the courts of justice; over which the judges, those venerable sages and interpreters of the law, presided, for determining the disputed rights and properties of men, as well as for the punishment of vice and protection of innocence. I mentioned the prudent management of our treasury; the valour and achievements of our forces, by sea and land. I computed the number of our people, by reckoning how many millions there might be of each religious sect, or political party among us. I did not omit even our sports and pastimes, or any other particular which I thought might redound to the honour of my country. And I finished all with a brief historical account of affairs and events in England for about a hundred years past.

This conversation was not ended under five audiences, each of several hours; and the king heard the whole with great attention, frequently taking notes of what I spoke, as well as memorandums of what questions he intended to ask me.

When I had put an end to these long discourses, his majesty, in a sixth audience, consulting his notes, proposed many doubts, queries, and objections, upon every article. He asked, "What methods were used to cultivate the minds and bodies of our young nobility, and in what kind of business they commonly spent the first and teachable parts of their lives? What course was taken to supply that assembly, when any noble family became extinct? What qualifications were necessary in those who are to be created new lords: whether the humour of the prince, a sum of money to a court lady, or a design of strengthening a party opposite to the public interest, ever happened to be the motive in those advancements? What share of knowledge these lords had in the laws of their country, and how they came by it, so as to enable them to decide the properties of their fellow-subjects in the last resort? Whether they were always so free from avarice, partialities, or want, that a bribe, or some other sinister view, could have no place among them? Whether those holy lords I spoke of were always promoted to that rank upon account of their knowledge in religious matters, and the sanctity of their lives; had never been compliers with the times, while they were common priests; or slavish prostitute chaplains to some nobleman, whose opinions they continued servilely to follow, after they were admitted into that assembly?"

He then desired to know, "What arts were practised in electing those whom I called commoners: whether a stranger, with a strong purse, might not influence the vulgar voters to choose him before their own landlord, or the most considerable gentleman in the neighbourhood? How it came to pass, that people were so violently bent upon getting into this assembly, which I allowed to be a great trouble and expense, often to the ruin of their families, without any salary or pension? because this appeared such an exalted strain of virtue and public spirit, that his majesty seemed to doubt it might possibly not be always sincere." And he desired to know, "Whether such zealous gentlemen could have any views of refunding themselves for the charges and trouble they were at by sacrificing the public good to the designs of a weak and vicious prince, in conjunction with a corrupted ministry?" He multiplied his questions, and sifted me thoroughly upon every part of this head, proposing numberless inquiries and objections, which I think it not prudent or convenient to repeat.

Upon what I said in relation to our courts of justice, his majesty desired to be satisfied in several points: and this I was the better able to do, having been formerly almost ruined by a long suit in chancery, which was decreed for me with costs. He asked, "What time was usually spent in determining between right and wrong, and what degree of expense? Whether advocates and orators had liberty to plead in causes manifestly known to be unjust, vexatious, or oppressive? Whether party, in religion or politics, were observed to be of any weight in the scale of justice? Whether those pleading orators were persons educated in the general knowledge of equity, or only in provincial, national, and other local customs? Whether they or their judges had any part in penning those laws, which they assumed the liberty of interpreting, and glossing upon at their pleasure? Whether they had ever, at different times, pleaded for and against the same cause, and cited precedents to prove contrary opinions? Whether they were a rich or a poor corporation? Whether they received any pecuniary reward for pleading, or delivering their opinions? And particularly, whether they were ever admitted as members in the lower senate?"

He fell next upon the management of our treasury; and said, "he thought my memory had failed me, because I computed our taxes at about five or six millions a-year, and when I came to mention the issues, he found they sometimes amounted to more than double; for the notes he had taken were very particular in this point, because he hoped, as he told me, that the knowledge of our conduct might be useful to him, and he could not be deceived in his calculations. But, if what I told him were true, he was still at a loss how a kingdom could run out of its estate, like a private person." He asked me, "who were our creditors; and where we found money to pay them?" He wondered to hear me talk of such chargeable and expensive wars; "that certainly we must be a quarrelsome people, or live among very bad neighbours, and that our generals must needs be richer than our kings." He asked, "what business we had out of our own islands, unless upon the score of trade, or treaty, or to defend the coasts with our fleet?" Above all, he was amazed to hear me talk of a mercenary standing army, in the midst of peace, and among a free people. He said, "if we were governed by our own consent, in the persons of our representatives, he could not imagine of whom we were afraid, or against whom we were to fight; and would hear my opinion, whether a private man's house might not be better defended by himself, his children, and family, than by half-a-dozen rascals, picked up at a venture in the streets for small wages, who might get a hundred times more by cutting their throats?"

He laughed at my "odd kind of arithmetic," as he was pleased to call it, "in reckoning the numbers of our people, by a computation drawn from the several sects among us, in religion and politics." He said, "he knew no reason why those, who entertain opinions prejudicial to the public, should be obliged to change, or should not be obliged to conceal them. And as it was tyranny in any government to require the first, so it was weakness not to enforce the second: for a man may be allowed to keep poisons in his closet, but not to vend them about for cordials."

He observed, "that among the diversions of our nobility and gentry, I had mentioned gaming: he desired to know at what age this entertainment was usually taken up, and when it was laid down; how much of their time it employed; whether it ever went so high as to affect their fortunes; whether mean, vicious people, by their dexterity in that art, might not arrive at great riches, and sometimes keep our very nobles in dependence, as well as habituate them to vile companions, wholly take them from the improvement of their minds, and force them, by the losses they received, to learn and practise that infamous dexterity upon others?"

He was perfectly astonished with the historical account gave him of our affairs during the last century; protesting "it was only a heap of conspiracies, rebellions, murders, massacres, revolutions, banishments, the very worst effects that avarice, faction, hypocrisy, perfidiousness, cruelty, rage, madness, hatred, envy, lust, malice, and ambition, could produce."

His majesty, in another audience, was at the pains to recapitulate the sum of all I had spoken; compared the questions he made with the answers I had given; then taking me into his hands, and stroking me gently, delivered himself in these words, which I shall never forget, nor the manner he spoke them in: "My little friend Grildrig, you have made a most admirable panegyric upon your country; you have clearly proved, that ignorance, idleness, and vice, are the proper ingredients for qualifying a legislator; that laws are best explained, interpreted, and applied, by those whose interest and abilities lie in perverting, confounding, and eluding them. I observe among you some lines of an institution, which, in its original, might have been tolerable, but these half erased, and the rest wholly blurred and blotted by corruptions. It does not appear, from all you have said, how any one perfection is required toward the procurement of any one station among you; much less, that men are ennobled on account of their virtue; that priests are advanced for their piety or learning; soldiers, for their conduct or valour; judges, for their integrity; senators, for the love of their country; or counsellors for their wisdom. As for yourself," continued the king, "who have spent the greatest part of your life in travelling, I am well disposed to hope you may hitherto have escaped many vices of your country. But by what I have gathered from your own relation, and the answers I have with much pains wrung and extorted from you, I cannot but conclude the bulk of your natives to be the most pernicious race of little odious vermin that nature ever suffered to crawl upon the surface of the earth."

7

THE AUTHOR'S LOVE OF HIS COUNTRY. HE MAKES A PROPOSAL OF MUCH ADVANTAGE TO THE KING, WHICH IS REJECTED. THE KING'S GREAT IGNORANCE IN POLITICS. THE LEARNING OF THAT COUNTRY VERY IMPERFECT AND CONFINED. THE LAWS, AND MILITARY AFFAIRS, AND PARTIES IN THE STATE.

Nothing but an extreme love of truth could have hindered me from concealing this part of my story. It was in vain to discover my resentments, which were always turned into ridicule; and I was forced to rest with patience, while my noble and beloved country was so injuriously treated. I am as heartily sorry as any of my readers can possibly be, that such an occasion was given: but this prince happened to be so curious and inquisitive upon every particular, that it could not consist either with gratitude or good manners, to refuse giving him what satisfaction I was able. Yet thus much I may be allowed to say in my own vindication, that I artfully eluded many of his questions, and gave to every point a more favourable turn, by many degrees, than the strictness of truth would allow. For I have always borne that laudable partiality to my own country, which Dionysius Halicarnassensis, with so much justice, recommends to an historian: I would hide the frailties and deformities of my political mother, and place her virtues and beauties in the most advantageous light. This was my sincere endeavour in those many discourses I had with that monarch, although it unfortunately failed of success.

But great allowances should be given to a king, who lives wholly secluded from the rest of the world, and must therefore be altogether unacquainted with the manners and customs that most prevail in other nations: the want of which knowledge will ever produce many prejudices, and a certain narrowness of thinking, from which we, and the politer countries of Europe, are wholly exempted. And it would be hard indeed, if so remote a prince's notions of virtue and vice were to be offered as a standard for all mankind.

To confirm what I have now said, and further to show the miserable effects of a confined education, I shall here insert a passage, which will hardly obtain belief. In hopes to ingratiate myself further into his majesty's favour, I told him of "an invention, discovered between three and four hundred years ago, to make a certain powder, into a heap of which, the smallest spark of fire falling, would kindle the whole in a moment, although it were as big as a mountain, and make it all fly up in the air together, with a noise and agitation greater than thunder. That a proper quantity of this powder rammed into a hollow tube of brass or iron, according to its bigness, would drive a ball of iron or lead, with such violence and speed, as nothing was able to sustain its force. That the largest balls thus discharged, would not only destroy whole ranks of an army at once, but batter the strongest walls to the ground, sink down ships, with a thousand men in each, to the bottom of the sea, and when linked together by a chain, would cut through masts and rigging, divide hundreds of bodies in the middle, and lay all waste before them. That we often put this powder into large hollow balls of iron, and discharged them by an engine into some city we were besieging, which would rip up the pavements, tear the houses to pieces, burst and throw splinters on every side, dashing out the brains of all who came near. That I knew the ingredients very well, which were cheap and common; I understood the manner of compounding them, and could direct his workmen how to make those tubes, of a size proportionable to all other things in his majesty's kingdom, and the largest need not be above a hundred feet long; twenty or thirty of which tubes, charged with the proper quantity of powder and balls, would batter down the walls of the strongest town in his dominions in a few hours, or destroy the whole metropolis, if ever it should pretend to dispute his absolute commands." This I humbly offered to his majesty, as a small tribute of acknowledgment, in turn for so many marks that I had received, of his royal favour and protection.

The king was struck with horror at the description I had given of those terrible engines, and the proposal I had made. "He was amazed, how so impotent and grovelling an insect as I" (these were his expressions) "could entertain such inhuman ideas, and in so familiar a manner, as to appear wholly unmoved at all the scenes of blood and desolation which I had painted as the common effects of those destructive machines; whereof," he said, "some evil genius, enemy to mankind, must have been the first contriver. As for himself, he protested, that although few things delighted him so much as new discoveries in art or in nature, yet he would rather lose half his kingdom, than be privy to such a secret; which he commanded me, as I valued any life, never to mention any more."

A strange effect of narrow principles and views! that a prince possessed of every quality which procures veneration, love, and esteem; of strong parts, great wisdom, and profound learning, endowed with admirable talents, and almost adored by his subjects, should, from a nice, unnecessary scruple, whereof in Europe we can have no conception, let slip an opportunity put into his hands that would have made him absolute master of the lives, the liberties, and the fortunes of his people! Neither do I say this, with the least intention to detract from the many virtues of that excellent king, whose character, I am sensible, will, on this account, be very much lessened in the opinion of an English reader: but I take this defect among them to have risen from their ignorance, by not having hitherto reduced politics into a science, as the more acute wits of Europe have done. For, I remember very well, in a discourse one day with the king, when I happened to say, "there were several thousand books among us written upon the art of government," it gave him (directly contrary to my intention) a very mean opinion of our understandings. He professed both to abominate and despise all mystery, refinement, and intrigue, either in a prince or a minister. He could not tell what I meant by secrets of state, where an enemy, or some rival nation, were not in the case. He confined the knowledge of governing within very narrow bounds, to common sense and reason, to justice and lenity, to the speedy determination of civil and criminal causes; with some other obvious topics, which are not worth considering. And he gave it for his opinion, "that whoever could make two ears of corn, or two blades of grass, to grow upon a spot of ground where only one grew before, would deserve better of mankind, and do more essential service to his country, than the whole race of politicians put together."

The learning of this people is very defective, consisting only in morality, history, poetry, and mathematics, wherein they must be allowed to excel. But the last of these is wholly applied to what may be useful in life, to the improvement of agriculture, and all mechanical arts; so that among us, it would be little esteemed. And as to ideas, entities, abstractions, and transcendentals, I could never drive the least conception into their heads.

No law in that country must exceed in words the number of letters in their alphabet, which consists only of two and twenty. But indeed few of them extend even to that length. They are expressed in the most plain and simple terms, wherein those people are not mercurial enough to discover above one interpretation: and to write a comment upon any law, is a capital crime. As to the decision of civil causes, or proceedings against criminals, their precedents are so few, that they have little reason to boast of any extraordinary skill in either.

They have had the art of printing, as well as the Chinese, time out of mind: but their libraries are not very large; for that of the king, which is reckoned the largest, does not amount to above a thousand volumes, placed in a gallery of twelve hundred feet long, whence I had liberty to borrow what books I pleased. The queen's joiner had contrived in one of Glumdalclitch's rooms, a kind of wooden machine five-and-twenty feet high, formed like a standing ladder; the steps were each fifty feet long. It was indeed a moveable pair of stairs, the lowest end placed at ten feet distance from the wall of the chamber. The book I had a mind to read, was put up leaning against the wall: I first mounted to the upper step of the ladder, and turning my face towards the book, began at the top of the page, and so walking to the right and left about eight or ten paces, according to the length of the lines, till I had gotten a little below the level of mine eyes, and then descending gradually till I came to the bottom: after which I mounted again, and began the other page in the same manner, and so turned over the leaf, which I could easily do with both my hands, for it was as thick and stiff as a pasteboard, and in the largest folios not above eighteen or twenty feet long.

Their style is clear, masculine, and smooth, but not florid; for they avoid nothing more than multiplying unnecessary words, or using various expressions. I have perused many of their books, especially those in history and morality. Among the rest, I was much diverted with a little old treatise, which always lay in Glumdalclitch's bed chamber, and belonged to her governess, a grave elderly gentlewoman, who dealt in writings of morality and devotion. The book treats of the weakness of human kind, and is in little esteem, except among the women and the vulgar. However, I was curious to see what an author of that country could say upon such a subject. This writer went through all the usual topics of European moralists, showing "how diminutive, contemptible, and helpless an animal was man in his own nature; how unable to defend himself from inclemencies of the air, or the fury of wild beasts: how much he was excelled by one creature in strength, by another in speed, by a third in foresight, by a fourth in industry." He added, "that nature was degenerated in these latter declining ages of the world, and could now produce only small abortive births, in comparison of those in ancient times." He said "it was very reasonable to think, not only that the species of men were originally much larger, but also that there must have been giants in former ages; which, as it is asserted by history and tradition, so it has been confirmed by huge bones and skulls, casually dug up in several parts of the kingdom, far exceeding the common dwindled race of men in our days." He argued, "that the very laws of nature absolutely required we should have been made, in the beginning of a size more large and robust; not so liable to destruction from every little accident, of a tile falling from a house, or a stone cast from the hand of a boy, or being drowned in a little brook." From this way of reasoning, the author drew several moral applications, useful in the conduct of life, but needless here to repeat. For my own part, I could not avoid reflecting how universally this talent was spread, of drawing lectures in morality, or indeed rather matter of discontent and repining, from the quarrels we raise with nature. And I believe, upon a strict inquiry, those quarrels might be shown as ill-grounded among us as they are among that people.

As to their military affairs, they boast that the king's army consists of a hundred and seventy-six thousand foot, and thirty-two thousand horse: if that may be called an army, which is made up of tradesmen in the several cities, and farmers in the country, whose commanders are only the nobility and gentry, without pay or reward. They are indeed perfect enough in their exercises, and under very good discipline, wherein I saw no great merit; for how should it be otherwise, where every farmer is under the command of his own landlord, and every citizen under that of the principal men in his own city, chosen after the manner of Venice, by ballot?

I have often seen the militia of Lorbrulgrud drawn out to exercise, in a great field near the city of twenty miles square. They were in all not above twenty-five thousand foot, and six thousand horse; but it was impossible for me to compute their number, considering the space of ground they took up. A cavalier, mounted on a large steed, might be about ninety feet high. I have seen this whole body of horse, upon a word of command, draw their swords at once, and brandish them in the air. Imagination can figure nothing so grand, so surprising, and so astonishing! it looked as if ten thousand flashes of lightning were darting at the same time from every quarter of the sky.

I was curious to know how this prince, to whose dominions there is no access from any other country, came to think of armies, or to teach his people the practice of military discipline. But I was soon informed, both by conversation and reading their histories; for, in the course of many ages, they have been troubled with the same disease to which the whole race of mankind is subject; the nobility often contending for power, the people for liberty, and the king for absolute dominion. All which, however happily tempered by the laws of that kingdom, have been sometimes violated by each of the three parties, and have more than once occasioned civil wars; the last whereof was happily put an end to by this prince's grand-father, in a general composition; and the militia, then settled with common consent, has been ever since kept in the strictest duty.

8

THE KING AND QUEEN MAKE A PROGRESS TO THE FRONTIERS. THE AUTHOR ATTENDS THEM. THE MANNER IN WHICH HE LEAVES THE COUNTRY VERY PARTICULARLY RELATED. HE RETURNS TO ENGLAND.

I had always a strong impulse that I should some time recover my liberty, though it was impossible to conjecture by what means, or to form any project with the least hope of succeeding. The ship in which I sailed, was the first ever known to be driven within sight of that coast, and the king had given strict orders, that if at any time another appeared, it should be taken ashore, and with all its crew and passengers brought in a tumbril to Lorbrulgrud. He was strongly bent to get me a woman of my own size, by whom I might propagate the breed: but I think I should rather have died than undergone the disgrace of leaving a posterity to be kept in cages, like tame canary-birds, and perhaps, in time, sold about the kingdom, to persons of quality, for curiosities. I was indeed treated with much kindness: I was the favourite of a great king and queen, and the delight of the whole court; but it was upon such a foot as ill became the dignity of humankind. I could never forget those domestic pledges I had left behind me. I wanted to be among people, with whom I could converse upon even terms, and walk about the streets and fields without being afraid of being trod to death like a frog or a young puppy. But my deliverance came sooner than I expected, and in a manner not very common; the whole story and circumstances of which I shall faithfully relate.

I had now been two years in this country; and about the beginning of the third, Glumdalclitch and I attended the king and queen, in a progress to the south coast of the kingdom. I was carried, as usual, in my travelling-box, which as I have already described, was a very convenient closet, of twelve feet wide. And I had ordered a hammock to be fixed, by silken ropes from the four corners at the top, to break the jolts, when a servant carried me before him on horseback, as I sometimes desired; and would often sleep in my hammock, while we were upon the road. On the roof of my closet, not directly over the middle of the hammock, I ordered the joiner to cut out a hole of a foot square, to give me air in hot weather, as I slept; which hole I shut at pleasure with a board that drew backward and forward through a groove.

When we came to our journey's end, the king thought proper to pass a few days at a palace he has near Flanflasnic, a city within eighteen English miles of the seaside.

Glumdalclitch and I were much fatigued: I had gotten a small cold, but the poor girl was so ill as to be confined to her chamber. I longed to see the ocean, which must be the only scene of my escape, if ever it should happen. I pretended to be worse than I really was, and desired leave to take the fresh air of the sea, with a page, whom I was very fond of, and who had sometimes been trusted with me. I shall never forget with what unwillingness Glumdalclitch consented, nor the strict charge she gave the page to be careful of me, bursting at the same time into a flood of tears, as if she had some forboding of what was to happen. The boy took me out in my box, about half an hours walk from the palace, towards the rocks on the sea-shore. I ordered him to set me down, and lifting up one of my sashes, cast many a wistful melancholy look towards the sea. I found myself not very well, and told the page that I had a mind to take a nap in my hammock, which I hoped would do me good. I got in, and the boy shut the window close down, to keep out the cold. I soon fell asleep, and all I can conjecture is, while I slept, the page, thinking no danger could happen, went among the rocks to look for birds' eggs, having before observed him from my window searching about, and picking up one or two in the clefts. Be that as it will, I found myself suddenly awaked with a violent pull upon the ring, which was fastened at the top of my box for the conveniency of carriage. I felt my box raised very high in the air, and then borne forward with prodigious speed. The first jolt had like to have shaken me out of my hammock, but afterward the motion was easy enough. I called out several times, as loud as I could raise my voice, but all to no purpose. I looked towards my windows, and could see nothing but the clouds and sky. I heard a noise just over my head, like the clapping of wings, and then began to perceive the woful condition I was in; that some eagle had got the ring of my box in his beak, with an intent to let it fall on a rock, like a tortoise in a shell, and then pick out my body, and devour it: for the sagacity and smell of this bird enables him to discover his quarry at a great distance, though better concealed than I could be within a two-inch board.

In a little time, I observed the noise and flutter of wings to increase very fast, and my box was tossed up and down, like a sign in a windy day. I heard several bangs or buffets, as I thought given to the eagle (for such I am certain it must have been that held the ring of my box in his beak), and then, all on a sudden, felt myself falling perpendicularly down, for above a minute, but with such incredible swiftness, that I almost lost my breath. My fall was stopped by a terrible squash, that sounded louder to my ears than the cataract of Niagara; after which, I was quite in the dark for another minute, and then my box began to rise so high, that I could see light from the tops of the windows. I now perceived I was fallen into the sea. My box, by the weight of my body, the goods that were in, and the broad plates of iron fixed for strength at the four corners of the top and bottom, floated about five feet deep in water. I did then, and do now suppose, that the eagle which flew away with my box was pursued by two or three others, and forced to let me drop, while he defended himself against the rest, who hoped to share in the prey. The plates of iron fastened at the bottom of the box (for those were the strongest) preserved the balance while it fell, and hindered it from being broken on the surface of the water. Every joint of it was well grooved; and the door did not move on hinges, but up and down like a sash, which kept my closet so tight that very little water came in. I got with much difficulty out of my hammock, having first ventured to draw back the slip-board on the roof already mentioned, contrived on purpose to let in air, for want of which I found myself almost stifled.

How often did I then wish myself with my dear Glumdalclitch, from whom one single hour had so far divided me! And I may say with truth, that in the midst of my own misfortunes I could not forbear lamenting my poor nurse, the grief she would suffer for my loss, the displeasure of the queen, and the ruin of her fortune. Perhaps many travellers have not been under greater difficulties and distress than I was at this juncture, expecting every moment to see my box dashed to pieces, or at least overset by the first violent blast, or rising wave. A breach in one single pane of glass would have been immediate death: nor could any thing have preserved the windows, but the strong lattice wires placed on the outside, against accidents in travelling. I saw the water ooze in at several crannies, although the leaks were not considerable, and I endeavoured to stop them as well as I could. I was not able to lift up the roof of my closet, which otherwise I certainly should have done, and sat on the top of it; where I might at least preserve myself some hours longer, than by being shut up (as I may call it) in the hold. Or if I escaped these dangers for a day or two, what could I expect but a miserable death of cold and hunger? I was four hours under these circumstances, expecting, and indeed wishing, every moment to be my last.

I have already told the reader that there were two strong staples fixed upon that side of my box which had no window, and into which the servant, who used to carry me on horseback, would put a leathern belt, and buckle it about his waist. Being in this disconsolate state, I heard, or at least thought I heard, some kind of grating noise on that side of my box where the staples were fixed; and soon after I began to fancy that the box was pulled or towed along the sea; for I now and then felt a sort of tugging, which made the waves rise near the tops of my windows, leaving me almost in the dark. This gave me some faint hopes of relief, although I was not able to imagine how it could be brought about. I ventured to unscrew one of my chairs, which were always fastened to the floor; and having made a hard shift to screw it down again, directly under the slipping-board that I had lately opened, I mounted on the chair, and putting my mouth as near as I could to the hole, I called for help in a loud voice, and in all the languages I understood. I then fastened my handkerchief to a stick I usually carried, and thrusting it up the hole, waved it several times in the air, that if any boat or ship were near, the seamen might conjecture some unhappy mortal to be shut up in the box.

I found no effect from all I could do, but plainly perceived my closet to be moved along; and in the space of an hour, or better, that side of the box where the staples were, and had no windows, struck against something that was hard. I apprehended it to be a rock, and found myself tossed more than ever. I plainly heard a noise upon the cover of my closet, like that of a cable, and the grating of it as it passed through the ring. I then found myself hoisted up, by degrees, at least three feet higher than I was before. Whereupon I again thrust up my stick and handkerchief, calling for help till I was almost hoarse. In return to which, I heard a great shout repeated three times, giving me such transports of joy as are not to be conceived but by those who feel them. I now heard a trampling over my head, and somebody calling through the hole with a loud voice, in the English tongue, "If there be any body below, let them speak." I answered, "I was an Englishman, drawn by ill fortune into the greatest calamity that ever any creature underwent, and begged, by all that was moving, to be delivered out of the dungeon I was in." The voice replied, "I was safe, for my box was fastened to their ship; and the carpenter should immediately come and saw a hole in the cover, large enough to pull me out." I answered, "that was needless, and would take up too much time; for there was no more to be done, but let one of the crew put his finger into the ring, and take the box out of the sea into the ship, and so into the captain's cabin." Some of them, upon hearing me talk so wildly, thought I was mad: others laughed; for indeed it never came into my head, that I was now got among people of my own stature and strength. The carpenter came, and in a few minutes sawed a passage about four feet square, then let down a small ladder, upon which I mounted, and thence was taken into the ship in a very weak condition.

The sailors were all in amazement, and asked me a thousand questions, which I had no inclination to answer. I was equally confounded at the sight of so many pigmies, for such I took them to be, after having so long accustomed mine eyes to the monstrous objects I had left. But the captain, Mr. Thomas Wilcocks, an honest worthy Shropshire man, observing I was ready to faint, took me into his cabin, gave me a cordial to comfort me, and made me turn in upon his own bed, advising me to take a little rest, of which I had great need. Before I went to sleep, I gave him to understand that I had some valuable furniture in my box, too good to be lost: a fine hammock, a handsome field-bed, two chairs, a table, and a cabinet; that my closet was hung on all sides, or rather quilted, with silk and cotton; that if he would let one of the crew bring my closet into his cabin, I would open it there before him, and show him my goods. The captain, hearing me utter these absurdities, concluded I was raving; however (I suppose to pacify me) he promised to give order as I desired, and going upon deck, sent some of his men down into my closet, whence (as I afterwards found) they drew up all my goods, and stripped off the quilting; but the chairs, cabinet, and bedstead, being screwed to the floor, were much damaged by the ignorance of the seamen, who tore them up by force. Then they knocked off some of the boards for the use of the ship, and when they had got all they had a mind for, let the hull drop into the sea, which by reason of many breaches made in the bottom and sides, sunk to rights. And, indeed, I was glad not to have been a spectator of the havoc they made, because I am confident it would have sensibly touched me, by bringing former passages into my mind, which I would rather have forgot.

I slept some hours, but perpetually disturbed with dreams of the place I had left, and the dangers I had escaped. However, upon waking, I found myself much recovered. It was now about eight o'clock at night, and the captain ordered supper immediately, thinking I had already fasted too long. He entertained me with great kindness, observing me not to look wildly, or talk inconsistently: and, when we were left alone, desired I would give him a relation of my travels, and by what accident I came to be set adrift, in that monstrous wooden chest. He said "that about twelve o'clock at noon, as he was looking through his glass, he spied it at a distance, and thought it was a sail, which he had a mind to make, being not much out of his course, in hopes of buying some biscuit, his own beginning to fall short. That upon coming nearer, and finding his error, he sent out his long-boat to discover what it was; that his men came back in a fright, swearing they had seen a swimming house. That he laughed at their folly, and went himself in the boat, ordering his men to take a strong cable along with them. That the weather being calm, he rowed round me several times, observed my windows and wire lattices that defended them. That he discovered two staples upon one side, which was all of boards, without any passage for light. He then commanded his men to row up to that side, and fastening a cable to one of the staples, ordered them to tow my chest, as they called it, toward the ship. When it was there, he gave directions to fasten another cable to the ring fixed in the cover, and to raise up my chest with pulleys, which all the sailors were not able to do above two or three feet." He said, "they saw my stick and handkerchief thrust out of the hole, and concluded that some unhappy man must be shut up in the cavity." I asked, "whether he or the crew had seen any prodigious birds in the air, about the time he first discovered me." To which he answered, "that discoursing this matter with the sailors while I was asleep, one of them said, he had observed three eagles flying towards the north, but remarked nothing of their being larger than the usual size:" which I suppose must be imputed to the great height they were at; and he could not guess the reason of my question. I then asked the captain, "how far he reckoned we might be from land?" He said, "by the best computation he could make, we were at least a hundred leagues." I assured him, "that he must be mistaken by almost half, for I had not left the country whence I came above two hours before I dropped into the sea." Whereupon he began again to think that my brain was disturbed, of which he gave me a hint, and advised me to go to bed in a cabin he had provided. I assured him, "I was well refreshed with his good entertainment and company, and as much in my senses as ever I was in my life." He then grew serious, and desired to ask me freely, "whether I were not troubled in my mind by the consciousness of some enormous crime, for which I was punished, at the command of some prince, by exposing me in that chest; as great criminals, in other countries, have been forced to sea in a leaky vessel, without provisions: for although he should be sorry to have taken so ill a man into his ship, yet he would engage his word to set me safe ashore, in the first port where we arrived." He added, "that his suspicions were much increased by some very absurd speeches I had delivered at first to his sailors, and afterwards to himself, in relation to my closet or chest, as well as by my odd looks and behaviour while I was at supper."

I begged his patience to hear me tell my story, which I faithfully did, from the last time I left England, to the moment he first discovered me. And, as truth always forces its way into rational minds, so this honest worthy gentleman, who had some tincture of learning, and very good sense, was immediately convinced of my candour and veracity. But further to confirm all I had said, I entreated him to give order that my cabinet should be brought, of which I had the key in my pocket; for he had already informed me how the seamen disposed of my closet. I opened it in his own presence, and showed him the small collection of rarities I made in the country from which I had been so strangely delivered. There was the comb I had contrived out of the stumps of the king's beard, and another of the same materials, but fixed into a paring of her majesty's thumb-nail, which served for the back. There was a collection of needles and pins, from a foot to half a yard long; four wasp stings, like joiner's tacks; some combings of the queen's hair; a gold ring, which one day she made me a present of, in a most obliging manner, taking it from her little finger, and throwing it over my head like a collar. I desired the captain would please to accept this ring in return for his civilities; which he absolutely refused. I showed him a corn that I had cut off with my own hand, from a maid of honour's toe; it was about the bigness of Kentish pippin, and grown so hard, that when I returned England, I got it hollowed into a cup, and set in silver. Lastly, I desired him to see the breeches I had then on, which were made of a mouse's skin.

I could force nothing on him but a footman's tooth, which I observed him to examine with great curiosity, and found he had a fancy for it. He received it with abundance of thanks, more than such a trifle could deserve. It was drawn by an unskilful surgeon, in a mistake, from one of Glumdalclitch's men, who was afflicted with the tooth-ache, but it was as sound as any in his head. I got it cleaned, and put it into my cabinet. It was about a foot long, and four inches in diameter.

The captain was very well satisfied with this plain relation I had given him, and said, "he hoped, when we returned to England, I would oblige the world by putting it on paper, and making it public." My answer was, "that we were overstocked with books of travels: that nothing could now pass which was not extraordinary; wherein I doubted some authors less consulted truth, than their own vanity, or interest, or the diversion of ignorant readers; that my story could contain little beside common events, without those ornamental descriptions of strange plants, trees, birds, and other animals; or of the barbarous customs and idolatry of savage people, with which most writers abound. However, I thanked him for his good opinion, and promised to take the matter into my thoughts."

He said "he wondered at one thing very much, which was, to hear me speak so loud;" asking me "whether the king or queen of that country were thick of hearing?" I told him, "it was what I had been used to for above two years past, and that I admired as much at the voices of him and his men, who seemed to me only to whisper, and yet I could hear them well enough. But, when I spoke in that country, it was like a man talking in the streets, to another looking out from the top of a steeple, unless when I was placed on a table, or held in any person's hand." I told him, "I had likewise observed another thing, that, when I first got into the ship, and the sailors stood all about me, I thought they were the most little contemptible creatures I had ever beheld." For indeed, while I was in that prince's country, I could never endure to look in a glass, after mine eyes had been accustomed to such prodigious objects, because the comparison gave me so despicable a conceit of myself. The captain said, "that while we were at supper, he observed me to look at every thing with a sort of wonder, and that I often seemed hardly able to contain my laughter, which he knew not well how to take, but imputed it to some disorder in my brain." I answered, "it was very true; and I wondered how I could forbear, when I saw his dishes of the size of a silver three-pence, a leg of pork hardly a mouthful, a cup not so big as a nut-shell;" and so I went on, describing the rest of his household-stuff and provisions, after the same manner. For, although he queen had ordered a little equipage of all things necessary for me, while I was in her service, yet my ideas were wholly taken up with what I saw on every side of me, and I winked at my own littleness, as people do at their own faults. The captain understood my raillery very well, and merrily replied with the old English proverb, "that he doubted mine eyes were bigger than my belly, for he did not observe my stomach so good, although I had fasted all day;" and, continuing in his mirth, protested "he would have gladly given a hundred pounds, to have seen my closet in the eagle's bill, and afterwards in its fall from so great a height into the sea; which would certainly have been a most astonishing object, worthy to have the description of it transmitted to future ages:" and the comparison of Phaëton was so obvious, that he could not forbear applying it, although I did not much admire the conceit.

The captain having been at Tonquin, was, in his return to England, driven north-eastward to the latitude of 44 degrees, and longitude of 143. But meeting a trade-wind two days after I came on board him, we sailed southward a long time, and coasting New Holland, kept our course west-south-west, and then south-south-west, till we doubled the Cape of Good Hope. Our voyage was very prosperous, but I shall not trouble the reader with a journal of it. The captain called in at one or two ports, and sent in his long-boat for provisions and fresh water; but I never went out of the ship till we came into the Downs, which was on the third day of June, 1706, about nine months after my escape. I offered to leave my goods in security for payment of my freight: but the captain protested he would not receive one farthing. We took a kind leave of each other, and I made him promise he would come to see me at my house in Redriff. I hired a horse and guide for five shillings, which I borrowed of the captain.

As I was on the road, observing the littleness of the houses, the trees, the cattle, and the people, I began to think myself in Lilliput. I was afraid of trampling on every traveller I met, and often called aloud to have them stand out of the way, so that I had like to have gotten one or two broken heads for my impertinence.

When I came to my own house, for which I was forced to inquire, one of the servants opening the door, I bent down to go in, (like a goose under a gate,) for fear of striking my head. My wife run out to embrace me, but I stooped lower than her knees, thinking she could otherwise never be able to reach my mouth. My daughter kneeled to ask my blessing, but I could not see her till she arose, having been so long used to stand with my head and eyes erect to above sixty feet; and then I went to take her up with one hand by the waist. I looked down upon the servants, and one or two friends who were in the house, as if they had been pigmies and I a giant. I told my wife, "she had been too thrifty, for I found she had starved herself and her daughter to nothing." In short, I behaved myself so unaccountably, that they were all of the captain's opinion when he first saw me, and concluded I had lost my wits. This I mention as an instance of the great power of habit and prejudice.

In a little time, I and my family and friends came to a right understanding: but my wife protested "I should never go to sea any more;" although my evil destiny so ordered, that she had not power to hinder me, as the reader may know hereafter. In the mean time, I here conclude the second part of my unfortunate voyages.

III
A VOYAGE TO LAPUTA, BALNIBARBI, LUGGNAGG, GLUBBDUBDRIB, AND JAPAN

I

THE AUTHOR SETS OUT ON HIS THIRD VOYAGE. IS TAKEN BY PIRATES. THE MALICE OF A DUTCHMAN. HIS ARRIVAL AT AN ISLAND. HE IS RECEIVED INTO LAPUTA.

I had not been at home above ten days, when Captain William Robinson, a Cornish man, commander of the Hopewell, a stout ship of three hundred tons, came to my house. I had formerly been surgeon of another ship where he was master, and a fourth part owner, in a voyage to the Levant. He had always treated me more like a brother, than an inferior officer; and, hearing of my arrival, made me a visit, as I apprehended only out of friendship, for nothing passed more than what is usual after long absences. But repeating his visits often, expressing his joy to find I me in good health, asking, "whether I were now settled for life?" adding, "that he intended a voyage to the East Indies in two months," at last he plainly invited me, though with some apologies, to be surgeon of the ship; "that I should have another surgeon under me, beside our two mates; that my salary should be double to the usual pay; and that having experienced my knowledge in sea-affairs to be at least equal to his, he would enter into any engagement to follow my advice, as much as if I had shared in the command."

He said so many other obliging things, and I knew him to be so honest a man, that I could not reject this proposal; the thirst I had of seeing the world, notwithstanding my past misfortunes, continuing as violent as ever. The only difficulty that remained, was to persuade my wife, whose consent however I at last obtained, by the prospect of advantage she proposed to her children.

We set out the 5th day of August, 1706, and arrived at Fort St. George the 11th of April, 1707. We staid there three weeks to refresh our crew, many of whom were sick. From thence we went to Tonquin, where the captain resolved to continue some time, because many of the goods he intended to buy were not ready, nor could he expect to be dispatched in several months. Therefore, in hopes to defray some of the charges he must be at, he bought a sloop, loaded it with several sorts of goods, wherewith the Tonquinese usually trade to the neighbouring islands, and putting fourteen men on board, whereof three were of the country, he appointed me master of the sloop, and gave me power to traffic, while he transacted his affairs at Tonquin.

We had not sailed above three days, when a great storm arising, we were driven five days to the north-north-east, and then to the east: after which we had fair weather, but still with a pretty strong gale from the west. Upon the tenth day we were chased by two pirates, who soon overtook us; for my sloop was so deep laden, that she sailed very slow, neither were we in a condition to defend ourselves.

We were boarded about the same time by both the pirates, who entered furiously at the head of their men; but finding us all prostrate upon our faces (for so I gave order), they pinioned us with strong ropes, and setting guard upon us, went to search the sloop.

I observed among them a Dutchman, who seemed to be of some authority, though he was not commander of either ship. He knew us by our countenances to be Englishmen, and jabbering to us in his own language, swore we should be tied back to back and thrown into the sea. I spoke Dutch tolerably well; I told him who we were, and begged him, in consideration of our being Christians and Protestants, of neighbouring countries in strict alliance, that he would move the captains to take some pity on us. This inflamed his rage; he repeated his threatenings, and turning to his companions, spoke with great vehemence in the Japanese language, as I suppose, often using the word *Christianos*.

The largest of the two pirate ships was commanded by a Japanese captain, who spoke a little Dutch, but very imperfectly. He came up to me, and after several questions, which I answered in great humility, he said, "we should not die." I made the captain a very low bow, and then, turning to the Dutchman, said, "I was sorry to find more mercy in a heathen, than in a brother christian." But I had soon reason to repent those foolish words: for that malicious reprobate, having often endeavoured in vain to persuade both the captains that I might be thrown into the sea (which they would not yield to, after the promise made me that I should not die), however, prevailed so far, as to have a punishment inflicted on me, worse, in all human appearance, than death itself. My men were sent by an equal division into both the pirate ships, and my sloop new manned. As to myself, it was determined that I should be set adrift in a small canoe, with paddles and a sail, and four days' provisions; which last, the Japanese captain was so kind to double out of his own stores, and would permit no man to search me. I got down into the canoe, while the Dutchman, standing upon the deck, loaded me with all the curses and injurious terms his language could afford.

About an hour before we saw the pirates I had taken an observation, and found we were in the latitude of 46 N. and longitude of 183. When I was at some distance from the pirates, I discovered, by my pocket-glass, several islands to the south-east. I set up my sail, the wind being fair, with a design to reach the nearest of those islands, which I made a shift to do, in about three hours. It was all rocky: however I got many birds' eggs; and, striking fire, I kindled some heath and dry sea-weed, by which I roasted my eggs. I ate no other supper, being resolved to spare my provisions as much as I could. I passed the night under the shelter of a rock, strewing some heath under me, and slept pretty well.

The next day I sailed to another island, and thence to a third and fourth, sometimes using my sail, and sometimes my paddles. But, not to trouble the reader with a particular account of my distresses, let it suffice, that on the fifth day I arrived at the last island in my sight, which lay south-south-east to the former.

This island was at a greater distance than I expected, and I did not reach it in less than five hours. I encompassed it almost round, before I could find a convenient place to land in; which was a small creek, about three times the wideness of my canoe. I found the island to be all rocky, only a little intermingled with tufts of grass, and sweet-smelling herbs. I took out my small provisions and after having refreshed myself, I secured the remainder in a cave, whereof there were great numbers; I gathered plenty of eggs upon the rocks, and got a quantity of dry sea-weed, and parched grass, which I designed to kindle the next day, and roast my eggs as well as I could, for I had about me my flint, steel, match, and burning-glass. I lay all night in the cave where I had lodged my provisions. My bed was the same dry grass and sea-weed which I intended for fuel. I slept very little, for the disquiets of my mind prevailed over my weariness, and kept me awake. I considered how impossible it was to preserve my life in so desolate a place, and how miserable my end must be: yet found myself so listless and desponding, that I had not the heart to rise; and before I could get spirits enough to creep out of my cave, the day was far advanced. I walked awhile among the rocks: the sky was perfectly clear, and the sun so hot, that I was forced to turn my face from it: when all on a sudden it became obscure, as I thought, in a manner very different from what happens by the interposition of a cloud. I turned back, and perceived a vast opaque body between me and the sun moving forwards towards the island: it seemed to be about two miles high, and hid the sun six or seven minutes; but I did not observe the air to be much colder, or the sky more darkened, than if I had stood under the shade of a mountain. As it approached nearer over the place where I was, it appeared to be a firm substance, the bottom flat, smooth, and shining very bright, from the reflection of the sea below. I stood upon a height about two hundred yards from the shore, and saw this vast body descending almost to a parallel with me, at less than an English mile distance. I took out my pocket perspective, and could plainly discover numbers of people moving up and down the sides of it, which appeared to be sloping; but what those people where doing I was not able to distinguish.

The natural love of life gave me some inward motion of joy, and I was ready to entertain a hope that this adventure might, some way or other, help to deliver me from the desolate place and condition I was in. But at the same time the reader can hardly conceive my astonishment, to behold an island in the air, inhabited by men, who were able (as it should seem) to raise or sink, or put it into progressive motion, as they pleased. But not being at that time in a disposition to philosophise upon this phenomenon, I rather chose to observe what course the island would take, because it seemed for awhile to stand still. Yet soon after, it advanced nearer, and I could see the sides of it encompassed with several gradations of galleries, and stairs, at certain intervals, to descend from one to the other. In the lowest gallery, I beheld some people fishing with long angling rods, and others looking on. I waved my cap (for my hat was long since worn out) and my handkerchief toward the island; and upon its nearer approach, I called and shouted with the utmost strength of my voice; and then looking circumspectly, I beheld a crowd gather to that side which was most in my view. I found by their pointing towards me and to each other, that they plainly discovered me, although they made no return to my shouting. But I could see four or five men running in great haste, up the stairs, to the top of the island, who then disappeared. I happened rightly to conjecture, that these were sent for orders to some person in authority upon this occasion.

The number of people increased, and, in less than half an hour, the island was moved and raised in such a manner, that the lowest gallery appeared in a parallel of less then a hundred yards distance from the height where I stood. I then put myself in the most supplicating posture, and spoke in the humblest accent, but received no answer. Those who stood nearest over against me, seemed to be persons of distinction, as I supposed by their habit. They conferred earnestly with each other, looking often upon me. At length one of them called out in a clear, polite, smooth dialect, not unlike in sound to the Italian: and therefore I returned an answer in that language, hoping at least that the cadence might be more agreeable to his ears. Although neither of us understood the other, yet my meaning was easily known, for the people saw the distress I was in.

They made signs for me to come down from the rock, and go towards the shore, which I accordingly did; and the flying island being raised to a convenient height, the verge directly over me, a chain was let down from the lowest gallery, with a seat fastened to the bottom, to which I fixed myself, and was drawn up by pulleys.

2

THE HUMOURS AND DISPOSITIONS OF THE LAPUTIANS DESCRIBED. AN ACCOUNT OF THEIR LEARNING. OF THE KING AND HIS COURT. THE AUTHOR'S RECEPTION THERE. THE INHABITANTS SUBJECT TO FEAR AND DISQUIETUDES. AN ACCOUNT OF THE WOMEN.

At my alighting, I was surrounded with a crowd of people, but those who stood nearest seemed to be of better quality. They beheld me with all the marks and circumstances of wonder; neither indeed was I much in their debt, having never till then seen a race of mortals so singular in their shapes, habits, and countenances. Their heads were all reclined, either to the right, or the left; one of their eyes turned inward, and the other directly up to the zenith. Their outward garments were adorned with the figures of suns, moons, and stars; interwoven with those of fiddles, flutes, harps, trumpets, guitars, harpsichords, and many other instruments of music, unknown to us in Europe. I observed, here and there, many in the habit of servants, with a blown bladder, fastened like a flail to the end of a stick, which they carried in their hands. In each bladder was a small quantity of dried peas, or little pebbles, as I was afterwards informed. With these bladders, they now and then flapped the mouths and ears of those who stood near them, of which practice I could not then conceive the meaning. It seems the minds of these people are so taken up with intense speculations, that they neither can speak, nor attend to the discourses of others, without being roused by some external action upon the organs of speech and hearing; for which reason, those persons who are able to afford it always keep a flapper (the original is *climenole*) in their family, as one of their domestics; nor ever walk abroad, or make visits, without him. And the business of this officer is, when two, three, or more persons are in company, gently to strike with his bladder the mouth of him who is to speak, and the right ear of him or them to whom the speaker addresses himself. This flapper is likewise employed diligently to attend his master in his walks, and upon occasion to give him a soft flap on his eyes; because he is always so wrapped up in cogitation, that he is in manifest danger of falling down every precipice, and bouncing his head against every post; and in the streets, of justling others, or being justled himself into the kennel.

It was necessary to give the reader this information, without which he would be at the same loss with me to understand the proceedings of these people, as they conducted me up the stairs to the top of the island, and from thence to the royal palace. While we were ascending, they forgot several times what they were about, and left me to myself, till their memories were again roused by their flappers; for they appeared altogether unmoved by the sight of my foreign habit and countenance, and by the shouts of the vulgar, whose thoughts and minds were more disengaged.

At last we entered the palace, and proceeded into the chamber of presence, where I saw the king seated on his throne, attended on each side by persons of prime quality. Before the throne, was a large table filled with globes and spheres, and mathematical instruments of all kinds. His majesty took not the least notice of us, although our entrance was not without sufficient noise, by the concourse of all persons belonging to the court. But he was then deep in a problem; and we attended at least an hour, before he could solve it. There stood by him, on each side, a young page with flaps in their hands, and when they saw he was at leisure, one of them gently struck his mouth, and the other his right ear; at which he startled like one awaked on the sudden, and looking towards me and the company I was in, recollected the occasion of our coming, whereof he had been informed before. He spoke some words, whereupon immediately a young man with a flap came up to my side, and flapped me gently on the right ear; but I made signs, as well as I could, that I had no occasion for such an instrument; which, as I afterwards found, gave his majesty, and the whole court, a very mean opinion of my understanding. The king, as far as I could conjecture, asked me several questions, and I addressed myself to him in all the languages I had. When it was found I could neither understand nor be understood, I was conducted by his order to an apartment in his palace (this prince being distinguished above all his predecessors for his hospitality to strangers), where two servants were appointed to attend me. My dinner was brought, and four persons of quality, whom I remembered to have seen very near the king's person, did me the honour to dine with me. We had two courses, of three dishes each. In the first course, there was a shoulder of mutton cut into an equilateral triangle, a piece of beef into a rhomboides, and a pudding into a cycloid. The second course was two ducks trussed up in the form of fiddles; sausages and puddings resembling flutes and hautboys, and a breast of veal in the shape of a harp. The servants cut our bread into cones, cylinders, parallelograms, and several other mathematical figures.

While we were at dinner, I made bold to ask the names of several things in their language, and those noble persons, by the assistance of their flappers, delighted to give me answers, hoping to raise my admiration of their great abilities if I could be brought to converse with them. I was soon able to call for bread and drink, or whatever else I wanted.

After dinner my company withdrew, and a person was sent to me by the king's order, attended by a flapper. He brought with him pen, ink, and paper, and three or four books, giving me to understand by signs, that he was sent to teach me the language. We sat together four hours, in which time I wrote down a great number of words in columns, with the translations over against them; I likewise made a shift to learn several short sentences; for my tutor would order one of my servants to fetch something, to turn about, to make a bow, to sit, or to stand, or walk, and the like. Then I took down the sentence in writing. He showed me also, in one of his books, the figures of the sun, moon, and stars, the zodiac, the tropics, and polar circles, together with the denominations of many plains and solids. He gave me the names and descriptions of all the musical instruments, and the general terms of art in playing on each of them. After he had left me, I placed all my words, with their interpretations, in alphabetical order. And thus, in a few days, by the help of a very faithful memory, I got some insight into their language. The word, which I interpret the flying or floating island, is in the original *Laputa*, whereof I could never learn the true etymology. *Lap*, in the old obsolete language, signifies high; and *untuh*, a governor; from which they say, by corruption, was derived *Laputa*, from *Lapuntuh*. But I do not approve of this derivation, which seems to be a little strained. I ventured to offer to the learned among them a conjecture of my own, that Laputa was *quasi lap outed*; *lap*, signifying properly, the dancing of the sunbeams in the sea, and *outed*, a wing; which, however, I shall not obtrude, but submit to the judicious reader.

Those to whom the king had entrusted me, observing how ill I was clad, ordered a tailor to come next morning, and take measure for a suit of clothes. This operator did his office after a different manner from those of his trade in Europe. He first took my altitude by a quadrant, and then, with a rule and compasses, described the dimensions and outlines of my whole body, all which he entered upon paper; and in six days brought my clothes very ill made, and quite out of shape, by happening to mistake a figure in the calculation. But my comfort was, that I observed such accidents very frequent, and little regarded.

During my confinement for want of clothes, and by an indisposition that held me some days longer, I much enlarged my dictionary; and when I went next to court, was able to understand many things the king spoke, and to return him some kind of answers. His majesty had given orders, that the island should move north-east and by east, to the vertical point over Lagado, the metropolis of the whole kingdom below, upon the firm earth. It was about ninety leagues distant, and our voyage lasted four days and a half. I was not in the least sensible of the progressive motion made in the air by the island. On the second morning, about eleven o'clock, the king himself in person, attended by his nobility, courtiers, and officers, having prepared all their musical instruments, played on them for three hours without intermission, so that I was quite stunned with the noise; neither could I possibly guess the meaning, till my tutor informed me. He said that, the people of their island had their ears adapted to hear "the music of the spheres, which always played at certain periods, and the court was now prepared to bear their part, in whatever instrument they most excelled."

In our journey towards Lagado, the capital city, his majesty ordered that the island should stop over certain towns and villages, from whence he might receive the petitions of his subjects. And to this purpose, several packthreads were let down, with small weights at the bottom. On these packthreads the people strung their petitions, which mounted up directly, like the scraps of paper fastened by school boys at the end of the string that holds their kite. Sometimes we received wine and victuals from below, which were drawn up by pulleys.

The knowledge I had in mathematics, gave me great assistance in acquiring their phraseology, which depended much upon that science, and music; and in the latter I was not unskilled. Their ideas are perpetually conversant in lines and figures. If they would, for example, praise the beauty of a woman, or any other animal, they describe it by rhombs, circles, parallelograms, ellipses, and other geometrical terms, or by words of art drawn from music, needless here to repeat. I observed in the king's kitchen all sorts of mathematical and musical instruments, after the figures of which they cut up the joints that were served to his majesty's table.

Their houses are very ill built, the walls bevil, without one right angle in any apartment; and this defect arises from the contempt they bear to practical geometry, which they despise as vulgar and mechanic; those instructions they give being too refined for the intellects of their workmen, which occasions perpetual mistakes. And although they are dexterous enough upon a piece of paper, in the management of the rule, the pencil, and the divider, yet in the common actions and behaviour of life, I have not seen a more clumsy, awkward, and unhandy people, nor so slow and perplexed in their conceptions upon all other subjects, except those of mathematics and music. They are very bad reasoners, and vehemently given to opposition, unless when they happen to be of the right opinion, which is seldom their case. Imagination, fancy, and invention, they are wholly strangers to, nor have any words in their language, by which those ideas can be expressed; the whole compass of their thoughts and mind being shut up within the two forementioned sciences.

Most of them, and especially those who deal in the astronomical part, have great faith in judicial astrology, although they are ashamed to own it publicly. But what I chiefly admired, and thought altogether unaccountable, was the strong disposition I observed in them towards news and politics, perpetually inquiring into public affairs, giving their judgments in matters of state, and passionately disputing every inch of a party opinion. I have indeed observed the same disposition among most of the mathematicians I have known in Europe, although I could never discover the least analogy between the two sciences; unless those people suppose, that because the smallest circle has as many degrees as the largest, therefore the regulation and management of the world require no more abilities than the handling and turning of a globe; but I rather take this quality to spring from a very common infirmity of human nature, inclining us to be most curious and conceited in matters where we have least concern, and for which we are least adapted by study or nature.

These people are under continual disquietudes, never enjoying a minute's peace of mind; and their disturbances proceed from causes which very little affect the rest of mortals. Their apprehensions arise from several changes they dread in the celestial bodies: for instance, that the earth, by the continual approaches of the sun towards it, must, in course of time, be absorbed, or swallowed up; that the face of the sun, will, by degrees, be encrusted with its own effluvia, and give no more light to the world; that the earth very narrowly escaped a brush from the tail of the last comet, which would have infallibly reduced it to ashes; and that the next, which they have calculated for one-and-thirty years hence, will probably destroy us. For if, in its perihelion, it should approach within a certain degree of the sun (as by their calculations they have reason to dread) it will receive a degree of heat ten thousand times more intense than that of red hot glowing iron, and in its absence from the sun, carry a blazing tail ten hundred thousand and fourteen miles long, through which, if the earth should pass at the distance of one hundred thousand miles from the nucleus, or main body of the comet, it must in its passage be set on fire, and reduced to ashes: that the sun, daily spending its rays without any nutriment to supply them, will at last be wholly consumed and annihilated; which must be attended with the destruction of this earth, and of all the planets that receive their light from it.

They are so perpetually alarmed with the apprehensions of these, and the like impending dangers, that they can neither sleep quietly in their beds, nor have any relish for the common pleasures and amusements of life. When they meet an acquaintance in the morning, the first question is about the sun's health, how he looked at his setting and rising, and what hopes they have to avoid the stroke of the approaching comet. This conversation they are apt to run into with the same temper that boys discover in delighting to hear terrible stories of spirits and hobgoblins, which they greedily listen to, and dare not go to bed for fear.

The women of the island have abundance of vivacity: they contemn their husbands, and are exceedingly fond of strangers, whereof there is always a considerable number from the continent below, attending at court, either upon affairs of the several towns and corporations, or their own particular occasions, but are much despised, because they want the same endowments. Among these the ladies choose their gallants: but the vexation is, that they act with too much ease and security; for the husband is always so rapt in speculation, that the mistress and lover may proceed to the greatest familiarities before his face, if he be but provided with paper and implements, and without his flapper at his side.

The wives and daughters lament their confinement to the island, although I think it the most delicious spot of ground in the world; and although they live here in the greatest plenty and magnificence, and are allowed to do whatever they please, they long to see the world, and take the diversions of the metropolis, which they are not allowed to do without a particular license from the king; and this is not easy to be obtained, because the people of quality have found, by frequent experience, how hard it is to persuade their women to return from below. I was told that a great court lady, who had several children,—is married to the prime minister, the richest subject in the kingdom, a very graceful person, extremely fond of her, and lives in the finest palace of the island,—went down to Lagado on the pretence of health, there hid herself for several months, till the king sent a warrant to search for her; and she was found in an obscure eating-house all in rags, having pawned her clothes to maintain an old deformed footman, who beat her every day, and in whose company she was taken, much against her will. And although her husband received her with all possible kindness, and without the least reproach, she soon after contrived to steal down again, with all her jewels, to the same gallant, and has not been heard of since.

This may perhaps pass with the reader rather for an European or English story, than for one of a country so remote. But he may please to consider, that the caprices of womankind are not limited by any climate or nation, and that they are much more uniform, than can be easily imagined.

In about a month's time, I had made a tolerable proficiency in their language, and was able to answer most of the king's questions, when I had the honour to attend him. His majesty discovered not the least curiosity to inquire into the laws, government, history, religion, or manners of the countries where I had been; but confined his questions to the state of mathematics, and received the account I gave him with great contempt and indifference, though often roused by his flapper on each side.

3

A PHENOMENON SOLVED BY MODERN PHILOSOPHY
AND ASTRONOMY. THE LAPUTIANS' GREAT
IMPROVEMENTS IN THE LATTER. THE KING'S
METHOD OF SUPPRESSING INSURRECTIONS.

I desired leave of this prince to see the curiosities of the island, which he was graciously pleased to grant, and ordered my tutor to attend me. I chiefly wanted to know, to what cause, in art or in nature, it owed its several motions, whereof I will now give a philosophical account to the reader.

The flying or floating island is exactly circular, its diameter 7837 yards, or about four miles and a half, and consequently contains ten thousand acres. It is three hundred yards thick. The bottom, or under surface, which appears to those who view it below, is one even regular plate of adamant, shooting up to the height of about two hundred yards. Above it lie the several minerals in their usual order, and over all is a coat of rich mould, ten or twelve feet deep. The declivity of the upper surface, from the circumference to the centre, is the natural cause why all the dews and rains, which fall upon the island, are conveyed in small rivulets toward the middle, where they are emptied into four large basins, each of about half a mile in circuit, and two hundred yards distant from the centre. From these basins the water is continually exhaled by the sun in the daytime, which effectually prevents their overflowing. Besides, as it is in the power of the monarch to raise the island above the region of clouds and vapours, he can prevent the falling of dews and rain whenever he pleases. For the highest clouds cannot rise above two miles, as naturalists agree, at least they were never known to do so in that country.

At the centre of the island there is a chasm about fifty yards in diameter, whence the astronomers descend into a large dome, which is therefore called *flandona gagnole*, or the astronomer's cave, situated at the depth of a hundred yards beneath the upper surface of the adamant. In this cave are twenty lamps continually burning, which, from the reflection of the adamant, cast a strong light into every part. The place is stored with great variety of sextants, quadrants, telescopes, astrolabes, and other astronomical instruments. But the greatest curiosity, upon which the fate of the island depends, is a loadstone of a prodigious size, in shape resembling a weaver's shuttle. It is in length six yards, and in the thickest part at least three yards over. This magnet is sustained by a very strong axle of adamant passing through its middle, upon which it plays, and is poised so exactly that the weakest hand can turn it. It is hooped round with a hollow cylinder of adamant, four feet yards in diameter, placed horizontally, and supported by eight adamantine feet, each six yards high. In the middle of the concave side, there is a groove twelve inches deep, in which the extremities of the axle are lodged, and turned round as there is occasion.

The stone cannot be removed from its place by any force, because the hoop and its feet are one continued piece with that body of adamant which constitutes the bottom of the island.

By means of this loadstone, the island is made to rise and fall, and move from one place to another. For, with respect to that part of the earth over which the monarch presides, the stone is endued at one of its sides with an attractive power, and at the other with a repulsive. Upon placing the magnet erect, with its attracting end towards the earth, the island descends; but when the repelling extremity points downwards, the island mounts directly upwards. When the position of the stone is oblique, the motion of the island is so too: for in this magnet, the forces always act in lines parallel to its direction.

By this oblique motion, the island is conveyed to different parts of the monarch's dominions. To explain the manner of its progress, let $A B$ represent a line drawn across the dominions of Balnibarbi, let the line $c\ d$ represent the loadstone, of which let d be the repelling end, and c the attracting end, the island being over C: let the stone be placed in position $c\ d$, with its repelling end downwards; then the island will be driven upwards obliquely towards D. When it is arrived at D, let the stone be turned upon its axle, till its attracting end points towards E, and then the island will be carried obliquely towards E; where, if the stone be again turned upon its axle till it stands in the position $E\ F$, with its repelling point downwards, the island will rise obliquely towards F, where, by directing the attracting end towards G, the island may be carried to G, and from G to H, by turning the stone, so as to make its repelling extremity to point directly downward. And thus, by changing the situation of the stone, as often as there is occasion, the island is made to rise and fall by turns in an oblique direction, and by those alternate risings and fallings (the obliquity being not considerable) is conveyed from one part of the dominions to the other.

But it must be observed, that this island cannot move beyond the extent of the dominions below, nor can it rise above the height of four miles. For which the astronomers (who have written large systems concerning the stone) assign the following reason: that the magnetic virtue does not extend beyond the distance of four miles, and that the mineral, which acts upon the stone in the bowels of the earth, and in the sea about six leagues distant from the shore, is not diffused through the whole globe, but terminated with the limits of the king's dominions; and it was easy, from the great advantage of such a superior situation, for a prince to bring under his obedience whatever country lay within the attraction of that magnet.

When the stone is put parallel to the plane of the horizon, the island stands still; for in that case the extremities of it, being at equal distance from the earth, act with equal force, the one in drawing downwards, the other in pushing upwards, and consequently no motion can ensue.

This loadstone is under the care of certain astronomers, who, from time to time, give it such positions as the monarch directs. They spend the greatest part of their lives in observing the celestial bodies, which they do by the assistance of glasses, far excelling ours in goodness. For, although their largest telescopes do not exceed three feet, they magnify much more than those of a hundred with us, and show the stars with greater clearness. This advantage has enabled them to extend their discoveries much further than our astronomers in Europe; for they have made a catalogue of ten thousand fixed stars, whereas the largest of ours do not contain above one third part of that number. They have likewise discovered two lesser stars, or satellites, which revolve about Mars; whereof the innermost is distant from the centre of the primary planet exactly three of his diameters, and the outermost, five; the former revolves in the space of ten hours, and the latter in twenty-one and a half; so that the squares of their periodical times are very near in the same proportion with the cubes of their distance from the centre of Mars; which evidently shows them to be governed by the same law of gravitation that influences the other heavenly bodies.

They have observed ninety-three different comets, and settled their periods with great exactness. If this be true (and they affirm it with great confidence) it is much to be wished, that their observations were made public, whereby the theory of comets, which at present is very lame and defective, might be brought to the same perfection with other arts of astronomy.

The king would be the most absolute prince in the universe, if he could but prevail on a ministry to join with him; but these having their estates below on the continent, and considering that the office of a favourite has a very uncertain tenure, would never consent to the enslaving of their country.

If any town should engage in rebellion or mutiny, fall into violent factions, or refuse to pay the usual tribute, the king has two methods of reducing them to obedience. The first and the mildest course is, by keeping the island hovering over such a town, and the lands about it, whereby he can deprive them of the benefit of the sun and the rain, and consequently afflict the inhabitants with dearth and diseases: and if the crime deserve it, they are at the same time pelted from above with great stones, against which they have no defence but by creeping into cellars or caves, while the roofs of their houses are beaten to pieces. But if they still continue obstinate, or offer to raise insurrections, he proceeds to the last remedy, by letting the island drop directly upon their heads, which makes a universal destruction both of houses and men. However, this is an extremity to which the prince is seldom driven, neither indeed is he willing to put it in execution; nor dare his ministers advise him to an action, which, as it would render them odious to the people, so it would be a great damage to their own estates, which all lie below; for the island is the king's demesne.

But there is still indeed a more weighty reason, why the kings of this country have been always averse from executing so terrible an action, unless upon the utmost necessity. For, if the town intended to be destroyed should have in it any tall rocks, as it generally falls out in the larger cities, a situation probably chosen at first with a view to prevent such a catastrophe; or if it abound in high spires, or pillars of stone, a sudden fall might endanger the bottom or under surface of the island, which, although it consist, as I have said, of one entire adamant, two hundred yards thick, might happen to crack by too great a shock, or burst by approaching too near the fires from the houses below, as the backs, both of iron and stone, will often do in our chimneys. Of all this the people are well apprised, and understand how far to carry their obstinacy, where their liberty or property is concerned. And the king, when he is highest provoked, and most determined to press a city to rubbish, orders the island to descend with great gentleness, out of a pretence of tenderness to his people, but, indeed, for fear of breaking the adamantine bottom; in which case, it is the opinion of all their philosophers, that the loadstone could no longer hold it up, and the whole mass would fall to the ground.

By a fundamental law of this realm, neither the king, nor either of his two eldest sons, are permitted to leave the island; nor the queen, till she is past child-bearing.

4

THE AUTHOR LEAVES LAPUTA; IS CONVEYED TO BALNIBARBI; ARRIVES AT THE METROPOLIS. A DESCRIPTION OF THE METROPOLIS, AND THE COUNTRY ADJOINING. THE AUTHOR HOSPITABLY RECEIVED BY A GREAT LORD. HIS CONVERSATION WITH THAT LORD.

Although I cannot say that I was ill treated in this island, yet I must confess I thought myself too much neglected, not without some degree of contempt; for neither prince nor people appeared to be curious in any part of knowledge, except mathematics and music, wherein I was far their inferior, and upon that account very little regarded.

On the other side, after having seen all the curiosities of the island, I was very desirous to leave it, being heartily weary of those people. They were indeed excellent in two sciences for which I have great esteem, and wherein I am not unversed; but, at the same time, so abstracted and involved in speculation, that I never met with such disagreeable companions. I conversed only with women, tradesmen, flappers, and court-pages, during two months of my abode there; by which, at last, I rendered myself extremely contemptible; yet these were the only people from whom I could ever receive a reasonable answer.

I had obtained, by hard study, a good degree of knowledge in their language: I was weary of being confined to an island where I received so little countenance, and resolved to leave it with the first opportunity.

There was a great lord at court, nearly related to the king, and for that reason alone used with respect. He was universally reckoned the most ignorant and stupid person among them. He had performed many eminent services for the crown, had great natural and acquired parts, adorned with integrity and honour; but so ill an ear for music, that his detractors reported, "he had been often known to beat time in the wrong place;" neither could his tutors, without extreme difficulty, teach him to demonstrate the most easy proposition in the mathematics. He was pleased to show me many marks of favour, often did me the honour of a visit, desired to be informed in the affairs of Europe, the laws and customs, the manners and learning of the several countries where I had travelled. He listened to me with great attention, and made very wise observations on all I spoke. He had two flappers attending him for state, but never made use of them, except at court and in visits of ceremony, and would always command them to withdraw, when we were alone together.

I entreated this illustrious person, to intercede in my behalf with his majesty, for leave to depart; which he accordingly did, as he was pleased to tell me, with regret: for indeed he had made me several offers very advantageous, which, however, I refused, with expressions of the highest acknowledgment.

On the 16th of February I took leave of his majesty and the court. The king made me a present to the value of about two hundred pounds English, and my protector, his kinsman, as much more, together with a letter of recommendation to a friend of his in Lagado, the metropolis. The island being then hovering over a mountain about two miles from it, I was let down from the lowest gallery, in the same manner as I had been taken up.

The continent, as far as it is subject to the monarch of the flying island, passes under the general name of *Balnibarbi*; and the metropolis, as I said before, is called *Lagado*. I felt some little satisfaction in finding myself on firm ground. I walked to the city without any concern, being clad like one of the natives, and sufficiently instructed to converse with them. I soon found out the person's house to whom I was recommended, presented my letter from his friend the grandee in the island, and was received with much kindness. This great lord, whose name was Munodi, ordered me an apartment in his own house, where I continued during my stay, and was entertained in a most hospitable manner.

The next morning after my arrival, he took me in his chariot to see the town, which is about half the bigness of London; but the houses very strangely built, and most of them out of repair. The people in the streets walked fast, looked wild, their eyes fixed, and were generally in rags. We passed through one of the town gates, and went about three miles into the country, where I saw many labourers working with several sorts of tools in the ground, but was not able to conjecture what they were about: neither did observe any expectation either of corn or grass, although the soil appeared to be excellent. I could not forbear admiring at these odd appearances, both in town and country; and I made bold to desire my conductor, that he would be pleased to explain to me, what could be meant by so many busy heads, hands, and faces, both in the streets and the fields, because I did not discover any good effects they produced; but, on the contrary, I never knew a soil so unhappily cultivated, houses so ill contrived and so ruinous, or a people whose countenances and habit expressed so much misery and want.

This lord Munodi was a person of the first rank, and had been some years governor of Lagado; but, by a cabal of ministers, was discharged for insufficiency. However, the king treated him with tenderness, as a well-meaning man, but of a low contemptible understanding.

When I gave that free censure of the country and its inhabitants, he made no further answer than by telling me, "that I had not been long enough among them to form a judgment; and that the different nations of the world had different customs;" with other common topics to the same purpose. But, when we returned to his palace, he asked me "how I liked the building, what absurdities I observed, and what quarrel I had with the dress or looks of his domestics?" This he might safely do; because every thing about him was magnificent, regular, and polite. I answered, "that his excellency's prudence, quality, and fortune, had exempted him from those defects, which folly and beggary had produced in others." He said, "if I would go with him to his country-house, about twenty miles distant, where his estate lay, there would be more leisure for this kind of conversation." I told his excellency "that I was entirely at his disposal;" and accordingly we set out next morning.

During our journey he made me observe the several methods used by farmers in managing their lands, which to me were wholly unaccountable; for, except in some very few places, I could not discover one ear of corn or blade of grass. But, in three hours travelling, the scene was wholly altered; we came into a most beautiful country; farmers' houses, at small distances, neatly built; the fields enclosed, containing vineyards, corn-grounds, and meadows. Neither do I remember to have seen a more delightful prospect. His excellency observed my countenance to clear up; he told me, with a sigh, "that there his estate began, and would continue the same, till we should come to his house: that his countrymen ridiculed and despised him, for managing his affairs no better, and for setting so ill an example to the kingdom; which, however, was followed by very few, such as were old, and wilful, and weak like himself."

We came at length to the house, which was indeed a noble structure, built according to the best rules of ancient architecture. The fountains, gardens, walks, avenues, and groves, were all disposed with exact judgment and taste. I gave due praises to every thing I saw, whereof his excellency took not the least notice till after supper; when, there being no third companion, he told me with a very melancholy air "that he doubted he must throw down his houses in town and country, to rebuild them after the present mode; destroy all his plantations, and cast others into such a form as modern usage required, and give the same directions to all his tenants, unless he would submit to incur the censure of pride, singularity, affectation, ignorance, caprice, and perhaps increase his majesty's displeasure; that the admiration I appeared to be under would cease or diminish, when he had informed me of some particulars which, probably, I never heard of at court, the people there being too much taken up in their own speculations, to have regard to what passed here below."

The sum of his discourse was to this effect: "That about forty years ago, certain persons went up to Laputa, either upon business or diversion, and, after five months continuance, came back with a very little smattering in mathematics, but full of volatile spirits acquired in that airy region: that these persons, upon their return, began to dislike the management of every thing below, and fell into schemes of putting all arts, sciences, languages, and mechanics, upon a new foot. To this end, they procured a royal patent for erecting an academy of projectors in Lagado; and the humour prevailed so strongly among the people, that there is not a town of any consequence in the kingdom without such an academy. In these colleges the professors contrive new rules and methods of agriculture and building, and new instruments, and tools for all trades and manufactures; whereby, as they undertake, one man shall do the work of ten; a palace may be built in a week, of materials so durable as to last for ever without repairing. All the fruits of the earth shall come to maturity at whatever season we think fit to choose, and increase a hundred fold more than they do at present; with innumerable other happy proposals. The only inconvenience is, that none of these projects are yet brought to perfection; and in the mean time, the whole country lies miserably waste, the houses in ruins, and the people without food or clothes. By all which, instead of being discouraged, they are fifty times more violently bent upon prosecuting their schemes, driven equally on by hope and despair: that as for himself, being not of an enterprising spirit, he was content to go on in the old forms, to live in the houses his ancestors had built, and act as they did, in every part of life, without innovation: that some few other persons of quality and gentry had done the same, but were looked on with an eye of contempt and ill-will, as enemies to art, ignorant, and ill common-wealth's men, preferring their own ease and sloth before the general improvement of their country."

His lordship added, "That he would not, by any further particulars, prevent the pleasure I should certainly take in viewing the grand academy, whither he was resolved I should go." He only desired me to observe a ruined building, upon the side of a mountain about three miles distant, of which he gave me this account: "That he had a very convenient mill within half a mile of his house, turned by a current from a large river, and sufficient for his own family, as well as a great number of his tenants; that about seven years ago, a club of those projectors came to him with proposals to destroy this mill, and build another on the side of that mountain, on the long ridge whereof a long canal must be cut, for a repository of water, to be conveyed up by pipes and engines to supply the mill, because the wind and air upon a height agitated the water, and thereby made it fitter for motion, and because the water, descending down a declivity, would turn the mill with half the current of a river whose course is more upon a level." He said, "that being then not very well with the court, and pressed by many of his friends, he complied with the proposal; and after employing a hundred men for two years, the work miscarried, the projectors went off, laying the blame entirely upon him, railing at him ever since, and putting others upon the same experiment, with equal assurance of success, as well as equal disappointment."

In a few days we came back to town; and his excellency, considering the bad character he had in the academy, would not go with me himself, but recommended me to a friend of his, to bear me company thither. My lord was pleased to represent me as a great admirer of projects, and a person of much curiosity and easy belief; which, indeed, was not without truth; for I had myself been a sort of projector in my younger days.

THE AUTHOR PERMITTED TO SEE THE GRAND ACADEMY OF LAGADO. THE ACADEMY LARGELY DESCRIBED. THE ARTS WHEREIN THE PROFESSORS EMPLOY THEMSELVES.

This academy is not an entire single building, but a continuation of several houses on both sides of a street, which growing waste, was purchased and applied to that use.

I was received very kindly by the warden, and went for many days to the academy. Every room has in it one or more projectors; and I believe I could not be in fewer than five hundred rooms.

The first man I saw was of a meagre aspect, with sooty hands and face, his hair and beard long, ragged, and singed in several places. His clothes, shirt, and skin, were all of the same colour. He has been eight years upon a project for extracting sunbeams out of cucumbers, which were to be put in phials hermetically sealed, and let out to warm the air in raw inclement summers. He told me, he did not doubt, that, in eight years more, he should be able to supply the governor's gardens with sunshine, at a reasonable rate: but he complained that his stock was low, and entreated me "to give him something as an encouragement to ingenuity, especially since this had been a very dear season for cucumbers." I made him a small present, for my lord had furnished me with money on purpose, because he knew their practice of begging from all who go to see them.

I went into another chamber, but was ready to hasten back, being almost overcome with a horrible stink. My conductor pressed me forward, conjuring me in a whisper "to give no offence, which would be highly resented;" and therefore I durst not so much as stop my nose. The projector of this cell was the most ancient student of the academy; his face and beard were of a pale yellow; his hands and clothes daubed over with filth. When I was presented to him, he gave me a close embrace, a compliment I could well have excused. His employment, from his first coming into the academy, was an operation to reduce human excrement to its original food, by separating the several parts, removing the tincture which it receives from the gall, making the odour exhale, and scumming off the saliva. He had a weekly allowance, from the society, of a vessel filled with human ordure, about the bigness of a Bristol barrel.

I saw another at work to calcine ice into gunpowder; who likewise showed me a treatise he had written concerning the malleability of fire, which he intended to publish.

There was a most ingenious architect, who had contrived a new method for building houses, by beginning at the roof, and working downward to the foundation; which he justified to me, by the like practice of those two prudent insects, the bee and the spider.

There was a man born blind, who had several apprentices in his own condition: their employment was to mix colours for painters, which their master taught them to distinguish by feeling and smelling. It was indeed my misfortune to find them at that time not very perfect in their lessons, and the professor himself happened to be generally mistaken. This artist is much encouraged and esteemed by the whole fraternity.

In another apartment I was highly pleased with a projector who had found a device of ploughing the ground with hogs, to save the charges of ploughs, cattle, and labour. The method is this: in an acre of ground you bury, at six inches distance and eight deep, a quantity of acorns, dates, chestnuts, and other mast or vegetables, whereof these animals are fondest; then you drive six hundred or more of them into the field, where, in a few days, they will root up the whole ground in search of their food, and make it fit for sowing, at the same time manuring it with their dung: it is true, upon experiment, they found the charge and trouble very great, and they had little or no crop. However it is not doubted, that this invention may be capable of great improvement.

I went into another room, where the walls and ceiling were all hung round with cobwebs, except a narrow passage for the artist to go in and out. At my entrance, he called aloud to me, "not to disturb his webs." He lamented "the fatal mistake the world had been so long in, of using silkworms, while we had such plenty of domestic insects who infinitely excelled the former, because they understood how to weave, as well as spin." And he proposed further, "that by employing spiders, the charge of dyeing silks should be wholly saved;" whereof I was fully convinced, when he showed me a vast number of flies most beautifully coloured, wherewith he fed his spiders, assuring us "that the webs would take a tincture from them; and as he had them of all hues, he hoped to fit everybody's fancy, as soon as he could find proper food for the flies, of certain gums, oils, and other glutinous matter, to give a strength and consistence to the threads."

There was an astronomer, who had undertaken to place a sun-dial upon the great weathercock on the town-house, by adjusting the annual and diurnal motions of the earth and sun, so as to answer and coincide with all accidental turnings of the wind.

I was complaining of a small fit of the colic, upon which my conductor led me into a room where a great physician resided, who was famous for curing that disease, by contrary operations from the same instrument. He had a large pair of bellows, with a long slender muzzle of ivory: this he conveyed eight inches up the anus, and drawing in the wind, he affirmed he could make the guts as lank as a dried bladder. But when the disease was more stubborn and violent, he let in the muzzle while the bellows were full of wind, which he discharged into the body of the patient; then withdrew the instrument to replenish it, clapping his thumb strongly against the orifice of then fundament; and this being repeated three or four times, the adventitious wind would rush out, bringing the noxious along with it, (like water put into a pump), and the patient recovered. I saw him try both experiments upon a dog, but could not discern any effect from the former. After the latter the animal was ready to burst, and made so violent a discharge as was very offensive to me and my companion. The dog died on the spot, and we left the doctor endeavouring to recover him, by the same operation.

I visited many other apartments, but shall not trouble my reader with all the curiosities I observed, being studious of brevity.

I had hitherto seen only one side of the academy, the other being appropriated to the advancers of speculative learning, of whom I shall say something, when I have mentioned one illustrious person more, who is called among them "the universal artist." He told us "he had been thirty years employing his thoughts for the improvement of human life." He had two large rooms full of wonderful curiosities, and fifty men at work. Some were condensing air into a dry tangible substance, by extracting the nitre, and letting the aqueous or fluid particles percolate; others softening marble, for pillows and pin-cushions; others petrifying the hoofs of a living horse, to preserve them from foundering. The artist himself was at that time busy upon two great designs; the first, to sow land with chaff, wherein he affirmed the true seminal virtue to be contained, as he demonstrated by several experiments, which I was not skilful enough to comprehend. The other was, by a certain composition of gums, minerals, and vegetables, outwardly applied, to prevent the growth of wool upon two young lambs; and he hoped, in a reasonable time to propagate the breed of naked sheep, all over the kingdom.

We crossed a walk to the other part of the academy, where, as I have already said, the projectors in speculative learning resided.

The first professor I saw, was in a very large room, with forty pupils about him. After salutation, observing me to look earnestly upon a frame, which took up the greatest part of both the length and breadth of the room, he said, "Perhaps I might wonder to see him employed in a project for improving speculative knowledge, by practical and mechanical operations. But the world would soon be sensible of its usefulness; and he flattered himself, that a more noble, exalted thought never sprang in any other man's head. Every one knew how laborious the usual method is of attaining to arts and sciences; whereas, by his contrivance, the most ignorant person, at a reasonable charge, and with a little bodily labour, might write books in philosophy, poetry, politics, laws, mathematics, and theology, without the least assistance from genius or study." He then led me to the frame, about the sides, whereof all his pupils stood in ranks. It was twenty feet square, placed in the middle of the room. The superfices was composed of several bits of wood, about the bigness of a die, but some larger than others. They were all linked together by slender wires. These bits of wood were covered, on every square, with paper pasted on them; and on these papers were written all the words of their language, in their several moods, tenses, and declensions; but without any order. The professor then desired me "to observe; for he was going to set his engine at work." The pupils, at his command, took each of them hold of an iron handle, whereof there were forty fixed round the edges of the frame; and giving them a sudden turn, the whole disposition of the words was entirely changed. He then commanded six-and-thirty of the lads, to read the several lines softly, as they appeared upon the frame; and where they found three or four words together that might make part of a sentence, they dictated to the four remaining boys, who were scribes. This work was repeated three or four times, and at every turn, the engine was so contrived, that the words shifted into new places, as the square bits of wood moved upside down.

Six hours a day the young students were employed in this labour; and the professor showed me several volumes in large folio, already collected, of broken sentences, which he intended to piece together, and out of those rich materials, to give the world a complete body of all arts and sciences; which, however, might be still improved, and much expedited, if the public would raise a fund for making and employing five hundred such frames in Lagado, and oblige the managers to contribute in common their several collections.

He assured me "that this invention had employed all his thoughts from his youth; that he had emptied the whole vocabulary into his frame, and made the strictest computation of the general proportion there is in books between the numbers of particles, nouns, and verbs, and other parts of speech."

I made my humblest acknowledgment to this illustrious person, for his great communicativeness; and promised, "if ever I had the good fortune to return to my native country, that I would do him justice, as the sole inventor of this wonderful machine;" the form and contrivance of which I desired leave to delineate on paper, as in the figure here annexed. I told him, "although it were the custom of our learned in Europe to steal inventions from each other, who had thereby at least this advantage, that it became a controversy which was the right owner; yet I would take such caution, that he should have the honour entire, without a rival."

We next went to the school of languages, where three professors sat in consultation upon improving that of their own country.

The first project was, to shorten discourse, by cutting polysyllables into one, and leaving out verbs and participles, because, in reality, all things imaginable are but norms.

The other project was, a scheme for entirely abolishing all words whatsoever; and this was urged as a great advantage in point of health, as well as brevity. For it is plain, that every word we speak is, in some degree, a diminution of our lungs by corrosion, and, consequently, contributes to the shortening of our lives. An expedient was therefore offered, "that since words are only names for things, it would be more convenient for all men to carry about them such things as were necessary to express a particular business they are to discourse on." And this invention would certainly have taken place, to the great ease as well as health of the subject, if the women, in conjunction with the vulgar and illiterate, had not threatened to raise a rebellion unless they might be allowed the liberty to speak with their tongues, after the manner of their forefathers; such constant irreconcilable enemies to science are the common people. However, many of the most learned and wise adhere to the new scheme of expressing themselves by things; which has only this inconvenience attending it, that if a man's business be very great, and of various kinds, he must be obliged, in proportion, to carry a greater bundle of things upon his back, unless he can afford one or two strong servants to attend him. I have often beheld two of those sages almost sinking under the weight of their packs, like pedlars among us, who, when they met in the street, would lay down their loads, open their sacks, and hold conversation for an hour together; then put up their implements, help each other to resume their burdens, and take their leave.

But for short conversations, a man may carry implements in his pockets, and under his arms, enough to supply him; and in his house, he cannot be at a loss. Therefore the room where company meet who practise this art, is full of all things, ready at hand, requisite to furnish matter for this kind of artificial converse.

Another great advantage proposed by this invention was, that it would serve as a universal language, to be understood in all civilised nations, whose goods and utensils are generally of the same kind, or nearly resembling, so that their uses might easily be comprehended. And thus ambassadors would be qualified to treat with foreign princes, or ministers of state, to whose tongues they were utter strangers.

I was at the mathematical school, where the master taught his pupils after a method scarce imaginable to us in Europe. The proposition, and demonstration, were fairly written on a thin wafer, with ink composed of a cephalic tincture. This, the student was to swallow upon a fasting stomach, and for three days following, eat nothing but bread and water. As the wafer digested, the tincture mounted to his brain, bearing the proposition along with it.

But the success has not hitherto been answerable, partly by some error in the *quantum* or composition, and partly by the perverseness of lads, to whom this bolus is so nauseous, that they generally steal aside, and discharge it upwards, before it can operate; neither have they been yet persuaded to use so long an abstinence, as the prescription requires.

6

A FURTHER ACCOUNT OF THE ACADEMY. THE AUTHOR PROPOSES SOME IMPROVEMENTS, WHICH ARE HONOURABLY RECEIVED.

In the school of political projectors, I was but ill entertained; the professors appearing, in my judgment, wholly out of their senses, which is a scene that never fails to make me melancholy. These unhappy people were proposing schemes for persuading monarchs to choose favourites upon the score of their wisdom, capacity, and virtue; of teaching ministers to consult the public good; of rewarding merit, great abilities, eminent services; of instructing princes to know their true interest, by placing it on the same foundation with that of their people; of choosing for employments persons qualified to exercise them, with many other wild, impossible chimeras, that never entered before into the heart of man to conceive; and confirmed in me the old observation, "that there is nothing so extravagant and irrational, which some philosophers have not maintained for truth."

But, however, I shall so far do justice to this part of the Academy, as to acknowledge that all of them were not so visionary. There was a most ingenious doctor, who seemed to be perfectly versed in the whole nature and system of government. This illustrious person had very usefully employed his studies, in finding out effectual remedies for all diseases and corruptions to which the several kinds of public administration are subject, by the vices or infirmities of those who govern, as well as by the licentiousness of those who are to obey. For instance: whereas all writers and reasoners have agreed, that there is a strict universal resemblance between the natural and the political body; can there be any thing more evident, than that the health of both must be preserved, and the diseases cured, by the same prescriptions? It is allowed, that senates and great councils are often troubled with redundant, ebullient, and other peccant humours; with many diseases of the head, and more of the heart; with strong convulsions, with grievous contractions of the nerves and sinews in both hands, but especially the right; with spleen, flatus, vertigos, and deliriums; with scrofulous tumours, full of fetid purulent matter; with sour frothy ructations: with canine appetites, and crudeness of digestion, besides many others, needless to mention. This doctor therefore proposed, "that upon the meeting of the senate, certain physicians should attend it the three first days of their sitting, and at the close of each day's debate feel the pulses of every senator; after which, having maturely considered and consulted upon the nature of the several maladies, and the methods of cure, they should on the fourth day return to the senate house, attended by their apothecaries stored with proper medicines; and before the members sat, administer to each of them lenitives, aperitives, abstersives, corrosives, restringents, palliatives, laxatives, cephalalgics, icterics, apophlegmatics, acoustics, as their several cases required; and, according as these medicines should operate, repeat, alter, or omit them, at the next meeting."

This project could not be of any great expense to the public; and might in my poor opinion, be of much use for the despatch of business, in those countries where senates have any share in the legislative power; beget unanimity, shorten debates, open a few mouths which are now closed, and close many more which are now open; curb the petulancy of the young, and correct the positiveness of the old; rouse the stupid, and damp the pert.

Again: because it is a general complaint, that the favourites of princes are troubled with short and weak memories; the same doctor proposed, "that whoever attended a first minister, after having told his business, with the utmost brevity and in the plainest words, should, at his departure, give the said minister a tweak by the nose, or a kick in the belly, or tread on his corns, or lug him thrice by both ears, or run a pin into his breech; or pinch his arm black and blue, to prevent forgetfulness; and at every levee day, repeat the same operation, till the business were done, or absolutely refused."

He likewise directed, "that every senator in the great council of a nation, after he had delivered his opinion, and argued in the defence of it, should be obliged to give his vote directly contrary; because if that were done, the result would infallibly terminate in the good of the public."

When parties in a state are violent, he offered a wonderful contrivance to reconcile them. The method is this: You take a hundred leaders of each party; you dispose them into couples of such whose heads are nearest of a size; then let two nice operators saw off the occiput of each couple at the same time, in such a manner that the brain may be equally divided. Let the occiputs, thus cut off, be interchanged, applying each to the head of his opposite party-man. It seems indeed to be a work that requires some exactness, but the professor assured us, "that if it were dexterously performed, the cure would be infallible." For he argued thus: "that the two half brains being left to debate the matter between themselves within the space of one skull, would soon come to a good understanding, and produce that moderation, as well as regularity of thinking, so much to be wished for in the heads of those, who imagine they come into the world only to watch and govern its motion: and as to the difference of brains, in quantity or quality, among those who are directors in faction, the doctor assured us, from his own knowledge, that it was a perfect trifle."

I heard a very warm debate between two professors, about the most commodious and effectual ways and means of raising money, without grieving the subject. The first affirmed, "the justest method would be, to lay a certain tax upon vices and folly; and the sum fixed upon every man to be rated, after the fairest manner, by a jury of his neighbours." The second was of an opinion directly contrary; "to tax those qualities of body and mind, for which men chiefly value themselves; the rate to be more or less, according to the degrees of excelling; the decision whereof should be left entirely to their own breast." The highest tax was upon men who are the greatest favourites of the other sex, and the assessments, according to the number and nature of the favours they have received; for which, they are allowed to be their own vouchers. Wit, valour, and politeness, were likewise proposed to be largely taxed, and collected in the same manner, by every person's giving his own word for the quantum of what he possessed. But as to honour, justice, wisdom, and learning, they should not be taxed at all; because they are qualifications of so singular a kind, that no man will either allow them in his neighbour or value them in himself.

The women were proposed to be taxed according to their beauty and skill in dressing, wherein they had the same privilege with the men, to be determined by their own judgment. But constancy, chastity, good sense, and good nature, were not rated, because they would not bear the charge of collecting.

To keep senators in the interest of the crown, it was proposed that the members should raffle for employment; every man first taking an oath, and giving security, that he would vote for the court, whether he won or not; after which, the losers had, in their turn, the liberty of raffling upon the next vacancy. Thus, hope and expectation would be kept alive; none would complain of broken promises, but impute their disappointments wholly to fortune, whose shoulders are broader and stronger than those of a ministry.

Another professor showed me a large paper of instructions for discovering plots and conspiracies against the government. He advised great statesmen to examine into the diet of all suspected persons; their times of eating; upon which side they lay in bed; with which hand they wipe their posteriors; take a strict view of their excrements, and, from the colour, the odour, the taste, the consistence, the crudeness or maturity of digestion, form a judgment of their thoughts and designs; because men are never so serious, thoughtful, and intent, as when they are at stool, which he found by frequent experiment; for, in such conjunctures, when he used, merely as a trial, to consider which was the best way of murdering the king, his ordure would have a tincture of green; but quite different, when he thought only of raising an insurrection, or burning the metropolis.

The whole discourse was written with great acuteness, containing many observations, both curious and useful for politicians; but, as I conceived, not altogether complete. This I ventured to tell the author, and offered, if he pleased, to supply him with some additions. He received my proposition with more compliance than is usual among writers, especially those of the projecting species, professing "he would be glad to receive further information."

I told him, "that in the kingdom of Tribnia,[1] by the natives called Langdon,[2] where I had sojourned some time in my travels, the bulk of the people consist in a manner wholly of discoverers, witnesses, informers, accusers, prosecutors, evidences, swearers, together with their several subservient and subaltern instruments, all under the colours, the conduct, and the pay of ministers of state, and their deputies. The plots, in that kingdom, are usually the workmanship of those persons who desire to raise their own characters of profound politicians; to restore new vigour to a crazy administration; to stifle or divert general discontents; to fill their coffers with forfeitures; and raise, or sink the opinion of public credit, as either shall best answer their private advantage. It is first agreed and settled among them, what suspected persons shall be accused of a plot; then, effectual care is taken to secure all their letters and papers, and put the owners in chains. These papers are delivered to a set of artists, very dexterous in finding out the mysterious meanings of words, syllables, and letters: for instance, they can discover a close stool, to signify a privy council; a flock of geese, a senate; a lame dog, an invader; the plague, a standing army; a buzzard, a prime minister; the gout, a high priest; a gibbet, a secretary of state; a chamber pot, a committee of grandees; a sieve, a court lady; a broom, a revolution; a mouse-trap, an employment; a bottomless pit, a treasury; a sink, a court; a cap and bells, a favourite; a broken reed, a court of justice; an empty tun, a general; a running sore, the administration.[3]

"When this method fails, they have two others more effectual, which the learned among them call acrostics and anagrams. First, they can decipher all initial letters into political meanings. Thus N, shall signify a plot; B, a regiment of horse; L, a fleet at sea; or, secondly, by transposing the letters of the alphabet in any suspected paper, they can lay open the deepest designs of a discontented party. So, for example, if I should say, in a letter to a friend, 'Our brother Tom has just got the piles,' a skilful decipherer would discover, that the same letters which compose that sentence, may be analysed into the following words, 'Resist —, a plot is brought home—The tour.' And this is the anagrammatic method."

The professor made me great acknowledgments for communicating these observations, and promised to make honourable mention of me in his treatise.

I saw nothing in this country that could invite me to a longer continuance, and began to think of returning home to England.

---

1. Britannia.—*Sir W. Scott.*
2. *London.—Sir W. Scott.*
3. This is the revised text adopted by Dr. Hawksworth (1766). The above paragraph in the original editions (1726) takes another form, commencing:—"I told him that should I happen to live in a kingdom where lots were in vogue," &c. The names Tribnia and Langdon are not mentioned, and the "close stool" and its signification do not occur.

7

THE AUTHOR LEAVES LAGADO: ARRIVES AT
MALDONADA. NO SHIP READY. HE TAKES A SHORT
VOYAGE TO GLUBBDUBDRIB. HIS RECEPTION BY
THE GOVERNOR.

The continent, of which this kingdom is apart, extends itself, as I have reason to believe, eastward, to that unknown tract of America westward of California; and north, to the Pacific Ocean, which is not above a hundred and fifty miles from Lagado; where there is a good port, and much commerce with the great island of Luggnagg, situated to the north-west about 29 degrees north latitude, and 140 longitude. This island of Luggnagg stands south-eastward of Japan, about a hundred leagues distant. There is a strict alliance between the Japanese emperor and the king of Luggnagg; which affords frequent opportunities of sailing from one island to the other. I determined therefore to direct my course this way, in order to my return to Europe. I hired two mules, with a guide, to show me the way, and carry my small baggage. I took leave of my noble protector, who had shown me so much favour, and made me a generous present at my departure.

My journey was without any accident or adventure worth relating. When I arrived at the port of Maldonada (for so it is called) there was no ship in the harbour bound for Luggnagg, nor likely to be in some time. The town is about as large as Portsmouth. I soon fell into some acquaintance, and was very hospitably received. A gentleman of distinction said to me, "that since the ships bound for Luggnagg could not be ready in less than a month, it might be no disagreeable amusement for me to take a trip to the little island of Glubbdubdrib, about five leagues off to the south-west." He offered himself and a friend to accompany me, and that I should be provided with a small convenient bark for the voyage.

Glubbdubdrib, as nearly as I can interpret the word, signifies the island of sorcerers or magicians. It is about one third as large as the Isle of Wight, and extremely fruitful: it is governed by the head of a certain tribe, who are all magicians. This tribe marries only among each other, and the eldest in succession is prince or governor. He has a noble palace, and a park of about three thousand acres, surrounded by a wall of hewn stone twenty feet high. In this park are several small enclosures for cattle, corn, and gardening.

The governor and his family are served and attended by domestics of a kind somewhat unusual. By his skill in necromancy he has a power of calling whom he pleases from the dead, and commanding their service for twenty-four hours, but no longer; nor can he call the same persons up again in less than three months, except upon very extraordinary occasions.

When we arrived at the island, which was about eleven in the morning, one of the gentlemen who accompanied me went to the governor, and desired admittance for a stranger, who came on purpose to have the honour of attending on his highness. This was immediately granted, and we all three entered the gate of the palace between two rows of guards, armed and dressed after a very antic manner, and with something in their countenances that made my flesh creep with a horror I cannot express. We passed through several apartments, between servants of the same sort, ranked on each side as before, till we came to the chamber of presence; where, after three profound obeisances, and a few general questions, we were permitted to sit on three stools, near the lowest step of his highness's throne. He understood the language of Balnibarbi, although it was different from that of this island. He desired me to give him some account of my travels; and, to let me see that I should be treated without ceremony, he dismissed all his attendants with a turn of his finger; at which, to my great astonishment, they vanished in an instant, like visions in a dream when we awake on a sudden. I could not recover myself in some time, till the governor assured me, "that I should receive no hurt:" and observing my two companions to be under no concern, who had been often entertained in the same manner, I began to take courage, and related to his highness a short history of my several adventures; yet not without some hesitation, and frequently looking behind me to the place where I had seen those domestic spectres. I had the honour to dine with the governor, where a new set of ghosts served up the meat, and waited at table. I now observed myself to be less terrified than I had been in the morning. I stayed till sunset, but humbly desired his highness to excuse me for not accepting his invitation of lodging in the palace. My two friends and I lay at a private house in the town adjoining, which is the capital of this little island; and the next morning we returned to pay our duty to the governor, as he was pleased to command us.

After this manner we continued in the island for ten days, most part of every day with the governor, and at night in our lodging. I soon grew so familiarized to the sight of spirits, that after the third or fourth time they gave me no emotion at all: or, if I had any apprehensions left, my curiosity prevailed over them. For his highness the governor ordered me "to call up whatever persons I would choose to name, and in whatever numbers, among all the dead from the beginning of the world to the present time, and command them to answer any questions I should think fit to ask; with this condition, that my questions must be confined within the compass of the times they lived in. And one thing I might depend upon, that they would certainly tell me the truth, for lying was a talent of no use in the lower world."

I made my humble acknowledgments to his highness for so great a favour. We were in a chamber, from whence there was a fair prospect into the park. And because my first inclination was to be entertained with scenes of pomp and magnificence, I desired to see Alexander the Great at the head of his army, just after the battle of Arbela: which, upon a motion of the governor's finger, immediately appeared in a large field, under the window where we stood. Alexander was called up into the room: it was with great difficulty that I understood his Greek, and had but little of my own. He assured me upon his honour "that he was not poisoned, but died of a bad fever by excessive drinking."

Next, I saw Hannibal passing the Alps, who told me "he had not a drop of vinegar in his camp."

I saw Cæsar and Pompey at the head of their troops, just ready to engage. I saw the former, in his last great triumph. I desired that the senate of Rome might appear before me, in one large chamber, and an assembly of somewhat a later age in counterview, in another.

The first seemed to be an assembly of heroes and demigods; the other, a knot of pedlars, pickpockets, highwayman, and bullies.

The governor, at my request, gave the sign for Cæsar and Brutus to advance towards us. I was struck with a profound veneration at the sight of Brutus, and could easily discover the most consummate virtue, the greatest intrepidity and firmness of mind, the truest love of his country, and general benevolence for mankind, in every lineament of his countenance. I observed, with much pleasure, that these two persons were in good intelligence with each other; and Cæsar freely confessed to me, "that the greatest actions of his own life were not equal, by many degrees, to the glory of taking it away." I had the honour to have much conversation with Brutus; and was told, "that his ancestor Junius, Socrates, Epaminondas, Cato the younger, Sir Thomas More, and himself were perpetually together:" a sextumvirate, to which all the ages of the world cannot add a seventh.

It would be tedious to trouble the reader with relating what vast numbers of illustrious persons were called up to gratify that insatiable desire I had to see the world in every period of antiquity placed before me. I chiefly fed mine eyes with beholding the destroyers of tyrants and usurpers, and the restorers of liberty to oppressed and injured nations. But it is impossible to express the satisfaction I received in my own mind, after such a manner as to make it a suitable entertainment to the reader.

8

A FURTHER ACCOUNT OF GLUBBDUBDRIB.
ANCIENT AND MODERN HISTORY CORRECTED.

Having a desire to see those ancients who were most renowned for wit and learning, I set apart one day on purpose. I proposed that Homer and Aristotle might appear at the head of all their commentators; but these were so numerous, that some hundreds were forced to attend in the court, and outward rooms of the palace. I knew, and could distinguish those two heroes, at first sight, not only from the crowd, but from each other. Homer was the taller and comelier person of the two, walked very erect for one of his age, and his eyes were the most quick and piercing I ever beheld. Aristotle stooped much, and made use of a staff. His visage was meagre, his hair lank and thin, and his voice hollow. I soon discovered that both of them were perfect strangers to the rest of the company, and had never seen or heard of them before; and I had a whisper from a ghost who shall be nameless, "that these commentators always kept in the most distant quarters from their principals, in the lower world, through a consciousness of shame and guilt, because they had so horribly misrepresented the meaning of those authors to posterity." I introduced Didymus and Eustathius to Homer, and prevailed on him to treat them better than perhaps they deserved, for he soon found they wanted a genius to enter into the spirit of a poet. But Aristotle was out of all patience with the account I gave him of Scotus and Ramus, as I presented them to him; and he asked them, "whether the rest of the tribe were as great dunces as themselves?"

I then desired the governor to call up Descartes and Gassendi, with whom I prevailed to explain their systems to Aristotle. This great philosopher freely acknowledged his own mistakes in natural philosophy, because he proceeded in many things upon conjecture, as all men must do; and he found that Gassendi, who had made the doctrine of Epicurus as palatable as he could, and the vortices of Descartes, were equally to be exploded. He predicted the same fate to *attraction*, whereof the present learned are such zealous asserters. He said, "that new systems of nature were but new fashions, which would vary in every age; and even those, who pretend to demonstrate them from mathematical principles, would flourish but a short period of time, and be out of vogue when that was determined."

I spent five days in conversing with many others of the ancient learned. I saw most of the first Roman emperors. I prevailed on the governor to call up Heliogabalus's cooks to dress us a dinner, but they could not show us much of their skill, for want of materials. A helot of Agesilaus made us a dish of Spartan broth, but I was not able to get down a second spoonful.

The two gentlemen, who conducted me to the island, were pressed by their private affairs to return in three days, which I employed in seeing some of the modern dead, who had made the greatest figure, for two or three hundred years past, in our own and other countries of Europe; and having been always a great admirer of old illustrious families, I desired the governor would call up a dozen or two of kings, with their ancestors in order for eight or nine generations. But my disappointment was grievous and unexpected. For, instead of a long train with royal diadems, I saw in one family two fiddlers, three spruce courtiers, and an Italian prelate. In another, a barber, an abbot, and two cardinals. I have too great a veneration for crowned heads, to dwell any longer on so nice a subject. But as to counts, marquises, dukes, earls, and the like, I was not so scrupulous. And I confess, it was not without some pleasure, that I found myself able to trace the particular features, by which certain families are distinguished, up to their originals. I could plainly discover whence one family derives a long chin; why a second has abounded with knaves for two generations, and fools for two more; why a third happened to be crack-brained, and a fourth to be sharpers; whence it came, what Polydore Virgil says of a certain great house, *Nec vir fortis, nec foemina casta*; how cruelty, falsehood, and cowardice, grew to be characteristics by which certain families are distinguished as much as by their coats of arms; who first brought the pox into a noble house, which has lineally descended scrofulous tumours to their posterity. Neither could I wonder at all this, when I saw such an interruption of lineages, by pages, lackeys, valets, coachmen, gamesters, fiddlers, players, captains, and pickpockets.

I was chiefly disgusted with modern history. For having strictly examined all the persons of greatest name in the courts of princes, for a hundred years past, I found how the world had been misled by prostitute writers, to ascribe the greatest exploits in war, to cowards; the wisest counsel, to fools; sincerity, to flatterers; Roman virtue, to betrayers of their country; piety, to atheists; chastity, to sodomites; truth, to informers: how many innocent and excellent persons had been condemned to death or banishment by the practising of great ministers upon the corruption of judges, and the malice of factions: how many villains had been exalted to the highest places of trust, power, dignity, and profit: how great a share in the motions and events of courts, councils, and senates might be challenged by bawds, whores, pimps, parasites, and buffoons. How low an opinion I had of human wisdom and integrity, when I was truly informed of the springs and motives of great enterprises and revolutions in the world, and of the contemptible accidents to which they owed their success.

Here I discovered the roguery and ignorance of those who pretend to write anecdotes, or secret history; who send so many kings to their graves with a cup of poison; will repeat the discourse between a prince and chief minister, where no witness was by; unlock the thoughts and cabinets of ambassadors and secretaries of state; and have the perpetual misfortune to be mistaken. Here I discovered the true causes of many great events that have surprised the world; how a whore can govern the back-stairs, the back-stairs a council, and the council a senate. A general confessed, in my presence, "that he got a victory purely by the force of cowardice and ill conduct;" and an admiral, "that, for want of proper intelligence, he beat the enemy, to whom he intended to betray the fleet." Three kings protested to me, "that in their whole reigns they never did once prefer any person of merit, unless by mistake, or treachery of some minister in whom they confided; neither would they do it if they were to live again:" and they showed, with great strength of reason, "that the royal throne could not be supported without corruption, because that positive, confident, restiff temper, which virtue infused into a man, was a perpetual clog to public business."

I had the curiosity to inquire in a particular manner, by what methods great numbers had procured to themselves high titles of honour, and prodigious estates; and I confined my inquiry to a very modern period: however, without grating upon present times, because I would be sure to give no offence even to foreigners (for I hope the reader need not be told, that I do not in the least intend my own country, in what I say upon this occasion,) a great number of persons concerned were called up; and, upon a very slight examination, discovered such a scene of infamy, that I cannot reflect upon it without some seriousness. Perjury, oppression, subornation, fraud, pandarism, and the like infirmities, were among the most excusable arts they had to mention; and for these I gave, as it was reasonable, great allowance. But when some confessed they owed their greatness and wealth to sodomy, or incest; others, to the prostituting of their own wives and daughters; others, to the betraying of their country or their prince; some, to poisoning; more to the perverting of justice, in order to destroy the innocent, I hope I may be pardoned, if these discoveries inclined me a little to abate of that profound veneration, which I am naturally apt to pay to persons of high rank, who ought to be treated with the utmost respect due to their sublime dignity, by us their inferiors.

I had often read of some great services done to princes and states, and desired to see the persons by whom those services were performed. Upon inquiry I was told, "that their names were to be found on no record, except a few of them, whom history has represented as the vilest of rogues and traitors." As to the rest, I had never once heard of them. They all appeared with dejected looks, and in the meanest habit; most of them telling me, "they died in poverty and disgrace, and the rest on a scaffold or a gibbet."

Among others, there was one person, whose case appeared a little singular. He had a youth about eighteen years old standing by his side. He told me, "he had for many years been commander of a ship; and in the sea fight at Actium had the good fortune to break through the enemy's great line of battle, sink three of their capital ships, and take a fourth, which was the sole cause of Antony's flight, and of the victory that ensued; that the youth standing by him, his only son, was killed in the action." He added, "that upon the confidence of some merit, the war being at an end, he went to Rome, and solicited at the court of Augustus to be preferred to a greater ship, whose commander had been killed; but, without any regard to his pretensions, it was given to a boy who had never seen the sea, the son of Libertina, who waited on one of the emperor's mistresses. Returning back to his own vessel, he was charged with neglect of duty, and the ship given to a favourite page of Publicola, the vice-admiral; whereupon he retired to a poor farm at a great distance from Rome, and there ended his life." I was so curious to know the truth of this story, that I desired Agrippa might be called, who was admiral in that fight. He appeared, and confirmed the whole account: but with much more advantage to the captain, whose modesty had extenuated or concealed a great part of his merit.

I was surprised to find corruption grown so high and so quick in that empire, by the force of luxury so lately introduced; which made me less wonder at many parallel cases in other countries, where vices of all kinds have reigned so much longer, and where the whole praise, as well as pillage, has been engrossed by the chief commander, who perhaps had the least title to either.

As every person called up made exactly the same appearance he had done in the world, it gave me melancholy reflections to observe how much the race of human kind was degenerated among us within these hundred years past; how the pox, under all its consequences and denominations had altered every lineament of an English countenance;

shortened the size of bodies, unbraced the nerves, relaxed the sinews and muscles, introduced a sallow complexion, and rendered the flesh loose and rancid.

I descended so low, as to desire some English yeoman of the old stamp might be summoned to appear; once so famous for the simplicity of their manners, diet, and dress; for justice in their dealings; for their true spirit of liberty; for their valour, and love of their country. Neither could I be wholly unmoved, after comparing the living with the dead, when I considered how all these pure native virtues were prostituted for a piece of money by their grand-children; who, in selling their votes and managing at elections, have acquired every vice and corruption that can possibly be learned in a court.

9

THE AUTHOR RETURNS TO MALDONADA. SAILS TO
THE KINGDOM OF LUGGNAGG. THE AUTHOR
CONFINED. HE IS SENT FOR TO COURT. THE
MANNER OF HIS ADMITTANCE. THE KING'S GREAT
LENITY TO HIS SUBJECTS.

The day of our departure being come, I took leave of his highness, the Governor of Glubbdubdrib, and returned with my two companions to Maldonada, where, after a fortnight's waiting, a ship was ready to sail for Luggnagg. The two gentlemen, and some others, were so generous and kind as to furnish me with provisions, and see me on board. I was a month in this voyage. We had one violent storm, and were under a necessity of steering westward to get into the trade wind, which holds for above sixty leagues. On the 21st of April, 1708, we sailed into the river of Clumegnig, which is a seaport town, at the south-east point of Luggnagg. We cast anchor within a league of the town, and made a signal for a pilot. Two of them came on board in less than half an hour, by whom we were guided between certain shoals and rocks, which are very dangerous in the passage, to a large basin, where a fleet may ride in safety within a cable's length of the town-wall.

Some of our sailors, whether out of treachery or inadvertence, had informed the pilots "that I was a stranger, and great traveller;" whereof these gave notice to a custom-house officer, by whom I was examined very strictly upon my landing. This officer spoke to me in the language of Balnibarbi, which, by the force of much commerce, is generally understood in that town, especially by seamen and those employed in the customs. I gave him a short account of some particulars, and made my story as plausible and consistent as I could; but I thought it necessary to disguise my country, and call myself a Hollander; because my intentions were for Japan, and I knew the Dutch were the only Europeans permitted to enter into that kingdom. I therefore told the officer, "that having been shipwrecked on the coast of Balnibarbi, and cast on a rock, I was received up into Laputa, or the flying island (of which he had often heard), and was now endeavouring to get to Japan, whence I might find a convenience of returning to my own country." The officer said, "I must be confined till he could receive orders from court, for which he would write immediately, and hoped to receive an answer in a fortnight." I was carried to a convenient lodging with a sentry placed at the door; however, I had the liberty of a large garden, and was treated with humanity enough, being maintained all the time at the king's charge. I was invited by several persons, chiefly out of curiosity, because it was reported that I came from countries very remote, of which they had never heard.

I hired a young man, who came in the same ship, to be an interpreter; he was a native of Luggnagg, but had lived some years at Maldonada, and was a perfect master of both languages. By his assistance, I was able to hold a conversation with those who came to visit me; but this consisted only of their questions, and my answers.

The despatch came from court about the time we expected. It contained a warrant for conducting me and my retinue to *Traldragdubh*, or *Trildrogdrib* (for it is pronounced both ways as near as I can remember), by a party of ten horse. All my retinue was that poor lad for an interpreter, whom I persuaded into my service, and, at my humble request, we had each of us a mule to ride on. A messenger was despatched half a day's journey before us, to give the king notice of my approach, and to desire, "that his majesty would please to appoint a day and hour, when it would by his gracious pleasure that I might have the honour to lick the dust before his footstool." This is the court style, and I found it to be more than matter of form: for, upon my admittance two days after my arrival, I was commanded to crawl upon my belly, and lick the floor as I advanced; but, on account of my being a stranger, care was taken to have it made so clean, that the dust was not offensive. However, this was a peculiar grace, not allowed to any but persons of the highest rank, when they desire an admittance. Nay, sometimes the floor is strewed with dust on purpose, when the person to be admitted happens to have powerful enemies at court; and I have seen a great lord with his mouth so crammed, that when he had crept to the proper distance from the throne; he was not able to speak a word. Neither is there any remedy; because it is capital for those, who receive an audience to spit or wipe their mouths in his majesty's presence. There is indeed another custom, which I cannot altogether approve of: when the king has a mind to put any of his nobles to death in a gentle indulgent manner, he commands the floor to be strewed with a certain brown powder of a deadly composition, which being licked up, infallibly kills him in twenty-four hours. But in justice to this prince's great clemency, and the care he has of his subjects' lives (wherein it were much to be wished that the Monarchs of Europe would imitate him), it must be mentioned for his honour, that strict orders are given to have the infected parts of the floor well washed after every such execution, which, if his domestics neglect, they are in danger of incurring his royal displeasure. I myself heard him give directions, that one of his pages should be whipped, whose turn it was to give notice about washing the floor after an execution, but maliciously had omitted it; by which neglect a young lord of great hopes, coming to an audience, was unfortunately poisoned, although the king at that time had no design against his life. But this good prince was so gracious as to forgive the poor page his whipping, upon promise that he would do so no more, without special orders.

To return from this digression. When I had crept within four yards of the throne, I raised myself gently upon my knees, and then striking my forehead seven times against the ground, I pronounced the following words, as they had been taught me the night before, *Inckpling gloffthrobb squut serummblhiop mlashnalt zwin tnodbalkuffh slhiophad gurdlubh asht*. This is the compliment, established by the laws of the land, for all persons admitted to the king's presence. It may be rendered into English thus: "May your celestial majesty outlive the sun, eleven moons and a half!" To this the king returned some answer, which, although I could not understand, yet I replied as I had been directed: *Fluft drin yalerick dwuldom prastrad mirpush*, which properly signifies, "My tongue is in the mouth of my friend;" and by this expression was meant, that I desired leave to bring my interpreter; whereupon the young man already mentioned was accordingly introduced, by whose intervention I answered as many questions as his majesty could put in above an hour. I spoke in the Balnibarbian tongue, and my interpreter delivered my meaning in that of Luggnagg.

The king was much delighted with my company, and ordered his *bliffmarklub*, or high-chamberlain, to appoint a lodging in the court for me and my interpreter; with a daily allowance for my table, and a large purse of gold for my common expenses.

I staid three months in this country, out of perfect obedience to his majesty; who was pleased highly to favour me, and made me very honourable offers. But I thought it more consistent with prudence and justice to pass the remainder of my days with my wife and family.

10

THE LUGGNAGGIANS COMMENDED. A PARTICULAR DESCRIPTION OF THE STRULDBRUGS, WITH MANY CONVERSATIONS BETWEEN THE AUTHOR AND SOME EMINENT PERSONS UPON THAT SUBJECT.

The Luggnaggians are a polite and generous people; and although they are not without some share of that pride which is peculiar to all Eastern countries, yet they show themselves courteous to strangers, especially such who are countenanced by the court. I had many acquaintance, and among persons of the best fashion; and being always attended by my interpreter, the conversation we had was not disagreeable.

One day, in much good company, I was asked by a person of quality, "whether I had seen any of their *struldbrugs*, or immortals?" I said, "I had not;" and desired he would explain to me "what he meant by such an appellation, applied to a mortal creature." He told me "that sometimes, though very rarely, a child happened to be born in a family, with a red circular spot in the forehead, directly over the left eyebrow, which was an infallible mark that it should never die." The spot, as he described it, "was about the compass of a silver threepence, but in the course of time grew larger, and changed its colour; for at twelve years old it became green, so continued till five and twenty, then turned to a deep blue: at five and forty it grew coal black, and as large as an English shilling; but never admitted any further alteration." He said, "these births were so rare, that he did not believe there could be above eleven hundred struldbrugs, of both sexes, in the whole kingdom; of which he computed about fifty in the metropolis, and, among the rest, a young girl born; about three years ago: that these productions were not peculiar to any family, but a mere effect of chance; and the children of the *struldbrugs* themselves were equally mortal with the rest of the people."

I freely own myself to have been struck with inexpressible delight, upon hearing this account: and the person who gave it me happening to understand the Balnibarbian language, which I spoke very well, I could not forbear breaking out into expressions, perhaps a little too extravagant. I cried out, as in a rapture, "Happy nation, where every child hath at least a chance for being immortal! Happy people, who enjoy so many living examples of ancient virtue, and have masters ready to instruct them in the wisdom of all former ages! but happiest, beyond all comparison, are those excellent *struldbrugs*, who, being born exempt from that universal calamity of human nature, have their minds free and disengaged, without the weight and depression of spirits caused by the continual apprehensions of death!" I discovered my admiration, "that I had not observed any of these illustrious persons at court; the black spot on the forehead being so remarkable a distinction, that I could not have easily overlooked it: and it was impossible that his majesty, a most judicious prince, should not provide himself with a good number of such wise and able counsellors. Yet perhaps the virtue of those reverend sages was too strict for the corrupt and libertine manners of a court: and we often find by experience, that young men are too opinionated and volatile to be guided by the sober dictates of their seniors. However, since the king was pleased to allow me access to his royal person, I was resolved, upon the very first occasion, to deliver my opinion to him on this matter freely and at large, by the help of my interpreter; and whether he would please to take my advice or not, yet in one thing I was determined, that his majesty having frequently offered me an establishment in this country, I would, with great thankfulness, accept the favour, and pass my life here in the conversation of those superior beings the *struldbrugs*, if they would please to admit me."

The gentleman to whom I addressed my discourse, because (as I have already observed) he spoke the language of Balnibarbi, said to me, with a sort of a smile which usually arises from pity to the ignorant, "that he was glad of any occasion to keep me among them, and desired my permission to explain to the company what I had spoke." He did so, and they talked together for some time in their own language, whereof I understood not a syllable, neither could I observe by their countenances, what impression my discourse had made on them. After a short silence, the same person told me, "that his friends and mine (so he thought fit to express himself) were very much pleased with the judicious remarks I had made on the great happiness and advantages of immortal life, and they were desirous to know, in a particular manner, what scheme of living I should have formed to myself, if it had fallen to my lot to have been born a *struldbrug*."

I answered, "it was easy to be eloquent on so copious and delightful a subject, especially to me, who had been often apt to amuse myself with visions of what I should do, if I were a king, a general, or a great lord: and upon this very case, I had frequently run over the whole system how I should employ myself, and pass the time, if I were sure to live for ever.

"That, if it had been my good fortune to come into the world a *struldbrug*, as soon as I could discover my own happiness, by understanding the difference between life and death, I would first resolve, by all arts and methods, whatsoever, to procure myself riches. In the pursuit of which, by thrift and management, I might reasonably expect, in about two hundred years, to be the wealthiest man in the kingdom. In the second place, I would, from my earliest youth, apply myself to the study of arts and sciences, by which I should arrive in time to excel all others in learning. Lastly, I would carefully record every action and event of consequence, that happened in the public, impartially draw the characters of the several successions of princes and great ministers of state, with my own observations on every point. I would exactly set down the several changes in customs, language, fashions of dress, diet, and diversions. By all which acquirements, I should be a living treasure of knowledge and wisdom, and certainly become the oracle of the nation.

"I would never marry after threescore, but live in a hospitable manner, yet still on the saving side. I would entertain myself in forming and directing the minds of hopeful young men, by convincing them, from my own remembrance, experience, and observation, fortified by numerous examples, of the usefulness of virtue in public and private life. But my choice and constant companions should be a set of my own immortal brotherhood; among whom, I would elect a dozen from the most ancient, down to my own contemporaries. Where any of these wanted fortunes, I would provide them with convenient lodges round my own estate, and have some of them always at my table; only mingling a few of the most valuable among you mortals, whom length of time would harden me to lose with little or no reluctance, and treat your posterity after the same manner; just as a man diverts himself with the annual succession of pinks and tulips in his garden, without regretting the loss of those which withered the preceding year.

"These *struldbrugs* and I would mutually communicate our observations and memorials, through the course of time; remark the several gradations by which corruption steals into the world, and oppose it in every step, by giving perpetual warning and instruction to mankind; which, added to the strong influence of our own example, would probably prevent that continual degeneracy of human nature so justly complained of in all ages.

"Add to this, the pleasure of seeing the various revolutions of states and empires; the changes in the lower and upper world; ancient cities in ruins, and obscure villages become the seats of kings; famous rivers lessening into shallow brooks; the ocean leaving one coast dry, and overwhelming another; the discovery of many countries yet unknown; barbarity overrunning the politest nations, and the most barbarous become civilized. I should then see the discovery of the longitude, the perpetual motion, the universal medicine, and many other great inventions, brought to the utmost perfection.

"What wonderful discoveries should we make in astronomy, by outliving and confirming our own predictions; by observing the progress and return of comets, with the changes of motion in the sun, moon, and stars!"

I enlarged upon many other topics, which the natural desire of endless life, and sublunary happiness, could easily furnish me with. When I had ended, and the sum of my discourse had been interpreted, as before, to the rest of the company, there was a good deal of talk among them in the language of the country, not without some laughter at my expense. At last, the same gentleman who had been my interpreter, said, "he was desired by the rest to set me right in a few mistakes, which I had fallen into through the common imbecility of human nature, and upon that allowance was less answerable for them. That this breed of *struldbrugs* was peculiar to their country, for there were no such people either in Balnibarbi or Japan, where he had the honour to be ambassador from his majesty, and found the natives in both those kingdoms very hard to believe that the fact was possible: and it appeared from my astonishment when he first mentioned the matter to me, that I received it as a thing wholly new, and scarcely to be credited. That in the two kingdoms above mentioned, where, during his residence, he had conversed very much, he observed long life to be the universal desire and wish of mankind. That whoever had one foot in the grave was sure to hold back the other as strongly as he could. That the oldest had still hopes of living one day longer, and looked on death as the greatest evil, from which nature always prompted him to retreat. Only in this island of Luggnagg the appetite for living was not so eager, from the continual example of the *struldbrugs* before their eyes.

"That the system of living contrived by me, was unreasonable and unjust; because it supposed a perpetuity of youth, health, and vigour, which no man could be so foolish to hope, however extravagant he may be in his wishes. That the question therefore was not, whether a man would choose to be always in the prime of youth, attended with prosperity and health; but how he would pass a perpetual life under all the usual disadvantages which old age brings along with it. For although few men will avow their desires of being immortal, upon such hard conditions, yet in the two kingdoms before mentioned, of Balnibarbi and Japan, he observed that every man desired to put off death some time longer, let it approach ever so late: and he rarely heard of any man who died willingly, except he were incited by the extremity of grief or torture. And he appealed to me, whether in those countries I had travelled, as well as my own, I had not observed the same general disposition."

After this preface, he gave me a particular account of the *struldbrugs* among them. He said, "they commonly acted like mortals till about thirty years old; after which, by degrees, they grew melancholy and dejected, increasing in both till they came to fourscore. This he learned from their own confession: for otherwise, there not being above two or three of that species born in an age, they were too few to form a general observation by. When they came to fourscore years, which is reckoned the extremity of living in this country, they had not only all the follies and infirmities of other old men, but many more which arose from the dreadful prospect of never dying. They were not only opinionative, peevish, covetous, morose, vain, talkative, but incapable of friendship, and dead to all natural affection, which never descended below their grandchildren. Envy and impotent desires are their prevailing passions. But those objects against which their envy seems principally directed, are the vices of the younger sort and the deaths of the old. By reflecting on the former, they find themselves cut off from all possibility of pleasure; and whenever they see a funeral, they lament and repine that others have gone to a harbour of rest to which they themselves never can hope to arrive. They have no remembrance of anything but what they learned and observed in their youth and middle-age, and even that is very imperfect; and for the truth or particulars of any fact, it is safer to depend on common tradition, than upon their best recollections. The least miserable among them appear to be those who turn to dotage, and entirely lose their memories; these meet with more pity and assistance, because they want many bad qualities which abound in others.

"If a *struldbrug* happen to marry one of his own kind, the marriage is dissolved of course, by the courtesy of the kingdom, as soon as the younger of the two comes to be fourscore; for the law thinks it a reasonable indulgence, that those who are condemned, without any fault of their own, to a perpetual continuance in the world, should not have their misery doubled by the load of a wife.

"As soon as they have completed the term of eighty years, they are looked on as dead in law; their heirs immediately succeed to their estates; only a small pittance is reserved for their support; and the poor ones are maintained at the public charge. After that period, they are held incapable of any employment of trust or profit; they cannot purchase lands, or take leases; neither are they allowed to be witnesses in any cause, either civil or criminal, not even for the decision of meers and bounds.

"At ninety, they lose their teeth and hair; they have at that age no distinction of taste, but eat and drink whatever they can get, without relish or appetite. The diseases they were subject to still continue, without increasing or diminishing. In talking, they forget the common appellation of things, and the names of persons, even of those who are their nearest friends and relations. For the same reason, they never can amuse themselves with reading, because their memory will not serve to carry them from the beginning of a sentence to the end; and by this defect, they are deprived of the only entertainment whereof they might otherwise be capable.

"The language of this country being always upon the flux, the *struldbrugs* of one age do not understand those of another; neither are they able, after two hundred years, to hold any conversation (farther than by a few general words) with their neighbours the mortals; and thus they lie under the disadvantage of living like foreigners in their own country."

This was the account given me of the *struldbrugs*, as near as I can remember. I afterwards saw five or six of different ages, the youngest not above two hundred years old, who were brought to me at several times by some of my friends; but although they were told, "that I was a great traveller, and had seen all the world," they had not the least curiosity to ask me a question; only desired "I would give them *slumskudask*," or a token of remembrance; which is a modest way of begging, to avoid the law, that strictly forbids it, because they are provided for by the public, although indeed with a very scanty allowance.

They are despised and hated by all sorts of people. When one of them is born, it is reckoned ominous, and their birth is recorded very particularly so that you may know their age by consulting the register, which, however, has not been kept above a thousand years past, or at least has been destroyed by time or public disturbances. But the usual way of computing how old they are, is by asking them what kings or great persons they can remember, and then consulting history; for infallibly the last prince in their mind did not begin his reign after they were fourscore years old.

They were the most mortifying sight I ever beheld; and the women more horrible than the men. Besides the usual deformities in extreme old age, they acquired an additional ghastliness, in proportion to their number of years, which is not to be described; and among half a dozen, I soon distinguished which was the eldest, although there was not above a century or two between them.

The reader will easily believe, that from what I had hear and seen, my keen appetite for perpetuity of life was much abated. I grew heartily ashamed of the pleasing visions I had formed; and thought no tyrant could invent a death into which I would not run with pleasure, from such a life. The king heard of all that had passed between me and my friends upon this occasion, and rallied me very pleasantly; wishing I could send a couple of *struldbrugs* to my own country, to arm our people against the fear of death; but this, it seems, is forbidden by the fundamental laws of the kingdom, or else I should have been well content with the trouble and expense of transporting them.

I could not but agree, that the laws of this kingdom relative to the *struldbrugs* were founded upon the strongest reasons, and such as any other country would be under the necessity of enacting, in the like circumstances. Otherwise, as avarice is the necessary consequence of old age, those immortals would in time become proprietors of the whole nation, and engross the civil power, which, for want of abilities to manage, must end in the ruin of the public.

11

THE AUTHOR LEAVES LUGGNAGG, AND SAILS TO JAPAN. FROM THENCE HE RETURNS IN A DUTCH SHIP TO AMSTERDAM, AND FROM AMSTERDAM TO ENGLAND.

I thought this account of the *struldbrugs* might be some entertainment to the reader, because it seems to be a little out of the common way; at least I do not remember to have met the like in any book of travels that has come to my hands: and if I am deceived, my excuse must be, that it is necessary for travellers who describe the same country, very often to agree in dwelling on the same particulars, without deserving the censure of having borrowed or transcribed from those who wrote before them.

There is indeed a perpetual commerce between this kingdom and the great empire of Japan; and it is very probable, that the Japanese authors may have given some account of the *struldbrugs*; but my stay in Japan was so short, and I was so entirely a stranger to the language, that I was not qualified to make any inquiries. But I hope the Dutch, upon this notice, will be curious and able enough to supply my defects.

His majesty having often pressed me to accept some employment in his court, and finding me absolutely determined to return to my native country, was pleased to give me his license to depart; and honoured me with a letter of recommendation, under his own hand, to the Emperor of Japan. He likewise presented me with four hundred and forty-four large pieces of gold (this nation delighting in even numbers), and a red diamond, which I sold in England for eleven hundred pounds.

On the 6th of May, 1709, I took a solemn leave of his majesty, and all my friends. This prince was so gracious as to order a guard to conduct me to Glanguenstald, which is a royal port to the south-west part of the island. In six days I found a vessel ready to carry me to Japan, and spent fifteen days in the voyage. We landed at a small port-town called Xamoschi, situated on the south-east part of Japan; the town lies on the western point, where there is a narrow strait leading northward into along arm of the sea, upon the north-west part of which, Yedo, the metropolis, stands. At landing, I showed the custom-house officers my letter from the king of Luggnagg to his imperial majesty. They knew the seal perfectly well; it was as broad as the palm of my hand. The impression was, *A king lifting up a lame beggar from the earth*. The magistrates of the town, hearing of my letter, received me as a public minister. They provided me with carriages and servants, and bore my charges to Yedo; where I was admitted to an audience, and delivered my letter, which was opened with great ceremony, and explained to the Emperor by an interpreter, who then gave me notice, by his majesty's order, "that I should signify my request, and, whatever it were, it should be granted, for the sake of his royal brother of Luggnagg." This interpreter was a person employed to transact affairs with the Hollanders. He soon conjectured, by my countenance, that I was a European, and therefore repeated his majesty's commands in Low Dutch, which he spoke perfectly well. I answered, as I had before determined, "that I was a Dutch merchant, shipwrecked in a very remote country, whence I had travelled by sea and land to Luggnagg, and then took shipping for Japan; where I knew my countrymen often traded, and with some of these I hoped to get an opportunity of returning into Europe: I therefore most humbly entreated his royal favour, to give order that I should be conducted in safety to Nangasac." To this I added another petition, "that for the sake of my patron the king of Luggnagg, his majesty would condescend to excuse my performing the ceremony imposed on my countrymen, of trampling upon the crucifix: because I had been thrown into his kingdom by my misfortunes, without any intention of trading." When this latter petition was interpreted to the Emperor, he seemed a little surprised; and said, "he believed I was the first of my countrymen who ever made any scruple in this point; and that he began to doubt, whether I was a real Hollander, or not; but rather suspected I must be a Christian. However, for the reasons I had offered, but chiefly to gratify the king of Luggnagg by an uncommon mark of his favour, he would comply with the singularity of my humour; but the affair must be managed with dexterity, and his officers should be commanded to let me pass, as it were by forgetfulness. For he assured me, that if the secret should be discovered by my countrymen the Dutch, they would cut my throat in the voyage." I returned my thanks, by the interpreter, for so unusual a favour; and some troops being at that time on their march to Nangasac, the commanding officer had orders to convey me safe thither, with particular instructions about the business of the crucifix.

On the 9th day of June, 1709, I arrived at Nangasac, after a very long and troublesome journey. I soon fell into the company of some Dutch sailors belonging to the Amboyna, of Amsterdam, a stout ship of 450 tons. I had lived long in Holland, pursuing my studies at Leyden, and I spoke Dutch well. The seamen soon knew whence I came last: they were curious to inquire into my voyages and course of life. I made up a story as short and probable as I could, but concealed the greatest part. I knew many persons in Holland. I was able to invent names for my parents, whom I pretended to be obscure people in the province of Gelderland. I would have given the captain (one Theodorus Vangrult) what he pleased to ask for my voyage to Holland; but understanding I was a surgeon, he was contented to take half the usual rate, on condition that I would serve him in the way of my calling. Before we took shipping, I was often asked by some of the crew, whether I had performed the ceremony above mentioned? I evaded the question by general answers; "that I had satisfied the Emperor and court in all particulars." However, a malicious rogue of a skipper went to an officer, and pointing to me, told him, "I had not yet trampled on the crucifix;" but the other, who had received instructions to let me pass, gave the rascal twenty strokes on the shoulders with a bamboo; after which I was no more troubled with such questions.

Nothing happened worth mentioning in this voyage. We sailed with a fair wind to the Cape of Good Hope, where we staid only to take in fresh water. On the 10th of April, 1710, we arrived safe at Amsterdam, having lost only three men by sickness in the voyage, and a fourth, who fell from the foremast into the sea, not far from the coast of Guinea. From Amsterdam I soon after set sail for England, in a small vessel belonging to that city.

On the 16th of April we put in at the Downs. I landed next morning, and saw once more my native country, after an absence of five years and six months complete. I went straight to Redriff, where I arrived the same day at two in the afternoon, and found my wife and family in good health.

IV
A VOYAGE TO THE COUNTRY OF THE HOUYHNHNMS

I

THE AUTHOR SETS OUT AS CAPTAIN OF A SHIP. HIS MEN CONSPIRE AGAINST HIM, CONFINE HIM A LONG TIME TO HIS CABIN, AND SET HIM ON SHORE IN AN UNKNOWN LAND. HE TRAVELS UP INTO THE COUNTRY. THE YAHOOS, A STRANGE SORT OF ANIMAL, DESCRIBED. THE AUTHOR MEETS TWO HOUYHNHNMS.

I continued at home with my wife and children about five months, in a very happy condition, if I could have learned the lesson of knowing when I was well. I left my poor wife big with child, and accepted an advantageous offer made me to be captain of the Adventurer, a stout merchantman of 350 tons: for I understood navigation well, and being grown weary of a surgeon's employment at sea, which, however, I could exercise upon occasion, I took a skilful young man of that calling, one Robert Purefoy, into my ship. We set sail from Portsmouth upon the 7th day of September, 1710; on the 14th we met with Captain Pocock, of Bristol, at Teneriffe, who was going to the bay of Campechy to cut logwood. On the 16th, he was parted from us by a storm; I heard since my return, that his ship foundered, and none escaped but one cabin boy. He was an honest man, and a good sailor, but a little too positive in his own opinions, which was the cause of his destruction, as it has been with several others; for if he had followed my advice, he might have been safe at home with his family at this time, as well as myself.

I had several men who died in my ship of calentures, so that I was forced to get recruits out of Barbadoes and the Leeward Islands, where I touched, by the direction of the merchants who employed me; which I had soon too much cause to repent: for I found afterwards, that most of them had been buccaneers. I had fifty hands onboard; and my orders were, that I should trade with the Indians in the South-Sea, and make what discoveries I could. These rogues, whom I had picked up, debauched my other men, and they all formed a conspiracy to seize the ship, and secure me; which they did one morning, rushing into my cabin, and binding me hand and foot, threatening to throw me overboard, if I offered to stir. I told them, "I was their prisoner, and would submit." This they made me swear to do, and then they unbound me, only fastening one of my legs with a chain, near my bed, and placed a sentry at my door with his piece charged, who was commanded to shoot me dead if I attempted my liberty. They sent me own victuals and drink, and took the government of the ship to themselves. Their design was to turn pirates and, plunder the Spaniards, which they could not do till they got more men. But first they resolved to sell the goods in the ship, and then go to Madagascar for recruits, several among them having died since my confinement. They sailed many weeks, and traded with the Indians; but I knew not what course they took, being kept a close prisoner in my cabin, and expecting nothing less than to be murdered, as they often threatened me.

Upon the 9th day of May, 1711, one James Welch came down to my cabin, and said, "he had orders from the captain to set me ashore." I expostulated with him, but in vain; neither would he so much as tell me who their new captain was. They forced me into the long-boat, letting me put on my best suit of clothes, which were as good as new, and take a small bundle of linen, but no arms, except my hanger; and they were so civil as not to search my pockets, into which I conveyed what money I had, with some other little necessaries. They rowed about a league, and then set me down on a strand. I desired them to tell me what country it was. They all swore, "they knew no more than myself;" but said, "that the captain" (as they called him) "was resolved, after they had sold the lading, to get rid of me in the first place where they could discover land." They pushed off immediately, advising me to make haste for fear of being overtaken by the tide, and so bade me farewell.

In this desolate condition I advanced forward, and soon got upon firm ground, where I sat down on a bank to rest myself, and consider what I had best do. When I was a little refreshed, I went up into the country, resolving to deliver myself to the first savages I should meet, and purchase my life from them by some bracelets, glass rings, and other toys, which sailors usually provide themselves with in those voyages, and whereof I had some about me. The land was divided by long rows of trees, not regularly planted, but naturally growing; there was great plenty of grass, and several fields of oats. I walked very circumspectly, for fear of being surprised, or suddenly shot with an arrow from behind, or on either side. I fell into a beaten road, where I saw many tracts of human feet, and some of cows, but most of horses. At last I beheld several animals in a field, and one or two of the same kind sitting in trees. Their shape was very singular and deformed, which a little discomposed me, so that I lay down behind a thicket to observe them better. Some of them coming forward near the place where I lay, gave me an opportunity of distinctly marking their form. Their heads and breasts were covered with a thick hair, some frizzled, and others lank; they had beards like goats, and a long ridge of hair down their backs, and the fore parts of their legs and feet; but the rest of their bodies was bare, so that I might see their skins, which were of a brown buff colour. They had no tails, nor any hair at all on their buttocks, except about the anus, which, I presume, nature had placed there to defend them as they sat on the ground, for this posture they used, as well as lying down, and often stood on their hind feet. They climbed high trees as nimbly as a squirrel, for they had strong extended claws before and behind, terminating in sharp points, and hooked. They would often spring, and bound, and leap, with prodigious agility. The females were not so large as the males; they had long lank hair on their heads, but none on their faces, nor any thing more than a sort of down on the rest of their bodies, except about the anus and pudenda. The dugs hung between their fore feet, and often reached almost to the ground as they walked. The hair of both sexes was of several colours, brown, red, black, and yellow. Upon the whole, I never beheld, in all my travels, so disagreeable an animal, or one against which I naturally conceived so strong an antipathy. So that, thinking I had seen enough, full of contempt and aversion, I got up, and pursued the beaten road, hoping it might direct me to the cabin of some Indian. I had not got far, when I met one of these creatures full in my way, and coming up directly to me. The ugly monster, when he saw me, distorted several ways, every feature of his visage, and stared, as at an object he had never seen before; then approaching nearer, lifted up his fore-paw, whether out of curiosity or mischief I could not tell; but I drew my hanger, and gave him a good blow with the flat side of it, for I durst not strike with the edge, fearing the inhabitants might be provoked against me, if they should come to know that I had killed or maimed any of their cattle. When the beast felt the smart, he drew back, and roared so loud, that a herd of at least forty came flocking about me from the next field, howling and making odious faces; but I ran to the body of a tree, and leaning my back against it, kept them off by waving my hanger. Several of this cursed brood, getting hold of the branches behind, leaped up into the tree, whence they began to discharge their excrements on my head; however, I escaped pretty well by sticking close to the stem of the tree, but was almost stifled with the filth, which fell about me on every side.

In the midst of this distress, I observed them all to run away on a sudden as fast as they could; at which I ventured to leave the tree and pursue the road, wondering what it was that could put them into this fright. But looking on my left hand, I saw a horse walking softly in the field; which my persecutors having sooner discovered, was the cause of their flight. The horse started a little, when he came near me, but soon recovering himself, looked full in my face with manifest tokens of wonder; he viewed my hands and feet, walking round me several times. I would have pursued my journey, but he placed himself directly in the way, yet looking with a very mild aspect, never offering the least violence. We stood gazing at each other for some time; at last I took the boldness to reach my hand towards his neck with a design to stroke it, using the common style and whistle of jockeys, when they are going to handle a strange horse. But this animal seemed to receive my civilities with disdain, shook his head, and bent his brows, softly raising up his right fore-foot to remove my hand. Then he neighed three or four times, but in so different a cadence, that I almost began to think he was speaking to himself, in some language of his own.

While he and I were thus employed, another horse came up; who applying himself to the first in a very formal manner, they gently struck each other's right hoof before, neighing several times by turns, and varying the sound, which seemed to be almost articulate. They went some paces off, as if it were to confer together, walking side by side, backward and forward, like persons deliberating upon some affair of weight, but often turning their eyes towards me, as it were to watch that I might not escape. I was amazed to see such actions and behaviour in brute beasts; and concluded with myself, that if the inhabitants of this country were endued with a proportionable degree of reason, they must needs be the wisest people upon earth. This thought gave me so much comfort, that I resolved to go forward, until I could discover some house or village, or meet with any of the natives, leaving the two horses to discourse together as they pleased. But the first, who was a dapple gray, observing me to steal off, neighed after me in so expressive a tone, that I fancied myself to understand what he meant; whereupon I turned back, and came near to him to expect his farther commands: but concealing my fear as much as I could, for I began to be in some pain how this adventure might terminate; and the reader will easily believe I did not much like my present situation.

The two horses came up close to me, looking with great earnestness upon my face and hands. The gray steed rubbed my hat all round with his right fore-hoof, and discomposed it so much that I was forced to adjust it better by taking it off and settling it again; whereat, both he and his companion (who was a brown bay) appeared to be much surprised: the latter felt the lappet of my coat, and finding it to hang loose about me, they both looked with new signs of wonder. He stroked my right hand, seeming to admire the softness and colour; but he squeezed it so hard between his hoof and his pastern, that I was forced to roar; after which they both touched me with all possible tenderness. They were under great perplexity about my shoes and stockings, which they felt very often, neighing to each other, and using various gestures, not unlike those of a philosopher, when he would attempt to solve some new and difficult phenomenon.

Upon the whole, the behaviour of these animals was so orderly and rational, so acute and judicious, that I at last concluded they must needs be magicians, who had thus metamorphosed themselves upon some design, and seeing a stranger in the way, resolved to divert themselves with him; or, perhaps, were really amazed at the sight of a man so very different in habit, feature, and complexion, from those who might probably live in so remote a climate. Upon the strength of this reasoning, I ventured to address them in the following manner: "Gentlemen, if you be conjurers, as I have good cause to believe, you can understand my language; therefore I make bold to let your worships know that I am a poor distressed Englishman, driven by his misfortunes upon your coast; and I entreat one of you to let me ride upon his back, as if he were a real horse, to some house or village where I can be relieved. In return of which favour, I will make you a present of this knife and bracelet," taking them out of my pocket. The two creatures stood silent while I spoke, seeming to listen with great attention, and when I had ended, they neighed frequently towards each other, as if they were engaged in serious conversation. I plainly observed that their language expressed the passions very well, and the words might, with little pains, be resolved into an alphabet more easily than the Chinese.

I could frequently distinguish the word *Yahoo*, which was repeated by each of them several times: and although it was impossible for me to conjecture what it meant, yet while the two horses were busy in conversation, I endeavoured to practise this word upon my tongue; and as soon as they were silent, I boldly pronounced *Yahoo* in a loud voice, imitating at the same time, as near as I could, the neighing of a horse; at which they were both visibly surprised; and the gray repeated the same word twice, as if he meant to teach me the right accent; wherein I spoke after him as well as I could, and found myself perceivably to improve every time, though very far from any degree of perfection. Then the bay tried me with a second word, much harder to be pronounced; but reducing it to the English orthography, may be spelt thus, *Houyhnhnm*. I did not succeed in this so well as in the former; but after two or three farther trials, I had better fortune; and they both appeared amazed at my capacity.

After some further discourse, which I then conjectured might relate to me, the two friends took their leaves, with the same compliment of striking each other's hoof; and the gray made me signs that I should walk before him; wherein I thought it prudent to comply, till I could find a better director. When I offered to slacken my pace, he would cry *hhuun hhuun*: I guessed his meaning, and gave him to understand, as well as I could, "that I was weary, and not able to walk faster;" upon which he would stand awhile to let me rest.

2

THE AUTHOR CONDUCTED BY A HOUYHNHNM TO HIS HOUSE. THE HOUSE DESCRIBED. THE AUTHOR'S RECEPTION. THE FOOD OF THE HOUYHNHNMS. THE AUTHOR IN DISTRESS FOR WANT OF MEAT. IS AT LAST RELIEVED. HIS MANNER OF FEEDING IN THIS COUNTRY.

Having travelled about three miles, we came to a long kind of building, made of timber stuck in the ground, and wattled across; the roof was low and covered with straw. I now began to be a little comforted; and took out some toys, which travellers usually carry for presents to the savage Indians of America, and other parts, in hopes the people of the house would be thereby encouraged to receive me kindly. The horse made me a sign to go in first; it was a large room with a smooth clay floor, and a rack and manger, extending the whole length on one side. There were three nags and two mares, not eating, but some of them sitting down upon their hams, which I very much wondered at; but wondered more to see the rest employed in domestic business; these seemed but ordinary cattle. However, this confirmed my first opinion, that a people who could so far civilise brute animals, must needs excel in wisdom all the nations of the world. The gray came in just after, and thereby prevented any ill treatment which the others might have given me. He neighed to them several times in a style of authority, and received answers.

Beyond this room there were three others, reaching the length of the house, to which you passed through three doors, opposite to each other, in the manner of a vista. We went through the second room towards the third. Here the gray walked in first, beckoning me to attend: I waited in the second room, and got ready my presents for the master and mistress of the house; they were two knives, three bracelets of false pearls, a small looking-glass, and a bead necklace. The horse neighed three or four times, and I waited to hear some answers in a human voice, but I heard no other returns than in the same dialect, only one or two a little shriller than his. I began to think that this house must belong to some person of great note among them, because there appeared so much ceremony before I could gain admittance. But, that a man of quality should be served all by horses, was beyond my comprehension. I feared my brain was disturbed by my sufferings and misfortunes. I roused myself, and looked about me in the room where I was left alone: this was furnished like the first, only after a more elegant manner. I rubbed my eyes often, but the same objects still occurred. I pinched my arms and sides to awake myself, hoping I might be in a dream. I then absolutely concluded, that all these appearances could be nothing else but necromancy and magic. But I had no time to pursue these reflections; for the gray horse came to the door, and made me a sign to follow him into the third room where I saw a very comely mare, together with a colt and foal, sitting on their haunches upon mats of straw, not unartfully made, and perfectly neat and clean.

The mare soon after my entrance rose from her mat, and coming up close, after having nicely observed my hands and face, gave me a most contemptuous look; and turning to the horse, I heard the word *Yahoo* often repeated betwixt them; the meaning of which word I could not then comprehend, although it was the first I had learned to pronounce. But I was soon better informed, to my everlasting mortification; for the horse, beckoning to me with his head, and repeating the *hhuun, hhuun*, as he did upon the road, which I understood was to attend him, led me out into a kind of court, where was another building, at some distance from the house. Here we entered, and I saw three of those detestable creatures, which I first met after my landing, feeding upon roots, and the flesh of some animals, which I afterwards found to be that of asses and dogs, and now and then a cow, dead by accident or disease. They were all tied by the neck with strong withes fastened to a beam; they held their food between the claws of their fore feet, and tore it with their teeth.

The master horse ordered a sorrel nag, one of his servants, to untie the largest of these animals, and take him into the yard. The beast and I were brought close together, and by our countenances diligently compared both by master and servant, who thereupon repeated several times the word *Yahoo*. My horror and astonishment are not to be described, when I observed in this abominable animal, a perfect human figure: the face of it indeed was flat and broad, the nose depressed, the lips large, and the mouth wide; but these differences are common to all savage nations, where the lineaments of the countenance are distorted, by the natives suffering their infants to lie grovelling on the earth, or by carrying them on their backs, nuzzling with their face against the mothers' shoulders. The fore-feet of the *Yahoo* differed from my hands in nothing else but the length of the nails, the coarseness and brownness of the palms, and the hairiness on the backs. There was the same resemblance between our feet, with the same differences; which I knew very well, though the horses did not, because of my shoes and stockings; the same in every part of our bodies except as to hairiness and colour, which I have already described.

The great difficulty that seemed to stick with the two horses, was to see the rest of my body so very different from that of a *Yahoo*, for which I was obliged to my clothes, whereof they had no conception. The sorrel nag offered me a root, which he held (after their manner, as we shall describe in its proper place) between his hoof and pastern; I took it in my hand, and, having smelt it, returned it to him again as civilly as I could. He brought out of the *Yahoos'* kennel a piece of ass's flesh; but it smelt so offensively that I turned from it with loathing: he then threw it to the *Yahoo*, by whom it was greedily devoured. He afterwards showed me a wisp of hay, and a fetlock full of oats; but I shook my head, to signify that neither of these were food for me. And indeed I now apprehended that I must absolutely starve, if I did not get to some of my own species; for as to those filthy *Yahoos*, although there were few greater lovers of mankind at that time than myself, yet I confess I never saw any sensitive being so detestable on all accounts; and the more I came near them the more hateful they grew, while I stayed in that country. This the master horse observed by my behaviour, and therefore sent the *Yahoo* back to his kennel. He then put his fore-hoof to his mouth, at which I was much surprised, although he did it with ease, and with a motion that appeared perfectly natural, and made other signs, to know what I would eat; but I could not return him such an answer as he was able to apprehend; and if he had understood me, I did not see how it was possible to contrive any way for finding myself nourishment. While we were thus engaged, I observed a cow passing by, whereupon I pointed to her, and expressed a desire to go and milk her. This had its effect; for he led me back into the house, and ordered a mare-servant to open a room, where a good store of milk lay in earthen and wooden vessels, after a very orderly and cleanly manner. She gave me a large bowlful, of which I drank very heartily, and found myself well refreshed.

About noon, I saw coming towards the house a kind of vehicle drawn like a sledge by four *Yahoos*. There was in it an old steed, who seemed to be of quality; he alighted with his hind-feet forward, having by accident got a hurt in his left fore-foot. He came to dine with our horse, who received him with great civility. They dined in the best room, and had oats boiled in milk for the second course, which the old horse ate warm, but the rest cold. Their mangers were placed circular in the middle of the room, and divided into several partitions, round which they sat on their haunches, upon bosses of straw. In the middle was a large rack, with angles answering to every partition of the manger; so that each horse and mare ate their own hay, and their own mash of oats and milk, with much decency and regularity. The behaviour of the young colt and foal appeared very modest, and that of the master and mistress extremely cheerful and complaisant to their guest. The gray ordered me to stand by him; and much discourse passed between him and his friend concerning me, as I found by the stranger's often looking on me, and the frequent repetition of the word *Yahoo*.

I happened to wear my gloves, which the master gray observing, seemed perplexed, discovering signs of wonder what I had done to my fore-feet. He put his hoof three or four times to them, as if he would signify, that I should reduce them to their former shape, which I presently did, pulling off both my gloves, and putting them into my pocket. This occasioned farther talk; and I saw the company was pleased with my behaviour, whereof I soon found the good effects. I was ordered to speak the few words I understood; and while they were at dinner, the master taught me the names for oats, milk, fire, water, and some others, which I could readily pronounce after him, having from my youth a great facility in learning languages.

When dinner was done, the master horse took me aside, and by signs and words made me understand the concern he was in that I had nothing to eat. Oats in their tongue are called *hlunnh*. This word I pronounced two or three times; for although I had refused them at first, yet, upon second thoughts, I considered that I could contrive to make of them a kind of bread, which might be sufficient, with milk, to keep me alive, till I could make my escape to some other country, and to creatures of my own species. The horse immediately ordered a white mare servant of his family to bring me a good quantity of oats in a sort of wooden tray. These I heated before the fire, as well as I could, and rubbed them till the husks came off, which I made a shift to winnow from the grain. I ground and beat them between two stones; then took water, and made them into a paste or cake, which I toasted at the fire and eat warm with milk. It was at first a very insipid diet, though common enough in many parts of Europe, but grew tolerable by time; and having been often reduced to hard fare in my life, this was not the first experiment I had made how easily nature is satisfied. And I cannot but observe, that I never had one hours sickness while I stayed in this island. It is true, I sometimes made a shift to catch a rabbit, or bird, by springs made of *Yahoo's* hairs; and I often gathered wholesome herbs, which I boiled, and ate as salads with my bread; and now and then, for a rarity, I made a little butter, and drank the whey. I was at first at a great loss for salt, but custom soon reconciled me to the want of it; and I am confident that the frequent use of salt among us is an effect of luxury, and was first introduced only as a provocative to drink, except where it is necessary for preserving flesh in long voyages, or in places remote from great markets; for we observe no animal to be fond of it but man, and as to myself, when I left this country, it was a great while before I could endure the taste of it in anything that I ate.

This is enough to say upon the subject of my diet, wherewith other travellers fill their books, as if the readers were personally concerned whether we fare well or ill. However, it was necessary to mention this matter, lest the world should think it impossible that I could find sustenance for three years in such a country, and among such inhabitants.

When it grew towards evening, the master horse ordered a place for me to lodge in; it was but six yards from the house and separated from the stable of the *Yahoos*. Here I got some straw, and covering myself with my own clothes, slept very sound. But I was in a short time better accommodated, as the reader shall know hereafter, when I come to treat more particularly about my way of living.

3

THE AUTHOR STUDIES TO LEARN THE LANGUAGE.
THE HOUYHNHNM, HIS MASTER, ASSISTS IN
TEACHING HIM. THE LANGUAGE DESCRIBED.
SEVERAL HOUYHNHNMS OF QUALITY COME OUT OF
CURIOSITY TO SEE THE AUTHOR. HE GIVES HIS
MASTER A SHORT ACCOUNT OF HIS VOYAGE.

My principal endeavour was to learn the language, which my master (for so I shall henceforth call him), and his children, and every servant of his house, were desirous to teach me; for they looked upon it as a prodigy, that a brute animal should discover such marks of a rational creature. I pointed to every thing, and inquired the name of it, which I wrote down in my journal-book when I was alone, and corrected my bad accent by desiring those of the family to pronounce it often. In this employment, a sorrel nag, one of the under-servants, was very ready to assist me.

In speaking, they pronounced through the nose and throat, and their language approaches nearest to the High-Dutch, or German, of any I know in Europe; but is much more graceful and significant. The emperor Charles V. made almost the same observation, when he said "that if he were to speak to his horse, it should be in High-Dutch."

The curiosity and impatience of my master were so great, that he spent many hours of his leisure to instruct me. He was convinced (as he afterwards told me) that I must be a *Yahoo*; but my teachableness, civility, and cleanliness, astonished him; which were qualities altogether opposite to those animals. He was most perplexed about my clothes, reasoning sometimes with himself, whether they were a part of my body: for I never pulled them off till the family were asleep, and got them on before they waked in the morning. My master was eager to learn "whence I came; how I acquired those appearances of reason, which I discovered in all my actions; and to know my story from my own mouth, which he hoped he should soon do by the great proficiency I made in learning and pronouncing their words and sentences." To help my memory, I formed all I learned into the English alphabet, and writ the words down, with the translations. This last, after some time, I ventured to do in my master's presence. It cost me much trouble to explain to him what I was doing; for the inhabitants have not the least idea of books or literature.

In about ten weeks time, I was able to understand most of his questions; and in three months, could give him some tolerable answers. He was extremely curious to know "from what part of the country I came, and how I was taught to imitate a rational creature; because the *Yahoos* (whom he saw I exactly resembled in my head, hands, and face, that were only visible), with some appearance of cunning, and the strongest disposition to mischief, were observed to be the most unteachable of all brutes." I answered, "that I came over the sea, from a far place, with many others of my own kind, in a great hollow vessel made of the bodies of trees: that my companions forced me to land on this coast, and then left me to shift for myself." It was with some difficulty, and by the help of many signs, that I brought him to understand me. He replied, "that I must needs be mistaken, or that I said the thing which was not;" for they have no word in their language to express lying or falsehood. "He knew it was impossible that there could be a country beyond the sea, or that a parcel of brutes could move a wooden vessel whither they pleased upon water. He was sure no *Houyhnhnm* alive could make such a vessel, nor would trust *Yahoos* to manage it."

The word *Houyhnhnm*, in their tongue, signifies a *horse*, and, in its etymology, the *perfection of nature*. I told my master, "that I was at a loss for expression, but would improve as fast as I could; and hoped, in a short time, I should be able to tell him wonders." He was pleased to direct his own mare, his colt, and foal, and the servants of the family, to take all opportunities of instructing me; and every day, for two or three hours, he was at the same pains himself. Several horses and mares of quality in the neighbourhood came often to our house, upon the report spread of "a wonderful *Yahoo*, that could speak like a *Houyhnhnm*, and seemed, in his words and actions, to discover some glimmerings of reason." These delighted to converse with me: they put many questions, and received such answers as I was able to return. By all these advantages I made so great a progress, that, in five months from my arrival I understood whatever was spoken, and could express myself tolerably well.

The *Houyhnhnms*, who came to visit my master out of a design of seeing and talking with me, could hardly believe me to be a right *Yahoo*, because my body had a different covering from others of my kind. They were astonished to observe me without the usual hair or skin, except on my head, face, and hands; but I discovered that secret to my master upon an accident which happened about a fortnight before.

I have already told the reader, that every night, when the family were gone to bed, it was my custom to strip, and cover myself with my clothes. It happened, one morning early, that my master sent for me by the sorrel nag, who was his valet. When he came I was fast asleep, my clothes fallen off on one side, and my shirt above my waist. I awaked at the noise he made, and observed him to deliver his message in some disorder; after which he went to my master, and in a great fright gave him a very confused account of what he had seen. This I presently discovered, for, going as soon as I was dressed to pay my attendance upon his honour, he asked me "the meaning of what his servant had reported, that I was not the same thing when I slept, as I appeared to be at other times; that his vale assured him, some part of me was white, some yellow, at least not so white, and some brown."

I had hitherto concealed the secret of my dress, in order to distinguish myself, as much as possible, from that cursed race of *Yahoos*; but now I found it in vain to do so any longer. Besides, I considered that my clothes and shoes would soon wear out, which already were in a declining condition, and must be supplied by some contrivance from the hides of *Yahoos*, or other brutes; whereby the whole secret would be known. I therefore told my master, "that in the country whence I came, those of my kind always covered their bodies with the hairs of certain animals prepared by art, as well for decency as to avoid the inclemencies of air, both hot and cold; of which, as to my own person, I would give him immediate conviction, if he pleased to command me: only desiring his excuse, if I did not expose those parts that nature taught us to conceal." He said, "my discourse was all very strange, but especially the last part; for he could not understand, why nature should teach us to conceal what nature had given; that neither himself nor family were ashamed of any parts of their bodies; but, however, I might do as I pleased." Whereupon I first unbuttoned my coat, and pulled it off. I did the same with my waistcoat. I drew off my shoes, stockings, and breeches. I let my shirt down to my waist, and drew up the bottom; fastening it like a girdle about my middle, to hide my nakedness.

My master observed the whole performance with great signs of curiosity and admiration. He took up all my clothes in his pastern, one piece after another, and examined them diligently; he then stroked my body very gently, and looked round me several times; after which, he said, it was plain I must be a perfect *Yahoo*; but that I differed very much from the rest of my species in the softness, whiteness, and smoothness of my skin; my want of hair in several parts of my body; the shape and shortness of my claws behind and before; and my affectation of walking continually on my two hinder feet. He desired to see no more; and gave me leave to put on my clothes again, for I was shuddering with cold.

I expressed my uneasiness at his giving me so often the appellation of *Yahoo*, an odious animal, for which I had so utter a hatred and contempt: I begged he would forbear applying that word to me, and make the same order in his family and among his friends whom he suffered to see me. I requested likewise, "that the secret of my having a false covering to my body, might be known to none but himself, at least as long as my present clothing should last; for as to what the sorrel nag, his valet, had observed, his honour might command him to conceal it."

All this my master very graciously consented to; and thus the secret was kept till my clothes began to wear out, which I was forced to supply by several contrivances that shall hereafter be mentioned. In the meantime, he desired "I would go on with my utmost diligence to learn their language, because he was more astonished at my capacity for speech and reason, than at the figure of my body, whether it were covered or not;" adding, "that he waited with some impatience to hear the wonders which I promised to tell him."

Thenceforward he doubled the pains he had been at to instruct me: he brought me into all company, and made them treat me with civility; "because," as he told them, privately, "this would put me into good humour, and make me more diverting."

Every day, when I waited on him, beside the trouble he was at in teaching, he would ask me several questions concerning myself, which I answered as well as I could, and by these means he had already received some general ideas, though very imperfect. It would be tedious to relate the several steps by which I advanced to a more regular conversation; but the first account I gave of myself in any order and length was to this purpose:

"That I came from a very far country, as I already had attempted to tell him, with about fifty more of my own species; that we travelled upon the seas in a great hollow vessel made of wood, and larger than his honour's house. I described the ship to him in the best terms I could, and explained, by the help of my handkerchief displayed, how it was driven forward by the wind. That upon a quarrel among us, I was set on shore on this coast, where I walked forward, without knowing whither, till he delivered me from the persecution of those execrable *Yahoos*." He asked me, "who made the ship, and how it was possible that the *Houyhnhnms* of my country would leave it to the management of brutes?" My answer was, "that I durst proceed no further in my relation, unless he would give me his word and honour that he would not be offended, and then I would tell him the wonders I had so often promised." He agreed; and I went on by assuring him, that the ship was made by creatures like myself; who, in all the countries I had travelled, as well as in my own, were the only governing rational animals; and that upon my arrival hither, I was as much astonished to see the *Houyhnhnms* act like rational beings, as he, or his friends, could be, in finding some marks of reason in a creature he was pleased to call a *Yahoo*; to which I owned my resemblance in every part, but could not account for their degenerate and brutal nature. I said farther, "that if good fortune ever restored me to my native country, to relate my travels hither, as I resolved to do, everybody would believe, that I said the thing that was not, that I invented the story out of my own head; and (with all possible respect to himself, his family, and friends, and under his promise of not being offended) our countrymen would hardly think it probable that a *Houyhnhnm* should be the presiding creature of a nation, and a *Yahoo* the brute."

4

THE HOUYHNHNM'S NOTION OF TRUTH AND FALSEHOOD. THE AUTHOR'S DISCOURSE DISAPPROVED BY HIS MASTER. THE AUTHOR GIVES A MORE PARTICULAR ACCOUNT OF HIMSELF, AND THE ACCIDENTS OF HIS VOYAGE.

My master heard me with great appearances of uneasiness in his countenance; because doubting, or not believing, are so little known in this country, that the inhabitants cannot tell how to behave themselves under such circumstances. And I remember, in frequent discourses with my master concerning the nature of manhood in other parts of the world, having occasion to talk of lying and false representation, it was with much difficulty that he comprehended what I meant, although he had otherwise a most acute judgment. For he argued thus: "that the use of speech was to make us understand one another, and to receive information of facts; now, if any one said the thing which was not, these ends were defeated, because I cannot properly be said to understand him; and I am so far from receiving information, that he leaves me worse than in ignorance; for I am led to believe a thing black, when it is white, and short, when it is long." And these were all the notions he had concerning that faculty of lying, so perfectly well understood, and so universally practised, among human creatures.

To return from this digression. When I asserted that the *Yahoos* were the only governing animals in my country, which my master said was altogether past his conception, he desired to know, "whether we had *Houyhnhnms* among us, and what was their employment?" I told him, "we had great numbers; that in summer they grazed in the fields, and in winter were kept in houses with hay and oats, where *Yahoo* servants were employed to rub their skins smooth, comb their manes, pick their feet, serve them with food, and make their beds." "I understand you well," said my master: "it is now very plain, from all you have spoken, that whatever share of reason the *Yahoos* pretend to, the *Houyhnhnms* are your masters; I heartily wish our *Yahoos* would be so tractable." I begged "his honour would please to excuse me from proceeding any further, because I was very certain that the account he expected from me would be highly displeasing." But he insisted in commanding me to let him know the best and the worst. I told him "he should be obeyed." I owned "that the *Houyhnhnms* among us, whom we called horses, were the most generous and comely animals we had; that they excelled in strength and swiftness; and when they belonged to persons of quality, were employed in travelling, racing, or drawing chariots; they were treated with much kindness and care, till they fell into diseases, or became foundered in the feet; but then they were sold, and used to all kind of drudgery till they died; after which their skins were stripped, and sold for what they were worth, and their bodies left to be devoured by dogs and birds of prey. But the common race of horses had not so good fortune, being kept by farmers and carriers, and other mean people, who put them to greater labour, and fed them worse." I described, as well as I could, our way of riding; the shape and use of a bridle, a saddle, a spur, and a whip; of harness and wheels. I added, "that we fastened plates of a certain hard substance, called iron, at the bottom of their feet, to preserve their hoofs from being broken by the stony ways, on which we often travelled."

My master, after some expressions of great indignation, wondered "how we dared to venture upon a *Houyhnhnm's* back; for he was sure, that the weakest servant in his house would be able to shake off the strongest *Yahoo*; or by lying down and rolling on his back, squeeze the brute to death." I answered "that our horses were trained up, from three or four years old, to the several uses we intended them for; that if any of them proved intolerably vicious, they were employed for carriages; that they were severely beaten, while they were young, for any mischievous tricks; that the males, designed for the common use of riding or draught, were generally castrated about two years after their birth, to take down their spirits, and make them more tame and gentle; that they were indeed sensible of rewards and punishments; but his honour would please to consider, that they had not the least tincture of reason, any more than the *Yahoos* in this country."

It put me to the pains of many circumlocutions, to give my master a right idea of what I spoke; for their language does not abound in variety of words, because their wants and passions are fewer than among us. But it is impossible to express his noble resentment at our savage treatment of the *Houyhnhnm* race; particularly after I had explained the manner and use of castrating horses among us, to hinder them from propagating their kind, and to render them more servile. He said, "if it were possible there could be any country where *Yahoos* alone were endued with reason, they certainly must be the governing animal; because reason in time will always prevail against brutal strength. But, considering the frame of our bodies, and especially of mine, he thought no creature of equal bulk was so ill-contrived for employing that reason in the common offices of life;" whereupon he desired to know "whether those among whom I lived resembled me, or the *Yahoos* of his country?" I assured him, "that I was as well shaped as most of my age; but the younger, and the females, were much more soft and tender, and the skins of the latter generally as white as milk." He said, "I differed indeed from other *Yahoos*, being much more cleanly, and not altogether so deformed; but, in point of real advantage, he thought I differed for the worse: that my nails were of no use either to my fore or hinder feet; as to my fore feet, he could not properly call them by that name, for he never observed me to walk upon them; that they were too soft to bear the ground; that I generally went with them uncovered; neither was the covering I sometimes wore on them of the same shape, or so strong as that on my feet behind: that I could not walk with any security, for if either of my hinder feet slipped, I must inevitably fall." He then began to find fault with other parts of my body: "the flatness of my face, the prominence of my nose, mine eyes placed directly in front, so that I could not look on either side without turning my head: that I was not able to feed myself, without lifting one of my fore-feet to my mouth: and therefore nature had placed those joints to answer that necessity. He knew not what could be the use of those several clefts and divisions in my feet behind; that these were too soft to bear the hardness and sharpness of stones, without a covering made from the skin of some other brute; that my whole body wanted a fence against heat and cold, which I was forced to put on and off every day, with tediousness and trouble: and lastly, that he observed every animal in this country naturally to abhor the *Yahoos*, whom the weaker avoided, and the stronger drove from them. So that, supposing us to have the gift of reason, he could not see how it were possible to cure that natural antipathy, which every creature discovered against us; nor consequently how we could tame and render them serviceable. However, he would," as he said, "debate the matter no farther, because he was more desirous to know my own story, the country where I was born, and the several actions and events of my life, before I came hither."

I assured him, "how extremely desirous I was that he should be satisfied on every point; but I doubted much, whether it would be possible for me to explain myself on several subjects, whereof his honour could have no conception; because I saw nothing in his country to which I could resemble them; that, however, I would do my best, and strive to express myself by similitudes, humbly desiring his assistance when I wanted proper words;" which he was pleased to promise me.

I said, "my birth was of honest parents, in an island called England; which was remote from his country, as many days' journey as the strongest of his honour's servants could travel in the annual course of the sun; that I was bred a surgeon, whose trade it is to cure wounds and hurts in the body, gotten by accident or violence; that my country was governed by a female man, whom we called queen; that I left it to get riches, whereby I might maintain myself and family, when I should return; that, in my last voyage, I was commander of the ship, and had about fifty *Yahoos* under me, many of which died at sea, and I was forced to supply them by others picked out from several nations; that our ship was twice in danger of being sunk, the first time by a great storm, and the second by striking against a rock." Here my master interposed, by asking me, "how I could persuade strangers, out of different countries, to venture with me, after the losses I had sustained, and the hazards I had run?" I said, "they were fellows of desperate fortunes, forced to fly from the places of their birth on account of their poverty or their crimes. Some were undone by lawsuits; others spent all they had in drinking, whoring, and gaming; others fled for treason; many for murder, theft, poisoning, robbery, perjury, forgery, coining false money, for committing rapes, or sodomy; for flying from their colours, or deserting to the enemy; and most of them had broken prison; none of these durst return to their native countries, for fear of being hanged, or of starving in a jail; and therefore they were under the necessity of seeking a livelihood in other places."

During this discourse, my master was pleased to interrupt me several times. I had made use of many circumlocutions in describing to him the nature of the several crimes for which most of our crew had been forced to fly their country. This labour took up several days' conversation, before he was able to comprehend me. He was wholly at a loss to know what could be the use or necessity of practising those vices. To clear up which, I endeavoured to give some ideas of the desire of power and riches; of the terrible effects of lust, intemperance, malice, and envy. All this I was forced to define and describe by putting cases and making suppositions. After which, like one whose imagination was struck with something never seen or heard of before, he would lift up his eyes with amazement and indignation. Power, government, war, law, punishment, and a thousand other things, had no terms wherein that language could express them, which made the difficulty almost insuperable, to give my master any conception of what I meant. But being of an excellent understanding, much improved by contemplation and converse, he at last arrived at a competent knowledge of what human nature, in our parts of the world, is capable to perform, and desired I would give him some particular account of that land which we call Europe, but especially of my own country.

5

THE AUTHOR AT HIS MASTER'S COMMAND, INFORMS HIM OF THE STATE OF ENGLAND. THE CAUSES OF WAR AMONG THE PRINCES OF EUROPE. THE AUTHOR BEGINS TO EXPLAIN THE ENGLISH CONSTITUTION.

The reader may please to observe, that the following extract of many conversations I had with my master, contains a summary of the most material points which were discoursed at several times for above two years; his honour often desiring fuller satisfaction, as I farther improved in the *Houyhnhnm* tongue. I laid before him, as well as I could, the whole state of Europe; I discoursed of trade and manufactures, of arts and sciences; and the answers I gave to all the questions he made, as they arose upon several subjects, were a fund of conversation not to be exhausted. But I shall here only set down the substance of what passed between us concerning my own country, reducing it in order as well as I can, without any regard to time or other circumstances, while I strictly adhere to truth. My only concern is, that I shall hardly be able to do justice to my master's arguments and expressions, which must needs suffer by my want of capacity, as well as by a translation into our barbarous English.

In obedience, therefore, to his honour's commands, I related to him the Revolution under the Prince of Orange; the long war with France, entered into by the said prince, and renewed by his successor, the present queen, wherein the greatest powers of Christendom were engaged, and which still continued: I computed, at his request, "that about a million of *Yahoos* might have been killed in the whole progress of it; and perhaps a hundred or more cities taken, and five times as many ships burnt or sunk."

He asked me, "what were the usual causes or motives that made one country go to war with another?" I answered "they were innumerable; but I should only mention a few of the chief. Sometimes the ambition of princes, who never think they have land or people enough to govern; sometimes the corruption of ministers, who engage their master in a war, in order to stifle or divert the clamour of the subjects against their evil administration. Difference in opinions has cost many millions of lives: for instance, whether flesh be bread, or bread be flesh; whether the juice of a certain berry be blood or wine; whether whistling be a vice or a virtue; whether it be better to kiss a post, or throw it into the fire; what is the best colour for a coat, whether black, white, red, or gray; and whether it should be long or short, narrow or wide, dirty or clean; with many more. Neither are any wars so furious and bloody, or of so long a continuance, as those occasioned by difference in opinion, especially if it be in things indifferent.

"Sometimes the quarrel between two princes is to decide which of them shall dispossess a third of his dominions, where neither of them pretend to any right. Sometimes one prince quarrels with another for fear the other should quarrel with him. Sometimes a war is entered upon, because the enemy is too strong; and sometimes, because he is too weak. Sometimes our neighbours want the things which we have, or have the things which we want, and we both fight, till they take ours, or give us theirs. It is a very justifiable cause of a war, to invade a country after the people have been wasted by famine, destroyed by pestilence, or embroiled by factions among themselves. It is justifiable to enter into war against our nearest ally, when one of his towns lies convenient for us, or a territory of land, that would render our dominions round and complete. If a prince sends forces into a nation, where the people are poor and ignorant, he may lawfully put half of them to death, and make slaves of the rest, in order to civilize and reduce them from their barbarous way of living. It is a very kingly, honourable, and frequent practice, when one prince desires the assistance of another, to secure him against an invasion, that the assistant, when he has driven out the invader, should seize on the dominions himself, and kill, imprison, or banish, the prince he came to relieve. Alliance by blood, or marriage, is a frequent cause of war between princes; and the nearer the kindred is, the greater their disposition to quarrel; poor nations are hungry, and rich nations are proud; and pride and hunger will ever be at variance. For these reasons, the trade of a soldier is held the most honourable of all others; because a soldier is a *Yahoo* hired to kill, in cold blood, as many of his own species, who have never offended him, as possibly he can.

"There is likewise a kind of beggarly princes in Europe, not able to make war by themselves, who hire out their troops to richer nations, for so much a day to each man; of which they keep three-fourths to themselves, and it is the best part of their maintenance: such are those in many northern parts of Europe."

"What you have told me," said my master, "upon the subject of war, does indeed discover most admirably the effects of that reason you pretend to: however, it is happy that the shame is greater than the danger; and that nature has left you utterly incapable of doing much mischief. For, your mouths lying flat with your faces, you can hardly bite each other to any purpose, unless by consent. Then as to the claws upon your feet before and behind, they are so short and tender, that one of our *Yahoos* would drive a dozen of yours before him. And therefore, in recounting the numbers of those who have been killed in battle, I cannot but think you have said the thing which is not."

I could not forbear shaking my head, and smiling a little at his ignorance. And being no stranger to the art of war, I gave him a description of cannons, culverins, muskets, carabines, pistols, bullets, powder, swords, bayonets, battles, sieges, retreats, attacks, undermines, countermines, bombardments, sea fights, ships sunk with a thousand men, twenty thousand killed on each side, dying groans, limbs flying in the air, smoke, noise, confusion, trampling to death under horses' feet, flight, pursuit, victory; fields strewed with carcases, left for food to dogs and wolves and birds of prey; plundering, stripping, ravishing, burning, and destroying. And to set forth the valour of my own dear countrymen, I assured him, "that I had seen them blow up a hundred enemies at once in a siege, and as many in a ship, and beheld the dead bodies drop down in pieces from the clouds, to the great diversion of the spectators."

I was going on to more particulars, when my master commanded me silence. He said, "whoever understood the nature of *Yahoos*, might easily believe it possible for so vile an animal to be capable of every action I had named, if their strength and cunning equalled their malice. But as my discourse had increased his abhorrence of the whole species, so he found it gave him a disturbance in his mind to which he was wholly a stranger before. He thought his ears, being used to such abominable words, might, by degrees, admit them with less detestation: that although he hated the *Yahoos* of this country, yet he no more blamed them for their odious qualities, than he did a *gnnayh* (a bird of prey) for its cruelty, or a sharp stone for cutting his hoof. But when a creature pretending to reason could be capable of such enormities, he dreaded lest the corruption of that faculty might be worse than brutality itself. He seemed therefore confident, that, instead of reason we were only possessed of some quality fitted to increase our natural vices; as the reflection from a troubled stream returns the image of an ill shapen body, not only larger but more distorted."

He added, "that he had heard too much upon the subject of war, both in this and some former discourses. There was another point, which a little perplexed him at present. I had informed him, that some of our crew left their country on account of being ruined by law; that I had already explained the meaning of the word; but he was at a loss how it should come to pass, that the law, which was intended for every man's preservation, should be any man's ruin. Therefore he desired to be further satisfied what I meant by law, and the dispensers thereof, according to the present practice in my own country; because he thought nature and reason were sufficient guides for a reasonable animal, as we pretended to be, in showing us what he ought to do, and what to avoid."

I assured his honour, "that the law was a science in which I had not much conversed, further than by employing advocates, in vain, upon some injustices that had been done me: however, I would give him all the satisfaction I was able."

I said, "there was a society of men among us, bred up from their youth in the art of proving, by words multiplied for the purpose, that white is black, and black is white, according as they are paid. To this society all the rest of the people are slaves. For example, if my neighbour has a mind to my cow, he has a lawyer to prove that he ought to have my cow from me. I must then hire another to defend my right, it being against all rules of law that any man should be allowed to speak for himself. Now, in this case, I, who am the right owner, lie under two great disadvantages: first, my lawyer, being practised almost from his cradle in defending falsehood, is quite out of his element when he would be an advocate for justice, which is an unnatural office he always attempts with great awkwardness, if not with ill-will. The second disadvantage is, that my lawyer must proceed with great caution, or else he will be reprimanded by the judges, and abhorred by his brethren, as one that would lessen the practice of the law. And therefore I have but two methods to preserve my cow. The first is, to gain over my adversary's lawyer with a double fee, who will then betray his client by insinuating that he hath justice on his side. The second way is for my lawyer to make my cause appear as unjust as he can, by allowing the cow to belong to my adversary: and this, if it be skilfully done, will certainly bespeak the favour of the bench. Now your honour is to know, that these judges are persons appointed to decide all controversies of property, as well as for the trial of criminals, and picked out from the most dexterous lawyers, who are grown old or lazy; and having been biassed all their lives against truth and equity, lie under such a fatal necessity of favouring fraud, perjury, and oppression, that I have known some of them refuse a large bribe from the side where justice lay, rather than injure the faculty, by doing any thing unbecoming their nature or their office.

"It is a maxim among these lawyers that whatever has been done before, may legally be done again: and therefore they take special care to record all the decisions formerly made against common justice, and the general reason of mankind. These, under the name of precedents, they produce as authorities to justify the most iniquitous opinions; and the judges never fail of directing accordingly.

"In pleading, they studiously avoid entering into the merits of the cause; but are loud, violent, and tedious, in dwelling upon all circumstances which are not to the purpose. For instance, in the case already mentioned; they never desire to know what claim or title my adversary has to my cow; but whether the said cow were red or black; her horns long or short; whether the field I graze her in be round or square; whether she was milked at home or abroad; what diseases she is subject to, and the like; after which they consult precedents, adjourn the cause from time to time, and in ten, twenty, or thirty years, come to an issue.

"It is likewise to be observed, that this society has a peculiar cant and jargon of their own, that no other mortal can understand, and wherein all their laws are written, which they take special care to multiply; whereby they have wholly confounded the very essence of truth and falsehood, of right and wrong; so that it will take thirty years to decide, whether the field left me by my ancestors for six generations belongs to me, or to a stranger three hundred miles off.

"In the trial of persons accused for crimes against the state, the method is much more short and commendable: the judge first sends to sound the disposition of those in power, after which he can easily hang or save a criminal, strictly preserving all due forms of law."

Here my master interposing, said, "it was a pity, that creatures endowed with such prodigious abilities of mind, as these lawyers, by the description I gave of them, must certainly be, were not rather encouraged to be instructors of others in wisdom and knowledge." In answer to which I assured his honour, "that in all points out of their own trade, they were usually the most ignorant and stupid generation among us, the most despicable in common conversation, avowed enemies to all knowledge and learning, and equally disposed to pervert the general reason of mankind in every other subject of discourse as in that of their own profession."

6

A CONTINUATION OF THE STATE OF ENGLAND UNDER QUEEN ANNE. THE CHARACTER OF A FIRST MINISTER OF STATE IN EUROPEAN COURTS.

My master was yet wholly at a loss to understand what motives could incite this race of lawyers to perplex, disquiet, and weary themselves, and engage in a confederacy of injustice, merely for the sake of injuring their fellow-animals; neither could he comprehend what I meant in saying, they did it for hire. Whereupon I was at much pains to describe to him the use of money, the materials it was made of, and the value of the metals; "that when a *Yahoo* had got a great store of this precious substance, he was able to purchase whatever he had a mind to; the finest clothing, the noblest houses, great tracts of land, the most costly meats and drinks, and have his choice of the most beautiful females. Therefore since money alone was able to perform all these feats, our *Yahoos* thought they could never have enough of it to spend, or to save, as they found themselves inclined, from their natural bent either to profusion or avarice; that the rich man enjoyed the fruit of the poor man's labour, and the latter were a thousand to one in proportion to the former; that the bulk of our people were forced to live miserably, by labouring every day for small wages, to make a few live plentifully."

I enlarged myself much on these, and many other particulars to the same purpose; but his honour was still to seek; for he went upon a supposition, that all animals had a title to their share in the productions of the earth, and especially those who presided over the rest. Therefore he desired I would let him know, "what these costly meats were, and how any of us happened to want them?" Whereupon I enumerated as many sorts as came into my head, with the various methods of dressing them, which could not be done without sending vessels by sea to every part of the world, as well for liquors to drink as for sauces and innumerable other conveniences. I assured him "that this whole globe of earth must be at least three times gone round before one of our better female *Yahoos* could get her breakfast, or a cup to put it in." He said "that must needs be a miserable country which cannot furnish food for its own inhabitants. But what he chiefly wondered at was, how such vast tracts of ground as I described should be wholly without fresh water, and the people put to the necessity of sending over the sea for drink." I replied "that England (the dear place of my nativity) was computed to produce three times the quantity of food more than its inhabitants are able to consume, as well as liquors extracted from grain, or pressed out of the fruit of certain trees, which made excellent drink, and the same proportion in every other convenience of life. But, in order to feed the luxury and intemperance of the males, and the vanity of the females, we sent away the greatest part of our necessary things to other countries, whence, in return, we brought the materials of diseases, folly, and vice, to spend among ourselves. Hence it follows of necessity, that vast numbers of our people are compelled to seek their livelihood by begging, robbing, stealing, cheating, pimping, flattering, suborning, forswearing, forging, gaming, lying, fawning, hectoring, voting, scribbling, star-gazing, poisoning, whoring, canting, libelling, freethinking, and the like occupations:" every one of which terms I was at much pains to make him understand.

"That wine was not imported among us from foreign countries to supply the want of water or other drinks, but because it was a sort of liquid which made us merry by putting us out of our senses, diverted all melancholy thoughts, begat wild extravagant imaginations in the brain, raised our hopes and banished our fears, suspended every office of reason for a time, and deprived us of the use of our limbs, till we fell into a profound sleep; although it must be confessed, that we always awaked sick and dispirited; and that the use of this liquor filled us with diseases which made our lives uncomfortable and short.

"But beside all this, the bulk of our people supported themselves by furnishing the necessities or conveniences of life to the rich and to each other. For instance, when I am at home, and dressed as I ought to be, I carry on my body the workmanship of a hundred tradesmen; the building and furniture of my house employ as many more, and five times the number to adorn my wife."

I was going on to tell him of another sort of people, who get their livelihood by attending the sick, having, upon some occasions, informed his honour that many of my crew had died of diseases. But here it was with the utmost difficulty that I brought him to apprehend what I meant. "He could easily conceive, that a *Houyhnhnm*, grew weak and heavy a few days before his death, or by some accident might hurt a limb; but that nature, who works all things to perfection, should suffer any pains to breed in our bodies, he thought impossible, and desired to know the reason of so unaccountable an evil."

I told him "we fed on a thousand things which operated contrary to each other; that we ate when we were not hungry, and drank without the provocation of thirst; that we sat whole nights drinking strong liquors, without eating a bit, which disposed us to sloth, inflamed our bodies, and precipitated or prevented digestion; that prostitute female *Yahoos* acquired a certain malady, which bred rottenness in the bones of those who fell into their embraces; that this, and many other diseases, were propagated from father to son; so that great numbers came into the world with complicated maladies upon them; that it would be endless to give him a catalogue of all diseases incident to human bodies, for they would not be fewer than five or six hundred, spread over every limb and joint—in short, every part, external and intestine, having diseases appropriated to itself. To remedy which, there was a sort of people bred up among us in the profession, or pretence, of curing the sick. And because I had some skill in the faculty, I would, in gratitude to his honour, let him know the whole mystery and method by which they proceed.

"Their fundamental is, that all diseases arise from repletion; whence they conclude, that a great evacuation of the body is necessary, either through the natural passage or upwards at the mouth. Their next business is from herbs, minerals, gums, oils, shells, salts, juices, sea-weed, excrements, barks of trees, serpents, toads, frogs, spiders, dead men's flesh and bones, birds, beasts, and fishes, to form a composition, for smell and taste, the most abominable, nauseous, and detestable, they can possibly contrive, which the stomach immediately rejects with loathing, and this they call a vomit; or else, from the same store-house, with some other poisonous additions, they command us to take in at the orifice above or below (just as the physician then happens to be disposed) a medicine equally annoying and disgustful to the bowels; which, relaxing the belly, drives down all before it; and this they call a purge, or a clyster. For nature (as the physicians allege) having intended the superior anterior orifice only for the intromission of solids and liquids, and the inferior posterior for ejection, these artists ingeniously considering that in all diseases nature is forced out of her seat, therefore, to replace her in it, the body must be treated in a manner directly contrary, by interchanging the use of each orifice; forcing solids and liquids in at the anus, and making evacuations at the mouth.

"But, besides real diseases, we are subject to many that are only imaginary, for which the physicians have invented imaginary cures; these have their several names, and so have the drugs that are proper for them; and with these our female *Yahoos* are always infested.

"One great excellency in this tribe, is their skill at prognostics, wherein they seldom fail; their predictions in real diseases, when they rise to any degree of malignity, generally portending death, which is always in their power, when recovery is not: and therefore, upon any unexpected signs of amendment, after they have pronounced their sentence, rather than be accused as false prophets, they know how to approve their sagacity to the world, by a seasonable dose.

"They are likewise of special use to husbands and wives who are grown weary of their mates; to eldest sons, to great ministers of state, and often to princes."

I had formerly, upon occasion, discoursed with my master upon the nature of government in general, and particularly of our own excellent constitution, deservedly the wonder and envy of the whole world. But having here accidentally mentioned a minister of state, he commanded me, some time after, to inform him, "what species of *Yahoo* I particularly meant by that appellation."

I told him, "that a first or chief minister of state, who was the person I intended to describe, was the creature wholly exempt from joy and grief, love and hatred, pity and anger; at least, makes use of no other passions, but a violent desire of wealth, power, and titles; that he applies his words to all uses, except to the indication of his mind; that he never tells a truth but with an intent that you should take it for a lie; nor a lie, but with a design that you should take it for a truth; that those he speaks worst of behind their backs are in the surest way of preferment; and whenever he begins to praise you to others, or to yourself, you are from that day forlorn. The worst mark you can receive is a promise, especially when it is confirmed with an oath; after which, every wise man retires, and gives over all hopes.

"There are three methods, by which a man may rise to be chief minister. The first is, by knowing how, with prudence, to dispose of a wife, a daughter, or a sister; the second, by betraying or undermining his predecessor; and the third is, by a furious zeal, in public assemblies, against the corruptions of the court. But a wise prince would rather choose to employ those who practise the last of these methods; because such zealots prove always the most obsequious and subservient to the will and passions of their master. That these ministers, having all employments at their disposal, preserve themselves in power, by bribing the majority of a senate or great council; and at last, by an expedient, called an act of indemnity" (whereof I described the nature to him), "they secure themselves from after-reckonings, and retire from the public laden with the spoils of the nation.

"The palace of a chief minister is a seminary to breed up others in his own trade: the pages, lackeys, and porters, by imitating their master, become ministers of state in their several districts, and learn to excel in the three principal ingredients, of insolence, lying, and bribery. Accordingly, they have a subaltern court paid to them by persons of the best rank; and sometimes by the force of dexterity and impudence, arrive, through several gradations, to be successors to their lord.

"He is usually governed by a decayed wench, or favourite footman, who are the tunnels through which all graces are conveyed, and may properly be called, in the last resort, the governors of the kingdom."

One day, in discourse, my master, having heard me mention the nobility of my country, was pleased to make me a compliment which I could not pretend to deserve: "that he was sure I must have been born of some noble family, because I far exceeded in shape, colour, and cleanliness, all the *Yahoos* of his nation, although I seemed to fail in strength and agility, which must be imputed to my different way of living from those other brutes; and besides I was not only endowed with the faculty of speech, but likewise with some rudiments of reason, to a degree that, with all his acquaintance, I passed for a prodigy."

He made me observe, "that among the *Houyhnhnms*, the white, the sorrel, and the iron-gray, were not so exactly shaped as the bay, the dapple-gray, and the black; nor born with equal talents of mind, or a capacity to improve them; and therefore continued always in the condition of servants, without ever aspiring to match out of their own race, which in that country would be reckoned monstrous and unnatural."

I made his honour my most humble acknowledgments for the good opinion he was pleased to conceive of me, but assured him at the same time, "that my birth was of the lower sort, having been born of plain honest parents, who were just able to give me a tolerable education; that nobility, among us, was altogether a different thing from the idea he had of it; that our young noblemen are bred from their childhood in idleness and luxury; that, as soon as years will permit, they consume their vigour, and contract odious diseases among lewd females; and when their fortunes are almost ruined, they marry some woman of mean birth, disagreeable person, and unsound constitution (merely for the sake of money), whom they hate and despise. That the productions of such marriages are generally scrofulous, rickety, or deformed children; by which means the family seldom continues above three generations, unless the wife takes care to provide a healthy father, among her neighbours or domestics, in order to improve and continue the breed. That a weak diseased body, a meagre countenance, and sallow complexion, are the true marks of noble blood; and a healthy robust appearance is so disgraceful in a man of quality, that the world concludes his real father to have been a groom or a coachman. The imperfections of his mind run parallel with those of his body, being a composition of spleen, dullness, ignorance, caprice, sensuality, and pride.

"Without the consent of this illustrious body, no law can be enacted, repealed, or altered: and these nobles have likewise the decision of all our possessions, without appeal."[1]

---

1. This paragraph is not in the original editions.

7

THE AUTHOR'S GREAT LOVE OF HIS NATIVE
COUNTRY. HIS MASTER'S OBSERVATIONS UPON THE
CONSTITUTION AND ADMINISTRATION OF
ENGLAND, AS DESCRIBED BY THE AUTHOR, WITH
PARALLEL CASES AND COMPARISONS. HIS MASTER'S
OBSERVATIONS UPON HUMAN NATURE.

The reader may be disposed to wonder how I could prevail on myself to give so free a representation of my own species, among a race of mortals who are already too apt to conceive the vilest opinion of humankind, from that entire congruity between me and their *Yahoos*. But I must freely confess, that the many virtues of those excellent quadrupeds, placed in opposite view to human corruptions, had so far opened my eyes and enlarged my understanding, that I began to view the actions and passions of man in a very different light, and to think the honour of my own kind not worth managing; which, besides, it was impossible for me to do, before a person of so acute a judgment as my master, who daily convinced me of a thousand faults in myself, whereof I had not the least perception before, and which, with us, would never be numbered even among human infirmities. I had likewise learned, from his example, an utter detestation of all falsehood or disguise; and truth appeared so amiable to me, that I determined upon sacrificing every thing to it.

Let me deal so candidly with the reader as to confess that there was yet a much stronger motive for the freedom I took in my representation of things. I had not yet been a year in this country before I contracted such a love and veneration for the inhabitants, that I entered on a firm resolution never to return to humankind, but to pass the rest of my life among these admirable *Houyhnhnms*, in the contemplation and practice of every virtue, where I could have no example or incitement to vice. But it was decreed by fortune, my perpetual enemy, that so great a felicity should not fall to my share. However, it is now some comfort to reflect, that in what I said of my countrymen, I extenuated their faults as much as I durst before so strict an examiner; and upon every article gave as favourable a turn as the matter would bear. For, indeed, who is there alive that will not be swayed by his bias and partiality to the place of his birth?

I have related the substance of several conversations I had with my master during the greatest part of the time I had the honour to be in his service; but have, indeed, for brevity sake, omitted much more than is here set down.

When I had answered all his questions, and his curiosity seemed to be fully satisfied, he sent for me one morning early, and commanded me to sit down at some distance (an honour which he had never before conferred upon me). He said, "he had been very seriously considering my whole story, as far as it related both to myself and my country; that he looked upon us as a sort of animals, to whose share, by what accident he could not conjecture, some small pittance of reason had fallen, whereof we made no other use, than by its assistance, to aggravate our natural corruptions, and to acquire new ones, which nature had not given us; that we disarmed ourselves of the few abilities she had bestowed; had been very successful in multiplying our original wants, and seemed to spend our whole lives in vain endeavours to supply them by our own inventions; that, as to myself, it was manifest I had neither the strength nor agility of a common *Yahoo*; that I walked infirmly on my hinder feet; had found out a contrivance to make my claws of no use or defence, and to remove the hair from my chin, which was intended as a shelter from the sun and the weather: lastly, that I could neither run with speed, nor climb trees like my brethren," as he called them, "the *Yahoos* in his country.

"That our institutions of government and law were plainly owing to our gross defects in reason, and by consequence in virtue; because reason alone is sufficient to govern a rational creature; which was, therefore, a character we had no pretence to challenge, even from the account I had given of my own people; although he manifestly perceived, that, in order to favour them, I had concealed many particulars, and often said the thing which was not.

"He was the more confirmed in this opinion, because, he observed, that as I agreed in every feature of my body with other *Yahoos*, except where it was to my real disadvantage in point of strength, speed, and activity, the shortness of my claws, and some other particulars where nature had no part; so from the representation I had given him of our lives, our manners, and our actions, he found as near a resemblance in the disposition of our minds." He said, "the *Yahoos* were known to hate one another, more than they did any different species of animals; and the reason usually assigned was, the odiousness of their own shapes, which all could see in the rest, but not in themselves. He had therefore begun to think it not unwise in us to cover our bodies, and by that invention conceal many of our deformities from each other, which would else be hardly supportable. But he now found he had been mistaken, and that the dissensions of those brutes in his country were owing to the same cause with ours, as I had described them. For if," said he, "you throw among five *Yahoos* as much food as would be sufficient for fifty, they will, instead of eating peaceably, fall together by the ears, each single one impatient to have all to itself; and therefore a servant was usually employed to stand by while they were feeding abroad, and those kept at home were tied at a distance from each other: that if a cow died of age or accident, before a *Houyhnhnm* could secure it for his own *Yahoos*, those in the neighbourhood would come in herds to seize it, and then would ensue such a battle as I had described, with terrible wounds made by their claws on both sides, although they seldom were able to kill one another, for want of such convenient instruments of death as we had invented. At other times, the like battles have been fought between the *Yahoos* of several neighbourhoods, without any visible cause; those of one district watching all opportunities to surprise the next, before they are prepared. But if they find their project has miscarried, they return home, and, for want of enemies, engage in what I call a civil war among themselves.

"That in some fields of his country there are certain shining stones of several colours, whereof the *Yahoos* are violently fond: and when part of these stones is fixed in the earth, as it sometimes happens, they will dig with their claws for whole days to get them out; then carry them away, and hide them by heaps in their kennels; but still looking round with great caution, for fear their comrades should find out their treasure." My master said, "he could never discover the reason of this unnatural appetite, or how these stones could be of any use to a *Yahoo*; but now he believed it might proceed from the same principle of avarice which I had ascribed to mankind. That he had once, by way of experiment, privately removed a heap of these stones from the place where one of his *Yahoos* had buried it; whereupon the sordid animal, missing his treasure, by his loud lamenting brought the whole herd to the place, there miserably howled, then fell to biting and tearing the rest, began to pine away, would neither eat, nor sleep, nor work, till he ordered a servant privately to convey the stones into the same hole, and hide them as before; which, when his *Yahoo* had found, he presently recovered his spirits and good humour, but took good care to remove them to a better hiding place, and has ever since been a very serviceable brute."

My master further assured me, which I also observed myself, "that in the fields where the shining stones abound, the fiercest and most frequent battles are fought, occasioned by perpetual inroads of the neighbouring *Yahoos*."

He said, "it was common, when two *Yahoos* discovered such a stone in a field, and were contending which of them should be the proprietor, a third would take the advantage, and carry it away from them both;" which my master would needs contend to have some kind of resemblance with our suits at law; wherein I thought it for our credit not to undeceive him; since the decision he mentioned was much more equitable than many decrees among us; because the plaintiff and defendant there lost nothing beside the stone they contended for: whereas our courts of equity would never have dismissed the cause, while either of them had any thing left.

My master, continuing his discourse, said, "there was nothing that rendered the *Yahoos* more odious, than their undistinguishing appetite to devour every thing that came in their way, whether herbs, roots, berries, the corrupted flesh of animals, or all mingled together: and it was peculiar in their temper, that they were fonder of what they could get by rapine or stealth, at a greater distance, than much better food provided for them at home. If their prey held out, they would eat till they were ready to burst; after which, nature had pointed out to them a certain root that gave them a general evacuation.

"There was also another kind of root, very juicy, but somewhat rare and difficult to be found, which the *Yahoos* sought for with much eagerness, and would suck it with great delight; it produced in them the same effects that wine has upon us. It would make them sometimes hug, and sometimes tear one another; they would howl, and grin, and chatter, and reel, and tumble, and then fall asleep in the mud."

I did indeed observe that the *Yahoos* were the only animals in this country subject to any diseases; which, however, were much fewer than horses have among us, and contracted, not by any ill-treatment they meet with, but by the nastiness and greediness of that sordid brute. Neither has their language any more than a general appellation for those maladies, which is borrowed from the name of the beast, and called *hnea-yahoo*, or *Yahoo's evil*; and the cure prescribed is a mixture of their own dung and urine, forcibly put down the *Yahoo's* throat. This I have since often known to have been taken with success, and do here freely recommend it to my countrymen for the public good, as an admirable specific against all diseases produced by repletion.

"As to learning, government, arts, manufactures, and the like," my master confessed, "he could find little or no resemblance between the *Yahoos* of that country and those in ours; for he only meant to observe what parity there was in our natures. He had heard, indeed, some curious *Houyhnhnms* observe, that in most herds there was a sort of ruling *Yahoo* (as among us there is generally some leading or principal stag in a park), who was always more deformed in body, and mischievous in disposition, than any of the rest; that this leader had usually a favourite as like himself as he could get, whose employment was to lick his master's feet and posteriors, and drive the female *Yahoos* to his kennel; for which he was now and then rewarded with a piece of ass's flesh. This favourite is hated by the whole herd, and therefore, to protect himself, keeps always near the person of his leader. He usually continues in office till a worse can be found; but the very moment he is discarded, his successor, at the head of all the *Yahoos* in that district, young and old, male and female, come in a body, and discharge their excrements upon him from head to foot. But how far this might be applicable to our courts, and favourites, and ministers of state, my master said I could best determine."

I durst make no return to this malicious insinuation, which debased human understanding below the sagacity of a common hound, who has judgment enough to distinguish and follow the cry of the ablest dog in the pack, without being ever mistaken.

My master told me, "there were some qualities remarkable in the *Yahoos*, which he had not observed me to mention, or at least very slightly, in the accounts I had given of humankind." He said, "those animals, like other brutes, had their females in common; but in this they differed, that the she *Yahoo* would admit the males while she was pregnant; and that the hes would quarrel and fight with the females, as fiercely as with each other; both which practices were such degrees of infamous brutality, as no other sensitive creature ever arrived at.

"Another thing he wondered at in the *Yahoos*, was their strange disposition to nastiness and dirt; whereas there appears to be a natural love of cleanliness in all other animals." As to the two former accusations, I was glad to let them pass without any reply, because I had not a word to offer upon them in defence of my species, which otherwise I certainly had done from my own inclinations. But I could have easily vindicated humankind from the imputation of singularity upon the last article, if there had been any swine in that country (as unluckily for me there were not), which, although it may be a sweeter quadruped than a *Yahoo*, cannot, I humbly conceive, in justice, pretend to more cleanliness; and so his honour himself must have owned, if he had seen their filthy way of feeding, and their custom of wallowing and sleeping in the mud.

My master likewise mentioned another quality which his servants had discovered in several Yahoos, and to him was wholly unaccountable. He said, "a fancy would sometimes take a *Yahoo* to retire into a corner, to lie down, and howl, and groan, and spurn away all that came near him, although he were young and fat, wanted neither food nor water, nor did the servant imagine what could possibly ail him. And the only remedy they found was, to set him to hard work, after which he would infallibly come to himself." To this I was silent out of partiality to my own kind; yet here I could plainly discover the true seeds of spleen, which only seizes on the lazy, the luxurious, and the rich; who, if they were forced to undergo the same regimen, I would undertake for the cure.

His honour had further observed, "that a female *Yahoo* would often stand behind a bank or a bush, to gaze on the young males passing by, and then appear, and hide, using many antic gestures and grimaces, at which time it was observed that she had a most offensive smell; and when any of the males advanced, would slowly retire, looking often back, and with a counterfeit show of fear, run off into some convenient place, where she knew the male would follow her.

"At other times, if a female stranger came among them, three or four of her own sex would get about her, and stare, and chatter, and grin, and smell her all over; and then turn off with gestures, that seemed to express contempt and disdain."

Perhaps my master might refine a little in these speculations, which he had drawn from what he observed himself, or had been told him by others; however, I could not reflect without some amazement, and much sorrow, that the rudiments of lewdness, coquetry, censure, and scandal, should have place by instinct in womankind.

I expected every moment that my master would accuse the *Yahoos* of those unnatural appetites in both sexes, so common among us. But nature, it seems, has not been so expert a school-mistress; and these politer pleasures are entirely the productions of art and reason on our side of the globe.

8

THE AUTHOR RELATES SEVERAL PARTICULARS OF
THE YAHOOS. THE GREAT VIRTUES OF THE
HOUYHNHNMS. THE EDUCATION AND EXERCISE OF
THEIR YOUTH. THEIR GENERAL ASSEMBLY.

As I ought to have understood human nature much better than I supposed it possible for my master to do, so it was easy to apply the character he gave of the *Yahoos* to myself and my countrymen; and I believed I could yet make further discoveries, from my own observation. I therefore often begged his honour to let me go among the herds of *Yahoos* in the neighbourhood; to which he always very graciously consented, being perfectly convinced that the hatred I bore these brutes would never suffer me to be corrupted by them; and his honour ordered one of his servants, a strong sorrel nag, very honest and good-natured, to be my guard; without whose protection I durst not undertake such adventures. For I have already told the reader how much I was pestered by these odious animals, upon my first arrival; and I afterwards failed very narrowly, three or four times, of falling into their clutches, when I happened to stray at any distance without my hanger. And I have reason to believe they had some imagination that I was of their own species, which I often assisted myself by stripping up my sleeves, and showing my naked arms and breasts in their sight, when my protector was with me. At which times they would approach as near as they durst, and imitate my actions after the manner of monkeys, but ever with great signs of hatred; as a tame jackdaw with cap and stockings is always persecuted by the wild ones, when he happens to be got among them.

They are prodigiously nimble from their infancy. However, I once caught a young male of three years old, and endeavoured, by all marks of tenderness, to make it quiet; but the little imp fell a squalling, and scratching, and biting with such violence, that I was forced to let it go; and it was high time, for a whole troop of old ones came about us at the noise, but finding the cub was safe (for away it ran), and my sorrel nag being by, they durst not venture near us. I observed the young animal's flesh to smell very rank, and the stink was somewhat between a weasel and a fox, but much more disagreeable. I forgot another circumstance (and perhaps I might have the reader's pardon if it were wholly omitted), that while I held the odious vermin in my hands, it voided its filthy excrements of a yellow liquid substance all over my clothes; but by good fortune there was a small brook hard by, where I washed myself as clean as I could; although I durst not come into my master's presence until I were sufficiently aired.

By what I could discover, the *Yahoos* appear to be the most unteachable of all animals: their capacity never reaching higher than to draw or carry burdens. Yet I am of opinion, this defect arises chiefly from a perverse, restive disposition; for they are cunning, malicious, treacherous, and revengeful. They are strong and hardy, but of a cowardly spirit, and, by consequence, insolent, abject, and cruel. It is observed, that the red haired of both sexes are more libidinous and mischievous than the rest, whom yet they much exceed in strength and activity.

The *Houyhnhnms* keep the *Yahoos* for present use in huts not far from the house; but the rest are sent abroad to certain fields, where they dig up roots, eat several kinds of herbs, and search about for carrion, or sometimes catch weasels and *luhimuhs* (a sort of wild rat), which they greedily devour. Nature has taught them to dig deep holes with their nails on the side of a rising ground, wherein they lie by themselves; only the kennels of the females are larger, sufficient to hold two or three cubs.

They swim from their infancy like frogs, and are able to continue long under water, where they often take fish, which the females carry home to their young. And, upon this occasion, I hope the reader will pardon my relating an odd adventure.

Being one day abroad with my protector the sorrel nag, and the weather exceeding hot, I entreated him to let me bathe in a river that was near. He consented, and I immediately stripped myself stark naked, and went down softly into the stream. It happened that a young female *Yahoo*, standing behind a bank, saw the whole proceeding, and inflamed by desire, as the nag and I conjectured, came running with all speed, and leaped into the water, within five yards of the place where I bathed. I was never in my life so terribly frightened. The nag was grazing at some distance, not suspecting any harm. She embraced me after a most fulsome manner. I roared as loud as I could, and the nag came galloping towards me, whereupon she quitted her grasp, with the utmost reluctance, and leaped upon the opposite bank, where she stood gazing and howling all the time I was putting on my clothes.

This was a matter of diversion to my master and his family, as well as of mortification to myself. For now I could no longer deny that I was a real *Yahoo* in every limb and feature, since the females had a natural propensity to me, as one of their own species. Neither was the hair of this brute of a red colour (which might have been some excuse for an appetite a little irregular), but black as a sloe, and her countenance did not make an appearance altogether so hideous as the rest of her kind; for I think she could not be above eleven years old.

Having lived three years in this country, the reader, I suppose, will expect that I should, like other travellers, give him some account of the manners and customs of its inhabitants, which it was indeed my principal study to learn.

As these noble *Houyhnhnms* are endowed by nature with a general disposition to all virtues, and have no conceptions or ideas of what is evil in a rational creature, so their grand maxim is, to cultivate reason, and to be wholly governed by it. Neither is reason among them a point problematical, as with us, where men can argue with plausibility on both sides of the question, but strikes you with immediate conviction; as it must needs do, where it is not mingled, obscured, or discoloured, by passion and interest. I remember it was with extreme difficulty that I could bring my master to understand the meaning of the word opinion, or how a point could be disputable; because reason taught us to affirm or deny only where we are certain; and beyond our knowledge we cannot do either. So that controversies, wranglings, disputes, and positiveness, in false or dubious propositions, are evils unknown among the *Houyhnhnms*. In the like manner, when I used to explain to him our several systems of natural philosophy, he would laugh, "that a creature pretending to reason, should value itself upon the knowledge of other people's conjectures, and in things where that knowledge, if it were certain, could be of no use." Wherein he agreed entirely with the sentiments of Socrates, as Plato delivers them; which I mention as the highest honour I can do that prince of philosophers. I have often since reflected, what destruction such doctrine would make in the libraries of Europe; and how many paths of fame would be then shut up in the learned world.

Friendship and benevolence are the two principal virtues among the *Houyhnhnms*; and these not confined to particular objects, but universal to the whole race; for a stranger from the remotest part is equally treated with the nearest neighbour, and wherever he goes, looks upon himself as at home. They preserve decency and civility in the highest degrees, but are altogether ignorant of ceremony. They have no fondness for their colts or foals, but the care they take in educating them proceeds entirely from the dictates of reason. And I observed my master to show the same affection to his neighbour's issue, that he had for his own. They will have it that nature teaches them to love the whole species, and it is reason only that makes a distinction of persons, where there is a superior degree of virtue.

When the matron *Houyhnhnms* have produced one of each sex, they no longer accompany with their consorts, except they lose one of their issue by some casualty, which very seldom happens; but in such a case they meet again; or when the like accident befalls a person whose wife is past bearing, some other couple bestow on him one of their own colts, and then go together again until the mother is pregnant. This caution is necessary, to prevent the country from being overburdened with numbers. But the race of inferior *Houyhnhnms*, bred up to be servants, is not so strictly limited upon this article: these are allowed to produce three of each sex, to be domestics in the noble families.

In their marriages, they are exactly careful to choose such colours as will not make any disagreeable mixture in the breed. Strength is chiefly valued in the male, and comeliness in the female; not upon the account of love, but to preserve the race from degenerating; for where a female happens to excel in strength, a consort is chosen, with regard to comeliness.

Courtship, love, presents, jointures, settlements have no place in their thoughts, or terms whereby to express them in their language. The young couple meet, and are joined, merely because it is the determination of their parents and friends; it is what they see done every day, and they look upon it as one of the necessary actions of a reasonable being. But the violation of marriage, or any other unchastity, was never heard of; and the married pair pass their lives with the same friendship and mutual benevolence, that they bear to all others of the same species who come in their way, without jealousy, fondness, quarrelling, or discontent.

In educating the youth of both sexes, their method is admirable, and highly deserves our imitation. These are not suffered to taste a grain of oats, except upon certain days, till eighteen years old; nor milk, but very rarely; and in summer they graze two hours in the morning, and as many in the evening, which their parents likewise observe; but the servants are not allowed above half that time, and a great part of their grass is brought home, which they eat at the most convenient hours, when they can be best spared from work.

Temperance, industry, exercise, and cleanliness, are the lessons equally enjoined to the young ones of both sexes: and my master thought it monstrous in us, to give the females a different kind of education from the males, except in some articles of domestic management; whereby, as he truly observed, one half of our natives were good for nothing but bringing children into the world; and to trust the care of our children to such useless animals, he said, was yet a greater instance of brutality.

But the *Houyhnhnms* train up their youth to strength, speed, and hardiness, by exercising them in running races up and down steep hills, and over hard stony grounds; and when they are all in a sweat, they are ordered to leap over head and ears into a pond or river. Four times a year the youth of a certain district meet to show their proficiency in running and leaping, and other feats of strength and agility; where the victor is rewarded with a song in his or her praise. On this festival, the servants drive a herd of *Yahoos* into the field, laden with hay, and oats, and milk, for a repast to the *Houyhnhnms*; after which, these brutes are immediately driven back again, for fear of being noisome to the assembly.

Every fourth year, at the vernal equinox, there is a representative council of the whole nation, which meets in a plain about twenty miles from our house, and continues about five or six days. Here they inquire into the state and condition of the several districts; whether they abound or be deficient in hay or oats, or cows, or *Yahoos*; and wherever there is any want (which is but seldom) it is immediately supplied by unanimous consent and contribution. Here likewise the regulation of children is settled: as for instance, if a *Houyhnhnm* has two males, he changes one of them with another that has two females; and when a child has been lost by any casualty, where the mother is past breeding, it is determined what family in the district shall breed another to supply the loss.

9

A GRAND DEBATE AT THE GENERAL ASSEMBLY OF THE HOUYHNHNMS, AND HOW IT WAS DETERMINED. THE LEARNING OF THE HOUYHNHNMS. THEIR BUILDINGS. THEIR MANNER OF BURIALS. THE DEFECTIVENESS OF THEIR LANGUAGE.

One of these grand assemblies was held in my time, about three months before my departure, whither my master went as the representative of our district. In this council was resumed their old debate, and indeed the only debate that ever happened in their country; whereof my master, after his return, give me a very particular account.

The question to be debated was, "whether the *Yahoos* should be exterminated from the face of the earth?" One of the members for the affirmative offered several arguments of great strength and weight, alleging, "that as the *Yahoos* were the most filthy, noisome, and deformed animals which nature ever produced, so they were the most restive and indocible, mischievous and malicious; they would privately suck the teats of the *Houyhnhnms'* cows, kill and devour their cats, trample down their oats and grass, if they were not continually watched, and commit a thousand other extravagancies." He took notice of a general tradition, "that *Yahoos* had not been always in their country; but that many ages ago, two of these brutes appeared together upon a mountain; whether produced by the heat of the sun upon corrupted mud and slime, or from the ooze and froth of the sea, was never known; that these *Yahoos* engendered, and their brood, in a short time, grew so numerous as to overrun and infest the whole nation; that the *Houyhnhnms*, to get rid of this evil, made a general hunting, and at last enclosed the whole herd; and destroying the elder, every *Houyhnhnm* kept two young ones in a kennel, and brought them to such a degree of tameness, as an animal, so savage by nature, can be capable of acquiring, using them for draught and carriage; that there seemed to be much truth in this tradition, and that those creatures could not be *yinhniamshy* (or *aborigines* of the land), because of the violent hatred the *Houyhnhnms*, as well as all other animals, bore them, which, although their evil disposition sufficiently deserved, could never have arrived at so high a degree if they had been *aborigines*, or else they would have long since been rooted out; that the inhabitants, taking a fancy to use the service of the *Yahoos*, had, very imprudently, neglected to cultivate the breed of asses, which are a comely animal, easily kept, more tame and orderly, without any offensive smell, strong enough for labour, although they yield to the other in agility of body, and if their braying be no agreeable sound, it is far preferable to the horrible howlings of the *Yahoos*."

Several others declared their sentiments to the same purpose, when my master proposed an expedient to the assembly, whereof he had indeed borrowed the hint from me. "He approved of the tradition mentioned by the honourable member who spoke before, and affirmed, that the two *Yahoos* said to be seen first among them, had been driven thither over the sea; that coming to land, and being forsaken by their companions, they retired to the mountains, and degenerating by degrees, became in process of time much more savage than those of their own species in the country whence these two originals came. The reason of this assertion was, that he had now in his possession a certain wonderful *Yahoo* (meaning myself) which most of them had heard of, and many of them had seen. He then related to them how he first found me; that my body was all covered with an artificial composure of the skins and hairs of other animals; that I spoke in a language of my own, and had thoroughly learned theirs; that I had related to him the accidents which brought me thither; that when he saw me without my covering, I was an exact *Yahoo* in every part, only of a whiter colour, less hairy, and with shorter claws. He added, how I had endeavoured to persuade him, that in my own and other countries, the *Yahoos* acted as the governing, rational animal, and held the *Houyhnhnms* in servitude; that he observed in me all the qualities of a *Yahoo*, only a little more civilized by some tincture of reason, which, however, was in a degree as far inferior to the *Houyhnhnm* race, as the *Yahoos* of their country were to me; that, among other things, I mentioned a custom we had of castrating *Houyhnhnms* when they were young, in order to render them tame; that the operation was easy and safe; that it was no shame to learn wisdom from brutes, as industry is taught by the ant, and building by the swallow (for so I translate the word *lyhannh*, although it be a much larger fowl); that this invention might be practised upon the younger *Yahoos* here, which besides rendering them tractable and fitter for use, would in an age put an end to the whole species, without destroying life; that in the mean time the *Houyhnhnms* should be exhorted to cultivate the breed of asses, which, as they are in all respects more valuable brutes, so they have this advantage, to be fit for service at five years old, which the others are not till twelve."

This was all my master thought fit to tell me, at that time, of what passed in the grand council. But he was pleased to conceal one particular, which related personally to myself, whereof I soon felt the unhappy effect, as the reader will know in its proper place, and whence I date all the succeeding misfortunes of my life.

The *Houyhnhnms* have no letters, and consequently their knowledge is all traditional. But there happening few events of any moment among a people so well united, naturally disposed to every virtue, wholly governed by reason, and cut off from all commerce with other nations, the historical part is easily preserved without burdening their memories. I have already observed that they are subject to no diseases, and therefore can have no need of physicians. However, they have excellent medicines, composed of herbs, to cure accidental bruises and cuts in the pastern or frog of the foot, by sharp stones, as well as other maims and hurts in the several parts of the body.

They calculate the year by the revolution of the sun and moon, but use no subdivisions into weeks. They are well enough acquainted with the motions of those two luminaries, and understand the nature of eclipses; and this is the utmost progress of their astronomy.

In poetry, they must be allowed to excel all other mortals; wherein the justness of their similes, and the minuteness as well as exactness of their descriptions, are indeed inimitable. Their verses abound very much in both of these, and usually contain either some exalted notions of friendship and benevolence or the praises of those who were victors in races and other bodily exercises. Their buildings, although very rude and simple, are not inconvenient, but well contrived to defend them from all injuries of cold and heat. They have a kind of tree, which at forty years old loosens in the root, and falls with the first storm: it grows very straight, and being pointed like stakes with a sharp stone (for the *Houyhnhnms* know not the use of iron), they stick them erect in the ground, about ten inches asunder, and then weave in oat straw, or sometimes wattles, between them. The roof is made after the same manner, and so are the doors.

The *Houyhnhnms* use the hollow part, between the pastern and the hoof of their fore-foot, as we do our hands, and this with greater dexterity than I could at first imagine. I have seen a white mare of our family thread a needle (which I lent her on purpose) with that joint. They milk their cows, reap their oats, and do all the work which requires hands, in the same manner. They have a kind of hard flints, which, by grinding against other stones, they form into instruments, that serve instead of wedges, axes, and hammers. With tools made of these flints, they likewise cut their hay, and reap their oats, which there grow naturally in several fields; the *Yahoos* draw home the sheaves in carriages, and the servants tread them in certain covered huts to get out the grain, which is kept in stores. They make a rude kind of earthen and wooden vessels, and bake the former in the sun.

If they can avoid casualties, they die only of old age, and are buried in the obscurest places that can be found, their friends and relations expressing neither joy nor grief at their departure; nor does the dying person discover the least regret that he is leaving the world, any more than if he were upon returning home from a visit to one of his neighbours. I remember my master having once made an appointment with a friend and his family to come to his house, upon some affair of importance: on the day fixed, the mistress and her two children came very late; she made two excuses, first for her husband, who, as she said, happened that very morning to *shnuwnh*. The word is strongly expressive in their language, but not easily rendered into English; it signifies, "to retire to his first mother." Her excuse for not coming sooner, was, that her husband dying late in the morning, she was a good while consulting her servants about a convenient place where his body should be laid; and I observed, she behaved herself at our house as cheerfully as the rest. She died about three months after.

They live generally to seventy, or seventy-five years, very seldom to fourscore. Some weeks before their death, they feel a gradual decay; but without pain. During this time they are much visited by their friends, because they cannot go abroad with their usual ease and satisfaction. However, about ten days before their death, which they seldom fail in computing, they return the visits that have been made them by those who are nearest in the neighbourhood, being carried in a convenient sledge drawn by *Yahoos*; which vehicle they use, not only upon this occasion, but when they grow old, upon long journeys, or when they are lamed by any accident: and therefore when the dying *Houyhnhnms* return those visits, they take a solemn leave of their friends, as if they were going to some remote part of the country, where they designed to pass the rest of their lives.

I know not whether it may be worth observing, that the *Houyhnhnms* have no word in their language to express any thing that is evil, except what they borrow from the deformities or ill qualities of the *Yahoos*. Thus they denote the folly of a servant, an omission of a child, a stone that cuts their feet, a continuance of foul or unseasonable weather, and the like, by adding to each the epithet of *Yahoo*. For instance, *hhnm Yahoo*; *whnaholm Yahoo*, *ynlhmndwihlma Yahoo*, and an ill-contrived house *ynholmhnmrohlnw Yahoo*.

I could, with great pleasure, enlarge further upon the manners and virtues of this excellent people; but intending in a short time to publish a volume by itself, expressly upon that subject, I refer the reader thither; and, in the mean time, proceed to relate my own sad catastrophe.

10

The author's economy, and happy life, among the Houyhnhnms. His great improvement in virtue by conversing with them. Their conversations. The author has notice given him by his master, that he must depart from the country. He falls into a swoon for grief; but submits. He contrives and finishes a canoe by the help of a fellow-servant, and puts to sea at a venture.

I had settled my little economy to my own heart's content. My master had ordered a room to be made for me, after their manner, about six yards from the house: the sides and floors of which I plastered with clay, and covered with rush-mats of my own contriving. I had beaten hemp, which there grows wild, and made of it a sort of ticking; this I filled with the feathers of several birds I had taken with springes made of *Yahoos'* hairs, and were excellent food. I had worked two chairs with my knife, the sorrel nag helping me in the grosser and more laborious part. When my clothes were worn to rags, I made myself others with the skins of rabbits, and of a certain beautiful animal, about the same size, called *nnuhnoh*, the skin of which is covered with a fine down. Of these I also made very tolerable stockings. I soled my shoes with wood, which I cut from a tree, and fitted to the upper-leather; and when this was worn out, I supplied it with the skins of *Yahoos* dried in the sun. I often got honey out of hollow trees, which I mingled with water, or ate with my bread. No man could more verify the truth of these two maxims, "That nature is very easily satisfied;" and, "That necessity is the mother of invention." I enjoyed perfect health of body, and tranquillity of mind; I did not feel the treachery or inconstancy of a friend, nor the injuries of a secret or open enemy. I had no occasion of bribing, flattering, or pimping, to procure the favour of any great man, or of his minion; I wanted no fence against fraud or oppression: here was neither physician to destroy my body, nor lawyer to ruin my fortune; no informer to watch my words and actions, or forge accusations against me for hire: here were no gibers, censurers, backbiters, pickpockets, highwaymen, housebreakers, attorneys, bawds, buffoons, gamesters, politicians, wits, splenetics, tedious talkers, controvertists, ravishers, murderers, robbers, virtuosos; no leaders, or followers, of party and faction; no encouragers to vice, by seducement or examples; no dungeon, axes, gibbets, whipping-posts, or pillories; no cheating shopkeepers or mechanics; no pride, vanity, or affectation; no fops, bullies, drunkards, strolling whores, or poxes; no ranting, lewd, expensive wives; no stupid, proud pedants; no importunate, overbearing, quarrelsome, noisy, roaring, empty, conceited, swearing companions; no scoundrels raised from the dust upon the merit of their vices, or nobility thrown into it on account of their virtues; no lords, fiddlers, judges, or dancing-masters.

I had the favour of being admitted to several *Houyhnhnms*, who came to visit or dine with my master; where his honour graciously suffered me to wait in the room, and listen to their discourse. Both he and his company would often descend to ask me questions, and receive my answers. I had also sometimes the honour of attending my master in his visits to others. I never presumed to speak, except in answer to a question; and then I did it with inward regret, because it was a loss of so much time for improving myself; but I was infinitely delighted with the station of an humble auditor in such conversations, where nothing passed but what was useful, expressed in the fewest and most significant words; where, as I have already said, the greatest decency was observed, without the least degree of ceremony; where no person spoke without being pleased himself, and pleasing his companions; where there was no interruption, tediousness, heat, or difference of sentiments. They have a notion, that when people are met together, a short silence does much improve conversation: this I found to be true; for during those little intermissions of talk, new ideas would arise in their minds, which very much enlivened the discourse. Their subjects are, generally on friendship and benevolence, on order and economy; sometimes upon the visible operations of nature, or ancient traditions; upon the bounds and limits of virtue; upon the unerring rules of reason, or upon some determinations to be taken at the next great assembly: and often upon the various excellences of poetry. I may add, without vanity, that my presence often gave them sufficient matter for discourse, because it afforded my master an occasion of letting his friends into the history of me and my country, upon which they were all pleased to descant, in a manner not very advantageous to humankind: and for that reason I shall not repeat what they said; only I may be allowed to observe, that his honour, to my great admiration, appeared to understand the nature of *Yahoos* much better than myself. He went through all our vices and follies, and discovered many, which I had never mentioned to him, by only supposing what qualities a *Yahoo* of their country, with a small proportion of reason, might be capable of exerting; and concluded, with too much probability, "how vile, as well as miserable, such a creature must be."

I freely confess, that all the little knowledge I have of any value, was acquired by the lectures I received from my master, and from hearing the discourses of him and his friends; to which I should be prouder to listen, than to dictate to the greatest and wisest assembly in Europe. I admired the strength, comeliness, and speed of the inhabitants; and such a constellation of virtues, in such amiable persons, produced in me the highest veneration. At first, indeed, I did not feel that natural awe, which the *Yahoos* and all other animals bear toward them; but it grew upon me by decrees, much sooner than I imagined, and was mingled with a respectful love and gratitude, that they would condescend to distinguish me from the rest of my species.

When I thought of my family, my friends, my countrymen, or the human race in general, I considered them, as they really were, *Yahoos* in shape and disposition, perhaps a little more civilized, and qualified with the gift of speech; but making no other use of reason, than to improve and multiply those vices whereof their brethren in this country had only the share that nature allotted them. When I happened to behold the reflection of my own form in a lake or fountain, I turned away my face in horror and detestation of myself, and could better endure the sight of a common *Yahoo* than of my own person. By conversing with the

Houyhnhnms, and looking upon them with delight, I fell to imitate their gait and gesture, which is now grown into a habit; and my friends often tell me, in a blunt way, "that I trot like a horse;" which, however, I take for a great compliment. Neither shall I disown, that in speaking I am apt to fall into the voice and manner of the *Houyhnhnms*, and hear myself ridiculed on that account, without the least mortification.

In the midst of all this happiness, and when I looked upon myself to be fully settled for life, my master sent for me one morning a little earlier than his usual hour. I observed by his countenance that he was in some perplexity, and at a loss how to begin what he had to speak. After a short silence, he told me, "he did not know how I would take what he was going to say: that in the last general assembly, when the affair of the *Yahoos* was entered upon, the representatives had taken offence at his keeping a *Yahoo* (meaning myself) in his family, more like a *Houyhnhnm* than a brute animal; that he was known frequently to converse with me, as if he could receive some advantage or pleasure in my company; that such a practice was not agreeable to reason or nature, or a thing ever heard of before among them; the assembly did therefore exhort him either to employ me like the rest of my species, or command me to swim back to the place whence I came: that the first of these expedients was utterly rejected by all the *Houyhnhnms* who had ever seen me at his house or their own; for they alleged, that because I had some rudiments of reason, added to the natural pravity of those animals, it was to be feared I might be able to seduce them into the woody and mountainous parts of the country, and bring them in troops by night to destroy the *Houyhnhnms'* cattle, as being naturally of the ravenous kind, and averse from labour."

My master added, "that he was daily pressed by the *Houyhnhnms* of the neighbourhood to have the assembly's exhortation executed, which he could not put off much longer. He doubted it would be impossible for me to swim to another country; and therefore wished I would contrive some sort of vehicle, resembling those I had described to him, that might carry me on the sea; in which work I should have the assistance of his own servants, as well as those of his neighbours." He concluded, "that for his own part, he could have been content to keep me in his service as long as I lived; because he found I had cured myself of some bad habits and dispositions, by endeavouring, as far as my inferior nature was capable, to imitate the *Houyhnhnms*."

I should here observe to the reader, that a decree of the general assembly in this country is expressed by the word *hnhloayn*, which signifies an exhortation, as near as I can render it; for they have no conception how a rational creature can be compelled, but only advised, or exhorted; because no person can disobey reason, without giving up his claim to be a rational creature.

I was struck with the utmost grief and despair at my master's discourse; and being unable to support the agonies I was under, I fell into a swoon at his feet. When I came to myself, he told me "that he concluded I had been dead;" for these people are subject to no such imbecilities of nature. I answered in a faint voice, "that death would have been too great a happiness; that although I could not blame the assembly's exhortation, or the urgency of his friends; yet, in my weak and corrupt judgment, I thought it might consist with reason to have been less rigorous; that I could not swim a league, and probably the nearest land to theirs might be distant above a hundred: that many materials, necessary for making a small vessel to carry me off, were wholly wanting in this country; which, however, I would attempt, in obedience and gratitude to his honour, although I concluded the thing to be impossible, and therefore looked on myself as already devoted to destruction; that the certain prospect of an unnatural death was the least of my evils; for, supposing I should escape with life by some strange adventure, how could I think with temper of passing my days among

Yahoos, and relapsing into my old corruptions, for want of examples to lead and keep me within the paths of virtue? that I knew too well upon what solid reasons all the determinations of the wise *Houyhnhnms* were founded, not to be shaken by arguments of mine, a miserable *Yahoo*; and therefore, after presenting him with my humble thanks for the offer of his servants' assistance in making a vessel, and desiring a reasonable time for so difficult a work, I told him I would endeavour to preserve a wretched being; and if ever I returned to England, was not without hopes of being useful to my own species, by celebrating the praises of the renowned *Houyhnhnms*, and proposing their virtues to the imitation of mankind."

My master, in a few words, made me a very gracious reply; allowed me the space of two months to finish my boat; and ordered the sorrel nag, my fellow-servant (for so, at this distance, I may presume to call him), to follow my instruction; because I told my master, "that his help would be sufficient, and I knew he had a tenderness for me."

In his company, my first business was to go to that part of the coast where my rebellious crew had ordered me to be set on shore. I got upon a height, and looking on every side into the sea; fancied I saw a small island toward the north-east. I took out my pocket glass, and could then clearly distinguish it above five leagues off, as I computed; but it appeared to the sorrel nag to be only a blue cloud: for as he had no conception of any country beside his own, so he could not be as expert in distinguishing remote objects at sea, as we who so much converse in that element.

After I had discovered this island, I considered no further; but resolved it should if possible, be the first place of my banishment, leaving the consequence to fortune.

I returned home, and consulting with the sorrel nag, we went into a copse at some distance, where I with my knife, and he with a sharp flint, fastened very artificially after their manner, to a wooden handle, cut down several oak wattles, about the thickness of a walking-staff, and some larger pieces. But I shall not trouble the reader with a particular description of my own mechanics; let it suffice to say, that in six weeks time with the help of the sorrel nag, who performed the parts that required most labour, I finished a sort of Indian canoe, but much larger, covering it with the skins of *Yahoos*, well stitched together with hempen threads of my own making. My sail was likewise composed of the skins of the same animal; but I made use of the youngest I could get, the older being too tough and thick; and I likewise provided myself with four paddles. I laid in a stock of boiled flesh, of rabbits and fowls, and took with me two vessels, one filled with milk and the other with water.

I tried my canoe in a large pond, near my master's house, and then corrected in it what was amiss; stopping all the chinks with *Yahoos'* tallow, till I found it staunch, and able to bear me and my freight; and, when it was as complete as I could possibly make it, I had it drawn on a carriage very gently by *Yahoos* to the sea-side, under the conduct of the sorrel nag and another servant.

When all was ready, and the day came for my departure, I took leave of my master and lady and the whole family, my eyes flowing with tears, and my heart quite sunk with grief. But his honour, out of curiosity, and, perhaps, (if I may speak without vanity,) partly out of kindness, was determined to see me in my canoe, and got several of his neighbouring friends to accompany him. I was forced to wait above an hour for the tide; and then observing the wind very fortunately bearing toward the island to which I intended to steer my course, I took a second leave of my master: but as I was going to prostrate myself to kiss his hoof, he did me the honour to raise it gently to my mouth. I am not ignorant how much I have been censured for mentioning this last particular. Detractors are pleased to think it improbable, that so illustrious a person should descend to give so great a mark of distinction to a creature so inferior as I. Neither have I forgotten how apt some travellers are to boast of extraordinary favours they have received. But, if these censurers were better acquainted with the noble and courteous disposition of the *Houyhnhnms*, they would soon change their opinion.

I paid my respects to the rest of the *Houyhnhnms* in his honour's company; then getting into my canoe, I pushed off from shore.

11

THE AUTHOR'S DANGEROUS VOYAGE. HE ARRIVES AT NEW HOLLAND, HOPING TO SETTLE THERE. IS WOUNDED WITH AN ARROW BY ONE OF THE NATIVES. IS SEIZED AND CARRIED BY FORCE INTO A PORTUGUESE SHIP. THE GREAT CIVILITIES OF THE CAPTAIN. THE AUTHOR ARRIVES AT ENGLAND.

I began this desperate voyage on February 15, 1714–15, at nine o'clock in the morning. The wind was very favourable; however, I made use at first only of my paddles; but considering I should soon be weary, and that the wind might chop about, I ventured to set up my little sail; and thus, with the help of the tide, I went at the rate of a league and a half an hour, as near as I could guess. My master and his friends continued on the shore till I was almost out of sight; and I often heard the sorrel nag (who always loved me) crying out, "*Hnuy illa nyha, majah Yahoo;*" "Take care of thyself, gentle *Yahoo.*"

My design was, if possible, to discover some small island uninhabited, yet sufficient, by my labour, to furnish me with the necessaries of life, which I would have thought a greater happiness, than to be first minister in the politest court of Europe; so horrible was the idea I conceived of returning to live in the society, and under the government of *Yahoos*. For in such a solitude as I desired, I could at least enjoy my own thoughts, and reflect with delight on the virtues of those inimitable *Houyhnhnms*, without an opportunity of degenerating into the vices and corruptions of my own species.

The reader may remember what I related, when my crew conspired against me, and confined me to my cabin; how I continued there several weeks without knowing what course we took; and when I was put ashore in the long-boat, how the sailors told me, with oaths, whether true or false, "that they knew not in what part of the world we were." However, I did then believe us to be about 10 degrees southward of the Cape of Good Hope, or about 45 degrees southern latitude, as I gathered from some general words I overheard among them, being I supposed to the south-east in their intended voyage to Madagascar. And although this were little better than conjecture, yet I resolved to steer my course eastward, hoping to reach the south-west coast of New Holland, and perhaps some such island as I desired lying westward of it. The wind was full west, and by six in the evening I computed I had gone eastward at least eighteen leagues; when I spied a very small island about half a league off, which I soon reached. It was nothing but a rock, with one creek naturally arched by the force of tempests. Here I put in my canoe, and climbing a part of the rock, I could plainly discover land to the east, extending from south to north. I lay all night in my canoe; and repeating my voyage early in the morning, I arrived in seven hours to the south-east point of New Holland. This confirmed me in the opinion I have long entertained, that the maps and charts place this country at least three degrees more to the east than it really is; which thought I communicated many years ago to my worthy friend, Mr. Herman Moll, and gave him my reasons for it, although he has rather chosen to follow other authors.

I saw no inhabitants in the place where I landed, and being unarmed, I was afraid of venturing far into the country. I found some shellfish on the shore, and ate them raw, not daring to kindle a fire, for fear of being discovered by the natives. I continued three days feeding on oysters and limpets, to save my own provisions; and I fortunately found a brook of excellent water, which gave me great relief.

On the fourth day, venturing out early a little too far, I saw twenty or thirty natives upon a height not above five hundred yards from me. They were stark naked, men, women, and children, round a fire, as I could discover by the smoke. One of them spied me, and gave notice to the rest; five of them advanced toward me, leaving the women and children at the fire. I made what haste I could to the shore, and, getting into my canoe, shoved off: the savages, observing me retreat, ran after me: and before I could get far enough into the sea, discharged an arrow which wounded me deeply on the inside of my left knee: I shall carry the mark to my grave. I apprehended the arrow might be poisoned, and paddling out of the reach of their darts (being a calm day), I made a shift to suck the wound, and dress it as well as I could.

I was at a loss what to do, for I durst not return to the same landing-place, but stood to the north, and was forced to paddle, for the wind, though very gentle, was against me, blowing north-west. As I was looking about for a secure landing-place, I saw a sail to the north-north-east, which appearing every minute more visible, I was in some doubt whether I should wait for them or not; but at last my detestation of the *Yahoo* race prevailed: and turning my canoe, I sailed and paddled together to the south, and got into the same creek whence I set out in the morning, choosing rather to trust myself among these barbarians, than live with European *Yahoos*. I drew up my canoe as close as I could to the shore, and hid myself behind a stone by the little brook, which, as I have already said, was excellent water.

The ship came within half a league of this creek, and sent her long boat with vessels to take in fresh water (for the place, it seems, was very well known); but I did not observe it, till the boat was almost on shore; and it was too late to seek another hiding-place. The seamen at their landing observed my canoe, and rummaging it all over, easily conjectured that the owner could not be far off. Four of them, well armed, searched every cranny and lurking-hole, till at last they found me flat on my face behind the stone. They gazed awhile in admiration at my strange uncouth dress; my coat made of skins, my wooden-soled shoes, and my furred stockings; whence, however, they concluded, I was not a native of the place, who all go naked. One of the seamen, in Portuguese, bid me rise, and asked who I was. I understood that language very well, and getting upon my feet, said, "I was a poor *Yahoo* banished from the *Houyhnhnms*, and desired they would please to let me depart." They admired to hear me answer them in their own tongue, and saw by my complexion I must be a European; but were at a loss to know what I meant by *Yahoos* and *Houyhnhnms*; and at the same time fell a-laughing at my strange tone in speaking, which resembled the neighing of a horse. I trembled all the while betwixt fear and hatred. I again desired leave to depart, and was gently moving to my canoe; but they laid hold of me, desiring to know, "what country I was of? whence I came?" with many other questions. I told them "I was born in England, whence I came about five years ago, and then their country and ours were at peace. I therefore hoped they would not treat me as an enemy, since I meant them no harm, but was a poor *Yahoo* seeking some desolate place where to pass the remainder of his unfortunate life."

When they began to talk, I thought I never heard or saw any thing more unnatural; for it appeared to me as monstrous as if a dog or a cow should speak in England, or a *Yahoo* in *Houyhnhnmland*. The honest Portuguese were equally amazed at my strange dress, and the odd manner of delivering my words, which, however, they understood very well. They spoke to me with great humanity, and said, "they were sure the captain would carry me *gratis* to Lisbon, whence I might return to my own country; that two of the seamen would go back to the ship, inform the captain of what they had seen, and receive his orders; in the mean time, unless I would give my solemn oath not to fly, they would secure me by force." I thought it best to comply with their proposal. They were very curious to know my story, but I gave them very little satisfaction, and they all conjectured that my misfortunes had impaired my reason. In two hours the boat, which went laden with vessels of water, returned, with the captain's command to fetch me on board. I fell on my knees to preserve my liberty; but all was in vain; and the men, having tied me with cords, heaved me into the boat, whence I was taken into the ship, and thence into the captain's cabin.

His name was Pedro de Mendez; he was a very courteous and generous person. He entreated me to give some account of myself, and desired to know what I would eat or drink; said, "I should be used as well as himself;" and spoke so many obliging things, that I wondered to find such civilities from a *Yahoo*. However, I remained silent and sullen; I was ready to faint at the very smell of him and his men. At last I desired something to eat out of my own canoe; but he ordered me a chicken, and some excellent wine, and then directed that I should be put to bed in a very clean cabin. I would not undress myself, but lay on the bed-clothes, and in half an hour stole out, when I thought the crew was at dinner, and getting to the side of the ship, was going to leap into the sea, and swim for my life, rather than continue among *Yahoos*. But one of the seamen prevented me, and having informed the captain, I was chained to my cabin.

After dinner, Don Pedro came to me, and desired to know my reason for so desperate an attempt; assured me, "he only meant to do me all the service he was able;" and spoke so very movingly, that at last I descended to treat him like an animal which had some little portion of reason. I gave him a very short relation of my voyage; of the conspiracy against me by my own men; of the country where they set me on shore, and of my five years residence there. All which he looked upon as if it were a dream or a vision; whereat I took great offence; for I had quite forgot the faculty of lying, so peculiar to *Yahoos*, in all countries where they preside, and, consequently, their disposition of suspecting truth in others of their own species. I asked him, "whether it were the custom in his country to say the thing which was not?" I assured him, "I had almost forgot what he meant by falsehood, and if I had lived a thousand years in *Houyhnhnmland*, I should never have heard a lie from the meanest servant; that I was altogether indifferent whether he believed me or not; but, however, in return for his favours, I would give so much allowance to the corruption of his nature, as to answer any objection he would please to make, and then he might easily discover the truth."

The captain, a wise man, after many endeavours to catch me tripping in some part of my story, at last began to have a better opinion of my veracity. But he added, "that since I professed so inviolable an attachment to truth, I must give him my word and honour to bear him company in this voyage, without attempting any thing against my life; or else he would continue me a prisoner till we arrived at Lisbon." I gave him the promise he required; but at the same time protested, "that I would suffer the greatest hardships, rather than return to live among *Yahoos*."

Our voyage passed without any considerable accident. In gratitude to the captain, I sometimes sat with him, at his earnest request, and strove to conceal my antipathy against human kind, although it often broke out; which he suffered to pass without observation. But the greatest part of the day I confined myself to my cabin, to avoid seeing any of the crew. The captain had often entreated me to strip myself of my savage dress, and offered to lend me the best suit of clothes he had. This I would not be prevailed on to accept, abhorring to cover myself with any thing that had been on the back of a *Yahoo*. I only desired he would lend me two clean shirts, which, having been washed since he wore them, I believed would not so much defile me. These I changed every second day, and washed them myself.

We arrived at Lisbon, Nov. 5, 1715. At our landing, the captain forced me to cover myself with his cloak, to prevent the rabble from crowding about me. I was conveyed to his own house; and at my earnest request he led me up to the highest room backwards. I conjured him "to conceal from all persons what I had told him of the *Houyhnhnms*; because the least hint of such a story would not only draw numbers of people to see me, but probably put me in danger of being imprisoned, or burnt by the Inquisition." The captain persuaded me to accept a suit of clothes newly made; but I would not suffer the tailor to take my measure; however, Don Pedro being almost of my size, they fitted me well enough. He accoutred me with other necessaries, all new, which I aired for twenty-four hours before I would use them.

The captain had no wife, nor above three servants, none of which were suffered to attend at meals; and his whole deportment was so obliging, added to very good human understanding, that I really began to tolerate his company. He gained so far upon me, that I ventured to look out of the back window. By degrees I was brought into another room, whence I peeped into the street, but drew my head back in a fright. In a week's time he seduced me down to the door. I found my terror gradually lessened, but my hatred and contempt seemed to increase. I was at last bold enough to walk the street in his company, but kept my nose well stopped with rue, or sometimes with tobacco.

In ten days, Don Pedro, to whom I had given some account of my domestic affairs, put it upon me, as a matter of honour and conscience, "that I ought to return to my native country, and live at home with my wife and children." He told me, "there was an English ship in the port just ready to sail, and he would furnish me with all things necessary." It would be tedious to repeat his arguments, and my contradictions. He said, "it was altogether impossible to find such a solitary island as I desired to live in; but I might command in my own house, and pass my time in a manner as recluse as I pleased."

I complied at last, finding I could not do better. I left Lisbon the 24th day of November, in an English merchantman, but who was the master I never inquired. Don Pedro accompanied me to the ship, and lent me twenty pounds. He took kind leave of me, and embraced me at parting, which I bore as well as I could. During this last voyage I had no commerce with the master or any of his men; but, pretending I was sick, kept close in my cabin. On the fifth of December, 1715, we cast anchor in the Downs, about nine in the morning, and at three in the afternoon I got safe to my house at Rotherhith.[1]

My wife and family received me with great surprise and joy, because they concluded me certainly dead; but I must freely confess the sight of them filled me only with hatred, disgust, and contempt; and the more, by reflecting on the near alliance I had to them. For although, since my unfortunate exile from the *Houyhnhnm* country, I had compelled myself to tolerate the sight of *Yahoos*, and to converse with Don Pedro de Mendez, yet my memory and imagination were perpetually filled with the virtues and ideas of those exalted *Houyhnhnms*. And when I began to consider that, by copulating with one of the *Yahoo* species I had become a parent of more, it struck me with the utmost shame, confusion, and horror.

As soon as I entered the house, my wife took me in her arms, and kissed me; at which, having not been used to the touch of that odious animal for so many years, I fell into a swoon for almost an hour. At the time I am writing, it is five years since my last return to England. During the first year, I could not endure my wife or children in my presence; the very smell of them was intolerable; much less could I suffer them to eat in the same room. To this hour they dare not presume to touch my bread, or drink out of the same cup, neither was I ever able to let one of them take me by the hand. The first money I laid out was to buy two young stone-horses, which I keep in a good stable; and next to them, the groom is my greatest favourite, for I feel my spirits revived by the smell he contracts in the stable. My horses understand me tolerably well; I converse with them at least four hours every day. They are strangers to bridle or saddle; they live in great amity with me and friendship to each other.

---

1. The original editions and Hawksworth's have Rotherhith here, though earlier in the work, Redriff is said to have been Gulliver's home in England.

12

THE AUTHOR'S VERACITY. HIS DESIGN IN PUBLISHING THIS WORK. HIS CENSURE OF THOSE TRAVELLERS WHO SWERVE FROM THE TRUTH. THE AUTHOR CLEARS HIMSELF FROM ANY SINISTER ENDS IN WRITING. AN OBJECTION ANSWERED. THE METHOD OF PLANTING COLONIES. HIS NATIVE COUNTRY COMMENDED. THE RIGHT OF THE CROWN TO THOSE COUNTRIES DESCRIBED BY THE AUTHOR IS JUSTIFIED. THE DIFFICULTY OF CONQUERING THEM. THE AUTHOR TAKES HIS LAST LEAVE OF THE READER; PROPOSES HIS MANNER OF LIVING FOR THE FUTURE; GIVES GOOD ADVICE, AND CONCLUDES.

Thus, gentle reader, I have given thee a faithful history of my travels for sixteen years and above seven months: wherein I have not been so studious of ornament as of truth. I could, perhaps, like others, have astonished thee with strange improbable tales; but I rather chose to relate plain matter of fact, in the simplest manner and style; because my principal design was to inform, and not to amuse thee.

It is easy for us who travel into remote countries, which are seldom visited by Englishmen or other Europeans, to form descriptions of wonderful animals both at sea and land. Whereas a traveller's chief aim should be to make men wiser and better, and to improve their minds by the bad, as well as good, example of what they deliver concerning foreign places.

I could heartily wish a law was enacted, that every traveller, before he were permitted to publish his voyages, should be obliged to make oath before the Lord High Chancellor, that all he intended to print was absolutely true to the best of his knowledge; for then the world would no longer be deceived, as it usually is, while some writers, to make their works pass the better upon the public, impose the grossest falsities on the unwary reader. I have perused several books of travels with great delight in my younger days; but having since gone over most parts of the globe, and been able to contradict many fabulous accounts from my own observation, it has given me a great disgust against this part of reading, and some indignation to see the credulity of mankind so impudently abused. Therefore, since my acquaintance were pleased to think my poor endeavours might not be unacceptable to my country, I imposed on myself, as a maxim never to be swerved from, that I would strictly adhere to truth; neither indeed can I be ever under the least temptation to vary from it, while I retain in my mind the lectures and example of my noble master and the other illustrious *Houyhnhnms* of whom I had so long the honour to be an humble hearer.

—*Nec si miserum Fortuna Sinonem*

Finxit, vanum etiam, mendacemque improba finget.

I know very well, how little reputation is to be got by writings which require neither genius nor learning, nor indeed any other talent, except a good memory, or an exact journal. I know likewise, that writers of travels, like dictionary-makers, are sunk into oblivion by the weight and bulk of those who come last, and therefore lie uppermost. And it is highly probable, that such travellers, who shall hereafter visit the countries described in this work of mine, may, by detecting my errors (if there be any), and adding many new discoveries of their own, justle me out of vogue, and stand in my place, making the world forget that ever I was an author. This indeed would be too great a mortification, if I wrote for fame: but as my sole intention was the public good, I cannot be altogether disappointed. For who can read of the virtues I have mentioned in the glorious *Houyhnhnms*, without being ashamed of his own vices, when he considers himself as the reasoning, governing animal of his country? I shall say nothing of those remote nations where *Yahoos* preside; among which the least corrupted are the *Brobdingnagians*; whose wise maxims in morality and government it would be our happiness to observe. But I forbear descanting further, and rather leave the judicious reader to his own remarks and application.

I am not a little pleased that this work of mine can possibly meet with no censurers: for what objections can be made against a writer, who relates only plain facts, that happened in such distant countries, where we have not the least interest, with respect either to trade or negotiations? I have carefully avoided every fault with which common writers of travels are often too justly charged. Besides, I meddle not the least with any party, but write without passion, prejudice, or ill-will against any man, or number of men, whatsoever. I write for the noblest end, to inform and instruct mankind; over whom I may, without breach of modesty, pretend to some superiority, from the advantages I received by conversing so long among the most accomplished *Houyhnhnms*. I write without any view to profit or praise. I never suffer a word to pass that may look like reflection, or possibly give the least offence, even to those who are most ready to take it. So that I hope I may with justice pronounce myself an author perfectly blameless; against whom the tribes of Answerers, Considerers, Observers, Reflectors, Detectors, Remarkers, will never be able to find matter for exercising their talents.

I confess, it was whispered to me, "that I was bound in duty, as a subject of England, to have given in a memorial to a secretary of state at my first coming over; because, whatever lands are discovered by a subject belong to the crown." But I doubt whether our conquests in the countries I treat of would be as easy as those of Ferdinando Cortez over the naked Americans. The *Lilliputians*, I think, are hardly worth the charge of a fleet and army to reduce them; and I question whether it might be prudent or safe to attempt the *Brobdingnagians*; or whether an English army would be much at their ease with the Flying Island over their heads. The *Houyhnhnms* indeed appear not to be so well prepared for war, a science to which they are perfect strangers, and especially against missive weapons. However, supposing myself to be a minister of state, I could never give my advice for invading them. Their prudence, unanimity, unacquaintedness with fear, and their love of their country, would amply supply all defects in the military art. Imagine twenty thousand of them breaking into the midst of an European army, confounding the ranks, overturning the carriages, battering the warriors' faces into mummy by terrible yerks from their hinder hoofs; for they would well deserve the character given to Augustus, *Recalcitrat undique tutus*. But, instead of proposals for conquering that magnanimous nation, I rather wish they were in a capacity, or disposition, to send a sufficient number of their inhabitants for civilizing Europe, by teaching us the first principles of honour, justice, truth, temperance, public spirit, fortitude, chastity, friendship, benevolence, and fidelity. The names of all which virtues are still retained among us in most languages, and are to be met with in modern, as well as ancient authors; which I am able to assert from my own small reading.

But I had another reason, which made me less forward to enlarge his majesty's dominions by my discoveries. To say the truth, I had conceived a few scruples with relation to the distributive justice of princes upon those occasions. For instance, a crew of pirates are driven by a storm they know not whither; at length a boy discovers land from the top-mast; they go on shore to rob and plunder, they see a harmless people, are entertained with kindness; they give the country a new name; they take formal possession of it for their king; they set up a rotten plank, or a stone, for a memorial; they murder two or three dozen of the natives, bring away a couple more, by force, for a sample; return home, and get their pardon. Here commences a new dominion acquired with a title by divine right. Ships are sent with the first opportunity; the natives driven out or destroyed; their princes tortured to discover their gold; a free license given to all acts of inhumanity and lust, the earth reeking with the blood of its inhabitants: and this execrable crew of butchers, employed in so pious an expedition, is a modern colony, sent to convert and civilize an idolatrous and barbarous people!

But this description, I confess, does by no means affect the British nation, who may be an example to the whole world for their wisdom, care, and justice in planting colonies; their liberal endowments for the advancement of religion and learning; their choice of devout and able pastors to propagate Christianity; their caution in stocking their provinces with people of sober lives and conversations from this the mother kingdom; their strict regard to the distribution of justice, in supplying the civil administration through all their colonies with officers of the greatest abilities, utter strangers to corruption; and, to crown all, by sending the most vigilant and virtuous governors, who have no other views than the happiness of the people over whom they preside, and the honour of the king their master.

But as those countries which I have described do not appear to have any desire of being conquered and enslaved, murdered or driven out by colonies, nor abound either in gold, silver, sugar, or tobacco, I did humbly conceive, they were by no means proper objects of our zeal, our valour, or our interest. However, if those whom it more concerns think fit to be of another opinion, I am ready to depose, when I shall be lawfully called, that no European did ever visit those countries before me. I mean, if the inhabitants ought to be believed, unless a dispute may arise concerning the two *Yahoos*, said to have been seen many years ago upon a mountain in *Houyhnhnmland*.

But, as to the formality of taking possession in my sovereign's name, it never came once into my thoughts; and if it had, yet, as my affairs then stood, I should perhaps, in point of prudence and self-preservation, have put it off to a better opportunity.

Having thus answered the only objection that can ever be raised against me as a traveller, I here take a final leave of all my courteous readers, and return to enjoy my own speculations in my little garden at Redriff; to apply those excellent lessons of virtue which I learned among the *Houyhnhnms*; to instruct the *Yahoos* of my own family, is far as I shall find them docible animals; to behold my figure often in a glass, and thus, if possible, habituate myself by time to tolerate the sight of a human creature; to lament the brutality to *Houyhnhnms* in my own country, but always treat their persons with respect, for the sake of my noble master, his family, his friends, and the whole *Houyhnhnm* race, whom these of ours have the honour to resemble in all their lineaments, however their intellectuals came to degenerate.

I began last week to permit my wife to sit at dinner with me, at the farthest end of a long table; and to answer (but with the utmost brevity) the few questions I asked her. Yet, the smell of a *Yahoo* continuing very offensive, I always keep my nose well stopped with rue, lavender, or tobacco leaves. And, although it be hard for a man late in life to remove old habits, I am not altogether out of hopes, in some time, to suffer a neighbour *Yahoo* in my company, without the apprehensions I am yet under of his teeth or his claws.

My reconcilement to the *Yahoo* kind in general might not be so difficult, if they would be content with those vices and follies only which nature has entitled them to. I am not in the least provoked at the sight of a lawyer, a pickpocket, a colonel, a fool, a lord, a gamester, a politician, a whoremonger, a physician, an evidence, a suborner, an attorney, a traitor, or the like; this is all according to the due course of things: but when I behold a lump of deformity and diseases, both in body and mind, smitten with pride, it immediately breaks all the measures of my patience; neither shall I be ever able to comprehend how such an animal, and such a vice, could tally together. The wise and virtuous *Houyhnhnms*, who abound in all excellences that can adorn a rational creature, have no name for this vice in their language, which has no terms to express any thing that is evil, except those whereby they describe the detestable qualities of their *Yahoos*, among which they were not able to distinguish this of pride, for want of thoroughly understanding human nature, as it shows itself in other countries where that animal presides. But I, who had more experience, could plainly observe some rudiments of it among the wild *Yahoos*.

But the *Houyhnhnms*, who live under the government of reason, are no more proud of the good qualities they possess, than I should be for not wanting a leg or an arm; which no man in his wits would boast of, although he must be miserable without them. I dwell the longer upon this subject from the desire I have to make the society of an English *Yahoo* by any means not insupportable; and therefore I here entreat those who have any tincture of this absurd vice, that they will not presume to come in my sight.

KIDNAPPED

ROBERT LOUIS STEVENSON

I

I SET OFF UPON MY JOURNEY TO THE HOUSE OF SHAWS

I will begin the story of my adventures with a certain morning early in the month of June, the year of grace 1751, when I took the key for the last time out of the door of my father's house. The sun began to shine upon the summit of the hills as I went down the road; and by the time I had come as far as the manse, the blackbirds were whistling in the garden lilacs, and the mist that hung around the valley in the time of the dawn was beginning to arise and die away.

Mr. Campbell, the minister of Essendean, was waiting for me by the garden gate, good man! He asked me if I had breakfasted; and hearing that I lacked for nothing, he took my hand in both of his and clapped it kindly under his arm.

"Well, Davie, lad," said he, "I will go with you as far as the ford, to set you on the way." And we began to walk forward in silence.

"Are ye sorry to leave Essendean?" said he, after awhile.

"Why, sir," said I, "if I knew where I was going, or what was likely to become of me, I would tell you candidly. Essendean is a good place indeed, and I have been very happy there; but then I have never been anywhere else. My father and mother, since they are both dead, I shall be no nearer to in Essendean than in the Kingdom of Hungary, and, to speak truth, if I thought I had a chance to better myself where I was going I would go with a good will."

"Ay?" said Mr. Campbell. "Very well, Davie. Then it behoves me to tell your fortune; or so far as I may. When your mother was gone, and your father (the worthy, Christian man) began to sicken for his end, he gave me in charge a certain letter, which he said was your inheritance. 'So soon,' says he, 'as I am gone, and the house is redd up and the gear disposed of' (all which, Davie, hath been done), 'give my boy this letter into his hand, and start him off to the house of Shaws, not far from Cramond. That is the place I came from,' he said, 'and it's where it befits that my boy should return. He is a steady lad,' your father said, 'and a canny goer; and I doubt not he will come safe, and be well lived where he goes.'"

"The house of Shaws!" I cried. "What had my poor father to do with the house of Shaws?"

"Nay," said Mr. Campbell, "who can tell that for a surety? But the name of that family, Davie, boy, is the name you bear—Balfours of Shaws: an ancient, honest, reputable house, peradventure in these latter days decayed. Your father, too, was a man of learning as befitted his position; no man more plausibly conducted school; nor had he the manner or the speech of a common dominie; but (as ye will yourself remember) I took aye a pleasure to have him to the manse to meet the gentry; and those of my own house, Campbell of Kilrennet, Campbell of Dunswire, Campbell of Minch, and others, all well-kenned gentlemen, had pleasure in his society. Lastly, to put all the elements of this affair before you, here is the testamentary letter itself, superscrived by the own hand of our departed brother."

He gave me the letter, which was addressed in these words: "To the hands of Ebenezer Balfour, Esquire, of Shaws, in his house of Shaws, these will be delivered by my son, David Balfour." My heart was beating hard at this great prospect now suddenly opening before a lad of seventeen years of age, the son of a poor country dominie in the Forest of Ettrick.

"Mr. Campbell," I stammered, "and if you were in my shoes, would you go?"

"Of a surety," said the minister, "that would I, and without pause. A pretty lad like you should get to Cramond (which is near in by Edinburgh) in two days of walk. If the worst came to the worst, and your high relations (as I cannot but suppose them to be somewhat of your blood) should put you to the door, ye can but walk the two days back again and risp at the manse door. But I would rather hope that ye shall be well received, as your poor father forecast for you, and for anything that I ken come to be a great man in time. And here, Davie, laddie," he resumed, "it lies near upon my conscience to improve this parting, and set you on the right guard against the dangers of the world."

Here he cast about for a comfortable seat, lighted on a big boulder under a birch by the trackside, sate down upon it with a very long, serious upper lip, and the sun now shining in upon us between two peaks, put his pocket-handkerchief over his cocked hat to shelter him. There, then, with uplifted forefinger, he first put me on my guard against a considerable number of heresies, to which I had no temptation, and urged upon me to be instant in my prayers and reading of the Bible. That done, he drew a picture of the great house that I was bound to, and how I should conduct myself with its inhabitants.

"Be soople, Davie, in things immaterial," said he. "Bear ye this in mind, that, though gentle born, ye have had a country rearing. Dinnae shame us, Davie, dinnae shame us! In yon great, muckle house, with all these domestics, upper and under, show yourself as nice, as circumspect, as quick at the conception, and as slow of speech as any. As for the laird—remember he's the laird; I say no more: honour to whom honour. It's a pleasure to obey a laird; or should be, to the young."

"Well, sir," said I, "it may be; and I'll promise you I'll try to make it so."

"Why, very well said," replied Mr. Campbell, heartily. "And now to come to the material, or (to make a quibble) to the immaterial. I have here a little packet which contains four things." He tugged it, as he spoke, and with some great difficulty, from the skirt pocket of his coat. "Of these four things, the first is your legal due: the little pickle money for your father's books and plenishing, which I have bought (as I have explained from the first) in the design of re-selling at a profit to the incoming dominie. The other three are gifties that Mrs. Campbell and myself would be blithe of your acceptance. The first, which is round, will likely please ye best at the first off-go; but, O Davie, laddie, it's but a drop of water in the sea; it'll help you but a step, and vanish like the morning. The second, which is flat and square and written upon, will stand by you through life, like a good staff for the road, and a good pillow to your head in sickness. And as for the last, which is cubical, that'll see you, it's my prayerful wish, into a better land."

With that he got upon his feet, took off his hat, and prayed a little while aloud, and in affecting terms, for a young man setting out into the world; then suddenly took me in his arms and embraced me very hard; then held me at arm's length, looking at me with his face all working with sorrow; and then whipped about, and crying good-bye to me, set off backward by the way that we had come at a sort of jogging run. It might have been laughable to another; but I was in no mind to laugh. I watched him as long as he was in sight; and he never stopped hurrying, nor once looked back. Then it came in upon my mind that this was all his sorrow at my departure; and my conscience smote me hard and fast, because I, for my part, was overjoyed to get away out of that quiet country-side, and go to a great, busy house, among rich and respected gentlefolk of my own name and blood.

"Davie, Davie," I thought, "was ever seen such black ingratitude? Can you forget old favours and old friends at the mere whistle of a name? Fie, fie; think shame."

And I sat down on the boulder the good man had just left, and opened the parcel to see the nature of my gifts. That which he had called cubical, I had never had much doubt of; sure enough it was a little Bible, to carry in a plaid-neuk. That which he had called round, I found to be a shilling piece; and the third, which was to help me so wonderfully both in health and sickness all the days of my life, was a little piece of coarse yellow paper, written upon thus in red ink:

"TO MAKE LILLY OF THE VALLEY WATER.—Take the flowers of lilly of the valley and distil them in sack, and drink a spoonful or two as there is occasion. It restores speech to those that have the dumb palsey. It is good against the Gout; it comforts the heart and strengthens the memory; and the flowers, put into a Glasse, close stopt, and set into ane hill of ants for a month, then take it out, and you will find a liquor which comes from the flowers, which keep in a vial; it is good, ill or well, and whether man or woman."

And then, in the minister's own hand, was added:

"Likewise for sprains, rub it in; and for the cholic, a great spoonful in the hour."

To be sure, I laughed over this; but it was rather tremulous laughter; and I was glad to get my bundle on my staff's end and set out over the ford and up the hill upon the farther side; till, just as I came on the green drove-road running wide through the heather, I took my last look of Kirk Essendean, the trees about the manse, and the big rowans in the kirkyard where my father and my mother lay.

2

I COME TO MY JOURNEY'S END

In the forenoon of the second day, coming to the top of a hill, I saw all the country fall away before me down to the sea; and in the midst of this descent, on a long ridge, the city of Edinburgh smoking like a kiln. There was a flag upon the castle, and ships moving or lying anchored in the firth; both of which, for as far away as they were, I could distinguish clearly; and both brought my country heart into my mouth.

Presently after, I came by a house where a shepherd lived, and got a rough direction for the neighbourhood of Cramond; and so, from one to another, worked my way to the westward of the capital by Colinton, till I came out upon the Glasgow road. And there, to my great pleasure and wonder, I beheld a regiment marching to the fifes, every foot in time; an old red-faced general on a grey horse at the one end, and at the other the company of Grenadiers, with their Pope's-hats. The pride of life seemed to mount into my brain at the sight of the red coats and the hearing of that merry music.

A little farther on, and I was told I was in Cramond parish, and began to substitute in my inquiries the name of the house of Shaws. It was a word that seemed to surprise those of whom I sought my way. At first I thought the plainness of my appearance, in my country habit, and that all dusty from the road, consorted ill with the greatness of the place to which I was bound. But after two, or maybe three, had given me the same look and the same answer, I began to take it in my head there was something strange about the Shaws itself.

The better to set this fear at rest, I changed the form of my inquiries; and spying an honest fellow coming along a lane on the shaft of his cart, I asked him if he had ever heard tell of a house they called the house of Shaws.

He stopped his cart and looked at me, like the others.

"Ay" said he. "What for?"

"It's a great house?" I asked.

"Doubtless," says he. "The house is a big, muckle house."

"Ay," said I, "but the folk that are in it?"

"Folk?" cried he. "Are ye daft? There's nae folk there—to call folk."

"What?" say I; "not Mr. Ebenezer?"

"Ou, ay" says the man; "there's the laird, to be sure, if it's him you're wanting. What'll like be your business, mannie?"

"I was led to think that I would get a situation," I said, looking as modest as I could.

"What?" cries the carter, in so sharp a note that his very horse started; and then, "Well, mannie," he added, "it's nane of my affairs; but ye seem a decent-spoken lad; and if ye'll take a word from me, ye'll keep clear of the Shaws."

The next person I came across was a dapper little man in a beautiful white wig, whom I saw to be a barber on his rounds; and knowing well that barbers were great gossips, I asked him plainly what sort of a man was Mr. Balfour of the Shaws.

"Hoot, hoot, hoot," said the barber, "nae kind of a man, nae kind of a man at all;" and began to ask me very shrewdly what my business was; but I was more than a match for him at that, and he went on to his next customer no wiser than he came.

I cannot well describe the blow this dealt to my illusions. The more indistinct the accusations were, the less I liked them, for they left the wider field to fancy. What kind of a great house was this, that all the parish should start and stare to be asked the way to it? or what sort of a gentleman, that his ill-fame should be thus current on the wayside? If an hour's walking would have brought me back to Essendean, I had left my adventure then and there, and returned to Mr. Campbell's. But when I had come so far a way already, mere shame would not suffer me to desist till I had put the matter to the touch of proof; I was bound, out of mere self-respect, to carry it through; and little as I liked the sound of what I heard, and slow as I began to travel, I still kept asking my way and still kept advancing.

It was drawing on to sundown when I met a stout, dark, sour-looking woman coming trudging down a hill; and she, when I had put my usual question, turned sharp about, accompanied me back to the summit she had just left, and pointed to a great bulk of building standing very bare upon a green in the bottom of the next valley. The country was pleasant round about, running in low hills, pleasantly watered and wooded, and the crops, to my eyes, wonderfully good; but the house itself appeared to be a kind of ruin; no road led up to it; no smoke arose from any of the chimneys; nor was there any semblance of a garden. My heart sank. "That!" I cried.

The woman's face lit up with a malignant anger. "That is the house of Shaws!" she cried. "Blood built it; blood stopped the building of it; blood shall bring it down. See here!" she cried again—"I spit upon the ground, and crack my thumb at it! Black be its fall! If ye see the laird, tell him what ye hear; tell him this makes the twelve hunner and nineteen time that Jennet Clouston has called down the curse on him and his house, byre and stable, man, guest, and master, wife, miss, or bairn—black, black be their fall!"

And the woman, whose voice had risen to a kind of eldritch sing-song, turned with a skip, and was gone. I stood where she left me, with my hair on end. In those days folk still believed in witches and trembled at a curse; and this one, falling so pat, like a wayside omen, to arrest me ere I carried out my purpose, took the pith out of my legs.

I sat me down and stared at the house of Shaws. The more I looked, the pleasanter that country-side appeared; being all set with hawthorn bushes full of flowers; the fields dotted with sheep; a fine flight of rooks in the sky; and every sign of a kind soil and climate; and yet the barrack in the midst of it went sore against my fancy.

Country folk went by from the fields as I sat there on the side of the ditch, but I lacked the spirit to give them a good-e'en. At last the sun went down, and then, right up against the yellow sky, I saw a scroll of smoke go mounting, not much thicker, as it seemed to me, than the smoke of a candle; but still there it was, and meant a fire, and warmth, and cookery, and some living inhabitant that must have lit it; and this comforted my heart.

So I set forward by a little faint track in the grass that led in my direction. It was very faint indeed to be the only way to a place of habitation; yet I saw no other. Presently it brought me to stone uprights, with an unroofed lodge beside them, and coats of arms upon the top. A main entrance it was plainly meant to be, but never finished; instead of gates of wrought iron, a pair of hurdles were tied across with a straw rope; and as there were no park walls, nor any sign of avenue, the track that I was following passed on the right hand of the pillars, and went wandering on toward the house.

The nearer I got to that, the drearier it appeared. It seemed like the one wing of a house that had never been finished. What should have been the inner end stood open on the upper floors, and showed against the sky with steps and stairs of uncompleted masonry. Many of the windows were unglazed, and bats flew in and out like doves out of a dove-cote.

The night had begun to fall as I got close; and in three of the lower windows, which were very high up and narrow, and well barred, the changing light of a little fire began to glimmer. Was this the palace I had been coming to? Was it within these walls that I was to seek new friends and begin great fortunes? Why, in my father's house on Essen-Waterside, the fire and the bright lights would show a mile away, and the door open to a beggar's knock!

I came forward cautiously, and giving ear as I came, heard some one rattling with dishes, and a little dry, eager cough that came in fits; but there was no sound of speech, and not a dog barked.

The door, as well as I could see it in the dim light, was a great piece of wood all studded with nails; and I lifted my hand with a faint heart under my jacket, and knocked once. Then I stood and waited. The house had fallen into a dead silence; a whole minute passed away, and nothing stirred but the bats overhead. I knocked again, and hearkened again. By this time my ears had grown so accustomed to the quiet, that I could hear the ticking of the clock inside as it slowly counted out the seconds; but whoever was in that house kept deadly still, and must have held his breath.

I was in two minds whether to run away; but anger got the upper hand, and I began instead to rain kicks and buffets on the door, and to shout out aloud for Mr. Balfour. I was in full career, when I heard the cough right overhead, and jumping back and looking up, beheld a man's head in a tall nightcap, and the bell mouth of a blunderbuss, at one of the first-storey windows.

"It's loaded," said a voice.

"I have come here with a letter," I said, "to Mr. Ebenezer Balfour of Shaws. Is he here?"

"From whom is it?" asked the man with the blunderbuss.

"That is neither here nor there," said I, for I was growing very wroth.

"Well," was the reply, "ye can put it down upon the doorstep, and be off with ye."

"I will do no such thing," I cried. "I will deliver it into Mr. Balfour's hands, as it was meant I should. It is a letter of introduction."

"A what?" cried the voice, sharply.

I repeated what I had said.

"Who are ye, yourself?" was the next question, after a considerable pause.

"I am not ashamed of my name," said I. "They call me David Balfour."

At that, I made sure the man started, for I heard the blunderbuss rattle on the window-sill; and it was after quite a long pause, and with a curious change of voice, that the next question followed:

"Is your father dead?"

I was so much surprised at this, that I could find no voice to answer, but stood staring.

"Ay," the man resumed, "he'll be dead, no doubt; and that'll be what brings ye chapping to my door." Another pause, and then defiantly, "Well, man," he said, "I'll let ye in;" and he disappeared from the window.

3

I MAKE ACQUAINTANCE OF MY UNCLE

Presently there came a great rattling of chains and bolts, and the door was cautiously opened and shut to again behind me as soon as I had passed.

"Go into the kitchen and touch naething," said the voice; and while the person of the house set himself to replacing the defences of the door, I groped my way forward and entered the kitchen.

The fire had burned up fairly bright, and showed me the barest room I think I ever put my eyes on. Half-a-dozen dishes stood upon the shelves; the table was laid for supper with a bowl of porridge, a horn spoon, and a cup of small beer. Besides what I have named, there was not another thing in that great, stone-vaulted, empty chamber but lockfast chests arranged along the wall and a corner cupboard with a padlock.

As soon as the last chain was up, the man rejoined me. He was a mean, stooping, narrow-shouldered, clay-faced creature; and his age might have been anything between fifty and seventy. His nightcap was of flannel, and so was the nightgown that he wore, instead of coat and waistcoat, over his ragged shirt. He was long unshaved; but what most distressed and even daunted me, he would neither take his eyes away from me nor look me fairly in the face. What he was, whether by trade or birth, was more than I could fathom; but he seemed most like an old, unprofitable serving-man, who should have been left in charge of that big house upon board wages.

"Are ye sharp-set?" he asked, glancing at about the level of my knee. "Ye can eat that drop parritch?"

I said I feared it was his own supper.

"O," said he, "I can do fine wanting it. I'll take the ale, though, for it slockens (moistens) my cough." He drank the cup about half out, still keeping an eye upon me as he drank; and then suddenly held out his hand. "Let's see the letter," said he.

I told him the letter was for Mr. Balfour; not for him.

"And who do ye think I am?" says he. "Give me Alexander's letter."

"You know my father's name?"

"It would be strange if I didnae," he returned, "for he was my born brother; and little as ye seem to like either me or my house, or my good parritch, I'm your born uncle, Davie, my man, and you my born nephew. So give us the letter, and sit down and fill your kyte."

If I had been some years younger, what with shame, weariness, and disappointment, I believe I had burst into tears. As it was, I could find no words, neither black nor white, but handed him the letter, and sat down to the porridge with as little appetite for meat as ever a young man had.

Meanwhile, my uncle, stooping over the fire, turned the letter over and over in his hands.

"Do ye ken what's in it?" he asked, suddenly.

"You see for yourself, sir," said I, "that the seal has not been broken."

"Ay," said he, "but what brought you here?"

"To give the letter," said I.

"No," says he, cunningly, "but ye'll have had some hopes, nae doubt?"

"I confess, sir," said I, "when I was told that I had kinsfolk well-to-do, I did indeed indulge the hope that they might help me in my life. But I am no beggar; I look for no favours at your hands, and I want none that are not freely given. For as poor as I appear, I have friends of my own that will be blithe to help me."

"Hoot-toot!" said Uncle Ebenezer, "dinnae fly up in the snuff at me. We'll agree fine yet. And, Davie, my man, if you're done with that bit parritch, I could just take a sup of it myself. Ay," he continued, as soon as he had ousted me from the stool and spoon, "they're fine, halesome food—they're grand food, parritch." He murmured a little grace to himself and fell to. "Your father was very fond of his meat, I mind; he was a hearty, if not a great eater; but as for me, I could never do mair than pyke at food." He took a pull at the small beer, which probably reminded him of hospitable duties, for his next speech ran thus: "If ye're dry ye'll find water behind the door."

To this I returned no answer, standing stiffly on my two feet, and looking down upon my uncle with a mighty angry heart. He, on his part, continued to eat like a man under some pressure of time, and to throw out little darting glances now at my shoes and now at my home-spun stockings. Once only, when he had ventured to look a little higher, our eyes met; and no thief taken with a hand in a man's pocket could have shown more lively signals of distress. This set me in a muse, whether his timidity arose from too long a disuse of any human company; and whether perhaps, upon a little trial, it might pass off, and my uncle change into an altogether different man. From this I was awakened by his sharp voice.

"Your father's been long dead?" he asked.

"Three weeks, sir," said I.

"He was a secret man, Alexander—a secret, silent man," he continued. "He never said muckle when he was young. He'll never have spoken muckle of me?"

"I never knew, sir, till you told it me yourself, that he had any brother."

"Dear me, dear me!" said Ebenezer. "Nor yet of Shaws, I dare say?"

"Not so much as the name, sir," said I.

"To think o' that!" said he. "A strange nature of a man!" For all that, he seemed singularly satisfied, but whether with himself, or me, or with this conduct of my father's, was more than I could read. Certainly, however, he seemed to be outgrowing that distaste, or ill-will, that he had conceived at first against my person; for presently he jumped up, came across the room behind me, and hit me a smack upon the shoulder. "We'll agree fine yet!" he cried. "I'm just as glad I let you in. And now come awa' to your bed."

To my surprise, he lit no lamp or candle, but set forth into the dark passage, groped his way, breathing deeply, up a flight of steps, and paused before a door, which he unlocked. I was close upon his heels, having stumbled after him as best I might; and then he bade me go in, for that was my chamber. I did as he bid, but paused after a few steps, and begged a light to go to bed with.

"Hoot-toot!" said Uncle Ebenezer, "there's a fine moon."

"Neither moon nor star, sir, and pit-mirk," * said I. "I cannae see the bed."

* Dark as the pit.

"Hoot-toot, hoot-toot!" said he. "Lights in a house is a thing I dinnae agree with. I'm unco feared of fires. Good-night to ye, Davie, my man." And before I had time to add a further protest, he pulled the door to, and I heard him lock me in from the outside.

I did not know whether to laugh or cry. The room was as cold as a well, and the bed, when I had found my way to it, as damp as a peat-hag; but by good fortune I had caught up my bundle and my plaid, and rolling myself in the latter, I lay down upon the floor under lee of the big bedstead, and fell speedily asleep.

With the first peep of day I opened my eyes, to find myself in a great chamber, hung with stamped leather, furnished with fine embroidered furniture, and lit by three fair windows. Ten years ago, or perhaps twenty, it must have been as pleasant a room to lie down or to awake in as a man could wish; but damp, dirt, disuse, and the mice and spiders had done their worst since then. Many of the window-panes, besides, were broken; and indeed this was so common a feature in that house, that I believe my uncle must at some time have stood a siege from his indignant neighbours—perhaps with Jennet Clouston at their head.

Meanwhile the sun was shining outside; and being very cold in that miserable room, I knocked and shouted till my gaoler came and let me out. He carried me to the back of the house, where was a draw-well, and told me to "wash my face there, if I wanted;" and when that was done, I made the best of my own way back to the kitchen, where he had lit the fire and was making the porridge. The table was laid with two bowls and two horn spoons, but the same single measure of small beer. Perhaps my eye rested on this particular with some surprise, and perhaps my uncle observed it; for he spoke up as if in answer to my thought, asking me if I would like to drink ale—for so he called it.

I told him such was my habit, but not to put himself about.

"Na, na," said he; "I'll deny you nothing in reason."

He fetched another cup from the shelf; and then, to my great surprise, instead of drawing more beer, he poured an accurate half from one cup to the other. There was a kind of nobleness in this that took my breath away; if my uncle was certainly a miser, he was one of that thorough breed that goes near to make the vice respectable.

When we had made an end of our meal, my uncle Ebenezer unlocked a drawer, and drew out of it a clay pipe and a lump of tobacco, from which he cut one fill before he locked it up again. Then he sat down in the sun at one of the windows and silently smoked. From time to time his eyes came coasting round to me, and he shot out one of his questions. Once it was, "And your mother?" and when I had told him that she, too, was dead, "Ay, she was a bonnie lassie!" Then, after another long pause, "Whae were these friends o' yours?"

I told him they were different gentlemen of the name of Campbell; though, indeed, there was only one, and that the minister, that had ever taken the least note of me; but I began to think my uncle made too light of my position, and finding myself all alone with him, I did not wish him to suppose me helpless.

He seemed to turn this over in his mind; and then, "Davie, my man," said he, "ye've come to the right bit when ye came to your uncle Ebenezer. I've a great notion of the family, and I mean to do the right by you; but while I'm taking a bit think to mysel' of what's the best thing to put you to—whether the law, or the meenistry, or maybe the army, whilk is what boys are fondest of—I wouldnae like the Balfours to be humbled before a wheen Hieland Campbells, and I'll ask you to keep your tongue within your teeth. Nae letters; nae messages; no kind of word to onybody; or else—there's my door."

"Uncle Ebenezer," said I, "I've no manner of reason to suppose you mean anything but well by me. For all that, I would have you to know that I have a pride of my own. It was by no will of mine that I came seeking you; and if you show me your door again, I'll take you at the word."

He seemed grievously put out. "Hoots-toots," said he, "ca' cannie, man—ca' cannie! Bide a day or two. I'm nae warlock, to find a fortune for you in the bottom of a parritch bowl; but just you give me a day or two, and say naething to naebody, and as sure as sure, I'll do the right by you."

"Very well," said I, "enough said. If you want to help me, there's no doubt but I'll be glad of it, and none but I'll be grateful."

It seemed to me (too soon, I dare say) that I was getting the upper hand of my uncle; and I began next to say that I must have the bed and bedclothes aired and put to sun-dry; for nothing would make me sleep in such a pickle.

"Is this my house or yours?" said he, in his keen voice, and then all of a sudden broke off. "Na, na," said he, "I didnae mean that. What's mine is yours, Davie, my man, and what's yours is mine. Blood's thicker than water; and there's naebody but you and me that ought the name." And then on he rambled about the family, and its ancient greatness, and his father that began to enlarge the house, and himself that stopped the building as a sinful waste; and this put it in my head to give him Jennet Clouston's message.

"The limmer!" he cried. "Twelve hunner and fifteen—that's every day since I had the limmer rowpit!* Dod, David, I'll have her roasted on red peats before I'm by with it! A witch —a proclaimed witch! I'll aff and see the session clerk."

* Sold up.

And with that he opened a chest, and got out a very old and well-preserved blue coat and waistcoat, and a good enough beaver hat, both without lace. These he threw on any way, and taking a staff from the cupboard, locked all up again, and was for setting out, when a thought arrested him.

"I cannae leave you by yoursel' in the house," said he. "I'll have to lock you out."

The blood came to my face. "If you lock me out," I said, "it'll be the last you'll see of me in friendship."

He turned very pale, and sucked his mouth in.

"This is no the way," he said, looking wickedly at a corner of the floor—"this is no the way to win my favour, David."

"Sir," says I, "with a proper reverence for your age and our common blood, I do not value your favour at a boddle's purchase. I was brought up to have a good conceit of myself; and if you were all the uncle, and all the family, I had in the world ten times over, I wouldn't buy your liking at such prices."

Uncle Ebenezer went and looked out of the window for awhile. I could see him all trembling and twitching, like a man with palsy. But when he turned round, he had a smile upon his face.

"Well, well," said he, "we must bear and forbear. I'll no go; that's all that's to be said of it."

"Uncle Ebenezer," I said, "I can make nothing out of this. You use me like a thief; you hate to have me in this house; you let me see it, every word and every minute: it's not possible that you can like me; and as for me, I've spoken to you as I never thought to speak to any man. Why do you seek to keep me, then? Let me gang back—let me gang back to the friends I have, and that like me!"

"Na, na; na, na," he said, very earnestly. "I like you fine; we'll agree fine yet; and for the honour of the house I couldnae let you leave the way ye came. Bide here quiet, there's a good lad; just you bide here quiet a bittie, and ye'll find that we agree."

"Well, sir," said I, after I had thought the matter out in silence, "I'll stay awhile. It's more just I should be helped by my own blood than strangers; and if we don't agree, I'll do my best it shall be through no fault of mine."

4

I RUN A GREAT DANGER IN THE HOUSE OF SHAWS

For a day that was begun so ill, the day passed fairly well. We had the porridge cold again at noon, and hot porridge at night; porridge and small beer was my uncle's diet. He spoke but little, and that in the same way as before, shooting a question at me after a long silence; and when I sought to lead him to talk about my future, slipped out of it again. In a room next door to the kitchen, where he suffered me to go, I found a great number of books, both Latin and English, in which I took great pleasure all the afternoon. Indeed, the time passed so lightly in this good company, that I began to be almost reconciled to my residence at Shaws; and nothing but the sight of my uncle, and his eyes playing hide and seek with mine, revived the force of my distrust.

One thing I discovered, which put me in some doubt. This was an entry on the fly-leaf of a chap-book (one of Patrick Walker's) plainly written by my father's hand and thus conceived: "To my brother Ebenezer on his fifth birthday." Now, what puzzled me was this: That, as my father was of course the younger brother, he must either have made some strange error, or he must have written, before he was yet five, an excellent, clear manly hand of writing.

I tried to get this out of my head; but though I took down many interesting authors, old and new, history, poetry, and story-book, this notion of my father's hand of writing stuck to me; and when at length I went back into the kitchen, and sat down once more to porridge and small beer, the first thing I said to Uncle Ebenezer was to ask him if my father had not been very quick at his book.

"Alexander? No him!" was the reply. "I was far quicker mysel'; I was a clever chappie when I was young. Why, I could read as soon as he could."

This puzzled me yet more; and a thought coming into my head, I asked if he and my father had been twins.

He jumped upon his stool, and the horn spoon fell out of his hand upon the floor. "What gars ye ask that?" he said, and he caught me by the breast of the jacket, and looked this time straight into my eyes: his own were little and light, and bright like a bird's, blinking and winking strangely.

"What do you mean?" I asked, very calmly, for I was far stronger than he, and not easily frightened. "Take your hand from my jacket. This is no way to behave."

My uncle seemed to make a great effort upon himself. "Dod man, David," he said, "ye should-nae speak to me about your father. That's where the mistake is." He sat awhile and shook, blinking in his plate: "He was all the brother that ever I had," he added, but with no heart in his voice; and then he caught up his spoon and fell to supper again, but still shaking.

Now this last passage, this laying of hands upon my person and sudden profession of love for my dead father, went so clean beyond my comprehension that it put me into both fear and hope. On the one hand, I began to think my uncle was perhaps insane and might be dangerous; on the other, there came up into my mind (quite unbidden by me and even discouraged) a story like some ballad I had heard folk singing, of a poor lad that was a rightful heir and a wicked kinsman that tried to keep him from his own. For why should my uncle play a part with a relative that came, almost a beggar, to his door, unless in his heart he had some cause to fear him?

With this notion, all unacknowledged, but nevertheless getting firmly settled in my head, I now began to imitate his covert looks; so that we sat at table like a cat and a mouse, each stealthily observing the other. Not another word had he to say to me, black or white, but was busy turning something secretly over in his mind; and the longer we sat and the more I looked at him, the more certain I became that the something was unfriendly to myself.

When he had cleared the platter, he got out a single pipeful of tobacco, just as in the morning, turned round a stool into the chimney corner, and sat awhile smoking, with his back to me.

"Davie," he said, at length, "I've been thinking;" then he paused, and said it again. "There's a wee bit siller that I half promised ye before ye were born," he continued; "promised it to your father. O, naething legal, ye understand; just gentlemen daffing at their wine. Well, I keepit that bit money separate—it was a great expense, but a promise is a promise—and it has grown by now to be a matter of just precisely—just exactly"—and here he paused and stumbled—"of just exactly forty pounds!" This last he rapped out with a sidelong glance over his shoulder; and the next moment added, almost with a scream, "Scots!"

The pound Scots being the same thing as an English shilling, the difference made by this second thought was considerable; I could see, besides, that the whole story was a lie, invented with some end which it puzzled me to guess; and I made no attempt to conceal the tone of raillery in which I answered—

"O, think again, sir! Pounds sterling, I believe!"

"That's what I said," returned my uncle: "pounds sterling! And if you'll step out-by to the door a minute, just to see what kind of a night it is, I'll get it out to ye and call ye in again."

I did his will, smiling to myself in my contempt that he should think I was so easily to be deceived. It was a dark night, with a few stars low down; and as I stood just outside the door, I heard a hollow moaning of wind far off among the hills. I said to myself there was something thundery and changeful in the weather, and little knew of what a vast importance that should prove to me before the evening passed.

When I was called in again, my uncle counted out into my hand seven and thirty golden guinea pieces; the rest was in his hand, in small gold and silver; but his heart failed him there, and he crammed the change into his pocket.

"There," said he, "that'll show you! I'm a queer man, and strange wi' strangers; but my word is my bond, and there's the proof of it."

Now, my uncle seemed so miserly that I was struck dumb by this sudden generosity, and could find no words in which to thank him.

"No a word!" said he. "Nae thanks; I want nae thanks. I do my duty. I'm no saying that everybody would have done it; but for my part (though I'm a careful body, too) it's a pleasure to me to do the right by my brother's son; and it's a pleasure to me to think that now we'll agree as such near friends should."

I spoke him in return as handsomely as I was able; but all the while I was wondering what would come next, and why he had parted with his precious guineas; for as to the reason he had given, a baby would have refused it.

Presently he looked towards me sideways.

"And see here," says he, "tit for tat."

I told him I was ready to prove my gratitude in any reasonable degree, and then waited, looking for some monstrous demand. And yet, when at last he plucked up courage to speak, it was only to tell me (very properly, as I thought) that he was growing old and a little broken, and that he would expect me to help him with the house and the bit garden.

I answered, and expressed my readiness to serve.

"Well," he said, "let's begin." He pulled out of his pocket a rusty key. "There," says he, "there's the key of the stair-tower at the far end of the house. Ye can only win into it from the outside, for that part of the house is no finished. Gang ye in there, and up the stairs, and bring me down the chest that's at the top. There's papers in't," he added.

"Can I have a light, sir?" said I.

"Na," said he, very cunningly. "Nae lights in my house."

"Very well, sir," said I. "Are the stairs good?"

"They're grand," said he; and then, as I was going, "Keep to the wall," he added; "there's nae bannisters. But the stairs are grand underfoot."

Out I went into the night. The wind was still moaning in the distance, though never a breath of it came near the house of Shaws. It had fallen blacker than ever; and I was glad to feel along the wall, till I came the length of the stairtower door at the far end of the unfinished wing. I had got the key into the keyhole and had just turned it, when all upon a sudden, without sound of wind or thunder, the whole sky lighted up with wild fire and went black again. I had to put my hand over my eyes to get back to the colour of the darkness; and indeed I was already half blinded when I stepped into the tower.

It was so dark inside, it seemed a body could scarce breathe; but I pushed out with foot and hand, and presently struck the wall with the one, and the lowermost round of the stair with the other. The wall, by the touch, was of fine hewn stone; the steps too, though somewhat steep and narrow, were of polished masonwork, and regular and solid underfoot. Minding my uncle's word about the bannisters, I kept close to the tower side, and felt my way in the pitch darkness with a beating heart.

The house of Shaws stood some five full storeys high, not counting lofts. Well, as I advanced, it seemed to me the stair grew airier and a thought more lightsome; and I was wondering what might be the cause of this change, when a second blink of the summer lightning came and went. If I did not cry out, it was because fear had me by the throat; and if I did not fall, it was more by Heaven's mercy than my own strength. It was not only that the flash shone in on every side through breaches in the wall, so that I seemed to be clambering aloft upon an open scaffold, but the same passing brightness showed me the steps were of unequal length, and that one of my feet rested that moment within two inches of the well.

This was the grand stair! I thought; and with the thought, a gust of a kind of angry courage came into my heart. My uncle had sent me here, certainly to run great risks, perhaps to die. I swore I would settle that "perhaps," if I should break my neck for it; got me down upon my hands and knees; and as slowly as a snail, feeling before me every inch, and testing the solidity of every stone, I continued to ascend the stair. The darkness, by contrast with the flash, appeared to have redoubled; nor was that all, for my ears were now troubled and my mind confounded by a great stir of bats in the top part of the tower, and the foul beasts, flying downwards, sometimes beat about my face and body.

The tower, I should have said, was square; and in every corner the step was made of a great stone of a different shape to join the flights. Well, I had come close to one of these turns, when, feeling forward as usual, my hand slipped upon an edge and found nothing but emptiness beyond it. The stair had been carried no higher; to set a stranger mounting it in the darkness was to send him straight to his death; and (although, thanks to the lightning and my own precautions, I was safe enough) the mere thought of the peril in which I might have stood, and the dreadful height I might have fallen from, brought out the sweat upon my body and relaxed my joints.

But I knew what I wanted now, and turned and groped my way down again, with a wonderful anger in my heart. About half-way down, the wind sprang up in a clap and shook the tower, and died again; the rain followed; and before I had reached the ground level it fell in buckets. I put out my head into the storm, and looked along towards the kitchen. The door, which I had shut behind me when I left, now stood open, and shed a little glimmer of light; and I thought I could see a figure standing in the rain, quite still, like a man hearkening. And then there came a blinding flash, which showed me my uncle plainly, just where I had fancied him to stand; and hard upon the heels of it, a great tow-row of thunder.

Now, whether my uncle thought the crash to be the sound of my fall, or whether he heard in it God's voice denouncing murder, I will leave you to guess. Certain it is, at least, that he was seized on by a kind of panic fear, and that he ran into the house and left the door open behind him. I followed as softly as I could, and, coming unheard into the kitchen, stood and watched him.

He had found time to open the corner cupboard and bring out a great case bottle of aqua vitae, and now sat with his back towards me at the table. Ever and again he would be seized with a fit of deadly shuddering and groan aloud, and carrying the bottle to his lips, drink down the raw spirits by the mouthful.

I stepped forward, came close behind him where he sat, and suddenly clapping my two hands down upon his shoulders—"Ah!" cried I.

My uncle gave a kind of broken cry like a sheep's bleat, flung up his arms, and tumbled to the floor like a dead man. I was somewhat shocked at this; but I had myself to look to first of all, and did not hesitate to let him lie as he had fallen. The keys were hanging in the cupboard; and it was my design to furnish myself with arms before my uncle should come again to his senses and the power of devising evil. In the cupboard were a few bottles, some apparently of medicine; a great many bills and other papers, which I should willingly enough have rummaged, had I had the time; and a few necessaries that were nothing to my purpose. Thence I turned to the chests. The first was full of meal; the second of moneybags and papers tied into sheaves; in the third, with many other things (and these for the most part clothes) I found a rusty, ugly-looking Highland dirk without the scabbard. This, then, I concealed inside my waistcoat, and turned to my uncle.

He lay as he had fallen, all huddled, with one knee up and one arm sprawling abroad; his face had a strange colour of blue, and he seemed to have ceased breathing. Fear came on me that he was dead; then I got water and dashed it in his face; and with that he seemed to come a little to himself, working his mouth and fluttering his eyelids. At last he looked up and saw me, and there came into his eyes a terror that was not of this world.

"Come, come," said I; "sit up."

"Are ye alive?" he sobbed. "O man, are ye alive?"

"That am I," said I. "Small thanks to you!"

He had begun to seek for his breath with deep sighs. "The blue phial," said he—"in the aumry—the blue phial." His breath came slower still.

I ran to the cupboard, and, sure enough, found there a blue phial of medicine, with the dose written on it on a paper, and this I administered to him with what speed I might.

"It's the trouble," said he, reviving a little; "I have a trouble, Davie. It's the heart."

I set him on a chair and looked at him. It is true I felt some pity for a man that looked so sick, but I was full besides of righteous anger; and I numbered over before him the points on which I wanted explanation: why he lied to me at every word; why he feared that I should leave him; why he disliked it to be hinted that he and my father were twins—"Is that because it is true?" I asked; why he had given me money to which I was convinced I had no claim; and, last of all, why he had tried to kill me. He heard me all through in silence; and then, in a broken voice, begged me to let him go to bed.

"I'll tell ye the morn," he said; "as sure as death I will."

And so weak was he that I could do nothing but consent. I locked him into his room, however, and pocketed the key, and then returning to the kitchen, made up such a blaze as had not shone there for many a long year, and wrapping myself in my plaid, lay down upon the chests and fell asleep.

5

I GO TO THE QUEEN'S FERRY

Much rain fell in the night; and the next morning there blew a bitter wintry wind out of the north-west, driving scattered clouds. For all that, and before the sun began to peep or the last of the stars had vanished, I made my way to the side of the burn, and had a plunge in a deep whirling pool. All aglow from my bath, I sat down once more beside the fire, which I replenished, and began gravely to consider my position.

There was now no doubt about my uncle's enmity; there was no doubt I carried my life in my hand, and he would leave no stone unturned that he might compass my destruction. But I was young and spirited, and like most lads that have been country-bred, I had a great opinion of my shrewdness. I had come to his door no better than a beggar and little more than a child; he had met me with treachery and violence; it would be a fine consummation to take the upper hand, and drive him like a herd of sheep.

I sat there nursing my knee and smiling at the fire; and I saw myself in fancy smell out his secrets one after another, and grow to be that man's king and ruler. The warlock of Essendean, they say, had made a mirror in which men could read the future; it must have been of other stuff than burning coal; for in all the shapes and pictures that I sat and gazed at, there was never a ship, never a seaman with a hairy cap, never a big bludgeon for my silly head, or the least sign of all those tribulations that were ripe to fall on me.

Presently, all swollen with conceit, I went up-stairs and gave my prisoner his liberty. He gave me good-morning civilly; and I gave the same to him, smiling down upon him, from the heights of my sufficiency. Soon we were set to breakfast, as it might have been the day before.

"Well, sir," said I, with a jeering tone, "have you nothing more to say to me?" And then, as he made no articulate reply, "It will be time, I think, to understand each other," I continued. "You took me for a country Johnnie Raw, with no more mother-wit or courage than a porridge-stick. I took you for a good man, or no worse than others at the least. It seems we were both wrong. What cause you have to fear me, to cheat me, and to attempt my life—"

He murmured something about a jest, and that he liked a bit of fun; and then, seeing me smile, changed his tone, and assured me he would make all clear as soon as we had breakfasted. I saw by his face that he had no lie ready for me, though he was hard at work preparing one; and I think I was about to tell him so, when we were interrupted by a knocking at the door.

Bidding my uncle sit where he was, I went to open it, and found on the doorstep a half-grown boy in sea-clothes. He had no sooner seen me than he began to dance some steps of the sea-hornpipe (which I had never before heard of far less seen), snapping his fingers in the air and footing it right cleverly. For all that, he was blue with the cold; and there was something in his face, a look between tears and laughter, that was highly pathetic and consisted ill with this gaiety of manner.

"What cheer, mate?" says he, with a cracked voice.

I asked him soberly to name his pleasure.

"O, pleasure!" says he; and then began to sing:

"For it's my delight, of a shiny night,
In the season of the year."

"Well," said I, "if you have no business at all, I will even be so unmannerly as to shut you out."

"Stay, brother!" he cried. "Have you no fun about you? or do you want to get me thrashed? I've brought a letter from old Heasyoasy to Mr. Belflower." He showed me a letter as he spoke. "And I say, mate," he added, "I'm mortal hungry."

"Well," said I, "come into the house, and you shall have a bite if I go empty for it."

With that I brought him in and set him down to my own place, where he fell-to greedily on the remains of breakfast, winking to me between whiles, and making many faces, which I think the poor soul considered manly. Meanwhile, my uncle had read the letter and sat thinking; then, suddenly, he got to his feet with a great air of liveliness, and pulled me apart into the farthest corner of the room.

"Read that," said he, and put the letter in my hand.

Here it is, lying before me as I write:

"The Hawes Inn, at the Queen's Ferry.

"Sir,—I lie here with my hawser up and down, and send my cabin-boy to informe. If you have any further commands for over-seas, to-day will be the last occasion, as the wind will serve us well out of the firth. I will not seek to deny that I have had crosses with your doer,* Mr. Rankeillor; of which, if not speedily redd up, you may looke to see some losses follow. I have drawn a bill upon you, as per margin, and am, sir, your most obedt., humble servant, "ELIAS HOSEASON." * Agent.

"You see, Davie," resumed my uncle, as soon as he saw that I had done, "I have a venture with this man Hoseason, the captain of a trading brig, the Covenant, of Dysart. Now, if you and me was to walk over with yon lad, I could see the captain at the Hawes, or maybe on board the Covenant if there was papers to be signed; and so far from a loss of time, we can jog on to the lawyer, Mr. Rankeillor's. After a' that's come and gone, ye would be swier (*unwilling*) to believe me upon my naked word; but ye'll believe Rankeillor. He's factor to half the gentry in these parts; an auld man, forby: highly respeckit, and he kenned your father."

I stood awhile and thought. I was going to some place of shipping, which was doubtless populous, and where my uncle durst attempt no violence, and, indeed, even the society of the cabin-boy so far protected me. Once there, I believed I could force on the visit to the lawyer, even if my uncle were now insincere in proposing it; and, perhaps, in the bottom of my heart, I wished a nearer view of the sea and ships. You are to remember I had lived all my life in the inland hills, and just two days before had my first sight of the firth lying like a blue floor, and the sailed ships moving on the face of it, no bigger than toys. One thing with another, I made up my mind.

"Very well," says I, "let us go to the Ferry."

My uncle got into his hat and coat, and buckled an old rusty cutlass on; and then we trod the fire out, locked the door, and set forth upon our walk.

The wind, being in that cold quarter the north-west, blew nearly in our faces as we went. It was the month of June; the grass was all white with daisies, and the trees with blossom; but, to judge by our blue nails and aching wrists, the time might have been winter and the whiteness a December frost.

Uncle Ebenezer trudged in the ditch, jogging from side to side like an old ploughman coming home from work. He never said a word the whole way; and I was thrown for talk on the cabin-boy. He told me his name was Ransome, and that he had followed the sea since he was nine, but could not say how old he was, as he had lost his reckoning. He showed me tattoo marks, baring his breast in the teeth of the wind and in spite of my remonstrances, for I thought it was enough to kill him; he swore horribly whenever he remembered, but more like a silly schoolboy than a man; and boasted of many wild and bad things that he had done: stealthy thefts, false accusations, ay, and even murder; but all with such a dearth of likelihood in the details, and such a weak and crazy swagger in the delivery, as disposed me rather to pity than to believe him.

I asked him of the brig (which he declared was the finest ship that sailed) and of Captain Hoseason, in whose praises he was equally loud. Heasyoasy (for so he still named the skipper) was a man, by his account, that minded for nothing either in heaven or earth; one that, as people said, would "crack on all sail into the day of judgment;" rough, fierce, unscrupulous, and brutal; and all this my poor cabin-boy had taught himself to admire as something seamanlike and manly. He would only admit one flaw in his idol. "He ain't no seaman," he admitted. "That's Mr. Shuan that navigates the brig; he's the finest seaman in the trade, only for drink; and I tell you I believe it! Why, look'ere;" and turning down his stocking he showed me a great, raw, red wound that made my blood run cold. "He done that —Mr. Shuan done it," he said, with an air of pride.

"What!" I cried, "do you take such savage usage at his hands? Why, you are no slave, to be so handled!"

"No," said the poor moon-calf, changing his tune at once, "and so he'll find. See'ere;" and he showed me a great case-knife, which he told me was stolen. "O," says he, "let me see him try; I dare him to; I'll do for him! O, he ain't the first!" And he confirmed it with a poor, silly, ugly oath.

I have never felt such pity for any one in this wide world as I felt for that half-witted creature, and it began to come over me that the brig Covenant (for all her pious name) was little better than a hell upon the seas.

"Have you no friends?" said I.

He said he had a father in some English seaport, I forget which.

"He was a fine man, too," he said, "but he's dead."

"In Heaven's name," cried I, "can you find no reputable life on shore?"

"O, no," says he, winking and looking very sly, "they would put me to a trade. I know a trick worth two of that, I do!"

I asked him what trade could be so dreadful as the one he followed, where he ran the continual peril of his life, not alone from wind and sea, but by the horrid cruelty of those who were his masters. He said it was very true; and then began to praise the life, and tell what a pleasure it was to get on shore with money in his pocket, and spend it like a man, and buy apples, and swagger, and surprise what he called stick-in-the-mud boys. "And then it's not all as bad as that," says he; "there's worse off than me: there's the twenty-pounders. O, laws! you should see them taking on. Why, I've seen a man as old as you, I dessay"—(to him I seemed old)—"ah, and he had a beard, too—well, and as soon as we cleared out of the river, and he had the drug out of his head—my! how he cried and carried on! I made a fine fool of him, I tell you! And then there's little uns, too: oh, little by me! I tell you, I keep them in order. When we carry little uns, I have a rope's end of my own to wollop 'em." And so he ran on, until it came in on me what he meant by twenty-pounders were those unhappy criminals who were sent over-seas to slavery in North America, or the still more unhappy innocents who were kidnapped or trepanned (as the word went) for private interest or vengeance.

Just then we came to the top of the hill, and looked down on the Ferry and the Hope. The Firth of Forth (as is very well known) narrows at this point to the width of a good-sized river, which makes a convenient ferry going north, and turns the upper reach into a landlocked haven for all manner of ships. Right in the midst of the narrows lies an islet with some ruins; on the south shore they have built a pier for the service of the Ferry; and at the end of the pier, on the other side of the road, and backed against a pretty garden of holly-trees and hawthorns, I could see the building which they called the Hawes Inn.

The town of Queensferry lies farther west, and the neighbourhood of the inn looked pretty lonely at that time of day, for the boat had just gone north with passengers. A skiff, however, lay beside the pier, with some seamen sleeping on the thwarts; this, as Ransome told me, was the brig's boat waiting for the captain; and about half a mile off, and all alone in the anchorage, he showed me the Covenant herself. There was a sea-going bustle on board; yards were swinging into place; and as the wind blew from that quarter, I could hear the song of the sailors as they pulled upon the ropes. After all I had listened to upon the way, I looked at that ship with an extreme abhorrence; and from the bottom of my heart I pitied all poor souls that were condemned to sail in her.

We had all three pulled up on the brow of the hill; and now I marched across the road and addressed my uncle. "I think it right to tell you, sir," says I, "there's nothing that will bring me on board that Covenant."

He seemed to waken from a dream. "Eh?" he said. "What's that?"

I told him over again.

"Well, well," he said, "we'll have to please ye, I suppose. But what are we standing here for? It's perishing cold; and if I'm no mistaken, they're busking the Covenant for sea."

6

WHAT BEFELL AT THE QUEEN'S FERRY

As soon as we came to the inn, Ransome led us up the stair to a small room, with a bed in it, and heated like an oven by a great fire of coal. At a table hard by the chimney, a tall, dark, sober-looking man sat writing. In spite of the heat of the room, he wore a thick sea-jacket, buttoned to the neck, and a tall hairy cap drawn down over his ears; yet I never saw any man, not even a judge upon the bench, look cooler, or more studious and self-possessed, than this ship-captain.

He got to his feet at once, and coming forward, offered his large hand to Ebenezer. "I am proud to see you, Mr. Balfour," said he, in a fine deep voice, "and glad that ye are here in time. The wind's fair, and the tide upon the turn; we'll see the old coal-bucket burning on the Isle of May before to-night."

"Captain Hoseason," returned my uncle, "you keep your room unco hot."

"It's a habit I have, Mr. Balfour," said the skipper. "I'm a cold-rife man by my nature; I have a cold blood, sir. There's neither fur, nor flannel—no, sir, nor hot rum, will warm up what they call the temperature. Sir, it's the same with most men that have been carbonadoed, as they call it, in the tropic seas."

"Well, well, captain," replied my uncle, "we must all be the way we're made."

But it chanced that this fancy of the captain's had a great share in my misfortunes. For though I had promised myself not to let my kinsman out of sight, I was both so impatient for a nearer look of the sea, and so sickened by the closeness of the room, that when he told me to "run down-stairs and play myself awhile," I was fool enough to take him at his word.

Away I went, therefore, leaving the two men sitting down to a bottle and a great mass of papers; and crossing the road in front of the inn, walked down upon the beach. With the wind in that quarter, only little wavelets, not much bigger than I had seen upon a lake, beat upon the shore. But the weeds were new to me—some green, some brown and long, and some with little bladders that crackled between my fingers. Even so far up the firth, the smell of the sea-water was exceedingly salt and stirring; the Covenant, besides, was beginning to shake out her sails, which hung upon the yards in clusters; and the spirit of all that I beheld put me in thoughts of far voyages and foreign places.

I looked, too, at the seamen with the skiff—big brown fellows, some in shirts, some with jackets, some with coloured handkerchiefs about their throats, one with a brace of pistols stuck into his pockets, two or three with knotty bludgeons, and all with their case-knives. I passed the time of day with one that looked less desperate than his fellows, and asked him of the sailing of the brig. He said they would get under way as soon as the ebb set, and expressed his gladness to be out of a port where there were no taverns and fiddlers; but all with such horrifying oaths, that I made haste to get away from him.

This threw me back on Ransome, who seemed the least wicked of that gang, and who soon came out of the inn and ran to me, crying for a bowl of punch. I told him I would give him no such thing, for neither he nor I was of an age for such indulgences. "But a glass of ale you may have, and welcome," said I. He mopped and mowed at me, and called me names; but he was glad to get the ale, for all that; and presently we were set down at a table in the front room of the inn, and both eating and drinking with a good appetite.

Here it occurred to me that, as the landlord was a man of that county, I might do well to make a friend of him. I offered him a share, as was much the custom in those days; but he was far too great a man to sit with such poor customers as Ransome and myself, and he was leaving the room, when I called him back to ask if he knew Mr. Rankeillor.

"Hoot, ay," says he, "and a very honest man. And, O, by-the-by," says he, "was it you that came in with Ebenezer?" And when I had told him yes, "Ye'll be no friend of his?" he asked, meaning, in the Scottish way, that I would be no relative.

I told him no, none.

"I thought not," said he, "and yet ye have a kind of gliff (*look*) of Mr. Alexander."

I said it seemed that Ebenezer was ill-seen in the country.

"Nae doubt," said the landlord. "He's a wicked auld man, and there's many would like to see him girning in the tow (*rope*). Jennet Clouston and mony mair that he has harried out of house and hame. And yet he was ance a fine young fellow, too. But that was before the sough (**report*) gaed abroad about Mr. Alexander, that was like the death of him."

"And what was it?" I asked.

"Ou, just that he had killed him," said the landlord. "Did ye never hear that?"

"And what would he kill him for?" said I.

"And what for, but just to get the place," said he.

"The place?" said I. "The Shaws?"

"Nae other place that I ken," said he.

"Ay, man?" said I. "Is that so? Was my—was Alexander the eldest son?"

"'Deed was he," said the landlord. "What else would he have killed him for?"

And with that he went away, as he had been impatient to do from the beginning.

Of course, I had guessed it a long while ago; but it is one thing to guess, another to know; and I sat stunned with my good fortune, and could scarce grow to believe that the same poor lad who had trudged in the dust from Ettrick Forest not two days ago, was now one of the rich of the earth, and had a house and broad lands, and might mount his horse tomorrow. All these pleasant things, and a thousand others, crowded into my mind, as I sat staring before me out of the inn window, and paying no heed to what I saw; only I remember that my eye lighted on Captain Hoseason down on the pier among his seamen, and speaking with some authority. And presently he came marching back towards the house, with no mark of a sailor's clumsiness, but carrying his fine, tall figure with a manly bearing, and still with the same sober, grave expression on his face. I wondered if it was possible that Ransome's stories could be true, and half disbelieved them; they fitted so ill with the man's looks. But indeed, he was neither so good as I supposed him, nor quite so bad as Ransome did; for, in fact, he was two men, and left the better one behind as soon as he set foot on board his vessel.

The next thing, I heard my uncle calling me, and found the pair in the road together. It was the captain who addressed me, and that with an air (very flattering to a young lad) of grave equality.

"Sir," said he, "Mr. Balfour tells me great things of you; and for my own part, I like your looks. I wish I was for longer here, that we might make the better friends; but we'll make the most of what we have. Ye shall come on board my brig for half an hour, till the ebb sets, and drink a bowl with me."

Now, I longed to see the inside of a ship more than words can tell; but I was not going to put myself in jeopardy, and I told him my uncle and I had an appointment with a lawyer.

"Ay, ay," said he, "he passed me word of that. But, ye see, the boat'll set ye ashore at the town pier, and that's but a penny stonecast from Rankeillor's house." And here he suddenly leaned down and whispered in my ear: "Take care of the old tod (*fox*); he means mischief. Come aboard till I can get a word with ye." And then, passing his arm through mine, he continued aloud, as he set off towards his boat: "But, come, what can I bring ye from the Carolinas? Any friend of Mr. Balfour's can command. A roll of tobacco? Indian feather-work? a skin of a wild beast? a stone pipe? the mocking-bird that mews for all the world like a cat? the cardinal bird that is as red as blood?—take your pick and say your pleasure."

By this time we were at the boat-side, and he was handing me in. I did not dream of hanging back; I thought (the poor fool!) that I had found a good friend and helper, and I was rejoiced to see the ship. As soon as we were all set in our places, the boat was thrust off from the pier and began to move over the waters: and what with my pleasure in this new movement and my surprise at our low position, and the appearance of the shores, and the growing bigness of the brig as we drew near to it, I could hardly understand what the captain said, and must have answered him at random.

As soon as we were alongside (where I sat fairly gaping at the ship's height, the strong humming of the tide against its sides, and the pleasant cries of the seamen at their work) Hoseason, declaring that he and I must be the first aboard, ordered a tackle to be sent down from the main-yard. In this I was whipped into the air and set down again on the deck, where the captain stood ready waiting for me, and instantly slipped back his arm under mine. There I stood some while, a little dizzy with the unsteadiness of all around me, perhaps a little afraid, and yet vastly pleased with these strange sights; the captain meanwhile pointing out the strangest, and telling me their names and uses.

"But where is my uncle?" said I suddenly.

"Ay," said Hoseason, with a sudden grimness, "that's the point."

I felt I was lost. With all my strength, I plucked myself clear of him and ran to the bulwarks. Sure enough, there was the boat pulling for the town, with my uncle sitting in the stern. I gave a piercing cry—"Help, help! Murder!"—so that both sides of the anchorage rang with it, and my uncle turned round where he was sitting, and showed me a face full of cruelty and terror.

It was the last I saw. Already strong hands had been plucking me back from the ship's side; and now a thunderbolt seemed to strike me; I saw a great flash of fire, and fell senseless.

7

I GO TO SEA IN THE BRIG "COVENANT" OF DYSART

I came to myself in darkness, in great pain, bound hand and foot, and deafened by many unfamiliar noises. There sounded in my ears a roaring of water as of a huge mill-dam, the thrashing of heavy sprays, the thundering of the sails, and the shrill cries of seamen. The whole world now heaved giddily up, and now rushed giddily downward; and so sick and hurt was I in body, and my mind so much confounded, that it took me a long while, chasing my thoughts up and down, and ever stunned again by a fresh stab of pain, to realise that I must be lying somewhere bound in the belly of that unlucky ship, and that the wind must have strengthened to a gale. With the clear perception of my plight, there fell upon me a blackness of despair, a horror of remorse at my own folly, and a passion of anger at my uncle, that once more bereft me of my senses.

When I returned again to life, the same uproar, the same confused and violent movements, shook and deafened me; and presently, to my other pains and distresses, there was added the sickness of an unused landsman on the sea. In that time of my adventurous youth, I suffered many hardships; but none that was so crushing to my mind and body, or lit by so few hopes, as these first hours aboard the brig.

I heard a gun fire, and supposed the storm had proved too strong for us, and we were firing signals of distress. The thought of deliverance, even by death in the deep sea, was welcome to me. Yet it was no such matter; but (as I was afterwards told) a common habit of the captain's, which I here set down to show that even the worst man may have his kindlier side. We were then passing, it appeared, within some miles of Dysart, where the brig was built, and where old Mrs. Hoseason, the captain's mother, had come some years before to live; and whether outward or inward bound, the Covenant was never suffered to go by that place by day, without a gun fired and colours shown.

I had no measure of time; day and night were alike in that ill-smelling cavern of the ship's bowels where I lay; and the misery of my situation drew out the hours to double. How long, therefore, I lay waiting to hear the ship split upon some rock, or to feel her reel head foremost into the depths of the sea, I have not the means of computation. But sleep at length stole from me the consciousness of sorrow.

I was awakened by the light of a hand-lantern shining in my face. A small man of about thirty, with green eyes and a tangle of fair hair, stood looking down at me.

"Well," said he, "how goes it?"

I answered by a sob; and my visitor then felt my pulse and temples, and set himself to wash and dress the wound upon my scalp.

"Ay," said he, "a sore dunt (*stroke). What, man? Cheer up! The world's no done; you've made a bad start of it but you'll make a better. Have you had any meat?"

I said I could not look at it: and thereupon he gave me some brandy and water in a tin pannikin, and left me once more to myself.

The next time he came to see me, I was lying betwixt sleep and waking, my eyes wide open in the darkness, the sickness quite departed, but succeeded by a horrid giddiness and swimming that was almost worse to bear. I ached, besides, in every limb, and the cords that bound me seemed to be of fire. The smell of the hole in which I lay seemed to have become a part of me; and during the long interval since his last visit I had suffered tortures of fear, now from the scurrying of the ship's rats, that sometimes pattered on my very face, and now from the dismal imaginings that haunt the bed of fever.

The glimmer of the lantern, as a trap opened, shone in like the heaven's sunlight; and though it only showed me the strong, dark beams of the ship that was my prison, I could have cried aloud for gladness. The man with the green eyes was the first to descend the ladder, and I noticed that he came somewhat unsteadily. He was followed by the captain. Neither said a word; but the first set to and examined me, and dressed my wound as before, while Hoseason looked me in my face with an odd, black look.

"Now, sir, you see for yourself," said the first: "a high fever, no appetite, no light, no meat: you see for yourself what that means."

"I am no conjurer, Mr. Riach," said the captain.

"Give me leave, sir," said Riach; "you've a good head upon your shoulders, and a good Scotch tongue to ask with; but I will leave you no manner of excuse; I want that boy taken out of this hole and put in the forecastle."

"What ye may want, sir, is a matter of concern to nobody but yoursel'," returned the captain; "but I can tell ye that which is to be. Here he is; here he shall bide."

"Admitting that you have been paid in a proportion," said the other, "I will crave leave humbly to say that I have not. Paid I am, and none too much, to be the second officer of this old tub, and you ken very well if I do my best to earn it. But I was paid for nothing more."

"If ye could hold back your hand from the tin-pan, Mr. Riach, I would have no complaint to make of ye," returned the skipper; "and instead of asking riddles, I make bold to say that ye would keep your breath to cool your porridge. We'll be required on deck," he added, in a sharper note, and set one foot upon the ladder.

But Mr. Riach caught him by the sleeve.

"Admitting that you have been paid to do a murder——" he began.

Hoseason turned upon him with a flash.

"What's that?" he cried. "What kind of talk is that?"

"It seems it is the talk that you can understand," said Mr. Riach, looking him steadily in the face.

"Mr. Riach, I have sailed with ye three cruises," replied the captain. "In all that time, sir, ye should have learned to know me: I'm a stiff man, and a dour man; but for what ye say the now—fie, fie!—it comes from a bad heart and a black conscience. If ye say the lad will die——"

"Ay, will he!" said Mr. Riach.

"Well, sir, is not that enough?" said Hoseason. "Flit him where ye please!"

Thereupon the captain ascended the ladder; and I, who had lain silent throughout this strange conversation, beheld Mr. Riach turn after him and bow as low as to his knees in what was plainly a spirit of derision. Even in my then state of sickness, I perceived two things: that the mate was touched with liquor, as the captain hinted, and that (drunk or sober) he was like to prove a valuable friend.

Five minutes afterwards my bonds were cut, I was hoisted on a man's back, carried up to the forecastle, and laid in a bunk on some sea-blankets; where the first thing that I did was to lose my senses.

It was a blessed thing indeed to open my eyes again upon the daylight, and to find myself in the society of men. The forecastle was a roomy place enough, set all about with berths, in which the men of the watch below were seated smoking, or lying down asleep. The day being calm and the wind fair, the scuttle was open, and not only the good daylight, but from time to time (as the ship rolled) a dusty beam of sunlight shone in, and dazzled and delighted me. I had no sooner moved, moreover, than one of the men brought me a drink of something healing which Mr. Riach had prepared, and bade me lie still and I should soon be well again. There were no bones broken, he explained: "A clour (*blow*) on the head was naething. Man," said he, "it was me that gave it ye!"

Here I lay for the space of many days a close prisoner, and not only got my health again, but came to know my companions. They were a rough lot indeed, as sailors mostly are: being men rooted out of all the kindly parts of life, and condemned to toss together on the rough seas, with masters no less cruel. There were some among them that had sailed with the pirates and seen things it would be a shame even to speak of; some were men that had run from the king's ships, and went with a halter round their necks, of which they made no secret; and all, as the saying goes, were "at a word and a blow" with their best friends. Yet I had not been many days shut up with them before I began to be ashamed of my first judgment, when I had drawn away from them at the Ferry pier, as though they had been unclean beasts. No class of man is altogether bad, but each has its own faults and virtues; and these shipmates of mine were no exception to the rule. Rough they were, sure enough; and bad, I suppose; but they had many virtues. They were kind when it occurred to them, simple even beyond the simplicity of a country lad like me, and had some glimmerings of honesty.

There was one man, of maybe forty, that would sit on my berthside for hours and tell me of his wife and child. He was a fisher that had lost his boat, and thus been driven to the deep-sea voyaging. Well, it is years ago now: but I have never forgotten him. His wife (who was "young by him," as he often told me) waited in vain to see her man return; he would never again make the fire for her in the morning, nor yet keep the bairn when she was sick. Indeed, many of these poor fellows (as the event proved) were upon their last cruise; the deep seas and cannibal fish received them; and it is a thankless business to speak ill of the dead.

Among other good deeds that they did, they returned my money, which had been shared among them; and though it was about a third short, I was very glad to get it, and hoped great good from it in the land I was going to. The ship was bound for the Carolinas; and you must not suppose that I was going to that place merely as an exile. The trade was even then much depressed; since that, and with the rebellion of the colonies and the formation of the United States, it has, of course, come to an end; but in those days of my youth, white men were still sold into slavery on the plantations, and that was the destiny to which my wicked uncle had condemned me.

The cabin-boy Ransome (from whom I had first heard of these atrocities) came in at times from the round-house, where he berthed and served, now nursing a bruised limb in silent agony, now raving against the cruelty of Mr. Shuan. It made my heart bleed; but the men had a great respect for the chief mate, who was, as they said, "the only seaman of the whole jing-bang, and none such a bad man when he was sober." Indeed, I found there was a strange peculiarity about our two mates: that Mr. Riach was sullen, unkind, and harsh when he was sober, and Mr. Shuan would not hurt a fly except when he was drinking. I asked about the captain, but I was told drink made no difference upon that man of iron.

I did my best in the small time allowed me to make something like a man, or rather I should say something like a boy, of the poor creature, Ransome. But his mind was scarce truly human. He could remember nothing of the time before he came to sea; only that his father had made clocks, and had a starling in the parlour, which could whistle "The North Countrie;" all else had been blotted out in these years of hardship and cruelties. He had a strange notion of the dry land, picked up from sailor's stories: that it was a place where lads were put to some kind of slavery called a trade, and where apprentices were continually lashed and clapped into foul prisons. In a town, he thought every second person a decoy, and every third house a place in which seamen would be drugged and murdered. To be sure, I would tell him how kindly I had myself been used upon that dry land he was so much afraid of, and how well fed and carefully taught both by my friends and my parents: and if he had been recently hurt, he would weep bitterly and swear to run away; but if he was in his usual crackbrain humour, or (still more) if he had had a glass of spirits in the roundhouse, he would deride the notion.

It was Mr. Riach (Heaven forgive him!) who gave the boy drink; and it was, doubtless, kindly meant; but besides that it was ruin to his health, it was the pitifullest thing in life to see this unhappy, unfriended creature staggering, and dancing, and talking he knew not what. Some of the men laughed, but not all; others would grow as black as thunder (thinking, perhaps, of their own childhood or their own children) and bid him stop that nonsense, and think what he was doing. As for me, I felt ashamed to look at him, and the poor child still comes about me in my dreams.

All this time, you should know, the Covenant was meeting continual head-winds and tumbling up and down against head-seas, so that the scuttle was almost constantly shut, and the forecastle lighted only by a swinging lantern on a beam. There was constant labour for all hands; the sails had to be made and shortened every hour; the strain told on the men's temper; there was a growl of quarrelling all day long from berth to berth; and as I was never allowed to set my foot on deck, you can picture to yourselves how weary of my life I grew to be, and how impatient for a change.

And a change I was to get, as you shall hear; but I must first tell of a conversation I had with Mr. Riach, which put a little heart in me to bear my troubles. Getting him in a favourable stage of drink (for indeed he never looked near me when he was sober), I pledged him to secrecy, and told him my whole story.

He declared it was like a ballad; that he would do his best to help me; that I should have paper, pen, and ink, and write one line to Mr. Campbell and another to Mr. Rankeillor; and that if I had told the truth, ten to one he would be able (with their help) to pull me through and set me in my rights.

"And in the meantime," says he, "keep your heart up. You're not the only one, I'll tell you that. There's many a man hoeing tobacco over-seas that should be mounting his horse at his own door at home; many and many! And life is all a variorum, at the best. Look at me: I'm a laird's son and more than half a doctor, and here I am, man-Jack to Hoseason!"

I thought it would be civil to ask him for his story.
He whistled loud.
"Never had one," said he. "I like fun, that's all." And he skipped out of the forecastle.

8

THE ROUND-HOUSE

One night, about eleven o'clock, a man of Mr. Riach's watch (which was on deck) came below for his jacket; and instantly there began to go a whisper about the forecastle that "Shuan had done for him at last." There was no need of a name; we all knew who was meant; but we had scarce time to get the idea rightly in our heads, far less to speak of it, when the scuttle was again flung open, and Captain Hoseason came down the ladder. He looked sharply round the bunks in the tossing light of the lantern; and then, walking straight up to me, he addressed me, to my surprise, in tones of kindness.

"My man," said he, "we want ye to serve in the round-house. You and Ransome are to change berths. Run away aft with ye."

Even as he spoke, two seamen appeared in the scuttle, carrying Ransome in their arms; and the ship at that moment giving a great sheer into the sea, and the lantern swinging, the light fell direct on the boy's face. It was as white as wax, and had a look upon it like a dreadful smile. The blood in me ran cold, and I drew in my breath as if I had been struck.

"Run away aft; run away aft with ye!" cried Hoseason.

And at that I brushed by the sailors and the boy (who neither spoke nor moved), and ran up the ladder on deck.

The brig was sheering swiftly and giddily through a long, cresting swell. She was on the starboard tack, and on the left hand, under the arched foot of the foresail, I could see the sunset still quite bright. This, at such an hour of the night, surprised me greatly; but I was too ignorant to draw the true conclusion—that we were going north-about round Scotland, and were now on the high sea between the Orkney and Shetland Islands, having avoided the dangerous currents of the Pentland Firth. For my part, who had been so long shut in the dark and knew nothing of head-winds, I thought we might be half-way or more across the Atlantic. And indeed (beyond that I wondered a little at the lateness of the sunset light) I gave no heed to it, and pushed on across the decks, running between the seas, catching at ropes, and only saved from going overboard by one of the hands on deck, who had been always kind to me.

The round-house, for which I was bound, and where I was now to sleep and serve, stood some six feet above the decks, and considering the size of the brig, was of good dimensions. Inside were a fixed table and bench, and two berths, one for the captain and the other for the two mates, turn and turn about. It was all fitted with lockers from top to bottom, so as to stow away the officers' belongings and a part of the ship's stores; there was a second store-room underneath, which you entered by a hatchway in the middle of the deck; indeed, all the best of the meat and drink and the whole of the powder were collected in this place; and all the firearms, except the two pieces of brass ordnance, were set in a rack in the aftermost wall of the round-house. The most of the cutlasses were in another place.

A small window with a shutter on each side, and a skylight in the roof, gave it light by day; and after dark there was a lamp always burning. It was burning when I entered, not brightly, but enough to show Mr. Shuan sitting at the table, with the brandy bottle and a tin pannikin in front of him. He was a tall man, strongly made and very black; and he stared before him on the table like one stupid.

He took no notice of my coming in; nor did he move when the captain followed and leant on the berth beside me, looking darkly at the mate. I stood in great fear of Hoseason, and had my reasons for it; but something told me I need not be afraid of him just then; and I whispered in his ear: "How is he?" He shook his head like one that does not know and does not wish to think, and his face was very stern.

Presently Mr. Riach came in. He gave the captain a glance that meant the boy was dead as plain as speaking, and took his place like the rest of us; so that we all three stood without a word, staring down at Mr. Shuan, and Mr. Shuan (on his side) sat without a word, looking hard upon the table.

All of a sudden he put out his hand to take the bottle; and at that Mr. Riach started forward and caught it away from him, rather by surprise than violence, crying out, with an oath, that there had been too much of this work altogether, and that a judgment would fall upon the ship. And as he spoke (the weather sliding-doors standing open) he tossed the bottle into the sea.

Mr. Shuan was on his feet in a trice; he still looked dazed, but he meant murder, ay, and would have done it, for the second time that night, had not the captain stepped in between him and his victim.

"Sit down!" roars the captain. "Ye sot and swine, do ye know what ye've done? Ye've murdered the boy!"

Mr. Shuan seemed to understand; for he sat down again, and put up his hand to his brow.

"Well," he said, "he brought me a dirty pannikin!"

At that word, the captain and I and Mr. Riach all looked at each other for a second with a kind of frightened look; and then Hoseason walked up to his chief officer, took him by the shoulder, led him across to his bunk, and bade him lie down and go to sleep, as you might speak to a bad child. The murderer cried a little, but he took off his sea-boots and obeyed.

"Ah!" cried Mr. Riach, with a dreadful voice, "ye should have interfered long syne. It's too late now."

"Mr. Riach," said the captain, "this night's work must never be kennt in Dysart. The boy went overboard, sir; that's what the story is; and I would give five pounds out of my pocket it was true!" He turned to the table. "What made ye throw the good bottle away?" he added. "There was nae sense in that, sir. Here, David, draw me another. They're in the bottom locker;" and he tossed me a key. "Ye'll need a glass yourself, sir," he added to Riach. "Yon was an ugly thing to see."

So the pair sat down and hob-a-nobbed; and while they did so, the murderer, who had been lying and whimpering in his berth, raised himself upon his elbow and looked at them and at me.

That was the first night of my new duties; and in the course of the next day I had got well into the run of them. I had to serve at the meals, which the captain took at regular hours, sitting down with the officer who was off duty; all the day through I would be running with a dram to one or other of my three masters; and at night I slept on a blanket thrown on the deck boards at the aftermost end of the round-house, and right in the draught of the two doors. It was a hard and a cold bed; nor was I suffered to sleep without interruption; for some one would be always coming in from deck to get a dram, and when a fresh watch was to be set, two and sometimes all three would sit down and brew a bowl together. How they kept their health, I know not, any more than how I kept my own.

And yet in other ways it was an easy service. There was no cloth to lay; the meals were either of oatmeal porridge or salt junk, except twice a week, when there was duff: and though I was clumsy enough and (not being firm on my sealegs) sometimes fell with what I was bringing them, both Mr. Riach and the captain were singularly patient. I could not but fancy they were making up lee-way with their consciences, and that they would scarce have been so good with me if they had not been worse with Ransome.

As for Mr. Shuan, the drink or his crime, or the two together, had certainly troubled his mind. I cannot say I ever saw him in his proper wits. He never grew used to my being there, stared at me continually (sometimes, I could have thought, with terror), and more than once drew back from my hand when I was serving him. I was pretty sure from the first that he had no clear mind of what he had done, and on my second day in the round-house I had the proof of it. We were alone, and he had been staring at me a long time, when all at once, up he got, as pale as death, and came close up to me, to my great terror. But I had no cause to be afraid of him.

"You were not here before?" he asked.

"No, sir," said I."

"There was another boy?" he asked again; and when I had answered him, "Ah!" says he, "I thought that," and went and sat down, without another word, except to call for brandy.

You may think it strange, but for all the horror I had, I was still sorry for him. He was a married man, with a wife in Leith; but whether or no he had a family, I have now forgotten; I hope not.

Altogether it was no very hard life for the time it lasted, which (as you are to hear) was not long. I was as well fed as the best of them; even their pickles, which were the great dainty, I was allowed my share of; and had I liked I might have been drunk from morning to night, like Mr. Shuan. I had company, too, and good company of its sort. Mr. Riach, who had been to the college, spoke to me like a friend when he was not sulking, and told me many curious things, and some that were informing; and even the captain, though he kept me at the stick's end the most part of the time, would sometimes unbuckle a bit, and tell me of the fine countries he had visited.

The shadow of poor Ransome, to be sure, lay on all four of us, and on me and Mr. Shuan in particular, most heavily. And then I had another trouble of my own. Here I was, doing dirty work for three men that I looked down upon, and one of whom, at least, should have hung upon a gallows; that was for the present; and as for the future, I could only see myself slaving alongside of negroes in the tobacco fields. Mr. Riach, perhaps from caution, would never suffer me to say another word about my story; the captain, whom I tried to approach, rebuffed me like a dog and would not hear a word; and as the days came and went, my heart sank lower and lower, till I was even glad of the work which kept me from thinking.

9

THE MAN WITH THE BELT OF GOLD

More than a week went by, in which the ill-luck that had hitherto pursued the Covenant upon this voyage grew yet more strongly marked. Some days she made a little way; others, she was driven actually back. At last we were beaten so far to the south that we tossed and tacked to and fro the whole of the ninth day, within sight of Cape Wrath and the wild, rocky coast on either hand of it. There followed on that a council of the officers, and some decision which I did not rightly understand, seeing only the result: that we had made a fair wind of a foul one and were running south.

The tenth afternoon there was a falling swell and a thick, wet, white fog that hid one end of the brig from the other. All afternoon, when I went on deck, I saw men and officers listening hard over the bulwarks—"for breakers," they said; and though I did not so much as understand the word, I felt danger in the air, and was excited.

Maybe about ten at night, I was serving Mr. Riach and the captain at their supper, when the ship struck something with a great sound, and we heard voices singing out. My two masters leaped to their feet.

"She's struck!" said Mr. Riach.

"No, sir," said the captain. "We've only run a boat down."

And they hurried out.

The captain was in the right of it. We had run down a boat in the fog, and she had parted in the midst and gone to the bottom with all her crew but one. This man (as I heard afterwards) had been sitting in the stern as a passenger, while the rest were on the benches rowing. At the moment of the blow, the stern had been thrown into the air, and the man (having his hands free, and for all he was encumbered with a frieze overcoat that came below his knees) had leaped up and caught hold of the brig's bowsprit. It showed he had luck and much agility and unusual strength, that he should have thus saved himself from such a pass. And yet, when the captain brought him into the round-house, and I set eyes on him for the first time, he looked as cool as I did.

He was smallish in stature, but well set and as nimble as a goat; his face was of a good open expression, but sunburnt very dark, and heavily freckled and pitted with the smallpox; his eyes were unusually light and had a kind of dancing madness in them, that was both engaging and alarming; and when he took off his great-coat, he laid a pair of fine silver-mounted pistols on the table, and I saw that he was belted with a great sword. His manners, besides, were elegant, and he pledged the captain handsomely. Altogether I thought of him, at the first sight, that here was a man I would rather call my friend than my enemy.

The captain, too, was taking his observations, but rather of the man's clothes than his person. And to be sure, as soon as he had taken off the great-coat, he showed forth mighty fine for the round-house of a merchant brig: having a hat with feathers, a red waistcoat, breeches of black plush, and a blue coat with silver buttons and handsome silver lace; costly clothes, though somewhat spoiled with the fog and being slept in.

"I'm vexed, sir, about the boat," says the captain.

"There are some pretty men gone to the bottom," said the stranger, "that I would rather see on the dry land again than half a score of boats."

"Friends of yours?" said Hoseason.

"You have none such friends in your country," was the reply. "They would have died for me like dogs."

"Well, sir," said the captain, still watching him, "there are more men in the world than boats to put them in."

"And that's true, too," cried the other, "and ye seem to be a gentleman of great penetration."

"I have been in France, sir," says the captain, so that it was plain he meant more by the words than showed upon the face of them.

"Well, sir," says the other, "and so has many a pretty man, for the matter of that."

"No doubt, sir," says the captain, "and fine coats."

"Oho!" says the stranger, "is that how the wind sets?" And he laid his hand quickly on his pistols.

"Don't be hasty," said the captain. "Don't do a mischief before ye see the need of it. Ye've a French soldier's coat upon your back and a Scotch tongue in your head, to be sure; but so has many an honest fellow in these days, and I dare say none the worse of it."

"So?" said the gentleman in the fine coat: "are ye of the honest party?" (meaning, Was he a Jacobite? for each side, in these sort of civil broils, takes the name of honesty for its own).

"Why, sir," replied the captain, "I am a true-blue Protestant, and I thank God for it." (It was the first word of any religion I had ever heard from him, but I learnt afterwards he was a great church-goer while on shore.) "But, for all that," says he, "I can be sorry to see another man with his back to the wall."

"Can ye so, indeed?" asked the Jacobite. "Well, sir, to be quite plain with ye, I am one of those honest gentlemen that were in trouble about the years forty-five and six; and (to be still quite plain with ye) if I got into the hands of any of the red-coated gentry, it's like it would go hard with me. Now, sir, I was for France; and there was a French ship cruising here to pick me up; but she gave us the go-by in the fog—as I wish from the heart that ye had done yoursel'! And the best that I can say is this: If ye can set me ashore where I was going, I have that upon me will reward you highly for your trouble."

"In France?" says the captain. "No, sir; that I cannot do. But where ye come from—we might talk of that."

And then, unhappily, he observed me standing in my corner, and packed me off to the galley to get supper for the gentleman. I lost no time, I promise you; and when I came back into the round-house, I found the gentleman had taken a money-belt from about his waist, and poured out a guinea or two upon the table. The captain was looking at the guineas, and then at the belt, and then at the gentleman's face; and I thought he seemed excited.

"Half of it," he cried, "and I'm your man!"

The other swept back the guineas into the belt, and put it on again under his waistcoat. "I have told ye sir," said he, "that not one doit of it belongs to me. It belongs to my chieftain," and here he touched his hat, "and while I would be but a silly messenger to grudge some of it that the rest might come safe, I should show myself a hound indeed if I bought my own carcase any too dear. Thirty guineas on the sea-side, or sixty if ye set me on the Linnhe Loch. Take it, if ye will; if not, ye can do your worst."

"Ay," said Hoseason. "And if I give ye over to the soldiers?"

"Ye would make a fool's bargain," said the other. "My chief, let me tell you, sir, is forfeited, like every honest man in Scotland. His estate is in the hands of the man they call King George; and it is his officers that collect the rents, or try to collect them. But for the honour of Scotland, the poor tenant bodies take a thought upon their chief lying in exile; and this money is a part of that very rent for which King George is looking. Now, sir, ye seem to me to be a man that understands things: bring this money within the reach of Government, and how much of it'll come to you?"

"Little enough, to be sure," said Hoseason; and then, "if they knew," he added, drily. "But I think, if I was to try, that I could hold my tongue about it."

"Ah, but I'll begowk* ye there!" cried the gentleman. "Play me false, and I'll play you cunning. If a hand is laid upon me, they shall ken what money it is."

*Befool.

"Well," returned the captain, "what must be must. Sixty guineas, and done. Here's my hand upon it."

"And here's mine," said the other.

And thereupon the captain went out (rather hurriedly, I thought), and left me alone in the round-house with the stranger.

At that period (so soon after the forty-five) there were many exiled gentlemen coming back at the peril of their lives, either to see their friends or to collect a little money; and as for the Highland chiefs that had been forfeited, it was a common matter of talk how their tenants would stint themselves to send them money, and their clansmen outface the soldiery to get it in, and run the gauntlet of our great navy to carry it across. All this I had, of course, heard tell of; and now I had a man under my eyes whose life was forfeit on all these counts and upon one more, for he was not only a rebel and a smuggler of rents, but had taken service with King Louis of France. And as if all this were not enough, he had a belt full of golden guineas round his loins. Whatever my opinions, I could not look on such a man without a lively interest.

"And so you're a Jacobite?" said I, as I set meat before him.

"Ay," said he, beginning to eat. "And you, by your long face, should be a Whig?"[1]

"Betwixt and between," said I, not to annoy him; for indeed I was as good a Whig as Mr. Campbell could make me.

"And that's naething," said he. "But I'm saying, Mr. Betwixt-and-Between," he added, "this bottle of yours is dry; and it's hard if I'm to pay sixty guineas and be grudged a dram upon the back of it."

"I'll go and ask for the key," said I, and stepped on deck.

The fog was as close as ever, but the swell almost down. They had laid the brig to, not knowing precisely where they were, and the wind (what little there was of it) not serving well for their true course. Some of the hands were still hearkening for breakers; but the captain and the two officers were in the waist with their heads together. It struck me (I don't know why) that they were after no good; and the first word I heard, as I drew softly near, more than confirmed me.

It was Mr. Riach, crying out as if upon a sudden thought: "Couldn't we wile him out of the round-house?"

"He's better where he is," returned Hoseason; "he hasn't room to use his sword."

"Well, that's true," said Riach; "but he's hard to come at."

"Hut!" said Hoseason. "We can get the man in talk, one upon each side, and pin him by the two arms; or if that'll not hold, sir, we can make a run by both the doors and get him under hand before he has the time to draw."

At this hearing, I was seized with both fear and anger at these treacherous, greedy, bloody men that I sailed with. My first mind was to run away; my second was bolder.

"Captain," said I, "the gentleman is seeking a dram, and the bottle's out. Will you give me the key?"

They all started and turned about.

"Why, here's our chance to get the firearms!"

Riach cried; and then to me: "Hark ye, David," he said, "do ye ken where the pistols are?"

"Ay, ay," put in Hoseason. "David kens; David's a good lad. Ye see, David my man, yon wild Hielandman is a danger to the ship, besides being a rank foe to King George, God bless him!"

I had never been so be-Davided since I came on board: but I said Yes, as if all I heard were quite natural.

"The trouble is," resumed the captain, "that all our firelocks, great and little, are in the round-house under this man's nose; likewise the powder. Now, if I, or one of the officers, was to go in and take them, he would fall to thinking. But a lad like you, David, might snap up a horn and a pistol or two without remark. And if ye can do it cleverly, I'll bear it in mind when it'll be good for you to have friends; and that's when we come to Carolina."

Here Mr. Riach whispered him a little.

"Very right, sir," said the captain; and then to myself: "And see here, David, yon man has a beltful of gold, and I give you my word that you shall have your fingers in it."

I told him I would do as he wished, though indeed I had scarce breath to speak with; and upon that he gave me the key of the spirit locker, and I began to go slowly back to the round-house. What was I to do? They were dogs and thieves; they had stolen me from my own country; they had killed poor Ransome; and was I to hold the candle to another murder? But then, upon the other hand, there was the fear of death very plain before me; for what could a boy and a man, if they were as brave as lions, against a whole ship's company?

I was still arguing it back and forth, and getting no great clearness, when I came into the round-house and saw the Jacobite eating his supper under the lamp; and at that my mind was made up all in a moment. I have no credit by it; it was by no choice of mine, but as if by compulsion, that I walked right up to the table and put my hand on his shoulder.

"Do ye want to be killed?" said I. He sprang to his feet, and looked a question at me as clear as if he had spoken.

"O!" cried I, "they're all murderers here; it's a ship full of them! They've murdered a boy already. Now it's you."

"Ay, ay," said he; "but they have n't got me yet." And then looking at me curiously, "Will ye stand with me?"

"That will I!" said I. "I am no thief, nor yet murderer. I'll stand by you."

"Why, then," said he, "what's your name?"

"David Balfour," said I; and then, thinking that a man with so fine a coat must like fine people, I added for the first time, "of Shaws."

It never occurred to him to doubt me, for a Highlander is used to see great gentlefolk in great poverty; but as he had no estate of his own, my words nettled a very childish vanity he had.

"My name is Stewart," he said, drawing himself up. "Alan Breck, they call me. A king's name is good enough for me, though I bear it plain and have the name of no farm-midden to clap to the hind-end of it."

And having administered this rebuke, as though it were something of a chief importance, he turned to examine our defences.

The round-house was built very strong, to support the breaching of the seas. Of its five apertures, only the skylight and the two doors were large enough for the passage of a man. The doors, besides, could be drawn close: they were of stout oak, and ran in grooves, and were fitted with hooks to keep them either shut or open, as the need arose. The one that was already shut I secured in this fashion; but when I was proceeding to slide to the other, Alan stopped me.

"David," said he—"for I cannae bring to mind the name of your landed estate, and so will make so bold as to call you David—that door, being open, is the best part of my defences."

"It would be yet better shut," says I.

"Not so, David," says he. "Ye see, I have but one face; but so long as that door is open and my face to it, the best part of my enemies will be in front of me, where I would aye wish to find them."

Then he gave me from the rack a cutlass (of which there were a few besides the firearms), choosing it with great care, shaking his head and saying he had never in all his life seen poorer weapons; and next he set me down to the table with a powder-horn, a bag of bullets and all the pistols, which he bade me charge.

"And that will be better work, let me tell you," said he, "for a gentleman of decent birth, than scraping plates and raxing (*reaching*) drams to a wheen tarry sailors."

Thereupon he stood up in the midst with his face to the door, and drawing his great sword, made trial of the room he had to wield it in.

"I must stick to the point," he said, shaking his head; "and that's a pity, too. It doesn't set my genius, which is all for the upper guard. And, now," said he, "do you keep on charging the pistols, and give heed to me."

I told him I would listen closely. My chest was tight, my mouth dry, the light dark to my eyes; the thought of the numbers that were soon to leap in upon us kept my heart in a flutter: and the sea, which I heard washing round the brig, and where I thought my dead body would be cast ere morning, ran in my mind strangely.

"First of all," said he, "how many are against us?"

I reckoned them up; and such was the hurry of my mind, I had to cast the numbers twice. "Fifteen," said I.

Alan whistled. "Well," said he, "that can't be cured. And now follow me. It is my part to keep this door, where I look for the main battle. In that, ye have no hand. And mind and dinnae fire to this side unless they get me down; for I would rather have ten foes in front of me than one friend like you cracking pistols at my back."

I told him, indeed I was no great shot.

"And that's very bravely said," he cried, in a great admiration of my candour. "There's many a pretty gentleman that wouldnae dare to say it."

"But then, sir," said I, "there is the door behind you, which they may perhaps break in."

"Ay," said he, "and that is a part of your work. No sooner the pistols charged, than ye must climb up into yon bed where ye're handy at the window; and if they lift hand against the door, ye're to shoot. But that's not all. Let's make a bit of a soldier of ye, David. What else have ye to guard?"

"There's the skylight," said I. "But indeed, Mr. Stewart, I would need to have eyes upon both sides to keep the two of them; for when my face is at the one, my back is to the other."

"And that's very true," said Alan. "But have ye no ears to your head?"

"To be sure!" cried I. "I must hear the bursting of the glass!"

"Ye have some rudiments of sense," said Alan, grimly.

---

1. Whig or Whigamore was the cant name for those who were loyal to King George.

10

THE SIEGE OF THE ROUND-HOUSE

But now our time of truce was come to an end. Those on deck had waited for my coming till they grew impatient; and scarce had Alan spoken, when the captain showed face in the open door.

"Stand!" cried Alan, and pointed his sword at him. The captain stood, indeed; but he neither winced nor drew back a foot.

"A naked sword?" says he. "This is a strange return for hospitality."

"Do ye see me?" said Alan. "I am come of kings; I bear a king's name. My badge is the oak. Do ye see my sword? It has slashed the heads off mair Whigamores than you have toes upon your feet. Call up your vermin to your back, sir, and fall on! The sooner the clash begins, the sooner ye'll taste this steel throughout your vitals."

The captain said nothing to Alan, but he looked over at me with an ugly look. "David," said he, "I'll mind this;" and the sound of his voice went through me with a jar.

Next moment he was gone.

"And now," said Alan, "let your hand keep your head, for the grip is coming."

Alan drew a dirk, which he held in his left hand in case they should run in under his sword. I, on my part, clambered up into the berth with an armful of pistols and something of a heavy heart, and set open the window where I was to watch. It was a small part of the deck that I could overlook, but enough for our purpose. The sea had gone down, and the wind was steady and kept the sails quiet; so that there was a great stillness in the ship, in which I made sure I heard the sound of muttering voices. A little after, and there came a clash of steel upon the deck, by which I knew they were dealing out the cutlasses and one had been let fall; and after that, silence again.

I do not know if I was what you call afraid; but my heart beat like a bird's, both quick and little; and there was a dimness came before my eyes which I continually rubbed away, and which continually returned. As for hope, I had none; but only a darkness of despair and a sort of anger against all the world that made me long to sell my life as dear as I was able. I tried to pray, I remember, but that same hurry of my mind, like a man running, would not

549

suffer me to think upon the words; and my chief wish was to have the thing begin and be done with it.

It came all of a sudden when it did, with a rush of feet and a roar, and then a shout from Alan, and a sound of blows and some one crying out as if hurt. I looked back over my shoulder, and saw Mr. Shuan in the doorway, crossing blades with Alan.

"That's him that killed the boy!" I cried.

"Look to your window!" said Alan; and as I turned back to my place, I saw him pass his sword through the mate's body.

It was none too soon for me to look to my own part; for my head was scarce back at the window, before five men, carrying a spare yard for a battering-ram, ran past me and took post to drive the door in. I had never fired with a pistol in my life, and not often with a gun; far less against a fellow-creature. But it was now or never; and just as they swang the yard, I cried out: "Take that!" and shot into their midst.

I must have hit one of them, for he sang out and gave back a step, and the rest stopped as if a little disconcerted. Before they had time to recover, I sent another ball over their heads; and at my third shot (which went as wide as the second) the whole party threw down the yard and ran for it.

Then I looked round again into the deck-house. The whole place was full of the smoke of my own firing, just as my ears seemed to be burst with the noise of the shots. But there was Alan, standing as before; only now his sword was running blood to the hilt, and himself so swelled with triumph and fallen into so fine an attitude, that he looked to be invincible. Right before him on the floor was Mr. Shuan, on his hands and knees; the blood was pouring from his mouth, and he was sinking slowly lower, with a terrible, white face; and just as I looked, some of those from behind caught hold of him by the heels and dragged him bodily out of the round-house. I believe he died as they were doing it.

"There's one of your Whigs for ye!" cried Alan; and then turning to me, he asked if I had done much execution.

I told him I had winged one, and thought it was the captain.

"And I've settled two," says he. "No, there's not enough blood let; they'll be back again. To your watch, David. This was but a dram before meat."

I settled back to my place, re-charging the three pistols I had fired, and keeping watch with both eye and ear.

Our enemies were disputing not far off upon the deck, and that so loudly that I could hear a word or two above the washing of the seas.

"It was Shuan bauchled (*bungled*) it," I heard one say.

And another answered him with a "Wheesht, man! He's paid the piper."

After that the voices fell again into the same muttering as before. Only now, one person spoke most of the time, as though laying down a plan, and first one and then another answered him briefly, like men taking orders. By this, I made sure they were coming on again, and told Alan.

"It's what we have to pray for," said he. "Unless we can give them a good distaste of us, and done with it, there'll be nae sleep for either you or me. But this time, mind, they'll be in earnest."

By this, my pistols were ready, and there was nothing to do but listen and wait. While the brush lasted, I had not the time to think if I was frighted; but now, when all was still again, my mind ran upon nothing else. The thought of the sharp swords and the cold steel was strong in me; and presently, when I began to hear stealthy steps and a brushing of men's clothes against the round-house wall, and knew they were taking their places in the dark, I could have found it in my mind to cry out aloud.

All this was upon Alan's side; and I had begun to think my share of the fight was at an end, when I heard some one drop softly on the roof above me.

Then there came a single call on the sea-pipe, and that was the signal. A knot of them made one rush of it, cutlass in hand, against the door; and at the same moment, the glass of the skylight was dashed in a thousand pieces, and a man leaped through and landed on the floor. Before he got his feet, I had clapped a pistol to his back, and might have shot him, too; only at the touch of him (and him alive) my whole flesh misgave me, and I could no more pull the trigger than I could have flown.

He had dropped his cutlass as he jumped, and when he felt the pistol, whipped straight round and laid hold of me, roaring out an oath; and at that either my courage came again, or I grew so much afraid as came to the same thing; for I gave a shriek and shot him in the midst of the body. He gave the most horrible, ugly groan and fell to the floor. The foot of a second fellow, whose legs were dangling through the skylight, struck me at the same time upon the head; and at that I snatched another pistol and shot this one through the thigh, so that he slipped through and tumbled in a lump on his companion's body. There was no talk of missing, any more than there was time to aim; I clapped the muzzle to the very place and fired.

I might have stood and stared at them for long, but I heard Alan shout as if for help, and that brought me to my senses.

He had kept the door so long; but one of the seamen, while he was engaged with others, had run in under his guard and caught him about the body. Alan was dirking him with his left hand, but the fellow clung like a leech. Another had broken in and had his cutlass raised. The door was thronged with their faces. I thought we were lost, and catching up my cutlass, fell on them in flank.

But I had not time to be of help. The wrestler dropped at last; and Alan, leaping back to get his distance, ran upon the others like a bull, roaring as he went. They broke before him like water, turning, and running, and falling one against another in their haste. The sword in his hands flashed like quicksilver into the huddle of our fleeing enemies; and at every flash there came the scream of a man hurt. I was still thinking we were lost, when lo! they were all gone, and Alan was driving them along the deck as a sheep-dog chases sheep.

Yet he was no sooner out than he was back again, being as cautious as he was brave; and meanwhile the seamen continued running and crying out as if he was still behind them; and we heard them tumble one upon another into the forecastle, and clap-to the hatch upon the top.

The round-house was like a shambles; three were dead inside, another lay in his death agony across the threshold; and there were Alan and I victorious and unhurt.

He came up to me with open arms. "Come to my arms!" he cried, and embraced and kissed me hard upon both cheeks. "David," said he, "I love you like a brother. And O, man," he cried in a kind of ecstasy, "am I no a bonny fighter?"

Thereupon he turned to the four enemies, passed his sword clean through each of them, and tumbled them out of doors one after the other. As he did so, he kept humming and singing and whistling to himself, like a man trying to recall an air; only what HE was trying was to make one. All the while, the flush was in his face, and his eyes were as bright as a five-year-old child's with a new toy. And presently he sat down upon the table, sword in hand; the air that he was making all the time began to run a little clearer, and then clearer still; and then out he burst with a great voice into a Gaelic song.

I have translated it here, not in verse (of which I have no skill) but at least in the king's English.

He sang it often afterwards, and the thing became popular; so that I have heard it and had it explained to me, many's the time.

"This is the song of the sword of Alan; The smith made it, The fire set it; Now it shines in the hand of Alan Breck.

"Their eyes were many and bright, Swift were they to behold, Many the hands they guided: The sword was alone.

"The dun deer troop over the hill, They are many, the hill is one; The dun deer vanish, The hill remains.

"Come to me from the hills of heather, Come from the isles of the sea. O far-beholding eagles, Here is your meat."

Now this song which he made (both words and music) in the hour of our victory, is something less than just to me, who stood beside him in the tussle. Mr. Shuan and five more were either killed outright or thoroughly disabled; but of these, two fell by my hand, the two that came by the skylight. Four more were hurt, and of that number, one (and he not the least important) got his hurt from me. So that, altogether, I did my fair share both of the killing and the wounding, and might have claimed a place in Alan's verses. But poets have to think upon their rhymes; and in good prose talk, Alan always did me more than justice.

In the meanwhile, I was innocent of any wrong being done me. For not only I knew no word of the Gaelic; but what with the long suspense of the waiting, and the scurry and strain of our two spirts of fighting, and more than all, the horror I had of some of my own share in it, the thing was no sooner over than I was glad to stagger to a seat. There was that tightness on my chest that I could hardly breathe; the thought of the two men I had shot sat upon me like a nightmare; and all upon a sudden, and before I had a guess of what was coming, I began to sob and cry like any child.

Alan clapped my shoulder, and said I was a brave lad and wanted nothing but a sleep.

"I'll take the first watch," said he. "Ye've done well by me, David, first and last; and I wouldn't lose you for all Appin—no, nor for Breadalbane."

So I made up my bed on the floor; and he took the first spell, pistol in hand and sword on knee, three hours by the captain's watch upon the wall. Then he roused me up, and I took my turn of three hours; before the end of which it was broad day, and a very quiet morning, with a smooth, rolling sea that tossed the ship and made the blood run to and fro on the round-house floor, and a heavy rain that drummed upon the roof. All my watch there was nothing stirring; and by the banging of the helm, I knew they had even no one at the tiller. Indeed (as I learned afterwards) there were so many of them hurt or dead, and the rest in so ill a temper, that Mr. Riach and the captain had to take turn and turn like Alan and me, or the brig might have gone ashore and nobody the wiser. It was a mercy the night had fallen so still, for the wind had gone down as soon as the rain began. Even as it was, I judged by the wailing of a great number of gulls that went crying and fishing round the ship, that she must have drifted pretty near the coast or one of the islands of the Hebrides; and at last, looking out of the door of the round-house, I saw the great stone hills of Skye on the right hand, and, a little more astern, the strange isle of Rum.

❊ II ❊

THE CAPTAIN KNUCKLES UNDER

Alan and I sat down to breakfast about six of the clock. The floor was covered with broken glass and in a horrid mess of blood, which took away my hunger. In all other ways we were in a situation not only agreeable but merry; having ousted the officers from their own cabin, and having at command all the drink in the ship—both wine and spirits—and all the dainty part of what was eatable, such as the pickles and the fine sort of bread. This, of itself, was enough to set us in good humour, but the richest part of it was this, that the two thirstiest men that ever came out of Scotland (Mr. Shuan being dead) were now shut in the fore-part of the ship and condemned to what they hated most—cold water.

"And depend upon it," Alan said, "we shall hear more of them ere long. Ye may keep a man from the fighting, but never from his bottle."

We made good company for each other. Alan, indeed, expressed himself most lovingly; and taking a knife from the table, cut me off one of the silver buttons from his coat.

"I had them," says he, "from my father, Duncan Stewart; and now give ye one of them to be a keepsake for last night's work. And wherever ye go and show that button, the friends of Alan Breck will come around you."

He said this as if he had been Charlemagne, and commanded armies; and indeed, much as I admired his courage, I was always in danger of smiling at his vanity: in danger, I say, for had I not kept my countenance, I would be afraid to think what a quarrel might have followed.

As soon as we were through with our meal he rummaged in the captain's locker till he found a clothes-brush; and then taking off his coat, began to visit his suit and brush away the stains, with such care and labour as I supposed to have been only usual with women. To be sure, he had no other; and, besides (as he said), it belonged to a king and so behoved to be royally looked after.

For all that, when I saw what care he took to pluck out the threads where the button had been cut away, I put a higher value on his gift.

He was still so engaged when we were hailed by Mr. Riach from the deck, asking for a parley; and I, climbing through the skylight and sitting on the edge of it, pistol in hand and with a bold front, though inwardly in fear of broken glass, hailed him back again and bade him speak out. He came to the edge of the round-house, and stood on a coil of rope, so that his chin was on a level with the roof; and we looked at each other awhile in silence. Mr. Riach, as I do not think he had been very forward in the battle, so he had got off with nothing worse than a blow upon the cheek: but he looked out of heart and very weary, having been all night afoot, either standing watch or doctoring the wounded.

"This is a bad job," said he at last, shaking his head.

"It was none of our choosing," said I.

"The captain," says he, "would like to speak with your friend. They might speak at the window."

"And how do we know what treachery he means?" cried I.

"He means none, David," returned Mr. Riach, "and if he did, I'll tell ye the honest truth, we couldnae get the men to follow."

"Is that so?" said I.

"I'll tell ye more than that," said he. "It's not only the men; it's me. I'm frich'ened, Davie." And he smiled across at me. "No," he continued, "what we want is to be shut of him."

Thereupon I consulted with Alan, and the parley was agreed to and parole given upon either side; but this was not the whole of Mr. Riach's business, and he now begged me for a dram with such instancy and such reminders of his former kindness, that at last I handed him a pannikin with about a gill of brandy. He drank a part, and then carried the rest down upon the deck, to share it (I suppose) with his superior.

A little after, the captain came (as was agreed) to one of the windows, and stood there in the rain, with his arm in a sling, and looking stern and pale, and so old that my heart smote me for having fired upon him.

Alan at once held a pistol in his face.

"Put that thing up!" said the captain. "Have I not passed my word, sir? or do ye seek to affront me?"

"Captain," says Alan, "I doubt your word is a breakable. Last night ye haggled and argle-bargled like an apple-wife; and then passed me your word, and gave me your hand to back it; and ye ken very well what was the upshot. Be damned to your word!" says he.

"Well, well, sir," said the captain, "ye'll get little good by swearing." (And truly that was a fault of which the captain was quite free.) "But we have other things to speak," he continued, bitterly. "Ye've made a sore hash of my brig; I haven't hands enough left to work her; and my first officer (whom I could ill spare) has got your sword throughout his vitals, and passed without speech. There is nothing left me, sir, but to put back into the port of Glasgow after hands; and there (by your leave) ye will find them that are better able to talk to you."

"Ay?" said Alan; "and faith, I'll have a talk with them mysel'! Unless there's naebody speaks English in that town, I have a bonny tale for them. Fifteen tarry sailors upon the one side, and a man and a halfling boy upon the other! O, man, it's peetiful!"

Hoseason flushed red.

"No," continued Alan, "that'll no do. Ye'll just have to set me ashore as we agreed."

"Ay," said Hoseason, "but my first officer is dead—ye ken best how. There's none of the rest of us acquaint with this coast, sir; and it's one very dangerous to ships."

"I give ye your choice," says Alan. "Set me on dry ground in Appin, or Ardgour, or in Morven, or Arisaig, or Morar; or, in brief, where ye please, within thirty miles of my own country; except in a country of the Campbells. That's a broad target. If ye miss that, ye must be as feckless at the sailoring as I have found ye at the fighting. Why, my poor country people in their bit cobles[1] pass from island to island in all weathers, ay, and by night too, for the matter of that."

"A coble's not a ship, sir," said the captain. "It has nae draught of water."

"Well, then, to Glasgow if ye list!" says Alan. "We'll have the laugh of ye at the least."

"My mind runs little upon laughing," said the captain. "But all this will cost money, sir."

"Well, sir," says Alan, "I am nae weathercock. Thirty guineas, if ye land me on the sea-side; and sixty, if ye put me in the Linnhe Loch."

"But see, sir, where we lie, we are but a few hours' sail from Ardnamurchan," said Hoseason. "Give me sixty, and I'll set ye there."

"And I'm to wear my brogues and run jeopardy of the red-coats to please you?" cries Alan. "No, sir; if ye want sixty guineas earn them, and set me in my own country."

"It's to risk the brig, sir," said the captain, "and your own lives along with her."

"Take it or want it," says Alan.

"Could ye pilot us at all?" asked the captain, who was frowning to himself.

"Well, it's doubtful," said Alan. "I'm more of a fighting man (as ye have seen for yoursel') than a sailor-man. But I have been often enough picked up and set down upon this coast, and should ken something of the lie of it."

The captain shook his head, still frowning.

"If I had lost less money on this unchancy cruise," says he, "I would see you in a rope's end before I risked my brig, sir. But be it as ye will. As soon as I get a slant of wind (and there's some coming, or I'm the more mistaken) I'll put it in hand. But there's one thing more. We may meet in with a king's ship and she may lay us aboard, sir, with no blame of mine: they keep the cruisers thick upon this coast, ye ken who for. Now, sir, if that was to befall, ye might leave the money."

"Captain," says Alan, "if ye see a pennant, it shall be your part to run away. And now, as I hear you're a little short of brandy in the fore-part, I'll offer ye a change: a bottle of brandy against two buckets of water."

That was the last clause of the treaty, and was duly executed on both sides; so that Alan and I could at last wash out the round-house and be quit of the memorials of those whom we had slain, and the captain and Mr. Riach could be happy again in their own way, the name of which was drink.

---

1. Coble: a small boat used in fishing.

12

I HEAR OF THE "RED FOX"

Before we had done cleaning out the round-house, a breeze sprang up from a little to the east of north. This blew off the rain and brought out the sun.

And here I must explain; and the reader would do well to look at a map. On the day when the fog fell and we ran down Alan's boat, we had been running through the Little Minch. At dawn after the battle, we lay becalmed to the east of the Isle of Canna or between that and Isle Eriska in the chain of the Long Island. Now to get from there to the Linnhe Loch, the straight course was through the narrows of the Sound of Mull. But the captain had no chart; he was afraid to trust his brig so deep among the islands; and the wind serving well, he preferred to go by west of Tiree and come up under the southern coast of the great Isle of Mull.

All day the breeze held in the same point, and rather freshened than died down; and towards afternoon, a swell began to set in from round the outer Hebrides. Our course, to go round about the inner isles, was to the west of south, so that at first we had this swell upon our beam, and were much rolled about. But after nightfall, when we had turned the end of Tiree and began to head more to the east, the sea came right astern.

Meanwhile, the early part of the day, before the swell came up, was very pleasant; sailing, as we were, in a bright sunshine and with many mountainous islands upon different sides. Alan and I sat in the round-house with the doors open on each side (the wind being straight astern), and smoked a pipe or two of the captain's fine tobacco. It was at this time we heard each other's stories, which was the more important to me, as I gained some knowledge of that wild Highland country on which I was so soon to land. In those days, so close on the back of the great rebellion, it was needful a man should know what he was doing when he went upon the heather.

It was I that showed the example, telling him all my misfortune; which he heard with great good-nature. Only, when I came to mention that good friend of mine, Mr. Campbell the minister, Alan fired up and cried out that he hated all that were of that name.

"Why," said I, "he is a man you should be proud to give your hand to."

"I know nothing I would help a Campbell to," says he, "unless it was a leaden bullet. I would hunt all of that name like blackcocks. If I lay dying, I would crawl upon my knees to my chamber window for a shot at one."

"Why, Alan," I cried, "what ails ye at the Campbells?"

"Well," says he, "ye ken very well that I am an Appin Stewart, and the Campbells have long harried and wasted those of my name; ay, and got lands of us by treachery—but never with the sword," he cried loudly, and with the word brought down his fist upon the table. But I paid the less attention to this, for I knew it was usually said by those who have the underhand. "There's more than that," he continued, "and all in the same story: lying words, lying papers, tricks fit for a peddler, and the show of what's legal over all, to make a man the more angry."

"You that are so wasteful of your buttons," said I, "I can hardly think you would be a good judge of business."

"Ah!" says he, falling again to smiling, "I got my wastefulness from the same man I got the buttons from; and that was my poor father, Duncan Stewart, grace be to him! He was the prettiest man of his kindred; and the best swordsman in the Hielands, David, and that is the same as to say, in all the world, I should ken, for it was him that taught me. He was in the Black Watch, when first it was mustered; and, like other gentlemen privates, had a gillie at his back to carry his firelock for him on the march. Well, the King, it appears, was wishful to see Hieland swordsmanship; and my father and three more were chosen out and sent to London town, to let him see it at the best. So they were had into the palace and showed the whole art of the sword for two hours at a stretch, before King George and Queen Carline, and the Butcher Cumberland, and many more of whom I havenae mind. And when they were through, the King (for all he was a rank usurper) spoke them fair and gave each man three guineas in his hand. Now, as they were going out of the palace, they had a porter's lodge to go by; and it came in on my father, as he was perhaps the first private Hieland gentleman that had ever gone by that door, it was right he should give the poor porter a proper notion of their quality. So he gives the King's three guineas into the man's hand, as if it was his common custom; the three others that came behind him did the same; and there they were on the street, never a penny the better for their pains. Some say it was one, that was the first to fee the King's porter; and some say it was another; but the truth of it is, that it was Duncan Stewart, as I am willing to prove with either sword or pistol. And that was the father that I had, God rest him!"

"I think he was not the man to leave you rich," said I.

"And that's true," said Alan. "He left me my breeks to cover me, and little besides. And that was how I came to enlist, which was a black spot upon my character at the best of times, and would still be a sore job for me if I fell among the red-coats."

"What," cried I, "were you in the English army?"

"That was I," said Alan. "But I deserted to the right side at Preston Pans—and that's some comfort."

I could scarcely share this view: holding desertion under arms for an unpardonable fault in honour. But for all I was so young, I was wiser than say my thought. "Dear, dear," says I, "the punishment is death."

"Ay" said he, "if they got hands on me, it would be a short shrift and a lang tow for Alan! But I have the King of France's commission in my pocket, which would aye be some protection."

"I misdoubt it much," said I.

"I have doubts mysel'," said Alan drily.

"And, good heaven, man," cried I, "you that are a condemned rebel, and a deserter, and a man of the French King's—what tempts ye back into this country? It's a braving of Providence."

"Tut!" says Alan, "I have been back every year since forty-six!"

"And what brings ye, man?" cried I.

"Well, ye see, I weary for my friends and country," said he. "France is a braw place, nae doubt; but I weary for the heather and the deer. And then I have bit things that I attend to. Whiles I pick up a few lads to serve the King of France: recruits, ye see; and that's aye a little moncy. But thc hcart of thc matter is the business of my chief, Ardshiel."

"I thought they called your chief Appin," said I.

"Ay, but Ardshiel is the captain of the clan," said he, which scarcely cleared my mind. "Ye see, David, he that was all his life so great a man, and come of the blood and bearing the name of kings, is now brought down to livc in a Frcnch town like a poor and private person. He that had four hundred swords at his whistle, I have seen, with these eyes of mine, buying butter in the market-place, and taking it home in a kale-leaf. This is not only a pain but a disgrace to us of his family and clan. There are the bairns forby, the children and the hope of Appin, that must be learned their letters and how to hold a sword, in that far country. Now, the tenants of Appin have to pay a rent to King George; but their hearts are staunch, they are true to their chief; and what with love and a bit of pressure, and maybe a threat or two, the poor folk scrape up a second rent for Ardshiel. Well, David, I'm the hand that carries it." And he struck the belt about his body, so that the guineas rang.

"Do they pay both?" cried I.

"Ay, David, both," says he.

"What! two rents?" I repeated.

"Ay, David," said he. "I told a different tale to yon captain man; but this is the truth of it. And it's wonderful to me how little pressure is needed. But that's the handiwork of my good kinsman and my father's friend, James of the Glens: James Stewart, that is: Ardshiel's half-brother. He it is that gets the money in, and does the management."

This was the first time I heard the name of that James Stewart, who was afterwards so famous at the time of his hanging. But I took little heed at the moment, for all my mind was occupied with the generosity of these poor Highlanders.

"I call it noble," I cried. "I'm a Whig, or little better; but I call it noble."

"Ay" said he, "ye're a Whig, but ye're a gentleman; and that's what does it. Now, if ye were one of the cursed race of Campbell, ye would gnash your teeth to hear tell of it. If ye were the Red Fox..." And at that name, his teeth shut together, and he ceased speaking. I have seen many a grim face, but never a grimmer than Alan's when he had named the Red Fox.

"And who is the Red Fox?" I asked, daunted, but still curious.

"Who is he?" cried Alan. "Well, and I'll tell you that. When the men of the clans were broken at Culloden, and the good cause went down, and the horses rode over the fetlocks in the best blood of the north, Ardshiel had to flee like a poor deer upon the mountains—he and his lady and his bairns. A sair job we had of it before we got him shipped; and while he still lay in the heather, the English rogues, that couldnae come at his life, were striking at his rights. They stripped him of his powers; they stripped him of his lands; they plucked the weapons from the hands of his clansmen, that had borne arms for thirty centuries; ay, and the very clothes off their backs—so that it's now a sin to wear a tartan plaid, and a man may be cast into a gaol if he has but a kilt about his legs. One thing they couldnae kill. That was the love the clansmen bore their chief. These guineas are the proof of it. And now, in there steps a man, a Campbell, red-headed Colin of Glenure——"

"Is that him you call the Red Fox?" said I.

"Will ye bring me his brush?" cries Alan, fiercely. "Ay, that's the man. In he steps, and gets papers from King George, to be so-called King's factor on the lands of Appin. And at first he sings small, and is hail-fellow-well-met with Sheamus—that's James of the Glens, my chieftain's agent. But by-and-by, that came to his ears that I have just told you; how the poor commons of Appin, the farmers and the crofters and the boumen, were wringing their very plaids to get a second rent, and send it over-seas for Ardshiel and his poor bairns. What was it ye called it, when I told ye?"

"I called it noble, Alan," said I.

"And you little better than a common Whig!" cries Alan. "But when it came to Colin Roy, the black Campbell blood in him ran wild. He sat gnashing his teeth at the wine table. What! should a Stewart get a bite of bread, and him not be able to prevent it? Ah! Red Fox, if ever I hold you at a gun's end, the Lord have pity upon ye!" (Alan stopped to swallow down his anger.) "Well, David, what does he do? He declares all the farms to let. And, thinks he, in his black heart, 'I'll soon get other tenants that'll overbid these Stewarts, and Maccolls, and Macrobs' (for these are all names in my clan, David); 'and then,' thinks he, 'Ardshiel will have to hold his bonnet on a French roadside.'"

"Well," said I, "what followed?"

Alan laid down his pipe, which he had long since suffered to go out, and set his two hands upon his knees.

"Ay," said he, "ye'll never guess that! For these same Stewarts, and Maccolls, and Macrobs (that had two rents to pay, one to King George by stark force, and one to Ardshiel by natural kindness) offered him a better price than any Campbell in all broad Scotland; and far he sent seeking them—as far as to the sides of Clyde and the cross of Edinburgh—seeking, and fleeching, and begging them to come, where there was a Stewart to be starved and a red-headed hound of a Campbell to be pleasured!"

"Well, Alan," said I, "that is a strange story, and a fine one, too. And Whig as I may be, I am glad the man was beaten."

"Him beaten?" echoed Alan. "It's little ye ken of Campbells, and less of the Red Fox. Him beaten? No: nor will be, till his blood's on the hillside! But if the day comes, David man, that I can find time and leisure for a bit of hunting, there grows not enough heather in all Scotland to hide him from my vengeance!"

"Man Alan," said I, "ye are neither very wise nor very Christian to blow off so many words of anger. They will do the man ye call the Fox no harm, and yourself no good. Tell me your tale plainly out. What did he next?"

"And that's a good observe, David," said Alan. "Troth and indeed, they will do him no harm; the more's the pity! And barring that about Christianity (of which my opinion is quite otherwise, or I would be nae Christian), I am much of your mind."

"Opinion here or opinion there," said I, "it's a kent thing that Christianity forbids revenge."

"Ay" said he, "it's well seen it was a Campbell taught ye! It would be a convenient world for them and their sort, if there was no such a thing as a lad and a gun behind a heather bush! But that's nothing to the point. This is what he did."

"Ay" said I, "come to that."

"Well, David," said he, "since he couldnae be rid of the loyal commons by fair means, he swore he would be rid of them by foul. Ardshiel was to starve: that was the thing he aimed at. And since them that fed him in his exile wouldnae be bought out—right or wrong, he would drive them out. Therefore he sent for lawyers, and papers, and red-coats to stand at his back. And the kindly folk of that country must all pack and tramp, every father's son out of his father's house, and out of the place where he was bred and fed, and played when he was a callant. And who are to succeed them? Bare-leggit beggars! King George is to whistle for his rents; he maun dow with less; he can spread his butter thinner: what cares Red Colin? If he can hurt Ardshiel, he has his wish; if he can pluck the meat from my chieftain's table, and the bit toys out of his children's hands, he will gang hame singing to Glenure!"

"Let me have a word," said I. "Be sure, if they take less rents, be sure Government has a finger in the pie. It's not this Campbell's fault, man—it's his orders. And if ye killed this Colin to-morrow, what better would ye be? There would be another factor in his shoes, as fast as spur can drive."

"Ye're a good lad in a fight," said Alan; "but, man! ye have Whig blood in ye!"

He spoke kindly enough, but there was so much anger under his contempt that I thought it was wise to change the conversation. I expressed my wonder how, with the Highlands covered with troops, and guarded like a city in a siege, a man in his situation could come and go without arrest.

"It's easier than ye would think," said Alan. "A bare hillside (ye see) is like all one road; if there's a sentry at one place, ye just go by another. And then the heather's a great help. And everywhere there are friends' houses and friends' byres and haystacks. And besides, when folk talk of a country covered with troops, it's but a kind of a byword at the best. A soldier covers nae mair of it than his boot-soles. I have fished a water with a sentry on the other side of the brae, and killed a fine trout; and I have sat in a heather bush within six feet of another, and learned a real bonny tune from his whistling. This was it," said he, and whistled me the air.

"And then, besides," he continued, "it's no sae bad now as it was in forty-six. The Hielands are what they call pacified. Small wonder, with never a gun or a sword left from Cantyre to Cape Wrath, but what tenty (*careful*) folk have hidden in their thatch! But what I would like to ken, David, is just how long? Not long, ye would think, with men like Ardshiel in exile and men like the Red Fox sitting birling the wine and oppressing the poor at home. But it's a kittle thing to decide what folk'll bear, and what they will not. Or why would Red Colin be riding his horse all over my poor country of Appin, and never a pretty lad to put a bullet in him?"

And with this Alan fell into a muse, and for a long time sate very sad and silent.

I will add the rest of what I have to say about my friend, that he was skilled in all kinds of music, but principally pipe-music; was a well-considered poet in his own tongue; had read several books both in French and English; was a dead shot, a good angler, and an excellent fencer with the small sword as well as with his own particular weapon. For his faults, they were on his face, and I now knew them all. But the worst of them, his childish propensity to take offence and to pick quarrels, he greatly laid aside in my case, out of regard for the battle of the round-house. But whether it was because I had done well myself, or because I had been a witness of his own much greater prowess, is more than I can tell. For though he had a great taste for courage in other men, yet he admired it most in Alan Breck.

13

THE LOSS OF THE BRIG

It was already late at night, and as dark as it ever would be at that season of the year (and that is to say, it was still pretty bright), when Hoseason clapped his head into the round-house door.

"Here," said he, "come out and see if ye can pilot."

"Is this one of your tricks?" asked Alan.

"Do I look like tricks?" cries the captain. "I have other things to think of—my brig's in danger!"

By the concerned look of his face, and, above all, by the sharp tones in which he spoke of his brig, it was plain to both of us he was in deadly earnest; and so Alan and I, with no great fear of treachery, stepped on deck.

The sky was clear; it blew hard, and was bitter cold; a great deal of daylight lingered; and the moon, which was nearly full, shone brightly. The brig was close hauled, so as to round the southwest corner of the Island of Mull, the hills of which (and Ben More above them all, with a wisp of mist upon the top of it) lay full upon the lar-board bow. Though it was no good point of sailing for the Covenant, she tore through the seas at a great rate, pitching and straining, and pursued by the westerly swell.

Altogether it was no such ill night to keep the seas in; and I had begun to wonder what it was that sat so heavily upon the captain, when the brig rising suddenly on the top of a high swell, he pointed and cried to us to look. Away on the lee bow, a thing like a fountain rose out of the moonlit sea, and immediately after we heard a low sound of roaring.

"What do ye call that?" asked the captain, gloomily.

"The sea breaking on a reef," said Alan. "And now ye ken where it is; and what better would ye have?"

"Ay," said Hoseason, "if it was the only one."

And sure enough, just as he spoke there came a second fountain farther to the south.

"There!" said Hoseason. "Ye see for yourself. If I had kent of these reefs, if I had had a chart, or if Shuan had been spared, it's not sixty guineas, no, nor six hundred, would have made me risk my brig in sic a stoneyard! But you, sir, that was to pilot us, have ye never a word?"

"I'm thinking," said Alan, "these'll be what they call the Torran Rocks."

"Are there many of them?" says the captain.

"Truly, sir, I am nae pilot," said Alan; "but it sticks in my mind there are ten miles of them."

Mr. Riach and the captain looked at each other.

"There's a way through them, I suppose?" said the captain.

"Doubtless," said Alan, "but where? But it somehow runs in my mind once more that it is clearer under the land."

"So?" said Hoseason. "We'll have to haul our wind then, Mr. Riach; we'll have to come as near in about the end of Mull as we can take her, sir; and even then we'll have the land to kep the wind off us, and that stoneyard on our lee. Well, we're in for it now, and may as well crack on."

With that he gave an order to the steersman, and sent Riach to the foretop. There were only five men on deck, counting the officers; these being all that were fit (or, at least, both fit and willing) for their work. So, as I say, it fell to Mr. Riach to go aloft, and he sat there looking out and hailing the deck with news of all he saw.

"The sea to the south is thick," he cried; and then, after a while, "it does seem clearer in by the land."

"Well, sir," said Hoseason to Alan, "we'll try your way of it. But I think I might as well trust to a blind fiddler. Pray God you're right."

"Pray God I am!" says Alan to me. "But where did I hear it? Well, well, it will be as it must."

As we got nearer to the turn of the land the reefs began to be sown here and there on our very path; and Mr. Riach sometimes cried down to us to change the course. Sometimes, indeed, none too soon; for one reef was so close on the brig's weather board that when a sea burst upon it the lighter sprays fell upon her deck and wetted us like rain.

The brightness of the night showed us these perils as clearly as by day, which was, perhaps, the more alarming. It showed me, too, the face of the captain as he stood by the steersman, now on one foot, now on the other, and sometimes blowing in his hands, but still listening and looking and as steady as steel. Neither he nor Mr. Riach had shown well in the fighting; but I saw they were brave in their own trade, and admired them all the more because I found Alan very white.

"Ochone, David," says he, "this is no the kind of death I fancy!"

"What, Alan!" I cried, "you're not afraid?"

"No," said he, wetting his lips, "but you'll allow, yourself, it's a cold ending."

By this time, now and then sheering to one side or the other to avoid a reef, but still hugging the wind and the land, we had got round Iona and begun to come alongside Mull. The tide at the tail of the land ran very strong, and threw the brig about. Two hands were put to the helm, and Hoseason himself would sometimes lend a help; and it was strange to see three strong men throw their weight upon the tiller, and it (like a living thing) struggle against and drive them back. This would have been the greater danger had not the sea been for some while free of obstacles. Mr. Riach, besides, announced from the top that he saw clear water ahead.

"Ye were right," said Hoseason to Alan. "Ye have saved the brig, sir. I'll mind that when we come to clear accounts." And I believe he not only meant what he said, but would have done it; so high a place did the Covenant hold in his affections.

But this is matter only for conjecture, things having gone otherwise than he forecast.

"Keep her away a point," sings out Mr. Riach. "Reef to windward!"

And just at the same time the tide caught the brig, and threw the wind out of her sails. She came round into the wind like a top, and the next moment struck the reef with such a dunch as threw us all flat upon the deck, and came near to shake Mr. Riach from his place upon the mast.

I was on my feet in a minute. The reef on which we had struck was close in under the southwest end of Mull, off a little isle they call Earraid, which lay low and black upon the larboard. Sometimes the swell broke clean over us; sometimes it only ground the poor brig upon the reef, so that we could hear her beat herself to pieces; and what with the great noise of the sails, and the singing of the wind, and the flying of the spray in the moonlight, and the sense of danger, I think my head must have been partly turned, for I could scarcely understand the things I saw.

Presently I observed Mr. Riach and the seamen busy round the skiff, and, still in the same blank, ran over to assist them; and as soon as I set my hand to work, my mind came clear again. It was no very easy task, for the skiff lay amidships and was full of hamper, and the breaking of the heavier seas continually forced us to give over and hold on; but we all wrought like horses while we could.

Meanwhile such of the wounded as could move came clambering out of the fore-scuttle and began to help; while the rest that lay helpless in their bunks harrowed me with screaming and begging to be saved.

The captain took no part. It seemed he was struck stupid. He stood holding by the shrouds, talking to himself and groaning out aloud whenever the ship hammered on the rock. His brig was like wife and child to him; he had looked on, day by day, at the mishandling of poor Ransome; but when it came to the brig, he seemed to suffer along with her.

All the time of our working at the boat, I remember only one other thing: that I asked Alan, looking across at the shore, what country it was; and he answered, it was the worst possible for him, for it was a land of the Campbells.

We had one of the wounded men told off to keep a watch upon the seas and cry us warning. Well, we had the boat about ready to be launched, when this man sang out pretty shrill: "For God's sake, hold on!" We knew by his tone that it was something more than ordinary; and sure enough, there followed a sea so huge that it lifted the brig right up and canted her over on her beam. Whether the cry came too late, or my hold was too weak, I know not; but at the sudden tilting of the ship I was cast clean over the bulwarks into the sea.

I went down, and drank my fill, and then came up, and got a blink of the moon, and then down again. They say a man sinks a third time for good. I cannot be made like other folk, then; for I would not like to write how often I went down, or how often I came up again. All the while, I was being hurled along, and beaten upon and choked, and then swallowed whole; and the thing was so distracting to my wits, that I was neither sorry nor afraid.

Presently, I found I was holding to a spar, which helped me somewhat. And then all of a sudden I was in quiet water, and began to come to myself.

It was the spare yard I had got hold of, and I was amazed to see how far I had travelled from the brig. I hailed her, indeed; but it was plain she was already out of cry. She was still holding together; but whether or not they had yet launched the boat, I was too far off and too low down to see.

While I was hailing the brig, I spied a tract of water lying between us where no great waves came, but which yet boiled white all over and bristled in the moon with rings and bubbles. Sometimes the whole tract swung to one side, like the tail of a live serpent; sometimes, for a glimpse, it would all disappear and then boil up again. What it was I had no guess, which for the time increased my fear of it; but I now know it must have been the roost or tide race, which had carried me away so fast and tumbled me about so cruelly, and at last, as if tired of that play, had flung out me and the spare yard upon its landward margin.

I now lay quite becalmed, and began to feel that a man can die of cold as well as of drowning. The shores of Earraid were close in; I could see in the moonlight the dots of heather and the sparkling of the mica in the rocks.

"Well," thought I to myself, "if I cannot get as far as that, it's strange!"

I had no skill of swimming, Essen Water being small in our neighbourhood; but when I laid hold upon the yard with both arms, and kicked out with both feet, I soon begun to find that I was moving. Hard work it was, and mortally slow; but in about an hour of kicking and splashing, I had got well in between the points of a sandy bay surrounded by low hills.

The sea was here quite quiet; there was no sound of any surf; the moon shone clear; and I thought in my heart I had never seen a place so desert and desolate. But it was dry land; and when at last it grew so shallow that I could leave the yard and wade ashore upon my feet, I cannot tell if I was more tired or more grateful. Both, at least, I was: tired as I never was before that night; and grateful to God as I trust I have been often, though never with more cause.

14

THE ISLET

With my stepping ashore I began the most unhappy part of my adventures. It was half-past twelve in the morning, and though the wind was broken by the land, it was a cold night. I dared not sit down (for I thought I should have frozen), but took off my shoes and walked to and fro upon the sand, bare-foot, and beating my breast with infinite weariness. There was no sound of man or cattle; not a cock crew, though it was about the hour of their first waking; only the surf broke outside in the distance, which put me in mind of my perils and those of my friend. To walk by the sea at that hour of the morning, and in a place so desert-like and lonesome, struck me with a kind of fear.

As soon as the day began to break I put on my shoes and climbed a hill—the ruggedest scramble I ever undertook—falling, the whole way, between big blocks of granite, or leaping from one to another. When I got to the top the dawn was come. There was no sign of the brig, which must have lifted from the reef and sunk. The boat, too, was nowhere to be seen. There was never a sail upon the ocean; and in what I could see of the land was neither house nor man.

I was afraid to think what had befallen my shipmates, and afraid to look longer at so empty a scene. What with my wet clothes and weariness, and my belly that now began to ache with hunger, I had enough to trouble me without that. So I set off eastward along the south coast, hoping to find a house where I might warm myself, and perhaps get news of those I had lost. And at the worst, I considered the sun would soon rise and dry my clothes.

After a little, my way was stopped by a creek or inlet of the sea, which seemed to run pretty deep into the land; and as I had no means to get across, I must needs change my direction to go about the end of it. It was still the roughest kind of walking; indeed the whole, not only of Earraid, but of the neighbouring part of Mull (which they call the Ross) is nothing but a jumble of granite rocks with heather in among. At first the creek kept narrowing as I had looked to see; but presently to my surprise it began to widen out again. At this I scratched my head, but had still no notion of the truth: until at last I came to a rising ground, and it burst upon me all in a moment that I was cast upon a little barren isle, and cut off on every side by the salt seas.

Instead of the sun rising to dry me, it came on to rain, with a thick mist; so that my case was lamentable.

I stood in the rain, and shivered, and wondered what to do, till it occurred to me that perhaps the creek was fordable. Back I went to the narrowest point and waded in. But not three yards from shore, I plumped in head over ears; and if ever I was heard of more, it was rather by God's grace than my own prudence. I was no wetter (for that could hardly be), but I was all the colder for this mishap; and having lost another hope was the more unhappy.

And now, all at once, the yard came in my head. What had carried me through the roost would surely serve me to cross this little quiet creek in safety. With that I set off, undaunted, across the top of the isle, to fetch and carry it back. It was a weary tramp in all ways, and if hope had not buoyed me up, I must have cast myself down and given up. Whether with the sea salt, or because I was growing fevered, I was distressed with thirst, and had to stop, as I went, and drink the peaty water out of the hags.

I came to the bay at last, more dead than alive; and at the first glance, I thought the yard was something farther out than when I left it. In I went, for the third time, into the sea. The sand was smooth and firm, and shelved gradually down, so that I could wade out till the water was almost to my neck and the little waves splashed into my face. But at that depth my feet began to leave me, and I durst venture in no farther. As for the yard, I saw it bobbing very quietly some twenty feet beyond.

I had borne up well until this last disappointment; but at that I came ashore, and flung myself down upon the sands and wept.

The time I spent upon the island is still so horrible a thought to me, that I must pass it lightly over. In all the books I have read of people cast away, they had either their pockets full of tools, or a chest of things would be thrown upon the beach along with them, as if on purpose. My case was very different. I had nothing in my pockets but money and Alan's silver button; and being inland bred, I was as much short of knowledge as of means.

I knew indeed that shell-fish were counted good to eat; and among the rocks of the isle I found a great plenty of limpets, which at first I could scarcely strike from their places, not knowing quickness to be needful. There were, besides, some of the little shells that we call buckies; I think periwinkle is the English name. Of these two I made my whole diet, devouring them cold and raw as I found them; and so hungry was I, that at first they seemed to me delicious.

Perhaps they were out of season, or perhaps there was something wrong in the sea about my island. But at least I had no sooner eaten my first meal than I was seized with giddiness and retching, and lay for a long time no better than dead. A second trial of the same food (indeed I had no other) did better with me, and revived my strength. But as long as I was on the island, I never knew what to expect when I had eaten; sometimes all was well, and sometimes I was thrown into a miserable sickness; nor could I ever distinguish what particular fish it was that hurt me.

All day it streamed rain; the island ran like a sop, there was no dry spot to be found; and when I lay down that night, between two boulders that made a kind of roof, my feet were in a bog.

The second day I crossed the island to all sides. There was no one part of it better than another; it was all desolate and rocky; nothing living on it but game birds which I lacked the means to kill, and the gulls which haunted the outlying rocks in a prodigious number. But the creek, or strait, that cut off the isle from the main-land of the Ross, opened out on the north into a bay, and the bay again opened into the Sound of Iona; and it was the neighbourhood of this place that I chose to be my home; though if I had thought upon the very name of home in such a spot, I must have burst out weeping.

I had good reasons for my choice. There was in this part of the isle a little hut of a house like a pig's hut, where fishers used to sleep when they came there upon their business; but the turf roof of it had fallen entirely in; so that the hut was of no use to me, and gave me less shelter than my rocks. What was more important, the shell-fish on which I lived grew there in great plenty; when the tide was out I could gather a peck at a time: and this was doubtless a convenience. But the other reason went deeper. I had become in no way used to the horrid solitude of the isle, but still looked round me on all sides (like a man that was hunted), between fear and hope that I might see some human creature coming. Now, from a little up the hillside over the bay, I could catch a sight of the great, ancient church and the roofs of the people's houses in Iona. And on the other hand, over the low country of the Ross, I saw smoke go up, morning and evening, as if from a homestead in a hollow of the land.

I used to watch this smoke, when I was wet and cold, and had my head half turned with loneliness; and think of the fireside and the company, till my heart burned. It was the same with the roofs of Iona. Altogether, this sight I had of men's homes and comfortable lives, although it put a point on my own sufferings, yet it kept hope alive, and helped me to eat my raw shell-fish (which had soon grown to be a disgust), and saved me from the sense of horror I had whenever I was quite alone with dead rocks, and fowls, and the rain, and the cold sea.

I say it kept hope alive; and indeed it seemed impossible that I should be left to die on the shores of my own country, and within view of a church-tower and the smoke of men's houses. But the second day passed; and though as long as the light lasted I kept a bright look-out for boats on the Sound or men passing on the Ross, no help came near me. It still rained, and I turned in to sleep, as wet as ever, and with a cruel sore throat, but a little comforted, perhaps, by having said good-night to my next neighbours, the people of Iona.

Charles the Second declared a man could stay outdoors more days in the year in the climate of England than in any other. This was very like a king, with a palace at his back and changes of dry clothes. But he must have had better luck on his flight from Worcester than I had on that miserable isle. It was the height of the summer; yet it rained for more than twenty-four hours, and did not clear until the afternoon of the third day.

This was the day of incidents. In the morning I saw a red deer, a buck with a fine spread of antlers, standing in the rain on the top of the island; but he had scarce seen me rise from under my rock, before he trotted off upon the other side. I supposed he must have swum the strait; though what should bring any creature to Earraid, was more than I could fancy.

A little after, as I was jumping about after my limpets, I was startled by a guinea-piece, which fell upon a rock in front of me and glanced off into the sea. When the sailors gave me my money again, they kept back not only about a third of the whole sum, but my father's leather purse; so that from that day out, I carried my gold loose in a pocket with a button. I now saw there must be a hole, and clapped my hand to the place in a great hurry. But this was to lock the stable door after the steed was stolen. I had left the shore at Queensferry with near on fifty pounds; now I found no more than two guinea-pieces and a silver shilling.

It is true I picked up a third guinea a little after, where it lay shining on a piece of turf. That made a fortune of three pounds and four shillings, English money, for a lad, the rightful heir of an estate, and now starving on an isle at the extreme end of the wild Highlands.

This state of my affairs dashed me still further; and, indeed my plight on that third morning was truly pitiful. My clothes were beginning to rot; my stockings in particular were quite worn through, so that my shanks went naked; my hands had grown quite soft with the continual soaking; my throat was very sore, my strength had much abated, and my heart so turned against the horrid stuff I was condemned to eat, that the very sight of it came near to sicken me.

And yet the worst was not yet come.

There is a pretty high rock on the northwest of Earraid, which (because it had a flat top and overlooked the Sound) I was much in the habit of frequenting; not that ever I stayed in one place, save when asleep, my misery giving me no rest. Indeed, I wore myself down with continual and aimless goings and comings in the rain.

As soon, however, as the sun came out, I lay down on the top of that rock to dry myself. The comfort of the sunshine is a thing I cannot tell. It set me thinking hopefully of my deliverance, of which I had begun to despair; and I scanned the sea and the Ross with a fresh interest. On the south of my rock, a part of the island jutted out and hid the open ocean, so that a boat could thus come quite near me upon that side, and I be none the wiser.

Well, all of a sudden, a coble with a brown sail and a pair of fishers aboard of it, came flying round that corner of the isle, bound for Iona. I shouted out, and then fell on my knees on the rock and reached up my hands and prayed to them. They were near enough to hear—I could even see the colour of their hair; and there was no doubt but they observed me, for they cried out in the Gaelic tongue, and laughed. But the boat never turned aside, and flew on, right before my eyes, for Iona.

I could not believe such wickedness, and ran along the shore from rock to rock, crying on them piteously even after they were out of reach of my voice, I still cried and waved to them; and when they were quite gone, I thought my heart would have burst. All the time of my troubles I wept only twice. Once, when I could not reach the yard, and now, the second time, when these fishers turned a deaf ear to my cries. But this time I wept and roared like a wicked child, tearing up the turf with my nails, and grinding my face in the earth. If a wish would kill men, those two fishers would never have seen morning, and I should likely have died upon my island.

When I was a little over my anger, I must eat again, but with such loathing of the mess as I could now scarce control. Sure enough, I should have done as well to fast, for my fishes poisoned me again. I had all my first pains; my throat was so sore I could scarce swallow; I had a fit of strong shuddering, which clucked my teeth together; and there came on me that dreadful sense of illness, which we have no name for either in Scotch or English. I thought I should have died, and made my peace with God, forgiving all men, even my uncle and the fishers; and as soon as I had thus made up my mind to the worst, clearness came upon me; I observed the night was falling dry; my clothes were dried a good deal; truly, I was in a better case than ever before, since I had landed on the isle; and so I got to sleep at last, with a thought of gratitude.

The next day (which was the fourth of this horrible life of mine) I found my bodily strength run very low. But the sun shone, the air was sweet, and what I managed to eat of the shell-fish agreed well with me and revived my courage.

I was scarce back on my rock (where I went always the first thing after I had eaten) before I observed a boat coming down the Sound, and with her head, as I thought, in my direction.

I began at once to hope and fear exceedingly; for I thought these men might have thought better of their cruelty and be coming back to my assistance. But another disappointment, such as yesterday's, was more than I could bear. I turned my back, accordingly, upon the sea, and did not look again till I had counted many hundreds. The boat was still heading for the island. The next time I counted the full thousand, as slowly as I could, my heart beating so as to hurt me. And then it was out of all question. She was coming straight to Earraid!

I could no longer hold myself back, but ran to the seaside and out, from one rock to another, as far as I could go. It is a marvel I was not drowned; for when I was brought to a stand at last, my legs shook under me, and my mouth was so dry, I must wet it with the sea-water before I was able to shout.

All this time the boat was coming on; and now I was able to perceive it was the same boat and the same two men as yesterday. This I knew by their hair, which the one had of a bright yellow and the other black. But now there was a third man along with them, who looked to be of a better class.

As soon as they were come within easy speech, they let down their sail and lay quiet. In spite of my supplications, they drew no nearer in, and what frightened me most of all, the new man tee-hee'd with laughter as he talked and looked at me.

Then he stood up in the boat and addressed me a long while, speaking fast and with many wavings of his hand. I told him I had no Gaelic; and at this he became very angry, and I began to suspect he thought he was talking English. Listening very close, I caught the word "whateffer" several times; but all the rest was Gaelic and might have been Greek and Hebrew for me.

"Whatever," said I, to show him I had caught a word.

"Yes, yes—yes, yes," says he, and then he looked at the other men, as much as to say, "I told you I spoke English," and began again as hard as ever in the Gaelic.

This time I picked out another word, "tide." Then I had a flash of hope. I remembered he was always waving his hand towards the mainland of the Ross.

"Do you mean when the tide is out—?" I cried, and could not finish.

"Yes, yes," said he. "Tide."

At that I turned tail upon their boat (where my adviser had once more begun to tee-hee with laughter), leaped back the way I had come, from one stone to another, and set off running across the isle as I had never run before. In about half an hour I came out upon the shores of the creek; and, sure enough, it was shrunk into a little trickle of water, through which I dashed, not above my knees, and landed with a shout on the main island.

A sea-bred boy would not have stayed a day on Earraid; which is only what they call a tidal islet, and except in the bottom of the neaps, can be entered and left twice in every twenty-four hours, either dry-shod, or at the most by wading. Even I, who had the tide going out and in before me in the bay, and even watched for the ebbs, the better to get my shellfish—even I (I say) if I had sat down to think, instead of raging at my fate, must have soon guessed the secret, and got free. It was no wonder the fishers had not understood me. The wonder was rather that they had ever guessed my pitiful illusion, and taken the trouble to come back. I had starved with cold and hunger on that island for close upon one hundred hours. But for the fishers, I might have left my bones there, in pure folly. And even as it was, I had paid for it pretty dear, not only in past sufferings, but in my present case; being clothed like a beggar-man, scarce able to walk, and in great pain of my sore throat.

I have seen wicked men and fools, a great many of both; and I believe they both get paid in the end; but the fools first.

15

THE LAD WITH THE SILVER BUTTON: THROUGH THE ISLE OF MULL

The Ross of Mull, which I had now got upon, was rugged and trackless, like the isle I had just left; being all bog, and brier, and big stone. There may be roads for them that know that country well; but for my part I had no better guide than my own nose, and no other landmark than Ben More.

I aimed as well as I could for the smoke I had seen so often from the island; and with all my great weariness and the difficulty of the way came upon the house in the bottom of a little hollow about five or six at night. It was low and longish, roofed with turf and built of unmortared stones; and on a mound in front of it, an old gentleman sat smoking his pipe in the sun.

With what little English he had, he gave me to understand that my shipmates had got safe ashore, and had broken bread in that very house on the day after.

"Was there one," I asked, "dressed like a gentleman?"

He said they all wore rough great-coats; but to be sure, the first of them, the one that came alone, wore breeches and stockings, while the rest had sailors' trousers.

"Ah," said I, "and he would have a feathered hat?"

He told me, no, that he was bareheaded like myself.

At first I thought Alan might have lost his hat; and then the rain came in my mind, and I judged it more likely he had it out of harm's way under his great-coat. This set me smiling, partly because my friend was safe, partly to think of his vanity in dress.

And then the old gentleman clapped his hand to his brow, and cried out that I must be the lad with the silver button.

"Why, yes!" said I, in some wonder.

"Well, then," said the old gentleman, "I have a word for you, that you are to follow your friend to his country, by Torosay."

He then asked me how I had fared, and I told him my tale. A south-country man would certainly have laughed; but this old gentleman (I call him so because of his manners, for his clothes were dropping off his back) heard me all through with nothing but gravity and pity.

When I had done, he took me by the hand, led me into his hut (it was no better) and presented me before his wife, as if she had been the Queen and I a duke.

The good woman set oat-bread before me and a cold grouse, patting my shoulder and smiling to me all the time, for she had no English; and the old gentleman (not to be behind) brewed me a strong punch out of their country spirit. All the while I was eating, and after that when I was drinking the punch, I could scarce come to believe in my good fortune; and the house, though it was thick with the peat-smoke and as full of holes as a colander, seemed like a palace.

The punch threw me in a strong sweat and a deep slumber; the good people let me lie; and it was near noon of the next day before I took the road, my throat already easier and my spirits quite restored by good fare and good news. The old gentleman, although I pressed him hard, would take no money, and gave me an old bonnet for my head; though I am free to own I was no sooner out of view of the house than I very jealously washed this gift of his in a wayside fountain.

Thought I to myself: "If these are the wild Highlanders, I could wish my own folk wilder."

I not only started late, but I must have wandered nearly half the time. True, I met plenty of people, grubbing in little miserable fields that would not keep a cat, or herding little kine about the bigness of asses. The Highland dress being forbidden by law since the rebellion, and the people condemned to the Lowland habit, which they much disliked, it was strange to see the variety of their array. Some went bare, only for a hanging cloak or great-coat, and carried their trousers on their backs like a useless burthen: some had made an imitation of the tartan with little parti-coloured stripes patched together like an old wife's quilt; others, again, still wore the Highland philabeg, but by putting a few stitches between the legs transformed it into a pair of trousers like a Dutchman's. All those makeshifts were condemned and punished, for the law was harshly applied, in hopes to break up the clan spirit; but in that out-of-the-way, sea-bound isle, there were few to make remarks and fewer to tell tales.

They seemed in great poverty; which was no doubt natural, now that rapine was put down, and the chiefs kept no longer an open house; and the roads (even such a wandering, country by-track as the one I followed) were infested with beggars. And here again I marked a difference from my own part of the country. For our Lowland beggars—even the gownsmen themselves, who beg by patent—had a louting, flattering way with them, and if you gave them a plaek and asked change, would very civilly return you a boddle. But these Highland beggars stood on their dignity, asked alms only to buy snuff (by their account) and would give no change.

To be sure, this was no concern of mine, except in so far as it entertained me by the way. What was much more to the purpose, few had any English, and these few (unless they were of the brotherhood of beggars) not very anxious to place it at my service. I knew Torosay to be my destination, and repeated the name to them and pointed; but instead of simply pointing in reply, they would give me a screed of the Gaelic that set me foolish; so it was small wonder if I went out of my road as often as I stayed in it.

At last, about eight at night, and already very weary, I came to a lone house, where I asked admittance, and was refused, until I bethought me of the power of money in so poor a country, and held up one of my guineas in my finger and thumb. Thereupon, the man of the house, who had hitherto pretended to have no English, and driven me from his door by signals, suddenly began to speak as clearly as was needful, and agreed for five shillings to give me a night's lodging and guide me the next day to Torosay.

I slept uneasily that night, fearing I should be robbed; but I might have spared myself the pain; for my host was no robber, only miserably poor and a great cheat. He was not alone in his poverty; for the next morning, we must go five miles about to the house of what he called a rich man to have one of my guineas changed. This was perhaps a rich man for Mull; he would have scarce been thought so in the south; for it took all he had—the whole house was turned upside down, and a neighbour brought under contribution, before he could scrape together twenty shillings in silver. The odd shilling he kept for himself, protesting he could ill afford to have so great a sum of money lying "locked up." For all that he was very courteous and well spoken, made us both sit down with his family to dinner, and brewed punch in a fine china bowl, over which my rascal guide grew so merry that he refused to start.

I was for getting angry, and appealed to the rich man (Hector Maclean was his name), who had been a witness to our bargain and to my payment of the five shillings. But Maclean had taken his share of the punch, and vowed that no gentleman should leave his table after the bowl was brewed; so there was nothing for it but to sit and hear Jacobite toasts and Gaelic songs, till all were tipsy and staggered off to the bed or the barn for their night's rest.

Next day (the fourth of my travels) we were up before five upon the clock; but my rascal guide got to the bottle at once, and it was three hours before I had him clear of the house, and then (as you shall hear) only for a worse disappointment.

As long as we went down a heathery valley that lay before Mr. Maclean's house, all went well; only my guide looked constantly over his shoulder, and when I asked him the cause, only grinned at me. No sooner, however, had we crossed the back of a hill, and got out of sight of the house windows, than he told me Torosay lay right in front, and that a hill-top (which he pointed out) was my best landmark.

"I care very little for that," said I, "since you are going with me."

The impudent cheat answered me in the Gaelic that he had no English.

"My fine fellow," I said, "I know very well your English comes and goes. Tell me what will bring it back? Is it more money you wish?"

"Five shillings mair," said he, "and hersel' will bring ye there."

I reflected awhile and then offered him two, which he accepted greedily, and insisted on having in his hands at once "for luck," as he said, but I think it was rather for my misfortune.

The two shillings carried him not quite as many miles; at the end of which distance, he sat down upon the wayside and took off his brogues from his feet, like a man about to rest.

I was now red-hot. "Ha!" said I, "have you no more English?"

He said impudently, "No."

At that I boiled over, and lifted my hand to strike him; and he, drawing a knife from his rags, squatted back and grinned at me like a wildcat. At that, forgetting everything but my anger, I ran in upon him, put aside his knife with my left, and struck him in the mouth with the right. I was a strong lad and very angry, and he but a little man; and he went down before me heavily. By good luck, his knife flew out of his hand as he fell.

I picked up both that and his brogues, wished him a good morning, and set off upon my way, leaving him barefoot and disarmed. I chuckled to myself as I went, being sure I was done with that rogue, for a variety of reasons. First, he knew he could have no more of my money; next, the brogues were worth in that country only a few pence; and, lastly, the knife, which was really a dagger, it was against the law for him to carry.

In about half an hour of walk, I overtook a great, ragged man, moving pretty fast but feeling before him with a staff. He was quite blind, and told me he was a catechist, which should have put me at my ease. But his face went against me; it seemed dark and dangerous and secret; and presently, as we began to go on alongside, I saw the steel butt of a pistol sticking from under the flap of his coat-pocket. To carry such a thing meant a fine of fifteen pounds sterling upon a first offence, and transportation to the colonies upon a second. Nor could I quite see why a religious teacher should go armed, or what a blind man could be doing with a pistol.

I told him about my guide, for I was proud of what I had done, and my vanity for once got the heels of my prudence. At the mention of the five shillings he cried out so loud that I made up my mind I should say nothing of the other two, and was glad he could not see my blushes.

"Was it too much?" I asked, a little faltering.

"Too much!" cries he. "Why, I will guide you to Torosay myself for a dram of brandy. And give you the great pleasure of my company (me that is a man of some learning) in the bargain."

I said I did not see how a blind man could be a guide; but at that he laughed aloud, and said his stick was eyes enough for an eagle.

"In the Isle of Mull, at least," says he, "where I know every stone and heather-bush by mark of head. See, now," he said, striking right and left, as if to make sure, "down there a burn is running; and at the head of it there stands a bit of a small hill with a stone cocked upon the top of that; and it's hard at the foot of the hill, that the way runs by to Torosay; and the way here, being for droves, is plainly trodden, and will show grassy through the heather."

I had to own he was right in every feature, and told my wonder.

"Ha!" says he, "that's nothing. Would ye believe me now, that before the Act came out, and when there were weepons in this country, I could shoot? Ay, could I!" cries he, and then with a leer: "If ye had such a thing as a pistol here to try with, I would show ye how it's done."

I told him I had nothing of the sort, and gave him a wider berth. If he had known, his pistol stuck at that time quite plainly out of his pocket, and I could see the sun twinkle on the steel of the butt. But by the better luck for me, he knew nothing, thought all was covered, and lied on in the dark.

He then began to question me cunningly, where I came from, whether I was rich, whether I could change a five-shilling piece for him (which he declared he had that moment in his sporran), and all the time he kept edging up to me and I avoiding him. We were now upon a sort of green cattle-track which crossed the hills towards Torosay, and we kept changing sides upon that like dancers in a reel. I had so plainly the upper-hand that my spirits rose, and indeed I took a pleasure in this game of blindman's buff; but the catechist grew angrier and angrier, and at last began to swear in Gaelic and to strike for my legs with his staff.

Then I told him that, sure enough, I had a pistol in my pocket as well as he, and if he did not strike across the hill due south I would even blow his brains out.

He became at once very polite, and after trying to soften me for some time, but quite in vain, he cursed me once more in Gaelic and took himself off. I watched him striding along, through bog and brier, tapping with his stick, until he turned the end of a hill and disappeared in the next hollow. Then I struck on again for Torosay, much better pleased to be alone than to travel with that man of learning. This was an unlucky day; and these two, of whom I had just rid myself, one after the other, were the two worst men I met with in the Highlands.

At Torosay, on the Sound of Mull and looking over to the mainland of Morven, there was an inn with an innkeeper, who was a Maclean, it appeared, of a very high family; for to keep an inn is thought even more genteel in the Highlands than it is with us, perhaps as partaking of hospitality, or perhaps because the trade is idle and drunken. He spoke good English, and finding me to be something of a scholar, tried me first in French, where he easily beat me, and then in the Latin, in which I don't know which of us did best. This pleasant rivalry put us at once upon friendly terms; and I sat up and drank punch with him (or to be more correct, sat up and watched him drink it), until he was so tipsy that he wept upon my shoulder.

I tried him, as if by accident, with a sight of Alan's button; but it was plain he had never seen or heard of it. Indeed, he bore some grudge against the family and friends of Ardshiel, and before he was drunk he read me a lampoon, in very good Latin, but with a very ill meaning, which he had made in elegiac verses upon a person of that house.

When I told him of my catechist, he shook his head, and said I was lucky to have got clear off. "That is a very dangerous man," he said; "Duncan Mackiegh is his name; he can shoot by the ear at several yards, and has been often accused of highway robberies, and once of murder."

"The cream of it is," says I, "that he called himself a catechist."

"And why should he not?" says he, "when that is what he is. It was Maclean of Duart gave it to him because he was blind. But perhaps it was a peety," says my host, "for he is always on the road, going from one place to another to hear the young folk say their religion; and, doubtless, that is a great temptation to the poor man."

At last, when my landlord could drink no more, he showed me to a bed, and I lay down in very good spirits; having travelled the greater part of that big and crooked Island of Mull, from Earraid to Torosay, fifty miles as the crow flies, and (with my wanderings) much nearer a hundred, in four days and with little fatigue. Indeed I was by far in better heart and health of body at the end of that long tramp than I had been at the beginning.

16

THE LAD WITH THE SILVER BUTTON:
ACROSS MORVEN

There is a regular ferry from Torosay to Kinlochaline on the mainland. Both shores of the Sound are in the country of the strong clan of the Macleans, and the people that passed the ferry with me were almost all of that clan. The skipper of the boat, on the other hand, was called Neil Roy Macrob; and since Macrob was one of the names of Alan's clansmen, and Alan himself had sent me to that ferry, I was eager to come to private speech of Neil Roy.

In the crowded boat this was of course impossible, and the passage was a very slow affair. There was no wind, and as the boat was wretchedly equipped, we could pull but two oars on one side, and one on the other. The men gave way, however, with a good will, the passengers taking spells to help them, and the whole company giving the time in Gaelic boat-songs. And what with the songs, and the sea-air, and the good-nature and spirit of all concerned, and the bright weather, the passage was a pretty thing to have seen.

But there was one melancholy part. In the mouth of Loch Aline we found a great sea-going ship at anchor; and this I supposed at first to be one of the King's cruisers which were kept along that coast, both summer and winter, to prevent communication with the French. As we got a little nearer, it became plain she was a ship of merchandise; and what still more puzzled me, not only her decks, but the sea-beach also, were quite black with people, and skiffs were continually plying to and fro between them. Yet nearer, and there began to come to our ears a great sound of mourning, the people on board and those on the shore crying and lamenting one to another so as to pierce the heart.

Then I understood this was an emigrant ship bound for the American colonies.

We put the ferry-boat alongside, and the exiles leaned over the bulwarks, weeping and reaching out their hands to my fellow-passengers, among whom they counted some near friends. How long this might have gone on I do not know, for they seemed to have no sense of time: but at last the captain of the ship, who seemed near beside himself (and no great wonder) in the midst of this crying and confusion, came to the side and begged us to depart.

Thereupon Neil sheered off; and the chief singer in our boat struck into a melancholy air, which was presently taken up both by the emigrants and their friends upon the beach, so that it sounded from all sides like a lament for the dying. I saw the tears run down the cheeks of the men and women in the boat, even as they bent at the oars; and the circumstances and the music of the song (which is one called "Lochaber no more") were highly affecting even to myself.

At Kinlochaline I got Neil Roy upon one side on the beach, and said I made sure he was one of Appin's men.

"And what for no?" said he.

"I am seeking somebody," said I; "and it comes in my mind that you will have news of him. Alan Breck Stewart is his name." And very foolishly, instead of showing him the button, I sought to pass a shilling in his hand.

At this he drew back. "I am very much affronted," he said; "and this is not the way that one shentleman should behave to another at all. The man you ask for is in France; but if he was in my sporran," says he, "and your belly full of shillings, I would not hurt a hair upon his body."

I saw I had gone the wrong way to work, and without wasting time upon apologies, showed him the button lying in the hollow of my palm.

"Aweel, aweel," said Neil; "and I think ye might have begun with that end of the stick, whatever! But if ye are the lad with the silver button, all is well, and I have the word to see that ye come safe. But if ye will pardon me to speak plainly," says he, "there is a name that you should never take into your mouth, and that is the name of Alan Breck; and there is a thing that ye would never do, and that is to offer your dirty money to a Hieland shentleman."

It was not very easy to apologise; for I could scarce tell him (what was the truth) that I had never dreamed he would set up to be a gentleman until he told me so. Neil on his part had no wish to prolong his dealings with me, only to fulfil his orders and be done with it; and he made haste to give me my route. This was to lie the night in Kinlochaline in the public inn; to cross Morven the next day to Ardgour, and lie the night in the house of one John of the Claymore, who was warned that I might come; the third day, to be set across one loch at Corran and another at Balachulish, and then ask my way to the house of James of the Glens, at Aucharn in Duror of Appin. There was a good deal of ferrying, as you hear; the sea in all this part running deep into the mountains and winding about their roots. It makes the country strong to hold and difficult to travel, but full of prodigious wild and dreadful prospects.

I had some other advice from Neil: to speak with no one by the way, to avoid Whigs, Campbells, and the "red-soldiers;" to leave the road and lie in a bush if I saw any of the latter coming, "for it was never chancy to meet in with them;" and in brief, to conduct myself like a robber or a Jacobite agent, as perhaps Neil thought me.

The inn at Kinlochaline was the most beggarly vile place that ever pigs were styed in, full of smoke, vermin, and silent Highlanders. I was not only discontented with my lodging, but with myself for my mismanagement of Neil, and thought I could hardly be worse off. But very wrongly, as I was soon to see; for I had not been half an hour at the inn (standing in the door most of the time, to ease my eyes from the peat smoke) when a thunderstorm came close by, the springs broke in a little hill on which the inn stood, and one end of the house became a running water. Places of public entertainment were bad enough all over Scotland in those days; yet it was a wonder to myself, when I had to go from the fireside to the bed in which I slept, wading over the shoes.

Early in my next day's journey I overtook a little, stout, solemn man, walking very slowly with his toes turned out, sometimes reading in a book and sometimes marking the place with his finger, and dressed decently and plainly in something of a clerical style.

This I found to be another catechist, but of a different order from the blind man of Mull: being indeed one of those sent out by the Edinburgh Society for Propagating Christian Knowledge, to evangelise the more savage places of the Highlands. His name was Henderland; he spoke with the broad south-country tongue, which I was beginning to weary for the sound of; and besides common countryship, we soon found we had a more particular bond of interest. For my good friend, the minister of Essendean, had translated into the Gaelic in his by-time a number of hymns and pious books which Henderland used in his work, and held in great esteem. Indeed, it was one of these he was carrying and reading when we met.

We fell in company at once, our ways lying together as far as to Kingairloch. As we went, he stopped and spoke with all the wayfarers and workers that we met or passed; and though of course I could not tell what they discoursed about, yet I judged Mr. Henderland must be well liked in the countryside, for I observed many of them to bring out their mulls and share a pinch of snuff with him.

I told him as far in my affairs as I judged wise; as far, that is, as they were none of Alan's; and gave Balachulish as the place I was travelling to, to meet a friend; for I thought Aucharn, or even Duror, would be too particular, and might put him on the scent.

On his part, he told me much of his work and the people he worked among, the hiding priests and Jacobites, the Disarming Act, the dress, and many other curiosities of the time and place. He seemed moderate; blaming Parliament in several points, and especially because they had framed the Act more severely against those who wore the dress than against those who carried weapons.

This moderation put it in my mind to question him of the Red Fox and the Appin tenants; questions which, I thought, would seem natural enough in the mouth of one travelling to that country.

He said it was a bad business. "It's wonderful," said he, "where the tenants find the money, for their life is mere starvation. (Ye don't carry such a thing as snuff, do ye, Mr. Balfour? No. Well, I'm better wanting it.) But these tenants (as I was saying) are doubtless partly driven to it. James Stewart in Duror (that's him they call James of the Glens) is half-brother to Ardshiel, the captain of the clan; and he is a man much looked up to, and drives very hard. And then there's one they call Alan Breck—"

"Ah!" I cried, "what of him?"

"What of the wind that bloweth where it listeth?" said Henderland. "He's here and awa; here to-day and gone to-morrow: a fair heather-cat. He might be glowering at the two of us out of yon whin-bush, and I wouldnae wonder! Ye'll no carry such a thing as snuff, will ye?"

I told him no, and that he had asked the same thing more than once.

"It's highly possible," said he, sighing. "But it seems strange ye shouldnae carry it. However, as I was saying, this Alan Breck is a bold, desperate customer, and well kent to be James's right hand. His life is forfeit already; he would boggle at naething; and maybe, if a tenant-body was to hang back he would get a dirk in his wame."

"You make a poor story of it all, Mr. Henderland," said I. "If it is all fear upon both sides, I care to hear no more of it."

"Na," said Mr. Henderland, "but there's love too, and self-denial that should put the like of you and me to shame. There's something fine about it; no perhaps Christian, but humanly fine. Even Alan Breck, by all that I hear, is a chield to be respected. There's many a lying sneck-draw sits close in kirk in our own part of the country, and stands well in the world's eye, and maybe is a far worse man, Mr. Balfour, than yon misguided shedder of man's blood.

Ay, ay, we might take a lesson by them.—Ye'll perhaps think I've been too long in the Hielands?" he added, smiling to me.

I told him not at all; that I had seen much to admire among the Highlanders; and if he came to that, Mr. Campbell himself was a Highlander.

"Ay," said he, "that's true. It's a fine blood."

"And what is the King's agent about?" I asked.

"Colin Campbell?" says Henderland. "Putting his head in a bees' byke!"

"He is to turn the tenants out by force, I hear?" said I.

"Yes," says he, "but the business has gone back and forth, as folk say. First, James of the Glens rode to Edinburgh, and got some lawyer (a Stewart, nae doubt—they all hing together like bats in a steeple) and had the proceedings stayed. And then Colin Campbell cam' in again, and had the upper-hand before the Barons of Exchequer. And now they tell me the first of the tenants are to flit to-morrow. It's to begin at Duror under James's very windows, which doesnae seem wise by my humble way of it."

"Do you think they'll fight?" I asked.

"Well," says Henderland, "they're disarmed—or supposed to be—for there's still a good deal of cold iron lying by in quiet places. And then Colin Campbell has the sogers coming. But for all that, if I was his lady wife, I wouldnae be well pleased till I got him home again. They're queer customers, the Appin Stewarts."

I asked if they were worse than their neighbours.

"No they," said he. "And that's the worst part of it. For if Colin Roy can get his business done in Appin, he has it all to begin again in the next country, which they call Mamore, and which is one of the countries of the Camerons. He's King's Factor upon both, and from both he has to drive out the tenants; and indeed, Mr. Balfour (to be open with ye), it's my belief that if he escapes the one lot, he'll get his death by the other."

So we continued talking and walking the great part of the day; until at last, Mr. Henderland after expressing his delight in my company, and satisfaction at meeting with a friend of Mr. Campbell's ("whom," says he, "I will make bold to call that sweet singer of our covenanted Zion"), proposed that I should make a short stage, and lie the night in his house a little beyond Kingairloch. To say truth, I was overjoyed; for I had no great desire for John of the Claymore, and since my double misadventure, first with the guide and next with the gentleman skipper, I stood in some fear of any Highland stranger. Accordingly we shook hands upon the bargain, and came in the afternoon to a small house, standing alone by the shore of the Linnhe Loch. The sun was already gone from the desert mountains of Ardgour upon the hither side, but shone on those of Appin on the farther; the loch lay as still as a lake, only the gulls were crying round the sides of it; and the whole place seemed solemn and uncouth.

We had no sooner come to the door of Mr. Henderland's dwelling, than to my great surprise (for I was now used to the politeness of Highlanders) he burst rudely past me, dashed into the room, caught up a jar and a small horn-spoon, and began ladling snuff into his nose in most excessive quantities. Then he had a hearty fit of sneezing, and looked round upon me with a rather silly smile.

"It's a vow I took," says he. "I took a vow upon me that I wouldnae carry it. Doubtless it's a great privation; but when I think upon the martyrs, not only to the Scottish Covenant but to other points of Christianity, I think shame to mind it."

As soon as we had eaten (and porridge and whey was the best of the good man's diet) he took a grave face and said he had a duty to perform by Mr. Campbell, and that was to inquire into my state of mind towards God. I was inclined to smile at him since the business of the snuff; but he had not spoken long before he brought the tears into my eyes. There are two things that men should never weary of, goodness and humility; we get none too much of them in this rough world among cold, proud people; but Mr. Henderland had their very speech upon his tongue. And though I was a good deal puffed up with my adventures and with having come off, as the saying is, with flying colours; yet he soon had me on my knees beside a simple, poor old man, and both proud and glad to be there.

Before we went to bed he offered me sixpence to help me on my way, out of a scanty store he kept in the turf wall of his house; at which excess of goodness I knew not what to do. But at last he was so earnest with me that I thought it the more mannerly part to let him have his way, and so left him poorer than myself.

17

THE DEATH OF THE RED FOX

The next day Mr. Henderland found for me a man who had a boat of his own and was to cross the Linnhe Loch that afternoon into Appin, fishing. Him he prevailed on to take me, for he was one of his flock; and in this way I saved a long day's travel and the price of the two public ferries I must otherwise have passed.

It was near noon before we set out; a dark day with clouds, and the sun shining upon little patches. The sea was here very deep and still, and had scarce a wave upon it; so that I must put the water to my lips before I could believe it to be truly salt. The mountains on either side were high, rough and barren, very black and gloomy in the shadow of the clouds, but all silver-laced with little watercourses where the sun shone upon them. It seemed a hard country, this of Appin, for people to care as much about as Alan did.

There was but one thing to mention. A little after we had started, the sun shone upon a little moving clump of scarlet close in along the water-side to the north. It was much of the same red as soldiers' coats; every now and then, too, there came little sparks and lightnings, as though the sun had struck upon bright steel.

I asked my boatman what it should be, and he answered he supposed it was some of the red soldiers coming from Fort William into Appin, against the poor tenantry of the country. Well, it was a sad sight to me; and whether it was because of my thoughts of Alan, or from something prophetic in my bosom, although this was but the second time I had seen King George's troops, I had no good will to them.

At last we came so near the point of land at the entering in of Loch Leven that I begged to be set on shore. My boatman (who was an honest fellow and mindful of his promise to the catechist) would fain have carried me on to Balachulish; but as this was to take me farther from my secret destination, I insisted, and was set on shore at last under the wood of Lettermore (or Lettervore, for I have heard it both ways) in Alan's country of Appin.

This was a wood of birches, growing on a steep, craggy side of a mountain that overhung the loch. It had many openings and ferny howes; and a road or bridle track ran north and south through the midst of it, by the edge of which, where was a spring, I sat down to eat some oat-bread of Mr. Henderland's and think upon my situation.

Here I was not only troubled by a cloud of stinging midges, but far more by the doubts of my mind. What I ought to do, why I was going to join myself with an outlaw and a would-be murderer like Alan, whether I should not be acting more like a man of sense to tramp back to the south country direct, by my own guidance and at my own charges, and what Mr. Campbell or even Mr. Henderland would think of me if they should ever learn my folly and presumption: these were the doubts that now began to come in on me stronger than ever.

As I was so sitting and thinking, a sound of men and horses came to me through the wood; and presently after, at a turning of the road, I saw four travellers come into view. The way was in this part so rough and narrow that they came single and led their horses by the reins. The first was a great, red-headed gentleman, of an imperious and flushed face, who carried his hat in his hand and fanned himself, for he was in a breathing heat. The second, by his decent black garb and white wig, I correctly took to be a lawyer. The third was a servant, and wore some part of his clothes in tartan, which showed that his master was of a Highland family, and either an outlaw or else in singular good odour with the Government, since the wearing of tartan was against the Act. If I had been better versed in these things, I would have known the tartan to be of the Argyle (or Campbell) colours. This servant had a good-sized portmanteau strapped on his horse, and a net of lemons (to brew punch with) hanging at the saddle-bow; as was often enough the custom with luxurious travellers in that part of the country.

As for the fourth, who brought up the tail, I had seen his like before, and knew him at once to be a sheriff's officer.

I had no sooner seen these people coming than I made up my mind (for no reason that I can tell) to go through with my adventure; and when the first came alongside of me, I rose up from the bracken and asked him the way to Aucharn.

He stopped and looked at me, as I thought, a little oddly; and then, turning to the lawyer, "Mungo," said he, "there's many a man would think this more of a warning than two pyats. Here am I on my road to Duror on the job ye ken; and here is a young lad starts up out of the bracken, and speers if I am on the way to Aucharn."

"Glenure," said the other, "this is an ill subject for jesting."

These two had now drawn close up and were gazing at me, while the two followers had halted about a stone-cast in the rear.

"And what seek ye in Aucharn?" said Colin Roy Campbell of Glenure, him they called the Red Fox; for he it was that I had stopped.

"The man that lives there," said I.

"James of the Glens," says Glenure, musingly; and then to the lawyer: "Is he gathering his people, think ye?"

"Anyway," says the lawyer, "we shall do better to bide where we are, and let the soldiers rally us."

"If you are concerned for me," said I, "I am neither of his people nor yours, but an honest subject of King George, owing no man and fearing no man."

"Why, very well said," replies the Factor. "But if I may make so bold as ask, what does this honest man so far from his country? and why does he come seeking the brother of Ardshiel? I have power here, I must tell you. I am King's Factor upon several of these estates, and have twelve files of soldiers at my back."

"I have heard a waif word in the country," said I, a little nettled, "that you were a hard man to drive."

He still kept looking at me, as if in doubt.

"Well," said he, at last, "your tongue is bold; but I am no unfriend to plainness. If ye had asked me the way to the door of James Stewart on any other day but this, I would have set ye right and bidden ye God speed. But to-day—eh, Mungo?" And he turned again to look at the lawyer.

But just as he turned there came the shot of a firelock from higher up the hill; and with the very sound of it Glenure fell upon the road.

"O, I am dead!" he cried, several times over.

The lawyer had caught him up and held him in his arms, the servant standing over and clasping his hands. And now the wounded man looked from one to another with scared eyes, and there was a change in his voice, that went to the heart.

"Take care of yourselves," says he. "I am dead."

He tried to open his clothes as if to look for the wound, but his fingers slipped on the buttons. With that he gave a great sigh, his head rolled on his shoulder, and he passed away.

The lawyer said never a word, but his face was as sharp as a pen and as white as the dead man's; the servant broke out into a great noise of crying and weeping, like a child; and I, on my side, stood staring at them in a kind of horror. The sheriff's officer had run back at the first sound of the shot, to hasten the coming of the soldiers.

At last the lawyer laid down the dead man in his blood upon the road, and got to his own feet with a kind of stagger.

I believe it was his movement that brought me to my senses; for he had no sooner done so than I began to scramble up the hill, crying out, "The murderer! the murderer!"

So little a time had elapsed, that when I got to the top of the first steepness, and could see some part of the open mountain, the murderer was still moving away at no great distance. He was a big man, in a black coat, with metal buttons, and carried a long fowling-piece.

"Here!" I cried. "I see him!"

At that the murderer gave a little, quick look over his shoulder, and began to run. The next moment he was lost in a fringe of birches; then he came out again on the upper side, where I could see him climbing like a jackanapes, for that part was again very steep; and then he dipped behind a shoulder, and I saw him no more.

All this time I had been running on my side, and had got a good way up, when a voice cried upon me to stand.

I was at the edge of the upper wood, and so now, when I halted and looked back, I saw all the open part of the hill below me.

The lawyer and the sheriff's officer were standing just above the road, crying and waving on me to come back; and on their left, the red-coats, musket in hand, were beginning to struggle singly out of the lower wood.

"Why should I come back?" I cried. "Come you on!"

"Ten pounds if ye take that lad!" cried the lawyer. "He's an accomplice. He was posted here to hold us in talk."

At that word (which I could hear quite plainly, though it was to the soldiers and not to me that he was crying it) my heart came in my mouth with quite a new kind of terror. Indeed, it is one thing to stand the danger of your life, and quite another to run the peril of both life and character. The thing, besides, had come so suddenly, like thunder out of a clear sky, that I was all amazed and helpless.

The soldiers began to spread, some of them to run, and others to put up their pieces and cover me; and still I stood.

"Jouk (*duck*) in here among the trees," said a voice close by.

Indeed, I scarce knew what I was doing, but I obeyed; and as I did so, I heard the firelocks bang and the balls whistle in the birches.

Just inside the shelter of the trees I found Alan Breck standing, with a fishing-rod. He gave me no salutation; indeed it was no time for civilities; only "Come!" says he, and set off running along the side of the mountain towards Balachulish; and I, like a sheep, to follow him.

Now we ran among the birches; now stooping behind low humps upon the mountain-side; now crawling on all fours among the heather. The pace was deadly: my heart seemed bursting against my ribs; and I had neither time to think nor breath to speak with. Only I remember seeing with wonder, that Alan every now and then would straighten himself to his full height and look back; and every time he did so, there came a great far-away cheering and crying of the soldiers.

Quarter of an hour later, Alan stopped, clapped down flat in the heather, and turned to me.

"Now," said he, "it's earnest. Do as I do, for your life."

And at the same speed, but now with infinitely more precaution, we traced back again across the mountain-side by the same way that we had come, only perhaps higher; till at last Alan threw himself down in the upper wood of Lettermore, where I had found him at the first, and lay, with his face in the bracken, panting like a dog.

My own sides so ached, my head so swam, my tongue so hung out of my mouth with heat and dryness, that I lay beside him like one dead.

18

I TALK WITH ALAN IN THE WOOD OF LETTERMORE

Alan was the first to come round. He rose, went to the border of the wood, peered out a little, and then returned and sat down.

"Well," said he, "yon was a hot burst, David."

I said nothing, nor so much as lifted my face. I had seen murder done, and a great, ruddy, jovial gentleman struck out of life in a moment; the pity of that sight was still sore within me, and yet that was but a part of my concern. Here was murder done upon the man Alan hated; here was Alan skulking in the trees and running from the troops; and whether his was the hand that fired or only the head that ordered, signified but little. By my way of it, my only friend in that wild country was blood-guilty in the first degree; I held him in horror; I could not look upon his face; I would have rather lain alone in the rain on my cold isle, than in that warm wood beside a murderer.

"Are ye still wearied?" he asked again.

"No," said I, still with my face in the bracken; "no, I am not wearied now, and I can speak. You and me must twine (*part*)," I said. "I liked you very well, Alan, but your ways are not mine, and they're not God's: and the short and the long of it is just that we must twine."

"I will hardly twine from ye, David, without some kind of reason for the same," said Alan, mighty gravely. "If ye ken anything against my reputation, it's the least thing that ye should do, for old acquaintance' sake, to let me hear the name of it; and if ye have only taken a distaste to my society, it will be proper for me to judge if I'm insulted."

"Alan," said I, "what is the sense of this? Ye ken very well yon Campbell-man lies in his blood upon the road."

He was silent for a little; then says he, "Did ever ye hear tell of the story of the Man and the Good People?"—by which he meant the fairies.

"No," said I, "nor do I want to hear it."

"With your permission, Mr. Balfour, I will tell it you, whatever," says Alan. "The man, ye should ken, was cast upon a rock in the sea, where it appears the Good People were in use to come and rest as they went through to Ireland. The name of this rock is called the Skerryvore, and it's not far from where we suffered ship-wreck. Well, it seems the man cried so sore, if he could just see his little bairn before he died! that at last the king of the Good People took peety upon him, and sent one flying that brought back the bairn in a poke (*bag*) and laid it down beside the man where he lay sleeping. So when the man woke, there was a poke beside him and something into the inside of it that moved. Well, it seems he was one of these gentry that think aye the worst of things; and for greater security, he stuck his dirk throughout that poke before he opened it, and there was his bairn dead. I am thinking to myself, Mr. Balfour, that you and the man are very much alike."

"Do you mean you had no hand in it?" cried I, sitting up.

"I will tell you first of all, Mr. Balfour of Shaws, as one friend to another," said Alan, "that if I were going to kill a gentleman, it would not be in my own country, to bring trouble on my clan; and I would not go wanting sword and gun, and with a long fishing-rod upon my back."

"Well," said I, "that's true!"

"And now," continued Alan, taking out his dirk and laying his hand upon it in a certain manner, "I swear upon the Holy Iron I had neither art nor part, act nor thought in it."

"I thank God for that!" cried I, and offered him my hand.

He did not appear to see it.

"And here is a great deal of work about a Campbell!" said he. "They are not so scarce, that I ken!"

"At least," said I, "you cannot justly blame me, for you know very well what you told me in the brig. But the temptation and the act are different, I thank God again for that. We may all be tempted; but to take a life in cold blood, Alan!" And I could say no more for the moment. "And do you know who did it?" I added. "Do you know that man in the black coat?"

"I have nae clear mind about his coat," said Alan cunningly, "but it sticks in my head that it was blue."

"Blue or black, did ye know him?" said I.

"I couldnae just conscientiously swear to him," says Alan. "He gaed very close by me, to be sure, but it's a strange thing that I should just have been tying my brogues."

"Can you swear that you don't know him, Alan?" I cried, half angered, half in a mind to laugh at his evasions.

"Not yet," says he; "but I've a grand memory for forgetting, David."

"And yet there was one thing I saw clearly," said I; "and that was, that you exposed yourself and me to draw the soldiers."

"It's very likely," said Alan; "and so would any gentleman. You and me were innocent of that transaction."

"The better reason, since we were falsely suspected, that we should get clear," I cried. "The innocent should surely come before the guilty."

"Why, David," said he, "the innocent have aye a chance to get assoiled in court; but for the lad that shot the bullet, I think the best place for him will be the heather. Them that havenae dipped their hands in any little difficulty, should be very mindful of the case of them that have. And that is the good Christianity. For if it was the other way round about, and the lad whom I couldnae just clearly see had been in our shoes, and we in his (as might very well have been), I think we would be a good deal obliged to him oursel's if he would draw the soldiers."

When it came to this, I gave Alan up. But he looked so innocent all the time, and was in such clear good faith in what he said, and so ready to sacrifice himself for what he deemed his duty, that my mouth was closed. Mr. Henderland's words came back to me: that we ourselves might take a lesson by these wild Highlanders. Well, here I had taken mine. Alan's morals were all tail-first; but he was ready to give his life for them, such as they were.

"Alan," said I, "I'll not say it's the good Christianity as I understand it, but it's good enough. And here I offer ye my hand for the second time."

Whereupon he gave me both of his, saying surely I had cast a spell upon him, for he could forgive me anything. Then he grew very grave, and said we had not much time to throw away, but must both flee that country: he, because he was a deserter, and the whole of Appin would now be searched like a chamber, and every one obliged to give a good account of himself; and I, because I was certainly involved in the murder.

"O!" says I, willing to give him a little lesson, "I have no fear of the justice of my country."

"As if this was your country!" said he. "Or as if ye would be tried here, in a country of Stewarts!"

"It's all Scotland," said I.

"Man, I whiles wonder at ye," said Alan. "This is a Campbell that's been killed. Well, it'll be tried in Inverara, the Campbells' head place; with fifteen Campbells in the jury-box and the biggest Campbell of all (and that's the Duke) sitting cocking on the bench. Justice, David? The same justice, by all the world, as Glenure found awhile ago at the roadside."

This frightened me a little, I confess, and would have frightened me more if I had known how nearly exact were Alan's predictions; indeed it was but in one point that he exaggerated, there being but eleven Campbells on the jury; though as the other four were equally in the Duke's dependence, it mattered less than might appear. Still, I cried out that he was unjust to the Duke of Argyle, who (for all he was a Whig) was yet a wise and honest nobleman.

"Hoot!" said Alan, "the man's a Whig, nae doubt; but I would never deny he was a good chieftain to his clan. And what would the clan think if there was a Campbell shot, and naebody hanged, and their own chief the Justice General? But I have often observed," says Alan, "that you Low-country bodies have no clear idea of what's right and wrong."

At this I did at last laugh out aloud, when to my surprise, Alan joined in, and laughed as merrily as myself.

"Na, na," said he, "we're in the Hielands, David; and when I tell ye to run, take my word and run. Nae doubt it's a hard thing to skulk and starve in the Heather, but it's harder yet to lie shackled in a red-coat prison."

I asked him whither we should flee; and as he told me "to the Lowlands," I was a little better inclined to go with him; for, indeed, I was growing impatient to get back and have the upper-hand of my uncle. Besides, Alan made so sure there would be no question of justice in the matter, that I began to be afraid he might be right. Of all deaths, I would truly like least to die by the gallows; and the picture of that uncanny instrument came into my head with extraordinary clearness (as I had once seen it engraved at the top of a pedlar's ballad) and took away my appetite for courts of justice.

"I'll chance it, Alan," said I. "I'll go with you."

"But mind you," said Alan, "it's no small thing. Ye maun lie bare and hard, and brook many an empty belly. Your bed shall be the moorcock's, and your life shall be like the hunted deer's, and ye shall sleep with your hand upon your weapons. Ay, man, ye shall taigle many a weary foot, or we get clear! I tell ye this at the start, for it's a life that I ken well. But if ye ask what other chance ye have, I answer: Nane. Either take to the heather with me, or else hang."

"And that's a choice very easily made," said I; and we shook hands upon it.

"And now let's take another peek at the red-coats," says Alan, and he led me to the northeastern fringe of the wood.

Looking out between the trees, we could see a great side of mountain, running down exceeding steep into the waters of the loch. It was a rough part, all hanging stone, and heather, and big scrogs of birchwood; and away at the far end towards Balachulish, little wee red soldiers were dipping up and down over hill and howe, and growing smaller every minute. There was no cheering now, for I think they had other uses for what breath was left them; but they still stuck to the trail, and doubtless thought that we were close in front of them.

Alan watched them, smiling to himself.

"Ay," said he, "they'll be gey weary before they've got to the end of that employ! And so you and me, David, can sit down and eat a bite, and breathe a bit longer, and take a dram from my bottle. Then we'll strike for Aucharn, the house of my kinsman, James of the Glens, where I must get my clothes, and my arms, and money to carry us along; and then, David, we'll cry, 'Forth, Fortune!' and take a cast among the heather."

So we sat again and ate and drank, in a place whence we could see the sun going down into a field of great, wild, and houseless mountains, such as I was now condemned to wander in with my companion. Partly as we so sat, and partly afterwards, on the way to Aucharn, each of us narrated his adventures; and I shall here set down so much of Alan's as seems either curious or needful.

It appears he ran to the bulwarks as soon as the wave was passed; saw me, and lost me, and saw me again, as I tumbled in the roost; and at last had one glimpse of me clinging on the yard. It was this that put him in some hope I would maybe get to land after all, and made him leave those clues and messages which had brought me (for my sins) to that unlucky country of Appin.

In the meanwhile, those still on the brig had got the skiff launched, and one or two were on board of her already, when there came a second wave greater than the first, and heaved the brig out of her place, and would certainly have sent her to the bottom, had she not struck and caught on some projection of the reef. When she had struck first, it had been bows-on, so that the stern had hitherto been lowest. But now her stern was thrown in the air, and the bows plunged under the sea; and with that, the water began to pour into the fore-scuttle like the pouring of a mill-dam.

It took the colour out of Alan's face, even to tell what followed. For there were still two men lying impotent in their bunks; and these, seeing the water pour in and thinking the ship had foundered, began to cry out aloud, and that with such harrowing cries that all who were on deck tumbled one after another into the skiff and fell to their oars. They were not two hundred yards away, when there came a third great sea; and at that the brig lifted clean over the reef; her canvas filled for a moment, and she seemed to sail in chase of them, but settling all the while; and presently she drew down and down, as if a hand was drawing her; and the sea closed over the Covenant of Dysart.

Never a word they spoke as they pulled ashore, being stunned with the horror of that screaming; but they had scarce set foot upon the beach when Hoseason woke up, as if out of a muse, and bade them lay hands upon Alan. They hung back indeed, having little taste for the employment; but Hoseason was like a fiend, crying that Alan was alone, that he had a great sum about him, that he had been the means of losing the brig and drowning all their comrades, and that here was both revenge and wealth upon a single cast. It was seven against one; in that part of the shore there was no rock that Alan could set his back to; and the sailors began to spread out and come behind him.

"And then," said Alan, "the little man with the red head—I havenae mind of the name that he is called."

"Riach," said I.

"Ay" said Alan, "Riach! Well, it was him that took up the clubs for me, asked the men if they werenae feared of a judgment, and, says he 'Dod, I'll put my back to the Hielandman's mysel'.' That's none such an entirely bad little man, yon little man with the red head," said Alan. "He has some spunks of decency."

"Well," said I, "he was kind to me in his way."

"And so he was to Alan," said he; "and by my troth, I found his way a very good one! But ye see, David, the loss of the ship and the cries of these poor lads sat very ill upon the man; and I'm thinking that would be the cause of it."

"Well, I would think so," says I; "for he was as keen as any of the rest at the beginning. But how did Hoseason take it?"

"It sticks in my mind that he would take it very ill," says Alan. "But the little man cried to me to run, and indeed I thought it was a good observe, and ran. The last that I saw they were all in a knot upon the beach, like folk that were not agreeing very well together."

"What do you mean by that?" said I.

"Well, the fists were going," said Alan; "and I saw one man go down like a pair of breeks. But I thought it would be better no to wait. Ye see there's a strip of Campbells in that end of Mull, which is no good company for a gentleman like me. If it hadnae been for that I would have waited and looked for ye mysel', let alone giving a hand to the little man." (It was droll how Alan dwelt on Mr. Riach's stature, for, to say the truth, the one was not much smaller than the other.) "So," says he, continuing, "I set my best foot forward, and whenever I met in with any one I cried out there was a wreck ashore. Man, they didnae stop to fash with me! Ye should have seen them linking for the beach! And when they got there they found they had had the pleasure of a run, which is aye good for a Campbell. I'm thinking it was a judgment on the clan that the brig went down in the lump and didnae break. But it was a very unlucky thing for you, that same; for if any wreck had come ashore they would have hunted high and low, and would soon have found ye."

19

THE HOUSE OF FEAR

Night fell as we were walking, and the clouds, which had broken up in the afternoon, settled in and thickened, so that it fell, for the season of the year, extremely dark. The way we went was over rough mountainsides; and though Alan pushed on with an assured manner, I could by no means see how he directed himself.

At last, about half-past ten of the clock, we came to the top of a brae, and saw lights below us. It seemed a house door stood open and let out a beam of fire and candle-light; and all round the house and steading five or six persons were moving hurriedly about, each carrying a lighted brand.

"James must have tint his wits," said Alan. "If this was the soldiers instead of you and me, he would be in a bonny mess. But I dare say he'll have a sentry on the road, and he would ken well enough no soldiers would find the way that we came."

Hereupon he whistled three times, in a particular manner. It was strange to see how, at the first sound of it, all the moving torches came to a stand, as if the bearers were affrighted; and how, at the third, the bustle began again as before.

Having thus set folks' minds at rest, we came down the brae, and were met at the yard gate (for this place was like a well-doing farm) by a tall, handsome man of more than fifty, who cried out to Alan in the Gaelic.

"James Stewart," said Alan, "I will ask ye to speak in Scotch, for here is a young gentleman with me that has nane of the other. This is him," he added, putting his arm through mine, "a young gentleman of the Lowlands, and a laird in his country too, but I am thinking it will be the better for his health if we give his name the go-by."

James of the Glens turned to me for a moment, and greeted me courteously enough; the next he had turned to Alan.

"This has been a dreadful accident," he cried. "It will bring trouble on the country." And he wrung his hands.

"Hoots!" said Alan, "ye must take the sour with the sweet, man. Colin Roy is dead, and be thankful for that!"

"Ay" said James, "and by my troth, I wish he was alive again! It's all very fine to blow and boast beforehand; but now it's done, Alan; and who's to bear the wyte (*blame*) of it? The accident fell out in Appin—mind ye that, Alan; it's Appin that must pay; and I am a man that has a family."

While this was going on I looked about me at the servants. Some were on ladders, digging in the thatch of the house or the farm buildings, from which they brought out guns, swords, and different weapons of war; others carried them away; and by the sound of mattock blows from somewhere farther down the brae, I suppose they buried them. Though they were all so busy, there prevailed no kind of order in their efforts; men struggled together for the same gun and ran into each other with their burning torches; and James was continually turning about from his talk with Alan, to cry out orders which were apparently never understood. The faces in the torchlight were like those of people overborne with hurry and panic; and though none spoke above his breath, their speech sounded both anxious and angry.

It was about this time that a lassie came out of the house carrying a pack or bundle; and it has often made me smile to think how Alan's instinct awoke at the mere sight of it.

"What's that the lassie has?" he asked.

"We're just setting the house in order, Alan," said James, in his frightened and somewhat fawning way. "They'll search Appin with candles, and we must have all things straight. We're digging the bit guns and swords into the moss, ye see; and these, I am thinking, will be your ain French clothes. We'll be to bury them, I believe."

"Bury my French clothes!" cried Alan. "Troth, no!" And he laid hold upon the packet and retired into the barn to shift himself, recommending me in the meanwhile to his kinsman.

James carried me accordingly into the kitchen, and sat down with me at table, smiling and talking at first in a very hospitable manner. But presently the gloom returned upon him; he sat frowning and biting his fingers; only remembered me from time to time; and then gave me but a word or two and a poor smile, and back into his private terrors. His wife sat by the fire and wept, with her face in her hands; his eldest son was crouched upon the floor, running over a great mass of papers and now and again setting one alight and burning it to the bitter end; all the while a servant lass with a red face was rummaging about the room, in a blind hurry of fear, and whimpering as she went; and every now and again one of the men would thrust in his face from the yard, and cry for orders.

At last James could keep his seat no longer, and begged my permission to be so unmannerly as walk about. "I am but poor company altogether, sir," says he, "but I can think of nothing but this dreadful accident, and the trouble it is like to bring upon quite innocent persons."

A little after he observed his son burning a paper which he thought should have been kept; and at that his excitement burst out so that it was painful to witness. He struck the lad repeatedly.

"Are you gone gyte (*mad*)?" he cried. "Do you wish to hang your father?" and forgetful of my presence, carried on at him a long time together in the Gaelic, the young man answering nothing; only the wife, at the name of hanging, throwing her apron over her face and sobbing out louder than before.

This was all wretched for a stranger like myself to hear and see; and I was right glad when Alan returned, looking like himself in his fine French clothes, though (to be sure) they were now grown almost too battered and withered to deserve the name of fine. I was then taken out in my turn by another of the sons, and given that change of clothing of which I had stood so long in need, and a pair of Highland brogues made of deer-leather, rather strange at first, but after a little practice very easy to the feet.

By the time I came back Alan must have told his story; for it seemed understood that I was to fly with him, and they were all busy upon our equipment. They gave us each a sword and pistols, though I professed my inability to use the former; and with these, and some ammunition, a bag of oatmeal, an iron pan, and a bottle of right French brandy, we were ready for the heather. Money, indeed, was lacking. I had about two guineas left; Alan's belt having been despatched by another hand, that trusty messenger had no more than seventeen-pence to his whole fortune; and as for James, it appears he had brought himself so low with journeys to Edinburgh and legal expenses on behalf of the tenants, that he could only scrape together three-and-five-pence-halfpenny, the most of it in coppers.

"This'll no do," said Alan.

"Ye must find a safe bit somewhere near by," said James, "and get word sent to me. Ye see, ye'll have to get this business prettily off, Alan. This is no time to be stayed for a guinea or two. They're sure to get wind of ye, sure to seek ye, and by my way of it, sure to lay on ye the wyte of this day's accident. If it falls on you, it falls on me that am your near kinsman and harboured ye while ye were in the country. And if it comes on me——" he paused, and bit his fingers, with a white face. "It would be a painful thing for our friends if I was to hang," said he.

"It would be an ill day for Appin," says Alan.

"It's a day that sticks in my throat," said James. "O man, man, man—man Alan! you and me have spoken like two fools!" he cried, striking his hand upon the wall so that the house rang again.

"Well, and that's true, too," said Alan; "and my friend from the Lowlands here" (nodding at me) "gave me a good word upon that head, if I would only have listened to him."

"But see here," said James, returning to his former manner, "if they lay me by the heels, Alan, it's then that you'll be needing the money. For with all that I have said and that you have said, it will look very black against the two of us; do ye mark that? Well, follow me out, and ye'll, I'll see that I'll have to get a paper out against ye mysel'; have to offer a reward for ye; ay, will I! It's a sore thing to do between such near friends; but if I get the dirdum (*blame*) of this dreadful accident, I'll have to fend for myself, man. Do ye see that?"

He spoke with a pleading earnestness, taking Alan by the breast of the coat.

"Ay" said Alan, "I see that."

"And ye'll have to be clear of the country, Alan—ay, and clear of Scotland—you and your friend from the Lowlands, too. For I'll have to paper your friend from the Lowlands. Ye see that, Alan—say that ye see that!"

I thought Alan flushed a bit. "This is unco hard on me that brought him here, James," said he, throwing his head back. "It's like making me a traitor!"

"Now, Alan, man!" cried James. "Look things in the face! He'll be papered anyway; Mungo Campbell'll be sure to paper him; what matters if I paper him too? And then, Alan, I am a man that has a family." And then, after a little pause on both sides, "And, Alan, it'll be a jury of Campbells," said he.

"There's one thing," said Alan, musingly, "that naebody kens his name."

"Nor yet they shallnae, Alan! There's my hand on that," cried James, for all the world as if he had really known my name and was foregoing some advantage. "But just the habit he was in, and what he looked like, and his age, and the like? I couldnae well do less."

"I wonder at your father's son," cried Alan, sternly. "Would ye sell the lad with a gift? Would ye change his clothes and then betray him?"

"No, no, Alan," said James. "No, no: the habit he took off—the habit Mungo saw him in." But I thought he seemed crestfallen; indeed, he was clutching at every straw, and all the time,

I dare say, saw the faces of his hereditary foes on the bench, and in the jury-box, and the gallows in the background.

"Well, sir," says Alan, turning to me, "what say ye to that? Ye are here under the safeguard of my honour; and it's my part to see nothing done but what shall please you."

"I have but one word to say," said I; "for to all this dispute I am a perfect stranger. But the plain common-sense is to set the blame where it belongs, and that is on the man who fired the shot. Paper him, as ye call it, set the hunt on him; and let honest, innocent folk show their faces in safety." But at this both Alan and James cried out in horror; bidding me hold my tongue, for that was not to be thought of; and asking me what the Camerons would think? (which confirmed me, it must have been a Cameron from Mamore that did the act) and if I did not see that the lad might be caught? "Ye havenae surely thought of that?" said they, with such innocent earnestness, that my hands dropped at my side and I despaired of argument.

"Very well, then," said I, "paper me, if you please, paper Alan, paper King George! We're all three innocent, and that seems to be what's wanted. But at least, sir," said I to James, recovering from my little fit of annoyance, "I am Alan's friend, and if I can be helpful to friends of his, I will not stumble at the risk."

I thought it best to put a fair face on my consent, for I saw Alan troubled; and, besides (thinks I to myself), as soon as my back is turned, they will paper me, as they call it, whether I consent or not. But in this I saw I was wrong; for I had no sooner said the words, than Mrs. Stewart leaped out of her chair, came running over to us, and wept first upon my neck and then on Alan's, blessing God for our goodness to her family.

"As for you, Alan, it was no more than your bounden duty," she said. "But for this lad that has come here and seen us at our worst, and seen the goodman fleeching like a suitor, him that by rights should give his commands like any king—as for you, my lad," she says, "my heart is wae not to have your name, but I have your face; and as long as my heart beats under my bosom, I will keep it, and think of it, and bless it." And with that she kissed me, and burst once more into such sobbing, that I stood abashed.

"Hoot, hoot," said Alan, looking mighty silly. "The day comes unco soon in this month of July; and to-morrow there'll be a fine to-do in Appin, a fine riding of dragoons, and crying of 'Cruachan!' (*the rallying-word of the Campbells*) and running of red-coats; and it behoves you and me to the sooner be gone."

Thereupon we said farewell, and set out again, bending somewhat eastwards, in a fine mild dark night, and over much the same broken country as before.

20

THE FLIGHT IN THE HEATHER: THE ROCKS

Sometimes we walked, sometimes ran; and as it drew on to morning, walked ever the less and ran the more. Though, upon its face, that country appeared to be a desert, yet there were huts and houses of the people, of which we must have passed more than twenty, hidden in quiet places of the hills. When we came to one of these, Alan would leave me in the way, and go himself and rap upon the side of the house and speak awhile at the window with some sleeper awakened. This was to pass the news; which, in that country, was so much of a duty that Alan must pause to attend to it even while fleeing for his life; and so well attended to by others, that in more than half of the houses where we called they had heard already of the murder. In the others, as well as I could make out (standing back at a distance and hearing a strange tongue), the news was received with more of consternation than surprise.

For all our hurry, day began to come in while we were still far from any shelter. It found us in a prodigious valley, strewn with rocks and where ran a foaming river. Wild mountains stood around it; there grew there neither grass nor trees; and I have sometimes thought since then, that it may have been the valley called Glencoe, where the massacre was in the time of King William. But for the details of our itinerary, I am all to seek; our way lying now by short cuts, now by great detours; our pace being so hurried, our time of journeying usually by night; and the names of such places as I asked and heard being in the Gaelic tongue and the more easily forgotten.

The first peep of morning, then, showed us this horrible place, and I could see Alan knit his brow.

"This is no fit place for you and me," he said. "This is a place they're bound to watch."

And with that he ran harder than ever down to the water-side, in a part where the river was split in two among three rocks. It went through with a horrid thundering that made my belly quake; and there hung over the lynn a little mist of spray. Alan looked neither to the right nor to the left, but jumped clean upon the middle rock and fell there on his hands and knees to check himself, for that rock was small and he might have pitched over on the far side. I had scarce time to measure the distance or to understand the peril before I had followed him, and he had caught and stopped me.

So there we stood, side by side upon a small rock slippery with spray, a far broader leap in front of us, and the river dinning upon all sides. When I saw where I was, there came on me a deadly sickness of fear, and I put my hand over my eyes. Alan took me and shook me; I saw he was speaking, but the roaring of the falls and the trouble of my mind prevented me from hearing; only I saw his face was red with anger, and that he stamped upon the rock. The same look showed me the water raging by, and the mist hanging in the air: and with that I covered my eyes again and shuddered.

The next minute Alan had set the brandy bottle to my lips, and forced me to drink about a gill, which sent the blood into my head again. Then, putting his hands to his mouth, and his mouth to my ear, he shouted, "Hang or drown!" and turning his back upon me, leaped over the farther branch of the stream, and landed safe.

I was now alone upon the rock, which gave me the more room; the brandy was singing in my ears; I had this good example fresh before me, and just wit enough to see that if I did not leap at once, I should never leap at all. I bent low on my knees and flung myself forth, with that kind of anger of despair that has sometimes stood me in stead of courage. Sure enough, it was but my hands that reached the full length; these slipped, caught again, slipped again; and I was sliddering back into the lynn, when Alan seized me, first by the hair, then by the collar, and with a great strain dragged me into safety.

Never a word he said, but set off running again for his life, and I must stagger to my feet and run after him. I had been weary before, but now I was sick and bruised, and partly drunken with the brandy; I kept stumbling as I ran, I had a stitch that came near to overmaster me; and when at last Alan paused under a great rock that stood there among a number of others, it was none too soon for David Balfour.

A great rock I have said; but by rights it was two rocks leaning together at the top, both some twenty feet high, and at the first sight inaccessible. Even Alan (though you may say he had as good as four hands) failed twice in an attempt to climb them; and it was only at the third trial, and then by standing on my shoulders and leaping up with such force as I thought must have broken my collar-bone, that he secured a lodgment. Once there, he let down his leathern girdle; and with the aid of that and a pair of shallow footholds in the rock, I scrambled up beside him.

Then I saw why we had come there; for the two rocks, being both somewhat hollow on the top and sloping one to the other, made a kind of dish or saucer, where as many as three or four men might have lain hidden.

All this while Alan had not said a word, and had run and climbed with such a savage, silent frenzy of hurry, that I knew that he was in mortal fear of some miscarriage. Even now we were on the rock he said nothing, nor so much as relaxed the frowning look upon his face; but clapped flat down, and keeping only one eye above the edge of our place of shelter scouted all round the compass. The dawn had come quite clear; we could see the stony sides of the valley, and its bottom, which was bestrewed with rocks, and the river, which went from one side to another, and made white falls; but nowhere the smoke of a house, nor any living creature but some eagles screaming round a cliff.

Then at last Alan smiled.

"Ay" said he, "now we have a chance;" and then looking at me with some amusement, "Ye're no very gleg (*brisk*) at the jumping," said he.

At this I suppose I coloured with mortification, for he added at once, "Hoots! small blame to ye! To be feared of a thing and yet to do it, is what makes the prettiest kind of a man. And then there was water there, and water's a thing that dauntons even me. No, no," said Alan, "it's no you that's to blame, it's me."

I asked him why.

"Why," said he, "I have proved myself a gomeral this night. For first of all I take a wrong road, and that in my own country of Appin; so that the day has caught us where we should never have been; and thanks to that, we lie here in some danger and mair discomfort. And next (which is the worst of the two, for a man that has been so much among the heather as myself) I have come wanting a water-bottle, and here we lie for a long summer's day with naething but neat spirit. Ye may think that a small matter; but before it comes night, David, ye'll give me news of it."

I was anxious to redeem my character, and offered, if he would pour out the brandy, to run down and fill the bottle at the river.

"I wouldnae waste the good spirit either," says he. "It's been a good friend to you this night; or in my poor opinion, ye would still be cocking on yon stone. And what's mair," says he, "ye may have observed (you that's a man of so much penetration) that Alan Breck Stewart was perhaps walking quicker than his ordinar'."

"You!" I cried, "you were running fit to burst."

"Was I so?" said he. "Well, then, ye may depend upon it, there was nae time to be lost. And now here is enough said; gang you to your sleep, lad, and I'll watch."

Accordingly, I lay down to sleep; a little peaty earth had drifted in between the top of the two rocks, and some bracken grew there, to be a bed to me; the last thing I heard was still the crying of the eagles.

I dare say it would be nine in the morning when I was roughly awakened, and found Alan's hand pressed upon my mouth.

"Wheesht!" he whispered. "Ye were snoring."

"Well," said I, surprised at his anxious and dark face, "and why not?"

He peered over the edge of the rock, and signed to me to do the like.

It was now high day, cloudless, and very hot. The valley was as clear as in a picture. About half a mile up the water was a camp of red-coats; a big fire blazed in their midst, at which some were cooking; and near by, on the top of a rock about as high as ours, there stood a sentry, with the sun sparkling on his arms. All the way down along the river-side were posted other sentries; here near together, there widelier scattered; some planted like the first, on places of command, some on the ground level and marching and counter-marching, so as to meet half-way. Higher up the glen, where the ground was more open, the chain of posts was continued by horse-soldiers, whom we could see in the distance riding to and fro. Lower down, the infantry continued; but as the stream was suddenly swelled by the confluence of a considerable burn, they were more widely set, and only watched the fords and stepping-stones.

I took but one look at them, and ducked again into my place. It was strange indeed to see this valley, which had lain so solitary in the hour of dawn, bristling with arms and dotted with the red coats and breeches.

"Ye see," said Alan, "this was what I was afraid of, Davie: that they would watch the burn-side. They began to come in about two hours ago, and, man! but ye're a grand hand at the sleeping! We're in a narrow place. If they get up the sides of the hill, they could easy spy us with a glass; but if they'll only keep in the foot of the valley, we'll do yet. The posts are thinner down the water; and, come night, we'll try our hand at getting by them."

"And what are we to do till night?" I asked.

"Lie here," says he, "and birstle."

That one good Scotch word, "birstle," was indeed the most of the story of the day that we had now to pass. You are to remember that we lay on the bare top of a rock, like scones upon a girdle; the sun beat upon us cruelly; the rock grew so heated, a man could scarce endure the touch of it; and the little patch of earth and fern, which kept cooler, was only large enough for one at a time. We took turn about to lie on the naked rock, which was indeed like the position of that saint that was martyred on a gridiron; and it ran in my mind how strange it was, that in the same climate and at only a few days' distance, I should have suffered so cruelly, first from cold upon my island and now from heat upon this rock.

All the while we had no water, only raw brandy for a drink, which was worse than nothing; but we kept the bottle as cool as we could, burying it in the earth, and got some relief by bathing our breasts and temples.

The soldiers kept stirring all day in the bottom of the valley, now changing guard, now in patrolling parties hunting among the rocks. These lay round in so great a number, that to look for men among them was like looking for a needle in a bottle of hay; and being so hopeless a task, it was gone about with the less care. Yet we could see the soldiers pike their bayonets among the heather, which sent a cold thrill into my vitals; and they would sometimes hang about our rock, so that we scarce dared to breathe.

It was in this way that I first heard the right English speech; one fellow as he went by actually clapping his hand upon the sunny face of the rock on which we lay, and plucking it off again with an oath. "I tell you it's 'ot," says he; and I was amazed at the clipping tones and the odd sing-song in which he spoke, and no less at that strange trick of dropping out the letter "h." To be sure, I had heard Ransome; but he had taken his ways from all sorts of people, and spoke so imperfectly at the best, that I set down the most of it to childishness. My surprise was all the greater to hear that manner of speaking in the mouth of a grown man; and indeed I have never grown used to it; nor yet altogether with the English grammar, as perhaps a very critical eye might here and there spy out even in these memoirs.

The tediousness and pain of these hours upon the rock grew only the greater as the day went on; the rock getting still the hotter and the sun fiercer. There were giddiness, and sickness, and sharp pangs like rheumatism, to be supported. I minded then, and have often minded since, on the lines in our Scotch psalm:—

"The moon by night thee shall not smite,
Nor yet the sun by day;"

and indeed it was only by God's blessing that we were neither of us sun-smitten.

At last, about two, it was beyond men's bearing, and there was now temptation to resist, as well as pain to thole. For the sun being now got a little into the west, there came a patch of shade on the east side of our rock, which was the side sheltered from the soldiers.

"As well one death as another," said Alan, and slipped over the edge and dropped on the ground on the shadowy side.

I followed him at once, and instantly fell all my length, so weak was I and so giddy with that long exposure. Here, then, we lay for an hour or two, aching from head to foot, as weak as water, and lying quite naked to the eye of any soldier who should have strolled that way. None came, however, all passing by on the other side; so that our rock continued to be our shield even in this new position.

Presently we began again to get a little strength; and as the soldiers were now lying closer along the river-side, Alan proposed that we should try a start. I was by this time afraid of but one thing in the world; and that was to be set back upon the rock; anything else was welcome to me; so we got ourselves at once in marching order, and began to slip from rock to rock one after the other, now crawling flat on our bellies in the shade, now making a run for it, heart in mouth.

The soldiers, having searched this side of the valley after a fashion, and being perhaps somewhat sleepy with the sultriness of the afternoon, had now laid by much of their vigilance, and stood dozing at their posts or only kept a look-out along the banks of the river; so that in this way, keeping down the valley and at the same time towards the mountains, we drew steadily away from their neighbourhood. But the business was the most wearing I had ever taken part in. A man had need of a hundred eyes in every part of him, to keep concealed in that uneven country and within cry of so many and scattered sentries. When we must pass an open place, quickness was not all, but a swift judgment not only of the lie of the whole country, but of the solidity of every stone on which we must set foot; for the afternoon was now fallen so breathless that the rolling of a pebble sounded abroad like a pistol shot, and would start the echo calling among the hills and cliffs.

By sundown we had made some distance, even by our slow rate of progress, though to be sure the sentry on the rock was still plainly in our view. But now we came on something that put all fears out of season; and that was a deep rushing burn, that tore down, in that part, to join the glen river. At the sight of this we cast ourselves on the ground and plunged head and shoulders in the water; and I cannot tell which was the more pleasant, the great shock as the cool stream went over us, or the greed with which we drank of it.

We lay there (for the banks hid us), drank again and again, bathed our chests, let our wrists trail in the running water till they ached with the chill; and at last, being wonderfully renewed, we got out the meal-bag and made drammach in the iron pan. This, though it is but cold water mingled with oatmeal, yet makes a good enough dish for a hungry man; and where there are no means of making fire, or (as in our case) good reason for not making one, it is the chief stand-by of those who have taken to the heather.

As soon as the shadow of the night had fallen, we set forth again, at first with the same caution, but presently with more boldness, standing our full height and stepping out at a good pace of walking. The way was very intricate, lying up the steep sides of mountains and along the brows of cliffs; clouds had come in with the sunset, and the night was dark and cool; so that I walked without much fatigue, but in continual fear of falling and rolling down the mountains, and with no guess at our direction.

The moon rose at last and found us still on the road; it was in its last quarter, and was long beset with clouds; but after awhile shone out and showed me many dark heads of mountains, and was reflected far underneath us on the narrow arm of a sea-loch.

At this sight we both paused: I struck with wonder to find myself so high and walking (as it seemed to me) upon clouds; Alan to make sure of his direction.

Seemingly he was well pleased, and he must certainly have judged us out of ear-shot of all our enemies; for throughout the rest of our night-march he beguiled the way with whistling of many tunes, warlike, merry, plaintive; reel tunes that made the foot go faster; tunes of my own south country that made me fain to be home from my adventures; and all these, on the great, dark, desert mountains, making company upon the way.

21

THE FLIGHT IN THE HEATHER: THE HEUGH OF CORRYNAKIEGH

Early as day comes in the beginning of July, it was still dark when we reached our destination, a cleft in the head of a great mountain, with a water running through the midst, and upon the one hand a shallow cave in a rock. Birches grew there in a thin, pretty wood, which a little farther on was changed into a wood of pines. The burn was full of trout; the wood of cushat-doves; on the open side of the mountain beyond, whaups would be always whistling, and cuckoos were plentiful. From the mouth of the cleft we looked down upon a part of Mamore, and on the sea-loch that divides that country from Appin; and this from so great a height as made it my continual wonder and pleasure to sit and behold them.

The name of the cleft was the Heugh of Corrynakiegh; and although from its height and being so near upon the sea, it was often beset with clouds, yet it was on the whole a pleasant place, and the five days we lived in it went happily.

We slept in the cave, making our bed of heather bushes which we cut for that purpose, and covering ourselves with Alan's great-coat. There was a low concealed place, in a turning of the glen, where we were so bold as to make fire: so that we could warm ourselves when the clouds set in, and cook hot porridge, and grill the little trouts that we caught with our hands under the stones and overhanging banks of the burn. This was indeed our chief pleasure and business; and not only to save our meal against worse times, but with a rivalry that much amused us, we spent a great part of our days at the water-side, stripped to the waist and groping about or (as they say) guddling for these fish. The largest we got might have been a quarter of a pound; but they were of good flesh and flavour, and when broiled upon the coals, lacked only a little salt to be delicious.

In any by-time Alan must teach me to use my sword, for my ignorance had much distressed him; and I think besides, as I had sometimes the upper-hand of him in the fishing, he was not sorry to turn to an exercise where he had so much the upper-hand of me. He made it somewhat more of a pain than need have been, for he stormed at me all through the lessons in a very violent manner of scolding, and would push me so close that I made sure he must run me through the body. I was often tempted to turn tail, but held my ground for all that, and got some profit of my lessons; if it was but to stand on guard with an assured countenance, which is often all that is required. So, though I could never in the least please my master, I was not altogether displeased with myself.

In the meanwhile, you are not to suppose that we neglected our chief business, which was to get away.

"It will be many a long day," Alan said to me on our first morning, "before the red-coats think upon seeking Corrynakiegh; so now we must get word sent to James, and he must find the siller for us."

"And how shall we send that word?" says I. "We are here in a desert place, which yet we dare not leave; and unless ye get the fowls of the air to be your messengers, I see not what we shall be able to do."

"Ay?" said Alan. "Ye're a man of small contrivance, David."

Thereupon he fell in a muse, looking in the embers of the fire; and presently, getting a piece of wood, he fashioned it in a cross, the four ends of which he blackened on the coals. Then he looked at me a little shyly.

"Could ye lend me my button?" says he. "It seems a strange thing to ask a gift again, but I own I am laith to cut another."

I gave him the button; whereupon he strung it on a strip of his great-coat which he had used to bind the cross; and tying in a little sprig of birch and another of fir, he looked upon his work with satisfaction.

"Now," said he, "there is a little clachan" (what is called a hamlet in the English) "not very far from Corrynakiegh, and it has the name of Koalisnacoan. There there are living many friends of mine whom I could trust with my life, and some that I am no just so sure of. Ye see, David, there will be money set upon our heads; James himsel' is to set money on them; and as for the Campbells, they would never spare siller where there was a Stewart to be hurt. If it was otherwise, I would go down to Koalisnacoan whatever, and trust my life into these people's hands as lightly as I would trust another with my glove."

"But being so?" said I.

"Being so," said he, "I would as lief they didnae see me. There's bad folk everywhere, and what's far worse, weak ones. So when it comes dark again, I will steal down into that clachan, and set this that I have been making in the window of a good friend of mine, John Breck Maccoll, a bouman[1] of Appin's."

"With all my heart," says I; "and if he finds it, what is he to think?"

"Well," says Alan, "I wish he was a man of more penetration, for by my troth I am afraid he will make little enough of it! But this is what I have in my mind. This cross is something in the nature of the crosstarrie, or fiery cross, which is the signal of gathering in our clans; yet he will know well enough the clan is not to rise, for there it is standing in his window, and no word with it. So he will say to himsel', THE CLAN IS NOT TO RISE, BUT THERE IS SOMETHING. Then he will see my button, and that was Duncan Stewart's. And then he will say to himsel', THE SON OF DUNCAN IS IN THE HEATHER, AND HAS NEED OF ME."

"Well," said I, "it may be. But even supposing so, there is a good deal of heather between here and the Forth."

"And that is a very true word," says Alan. "But then John Breck will see the sprig of birch and the sprig of pine; and he will say to himsel' (if he is a man of any penetration at all, which I misdoubt), ALAN WILL BE LYING IN A WOOD WHICH IS BOTH OF PINES AND BIRCHES. Then he will think to himsel', THAT IS NOT SO VERY RIFE HEREABOUT; and then he will come and give us a look up in Corrynakiegh. And if he does not, David, the devil may fly away with him, for what I care; for he will no be worth the salt to his porridge."

"Eh, man," said I, drolling with him a little, "you're very ingenious! But would it not be simpler for you to write him a few words in black and white?"

"And that is an excellent observe, Mr. Balfour of Shaws," says Alan, drolling with me; "and it would certainly be much simpler for me to write to him, but it would be a sore job for John Breck to read it. He would have to go to the school for two-three years; and it's possible we might be wearied waiting on him."

So that night Alan carried down his fiery cross and set it in the bouman's window. He was troubled when he came back; for the dogs had barked and the folk run out from their houses; and he thought he had heard a clatter of arms and seen a red-coat come to one of the doors. On all accounts we lay the next day in the borders of the wood and kept a close lookout, so that if it was John Breck that came we might be ready to guide him, and if it was the red-coats we should have time to get away.

About noon a man was to be spied, straggling up the open side of the mountain in the sun, and looking round him as he came, from under his hand. No sooner had Alan seen him than he whistled; the man turned and came a little towards us: then Alan would give another "peep!" and the man would come still nearer; and so by the sound of whistling, he was guided to the spot where we lay.

He was a ragged, wild, bearded man, about forty, grossly disfigured with the small pox, and looked both dull and savage. Although his English was very bad and broken, yet Alan (according to his very handsome use, whenever I was by) would suffer him to speak no Gaelic. Perhaps the strange language made him appear more backward than he really was; but I thought he had little good-will to serve us, and what he had was the child of terror.

Alan would have had him carry a message to James; but the bouman would hear of no message. "She was forget it," he said in his screaming voice; and would either have a letter or wash his hands of us.

I thought Alan would be gravelled at that, for we lacked the means of writing in that desert.

But he was a man of more resources than I knew; searched the wood until he found the quill of a cushat-dove, which he shaped into a pen; made himself a kind of ink with gunpowder from his horn and water from the running stream; and tearing a corner from his French military commission (which he carried in his pocket, like a talisman to keep him from the gallows), he sat down and wrote as follows:

"DEAR KINSMAN,—Please send the money by the bearer to the place he kens of.

"Your affectionate cousin,

"A. S."

This he intrusted to the bouman, who promised to make what manner of speed he best could, and carried it off with him down the hill.

He was three full days gone, but about five in the evening of the third, we heard a whistling in the wood, which Alan answered; and presently the bouman came up the waterside, looking for us, right and left. He seemed less sulky than before, and indeed he was no doubt well pleased to have got to the end of such a dangerous commission.

He gave us the news of the country; that it was alive with red-coats; that arms were being found, and poor folk brought in trouble daily; and that James and some of his servants were already clapped in prison at Fort William, under strong suspicion of complicity. It seemed it was noised on all sides that Alan Breck had fired the shot; and there was a bill issued for both him and me, with one hundred pounds reward.

This was all as bad as could be; and the little note the bouman had carried us from Mrs. Stewart was of a miserable sadness. In it she besought Alan not to let himself be captured, assuring him, if he fell in the hands of the troops, both he and James were no better than dead men. The money she had sent was all that she could beg or borrow, and she prayed heaven we could be doing with it. Lastly, she said, she enclosed us one of the bills in which we were described.

This we looked upon with great curiosity and not a little fear, partly as a man may look in a mirror, partly as he might look into the barrel of an enemy's gun to judge if it be truly aimed. Alan was advertised as "a small, pock-marked, active man of thirty-five or thereby, dressed in a feathered hat, a French side-coat of blue with silver buttons, and lace a great deal tarnished, a red waistcoat and breeches of black, shag;" and I as "a tall strong lad of about eighteen, wearing an old blue coat, very ragged, an old Highland bonnet, a long homespun waistcoat, blue breeches; his legs bare, low-country shoes, wanting the toes; speaks like a Lowlander, and has no beard."

Alan was well enough pleased to see his finery so fully remembered and set down; only when he came to the word tarnish, he looked upon his lace like one a little mortified. As for myself, I thought I cut a miserable figure in the bill; and yet was well enough pleased too, for since I had changed these rags, the description had ceased to be a danger and become a source of safety.

"Alan," said I, "you should change your clothes."

"Na, troth!" said Alan, "I have nae others. A fine sight I would be, if I went back to France in a bonnet!"

This put a second reflection in my mind: that if I were to separate from Alan and his tell-tale clothes I should be safe against arrest, and might go openly about my business. Nor was this all; for suppose I was arrested when I was alone, there was little against me; but suppose I was taken in company with the reputed murderer, my case would begin to be grave. For generosity's sake I dare not speak my mind upon this head; but I thought of it none the less.

I thought of it all the more, too, when the bouman brought out a green purse with four guineas in gold, and the best part of another in small change. True, it was more than I had. But then Alan, with less than five guineas, had to get as far as France; I, with my less than two, not beyond Queensferry; so that taking things in their proportion, Alan's society was not only a peril to my life, but a burden on my purse.

But there was no thought of the sort in the honest head of my companion. He believed he was serving, helping, and protecting me. And what could I do but hold my peace, and chafe, and take my chance of it?

"It's little enough," said Alan, putting the purse in his pocket, "but it'll do my business. And now, John Breck, if ye will hand me over my button, this gentleman and me will be for taking the road."

But the bouman, after feeling about in a hairy purse that hung in front of him in the Highland manner (though he wore otherwise the Lowland habit, with sea-trousers), began to roll his eyes strangely, and at last said, "Her nainsel will loss it," meaning he thought he had lost it.

"What!" cried Alan, "you will lose my button, that was my father's before me? Now I will tell you what is in my mind, John Breck: it is in my mind this is the worst day's work that ever ye did since ye was born."

And as Alan spoke, he set his hands on his knees and looked at the bouman with a smiling mouth, and that dancing light in his eyes that meant mischief to his enemies.

Perhaps the bouman was honest enough; perhaps he had meant to cheat and then, finding himself alone with two of us in a desert place, cast back to honesty as being safer; at least, and all at once, he seemed to find that button and handed it to Alan.

"Well, and it is a good thing for the honour of the Maccolls," said Alan, and then to me, "Here is my button back again, and I thank you for parting with it, which is of a piece with all your friendships to me." Then he took the warmest parting of the bouman. "For," says he, "ye have done very well by me, and set your neck at a venture, and I will always give you the name of a good man."

Lastly, the bouman took himself off by one way; and Alan and I (getting our chattels together) struck into another to resume our flight.

---

1. A bouman is a tenant who takes stock from the landlord and shares with him the increase.

22

THE FLIGHT IN THE HEATHER: THE MOOR

Some seven hours' incessant, hard travelling brought us early in the morning to the end of a range of mountains. In front of us there lay a piece of low, broken, desert land, which we must now cross. The sun was not long up, and shone straight in our eyes; a little, thin mist went up from the face of the moorland like a smoke; so that (as Alan said) there might have been twenty squadron of dragoons there and we none the wiser.

We sat down, therefore, in a howe of the hill-side till the mist should have risen, and made ourselves a dish of drammach, and held a council of war.

"David," said Alan, "this is the kittle bit. Shall we lie here till it comes night, or shall we risk it, and stave on ahead?"

"Well," said I, "I am tired indeed, but I could walk as far again, if that was all."

"Ay, but it isnae," said Alan, "nor yet the half. This is how we stand: Appin's fair death to us. To the south it's all Campbells, and no to be thought of. To the north; well, there's no muckle to be gained by going north; neither for you, that wants to get to Queensferry, nor yet for me, that wants to get to France. Well, then, we'll can strike east."

"East be it!" says I, quite cheerily; but I was thinking in to myself: "O, man, if you would only take one point of the compass and let me take any other, it would be the best for both of us."

"Well, then, east, ye see, we have the muirs," said Alan. "Once there, David, it's mere pitch-and-toss. Out on yon bald, naked, flat place, where can a body turn to? Let the redcoats come over a hill, they can spy you miles away; and the sorrow's in their horses' heels, they would soon ride you down. It's no good place, David; and I'm free to say, it's worse by daylight than by dark."

"Alan," said I, "hear my way of it. Appin's death for us; we have none too much money, nor yet meal; the longer they seek, the nearer they may guess where we are; it's all a risk; and I give my word to go ahead until we drop."

Alan was delighted. "There are whiles," said he, "when ye are altogether too canny and Whiggish to be company for a gentleman like me; but there come other whiles when ye show yoursel' a mettle spark; and it's then, David, that I love ye like a brother."

The mist rose and died away, and showed us that country lying as waste as the sea; only the moorfowl and the pewees crying upon it, and far over to the east, a herd of deer, moving like dots. Much of it was red with heather; much of the rest broken up with bogs and hags and peaty pools; some had been burnt black in a heath fire; and in another place there was quite a forest of dead firs, standing like skeletons. A wearier-looking desert man never saw; but at least it was clear of troops, which was our point.

We went down accordingly into the waste, and began to make our toilsome and devious travel towards the eastern verge. There were the tops of mountains all round (you are to remember) from whence we might be spied at any moment; so it behoved us to keep in the hollow parts of the moor, and when these turned aside from our direction to move upon its naked face with infinite care. Sometimes, for half an hour together, we must crawl from one heather bush to another, as hunters do when they are hard upon the deer. It was a clear day again, with a blazing sun; the water in the brandy bottle was soon gone; and altogether, if I had guessed what it would be to crawl half the time upon my belly and to walk much of the rest stooping nearly to the knees, I should certainly have held back from such a killing enterprise.

Toiling and resting and toiling again, we wore away the morning; and about noon lay down in a thick bush of heather to sleep. Alan took the first watch; and it seemed to me I had scarce closed my eyes before I was shaken up to take the second. We had no clock to go by; and Alan stuck a sprig of heath in the ground to serve instead; so that as soon as the shadow of the bush should fall so far to the east, I might know to rouse him. But I was by this time so weary that I could have slept twelve hours at a stretch; I had the taste of sleep in my throat; my joints slept even when my mind was waking; the hot smell of the heather, and the drone of the wild bees, were like possets to me; and every now and again I would give a jump and find I had been dozing.

The last time I woke I seemed to come back from farther away, and thought the sun had taken a great start in the heavens. I looked at the sprig of heath, and at that I could have cried aloud: for I saw I had betrayed my trust. My head was nearly turned with fear and shame; and at what I saw, when I looked out around me on the moor, my heart was like dying in my body. For sure enough, a body of horse-soldiers had come down during my sleep, and were drawing near to us from the south-east, spread out in the shape of a fan and riding their horses to and fro in the deep parts of the heather.

When I waked Alan, he glanced first at the soldiers, then at the mark and the position of the sun, and knitted his brows with a sudden, quick look, both ugly and anxious, which was all the reproach I had of him.

"What are we to do now?" I asked.

"We'll have to play at being hares," said he. "Do ye see yon mountain?" pointing to one on the north-eastern sky.

"Ay," said I.

"Well, then," says he, "let us strike for that. Its name is Ben Alder. it is a wild, desert mountain full of hills and hollows, and if we can win to it before the morn, we may do yet."

"But, Alan," cried I, "that will take us across the very coming of the soldiers!"

"I ken that fine," said he; "but if we are driven back on Appin, we are two dead men. So now, David man, be brisk!"

With that he began to run forward on his hands and knees with an incredible quickness, as though it were his natural way of going. All the time, too, he kept winding in and out in the lower parts of the moorland where we were the best concealed. Some of these had been burned or at least scathed with fire; and there rose in our faces (which were close to the ground) a blinding, choking dust as fine as smoke. The water was long out; and this posture of running on the hands and knees brings an overmastering weakness and weariness, so that the joints ache and the wrists faint under your weight.

Now and then, indeed, where was a big bush of heather, we lay awhile, and panted, and putting aside the leaves, looked back at the dragoons. They had not spied us, for they held straight on; a half-troop, I think, covering about two miles of ground, and beating it mighty thoroughly as they went. I had awakened just in time; a little later, and we must have fled in front of them, instead of escaping on one side. Even as it was, the least misfortune might betray us; and now and again, when a grouse rose out of the heather with a clap of wings, we lay as still as the dead and were afraid to breathe.

The aching and faintness of my body, the labouring of my heart, the soreness of my hands, and the smarting of my throat and eyes in the continual smoke of dust and ashes, had soon grown to be so unbearable that I would gladly have given up. Nothing but the fear of Alan lent me enough of a false kind of courage to continue. As for himself (and you are to bear in mind that he was cumbered with a great-coat) he had first turned crimson, but as time went on the redness began to be mingled with patches of white; his breath cried and whistled as it came; and his voice, when he whispered his observations in my ear during our halts, sounded like nothing human. Yet he seemed in no way dashed in spirits, nor did he at all abate in his activity, so that I was driven to marvel at the man's endurance.

At length, in the first gloaming of the night, we heard a trumpet sound, and looking back from among the heather, saw the troop beginning to collect. A little after, they had built a fire and camped for the night, about the middle of the waste.

At this I begged and besought that we might lie down and sleep.

"There shall be no sleep the night!" said Alan. "From now on, these weary dragoons of yours will keep the crown of the muirland, and none will get out of Appin but winged fowls. We got through in the nick of time, and shall we jeopard what we've gained? Na, na, when the day comes, it shall find you and me in a fast place on Ben Alder."

"Alan," I said, "it's not the want of will: it's the strength that I want. If I could, I would; but as sure as I'm alive I cannot."

"Very well, then," said Alan. "I'll carry ye."

I looked to see if he were jesting; but no, the little man was in dead earnest; and the sight of so much resolution shamed me.

"Lead away!" said I. "I'll follow."

He gave me one look as much as to say, "Well done, David!" and off he set again at his top speed.

It grew cooler and even a little darker (but not much) with the coming of the night. The sky was cloudless; it was still early in July, and pretty far north; in the darkest part of that night, you would have needed pretty good eyes to read, but for all that, I have often seen it darker in a winter mid-day. Heavy dew fell and drenched the moor like rain; and this refreshed me for a while. When we stopped to breathe, and I had time to see all about me, the clearness and sweetness of the night, the shapes of the hills like things asleep, and the fire dwindling away behind us, like a bright spot in the midst of the moor, anger would come upon me in a clap that I must still drag myself in agony and eat the dust like a worm.

By what I have read in books, I think few that have held a pen were ever really wearied, or they would write of it more strongly. I had no care of my life, neither past nor future, and I scarce remembered there was such a lad as David Balfour. I did not think of myself, but just of each fresh step which I was sure would be my last, with despair—and of Alan, who was the cause of it, with hatred. Alan was in the right trade as a soldier; this is the officer's part to make men continue to do things, they know not wherefore, and when, if the choice was offered, they would lie down where they were and be killed. And I dare say I would have made a good enough private; for in these last hours it never occurred to me that I had any choice but just to obey as long as I was able, and die obeying.

Day began to come in, after years, I thought; and by that time we were past the greatest danger, and could walk upon our feet like men, instead of crawling like brutes. But, dear heart have mercy! what a pair we must have made, going double like old grandfathers, stumbling like babes, and as white as dead folk. Never a word passed between us; each set his mouth and kept his eyes in front of him, and lifted up his foot and set it down again, like people lifting weights at a country play (*village fair*); all the while, with the moorfowl crying "peep!" in the heather, and the light coming slowly clearer in the east.

I say Alan did as I did. Not that ever I looked at him, for I had enough ado to keep my feet; but because it is plain he must have been as stupid with weariness as myself, and looked as little where we were going, or we should not have walked into an ambush like blind men.

It fell in this way. We were going down a heathery brae, Alan leading and I following a pace or two behind, like a fiddler and his wife; when upon a sudden the heather gave a rustle, three or four ragged men leaped out, and the next moment we were lying on our backs, each with a dirk at his throat.

I don't think I cared; the pain of this rough handling was quite swallowed up by the pains of which I was already full; and I was too glad to have stopped walking to mind about a dirk. I lay looking up in the face of the man that held me; and I mind his face was black with the sun, and his eyes very light, but I was not afraid of him. I heard Alan and another whispering in the Gaelic; and what they said was all one to me.

Then the dirks were put up, our weapons were taken away, and we were set face to face, sitting in the heather.

"They are Cluny's men," said Alan. "We couldnae have fallen better. We're just to bide here with these, which are his out-sentries, till they can get word to the chief of my arrival."

Now Cluny Macpherson, the chief of the clan Vourich, had been one of the leaders of the great rebellion six years before; there was a price on his life; and I had supposed him long ago in France, with the rest of the heads of that desperate party. Even tired as I was, the surprise of what I heard half wakened me.

"What," I cried, "is Cluny still here?"

"Ay, is he so!" said Alan. "Still in his own country and kept by his own clan. King George can do no more."

I think I would have asked farther, but Alan gave me the put-off. "I am rather wearied," he said, "and I would like fine to get a sleep." And without more words, he rolled on his face in a deep heather bush, and seemed to sleep at once.

There was no such thing possible for me. You have heard grasshoppers whirring in the grass in the summer time? Well, I had no sooner closed my eyes, than my body, and above all my head, belly, and wrists, seemed to be filled with whirring grasshoppers; and I must open my eyes again at once, and tumble and toss, and sit up and lie down; and look at the sky which dazzled me, or at Cluny's wild and dirty sentries, peering out over the top of the brae and chattering to each other in the Gaelic.

That was all the rest I had, until the messenger returned; when, as it appeared that Cluny would be glad to receive us, we must get once more upon our feet and set forward. Alan was in excellent good spirits, much refreshed by his sleep, very hungry, and looking pleasantly forward to a dram and a dish of hot collops, of which, it seems, the messenger had brought him word. For my part, it made me sick to hear of eating. I had been dead-heavy before, and now I felt a kind of dreadful lightness, which would not suffer me to walk. I drifted like a gossamer; the ground seemed to me a cloud, the hills a feather-weight, the air to have a current, like a running burn, which carried me to and fro. With all that, a sort of horror of despair sat on my mind, so that I could have wept at my own helplessness.

I saw Alan knitting his brows at me, and supposed it was in anger; and that gave me a pang of light-headed fear, like what a child may have. I remember, too, that I was smiling, and could not stop smiling, hard as I tried; for I thought it was out of place at such a time. But my good companion had nothing in his mind but kindness; and the next moment, two of the gillies had me by the arms, and I began to be carried forward with great swiftness (or so it appeared to me, although I dare say it was slowly enough in truth), through a labyrinth of dreary glens and hollows and into the heart of that dismal mountain of Ben Alder.

23

CLUNY'S CAGE

We came at last to the foot of an exceeding steep wood, which scrambled up a craggy hillside, and was crowned by a naked precipice.

"It's here," said one of the guides, and we struck up hill.

The trees clung upon the slope, like sailors on the shrouds of a ship, and their trunks were like the rounds of a ladder, by which we mounted.

Quite at the top, and just before the rocky face of the cliff sprang above the foliage, we found that strange house which was known in the country as "Cluny's Cage." The trunks of several trees had been wattled across, the intervals strengthened with stakes, and the ground behind this barricade levelled up with earth to make the floor. A tree, which grew out from the hillside, was the living centre-beam of the roof. The walls were of wattle and covered with moss. The whole house had something of an egg shape; and it half hung, half stood in that steep, hillside thicket, like a wasp's nest in a green hawthorn.

Within, it was large enough to shelter five or six persons with some comfort. A projection of the cliff had been cunningly employed to be the fireplace; and the smoke rising against the face of the rock, and being not dissimilar in colour, readily escaped notice from below.

This was but one of Cluny's hiding-places; he had caves, besides, and underground chambers in several parts of his country; and following the reports of his scouts, he moved from one to another as the soldiers drew near or moved away. By this manner of living, and thanks to the affection of his clan, he had not only stayed all this time in safety, while so many others had fled or been taken and slain: but stayed four or five years longer, and only went to France at last by the express command of his master. There he soon died; and it is strange to reflect that he may have regretted his Cage upon Ben Alder.

When we came to the door he was seated by his rock chimney, watching a gillie about some cookery. He was mighty plainly habited, with a knitted nightcap drawn over his ears, and smoked a foul cutty pipe. For all that he had the manners of a king, and it was quite a sight to see him rise out of his place to welcome us.

"Well, Mr. Stewart, come awa', sir!" said he, "and bring in your friend that as yet I dinna ken the name of."

"And how is yourself, Cluny?" said Alan. "I hope ye do brawly, sir. And I am proud to see ye, and to present to ye my friend the Laird of Shaws, Mr. David Balfour."

Alan never referred to my estate without a touch of a sneer, when we were alone; but with strangers, he rang the words out like a herald.

"Step in by, the both of ye, gentlemen," says Cluny. "I make ye welcome to my house, which is a queer, rude place for certain, but one where I have entertained a royal personage, Mr. Stewart—ye doubtless ken the personage I have in my eye. We'll take a dram for luck, and as soon as this handless man of mine has the collops ready, we'll dine and take a hand at the cartes as gentlemen should. My life is a bit driegh," says he, pouring out the brandy; "I see little company, and sit and twirl my thumbs, and mind upon a great day that is gone by, and weary for another great day that we all hope will be upon the road. And so here's a toast to ye: The Restoration!"

Thereupon we all touched glasses and drank. I am sure I wished no ill to King George; and if he had been there himself in proper person, it's like he would have done as I did. No sooner had I taken out the drain than I felt hugely better, and could look on and listen, still a little mistily perhaps, but no longer with the same groundless horror and distress of mind.

It was certainly a strange place, and we had a strange host. In his long hiding, Cluny had grown to have all manner of precise habits, like those of an old maid. He had a particular place, where no one else must sit; the Cage was arranged in a particular way, which none must disturb; cookery was one of his chief fancies, and even while he was greeting us in, he kept an eye to the collops.

It appears, he sometimes visited or received visits from his wife and one or two of his nearest friends, under the cover of night; but for the more part lived quite alone, and communicated only with his sentinels and the gillies that waited on him in the Cage. The first thing in the morning, one of them, who was a barber, came and shaved him, and gave him the news of the country, of which he was immoderately greedy. There was no end to his questions; he put them as earnestly as a child; and at some of the answers, laughed out of all bounds of reason, and would break out again laughing at the mere memory, hours after the barber was gone.

To be sure, there might have been a purpose in his questions; for though he was thus sequestered, and like the other landed gentlemen of Scotland, stripped by the late Act of Parliament of legal powers, he still exercised a patriarchal justice in his clan. Disputes were brought to him in his hiding-hole to be decided; and the men of his country, who would have snapped their fingers at the Court of Session, laid aside revenge and paid down money at the bare word of this forfeited and hunted outlaw. When he was angered, which was often enough, he gave his commands and breathed threats of punishment like any king; and his gillies trembled and crouched away from him like children before a hasty father. With each of them, as he entered, he ceremoniously shook hands, both parties touching their bonnets at the same time in a military manner. Altogether, I had a fair chance to see some of the inner workings of a Highland clan; and this with a proscribed, fugitive chief; his country conquered; the troops riding upon all sides in quest of him, sometimes within a mile of where he lay; and when the least of the ragged fellows whom he rated and threatened, could have made a fortune by betraying him.

On that first day, as soon as the collops were ready, Cluny gave them with his own hand a squeeze of a lemon (for he was well supplied with luxuries) and bade us draw in to our meal.

"They," said he, meaning the collops, "are such as I gave his Royal Highness in this very house; bating the lemon juice, for at that time we were glad to get the meat and never fashed for kitchen (*condiment*). Indeed, there were mair dragoons than lemons in my country in the year forty-six."

I do not know if the collops were truly very good, but my heart rose against the sight of them, and I could eat but little. All the while Cluny entertained us with stories of Prince Charlie's stay in the Cage, giving us the very words of the speakers, and rising from his place to show us where they stood. By these, I gathered the Prince was a gracious, spirited boy, like the son of a race of polite kings, but not so wise as Solomon. I gathered, too, that while he was in the Cage, he was often drunk; so the fault that has since, by all accounts, made such a wreck of him, had even then begun to show itself.

We were no sooner done eating than Cluny brought out an old, thumbed, greasy pack of cards, such as you may find in a mean inn; and his eyes brightened in his face as he proposed that we should fall to playing.

Now this was one of the things I had been brought up to eschew like disgrace; it being held by my father neither the part of a Christian nor yet of a gentleman to set his own livelihood and fish for that of others, on the cast of painted pasteboard. To be sure, I might have pleaded my fatigue, which was excuse enough; but I thought it behoved that I should bear a testimony. I must have got very red in the face, but I spoke steadily, and told them I had no call to be a judge of others, but for my own part, it was a matter in which I had no clearness.

Cluny stopped mingling the cards. "What in deil's name is this?" says he. "What kind of Whiggish, canting talk is this, for the house of Cluny Macpherson?"

"I will put my hand in the fire for Mr. Balfour," says Alan. "He is an honest and a mettle gentleman, and I would have ye bear in mind who says it. I bear a king's name," says he, cocking his hat; "and I and any that I call friend are company for the best. But the gentleman is tired, and should sleep; if he has no mind to the cartes, it will never hinder you and me. And I'm fit and willing, sir, to play ye any game that ye can name."

"Sir," says Cluny, "in this poor house of mine I would have you to ken that any gentleman may follow his pleasure. If your friend would like to stand on his head, he is welcome. And if either he, or you, or any other man, is not preceesely satisfied, I will be proud to step outside with him."

I had no will that these two friends should cut their throats for my sake.

"Sir," said I, "I am very wearied, as Alan says; and what's more, as you are a man that likely has sons of your own, I may tell you it was a promise to my father."

"Say nae mair, say nae mair," said Cluny, and pointed me to a bed of heather in a corner of the Cage. For all that he was displeased enough, looked at me askance, and grumbled when he looked. And indeed it must be owned that both my scruples and the words in which I declared them, smacked somewhat of the Covenanter, and were little in their place among wild Highland Jacobites.

What with the brandy and the venison, a strange heaviness had come over me; and I had scarce lain down upon the bed before I fell into a kind of trance, in which I continued almost the whole time of our stay in the Cage. Sometimes I was broad awake and understood what passed; sometimes I only heard voices, or men snoring, like the voice of a silly river; and the plaids upon the wall dwindled down and swelled out again, like firelight shadows on the roof. I must sometimes have spoken or cried out, for I remember I was now and then amazed at being answered; yet I was conscious of no particular nightmare, only of a general, black, abiding horror—a horror of the place I was in, and the bed I lay in, and the plaids on the wall, and the voices, and the fire, and myself.

The barber-gillie, who was a doctor too, was called in to prescribe for me; but as he spoke in the Gaelic, I understood not a word of his opinion, and was too sick even to ask for a translation. I knew well enough I was ill, and that was all I cared about.

I paid little heed while I lay in this poor pass. But Alan and Cluny were most of the time at the cards, and I am clear that Alan must have begun by winning; for I remember sitting up, and seeing them hard at it, and a great glittering pile of as much as sixty or a hundred guineas on the table. It looked strange enough, to see all this wealth in a nest upon a cliff-side, wattled about growing trees. And even then, I thought it seemed deep water for Alan to be riding, who had no better battle-horse than a green purse and a matter of five pounds.

The luck, it seems, changed on the second day. About noon I was wakened as usual for dinner, and as usual refused to eat, and was given a dram with some bitter infusion which the barber had prescribed. The sun was shining in at the open door of the Cage, and this dazzled and offended me. Cluny sat at the table, biting the pack of cards. Alan had stooped over the bed, and had his face close to my eyes; to which, troubled as they were with the fever, it seemed of the most shocking bigness.

He asked me for a loan of my money.

"What for?" said I.

"O, just for a loan," said he.

"But why?" I repeated. "I don't see."

"Hut, David!" said Alan, "ye wouldnae grudge me a loan?"

I would, though, if I had had my senses! But all I thought of then was to get his face away, and I handed him my money.

On the morning of the third day, when we had been forty-eight hours in the Cage, I awoke with a great relief of spirits, very weak and weary indeed, but seeing things of the right size and with their honest, everyday appearance. I had a mind to eat, moreover, rose from bed of my own movement, and as soon as we had breakfasted, stepped to the entry of the Cage and sat down outside in the top of the wood. It was a grey day with a cool, mild air: and I sat in a dream all morning, only disturbed by the passing by of Cluny's scouts and servants coming with provisions and reports; for as the coast was at that time clear, you might almost say he held court openly.

When I returned, he and Alan had laid the cards aside, and were questioning a gillie; and the chief turned about and spoke to me in the Gaelic.

"I have no Gaelic, sir," said I.

Now since the card question, everything I said or did had the power of annoying Cluny. "Your name has more sense than yourself, then," said he angrily, "for it's good Gaelic. But the point is this. My scout reports all clear in the south, and the question is, have ye the strength to go?"

I saw cards on the table, but no gold; only a heap of little written papers, and these all on Cluny's side. Alan, besides, had an odd look, like a man not very well content; and I began to have a strong misgiving.

"I do not know if I am as well as I should be," said I, looking at Alan; "but the little money we have has a long way to carry us."

Alan took his under-lip into his mouth, and looked upon the ground.

"David," says he at last, "I've lost it; there's the naked truth."

"My money too?" said I.

"Your money too," says Alan, with a groan. "Ye shouldnae have given it me. I'm daft when I get to the cartes."

"Hoot-toot! hoot-toot!" said Cluny. "It was all daffing; it's all nonsense. Of course you'll have your money back again, and the double of it, if ye'll make so free with me. It would be a singular thing for me to keep it. It's not to be supposed that I would be any hindrance to gentlemen in your situation; that would be a singular thing!" cries he, and began to pull gold out of his pocket with a mighty red face.

Alan said nothing, only looked on the ground.

"Will you step to the door with me, sir?" said I.

Cluny said he would be very glad, and followed me readily enough, but he looked flustered and put out.

"And now, sir," says I, "I must first acknowledge your generosity."

"Nonsensical nonsense!" cries Cluny. "Where's the generosity? This is just a most unfortunate affair; but what would ye have me do—boxed up in this bee-skep of a cage of mine—but just set my friends to the cartes, when I can get them? And if they lose, of course, it's not to be supposed——" And here he came to a pause.

"Yes," said I, "if they lose, you give them back their money; and if they win, they carry away yours in their pouches! I have said before that I grant your generosity; but to me, sir, it's a very painful thing to be placed in this position."

There was a little silence, in which Cluny seemed always as if he was about to speak, but said nothing. All the time he grew redder and redder in the face.

"I am a young man," said I, "and I ask your advice. Advise me as you would your son. My friend fairly lost his money, after having fairly gained a far greater sum of yours; can I accept it back again? Would that be the right part for me to play? Whatever I do, you can see for yourself it must be hard upon a man of any pride."

"It's rather hard on me, too, Mr. Balfour," said Cluny, "and ye give me very much the look of a man that has entrapped poor people to their hurt. I wouldnae have my friends come to any house of mine to accept affronts; no," he cried, with a sudden heat of anger, "nor yet to give them!"

"And so you see, sir," said I, "there is something to be said upon my side; and this gambling is a very poor employ for gentlefolks. But I am still waiting your opinion."

I am sure if ever Cluny hated any man it was David Balfour. He looked me all over with a warlike eye, and I saw the challenge at his lips. But either my youth disarmed him, or perhaps his own sense of justice. Certainly it was a mortifying matter for all concerned, and not least Cluny; the more credit that he took it as he did.

"Mr. Balfour," said he, "I think you are too nice and covenanting, but for all that you have the spirit of a very pretty gentleman. Upon my honest word, ye may take this money—it's what I would tell my son—and here's my hand along with it!"

24

THE FLIGHT IN THE HEATHER: THE QUARREL

Alan and I were put across Loch Errocht under cloud of night, and went down its eastern shore to another hiding-place near the head of Loch Rannoch, whither we were led by one of the gillies from the Cage. This fellow carried all our luggage and Alan's great-coat in the bargain, trotting along under the burthen, far less than the half of which used to weigh me to the ground, like a stout hill pony with a feather; yet he was a man that, in plain contest, I could have broken on my knee.

Doubtless it was a great relief to walk disencumbered; and perhaps without that relief, and the consequent sense of liberty and lightness, I could not have walked at all. I was but new risen from a bed of sickness; and there was nothing in the state of our affairs to hearten me for much exertion; travelling, as we did, over the most dismal deserts in Scotland, under a cloudy heaven, and with divided hearts among the travellers.

For long, we said nothing; marching alongside or one behind the other, each with a set countenance: I, angry and proud, and drawing what strength I had from these two violent and sinful feelings; Alan angry and ashamed, ashamed that he had lost my money, angry that I should take it so ill.

The thought of a separation ran always the stronger in my mind; and the more I approved of it, the more ashamed I grew of my approval. It would be a fine, handsome, generous thing, indeed, for Alan to turn round and say to me: "Go, I am in the most danger, and my company only increases yours." But for me to turn to the friend who certainly loved me, and say to him: "You are in great danger, I am in but little; your friendship is a burden; go, take your risks and bear your hardships alone——" no, that was impossible; and even to think of it privily to myself, made my cheeks to burn.

And yet Alan had behaved like a child, and (what is worse) a treacherous child. Wheedling my money from me while I lay half-conscious was scarce better than theft; and yet here he was trudging by my side, without a penny to his name, and by what I could see, quite blithe to sponge upon the money he had driven me to beg. True, I was ready to share it with him; but it made me rage to see him count upon my readiness.

These were the two things uppermost in my mind; and I could open my mouth upon neither without black ungenerosity. So I did the next worst, and said nothing, nor so much as looked once at my companion, save with the tail of my eye.

At last, upon the other side of Loch Errocht, going over a smooth, rushy place, where the walking was easy, he could bear it no longer, and came close to me.

"David," says he, "this is no way for two friends to take a small accident. I have to say that I'm sorry; and so that's said. And now if you have anything, ye'd better say it."

"O," says I, "I have nothing."

He seemed disconcerted; at which I was meanly pleased.

"No," said he, with rather a trembling voice, "but when I say I was to blame?"

"Why, of course, ye were to blame," said I, coolly; "and you will bear me out that I have never reproached you."

"Never," says he; "but ye ken very well that ye've done worse. Are we to part? Ye said so once before. Are ye to say it again? There's hills and heather enough between here and the two seas, David; and I will own I'm no very keen to stay where I'm no wanted."

This pierced me like a sword, and seemed to lay bare my private disloyalty.

"Alan Breck!" I cried; and then: "Do you think I am one to turn my back on you in your chief need? You dursn't say it to my face. My whole conduct's there to give the lie to it. It's true, I fell asleep upon the muir; but that was from weariness, and you do wrong to cast it up to me——"

"Which is what I never did," said Alan.

"But aside from that," I continued, "what have I done that you should even me to dogs by such a supposition? I never yet failed a friend, and it's not likely I'll begin with you. There are things between us that I can never forget, even if you can."

"I will only say this to ye, David," said Alan, very quietly, "that I have long been owing ye my life, and now I owe ye money. Ye should try to make that burden light for me."

This ought to have touched me, and in a manner it did, but the wrong manner. I felt I was behaving badly; and was now not only angry with Alan, but angry with myself in the bargain; and it made me the more cruel.

"You asked me to speak," said I. "Well, then, I will. You own yourself that you have done me a disservice; I have had to swallow an affront: I have never reproached you, I never named the thing till you did. And now you blame me," cried I, "because I cannae laugh and sing as if I was glad to be affronted. The next thing will be that I'm to go down upon my knees and thank you for it! Ye should think more of others, Alan Breck. If ye thought more of others, ye would perhaps speak less about yourself; and when a friend that likes you very well has passed over an offence without a word, you would be blithe to let it lie, instead of making it a stick to break his back with. By your own way of it, it was you that was to blame; then it shouldnae be you to seek the quarrel."

"Aweel," said Alan, "say nae mair."

And we fell back into our former silence; and came to our journey's end, and supped, and lay down to sleep, without another word.

The gillie put us across Loch Rannoch in the dusk of the next day, and gave us his opinion as to our best route. This was to get us up at once into the tops of the mountains: to go round by a circuit, turning the heads of Glen Lyon, Glen Lochay, and Glen Dochart, and come down upon the lowlands by Kippen and the upper waters of the Forth. Alan was little pleased with a route which led us through the country of his blood-foes, the Glenorchy Campbells. He objected that by turning to the east, we should come almost at once among the Athole Stewarts, a race of his own name and lineage, although following a different chief, and come besides by a far easier and swifter way to the place whither we were bound.

But the gillie, who was indeed the chief man of Cluny's scouts, had good reasons to give him on all hands, naming the force of troops in every district, and alleging finally (as well as I could understand) that we should nowhere be so little troubled as in a country of the Campbells.

Alan gave way at last, but with only half a heart. "It's one of the dowiest countries in Scotland," said he. "There's naething there that I ken, but heath, and crows, and Campbells. But I see that ye're a man of some penetration; and be it as ye please!"

We set forth accordingly by this itinerary; and for the best part of three nights travelled on eerie mountains and among the well-heads of wild rivers; often buried in mist, almost continually blown and rained upon, and not once cheered by any glimpse of sunshine. By day, we lay and slept in the drenching heather; by night, incessantly clambered upon breakneck hills and among rude crags. We often wandered; we were often so involved in fog, that we must lie quiet till it lightened. A fire was never to be thought of. Our only food was drammach and a portion of cold meat that we had carried from the Cage; and as for drink, Heaven knows we had no want of water.

This was a dreadful time, rendered the more dreadful by the gloom of the weather and the country. I was never warm; my teeth chattered in my head; I was troubled with a very sore throat, such as I had on the isle; I had a painful stitch in my side, which never left me; and when I slept in my wet bed, with the rain beating above and the mud oozing below me, it was to live over again in fancy the worst part of my adventures—to see the tower of Shaws lit by lightning, Ransome carried below on the men's backs, Shuan dying on the round-house floor, or Colin Campbell grasping at the bosom of his coat. From such broken slumbers, I would be aroused in the gloaming, to sit up in the same puddle where I had slept, and sup cold drammach; the rain driving sharp in my face or running down my back in icy trickles; the mist enfolding us like as in a gloomy chamber—or, perhaps, if the wind blew, falling suddenly apart and showing us the gulf of some dark valley where the streams were crying aloud.

The sound of an infinite number of rivers came up from all round. In this steady rain the springs of the mountain were broken up; every glen gushed water like a cistern; every stream was in high spate, and had filled and overflowed its channel. During our night tramps, it was solemn to hear the voice of them below in the valleys, now booming like thunder, now with an angry cry. I could well understand the story of the Water Kelpie, that demon of the streams, who is fabled to keep wailing and roaring at the ford until the coming of the doomed traveller. Alan I saw believed it, or half believed it; and when the cry of the river rose more than usually sharp, I was little surprised (though, of course, I would still be shocked) to see him cross himself in the manner of the Catholics.

During all these horrid wanderings we had no familiarity, scarcely even that of speech. The truth is that I was sickening for my grave, which is my best excuse. But besides that I was of an unforgiving disposition from my birth, slow to take offence, slower to forget it, and now incensed both against my companion and myself. For the best part of two days he was unweariedly kind; silent, indeed, but always ready to help, and always hoping (as I could very well see) that my displeasure would blow by. For the same length of time I stayed in myself, nursing my anger, roughly refusing his services, and passing him over with my eyes as if he had been a bush or a stone.

The second night, or rather the peep of the third day, found us upon a very open hill, so that we could not follow our usual plan and lie down immediately to eat and sleep. Before we had reached a place of shelter, the grey had come pretty clear, for though it still rained, the clouds ran higher; and Alan, looking in my face, showed some marks of concern.

"Ye had better let me take your pack," said he, for perhaps the ninth time since we had parted from the scout beside Loch Rannoch.

"I do very well, I thank you," said I, as cold as ice.

Alan flushed darkly. "I'll not offer it again," he said. "I'm not a patient man, David."

"I never said you were," said I, which was exactly the rude, silly speech of a boy of ten.

Alan made no answer at the time, but his conduct answered for him. Henceforth, it is to be thought, he quite forgave himself for the affair at Cluny's; cocked his hat again, walked jauntily, whistled airs, and looked at me upon one side with a provoking smile.

The third night we were to pass through the western end of the country of Balquhidder. It came clear and cold, with a touch in the air like frost, and a northerly wind that blew the clouds away and made the stars bright. The streams were full, of course, and still made a great noise among the hills; but I observed that Alan thought no more upon the Kelpie, and was in high good spirits. As for me, the change of weather came too late; I had lain in the mire so long that (as the Bible has it) my very clothes "abhorred me." I was dead weary, deadly sick and full of pains and shiverings; the chill of the wind went through me, and the sound of it confused my ears. In this poor state I had to bear from my companion something in the nature of a persecution. He spoke a good deal, and never without a taunt. "Whig" was the best name he had to give me. "Here," he would say, "here's a dub for ye to jump, my Whiggie! I ken you're a fine jumper!" And so on; all the time with a gibing voice and face.

I knew it was my own doing, and no one else's; but I was too miserable to repent. I felt I could drag myself but little farther; pretty soon, I must lie down and die on these wet mountains like a sheep or a fox, and my bones must whiten there like the bones of a beast. My head was light perhaps; but I began to love the prospect, I began to glory in the thought of such a death, alone in the desert, with the wild eagles besieging my last moments. Alan would repent then, I thought; he would remember, when I was dead, how much he owed me, and the remembrance would be torture. So I went like a sick, silly, and bad-hearted schoolboy, feeding my anger against a fellow-man, when I would have been better on my knees, crying on God for mercy. And at each of Alan's taunts, I hugged myself. "Ah!" thinks I to myself, "I have a better taunt in readiness; when I lie down and die, you will feel it like a buffet in your face; ah, what a revenge! ah, how you will regret your ingratitude and cruelty!"

All the while, I was growing worse and worse. Once I had fallen, my leg simply doubling under me, and this had struck Alan for the moment; but I was afoot so briskly, and set off again with such a natural manner, that he soon forgot the incident. Flushes of heat went over me, and then spasms of shuddering. The stitch in my side was hardly bearable. At last I began to feel that I could trail myself no farther: and with that, there came on me all at once the wish to have it out with Alan, let my anger blaze, and be done with my life in a more sudden manner. He had just called me "Whig." I stopped.

"Mr. Stewart," said I, in a voice that quivered like a fiddle-string, "you are older than I am, and should know your manners. Do you think it either very wise or very witty to cast my politics in my teeth? I thought, where folk differed, it was the part of gentlemen to differ civilly; and if I did not, I may tell you I could find a better taunt than some of yours."

Alan had stopped opposite to me, his hat cocked, his hands in his breeches pockets, his head a little on one side. He listened, smiling evilly, as I could see by the starlight; and when I had done he began to whistle a Jacobite air. It was the air made in mockery of General Cope's defeat at Preston Pans:

"Hey, Johnnie Cope, are ye waukin' yet?

And are your drums a-beatin' yet?"

And it came in my mind that Alan, on the day of that battle, had been engaged upon the royal side.

"Why do ye take that air, Mr. Stewart?" said I. "Is that to remind me you have been beaten on both sides?"

The air stopped on Alan's lips. "David!" said he.

"But it's time these manners ceased," I continued; "and I mean you shall henceforth speak civilly of my King and my good friends the Campbells."

"I am a Stewart—" began Alan.

"O!" says I, "I ken ye bear a king's name. But you are to remember, since I have been in the Highlands, I have seen a good many of those that bear it; and the best I can say of them is this, that they would be none the worse of washing."

"Do you know that you insult me?" said Alan, very low.

"I am sorry for that," said I, "for I am not done; and if you distaste the sermon, I doubt the pirliecue (*a second sermon*) will please you as little. You have been chased in the field by the grown men of my party; it seems a poor kind of pleasure to out-face a boy. Both the Campbells and the Whigs have beaten you; you have run before them like a hare. It behoves you to speak of them as of your betters."

Alan stood quite still, the tails of his great-coat clapping behind him in the wind.

"This is a pity," he said at last. "There are things said that cannot be passed over."

"I never asked you to," said I. "I am as ready as yourself."

"Ready?" said he.

"Ready," I repeated. "I am no blower and boaster like some that I could name. Come on!" And drawing my sword, I fell on guard as Alan himself had taught me.

"David!" he cried. "Are ye daft? I cannae draw upon ye, David. It's fair murder."

"That was your look-out when you insulted me," said I.

"It's the truth!" cried Alan, and he stood for a moment, wringing his mouth in his hand like a man in sore perplexity. "It's the bare truth," he said, and drew his sword. But before I could touch his blade with mine, he had thrown it from him and fallen to the ground. "Na, na," he kept saying, "na, na—I cannae, I cannae."

At this the last of my anger oozed all out of me; and I found myself only sick, and sorry, and blank, and wondering at myself. I would have given the world to take back what I had said; but a word once spoken, who can recapture it? I minded me of all Alan's kindness and courage in the past, how he had helped and cheered and borne with me in our evil days; and then recalled my own insults, and saw that I had lost for ever that doughty friend. At the same time, the sickness that hung upon me seemed to redouble, and the pang in my side was like a sword for sharpness. I thought I must have swooned where I stood.

This it was that gave me a thought. No apology could blot out what I had said; it was needless to think of one, none could cover the offence; but where an apology was vain, a mere cry for help might bring Alan back to my side. I put my pride away from me. "Alan!" I said; "if ye cannae help me, I must just die here."

He started up sitting, and looked at me.

"It's true," said I. "I'm by with it. O, let me get into the bield of a house—I'll can die there easier." I had no need to pretend; whether I chose or not, I spoke in a weeping voice that would have melted a heart of stone.

"Can ye walk?" asked Alan.

"No," said I, "not without help. This last hour my legs have been fainting under me; I've a stitch in my side like a red-hot iron; I cannae breathe right. If I die, ye'll can forgive me, Alan? In my heart, I liked ye fine—even when I was the angriest."

"Wheesht, wheesht!" cried Alan. "Dinna say that! David man, ye ken—" He shut his mouth upon a sob. "Let me get my arm about ye," he continued; "that's the way! Now lean upon me hard. Gude kens where there's a house! We're in Balwhidder, too; there should be no want of houses, no, nor friends' houses here. Do ye gang easier so, Davie?"

"Ay," said I, "I can be doing this way;" and I pressed his arm with my hand.

Again he came near sobbing. "Davie," said he, "I'm no a right man at all; I have neither sense nor kindness; I could nae remember ye were just a bairn, I couldnae see ye were dying on your feet; Davie, ye'll have to try and forgive me."

"O man, let's say no more about it!" said I. "We're neither one of us to mend the other—that's the truth! We must just bear and forbear, man Alan. O, but my stitch is sore! Is there nae house?"

"I'll find a house to ye, David," he said, stoutly. "We'll follow down the burn, where there's bound to be houses. My poor man, will ye no be better on my back?"

"O, Alan," says I, "and me a good twelve inches taller?"

"Ye're no such a thing," cried Alan, with a start. "There may be a trifling matter of an inch or two; I'm no saying I'm just exactly what ye would call a tall man, whatever; and I dare say," he added, his voice tailing off in a laughable manner, "now when I come to think of it, I dare say ye'll be just about right. Ay, it'll be a foot, or near hand; or may be even mair!"

It was sweet and laughable to hear Alan eat his words up in the fear of some fresh quarrel. I could have laughed, had not my stitch caught me so hard; but if I had laughed, I think I must have wept too.

"Alan," cried I, "what makes ye so good to me? What makes ye care for such a thankless fellow?"

"'Deed, and I don't know" said Alan. "For just precisely what I thought I liked about ye, was that ye never quarrelled:—and now I like ye better!"

25

IN BALQUHIDDER

At the door of the first house we came to, Alan knocked, which was of no very safe enterprise in such a part of the Highlands as the Braes of Balquhidder. No great clan held rule there; it was filled and disputed by small septs, and broken remnants, and what they call "chiefless folk," driven into the wild country about the springs of Forth and Teith by the advance of the Campbells. Here were Stewarts and Maclarens, which came to the same thing, for the Maclarens followed Alan's chief in war, and made but one clan with Appin. Here, too, were many of that old, proscribed, nameless, red-handed clan of the Macgregors. They had always been ill-considered, and now worse than ever, having credit with no side or party in the whole country of Scotland. Their chief, Macgregor of Macgregor, was in exile; the more immediate leader of that part of them about Balquhidder, James More, Rob Roy's eldest son, lay waiting his trial in Edinburgh Castle; they were in ill-blood with Highlander and Lowlander, with the Grahames, the Maclarens, and the Stewarts; and Alan, who took up the quarrel of any friend, however distant, was extremely wishful to avoid them.

Chance served us very well; for it was a household of Maclarens that we found, where Alan was not only welcome for his name's sake but known by reputation. Here then I was got to bed without delay, and a doctor fetched, who found me in a sorry plight. But whether because he was a very good doctor, or I a very young, strong man, I lay bedridden for no more than a week, and before a month I was able to take the road again with a good heart.

All this time Alan would not leave me though I often pressed him, and indeed his foolhardiness in staying was a common subject of outcry with the two or three friends that were let into the secret. He hid by day in a hole of the braes under a little wood; and at night, when the coast was clear, would come into the house to visit me. I need not say if I was pleased to see him; Mrs. Maclaren, our hostess, thought nothing good enough for such a guest; and as Duncan Dhu (which was the name of our host) had a pair of pipes in his house, and was much of a lover of music, this time of my recovery was quite a festival, and we commonly turned night into day.

The soldiers let us be; although once a party of two companies and some dragoons went by in the bottom of the valley, where I could see them through the window as I lay in bed.

What was much more astonishing, no magistrate came near me, and there was no question put of whence I came or whither I was going; and in that time of excitement, I was as free of all inquiry as though I had lain in a desert. Yet my presence was known before I left to all the people in Balquhidder and the adjacent parts; many coming about the house on visits and these (after the custom of the country) spreading the news among their neighbours. The bills, too, had now been printed. There was one pinned near the foot of my bed, where I could read my own not very flattering portrait and, in larger characters, the amount of the blood money that had been set upon my life. Duncan Dhu and the rest that knew that I had come there in Alan's company, could have entertained no doubt of who I was; and many others must have had their guess. For though I had changed my clothes, I could not change my age or person; and Lowland boys of eighteen were not so rife in these parts of the world, and above all about that time, that they could fail to put one thing with another, and connect me with the bill. So it was, at least. Other folk keep a secret among two or three near friends, and somehow it leaks out; but among these clansmen, it is told to a whole countryside, and they will keep it for a century.

There was but one thing happened worth narrating; and that is the visit I had of Robin Oig, one of the sons of the notorious Rob Roy. He was sought upon all sides on a charge of carrying a young woman from Balfron and marrying her (as was alleged) by force; yet he stepped about Balquhidder like a gentleman in his own walled policy. It was he who had shot James Maclaren at the plough stilts, a quarrel never satisfied; yet he walked into the house of his blood enemies as a rider (*commercial traveller*) might into a public inn.

Duncan had time to pass me word of who it was; and we looked at one another in concern. You should understand, it was then close upon the time of Alan's coming; the two were little likely to agree; and yet if we sent word or sought to make a signal, it was sure to arouse suspicion in a man under so dark a cloud as the Macgregor.

He came in with a great show of civility, but like a man among inferiors; took off his bonnet to Mrs. Maclaren, but clapped it on his head again to speak to Duncan; and having thus set himself (as he would have thought) in a proper light, came to my bedside and bowed.

"I am given to know, sir," says he, "that your name is Balfour."

"They call me David Balfour," said I, "at your service."

"I would give ye my name in return, sir," he replied, "but it's one somewhat blown upon of late days; and it'll perhaps suffice if I tell ye that I am own brother to James More Drummond or Macgregor, of whom ye will scarce have failed to hear."

"No, sir," said I, a little alarmed; "nor yet of your father, Macgregor-Campbell." And I sat up and bowed in bed; for I thought best to compliment him, in case he was proud of having had an outlaw to his father.

He bowed in return. "But what I am come to say, sir," he went on, "is this. In the year '45, my brother raised a part of the 'Gregara' and marched six companies to strike a stroke for the good side; and the surgeon that marched with our clan and cured my brother's leg when it was broken in the brush at Preston Pans, was a gentleman of the same name precisely as yourself. He was brother to Balfour of Baith; and if you are in any reasonable degree of nearness one of that gentleman's kin, I have come to put myself and my people at your command."

You are to remember that I knew no more of my descent than any cadger's dog; my uncle, to be sure, had prated of some of our high connections, but nothing to the present purpose; and there was nothing left me but that bitter disgrace of owning that I could not tell.

Robin told me shortly he was sorry he had put himself about, turned his back upon me without a sign of salutation, and as he went towards the door, I could hear him telling Duncan that I was "only some kinless loon that didn't know his own father." Angry as I was at these words, and ashamed of my own ignorance, I could scarce keep from smiling that a man who was under the lash of the law (and was indeed hanged some three years later) should be so nice as to the descent of his acquaintances.

Just in the door, he met Alan coming in; and the two drew back and looked at each other like strange dogs. They were neither of them big men, but they seemed fairly to swell out with pride. Each wore a sword, and by a movement of his haunch, thrust clear the hilt of it, so that it might be the more readily grasped and the blade drawn.

"Mr. Stewart, I am thinking," says Robin.

"Troth, Mr. Macgregor, it's not a name to be ashamed of," answered Alan.

"I did not know ye were in my country, sir," says Robin.

"It sticks in my mind that I am in the country of my friends the Maclarens," says Alan.

"That's a kittle point," returned the other. "There may be two words to say to that. But I think I will have heard that you are a man of your sword?"

"Unless ye were born deaf, Mr. Macgregor, ye will have heard a good deal more than that," says Alan. "I am not the only man that can draw steel in Appin; and when my kinsman and captain, Ardshiel, had a talk with a gentleman of your name, not so many years back, I could never hear that the Macgregor had the best of it."

"Do ye mean my father, sir?" says Robin.

"Well, I wouldnae wonder," said Alan. "The gentleman I have in my mind had the ill-taste to clap Campbell to his name."

"My father was an old man," returned Robin.

"The match was unequal. You and me would make a better pair, sir."

"I was thinking that," said Alan.

I was half out of bed, and Duncan had been hanging at the elbow of these fighting cocks, ready to intervene upon the least occasion. But when that word was uttered, it was a case of now or never; and Duncan, with something of a white face to be sure, thrust himself between.

"Gentlemen," said he, "I will have been thinking of a very different matter, whateffer. Here are my pipes, and here are you two gentlemen who are baith acclaimed pipers. It's an auld dispute which one of ye's the best. Here will be a braw chance to settle it."

"Why, sir," said Alan, still addressing Robin, from whom indeed he had not so much as shifted his eyes, nor yet Robin from him, "why, sir," says Alan, "I think I will have heard some sough (*rumour*) of the sort. Have ye music, as folk say? Are ye a bit of a piper?"

"I can pipe like a Macrimmon!" cries Robin.

"And that is a very bold word," quoth Alan.

"I have made bolder words good before now," returned Robin, "and that against better adversaries."

"It is easy to try that," says Alan.

Duncan Dhu made haste to bring out the pair of pipes that was his principal possession, and to set before his guests a mutton-ham and a bottle of that drink which they call Athole brose, and which is made of old whiskey, strained honey and sweet cream, slowly beaten together in the right order and proportion. The two enemies were still on the very breach of a quarrel; but down they sat, one upon each side of the peat fire, with a mighty show of politeness. Maclaren pressed them to taste his mutton-ham and "the wife's brose," reminding them the wife was out of Athole and had a name far and wide for her skill in that confection. But Robin put aside these hospitalities as bad for the breath.

"I would have ye to remark, sir," said Alan, "that I havenae broken bread for near upon ten hours, which will be worse for the breath than any brose in Scotland."

"I will take no advantages, Mr. Stewart," replied Robin. "Eat and drink; I'll follow you."

Each ate a small portion of the ham and drank a glass of the brose to Mrs. Maclaren; and then after a great number of civilities, Robin took the pipes and played a little spring in a very ranting manner.

"Ay, ye can blow" said Alan; and taking the instrument from his rival, he first played the same spring in a manner identical with Robin's; and then wandered into variations, which, as he went on, he decorated with a perfect flight of grace-notes, such as pipers love, and call the "warblers."

I had been pleased with Robin's playing, Alan's ravished me.

"That's no very bad, Mr. Stewart," said the rival, "but ye show a poor device in your warblers."

"Me!" cried Alan, the blood starting to his face. "I give ye the lie."

"Do ye own yourself beaten at the pipes, then," said Robin, "that ye seek to change them for the sword?"

"And that's very well said, Mr. Macgregor," returned Alan; "and in the meantime" (laying a strong accent on the word) "I take back the lie. I appeal to Duncan."

"Indeed, ye need appeal to naebody," said Robin. "Ye're a far better judge than any Maclaren in Balquhidder: for it's a God's truth that you're a very creditable piper for a Stewart. Hand me the pipes." Alan did as he asked; and Robin proceeded to imitate and correct some part of Alan's variations, which it seemed that he remembered perfectly.

"Ay, ye have music," said Alan, gloomily.

"And now be the judge yourself, Mr. Stewart," said Robin; and taking up the variations from the beginning, he worked them throughout to so new a purpose, with such ingenuity and sentiment, and with so odd a fancy and so quick a knack in the grace-notes, that I was amazed to hear him.

As for Alan, his face grew dark and hot, and he sat and gnawed his fingers, like a man under some deep affront. "Enough!" he cried. "Ye can blow the pipes—make the most of that." And he made as if to rise.

But Robin only held out his hand as if to ask for silence, and struck into the slow measure of a pibroch. It was a fine piece of music in itself, and nobly played; but it seems, besides, it was a piece peculiar to the Appin Stewarts and a chief favourite with Alan. The first notes were scarce out, before there came a change in his face; when the time quickened, he seemed to grow restless in his seat; and long before that piece was at an end, the last signs of his anger died from him, and he had no thought but for the music.

"Robin Oig," he said, when it was done, "ye are a great piper. I am not fit to blow in the same kingdom with ye. Body of me! ye have mair music in your sporran than I have in my head! And though it still sticks in my mind that I could maybe show ye another of it with the cold steel, I warn ye beforehand—it'll no be fair! It would go against my heart to haggle a man that can blow the pipes as you can!"

Thereupon that quarrel was made up; all night long the brose was going and the pipes changing hands; and the day had come pretty bright, and the three men were none the better for what they had been taking, before Robin as much as thought upon the road.

26

END OF THE FLIGHT: WE PASS THE FORTH

The month, as I have said, was not yet out, but it was already far through August, and beautiful warm weather, with every sign of an early and great harvest, when I was pronounced able for my journey. Our money was now run to so low an ebb that we must think first of all on speed; for if we came not soon to Mr. Rankeillor's, or if when we came there he should fail to help me, we must surely starve. In Alan's view, besides, the hunt must have now greatly slackened; and the line of the Forth and even Stirling Bridge, which is the main pass over that river, would be watched with little interest.

"It's a chief principle in military affairs," said he, "to go where ye are least expected. Forth is our trouble; ye ken the saying, 'Forth bridles the wild Hielandman.' Well, if we seek to creep round about the head of that river and come down by Kippen or Balfron, it's just precisely there that they'll be looking to lay hands on us. But if we stave on straight to the auld Brig of Stirling, I'll lay my sword they let us pass unchallenged."

The first night, accordingly, we pushed to the house of a Maclaren in Strathire, a friend of Duncan's, where we slept the twenty-first of the month, and whence we set forth again about the fall of night to make another easy stage. The twenty-second we lay in a heather bush on the hillside in Uam Var, within view of a herd of deer, the happiest ten hours of sleep in a fine, breathing sunshine and on bone-dry ground, that I have ever tasted. That night we struck Allan Water, and followed it down; and coming to the edge of the hills saw the whole Carse of Stirling underfoot, as flat as a pancake, with the town and castle on a hill in the midst of it, and the moon shining on the Links of Forth.

"Now," said Alan, "I kenna if ye care, but ye're in your own land again. We passed the Hieland Line in the first hour; and now if we could but pass yon crooked water, we might cast our bonnets in the air."

In Allan Water, near by where it falls into the Forth, we found a little sandy islet, overgrown with burdock, butterbur and the like low plants, that would just cover us if we lay flat. Here it was we made our camp, within plain view of Stirling Castle, whence we could hear the drums beat as some part of the garrison paraded. Shearers worked all day in a field on one side of the river, and we could hear the stones going on the hooks and the voices and even the words of the men talking. It behoved to lie close and keep silent. But the sand of the little isle was sun-warm, the green plants gave us shelter for our heads, we had food and drink in plenty; and to crown all, we were within sight of safety.

As soon as the shearers quit their work and the dusk began to fall, we waded ashore and struck for the Bridge of Stirling, keeping to the fields and under the field fences.

The bridge is close under the castle hill, an old, high, narrow bridge with pinnacles along the parapet; and you may conceive with how much interest I looked upon it, not only as a place famous in history, but as the very doors of salvation to Alan and myself. The moon was not yet up when we came there; a few lights shone along the front of the fortress, and lower down a few lighted windows in the town; but it was all mighty still, and there seemed to be no guard upon the passage.

I was for pushing straight across; but Alan was more wary.

"It looks unco' quiet," said he; "but for all that we'll lie down here cannily behind a dyke, and make sure."

So we lay for about a quarter of an hour, whiles whispering, whiles lying still and hearing nothing earthly but the washing of the water on the piers. At last there came by an old, hobbling woman with a crutch stick; who first stopped a little, close to where we lay, and bemoaned herself and the long way she had travelled; and then set forth again up the steep spring of the bridge. The woman was so little, and the night still so dark, that we soon lost sight of her; only heard the sound of her steps, and her stick, and a cough that she had by fits, draw slowly farther away.

"She's bound to be across now," I whispered.

"Na," said Alan, "her foot still sounds boss (*hollow*) upon the bridge."

And just then—"Who goes?" cried a voice, and we heard the butt of a musket rattle on the stones. I must suppose the sentry had been sleeping, so that had we tried, we might have passed unseen; but he was awake now, and the chance forfeited.

"This'll never do," said Alan. "This'll never, never do for us, David."

And without another word, he began to crawl away through the fields; and a little after, being well out of eye-shot, got to his feet again, and struck along a road that led to the eastward. I could not conceive what he was doing; and indeed I was so sharply cut by the disappointment, that I was little likely to be pleased with anything. A moment back and I had seen myself knocking at Mr. Rankeillor's door to claim my inheritance, like a hero in a ballad; and here was I back again, a wandering, hunted blackguard, on the wrong side of Forth.

"Well?" said I.

"Well," said Alan, "what would ye have? They're none such fools as I took them for. We have still the Forth to pass, Davie—weary fall the rains that fed and the hillsides that guided it!"

"And why go east?" said I.

"Ou, just upon the chance!" said he. "If we cannae pass the river, we'll have to see what we can do for the firth."

"There are fords upon the river, and none upon the firth," said I.

"To be sure there are fords, and a bridge forbye," quoth Alan; "and of what service, when they are watched?"

"Well," said I, "but a river can be swum."

"By them that have the skill of it," returned he; "but I have yet to hear that either you or me is much of a hand at that exercise; and for my own part, I swim like a stone."

"I'm not up to you in talking back, Alan," I said; "but I can see we're making bad worse. If it's hard to pass a river, it stands to reason it must be worse to pass a sea."

"But there's such a thing as a boat," says Alan, "or I'm the more deceived."

"Ay, and such a thing as money," says I. "But for us that have neither one nor other, they might just as well not have been invented."

"Ye think so?" said Alan.

"I do that," said I.

"David," says he, "ye're a man of small invention and less faith. But let me set my wits upon the hone, and if I cannae beg, borrow, nor yet steal a boat, I'll make one!"

"I think I see ye!" said I. "And what's more than all that: if ye pass a bridge, it can tell no tales; but if we pass the firth, there's the boat on the wrong side—somebody must have brought it—the country-side will all be in a bizz—"

"Man!" cried Alan, "if I make a boat, I'll make a body to take it back again! So deave me with no more of your nonsense, but walk (for that's what you've got to do)—and let Alan think for ye."

All night, then, we walked through the north side of the Carse under the high line of the Ochil mountains; and by Alloa and Clackmannan and Culross, all of which we avoided: and about ten in the morning, mighty hungry and tired, came to the little clachan of Limekilns. This is a place that sits near in by the water-side, and looks across the Hope to the town of Queensferry. Smoke went up from both of these, and from other villages and farms upon all hands. The fields were being reaped; two ships lay anchored, and boats were coming and going on the Hope. It was altogether a right pleasant sight to me; and I could not take my fill of gazing at these comfortable, green, cultivated hills and the busy people both of the field and sea.

For all that, there was Mr. Rankeillor's house on the south shore, where I had no doubt wealth awaited me; and here was I upon the north, clad in poor enough attire of an outlandish fashion, with three silver shillings left to me of all my fortune, a price set upon my head, and an outlawed man for my sole company.

"O, Alan!" said I, "to think of it! Over there, there's all that heart could want waiting me; and the birds go over, and the boats go over—all that please can go, but just me only! O, man, but it's a heart-break!"

In Limekilns we entered a small change-house, which we only knew to be a public by the wand over the door, and bought some bread and cheese from a good-looking lass that was the servant. This we carried with us in a bundle, meaning to sit and eat it in a bush of wood on the sea-shore, that we saw some third part of a mile in front. As we went, I kept looking across the water and sighing to myself; and though I took no heed of it, Alan had fallen into a muse. At last he stopped in the way.

"Did ye take heed of the lass we bought this of?" says he, tapping on the bread and cheese.

"To be sure," said I, "and a bonny lass she was."

"Ye thought that?" cries he. "Man, David, that's good news."

"In the name of all that's wonderful, why so?" says I. "What good can that do?"

"Well," said Alan, with one of his droll looks, "I was rather in hopes it would maybe get us that boat."

"If it were the other way about, it would be liker it," said I.

"That's all that you ken, ye see," said Alan. "I don't want the lass to fall in love with ye, I want her to be sorry for ye, David; to which end there is no manner of need that she should take you for a beauty. Let me see" (looking me curiously over). "I wish ye were a wee thing paler; but apart from that ye'll do fine for my purpose—ye have a fine, hang-dog, rag-and-tatter, clappermaclaw kind of a look to ye, as if ye had stolen the coat from a potato-bogle. Come; right about, and back to the change-house for that boat of ours."

I followed him, laughing.

"David Balfour," said he, "ye're a very funny gentleman by your way of it, and this is a very funny employ for ye, no doubt. For all that, if ye have any affection for my neck (to say nothing of your own) ye will perhaps be kind enough to take this matter responsibly. I am going to do a bit of play-acting, the bottom ground of which is just exactly as serious as the gallows for the pair of us. So bear it, if ye please, in mind, and conduct yourself according."

"Well, well," said I, "have it as you will."

As we got near the clachan, he made me take his arm and hang upon it like one almost helpless with weariness; and by the time he pushed open the change-house door, he seemed to be half carrying me. The maid appeared surprised (as well she might be) at our speedy return; but Alan had no words to spare for her in explanation, helped me to a chair, called for a tass of brandy with which he fed me in little sips, and then breaking up the bread and cheese helped me to eat it like a nursery-lass; the whole with that grave, concerned, affectionate countenance, that might have imposed upon a judge. It was small wonder if the maid were taken with the picture we presented, of a poor, sick, overwrought lad and his most tender comrade. She drew quite near, and stood leaning with her back on the next table.

"What's like wrong with him?" said she at last.

Alan turned upon her, to my great wonder, with a kind of fury. "Wrong?" cries he. "He's walked more hundreds of miles than he has hairs upon his chin, and slept oftener in wet heather than dry sheets. Wrong, quo' she! Wrong enough, I would think! Wrong, indeed!" and he kept grumbling to himself as he fed me, like a man ill-pleased.

"He's young for the like of that," said the maid.

"Ower young," said Alan, with his back to her.

"He would be better riding," says she.

"And where could I get a horse to him?" cried Alan, turning on her with the same appearance of fury. "Would ye have me steal?"

I thought this roughness would have sent her off in dudgeon, as indeed it closed her mouth for the time. But my companion knew very well what he was doing; and for as simple as he was in some things of life, had a great fund of roguishness in such affairs as these.

"Ye neednae tell me," she said at last—"ye're gentry."

"Well," said Alan, softened a little (I believe against his will) by this artless comment, "and suppose we were? Did ever you hear that gentrice put money in folk's pockets?"

She sighed at this, as if she were herself some disinherited great lady. "No," says she, "that's true indeed."

I was all this while chafing at the part I played, and sitting tongue-tied between shame and merriment; but somehow at this I could hold in no longer, and bade Alan let me be, for I was better already. My voice stuck in my throat, for I ever hated to take part in lies; but my very embarrassment helped on the plot, for the lass no doubt set down my husky voice to sickness and fatigue.

"Has he nae friends?" said she, in a tearful voice.

"That has he so!" cried Alan, "if we could but win to them!—friends and rich friends, beds to lie in, food to eat, doctors to see to him—and here he must tramp in the dubs and sleep in the heather like a beggarman."

"And why that?" says the lass.

"My dear," said Alan, "I cannae very safely say; but I'll tell ye what I'll do instead," says he, "I'll whistle ye a bit tune." And with that he leaned pretty far over the table, and in a mere breath of a whistle, but with a wonderful pretty sentiment, gave her a few bars of "Charlie is my darling."

"Wheesht," says she, and looked over her shoulder to the door.

"That's it," said Alan.

"And him so young!" cries the lass.

"He's old enough to——" and Alan struck his forefinger on the back part of his neck, meaning that I was old enough to lose my head.

"It would be a black shame," she cried, flushing high.

"It's what will be, though," said Alan, "unless we manage the better."

At this the lass turned and ran out of that part of the house, leaving us alone together. Alan in high good humour at the furthering of his schemes, and I in bitter dudgeon at being called a Jacobite and treated like a child.

"Alan," I cried, "I can stand no more of this."

"Ye'll have to sit it then, Davie," said he. "For if ye upset the pot now, ye may scrape your own life out of the fire, but Alan Breck is a dead man."

This was so true that I could only groan; and even my groan served Alan's purpose, for it was overheard by the lass as she came flying in again with a dish of white puddings and a bottle of strong ale.

"Poor lamb!" says she, and had no sooner set the meat before us, than she touched me on the shoulder with a little friendly touch, as much as to bid me cheer up. Then she told us to fall to, and there would be no more to pay; for the inn was her own, or at least her father's, and he was gone for the day to Pittencrieff. We waited for no second bidding, for bread and cheese is but cold comfort and the puddings smelt excellently well; and while we sat and ate, she took up that same place by the next table, looking on, and thinking, and frowning to herself, and drawing the string of her apron through her hand.

"I'm thinking ye have rather a long tongue," she said at last to Alan.

"Ay" said Alan; "but ye see I ken the folk I speak to."

"I would never betray ye," said she, "if ye mean that."

"No," said he, "ye're not that kind. But I'll tell ye what ye would do, ye would help."

"I couldnae," said she, shaking her head. "Na, I couldnae."

"No," said he, "but if ye could?"

She answered him nothing.

"Look here, my lass," said Alan, "there are boats in the Kingdom of Fife, for I saw two (no less) upon the beach, as I came in by your town's end. Now if we could have the use of a boat to pass under cloud of night into Lothian, and some secret, decent kind of a man to bring that boat back again and keep his counsel, there would be two souls saved—mine to all likelihood —his to a dead surety. If we lack that boat, we have but three shillings left in this wide world; and where to go, and how to do, and what other place there is for us except the chains of a gibbet—I give you my naked word, I kenna! Shall we go wanting, lassie? Are ye to lie in your warm bed and think upon us, when the wind gowls in the chimney and the rain tirls on the roof? Are ye to eat your meat by the cheeks of a red fire, and think upon this poor sick lad of mine, biting his finger ends on a blae muir for cauld and hunger? Sick or sound, he must aye be moving; with the death grapple at his throat he must aye be trailing in the rain on the lang roads; and when he gants his last on a rickle of cauld stanes, there will be nae friends near him but only me and God."

At this appeal, I could see the lass was in great trouble of mind, being tempted to help us, and yet in some fear she might be helping malefactors; and so now I determined to step in myself and to allay her scruples with a portion of the truth.

"Did ever you hear," said I, "of Mr. Rankeillor of the Ferry?"

"Rankeillor the writer?" said she. "I daur say that!"

"Well," said I, "it's to his door that I am bound, so you may judge by that if I am an ill-doer; and I will tell you more, that though I am indeed, by a dreadful error, in some peril of my life, King George has no truer friend in all Scotland than myself."

Her face cleared up mightily at this, although Alan's darkened.

"That's more than I would ask," said she. "Mr. Rankeillor is a kennt man." And she bade us finish our meat, get clear of the clachan as soon as might be, and lie close in the bit wood on the sea-beach. "And ye can trust me," says she, "I'll find some means to put you over."

At this we waited for no more, but shook hands with her upon the bargain, made short work of the puddings, and set forth again from Limekilns as far as to the wood. It was a small piece of perhaps a score of elders and hawthorns and a few young ashes, not thick enough to veil us from passersby upon the road or beach. Here we must lie, however, making the best of the brave warm weather and the good hopes we now had of a deliverance, and planing more particularly what remained for us to do.

We had but one trouble all day; when a strolling piper came and sat in the same wood with us; a red-nosed, bleareyed, drunken dog, with a great bottle of whisky in his pocket, and a long story of wrongs that had been done him by all sorts of persons, from the Lord President of the Court of Session, who had denied him justice, down to the Bailies of Inverkeithing who had given him more of it than he desired. It was impossible but he should conceive some suspicion of two men lying all day concealed in a thicket and having no business to allege. As long as he stayed there he kept us in hot water with prying questions; and after he was gone, as he was a man not very likely to hold his tongue, we were in the greater impatience to be gone ourselves.

The day came to an end with the same brightness; the night fell quiet and clear; lights came out in houses and hamlets and then, one after another, began to be put out; but it was past eleven, and we were long since strangely tortured with anxieties, before we heard the grinding of oars upon the rowing-pins. At that, we looked out and saw the lass herself coming rowing to us in a boat. She had trusted no one with our affairs, not even her sweetheart, if she had one; but as soon as her father was asleep, had left the house by a window, stolen a neighbour's boat, and come to our assistance single-handed.

I was abashed how to find expression for my thanks; but she was no less abashed at the thought of hearing them; begged us to lose no time and to hold our peace, saying (very properly) that the heart of our matter was in haste and silence; and so, what with one thing and another, she had set us on the Lothian shore not far from Carriden, had shaken hands with us, and was out again at sea and rowing for Limekilns, before there was one word said either of her service or our gratitude.

Even after she was gone, we had nothing to say, as indeed nothing was enough for such a kindness. Only Alan stood a great while upon the shore shaking his head.

"It is a very fine lass," he said at last. "David, it is a very fine lass." And a matter of an hour later, as we were lying in a den on the sea-shore and I had been already dozing, he broke out again in commendations of her character. For my part, I could say nothing, she was so simple a creature that my heart smote me both with remorse and fear: remorse because we had traded upon her ignorance; and fear lest we should have anyway involved her in the dangers of our situation.

27

I COME TO MR. RANKEILLOR

The next day it was agreed that Alan should fend for himself till sunset; but as soon as it began to grow dark, he should lie in the fields by the roadside near to Newhalls, and stir for naught until he heard me whistling. At first I proposed I should give him for a signal the "Bonnie House of Airlie," which was a favourite of mine; but he objected that as the piece was very commonly known, any ploughman might whistle it by accident; and taught me instead a little fragment of a Highland air, which has run in my head from that day to this, and will likely run in my head when I lie dying. Every time it comes to me, it takes me off to that last day of my uncertainty, with Alan sitting up in the bottom of the den, whistling and beating the measure with a finger, and the grey of the dawn coming on his face.

I was in the long street of Queensferry before the sun was up. It was a fairly built burgh, the houses of good stone, many slated; the town-hall not so fine, I thought, as that of Peebles, nor yet the street so noble; but take it altogether, it put me to shame for my foul tatters.

As the morning went on, and the fires began to be kindled, and the windows to open, and the people to appear out of the houses, my concern and despondency grew ever the blacker. I saw now that I had no grounds to stand upon; and no clear proof of my rights, nor so much as of my own identity. If it was all a bubble, I was indeed sorely cheated and left in a sore pass. Even if things were as I conceived, it would in all likelihood take time to establish my contentions; and what time had I to spare with less than three shillings in my pocket, and a condemned, hunted man upon my hands to ship out of the country? Truly, if my hope broke with me, it might come to the gallows yet for both of us. And as I continued to walk up and down, and saw people looking askance at me upon the street or out of windows, and nudging or speaking one to another with smiles, I began to take a fresh apprehension: that it might be no easy matter even to come to speech of the lawyer, far less to convince him of my story.

For the life of me I could not muster up the courage to address any of these reputable burghers; I thought shame even to speak with them in such a pickle of rags and dirt; and if I had asked for the house of such a man as Mr. Rankeillor, I suppose they would have burst out laughing in my face. So I went up and down, and through the street, and down to the harbour-side, like a dog that has lost its master, with a strange gnawing in my inwards, and every now and then a movement of despair. It grew to be high day at last, perhaps nine in the forenoon; and I was worn with these wanderings, and chanced to have stopped in front of a very good house on the landward side, a house with beautiful, clear glass windows, flowering knots upon the sills, the walls new-harled (*newly rough-cast*) and a chase-dog sitting yawning on the step like one that was at home. Well, I was even envying this dumb brute, when the door fell open and there issued forth a shrewd, ruddy, kindly, consequential man in a well-powdered wig and spectacles. I was in such a plight that no one set eyes on me once, but he looked at me again; and this gentleman, as it proved, was so much struck with my poor appearance that he came straight up to me and asked me what I did.

I told him I was come to the Queensferry on business, and taking heart of grace, asked him to direct me to the house of Mr. Rankeillor.

"Why," said he, "that is his house that I have just come out of; and for a rather singular chance, I am that very man."

"Then, sir," said I, "I have to beg the favour of an interview."

"I do not know your name," said he, "nor yet your face."

"My name is David Balfour," said I.

"David Balfour?" he repeated, in rather a high tone, like one surprised. "And where have you come from, Mr. David Balfour?" he asked, looking me pretty drily in the face.

"I have come from a great many strange places, sir," said I; "but I think it would be as well to tell you where and how in a more private manner."

He seemed to muse awhile, holding his lip in his hand, and looking now at me and now upon the causeway of the street.

"Yes," says he, "that will be the best, no doubt." And he led me back with him into his house, cried out to some one whom I could not see that he would be engaged all morning, and brought me into a little dusty chamber full of books and documents. Here he sate down, and bade me be seated; though I thought he looked a little ruefully from his clean chair to my muddy rags. "And now," says he, "if you have any business, pray be brief and come swiftly to the point. Nec gemino bellum Trojanum oritur ab ovo—do you understand that?" says he, with a keen look.

"I will even do as Horace says, sir," I answered, smiling, "and carry you in medias res." He nodded as if he was well pleased, and indeed his scrap of Latin had been set to test me. For all that, and though I was somewhat encouraged, the blood came in my face when I added: "I have reason to believe myself some rights on the estate of Shaws."

He got a paper book out of a drawer and set it before him open. "Well?" said he.

But I had shot my bolt and sat speechless.

"Come, come, Mr. Balfour," said he, "you must continue. Where were you born?"

"In Essendean, sir," said I, "the year 1733, the 12th of March."

He seemed to follow this statement in his paper book; but what that meant I knew not. "Your father and mother?" said he.

"My father was Alexander Balfour, schoolmaster of that place," said I, "and my mother Grace Pitarrow; I think her people were from Angus."

"Have you any papers proving your identity?" asked Mr. Rankeillor.

"No, sir," said I, "but they are in the hands of Mr. Campbell, the minister, and could be readily produced. Mr. Campbell, too, would give me his word; and for that matter, I do not think my uncle would deny me."

"Meaning Mr. Ebenezer Balfour?" says he.

"The same," said I.

"Whom you have seen?" he asked.

"By whom I was received into his own house," I answered.

"Did you ever meet a man of the name of Hoseason?" asked Mr. Rankeillor.

"I did so, sir, for my sins," said I; "for it was by his means and the procurement of my uncle, that I was kidnapped within sight of this town, carried to sea, suffered shipwreck and a hundred other hardships, and stand before you to-day in this poor accoutrement."

"You say you were shipwrecked," said Rankeillor; "where was that?"

"Off the south end of the Isle of Mull," said I. "The name of the isle on which I was cast up is the Island Earraid."

"Ah!" says he, smiling, "you are deeper than me in the geography. But so far, I may tell you, this agrees pretty exactly with other informations that I hold. But you say you were kidnapped; in what sense?"

"In the plain meaning of the word, sir," said I. "I was on my way to your house, when I was trepanned on board the brig, cruelly struck down, thrown below, and knew no more of anything till we were far at sea. I was destined for the plantations; a fate that, in God's providence, I have escaped."

"The brig was lost on June the 27th," says he, looking in his book, "and we are now at August the 24th. Here is a considerable hiatus, Mr. Balfour, of near upon two months. It has already caused a vast amount of trouble to your friends; and I own I shall not be very well contented until it is set right."

"Indeed, sir," said I, "these months are very easily filled up; but yet before I told my story, I would be glad to know that I was talking to a friend."

"This is to argue in a circle," said the lawyer. "I cannot be convinced till I have heard you. I cannot be your friend till I am properly informed. If you were more trustful, it would better befit your time of life. And you know, Mr. Balfour, we have a proverb in the country that evil-doers are aye evil-dreaders."

"You are not to forget, sir," said I, "that I have already suffered by my trustfulness; and was shipped off to be a slave by the very man that (if I rightly understand) is your employer?"

All this while I had been gaining ground with Mr. Rankeillor, and in proportion as I gained ground, gaining confidence. But at this sally, which I made with something of a smile myself, he fairly laughed aloud.

"No, no," said he, "it is not so bad as that. Fui, non sum. I was indeed your uncle's man of business; but while you (imberbis juvenis custode remoto) were gallivanting in the west, a good deal of water has run under the bridges; and if your ears did not sing, it was not for lack of being talked about. On the very day of your sea disaster, Mr. Campbell stalked into my office, demanding you from all the winds. I had never heard of your existence; but I had known your father; and from matters in my competence (to be touched upon hereafter) I was disposed to fear the worst. Mr. Ebenezer admitted having seen you; declared (what seemed improbable) that he had given you considerable sums; and that you had started for the continent of Europe, intending to fulfil your education, which was probable and praiseworthy. Interrogated how you had come to send no word to Mr. Campbell, he deponed that you had expressed a great desire to break with your past life. Further interrogated where you now were, protested ignorance, but believed you were in Leyden. That is a close sum of his replies. I am not exactly sure that any one believed him," continued Mr. Rankeillor with a smile; "and in particular he so much disrelished me expressions of mine that (in a word) he showed me to the door. We were then at a full stand; for whatever shrewd suspicions we might entertain, we had no shadow of probation. In the very article, comes Captain

Hoseason with the story of your drowning; whereupon all fell through; with no consequences but concern to Mr. Campbell, injury to my pocket, and another blot upon your uncle's character, which could very ill afford it. And now, Mr. Balfour," said he, "you understand the whole process of these matters, and can judge for yourself to what extent I may be trusted."

Indeed he was more pedantic than I can represent him, and placed more scraps of Latin in his speech; but it was all uttered with a fine geniality of eye and manner which went far to conquer my distrust. Moreover, I could see he now treated me as if I was myself beyond a doubt; so that first point of my identity seemed fully granted.

"Sir," said I, "if I tell you my story, I must commit a friend's life to your discretion. Pass me your word it shall be sacred; and for what touches myself, I will ask no better guarantee than just your face."

He passed me his word very seriously. "But," said he, "these are rather alarming prolocutions; and if there are in your story any little jostles to the law, I would beg you to bear in mind that I am a lawyer, and pass lightly."

Thereupon I told him my story from the first, he listening with his spectacles thrust up and his eyes closed, so that I sometimes feared he was asleep. But no such matter! he heard every word (as I found afterward) with such quickness of hearing and precision of memory as often surprised me. Even strange outlandish Gaelic names, heard for that time only, he remembered and would remind me of, years after. Yet when I called Alan Breck in full, we had an odd scene. The name of Alan had of course rung through Scotland, with the news of the Appin murder and the offer of the reward; and it had no sooner escaped me than the lawyer moved in his seat and opened his eyes.

"I would name no unnecessary names, Mr. Balfour," said he; "above all of Highlanders, many of whom are obnoxious to the law."

"Well, it might have been better not," said I, "but since I have let it slip, I may as well continue."

"Not at all," said Mr. Rankeillor. "I am somewhat dull of hearing, as you may have remarked; and I am far from sure I caught the name exactly. We will call your friend, if you please, Mr. Thomson—that there may be no reflections. And in future, I would take some such way with any Highlander that you may have to mention—dead or alive."

By this, I saw he must have heard the name all too clearly, and had already guessed I might be coming to the murder. If he chose to play this part of ignorance, it was no matter of mine; so I smiled, said it was no very Highland-sounding name, and consented. Through all the rest of my story Alan was Mr. Thomson; which amused me the more, as it was a piece of policy after his own heart. James Stewart, in like manner, was mentioned under the style of Mr. Thomson's kinsman; Colin Campbell passed as a Mr. Glen; and to Cluny, when I came to that part of my tale, I gave the name of "Mr. Jameson, a Highland chief." It was truly the most open farce, and I wondered that the lawyer should care to keep it up; but, after all, it was quite in the taste of that age, when there were two parties in the state, and quiet persons, with no very high opinions of their own, sought out every cranny to avoid offence to either.

"Well, well," said the lawyer, when I had quite done, "this is a great epic, a great Odyssey of yours. You must tell it, sir, in a sound Latinity when your scholarship is riper; or in English if you please, though for my part I prefer the stronger tongue. You have rolled much; quae regio in terris—what parish in Scotland (to make a homely translation) has not been filled with your wanderings? You have shown, besides, a singular aptitude for getting into false positions; and, yes, upon the whole, for behaving well in them. This Mr. Thomson seems to me a gentleman of some choice qualities, though perhaps a trifle bloody-minded. It would please me none the worse, if (with all his merits) he were soused in the North Sea, for the man, Mr. David, is a sore embarrassment. But you are doubtless quite right to adhere to him; indubitably, he adhered to you. It comes—we may say—he was your true companion; nor less paribus curis vestigia figit, for I dare say you would both take an orra thought upon the gallows. Well, well, these days are fortunately by; and I think (speaking humanly) that you are near the end of your troubles."

As he thus moralised on my adventures, he looked upon me with so much humour and benignity that I could scarce contain my satisfaction. I had been so long wandering with lawless people, and making my bed upon the hills and under the bare sky, that to sit once more in a clean, covered house, and to talk amicably with a gentleman in broadcloth, seemed mighty elevations. Even as I thought so, my eye fell on my unseemly tatters, and I was once more plunged in confusion. But the lawyer saw and understood me. He rose, called over the stair to lay another plate, for Mr. Balfour would stay to dinner, and led me into a bedroom in the upper part of the house. Here he set before me water and soap, and a comb; and laid out some clothes that belonged to his son; and here, with another apposite tag, he left me to my toilet.

28

I GO IN QUEST OF MY INHERITANCE

I made what change I could in my appearance; and blithe was I to look in the glass and find the beggarman a thing of the past, and David Balfour come to life again. And yet I was ashamed of the change too, and, above all, of the borrowed clothes. When I had done, Mr. Rankeillor caught me on the stair, made me his compliments, and had me again into the cabinet.

"Sit ye down, Mr. David," said he, "and now that you are looking a little more like yourself, let me see if I can find you any news. You will be wondering, no doubt, about your father and your uncle? To be sure it is a singular tale; and the explanation is one that I blush to have to offer you. For," says he, really with embarrassment, "the matter hinges on a love affair."

"Truly," said I, "I cannot very well join that notion with my uncle."

"But your uncle, Mr. David, was not always old," replied the lawyer, "and what may perhaps surprise you more, not always ugly. He had a fine, gallant air; people stood in their doors to look after him, as he went by upon a mettle horse. I have seen it with these eyes, and I ingenuously confess, not altogether without envy; for I was a plain lad myself and a plain man's son; and in those days it was a case of Odi te, qui bellus es, Sabelle."

"It sounds like a dream," said I.

"Ay, ay," said the lawyer, "that is how it is with youth and age. Nor was that all, but he had a spirit of his own that seemed to promise great things in the future. In 1715, what must he do but run away to join the rebels? It was your father that pursued him, found him in a ditch, and brought him back multum gementem; to the mirth of the whole country. However, majora canamus—the two lads fell in love, and that with the same lady. Mr. Ebenezer, who was the admired and the beloved, and the spoiled one, made, no doubt, mighty certain of the victory; and when he found he had deceived himself, screamed like a peacock. The whole country heard of it; now he lay sick at home, with his silly family standing round the bed in tears; now he rode from public-house to public-house, and shouted his sorrows into the lug of Tom, Dick, and Harry. Your father, Mr. David, was a kind gentleman; but he was weak, dolefully weak; took all this folly with a long countenance; and one day—by your leave!—

resigned the lady. She was no such fool, however; it's from her you must inherit your excellent good sense; and she refused to be bandied from one to another. Both got upon their knees to her; and the upshot of the matter for that while was that she showed both of them the door. That was in August; dear me! the same year I came from college. The scene must have been highly farcical."

I thought myself it was a silly business, but I could not forget my father had a hand in it. "Surely, sir, it had some note of tragedy," said I.

"Why, no, sir, not at all," returned the lawyer. "For tragedy implies some ponderable matter in dispute, some dignus vindice nodus; and this piece of work was all about the petulance of a young ass that had been spoiled, and wanted nothing so much as to be tied up and soundly belted. However, that was not your father's view; and the end of it was, that from concession to concession on your father's part, and from one height to another of squalling, sentimental selfishness upon your uncle's, they came at last to drive a sort of bargain, from whose ill results you have recently been smarting. The one man took the lady, the other the estate. Now, Mr. David, they talk a great deal of charity and generosity; but in this disputable state of life, I often think the happiest consequences seem to flow when a gentleman consults his lawyer, and takes all the law allows him. Anyhow, this piece of Quixotry on your father's part, as it was unjust in itself, has brought forth a monstrous family of injustices. Your father and mother lived and died poor folk; you were poorly reared; and in the meanwhile, what a time it has been for the tenants on the estate of Shaws! And I might add (if it was a matter I cared much about) what a time for Mr. Ebenezer!"

"And yet that is certainly the strangest part of all," said I, "that a man's nature should thus change."

"True," said Mr. Rankeillor. "And yet I imagine it was natural enough. He could not think that he had played a handsome part. Those who knew the story gave him the cold shoulder; those who knew it not, seeing one brother disappear, and the other succeed in the estate, raised a cry of murder; so that upon all sides he found himself evited. Money was all he got by his bargain; well, he came to think the more of money. He was selfish when he was young, he is selfish now that he is old; and the latter end of all these pretty manners and fine feelings you have seen for yourself."

"Well, sir," said I, "and in all this, what is my position?"

"The estate is yours beyond a doubt," replied the lawyer. "It matters nothing what your father signed, you are the heir of entail. But your uncle is a man to fight the indefensible; and it would be likely your identity that he would call in question. A lawsuit is always expensive, and a family lawsuit always scandalous; besides which, if any of your doings with your friend Mr. Thomson were to come out, we might find that we had burned our fingers. The kidnapping, to be sure, would be a court card upon our side, if we could only prove it. But it may be difficult to prove; and my advice (upon the whole) is to make a very easy bargain with your uncle, perhaps even leaving him at Shaws where he has taken root for a quarter of a century, and contenting yourself in the meanwhile with a fair provision."

I told him I was very willing to be easy, and that to carry family concerns before the public was a step from which I was naturally much averse. In the meantime (thinking to myself) I began to see the outlines of that scheme on which we afterwards acted.

"The great affair," I asked, "is to bring home to him the kidnapping?"

"Surely," said Mr. Rankeillor, "and if possible, out of court. For mark you here, Mr. David: we could no doubt find some men of the Covenant who would swear to your reclusion; but once they were in the box, we could no longer check their testimony, and some word of your friend Mr. Thomson must certainly crop out. Which (from what you have let fall) I cannot think to be desirable."

"Well, sir," said I, "here is my way of it." And I opened my plot to him.

"But this would seem to involve my meeting the man Thomson?" says he, when I had done.

"I think so, indeed, sir," said I.

"Dear doctor!" cries he, rubbing his brow. "Dear doctor! No, Mr. David, I am afraid your scheme is inadmissible. I say nothing against your friend, Mr. Thomson: I know nothing against him; and if I did—mark this, Mr. David!—it would be my duty to lay hands on him. Now I put it to you: is it wise to meet? He may have matters to his charge. He may not have told you all. His name may not be even Thomson!" cries the lawyer, twinkling; "for some of these fellows will pick up names by the roadside as another would gather haws."

"You must be the judge, sir," said I.

But it was clear my plan had taken hold upon his fancy, for he kept musing to himself till we were called to dinner and the company of Mrs. Rankeillor; and that lady had scarce left us again to ourselves and a bottle of wine, ere he was back harping on my proposal. When and where was I to meet my friend Mr. Thomson; was I sure of Mr. T.'s discretion; supposing we could catch the old fox tripping, would I consent to such and such a term of an agreement—these and the like questions he kept asking at long intervals, while he thoughtfully rolled his wine upon his tongue. When I had answered all of them, seemingly to his contentment, he fell into a still deeper muse, even the claret being now forgotten. Then he got a sheet of paper and a pencil, and set to work writing and weighing every word; and at last touched a bell and had his clerk into the chamber.

"Torrance," said he, "I must have this written out fair against to-night; and when it is done, you will be so kind as put on your hat and be ready to come along with this gentleman and me, for you will probably be wanted as a witness."

"What, sir," cried I, as soon as the clerk was gone, "are you to venture it?"

"Why, so it would appear," says he, filling his glass. "But let us speak no more of business. The very sight of Torrance brings in my head a little droll matter of some years ago, when I had made a tryst with the poor oaf at the cross of Edinburgh. Each had gone his proper errand; and when it came four o'clock, Torrance had been taking a glass and did not know his master, and I, who had forgot my spectacles, was so blind without them, that I give you my word I did not know my own clerk." And thereupon he laughed heartily.

I said it was an odd chance, and smiled out of politeness; but what held me all the afternoon in wonder, he kept returning and dwelling on this story, and telling it again with fresh details and laughter; so that I began at last to be quite put out of countenance and feel ashamed for my friend's folly.

Towards the time I had appointed with Alan, we set out from the house, Mr. Rankeillor and I arm in arm, and Torrance following behind with the deed in his pocket and a covered basket in his hand. All through the town, the lawyer was bowing right and left, and continually being button-holed by gentlemen on matters of burgh or private business; and I could see he was one greatly looked up to in the county. At last we were clear of the houses, and began to go along the side of the haven and towards the Hawes Inn and the Ferry pier, the scene of my misfortune. I could not look upon the place without emotion, recalling how many that had been there with me that day were now no more: Ransome taken, I could hope, from the evil to come; Shuan passed where I dared not follow him; and the poor souls that had gone down with the brig in her last plunge. All these, and the brig herself, I had outlived; and come through these hardships and fearful perils without scath. My only thought should have been of gratitude; and yet I could not behold the place without sorrow for others and a chill of recollected fear.

I was so thinking when, upon a sudden, Mr. Rankeillor cried out, clapped his hand to his pockets, and began to laugh.

"Why," he cries, "if this be not a farcical adventure! After all that I said, I have forgot my glasses!"

At that, of course, I understood the purpose of his anecdote, and knew that if he had left his spectacles at home, it had been done on purpose, so that he might have the benefit of Alan's help without the awkwardness of recognising him. And indeed it was well thought upon; for now (suppose things to go the very worst) how could Rankeillor swear to my friend's identity, or how be made to bear damaging evidence against myself? For all that, he had been a long while of finding out his want, and had spoken to and recognised a good few persons as we came through the town; and I had little doubt myself that he saw reasonably well.

As soon as we were past the Hawes (where I recognised the landlord smoking his pipe in the door, and was amazed to see him look no older) Mr. Rankeillor changed the order of march, walking behind with Torrance and sending me forward in the manner of a scout. I went up the hill, whistling from time to time my Gaelic air; and at length I had the pleasure to hear it answered and to see Alan rise from behind a bush. He was somewhat dashed in spirits, having passed a long day alone skulking in the county, and made but a poor meal in an alehouse near Dundas. But at the mere sight of my clothes, he began to brighten up; and as soon as I had told him in what a forward state our matters were and the part I looked to him to play in what remained, he sprang into a new man.

"And that is a very good notion of yours," says he; "and I dare to say that you could lay your hands upon no better man to put it through than Alan Breck. It is not a thing (mark ye) that any one could do, but takes a gentleman of penetration. But it sticks in my head your lawyer-man will be somewhat wearying to see me," says Alan.

Accordingly I cried and waved on Mr. Rankeillor, who came up alone and was presented to my friend, Mr. Thomson.

"Mr. Thomson, I am pleased to meet you," said he. "But I have forgotten my glasses; and our friend, Mr. David here" (clapping me on the shoulder), "will tell you that I am little better than blind, and that you must not be surprised if I pass you by to-morrow."

This he said, thinking that Alan would be pleased; but the Highlandman's vanity was ready to startle at a less matter than that.

"Why, sir," says he, stiffly, "I would say it mattered the less as we are met here for a particular end, to see justice done to Mr. Balfour; and by what I can see, not very likely to have much else in common. But I accept your apology, which was a very proper one to make."

"And that is more than I could look for, Mr. Thomson," said Rankeillor, heartily. "And now as you and I are the chief actors in this enterprise, I think we should come into a nice agreement; to which end, I propose that you should lend me your arm, for (what with the dusk and the want of my glasses) I am not very clear as to the path; and as for you, Mr. David, you will find Torrance a pleasant kind of body to speak with. Only let me remind you, it's quite needless he should hear more of your adventures or those of—ahem—Mr. Thomson."

Accordingly these two went on ahead in very close talk, and Torrance and I brought up the rear.

Night was quite come when we came in view of the house of Shaws. Ten had been gone some time; it was dark and mild, with a pleasant, rustling wind in the south-west that covered the sound of our approach; and as we drew near we saw no glimmer of light in any portion of the building. It seemed my uncle was already in bed, which was indeed the best thing for our arrangements. We made our last whispered consultations some fifty yards away; and then the lawyer and Torrance and I crept quietly up and crouched down beside the corner of the house; and as soon as we were in our places, Alan strode to the door without concealment and began to knock.

29

I COME INTO MY KINGDOM

For some time Alan volleyed upon the door, and his knocking only roused the echoes of the house and neighbourhood. At last, however, I could hear the noise of a window gently thrust up, and knew that my uncle had come to his observatory. By what light there was, he would see Alan standing, like a dark shadow, on the steps; the three witnesses were hidden quite out of his view; so that there was nothing to alarm an honest man in his own house. For all that, he studied his visitor awhile in silence, and when he spoke his voice had a quaver of misgiving.

"What's this?" says he. "This is nae kind of time of night for decent folk; and I hae nae trokings (*dealings*) wi' night-hawks. What brings ye here? I have a blunderbush."

"Is that yoursel', Mr. Balfour?" returned Alan, stepping back and looking up into the darkness. "Have a care of that blunderbuss; they're nasty things to burst."

"What brings ye here? and whae are ye?" says my uncle, angrily.

"I have no manner of inclination to rowt out my name to the country-side," said Alan; "but what brings me here is another story, being more of your affair than mine; and if ye're sure it's what ye would like, I'll set it to a tune and sing it to you."

"And what is't?" asked my uncle.

"David," says Alan.

"What was that?" cried my uncle, in a mighty changed voice.

"Shall I give ye the rest of the name, then?" said Alan.

There was a pause; and then, "I'm thinking I'll better let ye in," says my uncle, doubtfully.

"I dare say that," said Alan; "but the point is, Would I go? Now I will tell you what I am thinking. I am thinking that it is here upon this doorstep that we must confer upon this business; and it shall be here or nowhere at all whatever; for I would have you to understand that I am as stiffnecked as yoursel', and a gentleman of better family."

This change of note disconcerted Ebenezer; he was a little while digesting it, and then says he, "Weel, weel, what must be must," and shut the window. But it took him a long time to get down-stairs, and a still longer to undo the fastenings, repenting (I dare say) and taken with fresh claps of fear at every second step and every bolt and bar. At last, however, we heard the creak of the hinges, and it seems my uncle slipped gingerly out and (seeing that Alan had stepped back a pace or two) sate him down on the top doorstep with the blunderbuss ready in his hands.

"And, now" says he, "mind I have my blunderbush, and if ye take a step nearer ye're as good as deid."

"And a very civil speech," says Alan, "to be sure."

"Na," says my uncle, "but this is no a very chanty kind of a proceeding, and I'm bound to be prepared. And now that we understand each other, ye'll can name your business."

"Why," says Alan, "you that are a man of so much understanding, will doubtless have perceived that I am a Hieland gentleman. My name has nae business in my story; but the county of my friends is no very far from the Isle of Mull, of which ye will have heard. It seems there was a ship lost in those parts; and the next day a gentleman of my family was seeking wreck-wood for his fire along the sands, when he came upon a lad that was half drowned. Well, he brought him to; and he and some other gentleman took and clapped him in an auld, ruined castle, where from that day to this he has been a great expense to my friends. My friends are a wee wild-like, and not so particular about the law as some that I could name; and finding that the lad owned some decent folk, and was your born nephew, Mr. Balfour, they asked me to give ye a bit call and confer upon the matter. And I may tell ye at the off-go, unless we can agree upon some terms, ye are little likely to set eyes upon him. For my friends," added Alan, simply, "are no very well off."

My uncle cleared his throat. "I'm no very caring," says he. "He wasnae a good lad at the best of it, and I've nae call to interfere."

"Ay, ay," said Alan, "I see what ye would be at: pretending ye don't care, to make the ransom smaller."

"Na," said my uncle, "it's the mere truth. I take nae manner of interest in the lad, and I'll pay nae ransome, and ye can make a kirk and a mill of him for what I care."

"Hoot, sir," says Alan. "Blood's thicker than water, in the deil's name! Ye cannae desert your brother's son for the fair shame of it; and if ye did, and it came to be kennt, ye wouldnae be very popular in your country-side, or I'm the more deceived."

"I'm no just very popular the way it is," returned Ebenezer; "and I dinnae see how it would come to be kennt. No by me, onyway; nor yet by you or your friends. So that's idle talk, my buckie," says he.

"Then it'll have to be David that tells it," said Alan.

"How that?" says my uncle, sharply.

"Ou, just this way," says Alan. "My friends would doubtless keep your nephew as long as there was any likelihood of siller to be made of it, but if there was nane, I am clearly of opinion they would let him gang where he pleased, and be damned to him!"

"Ay, but I'm no very caring about that either," said my uncle. "I wouldnae be muckle made up with that."

"I was thinking that," said Alan.

"And what for why?" asked Ebenezer.

"Why, Mr. Balfour," replied Alan, "by all that I could hear, there were two ways of it: either ye liked David and would pay to get him back; or else ye had very good reasons for not wanting him, and would pay for us to keep him. It seems it's not the first; well then, it's the second; and blythe am I to ken it, for it should be a pretty penny in my pocket and the pockets of my friends."

"I dinnae follow ye there," said my uncle.

"No?" said Alan. "Well, see here: you dinnae want the lad back; well, what do ye want done with him, and how much will ye pay?"

My uncle made no answer, but shifted uneasily on his seat.

"Come, sir," cried Alan. "I would have you to ken that I am a gentleman; I bear a king's name; I am nae rider to kick my shanks at your hall door. Either give me an answer in civility, and that out of hand; or by the top of Glencoe, I will ram three feet of iron through your vitals."

"Eh, man," cried my uncle, scrambling to his feet, "give me a meenit! What's like wrong with ye? I'm just a plain man and nae dancing master; and I'm tryin to be as ceevil as it's morally possible. As for that wild talk, it's fair disreputable. Vitals, says you! And where would I be with my blunderbush?" he snarled.

"Powder and your auld hands are but as the snail to the swallow against the bright steel in the hands of Alan," said the other. "Before your jottering finger could find the trigger, the hilt would dirl on your breast-bane."

"Eh, man, whae's denying it?" said my uncle. "Pit it as ye please, hae't your ain way; I'll do naething to cross ye. Just tell me what like ye'll be wanting, and ye'll see that we'll can agree fine."

"Troth, sir," said Alan, "I ask for nothing but plain dealing. In two words: do ye want the lad killed or kept?"

"O, sirs!" cried Ebenezer. "O, sirs, me! that's no kind of language!"

"Killed or kept!" repeated Alan.

"O, keepit, keepit!" wailed my uncle. "We'll have nae bloodshed, if you please."

"Well," says Alan, "as ye please; that'll be the dearer."

"The dearer?" cries Ebenezer. "Would ye fyle your hands wi' crime?"

"Hoot!" said Alan, "they're baith crime, whatever! And the killing's easier, and quicker, and surer. Keeping the lad'll be a fashious (*troublesome*) job, a fashious, kittle business."

"I'll have him keepit, though," returned my uncle. "I never had naething to do with onything morally wrong; and I'm no gaun to begin to pleasure a wild Hielandman."

"Ye're unco scrupulous," sneered Alan.

"I'm a man o' principle," said Ebenezer, simply; "and if I have to pay for it, I'll have to pay for it. And besides," says he, "ye forget the lad's my brother's son."

"Well, well," said Alan, "and now about the price. It's no very easy for me to set a name upon it; I would first have to ken some small matters. I would have to ken, for instance, what ye gave Hoseason at the first off-go?"

"Hoseason!" cries my uncle, struck aback. "What for?"

"For kidnapping David," says Alan.

"It's a lee, it's a black lee!" cried my uncle. "He was never kidnapped. He leed in his throat that tauld ye that. Kidnapped? He never was!"

"That's no fault of mine nor yet of yours," said Alan; "nor yet of Hoseason's, if he's a man that can be trusted."

"What do ye mean?" cried Ebenezer. "Did Hoseason tell ye?"

"Why, ye donnered auld runt, how else would I ken?" cried Alan. "Hoseason and me are partners; we gang shares; so ye can see for yoursel' what good ye can do leeing. And I must plainly say ye drove a fool's bargain when ye let a man like the sailor-man so far forward in your private matters. But that's past praying for; and ye must lie on your bed the way ye made it. And the point in hand is just this: what did ye pay him?"

"Has he tauld ye himsel'?" asked my uncle.

"That's my concern," said Alan.

"Weel," said my uncle, "I dinnae care what he said, he leed, and the solemn God's truth is this, that I gave him twenty pound. But I'll be perfec'ly honest with ye: forby that, he was to have the selling of the lad in Caroliny, whilk would be as muckle mair, but no from my pocket, ye see."

"Thank you, Mr. Thomson. That will do excellently well," said the lawyer, stepping forward; and then mighty civilly, "Good-evening, Mr. Balfour," said he.

And, "Good-evening, Uncle Ebenezer," said I.

And, "It's a braw nicht, Mr. Balfour," added Torrance.

Never a word said my uncle, neither black nor white; but just sat where he was on the top door-step and stared upon us like a man turned to stone. Alan filched away his blunderbuss; and the lawyer, taking him by the arm, plucked him up from the doorstep, led him into the kitchen, whither we all followed, and set him down in a chair beside the hearth, where the fire was out and only a rush-light burning.

There we all looked upon him for a while, exulting greatly in our success, but yet with a sort of pity for the man's shame.

"Come, come, Mr. Ebenezer," said the lawyer, "you must not be down-hearted, for I promise you we shall make easy terms. In the meanwhile give us the cellar key, and Torrance shall draw us a bottle of your father's wine in honour of the event." Then, turning to me and taking me by the hand, "Mr. David," says he, "I wish you all joy in your good fortune, which I believe to be deserved." And then to Alan, with a spice of drollery, "Mr. Thomson, I pay you my compliment; it was most artfully conducted; but in one point you somewhat outran my comprehension. Do I understand your name to be James? or Charles? or is it George, perhaps?"

"And why should it be any of the three, sir?" quoth Alan, drawing himself up, like one who smelt an offence.

"Only, sir, that you mentioned a king's name," replied Rankeillor; "and as there has never yet been a King Thomson, or his fame at least has never come my way, I judged you must refer to that you had in baptism."

This was just the stab that Alan would feel keenest, and I am free to confess he took it very ill. Not a word would he answer, but stepped off to the far end of the kitchen, and sat down and sulked; and it was not till I stepped after him, and gave him my hand, and thanked him by title as the chief spring of my success, that he began to smile a bit, and was at last prevailed upon to join our party.

By that time we had the fire lighted, and a bottle of wine uncorked; a good supper came out of the basket, to which Torrance and I and Alan set ourselves down; while the lawyer and my uncle passed into the next chamber to consult. They stayed there closeted about an hour; at the end of which period they had come to a good understanding, and my uncle and I set our hands to the agreement in a formal manner. By the terms of this, my uncle bound himself to satisfy Rankeillor as to his intromissions, and to pay me two clear thirds of the yearly income of Shaws.

So the beggar in the ballad had come home; and when I lay down that night on the kitchen chests, I was a man of means and had a name in the country. Alan and Torrance and Rankeillor slept and snored on their hard beds; but for me who had lain out under heaven and upon dirt and stones, so many days and nights, and often with an empty belly, and in fear of death, this good change in my case unmanned me more than any of the former evil ones; and I lay till dawn, looking at the fire on the roof and planning the future.

30

GOOD-BYE

So far as I was concerned myself, I had come to port; but I had still Alan, to whom I was so much beholden, on my hands; and I felt besides a heavy charge in the matter of the murder and James of the Glens. On both these heads I unbosomed to Rankeillor the next morning, walking to and fro about six of the clock before the house of Shaws, and with nothing in view but the fields and woods that had been my ancestors' and were now mine. Even as I spoke on these grave subjects, my eye would take a glad bit of a run over the prospect, and my heart jump with pride.

About my clear duty to my friend, the lawyer had no doubt. I must help him out of the county at whatever risk; but in the case of James, he was of a different mind.

"Mr. Thomson," says he, "is one thing, Mr. Thomson's kinsman quite another. I know little of the facts, but I gather that a great noble (whom we will call, if you like, the D. of A.[1]) has some concern and is even supposed to feel some animosity in the matter. The D. of A. is doubtless an excellent nobleman; but, Mr. David, timeo qui nocuere deos. If you interfere to balk his vengeance, you should remember there is one way to shut your testimony out; and that is to put you in the dock. There, you would be in the same pickle as Mr. Thomson's kinsman. You will object that you are innocent; well, but so is he. And to be tried for your life before a Highland jury, on a Highland quarrel and with a Highland Judge upon the bench, would be a brief transition to the gallows."

Now I had made all these reasonings before and found no very good reply to them; so I put on all the simplicity I could. "In that case, sir," said I, "I would just have to be hanged—would I not?"

"My dear boy," cries he, "go in God's name, and do what you think is right. It is a poor thought that at my time of life I should be advising you to choose the safe and shameful; and I take it back with an apology. Go and do your duty; and be hanged, if you must, like a gentleman. There are worse things in the world than to be hanged."

"Not many, sir," said I, smiling.

"Why, yes, sir," he cried, "very many. And it would be ten times better for your uncle (to go no farther afield) if he were dangling decently upon a gibbet."

Thereupon he turned into the house (still in a great fervour of mind, so that I saw I had pleased him heartily) and there he wrote me two letters, making his comments on them as he wrote.

"This," says he, "is to my bankers, the British Linen Company, placing a credit to your name. Consult Mr. Thomson, he will know of ways; and you, with this credit, can supply the means. I trust you will be a good husband of your money; but in the affair of a friend like Mr. Thomson, I would be even prodigal. Then for his kinsman, there is no better way than that you should seek the Advocate, tell him your tale, and offer testimony; whether he may take it or not, is quite another matter, and will turn on the D. of A. Now, that you may reach the Lord Advocate well recommended, I give you here a letter to a namesake of your own, the learned Mr. Balfour of Pilrig, a man whom I esteem. It will look better that you should be presented by one of your own name; and the laird of Pilrig is much looked up to in the Faculty and stands well with Lord Advocate Grant. I would not trouble him, if I were you, with any particulars; and (do you know?) I think it would be needless to refer to Mr. Thomson. Form yourself upon the laird, he is a good model; when you deal with the Advocate, be discreet; and in all these matters, may the Lord guide you, Mr. David!"

Thereupon he took his farewell, and set out with Torrance for the Ferry, while Alan and I turned our faces for the city of Edinburgh. As we went by the footpath and beside the gateposts and the unfinished lodge, we kept looking back at the house of my fathers. It stood there, bare and great and smokeless, like a place not lived in; only in one of the top windows, there was the peak of a nightcap bobbing up and down and back and forward, like the head of a rabbit from a burrow. I had little welcome when I came, and less kindness while I stayed; but at least I was watched as I went away.

Alan and I went slowly forward upon our way, having little heart either to walk or speak. The same thought was uppermost in both, that we were near the time of our parting; and remembrance of all the bygone days sate upon us sorely. We talked indeed of what should be done; and it was resolved that Alan should keep to the county, biding now here, now there, but coming once in the day to a particular place where I might be able to communicate with him, either in my own person or by messenger. In the meanwhile, I was to seek out a lawyer, who was an Appin Stewart, and a man therefore to be wholly trusted; and it should be his part to find a ship and to arrange for Alan's safe embarkation. No sooner was this business done, than the words seemed to leave us; and though I would seek to jest with Alan under the name of Mr. Thomson, and he with me on my new clothes and my estate, you could feel very well that we were nearer tears than laughter.

We came the by-way over the hill of Corstorphine; and when we got near to the place called Rest-and-be-Thankful, and looked down on Corstorphine bogs and over to the city and the castle on the hill, we both stopped, for we both knew without a word said that we had come to where our ways parted. Here he repeated to me once again what had been agreed upon between us: the address of the lawyer, the daily hour at which Alan might be found, and the signals that were to be made by any that came seeking him. Then I gave what money I had (a guinea or two of Rankeillor's) so that he should not starve in the meanwhile; and then we stood a space, and looked over at Edinburgh in silence.

"Well, good-bye," said Alan, and held out his left hand.

"Good-bye," said I, and gave the hand a little grasp, and went off down hill.

Neither one of us looked the other in the face, nor so long as he was in my view did I take one back glance at the friend I was leaving. But as I went on my way to the city, I felt so lost and lonesome, that I could have found it in my heart to sit down by the dyke, and cry and weep like any baby.

It was coming near noon when I passed in by the West Kirk and the Grassmarket into the streets of the capital. The huge height of the buildings, running up to ten and fifteen storeys, the narrow arched entries that continually vomited passengers, the wares of the merchants in their windows, the hubbub and endless stir, the foul smells and the fine clothes, and a hundred other particulars too small to mention, struck me into a kind of stupor of surprise, so that I let the crowd carry me to and fro; and yet all the time what I was thinking of was Alan at Rest-and-be-Thankful; and all the time (although you would think I would not choose but be delighted with these braws and novelties) there was a cold gnawing in my inside like a remorse for something wrong.

The hand of Providence brought me in my drifting to the very doors of the British Linen Company's bank.

---

1. The Duke of Argyle.

MS. FOUND IN A BOTTLE

EDGAR ALLAN POE

MS. FOUND IN A BOTTLE

Qui n'a plus qu'un moment a vivre

N'a plus rien a dissimuler.

—Quinault—Atys.

Of my country and of my family I have little to say. Ill usage and length of years have driven me from the one, and estranged me from the other. Hereditary wealth afforded me an education of no common order, and a contemplative turn of mind enabled me to methodize the stores which early study very diligently garnered up.—Beyond all things, the study of the German moralists gave me great delight; not from any ill-advised admiration of their eloquent madness, but from the ease with which my habits of rigid thought enabled me to detect their falsities. I have often been reproached with the aridity of my genius; a deficiency of imagination has been imputed to me as a crime; and the Pyrrhonism of my opinions has at all times rendered me notorious. Indeed, a strong relish for physical philosophy has, I fear, tinctured my mind with a very common error of this age—I mean the habit of referring occurrences, even the least susceptible of such reference, to the principles of that science. Upon the whole, no person could be less liable than myself to be led away from the severe precincts of truth by the ignes fatui of superstition. I have thought proper to premise thus much, lest the incredible tale I have to tell should be considered rather the raving of a crude imagination, than the positive experience of a mind to which the reveries of fancy have been a dead letter and a nullity.

After many years spent in foreign travel, I sailed in the year 18— , from the port of Batavia, in the rich and populous island of Java, on a voyage to the Archipelago of the Sunda islands. I went as passenger—having no other inducement than a kind of nervous restlessness which haunted me as a fiend.

Our vessel was a beautiful ship of about four hundred tons, copper-fastened, and built at Bombay of Malabar teak. She was freighted with cotton-wool and oil, from the Lachadive islands. We had also on board coir, jaggeree, ghee, cocoa-nuts, and a few cases of opium. The stowage was clumsily done, and the vessel consequently crank.

We got under way with a mere breath of wind, and for many days stood along the eastern coast of Java, without any other incident to beguile the monotony of our course than the occasional meeting with some of the small grabs of the Archipelago to which we were bound.

One evening, leaning over the taffrail, I observed a very singular, isolated cloud, to the N.W. It was remarkable, as well for its color, as from its being the first we had seen since our departure from Batavia. I watched it attentively until sunset, when it spread all at once to the eastward and westward, girting in the horizon with a narrow strip of vapor, and looking like a long line of low beach. My notice was soon afterwards attracted by the dusky-red appearance of the moon, and the peculiar character of the sea. The latter was undergoing a rapid change, and the water seemed more than usually transparent. Although I could distinctly see the bottom, yet, heaving the lead, I found the ship in fifteen fathoms. The air now became intolerably hot, and was loaded with spiral exhalations similar to those arising from heat iron. As night came on, every breath of wind died away, an more entire calm it is impossible to conceive. The flame of a candle burned upon the poop without the least perceptible motion, and a long hair, held between the finger and thumb, hung without the possibility of detecting a vibration. However, as the captain said he could perceive no indication of danger, and as we were drifting in bodily to shore, he ordered the sails to be furled, and the anchor let go. No watch was set, and the crew, consisting principally of Malays, stretched themselves deliberately upon deck. I went below—not without a full presentiment of evil. Indeed, every appearance warranted me in apprehending a Simoom. I told the captain my fears; but he paid no attention to what I said, and left me without deigning to give a reply. My uneasiness, however, prevented me from sleeping, and about midnight I went upon deck.—As I placed my foot upon the upper step of the companion-ladder, I was startled by a loud, humming noise, like that occasioned by the rapid revolution of a mill-wheel, and before I could ascertain its meaning, I found the ship quivering to its centre. In the next instant, a wilderness of foam hurled us upon our beam-ends, and, rushing over us fore and aft, swept the entire decks from stem to stern.

The extreme fury of the blast proved, in a great measure, the salvation of the ship. Although completely water-logged, yet, as her masts had gone by the board, she rose, after a minute, heavily from the sea, and, staggering awhile beneath the immense pressure of the tempest, finally righted.

By what miracle I escaped destruction, it is impossible to say. Stunned by the shock of the water, I found myself, upon recovery, jammed in between the stern-post and rudder. With great difficulty I gained my feet, and looking dizzily around, was, at first, struck with the idea of our being among breakers; so terrific, beyond the wildest imagination, was the whirlpool of mountainous and foaming ocean within which we were engulfed. After a while, I heard the voice of an old Swede, who had shipped with us at the moment of our leaving port. I hallooed to him with all my strength, and presently he came reeling aft. We soon discovered that we were the sole survivors of the accident. All on deck, with the exception of ourselves, had been swept overboard;—the captain and mates must have perished as they slept, for the cabins were deluged with water. Without assistance, we could expect to do little for the security of the ship, and our exertions were at first paralyzed by the momentary expectation of going down. Our cable had, of course, parted like pack-thread, at the first breath of the hurricane, or we should have been instantaneously overwhelmed. We scudded with frightful velocity before the sea, and the water made clear breaches over us. The framework of our stern was shattered excessively, and, in almost every respect, we had received considerable injury; but to our extreme Joy we found the pumps unchoked, and that we had made no great shifting of our ballast. The main fury of the blast had already blown over, and we apprehended little danger from the violence of the wind; but we looked forward to its total cessation with dismay; well believing, that, in our shattered condition, we should inevitably perish in the tremendous swell which would ensue. But this very just apprehension seemed by no means likely to be soon verified. For five entire days and nights —during which our only subsistence was a small quantity of jaggeree, procured with great difficulty from the forecastle—the hulk flew at a rate defying computation, before rapidly succeeding flaws of wind, which, without equalling the first violence of the Simoom, were still more terrific than any tempest I had before encountered. Our course for the first four days was, with trifling variations, S.E. and by S.; and we must have run down the coast of New Holland.—On the fifth day the cold became extreme, although the wind had hauled round a point more to the northward.—The sun arose with a sickly yellow lustre, and clambered a very few degrees above the horizon—emitting no decisive light.—There were no clouds apparent, yet the wind was upon the increase, and blew with a fitful and unsteady fury. About noon, as nearly as we could guess, our attention was again arrested by the appearance of the sun. It gave out no light, properly so called, but a dull and sullen glow without reflection, as if all its rays were polarized. Just before sinking within the turgid sea, its central fires suddenly went out, as if hurriedly extinguished by some unaccountable power. It was a dim, sliver-like rim, alone, as it rushed down the unfathomable ocean.

We waited in vain for the arrival of the sixth day—that day to me has not arrived—to the Swede, never did arrive. Thenceforward we were enshrouded in patchy darkness, so that we could not have seen an object at twenty paces from the ship. Eternal night continued to envelop us, all unrelieved by the phosphoric sea-brilliancy to which we had been accustomed in the tropics. We observed too, that, although the tempest continued to rage with unabated violence, there was no longer to be discovered the usual appearance of surf, or foam, which had hitherto attended us. All around were horror, and thick gloom, and a black sweltering desert of ebony.—Superstitious terror crept by degrees into the spirit of the old Swede, and my own soul was wrapped up in silent wonder. We neglected all care of the ship, as worse than useless, and securing ourselves, as well as possible, to the stump of the mizen-mast, looked out bitterly into the world of ocean. We had no means of calculating time, nor could we form any guess of our situation. We were, however, well aware of having made farther to the southward than any previous navigators, and felt great amazement at not meeting with the usual impediments of ice. In the meantime every moment threatened to be our last—every mountainous billow hurried to overwhelm us. The swell surpassed anything I had imagined possible, and that we were not instantly buried is a miracle. My companion spoke of the lightness of our cargo, and reminded me of the excellent qualities of our ship; but I could not help feeling the utter hopelessness of hope itself, and prepared myself gloomily for that death which I thought nothing could defer beyond an hour, as, with every knot of way the ship made, the swelling of the black stupendous seas became more dismally appalling. At times we gasped for breath at an elevation beyond the albatross—at times became dizzy with the velocity of our descent into some watery hell, where the air grew stagnant, and no sound disturbed the slumbers of the kraken.

We were at the bottom of one of these abysses, when a quick scream from my companion broke fearfully upon the night. "See! see!" cried he, shrieking in my ears, "Almighty God! see! see!" As he spoke, I became aware of a dull, sullen glare of red light which streamed down the sides of the vast chasm where we lay, and threw a fitful brilliancy upon our deck.

Casting my eyes upwards, I beheld a spectacle which froze the current of my blood. At a terrific height directly above us, and upon the very verge of the precipitous descent, hovered a gigantic ship of, perhaps, four thousand tons. Although upreared upon the summit of a wave more than a hundred times her own altitude, her apparent size exceeded that of any ship of the line or East Indiaman in existence. Her huge hull was of a deep dingy black, unrelieved by any of the customary carvings of a ship. A single row of brass cannon protruded from her open ports, and dashed from their polished surfaces the fires of innumerable battle-lanterns, which swung to and fro about her rigging. But what mainly inspired us with horror and astonishment, was that she bore up under a press of sail in the very teeth of that supernatural sea, and of that ungovernable hurricane. When we first discovered her, her bows were alone to be seen, as she rose slowly from the dim and horrible gulf beyond her. For a moment of intense terror she paused upon the giddy pinnacle, as if in contemplation of her own sublimity, then trembled and tottered, and—came down.

At this instant, I know not what sudden self-possession came over my spirit. Staggering as far aft as I could, I awaited fearlessly the ruin that was to overwhelm. Our own vessel was at length ceasing from her struggles, and sinking with her head to the sea. The shock of the descending mass struck her, consequently, in that portion of her frame which was already under water, and the inevitable result was to hurl me, with irresistible violence, upon the rigging of the stranger.

As I fell, the ship hove in stays, and went about; and to the confusion ensuing I attributed my escape from the notice of the crew. With little difficulty I made my way unperceived to the main hatchway, which was partially open, and soon found an opportunity of secreting myself in the hold. Why I did so I can hardly tell. An indefinite sense of awe, which at first sight of the navigators of the ship had taken hold of my mind, was perhaps the principle of my concealment. I was unwilling to trust myself with a race of people who had offered, to the cursory glance I had taken, so many points of vague novelty, doubt, and apprehension. I therefore thought proper to contrive a hiding-place in the hold. This I did by removing a small portion of the shifting-boards, in such a manner as to afford me a convenient retreat between the huge timbers of the ship.

I had scarcely completed my work, when a footstep in the hold forced me to make use of it. A man passed by my place of concealment with a feeble and unsteady gait. I could not see his face, but had an opportunity of observing his general appearance. There was about it an evidence of great age and infirmity. His knees tottered beneath a load of years, and his entire frame quivered under the burthen. He muttered to himself, in a low broken tone, some words of a language which I could not understand, and groped in a corner among a pile of singular-looking instruments, and decayed charts of navigation. His manner was a wild mixture of the peevishness of second childhood, and the solemn dignity of a God. He at length went on deck, and I saw him no more.

A feeling, for which I have no name, has taken possession of my soul —a sensation which will admit of no analysis, to which the lessons of bygone times are inadequate, and for which I fear futurity itself will offer me no key. To a mind constituted like my own, the latter consideration is an evil. I shall never—I know that I shall never—be satisfied with regard to the nature of my conceptions. Yet it is not wonderful that these conceptions are indefinite, since they have their origin in sources so utterly novel. A new sense—a new entity is added to my soul.

. . .

MS. FOUND IN A BOTTLE

It is long since I first trod the deck of this terrible ship, and the rays of my destiny are, I think, gathering to a focus. Incomprehensible men! Wrapped up in meditations of a kind which I cannot divine, they pass me by unnoticed. Concealment is utter folly on my part, for the people will not see. It was but just now that I passed directly before the eyes of the mate—it was no long while ago that I ventured into the captain's own private cabin, and took thence the materials with which I write, and have written. I shall from time to time continue this Journal. It is true that I may not find an opportunity of transmitting it to the world, but I will not fall to make the endeavour. At the last moment I will enclose the MS. in a bottle, and cast it within the sea.

An incident has occurred which has given me new room for meditation. Are such things the operation of ungoverned Chance? I had ventured upon deck and thrown myself down, without attracting any notice, among a pile of ratlin-stuff and old sails in the bottom of the yawl. While musing upon the singularity of my fate, I unwittingly daubed with a tar-brush the edges of a neatly-folded studding-sail which lay near me on a barrel. The studding-sail is now bent upon the ship, and the thoughtless touches of the brush are spread out into the word DISCOVERY.

I have made many observations lately upon the structure of the vessel. Although well armed, she is not, I think, a ship of war. Her rigging, build, and general equipment, all negative a supposition of this kind. What she is not, I can easily perceive—what she is I fear it is impossible to say. I know not how it is, but in scrutinizing her strange model and singular cast of spars, her huge size and overgrown suits of canvas, her severely simple bow and antiquated stern, there will occasionally flash across my mind a sensation of familiar things, and there is always mixed up with such indistinct shadows of recollection, an unaccountable memory of old foreign chronicles and ages long ago.

I have been looking at the timbers of the ship. She is built of a material to which I am a stranger. There is a peculiar character about the wood which strikes me as rendering it unfit for the purpose to which it has been applied. I mean its extreme porousness, considered independently by the worm-eaten condition which is a consequence of navigation in these seas, and apart from the rottenness attendant upon age. It will appear perhaps an observation somewhat over-curious, but this wood would have every characteristic of Spanish oak, if Spanish oak were distended by any unnatural means.

In reading the above sentence a curious apothegm of an old weather-beaten Dutch navigator comes full upon my recollection. "It is as sure," he was wont to say, when any doubt was entertained of his veracity, "as sure as there is a sea where the ship itself will grow in bulk like the living body of the seaman."

About an hour ago, I made bold to thrust myself among a group of the crew. They paid me no manner of attention, and, although I stood in the very midst of them all, seemed utterly unconscious of my presence. Like the one I had at first seen in the hold, they all bore about them the marks of a hoary old age. Their knees trembled with infirmity; their shoulders were bent double with decrepitude; their shrivelled skins rattled in the wind; their voices were low, tremulous and broken; their eyes glistened with the rheum of years; and their gray hairs streamed terribly in the tempest. Around them, on every part of the deck, lay scattered mathematical instruments of the most quaint and obsolete construction.

I mentioned some time ago the bending of a studding-sail. From that period the ship, being thrown dead off the wind, has continued her terrific course due south, with every rag of canvas packed upon her, from her trucks to her lower studding-sail booms, and rolling every moment her top-gallant yard-arms into the most appalling hell of water which it can enter into the mind of a man to imagine. I have just left the deck, where I find it impossible to maintain a footing, although the crew seem to experience little inconvenience. It appears to me a miracle of miracles that our enormous bulk is not swallowed up at once and forever. We are surely doomed to hover continually upon the brink of Eternity, without taking a final plunge into the abyss. From billows a thousand times more stupendous than any I have ever seen, we glide away with the facility of the arrowy sea-gull; and the colossal waters rear their heads above us like demons of the deep, but like demons confined to simple threats and forbidden to destroy. I am led to attribute these frequent escapes to the only natural cause which can account for such effect.—I must suppose the ship to be within the influence of some strong current, or impetuous under-tow.

I have seen the captain face to face, and in his own cabin—but, as I expected, he paid me no attention. Although in his appearance there is, to a casual observer, nothing which might bespeak him more or less than man—still a feeling of irrepressible reverence and awe mingled with the sensation of wonder with which I regarded him. In stature he is nearly my own height; that is, about five feet eight inches. He is of a well-knit and compact frame of body, neither robust nor remarkably otherwise. But it is the singularity of the expression which reigns upon the face—it is the intense, the wonderful, the thrilling evidence of old age, so utter, so extreme, which excites within my spirit a sense—a sentiment ineffable. His forehead, although little wrinkled, seems to bear upon it the stamp of a myriad of years.— His gray hairs are records of the past, and his grayer eyes are Sybils of the future. The cabin floor was thickly strewn with strange, iron-clasped folios, and mouldering instruments of science, and obsolete long-forgotten charts. His head was bowed down upon his hands, and he pored, with a fiery unquiet eye, over a paper which I took to be a commission, and which, at all events, bore the signature of a monarch. He muttered to himself, as did the first seaman whom I saw in the hold, some low peevish syllables of a foreign tongue, and although the speaker was close at my elbow, his voice seemed to reach my ears from the distance of a mile.

The ship and all in it are imbued with the spirit of Eld. The crew glide to and fro like the ghosts of buried centuries; their eyes have an eager and uneasy meaning; and when their fingers fall athwart my path in the wild glare of the battle-lanterns, I feel as I have never felt before, although I have been all my life a dealer in antiquities, and have imbibed the shadows of fallen columns at Balbec, and Tadmor, and Persepolis, until my very soul has become a ruin.

When I look around me I feel ashamed of my former apprehensions. If I trembled at the blast which has hitherto attended us, shall I not stand aghast at a warring of wind and ocean, to convey any idea of which the words tornado and simoom are trivial and ineffective? All in the immediate vicinity of the ship is the blackness of eternal night, and a chaos of foamless water; but, about a league on either side of us, may be seen, indistinctly and at intervals, stupendous ramparts of ice, towering away into the desolate sky, and looking like the walls of the universe.

As I imagined, the ship proves to be in a current; if that appellation can properly be given to a tide which, howling and shrieking by the white ice, thunders on to the southward with a velocity like the headlong dashing of a cataract.

To conceive the horror of my sensations is, I presume, utterly impossible; yet a curiosity to penetrate the mysteries of these awful regions, predominates even over my despair, and will reconcile me to the most hideous aspect of death. It is evident that we are hurrying onwards to some exciting knowledge—some never-to-be-imparted secret, whose attainment is destruction. Perhaps this current leads us to the southern pole itself. It must be confessed that a supposition apparently so wild has every probability in its favor.

The crew pace the deck with unquiet and tremulous step; but there is upon their countenances an expression more of the eagerness of hope than of the apathy of despair.

In the meantime the wind is still in our poop, and, as we carry a crowd of canvas, the ship is at times lifted bodily from out the sea—Oh, horror upon horror! the ice opens suddenly to the right, and to the left, and we are whirling dizzily, in immense concentric circles, round and round the borders of a gigantic amphitheatre, the summit of whose walls is lost in the darkness and the distance. But little time will be left me to ponder upon my destiny—the circles rapidly grow small—we are plunging madly within the grasp of the whirlpool—and amid a roaring, and bellowing, and thundering of ocean and of tempest, the ship is quivering, oh God! and—going down.

NOTE.—The "MS. Found in a Bottle," was originally published in 1831, and it was not until many years afterwards that I became acquainted with the maps of Mercator, in which the ocean is represented as rushing, by four mouths, into the (northern) Polar Gulf, to be absorbed into the bowels of the earth; the Pole itself being represented by a black rock, towering to a prodigious height.

AMY FOSTER

JOSEPH CONRAD

AMY FOSTER

Kennedy is a country doctor, and lives in Colebrook, on the shores of Eastbay. The high ground rising abruptly behind the red roofs of the little town crowds the quaint High Street against the wall which defends it from the sea. Beyond the sea-wall there curves for miles in a vast and regular sweep the barren beach of shingle, with the village of Brenzett standing out darkly across the water, a spire in a clump of trees; and still further out the perpendicular column of a lighthouse, looking in the distance no bigger than a lead pencil, marks the vanishing-point of the land. The country at the back of Brenzett is low and flat, but the bay is fairly well sheltered from the seas, and occasionally a big ship, windbound or through stress of weather, makes use of the anchoring ground a mile and a half due north from you as you stand at the back door of the "Ship Inn" in Brenzett. A dilapidated windmill near by lifting its shattered arms from a mound no loftier than a rubbish heap, and a Martello tower squatting at the water's edge half a mile to the south of the Coastguard cottages, are familiar to the skippers of small craft. These are the official seamarks for the patch of trustworthy bottom represented on the Admiralty charts by an irregular oval of dots enclosing several figures six, with a tiny anchor engraved among them, and the legend "mud and shells" over all.

The brow of the upland overtops the square tower of the Colebrook Church. The slope is green and looped by a white road. Ascending along this road, you open a valley broad and shallow, a wide green trough of pastures and hedges merging inland into a vista of purple tints and flowing lines closing the view.

In this valley down to Brenzett and Colebrook and up to Darnford, the market town fourteen miles away, lies the practice of my friend Kennedy. He had begun life as surgeon in the Navy, and afterwards had been the companion of a famous traveller, in the days when there were continents with unexplored interiors. His papers on the fauna and flora made him known to scientific societies. And now he had come to a country practice—from choice. The penetrating power of his mind, acting like a corrosive fluid, had destroyed his ambition, I fancy. His intelligence is of a scientific order, of an investigating habit, and of that unappeasable curiosity which believes that there is a particle of a general truth in every mystery.

A good many years ago now, on my return from abroad, he invited me to stay with him. I came readily enough, and as he could not neglect his patients to keep me company, he took me on his rounds—thirty miles or so of an afternoon, sometimes. I waited for him on the roads; the horse reached after the leafy twigs, and, sitting in the dogcart, I could hear Kennedy's laugh through the half-open door left open of some cottage. He had a big, hearty laugh that would have fitted a man twice his size, a brisk manner, a bronzed face, and a pair of grey, profoundly attentive eyes. He had the talent of making people talk to him freely, and an inexhaustible patience in listening to their tales.

One day, as we trotted out of a large village into a shady bit of road, I saw on our left hand a low, black cottage, with diamond panes in the windows, a creeper on the end wall, a roof of shingle, and some roses climbing on the rickety trellis-work of the tiny porch. Kennedy pulled up to a walk. A woman, in full sunlight, was throwing a dripping blanket over a line stretched between two old apple-trees. And as the bobtailed, long-necked chestnut, trying to get his head, jerked the left hand, covered by a thick dog-skin glove, the doctor raised his voice over the hedge: "How's your child, Amy?"

I had the time to see her dull face, red, not with a mantling blush, but as if her flat cheeks had been vigorously slapped, and to take in the squat figure, the scanty, dusty brown hair drawn into a tight knot at the back of the head. She looked quite young. With a distinct catch in her breath, her voice sounded low and timid.

"He's well, thank you."

We trotted again. "A young patient of yours," I said; and the doctor, flicking the chestnut absently, muttered, "Her husband used to be."

"She seems a dull creature," I remarked listlessly.

"Precisely," said Kennedy. "She is very passive. It's enough to look at the red hands hanging at the end of those short arms, at those slow, prominent brown eyes, to know the inertness of her mind—an inertness that one would think made it everlastingly safe from all the surprises of imagination. And yet which of us is safe? At any rate, such as you see her, she had enough imagination to fall in love. She's the daughter of one Isaac Foster, who from a small farmer has sunk into a shepherd; the beginning of his misfortunes dating from his runaway marriage with the cook of his widowed father—a well-to-do, apoplectic grazier, who passionately struck his name off his will, and had been heard to utter threats against his life. But this old affair, scandalous enough to serve as a motive for a Greek tragedy, arose from the similarity of their characters. There are other tragedies, less scandalous and of a subtler poignancy, arising from irreconcilable differences and from that fear of the Incomprehensible that hangs over all our heads—over all our heads...."

The tired chestnut dropped into a walk; and the rim of the sun, all red in a speckless sky, touched familiarly the smooth top of a ploughed rise near the road as I had seen it times innumerable touch the distant horizon of the sea. The uniform brownness of the harrowed field glowed with a rosy tinge, as though the powdered clods had sweated out in minute pearls of blood the toil of uncounted ploughmen. From the edge of a copse a waggon with two horses was rolling gently along the ridge. Raised above our heads upon the sky-line, it loomed up against the red sun, triumphantly big, enormous, like a chariot of giants drawn by two slow-stepping steeds of legendary proportions. And the clumsy figure of the man plodding at the head of the leading horse projected itself on the background of the Infinite with a heroic uncouthness. The end of his carter's whip quivered high up in the blue. Kennedy discoursed.

"She's the eldest of a large family. At the age of fifteen they put her out to service at the New Barns Farm. I attended Mrs. Smith, the tenant's wife, and saw that girl there for the first time. Mrs. Smith, a genteel person with a sharp nose, made her put on a black dress every afternoon. I don't know what induced me to notice her at all. There are faces that call your attention by a curious want of definiteness in their whole aspect, as, walking in a mist, you peer attentively at a vague shape which, after all, may be nothing more curious or strange than a signpost. The only peculiarity I perceived in her was a slight hesitation in her utterance, a sort of preliminary stammer which passes away with the first word. When sharply spoken to, she was apt to lose her head at once; but her heart was of the kindest. She had never been heard to express a dislike for a single human being, and she was tender to every living creature. She was devoted to Mrs. Smith, to Mr. Smith, to their dogs, cats, canaries; and as to Mrs. Smith's grey parrot, its peculiarities exercised upon her a positive fascination. Nevertheless, when that outlandish bird, attacked by the cat, shrieked for help in human accents, she ran out into the yard stopping her ears, and did not prevent the crime. For Mrs. Smith this was another evidence of her stupidity; on the other hand, her want of charm, in view of Smith's well-known frivolousness, was a great recommendation. Her short-sighted eyes would swim with pity for a poor mouse in a trap, and she had been seen once by some boys on her knees in the wet grass helping a toad in difficulties. If it's true, as some German fellow has said, that without phosphorus there is no thought, it is still more true that there is no kindness of heart without a certain amount of imagination. She had some. She had even more than is necessary to understand suffering and to be moved by pity. She fell in love under circumstances that leave no room for doubt in the matter; for you need imagination to form a notion of beauty at all, and still more to discover your ideal in an unfamiliar shape.

"How this aptitude came to her, what it did feed upon, is an inscrutable mystery. She was born in the village, and had never been further away from it than Colebrook or perhaps Darnford. She lived for four years with the Smiths. New Barns is an isolated farmhouse a mile away from the road, and she was content to look day after day at the same fields, hollows, rises; at the trees and the hedgerows; at the faces of the four men about the farm, always the same—day after day, month after month, year after year. She never showed a desire for conversation, and, as it seemed to me, she did not know how to smile. Sometimes of a fine Sunday afternoon she would put on her best dress, a pair of stout boots, a large grey hat trimmed with a black feather (I've seen her in that finery), seize an absurdly slender parasol, climb over two stiles, tramp over three fields and along two hundred yards of road —never further. There stood Foster's cottage. She would help her mother to give their tea to the younger children, wash up the crockery, kiss the little ones, and go back to the farm. That was all. All the rest, all the change, all the relaxation. She never seemed to wish for anything more. And then she fell in love. She fell in love silently, obstinately—perhaps helplessly. It came slowly, but when it came it worked like a powerful spell; it was love as the Ancients understood it: an irresistible and fateful impulse—a possession! Yes, it was in her to become haunted and possessed by a face, by a presence, fatally, as though she had been a pagan worshipper of form under a joyous sky—and to be awakened at last from that mysterious forgetfulness of self, from that enchantment, from that transport, by a fear resembling the unaccountable terror of a brute...."

With the sun hanging low on its western limit, the expanse of the grass-lands framed in the counter-scarps of the rising ground took on a gorgeous and sombre aspect. A sense of penetrating sadness, like that inspired by a grave strain of music, disengaged itself from the silence of the fields. The men we met walked past slow, unsmiling, with downcast eyes, as if the melancholy of an over-burdened earth had weighted their feet, bowed their shoulders, borne down their glances.

"Yes," said the doctor to my remark, "one would think the earth is under a curse, since of all her children these that cling to her the closest are uncouth in body and as leaden of gait as if their very hearts were loaded with chains. But here on this same road you might have seen amongst these heavy men a being lithe, supple, and long-limbed, straight like a pine with something striving upwards in his appearance as though the heart within him had been buoyant. Perhaps it was only the force of the contrast, but when he was passing one of these villagers here, the soles of his feet did not seem to me to touch the dust of the road. He vaulted over the stiles, paced these slopes with a long elastic stride that made him noticeable at a great distance, and had lustrous black eyes. He was so different from the mankind around that, with his freedom of movement, his soft—a little startled, glance, his olive complexion and graceful bearing, his humanity suggested to me the nature of a woodland creature. He came from there."

The doctor pointed with his whip, and from the summit of the descent seen over the rolling tops of the trees in a park by the side of the road, appeared the level sea far below us, like the floor of an immense edifice inlaid with bands of dark ripple, with still trails of glitter, ending in a belt of glassy water at the foot of the sky. The light blur of smoke, from an invisible steamer, faded on the great clearness of the horizon like the mist of a breath on a mirror; and, inshore, the white sails of a coaster, with the appearance of disentangling themselves slowly from under the branches, floated clear of the foliage of the trees.

"Shipwrecked in the bay?" I said.

"Yes; he was a castaway. A poor emigrant from Central Europe bound to America and washed ashore here in a storm. And for him, who knew nothing of the earth, England was an undiscovered country. It was some time before he learned its name; and for all I know he might have expected to find wild beasts or wild men here, when, crawling in the dark over the sea-wall, he rolled down the other side into a dyke, where it was another miracle he didn't get drowned. But he struggled instinctively like an animal under a net, and this blind struggle threw him out into a field. He must have been, indeed, of a tougher fibre than he looked to withstand without expiring such buffetings, the violence of his exertions, and so much fear. Later on, in his broken English that resembled curiously the speech of a young child, he told me himself that he put his trust in God, believing he was no longer in this world. And truly—he would add—how was he to know? He fought his way against the rain and the gale on all fours, and crawled at last among some sheep huddled close under the lee of a hedge. They ran off in all directions, bleating in the darkness, and he welcomed the first familiar sound he heard on these shores. It must have been two in the morning then. And this is all we know of the manner of his landing, though he did not arrive unattended by any means. Only his grisly company did not begin to come ashore till much later in the day...."

The doctor gathered the reins, clicked his tongue; we trotted down the hill. Then turning, almost directly, a sharp corner into the High Street, we rattled over the stones and were home.

Late in the evening Kennedy, breaking a spell of moodiness that had come over him, returned to the story. Smoking his pipe, he paced the long room from end to end. A reading-lamp concentrated all its light upon the papers on his desk; and, sitting by the open window, I saw, after the windless, scorching day, the frigid splendour of a hazy sea lying motionless under the moon. Not a whisper, not a splash, not a stir of the shingle, not a footstep, not a sigh came up from the earth below—never a sign of life but the scent of climbing jasmine;

and Kennedy's voice, speaking behind me, passed through the wide casement, to vanish outside in a chill and sumptuous stillness.

"... The relations of shipwrecks in the olden time tell us of much suffering. Often the castaways were only saved from drowning to die miserably from starvation on a barren coast; others suffered violent death or else slavery, passing through years of precarious existence with people to whom their strangeness was an object of suspicion, dislike or fear. We read about these things, and they are very pitiful. It is indeed hard upon a man to find himself a lost stranger, helpless, incomprehensible, and of a mysterious origin, in some obscure corner of the earth. Yet amongst all the adventurers shipwrecked in all the wild parts of the world there is not one, it seems to me, that ever had to suffer a fate so simply tragic as the man I am speaking of, the most innocent of adventurers cast out by the sea in the bight of this bay, almost within sight from this very window.

"He did not know the name of his ship. Indeed, in the course of time we discovered he did not even know that ships had names—'like Christian people'; and when, one day, from the top of the Talfourd Hill, he beheld the sea lying open to his view, his eyes roamed afar, lost in an air of wild surprise, as though he had never seen such a sight before. And probably he had not. As far as I could make out, he had been hustled together with many others on board an emigrant-ship lying at the mouth of the Elbe, too bewildered to take note of his surroundings, too weary to see anything, too anxious to care. They were driven below into the 'tweendeck and battened down from the very start. It was a low timber dwelling—he would say—with wooden beams overhead, like the houses in his country, but you went into it down a ladder. It was very large, very cold, damp and sombre, with places in the manner of wooden boxes where people had to sleep, one above another, and it kept on rocking all ways at once all the time. He crept into one of these boxes and laid down there in the clothes in which he had left his home many days before, keeping his bundle and his stick by his side. People groaned, children cried, water dripped, the lights went out, the walls of the place creaked, and everything was being shaken so that in one's little box one dared not lift one's head. He had lost touch with his only companion (a young man from the same valley, he said), and all the time a great noise of wind went on outside and heavy blows fell—boom! boom! An awful sickness overcame him, even to the point of making him neglect his prayers. Besides, one could not tell whether it was morning or evening. It seemed always to be night in that place.

"Before that he had been travelling a long, long time on the iron track. He looked out of the window, which had a wonderfully clear glass in it, and the trees, the houses, the fields, and the long roads seemed to fly round and round about him till his head swam. He gave me to understand that he had on his passage beheld uncounted multitudes of people—whole nations—all dressed in such clothes as the rich wear. Once he was made to get out of the carriage, and slept through a night on a bench in a house of bricks with his bundle under his head; and once for many hours he had to sit on a floor of flat stones dozing, with his knees up and with his bundle between his feet. There was a roof over him, which seemed made of glass, and was so high that the tallest mountain-pine he had ever seen would have had room to grow under it. Steam-machines rolled in at one end and out at the other. People swarmed more than you can see on a feast-day round the miraculous Holy Image in the yard of the Carmelite Convent down in the plains where, before he left his home, he drove his mother in a wooden cart—a pious old woman who wanted to offer prayers and make a vow for his safety. He could not give me an idea of how large and lofty and full of noise and smoke and gloom, and clang of iron, the place was, but some one had told him it was called Berlin. Then they rang a bell, and another steam-machine came in, and again he was taken on and on through a land that wearied his eyes by its flatness without a single bit of a hill to be seen anywhere. One more night he spent shut up in a building like a good stable with a litter of straw on the floor, guarding his bundle amongst a lot of men, of whom not one could understand a single word he said. In the morning they were all led down to the stony shores of an extremely broad muddy river, flowing not between hills but between houses that seemed immense. There was a steam-machine that went on the water, and they all stood upon it packed tight, only now there were with them many women and children who made much noise. A cold rain fell, the wind blew in his face; he was wet through, and his teeth chattered. He and the young man from the same valley took each other by the hand.

"They thought they were being taken to America straight away, but suddenly the steam-machine bumped against the side of a thing like a house on the water. The walls were smooth and black, and there uprose, growing from the roof as it were, bare trees in the shape of crosses, extremely high. That's how it appeared to him then, for he had never seen a ship before. This was the ship that was going to swim all the way to America. Voices shouted, everything swayed; there was a ladder dipping up and down. He went up on his hands and knees in mortal fear of falling into the water below, which made a great splashing. He got separated from his companion, and when he descended into the bottom of that ship his heart seemed to melt suddenly within him.

"It was then also, as he told me, that he lost contact for good and all with one of those three men who the summer before had been going about through all the little towns in the foothills of his country. They would arrive on market days driving in a peasant's cart, and would set up an office in an inn or some other Jew's house. There were three of them, of whom one with a long beard looked venerable; and they had red cloth collars round their necks and gold lace on their sleeves like Government officials. They sat proudly behind a long table; and in the next room, so that the common people shouldn't hear, they kept a cunning telegraph machine, through which they could talk to the Emperor of America. The fathers hung about the door, but the young men of the mountains would crowd up to the table asking many questions, for there was work to be got all the year round at three dollars a day in America, and no military service to do.

"But the American Kaiser would not take everybody. Oh, no! He himself had a great difficulty in getting accepted, and the venerable man in uniform had to go out of the room several times to work the telegraph on his behalf. The American Kaiser engaged him at last at three dollars, he being young and strong. However, many able young men backed out, afraid of the great distance; besides, those only who had some money could be taken. There were some who sold their huts and their land because it cost a lot of money to get to America; but then, once there, you had three dollars a day, and if you were clever you could find places where true gold could be picked up on the ground. His father's house was getting over full. Two of his brothers were married and had children. He promised to send money home from America by post twice a year. His father sold an old cow, a pair of piebald mountain ponies of his own raising, and a cleared plot of fair pasture land on the sunny slope of a pine-clad pass to a Jew inn-keeper in order to pay the people of the ship that took men to America to get rich in a short time.

"He must have been a real adventurer at heart, for how many of the greatest enterprises in the conquest of the earth had for their beginning just such a bargaining away of the paternal cow for the mirage or true gold far away! I have been telling you more or less in my own words what I learned fragmentarily in the course of two or three years, during which I seldom missed an opportunity of a friendly chat with him. He told me this story of his adventure with many flashes of white teeth and lively glances of black eyes, at first in a sort of anxious baby-talk, then, as he acquired the language, with great fluency, but always with that singing, soft, and at the same time vibrating intonation that instilled a strangely penetrating power into the sound of the most familiar English words, as if they had been the words of an unearthly language. And he always would come to an end, with many emphatic shakes of his head, upon that awful sensation of his heart melting within him directly he set foot on board that ship. Afterwards there seemed to come for him a period of blank ignorance, at any rate as to facts. No doubt he must have been abominably sea-sick and abominably unhappy—this soft and passionate adventurer, taken thus out of his knowledge, and feeling bitterly as he lay in his emigrant bunk his utter loneliness; for his was a highly sensitive nature. The next thing we know of him for certain is that he had been hiding in Hammond's pig-pound by the side of the road to Norton six miles, as the crow flies, from the sea. Of these experiences he was unwilling to speak: they seemed to have seared into his soul a sombre sort of wonder and indignation. Through the rumours of the country-side, which lasted for a good many days after his arrival, we know that the fishermen of West Colebrook had been disturbed and startled by heavy knocks against the walls of weatherboard cottages, and by a voice crying piercingly strange words in the night. Several of them turned out even, but, no doubt, he had fled in sudden alarm at their rough angry tones hailing each other in the darkness. A sort of frenzy must have helped him up the steep Norton hill. It was he, no doubt, who early the following morning had been seen lying (in a swoon, I should say) on the roadside grass by the Brenzett carrier, who actually got down to have a nearer look, but drew back, intimidated by the perfect immobility, and by something queer in the aspect of that tramp, sleeping so still under the showers. As the day advanced, some children came dashing into school at Norton in such a fright that the schoolmistress went out and spoke indignantly to a 'horrid-looking man' on the road. He edged away, hanging his head, for a few steps, and then suddenly ran off with extraordinary fleetness. The driver of Mr. Bradley's milk-cart made no secret of it that he had lashed with his whip at a hairy sort of gipsy fellow who, jumping up at a turn of the road by the Vents, made a snatch at the pony's bridle. And he caught him a good one too, right over the face, he said, that made him drop down in the mud a jolly sight quicker than he had jumped up; but it was a good half-a-mile before he could stop the pony. Maybe that in his desperate endeavours to get help, and in his need to get in touch with some one, the poor devil had tried to stop the cart. Also three boys confessed afterwards to throwing stones at a funny tramp, knocking about all wet and muddy, and, it seemed, very drunk, in the narrow deep lane by the limekilns. All this was the talk of three villages for days; but we have Mrs. Finn's (the wife of Smith's waggoner) unimpeachable testimony that she saw him get over the low wall of Hammond's pig-pound and lurch straight at her, babbling aloud in a voice that was enough to make one die of fright. Having the baby with her in a perambulator, Mrs. Finn called out to him to go away, and as he persisted in coming nearer, she hit him courageously with her umbrella over the head and, without once looking back, ran like the wind with the perambulator as far as the first house in the village. She stopped then, out of breath, and spoke to old Lewis, hammering there at a heap of stones; and the old chap, taking off his immense black wire goggles, got up on his shaky legs to look where she pointed. Together they followed with their eyes the figure of the man running over a field; they saw him fall down, pick himself up, and run on again, staggering and waving his long arms above his head, in the direction of the New Barns Farm. From that moment he is plainly in the toils of his obscure and touching destiny. There is no doubt after this of what happened to him. All is certain now: Mrs. Smith's intense terror; Amy Foster's stolid conviction held against the other's nervous attack, that the man 'meant no harm'; Smith's exasperation (on his return from Darnford Market) at finding the dog barking himself into a fit, the back-door locked, his wife in hysterics; and all for an unfortunate dirty tramp, supposed to be even then lurking in his stackyard. Was he? He would teach him to frighten women.

"Smith is notoriously hot-tempered, but the sight of some nondescript and miry creature sitting cross-legged amongst a lot of loose straw, and swinging itself to and fro like a bear in a cage, made him pause. Then this tramp stood up silently before him, one mass of mud and filth from head to foot. Smith, alone amongst his stacks with this apparition, in the stormy twilight ringing with the infuriated barking of the dog, felt the dread of an inexplicable strangeness. But when that being, parting with his black hands the long matted locks that hung before his face, as you part the two halves of a curtain, looked out at him with glistening, wild, black-and-white eyes, the weirdness of this silent encounter fairly staggered him. He had admitted since (for the story has been a legitimate subject of conversation about here for years) that he made more than one step backwards. Then a sudden burst of rapid, senseless speech persuaded him at once that he had to do with an escaped lunatic. In fact, that impression never wore off completely. Smith has not in his heart given up his secret conviction of the man's essential insanity to this very day.

"As the creature approached him, jabbering in a most discomposing manner, Smith (unaware that he was being addressed as 'gracious lord,' and adjured in God's name to afford food and shelter) kept on speaking firmly but gently to it, and retreating all the time into the other yard. At last, watching his chance, by a sudden charge he bundled him headlong into the wood-lodge, and instantly shot the bolt. Thereupon he wiped his brow, though the day was cold. He had done his duty to the community by shutting up a wandering and probably dangerous maniac. Smith isn't a hard man at all, but he had room in his brain only for that one idea of lunacy. He was not imaginative enough to ask himself whether the man might not be perishing with cold and hunger. Meantime, at first, the maniac made a great deal of noise in the lodge. Mrs. Smith was screaming upstairs, where she had locked herself in her bedroom; but Amy Foster sobbed piteously at the kitchen door, wringing her hands and muttering, 'Don't! don't!' I daresay Smith had a rough time of it that evening with one noise and another, and this insane, disturbing voice crying obstinately through the door only added to his irritation. He couldn't possibly have connected this troublesome lunatic with the sinking of a ship in Eastbay, of which there had been a rumour in the Darnford marketplace. And I daresay the man inside had been very near to insanity on that night. Before his excitement collapsed and he became unconscious he was throwing himself violently about in the dark, rolling on some dirty sacks, and biting his fists with rage, cold, hunger, amazement, and despair.

"He was a mountaineer of the eastern range of the Carpathians, and the vessel sunk the night before in Eastbay was the Hamburg emigrant-ship *Herzogin Sophia-Dorothea*, of appalling memory.

"A few months later we could read in the papers the accounts of the bogus 'Emigration Agencies' among the Sclavonian peasantry in the more remote provinces of Austria. The object of these scoundrels was to get hold of the poor ignorant people's homesteads, and they were in league with the local usurers. They exported their victims through Hamburg mostly. As to the ship, I had watched her out of this very window, reaching close-hauled under short canvas into the bay on a dark, threatening afternoon. She came to an anchor, correctly by the chart, off the Brenzett Coastguard station. I remember before the night fell looking out again at the outlines of her spars and rigging that stood out dark and pointed on a background of ragged, slaty clouds like another and a slighter spire to the left of the Brenzett church-tower.

"In the evening the wind rose. At midnight I could hear in my bed the terrific gusts and the sounds of a driving deluge.

"About that time the Coastguardmen thought they saw the lights of a steamer over the anchoring-ground. In a moment they vanished; but it is clear that another vessel of some sort had tried for shelter in the bay on that awful, blind night, had rammed the German ship amidships (a breach—as one of the divers told me afterwards—'that you could sail a Thames barge through'), and then had gone out either scathless or damaged, who shall say; but had gone out, unknown, unseen, and fatal, to perish mysteriously at sea. Of her nothing ever came to light, and yet the hue and cry that was raised all over the world would have found her out if she had been in existence anywhere on the face of the waters.

"A completeness without a clue, and a stealthy silence as of a neatly executed crime, characterise this murderous disaster, which, as you may remember, had its gruesome celebrity. The wind would have prevented the loudest outcries from reaching the shore; there had been evidently no time for signals of distress. It was death without any sort of fuss. The Hamburg ship, filling all at once, capsized as she sank, and at daylight there was not even the end of a spar to be seen above water. She was missed, of course, and at first the Coastguardmen surmised that she had either dragged her anchor or parted her cable some time during the night, and had been blown out to sea. Then, after the tide turned, the wreck must have shifted a little and released some of the bodies, because a child—a little fair-haired child in a red frock—came ashore abreast of the Martello tower. By the afternoon you could see along three miles of beach dark figures with bare legs dashing in and out of the tumbling foam, and rough-looking men, women with hard faces, children, mostly fair-haired, were being carried, stiff and dripping, on stretchers, on wattles, on ladders, in a long procession past the door of the 'Ship Inn,' to be laid out in a row under the north wall of the Brenzett Church.

"Officially, the body of the little girl in the red frock is the first thing that came ashore from that ship. But I have patients amongst the seafaring population of West Colebrook, and, unofficially, I am informed that very early that morning two brothers, who went down to look after their cobble hauled up on the beach, found, a good way from Brenzett, an ordinary ship's hencoop lying high and dry on the shore, with eleven drowned ducks inside. Their families ate the birds, and the hencoop was split into firewood with a hatchet. It is possible that a man (supposing he happened to be on deck at the time of the accident) might have floated ashore on that hencoop. He might. I admit it is improbable, but there was the man—and for days, nay, for weeks—it didn't enter our heads that we had amongst us the only living soul that had escaped from that disaster. The man himself, even when he learned to speak intelligibly, could tell us very little. He remembered he had felt better (after the ship had anchored, I suppose), and that the darkness, the wind, and the rain took his breath away. This looks as if he had been on deck some time during that night. But we mustn't forget he had been taken out of his knowledge, that he had been sea-sick and battened down below for four days, that he had no general notion of a ship or of the sea, and therefore could have no definite idea of what was happening to him. The rain, the wind, the darkness he knew; he understood the bleating of the sheep, and he remembered the pain of his wretchedness and misery, his heartbroken astonishment that it was neither seen nor understood, his dismay at finding all the men angry and all the women fierce. He had approached them as a beggar, it is true, he said; but in his country, even if they gave nothing, they spoke gently to beggars. The children in his country were not taught to throw stones at those who asked for compassion. Smith's strategy overcame him completely. The wood-lodge presented the horrible aspect of a dungeon. What would be done to him next?... No wonder that Amy Foster appeared to his eyes with the aureole of an angel of light. The girl had not been able to sleep for thinking of the poor man, and in the morning, before the Smiths were up, she slipped out across the back yard. Holding the door of the wood-lodge ajar, she looked in and extended to him half a loaf of white bread—'such bread as the rich eat in my country,' he used to say.

"At this he got up slowly from amongst all sorts of rubbish, stiff, hungry, trembling, miserable, and doubtful. 'Can you eat this?' she asked in her soft and timid voice. He must have taken her for a 'gracious lady.' He devoured ferociously, and tears were falling on the crust. Suddenly he dropped the bread, seized her wrist, and imprinted a kiss on her hand. She was not frightened. Through his forlorn condition she had observed that he was good-looking. She shut the door and walked back slowly to the kitchen. Much later on, she told Mrs. Smith, who shuddered at the bare idea of being touched by that creature.

"Through this act of impulsive pity he was brought back again within the pale of human relations with his new surroundings. He never forgot it—never.

"That very same morning old Mr. Swaffer (Smith's nearest neighbour) came over to give his advice, and ended by carrying him off. He stood, unsteady on his legs, meek, and caked over in half-dried mud, while the two men talked around him in an incomprehensible tongue. Mrs. Smith had refused to come downstairs till the madman was off the premises; Amy Foster, far from within the dark kitchen, watched through the open back door; and he obeyed the signs that were made to him to the best of his ability. But Smith was full of mistrust. 'Mind, sir! It may be all his cunning,' he cried repeatedly in a tone of warning. When Mr. Swaffer started the mare, the deplorable being sitting humbly by his side, through weakness, nearly fell out over the back of the high two-wheeled cart. Swaffer took him straight home. And it is then that I come upon the scene.

"I was called in by the simple process of the old man beckoning to me with his forefinger over the gate of his house as I happened to be driving past. I got down, of course.

"'I've got something here,' he mumbled, leading the way to an outhouse at a little distance from his other farm-buildings.

"It was there that I saw him first, in a long low room taken upon the space of that sort of coach-house. It was bare and whitewashed, with a small square aperture glazed with one cracked, dusty pane at its further end. He was lying on his back upon a straw pallet; they had given him a couple of horse-blankets, and he seemed to have spent the remainder of his strength in the exertion of cleaning himself. He was almost speechless; his quick breathing under the blankets pulled up to his chin, his glittering, restless black eyes reminded me of a wild bird caught in a snare. While I was examining him, old Swaffer stood silently by the door, passing the tips of his fingers along his shaven upper lip. I gave some directions, promised to send a bottle of medicine, and naturally made some inquiries.

"'Smith caught him in the stackyard at New Barns,' said the old chap in his deliberate, unmoved manner, and as if the other had been indeed a sort of wild animal. 'That's how I came by him. Quite a curiosity, isn't he? Now tell me, doctor—you've been all over the world —don't you think that's a bit of a Hindoo we've got hold of here.'

"I was greatly surprised. His long black hair scattered over the straw bolster contrasted with the olive pallor of his face. It occurred to me he might be a Basque. It didn't necessarily follow that he should understand Spanish; but I tried him with the few words I know, and also with some French. The whispered sounds I caught by bending my ear to his lips puzzled me utterly. That afternoon the young ladies from the Rectory (one of them read Goethe with a dictionary, and the other had struggled with Dante for years), coming to see Miss Swaffer, tried their German and Italian on him from the doorway. They retreated, just the least bit scared by the flood of passionate speech which, turning on his pallet, he let out at them. They admitted that the sound was pleasant, soft, musical—but, in conjunction with his looks perhaps, it was startling—so excitable, so utterly unlike anything one had ever heard. The village boys climbed up the bank to have a peep through the little square aperture. Everybody was wondering what Mr. Swaffer would do with him.

"He simply kept him.

"Swaffer would be called eccentric were he not so much respected. They will tell you that Mr. Swaffer sits up as late as ten o'clock at night to read books, and they will tell you also that he can write a cheque for two hundred pounds without thinking twice about it. He himself would tell you that the Swaffers had owned land between this and Darnford for these three hundred years. He must be eighty-five to-day, but he does not look a bit older than when I first came here. He is a great breeder of sheep, and deals extensively in cattle. He attends market days for miles around in every sort of weather, and drives sitting bowed low over the reins, his lank grey hair curling over the collar of his warm coat, and with a green plaid rug round his legs. The calmness of advanced age gives a solemnity to his manner. He is clean-shaved; his lips are thin and sensitive; something rigid and monarchal in the set of his features lends a certain elevation to the character of his face. He has been known to drive miles in the rain to see a new kind of rose in somebody's garden, or a monstrous cabbage grown by a cottager. He loves to hear tell of or to be shown something that he calls 'outlandish.' Perhaps it was just that outlandishness of the man which influenced old Swaffer. Perhaps it was only an inexplicable caprice. All I know is that at the end of three weeks I caught sight of Smith's lunatic digging in Swaffer's kitchen garden. They had found out he could use a spade. He dug barefooted.

"His black hair flowed over his shoulders. I suppose it was Swaffer who had given him the striped old cotton shirt; but he wore still the national brown cloth trousers (in which he had been washed ashore) fitting to the leg almost like tights; was belted with a broad leathern belt studded with little brass discs; and had never yet ventured into the village. The land he looked upon seemed to him kept neatly, like the grounds round a landowner's house; the size of the cart-horses struck him with astonishment; the roads resembled garden walks, and the aspect of the people, especially on Sundays, spoke of opulence. He wondered what made them so hardhearted and their children so bold. He got his food at the back door, carried it in both hands carefully to his outhouse, and, sitting alone on his pallet, would make the sign of the cross before he began. Beside the same pallet, kneeling in the early darkness of the short days, he recited aloud the Lord's Prayer before he slept. Whenever he saw old Swaffer he would bow with veneration from the waist, and stand erect while the old man, with his fingers over his upper lip, surveyed him silently. He bowed also to Miss Swaffer, who kept house frugally for her father—a broad-shouldered, big-boned woman of forty-five, with the pocket of her dress full of keys, and a grey, steady eye. She was Church—as people said (while her father was one of the trustees of the Baptist Chapel)—and wore a little steel cross at her waist. She dressed severely in black, in memory of one of the innumerable Bradleys of the neighbourhood, to whom she had been engaged some twenty-five years ago—a young farmer who broke his neck out hunting on the eve of the wedding day. She had the unmoved countenance of the deaf, spoke very seldom, and her lips, thin like her father's, astonished one sometimes by a mysteriously ironic curl.

"These were the people to whom he owed allegiance, and an overwhelming loneliness seemed to fall from the leaden sky of that winter without sunshine. All the faces were sad. He could talk to no one, and had no hope of ever understanding anybody. It was as if these had been the faces of people from the other world—dead people—he used to tell me years afterwards. Upon my word, I wonder he did not go mad. He didn't know where he was. Somewhere very far from his mountains—somewhere over the water. Was this America, he wondered?

"If it hadn't been for the steel cross at Miss Swaffer's belt he would not, he confessed, have known whether he was in a Christian country at all. He used to cast stealthy glances at it, and feel comforted. There was nothing here the same as in his country! The earth and the water were different; there were no images of the Redeemer by the roadside. The very grass was different, and the trees. All the trees but the three old Norway pines on the bit of lawn before Swaffer's house, and these reminded him of his country. He had been detected once, after dusk, with his forehead against the trunk of one of them, sobbing, and talking to himself. They had been like brothers to him at that time, he affirmed. Everything else was strange. Conceive you the kind of an existence overshadowed, oppressed, by the everyday material appearances, as if by the visions of a nightmare. At night, when he could not sleep, he kept on thinking of the girl who gave him the first piece of bread he had eaten in this foreign land. She had been neither fierce nor angry, nor frightened. Her face he remembered as the only comprehensible face amongst all these faces that were as closed, as mysterious, and as mute as the faces of the dead who are possessed of a knowledge beyond the comprehension of the living. I wonder whether the memory of her compassion prevented him from cutting his throat. But there! I suppose I am an old sentimentalist, and forget the instinctive love of life which it takes all the strength of an uncommon despair to overcome.

"He did the work which was given him with an intelligence which surprised old Swaffer. By-and-by it was discovered that he could help at the ploughing, could milk the cows, feed the bullocks in the cattle-yard, and was of some use with the sheep. He began to pick up words, too, very fast; and suddenly, one fine morning in spring, he rescued from an untimely death a grand-child of old Swaffer.

"Swaffer's younger daughter is married to Willcox, a solicitor and the Town Clerk of Colebrook. Regularly twice a year they come to stay with the old man for a few days. Their only child, a little girl not three years old at the time, ran out of the house alone in her little white pinafore, and, toddling across the grass of a terraced garden, pitched herself over a low wall head first into the horse-pond in the yard below.

"Our man was out with the waggoner and the plough in the field nearest to the house, and as he was leading the team round to begin a fresh furrow, he saw, through the gap of the gate, what for anybody else would have been a mere flutter of something white. But he had straight-glancing, quick, far-reaching eyes, that only seemed to flinch and lose their amazing power before the immensity of the sea. He was barefooted, and looking as outlandish as the heart of Swaffer could desire. Leaving the horses on the turn, to the inexpressible disgust of the waggoner he bounded off, going over the ploughed ground in long leaps, and suddenly appeared before the mother, thrust the child into her arms, and strode away.

"The pond was not very deep; but still, if he had not had such good eyes, the child would have perished—miserably suffocated in the foot or so of sticky mud at the bottom. Old Swaffer walked out slowly into the field, waited till the plough came over to his side, had a good look at him, and without saying a word went back to the house. But from that time they laid out his meals on the kitchen table; and at first, Miss Swaffer, all in black and with an inscrutable face, would come and stand in the doorway of the living-room to see him make a big sign of the cross before he fell to. I believe that from that day, too, Swaffer began to pay him regular wages.

"I can't follow step by step his development. He cut his hair short, was seen in the village and along the road going to and fro to his work like any other man. Children ceased to shout after him. He became aware of social differences, but remained for a long time surprised at the bare poverty of the churches among so much wealth. He couldn't understand either why they were kept shut up on week days. There was nothing to steal in them. Was it to keep people from praying too often? The rectory took much notice of him about that time, and I believe the young ladies attempted to prepare the ground for his conversion. They could not, however, break him of his habit of crossing himself, but he went so far as to take off the string with a couple of brass medals the size of a sixpence, a tiny metal cross, and a square sort of scapulary which he wore round his neck. He hung them on the wall by the side of his bed, and he was still to be heard every evening reciting the Lord's Prayer, in incomprehensible words and in a slow, fervent tone, as he had heard his old father do at the head of all the kneeling family, big and little, on every evening of his life. And though he wore corduroys at work, and a slop-made pepper-and-salt suit on Sundays, strangers would turn round to look after him on the road. His foreignness had a peculiar and indelible stamp. At last people became used to see him. But they never became used to him. His rapid, skimming walk; his swarthy complexion; his hat cocked on the left ear; his habit, on warm evenings, of wearing his coat over one shoulder, like a hussar's dolman; his manner of leaping over the stiles, not as a feat of agility, but in the ordinary course of progression—all these peculiarities were, as one may say, so many causes of scorn and offence to the inhabitants of the village. *They* wouldn't in their dinner hour lie flat on their backs on the grass to stare at the sky. Neither did they go about the fields screaming dismal tunes. Many times have I heard his high-pitched voice from behind the ridge of some sloping sheep-walk, a voice light and soaring, like a lark's, but with a melancholy human note, over our fields that hear only the song of birds. And I should be startled myself. Ah! He was different: innocent of heart, and full of good will, which nobody wanted, this castaway, that, like a man transplanted into another planet, was separated by an immense space from his past and by an immense ignorance from his future. His quick, fervent utterance positively shocked everybody. 'An excitable devil,' they called him. One evening, in the tap-room of the Coach and Horses (having drunk some whisky), he upset them all by singing a love song of his country. They hooted him down, and he was pained; but Preble, the lame wheelwright, and Vincent, the fat blacksmith, and the other notables too, wanted to drink their evening beer in peace. On another occasion he tried to show them how to dance. The dust rose in clouds from the sanded floor; he leaped straight up amongst the deal tables, struck his heels together, squatted on one heel in front of old Preble, shooting out the other leg, uttered wild and exulting cries, jumped up to whirl on one foot, snapping his fingers above his head—and a strange carter who was having a drink in there began to swear, and cleared out with his half-pint in his hand into the bar. But when suddenly he sprang upon a table and continued to dance among the glasses, the landlord interfered. He didn't want any 'acrobat tricks in the taproom.' They laid their hands on him. Having had a glass or two, Mr. Swaffer's foreigner tried to expostulate: was ejected forcibly: got a black eye.

"I believe he felt the hostility of his human surroundings. But he was tough—tough in spirit, too, as well as in body. Only the memory of the sea frightened him, with that vague terror that is left by a bad dream. His home was far away; and he did not want now to go to America. I had often explained to him that there is no place on earth where true gold can be found lying ready and to be got for the trouble of the picking up. How then, he asked, could he ever return home with empty hands when there had been sold a cow, two ponies, and a bit of land to pay for his going? His eyes would fill with tears, and, averting them from the immense shimmer of the sea, he would throw himself face down on the grass. But sometimes, cocking his hat with a little conquering air, he would defy my wisdom. He had found his bit of true gold. That was Amy Foster's heart; which was 'a golden heart, and soft to people's misery,' he would say in the accents of overwhelming conviction.

"He was called Yanko. He had explained that this meant little John; but as he would also repeat very often that he was a mountaineer (some word sounding in the dialect of his country like Goorall) he got it for his surname. And this is the only trace of him that the succeeding ages may find in the marriage register of the parish. There it stands—Yanko Goorall—in the rector's handwriting. The crooked cross made by the castaway, a cross whose tracing no doubt seemed to him the most solemn part of the whole ceremony, is all that remains now to perpetuate the memory of his name.

"His courtship had lasted some time—ever since he got his precarious footing in the community. It began by his buying for Amy Foster a green satin ribbon in Darnford. This was what you did in his country. You bought a ribbon at a Jew's stall on a fair-day. I don't suppose the girl knew what to do with it, but he seemed to think that his honourable intentions could not be mistaken.

"It was only when he declared his purpose to get married that I fully understood how, for a hundred futile and inappreciable reasons, how—shall I say odious?—he was to all the countryside. Every old woman in the village was up in arms. Smith, coming upon him near the farm, promised to break his head for him if he found him about again. But he twisted his little black moustache with such a bellicose air and rolled such big, black fierce eyes at Smith that this promise came to nothing. Smith, however, told the girl that she must be mad to take up with a man who was surely wrong in his head. All the same, when she heard him in the gloaming whistle from beyond the orchard a couple of bars of a weird and mournful tune, she would drop whatever she had in her hand—she would leave Mrs. Smith in the middle of a sentence—and she would run out to his call. Mrs. Smith called her a shameless hussy. She answered nothing. She said nothing at all to anybody, and went on her way as if she had been deaf. She and I alone all in the land, I fancy, could see his very real beauty. He was very good-looking, and most graceful in his bearing, with that something wild as of a woodland creature in his aspect. Her mother moaned over her dismally whenever the girl came to see her on her day out. The father was surly, but pretended not to know; and Mrs. Finn once told her plainly that 'this man, my dear, will do you some harm some day yet.' And so it went on. They could be seen on the roads, she tramping stolidly in her finery—grey dress, black feather, stout boots, prominent white cotton gloves that caught your eye a hundred yards away; and he, his coat slung picturesquely over one shoulder, pacing by her side, gallant of bearing and casting tender glances upon the girl with the golden heart. I wonder whether he saw how plain she was. Perhaps among types so different from what he had ever seen, he had not the power to judge; or perhaps he was seduced by the divine quality of her pity.

"Yanko was in great trouble meantime. In his country you get an old man for an ambassador in marriage affairs. He did not know how to proceed. However, one day in the midst of sheep in a field (he was now Swaffer's under-shepherd with Foster) he took off his hat to the father and declared himself humbly. 'I daresay she's fool enough to marry you,' was all Foster said. 'And then,' he used to relate, 'he puts his hat on his head, looks black at me as if he wanted to cut my throat, whistles the dog, and off he goes, leaving me to do the work.' The Fosters, of course, didn't like to lose the wages the girl earned: Amy used to give all her money to her mother. But there was in Foster a very genuine aversion to that match. He contended that the fellow was very good with sheep, but was not fit for any girl to marry. For one thing, he used to go along the hedges muttering to himself like a dam' fool; and then, these foreigners behave very queerly to women sometimes. And perhaps he would want to carry her off somewhere—or run off himself. It was not safe. He preached it to his daughter that the fellow might ill-use her in some way. She made no answer. It was, they said in the village, as if the man had done something to her. People discussed the matter. It was quite an excitement, and the two went on 'walking out' together in the face of opposition. Then something unexpected happened.

"I don't know whether old Swaffer ever understood how much he was regarded in the light of a father by his foreign retainer. Anyway the relation was curiously feudal. So when Yanko asked formally for an interview—'and the Miss too' (he called the severe, deaf Miss Swaffer simply *Miss*)—it was to obtain their permission to marry. Swaffer heard him unmoved, dismissed him by a nod, and then shouted the intelligence into Miss Swaffer's best ear. She showed no surprise, and only remarked grimly, in a veiled blank voice, 'He certainly won't get any other girl to marry him.'

"It is Miss Swaffer who has all the credit of the munificence: but in a very few days it came out that Mr. Swaffer had presented Yanko with a cottage (the cottage you've seen this morning) and something like an acre of ground—had made it over to him in absolute property. Willcox expedited the deed, and I remember him telling me he had a great pleasure in making it ready. It recited: 'In consideration of saving the life of my beloved grandchild, Bertha Willcox.'

"Of course, after that no power on earth could prevent them from getting married.

"Her infatuation endured. People saw her going out to meet him in the evening. She stared with unblinking, fascinated eyes up the road where he was expected to appear, walking freely, with a swing from the hip, and humming one of the love-tunes of his country. When the boy was born, he got elevated at the 'Coach and Horses,' essayed again a song and a dance, and was again ejected. People expressed their commiseration for a woman married to that Jack-in-the-box. He didn't care. There was a man now (he told me boastfully) to whom he could sing and talk in the language of his country, and show how to dance by-and-by.

"But I don't know. To me he appeared to have grown less springy of step, heavier in body, less keen of eye. Imagination, no doubt; but it seems to me now as if the net of fate had been drawn closer round him already.

"One day I met him on the footpath over the Talfourd Hill. He told me that 'women were funny.' I had heard already of domestic differences. People were saying that Amy Foster was beginning to find out what sort of man she had married. He looked upon the sea with indifferent, unseeing eyes. His wife had snatched the child out of his arms one day as he sat on the doorstep crooning to it a song such as the mothers sing to babies in his mountains. She seemed to think he was doing it some harm. Women are funny. And she had objected to him praying aloud in the evening. Why? He expected the boy to repeat the prayer aloud after him by-and-by, as he used to do after his old father when he was a child—in his own country. And I discovered he longed for their boy to grow up so that he could have a man to talk with in that language that to our ears sounded so disturbing, so passionate, and so bizarre. Why his wife should dislike the idea he couldn't tell. But that would pass, he said. And tilting his head knowingly, he tapped his breastbone to indicate that she had a good heart: not hard, not fierce, open to compassion, charitable to the poor!

"I walked away thoughtfully; I wondered whether his difference, his strangeness, were not penetrating with repulsion that dull nature they had begun by irresistibly attracting. I wondered...."

The Doctor came to the window and looked out at the frigid splendour of the sea, immense in the haze, as if enclosing all the earth with all the hearts lost among the passions of love and fear.

"Physiologically, now," he said, turning away abruptly, "it was possible. It was possible."

He remained silent. Then went on—"At all events, the next time I saw him he was ill—lung trouble. He was tough, but I daresay he was not acclimatised as well as I had supposed. It was a bad winter; and, of course, these mountaineers do get fits of home sickness; and a state of depression would make him vulnerable. He was lying half dressed on a couch downstairs.

"A table covered with a dark oilcloth took up all the middle of the little room. There was a wicker cradle on the floor, a kettle spouting steam on the hob, and some child's linen lay drying on the fender. The room was warm, but the door opens right into the garden, as you noticed perhaps.

"He was very feverish, and kept on muttering to himself. She sat on a chair and looked at him fixedly across the table with her brown, blurred eyes. 'Why don't you have him upstairs?' I asked. With a start and a confused stammer she said, 'Oh! ah! I couldn't sit with him upstairs, Sir.'

"I gave her certain directions; and going outside, I said again that he ought to be in bed upstairs. She wrung her hands. 'I couldn't. I couldn't. He keeps on saying something—I don't know what.' With the memory of all the talk against the man that had been dinned into her ears, I looked at her narrowly. I looked into her shortsighted eyes, at her dumb eyes that once in her life had seen an enticing shape, but seemed, staring at me, to see nothing at all now. But I saw she was uneasy.

"'What's the matter with him?' she asked in a sort of vacant trepidation. 'He doesn't look very ill. I never did see anybody look like this before....'

"'Do you think,' I asked indignantly, 'he is shamming?'

"'I can't help it, sir,' she said stolidly. And suddenly she clapped her hands and looked right and left. 'And there's the baby. I am so frightened. He wanted me just now to give him the baby. I can't understand what he says to it.'

"'Can't you ask a neighbour to come in tonight?' I asked.

"'Please, sir, nobody seems to care to come,' she muttered, dully resigned all at once.

"I impressed upon her the necessity of the greatest care, and then had to go. There was a good deal of sickness that winter. 'Oh, I hope he won't talk!' she exclaimed softly just as I was going away.

"I don't know how it is I did not see—but I didn't. And yet, turning in my trap, I saw her lingering before the door, very still, and as if meditating a flight up the miry road.

"Towards the night his fever increased.

"He tossed, moaned, and now and then muttered a complaint. And she sat with the table between her and the couch, watching every movement and every sound, with the terror, the unreasonable terror, of that man she could not understand creeping over her. She had drawn the wicker cradle close to her feet. There was nothing in her now but the maternal instinct and that unaccountable fear.

"Suddenly coming to himself, parched, he demanded a drink of water. She did not move. She had not understood, though he may have thought he was speaking in English. He waited, looking at her, burning with fever, amazed at her silence and immobility, and then he shouted impatiently, 'Water! Give me water!'

"She jumped to her feet, snatched up the child, and stood still. He spoke to her, and his passionate remonstrances only increased her fear of that strange man. I believe he spoke to her for a long time, entreating, wondering, pleading, ordering, I suppose. She says she bore it as long as she could. And then a gust of rage came over him.

"He sat up and called out terribly one word—some word. Then he got up as though he hadn't been ill at all, she says. And as in fevered dismay, indignation, and wonder he tried to get to her round the table, she simply opened the door and ran out with the child in her arms. She heard him call twice after her down the road in a terrible voice—and fled.... Ah! but you should have seen stirring behind the dull, blurred glance of these eyes the spectre of the fear which had hunted her on that night three miles and a half to the door of Foster's cottage! I did the next day.

"And it was I who found him lying face down and his body in a puddle, just outside the little wicket-gate.

"I had been called out that night to an urgent case in the village, and on my way home at daybreak passed by the cottage. The door stood open. My man helped me to carry him in. We laid him on the couch. The lamp smoked, the fire was out, the chill of the stormy night oozed from the cheerless yellow paper on the wall. 'Amy!' I called aloud, and my voice seemed to lose itself in the emptiness of this tiny house as if I had cried in a desert. He opened his eyes. 'Gone!' he said distinctly. 'I had only asked for water—only for a little water....'

"He was muddy. I covered him up and stood waiting in silence, catching a painfully gasped word now and then. They were no longer in his own language. The fever had left him, taking with it the heat of life. And with his panting breast and lustrous eyes he reminded me again of a wild creature under the net; of a bird caught in a snare. She had left him. She had left him—sick—helpless—thirsty. The spear of the hunter had entered his very soul. 'Why?' he cried in the penetrating and indignant voice of a man calling to a responsible Maker. A gust of wind and a swish of rain answered.

"And as I turned away to shut the door he pronounced the word 'Merciful!' and expired.

"Eventually I certified heart-failure as the immediate cause of death. His heart must have indeed failed him, or else he might have stood this night of storm and exposure, too. I closed his eyes and drove away. Not very far from the cottage I met Foster walking sturdily between the dripping hedges with his collie at his heels.

"'Do you know where your daughter is?' I asked.

"'Don't I!' he cried. 'I am going to talk to him a bit. Frightening a poor woman like this.'

"'He won't frighten her any more,' I said. 'He is dead.'

"He struck with his stick at the mud.

"'And there's the child.'

"Then, after thinking deeply for a while—"'I don't know that it isn't for the best.'

"That's what he said. And she says nothing at all now. Not a word of him. Never. Is his image as utterly gone from her mind as his lithe and striding figure, his carolling voice are gone from our fields? He is no longer before her eyes to excite her imagination into a passion of love or fear; and his memory seems to have vanished from her dull brain as a shadow passes away upon a white screen. She lives in the cottage and works for Miss Swaffer. She is Amy Foster for everybody, and the child is 'Amy Foster's boy.' She calls him Johnny—which means Little John.

"It is impossible to say whether this name recalls anything to her. Does she ever think of the past? I have seen her hanging over the boy's cot in a very passion of maternal tenderness. The little fellow was lying on his back, a little frightened at me, but very still, with his big black eyes, with his fluttered air of a bird in a snare. And looking at him I seemed to see again the other one—the father, cast out mysteriously by the sea to perish in the supreme disaster of loneliness and despair."

THE OPEN BOAT

STEPHEN CRANE

THE OPEN BOAT

A TALE INTENDED TO BE AFTER THE FACT. BEING THE EXPERIENCE OF FOUR MEN FROM THE SUNK STEAMER 'COMMODORE'

I

None of them knew the colour of the sky. Their eyes glanced level, and were fastened upon the waves that swept toward them. These waves were of the hue of slate, save for the tops, which were of foaming white, and all of the men knew the colours of the sea. The horizon narrowed and widened, and dipped and rose, and at all times its edge was jagged with waves that seemed thrust up in points like rocks.

Many a man ought to have a bath-tub larger than the boat which here rode upon the sea. These waves were most wrongfully and barbarously abrupt and tall, and each froth-top was a problem in small boat navigation.

The cook squatted in the bottom and looked with both eyes at the six inches of gunwale which separated him from the ocean. His sleeves were rolled over his fat forearms, and the two flaps of his unbuttoned vest dangled as he bent to bail out the boat. Often he said: "Gawd! That was a narrow clip." As he remarked it he invariably gazed eastward over the broken sea.

The oiler, steering with one of the two oars in the boat, sometimes raised himself suddenly to keep clear of water that swirled in over the stern. It was a thin little oar and it seemed often ready to snap.

The correspondent, pulling at the other oar, watched the waves and wondered why he was there.

The injured captain, lying in the bow, was at this time buried in that profound dejection and indifference which comes, temporarily at least, to even the bravest and most enduring when, willy nilly, the firm fails, the army loses, the ship goes down. The mind of the master of a vessel is rooted deep in the timbers of her, though he commanded for a day or a decade, and this captain had on him the stern impression of a scene in the greys of dawn of seven turned faces, and later a stump of a top-mast with a white ball on it that slashed to and fro at the waves, went low and lower, and down. Thereafter there was something strange in his voice. Although steady, it was deep with mourning, and of a quality beyond oration or tears.

"Keep 'er a little more south, Billie," said he.

"'A little more south,' sir," said the oiler in the stern.

A seat in this boat was not unlike a seat upon a bucking broncho, and, by the same token, a broncho is not much smaller. The craft pranced and reared, and plunged like an animal. As each wave came, and she rose for it, she seemed like a horse making at a fence outrageously high. The manner of her scramble over these walls of water is a mystic thing, and, moreover, at the top of them were ordinarily these problems in white water, the foam racing down from the summit of each wave, requiring a new leap, and a leap from the air. Then, after scornfully bumping a crest, she would slide, and race, and splash down a long incline, and arrive bobbing and nodding in front of the next menace.

A singular disadvantage of the sea lies in the fact that after successfully surmounting one wave you discover that there is another behind it just as important and just as nervously anxious to do something effective in the way of swamping boats. In a ten-foot dingey one can get an idea of the resources of the sea in the line of waves that is not probable to the average experience which is never at sea in a dingey. As each slaty wall of water approached, it shut all else from the view of the men in the boat, and it was not difficult to imagine that this particular wave was the final outburst of the ocean, the last effort of the grim water. There was a terrible grace in the move of the waves, and they came in silence, save for the snarling of the crests.

In the wan light, the faces of the men must have been grey. Their eyes must have glinted in strange ways as they gazed steadily astern. Viewed from a balcony, the whole thing would doubtlessly have been weirdly picturesque. But the men in the boat had no time to see it, and if they had had leisure there were other things to occupy their minds. The sun swung steadily up the sky, and they knew it was broad day because the colour of the sea changed from slate to emerald-green, streaked with amber lights, and the foam was like tumbling snow. The process of the breaking day was unknown to them. They were aware only of this effect upon the colour of the waves that rolled toward them.

In disjointed sentences the cook and the correspondent argued as to the difference between a life-saving station and a house of refuge. The cook had said: "There's a house of refuge just north of the Mosquito Inlet Light, and as soon as they see us, they'll come off in their boat and pick us up."

"As soon as who see us?" said the correspondent.

"The crew," said the cook.

"Houses of refuge don't have crews," said the correspondent. "As I understand them, they are only places where clothes and grub are stored for the benefit of shipwrecked people. They don't carry crews."

"Oh, yes, they do," said the cook.

"No, they don't," said the correspondent.

"Well, we're not there yet, anyhow," said the oiler, in the stern.

"Well," said the cook, "perhaps it's not a house of refuge that I'm thinking of as being near Mosquito Inlet Light. Perhaps it's a life-saving station."

"We're not there yet," said the oiler, in the stern.

II

As the boat bounced from the top of each wave, the wind tore through the hair of the hatless men, and as the craft plopped her stern down again the spray slashed past them. The

THE OPEN BOAT

crest of each of these waves was a hill, from the top of which the men surveyed, for a moment, a broad tumultuous expanse, shining and wind-riven. It was probably splendid. It was probably glorious, this play of the free sea, wild with lights of emerald and white and amber.

"Bully good thing it's an on-shore wind," said the cook. "If not, where would we be? Wouldn't have a show."

"That's right," said the correspondent.

The busy oiler nodded his assent.

Then the captain, in the bow, chuckled in a way that expressed humour, contempt, tragedy, all in one. "Do you think we've got much of a show now, boys?" said he.

Whereupon the three were silent, save for a trifle of hemming and hawing. To express any particular optimism at this time they felt to be childish and stupid, but they all doubtless possessed this sense of the situation in their mind. A young man thinks doggedly at such times. On the other hand, the ethics of their condition was decidedly against any open suggestion of hopelessness. So they were silent.

"Oh, well," said the captain, soothing his children, "we'll get ashore all right."

But there was that in his tone which made them think, so the oiler quoth: "Yes! If this wind holds!"

The cook was bailing: "Yes! If we don't catch hell in the surf."

Canton flannel gulls flew near and far. Sometimes they sat down on the sea, near patches of brown sea-weed that rolled over the waves with a movement like carpets on a line in a gale. The birds sat comfortably in groups, and they were envied by some in the dingey, for the wrath of the sea was no more to them than it was to a covey of prairie chickens a thousand miles inland. Often they came very close and stared at the men with black bead-like eyes. At these times they were uncanny and sinister in their unblinking scrutiny, and the men hooted angrily at them, telling them to be gone. One came, and evidently decided to alight on the top of the captain's head. The bird flew parallel to the boat and did not circle, but made short sidelong jumps in the air in chicken-fashion. His black eyes were wistfully fixed upon the captain's head. "Ugly brute," said the oiler to the bird. "You look as if you were made with a jack-knife." The cook and the correspondent swore darkly at the creature. The captain naturally wished to knock it away with the end of the heavy painter; but he did not dare do it, because anything resembling an emphatic gesture would have capsized this freighted boat, and so with his open hand, the captain gently and carefully waved the gull away. After it had been discouraged from the pursuit the captain breathed easier on account of his hair, and others breathed easier because the bird struck their minds at this time as being somehow grewsome and ominous.

In the meantime the oiler and the correspondent rowed. And also they rowed.

They sat together in the same seat, and each rowed an oar. Then the oiler took both oars; then the correspondent took both oars; then the oiler; then the correspondent. They rowed and they rowed. The very ticklish part of the business was when the time came for the reclining one in the stern to take his turn at the oars. By the very last star of truth, it is easier to steal eggs from under a hen than it was to change seats in the dingey. First the man in the stern slid his hand along the thwart and moved with care, as if he were of Sèvres. Then the man in the rowing seat slid his hand along the other thwart. It was all done with the most extraordinary care. As the two sidled past each other, the whole party kept watchful eyes on the coming wave, and the captain cried: "Look out now! Steady there!"

The brown mats of sea-weed that appeared from time to time were like islands, bits of earth. They were travelling, apparently, neither one way nor the other. They were, to all intents, stationary. They informed the men in the boat that it was making progress slowly toward the land.

The captain, rearing cautiously in the bow, after the dingey soared on a great swell, said that he had seen the lighthouse at Mosquito Inlet. Presently the cook remarked that he had seen it. The correspondent was at the oars then, and for some reason he too wished to look at the lighthouse, but his back was toward the far shore and the waves were important, and for some time he could not seize an opportunity to turn his head. But at last there came a wave more gentle than the others, and when at the crest of it he swiftly scoured the western horizon.

"See it?" said the captain.

"No," said the correspondent slowly, "I didn't see anything."

"Look again," said the captain. He pointed. "It's exactly in that direction."

At the top of another wave, the correspondent did as he was bid, and this time his eyes chanced on a small still thing on the edge of the swaying horizon. It was precisely like the point of a pin. It took an anxious eye to find a lighthouse so tiny.

"Think we'll make it, captain?"

"If this wind holds and the boat don't swamp, we can't do much else," said the captain.

The little boat, lifted by each towering sea, and splashed viciously by the crests, made progress that in the absence of sea-weed was not apparent to those in her. She seemed just a wee thing wallowing, miraculously top-up, at the mercy of five oceans. Occasionally, a great spread of water, like white flames, swarmed into her.

"Bail her, cook," said the captain serenely.

"All right, captain," said the cheerful cook.

III

It would be difficult to describe the subtle brotherhood of men that was here established on the seas. No one said that it was so. No one mentioned it. But it dwelt in the boat, and each man felt it warm him. They were a captain, an oiler, a cook, and a correspondent, and they were friends, friends in a more curiously iron-bound degree than may be common. The hurt captain, lying against the water-jar in the bow, spoke always in a low voice and calmly, but he could never command a more ready and swiftly obedient crew than the motley three of the dingey. It was more than a mere recognition of what was best for the common safety. There was surely in it a quality that was personal and heartfelt. And after this devotion to the commander of the boat there was this comradeship that the correspondent, for instance, who had been taught to be cynical of men, knew even at the time was the best experience of his life. But no one said that it was so. No one mentioned it.

"I wish we had a sail," remarked the captain. "We might try my overcoat on the end of an oar and give you two boys a chance to rest." So the cook and the correspondent held the mast and spread wide the overcoat. The oiler steered, and the little boat made good way with her new rig. Sometimes the oiler had to scull sharply to keep a sea from breaking into the boat, but otherwise sailing was a success.

Meanwhile the lighthouse had been growing slowly larger. It had now almost assumed colour, and appeared like a little grey shadow on the sky. The man at the oars could not be prevented from turning his head rather often to try for a glimpse of this little grey shadow.

At last, from the top of each wave the men in the tossing boat could see land. Even as the lighthouse was an upright shadow on the sky, this land seemed but a long black shadow on

THE OPEN BOAT

the sea. It certainly was thinner than paper. "We must be about opposite New Smyrna," said the cook, who had coasted this shore often in schooners. "Captain, by the way, I believe they abandoned that life-saving station there about a year ago."

"Did they?" said the captain.

The wind slowly died away. The cook and the correspondent were not now obliged to slave in order to hold high the oar. But the waves continued their old impetuous swooping at the dingey, and the little craft, no longer under way, struggled woundily over them. The oiler or the correspondent took the oars again.

Shipwrecks are *à propos* of nothing. If men could only train for them and have them occur when the men had reached pink condition, there would be less drowning at sea. Of the four in the dingey none had slept any time worth mentioning for two days and two nights previous to embarking in the dingey, and in the excitement of clambering about the deck of a foundering ship they had also forgotten to eat heartily.

For these reasons, and for others, neither the oiler nor the correspondent was fond of rowing at this time. The correspondent wondered ingenuously how in the name of all that was sane could there be people who thought it amusing to row a boat. It was not an amusement; it was a diabolical punishment, and even a genius of mental aberrations could never conclude that it was anything but a horror to the muscles and a crime against the back. He mentioned to the boat in general how the amusement of rowing struck him, and the weary-faced oiler smiled in full sympathy. Previously to the foundering, by the way, the oiler had worked double-watch in the engine-room of the ship.

"Take her easy, now, boys," said the captain. "Don't spend yourselves. If we have to run a surf you'll need all your strength, because we'll sure have to swim for it. Take your time."

Slowly the land arose from the sea. From a black line it became a line of black and a line of white, trees and sand. Finally, the captain said that he could make out a house on the shore. "That's the house of refuge, sure," said the cook. "They'll see us before long, and come out after us."

The distant lighthouse reared high. "The keeper ought to be able to make us out now, if he's looking through a glass," said the captain. "He'll notify the life-saving people."

"None of those other boats could have got ashore to give word of the wreck," said the oiler, in a low voice. "Else the life-boat would be out hunting us."

Slowly and beautifully the land loomed out of the sea. The wind came again. It had veered from the north-east to the south-east. Finally, a new sound struck the ears of the men in the boat. It was the low thunder of the surf on the shore. "We'll never be able to make the lighthouse now," said the captain. "Swing her head a little more north, Billie," said he.

"'A little more north,' sir," said the oiler.

Whereupon the little boat turned her nose once more down the wind, and all but the oarsman watched the shore grow. Under the influence of this expansion doubt and direful apprehension was leaving the minds of the men. The management of the boat was still most absorbing, but it could not prevent a quiet cheerfulness. In an hour, perhaps, they would be ashore.

Their backbones had become thoroughly used to balancing in the boat, and they now rode this wild colt of a dingey like circus men. The correspondent thought that he had been drenched to the skin, but happening to feel in the top pocket of his coat, he found therein eight cigars. Four of them were soaked with sea-water; four were perfectly scatheless. After a search, somebody produced three dry matches, and thereupon the four waifs rode impudently in their little boat, and with an assurance of an impending rescue shining in their eyes, puffed at the big cigars and judged well and ill of all men. Everybody took a drink of water.

IV

"Cook," remarked the captain, "there don't seem to be any signs of life about your house of refuge."

"No," replied the cook. "Funny they don't see us!"

A broad stretch of lowly coast lay before the eyes of the men. It was of dunes topped with dark vegetation. The roar of the surf was plain, and sometimes they could see the white lip of a wave as it spun up the beach. A tiny house was blocked out black upon the sky. Southward, the slim lighthouse lifted its little grey length.

Tide, wind, and waves were swinging the dingey northward. "Funny they don't see us," said the men.

The surf's roar was here dulled, but its tone was, nevertheless, thunderous and mighty. As the boat swam over the great rollers, the men sat listening to this roar. "We'll swamp sure," said everybody.

It is fair to say here that there was not a life-saving station within twenty miles in either direction, but the men did not know this fact, and in consequence they made dark and opprobrious remarks concerning the eyesight of the nation's life-savers. Four scowling men sat in the dingey and surpassed records in the invention of epithets.

"Funny they don't see us."

The light-heartedness of a former time had completely faded. To their sharpened minds it was easy to conjure pictures of all kinds of incompetency and blindness and, indeed, cowardice. There was the shore of the populous land, and it was bitter and bitter to them that from it came no sign.

"Well," said the captain, ultimately, "I suppose we'll have to make a try for ourselves. If we stay out here too long, we'll none of us have strength left to swim after the boat swamps."

And so the oiler, who was at the oars, turned the boat straight for the shore. There was a sudden tightening of muscles. There was some thinking.

"If we don't all get ashore—" said the captain. "If we don't all get ashore, I suppose you fellows know where to send news of my finish?"

They then briefly exchanged some addresses and admonitions. As for the reflections of the men, there was a great deal of rage in them. Perchance they might be formulated thus: "If I am going to be drowned—if I am going to be drowned—if I am going to be drowned, why, in the name of the seven mad gods who rule the sea, was I allowed to come thus far and contemplate sand and trees? Was I brought here merely to have my nose dragged away as I was about to nibble the sacred cheese of life? It is preposterous. If this old ninny-woman, Fate, cannot do better than this, she should be deprived of the management of men's fortunes. She is an old hen who knows not her intention. If she has decided to drown me, why did she not do it in the beginning and save me all this trouble? The whole affair is absurd.... But no, she cannot mean to drown me. She dare not drown me. She cannot drown me. Not after all this work." Afterward the man might have had an impulse to shake his fist at the clouds: "Just you drown me, now, and then hear what I call you!"

The billows that came at this time were more formidable. They seemed always just about to break and roll over the little boat in a turmoil of foam. There was a preparatory and long growl in the speech of them. No mind unused to the sea would have concluded that the dingey could ascend these sheer heights in time. The shore was still afar. The oiler was a wily surfman. "Boys," he said swiftly, "she won't live three minutes more, and we're too far out to swim. Shall I take her to sea again, captain?"

"Yes! Go ahead!" said the captain.

This oiler, by a series of quick miracles, and fast and steady oarsmanship, turned the boat in the middle of the surf and took her safely to sea again.

There was a considerable silence as the boat bumped over the furrowed sea to deeper water. Then somebody in gloom spoke. "Well, anyhow, they must have seen us from the shore by now."

The gulls went in slanting flight up the wind toward the grey desolate east. A squall, marked by dingy clouds, and clouds brick-red, like smoke from a burning building, appeared from the south-east.

"What do you think of those life-saving people? Ain't they peaches?"

"Funny they haven't seen us."

"Maybe they think we're out here for sport! Maybe they think we're fishin'. Maybe they think we're damned fools."

It was a long afternoon. A changed tide tried to force them southward, but wind and wave said northward. Far ahead, where coast-line, sea, and sky formed their mighty angle, there were little dots which seemed to indicate a city on the shore.

"St. Augustine?"

The captain shook his head. "Too near Mosquito Inlet."

And the oiler rowed, and then the correspondent rowed. Then the oiler rowed. It was a weary business. The human back can become the seat of more aches and pains than are registered in books for the composite anatomy of a regiment. It is a limited area, but it can become the theatre of innumerable muscular conflicts, tangles, wrenches, knots, and other comforts.

"Did you ever like to row, Billie?" asked the correspondent.

"No," said the oiler. "Hang it."

When one exchanged the rowing-seat for a place in the bottom of the boat, he suffered a bodily depression that caused him to be careless of everything save an obligation to wiggle one finger. There was cold sea-water swashing to and fro in the boat, and he lay in it. His head, pillowed on a thwart, was within an inch of the swirl of a wave crest, and sometimes a particularly obstreperous sea came in-board and drenched him once more. But these matters did not annoy him. It is almost certain that if the boat had capsized he would have tumbled comfortably out upon the ocean as if he felt sure that it was a great soft mattress.

"Look! There's a man on the shore!"

"Where?"

"There! See 'im? See 'im?"

"Yes, sure! He's walking along."

"Now he's stopped. Look! He's facing us!"

"He's waving at us!"

"So he is! By thunder!"

"Ah, now we're all right! Now we're all right! There'll be a boat out here for us in half-an-hour."

"He's going on. He's running. He's going up to that house there."

The remote beach seemed lower than the sea, and it required a searching glance to discern the little black figure. The captain saw a floating stick and they rowed to it. A bath-towel was by some weird chance in the boat, and, tying this on the stick, the captain waved it. The oarsman did not dare turn his head, so he was obliged to ask questions.

"What's he doing now?"

"He's standing still again. He's looking, I think.... There he goes again. Towards the house.... Now he's stopped again."

"Is he waving at us?"

"No, not now! he was, though."

"Look! There comes another man!"

"He's running."

"Look at him go, would you."

"Why, he's on a bicycle. Now he's met the other man. They're both waving at us. Look!"

"There comes something up the beach."

"What the devil is that thing?"

"Why, it looks like a boat."

"Why, certainly it's a boat."

"No, it's on wheels."

"Yes, so it is. Well, that must be the life-boat. They drag them along shore on a wagon."

"That's the life-boat, sure."

"No, by ——, it's—it's an omnibus."

"I tell you it's a life-boat."

"It is not! It's an omnibus. I can see it plain. See? One of these big hotel omnibuses."

"By thunder, you're right. It's an omnibus, sure as fate. What do you suppose they are doing with an omnibus? Maybe they are going around collecting the life-crew, hey?"

"That's it, likely. Look! There's a fellow waving a little black flag. He's standing on the steps of the omnibus. There come those other two fellows. Now they're all talking together. Look at the fellow with the flag. Maybe he ain't waving it."

"That ain't a flag, is it? That's his coat. Why certainly, that's his coat."

"So it is. It's his coat. He's taken it off and is waving it around his head. But would you look at him swing it."

"Oh, say, there isn't any life-saving station there. That's just a winter resort hotel omnibus that has brought over some of the boarders to see us drown."

"What's that idiot with the coat mean? What's he signaling, anyhow?"

"It looks as if he were trying to tell us to go north. There must be a life-saving station up there."

"No! He thinks we're fishing. Just giving us a merry hand. See? Ah, there, Willie."

"Well, I wish I could make something out of those signals. What do you suppose he means?"

"He don't mean anything. He's just playing."

"Well, if he'd just signal us to try the surf again, or to go to sea and wait, or go north, or go south, or go to hell—there would be some reason in it. But look at him. He just stands there and keeps his coat revolving like a wheel. The ass!"

"There come more people."

"Now there's quite a mob. Look! Isn't that a boat?"

"Where? Oh, I see where you mean. No, that's no boat."

"That fellow is still waving his coat."

"He must think we like to see him do that. Why don't he quit it? It don't mean anything."

"I don't know. I think he is trying to make us go north. It must be that there's a life-saving station there somewhere."

"Say, he ain't tired yet. Look at 'im wave."

"Wonder how long he can keep that up. He's been revolving his coat ever since he caught sight of us. He's an idiot. Why aren't they getting men to bring a boat out? A fishing boat—one of those big yawls—could come out here all right. Why don't he do something?"

"Oh, it's all right, now."

"They'll have a boat out here for us in less than no time, now that they've seen us."

A faint yellow tone came into the sky over the low land. The shadows on the sea slowly deepened. The wind bore coldness with it, and the men began to shiver.

"Holy smoke!" said one, allowing his voice to express his impious mood, "if we keep on monkeying out here! If we've got to flounder out here all night!"

"Oh, we'll never have to stay here all night! Don't you worry. They've seen us now, and it won't be long before they'll come chasing out after us."

The shore grew dusky. The man waving a coat blended gradually into this gloom, and it swallowed in the same manner the omnibus and the group of people. The spray, when it dashed uproariously over the side, made the voyagers shrink and swear like men who were being branded.

"I'd like to catch the chump who waved the coat. I feel like soaking him one, just for luck."

"Why? What did he do?"

"Oh, nothing, but then he seemed so damned cheerful."

In the meantime the oiler rowed, and then the correspondent rowed, and then the oiler rowed. Grey-faced and bowed forward, they mechanically, turn by turn, plied the leaden oars. The form of the lighthouse had vanished from the southern horizon, but finally a pale star appeared, just lifting from the sea. The streaked saffron in the west passed before the all-merging darkness, and the sea to the east was black. The land had vanished, and was expressed only by the low and drear thunder of the surf.

"If I am going to be drowned—if I am going to be drowned—if I am going to be drowned, why, in the name of the seven mad gods who rule the sea, was I allowed to come thus far and contemplate sand and trees? Was I brought here merely to have my nose dragged away as I was about to nibble the sacred cheese of life?"

The patient captain, drooped over the water-jar, was sometimes obliged to speak to the oarsman.

"Keep her head up! Keep her head up!"

"'Keep her head up,' sir." The voices were weary and low.

This was surely a quiet evening. All save the oarsman lay heavily and listlessly in the boat's bottom. As for him, his eyes were just capable of noting the tall black waves that swept forward in a most sinister silence, save for an occasional subdued growl of a crest.

The cook's head was on a thwart, and he looked without interest at the water under his nose. He was deep in other scenes. Finally he spoke. "Billie," he murmured, dreamfully, "what kind of pie do you like best?"

V

"Pie," said the oiler and the correspondent, agitatedly. "Don't talk about those things, blast you!"

"Well," said the cook, "I was just thinking about ham sandwiches, and——"

A night on the sea in an open boat is a long night. As darkness settled finally, the shine of the light, lifting from the sea in the south, changed to full gold. On the northern horizon a new light appeared, a small bluish gleam on the edge of the waters. These two lights were the furniture of the world. Otherwise there was nothing but waves.

Two men huddled in the stern, and distances were so magnificent in the dingey that the rower was enabled to keep his feet partly warmed by thrusting them under his companions. Their legs indeed extended far under the rowing-seat until they touched the feet of the captain forward. Sometimes, despite the efforts of the tired oarsman, a wave came piling into the boat, an icy wave of the night, and the chilling water soaked them anew. They would twist their bodies for a moment and groan, and sleep the dead sleep once more, while the water in the boat gurgled about them as the craft rocked.

The plan of the oiler and the correspondent was for one to row until he lost the ability, and then arouse the other from his sea-water couch in the bottom of the boat.

The oiler plied the oars until his head drooped forward, and the overpowering sleep blinded him. And he rowed yet afterward. Then he touched a man in the bottom of the boat, and called his name. "Will you spell me for a little while?" he said, meekly.

"Sure, Billie," said the correspondent, awakening and dragging himself to a sitting position. They exchanged places carefully, and the oiler, cuddling down in the sea-water at the cook's side, seemed to go to sleep instantly.

The particular violence of the sea had ceased. The waves came without snarling. The obligation of the man at the oars was to keep the boat headed so that the tilt of the rollers would not capsize her, and to preserve her from filling when the crests rushed past. The black waves were silent and hard to be seen in the darkness. Often one was almost upon the boat before the oarsman was aware.

In a low voice the correspondent addressed the captain. He was not sure that the captain was awake, although this iron man seemed to be always awake. "Captain, shall I keep her making for that light north, sir?"

The same steady voice answered him. "Yes. Keep it about two points off the port bow."

The cook had tied a life-belt around himself in order to get even the warmth which this clumsy cork contrivance could donate, and he seemed almost stove-like when a rower, whose teeth invariably chattered wildly as soon as he ceased his labour, dropped down to sleep.

The correspondent, as he rowed, looked down at the two men sleeping under-foot. The cook's arm was around the oiler's shoulders, and, with their fragmentary clothing and haggard faces, they were the babes of the sea, a grotesque rendering of the old babes in the wood.

Later he must have grown stupid at his work, for suddenly there was a growling of water, and a crest came with a roar and a swash into the boat, and it was a wonder that it did not set the cook afloat in his life-belt. The cook continued to sleep, but the oiler sat up, blinking his eyes and shaking with the new cold.

"Oh, I'm awful sorry, Billie," said the correspondent contritely.

"That's all right, old boy," said the oiler, and lay down again and was asleep.

Presently it seemed that even the captain dozed, and the correspondent thought that he was the one man afloat on all the oceans. The wind had a voice as it came over the waves, and it was sadder than the end.

There was a long, loud swishing astern of the boat, and a gleaming trail of phosphorescence, like blue flame, was furrowed on the black waters. It might have been made by a monstrous knife.

Then there came a stillness, while the correspondent breathed with the open mouth and looked at the sea.

Suddenly there was another swish and another long flash of bluish light, and this time it was alongside the boat, and might almost have been reached with an oar. The correspondent saw an enormous fin speed like a shadow through the water, hurling the crystalline spray and leaving the long glowing trail.

The correspondent looked over his shoulder at the captain. His face was hidden, and he seemed to be asleep. He looked at the babes of the sea. They certainly were asleep. So, being bereft of sympathy, he leaned a little way to one side and swore softly into the sea.

But the thing did not then leave the vicinity of the boat. Ahead or astern, on one side or the other, at intervals long or short, fled the long sparkling streak, and there was to be heard the whiroo of the dark fin. The speed and power of the thing was greatly to be admired. It cut the water like a gigantic and keen projectile.

The presence of this biding thing did not affect the man with the same horror that it would if he had been a picnicker. He simply looked at the sea dully and swore in an undertone.

Nevertheless, it is true that he did not wish to be alone. He wished one of his companions to awaken by chance and keep him company with it. But the captain hung motionless over the water-jar, and the oiler and the cook in the bottom of the boat were plunged in slumber.

VI

"If I am going to be drowned—if I am going to be drowned—if I am going to be drowned, why, in the name of the seven mad gods who rule the sea, was I allowed to come thus far and contemplate sand and trees?"

During this dismal night, it may be remarked that a man would conclude that it was really the intention of the seven mad gods to drown him, despite the abominable injustice of it. For it was certainly an abominable injustice to drown a man who had worked so hard, so hard. The man felt it would be a crime most unnatural. Other people had drowned at sea since galleys swarmed with painted sails, but still——

When it occurs to a man that nature does not regard him as important, and that she feels she would not maim the universe by disposing of him, he at first wishes to throw bricks at the temple, and he hates deeply the fact that there are no bricks and no temples. Any visible expression of nature would surely be pelleted with his jeers.

Then, if there be no tangible thing to hoot he feels, perhaps, the desire to confront a personification and indulge in pleas, bowed to one knee, and with hands supplicant, saying: "Yes, but I love myself."

A high cold star on a winter's night is the word he feels that she says to him. Thereafter he knows the pathos of his situation.

The men in the dingey had not discussed these matters, but each had, no doubt, reflected upon them in silence and according to his mind. There was seldom any expression upon their faces save the general one of complete weariness. Speech was devoted to the business of the boat.

To chime the notes of his emotion, a verse mysteriously entered the correspondent's head. He had even forgotten that he had forgotten this verse, but it suddenly was in his mind.

"A soldier of the Legion lay dying in Algiers,There was lack of woman's nursing, there was dearth of woman's tears;But a comrade stood beside him, and he took that comrade's hand,And he said: 'I shall never see my own, my native land.'"

In his childhood, the correspondent had been made acquainted with the fact that a soldier of the Legion lay dying in Algiers, but he had never regarded the fact as important. Myriads of his school-fellows had informed him of the soldier's plight, but the dinning had naturally ended by making him perfectly indifferent. He had never considered it his affair that a soldier of the Legion lay dying in Algiers, nor had it appeared to him as a matter for sorrow. It was less to him than the breaking of a pencil's point.

Now, however, it quaintly came to him as a human, living thing. It was no longer merely a picture of a few throes in the breast of a poet, meanwhile drinking tea and warming his feet at the grate; it was an actuality—stern, mournful, and fine.

The correspondent plainly saw the soldier. He lay on the sand with his feet out straight and still. While his pale left hand was upon his chest in an attempt to thwart the going of his life, the blood came between his fingers. In the far Algerian distance, a city of low square forms was set against a sky that was faint with the last sunset hues. The correspondent, plying the oars and dreaming of the slow and slower movements of the lips of the soldier, was moved by a profound and perfectly impersonal comprehension. He was sorry for the soldier of the Legion who lay dying in Algiers.

The thing which had followed the boat and waited, had evidently grown bored at the delay. There was no longer to be heard the slash of the cut-water, and there was no longer the flame of the long trail. The light in the north still glimmered, but it was apparently no nearer to the boat. Sometimes the boom of the surf rang in the correspondent's ears, and he turned the craft seaward then and rowed harder. Southward, some one had evidently built a watch-fire on the beach. It was too low and too far to be seen, but it made a shimmering, roseate reflection upon the bluff back of it, and this could be discerned from the boat. The wind came stronger, and sometimes a wave suddenly raged out like a mountain-cat, and there was to be seen the sheen and sparkle of a broken crest.

The captain, in the bow, moved on his water-jar and sat erect. "Pretty long night," he observed to the correspondent. He looked at the shore. "Those life-saving people take their time."

"Did you see that shark playing around?"

"Yes, I saw him. He was a big fellow, all right."

"Wish I had known you were awake."

Later the correspondent spoke into the bottom of the boat.

"Billie!" There was a slow and gradual disentanglement. "Billie, will you spell me?"

"Sure," said the oiler.

As soon as the correspondent touched the cold comfortable sea-water in the bottom of the boat, and had huddled close to the cook's life-belt he was deep in sleep, despite the fact that his teeth played all the popular airs. This sleep was so good to him that it was but a moment before he heard a voice call his name in a tone that demonstrated the last stages of exhaustion. "Will you spell me?"

"Sure, Billie."

The light in the north had mysteriously vanished, but the correspondent took his course from the wide-awake captain.

Later in the night they took the boat farther out to sea, and the captain directed the cook to take one oar at the stern and keep the boat facing the seas. He was to call out if he should hear the thunder of the surf. This plan enabled the oiler and the correspondent to get respite together. "We'll give those boys a chance to get into shape again," said the captain. They curled down and, after a few preliminary chatterings and trembles, slept once more the dead sleep. Neither knew they had bequeathed to the cook the company of another shark, or perhaps the same shark.

As the boat caroused on the waves, spray occasionally bumped over the side and gave them a fresh soaking, but this had no power to break their repose. The ominous slash of the wind and the water affected them as it would have affected mummies.

"Boys," said the cook, with the notes of every reluctance in his voice, "she's drifted in pretty close. I guess one of you had better take her to sea again." The correspondent, aroused, heard the crash of the toppled crests.

As he was rowing, the captain gave him some whisky-and-water, and this steadied the chills out of him. "If I ever get ashore and anybody shows me even a photograph of an oar——"

At last there was a short conversation.

"Billie.... Billie, will you spell me?"

"Sure," said the oiler.

VII

When the correspondent again opened his eyes, the sea and the sky were each of the grey hue of the dawning. Later, carmine and gold was painted upon the waters. The morning appeared finally, in its splendour, with a sky of pure blue, and the sunlight flamed on the tips of the waves.

On the distant dunes were set many little black cottages, and a tall white windmill reared above them. No man, nor dog, nor bicycle appeared on the beach. The cottages might have formed a deserted village.

The voyagers scanned the shore. A conference was held in the boat. "Well," said the captain, "if no help is coming we might better try a run through the surf right away. If we stay out here much longer we will be too weak to do anything for ourselves at all." The others silently acquiesced in this reasoning. The boat was headed for the beach. The correspondent wondered if none ever ascended the tall wind-tower, and if then they never looked seaward. This tower was a giant, standing with its back to the plight of the ants. It represented in a degree, to the correspondent, the serenity of nature amid the struggles of the individual—nature in the wind, and nature in the vision of men. She did not seem cruel to him then, nor beneficent, nor treacherous, nor wise. But she was indifferent, flatly indifferent. It is, perhaps, plausible that a man in this situation, impressed with the unconcern of the universe, should see the innumerable flaws of his life, and have them taste wickedly in his mind and wish for another chance. A distinction between right and wrong seems absurdly clear to him, then, in this new ignorance of the grave-edge, and he understands that if he were given another opportunity he would mend his conduct and his words, and be better and brighter during an introduction or at a tea.

"Now, boys," said the captain, "she is going to swamp, sure. All we can do is to work her in as far as possible, and then when she swamps, pile out and scramble for the beach. Keep cool now, and don't jump until she swamps sure."

The oiler took the oars. Over his shoulders he scanned the surf. "Captain," he said, "I think I'd better bring her about, and keep her head-on to the seas and back her in."

"All right, Billie," said the captain. "Back her in." The oiler swung the boat then and, seated in the stern, the cook and the correspondent were obliged to look over their shoulders to contemplate the lonely and indifferent shore.

The monstrous in-shore rollers heaved the boat high until the men were again enabled to see the white sheets of water scudding up the slanted beach. "We won't get in very close," said the captain. Each time a man could wrest his attention from the rollers, he turned his glance toward the shore, and in the expression of the eyes during this contemplation there was a singular quality. The correspondent, observing the others, knew that they were not afraid, but the full meaning of their glances was shrouded.

As for himself, he was too tired to grapple fundamentally with the fact. He tried to coerce his mind into thinking of it, but the mind was dominated at this time by the muscles, and the muscles said they did not care. It merely occurred to him that if he should drown it would be a shame.

There were no hurried words, no pallor, no plain agitation. The men simply looked at the shore. "Now, remember to get well clear of the boat when you jump," said the captain.

Seaward the crest of a roller suddenly fell with a thunderous crash, and the long white comber came roaring down upon the boat.

"Steady now," said the captain. The men were silent. They turned their eyes from the shore to the comber and waited. The boat slid up the incline, leaped at the furious top, bounced over it, and swung down the long back of the wave. Some water had been shipped and the cook bailed it out.

But the next crest crashed also. The tumbling boiling flood of white water caught the boat and whirled it almost perpendicular. Water swarmed in from all sides. The correspondent had his hands on the gunwale at this time, and when the water entered at that place he swiftly withdrew his fingers, as if he objected to wetting them.

The little boat, drunken with this weight of water, reeled and snuggled deeper into the sea.

"Bail her out, cook! Bail her out," said the captain.

"All right, captain," said the cook.

"Now, boys, the next one will do for us, sure," said the oiler. "Mind to jump clear of the boat."

The third wave moved forward, huge, furious, implacable. It fairly swallowed the dingey, and almost simultaneously the men tumbled into the sea. A piece of life-belt had lain in the bottom of the boat, and as the correspondent went overboard he held this to his chest with his left hand.

The January water was icy, and he reflected immediately that it was colder than he had expected to find it off the coast of Florida. This appeared to his dazed mind as a fact important enough to be noted at the time. The coldness of the water was sad; it was tragic. This fact was somehow so mixed and confused with his opinion of his own situation that it seemed almost a proper reason for tears. The water was cold.

When he came to the surface he was conscious of little but the noisy water. Afterward he saw his companions in the sea. The oiler was ahead in the race. He was swimming strongly and rapidly. Off to the correspondent's left, the cook's great white and corked back bulged out of the water, and in the rear the captain was hanging with his one good hand to the keel of the overturned dingey.

There is a certain immovable quality to a shore, and the correspondent wondered at it amid the confusion of the sea.

It seemed also very attractive, but the correspondent knew that it was a long journey, and he paddled leisurely. The piece of life-preserver lay under him, and sometimes he whirled down the incline of a wave as if he were on a hand-sled.

But finally he arrived at a place in the sea where travel was beset with difficulty. He did not pause swimming to inquire what manner of current had caught him, but there his progress ceased. The shore was set before him like a bit of scenery on a stage, and he looked at it and understood with his eyes each detail of it.

As the cook passed, much farther to the left, the captain was calling to him, "Turn over on your back, cook! Turn over on your back and use the oar."

"All right, sir." The cook turned on his back, and, paddling with an oar, went ahead as if he were a canoe.

Presently the boat also passed to the left of the correspondent with the captain clinging with one hand to the keel. He would have appeared like a man raising himself to look over a board fence, if it were not for the extraordinary gymnastics of the boat. The correspondent marvelled that the captain could still hold to it.

They passed on, nearer to shore—the oiler, the cook, the captain—and following them went the water-jar, bouncing gaily over the seas.

The correspondent remained in the grip of this strange new enemy—a current. The shore, with its white slope of sand and its green bluff, topped with little silent cottages, was spread like a picture before him. It was very near to him then, but he was impressed as one who in a gallery looks at a scene from Brittany or Holland.

He thought: "I am going to drown? Can it be possible? Can it be possible? Can it be possible?" Perhaps an individual must consider his own death to be the final phenomenon of nature.

But later a wave perhaps whirled him out of this small deadly current, for he found suddenly that he could again make progress toward the shore. Later still, he was aware that the captain, clinging with one hand to the keel of the dingey, had his face turned away from the shore and toward him, and was calling his name. "Come to the boat! Come to the boat!"

In his struggle to reach the captain and the boat, he reflected that when one gets properly wearied, drowning must really be a comfortable arrangement, a cessation of hostilities accompanied by a large degree of relief, and he was glad of it, for the main thing in his mind for some moments had been horror of the temporary agony. He did not wish to be hurt.

Presently he saw a man running along the shore. He was undressing with most remarkable speed. Coat, trousers, shirt, everything flew magically off him.

"Come to the boat," called the captain.

"All right, captain." As the correspondent paddled, he saw the captain let himself down to bottom and leave the boat. Then the correspondent performed his one little marvel of the voyage. A large wave caught him and flung him with ease and supreme speed completely over the boat and far beyond it. It struck him even then as an event in gymnastics, and a true miracle of the sea. An overturned boat in the surf is not a plaything to a swimming man.

The correspondent arrived in water that reached only to his waist, but his condition did not enable him to stand for more than a moment. Each wave knocked him into a heap, and the under-tow pulled at him.

Then he saw the man who had been running and undressing, and undressing and running, come bounding into the water. He dragged ashore the cook, and then waded towards the captain, but the captain waved him away, and sent him to the correspondent. He was naked, naked as a tree in winter, but a halo was about his head, and he shone like a saint. He gave a strong pull, and a long drag, and a bully heave at the correspondent's hand. The correspondent, schooled in the minor formulæ, said: "Thanks, old man." But suddenly the man cried: "What's that?" He pointed a swift finger. The correspondent said: "Go."

In the shallows, face downward, lay the oiler. His forehead touched sand that was periodically, between each wave, clear of the sea.

The correspondent did not know all that transpired afterward. When he achieved safe ground he fell, striking the sand with each particular part of his body. It was as if he had dropped from a roof, but the thud was grateful to him.

It seems that instantly the beach was populated with men with blankets, clothes, and flasks, and women with coffee-pots and all the remedies sacred to their minds. The welcome of the land to the men from the sea was warm and generous, but a still and dripping shape was carried slowly up the beach, and the land's welcome for it could only be the different and sinister hospitality of the grave.

When it came night, the white waves paced to and fro in the moonlight, and the wind brought the sound of the great sea's voice to the men on shore, and they felt that they could then be interpreters.

THE "FRANCIS SPAIGHT"

A True Tale Retold

JACK LONDON

THE "FRANCIS SPAIGHT"

A TRUE TALE RETOLD

The Francis Spaight was running before it solely under a mizzentopsail, when the thing happened. It was not due to carelessness so much as to the lack of discipline of the crew and to the fact that they were indifferent seamen at best. The man at the wheel in particular, a Limerick man, had had no experience with salt water beyond that of rafting timber on the Shannon between the Quebec vessels and the shore. He was afraid of the huge seas that rose out of the murk astern and bore down upon him, and he was more given to cowering away from their threatened impact than he was to meeting their blows with the wheel and checking the ship's rush to broach to.

It was three in the morning when his unseamanlike conduct precipitated the catastrophe. At sight of a sea far larger than its fellows, he crouched down, releasing his hands from the spokes. The Francis Spaight sheered as her stern lifted on the sea, receiving the full fling of the cap on her quarter. The next instant she was in the trough, her lee-rail buried till the ocean was level with her hatch-coamings, sea after sea breaking over her weather rail and sweeping what remained exposed of the deck with icy deluges.

The men were out of hand, helpless and hopeless, stupid in their bewilderment and fear, and resolute only in that they would not obey orders. Some wailed, others clung silently in the weather shrouds, and still others muttered prayers or shrieked vile imprecations; and neither captain nor mate could get them to bear a hand at the pumps or at setting patches of sails to bring the vessel up to the wind and sea. Inside the hour the ship was over on her beam ends, the lubberly cowards climbing up her side and hanging on in the rigging. When she went over, the mate was caught and drowned in the after-cabin, as were two sailors who had sought refuge in the forecastle.

The mate had been the ablest man on board, and the captain was now scarcely less helpless than his men. Beyond cursing them for their worthlessness, he did nothing; and it remained for a man named Mahoney, a Belfast man, and a boy, O'Brien, of Limerick, to cut away the fore and main masts. This they did at great risk on the perpendicular wall of the wreck, sending the mizzentopmast overside along in the general crash. The Francis Spaight righted, and it was well that she was lumber laden, else she would have sunk, for she was already water-logged. The mainmast, still fast by the shrouds, beat like a thunderous sledge-hammer against the ship's side, every stroke bringing groans from the men.

Day dawned on the savage ocean, and in the cold gray light all that could be seen of the Francis Spaight emerging from the sea were the poop, the shattered mizzenmast, and a ragged line of bulwarks. It was midwinter in the North Atlantic, and the wretched men were half-dead from cold. But there was no place where they could find rest. Every sea breached clean over the wreck, washing away the salt incrustations from their bodies and depositing fresh incrustations. The cabin under the poop was awash to the knees, but here at least was shelter from the chill wind, and here the survivors congregated, standing upright, holding on by the cabin furnishings, and leaning against one another for support.

In vain Mahoney strove to get the men to take turns in watching aloft from the mizzenmast for any chance vessel. The icy gale was too much for them, and they preferred the shelter of the cabin. O'Brien, the boy, who was only fifteen, took turns with Mahoney on the freezing perch. It was the boy, at three in the afternoon, who called down that he had sighted a sail. This did bring them from the cabin, and they crowded the poop rail and weather mizzen shrouds as they watched the strange ship. But its course did not lie near, and when it disappeared below the skyline, they returned shivering to the cabin, not one offering to relieve the watch at the mast head.

By the end of the second day, Mahoney and O'Brien gave up their attempt, and thereafter the vessel drifted in the gale uncared for and without a lookout. There were thirteen alive, and for seventy-two hours they stood knee-deep in the sloshing water on the cabin floor, half-frozen, without food, and with but three bottles of wine shared among them. All food and fresh water were below, and there was no getting at such supplies in the water-logged condition of the wreck. As the days went by, no food whatever passed their lips. Fresh water, in small quantities, they were able to obtain by holding a cover of a tureen under the saddle of the mizzenmast. But the rain fell infrequently, and they were hard put. When it rained, they also soaked their handkerchiefs, squeezing them out into their mouths or into their shoes. As the wind and sea went down, they were even able to mop the exposed portions of the deck that were free from brine and so add to their water supply. But food they had none, and no way of getting it, though sea-birds flew repeatedly overhead.

In the calm weather that followed the gale, after having remained on their feet for ninety-six hours, they were able to find dry planks in the cabin on which to lie. But the long hours of standing in the salt water had caused sores to form on their legs. These sores were extremely painful. The slightest contact or scrape caused severe anguish, and in their weak condition and crowded situation they were continually hurting one another in this manner. Not a man could move about without being followed by volleys of abuse, curses, and groans. So great was their misery that the strong oppressed the weak, shoving them aside from the dry planks to shift for themselves in the cold and wet. The boy, O'Brien, was specially maltreated. Though there were three other boys, it was O'Brien who came in for most of the abuse. There was no explaining it, except on the ground that his was a stronger and more dominant spirit than those of the other boys, and that he stood up more for his rights, resenting the petty injustices that were meted out to all the boys by the men. Whenever O'Brien came near the men in search of a dry place to sleep, or merely moved about, he was kicked and cuffed away. In return, he cursed them for their selfish brutishness, and blows and kicks and curses were rained upon him. Miserable as were all of them, he was thus made far more miserable; and it was only the flame of life, unusually strong in him, that enabled him to endure.

As the days went by and they grew weaker, their peevishness and ill-temper increased, which, in turn, increased the ill-treatment and sufferings of O'Brien. By the sixteenth day all hands were far gone with hunger, and they stood together in small groups, talking in undertones and occasionally glancing at O'Brien. It was at high noon that the conference came to a head. The captain was the spokesman. All were collected on the poop.

"Men," the captain began, "we have been a long time without food—two weeks and two days it is, though it seems more like two years and two months. We can't hang out much longer. It is beyond human nature to go on hanging out with nothing in our stomachs. There is a serious question to consider: whether it is better for all to die, or for one to die. We are standing with our feet in our graves. If one of us dies, the rest may live until a ship is sighted. What say you?"

Michael Behane, the man who had been at the wheel when the Francis Spaight broached to, called out that it was well. The others joined in the cry.

"Let it be one of the b'ys!" cried Sullivan, a Tarbert man, glancing at the same time significantly at O'Brien.

"It is my opinion," the captain went on, "that it will be a good deed for one of us to die for the rest."

"A good deed! A good deed!" the men interjected.

"And it is my opinion that 'tis best for one of the boys to die. They have no families to support, nor would they be considered so great a loss to their friends as those who have wives and children."

"'Tis right." "Very right." "Very fit it should be done," the men muttered one to another.

But the four boys cried out against the injustice of it.

"Our lives is just as dear to us as the rest iv yez," O'Brien protested. "An' our famblies, too. As for wives an' childer, who is there savin' meself to care for me old mother that's a widow, as you know well, Michael Behane, that comes from Limerick? 'Tis not fair. Let the lots be drawn between all of us, men and b'ys."

Mahoney was the only man who spoke in favour of the boys, declaring that it was the fair thing for all to share alike. Sullivan and the captain insisted on the drawing of lots being confined to the boys. There were high words, in the midst of which Sullivan turned upon O'Brien, snarling—

"'Twould be a good deed to put you out of the way. You deserve it. 'Twould be the right way to serve you, an' serve you we will."

He started toward O'Brien, with intent to lay hands on him and proceed at once with the killing, while several others likewise shuffled toward him and reached for him. He stumbled backwards to escape them, at the same time crying that he would submit to the drawing of the lots among the boys.

The captain prepared four sticks of different lengths and handed them to Sullivan.

"You're thinkin' the drawin'll not be fair," the latter sneered to O'Brien. "So it's yerself'll do the drawin'."

To this O'Brien agreed. A handkerchief was tied over his eyes, blindfolding him, and he knelt down on the deck with his back to Sullivan.

"Whoever you name for the shortest stick'll die," the captain said.

Sullivan held up one of the sticks. The rest were concealed in his hand so that no one could see whether it was the short stick or not.

"An' whose stick will it be?" Sullivan demanded.

"For little Johnny Sheehan," O'Brien answered.

Sullivan laid the stick aside. Those who looked could not tell if it were the fatal one. Sullivan held up another stick.

"Whose will it be?"

"For George Burns," was the reply.

The stick was laid with the first one, and a third held up.

"An' whose is this wan?"

"For myself," said O'Brien.

With a quick movement, Sullivan threw the four sticks together. No one had seen.

"'Tis for yourself ye've drawn it," Sullivan announced.

"A good deed," several of the men muttered.

O'Brien was very quiet. He arose to his feet, took the bandage off, and looked around.

"Where is ut?" he demanded. "The short stick? The wan for me?"

The captain pointed to the four sticks lying on the deck.

"How do you know the stick was mine?" O'Brien questioned. "Did you see ut, Johnny Sheehan?"

Johnny Sheehan, who was the youngest of the boys, did not answer.

"Did you see ut?" O'Brien next asked Mahoney.

"No, I didn't see ut."

The men were muttering and growling.

"'Twas a fair drawin'," Sullivan said. "Ye had yer chanct an' ye lost, that's all iv ut."

"A fair drawin'," the captain added. "Didn't I behold it myself? The stick was yours, O'Brien, an' ye may as well get ready. Where's the cook? Gorman, come here. Fetch the tureen cover, some of ye. Gorman, do your duty like a man."

"But how'll I do it," the cook demanded. He was a weak-eyed, weak-chinned, indecisive man.

"'Tis a damned murder!" O'Brien cried out.

"I'll have none of ut," Mahoney announced. "Not a bite shall pass me lips."

"Then 'tis yer share for better men than yerself," Sullivan sneered. "Go on with yer duty, cook."

"'Tis not me duty, the killin' of b'ys," Gorman protested irresolutely.

"If yez don't make mate for us, we'll be makin' mate of yerself," Behane threatened. "Somebody must die, an' as well you as another."

Johnny Sheehan began to cry. O'Brien listened anxiously. His face was pale. His lips trembled, and at times his whole body shook.

"I signed on as cook," Gorman enounced. "An' cook I wud if galley there was. But I'll not lay me hand to murder. 'Tis not in the articles. I'm the cook—"

"An' cook ye'll be for wan minute more only," Sullivan said grimly, at the same moment gripping the cook's head from behind and bending it back till the windpipe and jugular were stretched taut. "Where's yer knife, Mike? Pass it along."

At the touch of the steel, Gorman whimpered.

"I'll do ut, if yez'll hold the b'y."

The pitiable condition of the cook seemed in some fashion to nerve up O'Brien.

"It's all right, Gorman," he said. "Go on with ut. 'Tis meself knows yer not wantin' to do ut. It's all right, sir"—this to the captain, who had laid a hand heavily on his arm. "Ye won't have to hold me, sir. I'll stand still."

"Stop yer blitherin', an' go an' get the tureen cover," Behane commanded Johnny Sheehan, at the same time dealing him a heavy cuff alongside the head.

The boy, who was scarcely more than a child, fetched the cover. He crawled and tottered along the deck, so weak was he from hunger. The tears still ran down his cheeks. Behane took the cover from him, at the same time administering another cuff.

THE "FRANCIS SPAIGHT"

O'Brien took off his coat and bared his right arm. His under lip still trembled, but he held a tight grip on himself. The captain's penknife was opened and passed to Gorman.

"Mahoney, tell me mother what happened to me, if ever ye get back," O'Brien requested.

Mahoney nodded.

"'Tis black murder, black an' damned," he said. "The b'y's flesh'll do none iv yez anny good. Mark me words. Ye'll not profit by it, none iv yez."

"Get ready," the captain ordered. "You, Sullivan, hold the cover—that's it—close up. Spill nothing. It's precious stuff."

Gorman made an effort. The knife was dull. He was weak. Besides, his hand was shaking so violently that he nearly dropped the knife. The three boys were crouched apart, in a huddle, crying and sobbing. With the exception of Mahoney, the men were gathered about the victim, craning their necks to see.

"Be a man, Gorman," the captain cautioned.

The wretched cook was seized with a spasm of resolution, sawing back and forth with the blade on O'Brien's wrist. The veins were severed. Sullivan held the tureen cover close underneath. The cut veins gaped wide, but no ruddy flood gushed forth. There was no blood at all. The veins were dry and empty. No one spoke. The grim and silent figures swayed in unison with each heave of the ship. Every eye was turned fixedly upon that inconceivable and monstrous thing, the dry veins of a creature that was alive.

"'Tis a warnin'," Mahoney cried. "Lave the b'y alone. Mark me words. His death'll do none iv yez anny good."

"Try at the elbow—the left elbow, 'tis nearer the heart," the captain said finally, in a dim and husky voice that was unlike his own.

"Give me the knife," O'Brien said roughly, taking it out of the cook's hand. "I can't be lookin' at ye puttin' me to hurt."

Quite coolly he cut the vein at the left elbow, but, like the cook, he failed to bring blood.

"This is all iv no use," Sullivan said. "'Tis better to put him out iv his misery by bleedin' him at the throat."

The strain had been too much for the lad.

"Don't be doin' ut," he cried. "There'll be no blood in me throat. Give me a little time. 'Tis cold an' weak I am. Be lettin' me lay down an' slape a bit. Then I'll be warm an' the blood'll flow."

"'Tis no use," Sullivan objected. "As if ye cud be slapin' at a time like this. Ye'll not slape, and ye'll not warm up. Look at ye now. You've an ague."

"I was sick at Limerick wan night," O'Brien hurried on, "an' the dochtor cudn't bleed me. But after slapin' a few hours an' gettin' warm in bed the blood came freely. It's God's truth I'm tellin' yez. Don't be murderin' me!"

"His veins are open now," the captain said. "'Tis no use leavin' him in his pain. Do it now an' be done with it."

They started to reach for O'Brien, but he backed away.

"I'll be the death iv yez!" he screamed. "Take yer hands off iv me, Sullivan! I'll come back! I'll haunt yez! Wakin' or slapin', I'll haunt yez till you die!"

"'Tis disgraceful!" yelled Behane. "If the short stick'd ben mine, I'd a-let me mates cut the head off iv me an' died happy."

Sullivan leaped in and caught the unhappy lad by the hair. The rest of the men followed, O'Brien kicked and struggled, snarling and snapping at the hands that clutched him from every side. Little Johnny Sheehan broke out into wild screaming, but the men took no notice of him. O'Brien was bent backward to the deck, the tureen cover under his neck. Gorman was shoved forward. Some one had thrust a large sheath-knife into his hand.

"Do yer duty! Do yer duty!" the men cried.

The cook bent over, but he caught the boy's eyes and faltered.

"If ye don't, I'll kill ye with me own hands," Behane shouted.

From every side a torrent of abuse and threats poured in upon the cook. Still he hung back.

"Maybe there'll be more blood in his veins than O'Brien's," Sullivan suggested significantly.

Behane caught Gorman by the hair and twisted his head back, while Sullivan attempted to take possession of the sheath-knife. But Gorman clung to it desperately.

"Lave go, an' I'll do ut!" he screamed frantically. "Don't be cuttin' me throat! I'll do the deed! I'll do the deed!"

"See that you do it, then," the captain threatened him.

Gorman allowed himself to be shoved forward. He looked at the boy, closed his eyes, and muttered a prayer. Then, without opening his eyes, he did the deed that had been appointed him. O'Brien emitted a shriek that sank swiftly to a gurgling sob. The men held him till his struggles ceased, when he was laid upon the deck. They were eager and impatient, and with oaths and threats they urged Gorman to hurry with the preparation of the meal.

"Lave ut, you bloody butchers," Mahoney said quietly. "Lave ut, I tell yez. Ye'll not be needin' anny iv ut now. 'Tis as I said: ye'll not be profitin' by the lad's blood. Empty ut overside, Behane. Empty ut overside."

Behane, still holding the tureen cover in both his hands, glanced to windward. He walked to the rail and threw the cover and contents into the sea. A full-rigged ship was bearing down upon them a short mile away. So occupied had they been with the deed just committed, that none had had eyes for a lookout. All hands watched her coming on—the brightly coppered forefoot parting the water like a golden knife, the headsails flapping lazily and emptily at each downward surge, and the towering canvas tiers dipping and curtsying with each stately swing of the sea. No man spoke.

As she hove to, a cable length away, the captain of the Francis Spaight bestirred himself and ordered a tarpaulin to be thrown over O'Brien's corpse. A boat was lowered from the stranger's side and began to pull toward them. John Gorman laughed. He laughed softly at first, but he accompanied each stroke of the oars with spasmodically increasing glee. It was this maniacal laughter that greeted the rescue boat as it hauled alongside and the first officer clambered on board.

THE WRECK OF THE DEUTSCHLAND

GERARD MANLEY HOPKINS

THE WRECK OF THE DEUTSCHLAND

To the
happy memory of five Franciscan Nuns
exiles by the Falk Laws
drowned between midnight and morning of
Dec. 7th. 1875

PART THE FIRST

Thou mastering me
God! giver of breath and bread;
World's strand, sway of the sea;
Lord of living and dead;
Thou hast bound bones and veins in me, fastened me flesh,
And after it almost unmade, what with dread,
Thy doing: and dost thou touch me afresh?
Over again I feel thy finger and find thee.

I did say yes
O at lightning and lashed rod;
Thou heardst me truer than tongue confess
Thy terror, O Christ, O God;
Thou knowest the walls, altar and hour and night:
The swoon of a heart that the sweep and the hurl of thee trod
Hard down with a horror of height:
And the midriff astrain with leaning of, laced with fire of stress.

The frown of his face
Before me, the hurtle of hell

GERARD MANLEY HOPKINS

Behind, where, where was a, where was a place?
I whirled out wings that spell
And fled with a fling of the heart to the heart of the Host.
My heart, but you were dovewinged, I can tell,
Carrier-witted, I am bold to boast,
To flash from the flame to the flame then, tower from the grace to the grace.

I am soft sift
In an hourglass—at the wall
Fast, but mined with a motion, a drift,
And it crowds and it combs to the fall;
I steady as a water in a well, to a poise, to a pane,
But roped with, always, all the way down from the tall
Fells or flanks of the voel, a vein
Of the gospel proffer, a pressure, a principle, Christ's gift.

I kiss my hand
To the stars, lovely-asunder
Starlight, wafting him out of it; and
Glow, glory in thunder;
Kiss my hand to the dappled-with-damson west:
Since, tho' he is under the world's splendour and wonder,
His mystery must be instressed, stressed;
For I greet him the days I meet him, and bless when I understand.

Not out of his bliss
Springs the stress felt
Nor first from heaven (and few know this)
Swings the stroke dealt—
Stroke and a stress that stars and storms deliver,
That guilt is hushed by, hearts are flushed by and melt—
But it rides time like riding a river
(And here the faithful waver, the faithless fable and miss),

It dates from day
Of his going in Galilee;
Warm-laid grave of a womb-life grey;
Manger, maiden's knee;
The dense and the driven Passion, and frightful sweat;
Thence the discharge of it, there its swelling to be,
Though felt before, though in high flood yet—
What none would have known of it, only the heart, being hard at bay,

Is out with it! Oh,
We lash with the best or worst
Word last! How a lush-kept plush-capped sloe
Will, mouthed to flesh-burst,
Gush!—flush the man, the being with it, sour or sweet,

THE WRECK OF THE DEUTSCHLAND

Brim, in a flash, full!—Hither then, last or first,
To hero of Calvary, Christ,'s feet—
Never ask if meaning it, wanting it, warned of it—men go.

Be adored among men,
God, three-numberèd form;
Wring thy rebel, dogged in den,
Man's malice, with wrecking and storm.
Beyond saying sweet, past telling of tongue,
Thou art lightning and love, I found it, a winter and warm;
Father and fondler of heart thou hast wrung:
Hast thy dark descending and most art merciful then.

With an anvil-ding
And with fire in him forge thy will
Or rather, rather then, stealing as Spring
Through him, melt him but master him still:
Whether at once, as once at a crash Paul,
Or as Austin, a lingering-out sweet skill,
Make mércy in all of us, out of us all
Mastery, but be adored, but be adored King.

PART THE SECOND

'Some find me a sword; some
The flange and the rail; flame,
Fang, or flood' goes Death on drum,
And storms bugle his fame.
But wé dream we are rooted in earth—Dust!
Flesh falls within sight of us, we, though our flower the same,
Wave with the meadow, forget that there must
The sour scythe cringe, and the blear share come.

On Saturday sailed from Bremen,
American-outward-bound,
Take settler and seamen, tell men with women,
Two hundred souls in the round—
O Father, not under thy feathers nor ever as guessing
The goal was a shoal, of a fourth the doom to be drowned;
Yet did the dark side of the bay of thy blessing
Not vault them, the million of rounds of thy mercy not reeve even them in?

Into the snows she sweeps,
Hurling the haven behind,
The Deutschland, on Sunday; and so the sky keeps,
For the infinite air is unkind,
And the sea flint-flake, black-backed in the regular blow,
Sitting Eastnortheast, in cursed quarter, the wind;

GERARD MANLEY HOPKINS

Wiry and white-fiery and whirlwind-swivellèd snow
Spins to the widow-making unchilding unfathering deeps.

She drove in the dark to leeward,
She struck—not a reef or a rock
But the combs of a smother of sand: night drew her
Dead to the Kentish Knock;
And she beat the bank down with her bows and the ride of
her keel:
The breakers rolled on her beam with ruinous shock;
And canvas and compass, the whorl and the wheel
Idle for ever to waft her or wind her with, these she endured.

Hope had grown grey hairs,
Hope had mourning on,
Trenched with tears, carved with cares,
Hope was twelve hours gone;
And frightful a nightfall folded rueful a day
Nor rescue, only rocket and lightship, shone,
And lives at last were washing away:
To the shrouds they took,—they shook in the hurling and horrible airs.

One stirred from the rigging to save
The wild woman-kind below,
With a rope's end round the man, handy and brave—
He was pitched to his death at a blow,
For all his dreadnought breast and braids of thew:
They could tell him for hours, dandled the to and fro
Through the cobbled foam-fleece, what could he do
With the burl of the fountains of air, buck and the flood of the wave?

They fought with God's cold—
And they could not and fell to the deck
(Crushed them) or water (and drowned them) or rolled
With the sea-romp over the wreck.
Night roared, with the heart-break hearing a heart-broke rabble,
The woman's wailing, the crying of child without check—
Till a lioness arose breasting the babble,
A prophetess towered in the tumult, a virginal tongue told.

Ah, touched in your bower of bone
Are you! turned for an exquisite smart,
Have you! make words break from me here all alone,
Do you!—mother of being in me, heart.
O unteachably after evil, but uttering truth,
Why, tears! is it? tears; such a melting, a madrigal start!
Never-eldering revel and river of youth,
What can it be, this glee? the good you have there of your own?

THE WRECK OF THE DEUTSCHLAND

Sister, a sister calling
A master, her master and mine!—
And the inboard seas run swirling and bawling;
The rash smart sloggering brine
Blinds her; but she that weather sees one thing, one;
Has one fetch in her: she rears herself to divine
Ears, and the call of the tall nun
To the men in the tops and the tackle rode over the storm's brawling.

She was first of a five and came
Of a coifèd sisterhood.
(O Deutschland, double a desperate name!
O world wide of its good!
But Gertrude, lily, and Luther, are two of a town,
Christ's lily and beast of the waste wood:
From life's dawn it is drawn down,
Abel is Cain's brother and breasts they have sucked the same.)

Loathed for a love men knew in them,
Banned by the land of their birth,
Rhine refused them. Thames would ruin them;
Surf, snow, river and earth
Gnashed: but thou art above, thou Orion of light;
Thy unchancelling poising palms were weighing the worth,
Thou martyr-master: in thy sight
Storm flakes were scroll-leaved flowers, lily showers—sweet
heaven was astrew in them.

Five! the finding and sake
And cipher of suffering Christ.
Mark, the mark is of man's make
And the word of it Sacrificed.
But he scores it in scarlet himself on his own bespoken,
Before-time-taken, dearest prizèd and priced—
Stigma, signal, cinquefoil token
For lettering of the lamb's fleece, ruddying of the rose-flake.

Joy fall to thee, father Francis,
Drawn to the Life that died;
With the gnarls of the nails in thee, niche of the lance, his
Lovescape crucified
And seal of his seraph-arrival! and these thy daughters
And five-livèd and leavèd favour and pride,
Are sisterly sealed in wild waters,
To bathe in his fall-gold mercies, to breathe in his all-fire glances.

Away in the loveable west,
On a pastoral forehead of Wales,

GERARD MANLEY HOPKINS

I was under a roof here, I was at rest,
And they the prey of the gales;
She to the black-about air, to the breaker, the thickly
Falling flakes, to the throng that catches and quails,
Was calling 'O Christ, Christ come quickly':
The cross to her she calls Christ to her, christens her wild-worn Best.

The majesty! what did she mean?
Breathe, arch and original Breath.
Is it love in her of the being as her lover had been?
Breathe, body of lovely Death.
They were else-minded then, altogether, the men
Woke thee with a *we are perishing* in the weather of Gennesareth.
Or is it that she cried for the crown then,
The keener to come at the comfort for feeling the combating keen?

For how to the heart's cheering
The down-dogged ground-hugged grey
Hovers off, the jay-blue heavens appearing
Of pied and peeled May!
Blue-beating and hoary-glow height; or night, still higher,
With belled fire and the moth-soft Milky Way,
What by your measure is the heaven of desire,
The treasure never eyesight got, nor was ever guessed what for the hearing?

No, but it was not these.
The jading and jar of the cart,
Time's tasking, it is fathers that asking for ease
Of the sodden-with-its-sorrowing heart,
Not danger, electrical horror; then further it finds
The appealing of the Passion is tenderer in prayer apart:
Other, I gather, in measure her mind's
Burden, in wind's burly and beat of endragonèd seas.

But how shall I ... make me room there;
Reach me a ... Fancy, come faster—
Strike you the sight of it? look at it loom there,
Thing that she ... there then! the Master,
Ipse, the only one, Christ, King, Head:
He was to cure the extremity where he had cast her;
Do, deal, lord it with living and dead;
Let him ride, her pride, in his triumph, despatch and have done with his doom there.

Ah! there was a heart right!
There was single eye!
Read the unshapeable shock night
And knew the who and the why;
Wording it how but by him that present and past,

THE WRECK OF THE DEUTSCHLAND

Heaven and earth are word of, worded by?—
The Simon Peter of a soul! to the blast
Tarpeian-fast, but a blown beacon of light.

Jesu, heart's light,
Jesu, maid's son,
What was the feast followed the night
Thou hadst glory of this nun?
Feast of the one woman without stain.
For so conceived, so to conceive thee is done;
But here was heart-throe, birth of a brain,
Word, that heard and kept thee and uttered thee outright.

Well, she has thee for the pain, for the
Patience; but pity of the rest of them!
Heart, go and bleed at a bitterer vein for the
Comfortless unconfessed of them—
No not uncomforted: lovely-felicitous Providence
Finger of a tender of, O of a feathery delicacy, the breast of the
Maiden could obey so, be a bell to, ring of it, and
Startle the poor sheep back! is the shipwrack then a harvest; does
tempest carry the grain for thee?

I admire thee, master of the tides,
Of the Yore-flood, of the year's fall;
The recurb and the recovery of the gulfs sides,
The girth of it and the wharf of it and the wall;
Stanching, quenching ocean of a motionable mind;
Ground of being, and granite of it: past all
Grasp God, throned behind
Death with a sovereignty that heeds but hides, bodes but abides;

With a mercy that outrides
The all of water, an ark
For the listener; for the lingerer with a love glides
Lower than death and the dark;
A vein for the visiting of the past-prayer, pent in prison,
The-last-breath penitent spirits—the uttermost mark
Our passion-plungèd giant risen,
The Christ of the Father compassionate, fetched in the storm of his strides.

Now burn, new born to the world,
Doubled-naturèd name,
The heaven-flung, heart-fleshed, maiden-furled
Miracle-in-Mary-of-flame,
Mid-numbered He in three of the thunder-throne!
Not a dooms-day dazzle in his coming nor dark as he came;
Kind, but royally reclaiming his own;

GERARD MANLEY HOPKINS

A released shower, let flash to the shire, not a lightning of fire hard-hurled.

Dame, at our door
Drowned, and among our shoals,
Remember us in the roads, the heaven-haven of the
Reward:
Our King back, oh, upon English souls!
Let him easter in us, be a dayspring to the dimness of us,
be a crimson-cresseted east,
More brightening her, rare-dear Britain, as his reign rolls,
Pride, rose, prince, hero of us, high-priest,
Our hearts' charity's hearth's fire, our thoughts' chivalry's throng's Lord.

Printed in Great Britain
by Amazon